Version 2.0

NEXT-GEN COMPUTER ARCHITECTURE

TILL THE END OF SILICON

SMRUTI R. SARANGI

White Falcon Publishing

Next-Gen Computer Architecture - Till the End of Silicon
Smruti R. Sarangi

Published by White Falcon Publishing
Chandigarh, India

Preface

Overview

This is a comprehensive book on all aspects of next-generation computer architecture. It is divided into three parts: processor design, the memory system, and advanced topics. The first part, processor design, covers all aspects of modern out-of-order processors and GPUs. The second part covers modern memory systems that include cache hierarchies, on-chip networks, memory systems for multi-processors, DRAM memories and nonvolatile memories. This area, in particular, has seen a lot of activity in both academia and industry in the last decade. The last part comprises four chapters on power and temperature, reliability, security, and architectures for machine learning, respectively. As of 2023, the last two topics are considered to be state-of-the-art topics. They are expected to play a very significant role in the development of the field in the coming decade.

Reasons for Writing this Book

Ever since my graduate days, I felt the need for a comprehensive textbook in computer architecture. The existing books were rather dated and captured the state of the field when it was still in its adolescence – many aspects were not fully formalized and a lot of much-needed mathematical rigor was missing. Books for teaching basic computer architecture did exist; however, courses on next-generation computer architecture were primarily taught from research papers and patents. Consequently, it was hard for students to appreciate the nuances of such a beautiful field, particularly while taking other courses in algorithms and compilers, which were comparatively much more developed. The field appeared to me to be really advanced as far as engineering contributions were concerned; however, formalizing those notions mathematically and presenting them in a simple-to-understand way was not commonplace. As a result, I graduated with a PhD in computer architecture without fully understanding how exactly memory models work or why virtual channels in on-chip networks are needed. These are very basic concepts, which were taught rather well by the instructors; in spite of that, the state of the field was not at the point at which these concepts could be absorbed to a sufficient depth by students taking the course.

I faced an even more acute problem in my teaching career when I was supposed to teach the concepts to students. They started having the same difficulty that I was having as an undergraduate student and later as a graduate student. We were primarily relying on texts that were originally written 30 years ago or on research papers, which are in any case not written from the perspective of teaching. As a result, teaching a course exclusively on the basis of research papers and patents proved to be rather difficult. Simultaneously, the field of computer architecture was advancing in leaps and bounds and thus it became necessary to teach larger classes and also teach employees in industry about recent developments in the field. Hence, I decided to undertake the mammoth exercise of trying to write a textbook in computer architecture. I along with my publishers subsequently realized that the field is too vast for a single textbook: hence I decided to write two. The first part that covers undergraduate computer architecture was published by McGraw-Hill in 2015 and later by WhiteFalcon in 2021. The latest version is titled, "Basic Computer Architecture" (official website: www.basiccomparch.com). The PDF of this book is freely downloadable from its official website. This book covers all aspects of assembly language programming, binary arithmetic, basic processor design, pipelining, caches, parallel programming, and I/O systems. This book is however not sufficient for senior undergraduates, graduate students, and engineers in the semiconductor industry.

Hence, I decided to write the next part of the book that covers advanced, next-generation aspects of computer architecture, which is this book. As of today, it is necessary to read most parts of this book to have a successful career in the semiconductor industry. In this book, I have made an effort to systematically track down all the major developments in the field and document them in a simple yet formal way. I have tried my best to add as much of mathematical rigor as possible such that definitions and results are as unambiguous as possible. Sadly, in traditional computer architecture teaching, seldom any references are made to other areas such as theoretical computer science and formal verification. In my view, this is not correct – the field has much to gain with some degree of cross-fertilisation with other fields. This is because in the last decade there are many results that other areas have produced, which make understanding and explaining computer architecture concepts, specifically memory models, far easier. Hence, I have amply borrowed results from other areas to explain difficult concepts in computer architecture. In many cases new theoretical constructs were created in this book to make it easier to explain concepts and prove results. These are fairly simple results, which can be understood by any student who has taken a basic course in data structures and algorithms.

Another important shortcoming was the nature of evaluations and assessments in computer architecture courses. I remember that throughout my student days, I was particularly concerned about the computer architecture exam (regardless of the university), primarily because the questions were more mechanical rather than conceptual. It is not that the universities that I had gone to were at fault; the problem lied in the way that the field was viewed. Comparatively, exams and quizzes in other courses such as algorithms, signal processing, operating systems, and compilers were far more *conceptually deeper*. This had a lasting impact on me. From my graduate days itself, I wanted to rearchitect the field such that we view computer architecture teaching differently and bring it in line with the way that more established computer science and electrical engineering courses are taught. The questions should be far more theoretical and conceptual, and not rely on specific artifacts of the implementation (the way it is presented in the book or a research paper). I have tried to bring this philosophy into life in this book by primarily focusing on conceptual questions in the exercises at the back of each chapter. They are not based on either rote learning or mechanically simulating algorithms. Specifically, the * and ** marked questions are difficult and have profound implications.

Target Readership

This book is meant to be the second book on computer architecture. Any student in computer science or electrical engineering who has taken a basic undergraduate course in computer architecture will be able to read and follow this book very easily. The book primarily targets senior undergraduate students, early graduate students, and professionals from industry. A short course on data structures and basic graph algorithms will prove to be beneficial. However, it is not mandatory; sufficient pointers are provided in the text to pick up any material that is required.

The material can be used to teach courses in computer architecture, cybersecurity, machine learning/intelligent systems, digital signal processing, and parallel programming.

Salient Features

- Comprehensive coverage of in-order pipelines and performance evaluation.
- Detailed descriptions of branch predictors, the fetch logic, and decode-stage optimisations.
- Extensive coverage of out-of-order pipelines: rename, schedule, and commit logic; advanced speculation; compiler optimisations.
- Coverage of the NVIDIA CUDA 10 language, and the design of GPUs.
- Large chapters on caches and on-chip networks that discuss the most popular optimisations.
- A novel theoretical treatment of memory models, coherence, data races, and transactional memory.
- Comprehensive description of the DDR-4 protocol and all popular nonvolatile memory technologies.
- Advanced topics: power and temperature modeling/management, reliability and process variation, and hardware security with focus on cryptographic primitives and trusted execution environments such as Intel SGX.
- Architectures for machine learning: a novel notation to describe loop transformations, broad classes of architectures, and systolic computation.
- Three appendices on state-of-the-art Intel, AMD, and Qualcomm processors.
- Software support: Tejas simulator® for architectural simulation.
- Pedagogy
  - Exercises: 193
  - Illustrations: 416

Organisation of the Chapters

Chapter 1 is an introductory chapter that discusses the landscape of processors. It makes the point that traditional in-order processors are insufficient when it comes to performance, and thus there is a need to design out-of-order (OOO) processors that have a far higher instruction throughput. Furthermore, it is like an expanded preface that summarises the rest of the chapters in the book.

Part I: Processor Design

This part comprises four chapters that describe OOO processors and GPUs in detail.

Chapter 2 starts out with providing an in-depth introduction of in-order pipelines. The treatment is exhaustive yet at the same time cursory. It assumes that the reader has a background of assembly language programming, programming experience in C/C++/Java, and some familiarity with processor design. After discussing the performance equation and the bottlenecks in in-order pipelines, it moves on to explain the basic concepts that underlie OOO pipelines.

Chapter 3 discusses the fetch and decode units in OOO pipelines in detail. Specifically, it describes the design of several branch predictors, the notion of saturating counters, and methods to handle *function call* and *return* instructions exclusively. This chapter should not be read to just learn about branch predictors; the implications are quite far-reaching in the sense that the same results can be used to design predictors across all the pipeline stages. It concludes with describing some optimisations that are typically made in the decode stage to leverage some common programming idioms, and optimise for CISC processors.

Chapter 4 describes the OOO pipeline in great detail starting from the rename stage until the commit stage. Reading this chapter is mandatory and it is not possible to appreciate the contents of the rest of the chapters without completing this chapter first. In this chapter, readers will appreciate the nuances of implementing renaming, instruction scheduling, managing loads and stores, and committing instructions correctly. It will be realised that regardless of the internal implementation, it should appear to an external observer that the processor executes a program instruction by instruction, in program order.

Chapter 5 is optional and thus it is not a part of the print copy of the book, it is available online. In this chapter, we start out by discussing additional features of advanced processors such as advanced speculation mechanisms that include load latency prediction and value prediction. In all such speculation mechanisms, recovering from a misspeculation is necessary and thus we need to design elaborate replay schemes. Alternatively, it is possible to simplify the design of a pipeline by storing temporary values in the ROB instead of using a physical register file. We can also perform many optimisations at the level of the compiler that include loop transformations like loop unrolling and software pipelining. We conclude with describing EPIC processors that lie at an extreme end of the spectrum, where the hardware is as simple as possible and the role of renaming and scheduling instructions is offloaded to the compiler to a large extent.

Chapter 6 describes the NVIDIA CUDA 10 language, design of traditional graphics processors, modern graphics pipelines, and contemporary GPGPUs. We shall appreciate the fact that the hardware in a GPU can be repurposed to also perform numerical and scientific computations. We do require additional support to manage a large number of threads and their complex synchronisation patterns; nevertheless, the gains outweigh the costs by a large margin.

Part II: The Memory System

This part comprises four chapters on caches, on-chip networks to route messages between different parts of the memory system, multiprocessor memory systems, and DRAM memories (includes nonvolatile memories as well).

Chapter 7 contains all the details of the on-chip memory system namely the caches and associated structures. It starts with introducing the basic structure of caches: tag and data arrays. The chapter then moves on to introducing direct mapped caches, set associative caches, fully associative caches, and virtual memory. The treatment of these topics is rather cursory because they are assumed to be a part of the standard undergraduate course in computer architecture. Subsequently, we discuss methods to model and optimally design large caches; in this context the CactI tool and the Elmore delay model are discussed. Subsequently, the chapter moves to different cache optimizations such as non-blocking caches, pipelined caches, VIPT caches, and way prediction. The chapter concludes with a discussion on instruction and data prefetching schemes.

Chapter 8 also starts with introductory material. This includes descriptions of common network topologies, basic concepts in on-chip networks (NoCs), and circuit-switched mechanisms. Subsequently, the discussion moves on to advanced flow-control schemes such as on-off flow control, credit-based flow control, store-and-forward, virtual cut through, wormhole protocols, and virtual channels. Once, the basic concepts in packet and flit-based routing are established, we subsequently discuss deadlock-free routing protocols starting from simple X-Y routing and oblivious routing. The discussion uses numerous theoretical concepts to mathematically explain the causes and implications of deadlocks. We describe a new mathematical technique called a *turn graph* that can be used to reason about deadlocks in terms of the turns that packets take. All the descriptions about turn-based adaptive routing protocols use these turn graphs as their basis. Subsequently, the chapter explains the design of a router and several optimisations for shortening the router's pipeline. Modern last-level cache access protocols are codesigned with the NoC such that it is possible to locate blocks easily and also migrate them towards the requesting core over time. These are known as NUCA protocols and are discussed in the next subsection. We finally conclude this chapter with discussing methods to measure and characterise the performance of an NoC.

Chapter 9 is the longest chapter in the book. It starts with basic introductory material that provides a light introduction to parallel programming using the shared memory and message passing paradigms. The treatment is by no means complete; the reader is requested to consult other sources. After discussing the Amdahl's law, Gustafson-Barsis's law, and the Flynn's taxonomy, we move on to discussing the theoretical background required to understand multiprocessor systems. This is the distinguishing feature of this book. We have distilled the formal verification literature and created a coherent framework to describe all the interactions between threads in multicore systems, and the space of different memory models. This part is theoretically heavy; however, for understanding we do not require any concept beyond simple graph algorithms especially cycle detection and topological sorting. Moreover, this part is inspired heavily from work in the formal verification community. For a long time, memory models were not properly understood because they were not formalised. Hence, we decided to import all the formal models that are required and present them in a manner that is easy to understand. Memory models naturally lead us towards results on data races. Here again, we prove many theorems that were hitherto not proven formally. Finally, the chapter concludes with a theoretical discussion on transaction memory and different software/hardware schemes to implement a practical transaction memory system.

Chapter 10 focuses on off-chip memory. As of 2020, the most popular off-chip memory technology is DRAM memory. Hence, this chapter starts with a detailed discussion of DRAM memory arrays, circuit technologies, and signalling protocols. Subsequently, we discuss different facets of the DDR family of protocols notably DDR-4 and subsequently explain its commands and timing contraints in detail. Then we move on to describe the design of memory controllers.

It is expected that in the near future, nonvolatile memories will become far more commonplace. Hence, this chapter describes the following technologies in detail starting from the basic physics to architecture level constructs: flash memories, Ferroelectric RAM (FeRAM), Magnetoresistive RAM (MRAM), phase change memory (PCM), and resistive RAM (ReRAM). There is a brief discussion on 3D memory technologies such as HBM and hybrid memory cubes as well. Finally, the chapter concludes with describing the Roofline model that nicely combines processor and memory performance.

Part III: Advanced Topics

This part comprises four assorted chapters that are mutually independent. They discuss power and temperature issues, reliability, security, and architectures for machine learning.

Chapter 11 is an online chapter that discusses power and temperature modeling as well as dynamic management. The aim is to provide a quick introduction to all power and temperature modelling mechanisms starting from transistor-level modelling to architecture-level modelling. Several schemes are discussed to manage dynamic power, leakage power, and stop temperature hotspots from forming.

Chapter 12 is also an online chapter that covers reliability and process variation. We discuss soft errors due to particle strikes, faults due to interactive noise, nondeterministic behavior, timing faults due to parameter variation, and errors due to aging. Along with the basic mechanisms, methods are discussed to mitigate the effects.

Chapter 13 is a very important chapter that discusses hardware security. An effort has been made to provide a comprehensive treatment of almost all aspects of hardware security in a short chapter. The chapter starts with basic cryptographic primitives such as encryption and one-way hashing. Once they are understood, the reader should move to the subsequent sections that talk about different encryption modes, methods to realise practical systems on the lines of Intel SGX, and efficiently storing encryption-related data in on and off-chip memory. The chapter also discusses common software-based attacks, methods to securely boot hardware and finally concludes with a description of side-channel attacks.

Chapter 14 is the star chapter of the book. Hence, it has been kept till the very end! It does not assume any background in machine learning; it starts from first principles and explains different mechanisms underlying linear and nonlinear models inclusive of neural networks. Subsequently, it introduces convolutional neural networks as simply a set of seven loops and looks at this 7-loop structure as a 7-dimensional space. We introduce a novel notation in this book that allows us to efficiently visualize and represent the way we compute a convolution (method of traversing the 7-dimensional space). Our succinct notation very effectively captures the control flow and the parallelism in a CNN accelerator. We subsequently provide different hardware implementations that cache different kinds of data within the individual processing elements. This discussion is continued by talking about the theory of systolic computation and designing a few systolic and semi-systolic arrays for 1D and 2D convolution. After discussing the compute part, we move on to the memory part where the design of the memory system in a CNN accelerator is discussed. The last subsection is devoted to methods that use analog circuits and emerging devices such as ReRAMs.

Appendices

There are five appendices in the book.

Appendix	Title
A	SimpleRisc ISA
B	The Tejas architectural simulator
C	Intel processors: Sunny Cove and Tremont architectures. Lakefield processor
D	AMD processors: Zen2 microarchitecture, Ryzen 3000 processor, EPYC 7742 processor
E	Qualcomm processors: Snapdragon 865 processor

Dependences between Chapters

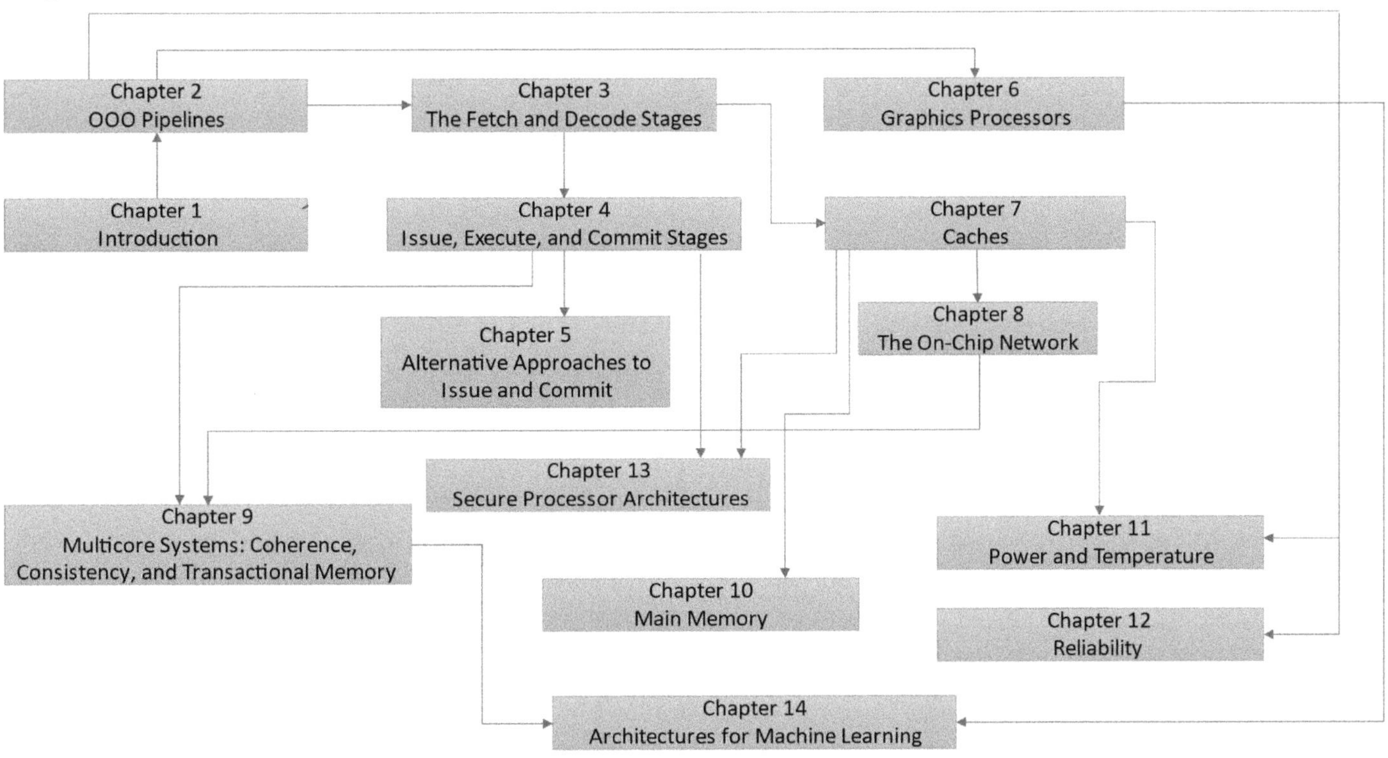

Pedagogical Features

The book has a host of pedagogical features. We define the following environments in the text.

- **Definition**: The definition environment is used the most frequently in the text. It is used to visually highlight the definition of important concepts. Note that there is often a repetition of the definition of a term. It is defined once in a paragraph, and then it is defined in a ``definition'' box at the end of the paragraph. While casually reading the book, it is per se not necessary to read both the definitions of a term. However, sometimes it might be useful to reinforce the learning. Secondly, while skimming through the book, or while preparing for an exam, the reader can just read all the definition boxes, and she will be able to recapitulate most of the concepts, and terms.

- **Example**: This environment is used for solved examples.
- **Theorem/Lemma/Corollary**: For theorems, and their proofs.
- **Question**: This environment is used to ask a thought-provoking question.
- **Point**: This environment is also frequently used to elucidate an important point in the text, or to discuss a profound insight. We use the ``Point'' environment to give a disproportionate amount of importance to a piece of text that contains vital information.
- **Historical Point**: Used to discuss historical anecdotes.
- **Way Point**: This environment summarises all the relevant concepts learnt in the previous chapters.
- **Trivia**: This environment presents a story, a fact, an anecdote, or the answer to a thought-provoking question. It is not integral to the text; however, it has been added to enrich the reading experience.
- **Design problems**: Every chapter has a couple of design problems that require the student to build a prototype. Such project-oriented assignments should ideally be done in groups. They have been designed to enhance the learning experience by providing a practical flavour to material covered in the book.

How to Use the Book

Instructors who wish to use this book as a textbook in a computer architecture course can follow one of the several course plans that we shall describe next.

Course Type	Chapters	Remarks
Light (1 semester)	1, 2, 3, 4, 6, 7	Provide adequate background in circuits and graph algorithms
Moderate (1 semester)	1, 2, 3, 4, 7, 8, 9	Transactional memory may be skipped.
Heavy (1 semester)	1, 2, 3, 4, 5, 7, 8, 9	EPIC processors may be skipped.
Very heavy (6-month semester)	1, 2, 3, 4, 5, 6, 7, 8, 9, 14	Optional topics: EPIC processors, transactional memory, NUCA caches
Two-semester course	Sem I: 1, 2, 3, 4, 5, 7, 8	Also cover the appendices as case studies.
	Sem II: 9, 10, 11, 12, 13, 6, 14	

Online Learning Materials

Slides, PDF of the book and **YouTube videos**: PowerPoint slides for all the chapters are available to both instructors and students on the book's official website. The PDF of the book is *freely* available on the official website including chapter-wise PDFs (can be <u>downloaded</u> for free). All the lecture videos are available on YouTube (pointers on the official website). The Tejas architectural simulator, which can be used to conduct the lab experiments is available at its official site: **http://www.cse.iitd.ac.in/tejas**

Official website of the book: http://www.nextgencomparch.com

Feedback

The author will be highly indebted to readers who can point out errors in the text, suggest changes, or contribute new insights. The readers can directly mail the author at: srsarangi@gmail.com with their valued feedback.

SmrutI Ranjan Sarangi

List of Trademarks

- AMD is a registered trademark of Advanced Micro Devices, Inc.

- AMD Phenom and ATI are trademarks of Advanced Micro Devices, Inc.

- Arm, Cortex, Neon, Thumb, and TrustZone are registered trademarks of Arm limited (or its subsidiaries).

- Arm7 and big.LITTLE are trademarks of Arm limited (or its subsidiaries).

- AutoCAD is a registered trademark of Autodesk, Inc.

- Facebook is a registered trademark of Facebook, Inc.

- FORMULA 1 is a registered trademark of Formula One Licensing BV.

- Google is a registered trademark of Google LLC.

- Google Maps is a trademark of Google LLC.

- HP is a registered trademark of Hewlett Packard, Inc.

- IBM, Power, and PowerPC are registered trademarks of International Business Machines Corporation.

- Intel, Pentium, Intel Xeon Phi, Intel Atom and Itanium are registered trademarks of Intel Corporation or its subsidiaries.

- Microsoft and Windows are registered trademarks of Microsoft Corporation.

- NVIDIA, CUDA, NVIDIA Tesla, NVIDIA Kepler, NVIDIA Maxwell and NVIDIA Turing are registered trademarks of NVIDIA Corporation.

- SPARC is a registered trademark of SPARC International, Inc.

- SPEC and SPEC CPU are registered trademarks of the Standard Performance Evaluation Corporation.

- Tejas Simulator is a trademark of IIT Delhi.

- Qualcomm, Snapdragon, Hexagon, and Adreno are trademarks of Qualcomm incorporated.

Contents

II The Memory System   251

7 Caches   253

8 The On-chip Network   335

III Advanced Topics   605

11 Power and Temperature   607

1

Introduction

Welcome to the study of advanced computer architecture. The first part [Sarangi, 2015] of this two-book series explains the basic concepts of computer organisation and architecture. In the first part, we discussed the basics of computer architecture: instruction sets (*SimpleRisc*, ARM, and x86), processor design (gates, memories, processor, pipeline), the memory system, multiprocessor systems, and I/O systems. We started from scratch and left the reader at a point where she could understand the essentials of a computer architecture, write simple assembly programs, understand the intricacies of pipelines, and appreciate the nuances of memory and I/O system design. Additionally, we also provided a foundation for understanding multiprocessor systems, which is the bedrock of a course on advanced computer architecture.

Unfortunately, the processor described in a basic course on computer architecture is hardly used today other than in some extremely simple and rudimentary devices. A processor used in a modern device starting from a smart watch to a server uses far more sophisticated techniques. These techniques are typically not covered in a basic course on computer architecture. Hence, we shall discuss such techniques in this book, and cover them in exquisite detail.

Let us start with understanding and appreciating the fact that the modern processor is not just a sophisticated pipeline. The pipeline is supplied data from the memory system. Unless the memory system is efficient and can provide high bandwidth, we cannot run a high performance pipeline. Moreover, modern processors do not necessarily have a single pipeline. They have multiple pipelines, where each pipeline along with its caches is known as a *core*. We thus are in the era of multi-core processors, where a processor chip has a multitude of cores, caches, and an elaborate network that connects them. In addition, this ensemble needs to be power-efficient, secure, and reliable.

Let us motivate our discussion further by considering the basic drivers of technological change in the world of computer architecture. A processor sits between the hardware and the software. Its aim is to leverage the features provided by the latest hardware technology to run software as efficiently as possible. As the underlying hardware keeps on improving, it becomes imperative to modify the computer architecture to exploit these improvements. The most important empirical law in this space is known as the *Moore's law*. It was proposed by Gordon Moore, the co-founder of Intel, in 1965. He postulated that because of advances in transistor technology, the number of transistors per chip will double roughly every year. He has been extremely prescient in his observation. Since 1965 the number of transistors per chip have doubled roughly every 1-2 years (see Figure 1.1). The processor industry went from generation to generation where the size of transistors decreased by a factor of $\sqrt{2}$. This ensured that the number of transistors per unit area doubled every generation. Till 2010 these transistors were being used to create more sophisticated processors and increase the on-chip memory. However, after 2010 the extra transistors are being used to increase the number of processors (cores) per chip mainly because the gains from increasing the complexity of a core are limited, and high power dissipation is a very major issue.

Off late, Moore's law is showing signs of saturation. Current feature sizes (smallest feature that can be fabricated) are at 7 nm as of 2020, and can only decrease till 5 nm. Beyond that, the size of a feature on silicon will become too small to fabricate. A 5 nm structure is only 25 silicon atoms wide! The trends seem to indicate that we will move to more application specific processors that will solve specific problems from different domains, particularly from the machine learning domain. Subsequently we need to move to non-silicon technologies.

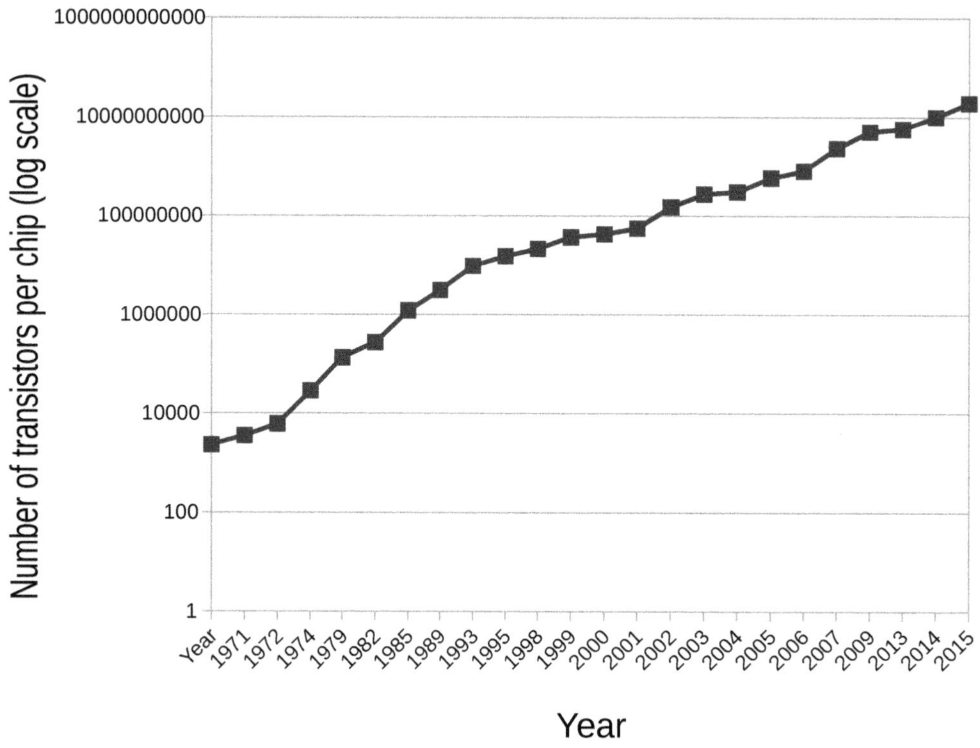

Figure 1.1: Transistors per chip over the last 50 years (adapted with modifications, source: [Rupp, 2017], licensed and distributed under the Creative Commons ShareAlike 4.0 license [ccs,])

Definition 1

It is an empirical observation that the number of transistors in a chip doubles every 1-2 years. Ever since it was proposed by Gordon Moore in 1965, it continued to hold till roughly 2012. Henceforth, the rate of technological change slowed down.

Most semiconductor companies move from one technology generation to another, where the feature size reduces by a factor of $\sqrt{2}$ every generation. The feature size is defined as the dimensions of the smallest possible structure that can be reliably fabricated on silicon.

In 1974 another empirical law was proposed by Robert Dennard, which is known as *Dennard scaling*. Dennard postulated that the performance per Watt also grows exponentially (tracks Moore's law). This will only happen if we can increase the frequency, and the total number of instructions processed per cycle every generation. This has ceased to happen since 2006 mainly because the power dissipation of chips outpaced gains in performance.

Let us now go through the organisation of the book keeping in mind that till roughly 2010 our main aim was to take advantage of Moore's law and Dennard scaling. The goal posts have changed henceforth.

1.1   Moving from In-order to Out-of-order Pipelines

A basic course on computer architecture talks about a simple 5-stage in-order pipeline (see Section 2.1 for more explanation). An in-order pipeline is a very basic pipeline where instructions are processed in program order (order in which they appear in the program). This is unfortunately an inefficient implementation. It is necessary to further complicate the processor.

A naive approach to do this is to issue multiple instructions in the same cycle. This augments our classic 5-stage pipeline that moved only one instruction from one stage to the next in a single cycle. In this case we move a bundle of k ($k = 2$, or $k = 4$) instructions from one stage to the next. This process does introduce complexities in the interlock and forwarding logic; however, for the time being let us assume that all of these are solved problems. Let us compare the increase in the instructions per cycle (IPC) for a standard set of SPEC benchmarks [Henning, 2006] with this technique. The SPEC benchmark suite is a standard set of programs that is used to evaluate the performance of processors.

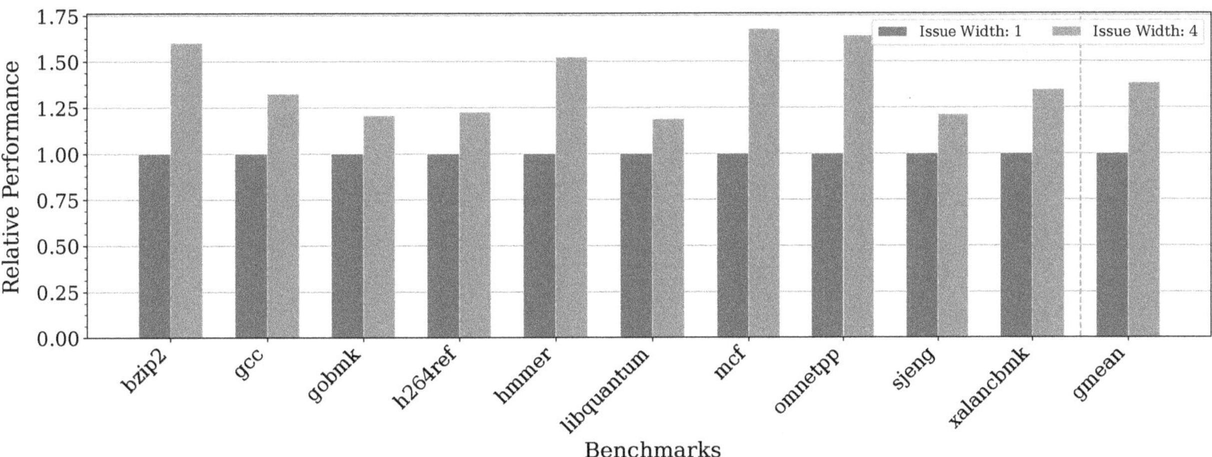

Figure 1.2: Performance comparison between 4-issue and 1-issue in-order processors (SPEC CPU® 2006 benchmarks(`https://www.spec.org`))

Figure 1.2 shows the comparison of the performance (inversely proportional to the simulated execution time) between a 4-issue and a 1-issue in-order pipeline. A 4-issue in-order pipeline creates bundles of at most four instructions and processes/executes all of them in one go. This requires four times the number of functional units. For example, if we want to execute four add instructions in parallel, we need four adders instead of just one adder as in a simple pipeline. We expect this pipeline to be much faster than traditional processors that we have all studied in a basic computer architecture course. The traditional pipeline is a 1-issue pipeline, where only one instruction is processed every cycle. However, as we see from Figure 1.2, this is not the case. The performance does not increase proportionately and it looks like our investment in adding more on-chip resources has not paid off. A 4-issue in-order pipeline just gives us 37.5% more performance on an average. Here, **performance** is defined as the

reciprocal of the execution time. The results were generated using an architectural simulator (the Tejas Simulator[TM]) that is discussed in Appendix B. An architectural simulator is a virtual processor that simulates the behaviour and timing of a real processor. It can be used to execute full programs (the SPEC CPU 2006 benchmarks in this case) and estimate their execution time and power. Additionally, we can get detailed statistics for each execution unit in the pipeline and in the memory system.

Let us thus move ahead and break the in-order assumption. This means that it is not necessary to execute instructions in program order. Consider the code shown in Figure 1.3. Assume that we can process/execute a maximum of two instructions per cycle. Given the fact that the code has strict dependences [1] between consecutive instructions, it is not possible to execute most pairs of consecutive instructions in parallel if we stick to in-order processors – executing them in program order. However, if we are allowed to pick instructions at will and execute them without affecting the correctness of the program, we could achieve a much higher performance. Such processors are known as out-of-order (OOO) processors. These processors do not execute instructions in program order; however, they respect all data and control dependences.

Figure 1.3 shows a code snippet written in the *SimpleRisc* assembly language (see Appendix A). The code with a 2-issue in-order pipeline takes 5 cycles, whereas with an OOO processor, we need 3 cycles. This is a performance improvement of 40%.

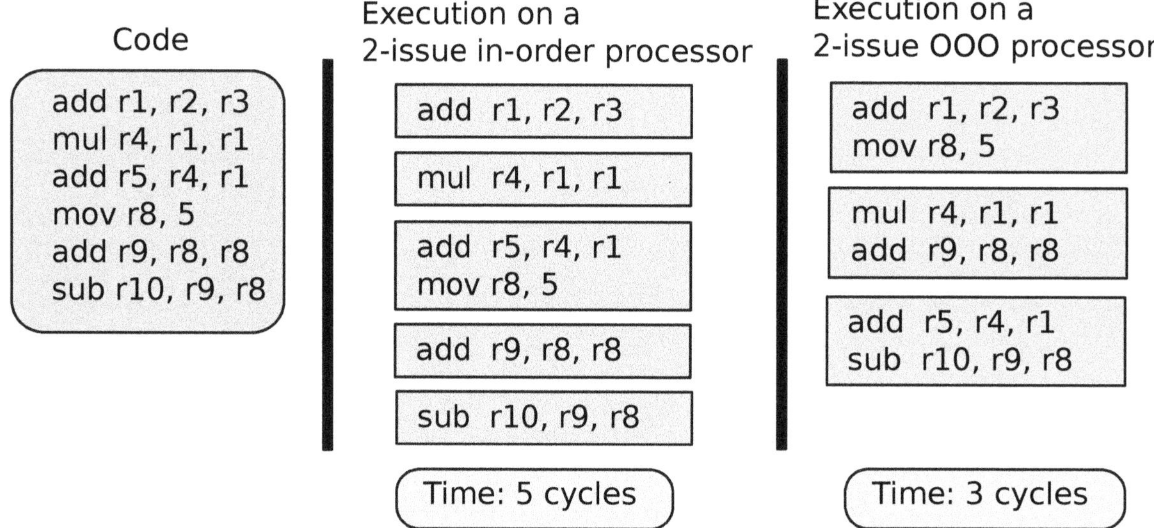

Figure 1.3: Execution on in-order and out-of-order processors

Clearly, in this case an OOO processor is the winner. To minimise the execution time, we need to increase the number of instructions we can process per cycle. This is quantified as the IPC (instructions per cycle) metric. To maximise the IPC, having more choice is better, and in this case OOO processors offer a far greater degree of freedom with respect to choosing instructions for execution. However, this sounds simpler than it actually is. Intelligently choosing instructions and executing them in parallel is very difficult to do in practice. We need to ensure the correctness of the program by ensuring that no dependences are being violated, all the branches are resolved correctly, and nothing wrong is being written to memory. We devote 4 chapters to study the intricate mechanisms involved in this process. Ensuring that we can pick as many independent instructions as possible without violating any correctness constraints is difficult and requires a complete redesign of our basic processor.

---

[1]Note that there are two English words, "dependence" and "dependency" – both refer to the quality of being dependent. However, we shall consistently use the term "dependence" in this book because "dependency" typical refers to a geopolitical entity that is controlled by a higher power. The plural form will be "dependences".

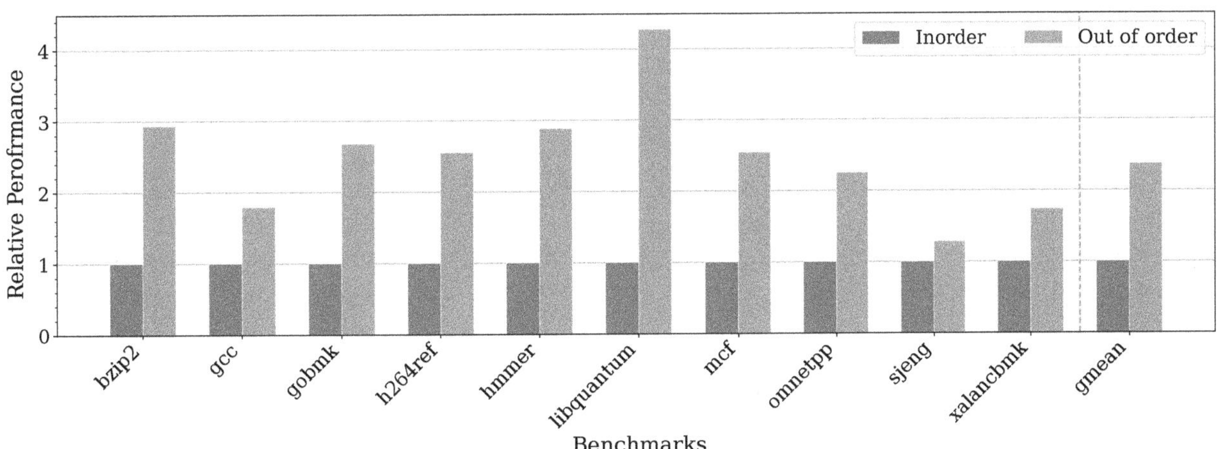

Figure 1.4: Performance comparison: in-order vs out-of-order processors

Figure 1.4 shows the comparison of the performance obtained for a 4-issue in-order pipeline and a 4-issue OOO pipeline. We observe that we get a mean performance improvement of 133% by using an OOO pipeline. This is significant in the world of processor design, and explains why most desktop and server processors today use OOO pipelines. We shall discuss OOO pipelines in Chapters 2, 3, 4, and 5.

1.2 Moving to Multicore Processors

Figure 1.5 shows the historical increase in processor (single core) performance over the last two decades. A *core* is defined as a single processing unit that has one pipeline and possibly a set of caches (data cache and instruction cache).

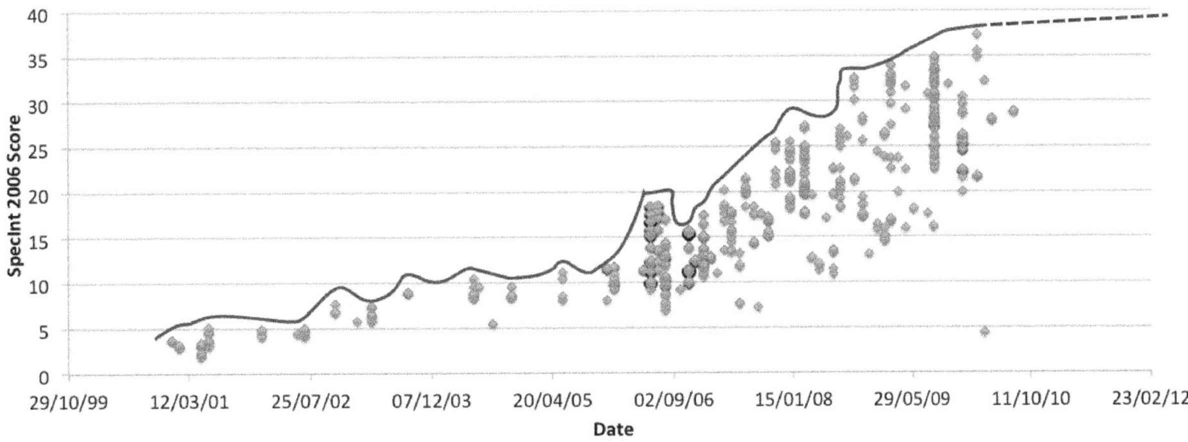

Figure 1.5: Improvement in processor performance over the years

As we can see, from 2009 onwards, the processor (single core) performance has saturated. Due to limitations imposed by power, temperature, and complexity, and sometimes the available amount of instruction level parallelism in the code, the performance could not increase further. Given the fact that investing on a single core produced little returns, we needed to move towards multicore processors, where we have many cores that can either work on their own, or cooperatively to solve a problem.

It was thus found to be necessary to move from sequential programs that we all love to write to parallel programs. In parallel programs, the programmer needs to tell the compiler and hardware which parts of the code can run in parallel. For example, consider a loop with N iterations, where the iterations are independent of each other – they do not have data dependences. In this case, we run the code corresponding to each of the N iterations, on a different core. We can use N cores for this purpose. In theory we can speedup up the program by N times. However, in practice the number will be much lower. This is because often there will be some dependences between the iterations. These need to be managed by complex hardware and software mechanisms. Such actions slow down the program.

Multicore processors and parallel processing are very rich areas. People have been working on parallel programming models for at least the last three decades, and have also been designing hardware to ensure that parallel programs running on different cores run efficiently. Furthermore, if there is a need for them to communicate with each other then the hardware needs to facilitate this with appropriate correctness guarantees.

1.2.1 GPUs

The first category of hardware that we describe in this space is the area of graphics processors (known as GPUs). GPUs were originally used for processing graphics and rendering complex scenes. Hence, GPUs have traditionally been used in games, CAD software, and software to create computer graphics videos. However, the last 10 years have seen a massive adoption of GPUs in conventional high performance computing such as numerical simulation, weather prediction, and finite element modelling of physical systems. GPUs are a very good fit for such applications because they consist of hundreds of very small cores – 512 to 4096 as of 2020. These cores are capable of performing arithmetic and logical calculations. If we have highly computation intensive numerical code without a lot of branches and irregular memory accesses, a GPU can be used. For example, if we want to compute the direction a cyclone will take, or its severity after three days, we need to perform a very large and complex weather simulation. Such programs are often based on large matrix operations, which have a lot of mutually independent computations, and this is where massively parallel GPUs can be used. A typical server processor can provide a maximum throughput of 10 GFLOPS (1 GFLOP $= 10^9$ floating point operations per second). In comparison the latest GPU can provide roughly 15 TFLOPS (1 TFLOP $= 1000$ GFLOPS) of computational throughput.

It should be, however, understood that GPUs are useful for a limited set of programs, particularly those that are based on large matrix operations. However, in general for parallel programs with complex communication patterns between different programs running on different cores, GPUs are not suitable. We shall delve into such issues in Chapter 6.

1.2.2 Large Multicore Processors

Since GPUs are not particularly very useful for complicated parallel programs, we need to create large multicore processors, where we have 10-20 cores on a single chip. These cores have complicated OOO pipelines. The OOO pipelines can support programs with complex branching and memory access patterns. However, for such processors to be effectively used, it is necessary to create hardware support for their communication model. Communication is typically done through reads and writes to the memory system. Hence, we need a fairly sophisticated memory system that can provide a set of intuitive correctness guarantees to parallel programs such that they behave more or less like equivalent sequential programs. Such mechanisms are known as cache coherence and memory consistency (see Chapter 9), and necessitate a lot of elaborate hardware support.

Transactional Memory

Parallel programming on multicore processors is regarded as difficult. As long as expert programmers in industry were writing such code, this was acceptable. However, to take parallel programming to the masses, it is necessary to have good programming models. These models need to ensure the correctness of programs, and also make it easy to write such programs. Furthermore, if there are some special programming mechanisms that are a part of these models, we might need additional hardware support.

Parallel programming models have been getting easier with time particularly with the parallel hardware becoming very cheap. The moment something needs to permeate to the masses, it needs to become very easy to use. Normally, programming languages have special functions and markers to mark regions as *parallel*.

However, to take things one step further, a new model that has been proposed, and is becoming increasingly popular is *transactional memory*. Here, we mark regions of code that need to be executed in parallel and should also appear to execute instantaneously. This is a very simple programming model, and even beginners can write a complex parallel program with little training. There are two kinds of transactional memory: software transactional memory (STM) and hardware transactional memory (HTM). STMs typically do not require any hardware support, whereas, HTMs require hardware support. The latter are far more efficient; however, they require complex hardware changes. We shall discuss such trade-offs in Chapter 9.

1.3 High Performance Memory System

To support high performance multi-core processors, we need a fast and high bandwidth memory system. The memory system needs to deliver both data and instructions to these cores such that they do not get stalled due to a lack of instructions or data. This requires us to design a large system of memories (known as *cache banks*), where we can quickly locate data, and supply it to the requesting cores. We shall see in Chapter 7 that there are many ways of very efficiently designing memories such that we can decrease their access times, and increase their bandwidth.

There are two kinds of memories that we typically have in modern architectures: on-chip caches based on SRAM (static RAM) cells, and off-chip memories made of DRAM (dynamic RAM) cells. We dedicate one chapter to study techniques to design efficient SRAM memories (Chapter 7), and one more chapter to study the design of DRAM memories (Chapter 10).

Just having a fast memory structure is not enough. It is important to route messages swiftly to these memory elements and get quick responses. We thus need an extremely responsive on-chip network that can provide low latency and high bandwidth. When the number of cores and on-chip memory elements was limited to single digits, the design of the on-chip network (referred to as the NoC, network-on-chip) was not very important. However, in modern processors with 20+ cores, and a similar number of memory elements, the NoC has suddenly become important.

Furthermore, we have processors such as the Intel® Xeon Phi™ processor with 70-80 cores. In such processors, the challenge of designing fast and power efficient interconnects is even more severe. Along with the traditional drivers – performance and power – we have several other issues with today's NoCs such as congestion, avoiding network traffic deadlocks, effective routing, and reliability. These issues will be covered in detail in Chapter 8.

1.4 Power, Temperature, Parameter Variation, and Reliability

Till the end of the late 90s, power was not considered an important design criteria. However, very soon power consumption became a first order design criteria. There were several reasons for this. The first was that increased power led to increased temperature. Unfortunately, leakage power (static power) is a super-linear function of the temperature. Thus, this leads to a positive feedback loop between power and temperature. Increased power dissipation leads to higher temperature, which in turn leads to increased leakage power, and so on. In extreme cases, this process might not converge and can lead to a condition called *thermal runaway* where the leakage power increases prohibitively. The results of this can be catastrophic. Additionally, there are other physical limitations: limits to conventional air cooling, and for embedded devices the battery capacity is limited. Hence, we need to design techniques to reduce power and energy consumption. This is discussed in Chapter 11.

To further compound the problem of high leakage power, we have the issue of *parameter variation* – variations in the fabrication process, supply voltage, and temperature. *Process variation* is the variation induced in the physical properties of transistors and interconnects due to the limitations in the physical processes used to create such devices. For example, to fabricate a 14 nm structure, we use light with a wavelength of 193 nm. This leads to non-uniformity in the design, and often when we are trying to print a rectangle on silicon, we actually fabricate a rounded rectangle with deformed edges. This leads to two pernicious effects: high leakage power and low performance. It is necessary to design fabrication methods and computer architectures to effectively combat this problem, and design hardware that is relatively immune to the negative effects of process variation. In addition, there can be fluctuations in the temperature of different regions of a chip due to a varying amount of power consumption. High temperature makes circuits dissipate more leakage power. We also can have fluctuations in the supply voltage because of resistive and inductive drops in the chip's power grid. If the supply voltage reduces, the transistors become slower. If we consider all of these effects, designing a high performance processor becomes fairly difficult unless we provide large margins for performance and power. We shall look at state of the art solutions in Chapter 12.

Other than increasing leakage power, there are many more reasons why high chip temperature is considered to be absolutely undesirable. High temperature increases the rate of failure of wires and transistors exponentially. If we have high temperature for a sustained period, then we can have permanent failures where for example a wire gets snapped, or a transistor gets destroyed. Furthermore, as we shall see in Chapter 12 high temperature can also induce transistor ageing, where its properties gradually degrade with time. Hence, there is now a large body of research dedicated to reducing power and temperature. Note that it is not necessary that a power control algorithm will always reduce the peak temperature. Here, the "peak temperature" is important because this is where we will have the highest rate of transistor and interconnect ageing. Similarly, temperature control algorithms need not be the best schemes to keep power consumption in check.

Other than faults caused by high temperature, there are sadly many other mechanisms that can cause a chip to malfunction either temporarily or permanently. One such cause is bit flips due to the impact of alpha particles or cosmic rays. These are known as *soft errors*. A soft error is typically a very short and transient phenomenon where an impact with a charged ion leads to a current pulse, which can flip the value of a bit that is either being computed by an ALU or stored in a latch. There are many ways to make circuits relatively more immune to soft errors. We shall look at such methods in Chapter 12 along with some other lesser known methods of failure.

1.5   Security

Nowadays, no processor design effort or course on computer architecture is complete without discussing the issue of security – both software and hardware. Security is gradually becoming more important because processors are beginning to get embedded everywhere. In the 70s computers were confined to either large companies or universities. However, today everybody has several computers with her: a phone, a tablet, and a smart watch. Small processors are embedded in smart glasses, and medical devices such as pacemakers. Performance and power efficiency are nevertheless still very worthy goals to pursue. However, we also need to ensure that these devices run correctly in the field. Even after taking all the steps to guarantee the reliability of the device, we need to ensure that malicious users cannot subvert its security measures, and either cause the device to malfunction, or steal sensitive data belonging to other users. Imagine a hacker breaking into a pacemaker. The hacker can cause it to fail, thus endangering the life of the patient.

Hence, it is very important to ensure that both code and data are secure. We shall discuss different methods to secure code and data in both the processor and the memory in Chapter 13.

1.6   Architectures for Machine Learning

General purpose computing is approaching its limits. The feature sizes have already reached 7 nm. They are not expected to go below 5 nm. Subsequently, traditional silicon based architectures will saturate because faster and more power efficient transistors may not be available unless there is a significant shift in the technology. Till now this was not a problem. Architects were always able to leverage improvements in process technology to design more efficient processor designs. For example, with reducing transistor sizes architects were able to place larger L2 caches on chip. They could then further propose many techniques to make caches and the interconnecting network more efficient. But with this process expected to come to a stop, the next frontier is to build application-specific processors. One of the most promising applications is machine learning (ML) accelerators. There are also many allied fields that use ML techniques such as computer vision, speech processing, and data analytics. All of them will benefit with such application-specific ML accelerators.

We shall discuss different architectures for machine learning in Chapter 14. This field has significantly grown and matured over the last 5 years. We now have numerous architectures for a host of machine learning algorithms. The most prominent class of architectures try to optimise the execution of CNNs (convolutional neural networks). CNNs have by far seen the maximum number of applications in the field of image, speech, and data processing. These techniques are generic in nature and can also be used to create a very large number of other ML architectures as well.

Part I

Processor Design

2

Out-of-order Pipelines

Processing an instruction is the most important task that modern processors perform. Hence, it is very important for us to understand the life cycle of an instruction from the time that it is fetched to the time that it is removed from the processor after completing its execution. As we shall see in this chapter, processing an instruction efficiently is a very complicated task, and we need very elaborate hardware structures to achieve this task.

We shall start our interesting journey in Section 2.1 where we shall understand the design of a simple conventional processor. The design of such a processor is typically taught in most first-level undergraduate courses. It is called an in-order processor because all the instructions are processed in program order. This processor is unfortunately very inefficient and as we shall see in Section 2.2, its performance can be significantly enhanced by processing more instructions simultaneously, and by executing them in an order that is different from their program order. Such kind of processors are known as out-of-order (OOO) processors (described in Section 2.3).

Designing an OOO processor that can process multiple instructions per cycle is a very difficult task. First, we need to handle branch instructions and try to predict their outcome (taken or not-taken) before they are executed. This will ensure that we are able to fill our processor with a large number of instructions. By buffering a large number of instructions within the processor we increase the likelihood of finding a set of mutually independent instructions whose operands are ready. These instructions can then be executed in parallel. We can thus increase the instruction execution throughput, and quickly execute large programs.

However, there are significant correctness issues that crop up. For example, we need to ensure that if an interrupt from a hardware device arrives, we can pause the execution of the program, handle the interrupt, and later on resume the execution of the program from exactly the same point. This requires us to maintain the state of the program in dedicated structures. This process of pause and recovery can be achieved seamlessly and without the explicit knowledge of the program. Finally, handling load and store operations is tricky because they are two-part operations: the first part computes the address, and the second part executes the memory instruction.

We shall not discuss all the techniques in this chapter. They will be discussed in the subsequent chapters. In this chapter, our aim is to introduce the issues, provide a broad overview of OOO pipelines, discuss the complexities, and motivate the reader to read the next few chapters. We do presume some background in instruction set architectures, assembly language programming, and the design of a simple processing unit (elaborated further in Section 2.1).

It is important for the reader to brush up her fundamentals on traditional in-order pipelines first. Then only she can understand the issues and nuances of more advanced designs. Hence, we discuss this topic first.

## 2.1	Overview of In-Order Pipelines

Let us start this section with a disclaimer. We expect the reader to be broadly familiar with basic computer architecture. The reader can refer to the entry level textbook on computer organisation and architecture by the author [Sarangi, 2015] for a deeper treatment of these topics. This section is only meant to provide a very cursory overview of processor design and pipelining.

Specifically, here are the list of topics that the reader should be familiar with.

- Instruction Set Architecture
  - RISC and CISC instruction sets
  - Memory, branch, and ALU instructions
  - Loads and stores to memory
  - Instruction set encoding

- Basics of Processor Design
  - Fetch, decode, execute, memory access and write-back stages
  - Notion of selecting data from multiple sources using multiplexers.
  - Basics of pipelining and the notion of stalls

- Memory system
  - Notion of caches: instruction and data cache.
  - Idea of a memory hierarchy

This section is meant to give the readers a brief overview of pipelining, in specific, conventional in-order pipelines. Even though this section is meant to be self contained; however, it does assume that the reader is broadly familiar with instruction set architectures and at least the design of a non-pipelined processor.

### 2.1.1	Processor Design

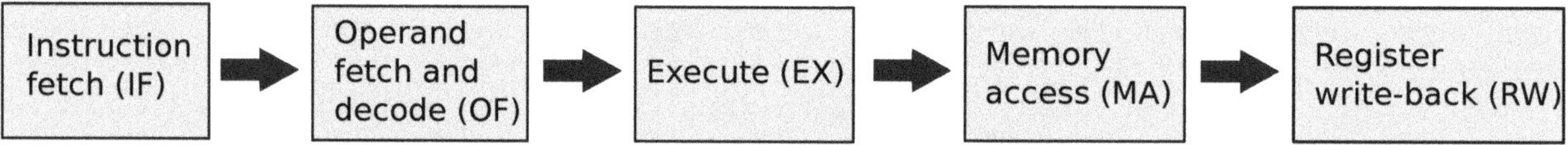

Figure 2.1: Five stages in a processor

Every basic processor consists of five stages as shown in Figure 2.1: instruction fetch (IF), decode and operand fetch (OF), execute (EX), memory access (MA), and register write-back (RW). We basically divide a processor's work into five logical stages such that the overlap between two stages in terms of functionality is negligible. Five is not a sacrosanct number. In alternative implementations of a processor, we can divide it into let's say three, four or six stages. The number of stages by itself is not important as long as the division of work between stages is done equitably, and with as little overlap as possible. We describe a representative example in this section.

Instruction Fetch Stage (IF)

In this stage, we fetch the contents of an instruction from instruction memory (often this is the instruction cache). Every instruction is uniquely indexed by the PC (program counter), which is a memory address.

In the fetch stage, we primarily do the following:

1. Given the PC, we fetch the instruction from memory. In most processors, this memory is a cache, known as the instruction cache (i-cache).

2. We compute the PC of the next instruction. This can either be the current PC plus the size of the instruction (4 or 8 bytes in most RISC processors) or if the instruction is a branch, the next PC can be the address of the branch's target.

3. If the instruction is a function return, then the PC is the value of the return address. The return address is typically stored in a register, or a location in memory.

The instruction fetch stage (IF) per se does not have a non-deterministic delay, and is meant to be simple in such in-order processors. Of course, complexities can get introduced if we assume a non-ideal memory. Recall that a cache contains a subset of all memory addresses. If we have a cache hit – we find an address in the cache – then the access is very fast. However, if we do not find the address in the cache leading to a cache miss, then it might take a long time to fetch the contents of the instruction. The IF stage needs to be stalled (kept idle) during that time.

Decode and Operand Fetch Stage (OF)

In this stage we decode the instruction. This means that we cleanly separate the different components of the instruction: opcode (operation code), ids of registers, and embedded constants.

Based on the instruction's opcode, we generate control signals to control the rest of the elements in the pipeline such that the instruction executes properly. A little bit of an explanation is due here. The part of the processor that generates all the control signals (single or multi-bit) is known as the *control logic*. The part of the processor's pipeline that creates, propagates, and uses the control signals is known as the *control path*. The rest of the processor that is involved with the storage of data, memory accesses, and computation is referred to as the *data path*.

After the ids of the registers are known, we access the register file (array of registers), and read the values of the source registers. There are some instructions such as the *return* instruction that often have an implicit operand – the return address register. This instruction is used to return from a function. Note that while calling a function we save the address of the next instruction. This is known as the *return address*. Most RISC processors save the return address in a dedicated return address register. Whereas, CISC processors store them on the stack. For a RISC ISA, we need to read the value of the return address from the register file while processing a return instruction in the operand fetch stage. Thus, the return address register is the implicit operand, whose value needs to be read.

Finally, some instructions embed constants in them. These constants can either be values that are to be used in arithmetic instructions or offsets from base registers (in load and store instructions), or offsets from the PC (in branches). In this stage, we need to extract these constants (known as *immediates*) and expand them to 32 or 64 bit values.

Thus, to summarise, in this stage we (1) generate all the control signals, (2) read values from the register file, and (3) and extract the constants embedded in the instruction. These values along with the contents of the instruction form the *instruction packet*. The instruction packet is forwarded to the subsequent stage.

Execute Stage (EX)

This stage has three major functions:

1. Perform the computation such as addition, subtraction, or multiplication.

2. If the instruction is a memory instruction (load or store), then compute the memory address. This is an addition operation. We add the offset to the contents of a register that contains the *base address* (base-offset addressing mode).

3. For a branch instruction compute the branch target. Most branches are relative. This means that the offset (embedded as a constant in the instruction) needs to be added to the PC to get the address of the branch target. This addition is performed in this stage. Subsequently, the branch target is sent to the fetch stage.

Memory Access Stage (MA)

Note that a memory access instruction is a two-stage operation. In the first stage, we need to compute the memory address by adding the offset to the contents of a base register. This was achieved in the EX (execute) stage. The next task is to access the data memory and perform the load or store.

1. A load operation has two arguments: memory address and destination register id. A dedicated circuit accesses the memory with the given address, retrieves 4 bytes or 8 bytes (depending upon the architecture), and stores it in the destination register.

2. A store operation does not have any destination registers. It has two arguments: memory address and source register id. A dedicated circuit takes the contents from the register, and stores it in memory at the given memory address.

For a memory instruction, we shall use the term *PC address* to indicate the address of the of the instruction in memory. To fetch the instruction, we need to set the program counter to the PC address. In comparison, the *memory address* is the address computed by the memory instruction in the EX stage. This instruction is sent to the memory system. In Section 7.2, we shall introduce the concept of address translation where the virtual address generated by the pipeline is translated into a physical address that is sent to the memory system. We shall use the term *memory address* to refer to either address – the connotation will be clear from the context.

Register Write-back Stage (RW)

This is the last stage of a typical 5-stage pipeline. In this stage, we write the final result – computed by the ALU or loaded from memory – to a register in the register file. If an instruction does not write to a register then nothing is done in this stage.

Additionally, we need to handle some special cases as well. Almost all ISAs have a *call* instruction, which jumps to the first line of a function, and simultaneously writes the return address to a register or a memory location. The latter depends on the instruction set. In instruction sets such as ARM® v7 the return address is saved in a dedicated register and in the Intel® x86 architecture the return address is saved in memory (top of the stack). Let us assume the former case where the return address is saved in a register. In this case, the return address will be written to the dedicated return address register in the RW stage.

Summary

A simple processor consists of these five stages. Here, a stage is being defined as a dedicated part of the processor's logic that has a very specialised function. Note that depending upon the instruction set, we can have more stages, or we might even remove or fuse a couple of stages.

The simplest type of such processors finish all of this work in a single clock cycle. The clock cycle begins with the instruction fetch stage getting activated, and ends when the results of the instruction

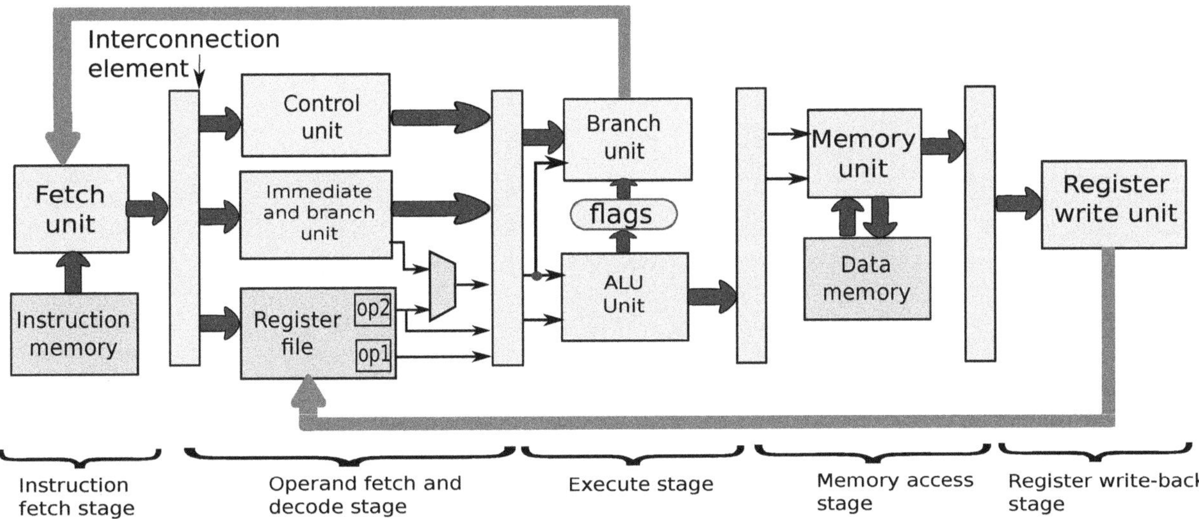

Figure 2.2: A simple RISC processor (adapted from [Sarangi, 2015]). Note the five stages in the design. The design has been purposefully simplified and a lot of the complex aspects of the processor have not been shown. Note the vertical rectangular boxes between stages. These are interconnection elements, where signals and values from the left stage move to components in the right stage.

have been written to the register file. We shall refer to such a processor as a *single-cycle processor* henceforth. Let us summarise our discussion by taking a look at Figure 2.2.

Figure 2.2 shows the design of a single-cycle RISC processor. The fetch stage reads in the instruction from the instruction memory. Subsequently, this is sent to the decode stage via an interconnection element, which in this case is essentially a set of copper wires and multiplexers that connects a set of sources in the left stage to a set of destinations in the right stage (vertical rectangle in the figure). In the second stage (decode and operand fetch), we compute the control signals, the values of immediates (constants) and branch offsets, and read the values of registers. For the second operand in a typical RISC instruction, there is a choice between an immediate and the value read from a register file. Hence, we need to add a multiplexer in this stage. For a much more detailed discussion the reader can refer to [Sarangi, 2015].

In the next stage, which is the execute stage, we perform arithmetic and logical computations, and we also compute the outcome of branch instructions. Conditional branch instructions in modern instruction sets are often evaluated on the basis of the outcome of the last compare instruction. The result of the last compare instruction is stored in a dedicated *flags* register. In addition, for processing return instructions, it is necessary to send the value of the return address read from the register file to the branch unit.

Subsequently, we forward the instruction to the memory access stage, where we perform a load or a store (if required). The last stage is the register write-back stage where we write to the registers (if we have to). Here, we need to handle the special case of the function *call* instruction, where we write the value of the next PC (current PC + ⟨*size of the instruction*⟩) to the return address register in the register file.

Finally, note the presence of two backward paths: one from the branch unit to the instruction fetch unit, and the other from the register write-back unit to the register file.

Important Point 1

A clock cycle *is a very basic concept in the world of digital electronics. A clock produces a periodic signal. It is typically a square wave; however, it need not be. We can think of a clock as a signal, where a particular event of interest happens periodically. The duration between two such consecutive events is defined as a* clock period. *The reciprocal of the clock period is defined as the* clock frequency. *The unit of clock frequency is Hz, where 1 Hz means that an event of interest happens once every second.*

A clock is a very useful feature in a digital circuit. It gives all the elements a time base. The computation of sub-circuits starts at the beginning of a clock cycle, and finishes by the end of the clock cycle. This helps us have a uniform notion of time across an electronic circuit (such as a processor). Finally, in most circuits the results computed in a clock cycle are stored in a storage element such as a flip-flop by the end of the cycle. The results are visible to another part of the circuit at the beginning of the next clock cycle.

2.1.2   Notion of Pipelining

Now that we know all about a single-cycle processor, we are ready to take a look at its intricacies and explore all of its nooks and crannies.

Consider the single-cycle processor as described in Section 2.1.1. It has five stages, and instructions pass from stage to stage. When the IF stage is active, the rest of the stages are inactive. Similarly, when the MA (memory access) stage is active, the rest of the stages are inactive. If we naively assume that each stage takes up 20% of the area of the overall processor, then at any point of time 80% of the processor is inactive. This clearly does not represent a situation where processing an instruction is happening in a very efficient manner. In an efficient system, all the parts of the processor are expected to be used at any point of time.

However, since one instruction has to move through the stages, the only way to increase efficiency is to process multiple instructions at the same time. When one instruction is in the RW stage, one more can be in the EX stage, and yet one more instruction might be getting fetched from instruction memory. This is the crux of the idea called *pipelining*.

Consider the following snippet of assembly code:

```
1   add r1, r2, r3
2   sub r4, r5, r6
3   mul r7, r8, r8
4   mov r9, r10
5   add r11, r12, r13
```

Here, we have five instructions. There are no dependences between them. Let us send the first instruction (instruction *1*) to the processor first. When it reaches the second stage (operand fetch (OF)), the IF stage will become free. At this point of time, let us use the IF stage instead of allowing it to remain idle. We can fetch instruction *2* when instruction *1* is in the second stage (OF stage). On similar lines, when instruction *2* reaches the second stage (OF) and instruction *1* reaches the third stage (EX), we can start fetching the third instruction (instruction *3*). Figure 2.3 graphically depicts the progress of instructions through the pipeline. Such diagrams are known as *pipeline diagrams*.

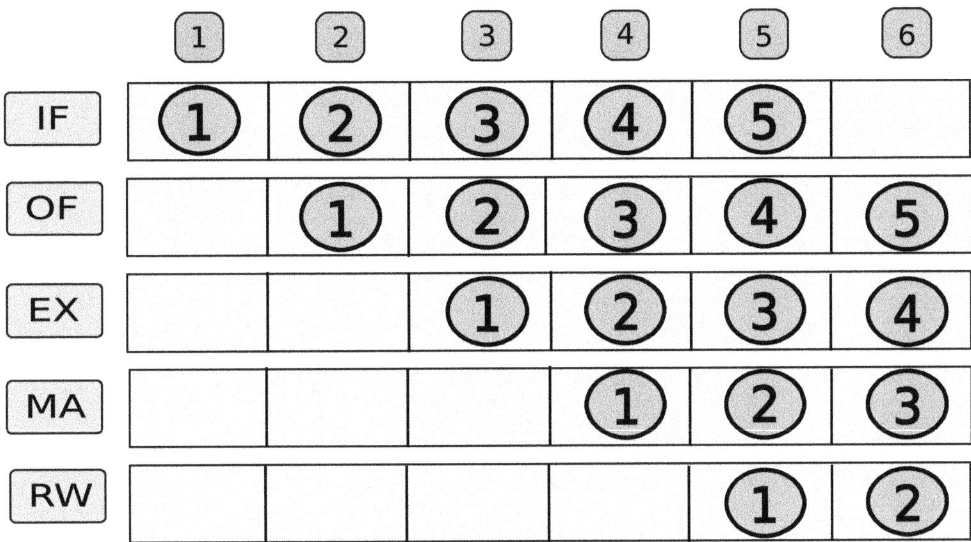

Figure 2.3: Sequence of actions in a pipeline

Implementing a Pipelined Processor

Pipelining in principle as shown in Figure 2.3 appears promising, where we can keep all parts of the processor busy. This should translate to higher efficiency. Sadly, at this point of time we are not in a position to evaluate exactly how much we gain in terms of efficiency.

Let us instead digress a little bit, and understand how to implement pipelining. Let us first consider a single-cycle processor (as described in Section 2.1.1), where the entire processing of an instruction finishes within a single processor cycle. We need to first demarcate different regions of the processor, where each region has a unique function and it overlaps as little as possible with other regions. We have already done that in Section 2.1.1 by defining five stages within a processor, where an instructions passes through the stages sequentially. Now, we need to ensure that an instruction can pass seamlessly from stage to stage. Imagine a person who changes his hotel every day. On day 1 he is in Hotel 1, and on day 2 he is in Hotel 2, and so on. Since he fully checks out, he needs to carry all his belongings with him, and move from one hotel to the other. The case with instructions is similar. In this case, an instruction needs to move from stage to stage with all its control signals (signals to control the data path) and temporary values.

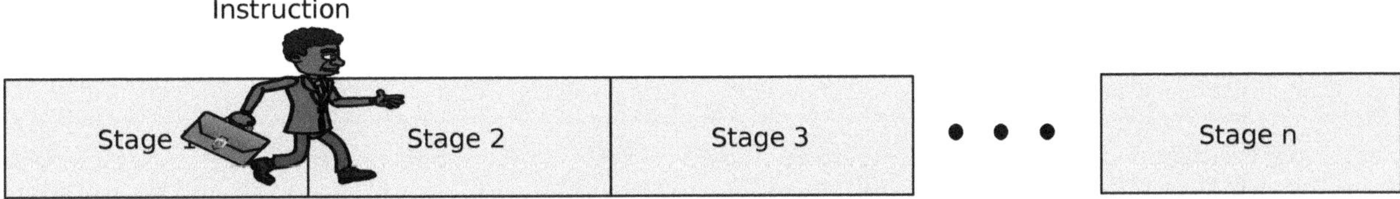

Figure 2.4: Instruction passing from stage to stage along with the instruction packet

An instruction along with its control signals and temporary values is referred to as the *instruction packet*. The instruction packet is like a traveller's briefcase that contains all the necessary information that an instruction requires to execute (see Figure 2.4).

Let us create a hardware mechanism for the instruction packet to move between stages. After every processor stage, we add a latch. A latch is a small memory that stores the instruction packet[1]. It can be made of flip-flops (refer to standard textbooks on digital logic such as [Taub and Schilling, 1977, Lin, 2011]). Each flip-flop typically reads in new data at the downward edge of the clock (when the clock transitions from 1 to 0 as shown in Figure 2.5). Subsequently, the data is stored inside the flip-flop and is visible as an input to the next stage.

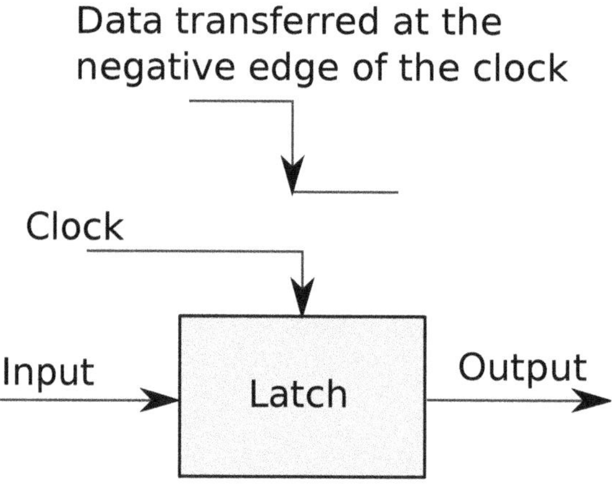

Figure 2.5: A simple clocked latch

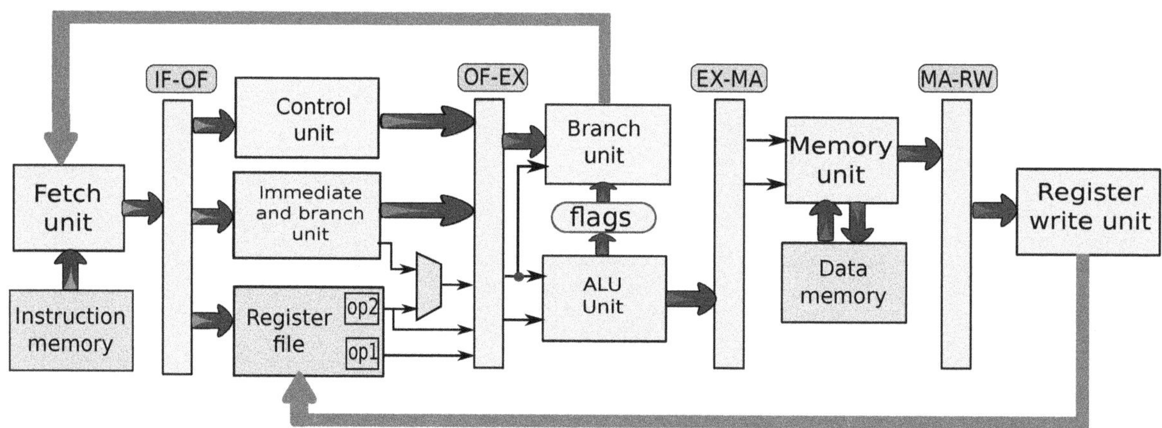

Figure 2.6: 5-stage pipeline with latches between stages

Let us refer to Figure 2.6, where we show the five stages of a typical pipeline. Note that there is a latch (also known as a pipeline register) between successive stages; we just replaced the interconnect element that was present in a single-cycle processor with a latch. The job of the latch is to buffer (or store) the instruction packet. Each of the stages are synchronised by a clock signal. It is provided as an input to each of the pipeline latches. When the clock signal has a negative edge $(1 \rightarrow 0)$, the outputs of stage i are stored in the latch at the end of the stage. They are subsequently visible as inputs to the next stage (stage $(i+1)$).

---

[1] A latch typically refers to a level triggered memory element. However, in this case it refers to an edge triggered memory element.

It is thus possible to ensure that we have five instructions being processed at the same time in the processor. Each instruction occupies a different stage in the pipeline.

2.1.3 Interlocks

Data Hazards

Sadly, the picture is not all that rosy. We can have dependences between instructions. Consider the following piece of code.

```
1   add r1, r2, r3
2   add r4, r1, r3
```

Here, there is a dependence between instructions *1* and *2*. Instruction *1* is writing to register $r1$ and instruction *2* is reading from it. This is called a read-after-write (RAW) dependence. There are problems executing this code.

Consider the fact that when instruction *2* is in the second stage (reading its operands), instruction *1* is in the third stage (execute stage). Since instruction *1* has not written the updated value of $r1$ to the register file, instruction *2* will get an outdated value for register $r1$. Thus, the execution will be **incorrect**. This means that unless we do something then we will have an incorrect execution. This situation is called a data hazard. Refer to Figure 2.7 for a graphical explanation. Recall that such types of diagrams are known as *pipeline diagrams*, where the rows represent pipeline stages, and the columns represent cycles.

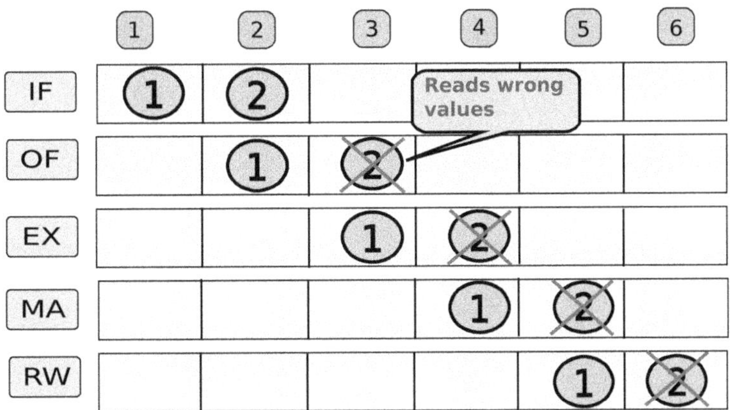

Figure 2.7: Graphical view of a data hazard

Definition 2
A data hazard *is defined as a risk of incorrect execution due to a data dependence not being respected.*

The only way for us to ensure correct execution in this case where there are producer-consumer dependences between instructions is as follows. The first instruction, which is the producer instruction (instruction *1*) can proceed as usual in the pipeline. The behaviour of the second instruction (instruction *2*), which is a consumer needs to be changed such that it gets the correct values of its source registers.

1. In the OF (operand fetch) stage, check for data dependences.

2. If there is a producer instruction in a later stage in the pipeline, then there is a data hazard. Stall the consumer instruction in the OF stage. Do not allow it to proceed.

3. This means that some pipeline stages will remain unused.

4. Finally, after the producer instruction writes to its destination register in its write-back(RW) stage, we can allow the consumer instruction to proceed.

This process will ensure that all data dependences are respected, and data hazards do not lead to incorrect execution. This process is shown in the pipeline diagram in Figure 2.8. We can see that between cycles 3 and 5, there is no activity in the operand fetch(OF) stage. Instruction *2* simply waits there for the operand to be ready. Sadly, later stages of the pipeline expect instructions from the earlier stages. In this case, we need to inject dummy instructions in the pipeline. Such dummy instructions are known as *pipeline bubbles*. A bubble basically refers to an instruction that does not perform any operation. We observe that in Figure 2.8, we insert 3 pipeline bubbles in the EX stage (cycles 4-6), and they subsequently propagate down the pipeline.

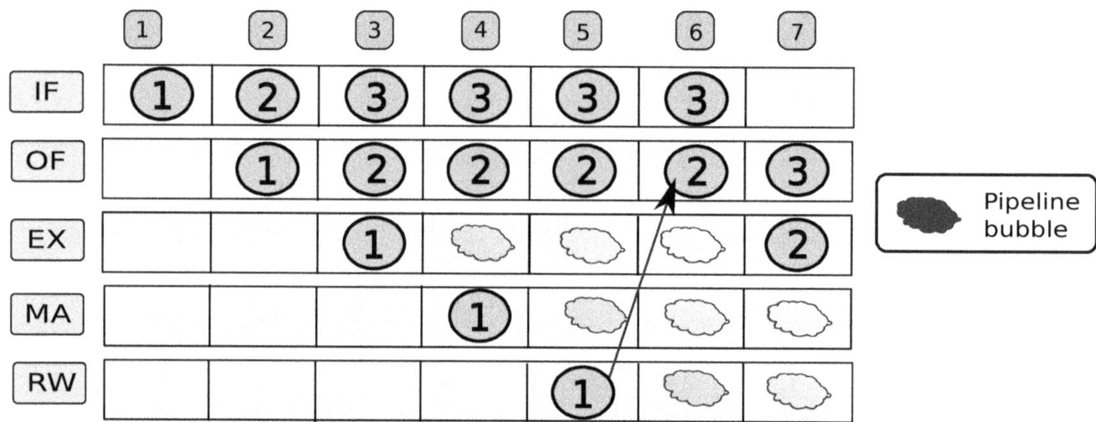

Figure 2.8: Pipeline diagram of a stall (RAW dependence between instructions 1 and 2)

Now assume that there is a RAW dependence between instructions *1* and instruction *3*, and there are no other dependences. In this case the dependence is not between consecutive instructions, but it is between a set of two instructions that have an instruction between them. In this case also, instruction *3* has to wait for instruction *1* to complete its RW (register write-back) stage. However, the time that instruction *3* needs to stall is lower. It is 2 cycles as compared to 3 cycles. Figure 2.9 shows this situation.

Now, it is true that we have avoided data hazards by this technique, which involves stalling the consumer instruction. This method is also known as a *data interlock*. Here, every consumer instruction waits for its producer instruction to produce its value, and write it to the register file before proceeding past the OF (operand fetch) stage. However, this comes at a price, and the price is *efficiency*. Let us see why.

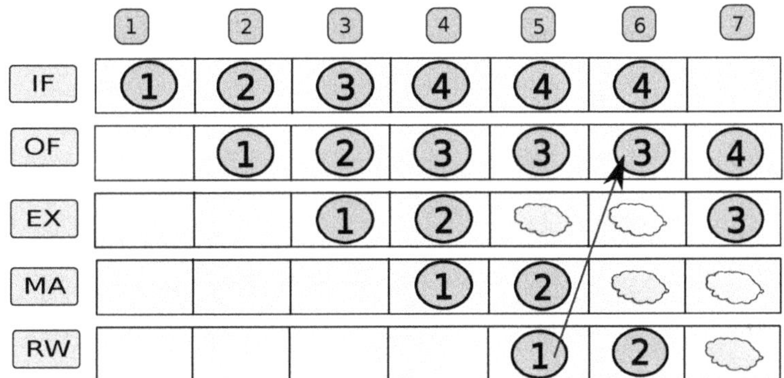

Figure 2.9: Pipeline diagram of a stall (RAW dependence between instructions 1 and 3)

Definition 3
A data interlock *is a method of stalling a consumer instruction in the OF stage till its producer instruction writes the value of the source operand to the register file. While the instruction is stalled, certain pipeline stages are idle (are not processing an active instruction). We can instead say that inactive stages execute invalid (or empty) instructions, which are popularly known as* pipeline bubbles.

Consider a person standing at the end of the last stage of the pipeline – the write-back stage (RW). Ideally, she will observe one instruction getting successfully executed every clock cycle. Thus, the CPI (clock cycles per instruction) will be 1. However, the moment we factor in dependences, we would have to stall the pipeline.

We thus have the following equation:

$$CPI = 1 + stall\_rate \times stall\_penalty \tag{2.1}$$

Here, the ideal CPI is 1 (also the CPI of a single-cycle processor). The term *stall_rate* denotes the probability of a stall per instruction, and the *stall_penalty* is measured in cycles. For example, it is 3 cycles if there is a RAW dependence between consecutive instructions. We see that as we have more dependences, the CPI will increase because of the increased number of stalls. An increase in the CPI basically means that it takes more time to process an instruction, and the processor thus effectively gets slower. This is a bad thing, and should be avoided. However, in the interest of correctness, this needs to be done unless we come up with a better idea.

Control Hazards

Sadly, data hazards are not the only kind of hazards. We also have control hazards, which arise because of specific complications while handling branch instructions.

Consider the following piece of code.

```
1  beq  .foo
2  add  r1,  r1,  r3
3  add  r4,  r5,  r6
4  ...
5  ...
6  .foo:
```

Here, the first instruction (instruction *1*) is a branch instruction. It is a conditional branch instruction, which is dependent on a previous comparison. If that comparison resulted in an equality, then we jump to the label (*.foo*). The next two instructions are regular arithmetic instructions without any dependences between them. Let us assume that the branch instruction, *beq*, is taken. Then, the point to note is that because of the branch instruction, we will not execute instructions *2* and *3*. We will instead branch to the label .foo. In this case, these two instructions are said to be on the *wrong path*.

Definition 4

- Wrong path instructions *are defined as the set of instructions after a branch in program order, which are not executed if the branch is taken. The correct path is defined on similar lines.*

- *A* control hazard *is a situation where there is a risk of executing instructions on the wrong path.*

The question is, "When do we know if instructions *2* and *3* are on the correct path or the wrong path?" We will only know that when instruction *1*, which is the branch, will reach stage 3 – the execute stage. Here, we will consider the result of the last comparison, and see if that resulted in an equality. If yes, then we need to jump to the branch target *.foo*. This means that in the next clock cycle, we will start fetching instructions from the instruction address corresponding to *.foo*.

However, in pipeline stages 1 and 2 (IF and OF), we have two instructions, which are unfortunately on the wrong path. They have been fetched, and unless something is done, they might very well execute and write their results to either the data memory or the register file. This will corrupt the program's state and lead to incorrect execution, which is definitely not desirable. Hence, when we realise that instruction *1* is a taken branch, we can automatically infer that instructions in the two previous stages (instructions *2* and *3*) are on the wrong path. They need to be cancelled. This means that we can set a bit in the instruction packet, which indicates that the instruction packet and the contained instruction is henceforth invalid. We thus convert instructions on the wrong path to pipeline bubbles. This is shown in Figure 2.10. Note that we need to retrospectively convert two instructions to bubbles, when we realise that they are on the wrong path.

We can alternatively say that we have incurred a stall of two cycles when we encounter a taken branch. We can infer a stall because we do not do any useful work in the two cycles after a taken branch. This is called a *branch interlock* where we are basically stalling the pipeline upon encountering a taken branch.

Definition 5
A branch interlock *is a method to stall a pipeline for several cycles to ensure that instructions on the correct path are fetched from instruction memory.*

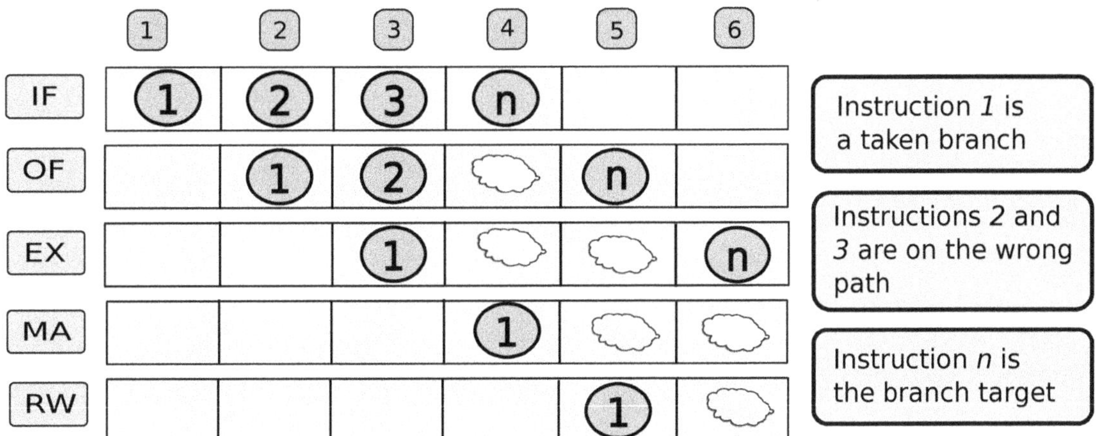

Figure 2.10: Nullifying two instructions on the wrong path

Thus, we can conclude that there are two ways of stalling processors: data interlocks and branch interlocks. Both of them increase the CPI as per Equation 2.1. There exists a trade-off between correctness and performance. To achieve correctness, we had to sacrifice performance.

Delayed Branches

Note that there are many ways of reducing the CPI while preserving correctness. Some of the approaches include (but are not limited to) branch prediction and delayed branches. We shall discuss branch prediction in great detail in Chapter 3. Let us take a very brief look at delayed branches here. Since we stand to lose the two successive cycles after fetching a taken branch, let us instead try to utilise these slots. Let us refer to these time slots as *delay slots*. The idea is to bring two instructions before the branch (which are on the correct path), and place them in the delay slots. This has to be done by the compiler while generating the machine code for the program. The caveat is that these instructions should not determine the direction of the branch instruction and should preferably not have any dependences between them.

Example 1
Reorder the following code snippet assuming that the hardware supports delayed branches. Assume two delay slots.

```
add  r1,  r2,  r3
sub  r4,  r2,  r3
beq  .foo
. . .
. . .
.foo:
```

Answer:

```
beq  .foo
add  r1,  r2,  r3
sub  r4,  r2,  r3
...
...
.foo:
```

Now, after fetching the branch instruction, let us execute the instructions in the delay slots as normal instructions. Since these instructions would have been executed anyway irrespective of the direction of the branch, we have not hampered correctness in any way. Once the direction of the branch is determined in the third cycle (EX stage), we can proceed to fetch instructions from the correct path. This approach does not require any stall cycles, because irrespective of the direction of the branch, we do not execute instructions on the wrong path. Please refer to Example 1 for an example of code reordering in the presence of delayed branches.

For a more extensive introduction to delayed branches, please refer to the book by Sarangi et al. [Sarangi, 2015]. However, the pitfalls of this approach lie in the fact that the compiler has to be aware of the details of the hardware, and this approach will constrain binaries to only work on only one kind of processors. For example, if a given processor has four delay slots, then such binaries will not work on them. This is not desirable. Let us search for a better method.

2.1.4 Forwarding

Data interlocks are inefficient mechanisms when it comes to eliminating the risk of incorrect execution due to data hazards. We stall the pipeline and insert bubbles. In the worst case when there is a data dependence between consecutive instructions, we need to stall for at the most 3 cycles. This represents wasted work. The important question that we need to answer is, "Are the stalls necessary?"

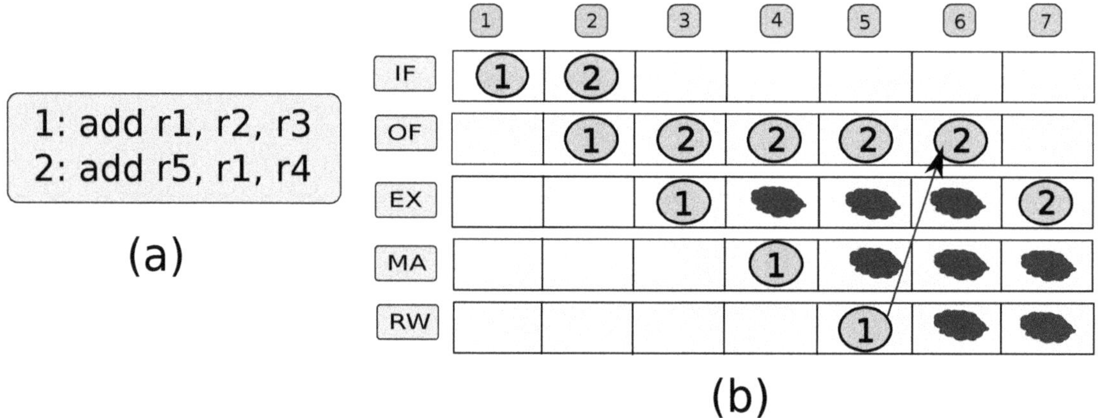

Figure 2.11: Example of a stall

Let us consider the piece of code in Figure 2.11(a), and its associated pipeline diagram in Figure 2.11(b). There is clearly a read-after-write (RAW) dependence between instructions *1* and *2* via register $r1$. With traditional data interlocks we need to stall instruction *2* till instruction *1* gets past the last stage (write-back (RW) stage). However, do we really need this delay?

Pay greater attention to Figure 2.11. Now, answer the following questions:

1. When does instruction *1* produce its destination value ($r1$)?

2. When does instruction *2* need the value of $r1$?

The answers are as follows.

1. Instruction *1* produces its result at the end of cycle 3 when it finishes executing its EX stage.

2. Instruction *2* needs the value of $r1$ at the beginning of cycle 4 – the beginning of its execution in the EX stage.

The important point to note is as follows: instruction *2* needs the value of $r1$ just after instruction *1* produces it. In real terms there are no data hazards. The result is available; it is albeit not present in the register file. That is not a big issue. Here is how we can solve the problem.

1. We can store the value of $r1$ that instruction *1* produces in its instruction packet.

2. This value will be present in the instruction packet at the beginning of cycle 4. At this point, instruction *1* will be in the MA stage (fourth stage).

3. We can **forward** the value of register $r1$ from the MA stage to the EX stage where instruction *2* needs it.

4. The value will arrive just in time for instruction *2* to execute correctly.

5. There will thus be no data hazards, and the code will execute correctly. Furthermore, there is no need to stall the pipeline. We have thus **eliminated stalls**.

This method is known as *forwarding*, or *bypassing*, where we pass results between pipeline stages.

Definition 6
A technique to pass results between pipeline stages to eliminate data hazards is known as forwarding *or* bypassing.

Forwarding Paths

To enable forwarding, we need to add a connection (forwarding path) between the beginning of the MA stage and the EX stage. This means that at the beginning of the EX stage, we need to choose between the operand that we have read from the register file in the previous stage (OF), and the forwarded value coming from the MA stage. We need to add a circuit that helps us choose between the two inputs. This is typically a multiplexer that helps us choose between the inputs (refer to Figure 2.12).

In Figure 2.12, we have two inputs and we need to choose the correct input based on whether we are forwarding inputs or not. We thus need a separate forwarding unit in the chip whose job is to compute the control signals for all the *forwarding multiplexers* in the processor. These control signals are used to choose between the value read in the OF stage and the forwarded value.

Figure 2.13 shows the modified pipeline diagram with forwarding. Note the arrow between the stage that forwards the value and the stage that uses it.

We have taken a look at only one example of forwarding, where we forward from the MA stage to the EX stage. However, this is not the only example of forwarding. We can have many more forwarding paths. For a deeper explanation of forwarding paths please refer to the textbook by Sarangi et al. [Sarangi, 2015]. We shall take a look at this issue very superficially in this book. A lot of concepts in this section

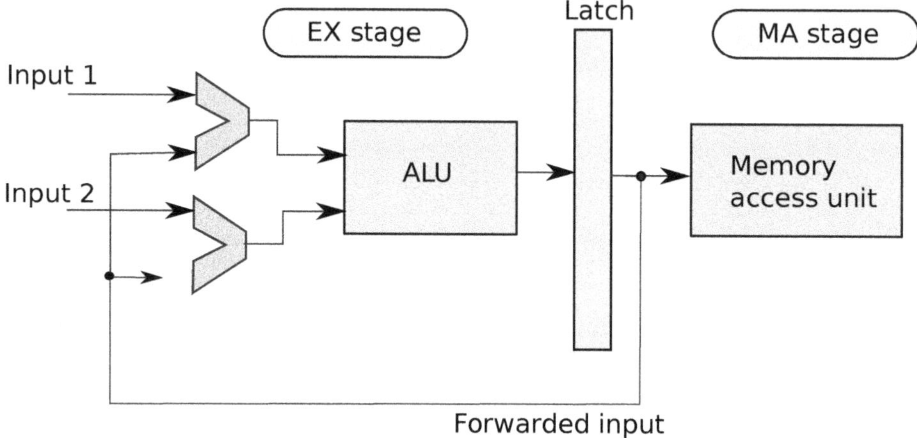

Figure 2.12: Circuit used to forward values from the MA stage to the EX stage

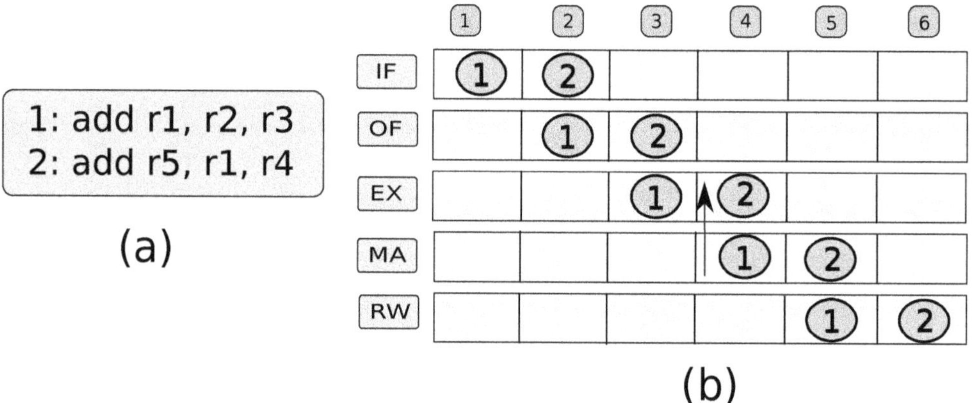

Figure 2.13: Modified pipeline diagram with forwarding

will be presented without proofs. The assumption is that readers will do their due diligence in picking up the background material from textbooks that look at in-order pipelines in detail.

Naively, we need forwarding paths between every pair of stages; however, this is overkill. Not all the paths are used. Let us settle on the following principles, while deciding on the forwarding paths.

Forwarding Principle 1 We forward from a later stage to an earlier stage.

Forwarding Principle 2 We forward as late as possible. This means that if we can delay forwarding by one or a few more cycles, then we do it. Note that we never compromise on correctness.

Now if we work out the details of the forwarding paths, we arrive at the following four forwarding paths:

Forwarding path	Example of code
RW → MA	`ld r1, 8[r2]` `st r1, 8[r3]`

RW → EX	`ld r1, 8[r2]`
	`sub r5, r6, r7`
	`add r3, r2, r1`

RW → OF	`ld r1, 8[r2]`
	`sub r5, r6, r7`
	`sub r8, r9, r10`
	`add r3, r2, r1`

MA → EX	`add r1, r2, r3` `sub r5, r1, r4`

We need to quickly understand, why these are the forwarding paths that we require, and no additional forwarding paths are needed. The forwarding paths need to always be from a later stage to an earlier stage (Forwarding Principle 1). Second, it makes no sense to forward from one stage to itself. Finally, it also makes no sense to forward a value to the IF stage. This is because in the IF stage we have not decoded the instruction and we are thus not aware of its contents. This leaves us with the following forwarding paths: $RW \rightarrow OF$, $RW \rightarrow EX$, $RW \rightarrow MA$, $MA \rightarrow EX$, $MA \rightarrow OF$, $EX \rightarrow OF$.

Now, consider the forwarding path $MA \rightarrow OF$. This is not required because we do not have an immediate need for any value in the OF stage. In accordance with *Forwarding Principle 2*, where we forward as late as possible, we can instead use the $RW \rightarrow EX$ forwarding path. We can argue on similar lines that we do not need to add the forwarding path $EX \rightarrow OF$. We can use the $MA \rightarrow EX$ path instead.

We are thus left with four forwarding paths, which are required: $RW \rightarrow OF$, $RW \rightarrow EX$, $RW \rightarrow MA$, and $MA \rightarrow EX$.

For each input in these stages, we need to have a multiplexer. In each multiplexer, we have several input terminals, where we choose between the default value (from the previous stage), and values forwarded from the forwarding paths. Figure 2.14 shows the augmented structure of the pipeline after adding forwarding paths.

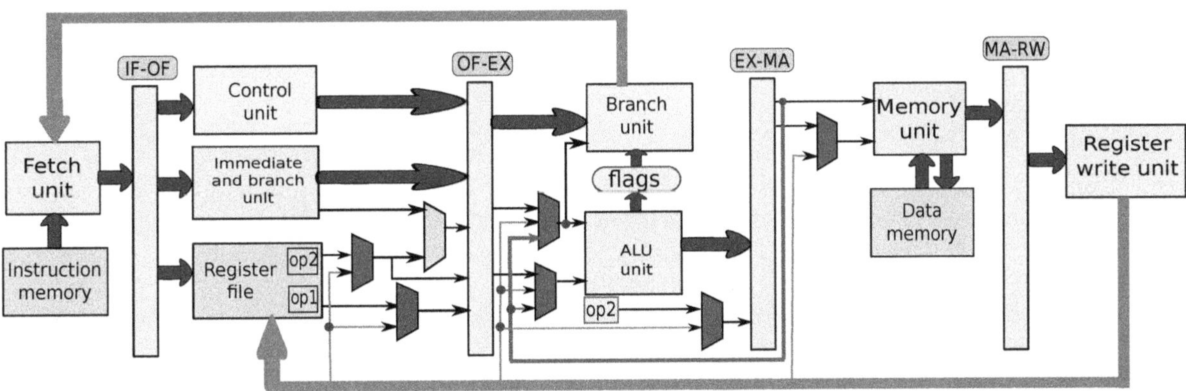

Figure 2.14: The pipeline with forwarding paths

Unfortunately, we cannot remove all RAW hazards using forwarding. There is one special case in a 5-stage pipeline that cannot be handled with forwarding. It is called a load-use hazard. Consider Figure 2.15.

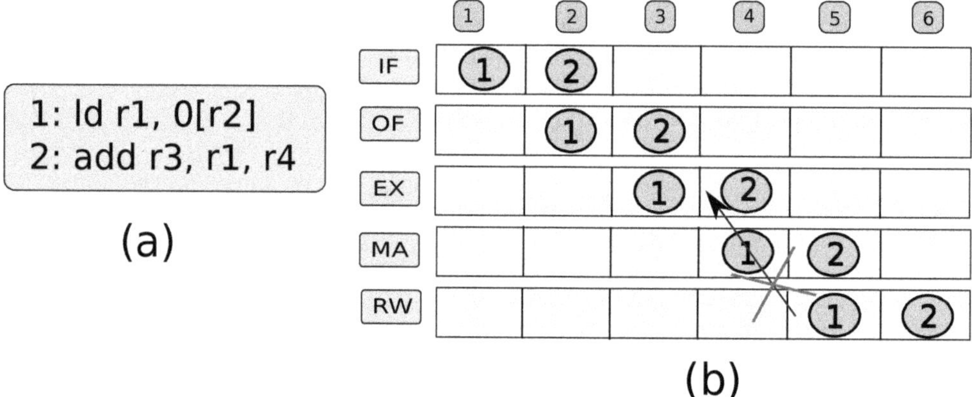

Figure 2.15: Pipeline diagram for a load-use hazard

Here we load a value and put it in register $r1$. Then this value is used by the subsequent add instruction. We can see in the corresponding pipeline diagram (see Figure 2.15(b)) that we produce the value of the load at the end of the 4th cycle, and it is available for forwarding at the beginning of the 5th cycle. However, the add instruction needs the value of $r1$ at the beginning of the 4th cycle. Thus, it is not possible to forward the value from the RW to the EX stage. This is the only case in a typical 5-stage pipeline where forwarding is not possible. The only way to solve this issue is by adding a one-cycle delay (one bubble) between instruction 1 and instruction 2. This is shown in Figure 2.16.

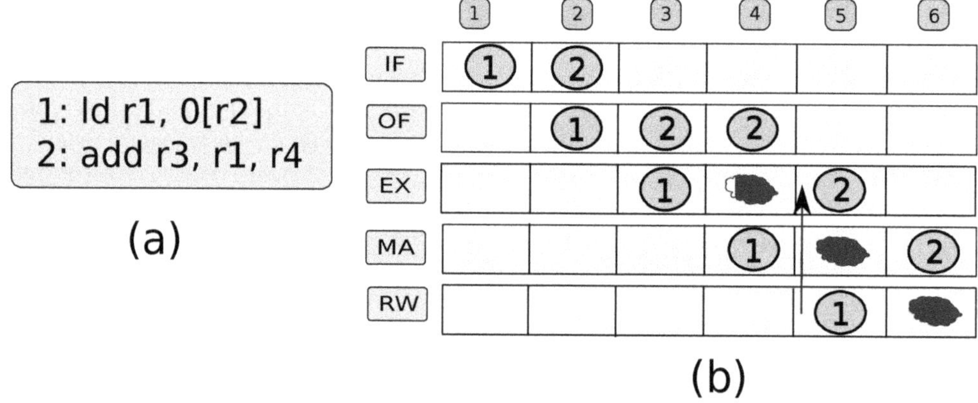

Figure 2.16: Pipeline diagram for a load-use hazard (we add a pipeline bubble here)

By using forwarding we have reduced the number of stall cycles to zero in most cases. Other than the case of load-use hazards, we do not need to stall the pipeline. If we use delayed branching, we can also eliminate the need for stalling for 2 cycles after a taken branch. However, as we discussed in Section 2.1.3 delayed branches reduce the portability of the code, and it may be difficult to find instructions that can be put in the delay slots. Our aim was to ideally reduce the CPI to 1 as far as possible. We have proposed a lot of fundamental mechanisms in this section; however, we are still short of this goal. Furthermore, in modern processors, we would like to also reduce the CPI to a number below 1 by issuing multiple instructions in parallel. In the subsequent sections, we shall discuss such designs.

2.2 Performance Considerations

2.2.1 The Performance Equation

The performance (P) of a program is defined as a quantity that is inversely proportional to the time that the program takes to execute. The units of performance are arbitrary (do not matter). We can always compare the relative performance of two programs as a ratio. In fact that is how the performance of programs and suites of programs in the popularly used SPEC benchmarks [Henning, 2006] is evaluated.

Let us assume that the constant of proportionality is 1 for ease of explanation. Now, let us derive the performance equation from first principles. Assume that a program takes $\#secs$ to execute (in seconds), and it has $\#insts$ dynamic instructions. Note that the term *dynamic instructions* refers to the actual number of instructions the processor executes. This is not the same as the term *static instructions*, which is the number of instructions in a program's binary.

$$
\begin{aligned}
P &= \frac{1}{\#secs} \\
&= \underbrace{\frac{\#insts}{\#cycles}}_{IPC} \times \underbrace{\frac{\#cycles}{\#secs}}_{f} \times \frac{1}{\#insts} \\
P &= \frac{IPC \times f}{\#insts}
\end{aligned}
\tag{2.2}
$$

The rest of the terms are defined as follows. IPC refers to the average number of instructions the processor executes per cycle, and f is the clock frequency.

The implications of the performance equation are very profound. The IPC is determined by the architecture. The more forwarding we have in a pipeline, better (higher) is the IPC. Additionally, it is also determined by the way the compiler organises the code. Consider the following assembly code snippet.

Unoptimised code

```
ld  r1, 4[r10]
add r3, r1, r2
ld  r5, 4[r11]
add r7, r6, r5
```

This code is clearly not optimal. There are two load-use hazards between the first and second statements, and the third and fourth statements respectively. There will thus be two stalls in a typical 5-stage pipeline. However, it is possible for the compiler to reorganise the code such that there are no load-use hazards.

Optimised code

```
ld  r1, 4[r10]
ld  r5, 4[r11]
add r3, r1, r2
add r7, r6, r5
```

This code snippet does not have any load-use hazards and will thus not have any stalls in a pipeline with forwarding. Thus, the compiler and the hardware have an important role in determining the IPC.

Let us come to the next variable in the performance equation: number of instructions ($\#insts$). This is predominantly determined by the compiler. Better compilers can generate shorter code sequences for the same snippet of high-level code.

The frequency, f, is determined by two factors namely the technology and the computer architecture. If we use smaller and more power efficient transistors, then we can run the circuit at a higher frequency. Note that power consumption is roughly proportional to the cube of the frequency, and thus using power efficient transistors are critical for running a chip at high frequencies. There are many other aspects to the *technology* aspect, which we shall study in later chapters. For example, it is possible to reduce the power consumption of a processor without actually using more power efficient transistors. We can use tricks at the level of the processor architecture.

The frequency is also very intimately related to the design of the processor. Before elaborating further, let us debunk a common myth associated with pipelined processors. The most common myth with regards to pipelining in a conventional pipelined processor is that since we can process more instructions at the same time, the performance is higher. This is **NOT CORRECT**, and neither is it according to the performance equation.

Let us compare the execution of the same program on two processors: one has a 5-stage pipeline, and the other does not have pipelining (single-cycle processor). Since they run the same program, the number of instructions is the same. The IPC of the single cycle processor is 1. The IPC of the pipelined processor is at the most 1, and is often less than 1. This is because of stalls in the pipeline. While most RAW hazards are avoidable, stalls associated with control hazards (on the wrong branch path) and load-use hazards are not avoidable and lead to wasted processor cycles. Thus, the IPC of the pipelined processor in all likelihood is less than 1. Now, if both the processors have the same frequency, then the performance of the single-cycle processor is more than that of the processor with pipelining. Where is the advantage of pipelining then?

The answer is that if we keep the frequency the same, there is no advantage of pipelining. The advantage of pipelining comes from the fact that we divide the processor into five smaller sub-processors (stages), where each sub-processor takes a lesser amount of time to complete its work. We can thus reduce the clock cycle period, where each clock period corresponds to the maximum time that it takes each stage to complete its work. If a pipeline with k stages is balanced (each stage takes roughly the same amount of time), then we can more or less reduce the clock period by a factor of k. This corresponds to a k times increase in the frequency(f). It is this increase in the frequency that allows us to realise the gains in pipelining. A mere implementation of pipelining does not give us the benefits, it is rather the opportunity to increase the frequency, which is more important. Keep in mind that the process of increasing the frequency has its limits: power consumption and pipeline latch delay.

Important Point 2

The gains in pipelining come from the fact that we can increase the clock frequency significantly.

Most beginners miss this point completely, and incorrectly assume that just processing multiple instructions in parallel (albeit in different stages) is good enough. This is far from the truth since neither the IPC nor the frequency increase. However, splitting the entire processor's circuit into several different sub-circuits helps us have a much faster clock.

Sadly, this approach does not take us very far. We cannot arbitrarily increase the frequency by creating more and more pipeline stages. We will very soon have diminishing returns because the latch delay (delay in the pipeline registers) will start to dominate the timing, and secondly we will greatly increase the number of stalled cycles. Additionally, there is a cubic dependence between frequency and power. Given the fact that power and temperature are extremely important issues today, we cannot expect to increase on-chip frequency (beyond the current levels of 3 to 3.5 GHz). Because of this reason the frequency has remained roughly static since 2005.

2.2.2   Multi-issue In-order Pipelines

Given the fact that we cannot increase the frequency any further due to power and temperature constraints, and it is also not possible to reduce the number of dynamic instructions significantly, we need to look at methods to increase the IPC. Sadly, after introducing pipelining, the IPC became less than 1 for most programs (due to the presence of stalls).

We can increase the IPC by processing more than one instruction per stage simultaneously. Here we focus on in-order pipelines where instructions are fetched and processed in program order. Note that the term *program order* refers to the order of dynamic instructions that a single-cycle processor will see.

Consider the following code sequence.

```
1   add r1, r2, r3
2   sub r4, r5, r6
3   mul r7, r8, r9
4   div r10, r11, r11
```

All the four instructions are independent of each other. We can treat instructions *1* and *2* as a single bundle and send them together in the pipeline. We just need to duplicate the resources. Instead of one decode unit, we need to have two. In a similar fashion, we can duplicate the execute and memory access units. The second bundle (instructions: *3* and *4*) has no conflicts with the first bundle. Both the instructions in the second bundle can be sent through the pipeline in the next cycle after the instructions in the first bundle are sent.

However, we shall seldom be that fortunate. Note that hardware designers need to be wary of Murphy's law. This law states that if something can go wrong, it will definitely go wrong.

Trivia 1
Murphy's law states that if something can go wrong, it will go wrong. It is not a scientific law, it is rather a pessimistic view of the world. For engineers, it means that they should always consider the worst possible case irrespective of its chance of occurrence while designing a system.

Example of Murphy's Law: *Imagine you fall down and break your leg, then you try to call the hospital, the phone is dead, then you knock your neighbour's door, nobody answers, then you somehow crawl to the street, no car stops for you, then you finally hop into your car and try to drive with the leg that is working, you get caught in a traffic jam, finally, when you reach the hospital, you find that it has closed down, and in its place a kids' amusement park has come up !!!*

Now, what can go wrong? We can have RAW hazards within instructions in a bundle, we can have RAW hazards across instructions from different bundles, we can have control hazards, and we can have two instructions in the same bundle accessing the same memory address. All of these issues will make the design of such a pipeline very difficult. Ensuring correctness will require a lot of additional circuitry. Always remember that additional circuitry implies more area, more power, and often more latency. The reason that additional circuitry slows down the execution of a processor is two-fold. First, it increases the length of the critical path. This means that signals need to travel for a longer duration – through more wires and transistors – to reach the end of a pipeline stage. Second, it increases the *routing* and *placement* overhead.

Let us briefly explain these terms. Circuit designers typically design their circuits in a hardware description language such as Verilog or VHDL. These tools are known as EDA (electronic design and automation) tools. Their job is to arrange transistors and wires in a circuit. The reasons for doing so are to reduce the area, decrease the signal propagation latency (alternatively the clock period), and reduce power consumption. Two of their main tasks are placement and routing. The process of *placement* refers to the proper arrangement of blocks of transistors in a circuit to increase its efficiency. For example, we should place the decode unit close to the execute unit in a processor, and the fetch unit should be far away from the memory access unit. If these constraints are not respected, then signals will take a long time to traverse along the wires, and the clock period needs to be unnecessarily increased. The process of *routing* arranges the wires in a circuit. A large processor with billions of transistors has billions of small copper wires also. No two wires can intersect. Additionally, we need to ensure that signals reach their destination as soon as possible. As a result, we need to reduce the length of wires as much as possible. This is a very complicated process.

Definition 7

Placement *It is the process of arranging electronic components in a chip to produce an efficient circuit. The criteria of efficiency can vary but typically focuses on reducing the area and the clock period.*

Routing *It is the process of laying out the wires in a circuit to make it more efficient.*

Now assume that we introduce a new piece of circuitry in a processor. We need to place it somewhere close to the other circuits that will use it. This will cause some amount of displacement of the other components, and most likely the placement tool will need to make compromises to accommodate this new circuit. The new piece of circuitry will also have its own wires, and this will complicate the routing process further. As a result, signals will take longer to reach their destination in the vicinity of the new circuit. Such effects can lead to a slowing down of the frequency, and an increase in the chip area. Hence, as far as possible, we try to avoid introducing new circuits in a high performance processor unless the gains outweigh the costs associated with placement and routing.

Adding a new feature clearly has issues in terms of complexity, routing, and placement. Let us gauge the expected benefits of such a scheme. Consider an in-order pipeline that fetches and executes multiple instructions at the same time. First, the onus of producing good code falls on the compiler. If the compiler produces code where instruction i is dependent on instruction $i+1$, then both of them cannot be a part of the same bundle, and we need to stall the pipeline. It is in general not a good idea to make the compiler do all the work because it becomes way too dependent on the architecture. Additionally, a program that runs well on one architecture will not run well on another architecture. For example, consider a processor A that can process two instructions at a time, and a processor B that can process three instructions at the same time. A program optimised for processor A might perform very poorly on processor B.

The more important question is, "How frequently will we find code sequences that can be rearranged to work optimally on such a multi-issue in-order processor?" Here the term, "multi-issue", means that we *issue* multiple instructions to the execution units simultaneously. The answer is that this will typically not happen. Most of the code that we write uses the results of the immediately previous statements, and thus we expect a lot of dependences across consecutive instructions to be present. As a result, the gains are expected to be limited. Other than a few processors such as the Intel® Pentium® processor, most of the other commercial processors have not adopted this approach.

2.3 Overview of Out-of-order Pipelines

2.3.1 Motivation

Given the fact that multi-issue in-order pipelines have limited benefits, we need to think of a new way of increasing IPC. To get inspiration for an idea, let us consider the following snippet of code.

```
1   add  r1,  r2,  r3
2   sub  r4,  r1,  r5
3   mul  r6,  r7,  r8
4   div  r9,  r6,  r7
```

Here the instructions have a dependence between them. Instruction *2* is dependent on the result of *1*, and *4* is dependent on the result of *3*. If the operator, $\rightarrow$, depicts the fact that the event on the left hand side needs to happen before the event on the right hand side, we have, $1 \rightarrow 2$ and $3 \rightarrow 4$.

The first solution is to rely on the compiler to re-organise the code. However, as discussed in Section 2.2.2, this is not a very good idea because it limits the generality of compilers, and makes programs very dependent on the type of processor that they are running on. We need a generic mechanism that can execute such code sequences without compiler support. The other issue with compilers is that they are great for pieces of code that they can analyse; however, a lot of code is dependent on run time parameters and cannot be analysed at compile time. For example, if we have a lot of code involving memory accesses, we will not know the values of the addresses till the code actually executes. It is very difficult for the compiler to optimise the code beforehand. We thus need a generic mechanism in hardware to optimise the execution sequence of dynamic instructions such that it is possible to execute as many instructions as possible in parallel. This is referred to as *instruction level parallelism* (ILP).

Definition 8
The term instruction level parallelism *(ILP) is a measure of the number of instructions that can be executed simultaneously. For two instructions to be executed simultaneously, they should not have any dependences between them.*

Let us take a second look at this piece of code and find out the degree of ILP. The dependences are *1* $\rightarrow$ *2*, and *3* $\rightarrow$ *4*. We can process instructions *1* and *3* together, and then process *2* and *4* together. In this case no dependence will be violated, and we can thus execute 2 instructions simultaneously without any issues. Figure 2.17 shows a conceptual view of such an execution. Note that this execution does not follow program order. The execution is *out of order*.

The main challenge is to automatically identify such sets of independent instructions in large instruction sequences, and execute them without causing any correctness issues. Note that the execution shown in Figure 2.17 has two distinguishing features.

1. We are processing multiple instructions in parallel.

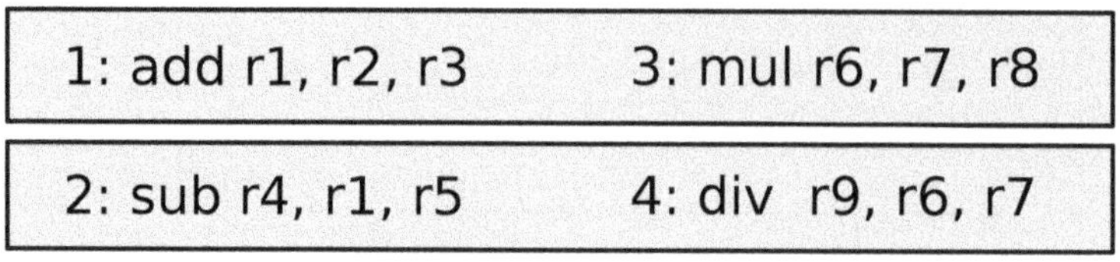

$$\boxed{\text{1: add r1, r2, r3} \qquad \text{3: mul r6, r7, r8}}$$
$$\boxed{\text{2: sub r4, r1, r5} \qquad \text{4: div r9, r6, r7}}$$

Figure 2.17: Parallel execution of instructions out of order

2. The instructions are not executing in program order. In this case instruction *3* is executing before instruction *2*. Instructions are executing *out of order*.

Let us take this opportunity to define two new terms: *superscalar* execution, and *out-of-order* execution. A superscalar processor fetches and executes multiple instructions simultaneously. In this case, we are exactly doing this. We are fetching and executing two instructions simultaneously. Now, there can be two kinds of superscalar processors. We can either execute instructions in program order (in-order processing as described in Section 2.2.2), or execute them in a different order. The latter approach is known as out-of-order processing, and a processor, which executes instructions out of order is known as an out-of-order processor. We shall often use the term OOO as an abbreviation for out-of-order.

Definition 9

Superscalar processor *A superscalar processor fetches and executes multiple instructions simultaneously.*

Out-of-order processor *An out-of-order processor executes instructions in an order that might not be the same as the program order. Note that data dependences are never violated. If instruction B is dependent on the output of instruction A, then an out-of-order processor will always execute B after A.*

Most high performance modern processors are out-of-order processors primarily because of their potential to increase the IPC. Let us consider our running example once again. We have the following dependences: *1 → 2* and *3 → 4*. If the instruction sequence from instructions *1* to *4* is executed by an in-order processor that can process two instructions simultaneously, the IPC will still be less than 2 because instructions *1,2* and instructions *3,4* have dependences between them. However, we can always execute them out of order and get an IPC of 2 as shown in Figure 2.17. If the frequency remains the same, we can improve the performance of the processor by a factor of 2.

2.3.2   Program Order versus Data Dependence Order

An in-order processor executes instructions in program order. This approach limits the ILP and thus leads to lower performance. We often cannot find enough independent instructions to execute in parallel. Even if we have a very smart compiler that can reorder code very efficiently, it is still very hard to extract high levels of ILP because a large part of the behaviour of programs is determined at run time.

It is much better to execute instructions out of order. Does it mean that we can arbitrarily execute instructions in parallel. The answer is, NO. If instruction B is dependent on the result of instruction A, then we still have to respect the order $A \rightarrow B$. This is known as the *data dependence order*. Let us formally define it.

Definition 10

The data dependence order *is defined as an ordering of instructions where instruction A must appear before B, if B is dependent on the results generated by instruction A.*

Note that the data dependence order is a transitive relationship. This means that $A \rightarrow B$ and $B \rightarrow C$ implies $A \rightarrow C$.

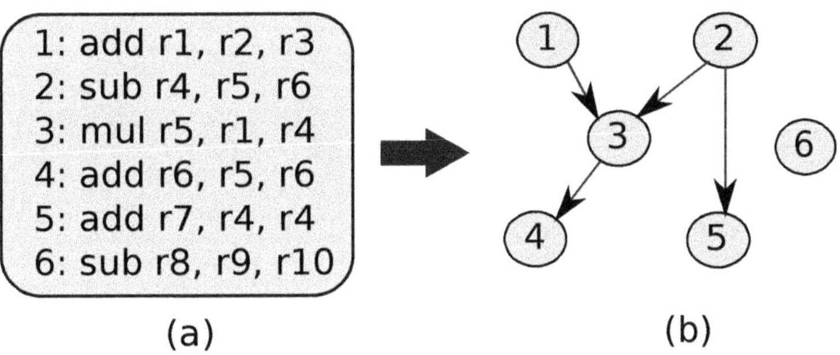

Figure 2.18: Code sequence modelled as a directed acyclic graph (DAG)

Definition 11

A graph *is a data structure in Computer Science. A data structure is a method of conveniently representing complex data. Consider the map of a city as shown below. Here the intersections are shown as rectangles with dotted boundaries. The intersections are numbered:* $I_1 \ldots I_8$.

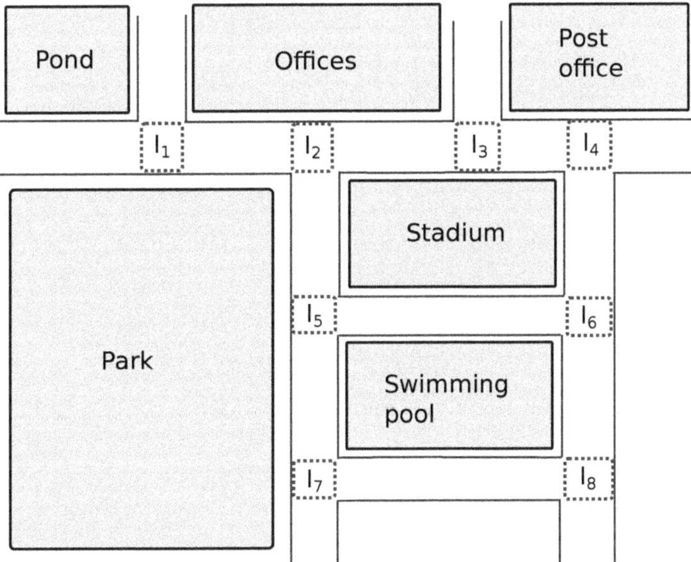

The main problem with such complicated scenarios is that they cannot be processed by a program. They need to be converted to a simpler format. We thus represent the map of a city as a graph. A

graph as shown below contains a set of nodes (or vertices), which in this case are the intersections. The intersections are connected by edges, where each edge is a segment of the road that connects the intersections. An edge can be annotated with additional information that indicates the length of the segment of the road, or other attributes.

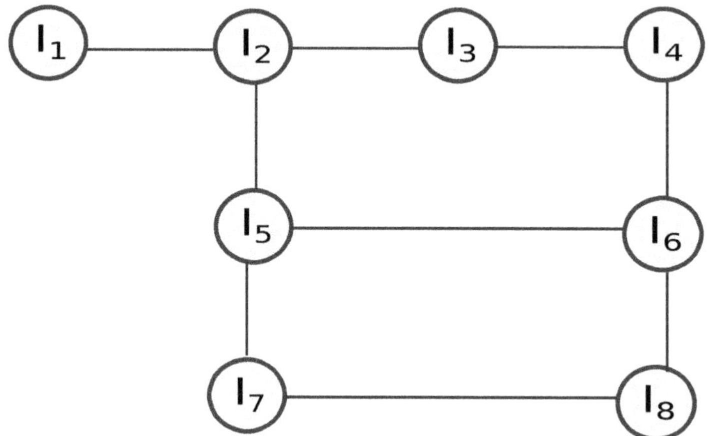

The advantage of modelling such a scenario as a graph is that this data structure can easily be analysed by a program. For example, we can find some interesting properties in the graph such as the shortest path between two points or the existence of cycles. We shall see in later chapters that a lot of problems can be modelled as graphs. The graphs can then be very intuitively analysed to provide important insights.

A directed acyclic graph or a DAG is a special type of graph where the edges are directed. They are like a city with one-way streets.

Let us explain the difference between the program order and the data dependence order. Consider Figure 2.18(a) and (b). Figure 2.18(a) shows a set of instructions arranged in program order. The arrows in Figure 2.18(b) indicate the dependences where the destination of the arrow needs to execute after the source. The same relationships are visualised in Figure 2.18(b) as a directed acyclic graph or DAG (also see Definition 11). In the DAG (Figure 2.18(b)) two instructions can be executed simultaneously only if there is no dependence between them. There is a dependence in the DAG between instructions A and B only if there is a path from A to B.

We can clearly see that in an out-of-order machine, it is much easier to find two instructions that can be executed simultaneously as compared to an in-order machine where we are restricted to strictly follow program order.

2.3.3   Basics of an Out-of-order Machine

Let us now try to build an out-of-order machine from scratch. What should the first stage be? Without doubt, in the first stage we need to fetch instructions from memory. To be specific, we fetch instructions from the instruction cache, which is the highest level in the memory hierarchy. Recall that if there is a miss in the instruction cache, then we need to access the lower levels of the memory hierarchy such as the L2 and L3 caches. After fetching the instruction, we need to decode it.

The process of fetching and decoding instructions needs to be done in program order because at this point we do not know the details of the instruction. As a result, we have no idea about the data dependence order at this point.

We have till now discussed two main stages: fetch and decode (see Figure 2.19). Note that for increasing performance we can further pipeline these stages.

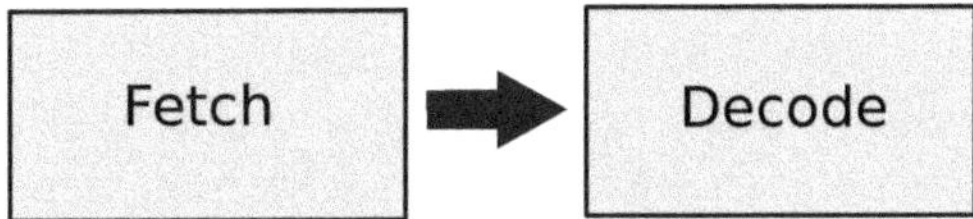

Figure 2.19: The front-end of the OOO pipeline (fetch and decode stages)

Once we get the instructions decoded we need to proceed to find dependences across instructions and find the sets of instructions that we can execute simultaneously. Let us consider an example, and try to prove that the more instructions we can simultaneously look at, the more ILP we shall find.

```
1: add r1, r2, r3        5: add r7, r8, r9
2: sub r4, r1, r2        6: sub r10, r7, r8
3: sub r5, r4, r1        7: sub r11, r10, r7
4: mul r6, r5, r1        8: mul r12, r11, r7
```

Figure 2.20: Two sets of 4 instructions with dependences between them

Consider Figure 2.20. Here, if we consider the first set of 4 instructions, the maximum amount of ILP is 1. There is a chain of dependence. However, if we consider all 8 instructions, we find that we can execute two instructions simultaneously: *1* and *5*, *2* and *6*, *3* and *7*, *4* and *8*. The larger is this pool of instructions, the higher is the expected ILP.

Now to create such a pool of instructions, do we fetch 8 instructions in one go? This is not possible because our fetch bandwidth (number of instructions that can be fetched simultaneously) is limited. We can at best fetch 4 or 8 instructions at once. A promising solution is to maintain a pool of instructions after the decode stage. Instructions that pass through the decode stage can be added to the pool. We can dynamically keep scanning this pool and then try to find instructions whose operands are ready and do not have dependences between each other. If the pool is large enough, there are high chances that we will always find more than one instruction to execute per cycle, and we can thus sustain an IPC of more than 1.

Our pipeline at the moment can be visualised as shown in Figure 2.21. Instructions pass through the fetch and decode stages. They then enter an instruction pool. We then choose sets of ready instructions without dependences between each other to execute in parallel. Note that a *ready* instruction is one whose operands have been computed and are available. The instructions then pass to the execution units, and finally write back their results. It is possible that an instruction might wait in this pool for a long time. It will wait till all the instructions that produce its source operands complete their execution. Alternatively, it is also possible that an instruction leaves the pool immediately because all of its inputs are available.

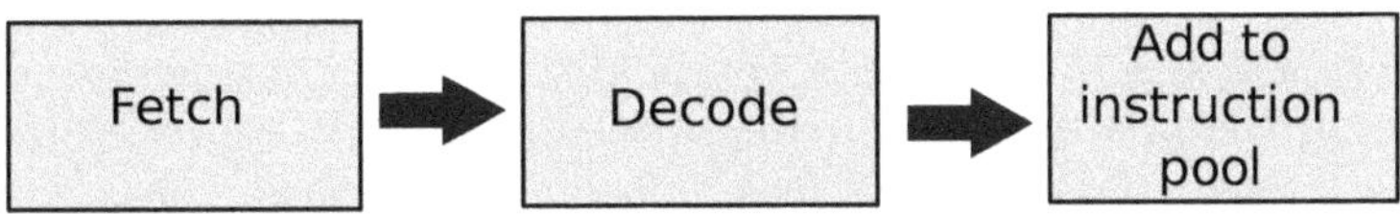

Figure 2.21: A part of the OOO pipeline with three stages

This instruction pool is referred to as the *instruction window* in computer architecture parlance. We shall refrain from formally defining this term now. We will have a lot of opportunity to look into the design of the instruction window later.

Ideally, the instruction window should be as large as possible. In this case, we can maximise the ILP because the larger is the instruction window higher are the chances of finding sets of ready instructions that do not have dependences between each other. But how large can the instruction window be? In modern processors, the instruction window contains somewhere between 64 to 256 entries. Note that it cannot be very small because the ILP needs to maximised, and it cannot be very large because in that case it will become a very slow structure and will consume a lot of power.

As a memory based structure such as the instruction window increases in size, it gets slower, and consumes more power. An instruction window is typically made of SRAM memory cells, and thus we cannot make it arbitrarily large.

Branch Prediction

Assume an instruction window with 128 entries (1 entry per instruction). We would ideally want to find as many instructions as possible to execute in parallel from this window. Thus, it is best if this window is close to being full almost all the time. Sadly, branch instructions have the potential of spoiling the party. In most programs, branch instructions are fairly frequent, and in most programs 1 in 5 instructions are branches. A window of 100+ instructions will have at least 20 branches.

What do we do about them? In an in-order pipeline we adopted several strategies. The simplest strategy was to stall the pipeline till the outcome of the branch was known. This is not possible in an out-of-order pipeline. It might take more than 10-20 cycles (at least) to know the outcome of a branch. We will never be able to fill our window if we adopt this strategy. The second strategy was to assume that the branch was not taken and proceed. If this assumption (not taken prediction) was found to be wrong, then we cancelled or nullified the instructions that were on the wrong path (see Definition 12 for a more generic definition). This is also not possible in our setup because the order of execution need not be consistent with the program order. Hence, in a sequence of 20 branches, we will have a lot of mispredictions and we will end up cancelling a lot of instructions because they will be on the wrong path. Note that the moment we have a misprediction, the rest of the instructions are pretty much useless.

Definition 12

Instructions that would have been executed if a branch would have had an outcome that is different from its real outcome, are said to be on the wrong path. *For example, instructions succeeding a branch instruction in the program are on the wrong path if the branch is taken. Valid instructions are said to be on the* correct path.

To avoid this, we need a very accurate method of predicting branches. If we can accurately predict the outcome of **all** the branch instructions in the window, and the targets of the taken branches in the window, then we can ensure that it has a lot of instructions that are on the correct path most of the time. This will help in maximising the ILP.

Let us get a quick idea of what the branch prediction accuracy should be. Assume that one in five instructions is a branch. To keep things simple, let the probability of misprediction of any given branch be p, and let us assume that the branch outcomes are independent of each other. If we consider n instructions, then the number of branches is $n/5$. The probability, P_n, of mispredicting at least one branch in a sequence of n instructions is shown in Equation 2.3. It can be derived as follows. The probability of predicting any given branch instruction correctly is $(1 - p)$; hence, the probability of predicting all $n/5$ branches correctly is $(1 - p)^{(n/5)}$. The probability of at least a single misprediction is thus 1 minus this number.

$$P_n = 1 - (1 - p)^{n/5} \tag{2.3}$$

A single misprediction in a large instruction window is rather lethal because we may end up flushing (removing from the pipeline) a large number of instructions. A lot of work might get wasted. Hence, we are interested in the probability P_n. Alternatively, we can interpret the probability $1 - P_n$ as the probability of all the $n/5$ branches being predicted correctly.

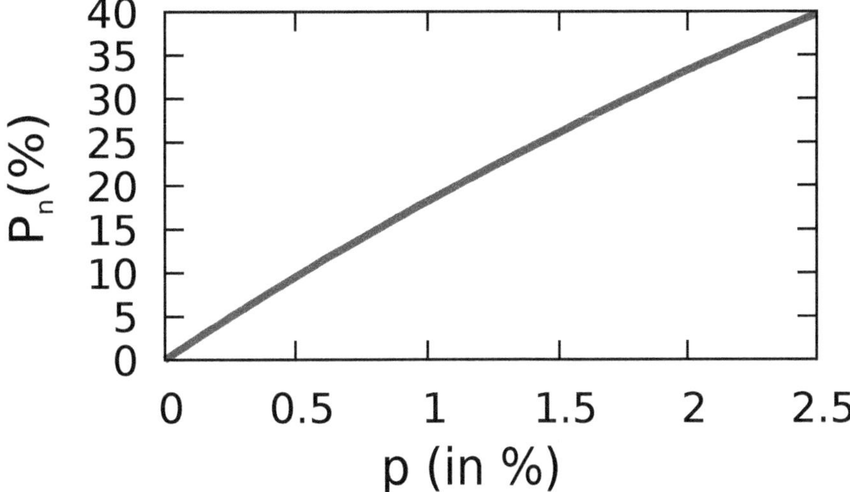

Figure 2.22: P_n versus p ($n = 100$)

Consider the results shown in Figure 2.22 for $n = 100$. We observe that even if the probability of a correct prediction is 99% ($p = 1\%$), there is a 17% chance that we shall have at least one branch misprediction in a sequence of 100 instructions. In that case, we will not be able to fill the instruction window. Even if the branch prediction rate (per branch) is as good as 99.5% (p=0.5%) we still have a roughly 7% probability of having at least a single misprediction. This gives us an idea of the kind of accuracies we need to ensure for having a window full of 100 instructions to be completely free of mispredicted branches. The per-branch prediction accuracy should be more than 99%. Creating a branch predictor that is 99% accurate is a very challenging task. We shall delve into this topic in Chapter 3.

Managing Anti and Output Dependences

The kind of dependences that we have been considering up till now are called real dependences, flow dependences, or RAW (read after write) dependences. This is because if we have, $A \to B$, then B cannot execute before A because it needs the results that A has generated.

Let us now consider some other classes of dependences that also need to be considered. Consider the following code snippet.

```
1  add  r5,  r1,  r6
2  add  r1,  r2,  r3
```

In this case instruction 2 cannot execute before instruction 1 because it will get the wrong value of $r1$. In the first instruction we are reading from $r1$, and in the second instruction we are writing to $r1$.

We have a write after read (WAR) dependence here. This is also called an *anti* dependence. We will use the $\xrightarrow{a}$ arrow to represent it. We thus have, $1 \xrightarrow{a} 2$.

We can have another dependence of the following form.

```
1  add r1, r2, r3
2  add r1, r4, r5
```

In this case both the instructions are writing to the register $r1$. Here also instruction 2 cannot execute before instruction 1. If this happens we will end up writing the wrong value to register $r1$. This type of a dependence is known as an output dependence. It is alternatively called a write after write (WAW) dependence. We will use the $\xrightarrow{o}$ arrow to represent it. We have, $1 \xrightarrow{o} 2$.

Definition 13

We have three kinds of data dependences between instructions in a program. Assume instruction B is after instruction A in program order.

- *A RAW dependence between instructions A and B means that A writes a value to a register that B reads from. It is represented as $A \rightarrow B$.*

- *A WAR dependence between instructions A and B means that B writes to a register that A reads from. It is represented as $A \xrightarrow{a} B$.*

- *A WAW dependence between instructions A and B means that both the instructions A and B write to the same register r, without any intervening writes to r. It is represented as $A \xrightarrow{o} B$.*

Register Renaming

It should be noted that WAW and WAR dependences are not real dependences. They are simply there because we have a finite number of registers.

Consider the following code snippet.

```
1  add r1, r2, r3
2  add r2, r5, r6
```

In this case, we cannot reorder instructions 1 and 2 because instruction 2 writes to $r2$, which is a source register for instruction 1. This WAR hazard is only arising because we are using $r2$ as the destination register for instruction 2. If we instead use another register in the place of $r2$ (not used before), we shall not have a WAR hazard.

Now, in practice the number of registers is limited; this number is also much lower than the number of entries in the instruction window. Thus, there will always be cases where we need to reuse registers, and we shall consequently have a lot of WAR and WAW hazards. Let us propose a solution to take care of this problem.

Let us call our traditional registers $(r1, r2, \ldots)$ as *architectural registers*. Let us also define a new set of registers $(p1, p2, \ldots)$ as *physical registers*. Let the physical registers be completely internal to the processor and be invisible to the compiler or the assembly language programmer. Furthermore, let us have many more physical registers than architectural registers. If we can map the architectural registers in an instruction to a set of physical registers, then we can possibly get rid of WAR and WAW hazards. This process is known as *renaming*. It will be explained in detail in Section 4.1. Right now, the important point to remember is that the process of renaming modifies an instruction such that its source and destination registers get converted from regular architectural registers to physical registers.

We need to ensure that the logic of the program does not change, if we convert our architectural registers into physical registers. Let us explain with an example. Assume that we already know that the data for the architectural registers $r1$ and $r2$ is saved in the physical registers $p1$ and $p2$ respectively. We can then take a piece of assembly code and convert it into equivalent assembly code that uses physical registers as follows.

<table>
<tr><td align="center">With arch. registers</td><td align="center">With physical registers</td></tr>
</table>

```
1  add  r3,  r1,  r2          1  add  p3,  p1,  p2
2  add  r4,  r3,  2           2  add  p4,  p3,  2
3  sub  r3,  r1,  1           3  sub  p5,  p1,  1
```

Let us consider the statements in order. In the first instruction we already know that $r1$ is mapped to $p1$ and $r2$ is mapped to $p2$. Let us use the $\leftrightarrow$ operator to indicate a mapping. We thus have $r1 \leftrightarrow p1$ and $r2 \leftrightarrow p2$. We map the architectural register $r3$ to $p3$. We thus convert the instruction *add r3, r1, r2* to *add p3, p1, p2*. For the second instruction, we already know that $r3$ is mapped to $p3$. We need to create a new mapping for $r4$. Let us map $r4$ to $p4$. We thus convert the instruction *add r4, r3, 2* to *add p4, p3, 2*. By using the same mapping for $r3$ ($r3 \leftrightarrow p3$), we reaffirm the fact that there is a RAW dependence between the first and second instructions. Recall that we are not allowed to change the logic of the program by creating such mappings. The only reason for mapping architectural registers to physical registers is to remove WAR and WAW dependences.

This is exactly what we have here. We have a WAW dependence between instructions *1* and *3*, and a WAR dependence between instructions *2* and *3*. We want to execute instructions *1* and *3*, or *2* and *3* in parallel if possible. This can be done by creating a new avatar for $r3$ in instruction *3*. Let us map it to a new physical register, $p5$. For the input operands of instruction *3*, we can use the earlier mappings. The only register input operand is $r1$, which has been mapped to $p1$. Thus *sub r3, r1, 1* becomes *sub p5, p1, 1*.

Now, we need to convince ourselves that the program with physical registers actually works, and does not change the logic of the original program with architectural registers. Consider the original program. The first instruction writes its result to $r3$ and then the second instruction needs to get this value. We have achieved this by using the same mapping for $r3$ in instructions *1* and *2* ($r3 \leftrightarrow p3$). Instruction *3* overwrites the value of $r3$. Any subsequent instruction will read the value of $r3$ written by instruction *3* or a newer value. Since instruction *3* does not read any value written by *1* and *2*, it does not have any RAW dependences, and thus it should be possible to execute it in parallel. However, there is a risk of it polluting the value of $r3$ if it executes and writes back its result before *1* and *2*. We thus create a new mapping for $r3$ ($r3 \leftrightarrow p5$). Now, there are no WAR or WAW dependences between instruction *3* and the previous instructions (*1* and *2*). We request the reader to look at both the code sequences thoroughly and convince herself that the renamed code (after register mapping) is correct.

The dependences in the original program were $1 \rightarrow 2$, $1 \overset{o}{\rightarrow} 3$, and $2 \overset{a}{\rightarrow} 3$. After renaming (mapping registers) the only dependence is $1 \rightarrow 2$. As we see, only the real (RAW) dependences are left in the renamed code. All WAW and WAR dependences have been removed! This increases the ILP, and can translate to a higher IPC if we start executing multiple instructions in the same cycle. Note that if we execute instructions *1* and *3* together in the first cycle, and then execute instruction *2*, we would be executing instructions **out of order**. Since we have removed WAR and WAW dependences, the execution will be correct.

Renaming can be done either in hardware or by the compiler. The latter is not a preferred option because in this case the compiler needs to be aware of the number of physical registers a processor has. We do not want to expose such internal details to the compiler. This is because across processor versions the number of internal physical registers can keep changing. We want to fix the ISA and then make as many changes as we want within the processor unbeknownst to the programmer and the compiler. As a result, almost all processors have a renaming unit in hardware that maps architectural registers to physical registers. The modified code does not have WAR and WAW dependences and thus has more ILP.

At this point our pipeline looks as shown in Figure 2.23.

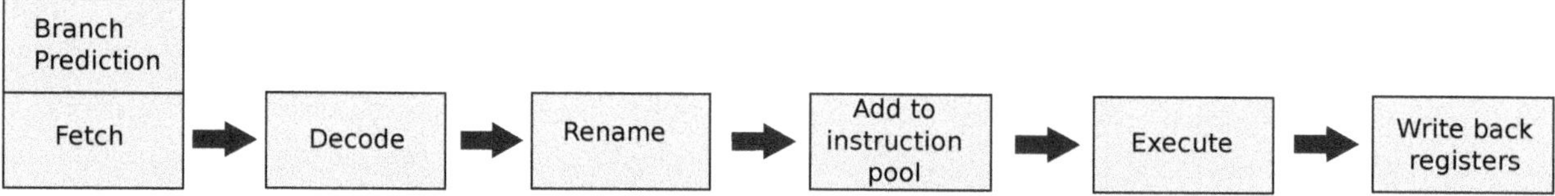

Figure 2.23: The OOO pipeline (as explained till now)

Ensuring Precise Exceptions

After renaming, we can execute multiple instructions out of order, and thus ensure a higher IPC. However, we shall have many problems in correctness particularly if we have an interrupt or exception.

Let us revisit this problem in the context of a traditional single-issue in-order pipeline. Now, recall that we define an *interrupt* as an external event such as a message from an I/O device, and an *exception* as an internal event such as an instruction dividing a number by 0. Typically during the execution of a long program the processor receives thousands or even millions of interrupts. It is necessary to stop the execution of the program, handle the interrupt/exception, and then come back and restart the program. We have several options here. For some types of events, we can restart the program at the instruction that immediately succeeds the last instruction whose results were written back, in the case of a page fault we can re-execute the faulting instruction, or we can restart the program at a different point. Regardless of the nature of the event, the correctness of the execution needs to be guaranteed.

Let the latest instruction (in program order) to write back its results to either the memory or register file be instruction I. Let us say that an instruction *completes* when it writes back its results to either the memory or the register file. To ensure correctness we need to ensure that the following conditions are met:

1. All the instructions before I in program order need to complete before the interrupt/exception handler begins to execute.

2. No instruction after I in program order should have completed at this point.

Let us intuitively explain the meaning of this definition. Assume that a user is looking at the execution of a program from outside. She does not care about the details of the processor. It can be a single-cycle processor, or a complex pipelined out-of-order processor. All that she wants to see is that the processor can stop a program $\mathcal{P}$ at any instruction in response to an event. It can then handle the event, run other programs, and then start $\mathcal{P}$ exactly at the point at which it had left it. Such an exception is called a *precise exception*. Note that this definition treats exceptions and interrupts interchangeably.

All processors support precise exceptions. Unless we have precise exceptions there will be serious violations in correctness. Consider this piece of code:

```
1  mov r4, 1
2  div r7, r5, r6
3  sub r4, r4, 1
```

Assume that after instruction *2*, the processor stops the program ($\mathcal{P}$) and proceeds to handle an interrupt. When we come back we expect $r4$ to be 1, and instruction *3* to have not executed. Assume that precise exceptions are not supported and the processor has already executed instruction *3* when $\mathcal{P}$ returns. We will incorrectly execute instruction *3* twice.

Given the fact that interrupts can happen any time, we need to ensure that the processor can suspend the execution of the current program very quickly, and jump to an interrupt handler. The interrupts/exceptions thus **have to be precise**.

To ensure precise exceptions in simple in-order pipelines we allow the instructions in the memory access and write-back stages to complete and we nullify the rest of the instructions in the pipeline. This gives us a clean point at which we can restart the program's execution. Given that we are executing instructions in program order, creating such a boundary between complete and incomplete instructions is very easy.

However, ensuring precise exceptions in an out-of-order pipeline is an entirely different issue. In this example, if we complete instructions *1* and *3* before completing instruction *2*, then we will not be able to ensure precise exceptions if an interrupt arrives before *2* is completed. In fact the whole idea of out-of-order machines is to issue instructions in an order that is possibly not consistent with the program order. It appears that the goal of ensuring precise exceptions and out-of-order execution are completely at odds with each other. We can only achieve one at the expense of the other. This situation is clearly undesirable; however, at this point we do not have a method to ensure both.

We need to think of an innovative solution to solve this problem without sacrificing the benefits of out-of-order execution. We need to somehow ensure that instructions write their results to the register file or the memory system in program order. This process is known as *committing* an instruction. We need a dedicated commit engine in hardware that ensures precise exceptions. It should appear to the outside world that instructions are committing in program order, even though they might be executing and computing their results out of order.

Let us take a look at the current shape of our out-of-order pipeline in Figure 2.24. Henceforth, we shall mostly use the acronym OOO to refer to an out-of-order pipeline.

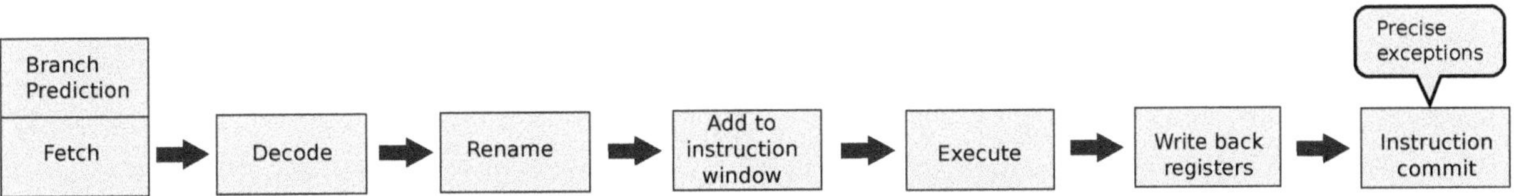

Figure 2.24: The OOO pipeline

We shall look at each of the stages in detail in the following chapters. The plan for the rest of the chapters in this area is as follows.

1. In Chapter 3, we shall look at branch prediction, and the fetch/decode logic.

2. In Chapter 4, we shall describe the rename unit, and the process of issuing instructions to execution units from the instruction window.

3. In Chapter 5, we shall describe alternative implementations of OOO pipelines.

2.4 Summary and Further Reading

2.4.1 Summary

Summary 1

1. A traditional 5-stage in-order pipeline processes instructions in program order. A later instruction never overtakes an earlier instruction in any stage of the pipeline.

2. It consists of 5 stages: Instruction Fetch (IF), Operand Fetch and Decode (OF), Execute (EX), Memory Access (MA), and Register Write-back (RW).

3. In-order pipelines primarily suffer from two kinds of stalls: stalls due to data hazards, and stalls due to control hazards. The need for such stalls are required (also called pipeline interlocks) to ensure that instructions read the correct values for their operands.

4. Almost all stalls can be eliminated by using forwarding techniques in such pipelines. Here, we pass results from a later stage to an earlier stage such that stalls are not required. The only exception is the load-use hazard, where we need to stall the pipeline for one cycle.

5. Control hazards typically require us to nullify the instructions in the IF and OF stages. Otherwise, we will end up executing instructions on the wrong path. One way to completely eliminate the need for doing this is by using the delayed branch mechanism where we assume that the two instructions after the branch instruction are on the correct path. This is ensured by the compiler that takes independent instructions before the branch and puts them just after the branch. The other way is to predict the direction of the branch.

6. The main problem with in-order pipelines is that their IPC (instructions per cycle) is less than 1 (due to stalls). Nevertheless, the primary advantage of pipelining is that we can increase the frequency because of the lesser amount of work we need to do per clock period as compared to a single-cycle pipeline.

7. The relationship between performance(P), IPC, frequency(f), and the number of instructions is given by the performance equation.

$$P \propto \frac{IPC \times f}{\#insts}$$

8. Due to limitations imposed by power consumption, it is very hard to increase the frequency further. We need to increase the IPC to get higher performance. Even though a multi-issue in-order pipeline can increase the IPC to a number above 1, it has limitations in terms of complexity. Additionally it suffers from the convoy effect, where one slow instruction can delay all the instructions after it.

9. The only other option is to create an out-of-order(OOO) pipeline that can execute instructions in an order that is not consistent with the program order. We can additionally fetch and execute multiple instructions per cycle to further increase the IPC. This is known as superscalar execution.

10. Instructions in such OOO processors suffer from three kinds of data hazards: RAW (read after write), WAW (write after write), and WAR (write after read). These hazards prevent us from reordering instructions unless additional steps are taken.

11. *The key steps in an OOO processor are as follows:*

    (a) We need an extremely accurate branch predictor such that we can create large sequences of instructions that are on the correct path. This is a part of the fetch stage. Subsequently, we decode the instructions and send them to the rename unit.

    (b) We rename instructions by replacing architectural registers with physical registers such that we can get rid of WAR and WAW hazards in the code.

    (c) The only dependences that we have between renamed instructions are RAW dependences.

    (d) We store a large set(50-100) of renamed instructions in the instruction window. In each cycle we try to find a set of instructions that are ready (operands are available in the register file), and are mutually independent. These instructions are sent for execution.

    (e) Finally, we write back the results, and remove the instruction from the pipeline (commit).

12. *We need to ensure that precise exceptions are guaranteed, which means that it is possible to pause a running program at any point, run another program, and again resume it at the same point seamlessly.*

2.4.2 Further Reading

For readers who are unfamiliar with the details of in-order pipelines, and would like to read further, we would like to recommend the book by Sarangi [Sarangi, 2015]. Subsequently, it is necessary to get a perspective of commercial processors that use in-order pipelines. Readers should refer to Saini [Saini, 1993] and Alpert et al. [Alpert and Avnon, 1993] for understanding the design of the Intel® Pentium® processor. After appreciating classical architectures, readers can move on to read about contemporary in-order ARM processors ARM® Cortex®-M3 [Yiu, 2009] and ARM® Cortex®-A8 [Williamson, 2007], and the Intel Atom® processor [Halfhill, 2008].

Exercises

Ex. 1 — Draw a pipeline diagram for the following code sequence. Assume we only have interlocks and no forwarding.

```
add  r1,  r2,  r3
add  r4,  r1,  r6
add  r5,  r6,  r7
add  r7,  r8,  r9
ld   r2,  8[r1]
sub  r1,  r2,  r2
```

Ex. 2 — Solve Exercise 1 assuming a pipeline that has forwarding enabled.

Ex. 3 — What is the performance equation? On the basis of that can we explain why a pipelined processor is faster than an equivalent non-pipelined processor? Justify your answer.

Ex. 4 — Draw a pipeline diagram for the following code sequence. Assume we have interlocks, no forwarding, and no support for delayed branches. Assume that the branch is taken.

```
add  r1, r2, r3
add  r7, r8, r9
beq  .loop
...
.loop:
sub  r5, r6, r7
mul  r8, r8, r1
```

Ex. 5 — Solve Exercise 4 for the case when we have delayed branches. Rest of the assumptions remain the same.

*** Ex. 6 —** Derive a set of conditions for creating instruction bundles in multi-issue in-order pipelines.

Ex. 7 — What are the advantages of OOO pipelines over in-order pipelines?

Ex. 8 — What is a superior mode of execution: execution in program order or in data dependence order? In a data dependence order, instruction B needs to execute after instruction A, if it reads a value that A produces. There are no other restrictions.

Ex. 9 — How does renaming remove WAR and WAW dependences? If we had a very large number of registers, would renaming still be required?

Ex. 10 — Why cannot RAW dependences be removed with renaming?

Ex. 11 — Why are precise exceptions required? Are they required in processors where we shall never have any interrupts or any other exceptional conditions where the intervention of another program is necessary?

Ex. 12 — In the case of an ISA where there are instructions that access the memory in the OF stage, what are the forwarding paths and dependences? Can we remove all dependences using forwarding?

Ex. 13 — Why is there a need for pipeline registers? Why can't we simply forward the instruction packet to the next stage and process it.

Ex. 14 — What will happen if we try to create a 1000-stage pipeline? Is it a good idea?

3

The Fetch and Decode Stages

The aim of this chapter is to design a fetch engine that has a very high bandwidth. This means that we can supply as many instructions as possible in a single cycle to the rest of the pipeline. A high bandwidth fetch engine can typically supply 4 or 6 instructions per cycle to the rest of the pipeline. If the fetch stage becomes a bottleneck, then the entire OOO processor will become very slow because irrespective of the speed of other stages, they will simply not have enough instructions to work with.

Designing a high bandwidth fetch engine is a classical problem in computer architecture and as of 2020 this field has matured. Let us take a brief look at the components of a modern fetch engine (see Figure 3.1).

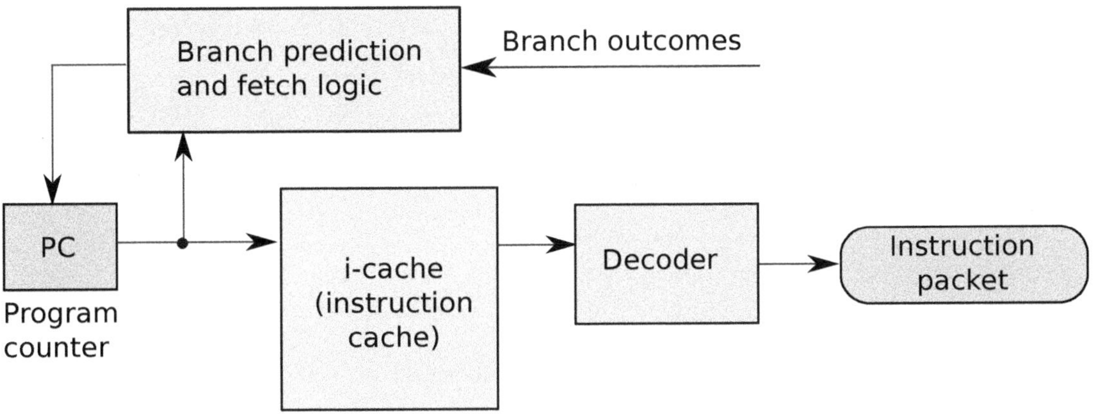

Figure 3.1: Fetch and decode stages in a modern pipeline

The components shown in Figure 3.1 are the instruction cache (i-cache), fetch logic, and the branch prediction unit. They send the fetched instructions to the decoder. The fetch engine reads its inputs from the instruction cache. The final output of the fetch and decode process is a set of instructions that have been decoded. Recall that the process of decoding extracts the information encoded in an instruction. This information includes register ids, immediates (constants), program counter based displacements for branches, and special instruction flags. The decode unit adds additional information to control the multiplexers along the data path such that the instruction can be executed properly by the execution units, and its results can be written back to either the data memory or the register file. The bundle of information that the decoder generates for each instruction is known as the *instruction packet*.

Definition 14

An instruction packet is defined as the bundle of information that is required to process an instruction in all the stages of a pipeline. It is generated in the decode stage and typically contains the ids of the source and destination registers, the values of constants embedded in the instruction (immediates), branch and memory offsets, special flags, and signals to control execution units throughout the pipeline.

3.1   Instruction Delivery from the I-Cache

The basic logic in the fetch engine of an OOO pipeline is no different from that of an in-order pipeline. If the size of each instruction is 4 bytes, then we need to fetch 4 bytes starting from the program counter (referred to as PC[1]). The addresses of the 4 bytes are in the range: PC, $PC + 3$. The next instruction starts at the address (PC + 4). Now, if we need to supply the pipeline with 4 instructions, we need to fetch 16 bytes from the i-cache.

Recall that a cache is a memory structure that contains data and instructions within the chip. We shall describe the internal details of caches in Chapter 7. For now, we can assume that a cache is a linear array of cache lines or cache blocks (the term *line* and *block* will be used interchangeably). A cache line or cache block is an atomic unit of data in a cache. It is read and written in one go. The typical instruction cache line size as of today is either 32 bytes or 64 bytes. The reason for using a cache is that these are fast memory structures unlike off-chip main memory that is very slow. We can quickly read data from such caches. Additionally, they can sustain a very high read throughput.

Let us now devise a mechanism to fetch these 16 bytes. Assume the simpler case first where there are no branches among these four instructions. In this case, we need to read 16 contiguous bytes from the i-cache.

Instruction caches are organised as regular caches with a block (line) size that is typically in the range of 32 to 64 bytes. Thus, each line contains 8 to 16 4-byte instructions. If we assume that the block size is 32 bytes, then each cache block or cache line contains 8 instructions. As of today most high performance i-caches allow us to read at least two blocks in parallel. Some caches can allow us to read even more blocks in parallel. However, two is considered a minimum, because any value less than that will severely limit the IPC of the OOO pipeline (reasons will be described in the next few paragraphs).

Now, the 4 instructions that we want to read can all be within the same cache line or they might straddle cache lines. In the latter case, we can always read two consecutive cache lines together. An example is shown in Figure 3.2.

Looking slightly deeper, we will all agree that it is necessary to be able to read at least two lines from the i-cache in parallel. Otherwise, we would not have been able to handle this case. In this case the i-cache is said to have two read ports. A *port* is defined as an external interface of an i-cache. A read port is a port through which we can only read data (and not write), and a write port is a port that allows only write accesses. Note that every memory structure needs at least one write port such that we can write data to it. Let us thus consider an i-cache with 2 read ports and 1 write port in our current discussion.

Now, let us look at the more difficult case. Assume that there is a *branch* in this set of four instructions. The probability of one among these four instructions being a branch is by no means low.

---

[1]We shall use the term, PC, to refer to the program counter as well as its contents (memory address). The reader needs to figure out the right meaning (l-value or r-value) from the context.

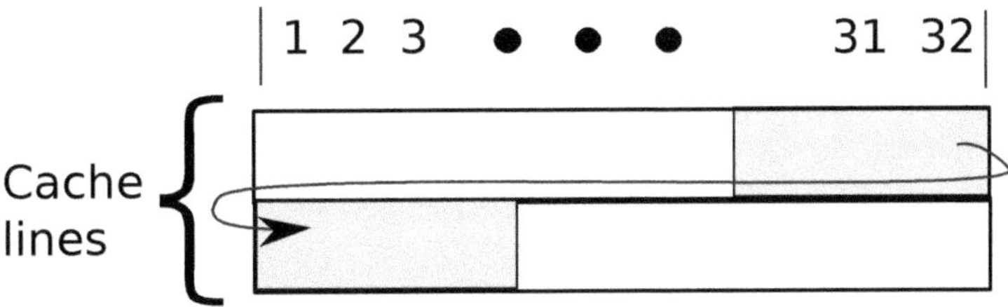

Figure 3.2: Accessing instruction bytes across two cache lines

Hence, we have to account for this case. If the branch is not taken then our problem is solved. A branch that is not taken is equivalent to a *nop* (instruction that does not do anything). The problem is that we do not know if a branch will be taken or not at the time of fetching the instruction. Assume that out of four instructions, the second instruction is a taken branch, and it is the only branch in this set of four instructions. In this case, the third and fourth instructions need to fetched from a different cache line. Figure 3.3 shows this situation.

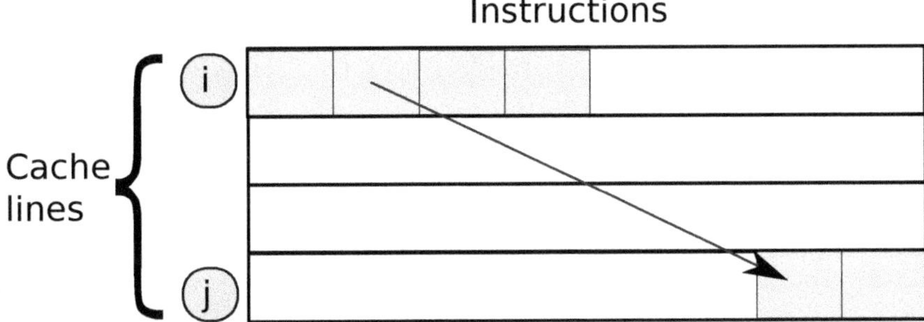

Figure 3.3: A taken branch in the middle of a 4-instruction sequence

In Figure 3.3, we see that we need to fetch the first and second instructions from cache line i, and the remaining two instructions from cache line j. Since we can fetch bytes only at the granularity of cache lines, we need to fetch line i and line j from the i-cache and pick the appropriate instructions from them.

There are some timing issues here. At any point of time, we know the address stored in the PC. Thus, we know about cache line i. There are several things that we do not know. Let us list them out:

1. We do not know which instructions in cache line i are branches. We have not had a chance to decode them.

2. We do not know if branches in line i (if there are any) are taken or not.

3. We do not know anything about the targets of the taken branches.

Given the fact that we do not know these important details before fetching the contents of cache line i, the processor would not know about line j, which contains the target instructions of a branch in line i. As a result with our current knowledge we can only design a processor that needs to work with only the instructions in line i. Since in the example we are considering, two instructions are there in line i, the maximum number of instructions that can be supplied to the remaining stages of the pipeline is two. We are thus not able to supply four instructions to the rest of the pipeline as we had originally intended to. The instruction throughput for this cycle is effectively reduced to 50% of the maximum value (4 instructions per cycle).

> **Important Point 3**
> *Note that any chain is only as strong as the weakest link. In this case, we can consider a pipeline as a chain of stages where the strength of a link is determined by the number of instructions that can be sent to the subsequent stage. If the fetch stage becomes a bottleneck, as we have just seen, then the rest of the pipeline stages will remain underutilised. This needs to be avoided, and thus it is imperative to have a high-throughput fetch engine.*

Now, what did we need to do to sustain a fetch throughput of four instructions per cycle? We needed to know the value of j before the current cycle. Thus, we need to design a mechanism such that the processor knows that it needs to fetch lines i and j from the i-cache. Assume that we know the value of line i from the value of the PC in the last instruction. To find out which line to fetch next (if any), we need to consider several points.

Let us outline them here.

- We need to first find if there are any branches in the instructions located at PC, PC+4, PC+8, and PC+12.

- If there are no branches, we can fetch the instructions from line i and $i + 1$ (if required).

- If any of the instructions is a branch, then we need to predict its outcome and target. Assume that we predict the instruction at (PC+4) to be a branch. We further predict the branch to be taken and its target to be at address K.

- Then we need to subsequently fetch the instructions at addresses K and (K+4).

Our strategy can handle almost all the cases where one of the four instructions is a branch. However, if we have two branches, then we will not be able to fetch from three cache lines in parallel because our i-cache does not have three read ports. The likelihood of having two branches in a sequence of four instructions is low. This probability can further be reduced by instructing the compiler to avoid generating such code. The other obvious solution is to have an i-cache with more read ports.

From this discussion, here are the important problems to be solved:

Problem 1 Predict if an instruction at a given address is a branch or not without looking at its contents.

Problem 2 Predict the outcome of a branch (taken or not-taken).

Problem 3 Predict the target of a branch.

3.2 Problem 1: Is an instruction with a given PC a branch?

The question that we need to answer is as follows. We are given the PC of an instruction. We need to figure out if it is a branch instruction or not without taking a look at its contents.

Now, it is not possible to guess that an instruction is a branch without ever looking at its contents. We have to take a look at the contents of the instruction at least once, remember it, and then use this fact to make a prediction the next time we see the same PC. This is exactly what we will do. In fact what we propose next is a standard approach in computer architecture and almost all predictors work on the same principle. We shall remember the fact that an instruction is a branch (or not) when we look at its contents for the first time, and then use this information the next time we need to fetch the instruction.

Let us explain with an example. Assume that we find out that the instruction at the address 0xFFFFFFCC is a branch. We can remember this information. Just before fetching an instruction from the address 0xFFFFFFCC we can look at the information that we have collected so far, and successfully predict that the instruction at this location is a branch. This will solve our problem.

Let us now look at a standard method for remembering such kind of information. We shall create a simple predictor. Figure 3.4 shows a black box where the input is the address and the output is a prediction: is the instruction a branch or not.

Figure 3.4: Basic structure of a predictor

A classical method for creating such a predictor is to use a table of entries, which we shall refer to as the Instruction Status Table(IST). The table is indexed by the least significant bits of the address. Each entry of the table contains the prediction: 0 (if the instruction is not a branch), and 1 (if the instruction is a branch). Let us explain with an example. Assume that the table has 1024 entries. Since $1024 = 2^{10}$, we can use the last 10 bits of the PC to locate the corresponding entry in the table.

Now, consider the fact that typically instructions are aligned to 4-byte boundaries. We can actually do better, because in this case the last two bits of the instruction's address will be 00. We can shift the address to the right by 2 places and use the shifted address to access the IST. This will unnecessarily complicate our explanation and we need to use the term shifted address everywhere. Hence, let us make a simplistic assumption in the remaining part of the text that instructions are not necessarily aligned to 4-byte boundaries. Their starting addresses can be arbitrary.

The prediction algorithm is as follows. Whenever we see an address, we extract the 10 least significant bits (LSB bits). We use these bits to index the IST and record the fact that an instruction is a branch or not. Whenever, we need to predict if an instruction is a branch, we extract the 10 LSB bits from the address, and read the IST. If the contents of the entry are equal to 1 then we predict the instruction to be a branch. This process is shown in Figure 3.5.

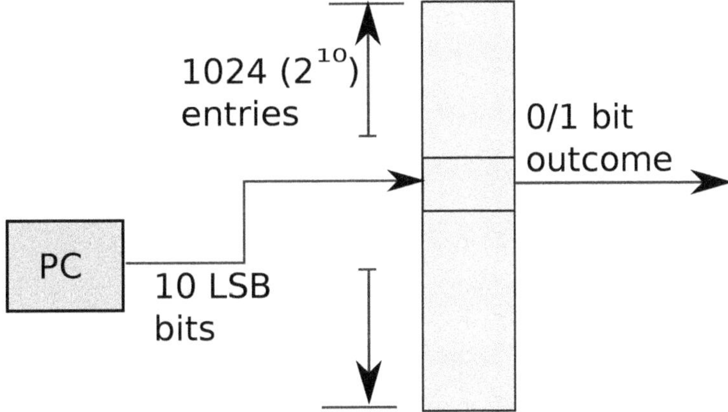

Figure 3.5: The instruction status table (IST)

Now, will this strategy work? The biggest criticism of such designs is based on the phenomenon of *destructive interference*. Let us proceed to define this term with an example. Consider addresses A and

A'. Assume that both of them have their 10 LSB bits in common. They will thus map to the same entry in the table. Let the instruction at A be a branch and the instruction at A' be a non-branch ALU instruction. If we have a code sequence that alternately accesses addresses A and A', we will always make the wrong prediction. Assume that when we make a wrong prediction we replace the entry in the table with the correct prediction. When we access A, we will record the entry in the table to be a branch. Subsequently, we will try to make a prediction before accessing the instruction at A'. We will predict it to be a branch, and the prediction will be wrong. We will then set the entry in the table to 0 because A' does not point to a branch instruction. Again before accessing the instruction at A we will try to predict and get a wrong prediction (we will read a 0, should be 1). We will thus always make a mistake and the predictor will never produce the correct value. This phenomenon is referred to as destructive interference in computer architecture.

Definition 15

When two computing units or computations share a storage element, and corrupt each other's state leading to a loss in performance, we refer to this phenomenon as destructive interference. *For example, when two branch instructions share entries in a predictor table and can overwrite each other's state, we observe destructive interference. In this case this phenomenon has a name – it is known as* branch aliasing.

One thing the reader should understand is that unlike theoretical computer science, in computer architecture we do not always rely on worst case situations. We are rather optimistic people and would like to look at the sunny side of life.

Fortunately, such cases as we just described are rare. Most programs have spatial locality. This means that if we access an address, we will access nearby addresses in the same interval of time. Given that we have 10 bits, it is unlikely that we will access an address that is 2^{10} (1024) bytes away in the same interval of time. Note that for the last 10 LSB bits to be common, the difference of the two addresses with these bits in common, has to be a multiple of 1024 bytes. Secondly, both the instructions with the common LSB bits should be executed fairly frequently to have a measurable effect. This is unlikely. As a result, this simple design will not be that bad in practice; we will still get a lot of correct predictions.

Can we do better? Yes, we can. Let us consider our running example. The basic problem is that we do not maintain sufficient information. We only maintain the last 10 bits, so two addresses that have their last 10 bits in common map to the same entry in the IST. This leads to destructive interference and the instructions end up corrupting each other's state. Let us add some more information to this table to make the prediction more accurate. Let us organise it as a cache.

Recall that a cache is a memory structure that saves a subset of blocks in the memory system. Each block is typically 32-128 bytes long, and has a unique address. We can uniquely address each block in a cache, read it, and modify it. Let us organise the IST as a simple direct mapped cache. Let us assume a 32-bit addressing system, and divide the memory address into two parts: a 22-bit tag, and a 10-bit index. Let us also divide each entry of the IST into two parts: a 22-bit tag, and a status bit indicating whether the instruction is a branch or not.

The access protocol is as follows. We first divide the address into two parts and use the index to access the corresponding entry in the IST. Each entry of the IST stores 23 bits (22-bit tag + a status bit). We compare the stored tag with the tag part of the address. If they match, then we use the status bit as the prediction. This process is pictorially shown in Figure 3.6. If the tags do not match, then we predict that the instruction is not a branch (reasons explained later).

This process will eliminate the problem of using the prediction of another address. This is because we are only using the status bit if the addresses match. We will never have the case that the instruction at A will use the prediction of the instruction at A'. It is true that the least significant 10 bits of A and A' might be the same and they may map to the same entry in the IST. However, the remaining 22 bits

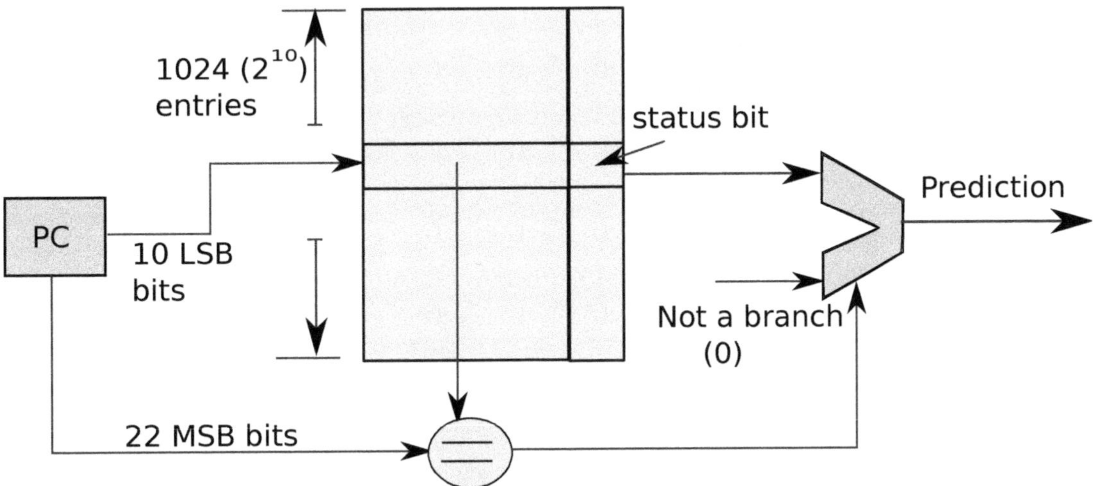

Figure 3.6: IST with tags

of the addresses (the tag part) will be different. Assume that the entry for the instruction at A' is there in the IST. When we try to make a prediction for the instruction at A, the upper (more significant) 22 bits of the address will not match with the 22 bits saved in the IST's entry. As a result we will not use the status bit to make a prediction.

Let us now consider the situation in which we do not find an entry in the IST where the remaining 22 bits of the address match. In this case, it is better if we predict that the instruction is not a branch. This is because if roughly 20% of the instructions are branches, we have a 4 in 5 chance of being right.

Let us now consider the access pattern: $A \to A' \to A \to \ldots$. With our simple IST the prediction rate was 0. With this version of the IST that is organised as a direct mapped cache, our hit rate will be better. The reasons are as follows. The instructions at A and A' will be overwriting each other's entries. When we access address A, we will not find its entry in the IST; we will instead find the entry for A'. The case for A' will be likewise. Since we will never find an entry, we will always predict that the instruction is not a branch. We will be right 50% of the time.

We have thus magically increased our hit rate from 0% to 50%!

This was a somewhat contrived example. The readers are invited to conduct simulations using real world benchmarks, implement both the predictors, and take a look at the results.

Activity 1
Get a trace of branch instructions using an architectural simulator such as the Tejas Simulator^{TM} [Sarangi et al., 2015], and do the following.

1. Get a trace of the program counters for branch instructions. The trace should have at least 1 million instructions.

2. Implement different versions of the IST and measure the accuracy of predicting whether a given PC corresponds to a branch instruction or not.

3. Vary the number of tag bits from 0 to 22.

3.2.1 Recording the Type of the Branch

We broadly have three kinds of branches: conditional, unconditional, and function calls/returns. They need to be handled differently. For conditional branches, we need to predict the outcome of the branch. For unconditional branches, the outcome is already known. All such unconditional branches are taken branches. Technically, function calls and returns are also unconditional branches because they are always taken. However, we choose to treat them as a separate category because we can create a really efficient mechanism to handle them (see Section 3.4.2).

In this section we are concerned with the mechanism that records and predicts the type of an instruction. We can implement this very easily by creating more status bits. Let us have 3 status bits, where the combination of bits indicates the type of the instruction. Refer to the following table.

Status Bits	Instruction type
000	Not a branch
001	Conditional branch instruction
010	Unconditional branch instruction
011	Function call
100	Function return

By having 3 status bits in each entry of the IST, we can correctly record the type of the instruction, and use it for further processing. We need the outcome of the branch, only if the instruction is a conditional branch. For unconditional branches, function calls and returns, we just need the target of the branch. We shall discuss methods to predict the branch target in Section 3.4.

3.3 Problem 2: Is a branch taken or not taken?

Now, that we know with some certainty that an instruction is a branch, we need to predict its direction (taken or not taken).

Let us first set the baseline. Assume that a branch's outcome is genuinely random akin to the outcome of a coin toss. It is possible to prove that irrespective of our approach we will never be able to successfully predict more than 50% of the outcomes. If we just simply guess that the branch is taken all the time, we will predict it successfully with a probability of 0.5. This statement can be theoretically proven using the Fano's inequality [Cover and Thomas, 2013] in information theory. This is beyond the scope of this book. Interested readers can always consult a book on information theory.

Let us now start our discussion by considering one of the simplest branch predictors namely the bimodal predictor.

3.3.1 Bimodal Predictor

We should shun the pessimistic point of view that states that branches are totally random. The reason is that branch outcomes are not totally random and thus it is possible to design much better predictors, whose accuracy is more than 90-95%. Let us consider a few examples. Consider the following C code snippet.

```
i = 0;
while (i < 100) {
        i = i + 1;
        . . .
}
```

Here, the branch corresponding to the *while* loop is not taken (control remains within the body of the *while* loop) for 100 times, and then it is taken (exits the *while* loop) just once. In this case the behaviour of the branch instruction is predictable. Let us assume that when we enter the body of the *while* loop the branch is predicted to be not taken. Thus, if we predict the branch to be not taken, we will be right 100 out of 101 times. Our accuracy will be close to 99%.

Let us now consider the following code snippet.

```
i = 0;
while (i < 100) {
    i = i + 1;
    if (i%10 == 0) {
        printf ("Multiple of 10");
    } else {
        printf ("Not a multiple of 10");
    }
}
```

We need a branch corresponding to the *if* statement. Assume that we enter the *else* part if the branch is taken, otherwise if the branch is not taken we enter the body of the *if* statement. We can clearly see in this example that 9 out of 10 times this branch will evaluate to taken.

In both these examples we have seen branches that most of the time evaluate to either taken or not-taken. It should be possible to design a predictor to predict them based on their activity in the past. We always do this in our lives. If a given store has historically been offering a discount, we choose it for shopping as compared to similar stores that do not offer discounts. There is no guarantee that on any given day the store will offer a discount. We can just make an intelligent guess based on its past behaviour.

Let us do something similar here. For each branch, let us save its history in a table. The next time that we encounter the branch instruction, we can read its history from the table and make a prediction. The history needs to be updated each time we become aware of the actual outcome of the branch.

Let us propose a simple design that is similar to the IST. Note that branch predictors need to be very simple structures because they lie on the critical path. Furthermore, we need to start predicting the outcome of a branch immediately after its PC is known and we need to finish the prediction before we proceed to fetch the instruction that can be the branch target. To avoid any pipeline stalls we need to ensure that the branch prediction finishes within one processor cycle.

Let us have a simple table similar to the IST with 2^n entries, which is indexed with the last n bits of the PC as shown in Figure 3.7. We can store the latest outcome of a branch: taken or not-taken. We thus need to store a single bit: 0 for not-taken and 1 for taken. We use this bit as the prediction (for the future). This means that if last time a given branch was taken, we predict it to be taken the next time. However, this is not a good approach.

Consider a function *foo* that contains a *for* loop with 5 iterations (refer to Figure 3.8). The branch associated with the *for* loop (*beq .exit*) will evaluate to not-taken 5 times, and the control will enter the body of the loop. The 6th time the branch will be taken and we will not enter the body of the loop. If we save the last outcome of the branch in each entry of the predictor table and use it to predict the outcome of the branch the next time we encounter it, we will make a misprediction the 6th time, because in the 5th iteration we would have recorded the fact that the branch was not taken. We will thus predict that the 6th time also, the branch will not be taken. This is wrong.

Now assume that we call the function *foo* that contains the *for* loop once again? We will mispredict the branch associated with the first iteration of the *for* loop because the last time we had encountered the branch, it was taken (not entering the *for* loop), and we would use this fact to make a prediction.

Let us now assume that we call the function *foo* repeatedly and there is no branch aliasing. The branch associated with the *for* loop will be invoked 6 times (5 times for entering the loop, and once for

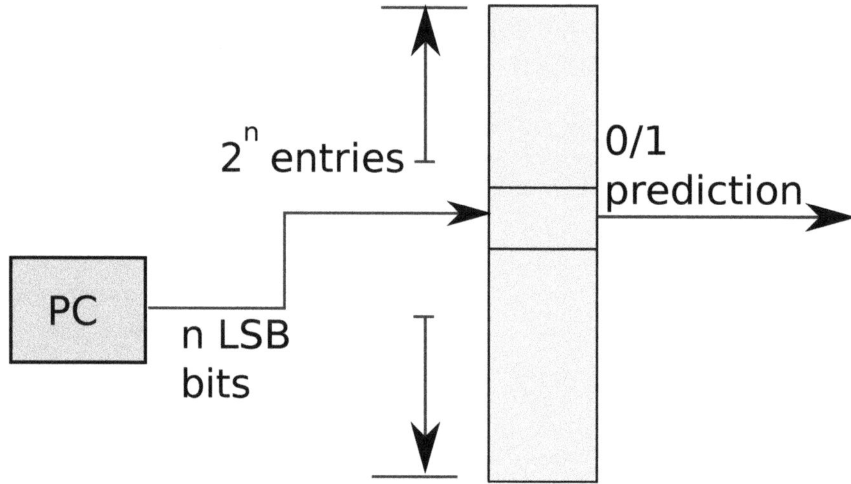

Figure 3.7: A simple single bit branch predictor

C code

```
void foo() {
    ...
        for(i=0; i < 5; i++){
            ...
        }
}
```

Assembly code

```
/* i mapped to r1 */
        mov r1, 0
.loop:
        cmp r1, 5
        beq .exit
        ...
        add r1, r1, 1
        b .loop
.exit:
        ret
```

Figure 3.8: A loop with 5 iterations

not entering it) for each function invocation. We will mispredict the branch twice (1st and 6th iterations). Thus, the misprediction rate is $2/6 = 1/3$, which is significant. Let us try to reduce it to $1/6$.

3.3.2 Predictor with Saturating Counters

The conditional branch in the *for* loop evaluates to not-taken 5 out of 6 times. The last invocation when the branch is taken can be thought of as an exception. The next time that we call the function *foo*, we should predict the branch (corresponding to the first iteration) to be not-taken based on its past behaviour. We should have a mechanism of either discarding or giving less weightage to exceptions.

Instead of keeping 1 bit to predict the outcome, let us instead use 2 bits in each entry of the predictor table. Let us refer to these 2 bits as a counter, where the count is the binary number represented by 2 bits. If the branch is taken, we increment the counter, and likewise if the branch is not taken, we decrement the counter. Since we have 2 bits, they can only be in the range of 00 to 11. If the count is equal to 11, and we find that the branch associated with it is taken, let us not further increment it. Let us instead maintain it at 11. Similarly, if the count is 00, and the branch is not taken, let us keep the count at 00. Such kind of a counter is known as a *saturating counter*.

Definition 16
A saturating counter is a special kind of counter that has the following fields: the count (C), a lower threshold (L), and an upper threshold (U). It supports two operations, increment *and* decrement, *which are defined as follows:*

increment:　$C \leftarrow min(C + 1, U)$

decrement:　$C \leftarrow max(C - 1, L)$

The counter thus cannot count beyond L on the lower side, and U on the higher side.

Let the prediction table have 2^n 2-bit saturating counters. We increment or decrement the counter once the outcome of a branch is known. Let us now use this array of saturating counters to predict the outcome of a branch.

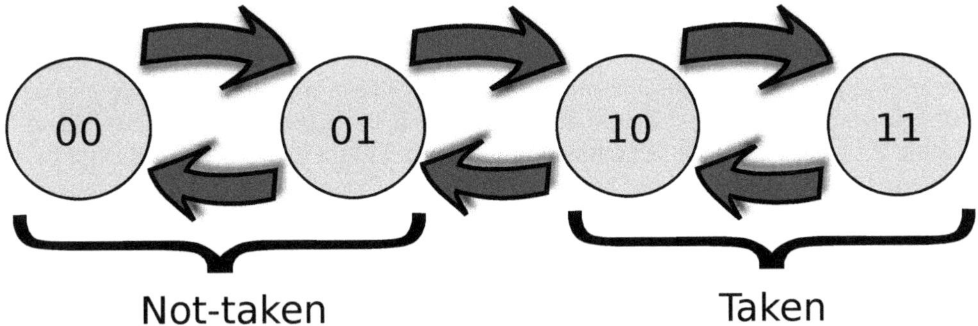

Figure 3.9: The state diagram of a saturating counter

Let us use the states 00 and 01 to predict not-taken, and the states 10 and 11 to predict taken. Figure 3.9 shows the state transition diagram of a saturating counter. If a branch is found to be taken, we move from left to right and keep on incrementing the counter. Once we reach the end (state 11), we do not further increment the counter. Similarly, if a branch is found to be not taken, we move to the left till we reach state 00. Let us use this array of predictors with our running example (function *foo* with a *for* loop in Figure 3.8).

Let us assume that we start in the state 01 (predict not-taken). After the first 5 iterations, the state of the counter will be 00. We will mispredict the branch in the 6th iteration, and the state of the counter will be set to 01 since it is a taken branch. Hence, our misprediction rate for this invocation of function *foo* is 1/6.

Let us see what happens when we call the function *foo* once again. We start with the state 01. For the first iteration of the *for* loop, we predict it to be not taken (value of the counter = 01), which is correct. Subsequently, the count remains at 00 till the 6th iteration when it again becomes 01. Here also the misprediction rate for the branch in the *for* loop is 1/6.

Note that if we would have started with a different value of the counter, the final value would have still been 01 because we encounter five consecutive not-taken branches. Irrespective of the starting value, the value of the counter at the end of the 5th iteration of the *for* loop will be 00. Subsequently, we encounter a taken branch, and the counter gets set to 01. If we call the function *foo* a large number of times the misprediction rate for the conditional branch in the *for* loop will stabilise to 1/6.

We can make an important conclusion here. By switching from the predictor with 1-bit counters to a predictor with 2-bit saturating counters we have halved the misprediction rate.

The states 00, 01, 10, and 11 also have the following alternative names.

State	Name
00	Strongly not-taken
01	Weakly not-taken
10	Weakly taken
11	Strongly taken

Given our discussion, we are in a position to understand why these states have been named in this manner. Let us assume that the counter is in state 00. We can tolerate one misprediction and still keep on predicting not-taken as we have done with our running example. Hence, this state is known as "strongly not-taken". Likewise is the case for state 11. The states 01 and 10 do not have that strong a bias. A single misprediction can change the subsequent prediction. For example, if the state is 01, and we have a misprediction (branch is taken), the new state is 10. We now predict the branch to be taken. Thus, this state is known as "weakly not-taken".

By replacing single bits with saturating counters, we have made the predictor slightly more intelligent. It can take a longer history of the branch into account, and it can effectively filter out the effects of infrequent outcomes. We can always extend this argument to have 3 or 4-bit saturating counters. However, there are negative aspects of increasing the number of bits. The first is the size of the predictor, and the associated area and latency overheads. The other is that the predictor becomes less responsive to changes in the branch outcomes. Assume that a branch for a long time was not being taken. The count will stabilise to 0. After that if suddenly we start taking the branch, a 2-bit counter will reach the weakly taken and strongly taken states sooner than a 3-bit counter. For a 3 or 4 bit counter, we will have many more intermediate states that will predict the branch to be not-taken. Computer architects typically run very extensive simulations with benchmarks to find the best possible configuration for a branch predictor.

3.3.3 Loop Predictor

Let us now look at designing a better predictor. The main problem with our running example is that we were not able to predict the last branch in the loop with a simple saturating counter based predictor. This is because the saturating counter associated with the branch gets set to the strongly not-taken state by the time we reach the end of the 5th iteration.

Let us first discuss a solution with limited applicability. Assume that we know the number of iterations at compile time. For example, we know that a loop will execute for only 100 times. We can create a simple circuit called a *loop predictor* that contains a register, and a small adder. When we enter the loop for the first time, the compiler can add an instruction to set the count in the register to 100. For every iteration of the loop we can decrement the count in the register. This can either be done via a dedicated instruction added to the program or the hardware can automatically figure out a loop iteration by looking at the contents of the instruction. Most loops are implemented using *backward branches*. These branches have a negative offset with respect to the program counter, which means that the control jumps to a point that is before the current instruction in the program. Most of the time, programs with loops use such branches to jump to the beginning of a loop. It is also possible for the compiler to add additional flags to an instruction to indicate that it is at the start of a loop iteration.

Now, if an instruction's PC is the same as that of the PC of the branch that decides if we need to iterate a loop, we can be sure that we are either entering a loop's iteration or exiting the loop. Once, the count reaches 0 we can predict that we need to exit the loop. In this case, when the count reaches 0, we can predict the branch (associated with the loop) to be taken and thus there will be no mispredictions. This solution undoubtedly sounds simple and effective. However, it is not generic. Most of the time, the number of iterations of a loop is not known at compile time. We can have *break* statements in a loop, loops inside a loop (nested loops), and loops might call complex functions with loops inside them. We can always make our simple design more complicated by having an array of registers indexed by the last few bits of the PC to accommodate multiple loops. Architects need to carefully evaluate the trade-offs while designing and using such predictors.

A general criticism of any approach that requires additional support from the compiler is that the approach does not remain generic anymore. A program that has special instructions might not run on a processor that does not support those instructions, but supports most of the other instructions in the ISA.

3.3.4   Predictors with Global History

We have looked at the local history of a branch, which is its behaviour in the past. Let us now look at the global history, which is the history of the last few branches of the program: they can either have the same PC or they can have different PCs.

Assume the code has an *if statement* before the end of the loop that does some further processing. It checks if the loop variable i is equal to 4. Assume that there are no other statements with branches inside the body of the *for* loop.

C code

```
void foo() {
    int i;
        for(i=0; i < 5; i++){
            ...
            if(i == 4){
                ...
            }
        }
}
```

Assembly code

```
/* i mapped to r1 */
mov r1, 0
.loop:
    cmp r1, 5
    beq .exit
    ...
    cmp r1, 4
    bne .cont
    /* Inside the body of the if
       statement */
    ...
.cont:
    add r1, r1, 1
    b .loop
.exit:
    ret
```

Clearly, the *if* statement's outcome is related to the outcome of the branch instruction in the *for* loop when we are exiting the loop (i is equal to 5). When i is equal to 4, we will enter the body of the *if* statement. We shall subsequently set i to 5, and conclude that we need to exit the loop. Let us create a circuit to capture this pattern.

We shall call this circuit the *branch history register* (BHR). This n-bit register records the outcome of the last n branches in a bit vector. For example, let us consider a 3-bit register. Let us refer to a taken branch by the bit 1, and a not-taken branch by the bit 0. If the last three branches are taken, the contents of the BHR will be 111. If the last branch was taken, and the branches before it were not taken, the contents of the vector will be 100. Whenever, we know the outcome of the branch we shift the contents of the BHR to the right by 1 position, and set the outcome of the latest branch as the MSB (most significant bit).

Let us now consider our *for* loop. Assume that we enter the *for* loop if the branch associated with it is not taken. Similarly, let us assume that we enter the body of the *if* statement if the branch associated with it is not taken. Let us assume a BHR with 3 bits. This means that the BHR contains the state of the last three branches encountered by the program. Note that the *bne* instruction refers to branch if not equal.

Let us compute the state of the BHR at the end of the 5th iteration. The last three branches and their outcomes are as follows:

Branch	Outcome
if statement in the 5th iteration	0 (not taken)
for loop branch at the beginning of the 5th iteration	0 (not taken)
if statement in the 4th iteration	1 (taken)

Thus the contents of the BHR are 001. This combination will only occur in the 5th iteration only. Thus, we can use the contents of the BHR to predict that we are done with the enclosing *for* loop and we can exit it. When we come to the branch that decides whether we need to enter the body of the *for* loop or exit it, we can use the contents of the BHR and safely predict that the branch should be taken, or in other words, we should not enter the *for* loop if the contents of the BHR are 001. This is known as the *global history*, because this information refers to the behaviour of other branches. In comparison, when we record the history of only a given branch instruction, this is known as the *local history*.

Definition 17

- *The global history captures the behaviour of the last k branches that have been encountered in program order.*

- *The local history captures the behaviour of only a single branch.*

Let us now design a predictor that uses this information to make a prediction.

3.3.5 A 2-Level Predictor

Such a predictor uses a BHR. Its design is shown in Figure 3.10.

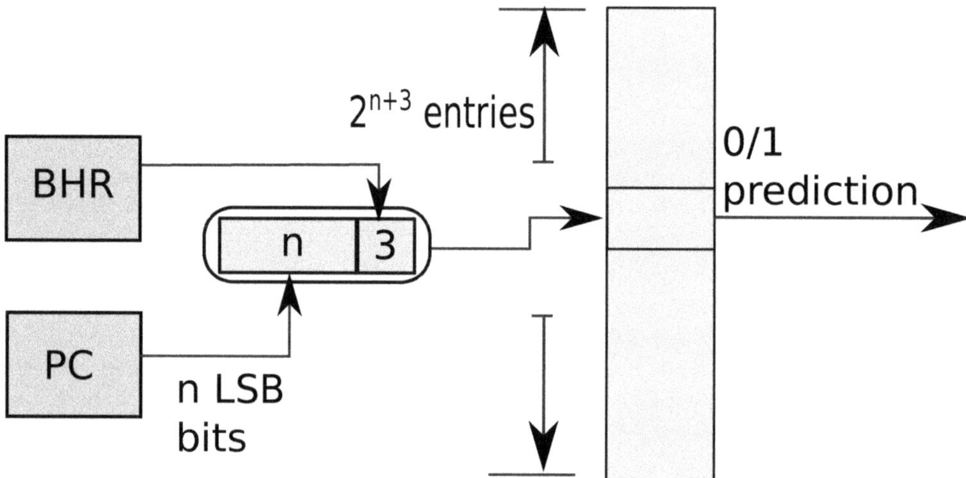

Figure 3.10: A global predictor that uses the BHR

Here, we combine two sources of information. We consider the contents of the 3-bit BHR (branch history), and the last n bits of the PC. Together, we have $n + 3$ bits. We use these $n + 3$ bits to index [2] a table with 2^{n+3} 2-bit saturating counters. The prediction and training steps are similar to that of the bimodal predictor with saturating counters. The only difference is that we are considering a tuple of the branch history and the PC bits to access the table.

Let us now argue that this is a better predictor than the bimodal predictor by considering our running example (*for* loop with 5 iterations). Let us consider the steady state where the code containing the *for* loop has been invoked many times. Now, consider the branch associated with the *for* loop. Only if the global history is equal to 001 (see Section 3.3.4), the branch should evaluate to taken. Otherwise, for the 7 other values of the global history the branch should evaluate to not-taken. Given that for each PC (represented by its last n bits), we have 8 entries (one for each combination of the bits in the BHR), we can store different outcomes for each value of the BHR. We store taken only for the combination 001. For the rest of the combinations we store not-taken.

Now, when we enter the first iteration of the *for* loop, it is highly unlikely that the BHR will contain 001. The likelihood of some other combination of bits being present in the BHR is high, and thus we will most likely predict not-taken. As we proceed till the last iteration, our predictions for the *for* loop will remain as not-taken. However, when we predict the outcome of the *for* loop's branch for the 6th time, the contents of the BHR will be 001, and we will predict taken (based on past behaviour), which is correct. After we exit the loop, the state of the corresponding BHR will be 100. The next time we enter the *for* loop, if the BHR remains the same (if there is no aliasing), we will make the correct prediction: not-taken. As a result, our current predictor will not make any mistakes. The rate of mistakes for the branch associated with the *for* loop will be 0.

Such kind of predictors are known as 2-level predictors. The first level reads the global history, the second level uses the global history, and bits of the PC to index a table of saturating counters. The table of saturating counters is also known as the *pattern history table* (PHT). For each pattern of bits (from the PC and BHR) it stores a saturating counter.

3.3.6   GAg, GAp, PAg, and PAp Predictors

Now, that we have seen the 2-level predictor, let us explore the space of all kinds of predictors that use a combination of bits from the PC and the BHR (branch history register).

Let us elaborate. In Section 3.3.5, the first level uses the BHR to record the behaviour of the last m ($m = 3$) branches. The second level predictor uses the contents of the BHR and n bits from the PC to create an $n + m$ bit number. This number is used to index a table of saturating counters. We argued that this is a good idea because it makes use of the behaviour of the last few branches. It is possible that the behaviour of the last m branches might give a clue about the behaviour of the next branch. This was indeed the case as we saw in the example code provided in Section 3.3.4.

Let us now classify each level into two categories: global(G), and local or per-address(P). A level is global if it uses structures that do not require bits from the PC to access it. For example, the BHR in the 2-level predictor that we saw in Section 3.3.5 is an example of a global structure. It is not indexed by bits from the PC – it is global in that sense. However, in the same predictor the next level uses bits from the PC. It stores some information that is specific to a set of instruction addresses. This is why the next level can be classified as *per-address*. Hence, the predictor described in Section 3.3.5 is a GAp predictor: global at the level of the BHR and local at the level of the PHT (table of 2-bit saturating counters).

On the same lines, we can have three more types of predictors – GAg, PAg, and PAp – as described by Yeh and Patt [Yeh and Patt, 1992]. Let us quickly look at them.

---

[2]Indexing a table in computer architecture means accessing an entry in the table with the given address.

GAg Predictor

This is a very simple predictor that does not use any bits from the PC. The first level is a BHR (similar to our 2-level predictor described in Section 3.3.5), and the second level is a table that is indexed by the bits stored in the BHR. This is shown in Figure 3.11. We assume that the BHR stores the behaviour of the last m branches. We use the contents of the BHR (m bits) to index the PHT (table of 2-bit saturating counters).

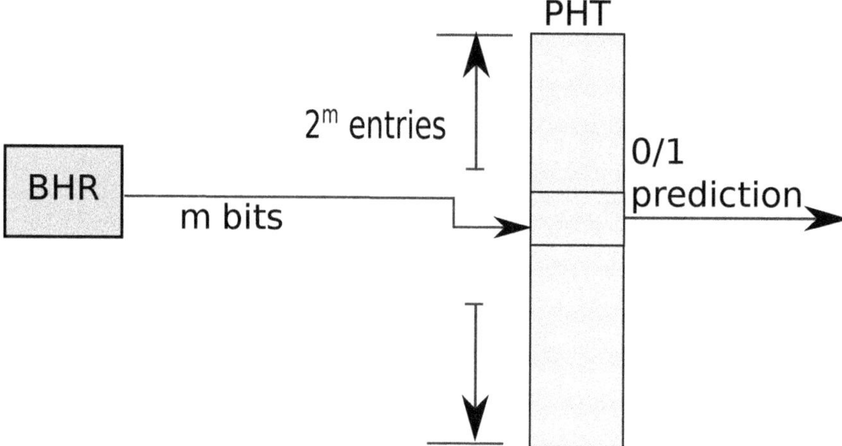

Figure 3.11: A GAg predictor

The advantage of this design is simplicity. However, the disadvantages are plenty. We are completely ignoring the past behaviour of any given branch. Assume it is always taken. We have no way of recording this information. We are completely basing our outcome on the behaviour of the m preceding branches, which is not the best thing to do in this case. This is because there can be many scenarios in a large program where the patterns for the last m branches will be identical. The associated outcomes might be very different though. This will cause an erroneous prediction for branches that are highly predictable (mostly taken or mostly not taken), and cases where the branch outcome is highly correlated with the past behaviour of the same branch.

The GAg predictor is thus not used in practice.

PAg Predictor

The first level in this case needs to use bits from the PC. Let us assume that we use 3 bits from the PC. There are thus 8 possible combinations. Each combination is associated with a set of program counters (PCs). Instead of one BHR, let us have eight BHRs – one for each set of PCs. This is shown in Figure 3.12. We show that we extract 3 bits from the PC address, and then access the appropriate BHR. Let us read an m-bit pattern P from the corresponding BHR.

We use this pattern P to access the pattern history table (PHT). Since this is a PAg predictor, we have a single table in the second level. Treating P as a binary number, we access the Pth entry in the PHT.

Note that as compared to the GAp predictor (Section 3.3.5), we do not use any bits from the PC to access the PHT. Let us understand the pros and cons of this design.

The PAg and GAg predictors have the same disadvantage. They do not take the past history of any given branch instruction into account. Considering the behaviour of other branches is not an effective substitute of the per-branch history. The same example as cited in the case of a GAg predictor holds here also. Assume a highly predictable branch (always taken or not taken), we might often be lead to

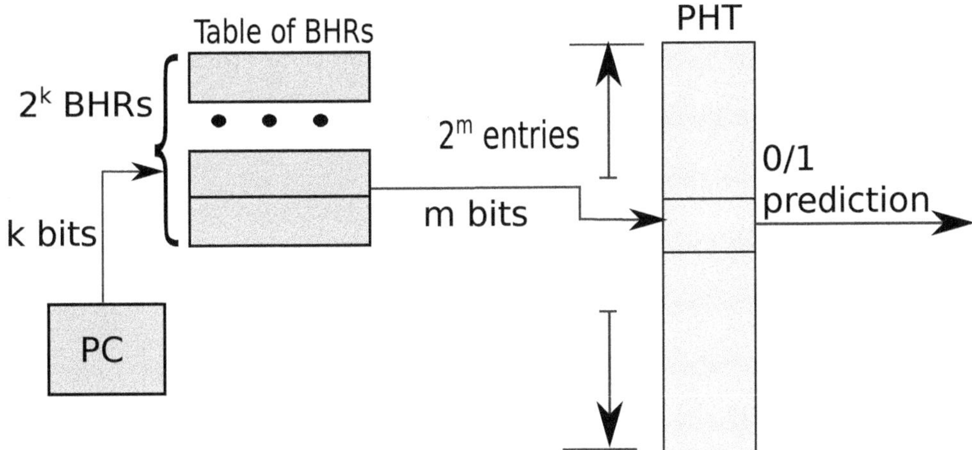

Figure 3.12: A PAg predictor

wrong conclusions if we just consider the behaviour of other branches. This information is not specific, and a lot of aliasing is possible.

However, the PAg predictor has some advantages as well. Let us see why. We use multiple BHRs, and this is often a good thing. To understand the reason behind this, let us look at the first level. We pick a couple of bits from the PC, and use them to choose the appropriate BHR. Which bits should they be? Should they be the least significant bits? The answer is probably no. Let us explain with an example. Assume we take 3 ($k = 3$ in Figure 3.12) bits from the PC. If they are the least significant bits then the 1st, 9th, and 17th branches in the program will map to the same BHR. There is little in common between them, and it is unlikely that we will get any benefits. Even worse, we will have the problem of aliasing, and the results will degrade.

Now, if we take the 3 most significant bits of the address, then all the branches in large regions of code will map to the same BHR. Again this is a bad idea, because effectively we have just one BHR. We are not reaping the advantages of having multiple BHRs. What is the solution?

The solution is to take 3 bits from somewhere in the middle of the address. Assume that these are bits 11, 12, and 13. In this case, all the branches in a 1 KB [3] region of code map to the same BHR. This is a good thing because this is in line with our original aim of having a BHR, which was to record the behaviour of recent branches. This is happening here. Let us now explain the logic of having different BHRs for different sets of addresses.

Because of spatial locality, in any window of time we are not expected to be touching a very large region of code. We will mostly be limited to small regions that contain loops. Assume that we are limited to a region of 5 KB. In our current mapping scheme, where each block of 1 KB is mapped to a separate BHR, we will map this 5 KB region to 5 separate BHRs. We will thus not have any aliasing and the consequent destructive interference. Furthermore, for every branch its corresponding BHR will contain the behaviour of the last n branches that are close to it in terms of the PC address (are in its neighbourhood). Branches that are far away and unrelated, will not be able to corrupt the state of the BHR. The BHR will thus capture more accurate information.

Let us try to summarise this argument. The aim of a BHR is to capture the behaviour of branches within a given neighbourhood of addresses. If we have a single BHR, then the possibility of destructive interference by branches in other regions of the program arises. Hence, it is the best to give a different BHR to each distinct neighbourhood of PC addresses. This is something that this predictor is trying to

---

[3]If we start the count from 1 (for the LSB), then each combination of the 11th, 12th, and 13th bits points to a region of code that takes 10 bits to address. The size of this region is thus 1024 bytes or 1 KB.

achieve.

When we move to a very different region of code, then the new branches will overwrite the contents of the BHRs. However, this is fine, because we expect to stay within the new region for a considerable duration of time given that most programs have a lot of temporal locality. The BHRs will get repopulated, and will capture the branch patterns in the new region.

PAp Predictor

This is the most generic predictor. It uses bits from the PC to access tables in both the levels. The first level looks like the first level of the PAg predictor (BHR selected by k PC bits). The second level looks like the second level of the GAp predictor: m bits from the relevant BHR concatenated with n bits from the PC. We use a combination of the pattern read from the BHR, and a few PC bits to access the second level table of saturating counters (the PHT). Refer to Figure 3.13.

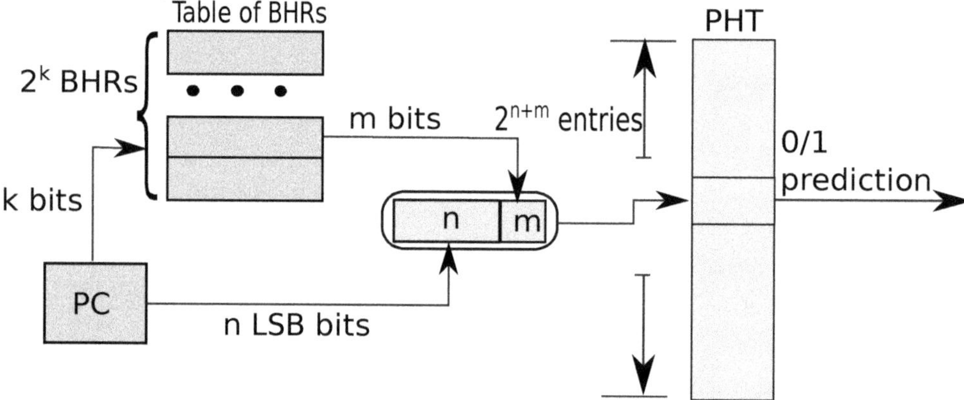

Figure 3.13: A PAp predictor

This scheme does not suffer from the disadvantages of the GAg and PAg predictors. It in fact, enjoys the advantages of both the GAp and PAg predictors. At each level, we need to very judiciously choose the the number and positions of bits that we want to take from the PC, and we also need to carefully choose the number of entries in the BHRs. If we are able to make a good choice, then such predictors typically have very high prediction rates.

A word of caution is due. Even though the PAp predictor has advantages, it need not always be the best choice. The first problem with it is that it is a large predictor – much larger than most of the other predictors that we have described. Large predictors are slow, are power consuming, and require a lot of area.

Additionally, it takes a lot of time to train such predictors. For example, a single-bit bimodal predictor can be trained very easily. If there are 1024 entries in the predictor, then all it takes is 1024 unique accesses to train it completely. If we have 2-bit saturating counters, then we require at the most 3 accesses to each entry to train it (e.g: strongly taken $\rightarrow$ strongly not taken). Now, if we have a BHR, we need to train the predictor for each access pattern in the BHR, which will require even more accesses. If our code size is small, or if we have a very high degree of locality where we are guaranteed to remain within the same region of code for millions of cycles, then the PAp predictor makes sense. However, for codes with low temporal locality, we will not be able to properly train the PAp predictor. By the time, we have trained the PAp predictor, we would have already moved to a different region of code, and all our previous work will get wasted.

3.3.7   GShare Predictor

We saw that the PAp predictor is the most powerful, yet suffers from various disadvantages. The primary disadvantage is the large size and the large training time. Even if we are not bothered about the training time, the on-chip area and power consumption are significant issues. Let us try to do the same thing in a different way.

The main aim while designing our predictors was to somehow combine global information stored in the BHRs with local (per branch) information. Let us extend the GAp predictor in a novel manner.

Let us have a single BHR in the first level. This will record the behaviour of the last n branches in a bit vector. In the GAp predictor, we were concatenating the pattern read from the BHR and m bits from the PC. In this case, let us instead do something else. Let us compute the XOR (exclusive OR) of the bits. The idea is to take the m-bit pattern from the BHR and perform a XOR operation between it and m PC bits.

In the second level, we access the PHT using the result of the XOR operation as an index (see Figure 3.14).

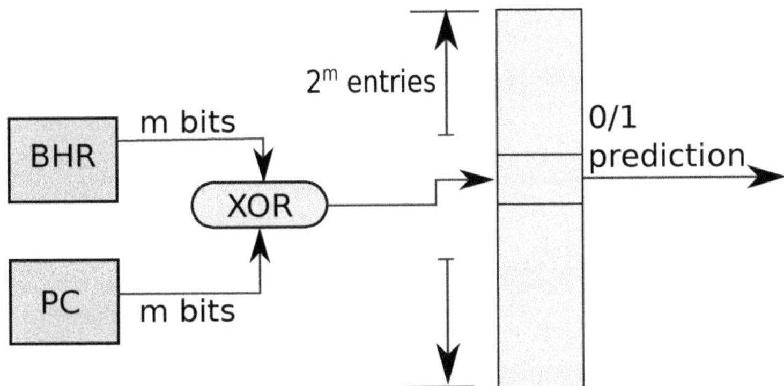

Figure 3.14: The GShare predictor

Using the XOR function as a method to combine two sources of information – PC bits and the global branch history – is an innovative idea. We can also choose n PC bits, and m BHR bits, and XOR them. When $n \neq m$, we need to pad the number with fewer bits with zeros while doing the XOR operation. The idea here is that after computing a XOR we will most likely arrive at a unique combination of PC bits and BHR bits. There is still a likelihood of aliasing. However, if n and m are large enough, and we have temporal and spatial locality in the code, then most likely in a small window of time the output of the XOR operation will uniquely represent the pair of bit vectors (PC bits and the branch history).

Recall that in the GAp and PAp designs, we were concatenating the PC bits with the branch history to get a unique combination; in this case, we are achieving something roughly similar by using a lesser number of bits. The trick is to use the XOR operation to combine two disparate sources of information.

Given that the probability of aliasing is relatively low in practical scenarios (as we have argued), using the GShare predictor is expected to be beneficial for performance. Furthermore, the number of rows in the PHT is $2^{max(m,n)}$ as compared to 2^{m+n} in the GAp and PAp predictors. This means that the table of saturating counters is smaller, faster, and more power efficient. This makes GShare a fast and efficient predictor.

3.3.8   Tournament Predictor

We have discussed a lot of predictors starting from the simple bimodal predictor to the GShare predictor. As we have argued, no predictor is good for all cases. For example, a PAg predictor is good when per-branch history does not matter and the behaviour of a branch is mostly dependent on the behaviour of the last n branches. As compared to that, a table of saturating counters is the best when branches are simply not dependent on other branches.

The accuracy of a predictor depends on the characteristics of the underlying code that the machine is executing. It is possible that one predictor might be good for one kind of code and another predictor might be the most suitable for another kind of code. There should be a mechanism of choosing one predictor for one region of the code, and another predictor for a different region.

Let us thus create a new kind of a predictor called a tournament predictor that contains multiple predictors. Refer to Figures 3.15 and 3.16. Here, we have two predictors: $Pred_1$ and $Pred_2$ (Predictor 1 and Predictor 2 in the figures). We then have an array of saturating counters called the selector array. It is a table of 2-bit saturating counters and is indexed by n bits of the PC. It is used to choose the outcome of one of the predictors.

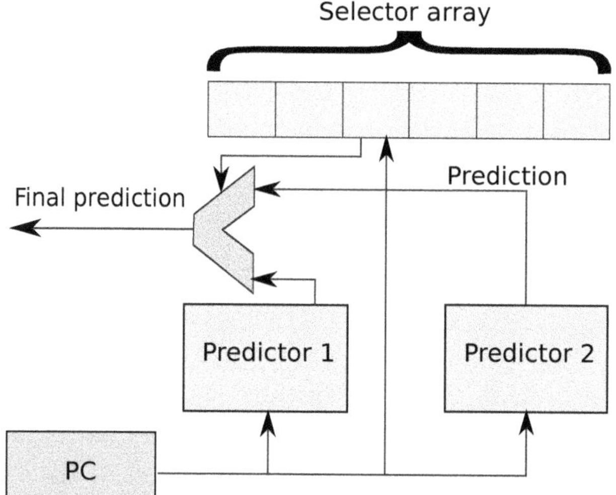

Figure 3.15: Branch prediction using the tournament predictor

The operation of the predictor is as follows. We first access the corresponding entry in the selector array for a given PC. If the value of the saturating counter is 00 or 01, we choose $Pred_1$, otherwise we choose $Pred_2$. Then we access the chosen predictor ($Pred_1$ or $Pred_2$), and use it to predict the branch. In parallel, we also run the other predictor (the one not chosen) and record its output.

Once the outcome of the branch (referred to as the Boolean value *result*) is known, we need to train the predictors. First, we train both the predictors separately using the outcome of the branch. The predictors internally update their tables. Now, we need to update the selector array. The logic is as follows. Assume that the function $outcome(Pred_1)$ refers to the outcome of $Pred_1$, and $\wedge$ represents a logical AND.

- $outcome(Pred_1) = outcome(Pred_2) \rightarrow$ Do not do anything.

- $(result = outcome(Pred_1)) \wedge (outcome(Pred_1) \neq outcome(Pred_2)) \rightarrow$ Decrement the saturating counter.

- $(result = outcome(Pred_2)) \wedge (outcome(Pred_1) \neq outcome(Pred_2)) \rightarrow$ Increment the saturating counter.

If both the predictors predict the same outcome, then there is no need to change the value of the corresponding saturating counter in the selector array. This situation basically means that we need to maintain status quo. However, if the outcomes are different, then the selector array's entry should be

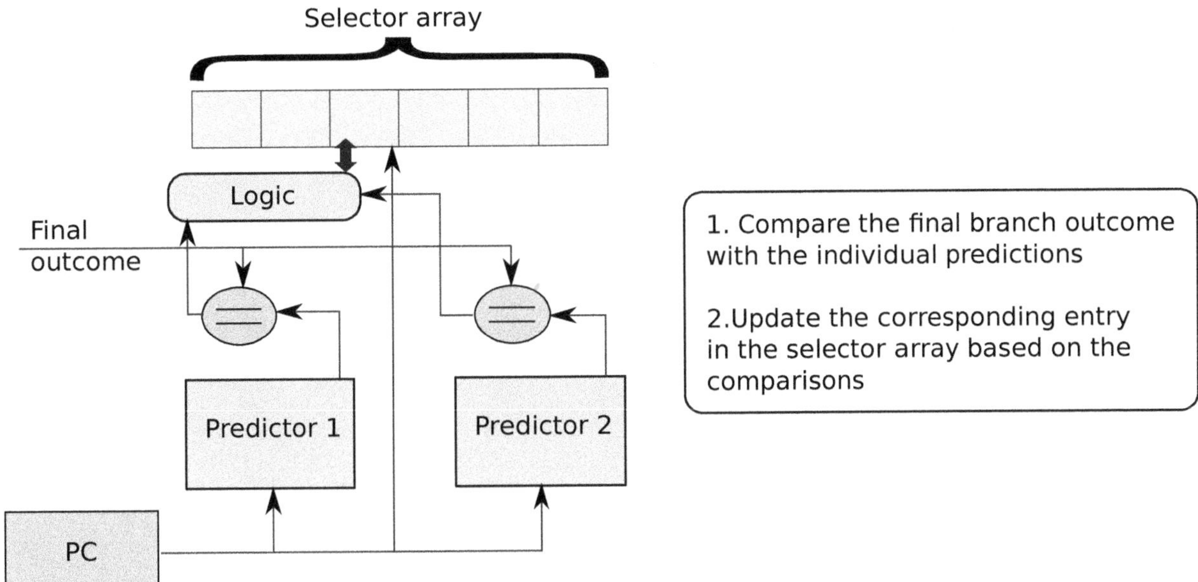

Figure 3.16: Training the tournament predictor

made to point towards that predictor, which gave the correct answer. If we assume that the states 00 and 01 correspond to $Pred_1$, then we need to decrement the saturating counter whenever $Pred_1$ is correct and $Pred_2$ is wrong. Likewise, we need to to do the reverse (i.e. increment the saturating counter), when $Pred_2$ is correct and $Pred_1$ is wrong. This mechanism ensures that we always choose the most accurate (and relevant) predictor for a given branch. This helps create the illusion that we have different branch predictors for different regions of code. Finally, the reason for choosing saturating counters is that we allow a certain amount of long term memory to be a part of the prediction process. We do not change predictors very frequently; we only do so when we make a given number of mistakes with the predictor that is currently chosen.

Tournament predictors have their fair share of overheads in terms of power, latency, and area. However, out of all the predictors that we have described, they are considered to be the most accurate, and are thus the predictors of choice in most cases.

Note that branch predictors in commercial chips use many more tables and combinations of bits, and use a hierarchy of different types of predictors. Discussing advanced designs is beyond the scope of this book.

3.4   Problem 3: What is the Target of a Branch?

Now, that we know if an instruction is a branch or not, and we can predict its outcome, let us predict the target of the branch. Let us here make a distinction between regular conditional and unconditional branches, and call/return statements. We claim that the latter two are special.

Consider the case of regular conditional and unconditional branches. Given the PC, we need to predict the target of the branch. In most ISAs, the address of the target is hard-coded into the instruction as a fixed offset with respect to the value of the PC. However, some ISAs support indirect branches where the target is contained in a register. In this case, predicting the branch target is more difficult.

Let us limit our discussion to cases where the offset is hard-coded in the instruction.

3.4.1 Branch Target Buffer (BTB)

Let us extend the IST to incorporate this information. We shall give it a new name and refer to it as the branch target buffer (BTB) henceforth. Let us add the branch target to each row of the BTB. The structure of the BTB is as shown in Figure 3.17. We use the least significant n bits of the PC to access a 2^n-entry BTB. Each entry of the BTB also contains the type of the branch (conditional/unconditional/call/return) and the target.

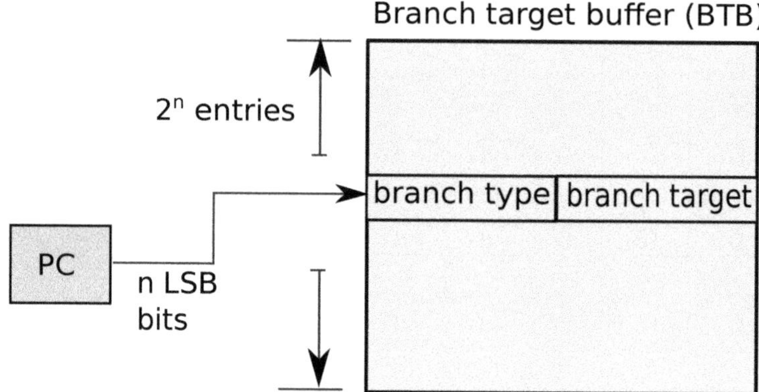

Figure 3.17: The branch target buffer

We can use the BTB for a dual purpose. It can be used to predict whether an instruction is a branch or not and the type of the branch. Furthermore, it can also be used to predict the target of a given branch.

To reduce the possibilities of destructive interference, we can adopt standard solutions as discussed in Section 3.2. Such solutions associate more information with each entry such that it is possible to differentiate between two branches that map to the same entry.

3.4.2 Call and Return Instructions

Let us now discuss the special case of function call and return instructions. They form a pattern. Consider the function call sequence shown in Figure 3.18.

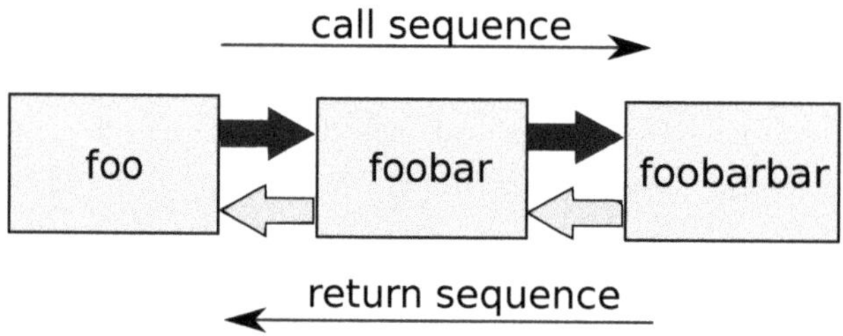

Figure 3.18: Call sequence ($foo \rightarrow foobar \rightarrow foobarbar$)

The function foo calls function $foobar$, which calls the function $foobarbar$. The return sequence is exactly the reverse $foobarbar \rightarrow foobar \rightarrow foo$. We can infer a last-in first-out behaviour. Computer architects and compiler writers have long exploited this pattern to optimise their designs. They start out with creating a stack of function calls. When we call a function we add an entry to the stack, and when we return from a function we pop the stack.

Let us thus create a stack of function call entries in hardware and refer to it as the *return address stack* (RAS). Each entry stores the return address (instruction immediately succeeding the function call) corresponding to the function call. Whenever, we encounter a call instruction, we insert its return address into the RAS. In our example, the state of the stack after calling the function *foobarbar* is as shown in Figure 3.19.

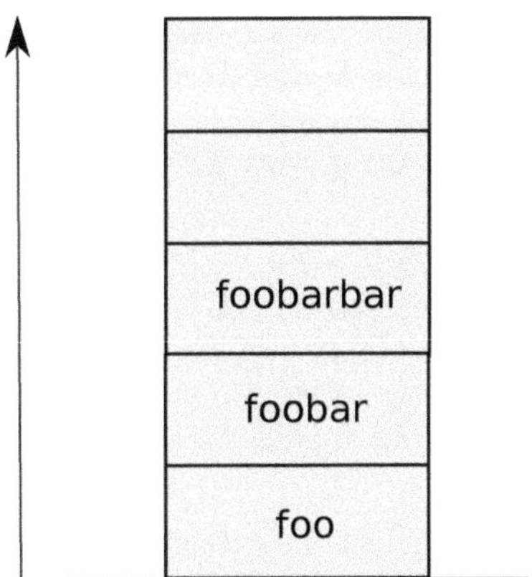

Figure 3.19: Function call stack

Now, when we encounter a return instruction, all that we need to do is just pop the stack. Since we return from instructions in a strictly reverse order, this simple strategy will always work. For our example, when we fetch the return instruction for the function *foobarbar*, we can just pop the topmost entry from the RAS stack, and use it. The topmost entry contains the return address for this function.

Specifically, the algorithm is as follows. Given the PC, if we predict that the instruction is a return instruction, then all that we need to do is use the element at the top of the RAS stack as the branch target of the return instruction. After decoding the instruction, if we find that the instruction was genuinely a return instruction, we can then pop the stack and remove the entry.

Using the RAS stack for return instructions is a far more accurate method of predicting branch targets than the BTB, primarily, because we do not suffer from destructive interference. However, this strategy does have its limitations. The first is that like the BTB the RAS has a finite size. It is possible that we might find the size of the RAS to be insufficient especially if we have a chain of recursive function calls.

In spite of these issues, the RAS stack is regarded as one of the most accurate methods of predicting the return address in modern processors. To increase its accuracy, researchers have proposed modifications to take care of recursive function calls, and furthermore it is possible to move a part of the RAS to memory if there is an overflow.

3.5   The Decode Stage

The process of instruction decoding is essential to most processors. The decode unit accepts an instruction encoded in a binary format, expands it such that all the fields are readable, and are easily accessible to all the units that process the instruction. Specifically, the roles of the decode unit (also see [Sarangi, 2015]) are as follows:

1. Expand all the immediate values embedded in the instruction to full 32 or 64-bit numbers.

2. Extract the branch offset (offset from the current PC), and expand it to a 32/64-bit field. Sometimes the decode unit is also used to compute the branch target by adding the current PC to the offset.

3. Extract the ids of all the registers.

4. Sometimes instructions might have an implicit source. For example the *ret* (return from function) instruction might read a certain return address register. The decode unit can make this explicit at this stage by recording the id of the return address register as a source register.

5. The decode unit creates the *instruction packet*. The instruction packet is defined as a bundle of information that contains all the details regarding the processing of the instruction. This includes its opcode (type), ids of source registers, constants, offsets, and control signals. Control signals are used to control the behaviour of different functional units in the data path (units that perform data processing and data storage operations). They are also used to choose one among multiple inputs for functional units, particularly, when we are choosing between inputs read from the register file, and forwarded inputs from other stages. A basic textbook on computer architecture (such as [Sarangi, 2015]) discusses the difference between the control path and the data path in great detail. It also talks about the way that control signals are generated and used to control different elements in the data path, notably, multiplexers that choose between different inputs.

The decoder is typically one of the most complex logic blocks in the processor. It consumes a lot of power, and also takes up a lot of area. The design of the decoder is in general very specific to an ISA, and thus it is seldom a subject of advanced study. However, let us nevertheless discuss some general ideas on how to make the process of decoding more efficient.

When is decoding likely to be a big issue? Recall that one great advantage of RISC instructions is that they make the process of decoding very easy. As compared to RISC instructions, CISC instructions are typically very hard to decode. In fact, the decode complexity is often cited as one of the biggest reasons behind the reasons to choose a RISC ISA. Let us see how this situation can be made better for CISC processors in Section 3.5.1.

We can also make a few modifications to the decode stage to efficiently leverage some simple patterns in the code. These will be discussed in Sections 3.5.2 and 3.5.3.

3.5.1   Predecoding CISC Instructions

In this section we shall discuss a scheme originally proposed by Narayan et al. [Narayan and Tran, 1999].

Let us first understand the issues at hand. CISC instructions such as Intel's x86 can be very complex. As of 2020, we have 1000+ x86 instructions and the number is growing with every new generation of processors. Moreover, the length of the instructions is also not fixed. In fact, the length can be highly variable. An x86 instruction's length as of 2020 can vary from 1 byte to 15 bytes. Thus, even figuring out the boundaries of instructions is a non-trivial problem. We need to decode the instruction to find this information. This causes several problems.

In general, when we are fetching multiple instructions at once, we can improve the throughput by decoding them in parallel. This is very easy to do in a RISC ISA because each instruction is of the same size, and thus we consequently know the starting address of each instruction. However, doing this in a CISC ISA is very challenging. We in fact need to do this serially. We need to read an instruction and figure out its length in bytes before we can read the next instruction. This makes a slow decoder even more slower.

There are additional complications in modern CISC processors. Most structures within the processor are designed to work optimally when the ISA is homogeneous. Flexibility is the enemy of high performance and low power. Hence, most processors that use CISC ISAs convert CISC instructions into RISC instructions internally. They are often referred to as microinstructions or micro-operations(μops). The process of conversion of CISC instructions into μops is typically done by the decoder. It would also be useful to know about the number of μops a given CISC instruction translates to, such that we can reserve enough space in different CPU structures. Again, without decoding the instruction it is not possible to find this information.

To solve all of these problems, let us consider an alternative organisation. Assume that when a cache line enters the i-cache for the first time we make it pass through a predecoder. The predecoder scans the set of bytes and marks the instruction boundaries. In addition, it annotates the instruction with some more information such that the effort required to decode the instruction reduces. The patent by Narayan et al. [Narayan and Tran, 1999] suggests a method where we add 5 bits to every byte in an i-cache line. The overall scheme is shown in Figure 3.20.

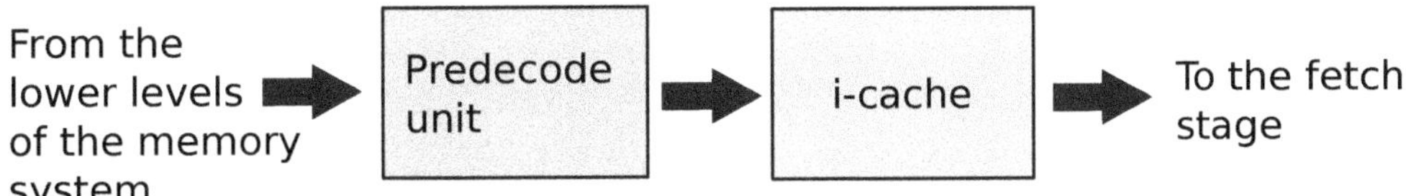

Figure 3.20: I-cache with a predecoder

The bits are as follows:

1. A start bit: indicates if the byte is the starting byte of an instruction.

2. An end bit: indicates if the byte is the last byte of an instruction.

3. A functional bit that indicates the type of the instruction and the type of its operands. This is specific to the instruction.

4. Two bits named *two-ROP* and *three-ROP* respectively. Their meaning is interpreted in conjunction with the end bit. They indicate the number of μops in an instruction.

Note that this is only one of the possible ideas in this space. It is possible to annotate a cache line in the i-cache in other ways also. For example, we may just want to store the indices (offsets within the line) for the starting bytes of each instruction. The general principle is that we are at least storing two pieces of information: positions of the start and end bytes of each instruction and the number of μops required to implement a CISC instruction. This is enough for us to do many things. For example, if we know the lengths of the instructions, we can decode them in parallel. If we know the number of μops that each instruction translates to, we can reserve space for the microinstructions in different architectural structures.

To summarise, when we fetch an i-cache line, we read the instruction bytes as well as the extra information written by the predecoder. The fetch unit passes this information to the decode unit, which can almost instantaneously figure out the boundaries of instructions, and the number of μops that will be required to execute each instruction. Specifically, the hardware has many parallel units that scan the cache line starting from different points. They look for start and end bits. They extract all the instructions in their part of the cache line, and then start decoding them.

Thus, by expending a little bit of additional storage, we can parallelise the process of decoding CISC instruction sets.

3.5.2 Optimising Operations on the Stack Pointer

Let us consider one of the most commonly occurring patterns in a program. We typically have instructions of this form:

```
st r1, 12[sp]
...
ld r1, 12[sp]
```

In this case, we are storing a value into the stack (indexed by the stack pointer sp) from register $r1$ and later loading it back. Recall that this is a very common pattern and is most often used while saving and restoring the values of registers before and after a function call. Since a function can overwrite registers it is often necessary to store the values of registers (that stand to be overwritten) on the stack, and later restore them. We also use such kind of a pattern when we perform register spilling. Recall that register spilling refers to the situation where the compiler runs out of registers, and it becomes necessary to free up some registers by writing their values on to the stack. Later on, when the values are required, they can be read from the stack.

Load and Store Instructions

Given that this pattern is so common, we can perform some optimisations at the decode stage itself to accelerate the execution of such instructions. Figure 3.21 shows the scheme. It was originally proposed by Bekerman et al. [Bekerman et al., 2000]. We shall describe a simplified version of their scheme in this section.

We maintain a register in the decode stage called the current stack pointer, csp. It is initialised to the starting value of the stack pointer. Every time we read the stack pointer, a small adder adds the memory offset to the csp to compute the memory address of the memory instruction. Thus, the memory address for all such instructions is available at the decode stage itself. We shall see in subsequent chapters that there are many more stages in the pipeline that an instruction needs to go through before we can compute the memory address. This is thus a quick shortcut.

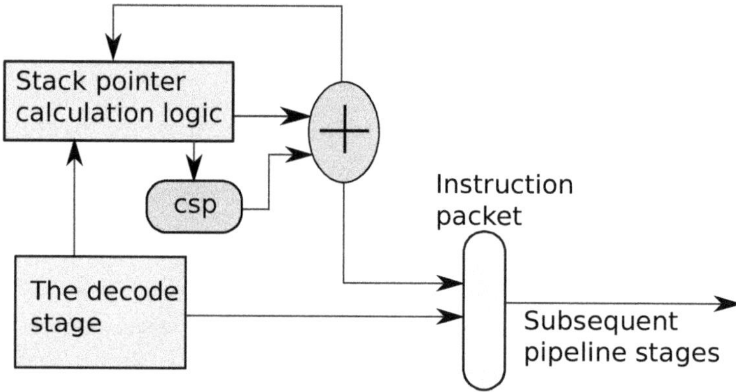

Figure 3.21: The stack pointer calculator

Refer to Figure 3.21 where we see that all we need is an adder to add the offset to the current value of the stack pointer. Since all the instructions till this point arrive in program order, we are sure that we are not reading wrong values.

Instructions that Update the Stack Pointer

Now, consider instructions that update the stack pointer. We typically have such instructions at the beginning and end of function calls. These instructions create an activation block (region in the stack) for the function to store its local variables, registers, and arguments. Before returning from a function, we destroy the activation block by updating the stack pointer. The stack pointer becomes the same as it was before the current function was called. These instructions are of the following type (assuming a downward growing stack).

```
/* create the activation block */
sub sp, sp, 24
...
...
/* delete the activation block */
add sp, sp, 24
```

We can add a quick shortcut to do this process as well. We can perform the same add or subtract operation on the contents of the *csp* register and update it. This process will ensure that the value of the stack pointer (stored in the *csp* register) is always up to date.

Tricky Corner Cases

Let us now consider an instruction of the type $\boxed{ld\ sp,\ 12[r1]}$.

In this case, we are loading a value from memory and saving it in the stack pointer. We cannot possibly process this instruction in the decode stage. The value of *12[r1]* will only be available to us after the load instruction gets the value from the memory system. This pattern is rare, nevertheless, we need to account for it. In this case, the *csp* register will contain a *null* value indicating that it does not contain the value of the stack pointer. All subsequent instructions that use the stack pointer will be aware of the fact that the value of the stack pointer is not currently available. They will read the value of the stack pointer using the regular process that treats the stack pointer as any other register.

Nevertheless, we can also do something very smart here. Assume we have the following code snippet.

```
ld   sp, 12[r1]
add  sp, sp, 24
...
add  sp, sp, 12
```

In this case, the load instruction sets the value of the *csp* register to *null*. Hence, the subsequent add instructions do not get the correct value of the stack pointer in the decode stage. Instead of not doing anything, we record the changes made to the stack pointer. For example, after the first add instruction, we record the fact that the value of the current stack pointer exceeds the value read by the load instruction by 24. After the second add instruction, we note that the value of the stack pointer has increased by 36. We thus record the difference between the current stack pointer, and the stack pointer computed by the latest instruction that nullified the content of the *csp*. Let us refer to this as Δ.

When the load instruction returns, we set the contents of the *csp* to:

$$csp \leftarrow addr + \Delta$$

where *addr* is the value returned by the load instruction. We can then continue the process of using and updating the stack pointer in the decode stage.

Benefits of Computing the Stack Pointer's Value Early

Let us now look at the benefits of this process. We might not be in a position to understand all the benefits because we have not read about most of the OOO pipeline. Just to give a sneak peek of what lies ahead, we shall see that the OOO pipeline is very complicated and consists of many stages. The stage that computes the memory address might be 20-30 cycles away. It is thus extremely beneficial, if we get the address on the stack early. Let us list some of the advantages.

1. We can issue a load to the memory system based on the stack pointer's value early (in the decode stage itself). This will ensure that the corresponding data arrives early and can be used to write to the register. We also do not have to issue a separate load instruction to the memory system later on.

2. For both load and store instructions, we can completely omit the process of address calculation. We shall already have the address with us.

3. We can also get rid of the instructions that add and subtract fixed constants to the stack pointer. They need not be sent down the pipeline. This will free up space in different structures in later stages of the pipeline, and also reduce one instruction.

3.5.3   Instruction Compression

One of the major bottlenecks in the fetch process is that only 8 to 16 instructions fit in a 64-byte cache line. Sometimes, we need to fetch multiple cache lines if a set of instructions straddle cache line boundaries, or if we have "taken branches" in the code. If we can somehow fit more instructions in an i-cache line, we can sustain a higher fetch bandwidth. Let us look at two common approaches.

Reduced-Width Instructions

Let us start out by describing a scheme that is currently implemented in commercial processors. ARM instructions are typically 32-bit (4 bytes) instructions. In general, having large instructions increases their fetch and decode overheads. We need to understand that most programs do not use all the instructions with the same frequency and sometimes an instruction has multiple variants. We only use one or two variants. It is thus possible to define a much simpler and compact ISA that captures most of the frequently occurring patterns in programs.

Consider the 16-bit Thumb ISA that is a subset of the regular 32-bit ARM ISA [Sloss et al., 2004]. Thumb programs typically take up 35% less space as compared to regular programs written using the full 32-bit ARM ISA. Moreover, once they enter the pipeline, Thumb instructions are decompressed into full 32-bit instructions. There is no measurable loss in performance in this process, and in addition it is not necessary to change the internals of the processor to support Thumb instructions.

Without discussing the details of the ARM ISAs, let us look at the general principles underlying the creation of an ISA that has shorter instructions.

1. Reduce the number of instructions supported in the reduced-width ISA. We will require fewer bits to encode the opcode(type) of the instruction.

2. Avoid encoding complicated flags in each instruction such as condition codes (dependent on the outcome of the last comparison).

3. We can show a reduced view of the architectural registers. Instead of exposing all the architectural registers, we can expose a subset of the architectural register space to the reduced ISA. For example, the Thumb ISA only sees 8 general purpose registers as compared to the full scale ARM-7 ISA that has access to 16 general purpose registers. This helps us save 1 bit while encoding registers.

4. We can reduce the size of the immediate fields. This will reduce the size of the constants that we can embed in instructions. Such constants include branch and memory offsets. In most cases, we do not need very large offsets given that we have a high degree of temporal and spatial locality in most programs.

5. Use an implicit operand in an instruction. This means that one of the source registers is the same as the destination register. We shall thus have instructions of the form $\boxed{add\ r1,\ r2}$.

This translates to *add r1, r1, r2* ($r1 \leftarrow r1 + r2$). In this case, the register $r1$ is known as an *accumulator*. To encode this instruction, we need to encode the ids of two registers instead of three (for most general purpose RISC ISAs). Using an accumulator reduces flexibility to some extent; however, since most ISA families have some support for accumulators (most notably the x86 ISA), there are very sophisticated compiler algorithms to generate code for ISAs with accumulators.

Compression Using Dictionaries

Let us consider an alternative approach. Let us identify frequently occurring sequences of instructions and replace them with a code word. At run time, we can retrieve the value of the code word in the decoder, and then retrieve the sequence of instructions by accessing a *dictionary*; it stores the mapping between the code word and the instruction sequence. This will increase the fetch bandwidth.

Let us discuss a scheme proposed by Lefurgy et al. [Lefurgy et al., 1997], albeit with some modifications. They propose a new pass after the compilation phase. Specifically, after the compiler has generated the binary, they introduce a pass where a program scans the instructions in the binary and figures out the most commonly used instruction sequences. It replaces each such sequence with a code word that uniquely identifies the code sequence. The mapping between the code words and the instruction sequences are saved in a dedicated region in the memory space of the program called the *dictionary*.

There are issues with regards to branches because now the code size changes. To keep things simple, the algorithm never encodes a branch instruction that uses relative offsets. Handling branch targets is complicated. If we are branching to a point that is in the middle of an encoded instruction sequence, then we need to specify the offset of the branch within the encoded instruction sequence. This creates an added layer of complexity. It is thus best to ensure that all branch targets are only at the beginning of encoded instruction sequences. This makes the scheme easy to use. Note that since the program effectively becomes shorter because instructions are now replaced with short code words, it is necessary to modify all the addresses that are used in the program, in specific, branch offsets. The post compilation pass needs to correct all of these offsets.

Once we run the program, and start fetching instructions, the first step is to see if we are fetching a regular instruction or a code word. If we are fetching a code word, then we need to access the dictionary, and fetch the instructions that correspond to the given code word. The subsequent stages of the pipeline run unmodified (see Figure 3.22).

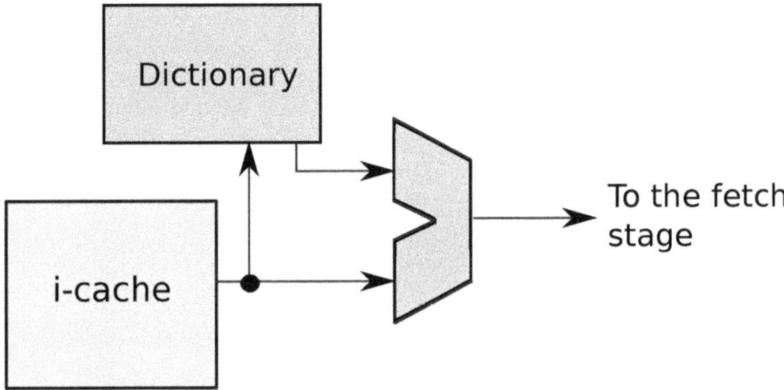

Figure 3.22: The fetch logic for a processor that uses compressed instructions stored in a dictionary

An astute reader may ask, "What is the benefit?" Previously we were reading uncompressed instructions directly from the i-cache, and now we are reading them from the dictionary. Let us mention the benefits.

1. The overall code size is lower. Assume one instruction sequence (containing 5 instructions) is found at 10 different locations in the program. Let the size of an instruction as well as that of a code word be 4 bytes. In this case, if we use the uncompressed version of the program we require $10 * 5 * 4 = 200$ bytes for these instructions. However, if we replace each instruction sequence with a 4-byte code word, then we require 20 $(4 * 5)$ bytes to store the sequence in the dictionary and $10 * 4$ bytes for the 10 corresponding code words in the program– one for each instance of the instruction sequence. We thus require a total storage space of 60 bytes. Given that the code size is lower, it will be easier to store such programs, particularly, in embedded systems where instruction memory is limited.

2. The dictionary can be stored on a separate storage structure, which is expected to be much smaller than the i-cache, and thus it can be much faster than the i-cache as well. If the encoded instruction sequence is long enough, then there will be a savings in terms of time if we fetch the constituent instructions from the dictionary.

3. We can extend this idea to store decoded instructions in the dictionary. We can thus effectively skip the decode stage using this optimisation.

3.6 Summary and Further Reading

3.6.1 Summary

Summary 2

1. We need a high-throughput mechanism to deliver instructions to the pipeline. We typically need to deliver 2-4 instructions to the pipeline in a single cycle. This is known as the fetch width.

2. The first problem is to decide if a given instruction is a branch or not. We can keep a table that is addressed by a subset of the bits of the PC. This table can contain the type of the instruction including the type of the branch – conditional, unconditional, call, or return.

3. We refer to this table as the IST (instruction status table).

4. The second problem is to predict the direction of a branch – taken or not-taken. The simplest method is to use the last n bits of the PC to access a table of bits. Each bit remembers the outcome of the branch when it was encountered for the last time. This is called a Bimodal Predictor.

5. Any such predictor that uses bits of the PC for addressing can suffer from the problem of aliasing or destructive interference. This refers to a phenomenon where multiple entries map to the same entry. A standard approach to solve such issues is to store additional bits of the PC (referred to as the tag) or to create a set associative structure. The latter is a standard technique used in the design of caches (small instruction or data memories) where we associate a given PC with a set of locations in a table. It can be present in any of the locations within the set. This gives us more flexibility.

6. We can further augment the bimodal approach by having a table of saturating counters. Each such counter incorporates a certain degree of hysteresis. One wrong prediction does not change the outcome of the predictor.

7. *We can further improve the accuracy of these predictors by incorporating global history where we consider the behaviour of the last few branches. This often determines the context of a prediction.*

8. *It is possible to further generalise this idea by considering the full design space of predictors that include different degrees of local history (same branch across time) and global history (last k branches in the same time window). They are referred to as the GAg, GAp, PAg, and PAp predictors.*

9. *The GShare predictor tries to reduce the amount of storage and still perform as well as a PAp predictor by indexing the table of saturating counters with a XOR of bits from the PC and the branch history.*

10. *The tournament predictor is composed of multiple predictors. The final outcome is equal to the outcome of the most accurate constituent predictor.*

11. *We can enhance the IST to create a structure called the branch target buffer (BTB) that also stores the branch target.*

12. *For return instructions, we prefer not to use the BTB mechanism. Instead it is a better idea to use a stack of return addresses known as the RAS (return address stack).*

13. *The fetch unit feeds its instructions to the decode unit. The decode unit is in general very simple for RISC ISAs. However, in variable length CISC ISAs, the decoder is very complex. It is often necessary to annotate cache lines with information to demarcate instruction boundaries.*

14. *We can do several decode time optimisations such as computing the value of the stack pointer in the decode stage.*

15. *We can also compress instructions offline, and dynamically decompress them at the time of execution. This will save us valuable space in the i-cache.*

3.6.2   Further Reading

The original papers on two-level branch predictors that incorporated global history were published by Yeh and Patt [Yeh and Patt, 1991, Yeh and Patt, 1992, Yeh and Patt, 1993]. Some advanced branch prediction mechanisms include the agree predictor [Sprangle et al., 1997], the YAGS predictor [Eden and Mudge, 1998], and the TAGE predictor [Seznec, 2007]. The paper on Alpha EV8 [Seznec et al., 2002] gives a perspective on branch predictors implemented in commercial processors.

Recent approaches have focused on novel methods for predicting branches. One of the most promising directions is based on neural networks [Jiménez, 2003, Seznec, 2004, Jiménez, 2011b]. Some of them even use analog electronics [Jiménez, 2011a] and memristors [Wang et al., 2013]. A recent survey by Mittal contains many more references of papers on branch predictors [Mittal, 2018] and also a detailed analysis of the design space.

There are some works that map the problem of branch prediction to predicting general sequences. Using information theoretic measures they derive an error bound, and also correlate this with the compressibility of the sequence (see [Federovsky et al., 1998]).

The area of instruction compression is very well studied. Some of the popular papers in this area are [Benini et al., 1999, Chen et al., 1997, Helkala et al., 2014].

Exercises

Ex. 1 — Show the working of a predictor with a 3-bit saturating counter.

Ex. 2 — How does a GShare predictor combine the PC bits and the branch history? What are the advantages of doing so? Do you expect it to be as effective as a PAp predictor?

Ex. 3 — Let us consider a tournament branch predictor with the following design.

- It contains an array of 3-bit saturating counters to choose between two predictors: $predictor A$ and $predictor B$. It uses the last n bits of the PC address to index this table.
- $predictor A$ is a simple branch predictor that uses m bits of the PC to access an array of 2-bit saturating counters.
- $predictor B$ is a global branch predictor that us the last k branches to access a table of 2-bit saturating counters.

How many bits are used in total?

Ex. 4 — Design a method to predict the targets of indirect branches. An indirect branch stores the branch target in a register.

Ex. 5 — Consider the code for regular matrix multiplication. What is the best branch predictor for this code pattern?

Ex. 6 — Is it a good idea to have saturating counters with 3 or 4 bits?

Ex. 7 — Design a two-level branch predictor with the following property. The branch predictor at the first level produces a confidence along with a prediction. If the confidence is low, then the more elaborate branch predictor at the second level is used. This design can save power if used correctly.

Ex. 8 — We have used the LSB bits of the address to access the branch predictors. Even if we have multiple predictors, this can cause destructive interference in all the predictors. Instead of using the LSB bits, can we use different hashing functions to map the PC with entries in the branch predictors? Comment on this design choice.

* **Ex. 9** — Let us say that we take a regular branch predictor and augment it with a biased coin that yields Heads with probability p. Every time that we need to make a prediction, we flip the coin, and if we get Heads, then we flip the prediction of the branch predictor. In the general case, will this design lead to a better prediction?

* **Ex. 10** — Show the detailed design of a fetch unit that can predict more than 1 branch per cycle. Explain the trade-offs.

* **Ex. 11** — Consider a structure called a *loop buffer*. This contains the decoded instructions inside a loop. While executing the instructions in a loop, the processor gets the instructions from the loop buffer instead of the i-cache. Answer the following questions.

1. How do we detect a loop in hardware?

2. How do you think the loop buffer works? Provide details of its design and operation.

3. What should the size of the loop buffer and associated structures be?

4. What are the advantages of a loop buffer?

** **Ex. 12** — Consider an OOO pipeline where the branch predictor takes 2 cycles (instead of 1). The BTB however takes just 1 cycle. How can we ensure back-to-back execution of instructions (including branches) in such a pipeline. Note that back-to-back execution means that consecutive instructions can be fetched and executed in consecutive cycles. Show all the details of your proposed solution, and prove its correctness. [HINT: We should be prepared to do some extra work that might potentially get wasted.]

Ex. 13 — What are the advantages of predecoding CISC instructions?

* **Ex. 14** — Is recursion a desirable feature in programs in the context of the Return Address Stack (RAS)? How can we make the RAS aware of a recursive pattern in the program? Can you propose an optimisation for the RAS when our workloads have a lot of recursive function calls.

Design Problems

Ex. 15 — Understand the implementation of branch predictors in an architectural simulator.

Ex. 16 — Implement a branch predictor based on neural networks in an architectural simulator.

Ex. 17 — Implement an instruction compression scheme in an architectural simulator.

Ex. 18 — There is an intimate connection between compressibility of a sequence and the predictability. This is captured by the Fano's inequality. Use it to find the upper bound on the prediction accuracy of branches for different workloads.

4

The Issue, Execute, and Commit Stages

The fetch and decode stages that we designed in Chapter 3 can deliver a steady stream of instructions with a very high throughput. Now, we need to create a high bandwidth instruction execution engine that can execute as many instructions in parallel as possible, subject to area and power constraints. This is the area of study in this chapter. Note that for understanding the contents of this chapter, Chapter 2 is an essential prerequisite. We need to be confident in the concepts listed in Way Point 1.

Way Point 1
At this point we are supposed to be confident with the following concepts.

- *In-order pipelines: 5 stages of instruction processing, interlocks, and forwarding.*

- *Data hazards: WAW, WAR, and RAW hazards. Special case of the load-use hazard.*

- *Basic idea of out-of-order pipelines: true and false dependences.*

- *Familiarity with the following concepts: branch prediction, instruction renaming, multi-instruction issue, and the instruction window.*

- *Knowledge of precise exceptions and in-order instruction completion.*

The first task is to remove all WAR (write after read) and WAW (write after write) dependences from the sequence of instructions. As we had discussed in Chapter 2, this will increase the available parallelism in the instruction stream significantly. This process is known as *renaming*, and requires elaborate hardware support. After renaming the only dependences in the code will be RAW (read after write) dependences. A RAW dependence enforces a strict order of execution between the producer and consumer instructions (see Section 4.1).

Such dependences have the potential to reduce the ILP (instruction level parallelism) unless we take additional measures. The standard approach to dealing with such issues is to take a look at a large set of instructions together, and then find a set of instructions that can be executed in parallel. They should not have any dependences between them. To find this set of independent instructions, we need hardware structures to track the dependences between instructions, and to find out when an instruction is ready to be executed. For an instruction to be ready, all of its input operands should be ready. It is possible that many instructions may become ready for execution in the same cycle. Given that we have a small set of execution units, we need to choose a subset of the ready instructions for execution. There are elaborate heuristics to *select* the appropriate set of instructions. This has implications in terms of the critical path of the program. Owing to their complexity, these structures are some of the most performance-critical units in the pipeline, and thus are designed very carefully (explained in Section 4.2).

Till now we have been discussing how to handle instructions that have only register based dependences. Handling memory instructions requires a different set of architectural structures. This is because register dependences can be figured out right after decoding the instructions; however, memory addresses are computed much later in the execution stage. Hence, most processors use an additional structure called the load-store queue (LSQ) to keep track of memory dependences. The LSQ as of today is a very sophisticated structure that enforces correctness, as well as implements many optimisations to improve performance. We shall delve into such issues in Section 4.3.

Finally, after processing all of these instructions out of order, it is necessary to create an illusion to an external observer that the instructions have actually been executing in program order. This is required to ensure precise exceptions (see Section 2.3.3) such that the program can transparently recover from faults, interrupts, and exceptions. Ensuring this in a complex system with branch prediction and out-of-order execution is fairly complex. We need to ensure that we restore the state of the program to exactly what it should have been right before the exception. This requires us to periodically take checkpoints of the state, and efficiently store them. In Section 4.4 we shall study the trade-offs between the overheads of taking periodic checkpoints and the time it takes to correctly restore the state.

4.1   Instruction Renaming

As we discussed in Section 2.3.3, instructions can have three kinds of dependences between them: WAR (write after read), WAW (write after write), and RAW (read after write). Out of these only the RAW dependence is a *true* dependence. In other words, if instruction B is dependent on the output of instruction A, B has to execute after A finishes. WAR and WAW dependences are in a sense *false* dependences because they arise due to the limited number of registers. If we would have had an infinite number of registers, then these dependences would not have been there. Note that in this discussion we are not talking about reads and writes to memory addresses. We shall discuss memory dependences in Section 4.3.

4.1.1   Overview of Renaming

Let us quickly recapitulate what we had learnt in Section 2.3.3. Consider two pieces of code as shown in Figure 4.1 (laid out side by side). The code on the left uses regular architectural registers. We note the presence of WAR and WAW hazards, whereas the code on the right has only RAW hazards. This was made possible because we replaced architectural registers by physical registers. This process was called *renaming*.

Before proceeding further, let us clarify the terminology that we shall use. All the architectural registers start with r. We have 16 architectural registers: $r0$ to $r15$. For the time being let us assume an unlimited number of physical registers. The architectural-to-physical register mapping scheme in Figure 4.1 is as follows. Initially, architectural register ri is mapped to physical register pi. However, every time we write to architectural register ri, we assign that avatar of ri to a new physical register. The physical registers are numbered as follows in our example: $pi1, pi2, \ldots$. For example, in Line 1 we write to $r1$. We thus assign it to a new physical register $p11$. When we write to $r1$ again in Line 2, we assign it to a new physical register $p12$. On similar lines, we assign $r7$ to the physical register $p71$ in Line 4. We can think of the first digit as the number of the architectural register that the physical register is mapped to, and the second digit as the version number. Every time we write to the register, we increment the version number. Note that this numbering is used in our running examples for the purpose of better explanation. In a real system, the numbering is done differently (see Section 4.1.5). Notwithstanding the limitations of our simple scheme, we clearly observe that the renamed code has only one dependence (between Lines 2 and 3), which is a RAW dependence.

Needless to say, during this assignment of architectural to physical registers, the correctness of the program is not affected. The producer-consumer relationships between instructions remain. The code looks like it is compiled for a machine that actually has a very large number of registers. We need to ensure that this is the case, when we discuss a more realistic implementation.

Original code   Renamed code

```
1  add r1, r2, r3                          add p11,  p2,   p3        1
2  add r1, r4, r5 /* WAW dep. r1 */        add p12,  p4,   p5        2
3  add r6, r1, r7 /* RAW dep. r1 */        add p61,  p12,  p7        3
4  add r7, r8, r9 /* WAR dep. r7 */        add p71,  p8,   p9        4
```

Figure 4.1: Original and renamed code

Now, in practice, we will never have an infinite number of registers. However, let us aim for a situation, where we will never fall short of physical registers. In this case, the number of such physical registers is practically infinite.

This is a very good vision, and we would all like to have a system where the performance nullifying effects of handling WAW and WAR hazards are not there. However, before proceeding, we need to answer a basic question: "Who does the renaming?"

Let us consider what we already know about this issue. Recall that we had argued in Chapter 2 that the programmer should not be aware if the processor is in-order or out-of-order. The programmer needs to see the same view of the registers, which is the architectural register set. Any physical register has to be defined exclusively inside the processor, and has to be visible only to elements within the processor. A physical register should be an undefined concept outside the processor.

This discussion naturally answers the question, "Who does the renaming?" The answer is that the processor does it, unbeknownst to the programmer and the compiler. All WAR and WAW hazards are eliminated by the processor on its own volition, and no cooperation is required by software entities such as the compiler. This is completely internal to the processor.

Let us thus proceed to answer the next question, "How does the processor rename instructions?"

4.1.2 Renaming using Physical Registers

Let us consider a typical ISA that has 16 architectural registers. Let us assume that there are 128 physical registers that are used to do renaming. This means that a piece of code that uses architectural registers is transformed into an equivalent piece of code that uses physical registers. The end result for both the pieces of the code is exactly the same. However, as we have argued in Chapter 2, the code with physical registers runs faster because it does not have WAR and WAW hazards.

Definition 18

A physical register file is a set of registers within a processor. Each physical register is used for the purpose of renaming. The physical registers are not visible to software or any other entity outside the processor.

To achieve this, let us create a register file with 128 registers. A register file is defined as an array of registers, where we access the contents of a register based on its id. In this case, since there are 128 registers, each register will have a 7-bit id ($2^7 = 128$).

Way Point 2

Up till now we have covered the following concepts.

- *A processor exposes a set of architectural registers, which are visible to the programmer, compiler, and assembler. Most ISAs typically have between 8 and 32 architectural registers.*

- *For renaming we also need a set of physical registers that are completely internal to the processor. They are not visible to the programmer or the compiler.*

We want to run code, written with architectural registers in mind, to run on a processor that uses physical registers. This is where there is a need to perform renaming. Let us illustrate this by one more example. In Figure 4.2, the code in the column on the left side uses architectural registers, and the code in the column on the right side uses physical registers. The register renaming scheme is the same as that used in Figure 4.1.

Original code   Renamed code

```
1  mov  r1, 1              mov  p11,  1          1
2  add  r1, r2, r3         add  p12,  p2,  p3    2
3  add  r4, r1, 1          add  p41,  p12,  1    3
4  mov  r2, 5              mov  p21,  5          4
5  add  r6, r2, r8         add  p61,  p21,  p8   5
6  mov  r1, 8              mov  p13,  8          6
7  add  r9, r1, r2         add  p91,  p13,  p21  7
```

Figure 4.2: Renaming with physical registers

4.1.3 The Rename Table

Let us now introduce the core idea of renaming. Let us *not have* an architectural register file. This means that let us not have a separate dedicated storage area for saving the architectural registers. **We shall instead designate a subset of the physical registers as architectural registers.** This mapping between physical registers and architectural registers is dynamic and will keep changing throughout the lifetime of the program. Note that this is a very important concept; hence, we would request the reader to read the next few paragraphs very attentively.

Important Point 4

The programmer, and the compiler see a set of architectural registers. They are typically small in number. Most processors have anywhere between 8 and 32 architectural registers. However, in our proposed design architectural registers only exist in theory. They are a concept. They do not have a permanent home.

> *Instead, we define the concept of physical registers. We typically have 100+ physical registers in OOO processors.*
>
> *The process of renaming creates a mapping between architectural registers and physical registers. This means that if we wish to read the value of a given architectural register, we shall find it in the physical register that is mapped to it. Note that this mapping is a function of time and keeps changing dynamically.*

Let us look at a few example mappings in Figure 4.3.

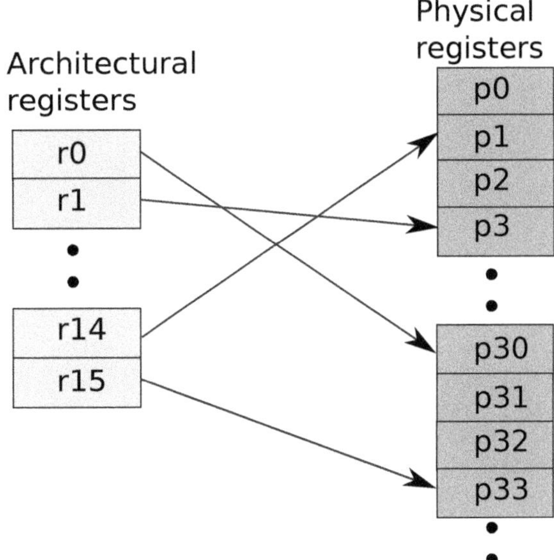

Figure 4.3: Example mapping between architectural and physical registers

We denote the architectural registers as $r0 \ldots r15$, and the physical registers as $p0 \ldots p127$. We assume that we have 128 physical registers. The need for that many physical registers is because we wish to have a lot of instructions in flight such that we can always find a set of instructions that can be issued to the execution units in parallel. The reasons for this will become clear as we read along. Even if readers at this point are not able to understand this logic, we would still urge them to read ahead.

Now, that we have 16 architectural registers and 128 physical registers, we need to create a mapping between architectural registers and physical registers. For example, a mapping would indicate that at a given point of time architectural register $r1$ is mapped to $p27$, and at a later point in time, it is mapped to $p32$, and so on. This means that if an assembly instruction wishes to read the contents of $r1$, the processor needs to read the value of its corresponding physical register. As we just described, this can be $p27$ at one point in the program and $p32$ at one more point in the program.

Figure 4.4 shows a high level overview of the mapping problem. We take an architectural register as input and the output is a physical register. Since in our running example we consider 16 architectural registers, we need 4 bits to encode architectural register ids. On similar lines, we require 7 bits to encode all the 128 physical register ids. Let us thus envision a simple 16-entry table where each entry corresponds to an architectural register (see Figure 4.5). We index the table using the 4-bit architectural register id. Each entry of the table stores a 7-bit physical register id. This is the current mapping between an architectural register and a physical register. Let us call this the rename table.

Figure 4.4: Renaming: replacing architectural register ids with physical register ids

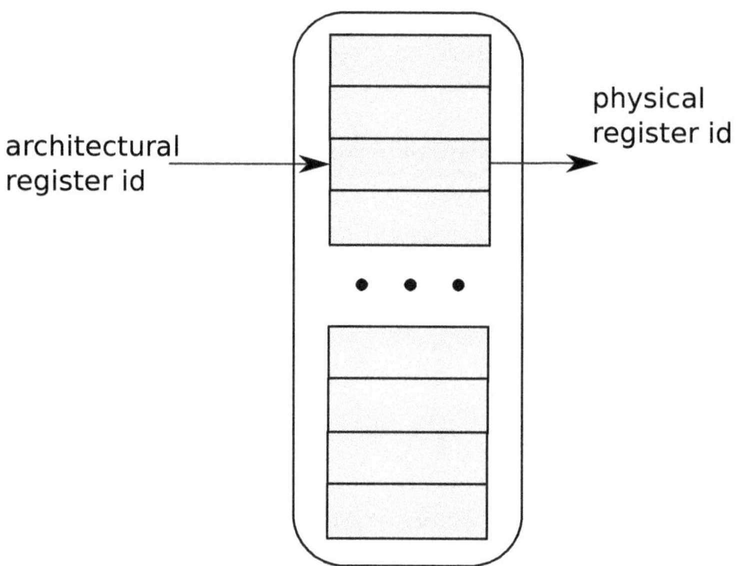

Figure 4.5: The rename table

Definition 19

A rename table *is a table in hardware that stores the mapping between architectural registers and physical registers. It is also known as the* register alias table (RAT table).

Renaming with a RAT table is very easy. We take a look at the source registers, read their corresponding physical register ids from the table, and use them for renaming. However, we need to do something extra for the destination register. Let us consider an add instruction of the form: *add* $r1, r2, r3$. Here, $r1$ is the destination register, $r2$ and $r3$ are the source registers. We need to access the rename table for the source registers $r2$ and $r3$. Subsequently, we need to replace $r2$ and $r3$ with the corresponding physical registers. However, for the destination register, $r1$, we need to follow a different approach. If we think about it, we are creating a new value (a fresh value) for $r1$. The lifetime of this new value starts after $r1$ is written, and continues till $r1$ is written the next time. Let us thus assign an unused physical register to $r1$ (elaborated in Example 2).

Example 2

Rename the following piece of code.

```
add  r1,  r2,  r3
sub  r4,  r1,  r2
```

Let r2 be initially mapped to p10 and r3 to p17.

Answer: *For r1, we assign a new physical register, which was hitherto unused. Let this be p5. Along with assigning the physical register p5 to r1, we need to make an entry in the rename table such that subsequent instructions get the mapping r1 ↔ p5 from the rename table.*

The subsequent instruction sub r4, r1, r2 needs to get the value of r1 from the physical register p5. The same mapping for r2 can be used as the previous instruction because its value has not been updated. We need to assign a new (hitherto unused) physical register to r4. Let this be p6.

The renamed code is thus as follows:

```
add  p5,  p10,  p17
sub  p6,  p5,   p10
```

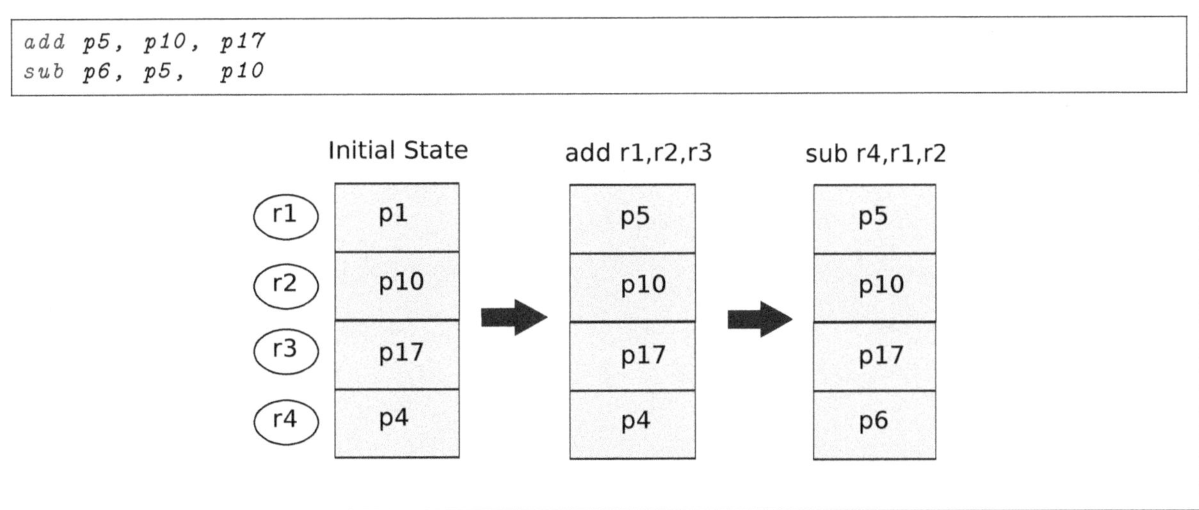

Let us summarise the major steps:

- Consider the source registers (registers that will be read) in the instruction. These are architectural registers.

- Find the corresponding physical registers from the rename table.

- Now, consider the destination register, if any. It needs to be assigned an unused physical register. Assign a free physical register (algorithms to be discussed later) and update the rename table with the new mapping.

The idea of renaming sounds easy in theory; however, there are still many practical challenges that need to be solved. Let us look at some of the tricky corner cases. Remember that life is not always nice and round. It does have *corners* ☻, and it is often these corner cases that make life very difficult. However, in every adversity lies an opportunity, and most of the time some of the most sophisticated techniques get developed because of these corner cases. Let us look at some corner cases in the idea of renaming that we have presented up till now.

The scheme that we have discussed is fine for a simple processor that renames only one instruction per cycle. However, for a processor that renames multiple instructions per cycle, there are additional problems.

Consider the following block of code.

```
add r1, r2, r3
sub r4, r1, r2
```

The second instruction uses the destination register of the first instruction as a source register. As a result, the renaming of the second instruction is dependent on the physical register that is assigned to the destination of the first register ($r1$). There is thus a dependence, and we need to wait for the first instruction to be fully renamed. This however will limit the amount of parallelism that we have in programs and will heavily restrict the ILP. Thus, there is a need for a better solution.

Now, think about the case where we rename four instructions together (rename width = 4). Here, there can be many dependences between the instructions. We clearly don't want to rename the instructions one after the other. There has to be a faster way of doing it.

4.1.4 Dependence Check Logic

Let us now solve the general renaming problem, where we have k instructions that need to be renamed together. Let us assume that we have enough free registers such that we can assign a free physical register to each of the destination registers.

The problem is that we can have a dependence where an earlier instruction writes to a register that is required by a later instruction as a source. In this case, the later instruction needs to know the id of the physical register that has been assigned. This is not possible to do (very easily) if they are all being renamed together. This makes the problem complex.

To solve this problem let us consider an example in Figure 4.6 with four instructions that need to be renamed together.

```
1   add r3, r1, r2
2   add r5, r3, r4
3   add r8, r6, r7
4   add r9, r8, r8
```

Figure 4.6: Example for the discussion on RAW dependences

Here, instruction *2* has a RAW dependence with instruction *1*. It is necessary to assign a physical register to $r3$ before we start renaming instruction *2*. Likewise, we have a similar dependence between instructions *3* and *4*. In the worst case, it is possible that we have dependences as follows: $1 \rightarrow 2 \rightarrow 3 \rightarrow 4$, where $a \rightarrow b$ indicates a RAW dependence between instructions a and b. Here, instruction a is the producer and instruction b is the consumer.

When we have such a dependence $1 \rightarrow 2 \rightarrow 3 \rightarrow 4$ between all four instructions, we need to rename the instructions serially (one after the other) as per the knowledge we have right now. This is clearly suboptimal, and we are not reaping any advantages of parallelism.

Let us assume that the time it takes to rename one instruction is T nanoseconds (ns). In the best case when there are no dependences between instructions, we can rename all the four instructions in T ns. However, if we have dependences between each pair of consecutive instructions, then there is a need to rename them serially, and the entire process will take $4T$ ns. We need to search for a better solution that is closer to T rather than $4T$.

It is important to first make certain key observations regarding the renaming process. Let us consider our running example once again (see Figure 4.6). We can rename instructions *1* and *3* in parallel. Let us now consider the case of instructions *2* and *4*. For instruction *2*, we do not really have to wait for the renaming of instruction *1* to finish completely. In fact an overlap exists. Let us take a look at Figure 4.7 to understand why.

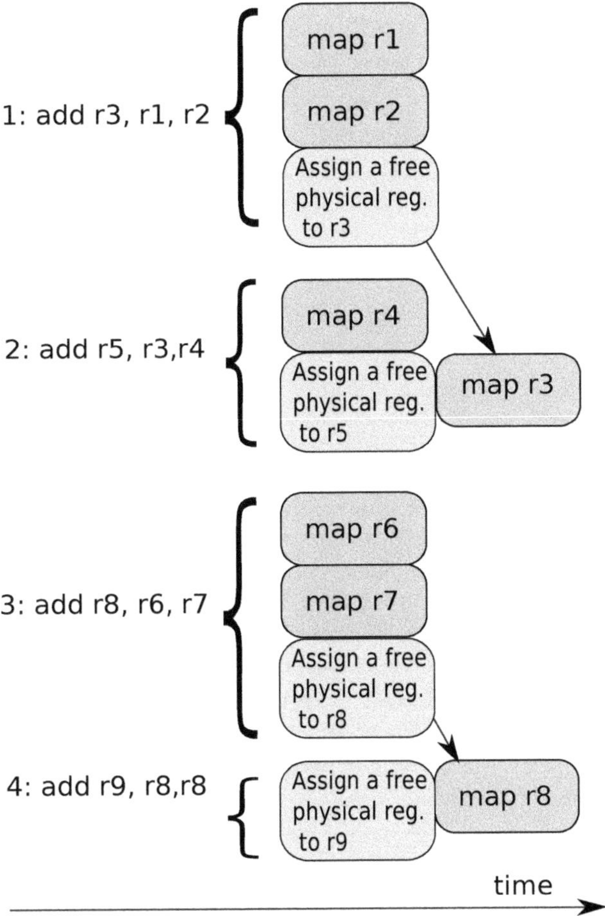

Figure 4.7: Flow of actions for simultaneously renaming four instructions

For instruction *1*, we can read the rename table for registers $r1$ and $r2$ in parallel. At the same time, we can also start reading the rename table for register $r4$, which is a source register for instruction *2*. The dependence exists for register $r3$. We need to wait for instruction *1* to assign a physical register to $r3$. This process can also be initiated in parallel as shown in Figure 4.7. Once we have assigned a physical register, this value can be forwarded to instruction *2*. There is per se no need for instruction *2* to access the rename table to get a mapping for $r3$. Akin to forwarding in pipelining, it can directly get the mapping from the hardware that is processing instruction *1*.

We thus observe that it is possible to perform a lot of actions in parallel while renaming. For example, instruction *2* does not have to wait for instruction *1*'s renaming to completely finish. In this case, instruction *2* simply needs to wait for a physical register to be assigned to *1*'s destination register.

We can have many more such cases, where for example in a 4-instruction bundle instruction *3* has RAW dependences with both instructions *1* and *2*. In that case the nature of actions will be different. We will have to wait for both instructions *1* and *2* to assign physical registers to their destination registers. Subsequently, instruction *3* can quickly use the values that have been forwarded to it by instructions *1* and *2*.

We can clearly see that the space of possibilities is very large. However, our goal is very clear – reduce the time required for renaming as much as possible.

For this we need to use a trick from our bag of architectural tricks. The specific technique that we shall use involves doing extra work that might be discarded later. However, we nevertheless need to do the additional (redundant) work because we might not be in a position to know if we need to do the additional work or not.

Using Redundant Work to Solve the Problem

Let us look at two of the instructions that we have been considering for renaming once again. We shall use the following piece of code as a running example.

```
1  add  r3,  r1,  r2
2  add  r5,  r3,  r4
```

We did outline a solution in Figure 4.7, where we try to create an overlap between the process of assigning physical registers, and accessing the rename table. It is not fully practical. This is because there is an assumption in this figure that we are already aware of the RAW dependences between the instructions. This is not the case; hence, we need to create a practical implementation that is conceptually similar to the flow of actions proposed in Figure 4.7.

Consider the following line of reasoning. The physical register assignment for $r3$ will be produced by the renaming process of instruction *1*. However, at the outset we have no way of knowing if at all there is a dependence between instructions *1* and *2*. The process of finding whether there is a dependence or not takes time, and during that time we would like to do useful work. It is possible that there might be a dependence, or it is alternatively possible that there is no dependence. There is no way of knowing without finding out, and that takes time.

We thus propose an alternative method of operation keeping our 2-instruction example in mind. Let us read the mappings for all the source registers from the rename table together. The source registers are $r1$, $r2$, $r3$, and $r4$. We will get valid mappings for three registers $r1$, $r2$, and $r4$. We will however not get a valid mapping for $r3$ because it is simultaneously updated by instruction *1*. Herein, lies the issue.

Let us simultaneously start a process of finding dependences between the instructions. We need to compare the source registers of instruction *2* with the destination register of instruction *1*. In this case, we compare 3 (from $r3$) with the numbers 3 (from $r3$) and 4 (from $r4$). There are two possibilities. Either there is no match, or there is a match. The former case is very easy to handle. It basically means that all the mappings from the rename table that we are simultaneously reading are all correct. However, the latter case is tricky. It means that some of the mappings that we are simultaneously reading are not correct. Let us just note down those mappings. In the case of this example, the mapping for $r3$ that is read from the rename table is not correct.

To ensure that we do not waste a lot of time, let us in parallel start a process to assign new mappings to the destinations of instructions *1* and *2*. This means that while we are reading the mappings of the sources from the rename table, we are simultaneously assigning new physical registers to the destinations. The latter is an independent activity. Let us assign $r3$ to the physical register $p22$.

Once, we have figured out the dependences between instructions, we are in a position to know that the mapping for $r3$ must come from the physical register assignment unit. It needs to be $p22$ in this case, and not the mapping that is contained in the rename table. We thus have a very simple problem on our hands. We have two options to choose from: a mapping from the previous instruction, and a mapping from the rename table. We can quickly choose between these options and get the final mapping between the architectural registers and the corresponding physical registers.

The timing is shown in Figure 4.8. We create an overlap between three actions: reading the rename table, assigning an unused physical register to an architectural register, and computing RAW dependences.

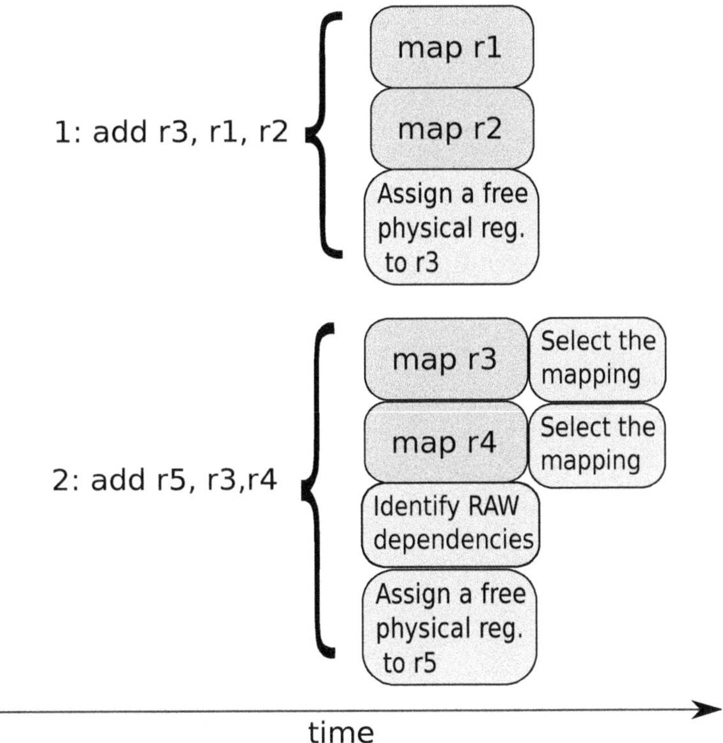

Figure 4.8: Flow of actions in a practical renaming system that tracks dependences

Final Solution for a 2-Issue Processor

Let us now implement this in hardware.

The first piece of hardware that we need is a circuit to choose between two options: mapping read from the rename table and the physical register assigned to the destination of a previous instruction. We need to choose one of the options based on whether there is a RAW dependence or not. The hardware structure that achieves exactly this is a **multiplexer** (see Figure 4.9).

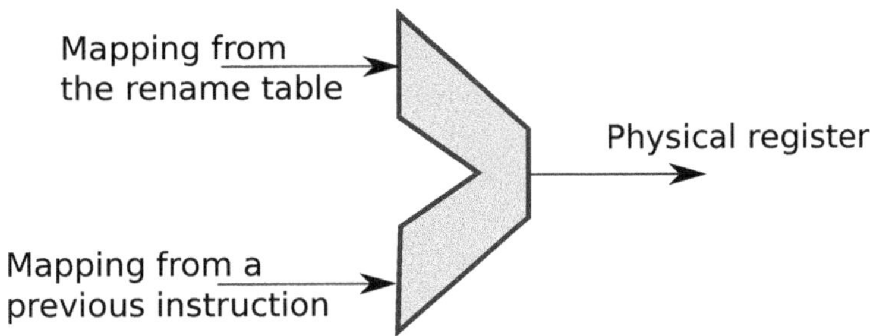

Figure 4.9: Multiplexer to choose between two options for the purpose of renaming

In Figure 4.9 we show a multiplexer with two inputs, one output (final register mapping), and one bit for selecting the input that is based on the comparison of the source register id and the previous instruction's destination register id. Let us now use this multiplexer to design the renaming stage. The logic is now complete because it traces RAW dependences between instructions that are being simultaneously renamed. It is referred to as the dependence check logic.

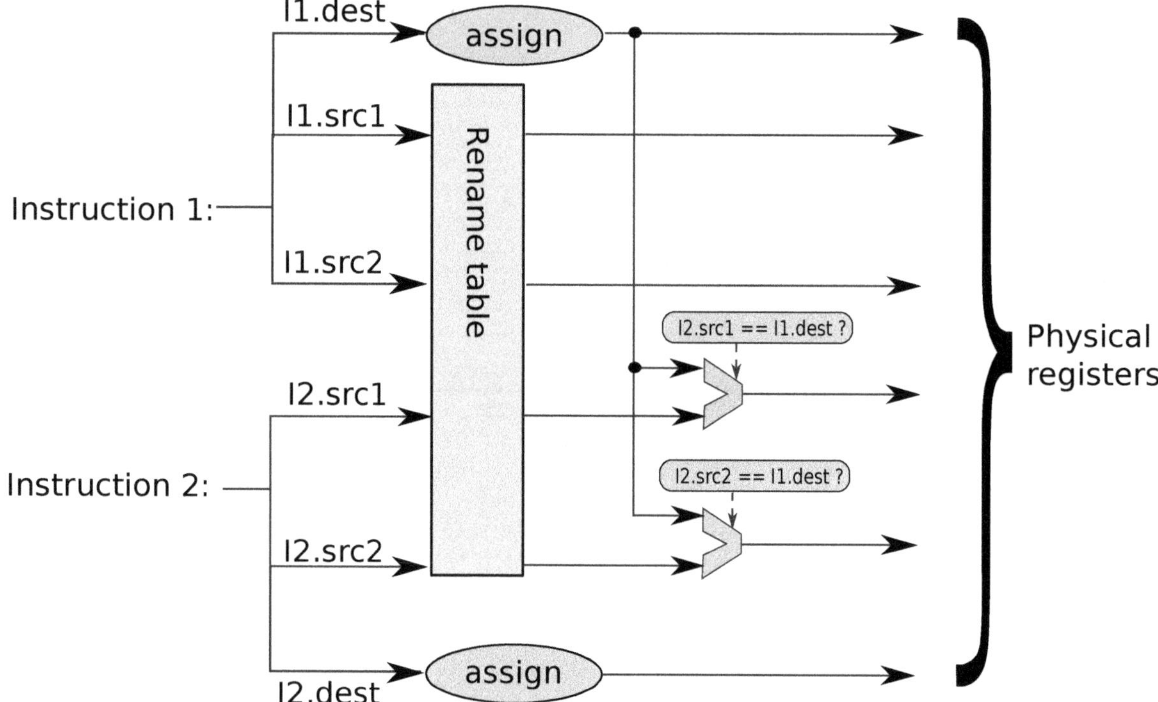

Figure 4.10: The rename stage with dependence check logic

Here is a textual description of our solution (also refer to Figure 4.10).

1: Parallel Activity: starts at t=0 Read the mappings of all the source registers.

2: Parallel Activity: starts at t=0 Assign physical registers to all the destination registers.

3: Parallel Activity: starts at t=0 Find RAW dependences between all the instructions.

4: Final Activity Once when activities (1), (2), and (3), are over $\rightarrow$ for each source register choose the right mapping with the help of a multiplexer.

We leave the process of extending our solution to a processor with a larger rename width as an exercise for the reader. All that we need is a wider multiplexer that takes in more inputs. Assume that we are renaming a set of instructions in parallel and we need to choose the mapping for a source operand of instruction k. We need to consider the mapping provided by the rename table and the physical registers assigned to the destinations of the previous $k-1$ instructions. Thus, we require a k-input multiplexer. Additionally, we need the logic to compute the control signals for these multiplexers. For a k-input multiplexer we need $\lceil log_2(k) \rceil$ bits.

4.1.5 The Free List

The only part that is remaining is how to assign a *free* physical register to an instruction's destination register. For this purpose we use a structure called a *free list*.

Definition 20
A free list is a hardware structure that maintains a list of physical registers that are currently free, and can be assigned to architectural registers.

Let us think of the free list as a black box. It takes in a request for a physical register, and returns the id of a free physical register. Similarly, we can also return a physical register to the free list. The quintessential way of designing a free list is by using a circular queue. The circular queue stores a list of registers as shown in Figure 4.11.

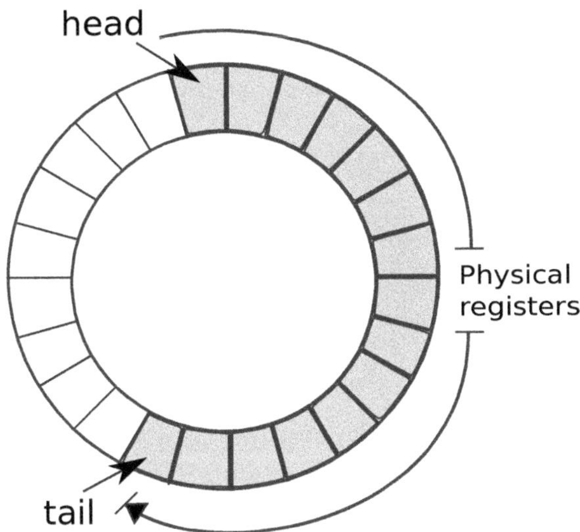

Figure 4.11: A circular queue of physical registers

A circular queue is an array of entries, where each entry contains the id of a physical register. When we add more entries, they wrap around the array and start getting added from the beginning. We maintain two pointers – *head* and *tail* – in hardware. Whenever we add a set of entries to the circular queue we add it to the tail and *increment* the *tail* pointer. Similarly, when we remove entries, we remove them from the side of the head. We also increment the *head* pointer.

The increment operation on the *head* pointer is $head = (head + 1)\%SIZE$. Here, $SIZE$ is the size of the queue. The reason we perform a '%' (remainder or modulo) operation is because the queue is supposed to wrap around (notion of a circular queue). Similarly, the corresponding operation for the tail is $tail = (tail + 1)\%SIZE$.

If the reader at this point is having difficulty, and finding it hard to understand the notion of a circular queue, then she can consult any of the classic texts on basic data structures and algorithms such as the book by Cormen et al. [Cormen et al., 2009].

To check if the queue is empty or not, we maintain a simple count of the number of entries currently present in the queue. When we add entries we increment the count, and when we remove entries we decrement the count. If the count becomes zero we can infer emptiness.

Such circular queues are very common structures, which find use in many architectural components. The free list is one such example, where we can keep track of unused physical registers, and assign them to architectural registers as and when required. When a free physical register is required we dequeue an entry from the free list, and similarly when we need to return a register we can add (enqueue) it to the free list. The benefits of using a circular queue are its simplicity and the ease of adding and deleting an entry.

There is one open question remaining.

Question 1
When do we add physical registers to the free list?

Unfortunately, we will have to wait till we discuss the process of committing instructions (see Section 4.4) to find the answer to this question. Till that point let us assume that we are never short of physical registers and we always find enough physical registers to satisfy our requirements.

Now, the set of renamed instructions, which don't have any false dependences need to be sent to the execution units.

4.2 Instruction Dispatch, Wakeup, and Select

Now that we have a stream of renamed instructions, we are sure of the following:

- The stream does not have any WAW and WAR dependences; we only have genuine RAW dependences.

- All the instructions access physical registers.

Now, the task at hand is to first provide a place to temporarily buffer the instructions. In this buffer, we need to find w instructions per cycle to be sent to the execution units. Here, the number w is known as the *issue width*. It is typically a number between 1 and 6.

Note that a renamed instruction might not find its input operands immediately. The instruction that is producing the value of the input operand might be in the temporary buffer awaiting execution. In this case the instruction needs to wait. In a similar manner many other instructions would be waiting. However, we will have some instructions whose operands are ready. We can then *issue* them to the execution units. The aim is to choose as many instructions as we can – subject to the issue width – and then issue them to the execution units. Let us define three terms here namely *instruction window, dispatch,* and *issue* (refer to Figure 4.12 and Definition 21). In addition, let the term *scheduling* encompass the process of dispatching and issuing an instruction.

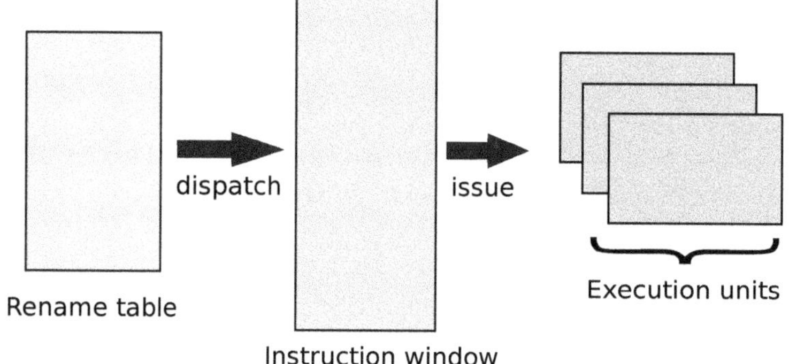

Figure 4.12: Instruction, dispatch, and issue

Definition 21

- *An* instruction window *is a storage structure that temporarily buffers instructions after they are renamed. Instructions wait in the instruction window till their source operands are ready and the execution unit is free.*

- *The process of sending instructions from the rename table to the instruction window is known as instruction* dispatch.

- *The process of sending instructions from the instruction window to the execution units is known as* instruction issue.

- *The entire process of dispatching the instruction, temporarily buffering it, and then issuing the instruction to the execution units is known as* scheduling.

4.2.1 Instruction Window

Before doing any further processing, let us temporarily buffer the instructions in a queue called the *instruction window*. Most hardware implementations of queues use circular queues as we had described in Section 4.1.5. Recall that such queues use an underlying array of entries; this is implemented in hardware. We have a head pointer, a tail pointer, and a count of the number of entries. A pointer in this case is an index in the underlying array.

Let us outline the need for having an instruction window or having a queue in general between pipeline stages. A queue is used to buffer instructions and provide a sense of *rate control*. Assume that at a given point of time, we are renaming four instructions per cycle and we are able to execute only two instructions per cycle. This situation can happen if we have a lot of RAW dependences between the instructions and we do not find enough instructions to execute every cycle.

In such cases, it is nice to have a queue that can absorb the excess instructions, albeit temporarily. Later on, when we can execute more instructions in parallel, the instructions can come from the instruction window. In other words, a queue can buffer instructions till they are consumed and thus try to reduce the mismatch between the rate of production and the rate of consumption. It can absorb spikes in excess production or excess consumption.

The other advantage is that if we are looking at a large set of instructions at a given point of time, the probability of finding more instructions that have all their inputs ready is higher. We should thus have a fairly large instruction window such that we can find a lot of instructions to send to the execution units in parallel.

If the issue width is w, then the best possible situation is when we can issue w instructions per cycle. However, most of the time, we will not find enough instructions primarily because we will be constrained by dependences.

Our aim is that in the instruction window we should be able to find all the instructions that can be issued simultaneously. This has to be an efficient process in terms of both performance and power. Figure 4.13 shows the pipeline of the processor that we have described till this point.

Structure of an Entry

Let us look at the structure of an entry in the instruction window. Its list of fields is shown in Table 4.1. We consider a 64-bit processor with 16 architectural, and 128 physical registers. Note that we are not showing all the fields that are typically associated with an instruction. For example, there are other fields

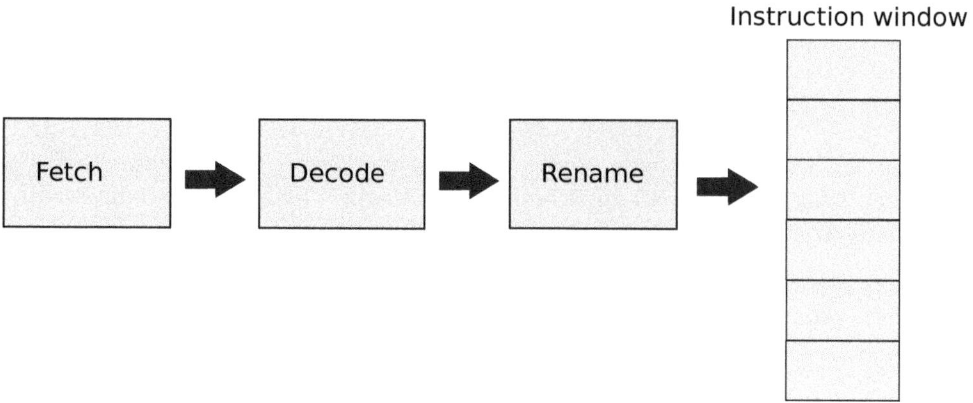

Figure 4.13: The instruction window

in the instruction packet that will be used later on such as the opcode, id of the destination register, and some control signals for controlling execution units. We have two options: either we can keep this information in the instruction window entry, or keep it in a separate location and ensure that the two parts of the instruction packet move together in the pipeline. A shortcoming of the former strategy is that it makes each entry in the instruction window very large, and a shortcoming of the latter scheme is that it makes the design of the pipeline more complicated. Designers typically make such difficult choices after detailed simulation based studies.

Field	Description	Width (in bits)
valid	validity of the entry	1
ready	instruction is ready to be executed	1
First source operand		
isreg1	register or immediate	1
ready1	value is present in the register file	1
rs1	id of the first source register	7
imm1	32-bit immediate	32
Second source operand		
isreg2	register or immediate	1
ready2	value is present in the register file	1
rs2	id of the second source register	7
imm2	32-bit immediate	32
Destination		
isregd	destination is a register	1
rd	destination register id	7

Table 4.1: List of fields in an instruction window entry

Let us now explain the fields in Table 4.1. Note that we consider instructions with two source operands and one destination operand (refer to Appendix A for the details of the ISA). A source operand can be a register or can be an immediate value calculated in an earlier stage of the pipeline (typically decode). There of course can be many other kinds of instructions such as branch instructions that need not have any source operands, or compare instructions that do not have any destination operands. Extending the current approach to handle such instructions is fairly trivial and is left as an exercise for the reader. Let us now focus on the broad concepts. The first row is self explanatory. The *valid* bit indicates if a given entry is valid or empty. Let us discuss the rest of the rows. We propose a *ready* bit that indicates whether the instruction is ready to be executed or not. If all the operands are either immediates or can be found in the register file, then we set the *ready* bit to 1. Otherwise, we set the *ready* bit to 0, and wait for the operands to be ready.

Going back to Table 4.1, let us consider the set of rows labelled as "First source operand". The field *isreg*1 indicates if the first source operand is a register or an immediate. If this field is 1, then the first source operand is a register. Next, we have the field *ready*1, which indicates if the operand is ready. If the operand is an immediate, then $ready = 1$, otherwise it indicates if the operand can be found in the register file or not. If the operand is a register, then the id of the register is stored in the field *rs*1. Finally, the field *imm*1 contains the 32-bit value of the immediate if the operand is an immediate. Note that these are all physical registers. We are not considering architectural registers here.

We use a similar terminology for the second source operand. The corresponding fields are *isreg*2, *ready*2, *rs*2, and *imm*2.

Finally, let us consider the last set of rows that correspond to the destination register. The field *isregd* indicates if we have a destination register or not, and the field *rd* is the id of the destination register. Note that some instructions notably the store instruction do not write to a register, or in other words, do not have a destination that is a register.

Let us now discuss the rules for populating an entry in the instruction window. After we decode an instruction we are aware of its type, and its nature of operands. We are also aware of which operand is a register, and which operand is not. All of this information is a part of the instruction packet that moves from stage to stage. Hence, while creating an instruction window entry, all this information is available. Here, we are making an assumption that physical register ids – obtained post renaming – are also a part of the instruction packet.

The *ready*1 and *ready*2 Bits

Let us explain the logic for setting the fields *ready*1 and *ready*2. Recall that these fields indicate whether the operand is ready or not. If the operand is an immediate, then the logic for setting these flags is obvious. Since we get the value of an immediate at the time of decoding an instruction, the operand is definitely ready. Hence, let us not consider this trivial case. Let us instead consider the more difficult case where the operand is a register.

In this case, there are a lot of possibilities. After the instruction enters the instruction window, it needs to know whether it needs to wait for a source register's value to be produced by an earlier instruction, or the instruction can be issued to the functional units. It will then read the value of the source register along the way from the physical register file. It is important for us to be armed with this information at the time of entering the instruction window such that we know whether we need to wait, or we can proceed.

Thus, setting the values of the fields *ready*1 and *ready*2 is important, and at the moment appears to be non-trivial. The problem at hand is to make a determination before entering the instruction window with regards to the value of these fields. The previous stage is the renaming stage. We clearly need to make a determination in this stage. Let us thus propose a small modification to the rename table.

Let us reconsider the structure of a rename table entry (see Figure 4.14). Let us add an additional bit to the mapping that indicates whether the value of a given register (at that point of time) exists in the physical register file or not. If it does not exist, then it means that the value is going to be produced by an earlier instruction in the pipeline. Let us call this bit the *available* bit, and represent it with the mnemonic *avlbl*. The *avlbl* bit thus indicates the availability of a source operand in an instruction, which is being renamed.

Assume that an instruction i is being renamed in the 10th cycle, then the *avlbl* bit for the source operand will indicate if the instruction expects to find the values of the source registers in the register file or not. This typically refers to the status of the source registers at the beginning of the 10th cycle. Once instruction i reads its corresponding *avlbl* bit it takes this information along with it to the next

avlbl bit	7-bit physical register id

Figure 4.14: A rename table entry with the *avlbl* bit

stage.

If the *avlbl* bit is 0 for a physical register px, then instruction i needs to wait in the instruction window for the value of px to get produced. This value will be produced by another instruction that is currently in the pipeline. However, if the *avlbl* bit is 1, then the value for px is ready. It can be read from the physical register file or it can be forwarded by another earlier instruction in the pipeline. Now the question that we need to answer is, "When do we set the *avlbl* bit?" This is set when the producer instruction writes the value of px to the register file. At the same time the producer can set the *avlbl* bit of px in the rename table.

It is true that adding a bit does solve the problem. However, it brings along a lot of complexity along with it. Assume that we are renaming and issuing 4 instructions per cycle. If we assume that each instruction has two sources and one destination, then our rename table requires 8 read ports (reading two sources) and 4 write ports (creating a mapping by reading the free list). Now, we have further burdened the rename table with the load of maintaining *avlbl* bits. We need 4 extra write ports such that we can update the available bits.

A structure with 8 read ports and 8 write ports is to say the least very complicated and difficult to design. However, we should get some relief from the fact that each entry is only a single bit. Since each entry is a single bit, we can design fast structures for achieving this. Sadly, at this point we are not in a position to understand the design issues associated with memory structures. We shall look at such issues in Chapter 7. Some of the broad approaches that we shall discuss in Chapter 7 include dividing a large array into several smaller sub-arrays. Each such sub-array will have a much lower number of read/write ports. Furthermore, we can also use simple flip-flops instead of expensive SRAM (static RAM) arrays. By a combination of such approaches we can design a fast structure that can be used to store the *avlbl* bits.

Important Point 5

- *The ready field in each instruction window entry is related to ready1 and ready2 as follows: ready = ready1 ∧ ready2. It is not strictly required because it can be inferred from ready1 and ready2. We have added it for the sake of simplicity.*

- *An operand can also be considered to be* ready *if we can read its value from the forwarding paths. This is a minor point and will be revisited later. The point to note is that when we say that an operand is "ready", its value is either available via a forwarding path or can be read from the register file.*

4.2.2   Broadcast and Wakeup

Now that we have enqueued all the renamed instructions in the instruction window, it is time to execute them. However, they may not be ready yet. Some of these instructions might be waiting for their source operands to be ready as we discussed in Section 4.2.1. Once the source operands are ready, the instructions can be sent for execution.

The problem that we wish to solve in this section is to create a mechanism to track and resolve dependences between instructions. There has to be some mechanism by which a producer instruction can let all its consumer instructions know that the value of its destination register is ready. It basically needs to *broadcast* the produced value to the consuming instructions. Furthermore, for this mechanism to work, each consumer instruction needs to wait for its operands to become ready. Once, all of its operands are ready, it is said to *wakeup* [1] Let us thus propose an architecture for the broadcast and wakeup mechanism, where a producer broadcasts information regarding its completion, and consumer instructions use this information to wakeup. We shall first discuss the architecture for broadcast (see Figure 4.15).

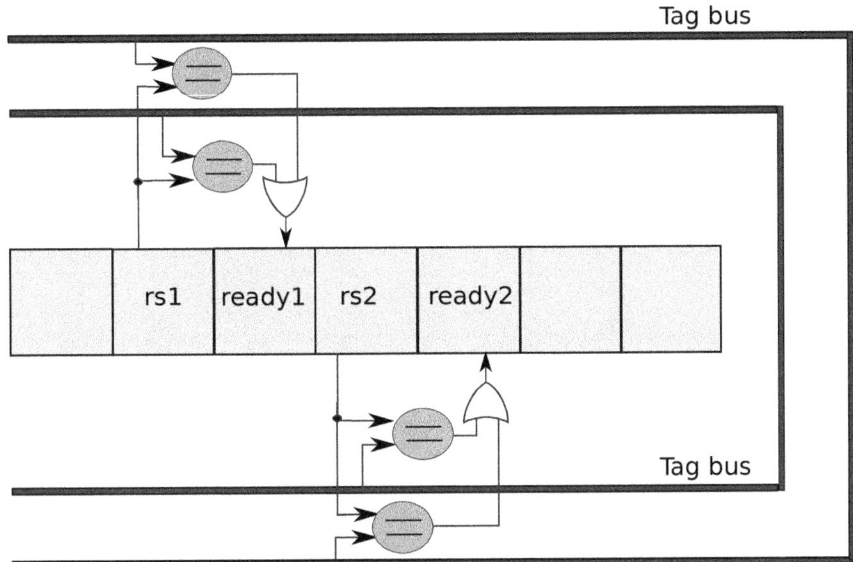

Figure 4.15: Instruction window with additional logic for tag broadcast and comparison

Each entry in the instruction window is connected to at least one set of copper wires called a *tag bus*. A tag bus is used to broadcast the id of the physical register whose value has been written to the register file. We alternatively refer to this id as a *tag*. The producer instruction broadcasts its tag (id of its destination register) on a tag bus: this is connected to both the source operands 1 and 2. If we have multiple instructions executing per cycle, then we need multiple tag buses. An instruction writes the id of its destination register to its corresponding tag bus. Figure 4.15 shows two tag buses: one for each producer instruction.

Let us elaborate. Consider the following code snippet.

```
1  add r1, r2, r3
2  add r4, r1, r5
```

Instruction *1* is the producer instruction. It produces the value for register $r1$. Assume that register $r1$ is mapped to physical register $p17$. Then 17 is the value of the tag that gets broadcasted on the corresponding tag bus. Each entry in the instruction window is connected to all the tag buses. For each source operand, we check to find out if it is equal to any of the broadcasted tags. This is done with the help of comparators and an OR gate as shown in Figure 4.15. If there is a match, then we get to know that the corresponding source operand is ready. For example, in the current scenario, instruction *2* is

---

[1] Note that we shall use the term "wakeup" rather than the regular English words "wake up" or "wake-up".

the consumer instruction. It waits for the value of register $r1$ (mapped to $p17$) to be produced and to be subsequently broadcast on a tag bus. Once there is a match in the comparator for the first source operand of instruction *2*, we can set the corresponding ready bit to 1. This means that we can proceed to read the value corresponding to architectural register $r1$ (physical register $p17$) from the register file.

Every producer instruction broadcasts its destination tag (if it has one) on one of the tag buses. This allows consumer instructions to see the broadcast and subsequently wakeup. We can further augment this mechanism to send the broadcast to the rename table. This will update the available bit (*avlbl*).

The process of waking up is simple. Once we observe the tag on a tag bus, we mark the corresponding operand as ready, and if all the operands are ready, we proceed to execute the instruction. This is in itself a multi-step process. We first need to set the *ready* bit in the instruction window's entry to indicate that the instruction is ready for execution. It is possible that multiple instructions might be ready for execution. For example, it is possible that five add instructions are ready; however, we have only two adders. In this case we need to choose two among the five instructions for execution. This process is called *instruction selection*.

4.2.3   Instruction Select

We can conceptually think of two kinds of valid instructions in the instruction window. One set of instructions have all their operands ready, and the other set of instructions are waiting for their operands to be ready. Let us consider the former set. Note that in any processor we cannot simultaneously execute all the instructions which are in the *woken up* state. It is theoretically possible that one instruction wakes up 100 other instructions. All of these 100 instructions will become immediately ready to execute. Given the fact that we have a limited number of functional units, we need to choose a subset of instructions that can execute simultaneously.

For example, if we have two adders and one multiplier, and have five instructions that are ready, we need to find two add instructions and one multiply instruction out of the five ready instructions. This involves a certain amount of decision making. The aim is to maximise the ILP.

Let us design a basic select unit that selects only one instruction (see Figure 4.16). Consider a theoretical version of the problem where we have n entries in the window. Each entry is connected to the select unit. If the instruction in an entry is ready (woken up), then it sets its *request* line to 1. However, if it is not ready, then its request line remains 0. Any subset of these n entries can have their request lines set to 1. The job of the select unit is to choose one of these n entries, which has a ready instruction. Once that entry is chosen (or selected), the select unit sets its grant line to 1. This lets the entry know that it is ready to be sent for execution.

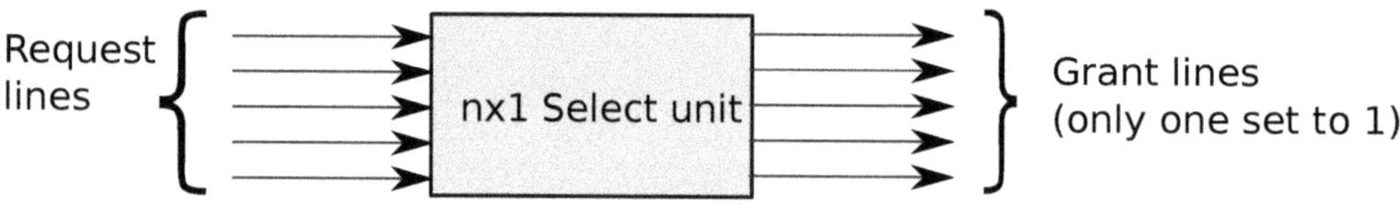

Figure 4.16: A basic select unit

Figure 4.16 basically shows a black box that takes in n 1-bit inputs (request lines), does some processing (unbeknownst to us at the moment), and then sets one of the grant lines. Let us elaborate.

Tree Based Select Unit

Let us consider one of the simplest designs for the select unit that has a tree-based shape. Please refer to Figure 4.17. Such a select unit is an $n \times 1$ select unit because we are choosing at most one out of n inputs.

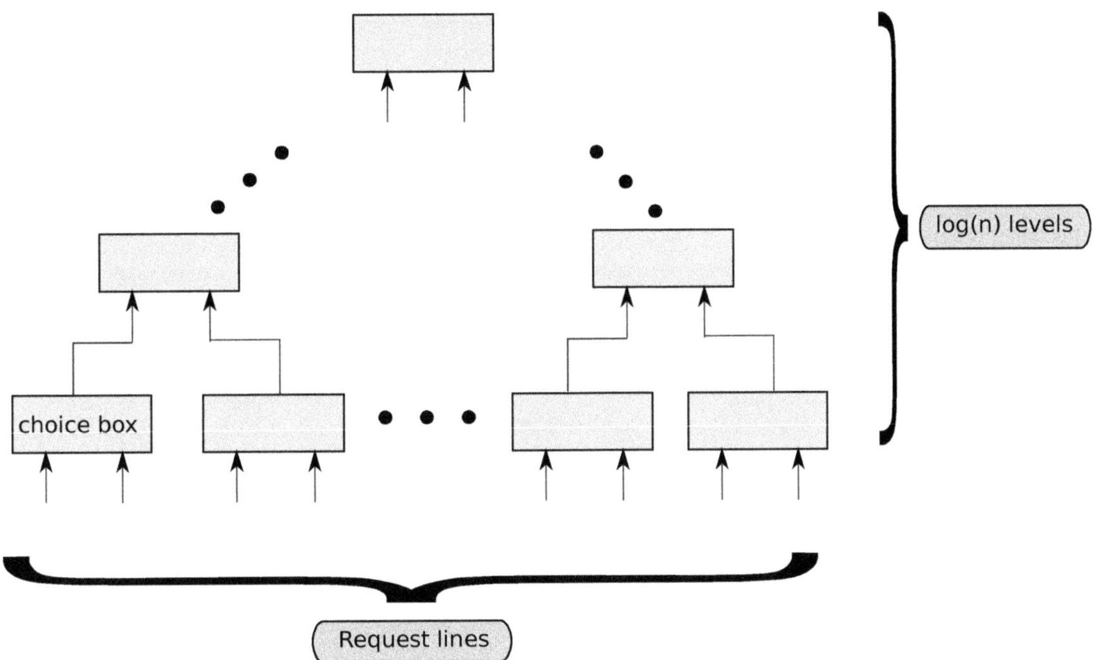

Figure 4.17: A tree based select unit

In this example, we have n request lines. At the lowest level (the leaves of the tree) successive pairs of consecutive request lines are routed to a set of $n/2$ elements. Each of these elements is a small select unit in its own right. Each such element has two inputs, and out of these, it needs to choose at most one. It is thus a 2×1 select unit. Instead of using the cryptic term, 2×1 select unit, we shall refer to these elements as *choice boxes*.

If we again take a look at Figure 4.17, we can make out that the choice boxes are organised in layers. The first layer of $n/2$ choice boxes choose a maximum of $n/2$ inputs for the next layer. In the next layer, we have $n/4$ choice boxes. They again choose at most half of the inputs as possible selections, which are forwarded to the next layer, and so on. Let us now delve into a choice box.

A choice box has two inputs (two request lines) as shown in Figure 4.18. Let us name the inputs i_0 and i_1. There are four possibilities. Either both of them are 1 (both interested), or one of them is 1 (two such possibilities), or none of them are 1. For the first case where both the inputs are 1, we need to make a choice. Let us at the moment choose one of the inputs arbitrarily. We shall discuss the policies for selection later. It is important to remember the choice. For this purpose, we can have a small state element (*choice*) inside each choice box such as a latch that remembers which input was chosen. For example, if we choose input i_0, then we store 0 in the latch, else we store 1. The choice box also has two grant lines corresponding to each input: g_0 and g_1.

Now, for the other two cases where only one input is asserted (set to 1), we choose that input. Subsequently, we set the output request line *result* to 1 thus indicating that the choice box has an input that is asserted. The output request line is an input to the next layer of choice boxes. If none of the inputs are asserted, then we set *result* to 0. This indicates to the next layer that there are no requests to be made.

Note that in every layer the number of choice boxes decreases by a factor of two (like a binary tree [Cormen et al., 2009]). We thus have a total of $log_2(n)$ levels. The final layer (the root node) has a single choice box. It chooses between its inputs and in a sense makes the final choice by asserting the corresponding grant signal for the chosen input. This information needs to propagate back to the

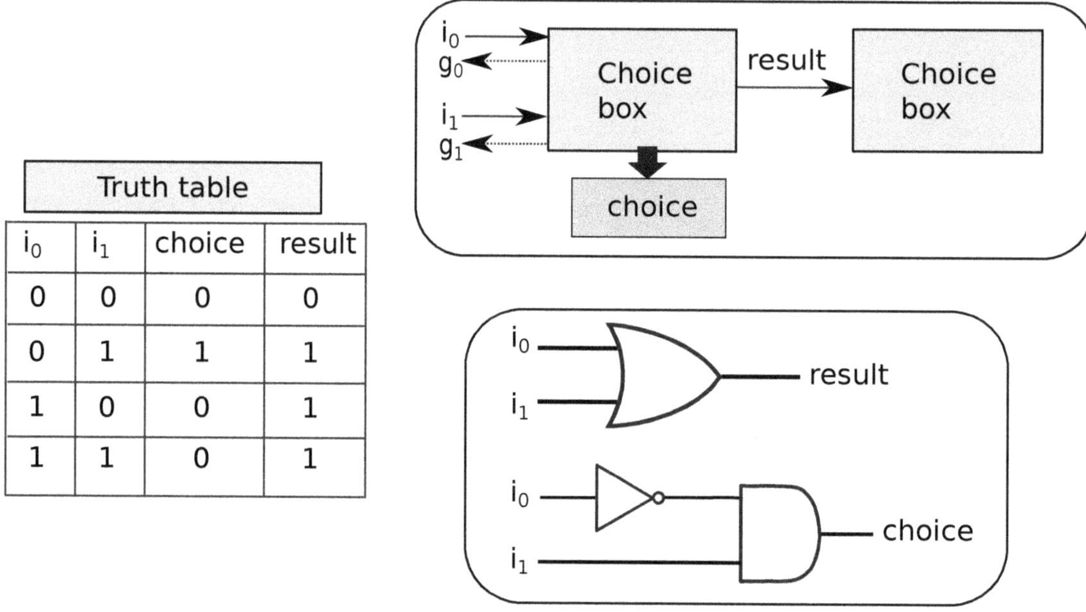

i_0	i_1	choice	result
0	0	0	0
0	1	1	1
1	0	0	1
1	1	0	1

Figure 4.18: A choice box (preference given to i_0)

original entry. The reverse path is followed. In each choice box along the way we set the appropriate grant signal.

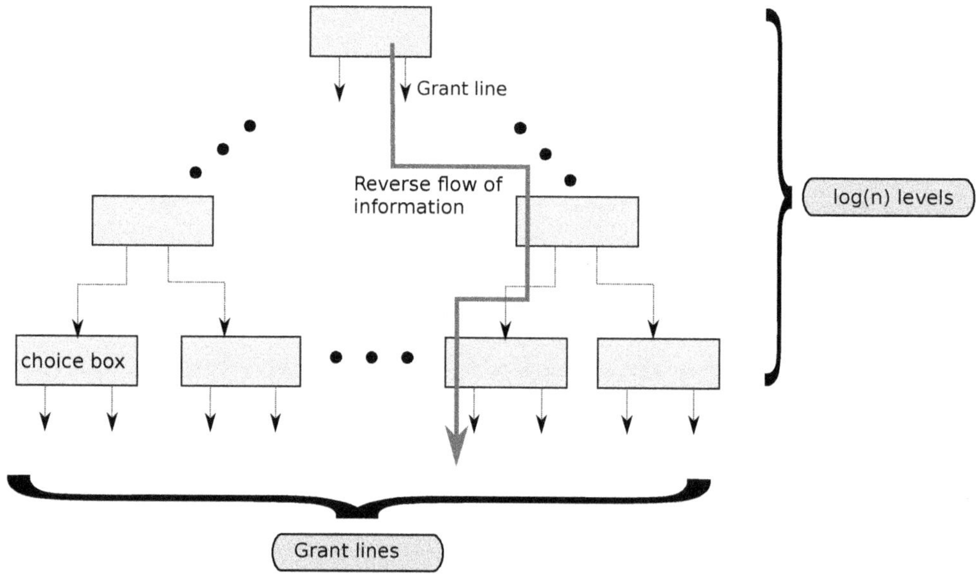

Figure 4.19: The path of grant requests

Figure 4.19 shows the path that is taken by the grant signal for one particular example. In this case, when a choice box finds that its input grant signal (coming from the root) is asserted, it finds out which input it had chosen, and asserts the corresponding grant signal. For example, if a choice box had chosen input i_1, and it subsequently finds that its input grant signal (coming from the root) is asserted, it sets the grant line associated with input i_1 to 1.

In this manner the grant signal propagates to the selected entry in the instruction window. Once an entry receives an asserted grant signal, it knows that it has been selected and should immediately proceed for execution.

$n \times m$ **Select Units**

We have discussed the design of an $n \times 1$ select unit. Let us now discuss the design of general $n \times m$ select units. Note that here m is typically not a very large number. After all, it is limited by the number of functional units. m is typically 2 or 3.

We have several options for designing an $n \times 2$ select unit.

Option 1: The first option is easier but slower. Here we cascade two $n \times 1$ select units. We first select one of the inputs. Then we de-assert (set to 0) its input request line, and proceed to select a request out of the rest of the requests using the second select unit. The schematic is shown in Figure 4.20.

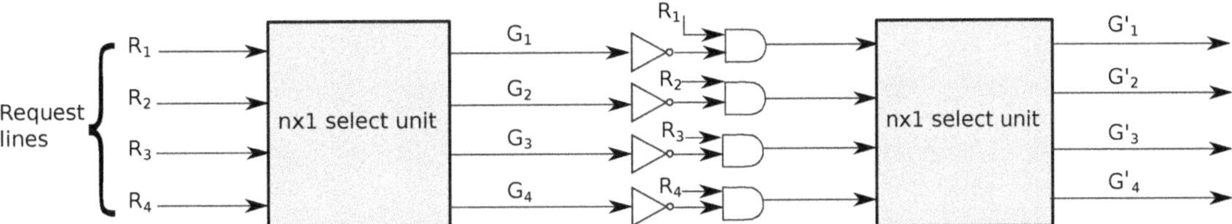

Figure 4.20: Two cascaded $n \times 1$ select units

With this design we take twice the time as a normal $n \times 1$ select unit. However, the design is simple, easy to create and understand. Note that there are issues with scalability. Designing an $n \times 3$ select unit on similar lines will be fairly slow.

Option 2: Let us now look at a slightly more direct approach. Let us modify a simple $n \times 1$ select unit to actually choose two instructions. We shall make the modification in each choice box. Each choice box now will have two 2-bit inputs (or request lines). Each input line will indicate the number of requests that have been selected in the subtree rooted at the choice box. This number can be either 0, 1, or 2. It is now possible that a choice box might be presented with four requests. Out of these, it needs to choose at most two and propagate this information towards the root of the tree. Finally, the root node will choose two requests and let the corresponding choice boxes know. This information will flow back towards the instruction window entry.

Refer to Figure 4.21 for a high level view.

Option 3: The select unit in Option 2 is complicated. There is no need to further underscore the fact that complicated units are also slow units. Let us instead divide the entries in the instruction window into disjoint sets. Each set can have an associated select unit. For example, we can divide the entries into two sets: entries at odd indices of the instruction window array and entries at even entries. We can have one $n \times 1$ select unit for each set. This strategy will ensure that we will never select more than two instructions and both the select units can act in parallel. However, the flip side is that if two entries at even locations are ready, and there are no entries at odd locations that are ready, we will only be able to select just one entry. This will lead to idleness and a consequent loss in performance. In spite of such concerns, having select entries work on disjoint portions of the instruction window is deemed to be a reasonably good solution primarily because of its simplicity.

Option 4: We can do slightly better. Let us have two select units, where each select unit is connected to all the instruction window entries. For each choice box let us refer to one of the inputs as *left* (i_0) and

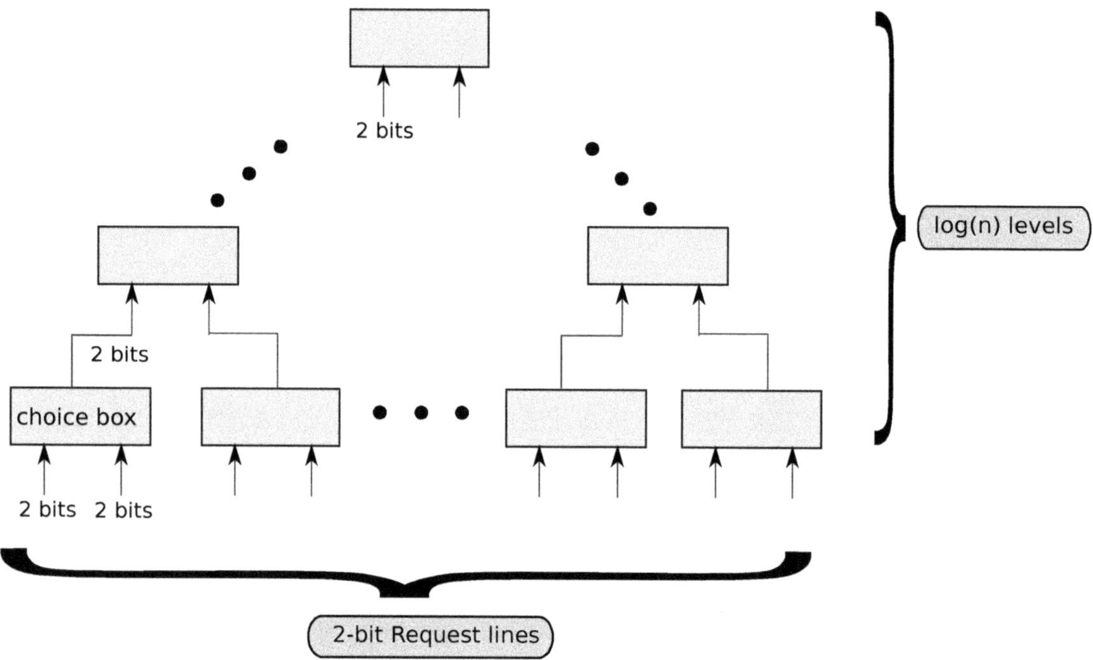

Figure 4.21: Non-cascaded design of an $n \times 2$ select unit (the grant lines are not shown)

the other one as *right* (i_1). Let us force the choice boxes in one select unit to always give a preference to their left inputs whenever there is a choice. Let us similarly force the choice boxes in the other select unit to always give a preference to their right inputs (whenever there is a choice). Let us now prove that it is never possible that the same input is chosen by both the select units when we have at least two requests – two instruction window entries that are ready.

Assume that we order the requests in a linear order from left to right. Consider any two requests R_0 and R_1. Furthermore, assume that in this order R_1 is to the right of R_0 (without loss of generality).

Consider the select unit where each choice box always prefers its right input. It is not possible for this select unit to choose R_0. It will either choose R_1 or some other request that is to right of R_1. Similarly, we can prove that the select unit where each choice box always prefers its left input chooses either R_0 or some other request that is to the left of R_0. Hence, we prove that both the select units can never choose the same request.

Important Point 6

There is a trade-off between Options 3 and 4. For the solution in Option 3, we connect half the entries in the instruction window to the first select unit and the rest half to the other select unit. However, in the more efficient solution (Option 4), we connect all the entries to both the select units. There is thus an increase in efficiency at the cost of doubling the number of connections. This is one more example of a general maxim: there is always a trade-off between efficiency and the number of resources.

Selecting Instructions for Different Types of Functional Units

The traditional solution for this problem is to have different select units for each class of instructions. For example, if we have adders and multipliers as the only functional units, then we can have one select unit for adders, and one more for multipliers. The problem of selecting instructions for these two classes of units is independent.

This approach is not scalable if we slightly complicate the situation. We can have functional units that can process instructions belonging to many different classes, or we might have a lot of classes of functional units. In this case, there is a need to complicate the select logic, where we need to send additional bits along with each request. We basically need to annotate each request with the type of the instruction. The choice boxes have to analyse the types of the requests, and make appropriate choices. This will slow down the select unit. Hence, it is wise to have a few classes of instructions and a set of functional units that can process only one class of instructions. Again, there are complex trade-offs in this case between the complexity of the ISA and the complexity of the select unit.

4.2.4   Early Broadcast

Let us begin by asking the question, "When should we broadcast?". A naive answer would be once we have finished executing the producer instruction. While writing to the register file, we can in parallel broadcast the tag. Unfortunately, this will lead to an extremely inefficient implementation.

Let us consider the following piece of code.

```
1   add r1, r2, r3
2   add r4, r1, r5
3   add r6, r4, r7
```

Instructions *1*, *2*, and *3* have RAW dependences between them. We have a RAW dependence between instructions *1* and *2* because register $r1$ is written to by instruction *1* and instruction *2* reads it. Similarly, there is a RAW dependence between instructions *2* and *3* (via register $r4$).

Now, let us see what happens if these instructions pass through our pipeline. Assume that instruction *1* wakes up in cycle 1. It is possible that multiple instructions might wake up in cycle 1, and we need to *select* which instructions shall proceed to execution. This will take one more cycle (cycle 2). Now in cycle 3, instruction *1* will proceed to read its operands from the register file, and in cycle 4 it will move to the execution units. Assuming it takes 1 cycle to execute the instruction, we will broadcast the tag in cycle 5, and in cycle 6 the consumer instruction will wake up. Along with broadcasting the tag, we can write the results to the register file. The chain of events is shown in Figure 4.22.

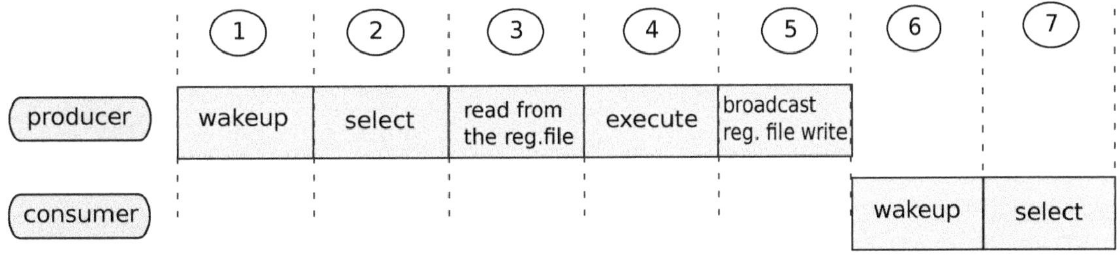

Figure 4.22: Chain of events between the execution of a producer and a consumer instruction

The main issue is that we have a delay of 5 cycles between executing instructions *1* and *2*. In other words, if instruction *1* executes in cycle 4, then instruction *2* will execute in cycle 9. Let us say that we are able to find a lot of independent instructions between cycles 4 and 9, then there is no problem: our pipeline will always be full with instructions.

However, this need not be the case always. Sometimes we might not find enough independent instructions. In this case, the pipeline will not have any work to do, and our performance will dip. In fact the situation is far worse than a simple in-order pipeline where for such execution sequences we would not have stalled. Clearly, we are not getting any benefit out of an OOO pipeline.

To ensure that we are able to get some gains out of an OOO pipeline we need to ensure that such instructions with a RAW dependence can execute in consecutive cycles. This will at least ensure that we are doing as well as an in-order pipeline. The additional benefits of OOO pipelines will accrue when we find enough independent instructions to fill up the rest of the issue slots. Nevertheless, waiting for 5 cycles to issue a consumer instruction seems to be a very bad idea. Let us aim for 1 cycle, which is the minimum (same as an in-order pipeline).

Let us thus summarise our new found objective. It is to execute instructions with a RAW dependence in consecutive cycles. Let us only confine our attention to regular arithmetic instructions, and keep memory instructions out of this discussion for the time being. Such kind of an execution, known as back-to-back execution, is very beneficial and will guarantee us some degree of minimum performance, even in programs with very little instruction level parallelism (ILP) (see Definition 8).

To ensure back-to-back execution, we need to take a very deep look at three actions namely broadcast, wakeup, and select. If a producer instruction wakes up in cycle i, then the consumer instruction has to wakeup in cycle $i + 1$. Before getting overly concerned with the exact mechanism, let us start drawing some diagrams to explain the process. We shall then add some meat to the bones by working on the mechanism.

At the moment, this is what we need to ensure:

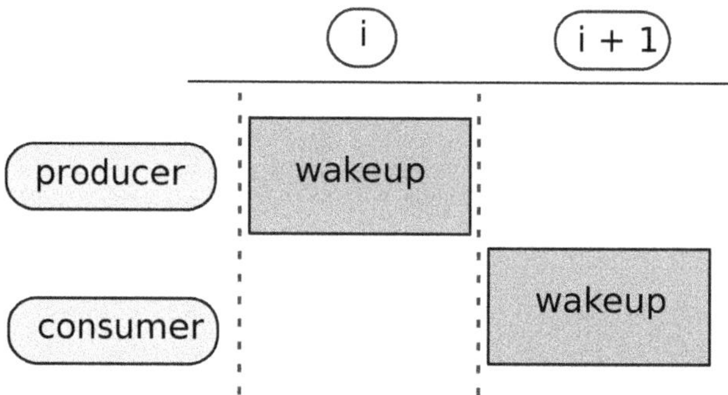

Now, given the fact that we need to perform a select operation, after an instruction wakes up, we have two options. Assume that we have slightly optimised our wakeup and select procedures such that they fit in a single cycle. In this case, the instruction can get selected in the same cycle. Assume it does get selected. We thus have arrived at the following pipeline diagram.

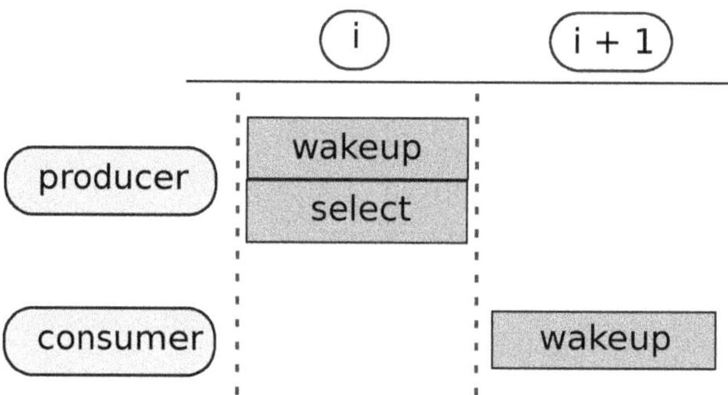

Once an instruction is selected, it knows that it is on its way to execution. There are no more roadblocks. It can proceed to the subsequent stages. In cycle $i+1$, it can broadcast the tag corresponding to its destination register. This is an early broadcast because we are broadcasting the tag before the producer instruction has computed its result and written it to the register file. We subsequently expect the consumer instruction to pick up the broadcasted tag (in the same cycle), and proceed through its wakeup and select stages. This is thus the final pipeline diagram:

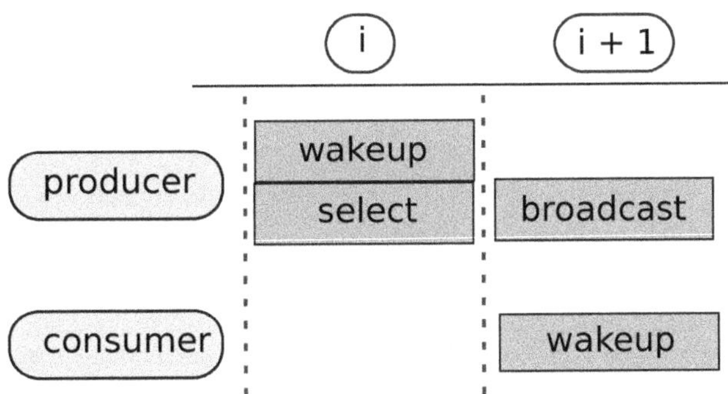

To summarise, for ensuring back-to-back execution, we have had to make significant changes to our design.

1. We have overlapped the broadcast of the producer instruction with the wake-up/select operations of consumer instructions. This requires us to ensure that these are very fast operations.

2. We do an *early broadcast*. This means that before the result of the producer is ready, we wake up the consumer instructions. They believe the producer, and proceed through the wakeup/select stages. The producer is expected to forward (or bypass) its result to the consumer instructions such that they can execute correctly. This is similar to classic forwarding in in-order processors, where the result of the producer is sent to the consumer. The consumer chooses between the value read from the register file, and the forwarded value using a multiplexer (see Section 2.1.4). **It is important to understand the forwarding technique in in-order processors before reading this section. We use exactly the same logic here.** In OOO processors forwarding is typically called *bypassing*.

3. The OOO pipeline from the dispatch stage to the register file write stage is thus as follows:

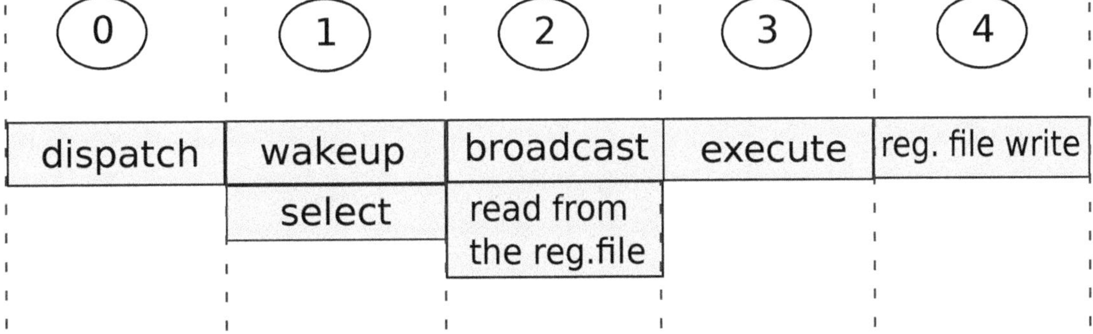

4. A question naturally arises: Is there a correctness issue in performing early broadcast? The reader should first try to answer this question on her own. The answer is given in Point 7.

Important Point 7

We are doing an early broadcast. This means that we are broadcasting the tag before the register has been written to. Is there a correctness issue?

Let us try to use the same logic that we used while discussing forwarding in in-order processors in Section 2.1.4. Let us look at the pipeline diagrams for a producer and consumer instruction issued back-to-back.

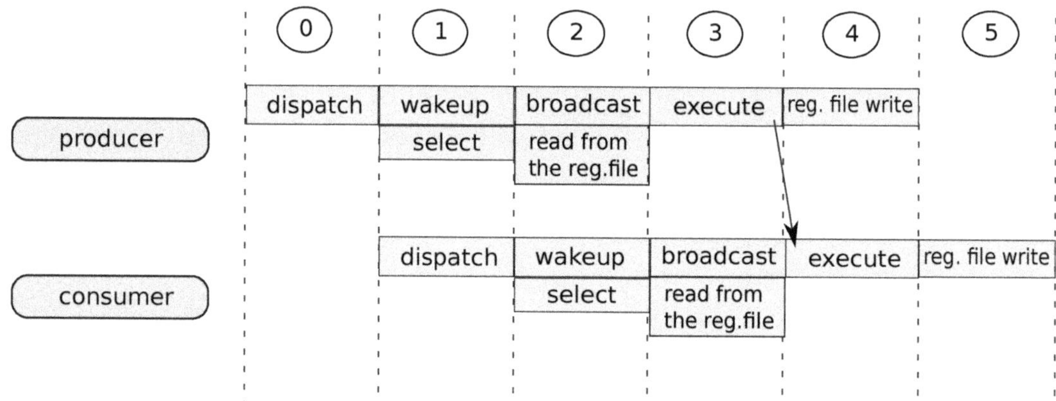

Here, we execute a producer-consumer instruction pair back-to-back, and we do an early broadcast. There is no problem in correctness, because the consumer instruction can always get the correct values from the producer. In this case, the consumer needs the producer's results at the beginning of cycle 4. The producer's results are ready by the end of cycle 3, and thus it can forward the results to the consumer. Similar to classic forwarding in in-order pipelines we require multiplexers.

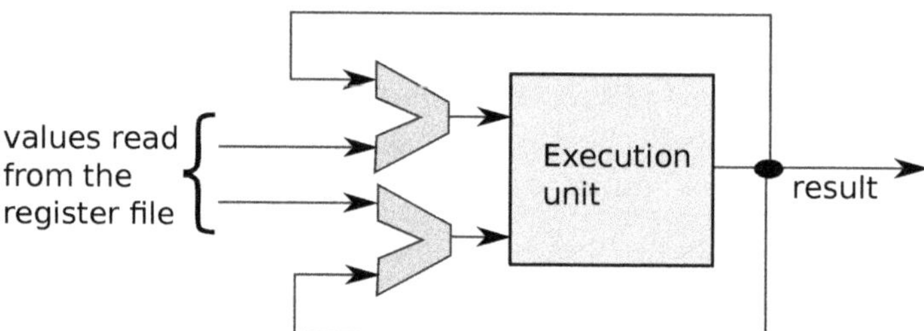

We know from our study of in-order pipelines that such kind of forwarding (also known as bypassing) can be done seamlessly (see [Sarangi, 2015] and Section 2.1.4) in most cases. All that we need to ensure is that when we need the data at the beginning of the execute stage, it is available somewhere in the pipeline. As long as we can ensure this, early broadcast will not introduce any correctness issues.

Let us now comment about the efficiency of this process. It is true that this method has enabled back-to-back execution, and thus we are guaranteed to at least get the same IPC as an in-order processor for codes that have a lot of such dependences. However, such optimisations come at a cost, and the cost is that we need to perform the broadcast-wakeup-select operations very quickly – all within one cycle (see Figure 4.23).

This might not be possible all the time, particularly when the instruction window has a large size. There are wire delays involved, and the wake-up/select operations can take more than one clock cycle particularly in high frequency processors. Hence, it might be a wise idea to forego the notion of back-

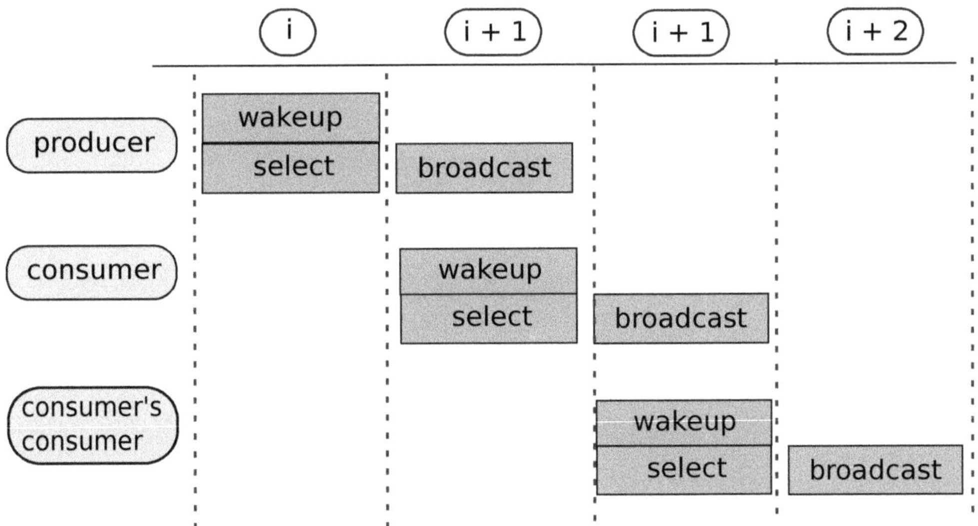

Figure 4.23: Back-to-back execution in an OOO pipeline

to-back execution if we desire a very high frequency processor. We will definitely lose IPC in codes with a lot of dependences; however for most general purpose programs we will always be able to find enough independent instructions to execute every cycle. There can be a net gain in performance because of the high frequency. Such kind of decisions illustrate the trade-off in designing high performance processors, where we cannot get high IPC and frequency at the same time. Again this also depends on the type of programs that we expect to run. If we expect that programs will have high ILP, then back-to-back execution is not a necessity, otherwise it is.

4.2.5 Tricky Issues with Early Broadcast

The Load-use Hazard

As we have discussed in Point 7, early broadcast per se is not an issue as long as it is possible to bypass values from one stage to the other. Of course, there are exceptions as we had discussed in Section 2.1.4 such as the load-use hazard, where if the producer instruction is a load, back-to-back execution is not possible. In the case of OOO processors, we have the same problem. The execute stage computes the address and then we need to perform a memory access, and thus bypassing is not possible. Let us visualise this.

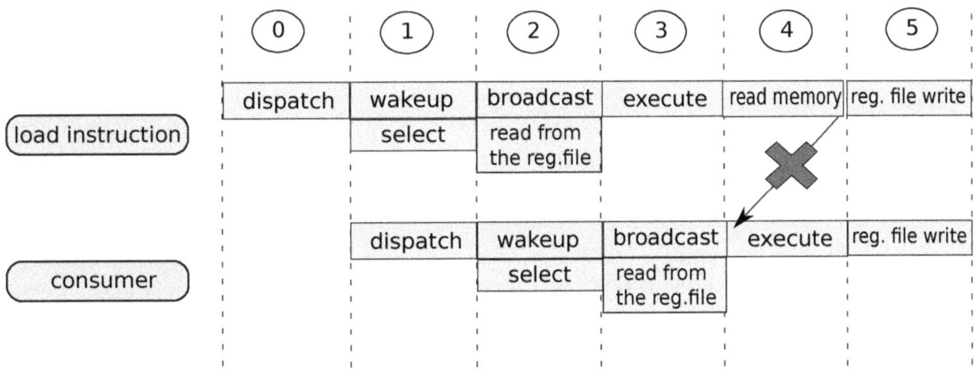

We add an extra stage after the execute stage to access memory. We make the simplistic assumption that a memory access takes one cycle. Then we try to forward the data. As we show in the diagram this is not possible. We are moving backwards in time. We need the results at the beginning of the 4th cycle, whereas they are produced at the end of the 4th cycle. Thus back-to-back execution is not possible. However, we can still broadcast the tag early, and get some benefits.

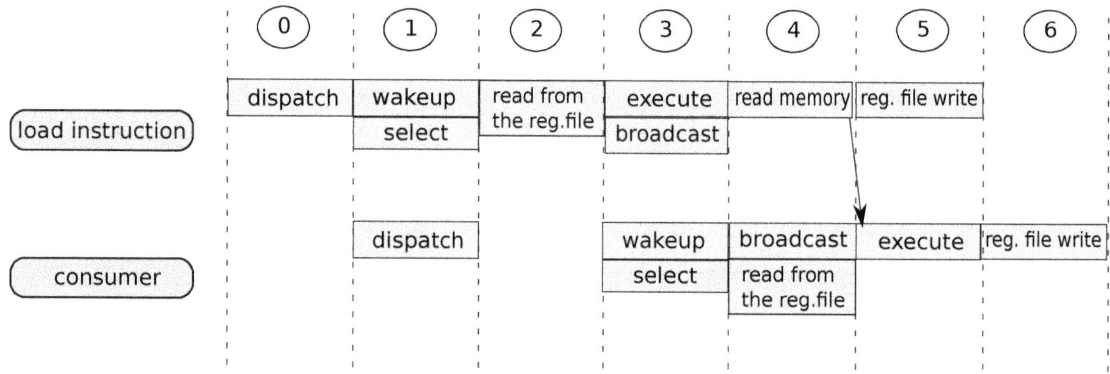

Instead of broadcasting the tag right after instruction select, let us instead broadcast the tag in the 3rd cycle as shown above. We thus broadcast one cycle later, and the consumer instruction needs to stall for an additional cycle. The rest of the processing for the consumer instruction remains the same. In this case, we do not have any correctness issues owing to the fact that the consumer instruction needs the result in the beginning of the 5th cycle, and it gets it. This is because the load returns with its value at the end of the 4th cycle.

To summarise, the method to handle a load-use hazard is to broadcast two cycles after selection. Let us generalise this. Let us club the execute and memory access stages into one large execute stage. In the current example this stage takes 2 cycles (1 for computing the address, and 1 for accessing memory). Assume it takes k cycles ($k \geq 1$). We claim that we need to do a broadcast k cycles after selecting the instruction to ensure that all the consumer instructions get the result exactly on time.

Let us prove this. Assume that the producer instruction wakes up and gets selected in cycle 1. It will then proceed to read the values of its register operands in the next cycle. Since the execution takes k cycles, the execution will finish in cycle $k+2$. Consider the next instruction. The worst case is that it is a consumer instruction. The earliest that it can execute is cycle $k+3$ (one cycle after the producer). Calculating backwards the consumer needs to wake up (and get selected) in cycle $k+1$ (one register read stage in the middle). This means that the producer needs to broadcast in cycle $k+1$, and that is the earliest. Recall that the producer had woken up in cycle 1, and we just proved that the earliest it can broadcast the tag is cycle $k+1$ (k cycles later). This proves our claim.

This means that for each class of instructions, we have different times at which we need to broadcast their tags. If an add instruction takes 1 cycle, then we can broadcast the tag immediately after the instruction gets selected (in the next cycle). However, if we have a slow divide or memory access operation, then we need to wait for k cycles. This is typically achieved by using a timer for each selected instruction that counts down from k to 0.

Setting the *avlbl* bit with Early Broadcast

We had discussed the *avlbl* bit in each entry of the rename table (see Figure 4.14). We had said in Section 4.2.1 that this bit indicates if a given source operand can be found in the register file or not. This needs to be revised in the light of our current discussion.

The *avlbl* bit should indicate if it is possible to get the value of the operand from either the register file or the bypass network (network of wires and multiplexers to transfer forwarded values). If it is so, then we can mark the operand to be ready, and the instruction can be issued if the rest of the operands are also ready. To summarise, when we say that an operand is available, it means that its value is present somewhere in the pipeline.

Regarding when we should set the *avlbl* bit, the answer should be obvious to us now. It should be set when the tag is being broadcasted on the tag buses. This is when the consuming instructions also get to know that the value corresponding to the tag is available (either from the register file or the bypass network). Along with doing this we can just forward the tags to the rename table, and set the appropriate *avlbl* bits.

Missing a Broadcast

Consider the following sequence of operations. For instruction I we read the rename table in cycle 1. We find that physical register $p1$ (one of the operands) is not available. Then in cycle 2 we dispatch this instruction to the instruction window. In cycle 2, the producer instruction (for $p1$) broadcasts the tag on the tag buses. If instruction I misses this broadcast because it is being simultaneously written to the instruction window, then there is a problem. The instruction window entry of I will continue to wait for the broadcast for $p1$, and this will never happen, because we have already broadcast the value in cycle 2.

Let us look at several ways to fix this problem.

- We write to the instruction window in the first half of the clock cycle, and we broadcast the tags in the second half of the clock cycle. This means that the instruction that is being dispatched (written to the instruction window) will not miss a broadcast. By the time that the tag is broadcast, the dispatched instruction is ready to wake up its operands. This is an easy solution. However, it is very inefficient. We are artificially reducing the time that we have for a broadcast and the subsequent wakeup. To accommodate this we need to elongate the duration of a clock cycle, which is not desirable.

- The other option is to store all the tags that were sent in a given cycle in a small buffer. We can compare these tags with the operands of the dispatched instructions in parallel. The *ready* bits for the operands can then be written later – either at the end of the current cycle or at the beginning of the next cycle – to the instruction window entries. This makes the circuit design complex in the sense that we need to create a separate structure to store the ready bits; however, in cases like this such complexities are inevitable.

- One more approach is to broadcast the tags that were missed once again. This will double the number of tag buses in the worst case. This can be done intelligently by broadcasting only those tags that have been genuinely missed and are needed to set the appropriate operands to the ready state. In the worst case, we need to double the number of tag buses, which is not desirable. In most cases, we can consider an average case; however, this depends on the benchmark, and is hard to predict.

4.3   The Load-Store Queue (LSQ)

We have up till now been discussing the execution of regular arithmetic instructions. Now we have acceptable solutions for renaming, selecting, and issuing instructions. Next, we need to turn our attention towards memory instructions. Sadly, we cannot use the mechanisms we have developed to process arithmetic instructions in the case of memory instructions. We need additional hardware. The most important structure that we add is known as the load-store queue (LSQ). Trivially speaking, it contains a list of load and store operations – arranged in FIFO (first-in first-out) order based on when they were fetched. Note that we shall use the terms "load-store queue" and "LSQ" interchangeably.

Let us motivate the need for an LSQ. Consider two memory instructions: *I1* and *I2*. We can have many kinds of dependences between them. Some of these dependences have been covered in previous sections, and some are new. We have considered dependences via registers in the previous sections. However, now let us consider dependences via memory. We shall have such kind of dependences, when the addresses of these instructions are the same.

4.3.1 Memory Dependences

Let us consider four separate cases. Let $I1$ and $I2$ be memory instructions that access the same address. Assume that $I1$ precedes $I2$ in program order ($I1 \rightarrow I2$). Finally, assume that there are no intervening memory instructions between $I1$ and $I2$ that access the same address.

load $\rightarrow$ *load* dependence: In this case a load instruction ($I1$) is followed by another load instruction ($I2$) from the same address: $I1$ is the earlier instruction and $I2$ is the later instruction. We can reorder $I1$ and $I2$. Of course, we shall have an issue when we consider multiprocessors (explained in Chapter 9); however, for single processors there is no issue. Furthermore, to reduce memory traffic, we need not send two instructions to memory. We can just send one instruction. For example, we can send $I1$ to memory first. Then we can forward the value ready by $I1$ to instruction $I2$. This will halve the memory traffic.

load $\rightarrow$ *store* dependence: In this case a load instruction ($I1$) is followed by another store instruction ($I2$) – both access the same address. We cannot reorder $I1$ and $I2$. If we do that, then the load will read the wrong value. It will read the value written by the store $I2$, which is wrong. As a result these instructions need to execute in program order. Recall that this is a classic WAR dependence in memory.

store $\rightarrow$ *load* dependence: In this case a store instruction ($I1$) is followed by another load instruction ($I2$). This is a classic RAW dependence in memory, where the store instruction is the producer and the load instruction is the consumer. Here again, it is not possible to reorder the instructions. Otherwise, the load instruction ($I2$) will get an older value, which is wrong.

store $\rightarrow$ *store* dependence: In this case a store instruction ($I1$) is followed by another store instruction ($I2$) to the same address (a WAW dependence). Akin to a similar case with registers, we cannot reorder the memory accesses.

The summary of all of this discussion is that there can be RAW, WAR, and WAW dependences between memory instructions the same way we have dependences between instructions with register operands. However, the sad part is that we cannot use the same techniques that we used to get rid of WAR and WAW hazards for registers in this case. For registers, we used renaming, and built an elaborate mechanism centred around the rename table. However, renaming memory is far more expensive. We can have thousands of memory locations, and maintaining such large rename tables is practically not feasible. Moreover, the memory address is not a 4-bit quantity, it is instead a 32-bit or 64-bit quantity. Thus, a memory renaming table will require millions of entries, and thus it is not practical.

As a result, whenever we have a dependence of any form that involves a write (WAR, RAW, or WAW), we need to ensure that the memory requests are sent to the memory system *in program order*.

This is not all. We sadly have more bad news. Register dependences are clearly visible after decoding the instruction. We know about the nature of dependences by taking a look at the ids of the source and destination registers. However, processing memory instructions is a multi-step process. The first step is, of course, to read the values of the source registers. The second step is to compute the address by adding the contents of the base address register and the offset. Only after address computation do we get to know the address of a memory instruction. This address needs to be subsequently used to find dependences between memory instructions. Unlike decisions that are taken right after the decode stage (such as register dependences), and that also in program order, the addresses of memory instructions are generated out of order, and need to be handled in the order in which they are generated. This out-of-order generation of memory addresses complicates the problem of managing and tracking memory dependences significantly.

Let us first try to solve this problem from a conceptual point of view. Subsequently, we shall propose a practical realisation of our method.

4.3.2   Conceptually Handling Loads and Stores

It should be noted that a memory instruction has two execution steps. The first step is to compute the address, and the next is the memory access itself. Insofar as the former step is concerned, it is a regular arithmetic addition. The memory instruction can happily pass through the dispatch and issue stages for this specific part of its processing. Now, consider the second execution step where we need to handle memory dependences.

Let us imagine a large conceptual first-in first-out queue that contains all the load and store instructions that are currently in the pipeline; let this be our LSQ (load-store queue). Whenever, we decode a memory instruction we create an entry for it in the LSQ. At this point, we do not have any knowledge of its memory address. This will be computed after the corresponding instruction is issued, and we add the contents of the base register to the offset (embedded in the instruction). Once, the address is generated, we can write it to the corresponding entry in the LSQ.

This is when the real processing starts. Every entry in the LSQ is marked *not ready* by default. However, once its address is generated it is ready to be executed – sent to the memory system. As we shall see in Section 4.4, stores cannot be sent to the memory system as soon as their address is computed. Otherwise, we will not be able to guarantee precise exceptions (see Section 2.3.3). Hence, stores are sent when the instruction is ready to be removed from the pipeline. As we shall see in Section 4.4, this is the point where the instruction is the oldest in the pipeline.

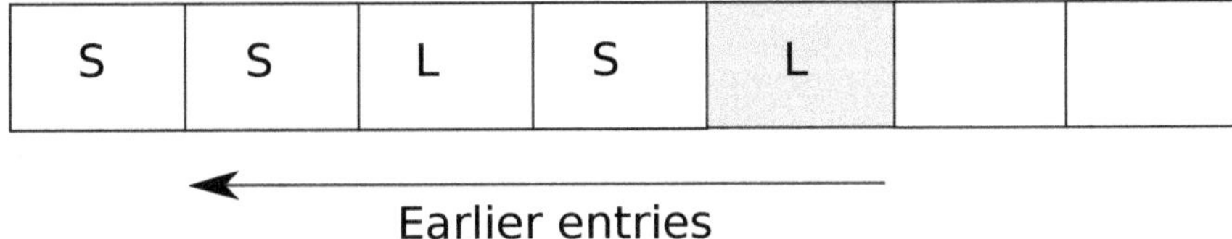

Figure 4.24: Example of a sequence of loads and stores (arranged in a queue as per the order in which they entered the pipeline).

Loads

Let us look at an entry right after its memory address is computed. We are ready to go to the memory system, if we are not violating any memory dependence as defined in Section 4.3.1. However, whether we do have dependences or not needs to be ascertained first.

Let us look at Figure 4.24 in detail. Assume that the shaded (or coloured) box in the load queue (load *A*) just got its address computed. Let us consider all the stores before it. There is a possibility of a *store → load* dependence. We need to read all the store entries before it and find if there is a store with the same address or with an unresolved (not computed) address. This means that in Figure 4.24, we need to search all the stores before the load – proceed in a leftward direction (towards earlier entries). There are three possible scenarios. Let us consider them in decreasing order of priority.

1. **While proceeding towards earlier entries we encounter a store with an unresolved address.** This means that in theory the address could be the same as the load. We cannot take the risk of ignoring this store instruction. If we ignore it and go ahead, it is possible that we might load the wrong data if the address of the store comes out to be the same as the address of load

A. Hence, we need to wait for the address of that store to be resolved (computed). The process terminates here, and we do not check for the rest of the scenarios.

2. **Assume that we encounter a store to the same address before encountering an unresolved store.** In this case, we can forward the value of the store to the load instruction. This is known as *load-store forwarding* or *forwarding in the LSQ*. In this case, the load can take the value of the store and proceed. Note that the store in consideration has not written its value to the memory system yet. However, since we know the value that it is going to write, we can happily let dependent load instructions proceed. This is similar to forwarding in an in-order pipeline.

3. **None of the above:** This means that we keep searching for previous store instructions; however, we do not encounter a store with an unresolved address or a store instruction with the same address as the load instruction. In this case, there is no reason to wait or forward from an earlier store. We can let the load instruction access the memory system and read its value from there.

To summarise, we need to search all the store entries before the load instruction *A* (in Figure 4.24). We need to keep searching till we find the first (latest before the load) store instruction that either stores to the same address or has an unresolved address. In the former case there is a *store → load* dependence and in the latter case there is a possibility of a dependence, and since we do not know, we need to wait. If there is a dependence, then we can directly forward the store's value to the load instruction. We are guaranteed to have the value in the LSQ because in our assumed RISC ISA, store instructions read the value, which is to be stored, from a register. We further assume that register file reads happen before the address of a store is computed. Thus, if a store's address is resolved, its value should also be present in the corresponding LSQ entry. With such forwarding, the load can continue its execution. This method effectively increases the IPC because it releases the load instruction as soon as possible and allows it to carry on with its execution. There will be less stalls in the future.

If there is no waiting or forwarding, then it means that we have searched all the earlier store entries, and there is no possibility of a memory dependence. The load instruction can be sent to the memory system.

Stores

Let us see what happens in the case of store instructions. Note that here there are two distinct points of time. The first point of time is when the store instruction is decoded and we create an entry for it in the LSQ. The second point of time is when we finish computing the address of the store instruction and update the address in the LSQ entry. We are assuming that at this point we know the value to be stored (contents of some register) as well. This is because we read the contents of the register that contains the base address and the contents of the register that holds the store value at the same time. Given that we have finished computing the address, the store value must also be present with us.

Now that we know the value that needs to be stored, and the address, a naive reader would think that we are ready to send the store to the memory system. However, as we shall see in Section 4.4, because of several reasons centred around correctness we can only send a store to the memory system when the instruction is being removed from the pipeline, and it is the oldest instruction in the pipeline. As long as we have earlier (older) instructions in the pipeline, we cannot send the store to memory. Since we do not have earlier instructions when the store instruction is sent to memory, it is guaranteed to be at the head of the LSQ, and there will be no memory dependences that can stop us from sending the store to memory.

Nevertheless, handling stores is not that simple. Initially, when an entry is created for a store at the time of decoding an instruction, the store's address is unresolved. Let us refer to this situation with a question mark (?) in our figures. Once its address is computed, the store's address is resolved. We shall use a tick mark to indicate this situation. Even though we cannot send the store to memory immediately after computing its address, we still have some work to do. Given that we have a store with a resolved address, new dependences will be created. The store can forward its value to newer loads as we can see in Figure 4.25. In this figure all the entries that are shaded (or coloured) have the same address.

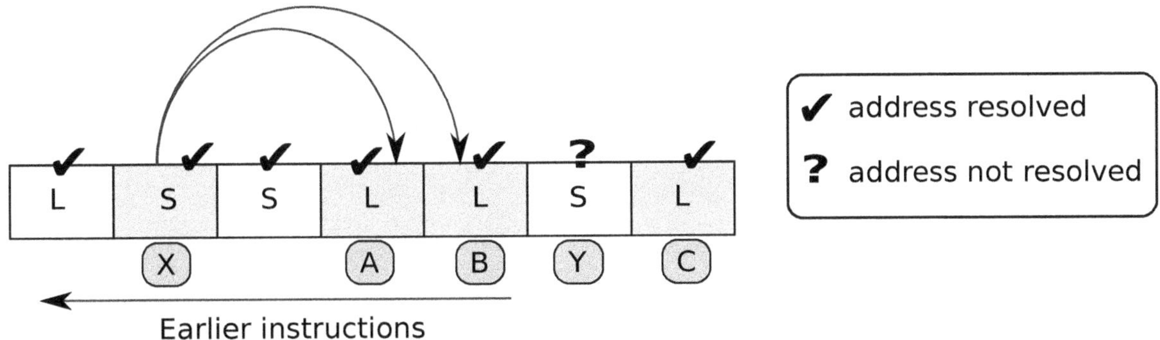

Figure 4.25: Forwarding in the LSQ (we cannot forward to C because of Y)

When store X in Figure 4.25 is resolved, suddenly loads A and B, which have the same address are eligible to get the forwarded data. They can take the forwarded value and continue their execution. However, load C is not eligible to get the forwarded value because it is preceded by the store instruction Y. Y's address has not been resolved, and it is possible that its address might be the same as X's and C's address. In that case, C should get the forwarded value from Y and not X. Since we do not know, load C needs to wait.

The algorithm is thus as follows:

- Search later entries. If we encounter a store to the same address or if a store is unresolved, then stop.

- Otherwise, if there is a load with the same address, forward the value, and then keep scanning later entries.

4.3.3 Design of the LSQ

Most common designs of the LSQ have a separate load queue and a store queue as shown in Figure 4.26. The queues by themselves are internally designed as circular queues, which as we have been seeing is almost always the case. Entries are added to the bottom of the corresponding queue (load or store), and they gradually move up. The logic for having two separate queues is efficiency. We typically need to find all the earlier stores, or later loads. Having smaller queues helps speed up the process.

Let us summarise the discussion that we had in Section 4.3.2 regarding the search operations that need to be performed (see Table 4.2) along with the conditions for terminating the search. Whenever we resolve the address of a load, we search all the stores before it till we find a store to the same address or a store with an unresolved address. In the former case we forward the value of the store to the load.

Whenever, we resolve the address of a store instruction we search all the loads and stores after it. We terminate the process when we encounter a store with the same address or an unresolved address. If we encounter a load to the same address before termination, then we forward the value of the store to the load, and mark the load instruction as ready.

The task now is to design basic hardware mechanisms to implement the logic in Table 4.2. Here are the basic primitives that we need to implement.

1. Search entries before or after a given entry.

2. Find entries with the same address.

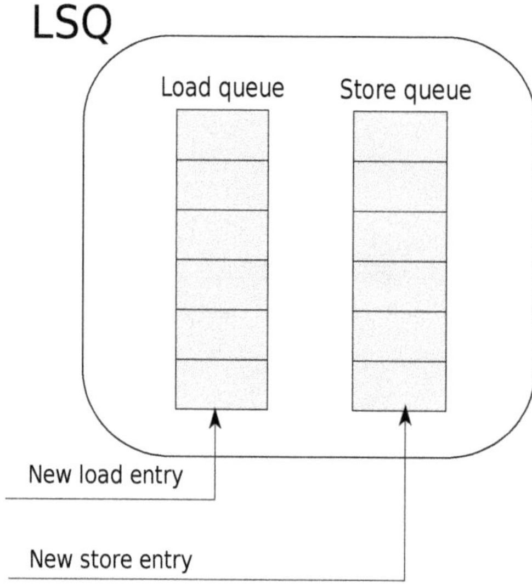

Figure 4.26: Design of the LSQ

Type	Search direction	Action: Condition
Loads	Search all stores before it	1. Terminate and forward value: Store to the same address 2. Terminate: Store with an unresolved address
Stores	Search all loads and stores after it	1. Terminate: Store to the same address 2. Terminate: Store with an unresolved address 3. Forward value: Load from the same address

Table 4.2: Rules for processing load and store entries after their address is resolved

3. Find the first (latest) entry before a given entry that satisfies a certain condition, or the first (earliest) entry after a given entry that satisfies a given condition.

Let us add the following fields to each entry (see Figure 4.27). Along with the address we create two additional fields: *valid* and *resvd*. *valid* indicates if the entry is valid (as the name suggests) and *resvd* indicates if the address has been resolved or not. If $resvd = 1$ then it means that the address has been computed (resolved).

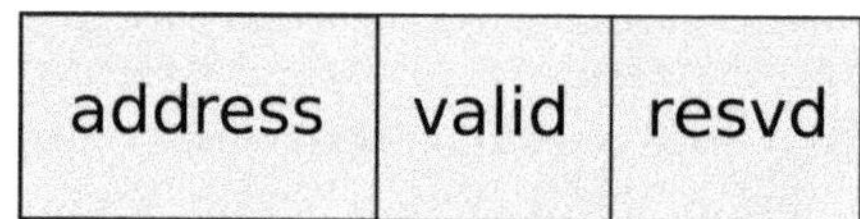

Figure 4.27: An entry in the LSQ

Finding Earlier or Later Loads and Stores

The basic question is, "Given a load or store how do we find the loads and stores before or after it ?" Since the load and store queues are implemented as circular queues, we have a *head* and a *tail* pointer associated with each queue. Every time we enqueue an entry, we increment the *tail* pointer (modulo the size of the queue). Similarly, every time we dequeue an entry, we increment the *head* pointer (modulo the size of the queue).

Let us create an abstract version of the problem. Let us consider an array v, which we shall use as a circular queue with a *head* and a *tail* pointer. In addition, we have a *size* field that indicates the number of entries in the queue. If $size = 0$, then it means that the queue is empty, and no processing needs to be done. Let us proceed with the assumption that $size \neq 0$. If $head = tail$, then it means that the queue has just one entry. If $tail < head$, then it means that the queue has wrapped around the end of the array. Here, we are not considering the possibility of overflows: more entries than the maximum size of the queue. Finally, note that we do not look at the *head* and *tail* pointers to decide whether a queue is empty or not, we simply look at the *size* field.

To record the relative ordering of loads and stores, we need to create a mechanism. We shall describe the mechanism for loads in this section. There is an analogous mechanism for stores. For each load entry we record the value of the *tail* pointer of the store queue when the load instruction was entered into the load queue. Recording the *tail* pointer of the store queue will help us find all the stores that came after the load, and the stores that were in the pipeline present before it.

Given an index j, we need to find all the entries that are either before it (towards *head*) or after it (towards *tail*). The assumption is of course that j is a valid index in the circular queue. The most trivial solution is to start at j and walk the array sequentially. This is a slow operation and is proportional to the size of the array in the average case. This is not acceptable. We need a parallel implementation.

Let us first fix the format of the output. Since the load queue or store queue typically have less than 64 entries, we can use this fact to significantly speed up operations by using some extra space. Let the output be a bit vector, where the number of bits is equal to the number of entries in the relevant queue (array v). A bit is 1, if the entry satisfies the predicate (before or after), otherwise it is 0. To create an efficient hardware implementation, we can store these bit vectors in registers. Additionally, let us assume that we have the following bit vectors available in registers: *valid* and *resvd*. The *valid* register contains all the *valid* bits of entries in the relevant queue. On similar lines we have a *resvd* register that contains one bit for each entry in the queue: 1 if the address is resolved and 0 if it is not.

Let us now show an example of how to compute a bit vector that contains a 1 for all the valid queue entries that are *before* a given j. Let the total number of entries in v be N. Let us first create a small N-entry array, where for a given index i (starts from 0) we store its unary representation using N bits. For example, when $N = 8$, we store 00000111 for 3. Basically, for a given number i, we store an N-bit number where the least significant i digits are 1 and the rest are 0. If $i = 17$, we store a number whose least significant 17 bits are 1, and the remaining $N - 17$ bits are 0. We can alternatively say that for each i we store $2^i - 1$. Such small arrays that store the precomputed results of functions (unary representations in this case) are known as lookup tables. These are really fast. In this case, let us represent this lookup table operation by the function *prec*.

First, consider the case where $j \geq head$ (no wraparound). The bit vector representing the elements before j – represented as $before(j)$ – is given as follows:

$$before(j) = \overline{prec(head)} \wedge prec(j) \tag{4.1}$$

This can also be viewed graphically. The first term captures all those entries that do not precede the *head* and the second term captures all those entries that precede entry number j. Note that in this diagram the least significant bit is the leftmost position and the most significant bit is the rightmost position (we go from left to right unlike the conventional way: right to left).

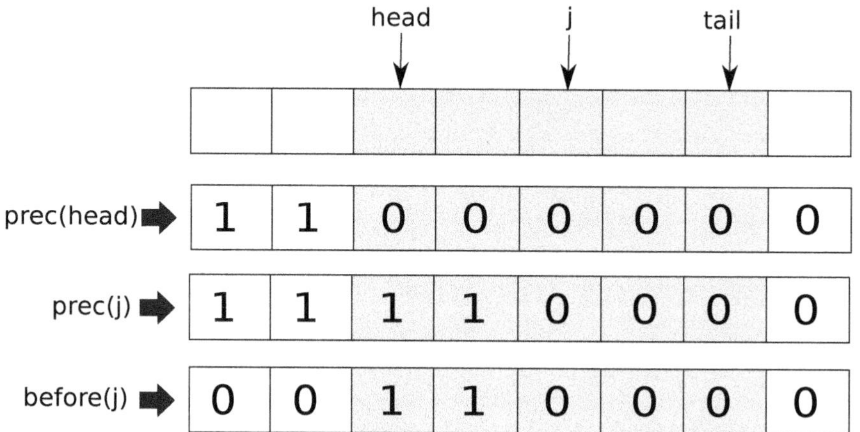

An analogous equation for the case when there is a wraparound ($j < head$) is as follows.

$$before(j) = \overline{prec(head)} \vee prec(j) \tag{4.2}$$

The first part, $\overline{prec(head)}$, captures all the entries from $head$ till the last $(N-1)^{th}$ entry of the array. The second part, $prec(j)$, comprises all the entries that are between the 0th and $(j-1)^{th}$ indices in the array. The proof of this case is left as an exercise for the reader.

Equations 4.1 and 4.2 are very easy to compute. They require simple logical operations and the bits can be processed in parallel. We do not have to sequentially scan any array. If we want to find all the resolved entries that are before a given index j, then we just need to compute $before(j) \wedge resvd$.

The corresponding equations for the function $after$ are as follows. The reader is encouraged to verify their correctness.

Case $j \leq tail$:

$$after(j) = \overline{prec(j)} \wedge \overline{map(j)} \wedge (prec(tail) \vee map(tail)) \tag{4.3}$$

Here, we use a function $map(i)$, which computes an N-bit bit vector where the ith bit is 1, and the rest of the bits are 0. Here, the first two terms set all the bits in the range $[j+1, \ldots, N-1]$ to 1. The last term $(prec(tail) \vee map(tail))$ computes a bit vector that has 1s at all the positions in the range $[0, \ldots, tail]$. The intersection gives us the correct result.

Case $j > tail$:

$$after(j) = (\overline{prec(j)} \vee prec(tail) \vee map(tail)) \wedge \overline{map(j)} \tag{4.4}$$

Note: In both the cases we are computing a logical AND operation with $\overline{map(j)}$ because we want to remove the jth entry from the result of the $after$ function. The rest of the proof is straightforward.

Finding Entries with the Same Address

To solve this problem, we need to implement the queues using a content addressable (CAM) array. We shall learn more about CAM arrays in Chapter 7. In such arrays we can access an entry both by its index as well as by its content. For example, if we designate the content to be the memory address, then we can search for all the entries that contain a matching address. The output will be an N-bit bit vector, where a value of 1 in the kth position indicates that the address matches with the kth entry in the array.

For small arrays we can get this bit vector in less than a cycle, and this can then be used to compute functions of the form: find the loads after a given store with a matching address.

Finding the Earliest or Latest Entries Satisfying a Given Property

Now that after we have computed the *before* and *after* functions, we can find the set of all the loads and stores before or after a given entry satisfying a certain property. For example, we can find all the stores after a certain store whose address is unresolved. We will get a bit vector as an output. As we saw in Table 4.2, it is often necessary to find the first entry before or after an entry that satisfies a given property. For example, for a load, we need to find the latest store before the load that has a matching or unresolved address.

Let us generalise this problem, and propose a solution. We have a bit vector where the entries of interest are set to 1, and the rest are set to 0. This bit vector has been computed after a series of logical operations. Each entry with a 1 satisfies a given property. Now, if $tail \geq head$, then there is no wraparound and we are fine. However, if $tail < head$, then we have a wraparound. In this case, let us create a modified bit vector that contains all the bits from *head* to *tail* in sequence. This needs a set of bit shift and copy operations that can be performed in less than a clock cycle. At the end of this operation our modified bit vector, v', will not have a wraparound.

We thus have a bit vector with a set of 0s and 1s. The aim is to find either the position of the leftmost or rightmost 1. We have seen such problems before. This is similar to an $n \times 1$ select operation, as we have seen in Section 4.2.3. We program the choice boxes as follows. If we want to choose the leftmost bit that is a 1, then we need to program the choice boxes to always choose their left input if there is a choice (when both inputs are 1). We can argue by mathematical induction that ultimately the leftmost 1 will be chosen as the output of the select unit. On similar lines we can find the position of the rightmost 1. Let us visualise this.

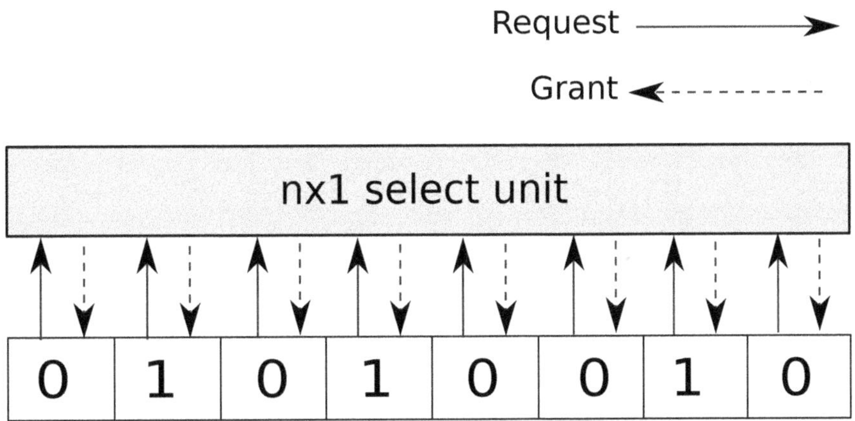

The request lines carry 1 if the corresponding bit is 1. Only one of the grant lines is set to 1, and this corresponds to the entry that is the leftmost or rightmost 1. We can thus very easily find the earliest or latest entries using a modification of the classic select unit that we have studied before.

Putting it all Together

The crucial insight that we can derive from this design is that it is often very expensive to process data one entry at a time. There is a need for parallel processing, and this requires the use of novel storage structures and algorithms. We often end up doing extra work; however, in high performance processors it is essential to do this additional work such that results can be computed in less than 1-2 cycles.

4.4 Instruction Commit

This is the last stage in an instruction's life. This stage is known as instruction commit, and is even known as the *instruction retirement* stage. The instruction is supposed to *logically complete* in this stage, and then subsequently leave the pipeline. The issue of an instruction logically completing needs to be further explained. It is a difficult concept and will require several pages of text before readers can fully appreciate what exactly this term means. It would be wise to go over Section 2.3.3 on precise exceptions once again before reading this section.

4.4.1 Notion of Precise Exceptions and In-order Commit

Let us take a second look at this topic (refer to Section 2.3.3). A precise exception was defined as a mechanism where all the instructions before (in program order) the faulting instruction execute completely, and none of the instructions after the faulty instruction appear to execute. We argued that having precise exceptions is vitally important for modern out-of-order processors. Otherwise, programs will appear to execute incorrectly and we will not be able to reason about them.

A common example that is given in this regard is the case of an instruction that accesses a piece of data that is not in memory (a page fault defined in Section 7.2). The CPU and the operating system do the following in response: (1) store the *execution state (context)* of the program and load the operating system, (2) execute a small function called an interrupt handler (part of the OS) that will bring the data into memory, (3) load the execution state of the original program back, and finally, (4) re-execute the faulting instruction. This process is shown in Figure 4.28. The interrupt handler loads the data into memory and then the OS restarts the original program. The original program re-executes the faulting instruction once again. This time it does not encounter a fault because its data is in memory. The entire process needs to happen seamlessly without the original program perceiving the interruption.

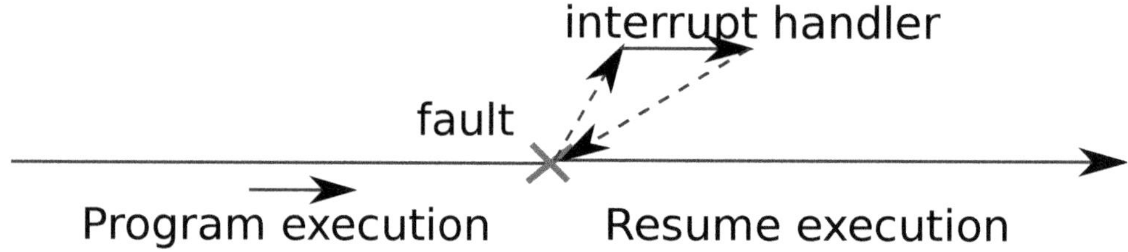

Figure 4.28: Life cycle of a faulting instruction

Let us look at the finer points. We are making an implicit assumption that before the faulting instruction all the instructions have fully executed – computed all their results, and written the results to the register file or memory. We are also assuming that no instruction after the faulting instruction has written its final result to the register file or memory. Basically, no permanent or visible changes have been made by instructions after the faulting instruction. We have in a sense *cleanly split* the execution of the original program, somehow stored its context (or execution state), executed other programs, and then restarted the same program magically from the same point. Such exceptions or interruptions in program execution are known as *precise exceptions*.

We further argued in Section 2.3.3 that to an outsider, a program should appear to execute in exactly the same way as if it was running on an in-order processor or a single-cycle processor. In such processors, precise exceptions are guaranteed because instructions write their results to the register file or main memory in program order. We can thus stop the program at any point fairly easily, flush the pipeline, and safely restart from either the faulting instruction (if there is a need) or from the instruction that appears after the faulting instruction in program order – depending upon the nature of the fault. For an out-of-order pipeline, to ensure similar behaviour, it will take more work.

Let us complicate the situation by adding a little bit more complexity. Till an instruction completes, we are not really sure if that instruction has any faults or not. It is possible that it might access an illegal address, perform some illegal arithmetic operation, have an illegal opcode, or do something else that is not allowed. Since we do not know sufficiently in advance which instruction will have a fault, it is a good idea to assume that any instruction might have a fault. This means that at any point in the execution of an instruction we might encounter an error – we still need to ensure that the notion of precise exceptions is maintained.

The crux of our discussion is thus as follows: an OOO processor should appear to be executing instructions in program order to an outsider. This idea can be visualised better in Figure 4.29.

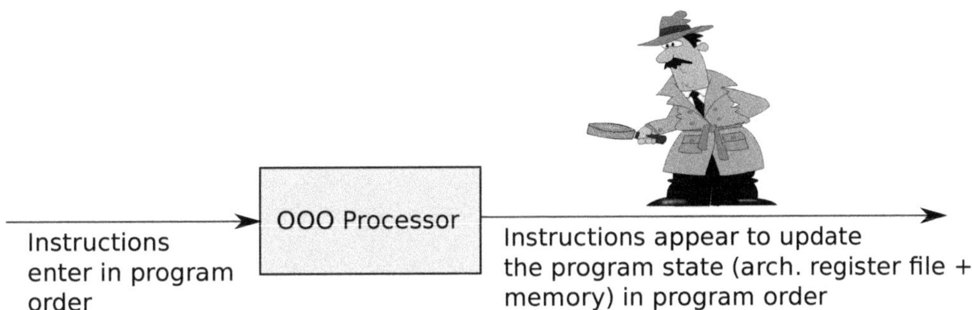

Figure 4.29: View of instruction execution from the point of view of an outsider

If we create a system where instructions are read in program order (this is already the case), and to an outsider sitting outside the processor, the instructions appear to complete also in program order, then we can achieve all our goals. This is shown in Figure 4.29. Within the processor, which we treat as a black box in the figure, instructions can compute their results and even write results to temporary storage out of order. However, for a hypothetical entity sitting just outside the processor, all instructions need to appear to make permanent changes to the register file and memory in program order.

Note that this is a stronger property than precise exceptions. If we can ensure this property, precise exceptions are automatically guaranteed, because now all instructions appear to in some sense *finish* or *complete* in program order. This model is followed by almost all processors today, and as we shall shortly see, there are no significant performance penalties.

This mechanism is known as *in-order commit*, which means that instructions finish and commit (permanently write) their results in program order. Let us try to design a hardware structure that ensures in-order commit. This is known as a Reorder Buffer. The notion of committing an instruction will become gradually clear over the next few sections.

4.4.2   The Reorder Buffer (ROB)

The Reorder Buffer or ROB is a queue of instructions. Like all our structures it is also designed as a circular queue in hardware. After an instruction is decoded, we create an entry for it in the ROB. Since instructions are decoded in program order, they are also inserted into the ROB in program order. Let us create a very basic ROB entry that contains the following fields: program counter of the instruction, the next PC, the type of the instruction, and a *finished* bit (initialised to 0).

Here, the next PC is either the branch target if the instruction is a branch or is the address of the next instruction in program order. If the instruction has completed its execution, and has computed its values, then we can set the *finished* bit to 1. After this we need to commit (or retire) the instruction, which means that at this point a hypothetical observer sitting outside the processor should be able to conclude that the instruction has fully finished its execution in the OOO pipeline and needs to be removed. After committing an instruction (in program order) we can remove it from the ROB and all other architectural structures. The claim is that we will be able to ensure precise exceptions with the help of the ROB. We will gradually realise this.

Definition 22

- *Immediately after committing (or retiring) an instruction, a hypothetical observer sitting outside the processor can conclude that the instruction has fully finished its execution in the OOO pipeline and needs to be removed. After committing an instruction we can remove it from the ROB and all other architectural structures.*

- *We commit instructions in program order such that precise exceptions are guaranteed. Moreover, to guarantee precise exceptions we need to ensure that no instruction makes permanent changes to the memory or the architectural register file before committing. Think of the point of committing an instruction as a point of no-return for that instruction.*

- *The* commit width *is defined as the maximum number of instructions that a processor can commit per cycle.*

The process of committing an instruction is very simple (at a high level). Let's say that we want to commit (or retire) four instructions in a cycle. This is also referred to as the *commit width* (defined as the maximum number of instructions that we can commit per cycle). We take a look at the *finished* bit of the earliest instruction (head of the ROB). If its *finished* bit is 1, then we can commit the instruction, and remove it from the ROB. Removing an instruction from the ROB, implies that we remove it from all other structures like the load-store queue and instruction window. The instruction is deemed to be removed from the pipeline at this point.

Then we move to the next instruction in the queue, and try to commit it. We stop when we either find an instruction that is still executing (*finished* bit set to 0), or when we have successfully committed κ instructions, where κ is the commit width. Ideally, if we are able to commit κ instructions every cycle, we have fully saturated the pipeline because the IPC will become equal to κ. However, life is never that ideal. Because of dependences and misses in memory, most processors typically have an IPC that is much lower than their commit width.

A ROB typically has anywhere between 100 to 200 entries in a modern OOO processor. If we aggressively fetch instructions, it is possible that the ROB might fill up. Recall that we can commit an instruction and remove it from the ROB only if all of its earlier instructions (in program order) have finished. It is thus possible for one instruction to block a lot of instructions after it. This can happen for many reasons such as a miss in the L2 or L3 cache. Since we have accepted in-order commit as the paradigm that we shall use, there is nothing that can be done in such a situation. If the ROB fills up, we should stop fetching instructions, and wait till there is space created in the ROB. This is thus a method to apply back-pressure on the decode and fetch stages such that they stop reading and fetching instructions.

We need to ensure that before an instruction commits, its results are not permanent, and after the instruction commits, its results become permanent. Along with this there are additional things that we need to do while committing an instruction such as releasing resources and some additional bookkeeping.

Thus there are two aspects to instruction commit – releasing resources and moving computed results to some form of permanent storage. Once both of these tasks are done, the instruction can be removed from the pipeline, and simultaneously from all the structures within the processor.

Let us look at releasing resources and doing bookkeeping. Subsequently, we shall look at methods to move computed results to some form of permanent storage, and restoring state to recover from faults, interrupts, and exceptions.

4.4.3   Releasing Resources and Bookkeeping

Arithmetic and Logical Instructions

Let us consider an instruction *I1* of the form: *add r1, r2, r3*. Here, $r1$, $r2$, and $r3$ are architectural registers. Let us map these to physical registers. Assume that the instruction gets converted to *add p1, p2, p3*, where $r1$ is mapped to $p1$, $r2$ to $p2$, and $r3$ to $p3$. The question that we had asked in Section 4.1 was, "When do we release physical registers and add them to the free list?" At that point we did not have an answer; however, we are in a position to answer this question now.

Let us assume that before instruction *I1* was renamed, $r1$ was mapped to the physical register px. After instruction *I1* got renamed, $r1$ got mapped to $p1$. We need to figure out when we can add the physical register px to the free list. Before answering this question, let us keep the following points in mind.

- Assume that $r1$ was mapped to px by instruction *Ix*. At a later point, $r1$ got mapped to $p1$ by instruction *I1*.

- *I1* is overwriting the value of $r1$ written by *Ix*.

- All the instructions that use the value of px written by *Ix* are between *Ix* and *I1* in program order.

- This means that once *I1* is ready to commit, all the instructions before it in program order have committed. It further means that there is no instruction in the pipeline that is going to use the value of $r1$ written by *Ix*. This is because all such instructions are before *I1* in program order, and all of them have committed.

- When we are ready to commit *I1*, there is no instruction in the pipeline that needs the value of $r1$ written by *Ix* (via the physical register px).

- We can thus release px at this point of time.

This reasoning clearly establishes that when we are committing instruction *I1*, we can release the register px. Here "releasing" means that we can return px to the free list such that it can be assigned to another instruction.

Let us now outline what we need to do to enable this mechanism. Whenever, we are renaming an instruction such as *I1*, we are creating a mapping. In this case we are mapping the architectural register $r1$ to the physical register $p1$. We need to remember the previous mapping, which is $r1 \leftrightarrow px$. The id of the physical register px can be stored in the ROB entry for *I1*. Thus the structure of an ROB entry is as follows.

The new field *preg* contains the id of the physical register that was previously mapped to the destination register. Once, the instruction is ready to commit, we can release the physical register *preg* and return it to the free list. This ends the life cycle of the physical register *preg*.

Important Point 8

A physical register is released (returned to the free list) after the instruction that overwrites its corresponding architectural register is ready to commit.

Branch Instructions

As we discussed in Chapter 3, we predict the direction of branches, and then we start fetching instructions from the predicted path. There is definitely a possibility of misprediction. The fact that we have mispredicted the branch will be discovered when we are executing the branch. For example, if it is a conditional branch we need to compare the value of a register with some value (typically 0). This will be done in the execute stage and the result of the comparison will indicate if the branch has been mispredicted or not.

If the branch has been predicted correctly, then there is no problem. However, if we discover that the branch has been mispredicted, then we need to treat this event as a *fault*. The instructions fetched after the mispredicted branch are on the *wrong path*. Their results should not be allowed to corrupt the program state. This is not different from an exception, where a given instruction leads to an error.

We can thus add another bit in each ROB entry called the *exception bit*. If a branch is found to be mispredicted, then we set the exception bit of its ROB entry to 1.

We proceed as usual and keep committing instructions till the mispredicted branch reaches the head of the ROB. At that point the commit logic will find out that the instruction's exception bit is set to 1. This means that all the instructions after it are on the wrong path and should not be executed. The commit logic needs to discard the branch instruction, and all the instructions after it by flushing the pipeline. In this case, flushing the pipeline means that all the structures of the pipeline are cleared. This includes the ROB, instruction window, and LSQ. We can then start execution from the mispredicted branch instruction. Since we know the direction of the branch, we need not do a prediction once again. Instead, we can use the direction of the branch to fetch the subsequent instructions and resume normal execution.

Of course, whenever there is a pipeline flush it is necessary to ensure that none of the instructions on the wrong path have written their results to permanent state. This is a separate issue and will be tackled in Section 4.4.4.

This mechanism can be used to process other events such as interrupts, exceptions, and system calls [2]. Whenever, we receive an interrupt from a device, we can mark the topmost instruction in the ROB by setting its exception bit. Then, the processor can flush the pipeline and load the interrupt handler. Similarly, if there is an exception such as a division by zero or an illegal memory access, then we can mark the instruction by setting its exception bit. Likewise, for system calls (asking the OS to intervene by suspending the current program), we can mark the instruction invoking the system call. When these instructions reach the head of the ROB, the processor will simply flush the pipeline, and then take appropriate action.

In such cases the next PC field of the ROB entry needs to be used. Recall that this field is set as either the branch target for a branch or the address of the next instruction for a non-branch instruction. We always keep track of the next PC field of the latest committed instruction. Now, let's say that the instruction at the head of the ROB has its exception bit set. Then it means that this instruction should not be committed. We thus flush the pipeline at this stage and store the "next PC" of the previously committed instruction in the context of the program.

Load Instructions

In our system, load instructions can get their value from earlier store instructions in the LSQ or can get it from the memory system. For the purpose of committing the instruction, we can treat a load instruction as a regular arithmetic or logical instruction with a destination register. Akin to arithmetic and logical instructions we remember the previous mapping of the destination register. We release the previously allocated physical register when the load instruction commits.

---

[2]A system call is a special instruction that allows the programmer to generate an exception. This mechanism is typically used to invoke routines within the operating system.

Store Instructions

Handling store instructions is tricky. This is because they directly make changes in the memory system – these are permanent changes. Hence, we cannot send a store to the memory system unless it is guaranteed to commit. We do not know in advance if a store instruction is guaranteed to commit or not. This will only be known when we are ready to commit a store instruction.

Hence, most processors send a store to memory only at commit time. Once the address of a store is resolved, they try to forward its value to load instructions that appear later in program order (see Section 4.3.2). However, they do not send the store to memory. Once the store instruction reaches the head of the ROB, it is sent to the memory system.

Let us analyse the pros and cons of this discussion. A clear disadvantage is that we keep a store instruction in the LSQ even after its address is resolved. We can in principle increase the IPC if we send the store instruction to the memory system as soon as its address is resolved. However, if we do this it will be impossible to guarantee precise exceptions.

However, the silver lining in the dark cloud is that we don't have to wait for the store instruction to finish the process of writing to the memory system. We just need to hand it over to the memory system. We shall discuss this issue in great detail in Chapter 9 and figure out when we can just hand over a store to the memory system, and when we need to wait for it to finish the write. The good news for us is that in most practical systems, we can simply hand over the store instruction to the memory system and proceed. This will not cause significant issues in performance.

Way Point 3

The final structure of each ROB entry is as follows.

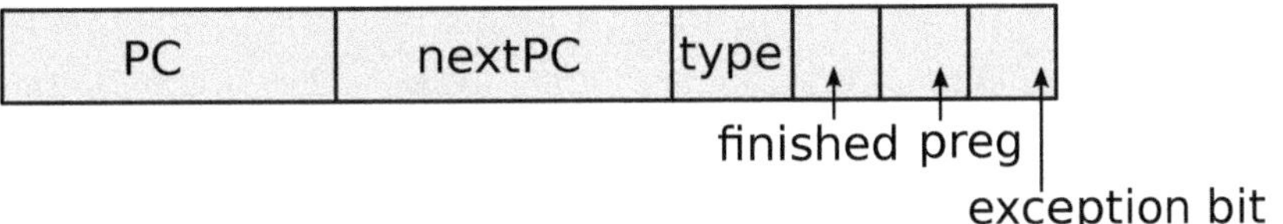

With an ROB, the context or the execution state or the program state is defined as the values of all the architectural registers, the contents of the memory, the PC and the next PC.

4.4.4   Checkpointing and Restoring the Program State

We have discussed the bookkeeping aspect of the commit process. Now, we need to discuss the correctness aspect. We need to ensure that the relevant program state (next PC, registers, and memory) is updated in program order. Precise exceptions are a direct consequence of this property. However, this is easier said than done. Let us consider a branch misprediction. It is possible that we fetch tens of instructions after we mispredict a branch. It is further possible that most of these instructions go through the renaming and register write stages before we detect that the branch has been mispredicted in the execute stage. In other words, when the branch is about to be committed, we shall have a lot of instructions in the wrong path that have expressed themselves by consuming rename table entries, and by writing to physical registers. This does not augur well for our aim of ensuring that only committed instructions write to permanent state – registers and memory.

Recall that we had discussed in Section 4.4.3 that we can stop uncommitted data from going to memory by allowing store instructions to update the memory system only after they have committed. We did not create any such mechanism for instructions with register destinations such as ALU instructions and loads; hence, we have this problem.

Let us clarify that we define the state of a program at any point of time as the state of the program after the last committed instruction. Let this be defined as the *precise state* or the *committed state*. It should be possible to pause the program, run some other program, and then restart the original program from this point.

Let us quickly recapitulate what we know and what we need to know.

1. For each instruction we record the current PC and the next PC in its ROB entry. Whenever we flush the pipeline we always keep a record of the next PC of the latest committed instruction. We resume the execution of the program at this point.

2. We ensure that only committed stores write their value to memory. This also ensures the notion of a precise state in memory. This issue will be revisited in Section 7.2. However, for the time being we can assume that the memory state remains safe in an environment where we switch between multiple programs by storing and restoring contexts.

3. We need to know the values of all the architectural registers in the precise state. Assume that the last committed instruction is instruction I. Now, assume that a single-cycle processor was executing the same program. Then the architectural state of the registers in the precise state (in our OOO processor) should be the same as that produced by executing the program till instruction I using the single-cycle processor. We can read the values of all the architectural registers, store them in the program's context, execute other programs, and then restore the original program's context. The original program needs to see exactly the same values of all the architectural registers.

Important Point 9

At any point of time, we need to only keep track of the contents of the architectural registers, the next PC, and the contents of the memory if we only consider all the committed instructions. We are assuming that none of the uncommitted instructions have even begun their execution. Since we have successfully solved the problem for the next PC and memory, we only need to create a method for architectural registers. Let us define this as the precise register state.

Let us look at some of the most common methods for tracking the precise register state at any point of time.

Retirement Register File (RRF)

Let us create a new structure called a retirement register file (RRF) as shown in Figure 4.30.

We maintain a small register file in the commit stage. It contains as many entries as the number of architectural registers. The moment an instruction with a register destination commits, we write its result to the corresponding architectural register in the RRF. As simple as that!

This mechanism ensures that the RRF always contains the precise state or the committed state of the program for the architectural registers. The RRF does not contain any values generated by uncommitted instructions. Let us summarise a few more salient points of the mechanism.

1. Each ROB entry needs to be augmented with the following fields: value produced by the instruction (64 bits), and the id of the destination register (4 bits)

2. Every time an instruction commits, we need to do a register write (to the RRF).

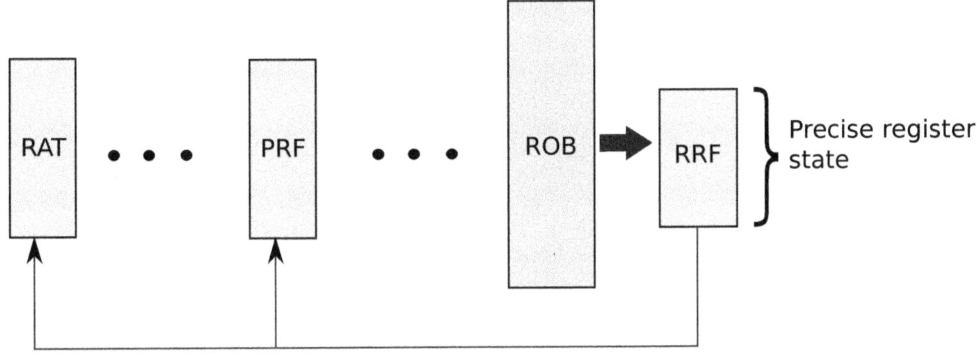

Figure 4.30: A retirement register file (RRF)

3. Restoring the state involves transferring the entire contents of the RRF to the regular register file with appropriate changes made to the rename table. Since we are initialising from a clean state, we can transfer the contents of architectural register ri (in the RRF) to physical register pi and create a corresponding mapping.

Let us try to do the same thing in another way.

Retirement Register Alias Table (RRAT)

Instead of a retirement register file, let us instead try to do something with the RAT table. Let us have an additional RAT table (rename table) in the commit stage as shown in Figure 4.31.

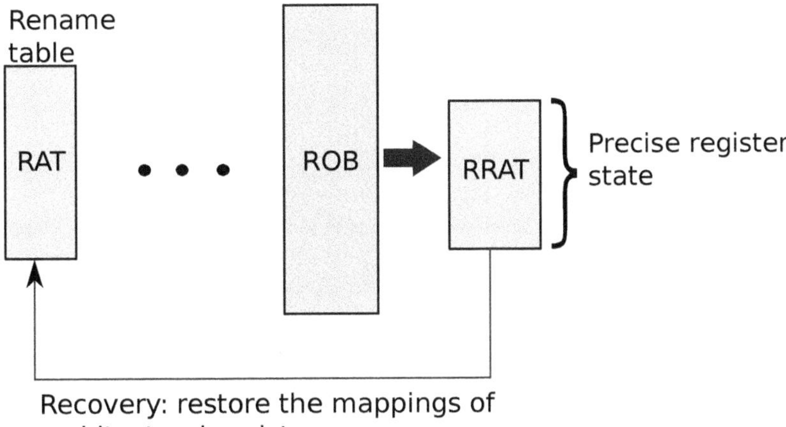

Figure 4.31: A retirement register alias table (RRAT)

In this case, each entry of the RRAT table maintains a mapping between the destination architectural register, and its mapped physical register for each committing instruction. Let us consider the instruction: *add r1, r2, r3*. Assume that the architectural register $r1$ is mapped to the physical register $p1$. When this instruction commits we add the mapping between $r1$ and $p1$. If we need to know the contents of the architectural register file in the committed state at any point of time, then we can just access the RRAT, get the corresponding physical registers, and access them. The mapping stored in the

RRAT stores the precise register state. The RRAT does not have mappings for instructions, which are not committed. Proving the correctness of this scheme is left as an exercise for the reader. Bear in mind that the physical registers pointed to by the RRAT will continue to maintain their values; they will not have been released.

The salient points of this scheme are as follows:

1. We need to maintain additional information in each ROB entry: id of the destination register and its corresponding physical register id.

2. For every instruction with a register destination we need to update the RRAT at commit time.

3. Restoring the state upon a pipeline flush involves performing N reads from the RRAT, and performing N writes to the actual RAT. Here, N is the number of architectural registers.

Nevertheless, this is a simple mechanism and has lower storage overheads than the RRF scheme: in this case, we just store the ids of the mapped physical registers instead of the full 64-bit values.

Checkpointing the RAT: SRAM Array

Instead of making changes to the commit stage, let us instead make changes to the rename stage. In this case, let us take a checkpoint of the RAT every time we encounter a branch instruction. A checkpoint is defined as a *snapshot* (a copy of all the entries, in this case it is a copy of the RAT table). Whenever, there is a branch misprediction of branch B we restore the RAT table to the checkpoint associated with it. This process is known as *recovery*. Every checkpoint captures the current mapping at that point of time. If all the instructions till instruction B are committed, then the registers mapped to the architectural registers in the checkpointed RAT table represent the committed state at that point of time. Note that subsequently, the registers will not be released because a physical register is released only when an instruction that overwrites the mapped architectural register commits. Since we restore the state when instruction B commits, we are guaranteed that no instruction after B would have committed. Thus, the physical registers containing the committed state would not have been released.

Note that other than branch mispredictions regular instructions can also suffer from faults, and we can receive hardware interrupts any time. In this case we will not have a precise checkpoint to roll back to. A naive option is to take a checkpoint of the RAT table after every instruction – this is too expensive. The other option is to rollback the state to the latest branch instruction. However, this introduces additional complexities in terms of correctness. Hence, let us proceed with the naive assumption that we are only dealing with branch mispredictions.

Consider a simple rename table, where we have N entries (N is the number of architectural registers). This can be constructed using simple static RAM (SRAM) cells (see Chapter 7 and [Sarangi, 2015]). Note that an SRAM cell is a memory cell consisting of 6 transistors. Each SRAM cell stores a single bit, and SRAM cells are organised as a matrix of cells (in rows and columns).

In this case, we can organise the SRAM array as follows. We organise each entry as a circular queue, where we insert new entries at one end and remove older entries at the other end. We always maintain two pointers: *head* and *tail* to the first and last entries respectively. Given that we are dealing with real hardware here, we can place a limit on the number of entries in the queue, and this should roughly be equal to the maximum number of branches we expect to have in the pipeline at any point of time. Figure 4.32 shows the design.

Whenever, we encounter a branch instruction, we create a new copy of the up to date entries of the RAT table and push them into the queues associated with the entries. This means that for a given entry, let's say architectural register $r4$, we read its latest mapping (let's say $r4 \leftrightarrow p10$), and insert $p10$ into the queue associated with the entry for $r4$. Subsequent instructions (after the branch) are free to update the mapping of $r4$. Now, let us assume that this branch (instruction B) gets mispredicted. We wait till instruction B commits. At that point, the checkpoint for each entry associated with B such as $r4 \leftrightarrow p10$ is guaranteed to be at the head of the respective queue. This is because no instruction older

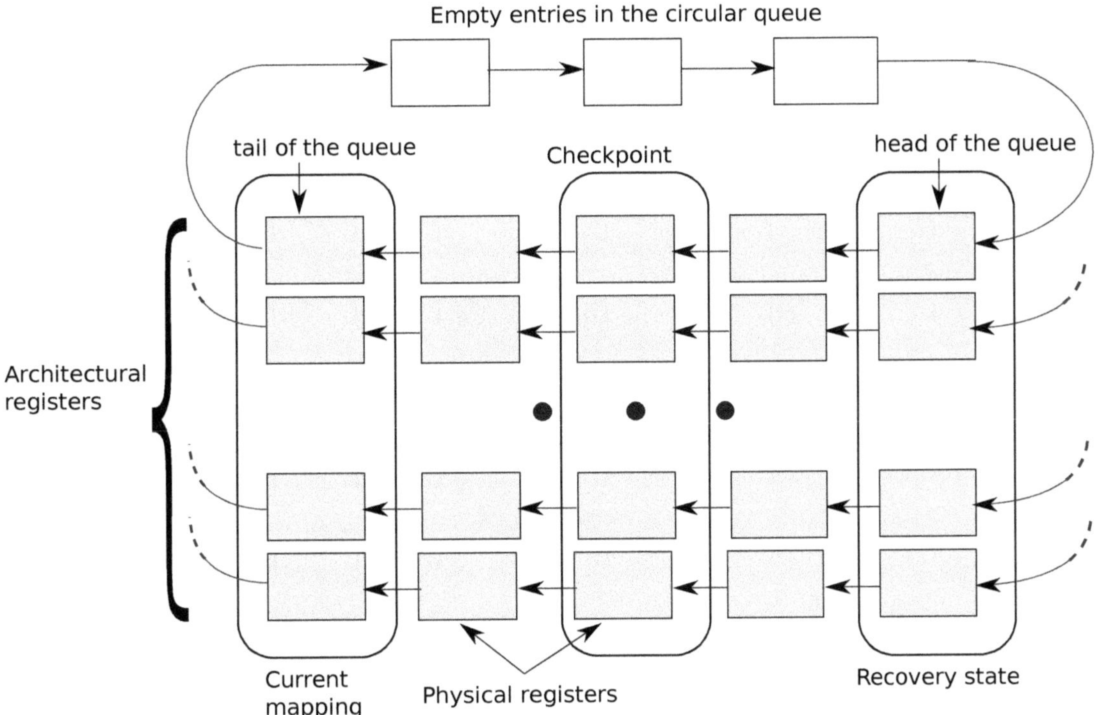

Figure 4.32: Checkpointing the RAT array with an SRAM-based implementation

than B will be in the pipeline, and thus its checkpoint will also not be there. This result can also be deduced from the FIFO (first in first out) property of each queue.

At this point to restore the checkpoint, we just need to discard the rest of the entries, which is very easy to do. We simply set the *head* pointer equal to the *tail* pointer – the rest of the entries get discarded on their own. This is how we can very easily restore a checkpoint.

The shortcomings of this scheme are as follows:

1. Every entry of the rename table needs to be organised as a circular queue.

2. We need to take a checkpoint (create a copy of the latest entry in each row) on every branch instruction. This means that we need to copy 7 bits (assuming there are 128 physical registers) between the tail of the queue and the memory cells that store the current mapping.

Checkpointing the RAT: CAM Array

A major problem with the previous solution was that we needed to move 7 bits between locations for creating a checkpoint. Secondly, if there are N entries in each circular queue, we need $7N$ bits of storage in each row of the SRAM array. Can we reduce this further such that the process of checkpoint creation becomes very easy?

Let us design the rename table (RAT table) in another way. Instead of using an SRAM array, let us use a CAM array (see Chapter 7 and [Sarangi, 2015]). A CAM (content-addressable memory) as discussed in Section 4.3 can be addressed in two ways: by the row index, and by the content in each row. We can design the RAT table as a CAM as follows. The content is the architectural register and an additional bit that indicates if the mapping is valid or not. Let us consider a scenario with 16 architectural registers and 128 physical registers. Instead of a traditional 16-entry table, let us have an

128-entry table. The contents in each row comprise a 4-bit architectural register id and 1 bit (valid bit). Note that at any point of time, only 16 entries will have their valid bits set. These 16 entries are mapped to each of the 16 architectural registers. For example, if we need to find the mapping corresponding to register $r4$, we create a 5-bit bit field: 4 bits from $r4$ that are 0100, and 1 as the valid bit. The bit field is thus 01001. We then lookup the CAM for a row with contents that match 01001. Only one row should match this value, and that row contains the current mapping for architectural register $r4$. Let this be row number 37 in the 128-entry RAT table. We can automatically infer that the physical register that is mapped to $r4$ is $p37$. We can use a simple Boolean encoder in this process.

Note that we made many statements in the previous paragraph without proof. The reader is invited to prove them. For example, why are we claiming that only 16 out of 128 entries will have their valid bit set to 1?

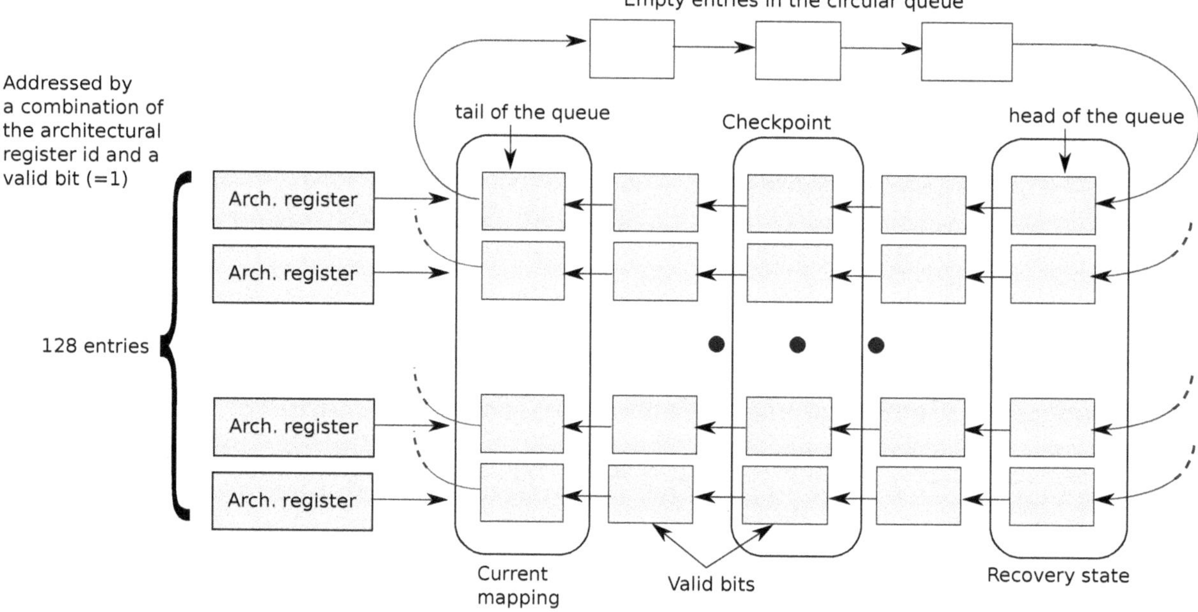

Figure 4.33: Checkpointing the RAT array with a CAM-based implementation

The important take-home point is that an array of valid bits contains the current mapping from architectural registers to physical registers. Now assume that $r4$ is mapped to $p37$. One more instruction comes by later that updates $r4$. It will be mapped to another physical register – let's say $p10$. The only change that needs to be done is that the valid bit for the 37th entry needs to be unset (set to 0) and for the 10th entry we need to set the contents to 4 (for $r4$), and then set the valid bit to 1.

Our design is similar to the checkpointing scheme with an SRAM array. In every row, we have a small circular queue that in this case stores a single bit per entry (valid bit). Before every branch, we take a checkpoint of the current mapping (128 valid bits). We do this by inserting the current valid bit of each row into its circular queue. Whenever, a mispredicted branch commits we remove its checkpoint from the head of the queue. To restore a checkpoint, and restart from that point we just restore the state of the RAT table to what it was before renaming the branch instruction. The head of each queue contains this state, and thus akin to the scheme with an SRAM array we can restore the checkpoint by making the entries at the head of the queues act as the current mapping. Note that in this scheme only the valid bits are a part of the queue (not 7-bit physical register ids). Refer to Figure 4.33.

Let us convince ourselves of one more fact. Consider the time at which we are restoring the checkpoint. At that point of time we wish to say that the architectural state is contained within a set of physical registers. Now, the entries corresponding to those registers will still be mapped to the same architectural registers, albeit their valid bits may not be 1 anymore. This is because we might have encountered a subsequent instruction that writes to the same architectural register. However, the mapping will still be there because to release the mapping, a later instruction that writes to the same architectural register needs to commit. Since the branch that owns this checkpoint has not committed, those later instructions would also have not committed – they would be after the branch. Hence, the mappings between physical and architectural registers would still be there. We just need to restore the set of valid bits. Recall that at any point of time only 16 out of 128 entries will be set to 1. The rest will be set to 0. This is because we shall always have an one-to-one mapping between the architectural registers and physical registers.

A clear advantage of this scheme is that instead of moving around 7 bits, we move just 1 bit. This means that taking a checkpoint is far easier, and also the overhead of storing checkpoints is much lower (7 times lower if we have 128 physical registers). However, there are other problems. Let us quickly review the shortcomings.

1. A CAM is far slower than an SRAM array of equivalent size. In this case, the CAM is expected to have many more rows than the equivalent SRAM based design. Considering these factors, a regular access to the RAT table will have a much higher latency.

2. A CAM also consumes more power. This needs to be taken into account when we opt for such designs.

3. We have the same issue of "taking checkpoints only at branches" as we had with the design that used SRAM arrays. If we want to take more checkpoints we need to increase the size of the circular queues. Otherwise, we lose the ability to recover at arbitrary points within the program, unless we do some additional bookkeeping.

Summary of Register Checkpointing Schemes

RRF	
+	Easy to implement. Transferring the checkpoint to the register file is easy.
-	Extra register writes every cycle. More power.
-	Need to store the result and destination register in the ROB. More space.

RRAT	
+	Requires less space in the ROB than the RRF.
-	Involves a few writes almost every cycle. More power.
-	Each entry of the ROB needs to be augmented with the id of the destination register and its associated physical register.

SRAM based RAT	
+	Activity only on a branch.
+	Checkpoint restoration is easier than RRF and RRAT based schemes.
-	Each row of the RAT is wider.
-	For every branch instruction we need to add an additional entry into the circular queue. It is hard to checkpoint and restore the state at arbitrary points in the program without additional bookkeeping.

CAM based RAT	
+	Checkpoint creation is very easy. Insert only 1 bit.
-	The CAM per se is a slower structure than an SRAM array. It has a higher latency, and consumes much more power.

4.5 Summary and Further Reading

4.5.1 Summary

Summary 3

1. *To remove WAW and WAR dependences in out-of-order (OOO) pipelines, it is necessary to perform instruction renaming.*

2. *The classical method to perform renaming assigns architectural registers to physical registers. We store a mapping between architectural registers and physical registers in a rename table (RAT table).*

3. *It is possible that there might be RAW dependences between different instructions that we are trying to simultaneously rename. We need to have dependence check logic, and forward the ids of assigned physical registers between instructions in this set.*

4. *The list of free (unassigned) physical registers is kept in a structure called a free list. When a physical register is released we add it to the free list.*

5. *A physical register is released when a subsequent instruction that writes to the same architectural register (that the physical register is mapped to) exits the pipeline.*

6. *The process of adding renamed instructions to the instruction window is known as instruction dispatch. Instructions wait in the instruction window till their operands are ready, and the functional units that they need are available.*

7. *Every instruction whose operand is ready waits for the tag to be broadcast on a tag bus. The tag is the id of the physical register assigned to the operand.*

8. *Once an instruction sees the tag on a tag bus, the operand is deemed to be ready. Once all the operands are ready, the instruction wakes up, and is ready to execute.*

9. *Since multiple instructions can be ready at the same time, we need to select a subset of instructions that can begin execution in a given cycle. The select unit is typically structured like a tree. The requests are the leaves, and in every level we discard some requests either based on priority, or randomly.*

10. *To ensure back-to-back execution (dependent instructions executing in consecutive cycles) it is necessary to execute the wakeup and select operations in the same cycle. In addition, we need to broadcast early (much before the instruction actually executes). In specific, if the instruction takes k cycles to execute, then we need to broadcast the tag k cycles after the instruction gets selected. This will ensure that instructions with RAW dependences can execute back to back.*

11. *To track the dependences between loads and stores, there is a need to create a separate structure called a load-store queue (LSQ). We create entries in this queue at the time of decoding an instruction. When we compute the address (in the execute stage), we update the respective LSQ entry.*

12. *At that point of time, the load instruction searches for earlier store instructions. If it finds a store instruction with a matching address, then it uses the value that it is going to store. Otherwise, if it finds a store with an unresolved address, then it waits.*

13. *Similarly, a store instruction searches for later load instructions until it encounters a store instruction that is either to the same address or is unresolved. If any of these load instructions have a matching address, then it forwards the value.*

14. *The LSQ is implemented as two separate queues: one load queue and one store queue. It uses parallel Boolean operations to speed up its operation.*

15. *We use a reorder buffer (ROB) to queue all the instructions that are active in the pipeline. An instruction commits (retires) when it reaches the head of the ROB. At that point of time it stores to memory, and its effects are said to be visible to the external world. The process of committing needs to be in program order to guarantee precise exceptions.*

16. *Whenever we mispredict a branch, or encounter an exception, we mark the instruction and wait for it to reach the head of the ROB. Once it does so we flush the pipeline, handle the exceptional event, and then restart the program from the same point.*

17. *To restart a program we need to store a checkpoint of the pipeline state – state of the architectural registers, and the next PC.*

18. *The state of the architectural registers can be stored in a retirement register file, or their mappings can be stored in an RRAT (retirement RAT). In addition, it is possible to achieve the same objective by storing checkpoints of the rename table at different points of interest such as right before a branch.*

The final pipeline from the rename to commit stages looks as follows.

rename	dispatch	wakeup	broadcast	execute	reg. file write	commit
		select	read from the reg.file			

4.5.2   Further Reading

Some of the earliest papers in the area of out-of-order execution were published by a few groups in the University of Wisconsin and the University of Illinois. A few of these landmark papers are [Hwu and Patt, 1987, Smith and Sohi, 1995]. A more detailed circuit level analysis can be found in [Palacharla et al., 1997]. After these research ideas, many processor vendors started building OOO processors. They published the details of their design. Some influential papers for industrial designs are descriptions of the Alpha 21264 [Leibholz and Razdan, 1997], Intel Pentium 4 [Hinton et al., 2001] and AMD Opteron [Keltcher et al., 2003] processors.

Let us now look at some of the promising ideas in the research community. [Brown et al., 2001] discuss instruction scheduling without the select operation, [Petric et al., 2005] perform standard compiler optimisations at the rename stage, and [Akkary et al., 2003] propose to create very large instruction windows.

To learn more about optimised LSQs, the reader should read the paper by Park et al. [Park et al., 2003]. There are two papers that we would like to recommend regarding releasing pipeline resources early: [Martínez et al., 2002] and [Ergin et al., 2004].

Exercises

Ex. 1 — Design the dependence check logic for a processor with a rename width of 4 (can rename 4 instructions per cycle).

Ex. 2 — Describe in detail how to set the *avlbl* bit for each entry in the rename table, and how to use it in the pipeline.

Ex. 3 — Why is the free list typically designed as a circular queue?

Ex. 4 — How do we free entries in the instruction window? Design an efficient scheme.

Ex. 5 — Assume that we want to create a scheme where we try to allocate physical registers uniformly. How can we modify the free list to support this feature?

Ex. 6 — Describe the wakeup mechanism in detail, particularly, when we are broadcasting multiple tags every cycle.

Ex. 7 — Do we need bypass and dependence check logic to access the register file? If yes, then provide an implementation.

Ex. 8 — Why do we need to broadcast the tags twice?

* **Ex. 9** — How do we perform an early broadcast if the execution duration is not predictable? Can we do better if we have a bound on the maximum number of cycles we require to execute an instruction?

* **Ex. 10** — We want to design a high performance OOO processor that has separate pipeline stages for the wakeup and select operations. Can you suggest modifications to the pipeline with physical registers. Your answer should address the following issues/points:

- What is the advantage of having separate stages for wakeup and select?
- What complications will it introduce to the simple design discussed in this chapter?
- When do we broadcast?
- What are the other changes that should be done to the rest of the stages in the pipeline?
- How do we take care of the issue of double broadcasts?

* **Ex. 11** — Let us design an OOO processor with a speculative select logic. In a regular OOO processor, an instruction might not necessarily get selected immediately after it wakes up. Assume that there is one adder, and three add instructions wake up at the same time. Only one of them will be immediately selected. The rest of the instructions need to wait.
Now let us speculate on this. We assume that the moment an instruction wakes up, it is eligible to be subsequently selected without any delays. It can thus go ahead and wake up consumer instructions. Design a scheme that has such a speculative select mechanism. Your answer should address the following issues (points).

- How do we realise the fact that we have speculatively selected more instructions than the number of functional units? This will lead to structural hazards unless corrected.
- How do we handle such situations?
- What do we do with instructions that have been speculatively selected?
- How do we reduce the number of misspeculations?

** **Ex. 12** — It is very frequently the case that we have single-shot instructions. An instruction i : $r1 \leftarrow r2 + r3$ is a single-shot instruction if there is only one instruction j that reads the value that i writes to its destination register $r1$, and after j executes, the value in $r1$ is not required. However, we cannot deallocate this register till a subsequent instruction that writes to $r1$ commits. This approach decreases the number of available physical registers in a pipeline because we have many such *short-lived* registers.
Can we speculate? Can we speculatively release a register before it should be actually released? How will this mechanism work? Explain in detail.

** **Ex. 13** — Assume we have an OOO processor with a PRF (physical register file). Given that we have 128 physical registers, what is the maximum possible size of the instruction window? In such processors, it is typical to have a large ROB. For example, the ROB in this case (with 128 physical registers) can be sized to contain 160 entries. Why is this the case?

* **Ex. 14** — In an in-order processor, the compare (*cmp*) instruction is used to compare the values in two registers. The result is saved in a *flags* register that is not accessible to software. Subsequent branch instructions use the value of the *flags* register to compute their decision. Will the same mechanism work in an OOO pipeline? If not, then how do we augment it to support this feature of the ISA?

Design Problems

Ex. 15 — Understand the wakeup, select, and broadcast logic in the Tejas simulator [TM].

Ex. 16 — Extend the simulator to make the delays of the wakeup, select, and broadcast stages configurable. They need not be done in the same cycle, and back-to-back execution is not a necessity.

5

Alternative Approaches to Issue and Commit

In Chapter 4 we learnt about the basic structure of an OOO pipeline. We further realised that a modern OOO machine is a very complex piece of hardware. To ensure performance without sacrificing on correctness, we need to add many additional hardware structures and do a lot of book keeping. The processor that was designed in Chapter 4 is very suitable for high performance implementations.

However, given that people have been designing processors for the last fifty years, there are many other designs of processors out there. Some of these techniques are for smaller embedded processors, some techniques are very power efficient at the cost of performance, and some techniques export the complexity to software. The aim of this chapter is to discuss all those *additional* techniques. Note that this chapter should be viewed as a sequel to Chapter 4. Unlike Chapter 4, this chapter discusses an assorted set of techniques, which are mostly unrelated to each other. Nevertheless, we have made a modest effort to classify these areas into the following categories:

Support for Aggressive Speculation and Replay Most OOO processors make guesses based on behaviours observed in the past for predicting different parameters such as the latency of memory operations – this information is used to optimistically assume that a given memory access always finds its value in the L1 cache. This is known as *speculation*. However, sometimes these guesses turn out to be wrong, then it is necessary to go back and fix the state. Some of the instructions, which might have potentially got wrong data, need to be *replayed*.

Simpler Designs of OOO Pipelines It is not necessary to have large physical register files, free lists, and separate ROBs in OOO pipelines. Depending on the workloads, we can merge some of these structures, and end up with a simpler and more power efficient design.

Software based Techniques It is not necessary to export all the complexity to hardware. It is possible to increase the ILP of the code by applying compiler based transformations. These *software approaches* are extremely useful and are an integral part of today's compiler tool chain. Some software based approaches require details of the underlying hardware, whereas, some others are generic.

EPIC Processors Most compiler based approaches are useful for generic OOO pipelines. However, there is a school of thought that advocates making the hardware significantly simpler and exporting the entire complexity to software. It is the software's job to sequence and schedule the

151

instructions. Simpler hardware translates to area and power efficiency. Such EPIC (Explicitly Parallel Instruction Computing) processors often require complex compiler infrastructure with some specialised hardware support to implement the directives produced by the compiler.

5.0.1 Organisation of this Chapter

At the outset, we shall discuss some more methods to increase the ILP in modern processors by aggressively speculating on load latencies, addresses, and values. We shall discuss some of the most common techniques in this space in Section 5.1. Recall that whenever we have speculation, there is always the possibility of an error. There is thus a need to *replay* some of the instructions, which might have been erroneously issued with wrong data (see Section 5.2).

Then, we shall proceed to discuss alternative designs of OOO pipelines in Section 5.3 that are less complicated. Instead of designing simpler hardware structures, we can also move some of the complexity to software. We will focus on compiler driven approaches to increase ILP in Section 5.4. As an extreme case, it is possible to keep hardware ultra-simple, and instead do all the scheduling, instruction sequencing, and renaming in software (by the compiler). We shall discuss such approaches in Section 5.5. Finally, in Section 5.6 we shall the discuss the design of the Intel® Itanium® processor, which is an EPIC processor.

5.1 Load Speculation

5.1.1 Introduction

Let us start out with making the design of the processor – introduced in Chapter 4 – more complicated and more realistic. Let us begin by taking into cognisance that one of the primary sources of non-determinism in execution is the memory system. A memory access such as a load or a store is a multi-step process. We first compute the memory address, and then we check for dependences in the load-store queue (see Section 4.3). We either forward a value from a store to a load or we send the requests to the memory system. The memory system is in itself a very complicated network of components. We have a hierarchy of caches, and then finally the main memory. A request can be serviced at any level in the memory system. Thus, the duration of a memory request is fundamentally non-deterministic in nature. It is very hard to predict if, for example, a load instruction will get its value from another store instruction, or from which level in the cache hierarchy. As we shall see, instead of adopting a very conservative stance where we wait for a step to fully complete before starting the next step, it is often wiser to speculate and go forward.

Speculation is a very common technique in computer architecture. Almost all kinds of speculation involve the following steps: make a prediction regarding the value of an input, use it to compute the output, and forward the output to other dependent instructions. Such predictions help us execute instructions *sooner*. However, the flip side is that it is possible that sometimes these predictions might be wrong. In that case we need to locate all the instructions that might have potentially received a wrong value, and cancel them. Then these instructions need to be re-executed with the correct values.

Speculation has many advantages. It helps break dependences. For example, consider a load-use dependence, where a load instruction L supplies its value to a consumer instruction I. If we can predict the value read by instruction L reliably, and give it to instruction I, we can execute L and I in parallel. This will break dependence chains, increase ILP, and tremendously increase performance. The crux of this mechanism lies in designing an accurate predictor, and to a lesser extent, we need to also have a fast method of recovering from the ill effects of a misprediction.

Definition 23

Speculation *is a very common technique in computer architecture where we predict something and proceed on the basis of the prediction. Consider the steps involved while predicting the input of an instruction.*

1. *We* predict *the value of an input.*

2. *The input is used to proceed with the execution of an instruction.*

3. *The instruction using the predicted input can forward its result to other instructions.*

4. *At a later point of time, the prediction is verified, and if we find that the prediction is incorrect, then all the influenced instructions are cancelled.*

5. *This technique breaks dependences between instructions and thus increases the available ILP. This leads to an increased IPC.*

Speculation is not limited to predicting the inputs of instructions, we can also predict the output of an instruction, or its duration.

Let us try to apply speculative techniques to load instructions. Before the astute reader asks, "Why load instructions?", let us answer this question. Load instructions typically have non-deterministic latencies and this can cause a lot of dependent instructions to get queued in the instruction window. This is also known as the *convoy effect* because the situation is similar to a road where a car breakdown can cause a huge traffic jam. Furthermore, these convoys of instructions can be fairly long because a load can take 100s of cycles if it needs to fetch its data from main memory.

Here are the primary methods for speculation with regards to load instructions.

Address Speculation Based on historical values, we try to predict the address of load instructions. If we know the address early, we can try to get forwarded values in the load-store queue, or fetch the value from the memory system in advance. This will save us valuable cycles, because we are in effect executing the load instruction and its dependent instructions early.

Load-Store Dependence Speculation We try to predict the dependence between loads and stores in the load-store queue. Based on predicted dependences, we can take decisions to forward values, wait for unresolved stores, or send requests to memory.

Latency Speculation We predict if a load hits in the L1 cache or not, and consequently the latency if it is a hit. If we predict a hit, we can wakeup dependent instructions early such that they can execute as early as possible (see Section 4.2 for a detailed discussion on instruction wakeup).

Value Prediction Finally, we can predict the value that a load instruction is expected to read. This can then be passed on to dependent instructions.

We shall present different methods of prediction in this section, and methods to replay instructions in Section 5.2.

5.1.2   Address Speculation

The aim here is to design a method to predict the address of a load instruction. The only information in our arsenal is the program counter (PC) of the load. Let us discuss two fairly straightforward solutions that work in most common cases. These solutions are similar to branch predictors. In fact, we shall

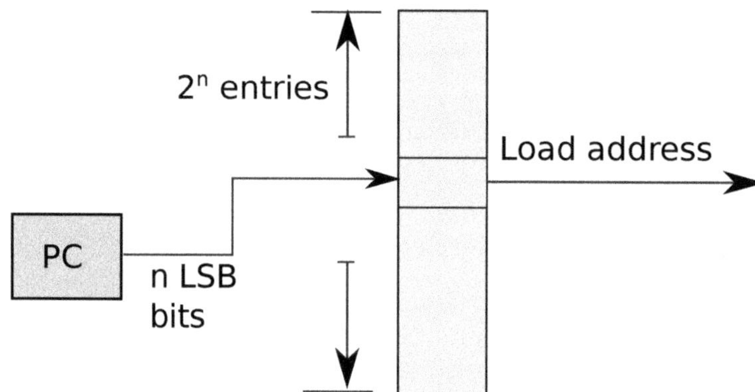

Figure 5.1: Load address predictor (based on the last computed address for this PC)

see that most predictors used to predict a host of different things are similar to our branch predictors presented in Chapter 3.

Predict Last Address

We maintain a table that is indexed by the least significant n bits of the PC address. In each entry, we store the memory address computed by the memory instruction the last time it was invoked.

As we can see in Figure 5.1, we use n bits from the PC address to index a 2^n entry table. Every time the memory address of a load is computed, we store it in this table. This is later on used for prediction.

We can use standard techniques that we had learnt in Chapter 3 to increase the accuracy of this process. For example, to avoid the effects of aliasing, we can keep some bits of the PC address in each entry. We will use the entry only if these bits match with the corresponding bits of the PC address. In addition, we can use a 2-bit saturating counter. The state 00 indicates that with a strong probability the address that we read is wrong. Likewise, the state 11 indicates that with a high probability, the address is correct. This shall work in exactly the same way. Every time the prediction is correct, we increment the counter, and every time the prediction is wrong, we decrement the counter. Depending upon our appetite for risk (captured by the saturating counters), we can use the predicted address accordingly.

Stride based Prediction

Let us now discuss a more sophisticated idea. Let us consider one of the most common scenarios where array accesses are used. One such example is a simple *for* loop used to iterate through all the elements of an array.

Consider the following piece of code (C code and equivalent assembly code).

C code

```
int sum = 0, arr[10];
for (i=0; i < 10; i++){
    sum += arr[i];
}
```

Assembly code

```
// Let us assume that the base address of arr is in r0
mov r1, 0              // i = 0
mov r2, 0              // sum = 0

.loop: cmp r1, 10      // compare i with 10
beq .exit              // if (r1 == 10) exit
ld   r3, [r0]          // load arr[i] to r3
add  r2, r2, r3        // sum += arr[i]
add  r0, r0, 4         // increment the memory address
add  r1, r1, 1         // increment the loop index
b .loop
```

In this case the load associated with accessing the array, *arr*, is called repeatedly. Every time the array index stored in register $r1$ increases by 1, the memory address gets incremented by 4 bytes (assuming the size of an integer is 4 bytes). Let's say, we want to predict the address of the single load instruction. In this case we shall perceive the address increasing by 4 every iteration. The address is thus predictable. There is a pattern, and if we are able to decipher the pattern, then we can successfully predict the address of the load for most of the iterations of the loop.

Whenever a given variable increases by a fixed value every iteration, this value is known as a *stride*. In this case we need to figure out the stride, and the fact that the memory access pattern is based on strides. Strides are a very common access pattern particularly when arrays are involved, and there are standard methods of handling them. Mathematically, we need a minimum of three iterations to identify a stride based access pattern.

We create a table with 2^n entries that can be accessed using the least significant n bits of the PC. In each entry, we need to store the following information: memory address that was computed the last time the load instruction was executed (A), the value of the stride (S), and a bit indicating if a stride based access pattern is followed or not (P). For a prediction, we simply predict $A + S$ if the access pattern is based on strides.

At a later point of time, when we compute the address of this load to be A'. We need to verify that we are following a stride based access pattern. We compute $S' = A' - A$. We compare this with the previous stride, S, stored in the entry. If the strides match, then we can conclude that we are following a stride based access pattern; we set $P = 1$ (stride access pattern bit set to 1). Otherwise, we set $P = 0$: do not make a prediction using strides. In either case, we set $A = A'$ and $S = S'$.

5.1.3   Load-Store Dependence Speculation

Let us look at another potential source of performance improvement. In Section 4.3, we indicated that a load cannot be sent to the memory system as long as it has an unresolved (address not computed) store before it in the load-store queue. This means that the load needs to wait for such stores. Let us assume that we have ten load instructions whose address has been computed. However, there is one store instruction before them whose address is yet to be computed. In this case, the ten load instructions have to wait. Later on if we find out that the address of the store does not conflict with the addresses of any of these load instructions, we would realise that we have waited in vain. This situation would represent a complete waste of time and ILP.

To handle all such situations, modern computer architectures typically *speculate*. For example, if in this case we can confidently predict if the store instruction will conflict with any of the resolved load instructions or not, then we can speculate. If the prediction is false, which means that the store is not expected to conflict, then we can send all the load instructions to the memory system before the store's address is resolved. Note that here we are making a guess. However, this is an intelligent guess because we have a mechanism to predict load-store dependences effectively. If there is a high probability of the prediction being correct, then we shall gain a lot of performance with this technique. A load will not wait for unresolved stores before it in program order, unless our load-store dependence predictor predicts a dependence. Such aggressive speculation mechanisms are indeed extremely helpful. However, there is a flip side to every good idea. Here again, we can have the problem of occasional mispredictions.

We use the solution described in a later section (Section 5.1), where we rely on a replay mechanism that identifies the instructions that have possibly read wrong values, nullifies them, and reissues them with the correct value. Let us now proceed to describe the design of such load-store dependence predictors.

Design of a Load-Store Dependence Predictor: Collision-based Predictor

Let us start with showing the design of a predictor that predicts if a given load collides (has the same address) with any of the preceding stores or not (see Yoaz et al. [Yoaz et al., 1999]). If a load is predicted to not collide with any of the preceding stores, then we can immediately execute the load.

The main insight here is that loads display roughly consistent and predictable behaviour. This means that if a given load is non-colliding in nature, it continues to remain so for some time. We can thus have a collision history table (CHT). The simplest design of a CHT is like a branch predictor. Here, we have a table of 2^n entries, which is addressed using the last n bits of the PC. In each location, we store the prediction: 0 or 1. We can further augment this table by having a saturating counter instead of a single bit. This will create some degree of hysteresis as we had done in the case of a branch predictor and also indicate the confidence of the prediction. For example, if a given load has been historically non-colliding, then one collision should not be able to change its behaviour. As we can observe, the saturating counter based predictor is a generic mechanism that can be reused in almost all cases where we need a binary prediction, as was done in this case.

The overall scheme is thus as follows.

1. When a load is either scheduled, or when its input operands are ready, we access the CHT. If we predict the load to be non-colliding, then as soon as the memory address is ready, the load instruction can be sent to the memory system.

2. However, if we predict the load to be colliding, then the load needs to wait in the LSQ till all the preceding stores are resolved.

3. Once we have computed the addresses of all the previous store instructions, we are in a position to determine if the load collided with any stores or not. We can then update the CHT accordingly with the correct value.

This mechanism is simple and works well in practice. However, it is possible to improve it even further. Let us consider a common access pattern: saving and restoring registers while calling functions. In this case, we store a register's value in memory before entering a function, and then restore its value from memory when the called function exits. Let us consider the loads that restore the state of the registers. The colliding stores for these loads are the stores that spill the registers to memory. If the behaviour of the function is roughly consistent and predictable, then we roughly know the distance between a conflicting load and store in terms of regular instructions or memory instructions. For example, if there are typically 10 memory instructions between the store that saves the value of a register, and the corresponding load that restores the value, then the distance between the load-store pair is 10 memory instructions. We can make use of this fact very effectively. When the load's address is computed, we can make it wait till there are less than 10 instructions before it in the LSQ. By this time if it has not gotten a forwarded value, then the load is ready to be sent to memory. This is because the chances of it colliding with a store are very little – we have predicted with high confidence that the distance between the load and store is 10 intervening memory instructions. This condition does not hold if there are less than 10 instructions preceding the load in the LSQ (refer to Figure 5.2).

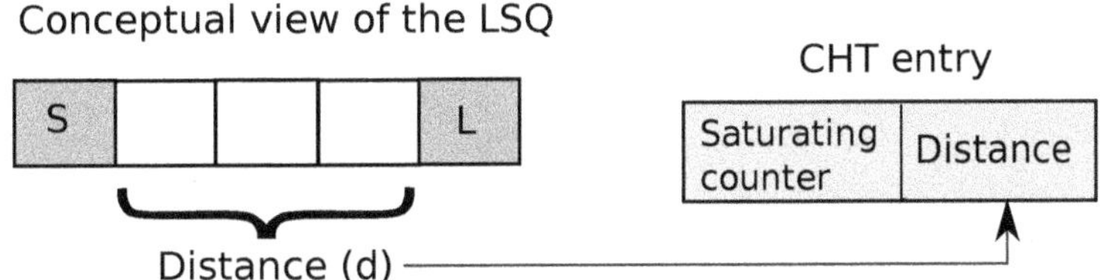

Figure 5.2: Load-store distance based prediction

We need to make a minor modification to the CHT. In each entry, we additionally store the distance between the load and store instruction. Whenever, we forward a value from a store to a load, we compute the distance between them in the LSQ (number of intervening entries), and store this in the CHT entry.

The prediction algorithm is thus as follows:

1. Either at the time of instruction dispatch, or at the time of computing the load's memory address, we access the CHT. If the load is not predictable as indicated by the saturating counter, then we make it wait till all prior stores are resolved. Subsequently, the load is sent to the memory system. Otherwise, we do the following.

2. If a load is predictable, we wait till there are less than N preceding entries in the LSQ. The value of N is stored in the CHT's entry, and denotes the predicted load-store distance.

3. If we get a forwarded value from a store, we use it and move forward.

4. Else, if there are less than N entries in the LSQ, then we send the load to the memory system.

This algorithm simply makes the load wait for some time in the hope of getting a forwarded value in the LSQ from an earlier store. However, loads do not wait forever. They wait till the number of preceding entries is below a threshold, and then the load is sent to the memory system. The main advantage of this improved scheme is that we reduce the number of replays

Load-Store Dependence Predictor: Store Sets

Now, that we have discussed methods to find if a load collides with other stores or not, let us move one step further. Let us also focus on stores, and see if we can predict load-store pairs that are expected to collide. If we can design such a predictor, then we can do two things:

1. We can delay a load from being sent to the memory system, if the predicted store is present in the LSQ or in the instruction window and precedes the load. This will reduce the number of replays and mispredictions.

2. Once the address of a store in a predicted load-store pair is resolved, we can forward the value from the store to the load if the addresses are the same. If there are no such stores, we can send the load instruction to memory at this stage.

As compared to the previous approach that predicted just on the basis of the PCs of loads, this approach uses more information. It takes the PCs of both loads and stores, and makes the predictions on the basis of load-store pairs. Whenever, we use more information, we expect the prediction to in general be better. Let us show the design of one such predictor that uses the concept of *store sets* [Chrysos and Emer, 1998]. Note that we always assume that a given load or store will behave the same way in the near future as it has been doing in the recent past.

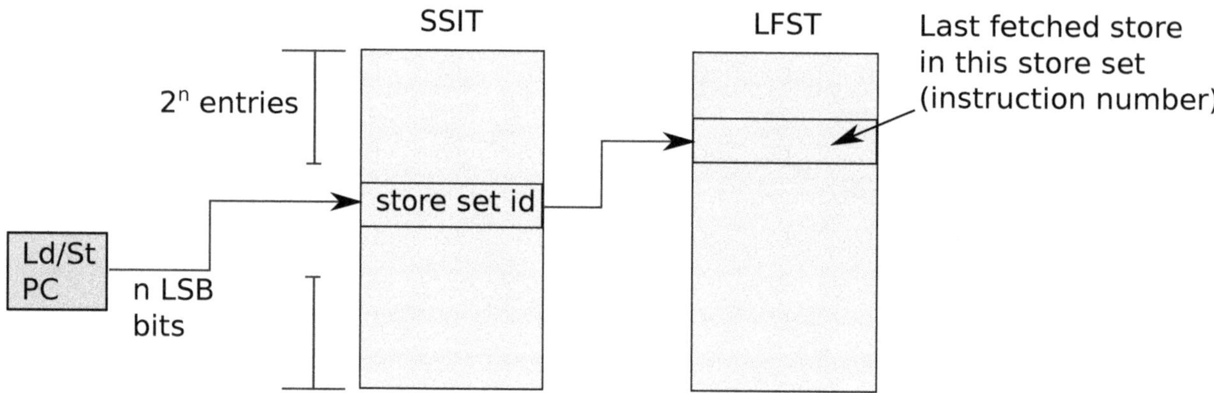

Figure 5.3: A predictor that uses store sets

For every load we associate a *store set*, which is the set of stores that have forwarded a value to the given load in the recent past. The exact mechanism is as follows. We have two tables: SSIT (Store Set Identifier Table), and LFST (Last Fetched Store Table).

The SSIT as shown in Figure 5.3 is a table that is indexed by either a load PC or a store PC. As usual, we consider the last n bits of the PC address, and access the SSIT table. Each entry of the SSIT table contains a store set identifier. It is a unique identifier that is assigned to each and every store set. If a load instruction accesses the SSIT, it reads the identifier of the store set that is associated with it. Similarly, if a store accesses the SSIT, it reads the identifier of the store set that it is a part of. There are two things to note. In both the cases (for a store and load), it is possible to read an invalid identifier. This means that the given load or store is not associated with a valid store set. Furthermore, to keep things simple, we can decide to make a store a part of only one store set. Otherwise, in each entry in the SSIT, we need to maintain multiple store set ids. This is a source of additional complexity. Note that later works [Moshovos et al., 1997, Moshovos and Sohi, 1999] did explore associating multiple store sets with a given store. However, let us explain the basic idea, where we assume that a store can only be a part of only one store set at a time.

Once we have read the id of the store set, we can use this id (if it is valid) to access the LFST. The corresponding entry in the LFST contains the instruction number of the store that was last fetched in the store set. The term *instruction number* is a unique identifier of an instruction in the pipeline. When an instruction enters the pipeline, we assign it a unique id, and it keeps this id till its retirement. Note that at any point of time, we cannot have two instructions in the pipeline with the same instruction number.

Let us now use the SSIT and LFST to create an algorithm that uses store sets. Consider the case of a load (L) first. After it is decoded, we access the SSIT with the PC of the load. There are two cases: either we get a valid store set id, or we do not. If we get a valid store set id, then we use it to access the LFST, otherwise we do not do anything. In the LFST (indexed by the store set id), we get the instruction number of the last fetched store in the load's store set. Let us refer to this store as S. Now, this means that there is a high probability that this store might supply its value to the load. Again, at this point, we are not sure because the address of the load has not been computed. Still there is a probability, and we should be aware of that. We thus add the instruction number of the store to the load's instruction packet.

Now, let us consider the case when a store (S) gets decoded. Similar to the case of the load, we lookup the address of the store in the SSIT. Recall that the SSIT has entries for both loads and stores. If the corresponding entry in the SSIT has a valid store set id, then we use it, otherwise we simply move ahead. If a valid id is found, we use it to access the LFST and write the instruction number of the current store to the entry in the LFST indexed by the store set id. This tells the LFST that the current store (S) is the most recent store in the store set.

There are several ways in which we can enforce a dependence. For example, we can proceed to find the instruction window entry of the store S, and then wait for S to be issued first. To find the instruction window entry we need a separate storage structure that maps the instruction number to the instruction window entry. By ensuring that there is an order in issuing the instructions, we can ensure that S is issued first, and then load L is issued. After the store is issued, we read the value it is going to write to the memory system from the register file. Since, we have predicted a load-store dependence, this value can be directly given to the load instruction. The load instruction can thus start early, albeit speculatively, and broadcast its result to instructions that are waiting for it. Another way of enforcing the dependence is to search in the LSQ for store S once load L is resolved. If S is present before L then we wait for it to get resolved before sending L to memory.

What did we gain in this process? We were able to significantly cut down on the latency of the load instruction. We did not have to send it to memory, nor wait for any value to be forwarded in the LSQ. We predicted a dependence with a store, and directly used the value that it is going to store. We were then able to wakeup the consumers of the load.

To enable this mechanism in the instruction window, wakeup and broadcast mechanisms have to be modified slightly. Any store with a valid store set id, can broadcast its instruction number. Any load waiting on that instruction number can wakeup and then get the value that the store is writing.

Recall that after the address for the store is computed, we do not send it to the memory system (Section 4.4), we rather wait for it to retire. This store will thus remain in the LSQ. Let us see what happens after we compute the address of the store. Since it has an entry in the LSQ, we can use it to forward values to any subsequent loads that come. Even if the address of the load is not computed, we can still speculatively forward the data if the store instruction is the latest instruction in the store set of the load. Upon retirement, we need to invalidate the LFST entry for the store, if it still points to it.

The last piece of the puzzle is the creation of an entry in the SSIT. There are several ways to do this, and there are different trade-offs associated with them. Let us discuss a simple scheme. Whenever we detect a dependence between a store S and a subsequent load L in the LSQ, we need to see if we need to create an SSIT entry or not. We first check the SSIT entry for S. If there is a valid entry then we do not do anything, otherwise we check the SSIT for L. If it is associated with a store set whose id is i then we set the store set of S to i. We write the instruction number of S to the ith entry of the LFST. Otherwise, if L does not have an associated store set entry we need to create a new store set id for both L and S and then populate the LFST.

Finally, let us discuss the issue of the instruction number. We chose to have a 7 or 8 bit instruction number as opposed to identifying a store by its 64-bit PC. This was done to reduce the required storage and the resources required to broadcast the id of the store. If there are 160 entries in the ROB, then we can simply create an 8-bit counter that is incremented (modulo 256) every time a new instruction is decoded. The instruction number of an instruction will be the value of this count; we are guaranteed to never have two instructions in the pipeline with the same instruction number.

5.1.4 Latency Speculation

Let us consider a simple system with a pipeline, an L1 cache, and an L2 cache. An access can either be a hit in the L1 cache or a miss. If it misses in the L1 cache, then it goes down the memory system, and it can either get its data from the L2 cache, or somewhere from deep within the memory system such as main memory or the swap space in the hard disk. The latency of a cache miss is not very predictable, and thus it is unwise to assume anything about the latency of a miss in a cache. However, we can assume that a very large percentage of our memory accesses will hit in the L1 cache. Furthermore, the latency of a hit in the L1 cache is almost always a constant. It is a very small number – typically between 1 to 3 cycles.

We have two options here. The first option is very conservative. Here, we wait for the load to read its data, before we wake up consumer instructions. In this case, we need to wait for the load instruction to hit or miss in the cache. The problem here is that it is not possible to ensure back-to-back execution (see Section 4.2.4) of a load instruction, and a subsequent instruction that uses the value read by the load. Instead, once we get the status from the cache (might take 1-2 cycles), we send a wakeup signal to the consumer instructions in the instruction window. This is an inefficient process because this ensures that instructions consuming the result of load instructions are ready to be executed after a delay of several cycles.

Instead, if we assume that every load instruction hits in the L1 cache, we might do much better. This is because most programs have a L1 hit rate of roughly 85-90% or more. This means that most of the time, our loads have a deterministic latency, and thus we can wakeup instructions such that they are ready just in time to consume the value read by the load (via the bypass network), and continue execution. This will allow us to significantly reduce the delay between issuing a load instruction and issuing the instructions that consume its value.

This is shown in Figure 5.4. For the pipeline shown in Figure 5.4, we have been able to save 2 cycles, in other words, we have been able to execute the consumer instruction 2 cycles early.

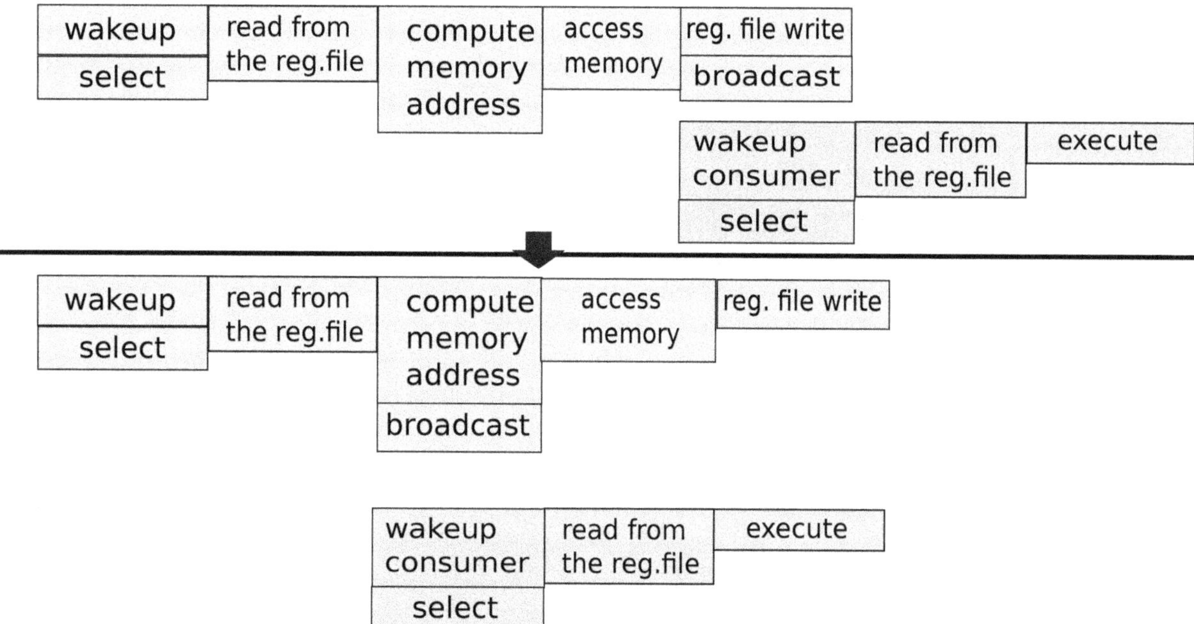

Figure 5.4: Load latency speculation

As of today, load latency speculation is a standard feature in almost all high performance OOO processors, particularly, in caches with multi-cycle hit times. We can gain a lot of performance by issuing consumer instructions early – before we determine if the load has had a hit or miss in the cache.

What about the remaining instructions (roughly 10%) that miss in the L1 cache? If we speculate on the latency of loads, we end up issuing dependent instructions before ascertaining if the load has hit in the L1 cache or not. Since these instructions are issued, they will try to pick up a value from the bypass network or the register file, and proceed. If the load has not completed, these instructions will pick up junk values and continue in the pipeline. There is a need to dynamically cancel these instructions, and reissue them once the correct value is read by the load instruction from the memory system. In this case, the load instruction will read its value from the lower levels of the memory system – L2 and beyond. This requires a replay mechanism (will be discussed in Section 5.2). Before that, let us discuss methods to optimise load latency speculation, and also discuss other forms of speculation in this space.

Hit-Miss Predictor

Let us discuss a basic hit-miss predictor (refer to [Yoaz et al., 1999]). Designing this is easy given all the designs that we have already seen. We need to take inspiration from the branch predictors that we had designed in Chapter 3. This is again a case of binary prediction, where we need to predict a hit (1), or a miss (0).

The simplest implementation of this predictor uses a 2^n entry table, where we index it using the last n bits of the PC of the load instruction. The assumption in all such cases is that the historic behaviour of a load instruction will continue to be predictive of the future, at least the near future. We can either use a simple 1-bit predictor, or a predictor that uses saturating counters. All the optimisations that we used in the case of branch predictors can be used here such as storing the tags for reducing aliasing.

In general having only one hit-miss predictor for the L1 cache is considered to be sufficient. We can in theory have more predictors for other caches such as the L2 and L3 caches. However, in such cases prediction accuracies are not known to be that great, and also the latency of a cache access at such levels is not very predictable. As we shall see in Chapter 7, an L2 or L3 cache is a fairly complex entity, and does not have a fixed latency.

5.1.5 Value Prediction

The idea here is to predict the value that the load instruction will read. Let us first list some of the main sources of value predictability. Some of the early studies in this area were performed by Lipasti et al. [Lipasti et al., 1996].

- **Input Sets**: In most programs, the inputs exhibit a tremendous amount of predictability. Assume we have an application that processes HTML files. A lot of the values, particularly, towards the beginning and end of the file (HTML tags) are expected to be the same. Moreover, two web pages from the same organisation will also have a lot of data in common.

- **Constants in the program**: Most programs rely on a lot of read-only data or data that is computed once and reused many times. These values are very predictable.

- **Base addresses**: Most of the time the base addresses of arrays, functions, and objects tend to remain the same throughout the execution of a program. When we load these addresses we can leverage the advantages of value prediction.

- **Virtual functions**: Programs in object oriented languages such as C++ often use a virtual function table that stores the addresses of the starting addresses of functions. Loads to read this table return very predictable values because this table typically does not change.

- **Register spilling:** Recall that when we run out of registers, or when we call a function, we need to write the values of some registers to memory. Their values are loaded later on. Many of these values remain constant, and are thus highly predictable.

Value Prediction Techniques

By this time most readers would have figured out the general pattern. We create a 2^n entry table that is indexed by n bits from the load instruction's PC. In this table we can store the predicted value, and then use the same optimisations that we have been using up till now. Lipasti et al. refer to this table as the LVPT (load value prediction table).

In some cases, we can leverage stride based patterns [Wang and Franklin, 1997] as we had studied in Section 5.1.2. Here, the value stored in a memory address changes by a fixed increment every time we issue the load instruction. There are fundamental reasons why such stride based patterns are more relevant for predicting memory addresses (see Section 5.1.2) as opposed to memory values. This is because most compilers try their best to put all the variables into registers. If a variable is getting regularly incremented, most likely the updates will remain confined to the register file. The updates will reach memory when the register is spilled either because of a function call or because we run out of registers. Most of the time such writes do not have a fixed and regular pattern. Hence, if we are predicting the values of memory values, we might not see a lot of benefits with stride-based prediction.

A promising set of techniques use some compiler support [Gabbay and Mendelson, 1997]. We add code to write the values of memory addresses to a file (this method is called *profiling*). Subsequently, we inspect these files to find the predictability of values. Predictability can be of two types: last value reuse and stride based. When the last value is reused we can use the LVPT based prediction scheme that uses the last value as the current prediction, whereas for a minority of cases we observe a stride based pattern. Here, we can use a regular stride based predictor as described in Section 5.1.2.

5.2 Replay Mechanisms

As we saw in Section 5.1, there are many ways of speculating. The common feature of all of these methods is to speculate on the basis of predictions. Note that the predictions are never 100% accurate. It is possible to have mispredictions. In this case, we need to dynamically locate all those instructions that have possibly gotten a wrong value, and *squash* (cancel or nullify) those instructions. For example, if we falsely predict the value returned by a load instruction, then all the instructions that have consumed the wrong value have to be squashed. This set of instructions is also known as the *forward slice*. Formally, the forward slice of an instruction I is defined as all the instructions that are data dependent either directly or indirectly (via other instructions) on the value produced by instruction I. It also includes instruction I.

Consider the following dependences ($\rightarrow$ indicates a RAW dependence): $I_0 \rightarrow I_1$, $I_1 \rightarrow I_2$ and $I_1 \rightarrow I_3$. In this case the forward slice of I_0 contains I_0, I_1, I_2, and I_3. If the result produced by I_0 is wrong, then its entire forward slice (I_0, I_1, I_2, I_3) also needs to be squashed.

Definition 24
The act of dynamically nullifying or cancelling an instruction in the pipeline is known as instruction squashing or just squashing.

What about control instructions? It is possible that the value returned by a load instruction might have influenced the direction of a branch. In this case, the branch will execute on the wrong path. However, in a modern OOO pipeline this will not happen. This is because we predict the outcome of branches at fetch time. We verify whether they were correctly predicted or not at commit time. This means that by this time all the instructions before the branch need to have fully executed, and written their results to the architectural state. All speculative loads before the branch would have completed, and their results would have been verified. We decide the outcome of a branch at commit time only on the basis of non-speculative data (data that is fully verified). Thus, there is no chance of a branch getting mispredicted because of load speculation.

Hence, we restrict our discussion to forward slices that are only created via data dependences.

Definition 25
The forward slice of instruction I_0 is defined as the set of instructions that are data-dependent on the value produced by instruction I_0 either directly or indirectly. An indirect dependence is established by a chain of direct data dependences between a pair of instructions. Refer to the following figure.

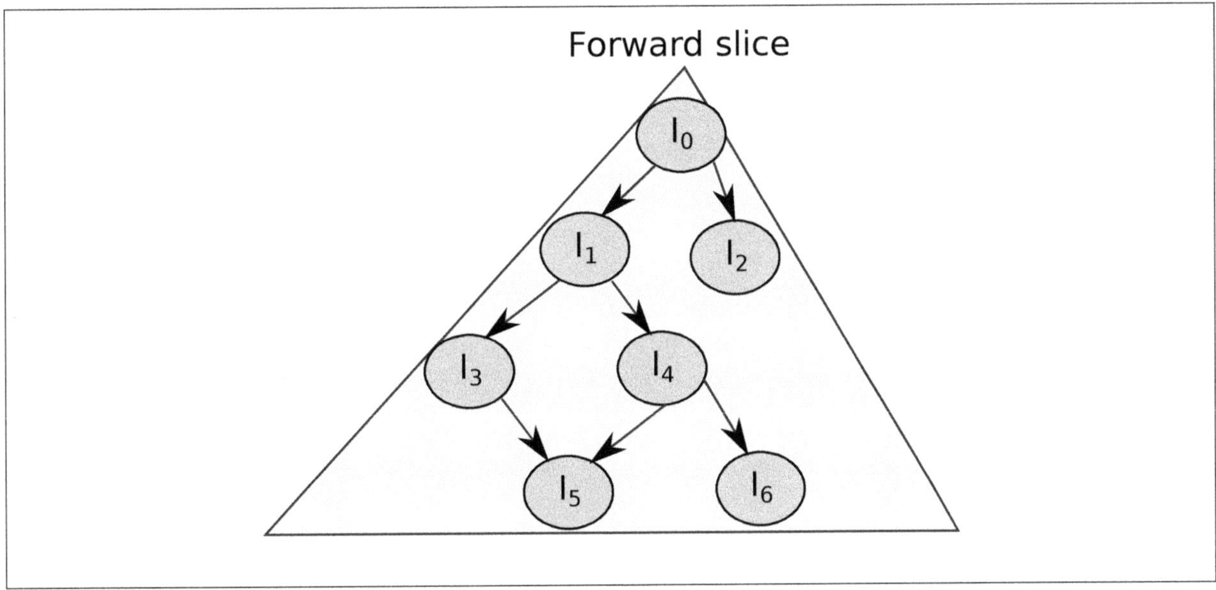

The main aim of the *replay* mechanism is to ensure that instructions in the *forward slice* of a misspeculated instruction are squashed and then re-executed..

5.2.1 Pipeline Flushing

The simplest method to fix the state of the pipeline is to flush the pipeline. Whenever we mispredict the outcome of an instruction, we mark it in the ROB. This marking is similar to marking mispredicted branches. Whenever the instruction with the mark reaches the head of the ROB, we do not allow the instruction to commit. We instead flush the pipeline, and restart execution from the instruction whose outcome was incorrectly predicted. Akin to the case of branch misprediction, we can fix the state of the pipeline and ensure that no misspeculated data gets written to the architectural state.

This method will no doubt work. It is a proven method, and does work wonderfully in the case of branch mispredictions. However, if we expect frequent mispredictions, then the overheads of this method are large. Note that flushing a pipeline is a very expensive operation. There might be 50 instructions fetched after a misspeculated instruction is fetched. All of these 50 instructions will be discarded if we flush the pipeline. This means that we will lose a lot of work that has been done. As a result, flushing the pipeline is not necessarily a good solution, even though it is very simple.

Typically forward slices of instructions are fairly small. Flushing the pipeline for cleaning up the effects of misspeculation is metaphorically like killing a mosquito with a cannon ball. We have to look for methods that can do the same with a significantly lower overhead. Let us look at a set of schemes originally proposed by Kim and Lipasti [Kim and Lipasti, 2004] in the rest of this section. Please note that we shall describe simplified adaptations.

5.2.2 Non-Selective Replay

This is a more efficient scheme as compared to a full pipeline flush. However, it is still not what we exactly want in the sense that it does not locate the exact forward slice and squash it. However, it is an important step in that direction. It chooses a superset of the forward slice. If we invalidate this set, then we are guaranteed to also have invalidated the forward slice. Then, we can reissue these instructions. Since we expect misspeculation events to be rare, we can afford a replay scheme with higher overheads.

Let us define the *window of vulnerability* (WV). Assume that a speculative load instruction broadcasts its tag in cycle 1. The nature of speculation can be diverse: speculating on the latency of the load or on its value. Now, assume that we shall get to know in the Nth cycle if the speculation is correct or not. Thus, it is possible that any instruction that marks any of its operands as ready between cycles 1 to N can be affected by the speculated load. Since we do an early broadcast, the consumers of the load instruction might get woken up, and they might subsequently wakeup their consumer instructions and so on. If in the Nth cycle, we realise that the speculation is wrong, the entire forward slice has to be squashed. **Since we do not explicitly keep track of the forward slice, we need to squash any instruction that has marked an operand as ready in the WV (cycles: 1 to N).** Note that a squashed instruction may either have already been issued, or may still be in the instruction window waiting to wake up or get selected.

The hardware support that is required is as follows. Along with every operand, which is not present in the register file, we associate a counter that is initialised to 0. This counter is set to N when we receive a broadcast for the tag associated with the operand. The counter thus starts the moment we see its tag on the tag bus, and then decrements itself by 1 every cycle till it reaches 0. Now, if the counter becomes 0, and we do not receive *bad news* (notification of a misspeculation), we can successfully conclude that the operand was read correctly. This scheme works on the principle that if there is a problem, instructions in the WV (window of vulnerability) will be informed, otherwise, all is well.

However, if there is a problem (misspeculation), then all the instructions in the WV (some operand has a non-zero counter) need to be squashed, and re-executed (replayed).

Let us explain with an example. Consider the following piece of assembly code.

```
1  ld   r1,  [r2]
2  add  r4,  r1,  r3
3  add  r5,  r6,  r7
4  add  r8,  r9,  r10
```

Assume that instruction *1*, which is a load instruction, is sent speculatively to the memory system. We predict that the value that it reads to be 7. Let's say we wait for 3 cycles and at the end of 3 cycles, we find out that the prediction was wrong. Let us further assume that instructions *2*, *3*, and *4* have been issued during that time frame because one of their operands was marked as ready. We then need to squash these three instructions: *2*, *3*, and *4*. Subsequently, we need to reissue instructions *1-4*. This is a non-selective replay mechanism because we decided to replay all the instructions in the window of vulnerability. Only instruction *2* is dependent on the result of the load. However, we are not selective, in the sense that we do not track dependences between instructions.

Let us look at the pros and cons of this scheme. The biggest advantage is that the scheme is simple. We do not have to track dependences between instructions. However, on the other hand, it can also be inefficient, particularly if N (size of the window of vulnerability) is high. In this case, we unnecessarily have to squash many instructions, even though the size of the forward slice may be really small. Of course, to choose a given replay mechanism we need to factor in many more things like the accuracy of the predictors, the number of instructions that are actually replayed, and the size of the replay hardware (as a fraction of the size of the rest of the hardware). Let us elaborate.

Dynamically Squashing Instructions

Whenever, we mark an operand as ready (because of a broadcast), we need to set a timer for that operand to N. The timer decrements every cycle (refer to Figure 5.5). Once the timer becomes 0, we are sure that this operand was read correctly. It is better to assume by default that things are all well, instead of the other way, because most of the time we expect the speculation to be correct.

Let us see what happens when we detect a misspeculation. Whenever we have such an event, we assert the kill wire (refer to Figure 5.5). Observe that the kill wire is connected to every entry of the instruction window. Here is the key idea: squash all the entries whose count for any operand is non-zero. These instructions are in the WV. For all such operands with a non-zero counter, we set their ready

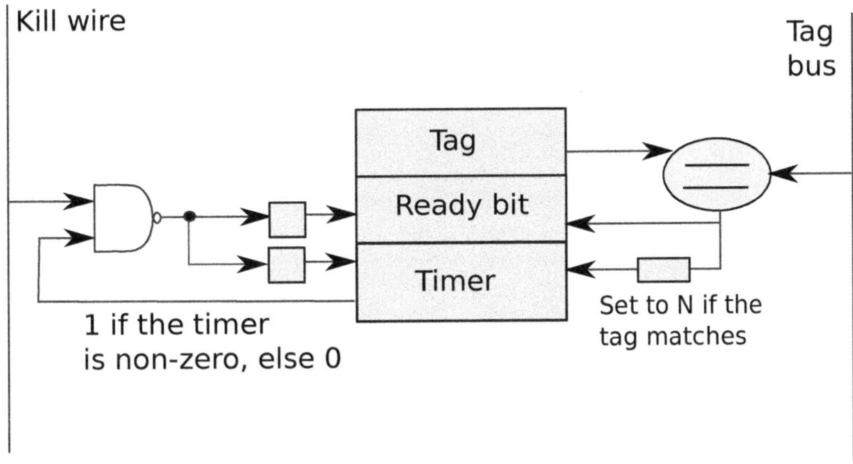

Figure 5.5: Structure of an instruction window entry with non-selective replay (only one tag bus is shown for the sake of simplicity)

bits to 0, and their counts to 0 as well. These instructions may have already been issued. In this case, they need to be replayed – re-executed with the correct values. If they have not been issued, then they need to wait till the tag is broadcasted again (corresponding to the correct value). Now, note that in Figure 5.5 we use a NAND gate that has two inputs: the kill wire and a bit that indicates if the timer's count is zero or non-zero. If both are 1 then the output of the NAND gate is a 0. This resets the ready bit and the timer. However, if the output of the NAND gate is 1, then no action is taken because in this case either the kill wire is deasserted or the timer's count is zero.

Let us look at the methods of re-execution, or in other words methods to replay the instructions.

5.2.3 Methods to Replay Instructions

Now, that we have dynamically squashed the instructions that might possibly have gotten a wrong value, it is time to re-execute or replay them. There are two ways of doing this.

Approach 1: Keep in the Instruction Window

The first approach is to keep instructions that have issued in the instruction window. We do not remove them after they are issued. Instead, we wait till the instructions get verified (all the predictions are correct). This means that the pipeline looks something like the one shown in Figure 5.6. Subsequently, when the instructions are *verified*, they are removed from the instruction window. Before discussing about what happens when instructions need to be replayed, let us delve into the details of the verification process.

An instruction is said to be verified, when it is issued, and the counters of all of its operands reach 0. This means that even if we assert the kill wire in the future, the current instruction will stay unaffected. At this point it can be removed from the instruction window.

However, if the instruction needs to be squashed, then we need to reset its state as described in Section 5.2.2. This becomes a fresh instruction, which needs to be woken up and issued once again. Note that the second time it will not get squashed because of the same speculative instruction. This is because for the same instruction we do not speculate twice. For example, if we predict the value of a load instruction, and then the prediction turns out to be incorrect, we do not predict once again. Instead, we wait for the right value to come from the memory system. Thus, it will never happen that the speculate-replay process will continue indefinitely with no progress.

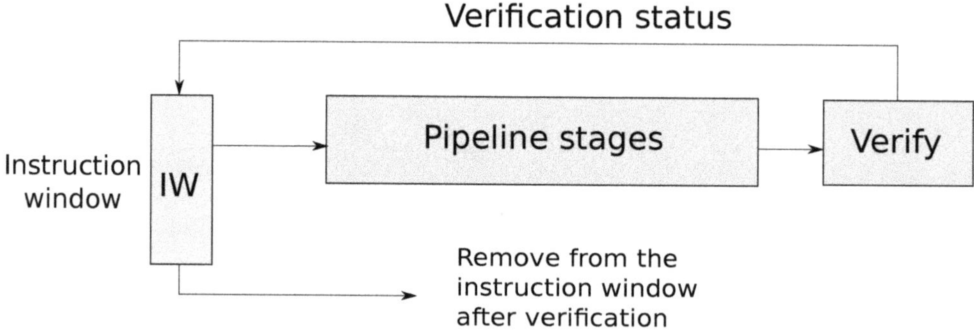

Figure 5.6: Instruction replay strategy: verify and remove

Once the right value comes from the memory system the misspeculated load instruction can re-execute, collect the right value from the memory system, and thus execute correctly. It can simultaneously broadcast the tag corresponding to its destination register to its consumer instructions that have also been squashed. They can wake up if the rest of their operands are available. In the next cycle, these consumer interactions can further wake up their consumers and so on. If the rest of the speculation is correct, this time the forward slice will execute correctly. Note that multiple misspeculations can happen concurrently, and thus a single instruction might get replayed multiple times if it is in the forward slice of multiple misspeculated instructions. However, the same instruction will suffer a misspeculation only once. We do not predict twice.

Approach 2: Create a Separate Replay Queue

If we keep all instructions in the instruction window till they are verified, it will create an otherwise complex instruction window even more complex. Furthermore, if there is very little speculation, then this mechanism simply adds to the overheads and is counterproductive. If the instruction window needs 100 entries, and because of the replay process, if we need to extend its size to let's say 150, it will unnecessarily become very slow.

Let us thus keep the size of the instruction window the same. We instead add a separate queue called the *replay queue* as shown in Figure 5.7.

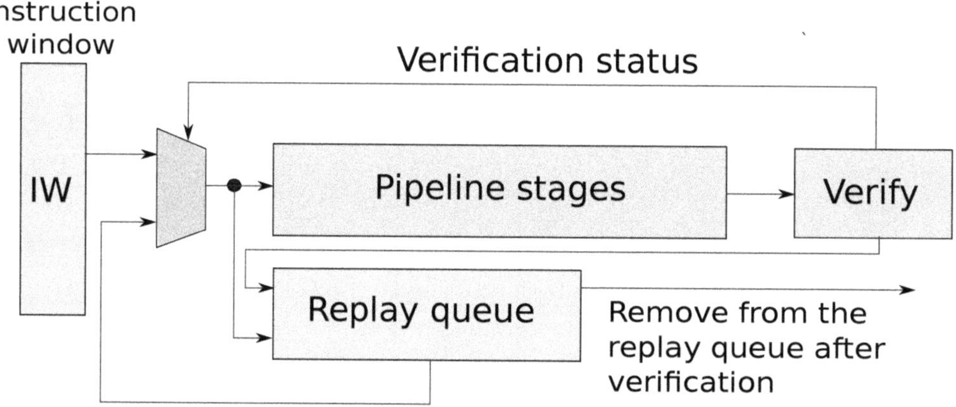

Figure 5.7: Instruction replay using the replay queue

After issuing an instruction, we move it to the replay queue. Thus, we do not need to increase the size of the instruction window unnecessarily. An instruction remains in the replay queue till it is verified. Once it is verified it can be removed from the replay queue. The rest of the logic remains the same.

Orphan Instructions

Let us summarise the situation that we have described till now. After we detect a misspeculation, we squash all the instructions that might have received a wrong value. We have looked at a simple method of creating this set of instructions using the non-selective replay approach. There are more sophisticated methods of creating this set, also known as the *squashed set*. Nevertheless, let us describe the basic principles that govern the correctness of the replay techniques.

If the squashed set is simply the forward slice of an instruction, then this situation is very easy to handle. We simply restart the instruction that was misspeculated with the correct value, and the entire forward slice shall get the right values through the broadcast-wakeup mechanism (over multiple cycles). Since we already guarantee that all instructions in the forward slice are squashed, we shall never miss an instruction, and the execution will be correct.

However, a problem arises when we squash a superset of the forward slice. Let us consider the following code fragment.

```
1  ld  r1,  8[r2]
2  sub r4,  r1,  r3
3  mul r5,  r6,  r7
```

Assume that we try to predict the latency of instruction *1* and speculate. Instruction *2* is dependent on *1*, and thus it is in its forward slice. However, instruction *3* is independent and not a part of its forward slice. Now assume that we have a misprediction while speculating on the latency of instruction *1*, and after asserting the kill signal, we squash all three instructions: *1*, *2* ,and *3*. In this case, we need to replay all three instructions. Replaying instructions *1* and *2* is easy. Instruction *1* gets replayed because we had mispredicted its latency. Once the load value is available we can broadcast the tag corresponding to register $r1$. This will wake up instruction *2*, and this time it will get the correct value of $r1$. However, there is nobody to wakeup instruction *3*!

Instruction *3* was unfortunately squashed because it was in the window of vulnerability (WV). Its only crime was that one or more of its operands became ready within the WV of instruction *1*. The producers of its operands $r6$ and $r7$ have long retired. We thus have a deadlock. No instruction is going to broadcast the tags corresponding to the physical registers mapped to $r6$ and $r7$, and thus instruction *3* will remain in the instruction window forever. Let us call such instructions as *orphan* instructions.

We can consider re-broadcasting the tags for instruction *3*. However, to do that we need to keep track of all the operands of all the instructions that have been squashed. We then need to keep track of the tags that have already been broadcast, and the ones that have not been broadcast yet. This is complicated, and requires fairly elaborate hardware. Here is a simple solution. Wait till instruction *3* reaches the head of the ROB. At that point of time all of its operands, should have gotten their correct values. This is because there will be no instruction in the pipeline that is earlier than instruction *3*. All such instructions would have executed correctly, written their values to the register file, and left the pipeline. Thus, at this point if instruction *3* is still waiting for some broadcasts, we can force it to execute with the values that are currently there in the register file. The result will be correct, because the values of the operands are correct. Let us extend this idea a little further.

5.2.4 Delayed Selective Replay

There are several disadvantages of non-selective replay. The forward slice can be a small portion of the squashed set. We might end up doing a lot of wasted work. Secondly, as we saw in Section 5.2.3, we can end up with orphan instructions.

Let us try to extend this scheme to solve some of these problems. Let us keep non-selective replay as the baseline scheme and make some enhancements.

Poison Bit

The first concept that we need to introduce is the *poison bit*. The aim is to keep track of the forward slice very accurately. We augment every register file entry, the instruction packet and the bypass network with an additional bit called the poison bit. Now, as an example, let us assume that we mispredict the value of a load instruction that writes to the physical register $p1$. It is possible that due to the early broadcast mechanism, other instructions in the pipeline will nevertheless read $p1$ because they have been eagerly issued. Let us thus attach a poison bit to the value stored in $p1$ and set it to 1. This means that regardless of how we get the value of $p1$ – via the register file or the bypass network – we always read the associated poison bit to be 1. All consuming instructions including those that have been issued because of the early broadcast mechanism will read this poison bit. If an instruction reads a source operand with its poison bit set, then it also sets the poison bit of its destination register.

This is how the poison bit propagates through the forward slice and thus we can dynamically mark an instruction's forward slice. Keep in mind that the poison bit propagates when we read a value either from the register file or the bypass network. It is not propagated while broadcasting tags or waking up instructions.

Now, when we misspeculate an instruction, we need to do two things:

1. Set the poison bit of the instruction packet and the destination register (physical register) to 1.

2. Set the kill wire and invalidate all the instructions in the window of vulnerability (non-selective replay scheme).

Basic Protocol

When an instruction finishes its execution, we do the following:

1. We check if the poison bit of the instruction is set. If it is, we squash the instruction by not allowing it to proceed further to the ROB. We however, set the poison bit in the physical register file for the destination register. Additionally, we also attach a poison bit along with the corresponding value on the bypass network.

2. If the poison bit is not set, then this means that this instruction has not received a speculative value. However, it is possible that this instruction might have been squashed because it is in the WV of a misspeculated instruction.

3. Let us make the instruction proceed towards the commit stage, and write its result to the register file. We also send its value on the bypass network to consumer instructions. Let us now proceed to handle such kind of corner cases.

Understanding of the Corner Cases

Let us first outline the problems associated with a window of vulnerability based replay scheme: it is false dependences. A *false dependence* arises when an instruction in the WV is squashed even though it is independent of the misspeculated instruction. Consider two instructions I and J. I is misspeculated and J is in the WV of I, even though it is not a part of I's forward slice. Assume that J is a safe instruction, which is not in the forward slice of any other misspeculated instruction. In this case there is a false dependence between I and J.

In the non-selective replay scheme such false dependences led to orphan instructions. In our current scheme – delayed selective replay – we have introduced a basic protocol that propagates the poison bit in the forward slice of the misspeculated instruction. Let us see what it achieves.

Assume that instruction J has been issued; it will pass through the execution units. Its poison bit will be 0. Since the instruction is safe, we need to let the replay queue know that the entry for J can be removed (similar logic for replay with the instruction window). This can be achieved by broadcasting the tag to all the elements in the replay queue. The entry for instruction J can mark itself to be free.

Now consider the tricky corner case when J has not been issued and we have ended up invalidating one of its ready operands. It is thus an *orphan* now. Similar to the case in Section 5.2.3 (for non-selective replay) there is no instruction to wake it up.

Dealing with Orphan Instructions

The fact that instruction J is an orphan basically means that when the kill wire for instruction I was asserted, one of J's operands was ready and its associated timer was non-zero. This operand's ready bit got unset. Now, there is nobody to set the operand's ready bit back to 1. Let us understand this process in some more detail. The fact that J's operand was ready means that some other instruction K must have set it to ready.

Let us now augment our design by adding a completion bus. It is similar to a tag bus that allows an instruction to broadcast its tag to all the entries in the instruction window. Now, assume that every instruction broadcasts its tag (id of its destination register) on the completion bus if it executes successfully without getting its poison bit set or getting misspeculated. This is done exactly N cycles after it has broadcasted its destination tag: there are two broadcasts in this scheme – the first is a regular broadcast for waking up consumers and the second broadcast is on the completion bus after the instruction's status is known. Assume that all the results of speculation are available within this time frame – within N cycles of broadcasting the tag (first broadcast). Finally, assume that the value of the timer associated with each source operand is set to N when the operand is woken up.

Consider the following timeline. Assume that in the Nth cycle, one of J's operands was ready, its counter was non-zero, and in this cycle instruction I asserted the kill wire. Since J was not issued yet, it got orphaned. This means that I must have broadcasted the tag any time t where $t \geq 1$ because it asserted the kill wire when $t = N$. Additionally, given that instruction K woke up the same operand, it must have also broadcasted its tag any time after $t \geq 1$ because at $t = N$ the timer of the operand was still non-zero.

Let instruction K signal its completion at any time $t \geq N + 1$. At this point of time, instruction J can read the tag off the completion bus and set the ready bit of the operand once again (see Figure 5.8).

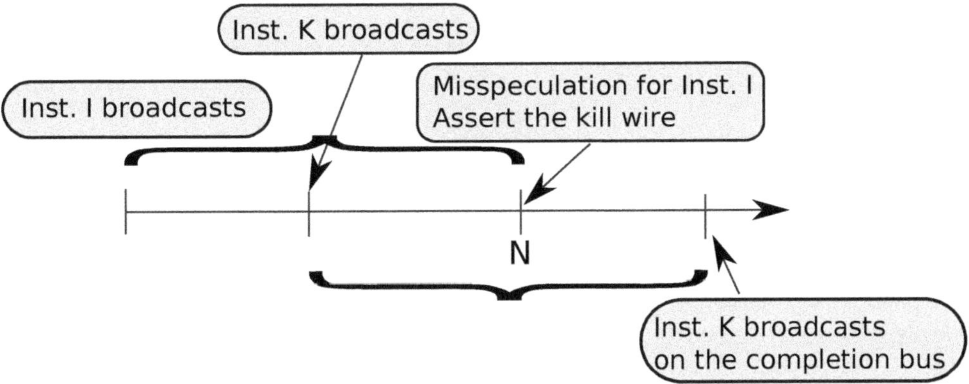

Figure 5.8: An example scenario that produces an orphan instruction

The summary of this discussion is that if an instruction has been orphaned because of a false dependence, then the instruction that had originally woken up the operand is going to again come back in the future to rescue it. In this case instruction K rescues instruction J. The completion bus is the additional overhead of this scheme.

5.2.5 Token based Replay

Let us now create a system that truly buffers the forward slice and no other instruction. As we have been observing, there is a trade-off between tracking dependences and the replay complexity. The more we track dependences, the easier it is to perform replays. If we are able to precisely mark the forward slice, performing a replay is easy – there are no false dependences. In token based replay the main idea is that for a load that is predicted to miss, we mark it, and propagate the mark to instructions in the forward slice (similar to a poison bit). With these marks it is very easy to identify the instructions that are there in the forward slice of a load.

Before proceeding, let us note a common pattern found in most programs. Let us consider the latency of loads in the data cache. Most of the time in such cases, the 90/10 thumb rule is found to operate. This is a thumb rule that basically says that 90% of the misses are accounted for by 10% of the instructions and 10% of the misses are accounted for by 90% of the instructions. A word of caution is due. This is not a hard and fast rule, it is a thumb rule. This means that we typically observe similar patterns in real programs. It has to do with the way that we write programs. Since most of the code executes within loops, we have a fair amount of temporal and spatial locality. As a result, we typically do not have a lot of misses in such phases. Moreover, for regular accesses such as walking through an array, we can very easily prefetch data, and this further reduces misses. Most of the misses happen when we access irregular data structures such as linked lists and execute portions of code that are rarely accessed.

Now, given this rule, let us try to leverage it. Given a load PC, let us try to predict if it will lead to a miss. We can use the hit-miss predictor described in Section 5.1.4. We can get a good accuracy, if our code uses data structures such as arrays. Let us create two sets of load instructions: S_1 and S_2. Instructions in S_1 are predicted to most likely miss in the L1 data cache, and instructions in S_2 are predicted to most likely hit in the L1 data cache.

At the time of decoding the instruction, we run the hit-miss predictor, and if an instruction is predicted to miss (part of S_1), then we proceed as follows.

Tokens and Token Vectors

Let us add a vector of tokens to the instruction packet of each instruction, each rename table entry, and to each source operand in an instruction window entry. This is a vector of k bits, where the bit at the ith position indicates the presence of token i. If the bit is 1, then it means that the given instruction or entry *holds* the token, and if the bit is 0, then it means that the token is not held. We will be using the token as a proxy for the forward slice. We have a total of k tokens.

Token Generation: When we predict an instruction to be in set S_1 in the decode stage, we collect a free token from a token allocator. Assume we get token i. Then we set the ith bit in the token vector of the instruction packet to 1. This instruction is said to be the *token head* for token i. We then proceed to the rename stage.

We add two additional fields to an entry in the rename table: *tokenId* and a token vector *tokenVec*. Let us explain with an example. Assume an instruction: *ld r1, 8[r4]*. In this case the destination register is $r1$. Assume it is mapped to the physical register $p1$. In the rename table entry of $p1$, we save the id of the token that the instruction owns in the field *tokenId*.

The logic for setting the field *tokenVec* is more elaborate.

Token Propagation:

Conceptual Idea
Now that we have a way to generate tokens, we need to design a method to propagate tokens along the

forward slice of an instruction. We can easily deduce that a producer needs to propagate its tokens to its consumers, and the consumers in turn need to propagate the tokens that they hold to their consumers. In this manner tokens need to propagate along the forward slice of an instruction. Note that we are using the word "tokens" in its plural form. This is because an instruction can be a part of the forward slices of many different load instructions. It will thus hold multiple tokens – one each for each load in S_1.

Let us consider our example instruction again. It was *ld r1, 8[r4]*. In this case register $r1$ was mapped to the physical register $p1$. We generated a token for this instruction and added it to its instruction packet as well as the *tokenId* field of its destination register $p1$ in the rename table.

Now consider the *tokenVec* field. It is supposed to contain a list of all the forward slices that the instruction is a part of. We use a token as a proxy for a forward slice and thus with each instruction and its destination register in the rename table we maintain a vector of tokens – *tokenVec*.

Implementation

Let us assume that the token vectors held by the source operands are $T_1 \ldots T_n$. Let t' refer to the token generated by the instruction. If the instruction does not generate a token then $t' = \phi$. Then the token vector for the instruction and its destination register in the rename table is given by Equation 5.1. Let us refer to the final vector of tokens as T_f .

$$T_f = T_1 \cup \ldots \cup T_n \cup t' \tag{5.1}$$

The process is shown graphically in Figure 5.9. We are essentially merging all the information – computing a union of all the token vectors. This is because now the current instruction is in the forward slice of many instructions – one forward slice per token. This computation can be done in the rename stage and then the computed token vector T_f can be used to set the token vector of the instruction and the *tokenVec* field of the rename table entry of the destination register. In this case $T_1 \ldots T_n$ correspond to the token vectors of each source register in the rename table.

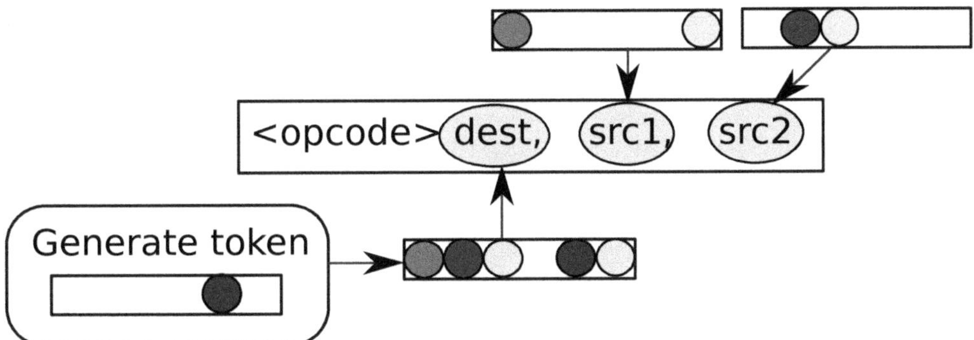

Figure 5.9: Token propagation (a coloured circle represents a token)

Subsequently, the instruction enters the instruction window. Let us keep two token vectors in each instruction window entry – one for each source operand. We can read these token vectors in the rename stage and populate the corresponding fields in the instruction window entry in the dispatch stage. If we have a replay queue then its entries will also be augmented with this information.

Verifying and Squashing Instructions

Let us continue our discussion. Note that we are only discussing instructions in set S_1 (predicted to suffer from a misspeculation).

Depending upon the type of speculation, we will have different methods of verifying the speculation. For example, if we are speculating on the latency of the load, then once a load completes, we can check if it took extra (more than its predicted value) cycles or not. If we are trying to predict a load-store dependence, we can always check whether this dependence exists or not, once the addresses of the corresponding loads and stores have been resolved. We can thus conclude that at a future point of time, we can expect a Boolean answer from the verification logic: True (speculation is correct) or False (speculation is false).

Speculation is Correct: In this case, we need to broadcast the token id that the load *owns* to all the entries in the rename table, the instruction window, and replay queue (if it exists). We need to set the bit corresponding to the token id in the token vectors to 0. This basically means that the respective token is being freed and removed from the system.

Broadcasting a token id to the entries in the rename table and instruction window requires some changes to the hardware. We need to create a new bus called the *token bus* that is connected to each entry. Furthermore, it is very well possible that multiple tokens might need to be released in each cycle. The simplest solution is to augment each entry with an AND gate. In each cycle we compute a logical AND operation between the $tokenVec$ of each entry and the value that is broadcast on the token bus. Let us assume that the token bus is as wide as the number of tokens in circulation. It transmits a mask that we shall refer to as $tokenMask$, and a single bit that indicates if we are freeing a token, or initiating a squash (referred to as the $squashBit$). Assume that we can have 8 tokens (numbered 1 to 8) in circulation and tokens 1, 2, and 4 are getting released. In this case, we will set the mask as 00001011 (counting from the right starting from 1). The logic is that if the ith token is being released we set the ith bit to 1, otherwise we set it to 0. After an AND operation between the bitwise complement of the token mask with the token vector $tokenVec$, the ith bit in $tokenVec$ will become 0. The respective token will thus get released.

We thus compute:

$$tokenVec = tokenVec \wedge \overline{tokenMask} \tag{5.2}$$

In this case the $squashBit = 0$ – the speculation is correct.

Speculation is Incorrect: In this case, we need to initiate a replay. The load that has had a misspeculation needs to be a token head (because it is a part of set S_1). Let it be the owner of token with id j. We need to broadcast j to all the entries in the instruction window and replay queue. We can use the same token bus mechanism with the squash bit set to 1. We can also support replays due to multiple misspeculations. Let us explain with an example.

Assume that in a system with 8 tokens, we have misspeculations for tokens 3 and 5. With $squashBit = 1$, we transmit the following $tokenMask$: 00010100. To find out if a given operand needs to be invalidated or not, we need to find if any of the tokens associated with the operand correspond to misspeculated instructions or not. This is possible by computing the result of the following equation.

$$result = tokenVec \wedge tokenMask \tag{5.3}$$

In this case, if any bit of $result$ is equal to 1, then it means that the given operand is a part of the forward slice of a squashed instruction. We thus need to squash that instruction. In this case, all that needs to be done is that we need to reset the ready bits and reissue these instructions when the operand becomes available again (similar to non-speculative replay).

Avoiding Orphan Instructions: It is easy to avoid orphan instructions in this scheme. We only invalidate those operands and instructions that are part of a misspeculated forward slice. We do not have false dependences in this scheme.

Instructions in Set S_2

Let us now consider instructions in set S_2. Instructions in this set are not expected to suffer from a misspeculation. Note that these instructions do not generate any tokens.

If they do not suffer from a misspeculation, then there is no problem. We continue as is. However, if they have a misspeculation, then we use a sledge hammer like approach as we had proposed in Section 5.2.1. We simply wait till the instruction reaches the head of the ROB, and then we flush the pipeline. This solution has a high overhead, yet is simple.

5.3 Simpler OOO Processor without a Register File

Let us now simplify things. We have invested a lot of silicon real estate in creating a high performance processor. However, since this chapter is about alternative designs, let us look at OOO processors that are less complex, and not necessarily very inefficient. Let us look at one of the most popular alternative designs that uses the ROB also as the physical register file (PRF)[1]. It leads to a simpler implementation. We need not have the paraphernalia associated with a physical register file. Even recovering from a branch misprediction is also much easier.

Let us first try to motivate this design by first taking a look at some aspects of the pipeline presented in Chapter 2, which are amenable to simplification. Here were the big sources of complexity.

Physical Register File To support large instruction window sizes, and remove all hazards, we needed large physical register files. To keep track of physical register file allocation it was necessary to have additional structures such as a free list. In addition, the logic for freeing a physical register is non-trivial. We need to wait for another instruction writing to the same architectural register to commit.

Maintaining Precise State Maintaining the correct architectural state (see Section 4.4) was difficult. We had to introduce many schemes to remember the mapping between physical registers and architectural registers at various points in the program. This was a slow and complicated mechanism. We would love to at least make this part simpler.

Recovery from Branch Mispredictions This point extends the previous point, where we discussed the complexity of maintaining architectural state. Recovery from a branch misprediction is also fairly involved in the scheme with physical register files. We need to restore a checkpoint, which can be a set of saved register values, or a set of mappings between architectural registers and physical registers. This process requires time and additional hardware.

Let us try to propose a new scheme that avoids the physical register file altogether and makes it easy to recover from branch mispredictions.

5.3.1 Overview of the Design

Main Insights

Let us ask the basic question: Why did we use a physical register file in the first place? We used it to avoid WAR and WAW hazards. This is not the only way of avoiding such hazards. Here is an alternative idea.

Instead of using the temporary storage provided by the physical register file, let us instead use an ROB entry to additionally play the role of a physical register. We can thus achieve both our aims with the same structure. It is true that this will increase the number of ROB accesses and make it a bottleneck. Let us entertain such considerations later. Let us first present the design.

---

[1]The terms *physical register file* and *PRF* will be used interchangeably

Design of the Pipeline

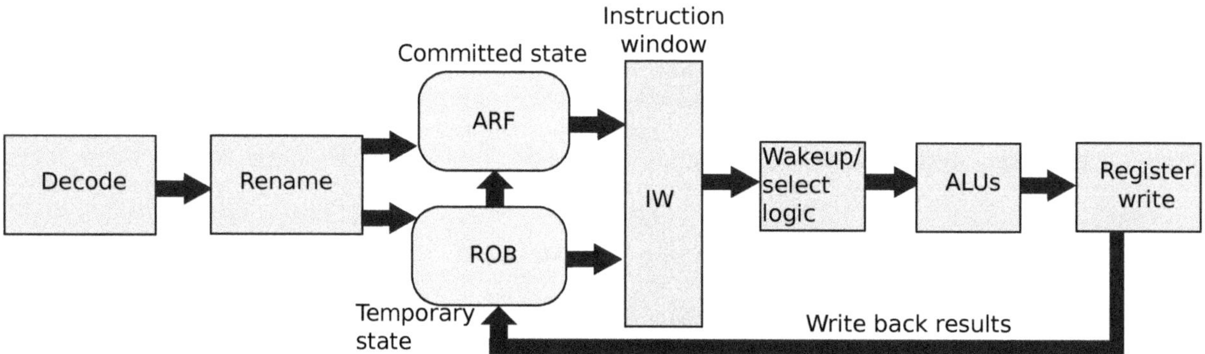

Figure 5.10: Overview of a simplified pipeline

Figure 5.10 provides an overview of our simplified pipeline. Instead of having a large physical register file, we have a smaller architectural register file (ARF). The number of entries in the ARF is the same as the number of architectural registers. Furthermore, the ARF also contains the precise architectural (committed) state. There is thus no need to create periodic checkpoints and restore them if there is a need. The ARF contains the committed state. The crucial assumption here is that committed values stay in the ARF and temporary (not committed) values reside in the ROB. Henceforth, we shall refer to the pipeline introduced in Chapter 4 as the PRF based pipeline, and the pipeline introduced in this section as the ARF based pipeline.

The crux of the idea is to change the renaming stage. Given an architectural register, the renaming stage needs to point out a location at which the value is available. Since there is no physical register file, the renaming stage in this case points to either the architectural register file (ARF) or the ROB (Reorder buffer). If the value that we want to read is a part of the committed state, then we need to read it from the ARF. However, if the instruction that has written the value to an architectural register has not committed yet, then we need to read its value from the ROB. The rename table points to the right location.

It is to be noted that once an instruction retires, we need to update the committed state. We write to the destination register in the ARF upon instruction retirement. The rest of the pipeline is roughly the same. The key difference is that in the PRF based design we read the register values after issuing the instruction. In this case, we read the operand values either from the ARF or ROB before the instruction enters the instruction window (IW).

5.3.2   Detailed Design

Rename Stage

Given that we have seen the overview of the design in Figure 5.10, let us look at the rename stage in some more detail. The structure of each entry in the rename table is as follows.

As before, the number of rows in the rename table is equal to the number of architectural registers. Let us assume that the architectural register that we want to rename is $r1$. The value of this architectural register can either be present in the ROB or ARF if it has already been computed. We thus add a bit in each entry of the rename table called $inARF$, which indicates if the value for the register $r1$ is in the ARF ($inARF = 1$) or in the ROB ($inARF = 0$). If the value is present in the ARF, then we can directly read the architectural register in the next cycle.

However, if the value is not present in the ARF, then we need to read the subsequent field $robEntry$. This is the number of the ROB entry that contains the value of the register. It contains the current value of the architectural register $r1$. Note that we are augmenting every ROB entry to contain additional data – result produced by the instruction.

Operand Read Stage

The major difference in this pipeline is that we read the values first and carry the values along with us in the pipeline. This is quite unlike the PRF based design, where we read the values from the register file or the bypass network just before execution. Here we try to read the values right after renaming the instruction and carry it through the processes of dispatch and issue. This is no doubt a source of inefficiency because a 7-bit PRF tag (assuming a 128-entry physical register file) is far easier to carry along as compared to a fat 64-bit value. However, if this is a 16-bit processor, where every value is 16 bits wide, then this idea does not look that bad.

Now, if the rename stage indicates that the value can be found in the ARF, we read the ARF, otherwise, we access the ROB.

Let us consider the case when the rename table indicates that the value of the operand (register $r1$) is present in the ROB. Each entry of the ROB contains the following fields: *avlbl* and *val*. *avlbl* is a 1-bit Boolean field that indicates if the instruction corresponding to the ROB entry has produced its result or not. The field *val* contains the result of the instruction after the completion of its execution.

There are two cases that we need to consider. If $avlbl = 1$, then it means that the ROB entry pointed to by the field *robEntry* in the rename table contains the value of $r1$; however if $avlbl = 0$ then this means that the value is not ready yet. Instead we need to wait in the instruction window for the value of $r1$ to be generated. Recall that we had relied on a broadcast-wakeup based mechanism in the PRF based pipeline. In that case we were broadcasting the PRF register id. This was also referred to as the *tag*. In this case, the tag is the index of the ROB entry that produces the value for $r1$, which is *robEntry*. We have to thus wait for the id of the ROB entry along with the value of the operand to be broadcasted. Subsequently, we can proceed for execution, if we have the values of the rest of the operands.

Dispatch Stage

In this stage, the instruction enters the instruction window. The only difference in this case is that an instruction enters the instruction window along with the values of operands. The structure of an entry in the instruction window is shown in Table 5.1. We assume that we have 128 entries in the ROB.

Field	Description	Width (in bits)
valid	validity of the entry	1
ready	instruction is ready to be executed	1
First source operand		
ready1	value is present	1
tag1	tag of the first source register	7
val1	value of the first operand	64
Second source operand		
ready2	value is present	1
tag2	tag of the second source register	7
val2	value of the second operand	64
Destination		
isregd	destination is a register	1
robTag	ROB entry of instruction	7

Table 5.1: List of fields in an instruction window entry

We have two additional fields in an instruction window entry: *val1* and *val2*. These are the values of the two source operands. If each value is 64 bits, then we are adding 128 bits to each instruction window entry. This is expensive; however, carrying the values along simplifies things to a great deal. It reduces dependences. Instead of waiting to read other structures such as the register file, we can directly execute the instruction if all the values have been read earlier, or can be obtained through the bypass network.

The bypass network also needs to change. The tag in this case is the index of the ROB entry that produces the value of the operand. The rest of the tag matching logic and wakeup logic remain the same. There is one more significant change as well. Along with broadcasting the tag, we also need to broadcast the value of the operand. Previously, this was not required because we could always read the value from the register file. This kept the bypass network relatively lean, and did not add a lot of wires and buffers. However, now we do not get a chance to read the register file after the instruction enters the instruction window. Hence, we need to broadcast the value also.

After an instruction picks up all of its operand values, it wakes up, is selected, and proceeds for execution.

Speculative Broadcast

Recall that in Section 4.2.4, we were broadcasting the tag in advance to ensure that instructions did not have to unnecessarily wait longer. They could pick up the values of operands on the way (from the bypass network). This enabled back-to-back execution.

Here also we can do the same. We can issue instructions *early* as long as they are guaranteed to get their operand values later in the pipeline. This aspect of the pipeline does not change.

Write-back Stage

After an instruction has executed, it is time to write its value back. We need to write this value to its ROB entry. The ROB entry buffers this value till the instruction is committed. We need to set $avlbl = 1$ in the ROB entry. This indicates that the value has been computed and can be read. Recall that by default we set $inARF$ to be 0 while creating an entry in the rename table; this means that by default we access the ROB unless instructed otherwise.

Commit Stage

This is the last stage. In this stage, we need to update the architectural state. For each instruction that is being committed, we write its result (stored in its ROB entry) to the ARF. This thus updates the architectural state.

Simultaneously, we need to update the $inARF$ bit in the rename table. However, this is easier said than done. Let us explain with an example. Assume a committing instruction I of the form *add r1, r2, r3*. In this case, the destination register is $r1$, which contains the result of the instruction. Let us first assume that after this instruction was renamed, no other instruction has passed through the rename stage with $r1$ as the destination register. In this case once instruction I commits, the value of $r1$ needs to be transferred from the ROB to the ARF, and in addition the rename table needs to be updated. We need to set the $inARF$ bit to 1 because now the value can be found in the ARF.

Let us now consider the other situation. In this situation, just after instruction I gets renamed, another instruction I' passes through the pipeline. It also writes to $r1$. In this case, the rename table entry for $r1$ gets updated – it points to the ROB entry for I'. When instruction I commits, it cannot set the $inARF$ bit to 1 for $r1$ in the rename table. This is because the latest value will be produced by instruction I' or a later instruction.

Let us thus summarise the logic. We need to compare the $robEntry$ field of the rename table's entry for $r1$ with the id of the ROB entry for instruction I. If they are equal, then it means that no instruction that also writes to $r1$ has been renamed after I. We can thus set $inARF$ in the rename table entry to 1. However, if they are not equal, then we can infer that there is another instruction in the pipeline that overwrites $r1$, and thus $inARF$ needs to remain 0. To summarise, an additional comparator is required

here. It needs to compare the *robEntry* field in the rename table entry with the id of the ROB entry of
the committing instruction.

Historical Note 1

*It is not necessary to have one unified instruction window. Indeed one of the earliest proposals for
designing an OOO processor by Robert Tomasulo in 1967 envisioned multiple instruction windows.
The rest of the design was conceptually similar to the ARF based OOO processor. He proposed
mini-instruction windows attached to each functional unit. Such instruction windows were known
as reservation stations. Each entry in a reservation station was similar to an entry in the instruction
window in our ARF based processor. All the reservation stations were connected to a common data
bus (CDB) where the tags and values were broadcasted. The reservation stations compared the tags
and upon a match buffered the value.*

*Modern designs often have different instruction windows for different classes of instructions. For
example, if the integer and floating point register set is completely disjoint, then separate instruction windows can be used for each class of functional units. We can also have such a separation
between regular integer/floating point instructions, and vector based SIMD instructions (instructions
that perform arithmetic instructions on multiple operands at a time). Having such a separation is
desirable because small instruction windows are faster and more power efficient. However, having
a unified window is also sometimes advantageous because it helps balance out the unevenness of the
load between different classes of functional units.*

5.3.3   Comparison

Let us now compare the PRF and ARF based designs by listing out their pros and cons (refer to
Table 5.2). Note that *IW* refers to the instruction window in the table.

Attribute	PRF based design	ARF based design
Values reside in only a single location	Only in the PRF	Multiple locations: ARF, IW, ROB
Size of an entry in the IW	small	large (contains operand values)
Restoring state after a misprediction	hard	very easy
Need for a free list	yes	no
Write ports in the ROB	decode_width	decode_width + is-sue_width
Read ports in the ROB	commit_width	commit_width + 2 * is-sue_width

Table 5.2: Comparison between the ARF and PRF based designs

The main drawbacks of the ARF based design are the size and complexity of the ROB. We write
to the ROB twice – while creating an entry in the decode stage and while writing the results of an
instruction. In the worst case, the number of ports required for writing the results can be equal to the
issue width.

We can always optimise this by populating the ROB entry lazily. We can write most of the contents
to the ROB entry at the time of writing the results. The ROB entry itself can be split across two

sub-arrays of memory cells (will be described in more detail in Chapter 7). Since the ROB also acts as a register file, in the worst case, we would need to read $\langle 2 \times issue\_width \rangle$ number of operands. In addition, we need to read the ROB while committing instructions. The number of simultaneous reads (for committing instructions) is equal to the commit width.

Note that even in the PRF based design we needed to update the ROB after the successful execution of each instruction. We needed to update a bit in each ROB entry to indicate that the instruction has completed successfully. To optimise, we can have a separate structure to store these bits. Moreover, since the size of each entry is a single bit, we can even have an array of flip-flops instead of an SRAM array. Hence, we have not added this source of overheads to Table 5.2.

Given that the ROB can be a bottleneck, and we need comparators with each rename table entry, this design will have significant performance overheads. It is simple, yet not expected to be as efficient as the PRF based designs particularly for large 64-bit server processors.

5.4   Compiler Based Techniques

We have looked at a lot of hardware starting from the basic in-order processor to an aggressive out-of-order processor with value prediction and token based replay. Adding such sophisticated features is no doubt a good thing. They ensure significant gains in performance. However, there is a flip side to everything. Adding extra hardware always has negative implications in terms of power consumption and complexity.

We did take a sharp turn towards simplicity in Section 5.3. We dismantled the physical register file, added more bits to the ROB, and simplified the processor. However, such processors have fairly large instruction window entries, a complex multi-ported ROB, and they move fat 64-bit values around. These are not particularly performance enhancing optimisations.

These are examples, where simplicity can give you some advantages, yet take some other advantages away. Let us now discuss a set of compiler based approaches that need not necessarily have a negative effect on performance.

Let us look at the compiler – something that we have been ignoring up till now. The role of a compiler is not just limited to converting a high level program to machine code, it is actually much more than that. Modern compilers spend most of their time in optimising code. This does increase the compilation time; however, at the same time it makes the code run efficiently on modern processors. The IPC increases, and in a lot of cases, the number of instructions also decreases. The only trade-off is the size, complexity, and time of execution of the compiler. These are not significant issues as of today.

Given the amount of physical memory we have, we don't mind if a compiler takes a couple of megabytes of more memory to do a good job in compilation. Same holds true for complexity and execution time. We need to run the compiler only once to produce a binary; however, we run the binary many times. Hence, the compilation speed per se does not matter. For example, at the moment, your author is typing this book using the *gvim* editor. The editor is really fast and allows the authors to achieve many complex tasks very quickly. It does not matter if it took 2 minutes to compile the source code of the editor or 2 hours.

We are definitely in a position to afford a very complex compiler that might possibly take a very long time to compile a given program. However, at the end, the compiler must do a very good job in creating a binary that has a lot of ILP, and in reducing the number and complexity of instructions. Let us look at some of the basic techniques that compilers use to produce efficient code.

5.4.1   Data Flow Optimisations

The main idea here is to optimise the process of data propagation between instructions, and see that we are able to reduce the number of instructions as well as their complexity. Recall that different instructions have different latencies, or in other words they take different amounts of time to execute. As a result, we are better off having simpler instructions such as add and subtract instead of more complex instructions such as multiply and divide.

Constant Folding

This is one of the simplest optimisations in our arsenal, yet is extremely effective. Consider the following piece of C code.

```c
int a = 4 + 6;
int b = a * 2;
int c = b * b;
```

A naive compiler will first add 4 and 6, then store the result in a, and then execute the rest of the statements in order. Is this required? The answer is absolutely not. A smart compiler can figure out at compile time that the value of a is a constant, and this constant is equal to 10. Similarly, it can also figure out that the values of b and c are also constants, and we can directly compute their values and update the registers that correspond to them. This saves us a lot of computation, and also decreases the number of instructions, which directly leads to an increase in performance.

Strength Reduction

Now that we have folded away our constants, let us look at operators. We need to understand that different arithmetic operations have different latencies. In particular multiplication and division are slow, with division being the slowest. It is best to replace such instructions with faster variants wherever possible. The faster instructions are add, subtract, and shift (left/right) instructions. Recall that shifting a value to the left by k places, is equivalent to multiplying it by 2^k. Similarly shifting a value to the right by k places, is equivalent to dividing it by 2^k.

Let us now consider an example.

```c
int b = a * 8;
int d = c / 4;
int e = b * 12;
```

We have two multiplication operations and one division operation here. These are expensive operations in terms of both power and time. Hence, it is highly advisable to replace these operations with simpler variants, if we have an option. In this case we do, because we can leverage the fact that the numbers 8, 4, and 12 are either powers of 2, or can be expressed as a sum of powers of 2. We can thus use shift operations here. Let us rewrite the code snippet to produce a more optimised variant.

```c
int b = a << 3;
int d = c >> 2;
int e = b << 2 + b << 3;
```

In this case, we have used far simpler shift operations, which can often be implemented in a single cycle and are far more power efficient.

What we see here is that we were able to replace multiply and divide operators with equivalent shift left and shift right operators. This *strength reduction* operation will lead to performance gains because of the lower latency of the shift instructions.

Common Subexpression Elimination

Consider the following snippet of C code.

```c
int c = (a + b) * 10;
int d = (a + b) * (a + b);
```

An unoptimised compiler will generate code to perform all the additions and multiplications. However, this is not required. We can alternately transform this code to a more optimised version.

```c
int t1 = a + b;
int c = t1 * 10;
int d = t1 * t1;
```

Instead of 3 additions and 2 multiplications, we are now doing 1 addition and 2 multiplications. We have definitely saved on 2 additions by a simple trick. Instead of computing the *common subexpression* $a + b$ again and again, we have computed it just once and saved it in a local variable $t1$, which can be mapped to a register. Subsequently, we use $t1$ to act as a substitute for $a + b$ in all subsequent instructions.

Compilers use this technique to reduce the number of instructions wherever possible. They try to compute the values of subexpressions before hand, and then they save it in registers. These values are then used over and over again in subsequent instructions. Since we decrease the number of instructions, we have a definite performance gain.

Dead Code Elimination

Consider the following program.

```c
int main (){
    int a=0, b=1, c;
    int vals[4];

    printf ("Hello World\n");
    c = a + b;
    vals[1] = c;
}
```

Is there a need to perform the last addition, $c = a + b$ and then set $vals[1]$ to c? There is no statement that is using the value of c and the array $vals$. These values are not influencing the output of the program, which is what most users care about. Unless, we explicitly want to run these instructions to measure the performance of the program with these instructions, in an overwhelming majority of the cases, we do not need these instructions.

We can thus label such instructions as *dead code*. This is code that does not have any purpose, and does not influence the output. Most compilers these days are fairly good at identifying and removing dead code. Other that the obvious advantage of reducing the number of instructions, another major advantage is that we can efficiently pack the useful instructions into instruction cache (i-cache) blocks. There is no wastage of space in the i-cache. Note that we do not want to waste valuable i-cache bandwidth in fetching instruction bytes that are not required.

Definition 26
Lines of code that do not influence the final output are referred to as dead code.

Silent Stores

Let us now increase the degree of sophistication. Consider the following piece of code.

```c
int arr[5], a, b, c;

arr[1] = 3;
a = 29;
b = a * arr[0];
arr[1] = 3;              /* Not required */
printf ("%d \n", (arr[1] + b));
```

Consider the second store to $arr[1]$. It is not required. It writes exactly the same value as the first store, even though it is not really dead code. However, the second store is a silent store, because it has no effect. It writes a value to a memory location, which is already present there. In that sense, it does not write a new value. Hence, we can happily get rid of the second store instruction to $arr[1]$. This is called *silent store elimination.*

Definition 27
Assume that a memory location at a given point of time contains the value v. If at that point of time, a store writes value v to that memory location, then it is called a silent store.

Such kind of data flow analyses can become increasingly sophisticated, and we can find a lot of redundancy in the program, which can be successfully eliminated. To understand how exactly these mechanisms work, the reader needs to take an advanced course on compilers.

5.4.2   Loop Optimisations

Most of the programs that we write use loops, and also most of the execution of a program is within loops. These are the repetitive structures that most often take up more than 90% of the execution time. Thus, optimising loops is essential. Even if we make a small change in the code of the loop, the benefits have the potential to multiply.

Loop Invariant based Code Motion

A variable or property that does not change across the iterations of a loop is known as a *loop invariant.* Assume that in every iteration we set the same variable to the same value, then that variable is a loop invariant. There is in fact no reason for it to be repeatedly updated to the same value within the body of the loop. The update statement can be moved outside the loop. Let us explain with an example.

```
for (i=0; i<N; i++){
    val = 5;
    A[i] = val;
}
```

There is no reason for the variable *val* to be updated within the loop. This update instruction can very well be moved by a smart compiler to a point before the loop. We will save a lot of dynamic instructions (N instructions in N iterations) by making this change. The code after moving the loop invariant to before the loop looks like this:

```
val = 5;
for (i=0; i<N; i++){
    A[i] = val;
}
```

This is a much faster implementation because we reduce the number of dynamic instructions.

Definition 28
A variable or property that does not change across the iterations of a loop is known as a loop *invariant.*

Induction Variable-based Optimisation

Let us now climb up the ladder of complexity. Consider the following *for* loop.

```
for (i=0; i<N; i++){
    j = 6*i;
    A[i] = B[j] + C[j];
}
```

This piece of code uses a loop variable i that gets incremented every cycle. However, let us concentrate our attention on the variable j. It is a multiple of i, and sadly we need to perform a multiplication to set j once every iteration. Is it possible to remove this multiplication? It turns out that the answer is yes. Consider the following piece of optimised code.

```
j = 0;
for (i=0; i<N; i++){
    A[i] = B[j] + C[j];
    j = j + 6;
}
```

The important observation that we need to make is that in every iteration we are incrementing the value of j by 6 because i is getting incremented by 1. We can thus replace a multiplication by an addition. In every iteration, we increment j by 6, which is mathematically the same thing. However, when we translate this to gains in performance, it can be significant, particularly if there is a large difference in the latencies of add and multiply instructions. For example, if a multiplication requires 4 cycles, and an addition requires 1 cycle, we can execute 4 times as many addition instructions as multiplication instructions in the same time.

Such analyses can be extended to nested loops with multiple induction variables and multiple constraints. We need to understand that most modern compilers are today constrained by the amount of information that is available to them at the time of compilation. This is because we do not know the values (or range of values) of all variables at compile time.

Loop Fusion

Let us now look at a slightly more complicated optimisation. Consider the following piece of code. In the next few examples we shall show assembly code written in the SimpleRisc assembly language (described in Appendix A).

C code

```
for (i=0; i<N; i++)   /* Loop 1 */
    A[i] = 0;

for (i=0; i<N; i++)   /* Loop 2 */
    B[i] = 0;
```

Assembly code

```
/* r0 and r1 contain the base addresses of A and B
   i is mapped to r2
   N is contained in r3 */

mov r10, 0              /* store 0 in r10 */
mov r2, 0               /* i = 0 */
.loop1:
    cmp r2, r3          /* compare i with N */
    beq .exit1          /* go to exit1 if i==N */
    lsl r4, r2, 2       /* r4 = i * 4, size of int is 4 bytes */
    add r5, r0, r4      /* address of A[i] */
    st  r10, [r5]       /* A[i] = 0 */
    add r2, r2, 1       /* i = i + 1 */
    b   .loop1          /* Jump to the beginning of loop1 */

.exit1:
mov r2, 0               /* i = 0 */
.loop2:
    cmp r2, r3          /* compare i with N */
    beq .exit2          /* go to exit2 if i==N */
    lsl r4, r2, 2       /* r4 = i * 4, size of int is 4 bytes */
    add r5, r1, r4      /* address of B[i] */
    st  r10, [r5]       /* B[i] = 0 */
    add r2, r2, 1       /* i = i + 1 */
    b .loop2            /* Jump to the beginning of loop2 */

.exit2:
```

This is a very standard piece of code where we initialise arrays. This pattern of writing code is also very common among programmers, particularly novice programmers. However, there are sub-optimal decisions in this code. We have two loops: *loop1* and *loop2*.

Notice that the only difference in the bodies of these loops is that we are updating different arrays. Otherwise, the code is identical. Instead of executing so many extra instructions, we can fuse loops 1 and 2, and create a larger loop. This will ensure that we execute as few extra instructions as possible. Most of the code to update the loop variable i and to check for loop termination can be shared. Let us thus try to rewrite the code.

C code

```c
for (i=0; i<N; i++){   /* Loop 1 */
    A[i] = 0;
    B[i] = 0;
}
```

Assembly code

```
/* r0 and r1 contain the base addresses of A and B
   i is mapped to r2
   N is contained in r3 */

mov r10, 0
mov r2, 0               /* i = 0 */
.loop1:
    cmp r2, r3          /* compare i with N */
    beq .exit1          /* go to exit1 if i==N */
    lsl r4, r2, 2       /* r4 = i * 4, size of int is 4 bytes */
    add r5, r0, r4      /* address of A[i] */
    st  r10, [r5]       /* A[i] = 0 */

    add r5, r1, r4      /* address of B[i] */
    st  r10, [r5]       /* B[i] = 0 */

    add r2, r2, 1       /* i = i + 1 */
    b   .loop1          /* Jump to the beginning of loop1 */

.exit1:
```

Let us see what we have achieved. In our original code, the body of loops 1 and 2 had 7 instructions each. Since each loop has N iterations, we shall execute $7N$ instructions per loop. In total, we shall execute $14N$ instructions.

However, now we execute far less instructions. Our loop body has just 9 instructions. We thus execute only $9N$ instructions. For large N, we save 36% of instructions, which can lead to a commensurate gain in performance. Note that we are ignoring instructions that initialise variables and instructions in the last iteration of the loop where we exit the loop (small constants).

Loop Unrolling

This is by far one of the most popular optimisations in this area. It has a very wide scope of applicability and is supported by almost all modern compilers.

The idea is as follows. Consider a loop with N iterations. We have multiple branch statements in the body of a loop. There are several ill effects of having these branch instructions. The first is that these are extra instructions in their own right. Executing them in the pipeline requires time. Additionally, they take up slots in the instruction window and ROB. If we can to a certain extent get rid of these additional branch instructions, we will be able to decrease the number of dynamic instructions appreciably.

The second effect is that every branch needs to be predicted and there is a finite chance of a misprediction. The number of mispredictions increases with the number of branches. A misprediction is very expensive in terms of time because we need to flush the pipeline. Hence, eliminating as many branches as possible is a good strategy.

To motivate the discussion, let us consider the following piece of C code.

C code

```
for (i=0; i<10; i++){
    sum = sum + i;
}
```

Assembly code

```
mov r0, 0          /* sum = 0 */
mov r1, 0          /* i = 0 */

.loop:
cmp r1, 10
beq .exit          /* if (i == 10) exit */
add r0, r0, r1     /* sum = sum + i */
add r1, r1, 1      /* i = i + 1 */
b .loop            /* next iteration */

.exit:
```

In this code, in each loop iteration we have 5 assembly instructions. Three of them are only for maintaining proper control flow within the loop and only the add instruction is for the data flow. It is pretty much the only instruction that is doing any real work.

This seems to be a rather inefficient use of the instructions in a typical loop. Most of the instructions in the body of the loop are just for ensuring that the loop's control flow is correct. However, we are not doing a lot of work inside the loop. Only 1 out of the 5 instructions is doing the useful work. Given that we already know that the number of iterations in the loop (i.e., 10), we should make an effort to do more useful work.

Hence, let us try to reduce the number of branches, and increase the amount of useful work done per iteration. Let us *unroll* the loop. This basically means that we need to fuse multiple iterations of a loop into a single iteration. Let us show the equivalent C code and assembly code.

C code

```
for (i=0; i<10; i+=2){
    sum = sum + i + (i+1);
}
```

Assembly code

```
mov r0, 0          /* sum = 0 */
mov r1, 0          /* i = 0 */

.loop:
cmp r1, 10
beq .exit          /* if (i == 10) exit */

add r0, r0, r1     /* sum = sum + i */
add r1, r1, 1      /* i = i + 1 */
add r0, r0, r1     /* sum = sum + i */

add r1, r1, 1      /* i = i + 1 */
b .loop            /* next iteration */

.exit:
```

We have basically fused two consecutive iterations into one single iteration. Let us now work out the math in terms of the number of instructions. To keep the maths elegant let us only count the 10 successful iterations, and not the one in which we don't enter the body of the loop because the comparison is successful. Before unrolling we executed 50 instructions (5 instructions in the body of the loop). However, now we execute 35 instructions because we have 5 iterations, and there are 7 instructions in the body of the loop. There is thus a savings of 30%, which is significant by all means.

Can we unroll further? Well, yes. We can fuse 4 or 8 iterations into one. However, this does not mean that we can unroll indefinitely. Otherwise, we will replace the entire loop with one large piece of unrolled code. There definitely are limits to unrolling. If we unroll too much, the code size will become very large, it will not fit in the instruction cache (small instruction memory), and we will simply have too many cache misses. If we have multiple programs resident in memory then we might also run out of memory. However, within limits, unrolling is a very effective technique.

5.4.3   Software Pipelining

Let us now come to one of the most difficult optimisations. Note that till now, we have not concerned ourselves with the details of the pipeline; however, this optimisation is very important in the context of modern pipelines. It takes into account instruction latencies and also the nature of hazards in a pipeline.

The key insight used in software pipelining is as follows. Loop iterations often execute inefficiently because of slow instructions. For example, if we have a load and a consumer instruction that uses its value, we have the possibility of a load-use hazard (see Section 2.1.4). Particularly, with a slow cache, waiting for a load instruction to return its value is a very expensive proposition. We would love to do useful work in the time being. However, we often might not have enough instructions in the loop iteration to execute between a load and its consumer. The key insight is to bring instructions from other iterations to fill this void. This will ensure that we waste as few cycles as possible. In addition, it is possible to optimise this technique to enable greater ILP, and make it possible to parallelise code with loops on multi-issue processors.

Let us consider the following piece of code.

C code

```c
int A[300], B[300];
...
for(i=0; i<300; i++){
    A[i] = B[i];
}
```

Assembly code

```
1   /* Assume the base address of A is in r0
2           and B is in r1 */
3   mov r2, 0              /* i = 0 */
4   mov r10, 0             /* offset = 0 */
5
6   .loop:
7       cmp r2, 300        /* termination check */
8       beq .exit
9
10      add r3, r1, r10 /* r3 = addr(B) + offset */
11      ld r5, 0[r3]       /* r5 = B[i] */
12
13      add r4, r0, r10 /* r4 = addr(A) + offset */
14      st r5, 0[r4]       /* A[i] = r5 (= B[i]) */
15
```

```
16       add r2, r2, 1    /* i = i + 1 */
17       lsl r10, r2, 2   /* offset = i * 4 */
18
19       b .loop
20
21   .exit:
```

We show the code of a simple loop that does an element wise copy from array B to array A. Note that we introduced the *offset* variable stored in $r10$ for the sake of readability. We could have incremented $r2$ by 4 in each iteration instead.

Other than the statements that manage the loop and compare the loop variable i with 300, we can divide the statements into three blocks.

Block	Lines	Statements	Role
L (load)	10 - 11	add r3, r1, r10 ld r5, 0[r3]	Read $B[i]$
S (store)	13 - 14	add r4, r0, r10 st r5, 0[r4]	Write to $A[i]$
I (increment)	16 - 17	add r2, r2, 1 lsl r10, r2, 2	Increment i

There are dependences between these blocks: $L \rightarrow S \xrightarrow{a} I$. Here "$\rightarrow$" denotes a RAW dependence and $\xrightarrow{a}$ denotes an anti or WAR dependence. Let us now introduce some new notation here. Let block L^k denote the load block in iteration k. Let the superscript represent the iteration number (starting from 0).

For such codes, we have a problem. In an in-order machine if we have a slow L1 cache that takes 3 cycles, we unnecessarily have to stall for one cycle between the load and store instructions. If we have an even slower L1 cache, we need to stall for more cycles. In an OOO machine, things can be slightly better. An OOO machine can automatically resolve WAR dependences. The only real dependence is the chain of increments to the loop variable. Let us make a very important observation here. **If we know the value of the loop variable for each iteration before hand, we can execute the iterations in parallel.** It turns out we can do something in the compiler to expose more instruction level parallelism.

Now, let us write all of these blocks in a linear (column wise fashion), and try to find a pattern. See Figure 5.11.

Let us explain Figure 5.11 very carefully. We first show 5 iterations of the loop. In each iteration, we show the value of the loop iterator, i, which increases from 0 to 4. In each iteration, we execute the three blocks of statements: L, S, and I. In the typical scheme of things, we first execute iteration 0, then iteration 1, and so on.

Let us change the order of execution of instructions. Let us execute instructions in the following order: $L^0 \rightarrow S^0 \rightarrow L^1 \rightarrow I^0 \rightarrow S^1 \rightarrow L^2 \rightarrow I^1 \ldots$. This method of execution is referred to as *software pipelining*. We will very soon explain its connection with real pipelining as we have studied in Chapter 2. Let us understand the way we are proposing to execute these statements. Refer to Figure 5.12, where we show a graphical view of the order of execution.

Let us first convince ourselves that we execute exactly the same set of blocks in Figure 5.12 and Figure 5.11. It is just that the order of evaluation is different. Now, how is this related to pipelining? Let us look at the diagram deeply. In a normal execution we proceed column-wise (iteration by iteration). However, in this case we proceed row-wise. This is the crux of the idea.

Consider iteration 2. The diagram looks as if iteration 2 is going from one stage (row) to the next. Let us see why. First we execute L^2. The we move to the next row, which we can consider to be a stage. In this stage we execute S^2. Then we move to the next row (or stage), where we execute I^2. Given that an iteration is logically seen to move between rows, we draw an analogy with pipelining, and refer to such coding styles as *software pipelining*. We treat each row in the figure as a pipeline stage.

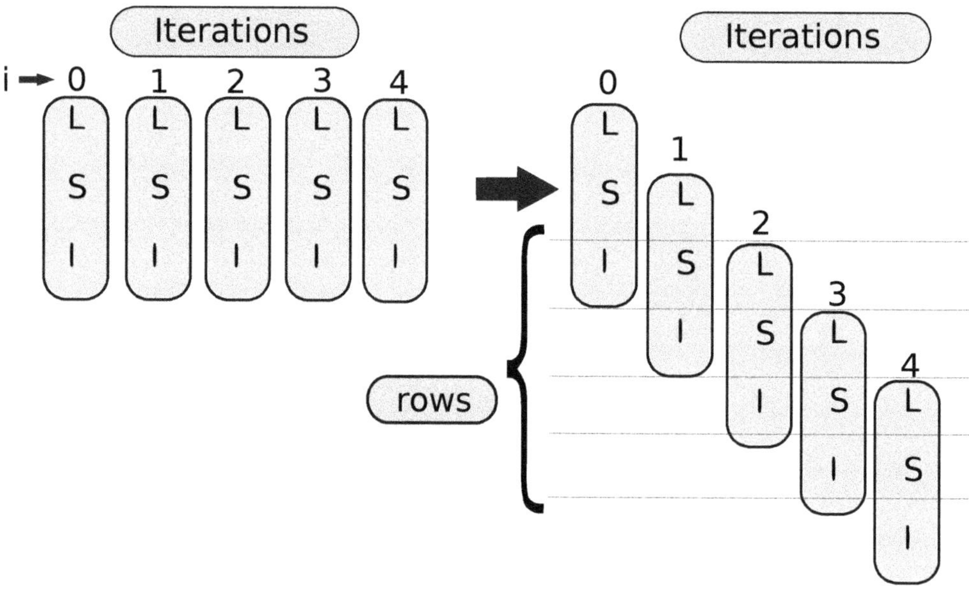

Figure 5.11: Overview of software pipelining

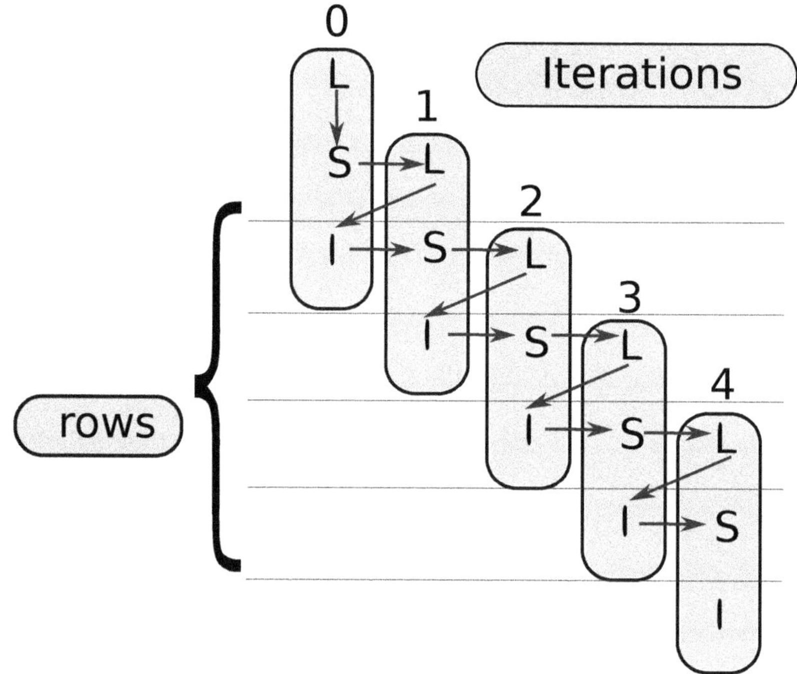

Figure 5.12: Flow of execution

Let us now look at correctness issues. Recall that there is a single loop variable i and the variable offset (stored in $r10$) that is derived from i. If we are executing I^0, then S^1, and then L^2, we have a problem. I^0 will increment i from 0 to 1. S^1 will see the right value of i and $offset$. However, L^2 needs to see $i = 2$ and $offset = 8$; it will however see $i = 1$ and $offset = 4$. This is a *loop-carried dependence*, where one iteration of a loop is dependent on the values (in this case it is i and $offset$) computed by another iteration of the loop. Thus, this execution style will be incorrect, unless we do something.

Definition 29
A loop-carried dependence is defined as a dependence between two statements within a loop, where the latter statement depends on a value that has been computed by the former statement in a previous iteration of the loop.

To solve this problem, let us create three loop variables, instead of one (i.e., i). Let us save them in registers $r6$, $r7$, and $r8$. Let us assign $r6$ (initialised to 0) to iteration 0, $r7$ (initialised to 1) to iteration 1, and $r8$ (initialised to 2) to iteration 2. Let their corresponding offsets be stored in the registers $r10$, $r11$, and $r12$. Now, there is no problem. There is no dependence between the instructions in the row that contains I^0, S^1, and L^2. Let us now move to the next row. It contains I^1, S^2, and L^3. I^1 and S^2 have their versions of the loop variable – in registers $r7$ and $r8$ respectively. What about iteration 3? Let us assume that it uses the same loop variable as iteration 0. Since iteration 0 is over, L^3 can use its loop variable, which is stored in register $r6$. This means that at this point $r6$ should contain 3 and the corresponding offset should be 12. We can indeed ensure this by modifying I^0. Instead of adding 1 to the loop variable stored in $r6$, it needs to add 3. In other words, we use three different loop variables stored in registers $r6$, $r7$, and $r8$ and corresponding offsets in registers $r10$, $r11$, and $r12$. When we increment the loop variable in the last block (I), instead of adding 1, we add 3. This value is then used by a subsequent iteration. For example, iteration 3 uses the loop variable of iteration 0, iteration 4 uses the loop variable of iteration 1, and so on. Note that in all cases the corresponding offsets get computed correctly because we just perform a left shift on the loop variable to compute the offset. Figure 5.13 shows this graphically. Note that since the loop variable and offset are intertwined we will not mention both of them all the time. Whenever, we mention loop variables, it should be inferred that we are also referring to the corresponding offset in the same context.

The three loop variables for iterations 0, 1, and 2 are stored in registers $r6$, $r7$, and $r8$ respectively. When the first block of iteration 3 runs, it needs to see the loop variable equal to 3. It uses $r6$, which has already been incremented by block I^0 to 3. Likewise, iteration 4, needs to see the loop variable (stored in $r7$) equal to 4. Block I^1 increments $r7$ (initialised to 1) by 3 to contain 4.

Before writing the code, we need to understand that we have one more constraint. All the iterations of a loop need to have the same code. We thus cannot make each row of Figure 5.13 an iteration of the loop. It does not have the same content. Let us thus unroll the loop and fuse three iterations into one. The content of each fused iteration (three rows) is as follows (also see Figure 5.14):

```
/* First Row */
add  r6,  r6,  3      /* I0 */
lsl  r10,  r6,  2

add  r4,  r0,  r11    /* S1 */
st   r5,  0[r4]

add  r3,  r1,  r12    /* L2 */
ld   r5,  0[r3]

/* Second Row */
add  r7,  r7,  3      /* I1 */
lsl  r11,  r7,  2

add  r4,  r0,  r12    /* S2 */
```

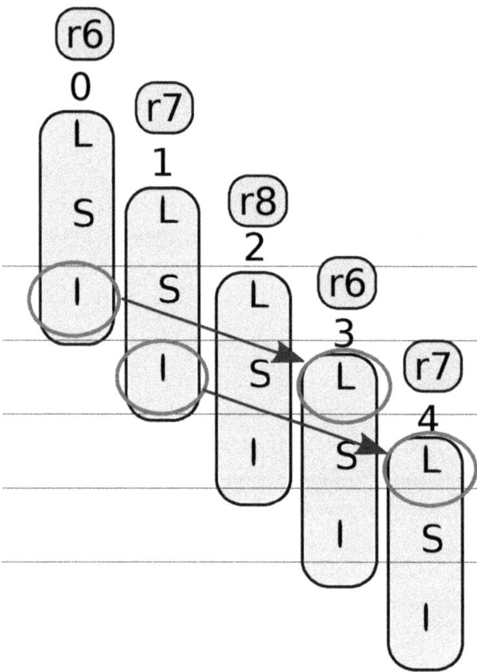

Figure 5.13: Updating the loop variables and corresponding offsets

```
st r5, 0[r4]

add r3, r1, r10   /* L3 */
ld r5, 0[r3]

/* Third Row */
add r8, r8, 3     /* I2  */
lsl r12, r8, 2

add r4, r0, r10   /* S3  */
st r5, 0[r4]

add r3, r1, r11   /* L4 */
ld r5, 0[r3]
```

Please take a look at the code in great detail and try to appreciate the fact that we are simply executing one row after the other. There is a dependence between instructions in the same iteration (same column); however, there is no dependence across instructions in the same row because we use three separate loop variables in registers $r6$, $r7$, and $r8$ respectively. Furthermore, in the same iteration $r5$ contains the value that is loaded, and subsequently stored in a different array. Between L^k and S^k, $r5$ is not overwritten by instructions from another iteration.

Let us discuss correctness by focusing on a row that has three entries. The ideal sequence of execution is $L^k \to S^k \to I^k$. However, now we execute $L^k \to I^{k-1} \to S^k \to L^{k+1} \to I^k$. We are basically executing extra instructions from other iterations in between two blocks of instructions in an iteration. This does not cause an issue because there are no dependences between L^k and I^{k-1}, or I^{k-1} and S^k. Similarly, the sequence $S^k \to L^{k+1} \to I^k$ does not violate any dependences primarily because we use different loop variables for different iterations. Since no dependences are violated, there is no difference between an

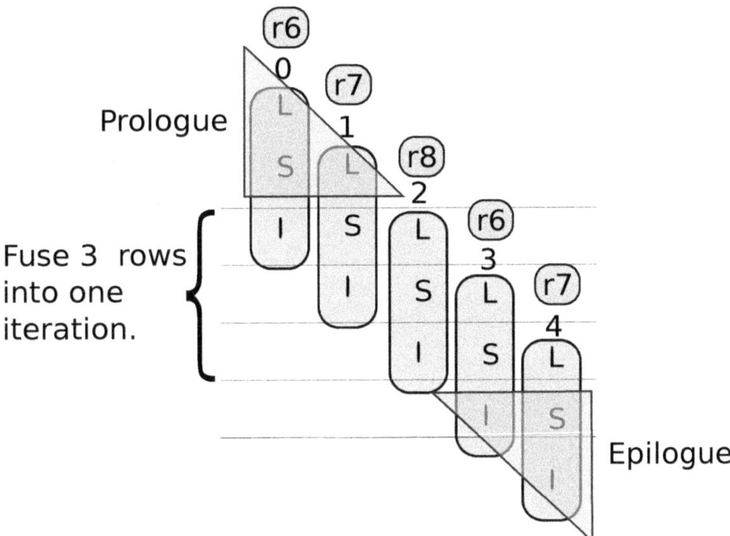

Figure 5.14: Fusing three iterations into one

execution without software pipelining and an execution with software pipelining. They are identical as far as correctness is concerned.

Let us now consider some corner cases. If a loop has a lot of iterations, we can unroll it by a factor of 3, and execute it in this fashion. However, there are some instructions that are not a part of this code. Look at the top of Figure 5.14. Instructions L^0, S^0, and L^1 are not a part of the fused loop. They need to be executed before the main loop starts. This piece of code is known as the prologue. Similarly, instructions I^3, S^4, and I^4 are a part of the epilogue that needs to execute separately, and in the correct sequence. In terms of correctness nothing changes; however in terms of overhead this is a minor overhead because we do not get the benefits of software pipelining for these codes. Nevertheless, when the number of iterations is large, this overhead is negligible. There is a rich theory of software pipelining to cater to the general case where we can have all kinds of dependences between instructions. The reader should refer to the work of Bob Rau [Rau, 1994] and Monica Lam [Lam, 1988].

We can do slightly better if we have more registers. There is a dependence between the L and S blocks even between different iterations because they use the same register $r5$. This precludes us from executing S^1 and L^2 in parallel. If we have a multi-issue in-order pipeline then we would want to execute S^1 and L^2 simultaneously. Let us try to do some renaming in software to take care of such issues. Similar to hardware renaming, the natural solution in this case will be to create three versions of $r5$ (one for each iteration).

Let us give ourselves some more room by considering a system that has 32 registers instead of the 16 that we have. For the 0th iteration let us use $r20$, and for the 1st and 2nd iterations let us use $r21$ and $r22$ respectively. The code thus looks as follows.

```
/* First Row */
add  r6, r6, 3    /* I0 */
lsl  r10, r6, 2

add  r4, r0, r11  /* S1 */
st   r21, 0[r4]
```

```
add  r3,  r1,  r12  /* L2 */
ld   r22,  0[r3]

/* Second Row */
add  r7,  r7,  3    /* I1 */
lsl  r11,  r7,  2

add  r4,  r0,  r12  /* S2 */
st   r22,  0[r4]

add  r3,  r1,  r10  /* L3 */
ld   r20,  0[r3]

/* Third Row */
add  r8,  r8,  3    /* I2  */
lsl  r12,  r8,  2

add  r4,  r0,  r10  /* S3  */
st   r20,  0[r4]

add  r3,  r1,  r11  /* L4 */
ld   r21,  0[r3]
```

Now, there are no dependences between the S, I, and L blocks. They can be executed in parallel. However, we cannot arbitrarily keep on doing this for larger loops because we will run out of registers. There is thus a trade-off between the number of registers and the degree of software pipelining. More are the registers in our code, less are the dependences, and more is the ILP.

Advantages of Software Pipelining:

Let us list out the advantages:

1. Between a load and its use there are 3 instructions, as opposed to 1 earlier. Thus, we can tolerate a slower L1 cache, and we do not have to introduce any pipeline bubbles in an in-order pipeline. This can be further increased by increasing the level of software pipelining (create rows of 6 instructions for example). Note that this is one of the biggest advantages of software pipelining in in-order machines. Instead of compulsorily introducing stalls in the case of load-use hazards, we can insert instructions from other loop iterations. This crucial insight allows us to get rid of the penalty associated with load-use hazards almost entirely.

2. By using more registers we can make the three blocks, I, S, and L, independent of each other. They can be executed in parallel on a machine that allows us to issue more than one instruction per cycle.

3. Assume that the original loop had N iterations. There was a chain of N RAW dependences between consecutive updates to the loop variable ($0 \rightarrow 1 \rightarrow 2 \rightarrow \ldots \rightarrow (N-1)$). In the case of software pipelining, this chain of dependences (critical path) got compressed to roughly a third: $0 \rightarrow 3 \rightarrow 6 \ldots \ldots \lfloor N/3 \rfloor$. Shorter dependence chains imply higher ILP, because it means that we can issue more instructions in parallel.

Software Pipelining Without Loop Unrolling

Note that loop unrolling is not a necessary feature of software pipelining. Even though most of the time both the optimisations are used together, we can have software pipelining that does not use loop unrolling. The main reason that we used loop unrolling is because when we brought together instructions from three different iterations, we needed three separate loop variables. We kept them in three separate registers.

Instead of keeping different variables for each iteration, we can instead **exploit the relationship between them**. Let us explain with the same example. To make things simple, let us modify the original C code such that each line corresponds to a block of 1-2 assembly instructions in a typical RISC ISA. In each block we never have two memory accesses.

Original C code

```
int A[300], B[300];
for(i=0; i<300; i++){
    A[i] = B[i];
}
```

Simpler C code

```
int A[300], B[300];
int i = 0;
.loop: if (i<300){
    t = B[i]; /* L */
    A[i] = t; /* S */
    i++;      /* I */
    goto .loop;
}
```

In a typical software pipelined execution the ordering is $I^0 \rightarrow S^1 \rightarrow L^2 \rightarrow I^1 \rightarrow S^2 \rightarrow L^3$. Let us try to change the code such that we overlap instructions of different iterations but we do not unroll the loop. Let us just write the body of the loop.

Body of the loop

```
    i++;          /* I */
    A[i] = t;     /* S */
    t = B[i+1];   /* L */

    goto .loop;
```

Let us analyse the sequence of operations when $i = 10$: $\boxed{\text{i=11}} \rightarrow \boxed{\text{A[11] = t}} \rightarrow \boxed{\text{t = B[12]}} \rightarrow \boxed{\text{i = 12}} \rightarrow \boxed{\text{A[12] = t}} \rightarrow \boxed{\text{t = B[13]}} \rightarrow \ldots$. Consider the operation $A[12] = B[12]$. In between them the only operation is $i = i + 1$, which sets i to 12. However, this does not induce any problems in correctness because the I block does not modify t. Similarly, for the loop variable, i, we increment it by 1 every cycle, and thus this is also correct. The only disadvantage is that we need an additional increment operation to compute the address $B[i + 1]$. We need to add 1 to i, and then add that to the register that contains the base address of B.

This code snippet is short and tricky. As we have more instructions, forming such loops can get very complicated. There is essentially a trade-off between keeping loop variables in registers (earlier approach), and using an arithmetic relationship between them to compute the array indices (this approach).

Alternative Method of Doing Software Pipelining

Consider the following example that uses an alternative method. We have deliberately written the C code in a way such that each line corresponds to roughly 1-2 lines of assembly code. There is only one memory operation per line.

SW pipelined version

```
int A[300], B[300];
for(i=0; i<300; i+= 3){
    t1 = B[i];
    t2 = B[i+1];
    t3 = B[i+2];

    t11 = t1 * 5;
    t12 = t2 * 5;
    t13 = t3 * 5;

    A[i]   = t11;
    A[i+1] = t12;
    A[i+2] = t13;
}
```

C code

```
int A[300], B[300];
for(i=0; i<300; i++){
    t1 = B[i];
    t2 = t1 * 5;
    A[i] = t2;
}
```

In this piece of code, we unroll the loop by a factor of 3, and then mix the instructions from the three iterations.

5.5 EPIC Processors

Can we do renaming at the level of the compiler and then schedule instructions in software akin to an OOO processor? If the compiler does renaming, it needs to be aware of the details of the hardware at a level that is lower than the instruction set. This further means that a compiled program (a binary) will not be able to run on a different machine (with a slightly different internal organisation). Indeed, there are processors of this type. They are known as EPIC machines (Explicitly Parallel Instruction Computing). A classic example of an EPIC processor was the Intel® Itanium® processor [Sharangpani and Arora, 2000]. It required sophisticated compilers to compile regular C code to Itanium compatible binaries. The compilers were aware of the details of the architecture.

Without going into the specific details of the Itanium architecture, let us highlight some of the advantages and disadvantages of such architectures. The advantage is based on the maxim – keep the hardware simple and move the complexity to software. This means that we don't need to have circuitry for taking care of stalls and our entire scheduling mechanism – dispatch, broadcast, wakeup, and select. Simpler hardware implies faster and more power efficient hardware.

5.5.1 Pros and Cons of EPIC and VLIW Processors

Even though this appears to be a worthy goal, there are problems. The first is that the compiler is not always aware of the dependences in a piece of code. Typical code is littered with *if* statements, *for* loops, and function calls. As a result, predicting all the dependences in advance and creating optimised code is difficult. Let us elaborate. Most EPIC processors follow the VLIW (Very Long Instruction Word) philosophy, where multiple instructions are packed together in a single *bundle* and the bundle is stored as a sequence of contiguous memory words [2]. The advantage of this approach is that we can fetch a bundle of instructions in one go and execute all the constituent instructions in parallel. Conceptually, this is similar to multi-issue in-order pipelines that we studied in Section 2.2.2. For now let us consider EPIC processors to be an advanced avatar of VLIW processors. We will explain the exact differences later.

Instructions in a bundle are fetched, decoded, and executed together (in parallel). However, creating such a bundle is difficult if there are branch instructions and memory instructions. Assume that we create a bundle of four instructions and the third instruction is a branch. Now at runtime if the branch is taken,

---

[2]A memory word is the minimum number of bytes that we can read or write in one go; it is typically 4 or 8 bytes.

then some of the instructions in the bundle will become invalid. It is thus necessary to have a mechanism to mark instructions as invalid, and either kill them or let them pass through the pipeline in the invalid state. In the latter case, when they are allowed to pass through the pipeline, such instructions will not be able to write to memory, the register file, or forward (bypass) values. This is called *predicated execution*. It simplifies the pipeline. We can just let instructions in the wrong path flow through the pipeline along with the correct instructions. The invalid instructions will not be processed by the functional units.

Now, let us consider the case of having multiple memory instructions in a bundle. For most memory instructions, we do not have an idea about their addresses at compile time. The addresses are computed at run time. There is always a possibility of a memory dependence (reads/writes to the same address) between different instructions in a bundle, or between instructions across bundles. We need elaborate hardware to take care of memory dependences, forward values between instructions if necessary, and also break a bundle if it is not possible to execute instructions together. Let us consider the following two-instruction bundle.

```
1  st r1, 8[r2]
2  ld r3, 8[r4]
```

In this case if instructions *1* and *2* have the same address then we cannot execute the load and store together. The store has to happen first, and the load later. The only issue is that it is not possible to figure out such dependences at compile time because we don't know the values that $r2$ and $r4$ will take. However, at runtime such issues will emerge, and dealing with each and every corner case requires extra hardware and extra power.

Along with performance and correctness issues, there are issues regarding the portability of the processor. By exposing details – beyond the instruction set – to the compiler, we are unnecessarily constraining the usability of compiled code. Code compiled for one processor might not work on another processor of the same family. Even if additional measures are taken to ensure mutual compatibility, there might be performance issues. As a result, the industry has by and large not adopted this solution. They have instead tried to do renaming and scheduling in hardware. Of course, this increases the complexity of the hardware, introduces concomitant power issues, and makes it hard to design a processor. Nevertheless, at least as of 2020 for general purpose programs, the benefits outweigh the costs.

Even though EPIC and VLIW processors are not used in modern laptops, desktops, and servers, they are still useful in certain situations. For example, such processors are still very common in the embedded domain particularly in digital signal processors [Eyre and Bier, 2000] and multimedia processors [Rathnam and Slavenburg, 1996]. In such cases, the code is fairly predictable, and thus it is possible to come up with good designs. Furthermore, reducing the power consumption of hardware is an important goal, and thus the EPIC and VLIW paradigms naturally fit in.

Before proceeding further, let us describe the difference between the terms VLIW and EPIC. They are often confused. Note that till now we have pretty much only mentioned that EPIC processors are modern avatars of VLIW processors: they have many features in common such as packing multiple independent instructions in a long memory word.

5.5.2 Difference between VLIW and EPIC Processors

The idea of moving all the complexity to software has been a very captivating idea for a long time. Way back in the mid eighties two important startups in this space came up: Cydrome and Multiflow. The main aim of these startups was to create a VLIW processor with very sophisticated compilers. There are some natural reasons for this thought to have come up. By the mid eighties, software had already attained a certain level of sophistication, the field of compilers had matured, and modern languages such as C and Pascal had arrived. However, hardware was slow. Intel's 386 processor had a 1μm feature size and could at best run at roughly 30 MHz. Coupled with a very low amount of memory, the hardware of those days was orders of magnitude slower than today's smart phones. Hence, increasing their performance using sophisticated compilers seemed to be a very worthy idea.

As we saw with software pipelining (Section 5.4.3), it is indeed possible to improve the available ILP significantly using compiler based techniques. Hence, early programmers logically extended the micro-programming paradigm. In this paradigm, we create a very long encoding of an instruction such that it need not be decoded, and furthermore micro-code can directly control the behaviour of different hardware units. With micro-programming, we need to know the details of the hardware including the interfaces of all of its components like the ALU and register file. We can create custom instructions by being able to directly program these components. Exposing such low-level hardware details is unthinkable as of today. It would be a very serious security risk.

However, in the good old days, this was considered acceptable. In continuation of this trend, the VLIW community proposed compilers that create large instruction words, which are similar to micro-programs, and have good visibility into the hardware. Components of the instruction's word (binary encoding) direct different functional units to perform different tasks. From packing a set of micro-instructions in a single memory word, this paradigm gradually evolved to co-locating multiple RISC instructions in the same group of memory words (referred to as a bundle). This entire bundle was sent down the pipeline. The obvious benefit was higher ILP, and the obvious shortcoming was the behaviour of branches and memory instructions in a bundle. Compilers were conservative and introduced nops (dummy instructions that don't do anything) to avoid stalls and interlocks. This strategy is alright for DSPs (digital signal processors) because their control flow and data flow are both predictable to a large extent.

However, for running general purpose programs, we need to make certain modifications to the basic VLIW design – it will be too inefficient otherwise. We thus arrived at EPIC processors, which are safe by design. This means that even if there are dependences within instructions in a bundle, or across two bundles, the processor handles them using a combination of stalls, speculation, and interlocks. VLIW processors unlike EPIC processors are not necessarily safe and correct by design. EPIC processors thus provide a virtual interface to programs, and internally also do a lot of virtualisation and translation. This ensures that a given program compiled for another EPIC processor with the same ISA but a different version, still runs correctly.

Definition 30

- *In a VLIW processor we create bundles of instructions that can either be regular RISC instructions or micro-instructions. The entire bundle of instructions is issued to the pipeline as an atomic unit, and then parallel execution units execute the constituent instructions. For programs that have a lot of ILP such as digital signal processing routines, this approach is very beneficial because we can achieve very high ILP. However, VLIW programs often rely on the compiler for correctness, and typically have limited portability.*

- *EPIC processors are modern versions of VLIW processors, which are correct by design. In other words, it is not possible to incorrectly execute a program. The hardware assures correctness sometimes at the cost of performance. In addition, programs compiled for one EPIC machine can often execute on other machines of the same processor family that have a different internal organisation. The designers of EPIC machines provide a virtual interface to software such that it is easy for compilers to generate code. The hardware internally tries to execute the code as efficiently as possible without compromising on correctness.*

5.6   Design of the Intel Itanium Processor

Let us now discuss the reference design of an EPIC processor – the Intel Itanium Processor. Intel and HP® together decided to work on a new EPIC processor and released the Itanium in 2001. Note that designing a VLIW processor would not have been the best thing to do because we never want to compromise on correctness. We need to ensure that irrespective of the compiler, the code always works correctly. Hence, creating an EPIC processor that works correctly in the face of nondeterminism due to branch misprediction, cache misses, and interrupts/exceptions, is the best way to go forward. Subsequently, Itanium 2 was released in 2002. However, since our aim is to describe the core concepts underlying an EPIC architecture, we shall mostly describe the architecture of the basic Itanium processor. We source most of the details from the paper by Sharangpani and Arora [Sharangpani and Arora, 2000]

Note that we take some creative liberties in this section particularly for the assembly code. Instead of showing proper Itanium assembly code, we have shown equivalent code in *SimpleRisc* for the sake of readability, and easier explanation. In addition, we try to generalise the architecture and describe multiple competing mechanisms wherever they exist.

5.6.1   Overview of the Constraints

Let us now start with some basic questions with regards to an EPIC architecture. What does a compiler do for us? It can find the dependences between instructions, and schedule them if it is aware of the latencies of execution units. We still need a branch predictor to sustain a high fetch bandwidth. Compilers cannot predict branches with 100% accuracy because the outcomes of branches depend on values obtained at run time. We need the decode unit as well because instructions have to be parsed, checked for errors, and converted into an internal representation that is easy to process. In fact, we conceptually need the rename stage as well. This is required because we still need to get rid of WAR and WAW hazards.

The unit that we can get rid off is the scheduler: instruction window, wakeup, broadcast, and select. Since we are supposed to know about the instructions in the pipeline (at compile time), we can schedule them such that all RAW dependences are taken care of. However, this is easier said than done because we have to very accurately take structural hazards into account.

Moreover, we do need the register file access stage and definitely the execution units. Figure 5.15 shows an overview of the Itanium architecture. It is necessary to keep referring to this figure throughout this section.

5.6.2   Fetch Stage

The design philosophy of the Itanium processor was to create a very high performance server processor. In line with this philosophy, the designers created a processor that could fetch up to six instructions per cycle. This requires two pieces of sophisticated hardware: a high bandwidth i-cache, and a very accurate branch predictor.

The key to having a high fetch bandwidth is to have an i-cache that supports a high throughput. The Itanium thus has a 16 KB 4-way set associative i-cache that can provide 32 bytes per cycle. In these 32 bytes, we can fit six instructions, which are grouped into bundles of three instructions each. There is a possibility of a rate mismatch between the fetch engine and subsequent stages of the pipeline. In such a case, it is advisable to have a buffer to store instructions that have been fetched, yet are not able to enter the pipeline. Itanium uses a *decoupling buffer* that can store up to 8 such bundles. Note that a *bundle* is an important concept in an EPIC architecture. We typically treat a bundle as an indivisible unit. The compiler creates bundles very carefully. In addition, the three instructions in a bundle should not have any mutual dependences between them.

Subsequently, a highly accurate branch predictor is required. This is because the branch misprediction penalty is nine cycles in Itanium. Given that the compiler has a significant involvement in such

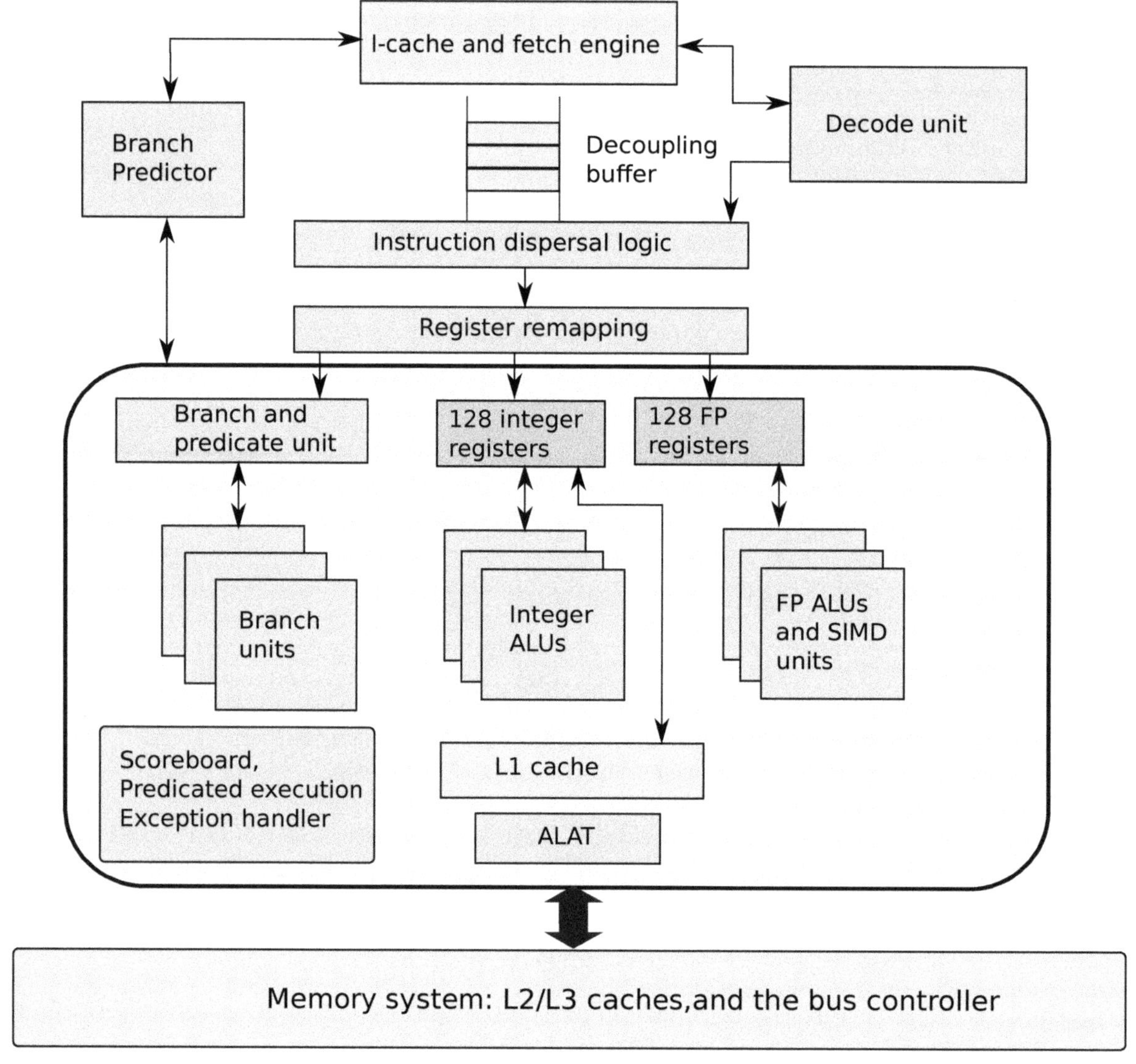

Figure 5.15: The Itanium processor (©[2000]IEEE. Reprinted, with permission, from [Sharangpani and Arora, 2000]).

architectures, we can send a lot of compile time information to the branch predictors. Let us briefly outline the various strategies followed by the designers of the Itanium processor.

Compiler Directed Since the compiler plays a very active role in such architectures, we spend much more time analysing the nature of loops particularly in numerically intensive code. In such codes, the behaviour of loops is often very predictable. We have four special registers called target address registers (TARs). It is the compiler's job to enter the branch targets into these registers via special instructions called *hints*. The hints contain the PC of the branch and the target address. Whenever the next program counter matches the PC contained in any of the TAR registers, we automatically predict taken, and extract the branch target from the corresponding TAR register. Thus, the entire process is very fast, and very energy efficient as well. We can easily accomplish this series of tasks within one cycle. How can the compiler be so sure? In most scientific codes, we exactly know the value of the loop index and the target addresses; hence, the compiler can easily analyse such loops and let the hardware know about the loop continuation and termination information.

Traditional Branch Prediction Not all branches are that well behaved. We thus do need high performance branch predictors. Itanium has a large PAp branch predictor that can predict branches very well.

Multi-way Branches Note that Itanium instructions are stored in 3-instruction bundles. Typically compilers ensure that the last instruction in a bundle is a branch. This means that just in case it is mispredicted, the earlier instructions in the bundle are still on the correct path. However, this is not always possible. Just in case there are multiple branches within a bundle, we need a method to handle this situation. Note that in this case, if we consider a bundle as a whole, it is a multi-way branch statement. It has many possible targets depending on the behaviour of the branches contained within it. Such a set of branches is also referred to as a *multi-way branch*.

We need to predict the first taken branch within a bundle. This means that if a bundle has three instructions, we have four possible choices for the first instruction that succeeds the current bundle: default, target of the first instruction, target of the second instruction, or the target of the third instruction. Itanium uses a history based predictor for each bundle. This predicts the first instruction that is most likely a taken branch. Once we predict this instruction, we can get its target from the branch target cache.

Itanium has other traditional modules such as the return address stack. They were already discussed in Chapter 3.

Loop Exit Prediction After we decode the instructions, we get to know of the opcodes of all the instructions including the branches within a bundle. At this stage Itanium uses a perfect loop-exit predictor, which can override earlier predictions. We need to initialise this predictor with the iteration count of the loop. The compiler marks the loop-branch (branch that takes us to the beginning of the loop) with a special instruction. The loop exit predictor keeps decrementing the loop count, every time we encounter this instruction. It can thus figure out the last iteration, and we can avoid mispredicting the last branch in a loop. This is not a very effective optimisation for large loops (large number of iterations). However, for small loops, this is a very good optimisation; it avoids a lot of mispredictions.

The last stage of the fetch unit also has the role of processing software initiated prefetch instructions. Itanium's compiler plays a fairly aggressive role in prefetching instructions.

5.6.3   Instruction Dispersal Stage

After fetching all our instructions, we keep the instruction bundles in the decoupling buffer. Having such buffers reduces the mismatch between the rate of fetching instructions and the rate of executing them.

Let us now look at instruction dispersal or instruction delivery – providing instructions to the execution units. Our explicit aim was to avoid the use of schedulers. Hence, we need to find a way to avoid data and structural hazards without using expensive hardware such as an instruction window, wakeup, select and broadcast hardware. We disperse (synonym of dispatch in the current context) two bundles of instructions (6 instructions) at a time via the issue ports. The Itanium processor has 9 issue ports: 2 for memory, 2 for integer, 2 for floating point, and 3 for branch instructions. Within each bundle, we disperse the instructions from the earlier to the later. For dispersing instructions, we need to respect both data as well as control dependences. Let us elaborate on how these are handled.

Data Hazards

Ideally, the compiler should find three instructions that are absolutely independent and place them in a bundle. However, this is not always possible. In such cases, we do have the option of putting *nop* instructions in the bundle; however, here again there are associated performance penalties because of wasted issue slots. Hence, it is sometimes wiser to have instructions within a bundle with data dependences between them – we get more performance than using *nop*s. There are two features in the IA-64 ISA (Itanium's ISA) that make this easier.

1. It is possible to have a compare instruction and a conditional branch that is dependent on its outcome in the same bundle. Itanium can internally forward the result of the comparison to the branch.

2. In the worst case, it is necessary to use *stop bits* in instructions. Let us consider the instructions in the order from the earliest instruction to the latest. Some instructions will have their stop bits set to 1, and the rest of the instructions will have their stop bits set to 0. The instructions between two instructions with their stop bits set to 1, are independent of each other. As a result, we do not need sophisticated hardware to check and mark dependences between instructions. Instructions between two stop bits are also referred to as an *instruction group*. Within an instruction group we have parallelism, and the instructions can be issued simultaneously. Instructions that are not marked by the compiler as independent, need to execute in program order.

Structural Hazards

Instead of using sophisticated decoding logic, Itanium has a very simple way of figuring out the resource requirements of instructions. It uses a 4-bit template field in each bundle. This indicates the type of instructions in a bundle: M (memory), I (integer), F (floating point) and B (branch). With these 8 bits (4 bits for each bundle), the processor can very quickly find the resource requirements of all the instructions, and schedule the issue ports accordingly.

5.6.4   Register Remapping Stage

We unfortunately do need register remapping (sophisticated form of renaming) here also. It would have been the best if we could have avoided this stage since with advanced compiler analyses it is possible to analyse the structure of dependences in a program very well. However, as we shall see, Itanium has extended the concept of register renaming and in fact the term that is used in the paper by Sharangpani and Arora [Sharangpani and Arora, 2000] is "register remapping", which is much more than renaming.

If we think about it, we would still need renaming in some form. This is because we need to get rid of false dependences. One approach is that the compiler is aware of the physical register file, and directly assigns architectural registers to physical registers while generating the binary itself. This approach limits portability and introduces dependences between instructions using the same physical register. This is because the compiler cannot predict with 100% accuracy, and moreover there are several sources of nondeterminism in the execution of modern programs: branch misprediction, and misses in the memory system. Let us look at what Itanium does.

Virtual Registers

Itanium solves this problem by using virtual registers. The software assumes that the hardware has a large number of virtual registers, and thus the software simply maps variables to virtual registers. This keeps the software simple and also the code remains portable. The hardware maps the virtual registers to physical registers. The Itanium architecture has a large 128-entry register file. These 128 entries are partitioned into two sets [Settle et al., 2003]: 32 *static* registers that are visible to all functions and 96 *stacked* registers that have limited visibility.

Specifically, Itanium optimises for two kinds of scenarios: argument passing to function calls and software pipelining. When we are making function calls, we often need to write the values of registers to memory. This is because the called function may overwrite the registers. Hence, it is a good idea to store the values of the registers in memory, and later restore them once the function returns. Assume that the function *foo* is calling the function *bar*. Now, there are two schemes: caller saved and callee saved. In the *caller saved* scheme, the code in the function *foo* is assigned the responsibility of saving and later restoring the registers that might possibly get overwritten. If we hand over this responsibility to the function *bar*, where it needs to save and restore the registers that might possibly get overwritten, then we have the *callee saved* scheme. Both of these schemes are expensive in terms of memory reads and writes.

Itanium solves this problem by allocating a different set of virtual registers to each function. This ensures that there is no possibility of different functions overwriting each other's registers unless there is an explicit intent to do so. We sometimes deliberately create an overlap between the register sets, when we want to pass arguments and return values between functions. If there is an overlap between the virtual register sets used by the caller (*foo*) and callee (*bar*) functions, then we can pass arguments and return values via virtual registers.

Let us explain with an example. In Figure 5.16, we show the example of a function call. Function *foo* calls the function *bar*. In Itanium it is possible to specify the virtual registers that contain the input arguments (in), the local variables (local), and the values to be sent to callee functions (out). In this case, let us assume that for the function *foo*, virtual registers 32 and 33 contain the input arguments, registers 34-39 contain the local variables, and register 40 contains the value that needs to be an input argument to the function *bar*. For the function *bar* we can create a different mapping. For example, we can assume that register 32 contains the input argument, and registers 33-36 contain the local variables. In this case, there is a need to map register 40 of function *foo* to register 32 of the function *bar* to pass the argument. This can be done by the hardware very easily. We just need to map these virtual registers to the same physical registers. Then unbeknownst to the functions *foo* and *bar*, arguments can be passed very easily between the functions. The need for saving and restoring registers is not there because the registers that are used by different function invocations are different. We only create an overlap in the register sets while passing parameters, otherwise, because the register sets are separate there is no need to spill registers to memory. This decreases the number of loads and stores.

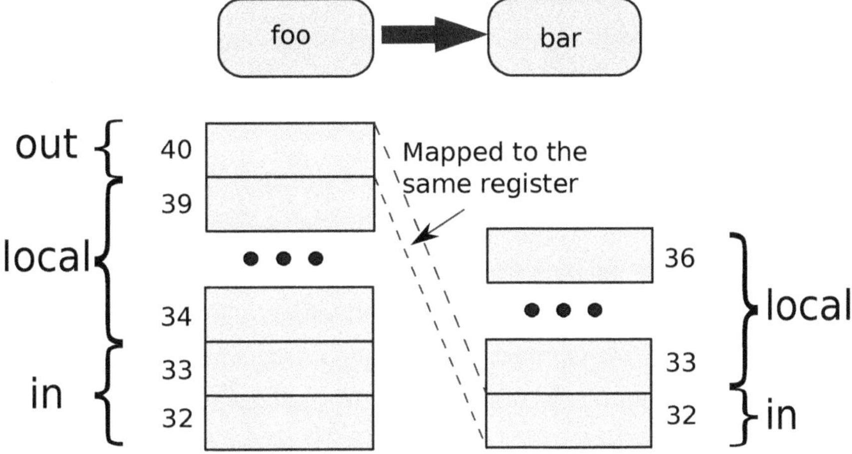

Figure 5.16: Using virtual registers for parameter passing

Register Stack Frame

We allocate a register stack frame for each function based on a special instruction added by the compiler called the *alloc* instruction. In the stack frame we store three kinds of registers: *in*, *local*, and *out*. There is a fourth optional kind called *rot*, which we shall discuss shortly. However, let us consider the first three kinds of registers first. The *in* and *local* registers are preserved across function calls. The *out* registers are meant to be accessed by callee functions and thus do not need to be preserved.

Once a function returns, the register stack frame for that function is destroyed. This is similar to a regular stack in programs that is stored in memory. Recall that a conventional stack stores the arguments and local variables of a function. It is destroyed once the function returns. Something very similar needs to be done here. We need to automatically destroy the stack frame after a return.

To summarise, we need to create a stack frame based on the number of virtual registers that the function requires (specified via the *alloc* instruction) when the function is invoked, and then destroy it once the function returns. This process of automatically managing registers across function calls reduces the work of the compiler significantly, and also reduces the unnecessary memory accesses that were happening because of saving and restoring registers.

Communicating Return Values

The last piece of the register remapping stage is communicating return values. The return value is typically communicated via a static register: $r8$. The main advantage of doing this is *tail recursion elimination*. Consider the following piece of code for the binary search routine.

```c
int bin_search(int arr[], int left, int right, int val){
        /* exit conditions */
        int mid;
        if (right < left) return -1;

        mid = (left + right) / 2;
        if(val == arr[mid])
                return mid;

        /* recursive conditions */
        if(val < arr[mid])
                return bin_search(arr, left, mid - 1, val);
        else
                return bin_search(arr, mid + 1, right, val);
}

int main(){
        ...
        result = bin_search ( ... );
next:
        printf("%d", result);
        ...
}
```

Here, we show a traditional binary search routine. All the parts of the code that are not relevant have been replaced with three dots (...). Let us consider the sequence of function calls. *main* calls *bin_search*, which is called recursively over and over again. The final answer is computed in the last call to *bin_search*, and then this answer is propagated to *main* via a sequence of return calls. This pattern is known as *tail recursion*, where the statement that produces the result is the last statement in the function. One way of optimising such patterns is to store the final answer at a known location, and return directly to the label that is after the call to *bin_search* in the *main* function (label *next* in the code). This will help us eliminate the overheads of tens of return calls. Most compilers are able to recognise such patterns very easily, and they directly replace a sequence of returns with a direct jump to the line after the first call to the recursive function (label *next* in this case). In such cases, it makes sense to store the return value in a fixed place that is outside the register stack. This is exactly what is done, and that's why we save the return value in a static register.

Support for Software Pipelining

Itanium has special support for software pipelining. Recall that in Section 5.4.3 we needed different sets of registers for different iterations of a software pipelined loop. Specifically, to store the loop variable we needed different registers, otherwise, there would have been a correctness issue. In fact one of the major limiting factors while doing software pipelining is that we run out of registers. The designers of the Itanium processor have very nicely solved this issue. They have created a rotating register set for storing the loop variable. There is a method to keep track of the iteration of a loop. For every iteration, the hardware automatically assigns new loop variables in a set of virtual registers. This ensures that we can seamlessly implement software pipelining without bothering about manually assigning different loop variables to different iterations. This also significantly simplifies the process of code generation.

Overflows

Let us now consider the case when we run out of registers. Recall that we only have 128 registers, and if we call a lot of functions, or have large loops, we will clearly run out of registers. The only option that we have is to store the registers in memory, and later on restore them. This is known as *register spilling*. Itanium thankfully has an automatic mechanism for doing this.

Definition 31
The process of saving registers in memory, when we run out of registers, is known as spilling (or register spilling). These spilled *registers are later on restored when they are required.*

Itanium has a dedicated Register Stack Engine (RSE). It keeps track of the number of registers we are using, and whenever there is an overflow it comes into action. It silently spills registers at the bottom of the register stack to a dedicated region in memory. When these registers are required, they are restored from memory back again. The programmer and compiler are blissfully unaware of this process. Unbeknownst to them, the RSE performs the task of saving and restoring registers. There is a performance penalty though. While this is happening, the pipeline is stalled for a couple of cycles, and this interferes with the execution of the current program.

5.6.5   High Performance Execution Engine

Ensuring high performance in such processors is the joint responsibility of the hardware, compiler, and the programmer. In EPIC processors, the compiler has a disproportionate role. Now, to create a high performance execution engine, the first and foremost requirement is to have a large array of functional units. At the same time, we need to ensure that control and data dependences do not get violated.

The Itanium processor uses a scoreboard based strategy to enforce dependences. Scoreboarding is a very old technique and has been around since the sixties. The first known use of scoreboarding was by the CDC 6600 machine way back in 1965. Let us look at different aspects of a modern scoreboard.

Scoreboarding

Scoreboarding [Thornton, 2000, Budde et al., 1990] is a technique that stalls instruction execution till it is guaranteed that the instructions will get the correct values for their operands. It explicitly takes WAW, WAR, and RAW hazards into account, and ensures that correctness is never compromised with.

The exact design of the Itanium Scoreboard is not available in the public domain. Let us thus try to create our own scoreboard.

Let us create a matrix (table in hardware), where the rows are the instructions listed in program order (see Figure 5.17). The columns are $finished$ (single bit), source register 1 ($rs1$), source register 2 ($rs2$), the destination register (rd), and the functional unit number (fu).

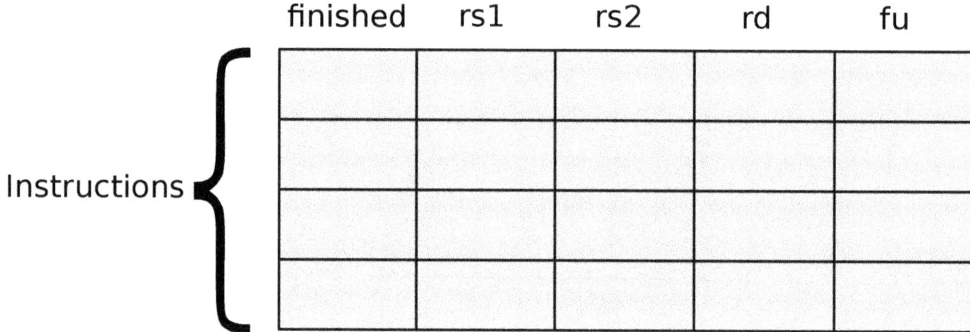

Figure 5.17: A simple scoreboard

Using this matrix, here is how we detect different hazards. We assume that this table is a content addressable array (refer to Chapter 7) that can be addressed by the content of a specific field of an entry. Furthermore, we use the same method to detect earlier instructions as in the load-store queue.

Let us introduce the terminology. For an instruction I, let the fields $I.finished$, $I.rs1$, $I.rs2$, $I.rd$, and $I.fu$ indicate the status of the instruction, ids of the source registers (1 and 2), id of the destination register, and the id of the functional unit respectively. Given a table entry E, let us use the same terminology for it as well. For example, the destination register of the instruction associated with the entry E is $E.rd$.

Now, given an instruction I, we need to create custom logic to ensure the following conditions are never violated.

WAW Hazards: Check all the earlier entries in the table. For each earlier entry E, the following expression should evaluate to false: $(E.finished = 0) \wedge (E.rd = I.rd))$. Otherwise, there is a potential WAW hazard.

WAR Hazards Similar to the earlier case, for each earlier entry E, the following expression should be false: $(E.finished = 0) \wedge ((E.rs1 = I.rd) \vee (E.rs2 = I.rd))$.

RAW Hazards Here is the corresponding expression that should always evaluate to false: $(E.finished = 0) \wedge ((E.rd = I.rs1) \vee (E.rd = I.rs2))$.

Structural Hazards The corresponding expression is $(E.finished = 0) \wedge (E.fu = I.fu)$.

The basic insight is that an unfinished earlier instruction can potentially conflict with the current instruction. Evaluating these expressions is not difficult. We need to access the matrix using different keys – destination register, source register, and functional unit number. Then we evaluate the aforementioned conditions, and if any of these conditions is true, then we stall the current instruction.

We can slightly optimise the scoreboard by avoiding costly CAM accesses for detecting RAW and WAW hazards. We can keep an array called $dest$ that is indexed by the register id. Instruction I sets $dest[rd] = I$ after getting decoded. This array is thus accessed in program order. Before issuing an instruction we read the arrays and get the instruction ids that will generate values for the source registers, and the latest instruction that writes to the destination register. An instruction thus depends on at the most three other instructions: two instructions that write to the source registers, and one that writes to the destination register. We wait for all of them to get finished. We thus automatically take care of RAW and WAW hazards in this process.

Important Point 10

Why do we need to use a CAM array for detecting WAR hazards? Why can't we use the same trick that we used for detecting WAW and RAW hazards?

Answer: *We need to write to a register in program order. Hence, there is a strict order between all the instructions that write to the same register. Thus, it suffices to remember just one instruction for let's say source 1 of instruction I. This will be the instruction that generates the value for source register 1 (rs1); it is also the most recent instruction that writes to rs1 (out of all the instructions fetched before I). We stored this information in the* dest *array and thus we created a very efficient technique to detect RAW and WAW hazards. However, this mechanism cannot be used for WAR hazards.*

For a WAR hazard, we need to find if there is any instruction in the pipeline fetched before the current instruction I that is unfinished, and reads from the register I.rd. This information is not stored in the dest *array. Thus it cannot be used in this case. Instead, we need to access every single entry in the CAM array and check if there is a WAR hazard.*

Predication

By now, we know that branch prediction is a very sensitive operation. Even a very tiny increase in the misprediction rate can severely degrade the performance. As a result a lot of processor companies spend a disproportionate amount of time designing branch predictors, and this is often one of their biggest trade secrets. Let us look at mechanisms that do not use branch prediction at all.

Consider a piece of code with a lot of loops, where the number of iterations is known in advance. Itanium has elaborate loop counters that ensure that we shall never have mispredictions in such loops. Now, consider (hypothetically) that we have a small piece of code within a very well behaved loop, which looks like this:

```
if(rand()%2 == 0)
        x = y;
else
        x = z;
```

We generate a random number. If it is even, we set x equal to y, and if it is odd, we set x equal to z. This branch is genuinely hard to predict because it is based on a random number, and thus finding a pattern is very difficult. In traditional OOO hardware, we still have to predict the direction, and statistically we will mispredict 50% of the time. Every misprediction will lead to a pipeline flush, which is a massive performance penalty. Furthermore, this is very unfair to the rest of the code, which is very well behaved. Maybe such kind of code is embedded inside a library, which is not visible to the programmer. In this case, the programmer in most cases will not even know the reason for poor performance.

We clearly need to do something to handle such cases. Flushing the pipeline is like burning down the house to kill just one mosquito inside it! Let us instead work on creating a different paradigm.

Here is the idea. Let us fully or partially execute a few more instructions in the pipeline than required. If by executing a few additional instructions, we can avoid a costly pipeline flush, which will cost us more than 20-30 cycles, it is well worth the effort. Also, the IPC for most programs is not equal to the issue width. For example, in the case of Itanium, the IPC will not be 6 most of the time because of limited ILP. We can thus find additional fetch, decode, and issue slots to send in a few more instructions for a large fraction of the time. To explain the idea, let us look at the corresponding *SimpleRisc* assembly code of an Itanium like EPIC processor.

```
1   /* mappings: x <-> r1, y <-> r2, z <-> r3 */
2
3   mod r0, r0, 2      /* assume r0 contains the output of rand(),
4                         compute the remainder when dividing it by 2 */
5
6   cmp r0, 0          /* compare */
7   beq .even
8   mov r1, r3         /* odd case */
9   b. exit
10  .even:
11  mov r1, r2         /* even case */
12
13  .exit:
```

From a cursory examination of this code, it does not look like that we can do anything. However, let us now introduce some additional hardware to open up an avenue of opportunity. Assume that the compare instruction sets two bits *po* and *pe* called the *predicate bits* corresponding to the result of the comparison. If $pe = 1$ we execute the even path (Line 11), and if $po = 1$, we execute the odd path (Lines 8 and 9).

Furthermore, let us augment each instruction in the even and odd paths with the predicate bits that need to be set to 1 for it to execute. The code thus looks as follows:

```
1   /* mappings: x <-> r1, y <-> r2, z <-> r3 */
2
3   mod r0, r0, 2      /* assume r0 contains the output of rand()
4                         compute the remainder when dividing it by 2 */
5
6   po,pe = cmp r0, 0  /* compare and set the predicates */
7   [po] mov r1, r3    /* odd case */
8   [pe] mov r1, r2    /* even case */
```

In Line 6, we set the predicate bits *po* and *pe*. Then, we use these bits for the subsequent instructions. We expect the compare instruction to be ordered before the execution of the instructions that use the predicates generated by it. Subsequently, in Line 7 and Line 8 we execute the instructions in the odd path and even path respectively.

How is this different? Note that we do not have any branch instructions. All the conditional and unconditional branch instructions have been removed. If there are no branch instructions, it implies that there are no mispredictions. The code is linear albeit for the fact that we have predicates. We fetch, decode, and issue the predicated move instructions as regular instructions. We even allow both of them to read the register file. However, the key difference lies in the execution stage. Instead of executing an instruction on the wrong path (predicate bit is 0) we nullify it. In no case, should we allow an instruction on the wrong path to update the register file or write to memory.

Thus, predication is a simple mechanism. It removes branches, and basically converts control dependences into data dependences. We simply need to read the values of the corresponding predicate registers and figure out if the instruction should execute and write back its result or not. For an instruction to do so, it needs to be on the correct branch path, and this will only happen if the values of all the predicates that the instruction depends on are 1. We thus need to compute a logical AND of all the predicate bits. In line with this argument, Itanium adds a high throughput 64-entry predicate register file, where each entry is 1 bit.

Predication sometimes is a very good mechanism, and can do wonders to the performance, particularly for cases that we have looked at. However, note that there are costs associated with this mechanism as well. It increases the number of instructions that need to be fetched, decoded, renamed, and issued. This decreases the effective throughput because a lot of these instructions might potentially be on the wrong path. Furthermore, we need a mechanism of generating and keeping track of predicates. This requires good compiler support.

5.6.6 Support for Aggressive Speculation

In Section 5.1, we introduced the notion of aggressive load speculation in OOO processors. Recall that we executed load instructions much before we were aware of their addresses and dependences. We claimed that if we could design accurate predictors, this approach would lead to large performance gains, and indeed this is so in most cases. Let us try to create a similar mechanism for EPIC processors.

Itanium has the notion of *load boosting*. Here, a load and a subset of its forward slice (dependent instructions) can be placed (boosted) at a point that is much before their actual position in the code; this is done by the compiler. This will increase the number of instructions between the load and the instructions that use its value. This means that even if the load misses in the L1 cache, and we need to go to the L2 cache or beyond, most of this delay will get hidden. By the time we encounter the use of the load, its value will mostly likely be in the L1 cache.

This mechanism can very effectively reduce the stalls associated with a read miss. However, there are several correctness issues. Assume that the load instruction encounters an exception. Maybe it accesses an illegal address. To maintain the notion of precise exceptions we need to remember this, and flag the exception only when we reach the original position of the load in the code.

Second, there might be stores between the original position of the load and the hoisted position that have the same address. In this case we will have a RAW dependence violation. Thus, we need to keep a record of all the stores between the two positions, and check for an address match. If we find such a match, the latest such store needs to forward its value to the load.

The summary of this entire discussion is that since Itanium does not have a load-store queue and we are still desirous of performing load dependence speculation, we need to implement the functionality of the LSQ using a combined software-hardware technique. Let us elaborate.

Itanium defines a hardware structure called an Advanced Load Address Table (ALAT). It contains the addresses of all the loads that have been boosted. EPIC processors such as Itanium need to define two instructions for loads: one for a normal load and one for a boosted load. Whenever the hardware encounters an instruction for a boosted load, it enters the load address into the ALAT. Subsequently, each store checks the entries of the ALAT for a match. If there is a match, then we can infer that there is a dependence violation. Thus we mark the ALAT entry as invalid.

At the original point of the load in the code, Itanium embeds a load check (ld.c) instruction. This checks the validity of the load in the ALAT. If the load is still valid, then it means that the speculation was successful, and nothing needs to be done. However, if the load is invalid, then we need to get the data from the latest store with a matching address. We thus need to reissue the load. This is exactly what is done. In such cases, the chances of getting the store data in the L1 cache itself is very high given the recency of the update. If the load had encountered an exception, then that also can be recorded in the ALAT, and the exception can be handled when the load check instruction is issued.

5.7 Summary and Further Reading

5.7.1 Summary

Summary 4

1. To further increase the performance of an out-of-order machine, we can perform four types of aggressive speculation.

   (a) Try to predict the address of a load instruction (address speculation).

   (b) Try to predict dependences between load-store instruction pairs (dependence speculation).

   (c) Try to predict the latency of a load instruction (latency speculation).

   (d) Try to predict the value returned by a load instruction (value speculation).

2. The standard approaches to make a prediction are:

   (a) Predict the last value if the prediction has a high confidence, otherwise do not predict at all.

   (b) If the value increases by a fixed increment every time it is predicted, then it follows a stride based access pattern. If we detect such an access pattern, then the next prediction is equal to the current value plus the stride.

3. Whenever there is a misspeculation (misprediction), we need to replay the instructions that have received wrong values.

4. There are three methods of performing a replay:

   (a) In non-selective replay we squash (kill or nullify) all instructions that have read an operand within W cycles of the faulting instruction being issued. Here, W is the duration of the window of vulnerability.

   (b) In delayed selective replay, we associate a poison bit with all the values that are computed by the forward slice of the misspeculated load instruction. For all the instructions that have a poison bit set for one of their operands, we squash them, otherwise we let the instruction successfully complete. In this scheme, dealing with orphan instructions is tricky.

   (c) This is solved by the token based replay scheme, where we associate one token for each speculated load. At the cost of additional hardware complexity, this is the most elegant out of our three schemes.

5. It is possible to design a fundamentally simpler OOO pipeline by avoiding the physical register file altogether. Instead, we can use the ROB to store uncommitted values. In this pipeline we do not need to store checkpoints. It is stored within the architectural register file, which is updated at commit time. The disadvantage of this pipeline is that we need to store values at multiple locations, and the ROB becomes very large and slow.

6. Instead of putting the onus on the hardware to increase performance, we can do a lot of analyses at the level of the compiler such that the branch prediction performance and register usage improves.

7. *The most complicated optimisation in this space is software pipelining. Here, we create an overlap between instructions of different loop iterations, and execute them in a manner such that it is not necessary to stall the pipeline for multi-cycle RAW dependences.*

8. *The epitome of compiler assisted execution is an EPIC processor. It relies on the compiler for generating and scheduling code. This keeps the hardware simple and power efficient.*

9. *The Intel Itanium processor is a classic EPIC processor that moves most of the work to the compiler. Some of its prominent features include compiler directed branch prediction, virtual registers with register windows for functions, hardware support for software pipelining, predicated execution, and support for latency speculation.*

5.7.2   Further Reading

For aggressive speculation, the reader can consult some highly cited papers in this area: survey of load speculation [Calder and Reinman, 2000], speculative memory cloaking and dynamic speculation [Moshovos and Sohi, 1999, Moshovos et al., 1997], and selective value prediction [Calder et al., 1999].

Over the years, researchers have proposed many novel methods for implementing processors; one of the most notable examples is the Transmeta Crusoe processor [Klaiber et al., 2000], whose core engine is a VLIW processor. It has a software layer that converts x86 instructions to the native VLIW instructions.

In the area of compiler optimisation, the best books are by Aho and Ulmann [Aho and Ullman, 1977, Aho, 2003], and the book on advanced compiler techniques by Muchnick [Muchnick et al., 1997]. For software pipelining, the two classic papers by Rau [Rau, 1994] and Lam [Lam, 1988] provide a very good introduction. Specifically, the paper by Bob Rau proposes modulo scheduling, which is one of the most efficient methods for software pipelining.

Rau's paper [Rau, 1993] on dynamic scheduling in VLIW processors tries to add features of regular pipelined processors such as scoreboarding and interlocks to VLIW processors. For a practical perspective, the paper on the iWarp processor [Peterson et al., 1991] is a good reference.

For EPIC processors, the best references are the papers [Sharangpani and Arora, 2000, Settle et al., 2003, McNairy and Soltis, 2003] on the design of the Itanium and Itanium 2 processors.

Exercises

Ex. 1 — Does aggressive speculation increase the IPC all the time?

* **Ex. 2** — In load latency speculation, how do we know that we have predicted the latency correctly or not. In which stage is this logic required?

Ex. 3 — Design a stride predictor with saturating counters that has some hysteresis. This means that if just one access does not fit the stride based pattern, we have a means of ignoring it.

Ex. 4 — Extend the design of the predictor that uses store sets such that one store can be associated with multiple store sets. What are the pros and cons of doing so?

Ex. 5 — Why are values predictable in programs?

Ex. 6 — How will you use a profiling based approach to improve the value prediction hit rates in programs? In a profiling based approach, we first do a dry run of the benchmark, and collect some run time information. This information is subsequently used to improve the performance of the regular run of the benchmark.

Ex. 7 — Assume a program, where we have many variables whose value alternates between two integer values across read operations. How do we design a value predictor to take care of this case?

Ex. 8 — Compare the advantages and disadvantages of the three replay schemes: non-selective replay, deferred selective replay, and token based replay.

Ex. 9 — What are the trade-offs between keeping instructions in the instruction window versus keeping them in a separate replay queue?

Ex. 10 — How do we deal with orphan instructions in the non-selective and delayed selective replay schemes?

Ex. 11 — Why do we need a kill wire when we already have the mechanism of poison bits in the delayed selective replay scheme?

Ex. 12 — Design an efficient scheme to separate instructions into predictable and non-predictable sets for the token based replay scheme. Use insights from the chapter on branch predictors.

* **Ex. 13** — The replay schemes are all about collecting the forward slice. Let us consider the backward slice, which is defined as the set of instructions that determine the value of the destination(result) of an instruction. It consists of the instruction itself, the producers of its source operands, the producers of the source operands of those instructions, and so on. Consider an example.

```
1: add r1, r2, r3
2: sub r4, r5, r6
3: add r7, r1, r0
4: ld r8, 4[r7]
5: add r9, r8, r10
6: add r10, r4, r3
```

The backward slice of instruction 5 comprises instructions 5, 4, 3, and 1. The backward slice of instruction 6 comprises instructions 6 and 2.

Let's say that we need to compute the backward slice of a given instruction in a window of the last κ instructions. Suggest an efficient method to do this given κ. This approach should be fully hardware based.

* **Ex. 14** — Can a backward slice be defined in terms of forward slices?

Ex. 15 — What is the problem in accessing registers after the instruction is dispatched in the ARF based design?

Ex. 16 — In programs with high ILP, is a scheme with a unified instruction window or a scheme with reservation stations expected to perform better? What about for programs with low ILP?

Ex. 17 — Consider the ARF based design. How many read and write ports do we need in the ROB? Provide an efficient implementation of the ROB.

* **Ex. 18** — Outline a scheme to perform strength reduction in hardware. Note that the first task is to identify those instructions where a multiplication or division operation can be replaced with a sequence of shift operations.

* **Ex. 19** — How do we create a loop detector in hardware with possible compiler support? What can it be used for?

* **Ex. 20** — In software pipelining, is the degree of loop unrolling related to the latency of operations?

Ex. 21 — What is the function of the ALAT?

** **Ex. 22** — Provide the outline of a compiler algorithm to insert stop bits.

Ex. 23 — How does Itanium avoid structural hazards?

Ex. 24 — What is the advantage of tail recursion elimination?

Ex. 25 — Is scoreboarding an efficient technique? Should it be used in regular OOO pipelines?

** **Ex. 26** — Under what conditions can a load be hoisted in Itanium?

Design Problems

Ex. 27 — Design a stride predictor using Logisim or Verilog/VHDL. Create a circuit to predict if the access pattern is based on strides, calculate the stride, and use it for different types of prediction.

Ex. 28 — Implement the replay based techniques (deferred selective and token based) in the Tejas architectural simulator. Compare and analyse the results.

Ex. 29 — Implement a load-store dependence predictor in the Tejas simulator.

6

Graphics Processors

Up till now we have discussed general purpose processors, which are used to run all kinds of code. However, they have their limitations. They can at best achieve an IPC of 4 or 6. However, this is the best case and in practice to reach an IPC of 4 or 6, we need a near-perfect branch predictor, a very accurate prefetcher, and copious amounts of ILP. It is very hard to find all of these highly desirable traits in regular integer programs; however, it is often easier to find them in numerical programs that use a lot of floating point operations. We also have issues with power consumption and complexity. Having large instruction windows, rename tables, and elaborate wakeup-select logic requires a lot of power, and since power is one of the largest bottlenecks in modern processors, it is often very difficult to scale the issue width beyond 6 instructions per cycle.

This means that we are naturally limited to an IPC of 4 or 6. However, there are programs (albeit in a fewer set of categories) that can sustain a far higher IPC. For example, if we are adding two matrices, then all the additions can be done in parallel. This means that if each matrix has 10,000 elements, we can in principle do 10,000 additions in parallel. Since most numerical/scientific programs such as weather prediction, temperature simulation, and earthquake modelling involve a lot of numerical algorithms that basically consist of matrix operations, the need for designing a new processor for such codes is there. These matrix operations (a subset of the broader area of linear algebra) form the crux of most scientific applications. Furthermore, they have a lot of operations that can be performed in parallel. If we can design a good branch predictor and prefetcher, we will be able to supply instructions to the parallel pipelines at a fast rate. Given the fact that we have high ILP, we should be able to achieve a high IPC.

However, the problem is that all of this is not achievable in a typical processor. A typical processor has a lot of overheads in terms of the decode logic, renaming logic, scheduling logic, the load-store queue, and commit logic. To increase the issue width we need more area such that we can place more functional units, and we also need much wider schedule and wakeup-select units. We are severely constrained by chip area and power, and thus there is a need to think of alternative solutions. Using general purpose processors to do specialised computations such as scientific programs, is thus not a wise idea. General purpose processors are not equipped to deal with such kind of programs.

We need a special kind of processor that is particularly suited for such programs. Before going further, let us understand the nature of such programs by taking a look at a very simple sample computation, where we are adding two $(N \times N)$ matrices: A and B.

```
for (i = 0; i < N; i++) {
    for (j=0; j < N; j++) {
        C[i][j] = A[i][j] + B[i][j];
    }
}
```

There are two loops: one for rows and one for columns. These loops are used to traverse large matrices. In other words, the parameter N can be very large (let's say > 1000), and thus the sophistication of the branch predictor does not matter because most branches are very predictable in this case. Secondly, in a lot of cases N is known in advance (during compile time). Thus, the programmer can manually optimise the program, and even break a large computation into several disjoint parts such that these individual parts can be run on different cores of a multiprocessor. It is true that the portability of code is an issue: a piece of code optimised for one computer will not run efficiently on another computer. However, given the fact that most scientific and numerical programs are not made to run on general purpose computers with ubiquitous usage in mind, this can be an affordable luxury.

We further observe that we have N^2 additions, where there are no dependences between these individual addition operations. They can be done in parallel, and thus we have a massive amount of ILP in this program. If we were to run this program on an aggressive out-of-order(OOO) processor, we will get a very high IPC (close to the fetch or issue width (minimum of the two)). However, to get even larger values of IPC, we need to create a processor that has many adders that can operate in parallel. If we have a processor with 100 adders, then we can perform 100 additions in parallel. If we have 1000 adders, then we can do 1000 additions in parallel.

In principle, this sounds to be a very enticing idea. If we have a different kind of processor that has hundreds of simple ALUs, then we can perform hundreds of arithmetic operations per second. This will give us the required throughput to execute large scientific applications very quickly. As we can see from the example of matrix addition, such codes are relatively simpler as compared to normal programs, which have a lot of complex constructs, conditionals, and pointer arithmetic.

Way Point 4

1. *There are a class of programs that have a lot of numerical computations. They are relatively simpler in terms of the number and nature of operations as compared to traditional general purpose programs.*

2. *These programs have high ILP. Most linear algebra operations fall in this category.*

Now, for such programs, we would definitely benefit if we have a processor with let's say a 100 ALUs. This means that at least in theory we can execute 100 operations simultaneously, which is way better than an aggressive OOO processor that can at best provide a throughput of 4-6 operations per cycle. There is a flip side, which is that once we dedicate all our resources to these ALUs, and math processing engines, we are left with little area and energy to implement traditional functionalities of a processor such as fetch, decode, schedule, memory access, and commit. This implies that we need to simplify all of this logic, and create a processor that can execute a limited set of operations very efficiently. We essentially need to constrain the scope of the programs, and provide extremely high instruction throughput for the programs in this limited set.

Let us thus list out a few basic principles from what we have just learnt.

1. We need to design a processor with possibly hundreds of ALUs. This processor should be able to execute hundreds of arithmetic operations per clock cycle.

2. We need not support a very expressive ISA. We can have a small custom ISA explicitly tailored for numerical programs.

3. Conditional instructions, long dependence chains, and irregular memory accesses make conventional programs complicated in terms of their structure and the hardware that is necessary to execute them. We can have limited support for such instructions and programmatic constructs.

By now, the broad contours of a processor explicitly tailored for numerical operations is more or less clear. We now need to find the best way to design one such processor. We at this stage might not know what to do, but we at least know what not to do – we cannot use a general purpose OOO processor for this purpose.

6.1 Traditional Technologies

Let us look at some of the conventional alternatives that have been there for at least the last three decades.

6.1.1 ASICs and ASIPs

We can use a custom made silicon chip called an ASIC (application specific integrated circuit). This is a silicon chip that is specifically designed for a single class of programs. Here, the algorithms are hard-coded in RTL and the degree of flexibility is very low. For example, we can have an ASIC to add two matrices, or multiply two matrices. In this case, we need to provide the matrices to the chip, and their dimensions. The chip will add (or multiply) these matrices, and store the result in memory. Even though such processors can be tailor made for a problem, they have extremely limited applicability. A circuit designed to multiply matrices will not be able to find the inverse of a matrix. ASICs at best can be useful in very targeted applications. For example, we can have an ASIC in a video camera to compress the captured video. This will be an extremely fast and power efficient circuit. However, the ASIC cannot be used to do anything else. There is a clear trade-off between efficiency and flexibility.

In general, ASICs are very useful for specialised applications. The ASIC market as of 2020 is hundreds of billions of US dollars. However, it should be noted that ASICs are not full fledged processors because they are not programmable. Hence, they cannot be used for solving generic numerical problems. We can try to make the ASICs more programmable by introducing an instruction set, and by bringing in some of the components present in regular processors. Such interventions will make an ASIC an ASIP (application specific instruction set processor). An ASIP provides a very restricted ISA. In terms of flexibility it lies in between an ASIC and a general purpose processor. We can view the range of options from an ASIC to a regular processor as a spectrum; ASIPs fall somewhere in the middle.

Our aim is to operate at a sweet spot in this spectrum where we can optimally balance flexibility, programmability, power and performance.

6.1.2 FPGAs

No text on application specific computers is complete without a reference to FPGAs (field programmable gate arrays). An FPGA contains a large set of programmable logic circuits (or blocks), and a reconfigurable interconnection network. We can program the reconfigurable interconnect to make specific connections between logic blocks. It is possible to realise almost any kind of a digital circuit using an FPGA. FPGAs are logical successors of programmable logic arrays. Recall that a PLA (programmable logic array) consists of a large set of AND gates and OR gates, and it can be used to implement any type of Boolean function. An FPGA goes one step further and incorporates a lot of state elements and SRAM memories as well. We can program all of these blocks, and their interconnecting network at run time to realise an actual processor. This basically means that we can take an unprogrammed FPGA and convert it to a working processor on the fly (at run time).

It is true that we can dynamically create sophisticated processing elements on the fly using FPGAs. However, given the fact that they are being created from generic processing blocks using a generic interconnection network, they have performance limitations. As of 2020, FPGAs cannot be clocked at a frequency more than 600 MHz (general purpose processors can be clocked at 3-4 GHz). Furthermore, for most of their logic, they rely on lookup tables (LUTs). Lookup tables are large arrays that are used to compute the values of Boolean expressions (logic functions). A naive version of an LUT for a function with 16 variables contains 2^{16} (65,536) entries. Each row represents a Boolean combination of inputs, and each entry in a row contains the result of the function that is being evaluated. We can use such LUTs to compute the values of Boolean functions.

The advantage of an LUT is that we can implement any Boolean function using it. We simply need to change its contents. Of course, there are limitations in the scalability of this approach. If a function takes two values – 64 bits each – then we cannot afford to have a single LUT. Instead, we need to break the computation into several sub-computations, and we can have an LUT for each sub-computation.

Having a network of such LUTs, and a generic programmable interconnect is a very good idea for creating a high throughput system for a particular set of algorithms such as gene mapping or image reconstruction. However, FPGAs again have limited applicability, and also require fairly sophisticated programming tools. We desire a piece of hardware, which is reasonably generic, can be programmed with a fairly general purpose programming language, and delivers great performance.

This is precisely where GPUs (graphics processing units) come in to the picture. Let us understand traditional GPUs before moving to their modern avatars – general purpose GPUs (GPGPUs). Traditional GPUs were exclusively used for accelerating graphics computations; however, modern GPGPUs are used for general purpose numerical codes.

6.2   Traditional GPUs

In the good old days of MS-DOS and other operating systems that primarily operated via the command line, computer graphics had a very limited role to play. Most personal computer users as well as business users primarily used text-only terminals and were happy with predominantly textual interfaces. Even popular computer games like Tetris (see Figure 6.1) did not use a great amount of animation and graphics.

However, the entire situation changed with the introduction of operating systems such as Windows® that did not rely on the command line, and highly graphics intensive games. To sustain the requirements for such applications, there was a concomitant increase in the resolution of monitors. We started seeing monitors with a resolution of (1024x768 pixels and more) that used displays with vivid colours. Current monitors support 16 million colours. Even the nature and quality of animation increased, and suddenly car racing games felt like actually racing a real car in a FORMULA 1^{TM} race.

Let us figure out the cost of doing all of this computation. A car racing game requires a lot of computation; consider something simpler – minimising a window. In a modern system, we see the window artistically minimising itself and becoming an icon on the taskbar at the bottom of the screen. The space that is left behind is used to show the contents of other windows or the Desktop. This much of computation definitely does take a toll on the processor. Consider a relatively old display with a resolution of 1024x768 pixels. This makes a total of 786,432 pixels.

If we consider a 3 GHz processor with an IPC equal to 2 (floating point + memory operations), then we are only allowed to execute 7633 instructions per pixel per second. If we consider a 60 Hz monitor that displays 60 frames per second, it means that we can only run 127 instructions per pixel per frame. This might be enough for minimising a window; however, this is clearly not enough for all the games that we play. Some such games have multiple characters shooting bullets, cracking windows, and characters jumping across ledges and crevasses. We need to calculate a lot of things such as scenes, animations, shadows, illumination, and even the way that the hair of the characters will bounce when they jump. Sadly, the resources of a general purpose processor falls short for the requirements of modern games,

Figure 6.1: The DOS based Tetris game

which run on extremely high resolution displays (e.g. 3840×2160 UHD displays). Even if we can barely process the scenes in a game, we cannot do anything else like simultaneously browsing the web.

Highly aesthetic windowing systems, or games are not the only applications that require advanced graphics processing. Most of us regularly watch HD quality videos on our computers that require sophisticated video decoding engines, and we regularly visit highly interactive web pages. In addition, most engineers typically do their work using graphics intensive software such as AutoCAD®, which help us in designing complex 3D objects. Such diverse uses highly stress the processor, and most single or multicore processors simply do not support a large enough instruction throughput to run such applications. Furthermore, when we are playing a game, we would like to do other tasks in the background as well such as take backups, or run anti-virus programs. This requires additional computational throughput.

In response to such requirements, processor manufacturers increasingly started to ship their system with an additional *graphics processor* abbreviated as a GPU (graphics processing unit) along with regular processors. The job of the GPU was to process the graphics operations. This required support at multiple levels.

1. Programmers had to write their code such that a part of it ran on the CPU and a part of it ran on the GPU.

2. It was necessary to design new motherboards, where there was a fast and high bandwidth connection between the CPU and GPU.

3. Some new languages and compilers were created to write code for GPUs and optimally compile it for a given GPU.

It is important to note that till 2007 GPUs were predominantly used for graphics intensive tasks. There was no explicit thought of using GPUs for other generic tasks as well. This actually came gradually after 2010, when the community realised that GPUs could be re-purposed for general purpose computations as well. Thus the idea of a GPGPU (general purpose GPU) was born. However, before delving into the details of a GPGPU, let us concentrate on traditional GPUs and understand them.

6.2.1   Early Days of GPUs

Graphics applications can trace their origin to the 70s when the main applications of computer graphics were in CAD (computer aided design) and flight simulation. Gradually, with an increase in computing power, many of these applications started migrating to workstations and desktops. By the late eighties, some new applications such as video editing and computer games had also arrived, and there was a fairly large market for them as well. This is when a gradual transition from CPUs to GPUs began. The modern GPU can trace its origin from early designs proposed by NVIDIA® and ATI® in the late nineties.

Before we proceed forward, it is important to define two terms here – *vector* and *raster*. These concepts can be explained as follows. There are two ways to define a rectangle. First, we can define it by the coordinates of its top-left corner, its height and width. In this case, each rectangle can be defined by 4 floating point values. This is a vector graphics system. We can optionally specify the colour and width of the boundary of the rectangle, and maybe the colour that is used to fill the inside of the rectangle. These will be a few more values. In comparison, in a raster system we store a rectangle as a matrix of pixels. Each value in the matrix represents the colour of the pixel. This means that if a rectangle contains 10,000 pixels, we need to store 10,000 values.

Both the systems have their relative advantages and disadvantages. If we take an image (drawn using a vector graphics software) and enlarge it, then it will still retain its visual appeal. On the enlarged display, the system will still be able to draw the rectangle correctly. However, if we do the same with raster graphics, then it is possible that the image might actually look very grainy (see Figure 6.2 and 6.3). Also, for stretching and transforming an object, vector graphics is much better. In comparison, if we need to add effects such as illumination, shadows, or blurring, then raster graphics is more preferable. In general, we prefer raster graphics when we work with photographs.

Figure 6.2: Vector graphics

Figure 6.3: Raster graphics

Given the fact that there is no clear winner, it is advisable to actually support both the methods while creating a *graphics processing engine*. This engine needs to have multiple types of units for performing different kinds of tasks. Early systems were multi-pass systems [Blythe, 2008] – multiple computational passes were made on the same image. Each pass added a particular kind of transformation. This becomes particularly difficult, when images require a large amount of memory. Hence, a single-pass method is desired, where we can conceptually create a *graphics pipeline*. Images, scenes, or videos enter the pipeline at one end, undergo a process of transformation, and then exit from the other end. The end of the pipeline is typically connected to a display device such as a monitor.

By the beginning of this millennium the idea of creating a graphics pipeline with many specialised units, as well as many general purpose units that could be programmed, started to take shape. Also by that time a lot of graphics applications had emerged, and the space of applications was just not limited to a few well defined tasks . *Fixed function pipelines* that consisted of a set of simple units that could just perform basic vertex and pixel transformation tasks were not powerful enough for these new classes of applications.

As a result, the best option was to provide users much more flexibility in terms of what they could do. Thus the idea of a *shader* program was born. A *shader* is a small program that processes a fixed set of vertices or pixels. It is typically used to apply transformations to images, and add specialised effects such as rotation, shading, or illumination. The conceptual diagram of a shader is shown in Figure 6.4. Researchers further started working on custom languages for writing shaders. There was a need to make these languages independent of the underlying hardware such that they could run on different kinds of GPUs.

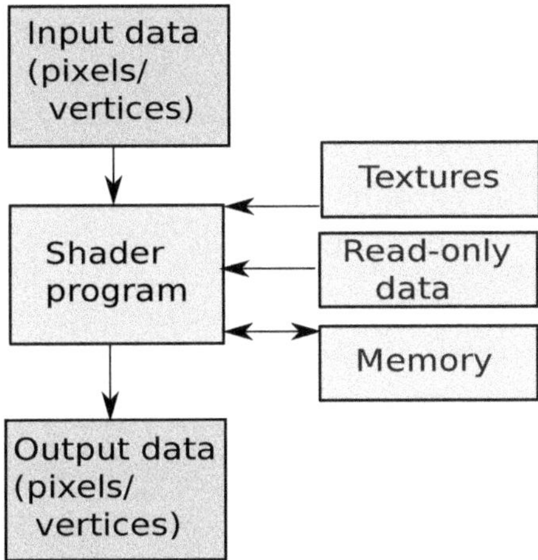

Figure 6.4: Conceptual diagram of a shader [Blythe, 2008]

Shaders have matured over the years. Starting from very rudimentary vertex and pixel processing operations, they have become significantly sophisticated. They are used for all kinds of applications: motion detection, adding texture, lighting, shadows, edge detection, and blurring. Much of today's research into the graphics aspect of GPUs is focused on designing and supporting more sophisticated shaders. Note that even though a shader is a program written in software, to run efficiently, it needs elaborate hardware support. This is where architectural techniques become important.

6.2.2   High Level View of a Graphics Pipeline

Before we discuss the high level view of a graphics pipeline, let us emphasise one thing. A graphics pipeline is meant to synthesise images, it is not meant to only display images. Most of the units in a graphics pipeline are dedicated to image synthesis. This process is also known as *rendering*.

Definition 32
Rendering *is a process of automatically creating an image (2D or 3D) from some rules and models. For example, a rendering engine can create a nice looking window on the screen based on some simple rules, models, and image files.*

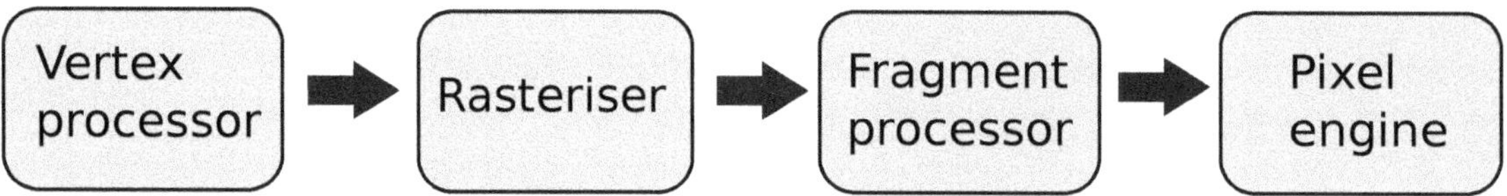

Figure 6.5: A basic rendering pipeline

A basic rendering pipeline is shown in Figure 6.5. We have four units. The programmer specifies a scene as a set of objects and a set of rules to manipulate those objects. These objects correspond to different distinct parts of a scene. These rules are written in high level graphics programming languages or APIs such as DirectX or OpenGL. Then, there are dedicated compilers that translate directives written in these high level languages to device specific commands. Graphics processors have their own assembly language and instruction formats. The NVIDIA family of graphics processors compile programs written in C/C++ (using the CUDA library) to a virtual instruction set called PTX (Portable Thread eXecution). PTX is a generic instruction set that is compatible with a broad line of NVIDIA processors. At runtime PTX is compiled to SASS (Shader ASSembler). SASS is a device specific ISA and is typically not compatible across different lines of processors, even from the same vendor.

Let us describe a generic pipeline that is broadly inspired from the NVIDIA® Tesla® [Lindholm et al., 2008] and NVIDIA Fermi [Wittenbrink et al., 2011] processors. For the exact description of the pipeline, please refer to the original sources. Our aim in the next few sections is to describe the main parts of the graphics processing pipeline. It is possible that individual processors might have slightly different implementations.

6.2.3 Vertex Processor

We start out by dispatching a set of instructions and a set of objects (to be manipulated) from the CPU to the GPU. The first box in Figure 6.5 is called a *Vertex Processor*. It accepts several objects as inputs along with rules for manipulating them. Even though it is more intuitive to represent objects as polygons; however, in the world of computer graphics it is often much more easier to represent them as a set of triangles. For each triangle, we simply need to specify the coordinates of its three vertices, and optionally the colour of its interior. Note that more efficient storage mechanisms are also possible; however, this is beyond the scope of the book.

There are several advantages of using triangles.

- When we want to represent a 3D surface, decomposing it into triangles is always preferred. This is because the three vertices of a triangle will always be on the same plane. However, this is not true for a quadrilateral. Hence, even if the surface has many bumps, twists, bends, and holes, it can still be efficiently represented by a set of triangles.

- The technique of using triangles is the simplest method to represent a surface. Hence, we can design many fast algorithms in hardware to quickly process them.

- To generate realistic images it is often necessary to treat a light source as consisting of many rays of light. For each ray, we need to find its point of intersection with a surface. If a surface is decomposed into triangles, then this is very easy because there are very efficient methods for computing the point of intersection between a ray and a triangle.

- A lot of algorithms to add colour and texture to a surface assume a very simple surface that is easy to work with. The surface of a triangle is very easy to work with in this regard.

- Moving, rotating, and scaling triangles can be represented as matrix operations. If we can quickly process such matrix operations, then we can quickly do many complex operations with sets of triangles.

Since complex rendering tasks can be achieved by manipulating the humble triangle, we can design the vertex processor by having a lot of small triangle processing engines. Each such engine can further support primitives such as translating, rotating, scaling, and re-shaping triangles. Such geometrical operations can be done in parallel for different objects and even for different triangles within an object.

Each triangle can additionally be augmented with more information such as the colour associated with each vertex, and the depth of the triangle (how far is an object from the eye in a 3D image).

6.2.4 Polymorph Engine

In modern GPUs [Wittenbrink et al., 2011], the Vertex Processor has been replaced by a more sophisticated Polymorph Engine. This is because the demands of modern applications such as 3D scene rendering and virtual reality require complex 3D operations that are well beyond the capabilities of traditional Vertex Processors. Hence, there is a need to create a new pipeline with new functional units.

The key idea of this engine is to focus on what is called "geometry processing". We divide the surface of an object into a set of polygons (often triangles). This process is known as *tessellation*. Subsequently, we perform very complex operations on these polygons in parallel. Figure 6.6 shows the 5-stage pipeline of the Polymorph Engine (source: NVIDIA GF100 [Wittenbrink et al., 2011]). Let us proceed to describe the Polymorph engine that is a part of most modern GPUs today. In specific, let us look at the pipeline of the NVIDIA Fermi processor [Wittenbrink et al., 2011].

Figure 6.6: Stages in the Polymorph Engine

Vertex Fetch

The input to this stage is a set of objects with 3D coordinates. The coordinates are in the *object space*, where the coordinates are local to the object. At the end of this stage, all the vertices are in *world coordinates*; this means that all of them use the same reference axes and the same 3D coordinate system.

We start out with fetching the vertex data from memory. Subsequently we perform two actions: vertex shading and hull shading. We shall see in Section 6.4.2 that GPUs consist of groups of cores known as streaming multiprocessors (SMs). The Polymorph Engine delegates a lot of its work to different SMs. Specifically, SMs perform two tasks in this stage: vertex shading and hull shading.

Vertex shaders are particularly useful in 3D scenes. They are used to add visual effects to a scene. For example, a vertex shader can be used to compute the effect of lighting a surface, or to simulate bones in a lifelike character. In the latter case, we need to compute the new position of each vertex in the bone as the arm that contains the bones moves. This can be done by the vertex position translation feature of a vertex shader. Thus to summarise, the vertex shader works at the level of vertices, and can primarily change the coordinates, colour, and the texture associated with each vertex.

The hull shader divides polygons into several smaller polygons. This is because we want different degrees of granularity at different points in the generated image. The objects that are closer to the viewpoint need a finer granularity as compared to objects that are far away.

Tessellation

The process of tessellation involves breaking down every polygon in the image into several smaller structures: triangles and line segments. The tessellation stage uses inputs from the hull shader. The main reason for doing tessellation is to create more detail on the surface and to also enable later stages of the pipeline to create an elaborate surface texture.

Viewport Transformation

In general, when we create a scene we are more interested in the objects and the rules that govern the interaction between them. For example, if we are rendering a scene in a game, we care about the position of the characters, and how they interact with their environment. However, we do not want to show the entire scene on the screen. It might be too large, and also all the parts of the scene may not be relevant. Let us refer to the scene that we have worked with up till now as the *window*.

Let us define a *viewport*, which is a portion of the coordinate space that we would like to show. There is thus a need to transform the 3D scene in the window to the scene that will be visible in the viewport. We first need to clip the scene (select a portion of it) and then perform scaling if the aspect ratio (width/height) of the viewport is different from that of the display device.

Attribute Setup

Now that we have created a scene in the viewport, we need to ensure that it renders correctly, particularly when we create the final 2D image. We do not want the backs of objects to be visible. Furthermore, if there is a light source, the illumination depends on the direction of the light rays, and the outward normal of the surface at each point. The dot product between the outward normal and the light rays determines the degree of illumination.

For each constituent triangle in the image, we compute the image of the plane (known as the plane equation) that it belongs to, and annotate each triangle with this information. This attribute will be useful later when we want to compute the visibility of different sides of an object and the degree of illumination.

Stream Output

The list of triangles is finally written to memory such that it can be used by subsequent stages. We typically do not have sufficient storage on the GPU to store all this information.

6.2.5 Rasterisation

This process converts all the triangles to sets of pixels. Each such set of pixels is known as a *fragment*. This can be achieved by overlaying an uniform grid over each graphical object. Each cell of this grid consists of multiple pixels and can be considered as the fragment. In this stage, we can optionally compute a colour for the fragment by considering its centre point. We can interpolate its colour by considering the colours of the vertices of the triangle, which this point is a part of.

Note that we do not discard all the information about triangles that comes from the Vertex Processor. Often all of this information is passed to the subsequent stage (Fragment Processor). Since the process of rasterisation typically is not associated with a lot of flexibility, we can have a dedicated unit for rasterisation. It need not be very programmable.

Furthermore, there is some degree of variance in the rasterisation stage among different processors. In earlier processors such as NVIDIA Tesla this stage was relatively smaller. However, in NVIDIA Fermi and beyond, this unit does visibility calculations as well. This means that we compute which parts of objects are visible in a scene. There is no hard and fast rule on which action needs to be performed in which stage as long as all the actions that it is dependent upon are done. Readers should thus interpret the design presented in this section as broadly suggestive.

6.2.6　Fragment Processor

Subsequently, we need to compute the final colour value of each pixel fragment. We need to take all kinds of visual effects and textures before computing this value. The job of the fragment processor is to perform all these computations.

The simplest method is to use the interpolated colour value of the centroid of the entire fragment. However, this produces fairly grainy and uneven images. Instead, we can use a more elaborate process. This often requires solving complex equations and performing a lot of linear algebra operations. Let us look at some of the common operations in this stage.

Interpolation How do we compute the value of the colour at each pixel? There are several interpolation techniques that allow us to do this. Some of the common techniques in this space are Goraud shading and Phong shading. Goraud shading is a simple linear interpolation based model where we can compute colour values based on the colours of the vertices, the nature of the ambient light source, and a model of reflectivity of the surface. It assumes that a triangle is a flat surface, whereas Phong shading, which is a more involved technique does not make this assumption. It assumes a smoothly varying normal vector (perpendicular to the surface) across the surface of the triangle, and has a much more complex model for reflectivity.

Texture Mapping Consider a realistic image. It is very unlikely that its surface will be a single colour, or even be a gradient. For example, the colour of a tree's surface is not exactly brown, neither does the colour uniformly vary between different shades of brown. A tree's colour has a *texture*. Refer to Figure 6.7 for examples of different kinds of textures.

(a) brick

(b) dirt

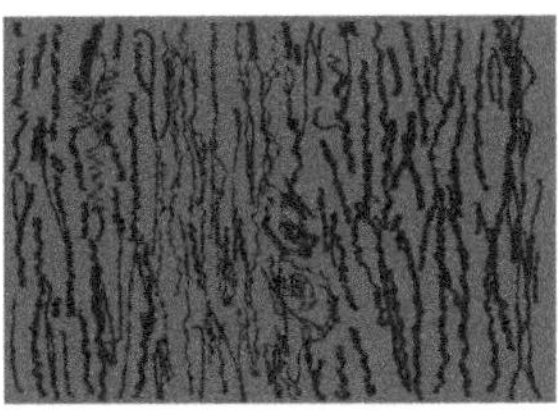

(c) wood

Figure 6.7: Different kinds of textures

Based on rules specified by the programmer, the GPU maps textures to triangles such that the surface of a tree looks realistic. We show the effect of adding a wooden texture to an object in the following figure.

In modern graphics processors it is possible to apply several textures and nicely blend them to produce a combined effect.

Fog Computation Distance Fog is a 3D rendering technique where pixels that have a greater depth
(further away from the eye) are shaded (coloured) differently to give a perception of distance.
Recall that the vertex processor computes the distance information. This information can be used
here to colour objects farther away slightly differently.

6.2.7 Pixel Engine

The job of the Pixel Engine is to take the output of the Fragment Processor and populate the frame
buffer. The frame buffer is a simple 2D matrix that holds only the colour information for each pixel on
the screen. The frame buffer is directly sent to the monitor for display.

To populate the frame buffer it is necessary to take all the fragments, and create a 2D image – image
that is seen on the screen.

Depth and colour buffering Fragments have different depths (known as the *Z-depth*). While rendering 3D images, one fragment might block the view of another fragment. It is possible to find out
if this is happening by comparing their coordinates and Z-depths. Once this computation is done,
we can find the fragments that should be visible and the fragments that should not be visible. We
can then look at their colours (computed from the previous stage) and use them to create a 2D
image out of the visible fragments.

Transparency effects Modern colouring systems are based on three colours: red, green, and blue
(RGB). In addition, they take an additional value called *alpha* that specifies the degree of transparency. It varies from 0.0 (fully transparent) to 1.0 (fully opaque). If a translucent object
(semi-transparent) is in front of an opaque object, then we should actually be able to see both.
This part of the graphics pipeline ensures that this is indeed the case.

Once the frame buffer is populated, it is ready to be sent to the display device.

6.2.8 Other Uses of a GPU

Till now we have discussed the different structures inside a traditional GPU. The crux of the discussion
centred around the concept of breaking complex structures into triangles and then operating on sets of
triangles. This was achieved by converting operations on triangles to different kinds of matrix operations.
Note that many such linear algebra based operations form the backbone of a lot of scientific code starting
from weather simulation to finding the drag experienced by a wing of an aircraft. The users of such
simulation software were traditionally using expensive workstations and large supercomputers.

Starting from 2006, the scientific community gradually woke up to the fact that graphics processors
are almost as powerful as large servers if we simply compare the number of floating point operations that
they can execute per second (FLOPs). For example, in April 2004, high end desktop processors had a
peak throughput of roughly 20 GFLOPs (giga FLOPs), whereas some of NVIDIA's GPUs had a peak
throughput of 50 GFLOPs [Geer, 2005]. By May 2005, the peak GPU throughput had increased to
170 GFLOPs with the CPU performance remaining more or less the same. This is where programmers
sensed an opportunity. They started thinking on how to commandeer the resources of a GPU to perform
their numerical calculations.

Some early pioneers started mapping their calculations to scenes and textures. Then they used vertex
and fragment processing operations to perform operations on their matrices as described by Rumpf et
al. [Rumpf and Strzodka, 2006]. This is like using the engine of a car to run a boat.

Gradually, GPU designers understood that it is better to make the GPU far more flexible and
programmable. This is the most beneficial: it opens up new markets because now a GPU can be used
for many other purposes other than rendering scenes. Vendors of GPUs also realised that many of the
operations in vertex and fragment processing are in reality massively parallel computations mostly based
on linear algebra. To increase the degree of programmability, it is wiser to make these units more generic

in character. Furthermore, since engineers working on high performance computing also require such capabilities, it is advisable to create features such that they can write and run their algorithms on a GPU. Anticipating such trends, NVIDIA released the CUDA (Compute Unified Device Architecture) framework in February 2007, which was the first widely available software development kit (SDK) that could be used to program a GPU.

Thus, the modern GPGPU (general purpose GPU) was born. It is a very programmable and flexible processor that can be used to perform almost all kinds of high performance numerical computations. GPUs today are no more limited to just processing and creating computer graphics, instead, graphics is just one of the applications that is supported by a GPU.

6.3   Programming GPGPUs

As we saw in Section 6.2 graphics processors have elaborate structures to perform graphics intensive tasks. However, they can also be effectively used for regular scientific code such as weather simulation, or computing the distribution of temperature in an object using finite element analysis techniques. Such computations more or less share the same characteristics. They involve complex linear algebra based operations and a lot of predominantly numerical operations.

Using GPUs for numerical and scientific computation might sound as an obvious idea particularly after we have described the motivation for doing so; however, for its time it was a very revolutionary idea. Your author recalls a fair amount of skepticism among people from both industry and academia when this idea was first proposed by some GPU evangelists. It took time to sink in. Now, nobody bats an eyelid if they hear that GPUs are being used for high performance computing. In fact, today GPUs can do most of the heavy lifting when it comes to computational work.

In this section, we shall introduce the CUDA programming language, analyse its constructs, and briefly cover some advanced features. Note that this section just provides a cursory introduction to the CUDA language and runtime. For a much more detailed treatment, readers should consult books on the CUDA programming language [Farber, 2011].

6.3.1   GPU ISAs

As mentioned in Section 6.2.2, the process of compiling a program on a GPU is a two-step process. The user writes her program using a variant of C++which can be one of the popular GPU programming languages: CUDA or OpenCL. Let us describe NVIDIA's CUDA toolkit. CUDA is an abbreviation for *Compute Unified Device Architecture*. It is an extension of C++ where a user writes a program for NVIDIA's entire line of GPUs. A typical CUDA program looks almost like a C++ program with some additional directives that specify which part of the code needs to run on the CPU, and which part of the code is meant for the GPU.

NVIDIA provides a dedicated compiler called *nvcc* that can be used to compile CUDA code. It uses separate tools to compile the CPU code and the GPU code (see Figure 6.8). The GPU code is first processed by a C++ preprocessor that replaces macros. Then a compilation pass compiles the code meant for the GPU into the PTX instruction set, which is a virtual instruction set. PTX stands for Parallel Thread eXecution. It is a RISC-like ISA with an infinite set of registers, where the compiler generates code mostly in the single assignment form – each variable is assigned a value exactly once. Using a virtual instruction set is preferable because there is a large diversity in the underlying hardware, and if we generate code for one kind of hardware, the code will lose its portability. Subsequently, we generate a fat binary, which contains the PTX code, and also contains the machine code for different popular models of GPUs. In other words, a single binary contains different images, where each image corresponds to a specific GPU ISA. Simultaneously, we compile the C++ part of the code using standard C++ compilers, embed references to GPU functions, and link functions provided by the CUDA library. *nvcc* finally produces one executable that contains both the CPU and the GPU code.

When the program is run, the runtime dispatches the PTX code to the GPU driver that also contains a compiler. If we are not using a pre-compiled binary, then this compiler performs just-in-time (JIT) compilation. The advantages of just-in-time compilation is that the code can be optimised for the specific GPU. Given that PTX assumes a virtual machine, specific optimisations need to be made at a later stage to generate the final machine code. Furthermore, unlike general purpose processors, GPGPUs are still not completely standardised; fairly invasive changes are happening every generation. Hence, to ensure that code written in the past runs efficiently is a challenge, and this necessitates compilation at runtime. The PTX code is compiled to SASS (Shader ASSembler) code, which is native to the machine. It can be generated separately from the PTX binary using the CUDA utility *ptxas* as well.

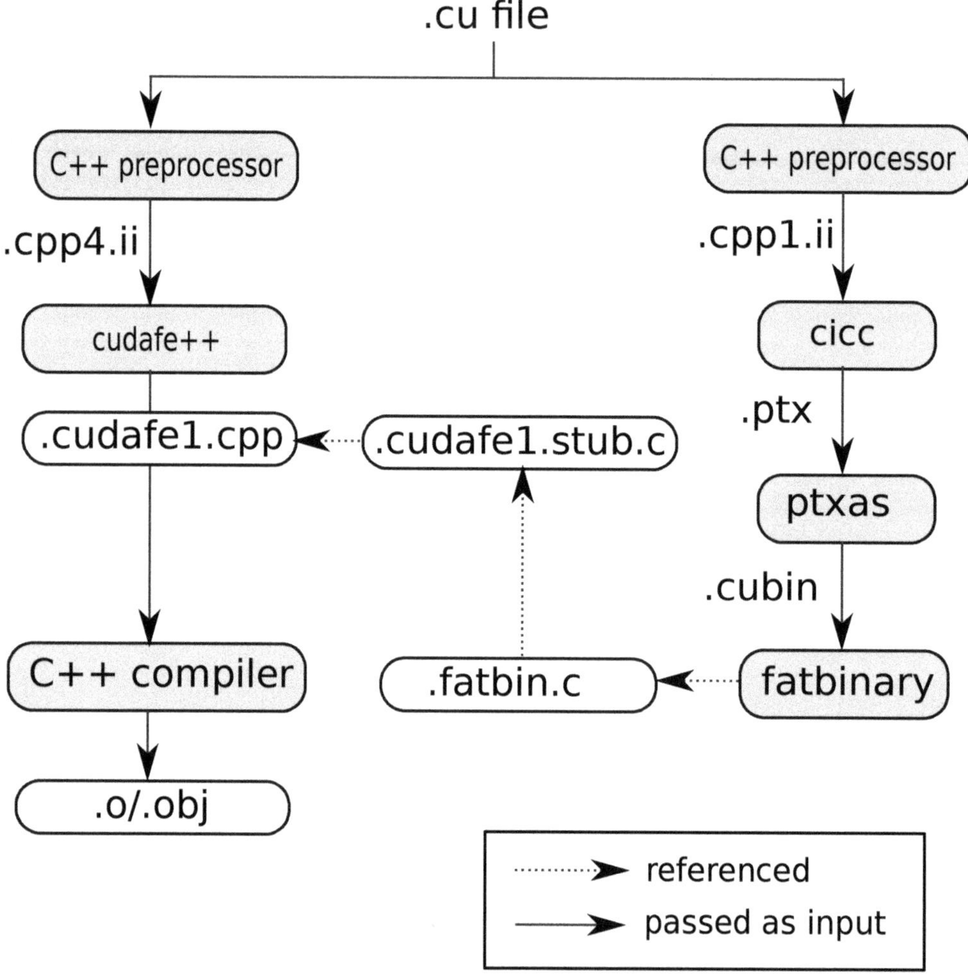

Figure 6.8: Compilation flow of *nvcc* (source [NVIDIA Inc., 2020])

6.3.2   Kernels, Threads, Blocks, and Grids

Let us now look at the basics of writing CUDA code. In this section we shall describe some of the basic concepts. The source of this material is NVIDIA's documentation for the CUDA 10 toolkit [NVIDIA, 2018].

A basic function that is to be executed on a GPU is known as a *kernel*. It typically represents a function that needs to be invoked for each item in a list of items. For example, if we are adding two vectors, then the kernel can be a simple add function that adds two elements in a vector. Each kernel is called by a CUDA thread, where a thread is defined as a process (running instance of a program) that can share a part of its address space with other threads. In a GPU we can think of the threads as separate programs that execute the same code, share data via shared memory structures, and execute in parallel. Each such thread has a unique thread id, which can be obtained by accessing the *threadIdx* variable. To better explain these concepts, let us write our first CUDA code that uses multiple parallel threads to compute the sum of two vectors. Let us show only the function that will run on a GPU. We will gradually reveal the rest of the code.

```
__global__ void vecAdd (float *A, float *B, float *C){
    int idx = threadIdx.x;
    C[idx] = A[idx] + B[idx];
}
```

The *__global__* directive precedes every kernel indicating that it should run on a GPU. Let us now explain the built-in *threadIdx* variable. In the CUDA programming language threads are grouped into blocks of threads. A *block* of threads contains a set of threads, where each thread operates on a set of variables assigned to it. The threads in a block can be arranged along 1D, 2D, and 3D axes. For example if we are working on a cube, it makes sense to arrange the threads as per their x, y, and z coordinates. *threadIdx* in this case has three components: *threadIdx.x*, *threadIdx.y*, and *threadIdx.z*. For the code that we have shown, threads are arranged along a single dimension, hence we only use *threadIdx.x* to get the index of the thread. We further assume that if we have N threads, then each vector also has N elements: assign one element to each thread. For each thread we read the corresponding array index, get the data values, add them, and write the result to the array C. If all of the threads work in parallel, then we can potentially get an N times speedup.

The main advantage of arranging threads as a 1D chain, 2D matrix, or a 3D cuboid is that it is easy to partition the data among the threads because the arrangement of the threads mimics the structure of the data. Thread blocks typically cannot contain more than 768 or 1024 threads (depending on the architecture). On similar lines we can group blocks of threads into a grid.

Let us now show an example of a matrix addition kernel that uses a 2D block of threads. In this case we shall show a part of the *main* function that invokes the kernel.

```
__global__ void matAdd(float A[N][N], float B[N][N], float C[N][N]){
    int idx = threadIdx.x;
    int jdx = threadIdx.y;
    C[idx][jdx] = A[idx][jdx] + B[idx][jdx];
}

int main(){
    ...
    dim3 threadsPerBlock(N, N);
    matAdd<<<1, threadsPerBlock>>>(A, B, C);
    ...
}
```

In the *main* function we define an object called *threadsPerBlock* of type *dim3*. *dim3* is a built-in type, which is a 3-tuple that can contain up to 3 integers: x, y, and z. If any integer is unspecified, its value defaults to 1. In this case, we are defining *threadsPerBlock* to be a pair of integers, which has two elements: N and N. The third element has a default value of 1. Thus the value of the variable *threadsPerBlock* is $\langle N, N, 1 \rangle$. Subsequently, we invoke the kernel function *matAdd* that will be executed on the GPU. Between the angle brackets, $<<<$ and $>>>$, we specify the arrangement of blocks in the grid, and the arrangement of the threads per block. In this case we have a single block in the grid, hence the first argument is 1; however, we arrange the threads within the block as an $N \times N$ array. This is because the second argument is the *threadsPerBlock* variable, which we set to $\langle N, N, 1 \rangle$. The GPU subsequently creates N^2 threads.

In the code of the kernel (function *matAdd*), we find the x and y coordinates of each thread by accessing the variables *threadIdx.x* and *threadIdx.y*. They are stored in the variables *idx* and *jdx* respectively. Since the threads are arranged the same way as the data, we can use *idx* and *jdx* to find the elements in each matrix that correspond to a given thread. Then we add the elements and set the corresponding element in the result matrix C to the sum. We thus have parallelism at the level of elements, which is elegantly exploited by arranging our threads in the same way as the underlying data.

We can subsequently group blocks into a grid using a similar mechanism. A grid is in principle a 3D structure of blocks, where every block has an x, y, and z coordinate. However, by setting a subset of these coordinates to 1 we can think of a grid as a 1D chain or a 2D matrix of blocks.

Let's say we want to add two $N \times N$ matrices, where $N = 1024$. Furthermore, assume that we cannot create more than 768 threads. In this case let us limit ourselves to 16 threads per dimension (assuming 2 dimensions). We can then create $N/16 \times N/16$ blocks, where each block's dimensions are 16×16. The resultant code is shown below.

```
__global__ void matAdd(float A[N][N], float B[N][N], float C[N][N]){
    int idx = blockIdx.x * blockDim.x + threadIdx.x;
    int jdx = blockIdx.y * blockDim.y + threadIdx.y;
    C[idx][jdx] = A[idx][jdx] + B[idx][jdx];
}

int main(){
    ...
    dim3 blockDimensions (N/16, N/16);
    dim3 threadsPerBlock(16, 16);
    matAdd<<<blockDimensions, threadsPerBlock>>>(A, B, C);
    ...
}
```

Similar to *threadIdx*, *blockIdx* stores the coordinates of the block. The variable *blockDim* stores the dimensions of each block. It has an x, y, and z component, which are represented as *blockDim.x*, *blockDim.y*, and *blockDim.z* respectively. Blocks of threads are meant to execute completely independently on the GPU. They can be scheduled in any order. However, threads within a block can synchronise between themselves and share data. For synchronising threads, we can call the *__syncthreads()* function, which acts as a barrier for all the threads in the block. Let us define a barrier. A *barrier* is a point in the code where all the threads must reach before any of the threads is allowed to proceed past it. This is graphically shown in Figure 6.9.

Definition 33

A barrier *is a point in the code where all the threads must reach before any of the threads is allowed to proceed past it.*

Definition 34

- *A kernel is a function in CUDA code that executes on a GPU. It is invoked by the host (CPU) code.*

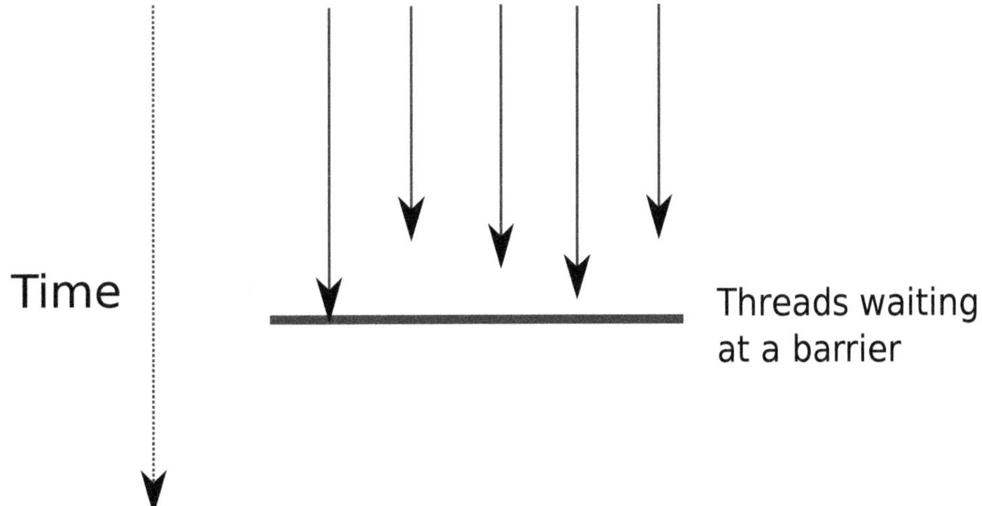

Figure 6.9: A barrier in the code

> - *A thread in the context of a GPU is a process running on the GPU that is spawned at runtime. Similar to CPU threads, different GPU threads can share data amongst each other. However, the rules for sharing data are far more complex. While invoking a kernel we typically specify the number of threads that need to be created. They are created by the runtime. Each thread is assigned some data for performing its computation. This depends on its position within the block. In general, the threads execute in parallel, and this is why GPUs provide very large speedups.*
>
> - *A block is a group of threads, where the threads can be organised in a 1D, 2D, or 3D arrangement. The threads in a block can share data, and can synchronise with each other.*
>
> - *Similar to threads in a block, blocks are arranged in a grid in a 1D, 2D, or 3D arrangement. Blocks within a grid are supposed to execute independently without any form of synchronisation.*

6.3.3   Memory Access

In GPUs there are two separate memory spaces: one on the CPU, and one on the GPU. We need to explicitly manage the flow of data between these spaces, and ensure that the process of transferring data is overlapped with computation as much as possible.

GPUs have many kinds of memories. Each thread has a per-thread local memory, then it has a shared memory that is visible to the rest of the threads in the block, and the lowest level is called the global memory, which is visible to all the threads. Additionally, many GPUs provide access to different read-only memories. Two of the popular memories in this class are the constant memory (for read-only constants) and the texture memory. The latter is used to store the details of textures in graphics oriented tasks.

In CUDA while allocating a region in memory, we can optionally add a memory specifier, which indicates where the bytes will be stored. The list of valid specifiers are as follows.

Specifier	Meaning
device	The region resides in the GPU (device)
constant	Resides in the constant caches of the GPU
shared	Resides in the per-block shared memory
managed	Can be used from both the host (CPU) and the device

Let us now show the complete code for vector addition, which includes statements to allocate memory, transfer data between the CPU's memory and the GPU's memory, and free memory on the GPU.

Listing 6.1: CUDA code to add two vectors

```
1   __global__ void vecAdd (float *A, float *B, float *C){
2       int idx = threadIdx.x;
3       C[idx] = A[idx] + B[idx];
4   }
5
6   int main() {
7       ...
8       /* Allocate the arrays A, B, and C on the CPU */
9       int size = N * sizeof(float);
10      A = (int *) malloc (size);
11      B = (int *) malloc (size);
12      C = (int *) malloc (size);
13
14      /* Initialise the arrays */
15      ...
16
17      /* Allocate A, B, and C on the GPU */
18      float *g_A = cudaMalloc (&g_A, size);
19      float *g_B = cudaMalloc (&g_B, size);
20      float *g_C = cudaMalloc (&g_C, size);
21
22      /* Copy vectors from the host to the device */
23      cudaMemcpy (g_A, A, cudaMemcpyHostToDevice);
24      cudaMemcpy (g_B, B, cudaMemcpyHostToDevice);
25
26      /* invoke the kernel */
27      vecAdd<<<1,N>>> (g_A, g_B, g_C);
28
29      /* Transfer from the device to the host */
30      cudaMemcpy (C, g_C, cudaMemcpyDeviceToHost);
31
32      /* Free the space on the GPU */
33      cudaFree(g_A);
34      cudaFree(g_B);
35      cudaFree(g_C);
36
37  }
```

First we allocate memory on the host for the three arrays (Lines 10 to 12). Then we create three arrays on the device (GPU) with the same dimensions. These arrays need to be allocated space on the GPU (Lines 18 to 20). We use the function *cudaMalloc* for this purpose, which allocates space in the global memory. Then, we need to copy the contents of the arrays from the host's memory space to the device's (GPU's) memory space. We use the *cudaMemcpy* function to copy the arrays; this function takes three arguments: destination array, source array, and the direction of the transfer. The third argument (direction of the transfer) specifies whether we are transferring data from the host to the device or from the device to the host. It thus can have two values: *cudaMemcpyHostToDevice* and *cudaMemcpyDeviceToHost*.

Then we invoke the kernel in Line 27. We are using N threads and 1 block. Furthermore, this is a synchronous call, which means that we wait till the GPU has computed the result. Once this is done, we transfer the contents of the array g_C from the device to the host. We again call the *cudaMemcpy* function; however, this time data is transferred in the reverse direction. Finally, we free the arrays on the device in Lines 33-35 using the function *cudaFree*.

For multi-dimensional arrays we can use the function calls *cudaMallocPitch()* and *cudaMalloc3D()*, which are used to allocate 2D and 3D arrays respectively. It is recommended to use these functions rather than using *cudaMalloc* because these functions take care of the alignment issues in data. Additionally, we have similar functions to copy data from the device to the host and vice versa: *cudaMemcpy2D* and *cudaMemcpy3D*.

6.3.4 Streams, Graphs, and Events

Streams

The code in Listing 6.1 is to a certain degree inefficient because it has three well defined phases – transfer the data to the GPU, perform the computation, and transfer the results back to the CPU – that execute sequentially even when they are not required to. It would have been much better if we could pipeline these phases such that the GPU's compute engines are not idle when the data is being transferred to them. Additionally, if we consider multiple kernels, then one kernel needs to wait till all the outputs of the previously executed kernel have been transferred to the CPU. This is again inefficient.

To solve problems of such a nature, the designers of CUDA introduced the concept of streams. A *stream* is defined as a sequence of commands that are meant to execute in order. The commands can be initiated by different threads on the host.

We can create different streams. There is no ordering of commands across the streams – they are independent. Depending on the compute capabilities of the device it might allow different kinds of overlaps to occur or it might preclude them.

Let us explain with an example. Consider the code in Listing 6.1 once again. It has three distinct phases: transfer to the GPU (ToGPU), compute the result (*Compute*), and transfer to the host (*ToCPU*). Without any streams, their execution is as shown in Figure 6.10(a). There is no overlap between the phases. Let us now create two streams where we partition the arrays into two parts. If the arrays have N elements each, let the two parts cover the indices $[0, \lfloor N/2 \rfloor]$, and $[\lfloor N/2 \rfloor + 1, N - 1]$ respectively. Stream 1 is assigned the first half of indices, and stream 2 is assigned the second half. In our code that performs simple addition, stream 1 and stream 2 do not have any dependences between them.

Figure 6.10(b) shows the timeline of the execution with streams. We divide each phase into two parts, and distribute it among the two streams. Let us quantitatively compare the difference in the execution time. Assume that the three phases take 1 unit of time each. In Figure 6.10(b), each phase takes 0.5 units of time. Stream 1 starts at time $t = 0$ and ends at $t = 1.5$. Stream 2 starts at $t = 0.5$, and ends at $t = 2.0$. We thus observe that by using streams, we speedup the execution from 3 units of time to 2 units of time. We reduced the time of execution by one-third. Depending on the amount of resources, and the nature of overlaps that are allowed, we can increase the speedup even more by having more streams. For example, some devices allow the concurrent execution of kernels and some allow concurrent data transfers.

Graphs

In the CUDA framework, the costs of launching a kernel and managing the data transfers between the CPU and GPU are high. This cost is even more pronounced when we have a lot of kernels that run for a short duration. Even if we group kernels into streams, the static overhead of setting up the kernels in

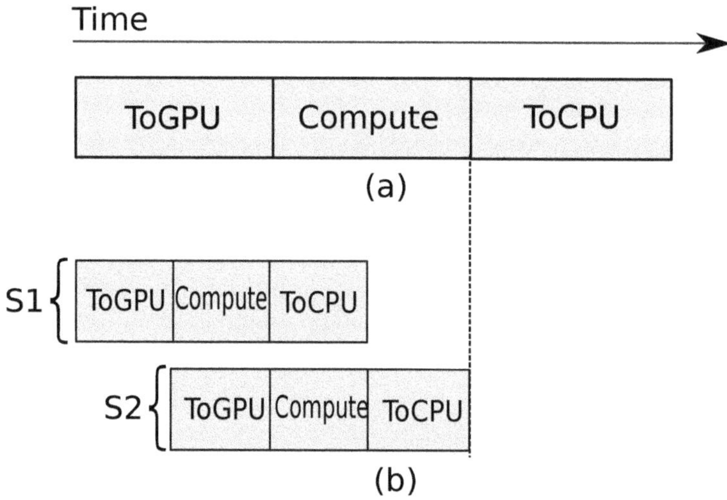

Figure 6.10: A sample execution with two streams

the GPU, loading their instructions, and initialising the GPU's hardware structures, does not reduce. In such scenarios CUDA graphs are useful.

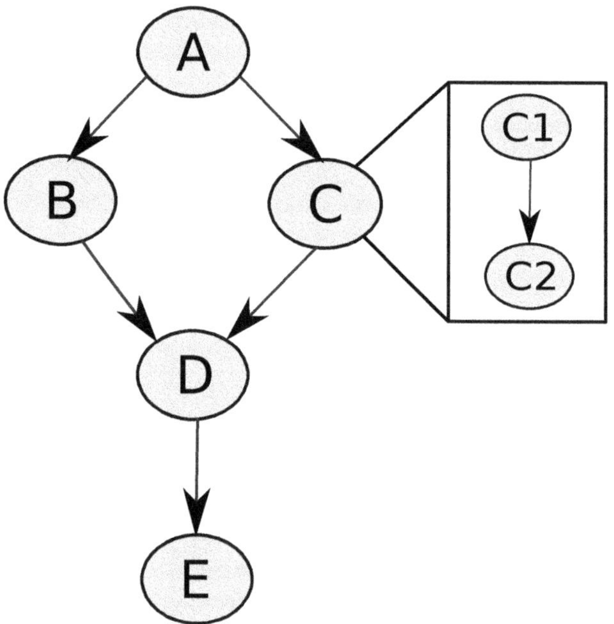

Figure 6.11: A graph in CUDA (the example shows a graph where node C is a subgraph)

A graph is a data structure that contains a set of vertices (nodes) and edges (see Definition 11 in Section 2.3.2). As shown in Figure 6.11, each edge joins two nodes. In CUDA, a graph can contain the following types of nodes:

1. Kernel (runs on the GPU)

2. Function call on the CPU

3. Memory copy and initialisation

4. Another child graph

The programmer creates a graph by specifying the kernels, the nature of the data transfer, the CPU function calls, and the dependences between them. If there is an edge from node A to node B, then it means that task B starts only after task A executes completely. This graph is first validated and then the CUDA runtime prepares itself for running the tasks associated with the graph. The advantage of this approach is that when an ensemble of tasks is presented to the CUDA runtime, it can reduce the cost of launching kernels, and setting up data transfers, significantly. This is done by pre-computing the schedule of actions, prefetching data and code, and allocating resources for intermediate values and prefetched data.

Events

Programming a GPU is a skillful job. Unlike programming regular multicore processors, a GPU is a very complex framework. Programmers need to be aware of the details of the hardware, the way in which CUDA programs leverage the features of the hardware, and have an accurate knowledge of the performance bottlenecks in their program. Let us focus on the last point. CUDA programmers should know how much time different portions of their program are taking to execute. They can use CUDA events for this purpose. The programmer can create CUDA events that record the time at which a stream of commands started, and when it ended. The function *cudaEventElapsedTime* can be used to find the time between the two events: start of a stream's execution and end of a stream's execution. This information can be used to optimise the CUDA program.

6.4   General Purpose Graphics Processors

Over the last 10-15 years (as of 2020) many new designs of GPUs have come up; however, the broad architecture of a GPU has more or less stayed the same barring small modifications and improvements made every new generation. We shall describe a representative architecture in this section, which is broadly similar to NVIDIA Volta, even though it is not exactly the same.

6.4.1   Overview of the Architecture of a GPU

Figure 6.12 shows the reference architecture of a GPU. Let us start with the interface. There are several ways in which the GPU can be connected with the CPU. It can be on the same die as the CPU like Intel Sandy Bridge or it can be housed separately. In the latter case, the CPU and GPU need to be connected with a high bandwidth interconnect such as PCI Express.

The interconnect is connected to the Thread Engine (GigaThread Engine in Figure 6.12) whose role is to schedule the computation (graphics and general purpose) on different compute units. Given that a GPU has a lot of compute units, programmers typically run a lot of multithreaded code on the GPU. It is too expensive to let the operating system or other software units schedule the threads as is the case in a normal CPU. It is best to have a hardware scheduler that can very quickly schedule the threads among the compute units.

In the architecture shown in Figure 6.12, we divide the compute units in a GPU into six separate clusters – each cluster is known as a GPC (Graphics processing cluster). Since a GPU is expected to have a lot of cores, we shall quickly see that it is a wise idea to divide it into clusters of cores for more efficient management of the tasks assigned to the cores.

Finally, in the high level picture, we have a large L2 cache, which as of 2020 is between 4-6 MB. The GPU has multiple on-chip memory controllers to read and write to off-chip DRAM modules. In this case the High Bandwidth Memory 2 (HBM2) technology is used.

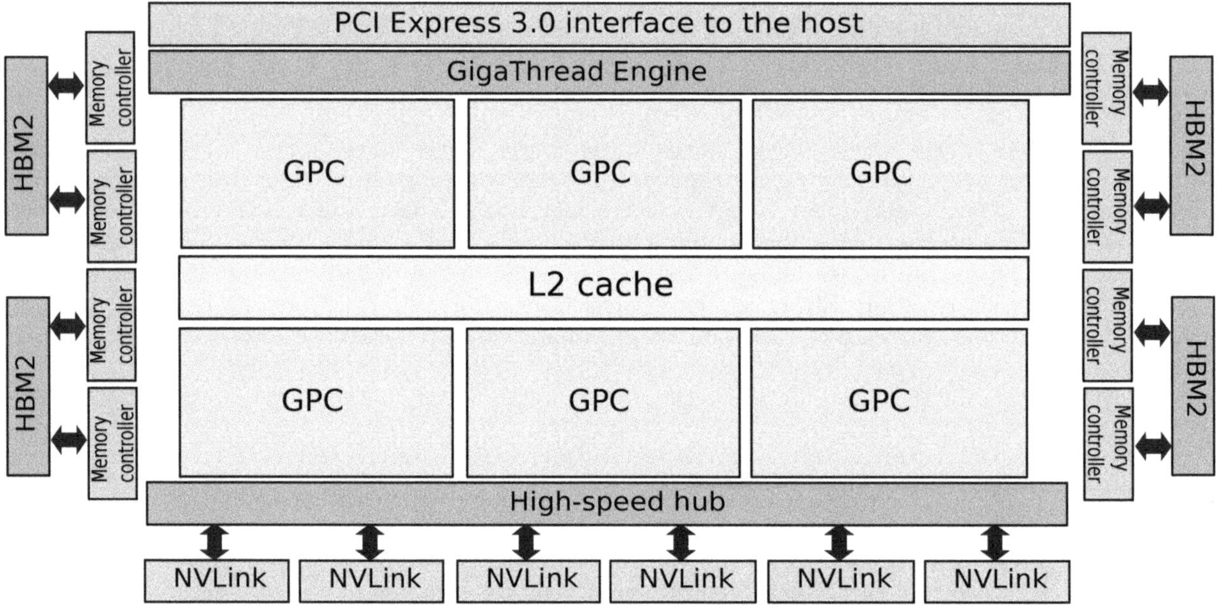

Figure 6.12: Architecture of a GPU (adapted from [NVIDIA Inc., 2017])

Most high performance systems today are multi-GPU systems. A large problem is split into multiple parts and each part is assigned to a separate GPU. The GPUs need to coordinate among themselves to execute the problem. As a result a very high bandwidth interconnect is required to connect the GPUs. NVIDIA created the NVLink interconnect that can be used to create such multi-GPU systems. The architecture shown in Figure 6.12 has six NVLink controllers that can be used to communicate with other sister GPUs.

6.4.2   Structure of a GPC

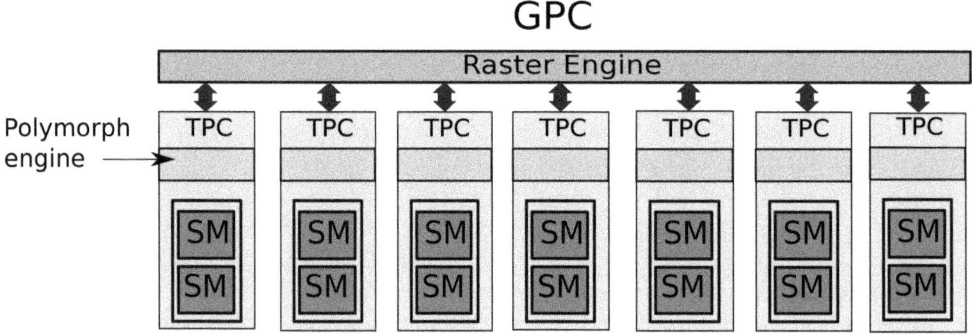

Figure 6.13: Architecture of a GPC (adapted from [NVIDIA Inc., 2017])

Let us now look at the structure of a GPC in Figure 6.13. Each GPC has a rasterisation engine (referred to as the *Raster Engine*), which does the job of pixel rasterisation (see Section 6.2.5). This unit is connected to seven Texture Processing Clusters (TPCs). Even though the TPC has maintained its historical name – as of today it consists of two distinct parts. The first is a vertex processor called the

Polymorph Engine (see Section 6.2.4) and the second is a set of two compute engines called Streaming Multiprocessors (SMs).

Way Point 5

- *In our reference architecture the GPU has six GPCs.*

- *Each GPC has a large Raster Engine for rasterisation, and seven TPCs.*

- *Each TPC has a vertex processor called the Polymorph Engine, and two SMs (Streaming Multiprocessors).*

- *We thus have a total of 84 SMs.*

6.4.3   Structure of an SM

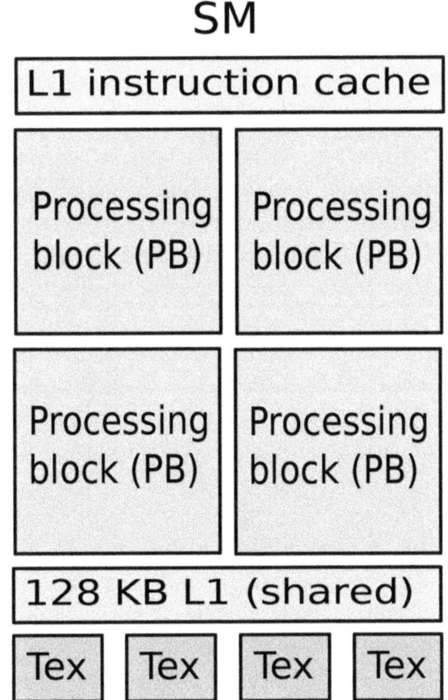

Figure 6.14: Layout of an SM (adapted from [NVIDIA Inc., 2017])

Figure 6.14 shows the structure of an SM. An SM can be further sub-divided into two parts: memory structures and groups of simple cores. Let us look at memory structures first. In GPUs, we have the following types of memory structures within an SM. Note that they need not be separate structures in every design. Some designs use the same structure for multiple functions.

Instruction Cache This is very similar to an i-cache in a regular processor. It contains the instructions that need to be executed.

L1 Cache This cache stores regular data that cores write (similar to a regular data cache).

Texture Cache This cache contains texture information. This information is provided to the texture units that colour the fragment with a given texture.

Constant Cache Stores read-only constants.

Shared Memory This is a small piece of memory (64-128 KB) that all the cores in an SM can access. This can explicitly be used to store data that all the cores can quickly reference. CUDA programs can be directed to store arrays in the shared memory by using the _shared_ specifier. The latency of this shared memory unit is typically far lower than that of the L2 cache, and other memory structures beyond it.

Some of the older GPUs had many kinds of such memories. However, there is a trend to unify them and have fewer memory structures. In our reference architecture each SM has an 128 KB L1 data cache that also acts as the shared memory. It is used to store all the data that the SMs need. Additionally, we have a single L1 instruction cache that is shared by all the cores in the SM.

Let us now focus on the compute parts of an SM. Each SM has four processing blocks (PBs) that contain cores and special computing units. They are used to do all the mathematical processing in a GPU. Additionally, each SM has four texture processing units that process texture information (shown as *Tex* in the Figure). The job of each such unit is to fetch, process, and add textures to the rendered image.

The Compute Part of an SM: Processing Block

Figure 6.15 shows the detailed structure of a processing block (PB) in an SM. It is a simple in-order pipeline. Instructions pass through an instruction buffer (L0 i-cache), a scheduler based on a scoreboard (see Section 5.6.5), a dispatch unit, a large register file, and then they enter the compute cores. Other than the scheduler, the rest is similar to a regular in-order pipeline. We shall discuss the scheduling aspect shortly in Section 6.4.4.

In our reference architecture, a PB consists of 16 integer cores, 16 single precision floating point cores, 8 double precision floating point cores, and two tensor processing cores (for matrix operations). Each core is very simple: slightly more sophisticated than a regular ALU. When we have so many cores, they are bound to have a large memory requirement. We thus need 8 Ld/St units for accessing memory. In addition, scientific programs use a lot of transcendental and trigonometric functions. As a result, we need a special function unit (SFU) to compute the results of all of these functions. Additionally, SFUs have special support for interpolating the colour of pixels. Recall that we had discussed in Section 6.2.6 that in the fragment processing stage, we need to interpolate the colour of pixels based on the colours of adjoining pixels or the colours of the vertices of the triangle that the pixel is a part of. SFUs have special hardware to support these operations.

The cores are typically referred to as SPs (streaming processors). They contain fully pipelined functional units. Additionally, most GPUs support the multiply-and-add (MAD) instruction, which is of the form: $a = a + b * c$. Such instructions are very useful while performing linear algebra operations such as matrix multiplication.

Before delving into the details of the pipeline, let us understand the concept of a *warp*.

6.4.4   Concept of a Warp

We need to understand that we are not running a single pipeline. Instead we are running a complex system with 40+ computing units. If we make this a free-for-all system, where any instruction from any thread can execute, then the entire system of threads will become very complex. We will need complex logic to handle branch statements, memory accesses, and dependences between the threads. This extra

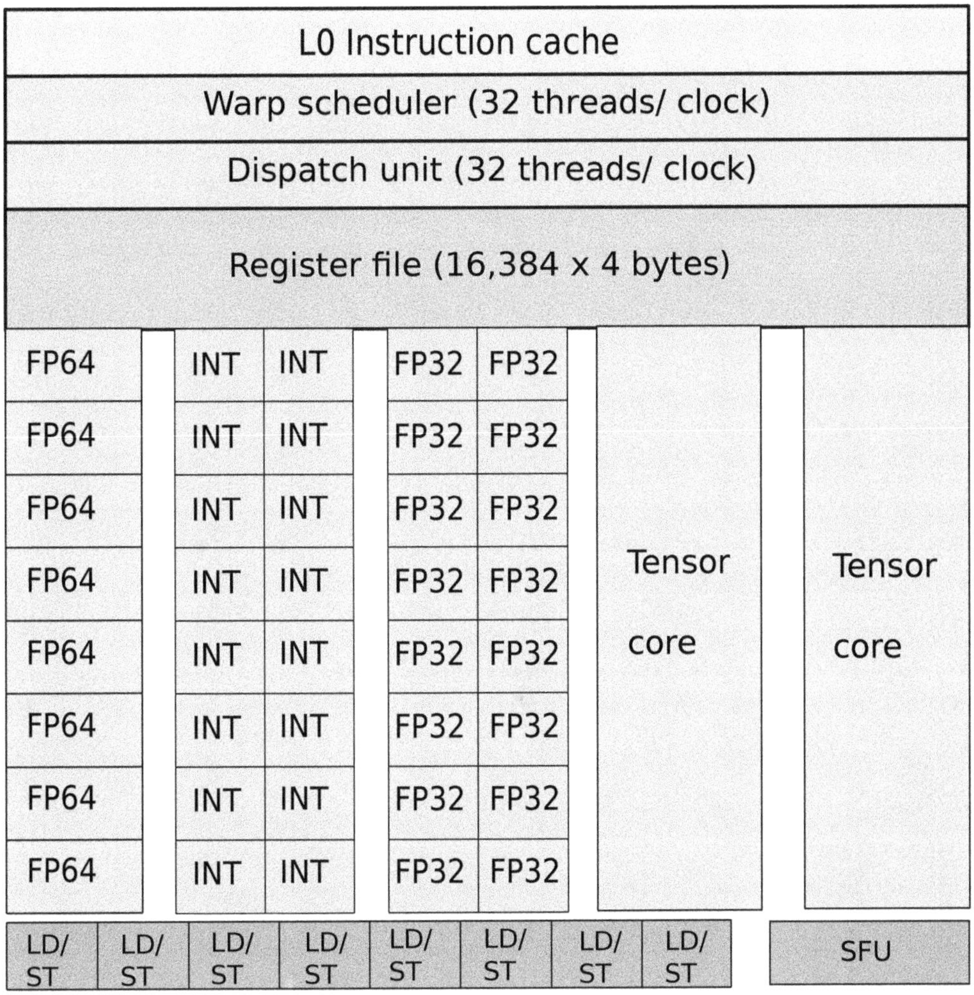

L0 Instruction cache							
Warp scheduler (32 threads/ clock)							
Dispatch unit (32 threads/ clock)							
Register file (16,384 x 4 bytes)							
FP64		INT	INT	FP32	FP32		
FP64		INT	INT	FP32	FP32	Tensor core	Tensor core
FP64		INT	INT	FP32	FP32		
FP64		INT	INT	FP32	FP32		
FP64		INT	INT	FP32	FP32		
FP64		INT	INT	FP32	FP32		
FP64		INT	INT	FP32	FP32		
FP64		INT	INT	FP32	FP32		
LD/ST	LD/ST	LD/ST	LD/ST	LD/ST	LD/ST	LD/ST	LD/ST	SFU

Figure 6.15: Layout of a processing block (adapted from [NVIDIA Inc., 2017])

logic will increase the area of each core, and also increase its power consumption. In a system with hundreds of cores, we cannot afford this. As a result, some order needs to be imposed on the threads.

Modern GPUs (notably NVIDIA's GPUs) follow a SIMT model (single instruction, multiple thread) model. Here, we group a set of threads into *warps*, where a warp typically contains 32 threads. Each thread has the same set of instructions (this is where *single instruction* comes from). When the threads in a warp execute, all of them start from the same point (same program counter). The scheduler maps each thread in the warp to an individual core, and then the threads start executing. However, note that the execution takes place in a special way. Threads do not run uncoordinated; they run in lockstep. This means that after a warp begins, the PB executes the first instruction in the warp for all the threads. Once the first instruction has finished executing for all the threads, it executes the second instruction for all the threads, and so on. The threads, of course, work on different pieces of data.

This is a very simple model of execution and we do not need to have sophisticated hardware to ensure that all the threads are synchronised. The scheduler simply picks the next instruction in a warp and sends it to all the cores. Since all the cores execute the same instruction – albeit on different pieces of data – instruction fetch and dispatch are not difficult tasks. After all the cores finish an instruction, we send the next instruction. Now, this simple picture is riddled with corner cases. Let us see why.

Definition 35

- *The SIMT model – single instruction, multiple thread – is followed in most modern GPUs. Here, the threads run in lockstep. Conceptually, this is like all the threads executing an instruction, waiting till all the threads complete, and then moving on to the next instruction.*

- *The concept of the* warp *is integral to the SIMT model. It is a group of threads that are scheduled together on a PB and executed in lockstep.*

Varying Execution Times

First, instructions might take different amounts of time to execute. For example, it is possible that a memory instruction might not find its data in the L1 cache, and hence it needs to access the L2 cache. In this case it will take more time to complete than the rest of the instructions who possibly find their data in the L1 cache. Instead of letting the rest of the threads continue as in an OOO processor, we make all the threads wait till all the lagging instructions have completed. In general, this is not a very serious problem because all the data for graphical and numerical tasks is typically co-located. We normally do not deal with a lot of irregular memory accesses where data can be present at arbitrary locations. Nevertheless, it is always possible that accesses straddle cache lines and a few of these lines are not present in the cache. In such cases, the SIMT model will lead to a severe performance degradation.

Branch Divergence and Predicated Execution

There is another problem is even more pernicious and difficult to solve. What if we have branches? In this case, different threads will clearly execute different sets of instructions. It will be hard to maintain the SIMT and lockstep properties. Consider an if-else statement. It is possible that based on the data one thread might execute the *if* portion of the code, and the other thread might execute the *else* portion of the code. In this case the lockstep property will be violated. Furthermore, we need to have a mechanism to wait for the threads to converge. Let us explain with an example. Consider the code in Listing 6.2.

Listing 6.2: If-else statements in GPU code

```
1  if (x > 0) {
2      a = 1;
3      b = a + 3;
4      c = b * b;
5  } else {
6      d = 3;
7      c = d * d;
8  }
9  x = c;
```

If we just consider two threads, it is possible that one thread enters the *if* portion and the other thread enters the *else* portion. Let us refer to the threads as threads 1 and 2 respectively. A normal processor would make thread 1 execute Lines 2-4 and then directly jump to Line 9. Similarly, it would make thread 2 execute Lines 6 and 7 and then proceed to Line 9. However, this requires complex logic to compute branch targets, and add offsets to program counters. The two threads will follow divergent paths till they reconverge at Line 9.

Given the fact that thread 1 needs to execute one more instruction as compared to thread 2, we need to make thread 2 wait for the time it takes to execute one instruction. Subsequently, both the threads can start to execute the instruction at Line 9 (point of reconvergence) at the same point of time in lockstep. This is a very complex mechanism and is expensive. Furthermore, it is possible to have nested branches within the *if* portion or the *else* portion. This will further complicate matters.

To keep things simple, GPUs use predicated execution. In this model, all the threads follow the same path. This means that thread 1 processes all the instructions – Lines 2 to 9 – and so does thread 2. However, processing an instruction does not mean executing it. Here is what we mean.

- Thread 1 executes the instructions at Lines 2 – 4.

- However, when it comes to the instructions at Lines 6 and 7, it ignores them. Nevertheless it waits for other threads to finish executing them, if they have to.

- On similar lines, thread 2 ignores the instructions at Lines 2 – 4. It is not the case that it ignores these instructions and moves ahead. Instead it waits for thread 1 to finish executing these instructions. **The threads still move in lockstep.**

- Thread 2 executes the instructions at Lines 6 and 7.

- Finally, both the threads reconverge at the instruction in Line 9.

Definition 36 summarises this discussion and formally defines predicated execution in the context of GPUs.

Definition 36

Predicated execution *refers to a paradigm where a thread executes (processes) instructions belonging to both the paths of a branch instruction. The instructions on the correct path are fully executed, and they are allowed to modify the architectural state. However, the instructions on the* wrong path *are discarded, and not allowed to modify the architectural state.*

In the context of GPUs, predicated execution is heavily used in the SIMT model. All the threads execute all the paths of branches in lockstep. They pretty much treat the instructions in a warp as a sequential piece of code. However, some of these instructions are on the wrong path. The hardware keeps track of these instructions and does not allow them to modify the architectural state. However, this does not mean that the thread moves ahead. The thread still follows the lockstep property, and waits for all the other threads to finish executing that instruction. The instruction scheduler maintains a mask for threads in a warp. Only those threads whose bit in the mask is 1 execute the instruction and the rest ignore it. Alternatively, we can say that if the ith bit in the mask is 1, then it means that the current instruction is in the correct branch path for thread i.

For our running example (Listing 6.2), Figure 6.16 shows a graphical view of the predicated execution. The cross marks indicate that a given instruction is being ignored by a thread.

Using this method threads execute instructions in a warp very easily. Let us now briefly look at how predication is implemented. Let us associate a stack with every thread. Every time we enter the code of a branch (branch path) we push an entry on the stack. If we are on the correct path we push a 1, otherwise we push a 0. If we have nested branches (branches within branches), we do the same. Similarly, when we exit a branch path, we pop the stack. This means that for every line of code in a warp, we maintain a small stack with 1-bit entries. We execute a given instruction and commit it if all the entries in its associated stack are 1. This means that we are on the correct path of all the branches encountered so far. However, if this is not the case, then we ignore the instruction because we are on

	Thread 1	Thread 2
if (x > 0) {	✓	✓
a = 1;	✓	✗
b = a + 3;	✓	✗
c = b * b;	✓	✗
} **else** {		
d = 3;	✗	✓
c = d * d;	✗	✓
}		
x = c;	✓	✓

Figure 6.16: Graphical view of predicated execution

the wrong path of at least one branch. Note that if the stack is empty, then we execute and commit the instruction because this corresponds to the case, where the code is outside the scope of any branch. Before executing every instruction it is not possible to read the contents of the entire stack and compute a logical AND of the bits. We can succinctly store this information in a bit mask that contains 32 bits – one for each thread. If the ith bit is 1, then it means that thread i can correctly execute the instruction. This bit mask is updated when we either enter the body of a conditional statement or exit it.

We show an example in Figure 6.17. Here, we consider three threads: 1A, 1B, and 2. We modify the code in Listing 6.2 (our running example) to add another nested *if* statement in the body of the first *if* statement. Threads 1A and 1B execute the body of the first *if* statement, whereas thread 2 does not. Inside the body of the first *if* statement, thread 1A executes the body of the second *if* statement, whereas thread 1B does not. The stack associated with the branch paths is shown in the figure beside the tick/cross marks. Please note how we push and pop entries into the stack as we enter and exit a group of conditional statements.

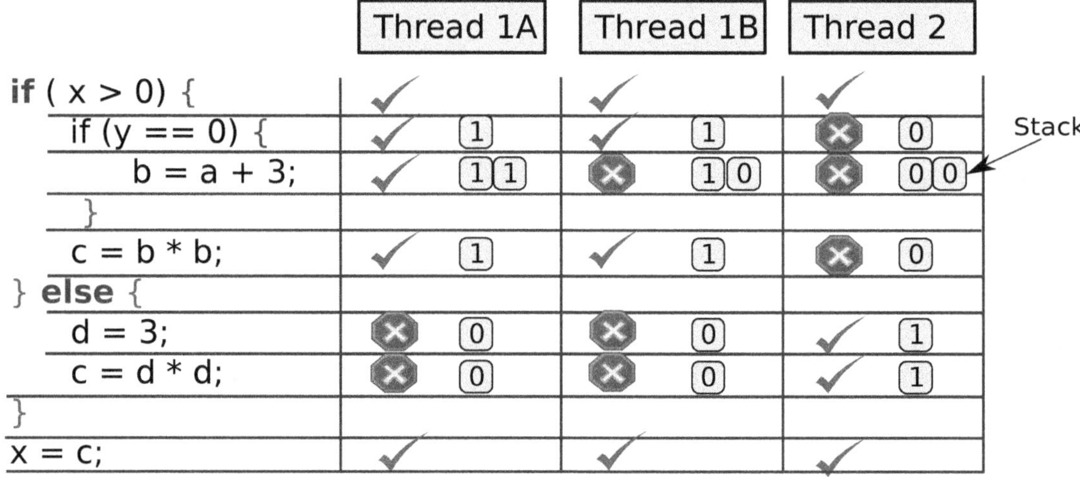

Figure 6.17: Using a stack for predicated execution in GPUs

Finally, we reach the point of reconvergence for all threads.

Definition 37

A point of reconvergence *is an instruction (point in the program) that is executed by all the threads in the warp and is just outside the scope of all previous conditional statements.*

Warp Scheduling

We need to appreciate that it is necessary to group computations into warps in a GPU. This keeps things simple and manageable. Otherwise, if we schedule every instruction independently, the overheads will be prohibitive; it will simply be impractical to do so. Hence, we have the concept of warps. However, we need to schedule warps and this requires a scheduler.

It is the job of the warp scheduler (typically a part of the PB or SM) to schedule the warps. It keeps a set of warps in a buffer. Every few cycles it selects a new warp and executes a few instructions from it. For example in the NVIDIA Tesla [Lindholm et al., 2008] GPU, the warp scheduler stores a maximum of 24 warps. Every cycle it can choose one of the warps and make it run. Later designs have modified this basic design, and have made the warp scheduler more complicated. For example, the NVIDIA Fermi GPU can select two warps at a time, and execute them simultaneously – each warp has 16 cores, 16 load/store units, or 4 SFUs at its disposal [Wittenbrink et al., 2011]. Later designs such as NVIDIA Kepler [GTX, 2014] have four warp schedulers per SM. In our reference architecture inspired by NVIDIA Volta [NVIDIA Inc., 2017], we divide an SM into four PBs, and we have one warp scheduler per PB.

The simplest strategy is to run a single warp at a time. However, running multiple warps at a time has some inherent advantages. Let us explain with an example. Consider an SM with 16 load/store units, and 16 ALUs. Furthermore, assume that a warp has 32 threads. Given that we execute the instructions in lockstep, all the instructions will be of the same type. Let us assume that we can either have memory instructions (load/store) or ALU instructions. This means that we can keep only half the number of functional units busy: either 16 ALUs or 16 load/store units. However, if we are able to schedule two unrelated warps at the same time, then we can do better. It is possible to make full use of the resources if we can overlap the execution of ALU instructions of one warp with the memory instructions of the other warp. In this case, one warp will use 16 ALUs, and the other warp will use the 16 load/store units. We will thus have 100% utilisation.

Another possible option is to have a single warp scheduler with 32 ALUs and 32 load/store units. From the point of view of execution latency, this is a good idea; however, this is wasteful in terms of resources. It is best to have a heterogeneous set of units, and have the capability to schedule threads from multiple unrelated warps in the same cycle. If we have a good scheduler it will be able to ensure a high utilisation rate of the functional units, and thus increase the overall execution throughput.

We can go a step further and schedule warps from different applications together, which is done in the NVIDIA Pascal architecture and later architectures. It does not strictly separate resources as previous architectures do. It allows a flexible allocation of functional units to threads of different warps depending upon the warp's criticality. Furthermore, NVIDIA Pascal also supports quick preemption. It is possible to quickly save the work of a warp, and switch to another task. Once that task finishes we can quickly resume the work of the unfinished warp.

Independent Scheduling of Threads in a Warp

Till now we have treated a warp as a group of 32 threads that have a single program counter. Furthermore, we have a 32-bit mask associated with each warp. For an instruction, if the ith bit is set, then only thread i executes it and commits the results to the architectural state. Otherwise, for thread i this instruction is on the wrong path, and it is not executed. This architecture unfortunately has a problem. Consider the code in Listing 6.3 in a system with a hypothetical 4-thread warp.

Listing 6.3: Deadlocks in a CUDA program

```
1  x = 0;
2  if (threadIdx.x < 2) {
3      while (x == 0) {}
4  } else {
5      x = 1;
6      y = 1;
7  }
```

We have four threads with ids 0, 1, 2, and 3 respectively. Two of the threads will execute the *while* loop (Line 3), and two threads will execute the code in Lines 5 and 6. If we run the code on a regular multicore processor, then there will be no deadlock. This is because first threads 0 and 1 will wait at the *while* loop. Then either thread 2 or thread 3 will set x equal to 1 in Line 5. This will release threads 0 and 1. However, in the case of a GPU with our lockstepped threading model, this code will have a deadlock. All the four threads will first arrive at the *while* loop in Line 3. For two threads (0 and 1) the *while* loop is on the correct path, and for the other two threads (2 and 3), it is on the wrong path. Threads 2 and 3 will not execute the loop; however, they will wait for threads 0 and 1 to finish executing the *while* loop. Unfortunately, this is where the problem lies. Threads 0 and 1 will never come out of the loop. They will be stuck forever because $x = 0$. Threads 2 and 3 will never reach Line 5 where they can set x to 1. This is an unacceptable situation. We can perform such synchronising accesses between threads across different warps but not between threads in the same warp!

The solution is to maintain separate execution state for each thread. This includes a separate thread specific program counter, and a call stack. This however does break the notion of threads executing in lockstep, and has the potential for increasing the overheads significantly. Let us look at how the designers of NVIDIA Volta solved this problem.

They introduced the notion of *restricted lockstep* execution. This is shown in Figure 6.18. In the figure we define three blocks of instructions: W (while loop), X ($x = 1$), and Y ($y = 1$).

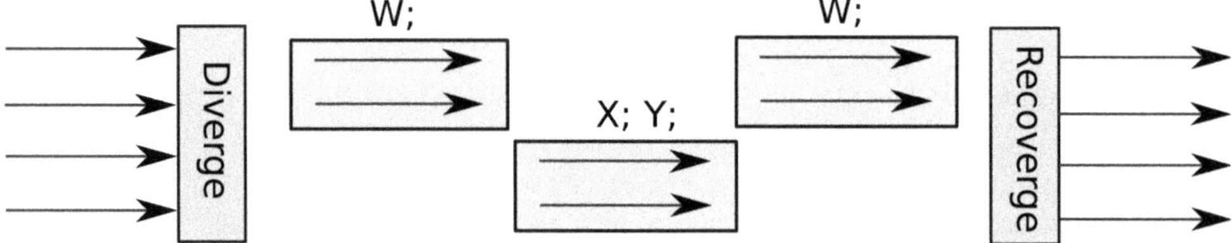

Figure 6.18: SIMT execution with per thread state

As we can see, the execution model is still SIMT. In any cycle, all the **active threads** in the warp still execute the same instruction. However, unlike our previous model, we do not proceed sequentially. We increase the degree of concurrency by executing the code blocks X and Y concurrently with the code block W. Let us follow the timeline. We first execute the code block W. We are not able to make progress because $x = 0$. Then we execute the code blocks X and Y. Subsequently, we execute the code block W once again. This time we are able to make progress because x has been set to 1. We thus leave the *if-else* block and our divergent threads reconverge.

We can also force reconvergence between the threads by calling the CUDA function _*syncwarp*(). In general, the role of the GPU is to ensure as much of SIMT execution as possible. This means that it needs to group together as many active threads as it can per instruction, and also ensure that all threads make forward progress. The latter ensures that we do not have deadlocks as we showed in Listing 6.18.

The reader needs to convince herself that this method allows us to use lock and unlock functions in GPU threads similar to regular CPU threads.

6.4.5   The GPU Pipeline

Way Point 6

- *In our reference architecture, the GPU consists of a set of 6 GPCs, a large 6MB L2 cache, 8 memory controllers, and 6 NVLink controllers.*

- *Each GPC consists of 14 SMs (streaming multiprocessors).*

- *Each SM consists of 4 processing blocks, an L1 instruction cache, and a 128 KB data cache.*

- *Each processing block (PB) contains 16 integer cores, 16 single precision FP cores, and 8 double precision FP cores. It additionally contains two tensor cores for matrix operations, 8 load/store units, and a dedicated special function unit.*

- *Each PB executes a warp of threads in parallel. The threads in the warp access the large 64 KB register file, and the L1 cache of the SM most of the time. If they record misses in these top level memories, then they access the L2 cache and finally the off-chip DRAM.*

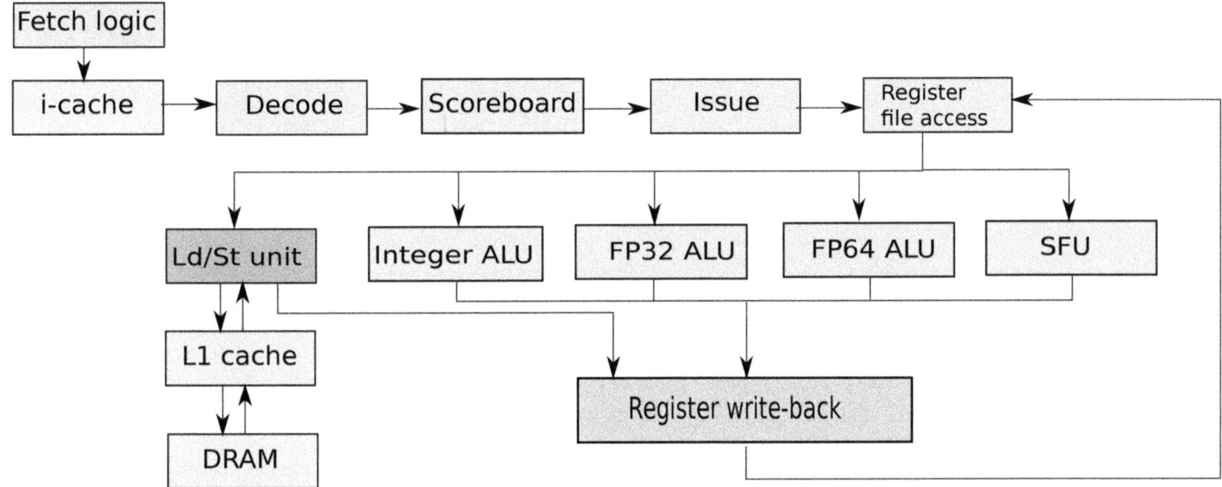

Figure 6.19: A GPGPU's pipeline

Figure 6.19 shows the pipeline of a GPGPU core. It is similar to a regular in-order pipeline as described in Section 2.1. Let us elaborate.

Once we have decided to schedule a warp, we read its instructions from the i-cache. We decode the instructions and while dispatching the instructions we check for dependences. We typically do not use expensive mechanisms like the rename table or reservation stations. They consume excessive amounts of power and are also not efficient in terms of area. We use the simple scoreboard based mechanism as described in Section 5.6.5. Recall that a scoreboard is a simple table that we use to track dependences between instructions. Once the instructions in a warp are ready to be issued, we send them to the register file. Unlike a CPU's register file, a register file in a GPU is a very large structure. It is almost as large as a cache – 64 KB in our reference architecture. We shall look at the design of a GPU's register file in Section 6.4.6.

To support lockstep execution of all the active threads, we need to read all their data at once. This requires a very high throughput register file. Once we have read all the data, we send it to the functional units. They compute the result, access memory (if required), and finally write the results back to the register file or the relevant memory structure.

6.4.6 The Register File

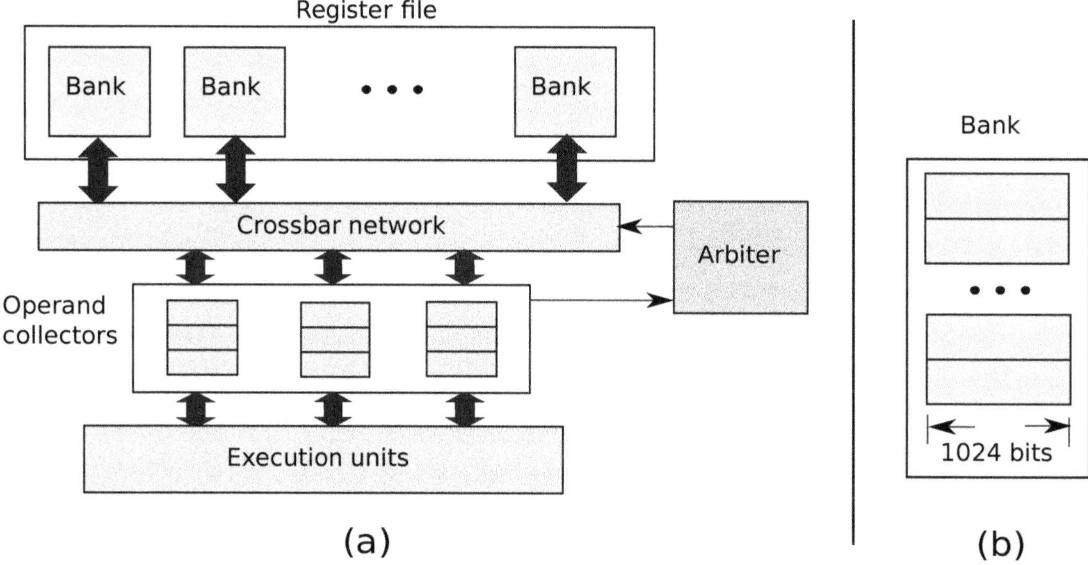

Figure 6.20: The register file in a GPU

The PTX ISA assumes an infinite number of registers. The advantage of this is that the PTX code can remain platform independent, and the code can be written in terms of virtual registers, which improves the effectiveness of a host of compiler optimisations. While generating the binary code we can assign real registers to the virtual registers. This can be done by the PTX assembler, *ptxas*, or in the process of JIT (just-in-time) compilation of the binary.

Let us now consider the design of the register file. In a GPU we need a very high-throughput register file given the bandwidth requirements. It is impractical to read and write data at the granularity of 4-byte words given that we have at least 32 threads running at the same time in a processing block. Consider a piece of code where all the threads in a warp use a 32-bit local variable. We need to create 32 copies of this variable. The total number of bytes that we need to allocate is $32 \times 32 = 1024$ bits. We thus set the block size in the register file to 1024 bits (or 128 bytes). This is shown in Figure 6.20(b) that shows a bank in a register file with a 1024-bit block size. A bank is defined as a subcache (see Section 7.3.2). We typically divide a large cache into multiple banks to increase the performance and reduce power consumption.

Let us now design a register file (see Figure 6.20(a)). Assume we have a 64 KB register file. We can divide it into 16 banks, where the size of each bank is 4 KB. If the size of a single entry is 128 bytes, we shall have 32 such entries in each register file bank. In a lot of modern GPUs that have many outstanding instructions and frequent warp switches, there are many memory instructions in flight. There is thus an elevated chance of *bank conflicts* – conflicting accesses to the same bank. This will further cause delays because we can process only one memory request at a time per bank. In addition, we cannot read and transfer 1024 bits at the same time; we need to read 1024 bits over several cycles. Moreover, we may have wider operands such as double precision values. In this case, we need to store the set of 32 values in multiple banks. All of these values have to be read, collected, and then sent to the execution units within the PB.

We thus create a set of buffers known as operand collectors, where each entry is associated with an instruction. It stores the values of all the source operands. We connect the banks and the operand collectors with a crossbar switch, which is an $N \times M$ switch. We have N ports for the banks in the register file, and M ports for the operand collectors. We can route data from any bank to any operand collector (all-to-all traffic). Once each entry in the operand collector receives all its source operands in entirety, the values are sent to the arrays of execution units within the PB.

6.4.7 L1 Caches

Similar to the register file, the memory bandwidth demands are very high for the caches particularly the L1 cache that sees all the accesses. If the L1 hit rate is high, then the traffic that reaches the L2 cache is significantly reduced. Furthermore, since the L2 cache is much larger, we can afford to create many more banks to sustain more parallelism. Hence, out of all the memory structures the L1 cache is the most critical.

In the case of memory accesses, we will have a set of accesses: one for each thread. Since we have 8 load/store units in our reference architecture, we can issue 8 or 16 memory accesses per cycle depending upon the parallelism in the load/store units. The second stage is an arbiter, which figures out the bank conflicts between the accesses. It splits the set of accesses into two subsets. The first subset does not have any bank conflicts between the accesses, and the second set of accesses have bank conflicts with the first subset, and might have more conflicts between them. The addresses in the first subset are then routed to the L1 cache. If the accesses are writes, then the process ends here. If the accesses are reads, we read the data and route them to the operand collectors associated with the register file. Subsequently, we send the requests from the second set that do not have bank conflicts, and so on.

Let us now look at some special cases. Assume we have a miss in the cache. We then use a structure like an MSHR (miss status handling register) to record the miss (see Section 7.4.2 for the definition of an MSHR). Similar to a traditional MSHR, we can merge requests if they are for different words in the same block. Once the block arrives into the cache, we lock the corresponding line to ensure that it is not evicted, and *replay* the load/store accesses for different words within that block from the MSHR. Similarly, we replay the instructions that access words within the block and could not be sent to the cache because of bank conflicts. Once the accesses are done, we unlock the line.

6.5   Summary and Further Reading

6.5.1   Summary

Summary 5

1. *General purpose processors are limited by their power consumption and IPC. In practice, the IPC almost never exceeds 4.*

2. *Linear algebra operations that form the core of much of today's scientific computing are often embarrassingly parallel and have a high ILP. This parallelism cannot be exploited by general purpose processors. Hence, we need specialised hardware.*

3. *Graphics processors (GPUs) were initially used for rendering graphics. Their core was a shader program whose job was to translate users' directives into graphical objects.*

4. *The input to shaders was a list of triangles, and the output was a set of triangles or pixels after applying various graphical effects.*

5. *The four parts of a basic rendering pipeline are the Vertex processor, Rasteriser, Fragment processor, and the Pixel engine.*

    (a) *The Vertex processor accepts a list of triangles as input, and then performs geometric transformations on them.*

    (b) *The Rasteriser converts all the triangles to a set of pixels. It can also optionally perform visibility calculations to determine which set of pixels (fragments) are visible in the final scene.*

    (c) *The Fragment processor has three major functions: interpolation of colours, texture mapping, and fog computation.*

        i. *It computes the colour of each pixel using interpolation based techniques. There are two common approaches to do this: Goraud shading and Phong shading.*
        ii. *It adds texture information to each fragment.*
        iii. *Based on the distance of an object from the view point, it shades objects differently (fog computation). This provides a perception of distance to the human eye.*

    (d) *Then we have the pixel engine that computes the depth and visibility of each object, and applies transparency effects. If an object is transparent or translucent, then objects behind it are also visible.*

6. *The Vertex processor in modern GPUs has been replaced by a Polymorph engine. It performs the following roles.*

    (a) *Vertex fetching: It computes the coordinates of the objects in the scene and their orientation, and can add visual or geometric effects to the objects in the scene.*

    (b) *Tessellation: Break down all the objects into a set of triangles and creates a degree of fine detail on the surface.*

    (c) *Viewport Transformation: We typically render large scenes in a virtual coordinate system. However, all the objects need not be entirely visible on the screen (the viewport). In this stage we compute the parts of the objects that are visible.*

(d) *Attribute setup: Annotate each triangle with the depth information for visibility calculations.*

(e) *Stream output: Write the information computed by the Polymorph engine to memory.*

7. *Most GPUs have their own ISAs. NVIDIA GPUs can be programmed using the CUDA framework, which uses an extension of C++. The code is separately compiled for the CPU and the GPU, respectively.*

8. *CUDA programs are typically compiled to the PTX ISA, which is a virtual ISA. At runtime the compiler that is a part of the GPU driver converts PTX to native GPU code (SASS code).*

9. *A CUDA function that is invoked by the host CPU and runs on the GPU is known as a kernel. A GPU spawns multiple instances of the kernel, and assigns each instance to a thread. In the general case, the threads are organised as a 3D matrix – this is known as a block. The blocks can further be arranged in a 3D form – this is known as a grid. Every thread knows its coordinates in its block, and its block's coordinates in the grid. This information is used to split the input data among the threads.*

10. *A CUDA program has access to four types of memory: device (on the GPU), host (on the CPU), shared (resides in per-block shared memory), and managed (can be used from both the CPU and GPU).*

11. *The design of a GPGPU is as follows:*

    (a) *A GPGPU has a multitude of GPCs (graphics processing clusters), an L2 cache, and high speed links to memory.*

    (b) *A GPC further contains multiple TPCs (texture processing clusters), and each TPC contains multiple SMs (streaming multiprocessors).*

    (c) *Each SM consists of multiple processing blocks, where each processing block contains an i-cache, warp scheduler, dispatch unit, register file, a set of integer and floating point ALUs, load-store units, special function units, and a few tensor cores.*

    (d) *Typically, 32 GPU threads are grouped together as a warp. They execute together in lockstep.*

    (e) *The tensor cores contain units for performing matrix multiplication. This is useful in linear algebra and machine learning algorithms.*

12. *Most GPUs implement predicated execution where each thread processes instructions in both the correct and wrong paths of a branch. The instructions on the wrong path are dynamically converted to nops. This is known as predicated execution.*

13. *Efficient warp scheduling is very important. Scheduling multiple warps at a time makes better use of resources.*

14. *GPUs have very large and sophisticated register files. Their size is typically between 32 and 128 KB.*

15. *The L1 cache is divided into multiple banks. We divide the set of accesses by a warp into two sets: accesses that do not have bank conflicts between them, and accesses that have conflicts. The latter set of accesses are sent to the cache after the first set of accesses. They are said to be replayed.*

16. *The L2 cache in a GPU is connected to external DRAM using a high bandwidth interconnect.*

6.5.2   Further Reading

Readers should start with the CUDA programming language. The most authentic CUDA programming resources are available on NVIDIA's website [NVIDIA, 2018]. Readers can additionally consult the book by Rob Farber [Farber, 2011] on developing GPU applications. In addition to CUDA, interested readers can also learn OpenCL if they wish to program AMD GPUs. The book by Kaeli et al. [Kaeli et al., 2015] is a good starting point.

For the architecture of GPUs, the starting point is NVIDIA's documentation for their architectures: Tesla [Lindholm et al., 2008], Fermi [Wittenbrink et al., 2011], Kepler [Corporation, 2014b], Maxwell [GTX, 2014], Pascal [Corporation, 2014a], and Volta [NVIDIA Inc., 2017]. To conduct research in this area users need a software based GPU simulator. Some of the popular simulators are GPUTejas [Malhotra et al., 2014], and GPGPU-Sim [Bakhoda et al., 2009]. GPUWattch [Leng et al., 2013] is a power model that can be plugged into the GPGPU-Sim simulator. Programming GPUs is increasingly getting easier. The Theano [Bergstra et al., 2010] project proposes a Python based framework to run code on the GPU. For studying GPUs further we can write specialised micro-benchmarks to understand their performance characteristics using the approach proposed by Wong et al. [Wong et al., 2010] or we can use Hong et al.'s analytical models [Hong and Kim, 2009].

Exercises

Ex. 1 — What is a better idea: have more threads per block and less blocks per grid or have less threads per block and more blocks per grid? Assume that the total number of threads is the same.

Ex. 2 — Write CUDA code to implement the following algorithms:

1.Matrix multiplication.

2.Matrix multiplication using the Tensor Processing Units of the NVIDIA Turing GPU.

3.Solution of the Fourier heat equation.

4.Sorting 10 million numbers.

5.Find edges in an image.

Ex. 3 — How does a GPU core handle WAW and WAR hazards?

Ex. 4 — What are the pros and cons of having a large register file in the context of a CPU and a GPU?

Ex. 5 — Theoretically analyse the computation time of a matrix multiplication operation on a GPU and a CPU.

Ex. 6 — What is the *_syncthreads()* instruction in CUDA? When is it useful?

Ex. 7 — Can we replace the register file of a GPU with a block of shared memory? Explain you answer.

Ex. 8 — How do we detect and handle bank conflicts while accessing the first level cache in a GPU?

*** Ex. 9** — Describe the architectural mechanism for SIMT execution with per-thread state.

Design Problems

Ex. 10 — Understand the working of the GPU simulator *GPUTejas*™.

Ex. 11 — Implement predicated execution in *GPUTejas*.

Part II

The Memory System

7

Caches

In the second part of this book, we shall focus on the design of the memory system. To sustain a high performance pipeline, we need a high performance memory system. Otherwise, we will not be able to realise the gains of having a high performance pipeline. It is like having a strong body and a strong mind. Unless we have a strong body, we cannot have a strong mind, and vice versa.

The most important element in the on-chip memory system is the notion of a cache that stores a subset of the memory space, and the hierarchy of caches. In this section, we assume that the reader is well aware of the basics of caches, and is also aware of the notion of virtual memory. We shall provide a very brief introduction to these topics in this section for the sake of recapitulation. However, this might be woefully insufficient for readers with no prior background. Hence, readers are requested to take a look at some basic texts such as [Sarangi, 2015] to refresh their basics.

In line with this thinking, we shall provide a very quick overview of cache design in Section 7.1 and virtual memory in Section 7.2. Then, we shall move on to discuss methods to analytically estimate the area, timing, and power consumption of caches in Section 7.3. This will give us a practical understanding of the issues involved in designing caches. We shall then extend this section to consider advanced cache design techniques in Section 7.4.

We will then proceed to look at a very unconventional design – Intel's trace cache – in Section 7.5. It is designed to store sequences of instructions, whereas conventional caches are designed to store just blocks of bytes. Storing traces gives us a lot of benefits. In most cases we can completely skip the fetch and decode stages.

The next half of the chapter focuses on using methods to improve the efficiency of the memory system by using complicated logic that resides outside the caching structures. In Sections 7.6 and 7.7, we shall focus on prefetching mechanisms where we try to predict the memory blocks that are required in the near future and try to fetch them in advance. This reduces the average memory latency. Prefetching techniques are highly effective for both instructions and data.

7.1 Memory Hierarchy and the Notion of Caches

Let us provide a quick introduction to the memory systems in today's processors. Let us start by noting that we need memory to store instructions and data. At the level of the memory system it does not matter if we are storing instructions or data. We treat everything as data, and the memory system with some exceptions is oblivious of the contents of the bytes that it stores. In fact storing instructions as data was one of the most revolutionary ideas in the history of computing. The credit goes to early pioneers such as Alan Turing and John von Neumann.

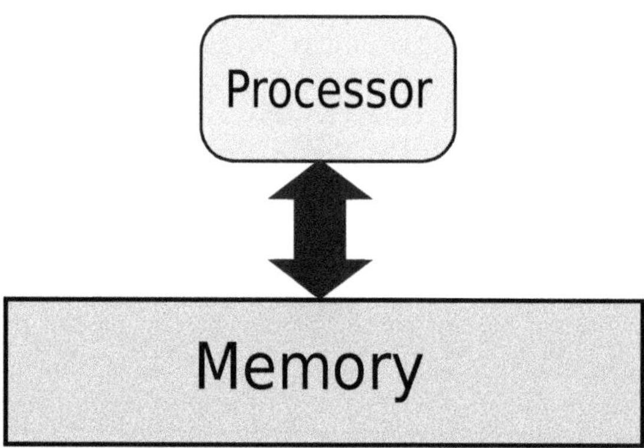

Figure 7.1: A simple processor-memory system (Von Neumann architecture)

In a simplistic model we have the processor connected to the memory system as shown in Figure 7.1: the memory system stores both instructions and data. This is the Von Neumann architecture. The main problem with this organisation is that a single unified memory is too large and too slow. If every memory access takes 100s of cycles, the IPC will be less than 0.01. A ready fix to this issue is to use registers, which are named storage locations within the processor. Each register takes less than a cycle to access and this is why we use registers for most instructions. However, to keep the register file fast, we need to keep it small. Hence, we have a limited number of on-chip registers. The number is typically limited to 8 or 16.

Compilers often run out of registers while mapping variables to registers. It is thus necessary to spill the values of some registers to memory to free them. The spilled values can then be read back from memory, whenever we need to use them. Additionally, it is also necessary to store the registers to memory before calling a function. This is because the function may overwrite some of the registers, and their original contents will be lost. Finally, we need to restore their values once the function returns. Along with local variables in functions, most programs also use large arrays and data structures that need to be stored in the memory system. Because of multiple such reasons, memory accesses are an integral part of program execution. In fact, memory instructions account for roughly a third of all the instructions in most programs.

We have till now discussed only data accesses. However, instructions are also stored in the memory system, and every cycle we need to fetch them from the memory system. The part of the memory system that stores the instructions is traditionally known as the instruction memory. Having one single memory for both instructions and data is an inefficient solution because it needs to simultaneously provide both instructions and data. This increases the overheads significantly. Hence, a more practical method is to split the unified memory into separate instruction and data memories as shown in Figure 7.2. This is known as the Harvard architecture.

To store all the instructions and data in a modern program, we need large memories. Large memories are slow, have large area, and consume a lot of power. Another direct consequence of a large memory size is that such memories cannot be fit within the CPU. They need to reside outside the CPU (off-chip). Accessing off-chip memory (also referred to as *main memory*) for both instructions and data is simply not practical, neither feasible. In most processors, it takes 200-300 cycles to get data back from off-chip memory. This will decrease our IPC significantly.

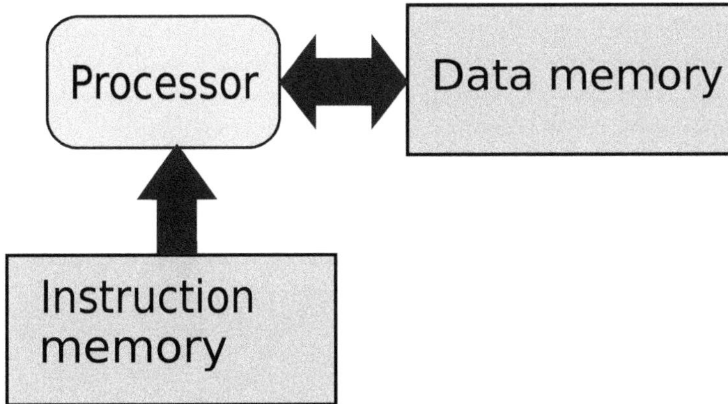

Figure 7.2: The Harvard architecture

7.1.1 Temporal and Spatial Locality

There is thus a dire need to fix this situation. Let us make use of some common patterns in programs to suggest an organisation of the memory system. Most programs contain loops, and also spend most of their time executing loops. Loops are typically small pieces of code, particularly when we consider the entire program. Most programs typically move from function to function. In each function they do some intense activity within a hierarchy of loops, and then move to another function where they do the same. Such kind of patterns are very common in programming languages, and are often referred to using two very special names: *spatial locality* and *temporal locality*.

Spatial Locality

Spatial locality refers to a pattern where we access objects that are in some sense proximate (close by) in a small interval of time. Before looking at deeper aspects of this definition, let us explain with an example. Consider the instructions in a loop. In terms of PC addresses, we access instructions that have addresses that are close by. Thus, we have spatial locality. Similarly, when we are accessing an array, we also have spatial locality if we are accessing it sequentially – from indices 0 to N. Spatial locality is an inherent property of most programs that we use in our everyday life. As a result, most computer architects take spatial locality in programs for granted.

Note that there is some vagueness in the definition. We have not precisely defined what exactly we mean by "a small interval of time". Is it in nanoseconds, microseconds, or hours? This is subjective, and depends on the scenario.

Consider a loop. If in every iteration of a loop we access an array location in sequence, we have spatial locality because of the way we are accessing the array. Now assume that we take the same loop and in every iteration we insert a function call that takes a few thousand cycles to complete. Do we still have spatial locality? The answer is, no. This is because it is true that we are accessing nearby addresses in the array; however, this is being done across thousands of cycles. This is by no means a small interval of time as compared to the time it takes to access a single location in an array. Hence, we do not have spatial locality.

Let us further augment the code of the loop to include an access to the hard disk that takes a million cycles. Let the hard disk accesses be to consecutive sectors (blocks of 512 bytes on the disk). Do we have spatial locality? We do not have spatial locality for the array accesses; however, we do have spatial locality for the disk accesses. This is because in the time scale of a disk access (a few million cycles), the instructions of the loop qualify as a "small interval of time". The summary of this discussion is that we need to deduce spatial locality on a case by case basis. The accesses that we are considering to be "spatially local" should occupy a non-trivial fraction of the interval under consideration.

A related concept is the notion of the *working set*. It is defined as the set of memory addresses that a program accesses repeatedly in a short time interval. Here again, the definition of *short* is on the same lines as the definition for spatial locality – there is a degree of subjectivity. This subjectivity can be reduced if we realise that program execution can typically be divided into phases: in each phase a program executes the same piece of code and accesses the same region of data over and over again, and then moves to another region of the code – the next phase begins. We typically have spatial locality for accesses within a phase, and the set of addresses accessed repeatedly in a phase comprise the working set at that point of time.

Definition 38

We can divide program execution into phases, where each phase has a distinct pattern in terms of instruction and data accesses. Within a phase, we typically access data that is proximate in terms of memory addresses – this is known as spatial locality. The set of addresses accessed repeatedly in a phase comprises the working set of the program at that point of time.

Temporal Locality

Let us consider a program with loops once again. There are some variables and regions of memory that we tend to access frequently in a small interval of time. For example, in a loop we access the loop variables frequently, and also we execute the instructions in the loop in every iteration. Even while walking through an array we access the base register of the array on every access. Such patterns, where we keep accessing the same memory locations over and over again, is referred to as *temporal locality*. Note that temporal locality has been found to be a general property in most programs. Temporal locality is observed while accessing instructions or data. In fact, we can see temporal locality in almost all memory and storage structures inside the chip.

Most schemes in computer architecture are designed to make use of temporal locality. For example, a branch predictor uses this fact to keep a small table of saturating counters. The expectation is that the hit rate (probability of finding an entry) in this table will be high; this is guaranteed by temporal locality. The branch target buffer operates on a similar principle. Even predictors such as value predictors or dependence predictors rely on the same phenomenon. Had we not had temporal locality, most of our architectural structures would have never come into being. In the case of of the memory system as well, we shall explicitly rely on temporal locality in our memory access patterns.

Definition 39

Temporal locality refers to an access pattern where we repeatedly access the same locations over and over again in a small interval of time.

7.1.2 Notion of a Cache

We now know that a typical memory access stream has both temporal locality and spatial locality. We also know that we cannot afford large memories. What do we do?

We can take inspiration from registers, and create a structure that can be conceptually thought of as a larger register file. This structure can keep the data corresponding to the most frequently accessed memory addresses close to the processor. It will also be small, fast, and power efficient. Since we have temporal locality, we can expect to find most of our data in this structure. Let us call such a structure a *cache*. Formally, a cache is a memory structure that stores a subset of the memory values used by a program. We can also say that a cache stores a subset of the program's address space, where the address space is defined as the set of addresses that a program uses. Finally, note that this is a non-contiguous subset. For example, we can have addresses 8, 100, and 400 in the cache, and not have a lot of intervening addresses. The bottom line is that caches store frequently accessed data and instructions. Hence, due to temporal locality, we are guaranteed to see a high cache hit rate (probability of successfully finding a value).

> **Definition 40**
> *If we find a value in the cache, then this event is known as a cache* hit, *otherwise it is known as a cache* miss.

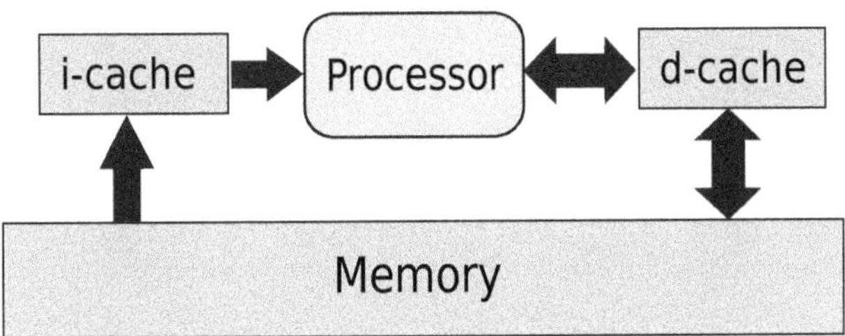

Figure 7.3: The i-cache and d-cache

Taking inspiration from the Harvard and Von Neumann architectures, we arrive at the design in Figure 7.3, where the pipeline reads in data from the instruction cache (i-cache), and reads or writes data to the data cache (d-cache). These are small caches, which as of 2020 are from 16 KB to 64 KB in size. They are referred to as the level 1 or L1 caches. Often when people use the word "L1 cache" they refer to the data cache. We shall sometimes use this terminology. The usage will be clear from the context.

Observe that in Figure 7.3, we have the processor, two caches, and a combined memory that stores instructions and data: we have successfully combined the Harvard and Von Neumann paradigms. The access protocol is as follows. For both instructions and data, we first access the respective caches. If we find the instruction or data bytes, then we use them. This event is known as a *cache hit*. Otherwise, we have a *cache miss*. In this case, we go down to the lower level, which is a large memory that contains all the code and data used by the program. It is guaranteed to contain everything (all code and data bytes). Recall that we store instructions as data in structures that store both kinds of information. Finally, note that this is a very simplistic picture. We shall keep on refining it, and adding more detail in the subsequent sections.

Up till now we have not taken advantage of spatial locality. Let us take advantage of it by grouping bytes into blocks. Instead of operating on small groups of bytes at a time, let us instead create blocks of 32 or 64 bytes. Blocks are atomic units in a cache. We always fetch or evict an entire block in one go – not in smaller units. One advantage of this is that we automatically leverage spatial locality. Let's say we are accessing an array, and the array elements are stored in contiguous memory locations as is most often the case. We access the first element, which is 4 bytes wide. If the block containing the element is not in the cache, then we fetch the entire block from the memory to the cache. If this element was at the beginning of the 32-byte block, then the remaining 28 bytes are automatically fetched because they are a part of the same block. This means that for the next 7 accesses (28 bytes = 7 accesses * 4 bytes/access), we have the elements in the cache. They can be quickly accessed. In this case, by creating blocks, we have taken advantage of spatial locality, and consequently reduced the time it takes to access the array elements.

Way Point 7

We now know that memory access patterns exhibit both temporal and spatial locality. Most modern memory systems take advantage of these properties. This is done as follows:

- *We create a small structure called a cache that stores the values corresponding to a subset of the memory addresses used by the program. Because of temporal locality, we are guaranteed to find our data or instructions in the caches most of the time. Two such structures that most processors typically use are the instruction cache (i-cache) and the data cache (d-cache).*

- *To take advantage of spatial locality, we group consecutive bytes into blocks. Furthermore, we treat blocks atomically, and fetch or evict data at the granularity of blocks within the memory system. The advantage of fetching 32-64 bytes at once is conspicuously visible when we are accessing a sequence of contiguous instructions or accessing an array. If we read a memory word (4 bytes), then with a very high probability we shall find the next memory word in the same block. Since the block has already been fetched from memory, and kept in the cache, the access time for other memory words in the same block will get reduced significantly. In other words, if our access pattern has spatial locality, then we will find many memory words in the cache because other words in the same blocks would have already been fetched. This will reduce our overall memory access time.*

7.1.3   Hierarchy of Caches

Till now we have discussed the need and use of an i-cache and a d-cache. However, we can stretch our line of argument further and have another larger cache between them and the off-chip main memory. This cache can contain both data as well as instructions – at this level we do not differentiate between data and instructions, they are both treated as data. This is typically known as the L2 (level 2) cache, and as of 2020, it is roughly between 256 KB and 8 MB. The L2 cache is larger and slower as compared to the L1 caches.

The access protocol is as follows. The processor first accesses the L1 caches (i-cache and d-cache). Because of temporal locality, we expect most of the accesses to be hits. Just in case we miss in the L1 caches, then we need to fetch the data from the lower level in the memory system, which will be an L2 cache. The L1 caches are typically very fast, and often provide the data in 1-3 clock cycles. In comparison, L2 caches are much slower and can take anywhere from 10-50 cycles depending on how much time it takes to send a message to the cache, execute the operation, and get the data back. However, this is still better than main memory that typically takes 200-400 cycles to access. Owing to temporal and spatial locality, we expect a good hit rate at this level as well.

Most embedded and laptop processors do not have any more levels in the cache hierarchy. If there is a miss in the L2 cache, then they send the request to the main memory. However, in most modern processors that are used in servers and high-end desktops, we have an additional L3 (level 3) cache, which is much larger (2-16 MB), and consequently slower as well (access time: 20-80 cycles). Because of similar reasons, the L3 level can particularly be beneficial if we are accessing a large amount of data. As of 2020 some servers have started including an L4 cache as well.

We thus have a memory system that consists of a hierarchy of caches as shown in Figure 7.4.

It is important to mention at this stage that the caches are inclusive. This means that if a block exists in the L1 cache, it has to be present in the caches at all the lower levels: L2, L3, and main memory. This property is known as *inclusion*, and caches with this property are known as inclusive caches. The

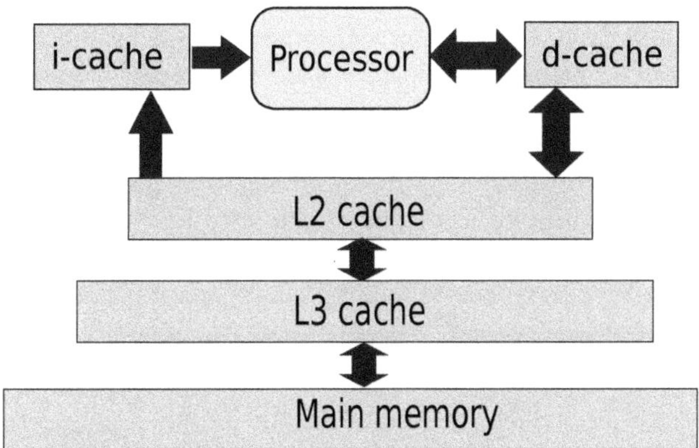

Figure 7.4: Hierarchy of caches

same holds true for the L2 cache as well. If we have a block in the L2 cache, then it has to be present in the L3 cache and main memory.

Inclusion simplifies things significantly. If we evict a block in the L1 cache, then the changes can be seamlessly written to the possibly older copy of the block present in the L2 cache. However, if the block is not present in the L2 cache, and we have modified its contents, the situation becomes tricky. We need to search in the L3 cache, and main memory to find if they contain the block. This increases the complexity of the cache logic significantly. However, inclusion has its costs. If the processor is fetching a block for the first time, then it needs to come from main memory and be stored in each of the levels of the cache hierarchy.

Example 3
A natural question that might arise is why do we stop at 2 or 3 cache levels. Why do not we have 7 or 8 levels of caches?

Answer: *Caches are not particularly free. They have costs in terms of the transistor area. Given that we cannot synthesise very large silicon dies, we have to limit the number of transistors that we place on the chip. The typical silicon die size is about 200 mm^2 for desktop processors and 400-500 mm^2 for server class processors. In larger dies, we can place more transistors; however, we cannot place enough to create additional caching levels.*

Also note that as we go to lower and lower cache levels the miss rates typically become high and saturate. The incremental benefit of having more cache levels goes down.

Finally, additional layers of caches introduce additional overheads in terms of the area and power consumed by the caches. Moreover, the miss penalty increases for a block that is being accessed for the first time, because now the request has to pass through multiple caches.

7.1.4   Organisation of a Cache

Let us provide an overview of how a cache is organised. A cache stores a subset of the blocks used in the memory system. For example, if a program requires 10,000 blocks, we may store 1024 blocks in the cache. Their addresses are not necessarily contiguous. Given a block address, we need to find out if it exists within a cache or not.

Let us consider a running example. Assume a 32-bit memory system (memory addresses are 32 bits) for the sake of simplicity. We want to design a 64 KB cache with 64-byte blocks. Let us first separate the block address from the memory address. Given that a block consists of consecutive bytes, we can easily conclude that the last 6 bits of the memory address give the address of the byte within the block. This is because $2^6 = 64$, and thus we require 6 bits to uniquely index a byte within a block. This is shown in Figure 7.5, where we divide a 32-bit memory address into two parts: 26 bits for the block address, and 6 bits for the offset (required for uniquely indexing a byte within a block).

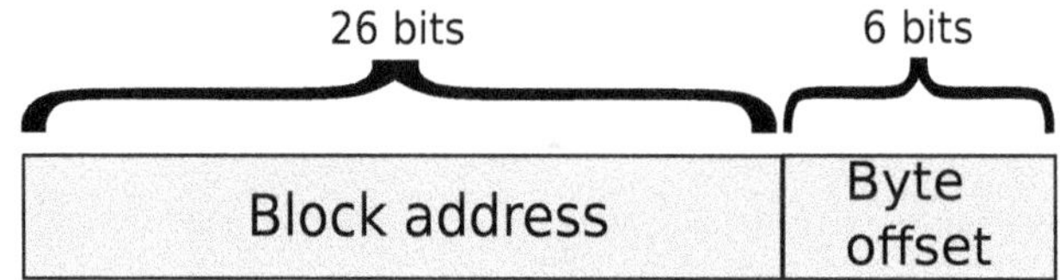

Figure 7.5: Splitting a memory address into two parts: block address and byte offset

Let us now consider the 26-bit block address, and the fact that we have 1024 blocks in the cache (64 KB / 64 B). We need to search these 1024 entries, and find out if the given block address is present in the cache. Conceptually, we can think of this cache as a 1024-entry array. Each entry is also known as a *cache line*. Typically, the terms "cache line" and "cache block" are used synonymously and interchangeably. However, we shall use the term "cache line" to refer to the entire entry in the cache and the term "cache block" to refer to the actual, usable contents: 64 bytes in the case of our running example. A cache line thus contains the cache block along with some additional information. Typically, this subtle distinction does not matter in most cases; nevertheless, if there are two terms, it is a wise idea to precisely define them and use them carefully.

Now, we are clearly not going to search all 1024 entries for a given block address. This is too slow, and too inefficient. Let us take a cue from a course in computer algorithms, and design a method based on the well known technique called *hashing* [Cormen et al., 2009]. Hashing is a technique where we map a large set of numbers to a much smaller set of numbers. This is a many-to-one mapping. Here, we need to map a 26-bit space of block addresses to a 10-bit space of cache lines ($1024 = 2^{10}$).

The simplest solution is to extract the 10 LSB (least significant) bits from the block address, and use them to access the corresponding entry in the cache, which we are currently assuming to be a simple one-dimensional table. Each entry is identified by its row number: 0 to 1023. This is a very fast scheme, and is very efficient. Extracting the 10 LSB bits, and on the basis of that accessing a hardware table is a very quick and power efficient operation. Recall that this is similar to how we were accessing the branch predictor.

However, there is a problem. We can have aliasing, which means that two block addresses can map to the same entry. We need to have a method to disambiguate this process. We can do what was suggested way back in Section 3.2, which is to store some additional information with each entry. We can divide a 32-bit address into three parts: 16-bit tag, 10-bit index, and 6-bit offset.

The 10-bit index is used to access the corresponding line in the cache, which for us is a one-dimensional table (or an array). The 6-bit offset will be used to fetch the byte within the block. And, finally the 16-bit tag will be used to uniquely identify a block. Even if two separate blocks have the last 10 bits of the block address (index) in common, they will have different tags. Otherwise, the block addresses are the same, and the blocks are not different (all 26 bits of the block address are common). This is pictorially shown in Figure 7.6.

Let us explain this differently. Out of a 32-bit memory address, the upper 26 bits (more significant) comprise the block address. Out of this, the lower 10 bits form the index that we use to access our cache. The upper 16 bits can thus vary between two block addresses that map to the same line in the cache. However, if this information is also stored along with each line in the cache, then while accessing the cache we can compare these 16 bits with the tag part of the memory address, and decide if we have

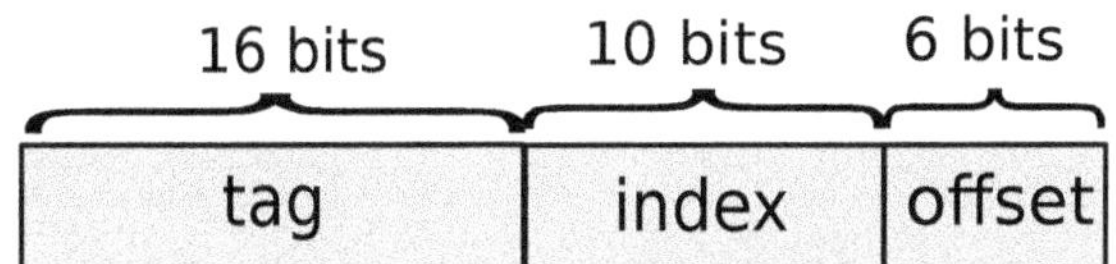

Figure 7.6: The concept of the tag

a cache hit or miss. We are thus comparing and using all the information that is present in a memory address. There is no question of aliasing here. Figure 7.7 explains this concept graphically.

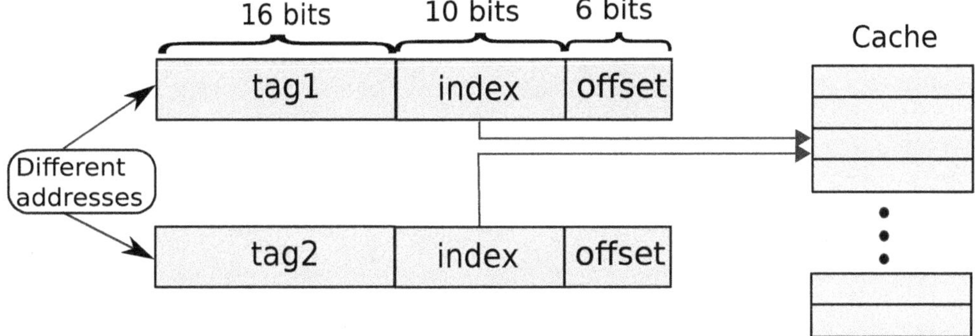

Figure 7.7: The concept of the tag explained along with aliasing

Let us now take a look at one of the simplest cache designs that uses this concept.

Direct Mapped Cache

A direct mapped cache contains two arrays: a tag array and a data array. The tag array in the case of our running example stores 1024 tags, and the data array stores the contents of 1024 blocks as shown in Figure 7.8.

In the case of a direct mapped cache, we index the tag and data array bits using the n least significant bits of the block address, where 2^n is equal to the number of entries in either array. Thus, in this case, we extract the 10 least significant bits of the block address, and use them to access both the arrays. Assume that we want to access the cache and fetch the block, whose block address is A. We proceed as discussed by extracting the 10 LSB bits, and use them to index the data and tag arrays. Assume that the entry that is present in the arrays is for a block address A'. Now, if $A = A'$, we have a hit, otherwise we have a miss.

Let us summarise the process with a set of bullet points. Assume that the function $tag(A)$ provides the tag part (upper 16 bits in this case) of the block address. We will use the block addresses A and A' (as defined in the previous paragraph) in the following description.

- Every byte is uniquely identified by a 32-bit memory address.

- Out of these 32 bits, we have taken out the 6 least significant bits because they specify the offset of a byte within a block. We are left with 26 bits.

- Out of these 26 bits, we have used the 10 least significant bits to index the tag and data arrays. By this point, we have used 16 bits out of the 32-bit address. This means that between addresses A and A', we have the lower 16 bits in common. We are not sure of the upper (more significant) 16 bits. If they match, then the addresses are the same.

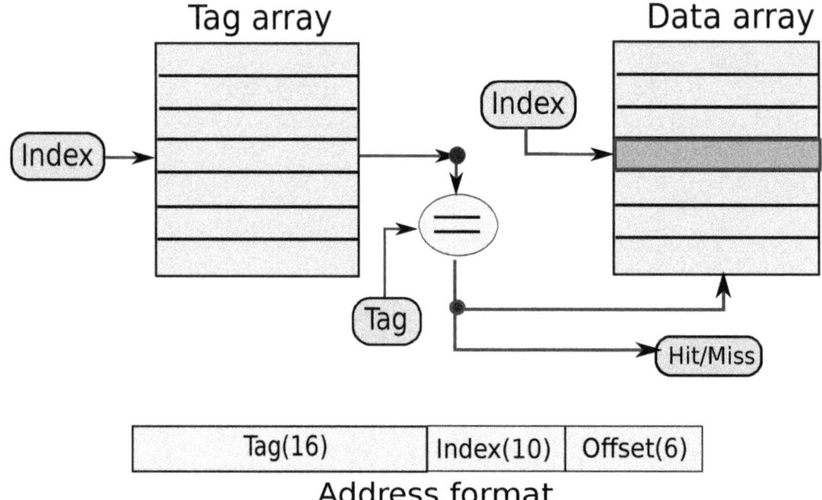

Figure 7.8: A direct mapped cache

- The upper 16 bits are the tag part of the address. Thus, the problem gets reduced to a simpler problem: check if $tag(A) = tag(A')$.

- The upper 16 bits of A' are stored in the tag array. We need to compare them with the upper 16 bits of A, which is $tag(A)$. These bits can be easily extracted from the address A and sent to a comparator for comparison, as shown in Figure 7.8.

Thus, accessing a direct mapped cache is per se rather simple. We access the data and tag arrays in parallel. Simultaneously, we compute the tag part of the address. If there is a tag match – the tag part of the address matches the corresponding contents of the tag array – then we declare a hit, and use the contents of the corresponding entry in the data array. Otherwise, we declare a miss.

The logic for having separate tag and data arrays will be clear in Section 7.3. Let us proceed to look at other variants of caches.

Fully Associative Cache

A direct mapped cache is a good idea. However, it suffers from a major flaw. Assume we access two memory locations very frequently, and their corresponding addresses map to the same entry in the tag and data arrays. The hit rate in the case of direct mapped caches will be very low, because these accesses will constantly displace each other's data. Let us instead design a cache where an entry can reside anywhere in the cache. This means that for our running example, we have 1024 possible locations for a given block. Performance considerations aside, this can completely mitigate the problem of aliasing. In theory, we can have 1024 blocks that map to the same location reside in the cache without causing any misses.

The idea definitely does look very appealing; however, the devil is in the details. We need to appreciate that we never get anything for free in life, and this rule is particularly important in computer architecture.

We shall discuss the details of this design in Section 7.3 including a description of the hardware. In this section, we shall offer a superficial treatment of this area.

As we shall see in Section 7.3, such caches use a different kind of basic memory cell known as the CAM (content addressable memory) cell. It is typically made of 10 transistors. In comparison, regular

SRAM (static RAM) cells have 6 transistors. The main advantage of CAM cells is that it is possible to compare a set of bits pairwise with the bits stored in an array of CAM cells. If all of them match, then the match line in Figure 7.9 is set to 1.

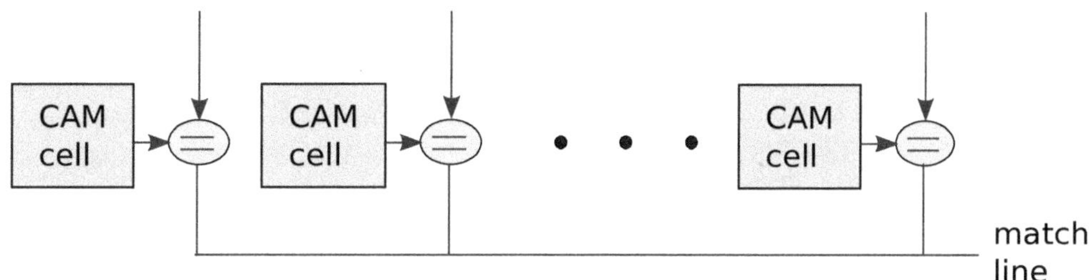

Figure 7.9: A set of CAM cells. The match line is a wired-AND bus (computes a logical AND of all the inputs).

Using such CAM cells, we can create a content addressable memory (CAM memory). This term deserves some more explanation. In a normal memory such as the data and tag arrays of a direct mapped cache, we access each entry based on the index. The index is the number of the entry. It starts from 0, and monotonically increases by 1 for each subsequent entry. This is similar to an array in programming languages. However, a CAM array or CAM memory is more like a hash table in C++ or Java. We typically access an entry based on its contents. Let us explain with an example. Consider an array of numbers: *vals[]* = {*5, 6, 2, 10, 3, 1* }. The expression *vals[3]* refers to accessing the array *vals* by its index, which is 3. In this case, the result of this expression is 10.

However, we can also access the array by the contents of an array element, and get the index if the array contains the value. For example, we can issue the statement *get(vals, 10)*. In this case, the answer will be 3 because the value 10 exists at the array index 3 (we start counting from 0). CAM arrays can be used to see if a given value exists within an array, and for finding the index of the row that contains the value. If there are multiple copies of the same value, then we can either return the lowest index, or any of the indices at random. The behaviour in such cases is often undefined.

Now let us use the CAM array to build a cache (refer to Figure 7.10). We show a simple example with only 4 entries (can be scaled for larger designs). For our problem at hand, the CAM array is the best structure to create the tag array. The input is the tag part of the memory address; we need to quickly search if it is contained within any row of the tag array. In this case, we do not have an index. Instead, the address is split into two parts: 6-bit offset and 26-bit tag. The tag is large because we are not dedicating any bits to index the tag array. The output will be the index of the entry that contains the same tag or a miss signal (tag not present). Once we get the index, we can access the data array with that index, and fetch the contents of the block. Note that there is a one-to-one correspondence between the entries of the tag array and the data array.

The main technological innovation that allowed us to build this cache, which is called a *fully associative cache*, is the CAM array. It allows for a quick comparison with the contents of each entry, and thus we gain the flexibility of storing an entry any where in the array. Even though such an approach can reduce the miss rate by taking care of aliasing, it has its share of pitfalls.

The CAM cell is large and slow. In addition, the process of comparing with each entry in the CAM array is extremely inefficient when it comes to power. This approach is not scalable, and it is often very difficult to construct CAM arrays of any practical significance beyond 64 entries. It is a very good structure when we do not have a large number of entries ($\leq$ 64).

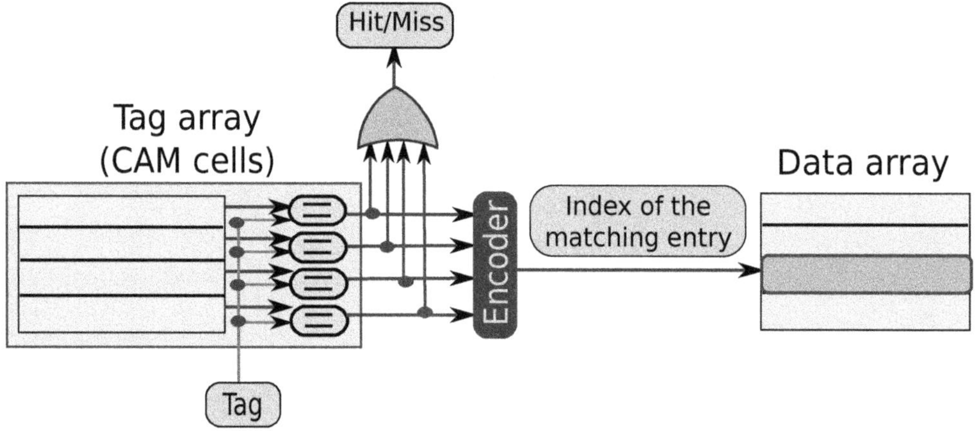

Figure 7.10: Fully associative cache

Set Associative Cache

We have seen a direct mapped cache and a fully associative cache. The former has a low access time, and the latter has a low miss rate at the cost of access time and power. Is a compromise possible?

Indeed, it is possible. Such a design is called a *set associative cache*. Here, we offer limited flexibility, and do not significantly compromise on the access time and power. The idea is as follows. Instead of offering the kind of flexibility that the fully associative cache provides, let us restrict a given block address to a few locations instead of all the locations. For example, we can restrict a given address to 2 or 4 locations in the tag and data arrays.

Let us proceed as follows. Let us divide the tag array into groups of equal sized sets. Sets often contain 2, 4, or 8 blocks. Let us implement our running example by creating a 4-way set associative cache, where each set contains 4 entries. In general, if a set contains k entries, we call it a k-way set associative cache. Each entry in the set is called a *way*. In other words, a way corresponds to an entry in the tag array and data array that belongs to a given set. In a k-way set associative cache we have k ways per set.

Definition 41

If a set contains k entries, we call it a k-way set associative cache. Each entry in the set is called a way.

Recall that we needed to create a 64 KB cache with a 64-byte block size in a 32-bit memory system. The number of blocks in the data array and the number of entries in the tag array is equal to 1024 (64 KB/ 64 B). As we had done with direct mapped caches, we can split the 32-bit memory address into a 6-bit offset and 26-bit block address.

Let us now perform a different kind of calculation. Each set has 4 entries. We thus have $1024/4 = 256$ sets. The number of bits required to index each set is $log_2(256)$, which is 8. We can thus use the 8 LSB bits of the block address to find the number or index of the set. Once we get the number of the set we can access all the entries in the set. We can trivially map the entries in the tag array to sets as follows. For a 4-way set associative cache, we can assume that entries 0 to 3 belong to set 1, entries 4 to 7 belong to set 2, and so on. To find the starting entry of each set, we just need to multiply the set index by 4, which is very easy to do in binary (left shift by 2 positions).

Till now we have used 6 bits for the offset within the block and 8 bits for the set id. We are left with 18 (32 - 14) bits. This is the part of the address that is not common to different addresses that map to the same set, and thus by definition it is the *tag*. The size of the tag is thus 18 bits. The breakup of an address for a 4-way set associative cache in our running example is shown in Figure 7.11.

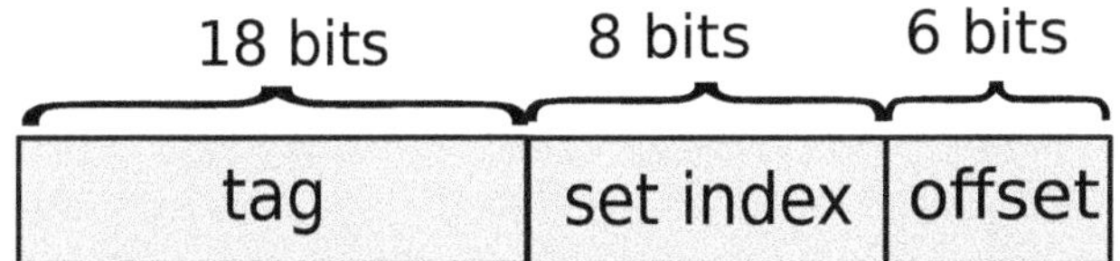

Figure 7.11: Breakup of the address in a 4-way set associative cache

To access (read/write) a data block, we first send the address to the tag array. We compute the set index, and access all the entries belonging to that set in parallel. In this case, we read out 4 tags (corresponding to each way) from the tag array, and compare each of them with the tag part of the address using a set of comparators. If there is no match, then we have a miss, otherwise we have a hit. If the tags match, then we can easily compute the index in the tag array that contains the matching tag with an encoder. Refer to Figure 7.12 for a representative design of a set associative cache.

We subsequently index the data array with the index and read out the data block. Some times for the sake of efficiency we can read out the contents of the 4 corresponding data blocks in parallel. After computing the tag match, we can choose one of the blocks as the final output. This is faster because it creates an overlap between accessing the tag array and reading the data blocks; however, it is inefficient in terms of power because it involves extra work.

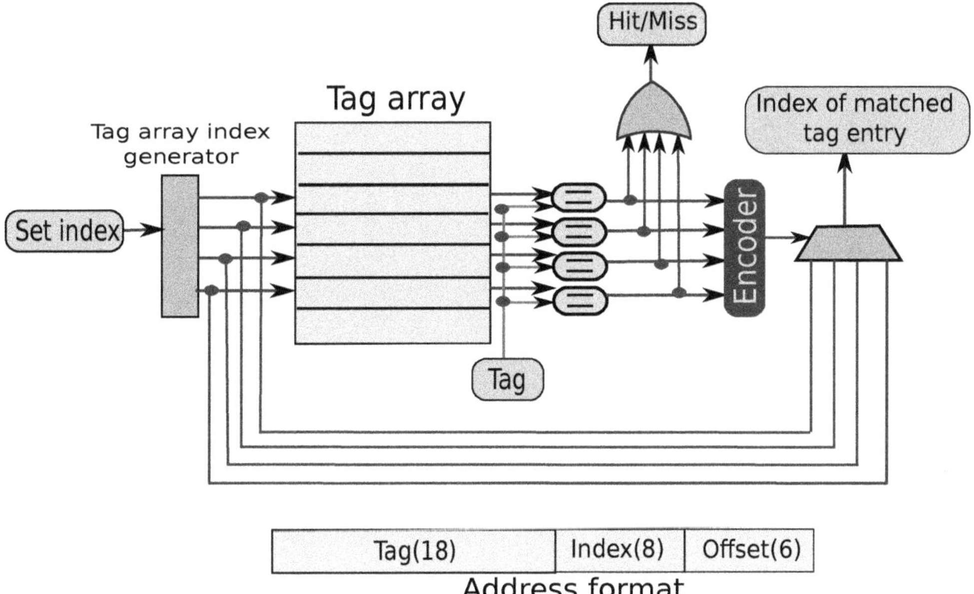

Figure 7.12: A set associative cache

> **Important Point 11**
>
> *If we think about it, a direct mapped cache is also a set associative cache. Here, the size of each set is 1. A fully associative cache is also a set associative cache, where the size of the set is equal to the number of blocks in the cache.*

The set associative cache represents an equitable trade-off between direct mapped and fully associative caches. It is not as slow as fully associative caches, because it still uses the faster SRAM cells. Additionally, its miss rate is not as low as direct mapped caches. This is because there is some degree of immunity against aliasing. If two addresses conflict (map to the same block) in a direct mapped cache, they can be placed in different ways of a set in a set associative cache. In many such cases, we can avoid misses altogether as compared to a direct mapped cache.

7.1.5 Basic Operations in a Cache

Let us quickly look at the basic operations that a cache supports. The most basic primitive that the cache needs to support is the lookup operation. The lookup operation tells us if the cache contains the block corresponding to a given memory address or not. If it does, then it returns a hit/miss signal and the location of the block if it exists in the cache. Subsequently, we can either read or modify the contents of the block.

Let us consider the situation in which a lookup operation indicates that we have a cache miss. In this case, we need to fetch the contents of the block from the lower levels of the memory system. For example, if we have a cache miss in the L1 cache, then we will try to fetch the block from the L2 cache. If we do not find the block in the L2 cache, then we need to fetch it from an even lower level such as the L3 cache (if it exists) or the main memory. After we fetch the contents of the block, we need to write it to all the levels of the memory system that did not have a copy of it. This is because we wish to support the property of inclusiveness in a cache.

Subsequently, we can read and write to the block in the L1 cache. Reading is a very easy operation. Writing is tricky. Let us thus look at the process of writing in some more detail. After completing a store operation, the L1 cache will have the most up to date copy of the block. The other caches such as L2 and L3 will have possibly *stale* copies of the block. Nevertheless, to support the property of inclusive caches we need to maintain such stale copies. We shall discuss this issue in some more detail in Section 7.1.5.

> **Important Point 12**
>
> *Why is it necessary to first fetch a block to the L1 cache before writing to it?*
>
> ***Answer:***   *A block is typically 32 or 64 bytes long. However, most of the time we write 4 bytes or 8 bytes at a time. If the block is already present in the cache, then there is no problem. However, if there is a cache miss, then the question that we need to answer is, "Do we wait for the entire contents of the block to arrive from the lower levels of the memory hierarchy?" A naive and incorrect way of doing so will be to go ahead and write the data at the appropriate positions within an empty cache block, even though the rest of the contents of the actual block are not present in the cache. However, this method is fraught with difficulties. We need to keep track of the bytes within a block that we have updated. Later on, these bytes have to be merged with the rest of the contents of the block (after they arrive). The process of merging is complicated because some of the bytes would have been updated, and the rest would be the same. We need to maintain information at the byte level with regards to whether a given byte has been updated or not. Keeping these complexities in mind, we treat a block as an atomic unit, and do not keep track of any information at the intra-block level. Hence, before writing to a block, we ensure that it is present in the cache first.*

Replacement and Eviction

Consider a set associative cache with k ways. It is possible that $k + 1$ block addresses might map to the set. In this case, we cannot store all of them in the set. Whenever we need to add a block to the set, one of the blocks in the set has to be evicted (thrown out) to make room for the new block.

We have k possible options. Any of these blocks may be *replaced* with the new block. There are many algorithms to choose the best candidate for replacement. The most effective algorithm is typically a variant of the classic LRU (least recently used) algorithm. Here we try to find the block that has been used the least in the recent past. Based on this we predict that the probability of this block being used in the future is the least among all the blocks in the set. Implementing an accurate LRU algorithm is impractical. Most systems thus implement a pseudo-LRU algorithm. In this algorithm, we associate a saturating counter with each way in the set. Every time we access the way, we increment the counter. This gives us a measure of how many times the block has been used.

This is sadly not enough because over time the counters will tend to saturate, and all the blocks within a set will hold the maximum count. To ensure that this does not happen and we capture recent history, we need to periodically decrement the values of all the counters such that the counts of unused blocks move towards 0. We can thus deduce that higher the count, higher is the probability of accesses in the recent past. The least recently used block is expected to have the least count. Note that periodically decrementing counters is absolutely necessary, otherwise we cannot maintain information about the recent past.

Since this approach approximates the LRU scheme, it does not always identify the least recently used block; however, in all cases it identifies one of the least used blocks in the recent past. This is a good candidate for replacement.

To replace a block, we evict the block that has the least count, and in its place we bring in the new block. The process of eviction is not easy, and there are various complexities. Let us quickly understand the trade-offs between different approaches.

Write-Through and Write-Back Schemes

There are two paradigms: write-through and write-back. In a write-through cache, whenever we perform a write operation, we write the data to the lower level immediately. Because our memory system is inclusive, we are guaranteed to find the block in the lower level as well. Also recall that we never write to all the bytes of a typical 64-byte block together. Instead we write at a much finer granularity – 2 to 8 bytes at a time. These small writes are sent to the lower level cache, where the corresponding block is updated. Thus, we never have stale copies while using a write-through cache. In this case, eviction is very easy. We do not have the concept of fresh and stale copies. Since all the writes have been forwarded to the lower level, the block is up to date in the lower level cache. We can thus seamlessly evict the block and not do anything more.

However, a write-back cache is more complicated: here we do not send writes automatically to the lower level. We keep a bit known as the *modified bit* with each cache line that indicates if the line has been *modified* with a write operation or not. If it is modified, then we need to perform additional steps, when this line is going to be evicted. Note that in this case, the write-back cache will contain the up to date copy of the data, whereas the cache at the immediately lower level will contain a stale copy because it has not received any updates. Hence, whenever we observe the modified bit to be 1 during eviction, we write the block to the lower level. This ensures that the lower level cache contains all the modifications made to the contents of the block. However, if the modified bit is 0, then it means that the block has not been written to. There is thus no need to write back the block to the lower level. It can be seamlessly evicted.

The write-back cache basically defers writing back the block till the point of eviction. In comparison, a write-through cache writes back the block every time it is written. In a system with high temporal locality and a lot of writes, a write-through cache is clearly very inefficient. First, because of temporal locality we expect the same block to be accessed over and over again. Additionally, because of the high write traffic in some workloads, we will need to write a lot of blocks back to the lower level – every time they are modified at the upper level. These writes are unnecessary and can be avoided if we use a write-back cache. However, on the flip side, write-through caches are simple and support seamless eviction.

There is one more subtle advantage of write-through caches. Assume we have a three level cache hierarchy. Because of the property of inclusiveness, we will have three entries for a given block in all the three caches: L1, L2, and L3. Now, assume that there is an eviction in L3, or an I/O device wishes to write to the block. Many I/O devices write directly to main memory, and not to the caches. In this case, it is necessary to evict the block from all three caches. In the case of write-through caches, this is simple. The blocks can be seamlessly evicted. However, in the case of a write-back cache, we need to check the modified bits at each level, and perform a write back to main memory if necessary. This has high overheads.

Given the nature of the requirements, we need to make a judicious choice.

7.1.6 Mathematical Analysis

Let us compute the formula for the average memory access time (AMAT) of a given memory request. Let us start with the L1 cache. It is equal to:

$$AMAT = L1_{hit\_time} + L1_{miss\_rate} \times L1_{miss\_penalty} \tag{7.1}$$

Irrespective of a hit or a miss, we need to spend some time in accessing the cache. If we get back the data, we declare a hit, else we declare a miss. We can consider this to be the $L1_{hit\_time}$. Note that this is a simplistic model. We shall see in Section 7.3 that the equations can get more elaborate. However, for the sake of a simplistic model, this is sufficient. If we have a miss with a probability equal to $L1_{miss\_rate}$, then we need to pay the miss penalty in terms of time, which is denoted by $L1_{miss\_penalty}$. This is a fairly simple equation that requires little explanation. It can be directly derived from the formula of the expected value of a random variable.

Let us now compute $L1_{miss\_penalty}$. This is nothing but the average memory access time for the L2 cache. This is because once we have a miss in the L1 cache, we go to the L2 cache and we initiate a fresh cache access. Similar to Equation 7.1, the average access time of the L2 cache ($L2_{access\_time}$) is given by

$$\begin{aligned} L1_{miss\_penalty} &= L2_{access\_time} \\ &= L2_{hit\_time} + L2_{miss\_rate} \times L2_{miss\_penalty} \end{aligned} \tag{7.2}$$

We can write similar equations for the rest of the levels of the memory system. This process will terminate when we reach the main memory, or the hard disk. At this stage, the miss rate will be 0, and thus this recursive process will terminate. The set of equations for a memory system with three levels of caches and a main memory that contains all the data are as follows:

$$\begin{aligned} AMAT &= L1_{hit\_time} + L1_{miss\_rate} \times L1_{miss\_penalty} \\ L1_{miss\_penalty} &= L2_{hit\_time} + L2_{miss\_rate} \times L2_{miss\_penalty} \\ L2_{miss\_penalty} &= L3_{hit\_time} + L3_{miss\_rate} \times L3_{miss\_penalty} \\ L3_{miss\_penalty} &= MainMem_{access\_time} \end{aligned} \tag{7.3}$$

Note that the term, "miss rate", refers to the local miss rate, which is defined as follows. For example, the L3 miss rate (or local miss rate) is defined as the number of L3 misses divided by the number of L3 accesses. In comparison, the L3 global miss rate is defined as then number of L3 misses divided by the total number of memory accesses.

Finally, let us put the pieces together. The AMAT can be used to compute the CPI (cycles per instruction) of an in-order machine (also see Equation 2.1). For an OOO machine, the formula does not hold exactly; however, it can be calibrated with a real system to provide numbers that are suggestive of broad trends. We have

$$CPI = CPI_{base} + f_{mem} * (AMAT - L1_{hit\_time}) \tag{7.4}$$

Here, CPI_{base} is the baseline CPI with a perfect memory system and f_{mem} is the fraction of memory instructions. In this equation, we account for the additional delay of the memory instructions. The additional delay is equal to $(AMAT - L1_{hit\_time})$. We multiply this with the fraction of memory instructions and add it to the baseline CPI. Note that we subtract $L1_{hit\_time}$ from $AMAT$ because we assume that the L1 hit time is already accounted for while computing CPI_{base}. The formula is derived by using the fact that the expected CPI is a sum of the expected values of its components.

7.1.7   Optimising the Cache Design

The formula for the average memory access time does teach us something. It teaches us that to reduce the average memory access time we can either reduce the hit time, the miss rate, or the miss penalty. Let us discuss a few basic methods to reduce each of these factors.

Reducing the Hit Time

The hit time can be reduced by designing a smaller and faster cache. We can also reduce the associativity. However, we need to pay a price in terms of an increased miss rate. If the AMAT (average memory access time) decreases for the programs we are interested in, then such trade-offs are justified, otherwise such design choices are not justified.

Reducing the Miss Rate

Now that we know about the design of caches, particularly, set associative caches, let us look at the types of cache misses that we can have. These are typically known as the three Cs; misses can be classified into three categories.

Compulsory or Cold Misses These misses happen when we read in instructions or data for the first time. In this case, misses are inevitable, unless we can design a predictor that can predict future accesses and prefetch them in advance. Such mechanisms are known as prefetchers. We shall discuss prefetching schemes in detail in Sections 7.6 and 7.7. Prefetching is a general technique and is in fact known to reduce all kinds of misses.

Capacity Misses Assume we have a 16 KB L1 cache. However, we wish to access 32 KB of data on a frequent basis. Then we shall inevitably have a lot of misses, because the amount of data that the program wants to access will not fit in the cache. Other than generic schemes such as prefetching, better compiler algorithms or optimisations at the level of the code are more effective. For example, if we are multiplying two large matrices, we shall have capacity misses. It is possible to reduce this by reorganising the code such that we always consider small blocks of data and operate on them (we shall look at such compiler driven schemes in Section 7.4.5).

Conflict Misses This is an artefact of having finite sized sets. Assume that we have a 4-way set associative cache and we have 5 blocks in our access pattern that map to the same set. Since we cannot fit more than 4 blocks in the same set, the moment the 5th block arrives, we shall have a miss. Such misses can be reduced by increasing the associativity. This will increase the hit time and thus may not always be desirable.

The standard way to reduce the miss rate is to have better prefetching schemes, increase the cache size or the associativity. However, they increase the hardware overheads. Here is a low-overhead scheme that is very effective.

Victim Cache A victim cache is a small cache that is normally added between the L1 and L2 caches. The insight is that sometimes we have some sets in the L1 cache that see a disproportionate number of accesses, and we thus have conflict misses. For example, in a 4-way set associative cache, we might have 5 frequently used blocks mapping to the same set. In this case, one of the blocks will frequently get evicted from the cache. Instead of going to the lower level, which is a slow process, we can add a small cache between L1 and L2 that contains such *victim blocks*. It can have 8-64 entries making it very small and very fast. For a large number of programs, victim caches prove to be extremely beneficial in spite of their small size. It is often necessary to wisely choose which blocks need to be added to a victim cache. We would not like to add blocks that have a very low probability of being accessed in the future. We can track the usage of sets with counters and only store evicted blocks of those sets that are frequently accessed.

Reducing the Miss Penalty

Reducing the miss penalty is equivalent to reducing the memory access time at the lower level. This includes reducing the hit time or the miss rate at the lower level. However, there are schemes that are particularly tailored towards reducing the miss penalty.

One such scheme is *critical word first and early restart*. The insight is as follows. Almost always reads are on the critical path because we have waiting instructions and writes are not on the critical path. Furthermore, we often read data at the granularity of 4 bytes or 8 bytes, whereas a block is 32-128 bytes. This means that we often read a very small part of every block. We thus need not pay the penalty of fetching the entire block. Consider a 64-byte block. In most on-chip networks we can only transfer 8 bytes in a single cycle, and it thus takes 8 cycles to transfer a full block. The 8-byte packets are ordered as per their addresses.

We can instead transfer them in a different order. We can transfer the memory word (4 or 8 bytes) that is immediately needed by the processor first, and transfer the rest of the words in the block in later cycles. This optimisation is known as fetching the *critical word first*. Subsequently, the processor can process the memory word, and start executing the consumer instructions. This is known as *early restart* because we are not waiting to fetch the rest of the bytes in the block.

This optimisation helps reduce the miss penalty because we are prioritising the data that needs to be sent first. This is easy to implement, and is heavily used. Furthermore, this technique is the most useful when applied between the L1 and L2 caches. It fails to show appreciable benefits when the miss penalty is large. The savings in the miss penalty do not significantly affect the AMAT in this case.

Next, let us discuss the write buffer that reduces the latency of writes to the lower level. It temporarily buffers the write and allows other accesses to go through.

Write Buffer A write buffer is a small fully associative cache for writes that we add between levels in the memory hierarchy, or attach with the store unit of the pipeline. It typically contains 4-8 entries where each entry stores a block. The insight is as follows. Due to spatial locality we tend to write to multiple words in a block one after the other. If we have repeated misses for different words in the same block, we do not want to send separate write-miss requests to the lower level. We should ideally send a single write-miss message for the block, and *merge* all the writes. This is the job of the write buffer's entry. For every write operation, we allocate a write buffer entry, which absorbs the flurry of writes to the same block. It is managed like a regular cache, where older entries are purged out and written to the lower level of the memory hierarchy. Subsequent read operations to the same block get their value from the write buffer entry. Other read operations that do not find their blocks in the write buffer can bypass the write buffer and can directly be sent to the lower levels of the memory system. To summarise, write buffers allow the processor to move ahead with other memory requests, reduce the pressure on the memory system by merging write operations to the same block, and can quickly serve read requests if their data is found in the write buffer.

Now that we have gained a good high level understanding of caches in modern processors, let us proceed to understand the internals of modern caches in Section 7.3. Before that we need to understand the concept of virtual memory.

7.2   Virtual Memory

This section provides a quick introduction to virtual memory. The treatment is cursory. For a detailed explanation the reader is requested to consult a basic textbook in architecture or operating systems.

Up till now we have conceptually assumed that the memory space is one large contiguous array of bytes. Each index of this array is the memory address. Figure 7.13 shows this conceptual view, where we have the processor and a large physical array of bytes. Of course, we have created a cache hierarchy to store parts of the address space closer to the processor; the key abstraction is that the entire memory space is nevertheless just one large array of bytes.

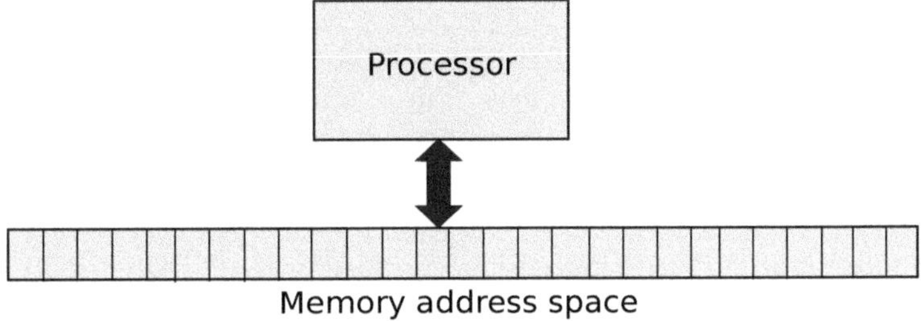

Figure 7.13: Conceptual view of the address space

Even though this abstraction suffices for a programmer and the compiler, it is not practical. Hence, as we have argued in Section 7.1, we need to create a memory hierarchy that consists of a set of caches. We have layers of caches that increasingly store larger and larger subsets of the memory address space. The reason that the memory hierarchy works is because of temporal locality. In the rare instances, where we cannot find some data in the caches, we need to access the off-chip main memory, which we assume contains all the data and instructions for the program. We never have a miss in the main memory.

Let us now systematically take the peel off all of these assumptions, and argue about the problems that we shall face in a real situation. As described in the introductory text by Sarangi [Sarangi, 2015], there are two problems in such implementations: the *overlap problem* and the *size problem*.

7.2.1   Overlap and Size Problems

The overlap problem is elaborated as follows. Even though we have been assuming that a single program is running on the processor, this is seldom the case. If we have multiple cores (processors on chip), then each core runs a separate program. Even if we have a single core, then also we share the core among different processes. Here a *process* is defined as the running instance of a program. The processes time-share the CPU. This means that after one process runs for some time, an external device called a timer signals an interrupt. The CPU loads the operating system (OS). The OS finds a process that is ready to execute and starts executing it on the core. In this manner a plurality of processes share the same CPU and operate in a time-multiplexed fashion.

Definition 42

A process is defined as a running instance of a program. Note that for one program we can create any number of processes. All of them are independent of each other, unless we use sophisticated mechanisms to pass messages between them. A process has its own memory space, and it further assumes that it has exclusive access to all the regions within its memory space.

The reader can click Ctrl-Alt-Del on her Microsoft® Windows® machine and see the list of processes that are currently active. She will see that there will be tens of processes that are active even if she has just one core on her laptop. This is because the processor is being time shared across all the processes. Furthermore, these programs are switching so quickly (tens of times a second) that the human brain is not able to perceive this. This is why we can have an editor, web browser, and video player running at the same time.

Note that these programs running on the processor have been compiled at different places by different compilers. All of them assume that they have complete and exclusive control over the entire memory space. This means that they can write to any memory location that they please. The problem arises if these sets of memory addresses overlap across processes. It is very much possible that process A and process B access the same memory address. In this case, one process may end up overwriting the other process's data, and this will lead to incorrect execution. Even worse, one process can steal secret data such as credit card numbers from another process. Such overlaps fortunately do not happen in real systems. This is because additional steps are taken to ensure that processes do not inadvertently or maliciously corrupt each other's memory addresses. This means that even if we maintain the abstraction that each process's memory space belongs to it exclusively, we somehow ensure that two processes do not corrupt each other's data. We need to somehow ensure that in reality the memory spaces do not unintentionally overlap.

Let us now look at the *size problem*. Assume that the size of the main memory is 1 GB. We have been assuming till now that all the accesses find their data in the main memory (miss rate is 0). This means that the maximum amount of memory that any process is allowed to use is limited to 1 GB. This is too restrictive in practice. It should be possible to run larger programs. In this case, we need to treat the main memory as the cache, and create a lower level beneath it. This is exactly how modern systems are organised as shown in Figure 7.14. The level beneath the main memory is the hard disk, which is a large magnetic storage device that typically has 10-100 times more capacity than main memory. We dedicate a part of the hard disk known as the *swap space* to store data that does not fit in the main memory.

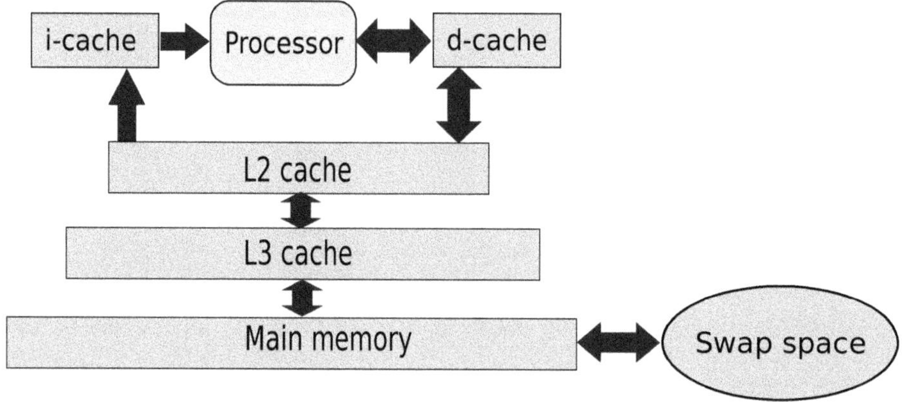

Figure 7.14: The memory hierarchy with the swap space

This should happen seamlessly, and the programmer or the compiler should not be able to know about the movement of data between main memory and the swap space. It should thus be possible for the programmer to use more memory than the capacity of the off-chip main memory. In this specific case, it should for example be possible to run a program that uses 3 GB of memory. Some of the data blocks will be in main memory, and the rest need to be in the swap space. The relationship is typically not *inclusive*.

Such a pristine view of the memory space is known as *virtual memory*. Every process has a *virtual view* of memory where it assumes that the size of the memory that it can access is 2^N bytes, where we assume that valid memory addresses are N bits wide. For example, in a 32-bit machine the size of the virtual address space is 2^{32} bytes and on a 64-bit machine the size of the virtual address space is 2^{64} bytes. Furthermore, the process can unreservedly write to any location within its memory space without any fear of interference from other programs and the total amount of memory that a process can use is limited by the size of the main memory and the swap space. This memory space is known as the *virtual address space.*

Definition 43

Virtual memory is defined as a view of the memory space that is seen by each process. A process assumes its memory space (known as the virtual address space) is as large as the range of valid memory addresses. The process has complete and exclusive control over the virtual address space, and it can write to any location in the virtual address space at will without any fear of interference from other programs.

Note that at this point of time, *virtual memory* is just a concept. We are yet to provide a physical realisation for it. Any physical implementation has to be consistent with the memory hierarchy that we have defined. Before proceeding further, let us enumerate the advantages of virtual memory:

1. It automatically solves the overlap problem. A process cannot unknowingly or even maliciously write in the memory space of another process.

2. It also automatically solves the size problem. We can store data in an area that is as large as the swap space and main memory combined. We are not limited by the size of the main memory.

3. Since we can write to any location at will within the virtual address space, the job of the programmer and the compiler become very easy. They can create code that is not constrained by a restrictive set of allowed memory addresses.

Important Point 13

Many students often argue that virtual memory is not required. We can always ask a process to use a region of memory that is currently unused, or we can force different programs at run time to use a different set of memory addresses. All of these approaches that seek to avoid the use of virtual memory have problems.

A program is compiled once, and run millions of times. It is not possible for the compiler to know about the set of memory addresses that a program needs to use in a target system to avoid interference from other programs. What happens if we run two copies of the same program? They will have clashing addresses.

Another school of thought is to express all addresses in a program as an offset from a base address, which can be set at runtime. The sad part is that this still does not manage to solve the overlap problem completely. This will work if the set of memory addresses in a program are somewhat contiguous. Again, if the memory footprint grows with time, we need to ensure that irrespective of how much it grows it will never encroach into the memory space of another process. This is fairly hard to ensure in practice.

7.2.2   Implementation of Virtual Memory

Virtual memory is extremely alluring as a concept. However, it needs a physical implementation and this physical implementation has to be reconciled with our existing hierarchy of caches. Let us make the following assumptions. All programs are written and compiled with virtual memory in mind. The compiler generates code that uses virtual addresses. In fact the programmer and compiler are only aware of the virtual address space. They are not aware of the physical memory hierarchy and the details of the caches.

Moreover, the address that is computed in the execute stage by the processor is also the virtual address because it is computed based on values supplied by the programmer. However, this address is not presented to the memory system. This is because the virtual addresses of two processes can be the same even though we are not referring to the same piece of data. Hence, it is necessary for the addresses to undergo a process of translation where virtual addresses are converted to physical addresses. Physical addresses are the same addresses that we use to access the memory hierarchy: this includes all the caches and the main memory itself.

Definition 44
A physical address refers to an actual location of a byte or a set of bytes in the on-chip or off-chip memory structures such as the caches, main memory, and swap space. The available range of physical addresses is known as the physical address space.

This process is shown in Figure 7.15. If we assume a 32-bit address then the input to the translator is a 32-bit address, and let's say the output is also a 32-bit address[1]. The only distinction is that the former is a virtual address, and the latter is a physical address, which can be used to access the memory system. Let us delve into this further.

Figure 7.15: Virtual to physical address translation

Pages and Frames

Let us divide the virtual address space into fixed size chunks called pages. Typically, each page is 4 KB in size. Thus, to address a byte within a page, it takes 12 bits ($2^{12} = 4096$). If we remove these bits that specify the offset of a byte in a page (similar to the offset of a byte within a cache block), we are left with 20 bits. Let us refer to these 20 bits as the page id.

On similar lines let us break the physical address space into 4 KB chunks, and call them frames. *The main aim of the translation process is to map a page to a frame.* Note that we map a page to only one frame, and almost all the time we map a frame to only one page of a given process. Unlike the page, which is just a programmatic concept, a frame is associated with 4096 physical locations that store 1 byte each. Let us now understand why using pages and frames solves all the problems for us.

Consider the mapping shown in Figure 7.16. Here, we map the pages of two processes to frames. Note that even though the pages are contiguous, the frames are not. The mapping looks haphazard,

---

[1]The virtual and physical addresses need not have the same size.

because we genuinely have the flexibility of mapping a page to any frame, and there is no restriction on the order of the frames. They need not necessarily be arranged sequentially in the physical address space.

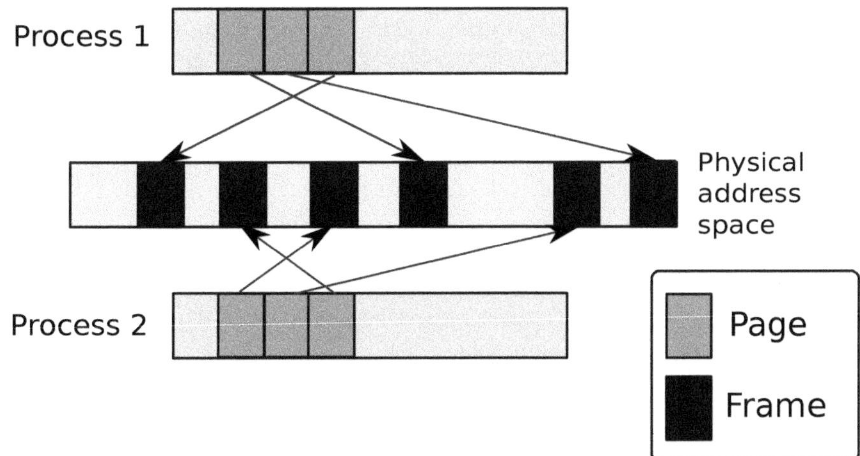

Figure 7.16: Mapping of pages to frames

It is easy to realise that we are solving the overlap problem seamlessly. If we never map the same frame to two different pages, then there is no way that writes from one process will be visible to another process. The virtual memory system will never translate addresses such that this can happen.

Solving the size problem is also straightforward (refer to Figure 7.17). Here, we map some of the pages to frames in memory and some to frames in the swap space. Even if the virtual address space is much larger than the physical address space, this will not pose a problem.

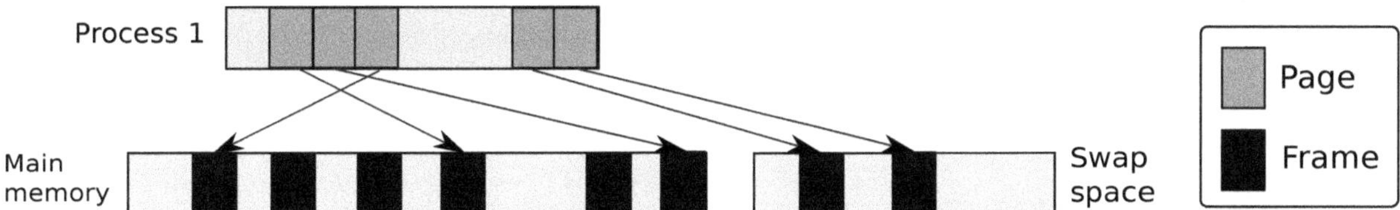

Figure 7.17: Mapping to the main memory and swap space

Mapping between Pages and Frames

In a 32-bit memory system with 4-KB pages, each page id is 20 bits. This is because we require 12 bits to address a byte in a page, and the remaining 20 bits specify the id of the page. Further, assume that we have 1 GB of main memory, and 1 GB of swap space. The total physical space thus available to a process is 2 GB. To address 2 GB of physical memory we require 31 bits ($2GB = 2^{31}$ bytes). Given that the frame size is equal to the page size, we require 19 (=31 - 12) bits to address each frame. We thus need to create a mapping that converts a 20-bit page id to a 19-bit frame id. Note that it is possible that we might later on add memory into the system by inserting additional memory chips in the motherboard, or we can dynamically increase the size of the swap space. In this case, we will need more bits for the frame ids. In such cases, 19 bits will not be enough. Since the size of a frame id can never be more than the size of a page id, we thus conservatively set the size of a frame id to the maximum value: 20

bits. Even if we actually require 19 bits in this case, we still use 20 bits keeping in mind that we might add more physical memory or swap space later, even at runtime. This is a standard assumption that is made in all practical systems. If some MSB bits are unused, they can be set to 0. Hence, to summarise, our mapping process needs to convert a 20-bit page id to a 20-bit frame id.

We need to maintain a data structure in software to store such mappings for each process. Such a data structure is known as the page table. There are different ways of efficiently implementing page tables. The reader can refer to books on operating systems [Silberschatz et al., 2018] or the background text by Sarangi [Sarangi, 2015] for a deeper discussion on page tables. A naive approach is to have a single level page table with 2^{20} entries, where each entry stores the id of a frame: 20 bits. The total space requirement is 2.5 MB per process, which is prohibitive.

To save space, most page tables are organised as 2-level tables, where we use the upper 10 bits to access a primary page table. Each entry of the primary page table points to a secondary page table. We use the subsequent 10 bits of the page id to access the secondary page table that contains the mapping. Note that all the primary page table entries will not point to valid secondary page tables. This is because most of the entries will correspond to portions of the address space that are unused. As a result, we can save a lot of space by creating only those secondary page tables that are required. For a 64-bit address space we can design a 3-level or 4-level page table. The reader is invited to study the space requirements of different page tables; she needs to convince herself that having multi-level page tables is a very good idea for large virtual address spaces.

Sadly, with such page tables we require multiple accesses to the memory system to read a single entry. Some of these entries maybe there in the cache; however, in the worst case we might need to make several accesses to main memory. Given that each main memory access takes roughly 200 to 400 cycles depending on the technology, this is a very expensive operation. Now if we look at these numbers in the light of the fact that we need to perform a virtual-to-physical mapping for every single memory access, the performance is expected to be abysmally poor. We clearly cannot afford such costly operations for every single memory access. This will offset all the gains that we have made in creating a sophisticated out-of-order pipeline and an advanced memory system.

Thankfully, a simple solution exists. We can use the same ideas that we used in caching: temporal locality and spatial locality. We keep a small hardware cache known as the Translation Lookaside Buffer (TLB) with each core. This keeps a set of the most recently used mappings from virtual pages to physical frame ids. Given the property of temporal locality, we expect to have a very high hit rate in the TLB. This is because most programs tend to access the same set of pages repeatedly. In addition, we can also exploit spatial locality. Since most accesses will be to nearby addresses, they are expected to be within the same page. Hence, saving a mapping at the level of pages is expected to be very beneficial because it has a potential for significant reuse.

Definition 45

- *The page table is a data structure that maintains a mapping between page ids and their corresponding frame ids. In most cases this data structure is maintained in a dedicated memory region by software. Specialised modules of the operating system maintain a separate page table for each process. However, in some architectures, notably latest Intel processors, the process of looking up a mapping (also referred to as a* page walk*) is performed by hardware.*

- *To reduce the overheads of address translation, we use a small cache of mappings between pages and frames. This is known as the Translation Lookaside Buffer or the TLB. It typically contains 32-128 entries, and can be accessed in less than 1 clock cycle. It is necessary to access the TLB every time we issue a load/store request to the memory system.*

The process of memory address translation is thus as follows. The virtual address first goes to the TLB where it is translated to the physical address. Since the TLB is typically a very small structure that contains 32-128 entries its access time is typically limited to a single cycle. Once we have the translated address, it can be sent to the memory system, which is either the i-cache (for instructions) or the d-cache (for data).

TLB Misses and Page Faults

We expect a very high hit rate in the TLB (more than 99%). In rare cases, when we have a miss in the TLB, we need to fetch the mapping from the page table. This is an expensive operation because it may involve accesses to main memory, which take hundreds of cycles. If the mapping does not exist yet the virtual address is valid, then we create a new mapping and proceed to allocate an empty frame in main memory. If the mapping exists, there are two cases: the frame is either present in memory, or it is present in the swap space on the hard disk. In the former case, nothing needs to be done other than simply updating the TLB with the mapping. However, in the latter case, we additionally need to allocate a frame in memory, and read in its contents from the disk. To summarise, whenever we do not find a frame in main memory, we need to perform some costly operations in terms of creating space in main memory, and possibly reading the data of the frame from the swap space. This event is known as a *page fault*.

The first step in servicing a page fault is to allocate a frame in main memory. If free space is available, then we can choose an empty frame, and use it. However, if such a frame is not available, there is a need to evict a frame from main memory by writing its contents to the swap space. This requires a method for page (or frame) replacement. There are many common algorithms to achieve this such as FIFO (first in first out) and LRU (least recently used). Once a frame is allocated, we either need to initialise it with all zeros (for security reasons) if we are creating a new mapping, or read in its contents from the disk. The latter is a slow operation. Hard disk access times are of the order of milliseconds. This translates to several million cycles for a single page fault.

The flowchart for the entire process is shown in Figure 7.18.

Definition 46
A page fault is defined as an event where a page's corresponding frame is not found in main memory. It either needs to be initialised in main memory, or its contents need to be read from the hard disk and stored in the main memory.

7.3 Modelling and Designing a Cache

Let us now delve deeper into the components of a cache's performance, which are area, power, and latency. The most widely used tool to model a cache and compute its parameters is the Cacti tool [Wilton and Jouppi, 1993]. It has been around for almost the last 25 years, and is still the tool of choice for modelling a cache. In this section, we shall heavily cite concepts from the Cacti research reports (versions 1 to 6). Note that we shall take liberties to simplify and generalise concepts wherever possible.

7.3.1 Memory Technologies used in a Cache: SRAM and CAM Arrays

Let us briefly explain how a cache is designed. Note that this is a superficial introduction to this topic. Interested readers can consult textbooks on the design of memory systems for more in-depth coverage.

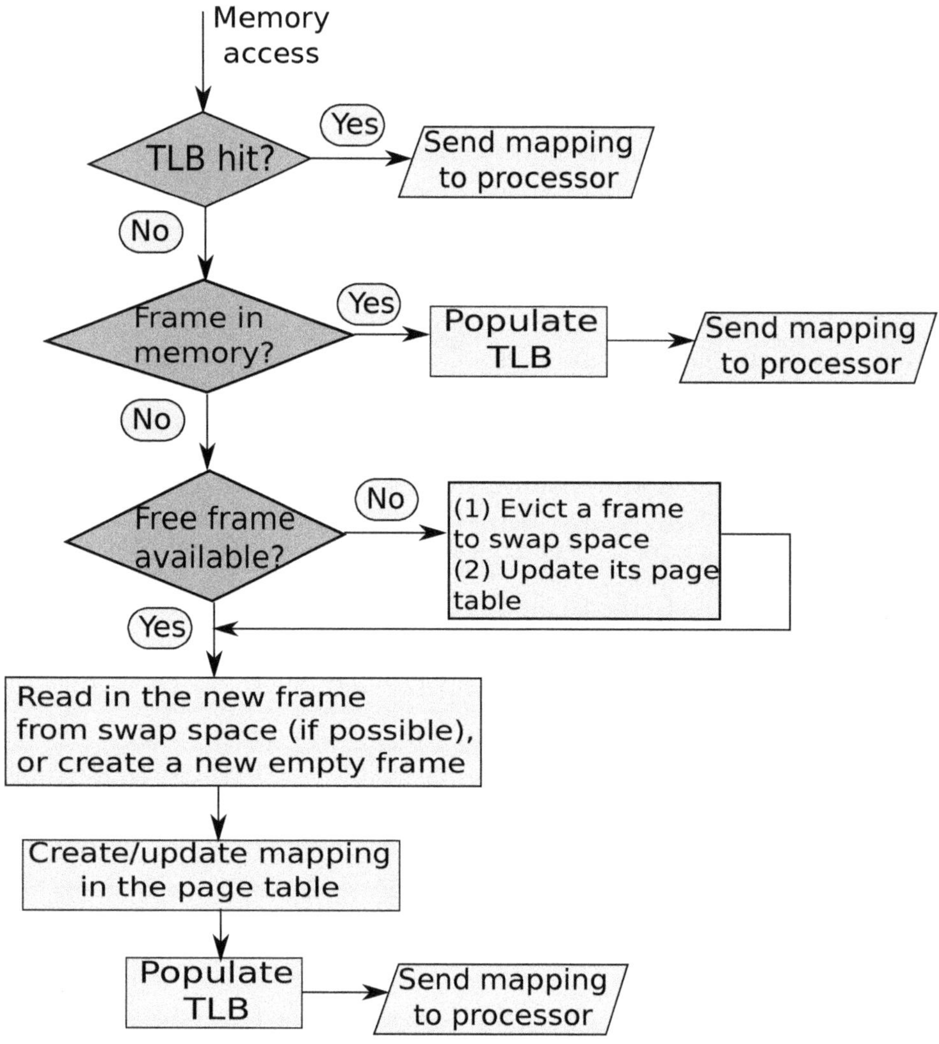

Figure 7.18: Flowchart for memory accesses

The basic element of any memory structure is a memory cell that stores 1 bit of information. There are many kinds of memory cells. In this book, we shall mainly use the 6-transistor SRAM cell, and the 10-transistor CAM cell. Let us quickly describe these memory technologies.

SRAM Cell

The question that we wish to answer is how do we store 1 bit of information? We can always use latches and flip-flops. However, these are area intensive structures and cannot be used to store thousands of bits. We need a structure that is far smaller.

Let us extend the idea of a typical SR latch as shown in Figure 7.19. An SR latch can store a single bit. If we set S to 1 and R to 0, then we store a 1. Conversely, if we set $S = 0$ and $R = 1$, we store a 0.

Let us appreciate the basic structure of this circuit. We have a cross-coupled pair of NAND gates.

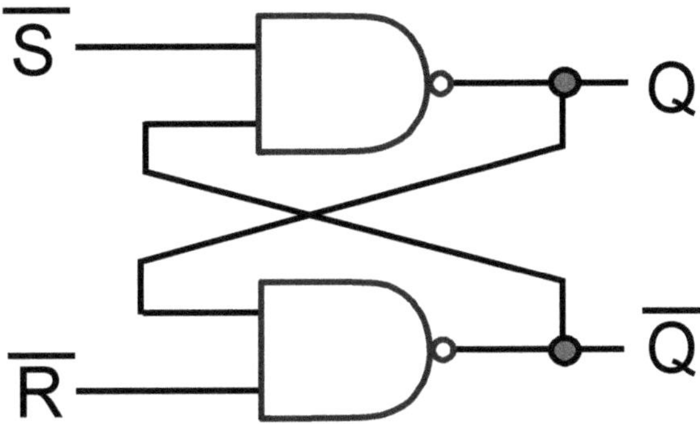

Figure 7.19: A basic SR latch

By cross-coupling, we mean that the output of one NAND gate is connected to the input of the other and likewise for the other gate. Unfortunately, a NAND gate has four transistors, and thus this circuit is not area efficient. Let us take this idea, and build a circuit that has two cross-coupled inverters as shown in Figure 7.20.

This structure can also store a bit. It just uses four transistors, because one CMOS inverter can be made out of one NMOS transistor and one PMOS transistor. To write a value, we can simply set the value of node Q to the value that we want to write. The other node will always have $\overline{Q}$ because of the two inverters. Reading a value is also easy. It is the output at node Q.

However, this circuit has a drawback. There is no way to enable or disable the circuit. Enabling and disabling a memory cell is very important because we are not reading or writing to the cell in every cycle. We want to maintain the value in the cell when we are not accessing it. During this period, its access should be disabled. Otherwise, whenever there is a change in the voltages of nodes Q or $\overline{Q}$, the value stored in the cell will change. If we can effectively disconnect the cell from the outside world, then we are sure that it will maintain its value.

This is easy to do. We can use the most basic property of a transistor, which is that it works like a switch. We can connect two transistors to both the nodes of the cross-coupled inverter. This design in shown in Figure 7.21. We add two transistors – W_1 and W_2 – at the terminals Q and $\overline{Q}$, respectively.These are called *word line transistors*; they connect the inverter pair to two bit lines on either side. The gates of W_1 and W_2 are connected to a single wire called the *word line*. If the word line is set to 1, both the transistors get enabled (the switch closes). In this case, the bit lines get connected to the terminals Q and $\overline{Q}$ respectively. We can then read the value stored in the inverter pair and also write to it. If we set the word line to 0, then the switch gets disconnected, and the 4-transistor inverter pair is disconnected from the bit lines. We cannot read the value stored in it, or write to it. Thus, we have a 6-transistor memory cell; this is known as an SRAM (static random access memory) cell. This is a big improvement as compared to the SR latch in terms of the number of transistors that are used.

SRAM Array

Now that we have designed a memory cell that can store a single bit, let us create an array of SRAM cells. We can use this array to store data.

To start with, let us create a matrix of cells as shown in Figure 7.22. We divide the address used to access the SRAM array into two parts: row address, and column address. We send the row address to the row decoder. Assume that it contains r bits. The decoder takes in these r bits, and it sets one out of 2^r output lines that are the word lines to 1. Each word line is identified by the binary number represented by the row address. For example, if the row address is 0101, then the fifth output of the

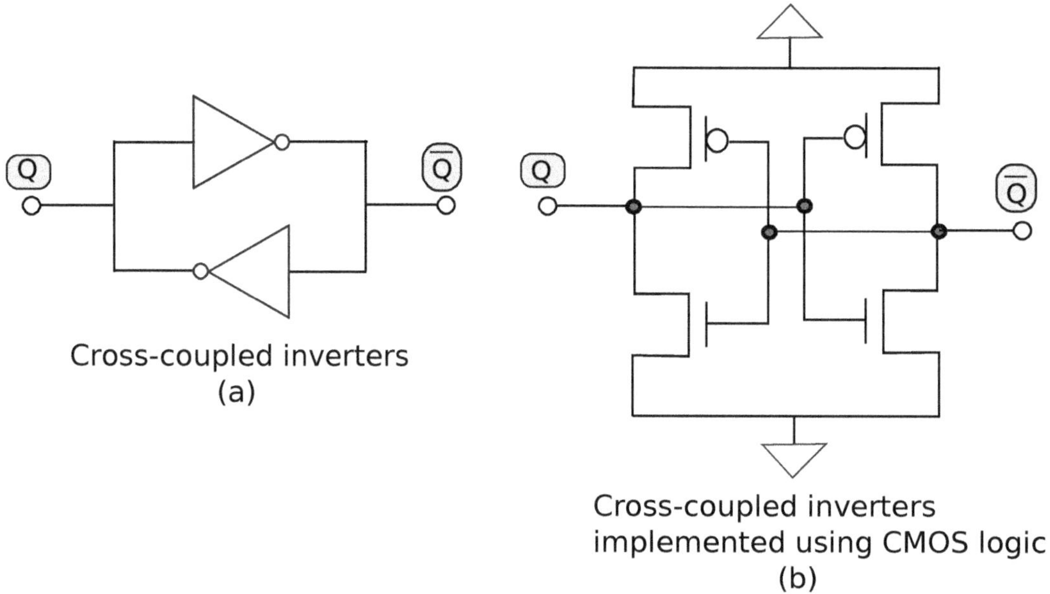

Figure 7.20: Cross-coupled inverters

decoder is set to 1 or the fifth word line is set to 1. The rest of the output lines (word lines) are set to 0.

The decoder is a standard electronic circuit, and can be easily constructed out of logic gates. The benefit of using the decoder is that it enables only one of the word lines. This word line subsequently enables a row of cells in the 2D array (matrix) of memory cells. All the memory cells in a row can then be accessed.

Let us consider the process of writing first. Every cell is connected to two wires that are called bit lines. Each bit line is connected to a node of the memory cell (Q or $\overline{Q}$) via a transistor switch that is enable by a word line. The bit lines carry complementary logic values. Let us refer to the left bit line as BL and the right bit line as $\overline{BL}$. To write values we use fast write drivers that can quickly set the voltage of the bit lines. If we want to write a 1 to a given cell, then we set its bit lines as follows: BL to a logical 1 and $\overline{BL}$ to a logical 0. We do the reverse, if we wish to write a logical 0. The pair of inverters get reprogrammed once we set the voltages of BL and $\overline{BL}$.

The more difficult operation is reading the SRAM array. In this case, once we enable the memory cell, the bit lines get charged to the values that are contained in the memory cell. For example, if the value of a node of the memory cell is a logical 1 (assume a logical 1 is 1 V), then the voltage on the corresponding bit line increases towards 1 V. Similarly, the voltage on the other bit line starts moving towards 0 V. This situation is not the same as writing a value. While writing a value we could use large

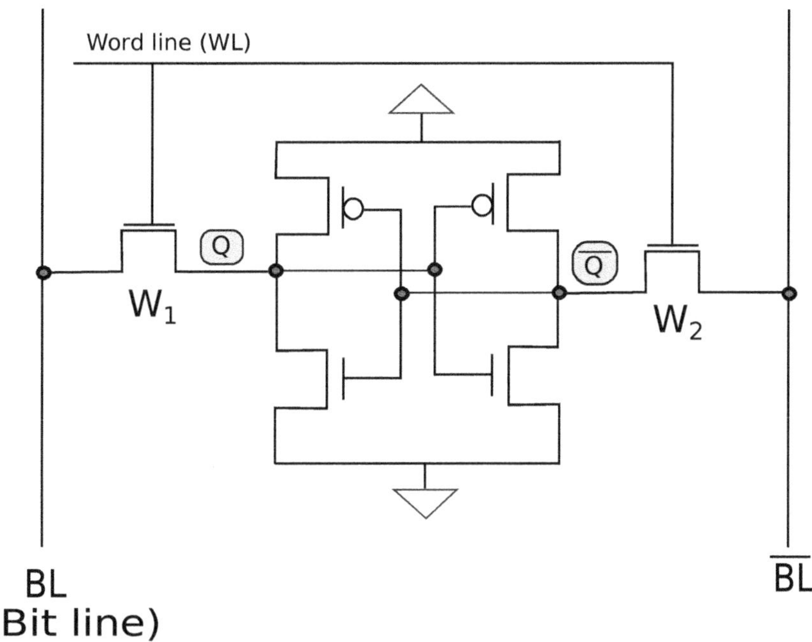

Figure 7.21: Cross-coupled inverters with enabling transistors

write drivers that can pump in a lot of current into the bit lines. In this case, we only have a small 6-transistor cell that is charging the bit lines. It is far weaker than the powerful write drivers. As a result, the process of charging (towards a logical 1) or discharging (towards a logical 0) is significantly slower. Note that the process of reading is crucial. It is often on the critical path because there are instructions waiting for the value read by a load instruction. Hence, we need to find ways to accelerate the process.

A standard method of doing this is called *precharging*. We set the value of both the bit lines to a value that is midway between the voltages between logical 0 and 1. Since we have assumed that the voltage corresponding to a logical 1 is 1 V, the precharge voltage is 0.5 V. We use strong precharge drivers to precharge both the bit lines to 0.5 V. Akin to the case with write drivers, this process can be done very quickly. Once the lines are precharged, we enable a row of memory cells. Each memory cell starts setting the values of the bit lines that it is connected to. For one bit line the voltage starts moving to 1 V and for the other the voltage starts moving towards 0 V. We monitor the difference in voltage between the two bit lines.

Assume the cell stores a logical 1. In this case, the voltage on the bit line BL will try to move towards 1 V, and the voltage on the bit line $\overline{BL}$ will try to move towards 0 V. The difference between the voltages of BL and $\overline{BL}$ will start at 0 V and gradually increase to 1 V. However, the key idea is that we do not have to wait till the difference reaches 1 V or -1 V (when we store a logical 0). Once the difference crosses a certain threshold, we can infer the final direction in which the voltages on both the bit lines are expected to progress. Thus, much before the voltages on the bit lines reach their final values, we can come to the correct conclusion.

Let us represent this symbolically. Let us define the function V to represent the voltage. For example, $V(BL)$ represents the instantaneous voltage of the bit line BL. Here are the rules for inferring a logical 0 or 1 after we enable the cell for reading.

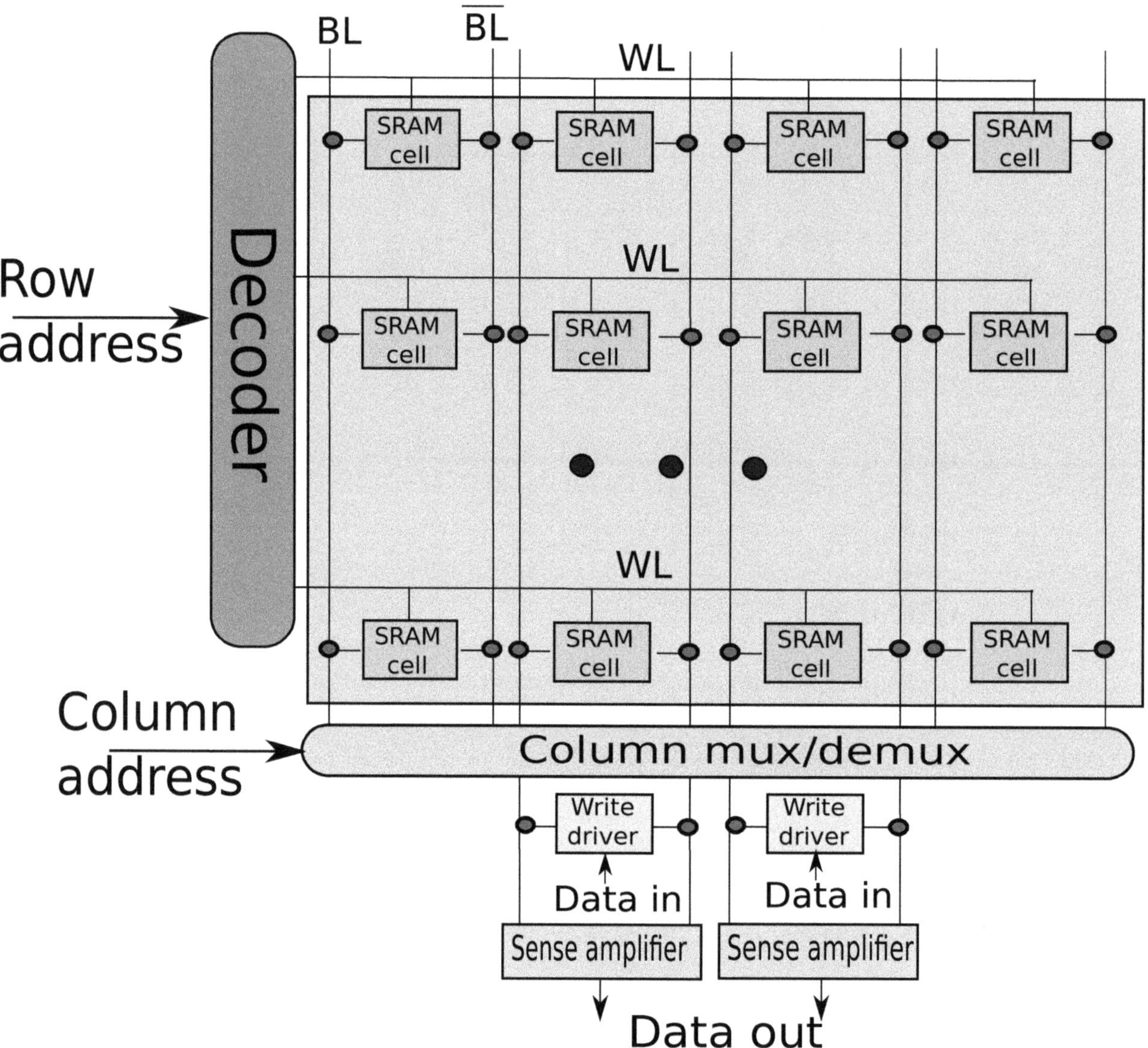

Figure 7.22: An SRAM array

$$value = \begin{cases} 1 & V(BL) - V(\overline{BL}) > \Delta \\ 0 & V(\overline{BL}) - V(BL) > \Delta \end{cases}$$

In this case, we define a threshold Δ that is typically of the order of tens of millivolts. An astute reader might ask a question about the need for the threshold, Δ. One of the reasons is that long copper wires such as bit lines can often accumulate an EMF due to impinging electromagnetic radiation. In fact, unbeknownst to us a long copper wire can act as a miniature antenna and pick up electric fields. This might cause a potential to build up along the copper wire. In addition, we might have crosstalk between copper wires where because of some degree of inductive and capacitive coupling adjacent wires might get charged. Due to such types of *noise*, it is possible that we might initially see the voltage on a bit line swaying in a certain direction. To completely discount such effects, we need to wait till the absolute value of the voltage difference exceeds a threshold. This threshold is large enough to make us sure that the voltage difference between the bit lines is not arising because of transient effects such as picking up random electric fields. We should be sure that the difference in voltages is because one bit line is moving towards logical 1 and the other towards logical 0.

At this point, we can confidently declare the value contained in the memory cell. We do not have to wait for the voltages to reach their final values. This is thus a much faster process. The lower we set Δ, faster is our circuit. We are limited by the amount of noise.

Note that there is one hidden advantage of SRAM arrays. Both BL and $\overline{BL}$ are spaced close together. Given their spatial proximity, the effects of noise will be similar, and thus if we consider the difference in voltages, we shall see that the effects of electromagnetic or crosstalk noise will mostly get cancelled out. This is known as *common mode rejection* and works in our favour. Had we had a single bit line, this would not have happened.

In our SRAM array (shown in Figure 7.22) we enable the entire row of cells. However, we might not be interested in all of this data. For example, if the entire row contains 64 bytes of data, and we are only interested in 16 bytes, then we need to choose the component of the row that we are interested in. This is done using the column multiplexers that read in only those columns that are we are interested in. The column address is the input to these column multiplexers. For example, in this case since there are four 16 byte chunks in a 64 byte row, there are four possible choices for the set of columns. We thus need 2 bits to encode this set of choices. Hence, the column address is 2 bits wide.

Column Multiplexers

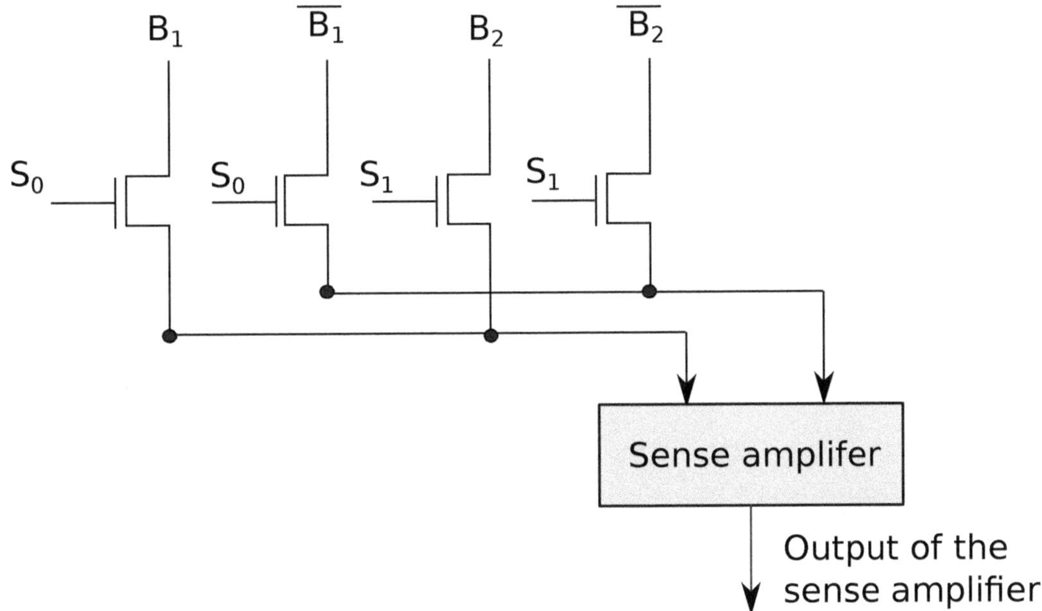

Figure 7.23: A column multiplexer

Let us look at the design of the column multiplexers. Figure 7.23 shows a simple example. We have two pairs of bit lines: $(B_1, \overline{B_1})$ and $(B_2, \overline{B_2})$. We need to choose one of the pairs. We connect each wire to an NMOS transistor, which is known as a *pass transistor*. If the input at its gate is a logical 1, then the transistor conducts, and the voltage at the drain is reflected at the source. However, if the voltage at the gate is a logical 0, then the transistor behaves as an open circuit.

In this case, we need a single column address bit because there are two choices. We send this bit to a decoder and derive two outputs: S_0 and S_1. Only one of them can be true. Depending upon the output that is true, the corresponding pass transistors get enabled. We connect B_1 and B_2 to the same wire, and we do the same with $\overline{B_1}$ and $\overline{B_2}$. Only one bit line from each pair will get enabled. The enabled signals are then sent to the sense amplifier that senses the difference in the voltage and determines the logic level of the bit stored in the SRAM cell.

Sense Amplifiers

After we have chosen the columns that we are interested in, we need to compare BL and $\overline{BL}$ for each cell, and then ascertain which way the difference is going (positive or negative). We use a specialised circuit called a sense amplifier for this purpose. The circuit diagram of a typical sense amplifier is shown in Figure 7.24.

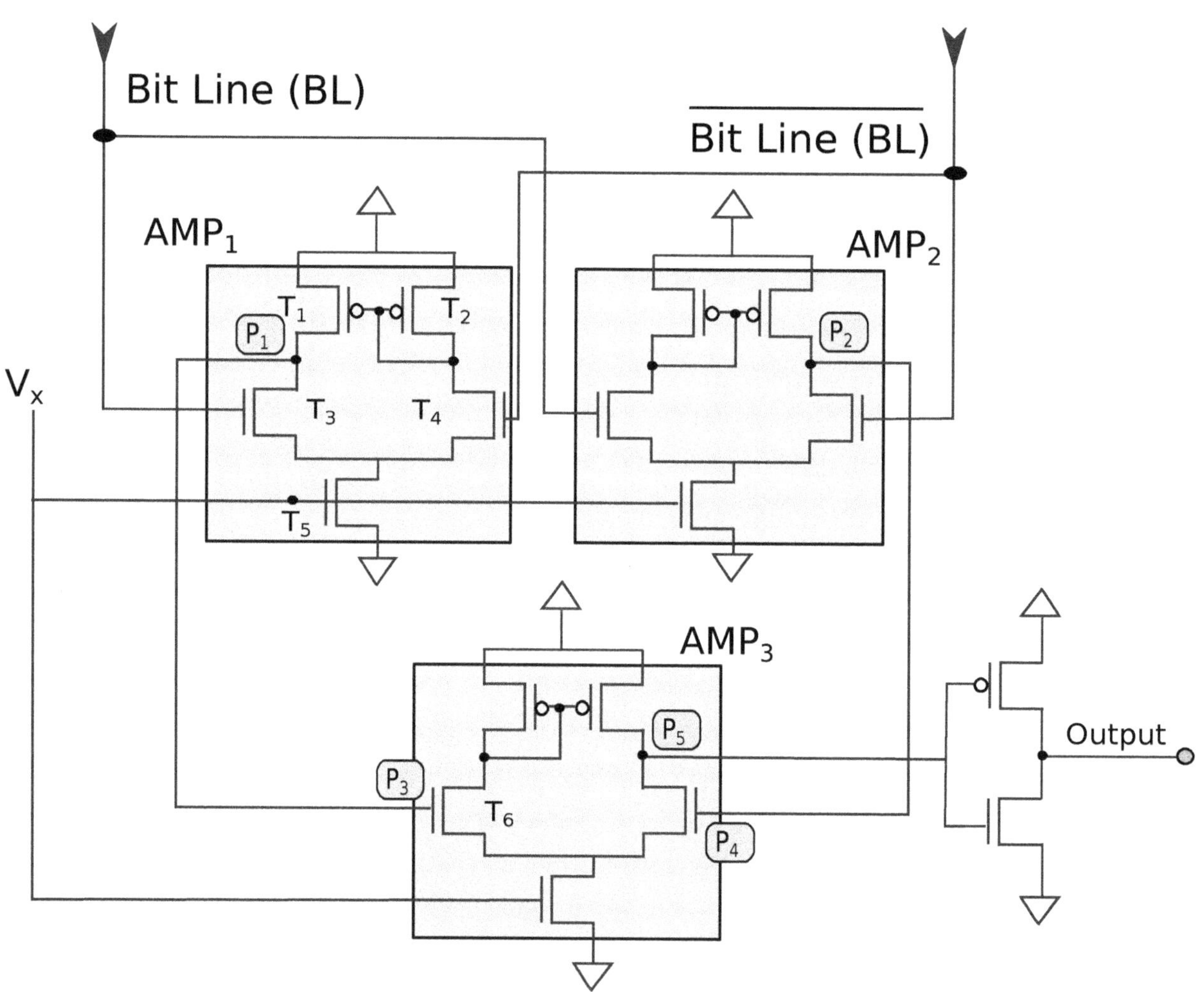

Figure 7.24: A sense amplifier

Let us describe the operation of a sense amplifier as shown in Figure 7.24. A sense amplifier is made up of three differential amplifiers. In Figure 7.24, each shaded box represents a differential amplifier. Let us consider the amplifier at the left top and analyse it. We shall provide an informal treatment in this book. For a better understanding of this circuit, readers can perform circuit simulation or analyse the circuit mathematically. First, assume that $V(BL) = V(\overline{BL})$. Transistors T_1 and T_2 form a circuit known as a current mirror, where the current flowing through both the transistors is the same. Furthermore, transistor T_2 is in saturation ($V_{SD} > V_{SG} - V_T$), which fixes the current flowing through the transistor.

Now assume that $V(BL)$ is slightly lower than $V(\overline{BL})$, specifically $V(\overline{BL}) - V(BL) = \Delta$, which is the difference threshold for detecting a logic level. In this case transistor T_4 will draw slightly more current as compared to the equilibrium state. Let this current be I_d mA. This means an additional current of I_d mA will pass through T_2. Because we have a current mirror, the same additional current I_d will also pass through T_1. However, the current through T_5 will remain constant because it is set to operate in the saturation region (the reader should verify this by considering possible values of V_x). This means that since the current through T_4 has increased by I_d, the current through T_3 needs to decrease by I_d to ensure that the sum (flowing through T_5) remains constant.

The summary of this discussion is that an additional I_d mA flows through T_1 and the current in T_3 decreases by I_d mA. There is thus a total shortfall of $2I_d$ mA, which must flow from terminal P_1 to P_3. Terminal P_3 is the gate of transistor T_6. This current will serve the purpose of increasing its gate voltage. Ultimately, the current will fall of to zero once the operating conditions of transistors $T_1 \ldots T_5$ change. Thus, the net effect of a small change in the voltage between the bit lines is that the voltage at terminal P_3 increases significantly. Consider the reverse situation where $V(\overline{BL})$ decreases as compared to $V(BL)$. It is easy to argue that we shall see a reverse effect at terminal P_3. Hence, we can conclude that transistors $T_1 \ldots T_5$ make up a differential amplifier (AMP_1 in the figure).

Similarly, we have another parallel differential AMP_2 where the bit lines are connected to the amplifier in a reverse fashion. Let us convince ourselves that the directions in which the voltages increase at terminals P_1 and P_2 are opposite. When one decreases, the other increases and vice versa. The role of the parallel differential amplifiers(AMP_1 and AMP_2) is to amplify the difference between the voltages at the bit lines; this shows up at terminals P_3 and P_4.

Terminals P_3 and P_4 are the inputs to another differential amplifier AMP_3, which further amplifies the voltage difference between the terminals. We thus have a two-stage differential amplifier. Note that as $V(\overline{BL})$ increases, the voltage at terminal P_3 increases and this increases the voltage at terminal P_5 (using a similar logic). However, with an increase in $V(\overline{BL})$ we expect the output to become 0, and vice versa. To ensure that this happens, we need to connect an inverter to terminal P_5. The final output of the sense amplifier is the output of the inverter.

Sense amplifiers are typically connected to long copper wires that route the output to other functional units. Sense amplifiers are typically very small circuits and are not powerful enough to charge long copper wires. Hence, we need another circuit called the *output driver* that takes the output of a sense amplifier, and stabilises it such that it can provide enough charge to set the potential of long copper wires to a logical 1 if there is a need. Note that this is a basic design. There are many modern power-efficient designs. We shall discuss another variant of sense amplifiers that are used in DRAMs in Chapter 10.

CAM Cell

In Section 7.1.4 we had discussed the notion of a CAM (content-addressable memory) array, where we address a row in the matrix of memory cells based on its contents and not on the basis of its index. Let us now proceed to design such an array. The basic component of a CAM array is the CAM cell (defined on the same lines as a 6-transistor SRAM cell).

Figure 7.25 shows the design of a CAM cell with 10 transistors. Let us divide the diagram into two halves: above and below the match line. The top half looks the same as an SRAM cell. It contains 6 transistors and stores a bit using a pair of inverters. The extra part is the 4 extra transistors at the bottom. The two output nodes of the inverter pair are labelled Q and $\overline{Q}$ respectively. In addition, we have two inputs, A and $\overline{A}$. Our job is to find out if the input bit A matches the value stored in the inverter pair, Q.

The four transistors at the bottom have two pairs of two NMOS transistors each connected in series. Let us name the two transistors in the first pair T_1 and T_2 respectively. The drain terminal of T_1 is connected to the *match line*, which is initially precharged to the supply voltage. The first pair of NMOS

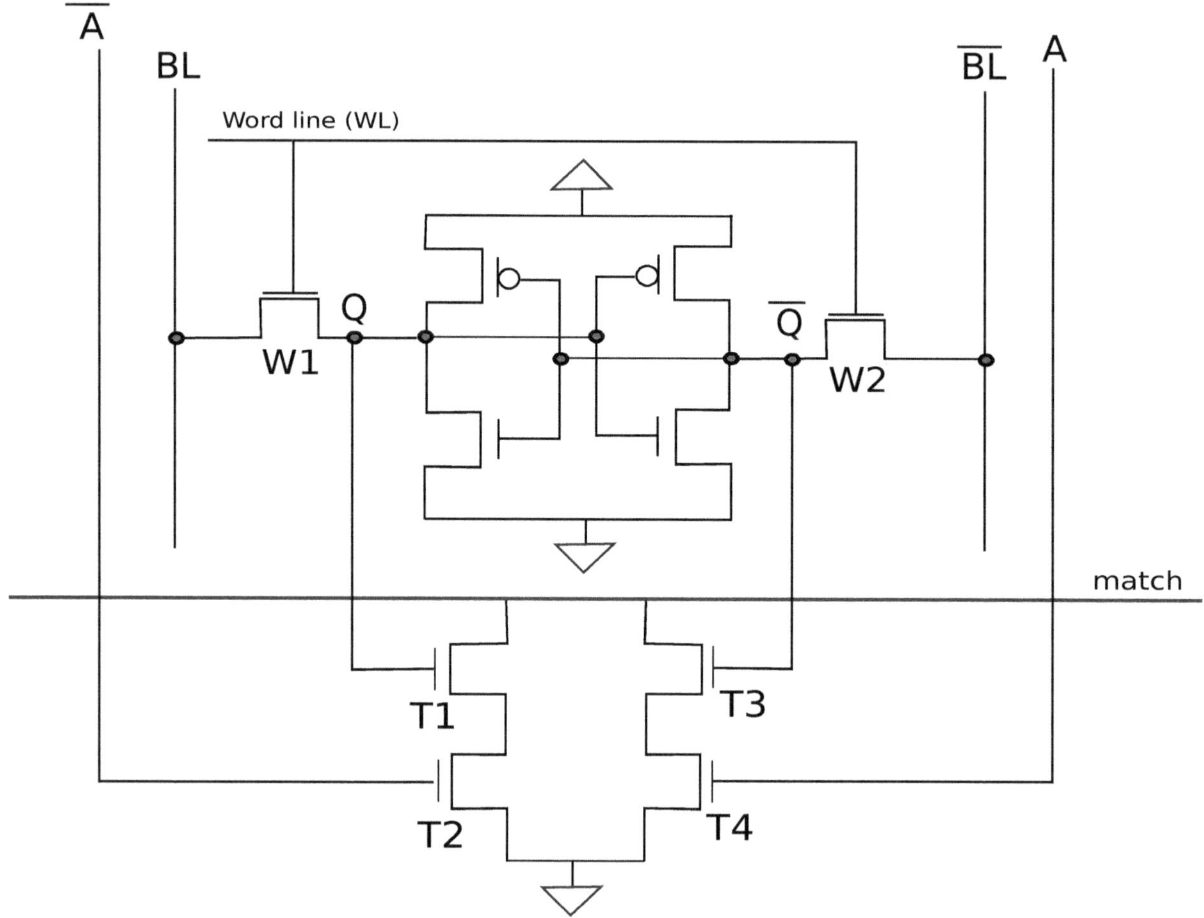

Figure 7.25: A CAM cell

transistors is connected to Q and $\overline{A}$ respectively. Let us create a truth table based on the inputs and the states of the transistors T_1 and T_2.

Q	$\overline{A}$	T_1	T_2
0	0	off	off
0	1	off	on
1	0	on	off
1	1	on	on

If the inputs Q and $\overline{A}$ are both 1, then only do both the transistors conduct. Otherwise, at least one of the transistors does not conduct. In other words if $Q = 1$ and $A = 0$, there is a straight conducting path between the match line and the ground node. Thus, the voltage of the match line becomes zero. Otherwise, the voltage of the match line will continue to remain the same as its precharged value because there is no conducting path to the ground.

Let us now look at the other pair of transistors, T_3 and T_4, that are connected in the same way albeit to different inputs: $\overline{Q}$ and A (complements of the inputs to transistors T_1 and T_2). Let us build a similar truth table.

$\overline{Q}$	A	T_3	T_4
0	0	off	off
0	1	off	on
1	0	on	off
1	1	on	on

Here also, the only condition for a conducting path is $\overline{Q} = A = 1$. If we combine the results of both the truth tables, then we have the following conditions for the match line to get set to 0. Either $Q = \overline{A} = 1$, or $\overline{Q} = A = 1$. We should convince ourselves that this will only happen if $A \neq Q$. If $A = Q$, then both of these conditions will always be false. One of the values will be 1 and the other will be 0. However, if $A \neq Q$, then only this is possible.

Let us thus summarise. A CAM cell stores a value Q. In addition, it takes as input the bit A that is to be compared with Q. If the values are equal, then the match line maintains its precharged value. However, if they are not equal then a direct conducting path forms between the match line and ground. Its value gets set to a logical 0. Thus, by looking at the potential of the match line, we can infer if there has been a match or not.

CAM Array

Let us build a CAM array the same way we built the SRAM array. Figure 7.26 shows the design.

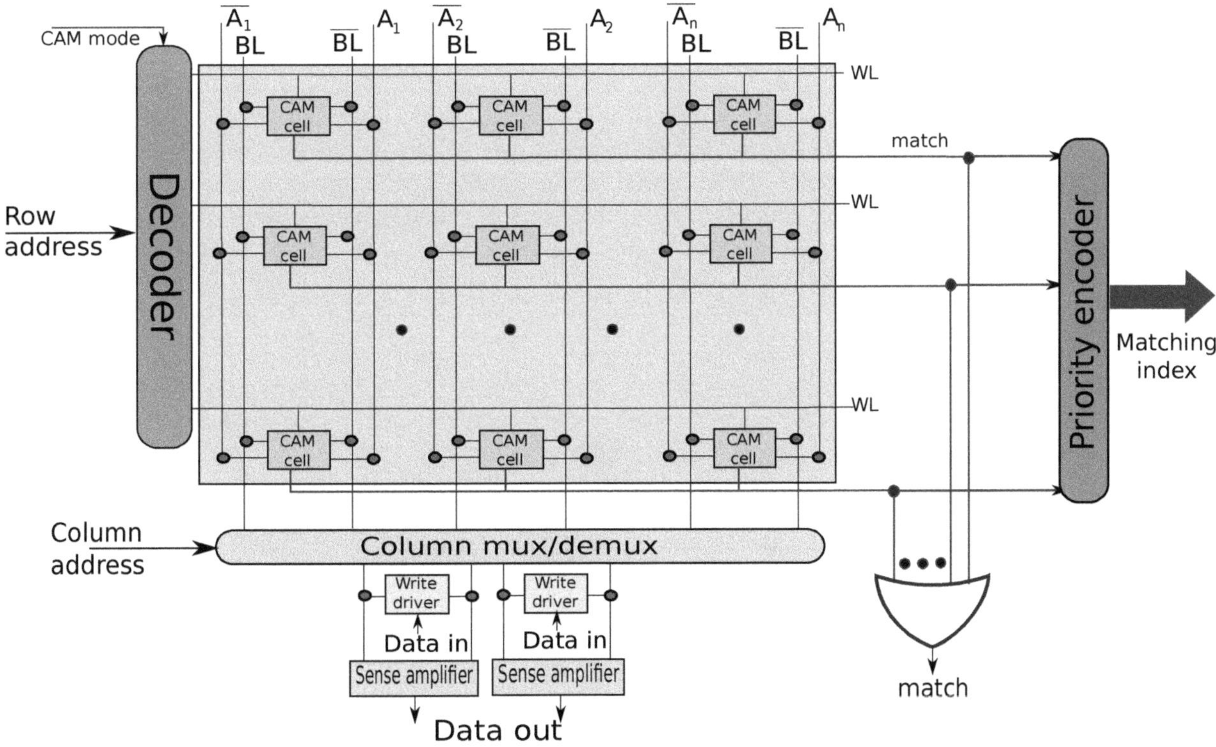

Figure 7.26: A CAM array

Typically, a CAM array has all the features of an SRAM array, and in addition it has more features such as content-based addressability. The row address decoder, column multiplexers, sense amplifiers, precharge circuits, write and output drivers are the parts that the CAM array inherits from the SRAM array. To use the CAM array like a regular SRAM array, we just simply enable the row decoder nd proceed with a regular array access. In this case, we do not set the match line or read its value.

Let us now focus on the extra components that are useful when we are searching for an entry based on its contents. To keep the discussion simple, we assume that we wish to match an entire row. Extending this idea to cases where we wish to match a part of the row is trivial. Now, observe that all the transistors in the same row are connected to the same match line (see Figure 7.26). We provide a vector V as input such that it can be compared with each row bit by bit. Thus, the ith bit in the vector is compared with the value stored in the ith CAM cell in the row. In other words, at each cell we compare a pair of bits: one from the vector V (bit A_i in the figure) and the value stored in the CAM cell. First, assume that all the bits match pairwise. In this case, we observe the bits to be equal at each cell, and thus a conducting path between the match line and ground does not form. This happens for all the cells in the row. Thus, the match line continues to maintain its precharged value: a logical 1.

Now, consider the other case, where at least one pair of bits does not match. In this case at that CAM cell, a conducting path forms to the ground, and the match line gets discharged; the voltage gets set to a logical 0.

Thus, to summarise, we can infer if the entire row has matched the input vector V or not by basically looking at the voltage of the match line after the compare operation. If it is the same as its precharged value (logical 1), then there has been a full match. Otherwise, if the match line has been discharged, then we can be sure that at least one pair of bits has not matched.

Hence, the process of addressing a CAM memory based on the contents of its cells is as follows. We first enable all the word lines. Then, we set the bits of the input vector (bits $A_1 \ldots A_n$ in the figure) and then allow the comparisons to proceed. We always assume that we do not have any duplicates. There are thus two possible choices: none of the match lines are at a logical 1 or only one of the match lines is set to 1. This is easy to check. We can create an OR circuit that checks if any of the match lines is a logical 1 or not. If the output of this circuit is 1, then it means that there is a match, otherwise there is no match. Note that it is impractical to create a large OR gate using NMOS transistors. We can either create a tree of OR gates with a limited fan-in (number of inputs), or we can use wired-OR logic, where all the match lines are connected to a single output via diodes (as shown in Figure 7.27). If any of the match lines is 1, it sets the output to 1. Because of the diodes current cannot flow from the output terminal to the match lines.

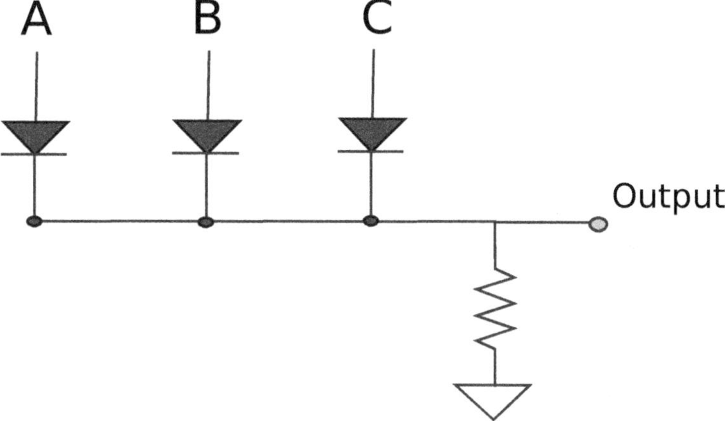

Figure 7.27: Wired-or logic

Now, if we know that one of the match lines is set (equal to 1), we need to find the number of the row that matches the contents. Note that our count starts from 0 in this case (similar to arrays in programming languages). We can use an encoder for this that takes N inputs and has $log_2(N)$ outputs.

The output gives the id (Boolean encoding) of the input that is set to 1. For example, if the 9th input out of a set of 16 inputs is set to 1 its encoding will be 1001 (assume that the count starts at 0).

In a fully associative cache whose tag array is implemented as a CAM array, once we get the id of the row whose match line is set to 1, we can access the corresponding entry of the data array and read or write to the corresponding block. A CAM array is thus an efficient way of creating a hash table in hardware. The tag array of a fully associative cache is typically implemented as a CAM array, whereas the data array is implemented as a regular SRAM array.

7.3.2 Designing a Cache

To design a real cache using our basic technologies, we need to consider the inputs that a typical cache modelling tool such as Cacti takes ([Wilton and Jouppi, 1993]).

Field	Description
A	Associativity
B	Block size (in bytes)
C	Cache size (in bytes)
b_o	Width of the output (in bits)
b_{addr}	Width of the input address (in bits)

These are the most basic parameters for any set associative cache. Note that direct mapped caches and fully associative caches are specific instances of set associative caches. Hence, we use the set associative cache as a basis for all our subsequent discussion. Using the ABC parameters (associativity, block size, and cache size), we can compute the size of the set index and the size of the tag (refer to Example 4).

Example 4

Given A (associativity), B (block size in bytes), W (width of the input address in bits), and C (cache size), compute the number of bits in the set index and the size of the tag.

Answer: *The number of blocks that can be stored in the cache is equal to C/B. The size of each set is A. Thus, the number of sets is equal to $C/(BA)$. Therefore, the number of bits required to index each set is $log_2(C/(BA))$.*

Let us now compute the size of the tag. We know that the number of bits in the memory address is W. Furthermore, the block size is B bytes, and we thus require $log_2(B)$ bits to specify the index of a byte within a block (block address bits).

Hence, the number of bits left for the tag is as follows:

$$tag\ bits = address\ size - \#set\ index\ bits - \#block\ address\ bits$$
$$= W - log_2(C/(BA)) - log_2(B)$$
$$= W - log_2(C) + log_2(A)$$

A naive organisation with the ABC parameters might result in a very skewed design. For example, if we have a large cache, then we might end up with a lot of rows and very few columns. In this case, the load on the row decoder will be very large and this will become a bottleneck. Additionally, the number of devices connected to each bit line would increase and this will increase its capacitance, thus making it slower because of the increased RC delay.

On the other hand, if we have a lot of columns then the load on the column multiplexers and the word lines will increase. They will then become a bottleneck. In addition, placing a highly skewed structure on the chip is difficult. It conflicts with other structures. Having an aspect ratio (width/length) that is close to that of a square is almost always the best idea from the point of view of placing a component on the chip. Hence, having a balance between the number of rows and columns is a desirable attribute.

It is thus necessary to break down a large array of SRAM transistors into smaller arrays such that they are faster and more manageable. We refer to the large original array as the *undivided array* and the smaller arrays as *subarrays*. Cacti thus introduces two additional parameters: N_{dwl} and N_{dbl}. N_{dwl} indicates the number of segments that we create by splitting each word line or alternatively the number of partitions that we create by splitting the set of columns of the undivided array. On similar lines, N_{dbl} indicates the number of segments that we create by splitting each bit line or the set of rows. After splitting, we create a set of subarrays. In this case, the number of subarrays is equal to $N_{dwl} \times N_{dbl}$.

Additionally, the Cacti tool introduces another parameter called N_{spd}, which basically sets the aspect ratio of the undivided array. It indicates the number of sets that are mapped to a single word line. Let us do some math using our *ABC* parameters. The size of a block is B, and if the associativity is A, then the size of a set in bytes is $A \times B$. Thus, the number of bytes that are stored in a row (for a single word line) is $A \times B \times N_{spd}$.

Example 5 *Compute the number of rows and columns in a subarray using Cacti's parameters.*

Answer: *Let us compute the number of columns as follows. We have $A \times B \times N_{spd}$ bytes per row in the undivided cache. This is equal to $8 \times A \times B \times N_{spd}$ bits. Now, if we divide the set of columns into N_{dwl} parts, the number of columns in each subarray is equal to $\frac{8 \times A \times B \times N_{spd}}{N_{dwl}}$.*

Let us now compute the number of rows in a subarray. The number of bytes in each row of the undivided cache is equal to $A \times B \times N_{spd}$. Thus, the number of rows is equal to the size of the cache C divided by this number, which is equal to $\frac{C}{A \times B \times N_{spd}}$. Now, if we divide this into N_{dbl} segments, we get the number of rows in each subarray as $\frac{C}{A \times B \times N_{spd} \times N_{dbl}}$.

Thus, given a cache, the task is to compute these three parameters – N_{dwl}, N_{dbl}, and N_{spd}. We need to first figure out a goal such as minimising the access time or the energy per access. Then, we need to compute the optimal values of these parameters. These parameters were for the data array (d in the subscript). We can define similar parameters for the tag array: N_{twl}, N_{tbl}, and N_{tspd} respectively.

Let us now summarise our discussion. We started out with an array or rather a matrix of SRAM cells. We quickly realised that we cannot have a skewed ratio (disproportionate number of rows or columns). In one case, we will have very slow word lines, and in the other case we will have very slow bit lines. Both are undesirable. Hence, to strike a balance we divide an array of memory cells into a series of subarrays. This is graphically shown in Figure 7.28.

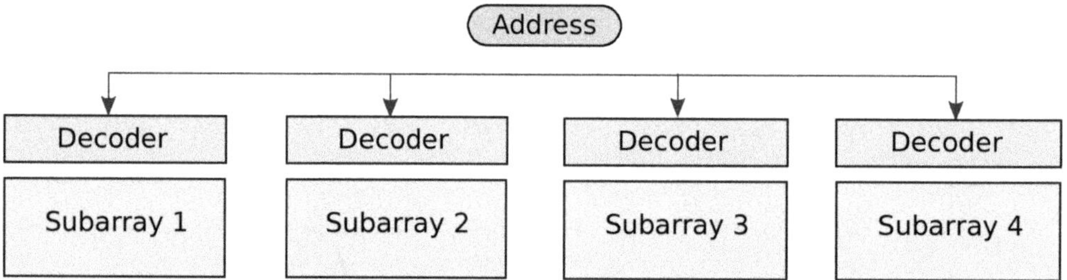

Figure 7.28: An array broken into several subarrays

Each subarray has its own decoder. Recall that the input to the decoder is the set index. If we have 4 subarrays then we can use the last two bits of the set index to index the proper subarray. Subsequently, we expect to find a full set in the row of the subarray. However, in theory it is possible that the set of blocks maybe split across multiple subarrays. In this case, we need to read all the subarrays that contain the blocks in the set. Given that we can divide a large SRAM array in this manner, we will end up accessing subarrays, which are much smaller and faster.

Multiple Parallel Accesses

Let us now complicate the model of our cache. Assume that we need to send multiple read and write requests each cycle. In this case, we need to define a multi-ported structure. A *port* is defined as an interface for accepting a read or write request. We can have a read port, a write port, or a read/write port.

> **Definition 47**
> *A* port *is defined as an interface for accepting a read or write request. We can have a read port, a write port, or a read/write port.*

The traditional approach for creating a multi-ported structure is to connect each SRAM cell to an additional pair of bit lines as shown in Figure 7.29. We thus introduce two additional word line transistors W_3 and W_4 that are enabled by a different word line – this creates a 2-ported structure. Now, since we have two pairs of bit lines, it means that we can make two parallel accesses to the SRAM array. One access will use all the bit lines with subscript 1, and the other access will use all the bit lines with subscript 2. Each pair of bit lines needs its separate set of column multiplexers, sense amplifiers, write, precharge, and output drivers. Additionally, we need two decoders – one for each address. This increases the area of each array significantly. A common thumb rule that is used is that the area of an array increases as the square of the number of ports – proportional increase in the number of word/bit lines in both the axes.

A better solution is a multi-banked cache. A bank is defined as an independent array with its own subarrays and decoders. If a cache has 4 banks, then we split the physical address space between the 4 banks. This can be done by choosing 2 bits in the physical address and then using them to access the right bank. Each bank may be organised as a cache with its own tag and data arrays, alternatively we can divide the data and tag arrays into banks separately. For performance reasons, each bank typically has a single port.

The advantage of dividing a cache into banks is that we can seamlessly support concurrent accesses to different banks. Now, for 4 banks there is a 25% chance of two simultaneous accesses accessing the same bank – assuming a uniformly random distribution of accesses across the banks. This is known as a *bank conflict*, and in this case we need to serialise the accesses. This means that one memory access needs to wait for the other. There is an associated performance penalty. However, this is often outweighed by the fast access time of banks. Finally, note that each bank has its own set of subarrays. However, subarrays cannot be accessed independently.

Hierarchical Organisation of Caches

As caches increase in size, the simple organisation that we have presented does not remain efficient. Recall that we have shown how to divide a cache into multiple banks and then divide each bank into multiple subarrays.

Let us now look at even larger caches, where we need to further optimise the data and tag arrays [Thoziyoor et al., 2007] separately. Let us focus on the data array, which is much larger than the

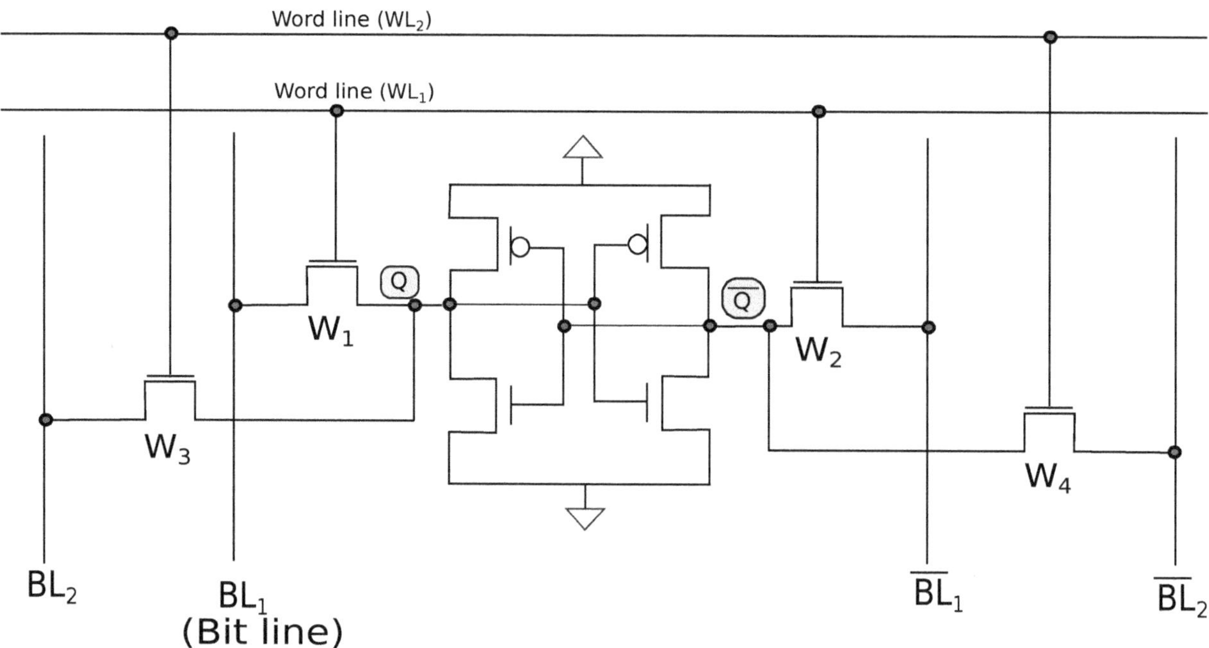

Figure 7.29: SRAM cell with 2 ports

tag array. In Cacti 5.0, the authors propose to divide an array into multiple banks, then further sub-divide a bank into subbanks. Banks can be accessed independently by concurrent requests. However, one bank can process only one memory request at any given point of time. Each bank consists of multiple subbanks, and only one of the subbanks can be enabled for a memory request. A subbank contains an entire data block, which is typically either 64 bytes or 128 bytes. Following the maxim, "smaller is faster", we divide a subbank into multiple mats, and each mat into 4 subarrays. The structure is shown in Figure 7.30. The hierarchy is $Array \rightarrow Bank \rightarrow Subbank \rightarrow Mat \rightarrow Subarray$.

The logic for such a deep hierarchy is as follows. If a subbank is one large array, it will be very big and very slow. Hence, we divide a subbank into multiple mats, and we divide each mat into multiple subarrays. We store a part of each block in each mat. For a read operation, each mat supplies the part of the block that it contains and at the subbank level we join all the parts to get the block. We do the same for the subarrays within mats. This process ensures that the mats and their constituent subarrays are small and hence fast. This also parallelises the process of reading and writing. We can thus quickly read or write an entire data block. Another advantage of this design is that different subarrays within a mat share their decoding logic, which increases the overall speed of operation and minimises the area.

Routing messages between the cache controller, which is a small piece of logic in each bank, and the subarrays can be complicated in large caches that have long wire delays. Let us outline an approach to solve this problem.

H-Trees

The memory address needs to be sent to all the mats and subarrays. Because wire delays in large caches can be of the order of a few cycles, it is possible that the request might not reach all the mats and subarrays at the same time, particularly if there is a mismatch in the length of wires. If this happens, the responses will not arrive at the same time. To ensure that all the requests reach the subarrays at the same time, we create a network that looks like an H-tree as shown in Figure 7.31. The sender is at the centre of the figure. Observe that it is located at the centre of the middle bar of a large 'H' shaped

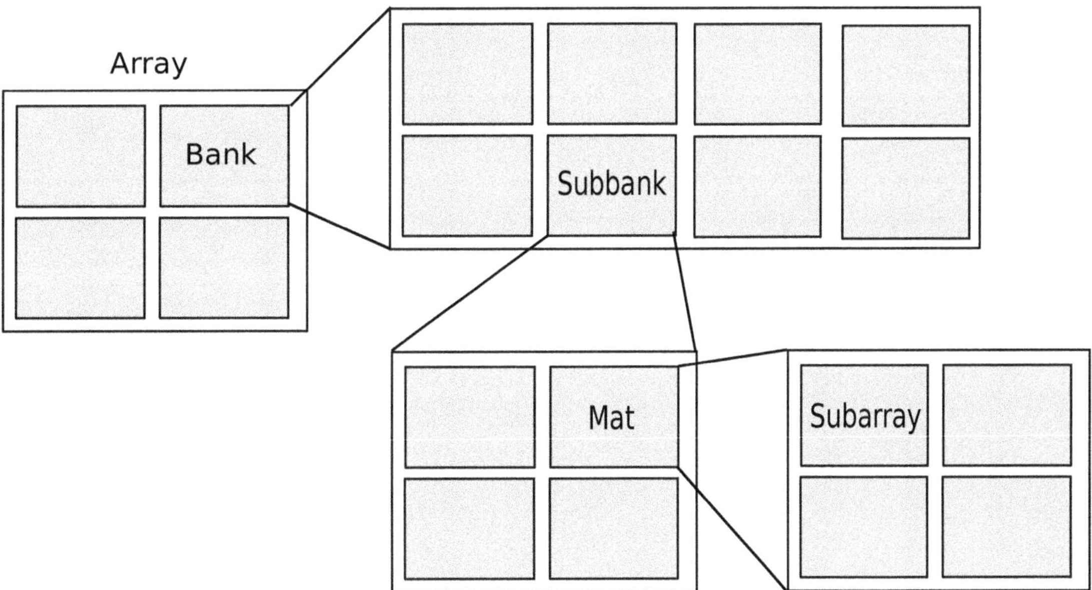

Figure 7.30: Bank $\rightarrow$ Subbank $\rightarrow$ Mat $\rightarrow$ Subarray

subnetwork. Each corner of the large 'H' shaped subnetwork is the centre of another smaller 'H' shaped network. This process continues till all the receivers are connected. The reader needs to convince herself that the distance from the centre to each receiving node (dark circle) is the same. The address and data are sent along the edges of the H-tree. They reach each subarray at exactly the same time.

7.3.3 Circuit Level Modelling of a Cache: Elmore Delay Model

The challenge now is to model the delay and power consumption of an array of SRAM and CAM cells. There are many components in these cells: transistors in the memory cell, pass transistors, long wires, and complex circuits such as sense amplifiers, decoders, and driver circuits. In general, to simulate such circuits, we use circuit simulation tools. However, using such tools for a large structure such as a cache will take a lot of time. We need simpler and faster models. We are willing to trade accuracy for simulation speed.

Let us make our analysis simpler. Let us replace every circuit element with an equivalent RC circuit made of just resistors and capacitors, which is small and simple. For example, we can replace a long wire with a sequence of resistors and capacitors as shown in Figure 7.32. The logic is that every segment of a wire will have a resistance because it has a finite resistivity, length, and cross-sectional area. In addition, it will also have a capacitance associated with each segment. This is because whenever we have two metallic conductors in proximity, they will act like a classic capacitor – two parallel plates separated by a dielectric. Such a pair of conductors will store some charge across a potential difference. We can model this as a capacitor between the segment of the wire and ground. A wire can thus be visualised as a ladder network of such R and C elements (see Figure 7.32).

Similarly, we can replace a transistor with a set of resistors and capacitors as shown in Figure 7.33. We have a gate capacitance because the gate is comprised of a conducting plate that is set to a given potential. Thus it is going to store charge, and this can be modelled as the gate capacitance. Using a similar argument, both the drain and source nodes will also have a capacitance associated with them. When the transistor is in the linear region, the resistance across the channel will not be 0. For a given drain-source and gate voltage, the drain current is given by the Id-Vg curve of the transistor.

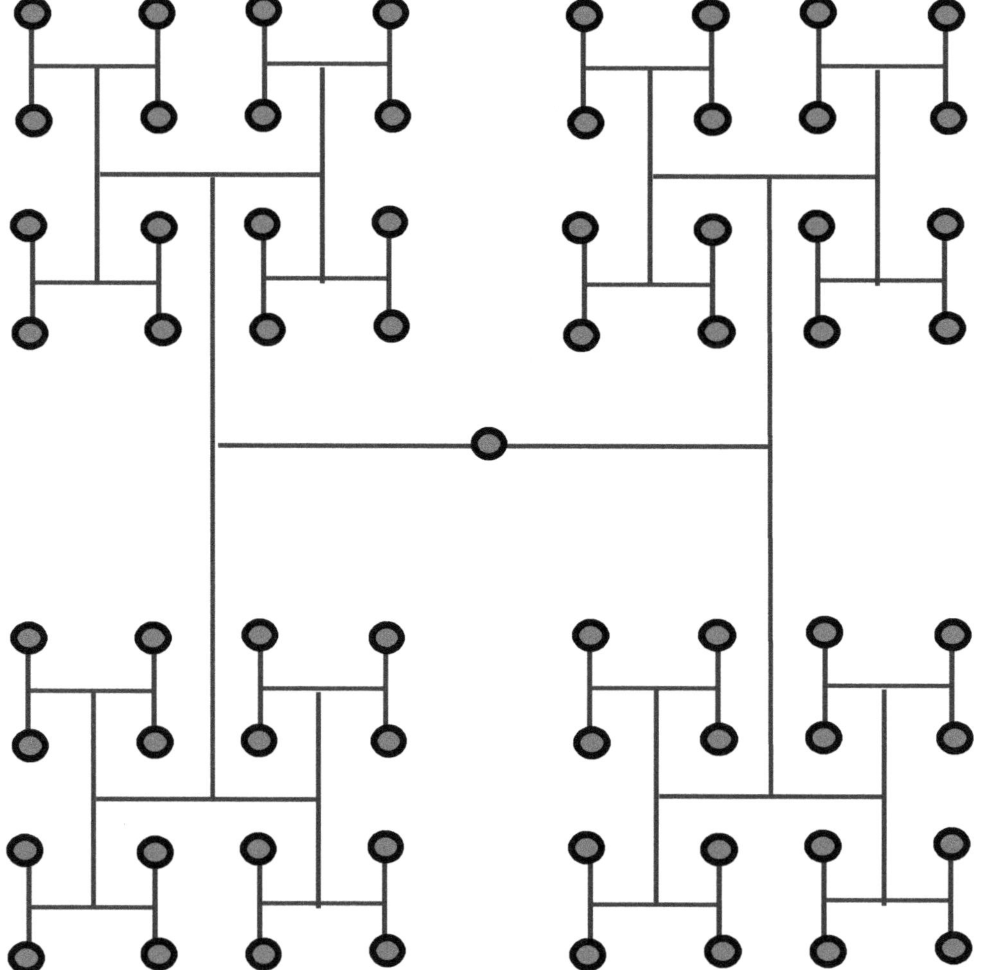

Figure 7.31: H-tree network

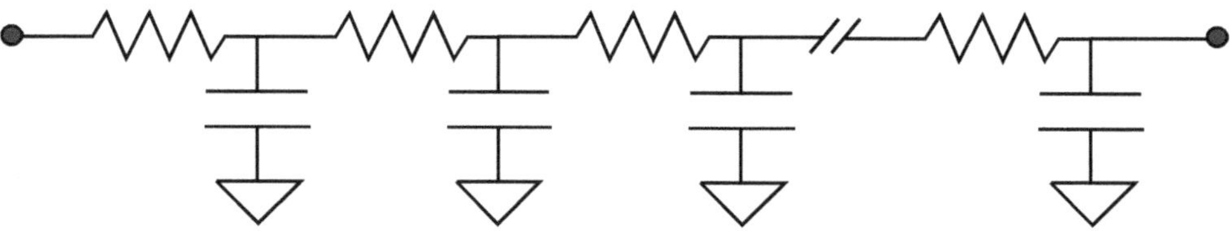

Figure 7.32: Equivalent RC circuit for a wire

This relationship can be modelled by placing a resistor between the drain and the source. When the transistor is in saturation it behaves as a current source and the drain-source resistor can be replaced with a regular current source.

Using such RC networks is a standard approach in the analysis of electronic circuits, particularly when we want to leverage the power of fast circuit simulation tools to compute the voltage at a few given nodes in the circuit. We sometimes need to add an inductance term if long wires are involved. Subsequently, to compute the voltages and currents, it is necessary to perform circuit simulation on

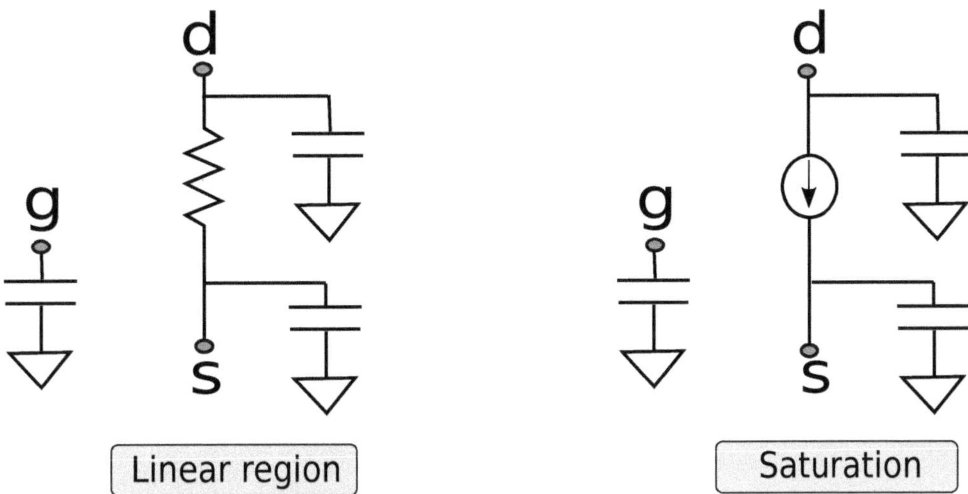

Figure 7.33: Equivalent RC circuit for an NMOS transistor

these simplified RC networks.

The Cacti 1.0 [Wilton and Jouppi, 1993] model proposes to replace all the elements in a cache inclusive of the wires, transistors, and specialised circuits with simple RC circuits. Once we have a circuit consisting of just voltage sources, current sources, and RC elements, we can then use quick approximations to compute the voltage at points of interest. In this section, we shall mainly present the results from Horowitz's paper [Horowitz, 1983] on modelling the delay of MOS circuits. This paper in turn bases its key assumptions on Elmore's classic paper [Elmore, 1948] published in 1948. This approach is often referred to as the Elmore delay model.

RC Trees

Let us consider an RC network, and try to compute the time it takes for a given output to either rise to a certain voltage (rise time), or fall to a certain voltage (fall time). For example, our model should allow us to compute how long it will take for the input of the sense amplifier to register a certain voltage after we enable the word lines.

Let us make two assumptions. The first is that we consider an RC tree and not a general RC network. This means that there are no cycles in our network. Most circuits can be modelled as RC trees and only in rare cases where we have a feedback mechanism, we have cycles in our network. Hence, we are not losing much by assuming only RC trees.

The second assumption that we make is that we consider only a single type of voltage sources that provide a step input (see Figure 7.34).

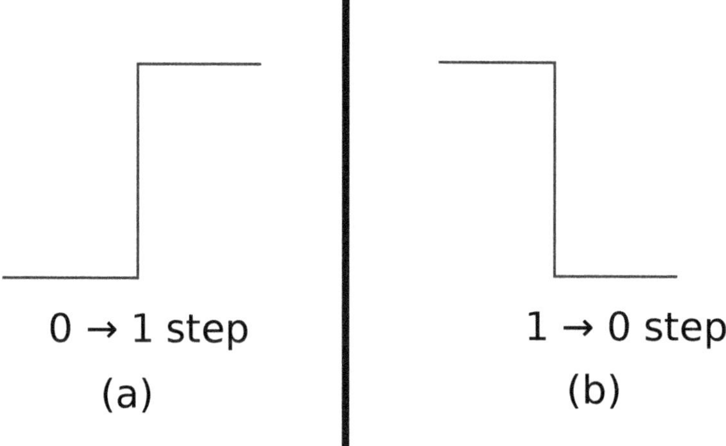

Figure 7.34: A step input

We consider two kinds of such inputs: a $0 \to 1$ transition and a $1 \to 0$ transition. In digital circuits we typically have such transitions. We do not transition to any intermediate values. Thus, the usage of the step function is considered to be standard practice. For the sake of simplicity, we assume that a logical 0 is at 0 V and a logical 1 is at 1 V.

Analysis of an RC Tree

Let us consider a generic RC tree as described by Horowitz [Horowitz, 1983]. Consider a single voltage source that can be treated as the input. As discussed, it is a step input that can either make a $0 \to 1$ transition or a $1 \to 0$ transition. Let us assume that it makes a $1 \to 0$ transition (the reverse case is analogous).

Let us draw an RC tree and number the resistors and capacitors (see Figure 7.35). Note that between an output node and the voltage sources we only have a series of resistors, we do not have any capacitors. All the capacitors are between a node and ground.

Each capacitor can be represented as a current source. For a capacitor with capacitance C, the charge that it stores is $V(t)C$, where $V(t)$ is the voltage at time t. We assume that the input voltage makes a transition at $t = 0$. Now, the current leaving the capacitor is equal to $-CdV(t)/dt$. Let us draw an equivalent figure where our capacitors are replaced by current sources. This is shown in Figure 7.36.

The goal is to compute $V_x(t)$, where x is the number of the output node (shown in an oval shaped box in the figure). Let us show how to compute the voltage at node 3 using the principle of superposition. If we have n current sources, we consider one at a time. When we are considering the kth current source we disconnect (replace with an open circuit) the rest of the $n - 1$ current sources. This reduced circuit has just one current source. We then proceed to compute the voltage at node 3.

In this RC tree, only node 0 is connected to a voltage source, which makes a $1 \to 0$ transition at $t = 0$. The rest of the nodes are floating. As a result the current will flow towards node 0 via a path consisting exclusively of resistors.

Now, assume that the current source at node 4 is connected, and the rest of the current sources are replaced with open circuits. The current produced by the current source is equal to $-C_4 dV_4^4/dt$. The term V_i^j refers to the voltage at terminal i because of the effect of the current source placed at terminal j using our methodology. The voltage at node 1 is therefore $-R_1 C_4 dV_4^4/dt$. Since the rest of the nodes are floating, this is also equal to the voltage at node 3. We thus have:

$$V_3^4 = -R_1 C_4 \frac{dV_4^4}{dt} \tag{7.5}$$

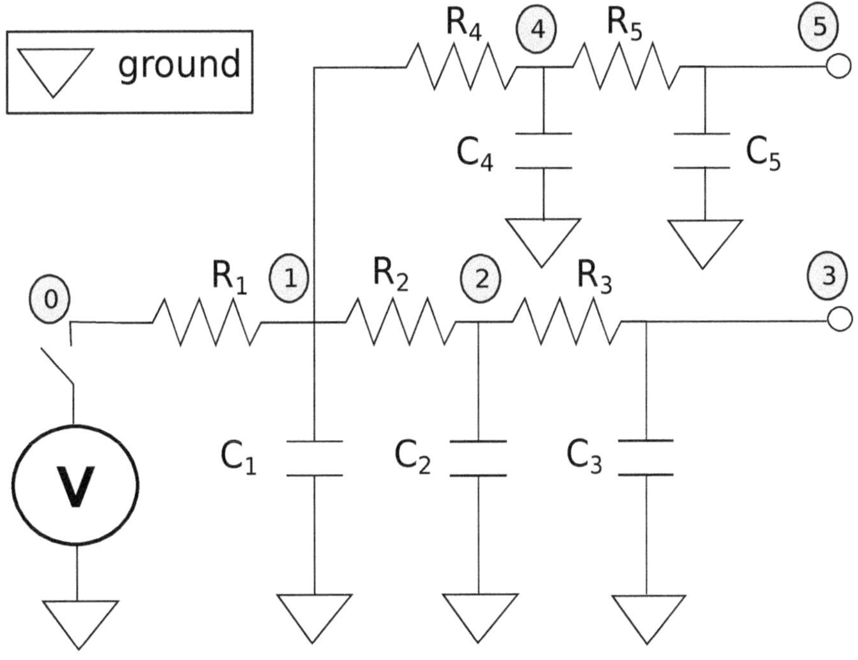

Figure 7.35: RC tree

Let us do a similar analysis when the current source attached to node 2 is connected. In this case, the voltage at node 2 is equal to the voltage at node 3. The voltage at node 2 or 3 is given by the following equation:

$$V_2^2 = V_3^2 = -(R_1 + R_2)C_2 \frac{dV_2^2}{dt} \tag{7.6}$$

Let us generalise these observations. Assume we want to compute the voltage at node i, when the current source attached to node j is connected. Now consider the path between node 0 (voltage source) and node i. Let the set of resistors on this path be P_{0i}. Similarly, let the set of resistors in the path from node 0 to node j be P_{0j}. Now, let us consider the intersection of these paths and find all the resistors that are in common. These resistors are given by

$$P_{ij} = P_{0i} \cap P_{0j} \tag{7.7}$$

We can easily verify that $P_{34} = \{R_1\}$, and $P_{23} = \{R_1, R_2\}$. Let R_{ij} be equal to the sum of all the resistors in P_{ij}. Formally,

$$R_{ij} = \sum_{R \in P_{ij}} R \tag{7.8}$$

Now, please convince yourself that Equations 7.5 and 7.6 are special cases of the following equation. Assume that we only consider the current source at node j.

$$V_i^j = -R_{ij}C_j \frac{dV_j^j}{dt} \tag{7.9}$$

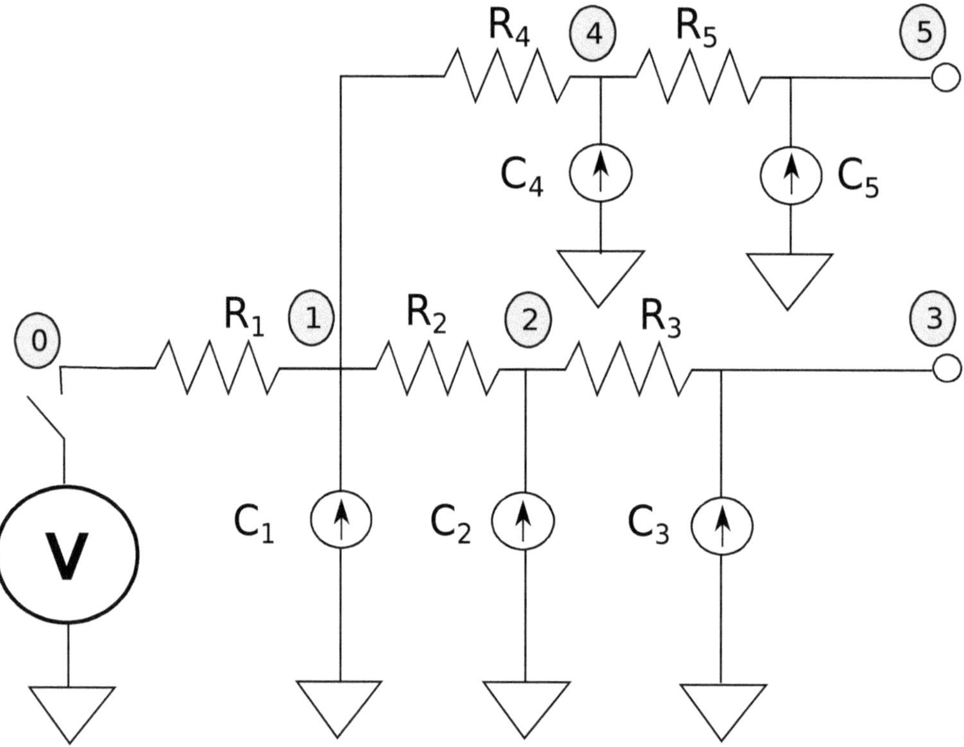

Figure 7.36: Equivalent RC tree (replacing capacitors with current sources)

Now, if we consider all the capacitors one by one and use the principle of superposition, we compute V_i to be a sum of the voltages at i computed by replacing each capacitor with a current source.

$$V_i = \sum_j V_i^j = \sum_j -R_{ij} C_j \frac{dV_j^j}{dt} \tag{7.10}$$

Unfortunately, it is hard to solve a system of simultaneous differential equations, that too quickly and accurately. It is therefore imperative that we make some approximations.

This is exactly where Elmore [Elmore, 1948] proposed his famous approximation. Let us assume that $dV_j^j/dt = \alpha dV_i/dt$, where α is a constant. This is also referred to as the single pole approximation (refer to the concept of poles and zeros in electrical networks). Using this approximation, we can compute the voltage at node i to be

$$V_i^* = \sum_j -\alpha R_{ij} C_j \frac{dV_i}{dt} \tag{7.11}$$

Here, V_i^* is the voltage at node i computed using our approximation. Let us now consider the error

$\int (V_i - V_i^*)dt$. Assume $\alpha = 1$ in the subsequent equation. We have

$$V_i - V_i^* = \sum_j -R_{ij}C_j \frac{dV_j^j}{dt} - \sum_j -R_{ij}C_j \frac{dV_i}{dt}$$

$$= \sum_j -R_{ij}C_j \left(\frac{dV_j^j}{dt} - \frac{dV_i}{dt} \right)$$

$$\int (V_i - V_i^*)dt = \sum_j -R_{ij}C_j \int \left(\frac{dV_j^j}{dt} - \frac{dV_i}{dt} \right) dt \qquad (7.12)$$

$$= \sum_j -R_{ij}C_j (V_j^j - V_i) \Big|_0^\infty$$

$$= 0$$

Note that the expression, $(V_j^j - V_i)\big|_0^\infty = 0$, because both V_i and V_j^j start from the same voltage (1 V in this case) and end at the same voltage (0 V in this case). Thus, we can conclude that the error $\int (V_i - V_i^*)dt = 0$, when we assume that $dV_j^j/dt = dV_i/dt$ for all i and j. This is the least possible error, and thus we can conclude that our approximation with $\alpha = 1$ minimises the error as we have defined it (difference of the two functions). Let us now try to solve the equations for any V_i using our approximation. Let us henceforth not use the term V_i^*. We shall use the term V_i (voltage as a function of time) to refer to the voltage at node i computed using Elmore's approximations.

We thus have

$$V_i = \sum_j -R_{ij}C_j \frac{dV_i}{dt}$$

$$= -\tau_i \frac{dV_i}{dt} \qquad (\tau_i = \sum_j R_{ij}C_j)$$

$$\Rightarrow \frac{dt}{\tau_i} = -\frac{dV_i}{V_i} \qquad (7.13)$$

$$\Rightarrow \frac{t}{\tau_i} - ln(k) = -ln(V_i) \qquad \text{ln(k) is the constant of integration}$$

$$\Rightarrow V_i = ke^{-\frac{t}{\tau_i}}$$

$$\Rightarrow V_i = V_0 e^{-\frac{t}{\tau_i}} \qquad \text{at } t = 0,\ V_i = V_0 = k$$

V_i thus reduces exponentially with time constant τ_i. Recall that this equation is similar to a capacitor discharging in a simple RC network consisting of a single resistor and capacitor. Let us now use this formula to compute the time it takes to discharge a long copper wire (see Example 6).

Example 6
Compute the delay of a long copper wire.

Answer: *Let us divide a long copper wire into n short line segments. Each segment has an associated resistance and capacitance, which are assumed to be the same for all the segments.*

Let the total resistance of the wire be R and the total capacitance be C. Then the resistance and capacitance of each line segment is R/n and C/n respectively. Let terminal i be the end point of segment i. The time constant measured at terminal n is given by Equation 7.13. It is equal to

$$V_n = \sum_j -R_{nj}C_j \frac{dV_n}{dt} \tag{7.14}$$

Any R_{nj} in this network is equal to $\sum_{i=1}^{j} R_i$. R_i and C_i correspond to the resistance and capacitance of the ith line segment respectively. We can assume that $\forall i, R_i = R/n$ and $\forall i, C_i = C/n$. Hence, $R_{nj} = jR/n$. The time constant of the wire is therefore equal to

$$\begin{aligned}
\tau &= \sum_{j=1}^{n} R_{nj}C_j = \frac{C}{n} \sum_{j=1}^{n} \frac{R}{n} \times j \\
&= \frac{C}{n} \times \frac{R}{n} \times \frac{n(n+1)}{2} = \frac{C}{n} \times R \times \frac{n+1}{2} \\
&= RC \times \frac{n+1}{2n}
\end{aligned} \tag{7.15}$$

As $n \to \infty$, $\tau \to \frac{RC}{2}$. We can assume that the time constant of a wire is equivalent to that of a simple RC circuit that has the same capacitance and half the resistance of the wire (or vice versa).

We can draw some interesting conclusions from Example 6. The first is that the time constant of a wire is equal to $RC/2$, where R and C are the resistance and capacitance of the entire wire respectively. Let the resistance and capacitance for a small segment of the wire be r and c respectively. Then, we have the following relations.

$$\begin{aligned}
R &= nr \\
C &= nc
\end{aligned} \tag{7.16}$$

Hence, the time constant, τ, is equal to $rcn^2/2$. Recall that the time constant is the time it takes for the input to rise to 63% of its final value $(1 - 1/e)$, or the output to fall to 37% of the maximum value $(1/e)$. We can extend this further. A typical RC circuit charges or discharges by 98% after 4τ units of time. After 5τ units of time, the final voltage is within 0.7% of its final value. If we set a given threshold for the voltage for deciding whether it is a logical 0 or 1, then the time it takes to reach that threshold can be expressed in terms of time constants. It is common to refer to the time a circuit takes to respond to an input in terms of time constants.

Now, given that $\tau = rcn^2/2$ for a long wire, we can quickly deduce that **the delay is proportional to the square of the wire's length**. This is bad news for us because it means that long wires are not scalable and thus should not be used.

Dealing with Slow Inputs

Up till now we have been making two critical assumptions. First, the input is a step function, and second, the devices can be replaced with linear elements such as resistors and capacitors. Unfortunately, both these assumptions do not exactly hold with real MOS transistors, and sometimes the errors can be unacceptably large. Let us thus replace step sources with arbitrary sources, and call them *slow inputs* (same terminology used by Horowitz [Horowitz, 1983]).

To consider circuits that do not have step inputs and have a non-linear response, the authors of the Cacti tool use the Horowitz approximation for non-linear circuits. This is the equation of the rise time for an inverter.

$$delay_{rise} = \tau \sqrt{(log(v_{th})^2 + 2t_{rise}b(1 - v_{th})/\tau}$$ (7.17)

τ is the time constant assuming a step input, v_{th} is the threshold voltage as a fraction of the supply voltage, t_{rise} is the rise time of the input, and b is the fraction of the input's swing at which the output changes (Cacti 1 uses a value of $b = 0.5$). We have a similar equation for the time it takes for an input to fall.

$$delay_{fall} = \tau \sqrt{(log(v_{th})^2 + 2t_{fall}b(1 - v_{th})/\tau}$$ (7.18)

Equations 7.17 and 7.18 are primarily based on empirical models that describe the behaviour of transistors in the linear and saturation regions. These equations can change with the transistor technology and are thus not fundamental principles. Hence, it is necessary to change these equations appropriately if we are trying to use a different kind of transistors.

Example: Delay of a Bit Line

Let us show the calculation of the delay of a bit line in the Cacti 1 model when the bit line goes low (towards 0 V). The equivalent circuit used by the Cacti model is shown in Figure 7.37.

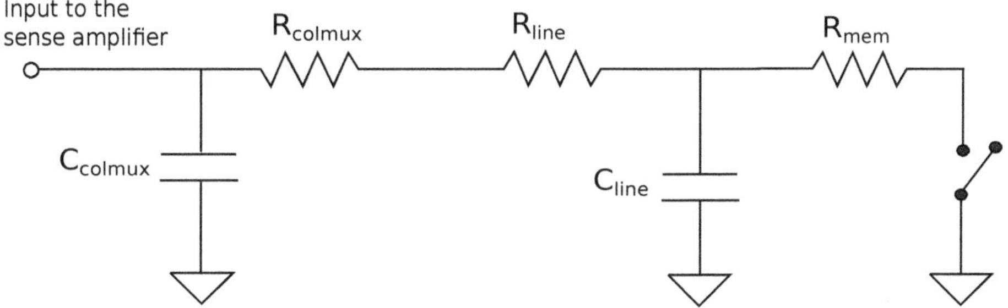

Figure 7.37: Equivalent circuit of a bit line(adapted from [Wilton and Jouppi, 1993])

R_{mem} is the combined resistance of the word line transistor and the NMOS transistor in the memory cell (via which the bit line discharges). These transistors connect the bit line to the ground. C_{line} is the effective capacitance of the entire bit line. This includes the drain capacitance of the pass transistors (controlled by the word lines), the capacitance that arises due to the metallic portion of the bit line, and the drain capacitances of the precharge circuit and the column multiplexer.

R_{colmux} and C_{colmux} represent the resistance of the pass transistor in the column multiplexer and the output capacitance of the column multiplexer respectively.

R_{line} needs some explanation. Refer to Example 6, where we had computed the time constant of a long wire to be approximately $RC/2$, where R and C are its resistance and capacitance respectively. A model that treats a large object as a small object with well defined parameters is known as a lumped model. In this case, the lumped resistance of the entire bit line is computed as follows:

$$R_{line} = \frac{\#rows}{2} \times R_{segment}$$ (7.19)

Here, $R_{segment}$ is the resistance of the segment of a bit line corresponding to one row of SRAM cells. We divide it by 2 because the time constant in the lumped model of a wire is $RC/2$. We need to divide either the total resistance or capacitance by 2.

Using the Elmore delay model the time constant (τ) is equal to $R_{mem}C_{line} + (R_{mem} + R_{line} + R_{colmux})C_{colmux}$.

Example: Delay of a Word Line

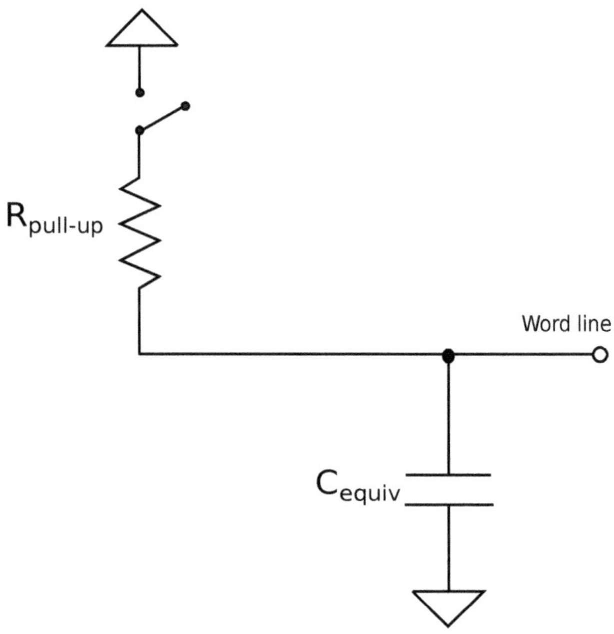

Figure 7.38: Equivalent circuit for a word line (adapted from [Wilton and Jouppi, 1993])

Figure 7.38 shows the equivalent circuit for a word line. In this circuit $R_{pull-up}$ is the pull-up resistance. The internal resistance of the word line drivers determine the value of this parameter. C_{equiv} is the equivalent capacitance of the word line. It is given by the following equation.

$$C_{equiv} = \#cols \times (2 \times C_{gatewl} + C_{metal}) \tag{7.20}$$

The parameter $\#cols$ refers to the number of columns in a row. C_{gatewl} is the gate capacitance of each pass transistor that is controlled by the word line. Since there are two such transistors per memory cell, we need to multiply this value by 2. Finally, C_{metal} is the capacitance of just the metallic portion of the word line. C_{equiv} is a sum of all these parameters.

The time constant in this case is simply $R_{pull-up} \times C_{equiv}$.

7.4   Advanced Cache Design

In this section we shall look at some common methods to increase the performance of a cache.

7.4.1   Pipelined Caches

Assume that the L1 d-cache (data cache) has a hit latency of 3 cycles. In this case, there are two options. The first is that if a cache is processing a request, then it does not process any other requests till it is done. This is not efficient in terms of performance. The other scheme is that the cache itself is pipelined. This means that it can accept a new request every cycle akin to normal processor pipelines. The pipelined design is needless to say more efficient because it provides a greater throughput. In other words, if a cache can start the processing of a new set of requests every cycle, it can match the rate at which the processor produces memory requests in the worst case. Thus, memory requests will not queue up at the side of the processor.

Let us look at the set of steps that need to be performed to pipeline a cache. The first task is to decompose the work of a cache into multiple subtasks. Figure 7.39 shows a representative example for a read operation. We first perform a data array access and a tag array access in parallel. This is done for performance reasons. At the outset we don't know which way of a set will match. Hence, we read all the data blocks in parallel, and choose one of them later if there is a match. The advantage in this case is that the process of reading the data blocks is off the critical path. It can be overlapped with reading the tags. Subsequently, we start the process of tag comparison, and immediately after that we choose the right data block based on the results of the tag comparison. Since we have read all the data blocks in the set in advance, we need not access the data array again. We simply choose one of the blocks that has been read.

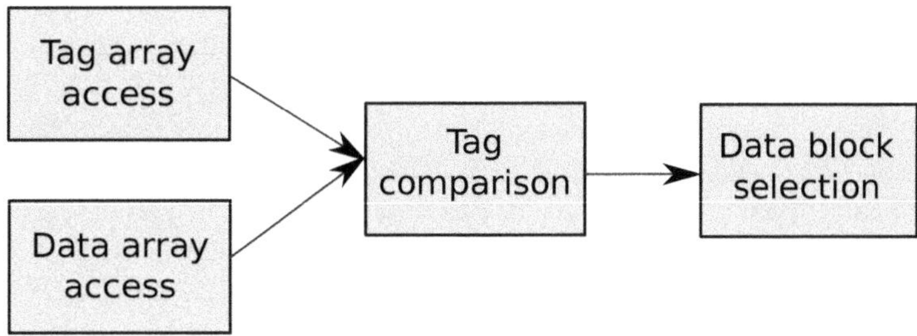

Figure 7.39: Subtasks in a read operation

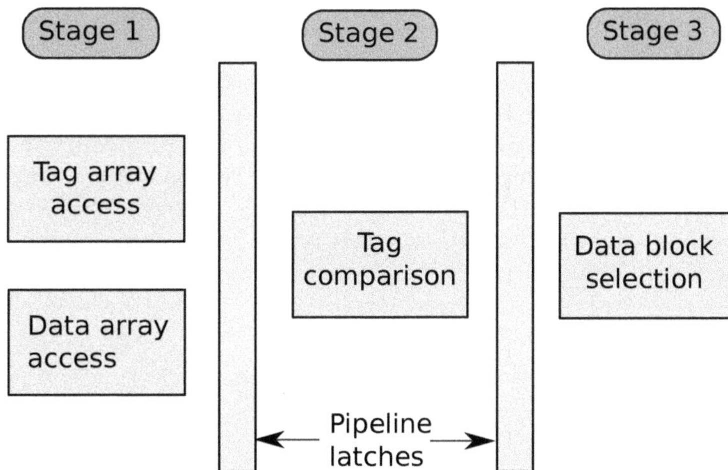

Figure 7.40: Design of a pipelined cache (for the read operation)

We need to add pipeline latches or buffers between these stages (similar to what we had done in an in-order pipeline) to create a pipelined cache. The resulting structure is shown in Figure 7.40. Of course, we are making many simplistic assumptions in this process, notably that the time it takes to complete each subtask (stage) is roughly the same. Sometimes we might wish to create more pipeline stages.

In pursuance of this goal, it is possible to break the SRAM array access process into two stages: address decode and row access. If the decoder has N outputs, then we can create a large N-bit pipeline latch to temporarily store its output. In the next stage we can access the target row of the SRAM array. This will increase the depth of the pipeline to 4 stages. It is typically not possible to pipeline the row access process because it is basically an analog circuit.

Even though the exact nature of pipelining may differ, the key idea here is that we need to pipeline the cache to ensure that it does not lock up while processing a request. The process of pipelining ensures a much larger throughput, which is mandatory in high performance systems.

Now, if we consider write accesses as well, then they can be pipelined in a similar fashion: first access the tag array, then compare the tag part of the address with all the tags in the set, and finally perform the write. If the subsequent access is a read, then we require forwarding; therefore forwarding paths similar to in-order processors are required here as well. Working out the details of these forwarding paths is left as an exercise for the reader.

7.4.2   Non-blocking Caches

Let us consider the interface between the core and the memory system. After we issue a load or a store to the memory system, we access the i-cache for instructions and the d-cache for data. If there is a hit, then we can immediately supply the data to the processor. In Section 7.4.1, we discussed how to increase the throughput of a cache by pipelining it. However, all of this was done to make cache hits faster. We did not talk about misses. Let us now see what happens in the case of misses.

Whenever there is a miss in the cache, we need to fetch the block from the lower level, irrespective of whether we need to perform a read or a write operation. The key question is, "Do we block the cache during this time?" or do we proceed with other requests. In modern processors, we always choose the latter option, where we proceed with other requests. Even if there is a miss, or there are several outstanding misses that are waiting to get their data, we proceed with other requests. This is also known as the, "access under multiple misses," assumption. Such kind of a cache that never blocks is known as a non-blocking cache. It is an essential part of all high performance processors as of 2020.

Note that even if this sounds as a very worthy goal, implementing such a cache is difficult. Assume that we suffer a miss because we wanted to access the fourth word (4 or 8 bytes) in a block. In a non-blocking cache, we do not lock the cache till the miss returns. Instead, we let other accesses go through. Assume that at a later point in time we suffer a miss for the fifth word in the same block. In this case, if we also allow this miss to go through then we are in a sense doubling the requests made to the lower level as compared to a blocking cache. Since we have spatial locality, we are expected to access many more words in the block before the original miss returns with the data. The unwanted side effect of a non-blocking cache is that we significantly increase the requests made to the lower level cache. We stand to lose all the gains we wanted to make by having non-blocking caches.

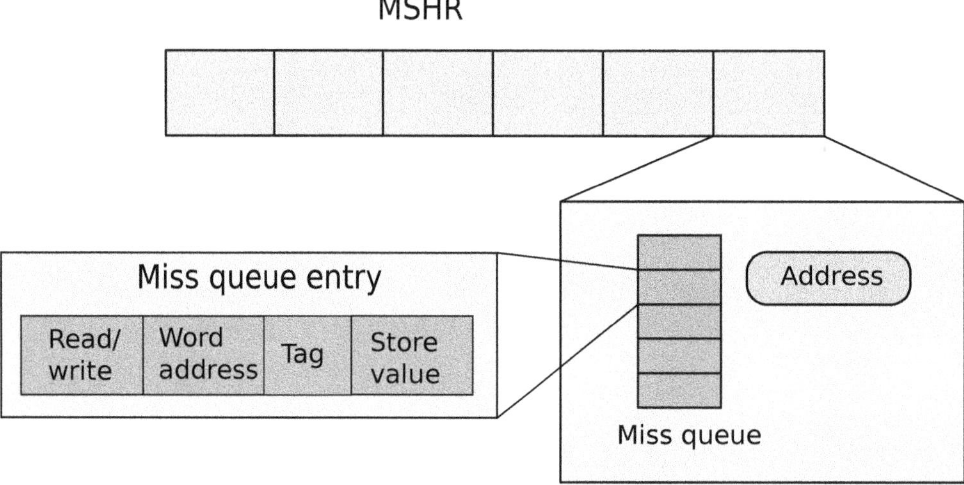

Figure 7.41: Design of an MSHR

Let us thus propose a new structure called an MSHR (miss status holding register) [Kroft, 1981,

Scheurich and Dubois, 1988]. We associate an MSHR with each cache. The structure of an MSHR is shown in Figure 7.41. It consists of a set of arrays. Whenever we miss in the cache, and there are no other pending misses for that block, we refer to such a miss as a *primary miss*. Upon a primary miss, we allocate an empty array in the MSHR to this miss. In the MSHR entry, we store the block address. Then, we initialise the first array entry that stores the type of the access (read or write), address of the word within the block (word address) that the current access refers to, and the destination register (*tag*) of a load instruction or the *value* that a store instruction writes to memory. The miss request is subsequently dispatched to the lower level. Let us refer to each such array as a miss queue. The reason for calling it a miss queue will be clear after we have described the operation of the MSHR.

Before the miss has returned, we might have several additional misses for other words in the block. These are called *secondary misses*. The method to handle secondary misses is conceptually similar to the way we handled memory requests in the LSQ. Assume that a secondary miss is a write. We create an entry at the tail of the miss queue, which contains the value that is to be written along with the address of the word within the block. Now, assume that the secondary miss is a read. In this case, if we are reading a single memory word, then we first check the earlier entries in the miss queue to see if there is a corresponding write. If this is the case, then we can directly forward the value from the write to the read. There is no need to queue the entry for the read. However, if such forwarding is not possible, then we create a new entry at the tail of the miss queue and add the parameters of the read request to it. This includes the details of the memory request such as the id of the destination register (in the case of the L1 cache) or the id of the requesting cache (at other levels) – referred to as the *tag* in Figure 7.41.

The advantage of an MSHR is that instead of sending multiple miss requests to the lower level, we send just one. In the time being the cache continues to serve other requests. Then, when the primary miss returns with the data, we need to take a look at all the entries in the miss queue, and start applying them in order. After this process, we can write the modified block to the cache, and return all the read/write requests to the upper level.

Now let us account for the corner cases. We might have a lot of outstanding memory requests, which might exhaust the number of entries in a miss queue, or we might run out of miss queues. In such a scenario, the cache needs to lock up and stop accepting new requests.

7.4.3   Skewed Associative Caches

The basic philosophy in a regular k-way set associative cache is that given the address of a block, there are k locations in the cache that might potentially keep its data. We check all the k locations and compare the tag part of the address with the tags that are stored in these locations. The problem with this approach is as follows. Assume there are $k + 1$ blocks that map to the same set, and are frequently accessed. They will continue to create conflict misses. Some of these penalties can be absorbed by using a victim cache (see Section 7.1.7); however, if there are many such sets, then a victim cache is useless.

This is not a contrived scenario. Even if we consider a workload with a small working set (see Section 7.1.1), there will always be some sets that see a lot of contention. There is no way to offload this contention to sets that are relatively less contended. This is where a skewed associative cache [Seznec, 1993] can help. It introduces a different kind of thinking.

To start the discussion, let us consider a traditional 2-way set associative cache first. Given a block, we first find its set index, which is a subset of the bits in the block address. Let it set index be I. Then, the two locations that can potentially contain a copy of the block are $2I$ and $2I + 1$. If two blocks with addresses A_1 and A_2 have the same set index, then both of them will vie for the same locations on the cache: $2I$ and $2I + 1$. If we have three such blocks that are accessed frequently, then we will have a large number of misses. Let us do something to minimise the contention by designing a skewed associative cache.

Let us partition a cache into two subcaches. Let us use two different functions – f_1 and f_2 – to map a block to lines in the different subcaches. This means that if a block has address A, we need to search for it in the lines $f_1(A)$ and $f_2(A)$ in the two subcaches, respectively. Let function f_k refer to a line in the kth subcache. The crux of the idea is to ensure that for two block addresses, A_1 and A_2, if $f_1(A_1) = f_1(A_2)$ (in subcache 1), then $f_2(A_1) \neq f_2(A_2)$ (in subcache 2). In simple terms, if two blocks have a conflict in one subcache, they should have a very high likelihood of not conflicting in the other subcache. We can easily extend this idea to a cache with k subcaches. We can create separate mapping functions for each subcache to ensure that even if a set of blocks have conflicts in a few subcaches, they do not conflict in the rest of the subcaches. To implement such a scheme, we can treat each bank as a subcache.

The operative part of the design is the choice of functions to map block addresses to lines in subcaches. The main principle that needs to be followed is that if two blocks map to the same line in subcache 1, then their probability of mapping to the same line in subcache 2 will be $1/N$, where N is the number of lines in a subcache. The functions $f_1()$ and $f_2()$ are known as *skewing functions*.

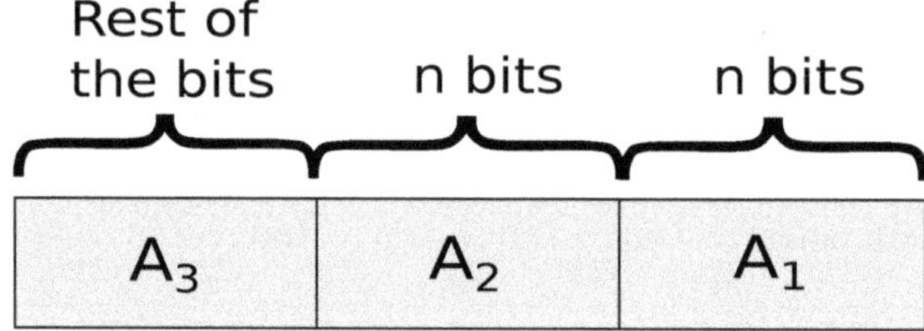

Figure 7.42: Breakup of a memory address in a skewed associative cache

Let us discuss the skewing functions described by Bodin and Seznec [Bodin and Seznec, 1997]. We divide a block address into three parts as shown in Figure 7.42. Assume each subcache has 2^n cache lines. We create three chunks of bits: A_1 (lowest n bits), A_2 (n bits after the bits in A_1), and A_3 (rest of the MSB bits).

The authors use a function σ that shuffles the bits similar to shuffling a deck of playing cards. There are several fast algorithms in hardware to shuffle a set of bits. Discussing them is out of the scope of the book. For a deeper understanding of this process, readers can refer to the seminal paper by Diaconis [Diaconis et al., 1983]. For a 4-way skewed associative cache (see Figure 7.43), where each logical subcache is mapped to a separate bank, the four mapping functions for block address A are as follows. The $\oplus$ sign refers to the XOR function.

Bank 1 $f_1(A) = A_1 \oplus A_2$

Bank 2 $f_2(A) = \sigma(A_1) \oplus A_2$

Bank 3 $f_3(A) = \sigma(\sigma(A_1)) \oplus A_2$

Bank 4 $f_4(A) = \sigma(\sigma(\sigma(A_1))) \oplus A_2$

These functions can be computed easily in hardware, and we can thus reduce the probability of conflicts to a large extent as observed by Bodin and Seznec. In a skewed associative cache, let us refer to the locations at which a block can be stored as its *set*. A set is distributed across subcaches.

The last piece remaining is the replacement policy. Unlike a traditional cache, where we can keep LRU timestamps for each set, here we need a different mechanism. We can opt for a very simple pseudo-LRU policy. Assume we want to insert a new block, and all the cache lines in its set are non-empty. We ideally need to find the line that has been accessed the least. One approach to almost achieve this is to have a bit along with each cache line. When the cache line is accessed this bit is set to 1. Periodically, we clear all such bits. Now, when we need to evict a line out of the set of k lines in a k-way skewed associative cache, we can choose that line whose bit is 0. This means that it has not been accessed in the recent past. However, if the bits for all the lines where the given block can be inserted are set to 1, then we can randomly pick a block as a candidate for replacement.

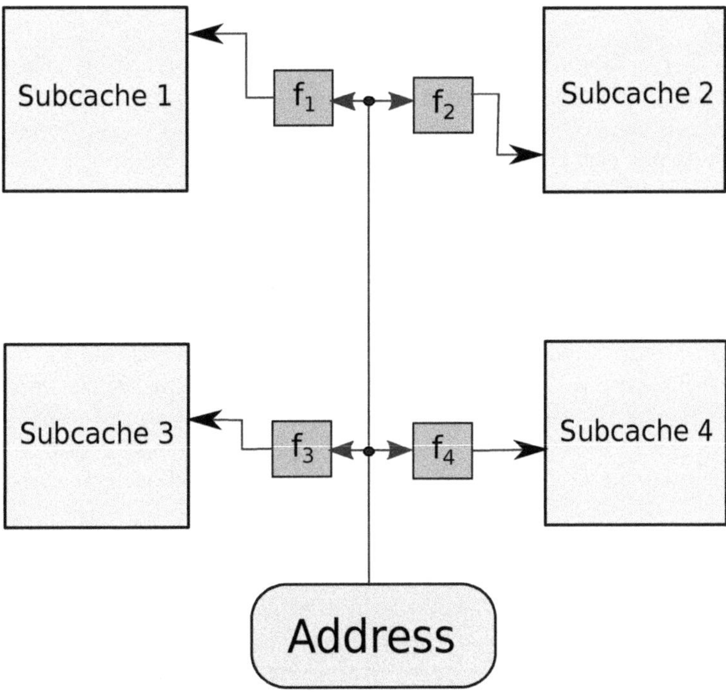

Figure 7.43: Skewed associative cache

We can always do something more sophisticated. This includes associating a counter with each line, which is decremented periodically, and incremented when the line is accessed (similar to classical pseudo-LRU). We can also implement *Cuckoo hashing*. Assume that for address A, all the lines in its set are non-empty. Let a block with address A' be present in its set (in subcache 2). It is possible that the line $f_1(A')$ in subcache 1 is empty. Then the block with address A' can be moved to subcache 1. This will create an empty line in the set, and the new block with address A can be inserted there. This process can be made a cascaded process, where we remove one block, move it to one of its alternative locations, remove the existing block in the alternative location, and try to place it in another location in its set, until we find an empty line.

7.4.4 Way Prediction

We have discussed two kinds of cache addressing schemes: a regular set-index based approach, and the skewed associative approach. In both the cases there are multiple ways associated with each set, and we unfortunately need to read the tags in all of the ways to compute a tag match. This is wasteful in terms of both time as well as energy. It would be a much better idea to predict the way in the set that most likely contains the data and access it first. If there is a miss, then we access the rest of the ways using the regular method. The efficacy of this approach completely depends on the accuracy of the predictor.

Let us describe two simple way predictors (see [Powell et al., 2001]). The main idea is to predict the way in which we expect to find the contents of a block before we proceed to access the cache. If after computing the memory address, it will take a few cycles to translate it and check the LSQ for a potential forwarding opportunity, then we can use the memory address itself for way prediction. Let us thus consider the more difficult case where we can access the cache almost immediately because address translation and LSQ accesses are not on the critical path either because of speculation or because they are very fast. In this case, we need to use information other than the memory address to predict the way.

For predicting the way in advance, the only piece of information that we have at our disposal is the PC of the load or the store. This is known well in advance and thus we can use a similar table as we had used for branch prediction or value prediction to predict the way. For a k-way set associative cache, we need to store $log_2(k)$ bits per entry. Whenever we access the cache, we first access the predicted way. If we do not find the entry there, then we check the rest of the ways using the conventional approach. Let us take a look at the best case and the worst case. The best case is that we have a 100% hit rate with the way predictor. In this case, our k-way set associative cache behaves as a direct mapped cache. We access only a single way. The energy is also commensurately lower.

Let us consider the worst case at the other end of the spectrum, where the hit rate with the predicted way is 0%. In this case, we first access the predicted way, and then realise that the block is not contained in that way. Subsequently, we proceed to access the rest of the ways using the conventional cache access mechanism. This is both a waste of time and a waste of energy. We unnecessarily lost a few cycles in accessing the predicted way, which proved to be absolutely futile. The decision of whether to use a way predictor or not is thus dependent on its accuracy and the resultant performance gains (or penalties).

XOR based Approach

Let us now discuss another method that has the potential to be more accurate than the PC based predictor. The main problem with the PC based predictor is that the computed memory addresses can keep changing. For example, with an array access, the memory address keeps getting incremented, and thus predicting the way becomes more difficult. It is much easier to do this with the memory address of the load or store. However, we do not want to introduce another way prediction stage between the stage that computes the value of the memory address and the cache access because this is on the critical path.

Let us find a solution in the middle, where we can compute the prediction just before the cache access. Recall that after we read the registers, the values are sent to the execution unit. There is thus at least a single cycle gap between the time at which the value of the base register is available, and the time at which the address reaches the L1 cache. We have the execute stage in the middle that adds the offset to the address stored in the base register. Let us use this time productively. Once we have the value of the base register, let us compute a XOR between this value and the offset.

Consider an example: a load instruction *ld r2, 12[r1]*. In this case, the base register is $r1$. We read the value V of $r1$ in the register read stage. Subsequently, we add 12 to V and this becomes the memory address of the load instruction. Next, we need to update the corresponding entry in the LSQ and check for store→load forwarding. Meanwhile, let us compute the XOR of V and 12. We compute $R = V \oplus 12$. Similar to what we had done in the GShare predictor, the result R of the XOR instruction in some sense captures the value of the base register and the offset. Computing a XOR is much faster than doing an addition and possibly checking for forwarding in the LSQ. Thus, in the remaining part of the clock cycle we can access a 2^n-entry way prediction cache that is organised in a manner similar to a last value predictor (see Section 5.1.5) using n bits from the result, R. Once the address has been computed, we can access the cache using the predicted way. This approach uses a different source of information, which is not the memory address, but is a quantity that is similar to it in terms of information content.

7.4.5 Loop Tiling

We have looked at several designs based exclusively in hardware. Let us now look at software based approaches, and consider the most popular optimisation technique in this space. It is known as *loop tiling* or *blocking*. It is a compiler based technique to improve the temporal locality of data accesses in matrices.

Let us provide a brief background. Linear algebra operations using matrices are integral to many scientific and numerical computations. They are also the core operations in image processing and computer graphics. As a result, there is a lot of demand for processors that execute matrix operations very quickly. Since such operations form the kernel of most numerical algorithms, a lot of end-user applications will gain from speeding up such operations.

One of the most important matrix based operations is matrix multiplication. Let us look at a naive implementation of matrix multiplication as shown in Listing 7.1. Here, we are multiplying two $N \times N$ matrices referred to as A and B to produce a matrix C.

Listing 7.1: Matrix multiplication

```
for (i=0; i<N; i++) {
    for (j=0; j<N; j++) {
        sum = 0;
        for (k=0; k<N; k++)
                sum +=  A[i][k] * B[k][j];
        C[i][j] = sum;
    }
}
```

This is the classic matrix multiplication algorithm – nice and simple. However, this code is not efficient from the point of view of cache accesses for large values of N, which is most often the case. Let us understand why. Assume that N is a very large number; hence, none of the matrices fit within the L1 cache. In the case of this algorithm, we multiply a row in A with a column in B, element by element. Subsequently, we move to the next column in B till we reach the end of the matrix. Even though we have temporal locality for the elements of the row in A, we essentially touch all the elements in B column by column. The N^2 accesses to elements in B do not exhibit any temporal locality, and if the size of N is large, we shall have a lot of capacity misses. Thus the cache performance of this code is expected to be very poor.

Let us now see what happens in the subsequent iteration of the outermost loop. We choose the next row of A and then again scan through the entire matrix B. We do not expect any elements of B to have remained in the cache after the last iteration because these entries would have been displaced from the cache given B's size. Thus there is a need to read the elements of the entire matrix (B in this case) again. We can thus conclude that the main reason for poor temporal locality and consequently poor cache hit rates is because in every iteration of the outermost loop, we need to read the entire matrix B from the lowest levels of memory. This is because it does not fit in the higher level caches. If we can somehow increase the degree of temporal locality, then we can improve the cache hit rates as well as the overall performance.

The key insight here is to not read the entire matrix B in every iteration. We need to consider small regions of A and small regions of B, process them, and then move on to other regions. We do not have the luxury of reading large amounts of data every iteration. Instead, we need to look at small regions of both the matrices simultaneously. Such regions are also called *tiles*, and thus the name of our algorithm is called *loop tiling*.

Let us start by looking at matrix multiplication graphically as depicted in Figure 7.44. In traditional matrix multiplication (Figure 7.44(a)), we take a row of matrix A and multiply it with a column of matrix B. If the size of each row or column is large, then we shall have a lot of cache misses. In comparison, the approach with tiling is significantly different. We consider a $b \times b$ tile in matrix A, and a same-sized tile in matrix B. Then we multiply them using our conventional matrix multiplication technique to produce a $b \times b$ tile (see Figure 7.44(b)). The advantage of this approach is that at any point of time, we are only considering three matrices of b^2 elements each. Thus, the total amount of working memory that we require is $3b^2$. If this data fits in the cache, then we can have a great degree of temporal locality in our computations.

Now, that we have looked at the insight, let us look at the code of an algorithm that uses such kind of loop tiling or blocking (refer to Listing 7.2). Assume that the result matrix C is initialised to all zeros. Additionally, assume that both the input matrices, A and B, are $N \times N$ matrices, where N is divisible

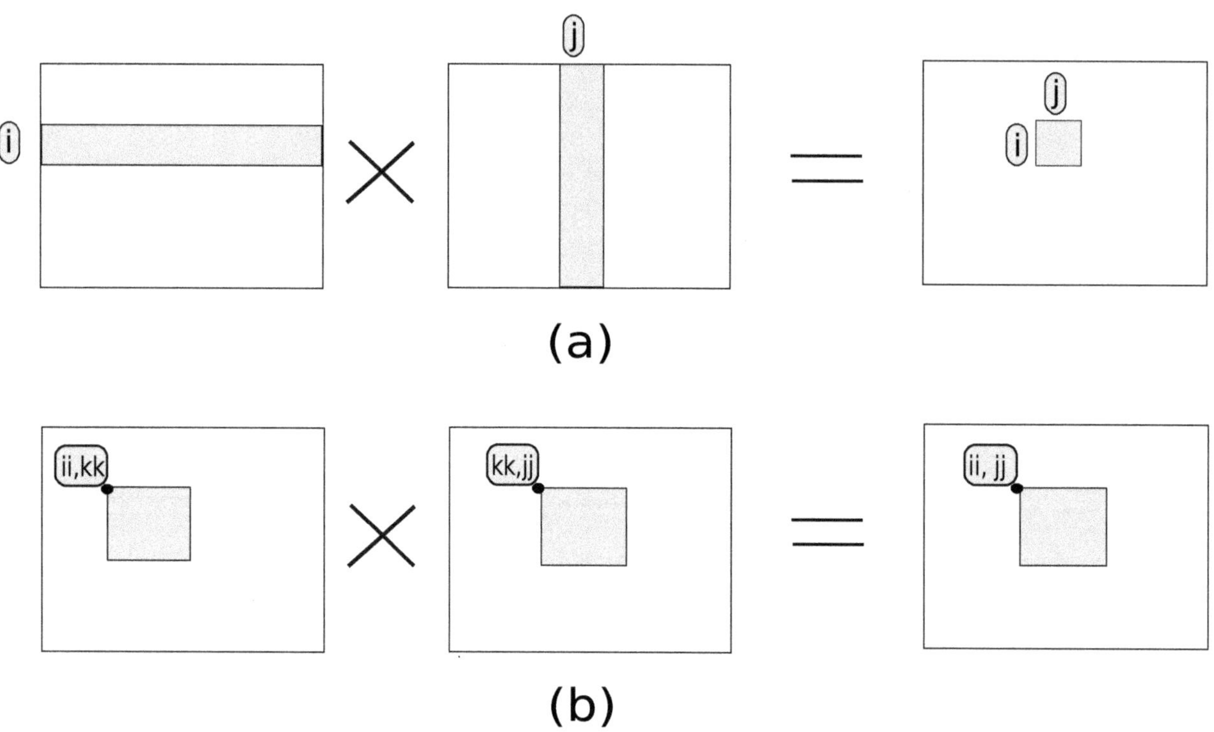

(a)

(b)

Figure 7.44: Matrix multiplication: (a) normal (b) with tiling

by the tile size b.

Listing 7.2: Matrix multiplication using tiling or blocking

```
/* Iterate through the tiles */
for (ii=0; ii<N; ii+=b) {
    for (jj=0; jj<N; jj+=b) {
        for (kk=0; kk<N; kk+=b) {

/* iterate within a tile */
            for (i=ii; i<(ii+b); i++) {
                for (j=jj; j<(jj+b); j++) {
                    for (k=kk; k<(kk+b); k++) {
                        C[i][j] += A[i][k] * B[k][j];
                    }
                }
            }
        }
    }
}
```

There are many implementations of tiling. There are variants that have 5 nested loops. We show a simpler implementation with 6 nested loops. First we consider the three matrices consisting of arrays of tiles, where each tile has $b \times b$ elements. Similar to traditional matrix multiplication, we iterate through all combinations of tiles in the three outermost loops. We essentially choose two tiles from the matrices A and B in the three outermost loops. The first tile starts at (ii, kk); it is b elements deep and b elements wide. Similarly, the second tile starts at (kk, jj) – its dimensions are also $b \times b$.

Next, let us move our attention to the three innermost loops. This is similar to traditional matrix multiplication where we iterate through each and every individual element in these tiles, multiply the corresponding elements from the input matrices, and add the product to the result element's value – value of $C[i][j]$. Let us convince ourselves that this algorithm is correct, and it is equivalent to the traditional matrix multiplication algorithm.

This is easy to prove. Consider the traditional matrix multiplication algorithm. We consider all combinations of i, j, and k. For each combination we multiply $A[i][k]$ and $B[k][j]$, and add the result to the current value of the result element $C[i][j]$. There are N^3 possible values of such combinations and that's the reason we need three loops.

In this case, we simply need to prove that the same thing is happening. We need to show that we are considering all combinations of i, j, and k, and the result is being computed in the same manner. To prove this, let us start out by observing that the three outermost loops ensure that we consider all combinations of $b \times b$ tiles across matrices A and B. The three innermost loops ensure that for each pair of input tiles, we consider all the values that the 3-tuple (i, j, k) can take. Combining both of these observations, we can conclude that all the combinations of i, j, and k are being considered. Furthermore, the reader should also convince herself that no combination is being considered twice. Finally, we perform the multiplication between elements in the same way, and also compute the result matrix C in the same way. A formal proof of correctness is left as an exercise for the reader.

The advantage of such techniques is that it confines the execution to small sets of tiles. Thus, we can take advantage of temporal locality, and consequently reduce cache miss rates. Such techniques have a very rich history, and are considered vitally important for designing commercial implementations of linear algebra subroutines.

7.4.6 Virtually Indexed Physically Tagged (VIPT) Caches

Up till now we have blissfully ignored the fact that we actually need to translate virtual to physical addresses before accessing the cache. The reason was that we assumed that the LSQ stores physical addresses, and the translation happens prior to accessing the LSQ. However, we can have an alternative design where the LSQ stores virtual addresses, and no two virtual pages map to the same physical frame. In this case, we can defer address translation till we access the cache. This introduces an additional overhead in terms of time. It lengthens the critical path by introducing an additional stage – virtual to physical address translation.

Let us try to reduce this overhead by creating a virtually indexed physically tagged (VIPT) cache, which is indexed with the virtual address, and the tag comes from the physical address. Let us first discuss the design of this cache, and then we shall discuss its benefits. Consider the way we access a cache in a 32-bit machine. We divide a memory address into three parts as shown in Figure 7.45(a). The three parts are the bits required to address the byte within the block (block offset), the bits for indexing the set (index), and the tag (rest of the bits). Note that in this section, we will use two terms: block offset (bits used to address a byte within a cache block), and page offset (bits used to address a byte within a page).

Just below Figure 7.45(a), we have Figure 7.45(b) that shows the way that we split a virtual memory address into the 12-bit offset (address of a byte within a page) and the 20-bit page number (see Section 7.2). Immediately below Figure 7.45(b), we have Figure 7.45(c) that shows the breakup of a physical address into two components: offset of a byte within the frame (or page) and the frame address. Let us now notice a pattern that is staring at us. If the size of the block offset and the set index is less than 12 bits, then there is an opportunity for an interesting optimisation. Consider an example. Assume we have a 64-byte block size, and 64 sets in a cache. In this case, we need 6 bits to specify the address of a byte within the block, and we need 6 bits to uniquely index a set. Thus, in total, we need 12 bits.

How do we connect this to the fact that we need the same 12 bits to specify the address of a byte within a page or a frame? Here, the key insight is that in the process of address translation, the 12 LSB bits do not change. They remain the same because the size of a page or a frame is 4 KB (as per our

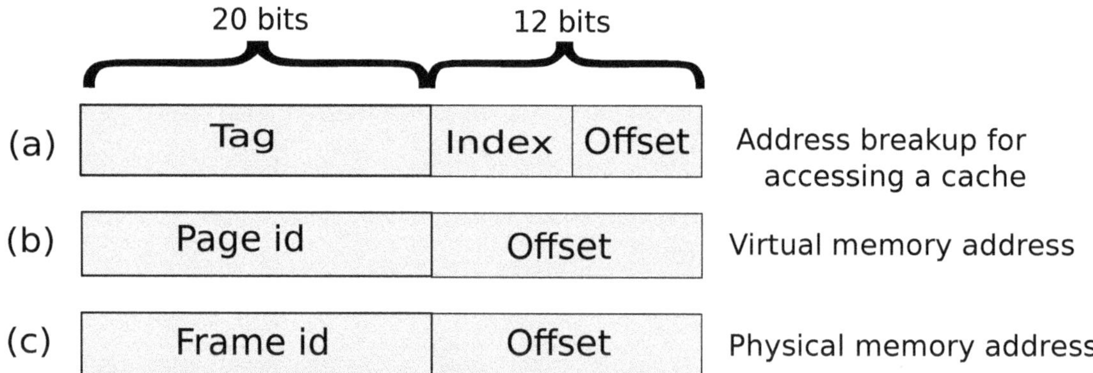

Figure 7.45: Breakup of a memory address for accessing a set associative cache. This example is for a 32-bit memory system with 4 KB pages.

assumptions). However, the remaining 20 MSB bits change according to the mapping between pages and frames. The crucial insight is that the **12 LSB bits** remain the same in the virtual and physical addresses. If we can find the set index using these 12 bits, then it does not matter if we are using the physical address or the virtual address. We can index the correct set before translating the address.

In this particular case, where we are using 12 bits to find the set index and block offset, we can use the virtual address to access the set. Refer to the VIPT cache in Figure 7.46. When the memory address is ready, and we are sure that there are no chances of store→load forwarding in the LSQ, we can proceed to access the L1 cache. We first extract the 6 set index bits, and read out all the tags in the set. Simultaneously (see the timing diagram in Figure 7.46) we perform the virtual to physical address translation by accessing the TLB. The greatness of the VIPT cache is that it allows us to overlap the tag accesses with the process of translation. In the next stage of the access, we have the physical address with us, and then we can extract its tag and compare the tag portion of the address with the tags stored in the ways. The rest of the access (read or write) proceeds as usual.

Note that the VIPT scheme has its limitations. If we have a large number of sets, then it is possible that the set index bits are split between the page offset, and the page/frame number. Then, this approach is not feasible. The only reason this approach works is because it is possible to access the set and read out all of its constituent ways in parallel without translating the address.

Let us now extend this idea. Assume that the number of block offset bits and set index bits adds up to 14. Since a page is 4 KB (12 bits), our VIPT scheme will not work. This is because we have two extra bits, and they will not be the same after the mapping process. This is where we can get some help from either software or hardware.

Let us discuss the software approach first. Assume that our process of translation is such that the least significant 14 bits are always the same between physical and virtual addresses. This requires minimal changes to the OS's page mapping algorithms. However, the advantage is that we can then use the 14 LSB bits to read out all the tags from the set (similar to the original VIPT scheme). We shall thus have all the advantages of a virtually indexed physically tagged cache. However, there is a flip side to this. This is that in this case, we are creating a super-page (larger than a page) that is 16 KB (2^{14} $bytes = 16\,KB$). Frames in memory need to be reserved at granularities of 16 KB each. This might cause wastage of memory space. Assume that in a frame, we are only using 8 KB; the remaining 8 KB will get wasted. We thus have a trade-off between memory usage and performance. For some programs, such a trade-off might be justified. This needs to be evaluated on a case-by-case basis.

The other method of dealing with such cases is with a hardware trick. We start out by noting that most of the time we have a good amount of temporal and spatial locality. Most consecutive accesses are expected to be to the same page. We can thus keep the corresponding frame number in a small register.

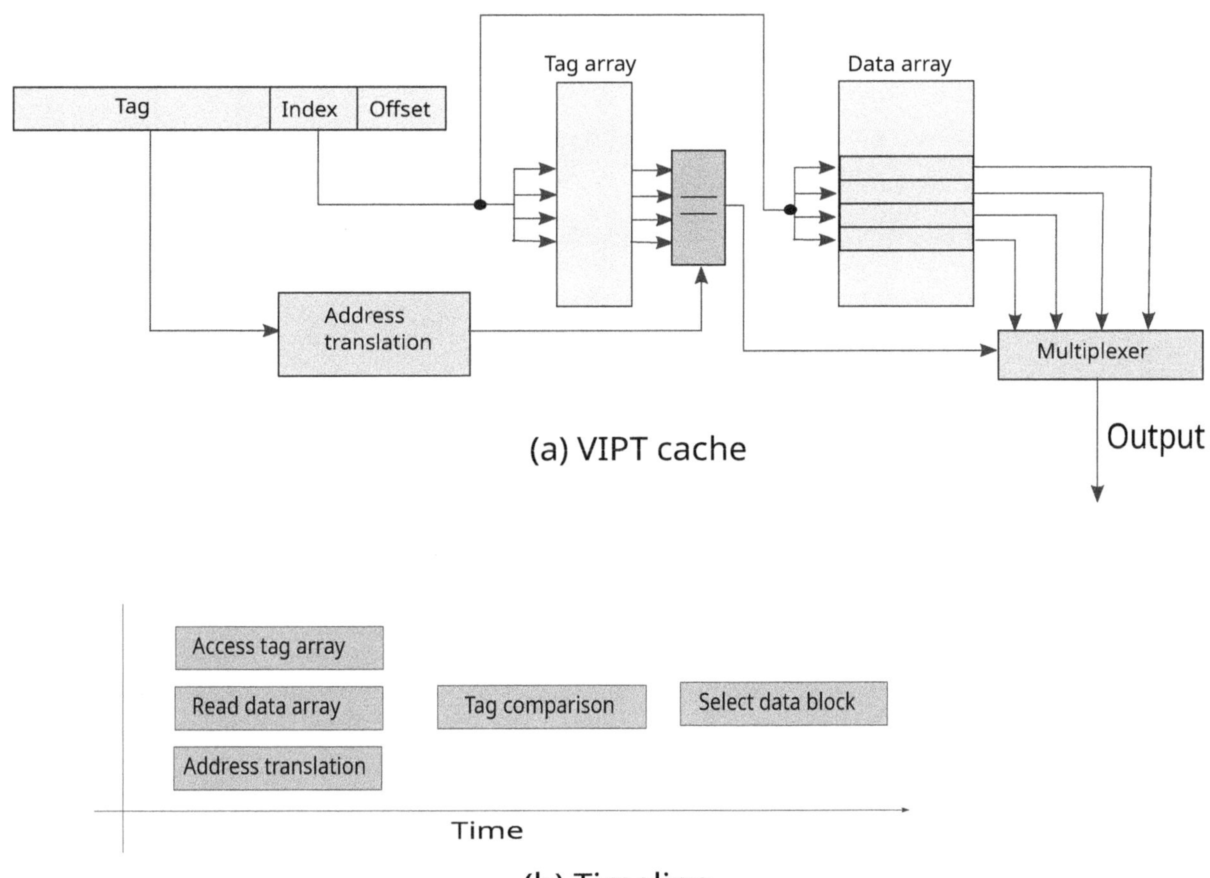

(a) VIPT cache

(b) Timeline

Figure 7.46: Virtually indexed physically tagged (VIPT) cache

We can speculatively read the translation from the register, create a physical address, and start accessing the cache. This is a very fast operation as compared to a full TLB access. In parallel, we need to access the TLB, and verify if the speculation is correct or not. If we have a high chance of success, then we have effectively minimised the address translation overhead. The accuracy of this process can further be enhanced by having a more sophisticated predictor that uses the PC, and possibly the memory address of the load. The prediction however must be done before the request is ready to be sent to the L1 cache.

7.5 Trace Caches

Let us sit back for a minute, and think about what we really want. We need a stream of instructions on the correct path at a rate that is more than the issue or commit width of the processor. This would ensure that the fetch stage is not a bottleneck. In CISC processors, we need a high-bandwidth decode unit as well. In most CISC ISAs as of 2020 such as Intel x86, instructions are converted from CISC to RISC micro-instructions inside the processor such that they can easily be processed in the pipeline. They are then sent to the decode unit. Sometimes this process can become very slow, and as a result, the decode stage can also become a bottleneck. To create a high-throughput decode stage, processors typically have multiple decoders that operate in parallel.

All this circuitry consumes a fair amount of chip area, and consumes a disproportionate amount of power. If we can somehow get rid of all of this circuitry, and manage to get decoded RISC micro-instructions directly from the caches, then we can radically decrease the power consumption and improve performance. In other words, we can completely skip the fetch and decode stages of the pipeline.

This does sound too good to be true. However, it is possible to get close. Designers at Intel tried to realise this goal in early 2000, when they designed a novel structure called a *trace cache* for the Intel® Pentium® 4 processor. In this section, we shall present the ideas contained in the patent filed by Krick et al. [Krick et al., 2000]. We shall simplify some sections for the sake of readability. For all the details please refer to the original patent.

Let us first explain the concept of a trace. A trace is a sequence of dynamic instructions that subsumes branches and loop iterations. Let us explain with an example. Consider the following piece of C code.

```c
int sum = 0;

for (i=0; i<3; i++){
        if (i == 1)
                continue;
        sum = sum + arr[i];
}
```

We have a loop with 3 iterations and an *if* statement that skips the body of the second loop iteration. Let us look at the sequence of instructions that the processor will execute. For the sake of readability we show C statements instead of x86 assembly code. Let the label *.loop* point to the beginning of the loop, and the label *.exit* point to the statement immediately after the loop. Note that we are not showing a well-formed assembly program, we are instead just showing a dynamic sequence of instructions that the processor will see (simplifications made to increase readability).

```c
/* initial part */
sum = 0;
i = 0;

/* first iteration */
if (i >= 3) goto .exit;
if (i == 1) goto .temp;
sum = sum + arr[i]; // i = 0
.temp: i = i + 1;
goto .loop;

/* second iteration: starts at .loop */
if (i >= 3) goto .exit;
if (i == 1) goto .temp;  /* next iteration */
.temp: i = i + 1;
goto .loop;


/* third iteration: starts at .loop */
if (i >= 3) goto .exit;
if (i == 1) goto .temp;
sum = sum + arr[i]; // i = 2
.temp: i = i + 1;
goto .loop;


/* fourth iteration */
if (i >= 3) goto .exit;  /* exit the for loop */
```

The instructions in this unrolled loop form a trace. It is the sequence of instructions that the processor is going to fetch to execute the code. If we can store the instructions corresponding to the entire trace in a trace cache, then all that we need to do is to simply fetch the instructions in the trace and process them. Furthermore, if we can also store them in their decoded format, then we can skip the power-hungry decode stage. In the case of CISC processors, it is desirable if the trace cache stores micro-instructions instead of full CISC instructions. If we observe a good hit rate in the trace cache, then we can save all the energy that would have been consumed in the fetch and decode stages. In addition, the trace cache is also serving as a branch predictor. We are using the information about subsequent trace segments as branch predictions. Finally, note that we still need an i-cache in a system with a trace cache. We always prefer reading instructions from the trace cache; however, if we do not find an entry, we need to access the conventional i-cache.

7.5.1 Design of the Trace Cache

The basic structure of a trace cache is shown in Figure 7.47. Akin to a normal cache, we have a tag array, a data array, and a cache controller. The only extra structure that we see is the fill buffer, which is used while constructing a trace.

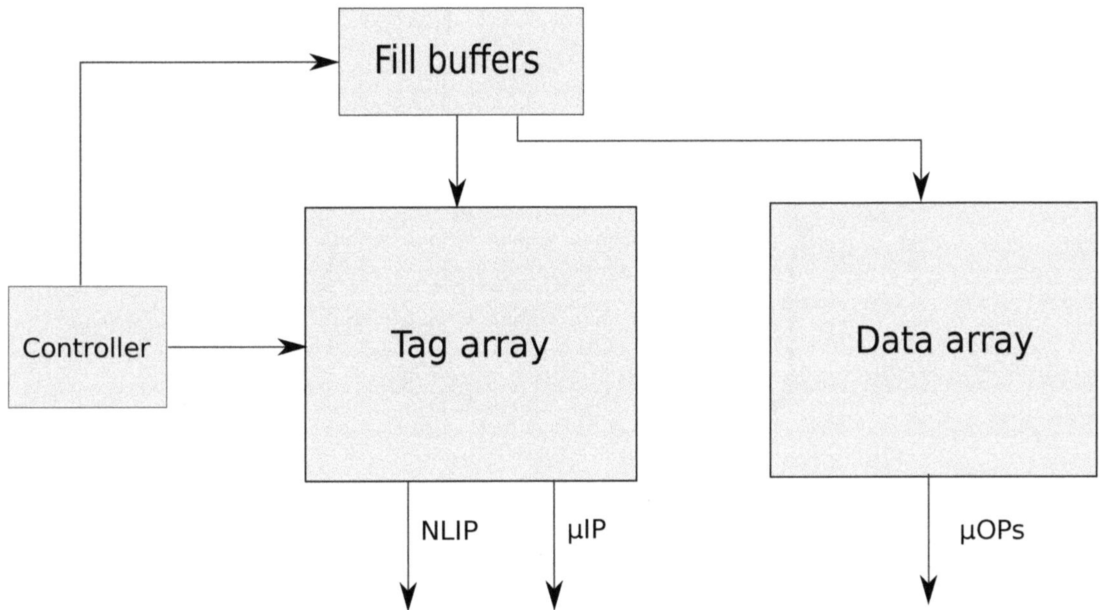

Figure 7.47: Overview of the trace cache

The data array is a regular k-way set associative cache. Let us assume that it is a 4-way set associative cache with 4 ways per set. Instead of defining traces at the granularity of instructions, let us define a trace as a sequence of cache lines. For example, it is possible that a trace many contain 5 cache lines. Each such line is known as a *trace segment*. We can have three kinds of segments: head, body, and tail. Every trace is organised as a linked list as shown in Figure 7.48. It starts with the head segment, and ends with the tail segment.

Next, we need to store the trace in the trace cache. We start with the head of the trace. We create a tag array entry with the head of the trace. The rest of the segments in the trace are organised as a linked list (see Figure 7.48). Each segment is stored in a separate data line, and has a dedicated entry in the tag array. The standard way of representing a linked list is by storing a pointer to the next node within the current node. However, this is not space efficient. If a data block is 64 bytes, and a pointer

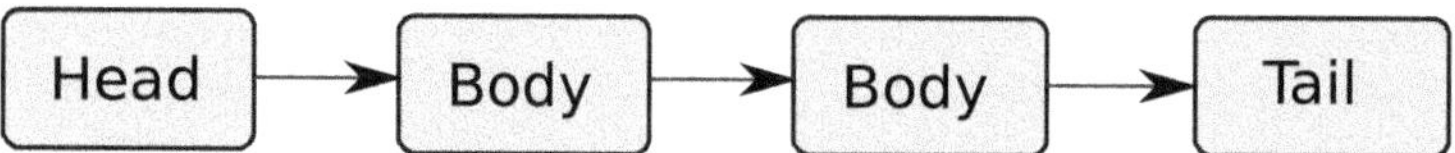

Figure 7.48: A trace consisting of multiple segments

is 64 bits (8 bytes), then the space overhead is equal to 12.5%. This is significant. Hence, let us restrict the way a trace is stored.

Let us store a trace in contiguous cache sets. For example, if a trace has 5 segments, we can store the segments in sets s, $s+1$, ..., $s+4$, where s is the index of the set that stores the trace head. Consider a 4-way set associative cache. Each trace segment can be stored in any of the 4 ways of a set. Given that we have stored a trace segment in a given set, we know that the next trace segment is stored in the next set. The only information that we need to store is the index of the way in that set. This requires just 2 bits, and thus the additional storage overhead is minimal. Figure 7.49 shows how we store multiple traces in the data array. In this figure, each column is a way in a set. A trace cache can be visualised as a packet of noodles, where each individual strand represents a trace.

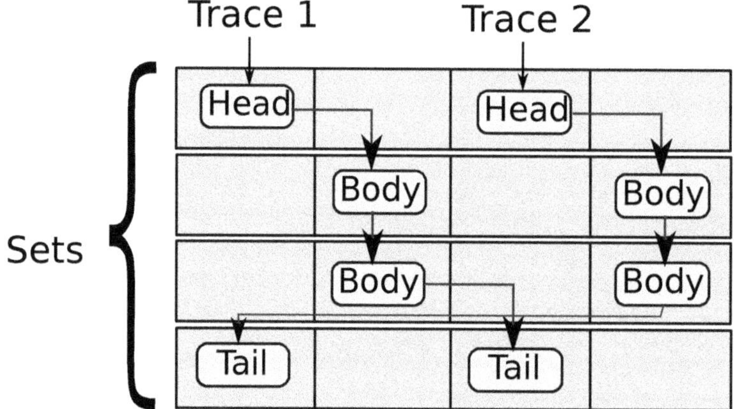

Figure 7.49: Visualisation of traces stored in the data array

Traces cannot be arbitrarily long. Their length is limited by the number of sets in the cache. However, there are a few additional conditions that govern the length of a trace.

Let us first look at conditions for terminating the creation of a trace segment, we shall then move on to the rules for terminating the creation of a trace. Let us henceforth refer to a microinstruction as a μOP (micro-op).

1. If we encounter a complex CISC instruction that translates to many more μOPs than what a single data line can store, then we store all the μOPs that can be stored in the data line, and then terminate the trace segment. The remaining μOPs need to be generated by the decode unit by reading the microcode memory. The microcode memory contains all the microinstructions for complex CISC instructions.

2. We allow a limited number of branch instructions per trace segment. If we encounter more than that, we terminate the trace segment. This is to avoid structural hazards.

3. We never distribute the μOPs of a CISC instruction across trace segments. We terminate the segment if we do not have enough space to store all the μOPs of the next CISC instruction.

Let us now look at the criteria to terminate the process of trace creation.

1. In an indirect branch, a call, or a return statement, the branch's target may be stored in a register. Since the address is not based on a fixed PC-relative offset, the next CISC instruction tends to change for every trace. Consider a function return statement. Depending on the caller function, we may return to a possibly different address in each invocation. This is hard to capture in a trace. Hence, it is better to terminate a trace after we encounter such instructions.

2. If we receive a branch misprediction or an interrupt alert, then we terminate the trace. This is because the subsequent instructions will be discarded from the pipeline and thus will not be checked for correctness.

3. The length of every trace is limited by the number of sets in the cache, and this is thus a hard limit on the length of the trace.

Tag Array

Let us now look at the trace cache in greater detail. Each entry in the tag array contains the following fields: address tag, valid bit, type (head or body or tail), next way, previous way, NLIP (next line's instruction pointer), and μIP. Let us describe them in sequence (also see Figure 7.50).

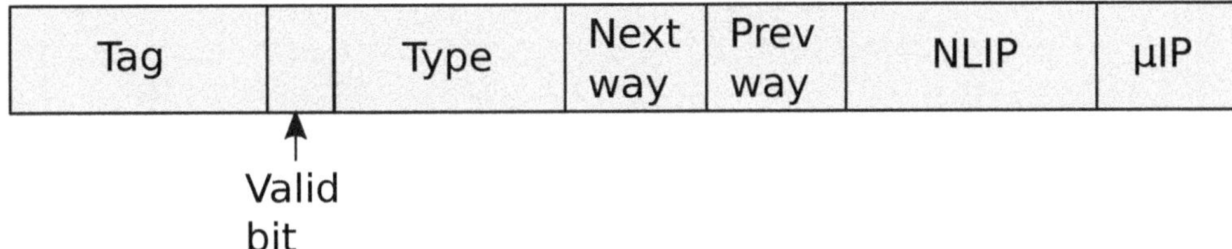

Figure 7.50: Entry in the tag array of the trace cache

When we are performing a lookup in the tag array to locate the head of the trace, we send the address to the tag array. This is similar to a regular cache access, where the tag portion of the address needs to be compared with the tag stored in the entry. Hence, the first entry that we store is the tag. Subsequently, we have a customary valid bit that indicates the validity of the entry.

For each data line that stores one trace segment, we need to store whether it is a trace head, body or tail. This requires 2 bits (type field). Since we store consecutive trace segments in consecutive sets, the only information that we need to store is the id of the next and previous ways such that we can create a doubly linked list comprising trace segments. Previous pointers are required to delete the trace at a later point of time starting from a body or a tail segment. The next field is NLIP, which stores the address of the next CISC instruction. This is only required for the tail segment such that we can locate the address of the next CISC instruction. The last field, μIP, is used to read microinstructions for a complex CISC instruction. We use it to index a table of microinstructions known as the *microcode memory*.

Data Array

Each line in the data array can store up to a maximum of 6 microinstructions (μOPs). We have a valid bit for each μOP. To skip the decode stage, we store the μOPs in a decoded format such that the microinstruction does not have to be decoded in the pipeline. In addition, each μOP also stores a branch target such that it does not have to be computed. This saves us an addition operation for every instruction that has a PC-relative branch.

7.5.2 Operation

To fetch a trace, the trace cache runs a state machine as shown in Figure 7.51. During execution, we run a state machine that starts in the *Head lookup* state. Given the program counter of an instruction, we search for it in the trace cache.

Assume that we find an entry. We then transition to the *Body lookup* state, where we keep reading all the trace segments in the body of the trace and supplying them to the pipeline. Once we reach the tail, we transition to the *Tail* state. In the *Body lookup* state, if there is a branch misprediction, or we receive an interrupt, we abort reading the trace, and move to the *Head lookup* state to start anew. Furthermore, if at any point, we encounter a complex macroinstruction, we read all its constituent microinstructions from a dedicated microcode memory (*Read microinstructions* state), and then continue executing the trace. If at any point, we do not find a trace segment in the trace cache, we transition to the *body miss* state, which means that our trace has snapped in the middle. This is because while building another trace we evicted a data block in the current trace. Whenever we terminate executing a trace either because of an unanticipated event such as an external interrupt, we reached the *Tail* state, or we reached the *Body miss* state, we start from the *Head lookup* state once again.

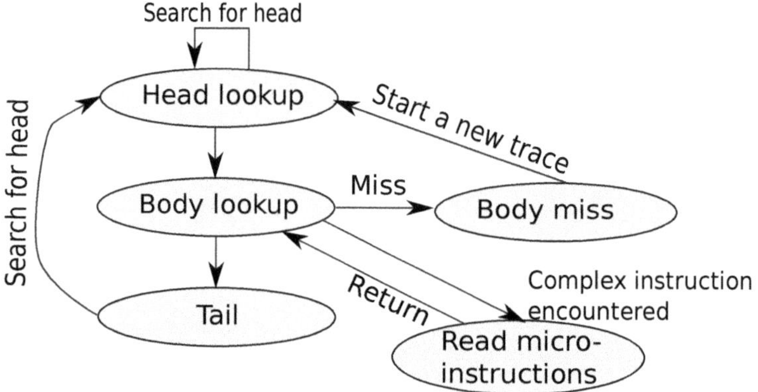

Figure 7.51: FSM (finite state machine) used for reading a trace

Let us now look at the process of creating a trace. The flowchart is shown in Figure 7.52. We trigger such an operation when we find that a fetched instruction is not a part of any trace. We treat it as the head of a trace, and try to build a trace. The first step is to issue a fetch request to the i-cache. Then the state changes to the *wait for μOPs* state, where we wait for the decoder to produce a list of decoded μOPs. Once the instruction is decoded, the μOPs are sent to the fill buffer. Then we transition to the *bypass μOPs* state, where we send the μOPs to the rest of the pipeline. This continues till we encounter a trace segment terminating condition. There are two common cases that can disrupt the flow of events.

The first is that we encounter a complex instruction, where we need a list of microinstructions from microcode memory. In this case, we transition to the *Read microinstructions* state. The second is a normal trace segment terminating condition. In this case, we move to the *Transfer* state where the data line created in the fill buffer is transferred to the tag and data arrays. Then we transition back to the *Wait for μOPs* state, if we have not reached the end of the trace. However, if we have encountered a condition to end the trace, then we mark the data line as the tail of the trace, and finish the process of creating the trace.

We subsequently fetch the next instruction, and check if it is the head of a trace. If it is not the head of any trace, then we start building a new trace.

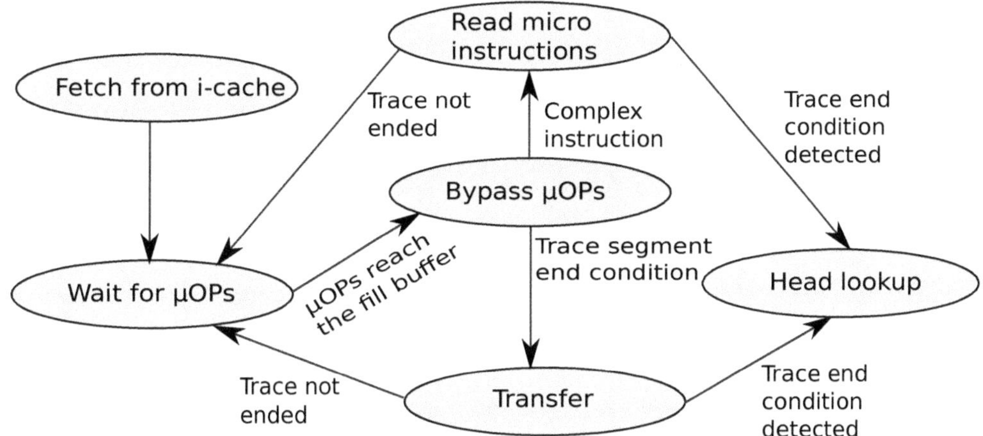

Figure 7.52: FSM used for building a trace

7.6 Instruction Prefetching

If we go back to our discussion in Section 7.1.7, we shall recall that prefetching can solve most of the problems that lead to frequent cache misses. They can reduce all three types of misses: cold misses, capacity misses, and conflict misses. Predicting memory accesses in advance is a very powerful mechanism, and in theory, it can hide the memory access latency almost completely. We shall discuss instruction prefetching in this section; we will discuss data prefetching in the next section.

The basic idea of prefetching is very simple. We predict the misses before hand, and issue memory requests to "prefetch" data to higher levels in the memory hierarchy. If we are able to predict misses with a reasonable accuracy, then we are effectively increasing the hit rate of caches at higher levels of the memory hierarchy. This increases the performance, and reduces the traffic to the lower levels of the memory system such as the LLC (last level cache) and off-chip memory.

The two key questions that need to be asked are (1) "When to prefetch," and (2) "What to prefetch." Regarding the first question, we can neither prefetch too soon nor too late. If we prefetch too soon, then the prefetched block needs to wait for a long time till it is used. During this time, some other accesses can evict this block. Additionally, prefetching may displace other blocks with useful data from the cache. These displaced blocks might be used in the near future, and thus we might actually be increasing the miss rate by prefetching a lot of blocks too soon. It is possible that we might be displacing useful data with useless data.

In comparison, if we prefetch a block too late, then it will not be available in the caches when the core needs it. It is true that the time a memory request needs to wait might get reduced because of an outstanding prefetch request, however this situation is not optimal. Hence, the golden rule for prefetching is that we need to prefetch the right set of addresses at exactly the right time. If we prefetch too soon or too late, too little or too much, there is an associated performance penalty.

Keeping these broad principles in mind, let us look at some of the most common prefetching strategies.

7.6.1 Next Line Prefetching

Let us consider the simplest method of prefetching known as *next line prefetching*. The basic insight is as follows. If we have accessed a cache block with block address X, then there is a very high probability that the next few blocks that we shall access will have their block addresses equal to $X + 1$, $X + 2$, and so on. This means that after we access address X, we need to prefetch the subsequent blocks. Even though the high-level idea looks simple, there is an important point to note here.

Most prefetchers actually base their decisions on the miss sequence and not the access sequence. This means that a prefetcher for the L1 cache takes a look at the L1 misses, but not at the L1 accesses. This is because we are primarily concerned with L1 misses, and there is no point in considering accesses for blocks that are already there in the cache. It is not power efficient, and this information is not particularly useful. Hence, we shall assume from now on that all our prefetchers consider the miss sequence only while computing their prefetching decisions. Furthermore, we shall only consider block addresses while discussing prefetchers – the bits that specify the addresses of words in a block are not important while considering cache misses.

Important Point 14

Prefetchers operate on the miss sequence of a cache, and not on the access sequence. This means that if a prefetcher is associated with a cache, it only takes a look at the misses that are happening in the cache; it does not look at all the accesses. This is because most cache accesses are typically hits, and thus there is no need to consider them for the sake of prefetching data/instructions into the cache. We only need to prefetch data/instructions for those block addresses that may record misses in the cache. Additionally, operating on the access sequence will consume a lot of power.

Hence, in the case of a next line or next block prefetcher, we look at misses. If we record a miss for block address X, we predict a subsequent *miss* for block address $X + 1$ – we thus prefetch it.

This is a simple approach for instruction prefetching and often works well in practice. Even if we have branches, this method can still work. Note that most branches such as *if-else* statements, or the branches in *for* loops have targets that are nearby (in terms of memory addresses). Hence, fetching additional cache blocks, as we are doing in this scheme, is helpful.

There can be an issue with fetching blocks too late. This can be fixed by prefetching the block with address $X + k$, when we record a miss for block address X. If we record a miss for a new block every n cycles, and the latency to access the lower level memory is L cycles, k should be equal to L/n. This means that the block $X + k$ will arrive just before we need to access it.

7.6.2 Markov Prefetching

Let us now design something more sophisticated. The main problem with next line prefetching is that it relies on an assumption that if an access with address X misses in the cache, then there is a high likelihood of an access with address $X + 1$ also suffering from a miss in the near future (note that these are block addresses). This need not necessarily be the case all the time. We can have branches to blocks that are far away. Next line prefetching will not be able to cover such cases. Let us thus use a different algorithm called *Markov prefetching*, which is inspired from the concept of Markov chains. A Markov chain is a type of random process that moves from state to state. We can make predictions about future states solely based on the current state. This is also known as the *Markov property*.

We can use the same property here. Consider two cache blocks A and B. Further assume that every time we record a miss for cache block A, the next miss that we observe is for cache block B. Can this pattern be used to design a good prefetcher? Such a pattern does indeed follow the Markov property. If we record a miss for block A, we can immediately deduce that we need to prefetch cache block B. We can thus immediately issue a prefetch request to the memory system to fetch cache block B. This is the basic idea of a Markov prefetcher.

Let us thus create a miss table as shown in Figure 7.53, where we record the pattern of misses. Each row of the miss table corresponds to a cache block. Consider the row that corresponds to the cache block with address X. In each row we have multiple columns that record the access frequencies of other cache blocks that have recorded a miss just after a miss was recorded for block X. Let us explain in the context of the example shown in Figure 7.53. Here, we keep data for two other blocks that suffered from a cache miss, after we failed to find X in the cache. Let them be Y and Z. For each block, we store the corresponding miss count. We associate a saturating counter with each column that indicates the miss count. To ensure that the information stays fresh, we periodically decrement these counters.

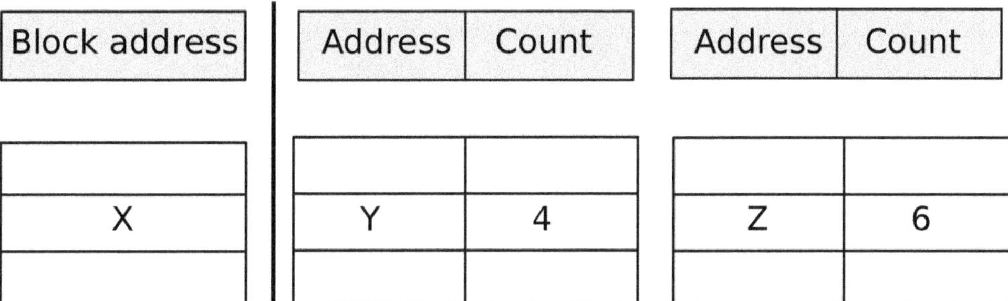

Figure 7.53: The miss table

Now, when we have a cache miss, we look up the address in this table. Assume we suffer a miss for block X. In the table we find two entries: one each for blocks Y and Z respectively. There are several choices. The most trivial option is to issue prefetch requests for both Y and Z. However, this is not power efficient and might increase the pressure on the lower level cache. Sometimes it might be necessary to adopt a better solution to conserve bandwidth. We can compare the miss counts of Y and Z and choose the block that has a higher miss count.

After issuing the prefetch request, we continue with normal operation. Assume that for some reason the prefetch request suffers from an error. This could be because the virtual memory region corresponding to the address in the request has not been allocated. Then we will get an "illegal address" error. Such errors for prefetch requests can be ignored. Now, for the next cache miss, we need to record its block address. If the miss happened for block Y or block Z, we increment the corresponding count in the table. For a new block we have several options.

The most intuitive option is to find the entry with the lowest miss count in the table among the blocks in the row corresponding to the cache miss, and replace that entry with an entry for the new block. However, this can prove to be a bad choice, particularly, if we are disturbing a stable pattern. In such cases, we can replace the entry probabilistically. This provides some hysteresis to entries that are already there in the table; however, it also allows a new entry to come into the miss table with a finite probability. The choice of the probability depends on the nature of the target workload and the architecture.

7.6.3   Call Graph Prefetching

Till now we had been looking at instructions at the granularity of cache blocks. However, let us now consider some of the modern approaches for prefetching, where we consider instructions at the granularity of functions. In such approaches, we directly prefetch the entire function. If the function is large, we only prefetch the first N lines of the function. Let us discuss one of the early approaches in this space. It is known as call graph prefetching (CGP) [Annavaram et al., 2003]. The basic idea is that when we are executing one function, we predict the functions that it will call and prefetch their instructions. This reduces the number of instruction cache misses.

There are two approaches: one in software and one in hardware. Let us discuss the software approach first.

Software Approach

We first start out by creating a *call graph* of a program. A call graph is created as follows. We run the program in profiling mode, which is defined as a *test run* of the program before the actual run, where we collect important statistics regarding the program's execution. These statistics are known as the program's *profile*, and this process is known as *profiling*. In the profiling phase, we create a graph (defined in Section 2.3.2) in which each node represents a function. If function A calls function B, then we add an edge between the nodes representing A and B respectively. Note that it is possible for node A to call different functions across its invocations. One option is to only consider the first invocation of function A; in this case, we do not collect any data for subsequent invocations. Based on this information, we can create a graph of function calls, which is referred to as the *call graph*. From the call graph, we can create a list of $\langle caller, callee \rangle$ function pairs, and write them to a file. Note that if function A calls function B, then A is the caller and B is the callee.

Let us explain this process with an example. Consider the set of function invocations shown in Figure 7.54(a). The associated call graph is shown in Figure 7.54(b). In addition, we label the edges based on the order in which the parent function invokes the child functions. For example, in Figure 7.54(a), *foo2* is called after *foo1*, and thus we have labelled the edges to indicate this fact.

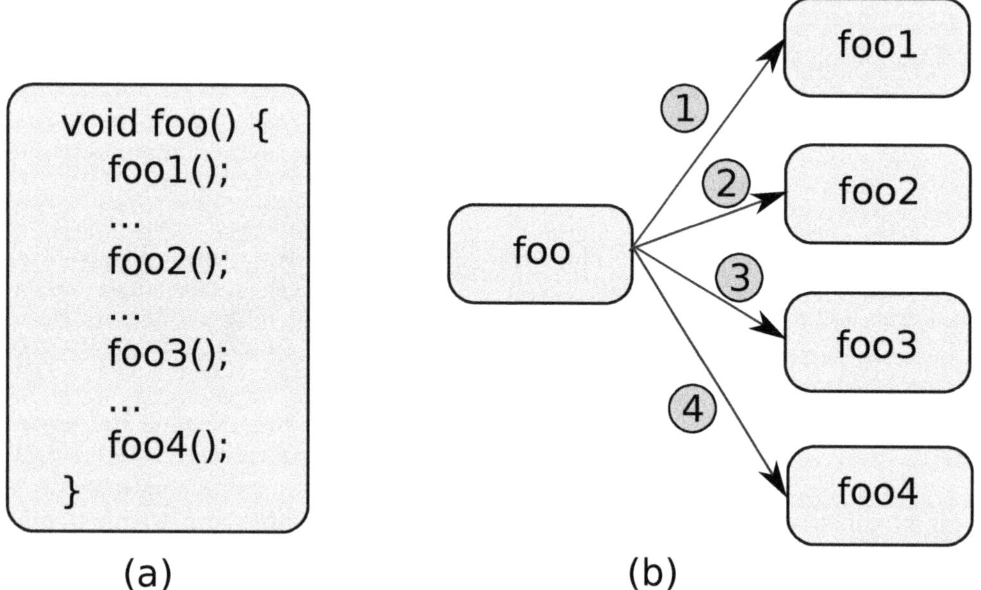

Figure 7.54: Example of a call graph

Subsequently, we can use a binary instrumentation engine, or even a compiler to generate code that prefetches instructions. The algorithm to insert prefetch statements is as follows. Assume function A calls function B and then function C. We insert prefetch code for function B at the beginning of function A. We assume that it will take some time to setup the arguments for B, and then we shall invoke the function. During this time, the memory system can fetch the instructions for function B.

After the call instruction that calls function B, we insert prefetch code for function C. Again the logic is the same. We need some time to prepare the arguments for function C after B returns. During this time, the memory system can in parallel prefetch the instructions for C. If after C, we would have invoked another function D, then we would have continued the same process.

The software approach is effective and is generic. However, it necessitates a profiling run. This is an additional overhead. In addition, it is not necessary that the inputs remain the same for every run of the program. Whenever, the input changes substantially, we need to perform the process of profiling once again. In addition, for large programs, we can end up generating large files to store these profiles. This represents a large storage overhead also. Finally, the profiling run need not be representative. A function might be called many times and its behaviour might vary significantly, and all of these might not be effectively captured in the profile. Hence, whenever we have the luxury, a hardware based approach is preferable.

Hardware based Approach

Let us create a call graph history cache (CGHC) as originally proposed by [Annavaram et al., 2003]. In this case, we maintain a dynamic subset of the call graph. Unlike the software approach, the execution is not preceded by a profiling phase.

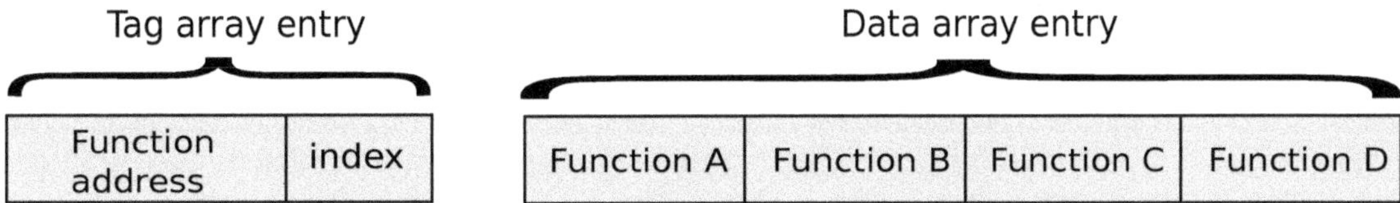

Figure 7.55: Tag and data array entries in the CGHC

Figure 7.55 shows the structure of a call graph history cache. It consists of a tag array and data array similar to a normal cache. The tag array stores the tags corresponding to the PCs of the first (starting) instructions of the functions. Along with each entry in the tag array, we store an integer called an index, which is initialised to 1. The data array can contain up to N entries, where each entry is the starting PC of a function that can be invoked by the current function.

Assume function A invokes the functions B, C, and D, in sequence. We store the starting PCs of B, C, and D, respectively, in the data array row. Note that we store the starting PCs of functions in the same order in which they are invoked. This order is also captured by the *index*. If the *index* is k, then it means that we are referring to the kth function in the data array row.

Similar to software prefetching, whenever we invoke function A, we start prefetching the instructions of function B. When B returns, we prefetch the instructions of function C, and so on. We use the *index* field in the tag array for this purpose. Initially, the index is 1, hence, we prefetch the first function in the data array row. On every subsequent return, we increment the *index* field, and this is how we identify the next function to prefetch: if the *index* is i, then we prefetch the instructions for the ith function in the row. When A returns, we reset its *index* field to 1.

Whenever A invokes a new function, we have two cases. If the function is invoked after the last function in the data array row, then we need to just create a new entry in the row, and store the address of the first instruction of the newly invoked function. However, if we invoke a new function that needs to be in the middle of the row, then there is a problem: it means that the control flow path has changed. We have two options. The first is that we adopt a more complicated structure for the data array row. In the first few bytes, we can store a mapping between the function's index and its position in the data array row. This table can be updated at run time such that it accurately tracks the control flow. The other option is to discard the rest of the entries in the data array row, and then insert the new entry. The former is a better approach because it allows changes to propagate faster; however, the latter is less complex.

In addition, we can borrow many ideas from the notion of saturated counters to keep track of the functions that are a part of the call sequence in the current phase of the program. Whenever A calls B, we can increment the saturating counter for B in A's row of the CGHC. This indicates that the entry is still fresh. Periodically, we can decrement the counters to indicate the fact that the information that we have stored is ageing. Once a counter becomes zero, we can remove the entry from the row.

7.6.4 Other Approaches

Instruction prefetching per se is a very rich area, and there are many recent research proposals in this area. Most of the advanced proposals prefetch instructions at the granularity of functions, and in addition try to group the functions into larger units.

Recent works [Ferdman et al., 2011, Kolli et al., 2013, Kallurkar and Sarangi, 2017] create instruction groups called streams, tasks, or super-functions, where the idea is that we group together functions that are typically executed in sequence. Such approaches deduce a high level structure in the program. For example, if we are executing a large program, we divide it into large and distinct subtasks. If we are executing subtask 1, we can predict that we will execute subtask 2 once it ends. We can then start prefetching the starting functions of subtask 2.

7.7 Data Prefetching

In Section 7.6, we looked at instruction prefetching algorithms. In this section, let us look at data prefetching algorithms. Instruction prefetching and data prefetching have similarities, as well as many differences. The first is that instructions have much more temporal and spatial locality as compared to data. The most common access patterns for instructions are as follows: we access them in sequence or we access instructions as a part of loops. Both of these access patterns have a significant amount of temporal and spatial locality.

However, data access has a different kind of pattern. The primary sources of data are the stack, heap, and data sections (specific to Linux) in the memory map of a process. The stack is used to store function arguments, return addresses, and local variables. Ideally we would like to keep all of these variables in registers. However, because of a paucity of registers, we often face the need to spill these registers into memory, and this requires data accesses. Local variables and function arguments do not take up a lot of space. Even if something is spilled to memory, its likelihood of still being in the L1 cache is fairly high. Hence, prefetching such data that resides in the stack is not very beneficial.

However, we often allocate large data structures in the heap and sometimes in the *data* section of the memory map, which contain dynamically allocated and global variables, respectively. Prefetching these data structures can prove to be extremely beneficial.

Let us classify data memory accesses as either *regular* or *irregular*. A regular access is a traversal of an array or a matrix element-by-element. In comparison, we perform irregular accesses when we traverse a tree or a linked list. These are based on pointers and the sequence of memory addresses that we access does not follow a simple and well defined pattern. We can access an array using irregular accesses as well. Consider two arrays A and B. An access pattern of the form $A[B[i]]$ is an irregular access pattern for A because the array indices are not necessarily consecutive.

On the lines of our discussion in the section on instruction prefetching, a good data prefetching algorithm should be accurate, timely (not issue prefetches too soon or too fast), and additionally be able to cater to all kinds of data accesses: regular and irregular.

7.7.1 Stride based Prefetching

Notion of a Stride

The most common regular access is an array access, when we traverse the array in the sequence of increasing indices. Most programs often sequentially access array elements. Hence, such instructions should be first targeted for the purpose of prefetching. Let us create a predictor to detect this pattern..

Let us start with the definition of the term *stride* (also defined in Section 5.1.2). Consider the following piece of code.

```
for (i=0; i<N; i++){
    ...
    sum += A[i];
    ...
}
```

Here, A is an array. Depending on the data type of the array, the memory address of the array is calculated for the statement, *sum += A[i];* . If A is an array of integers, then in each iteration we increment i by 4. If it is an array of double precision numbers, then we increment i by 8. Let us now look at the assembly code for the statement *sum += A[i];* .

```
1   /* r0 contains the base address of A */
2   /* r1 contains the index i */
3   /* r2 contains the sum */
4   add r3, r1, r0
5   ld  r4, 0[r3]      /* r4 contains A[i] */
6   add r2, r2, r4     /* sum = sum + A[i] */
```

Consider the load instruction (Line 5). Every time that it is invoked, it will have a different address. Let us define the difference in the memory addresses between consecutive calls to a memory instruction (load or store) as the *stride*. In this case , the stride depends on the data type stored in array A. Alternatively, it is possible that the enclosing *for* loop does not visit array locations consecutively, instead it only traverses the even indices within the array. The value of the stride will double in this case.

Definition 48
Let us define the difference in the memory addresses between consecutive calls to a memory instruction (load or store) as the stride.

We thus observe that the value of the stride is dependent on two factors: the data type and the array access pattern. However, the only thing that we require is to know if a given stride is relatively stable and predictable. This means that the stride, irrespective of its value, should not change often. Otherwise we will not be able to predict the addresses of future memory accesses. Let us design a stride predictor, and a stride based prefetcher.

Stride Predictor

Let us design a stride predictor on the lines of the predictors that we have been seeing up till now. We create an array indexed by the least significant bits of the PC. In each row, we can optionally have a tag for increasing the accuracy. In addition, we have the following fields (also see Figure 7.56): last address, stride, confidence bits.

The *last address* field stores the value of the memory address that was computed by the last invocation of the memory instruction. The *stride* field stores the current stride, and the confidence bits (implemented using a saturating counter) show the confidence that we have in the value of the stride that is stored in the entry.

Let us now discuss the logic. Whenever, we record a miss in a cache, we access the stride predictor. First, we subtract the last address from the current address to compute the current stride. If this is equal to the value of the stride stored in the table, then we increment the saturating counter that represents

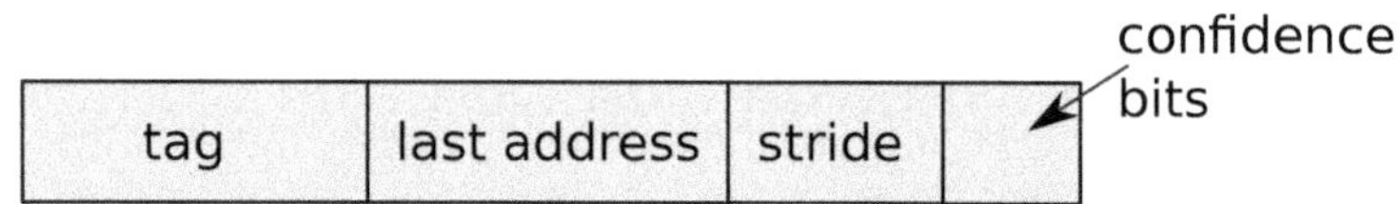

Figure 7.56: Contents of each row in the stride predictor

the confidence bits. If the strides do not match, then we decrement the confidence bits. The confidence bits provide a degree of hysteresis to the stride. Even if there is one irregular stride, we still maintain the old value till we make a sufficient number of such observations. At the end, we set the last address field to the memory address of the current instruction.

As long as the stride is being observed to be the same, this is good news. We keep incrementing the confidence bits till they saturate. However, if the value of the stride changes, then ultimately the saturating counter will reach 0, and once it does so, we replace the value of the stride stored in the entry with the current stride. In other words, our predictor can dynamically learn the current stride, and adapt to changes over time.

Process of Prefetching

Now, the process of prefetching is as follows. Whenever, we record a miss for a given block, we access its corresponding entry in the stride predictor. If the value of the confidence is high (saturating counter above a certain threshold), we decide to prefetch. If the value of the stride is S and the current address is A, we issue a prefetch instruction for address $A' = A + \kappa S$. Note that κ in this case is a constant whose value can either be set dynamically or at design time. The basic insight behind this parameter is that the prefetched data should arrive just before it is actually required. It should not arrive too soon nor too late. If we do not expect a huge variance in the nature of the workloads, then κ can be set at design time.

However, if we have a lot of variation, and we are not sure where the prefetched values are coming from, then we are not in a position to predict how long it will take to prefetch the values. If they are coming from the immediately lower level of memory, they will quickly arrive; however, if the values are coming from main memory, then they will take hundreds of cycles. This can be dynamically estimated by maintaining a set of counters. For example, we can have a counter that starts counting after a prefetch request for block A' is sent to the memory system. The counter increments every cycle. Once the data arrives, we note the value of the counter. Let the count be $T_{prefetch}$ – this gives us an estimate of the time it takes to prefetch a block.

We can have another counter to keep track of the duration between prefetching the block A' and accessing it. This counter starts when a prefetch request is sent to the memory system. The counter stops when subsequently the first memory request for a word in the block A' is sent to the memory system. Let this duration be referred to as T_{access}.

Ideally, $T_{prefetch}$ should be equal to T_{access}. If $T_{prefetch} < T_{access}$, then it means that the data has arrived too soon. We could have possibly prefetched later. This can be done by decreasing κ. Similarly, $T_{prefetch} > T_{access}$ means that the data arrived too late. In this case, we need to increase κ. We can dynamically learn the relationship between κ and T_{access} by dynamically changing the value of κ for different blocks and measuring the corresponding values of T_{access}. This approximate relationship can be used to tune κ accordingly.

As of today, stride based prediction is the norm in almost all high-end processors. This is a very simple prefetching technique, and is very useful in codes that use arrays and matrices.

7.7.2 Pointer Chasing

Let us now look at irregular accesses. A typical example of an irregular access is traversing a linked list.
Consider a representative code snippet.

```c
struct node_t {
    int val;
    struct node_t *next;
};

typedef struct node_t node;

void foo() {
    ...
    /* traverse the linked list */
    node* temp = start_node;
    while (temp != NULL) {
        process(temp);
        temp = temp->next;
    }
    ...
}
```

In this piece of code, we define a linked list node (*struct node_t*). To traverse the linked list, we
keep reading the next pointer of the linked list, which gives us the address of the next node in the
linked list. The addresses of subsequent nodes need not be arranged contiguously in memory, and thus
standard prefetching algorithms do not work. A simple way of solving this problem is to insert a prefetch
instruction in software for the linked list traversal code.

```c
    ...
    /* traverse the linked list */
    node* temp = start_node;
    while (temp != NULL) {
        prefetch(temp->next);   /* prefetch the next node */
        process(temp);
        temp = temp->next;
    }
    ...
```

We add a set of prefetch instructions for fetching the next node in the linked list before we process
the current node. If the code to process the current node is large enough, it gives us enough time to
prefetch the next node, and this will reduce the time we need to stall for data to come from memory.
Such a prefetching strategy is known as *pointer chasing*. We are literally chasing the next pointer and
trying to prefetch it. We can extend this scheme by traversing a few more nodes in the linked list and
prefetching them. Since prefetch instructions do not lead to exceptions, there is no possibility of having
null pointer exceptions or illegal memory access issues in such code.

The compiler and memory allocator can definitely help in this regard. If on a best-effort basis, the
memory allocator tries to allocate new nodes in the linked list in contiguous cache lines, then traditional
prefetchers will still work. Of course the situation can get very complicated if we have many insertions
or deletions in the linked list. However, parts of the linked list that are untouched will still maintain a
fair amount of spatial locality.

7.7.3   Runahead Execution and Helper Threads

Let us now do some thing similar to pointer chasing in hardware. Unlike software, where we have a lot of visibility, and with explicit support from the programmer we can add prefetch instructions at the right places, hardware has very limited capabilities. It is not possible for it to make sense of the billions of instructions that pass through it every second. Hence, our hardware interventions will in a sense be less intelligent; however, they can still be effective. Let us discuss a space of such ideas.

Consider a miss in the L2 cache. Upon an L2 miss, the request needs to go to main memory, which often has a very high access latency. This is typically between 200-400 clock cycles. During this time the processor pipeline will fill up, and stall the fetch process. The processor will just wait for the data to come back from memory, and in the meanwhile it will not do anything. Hence, such L2 or L3 misses are very expensive – they lead to a lot of stalled cycles.

Keeping this in mind, let us try to do something when the processor is stalled. There are many similar ideas in this space. We shall discuss some of the major proposals in this area. They are collectively known as *pre-execution techniques*.

Runahead Execution

Let us discuss one of the earliest ideas in this space known as runahead execution [Mutlu et al., 2003]. In this case, whenever we have a high-latency L2 miss, we let the processor proceed with a possibly predicted value of the data. This is known as the *runahead mode*. In this mode, we do not change the architectural state. Once the data from the miss comes back, the processor exits the runahead mode, and enters the normal mode of operation. All the changes made in the runahead mode are discarded. The advantage of the runahead mode is that we still execute a lot of instructions with correct values, and in specific, we execute many memory instructions with correct addresses. This effectively prefetches the data for those instructions from the memory system. When we restart normal execution, we shall find many much-needed blocks in the caches, and thus the overall performance is expected to increase. Let us elaborate further.

Whenever we have an L2 miss, we enter runahead mode. We take a checkpoint of the architectural register file and the branch predictors. Similar to setting the poison bit in the delayed selective replay scheme (see Section 5.2.4), we set the invalid bit for the destination register of the load that missed in the L2 cache. We subsequently propagate this poison bit to all the instructions in the load's forward slice. Recall that the forward slice of an instruction consists of its consumers, its consumers' consumers and so on. The invalid bit is propagated via the bypass paths, the LSQ, and the register file. This ensures that all the consumers of an instruction receive an operand marked as invalid. If any of the sources are invalid, the entire instruction including its result is marked as invalid. An instruction that is not marked invalid, is deemed to be valid.

We execute instructions in the runahead mode as we execute them in the normal mode. The only difference is that we always keep track of the valid/invalid status of instructions. Second, we do not update the branch predictor when we resolve the direction of a branch that is invalid.

Runahead execution introduces the notion of *pseudo-retirement*, which means retirement in runahead mode. Once an instruction reaches the head of the ROB, we inspect it. If it is invalid, we can remove it immediately, otherwise we wait for it to complete. We never let stores in the runahead mode write their values to the normal cache. Instead, we keep a small runahead L1 cache, where the stores in runahead mode write their data. All the loads in the runahead mode first access the runahead cache, and if there is a miss, they are sent to the normal cache. Furthermore, whenever we evict a line from the runahead cache, we never write it to the lower level.

Once the value of the load that missed in the L2 cache arrives, we exit the runahead mode. This is accompanied by flushing the pipeline and cleaning up the runahead cache. We reset all the invalid bits, and restore the state to the checkpointed state that was collected before we entered the runahead mode.

There are many advantages of this scheme. The first is that we keep track of the forward slice of the load that has missed in the L2 cache. The entire forward slice is marked as invalid, and we do not allow instructions in the forward slice to corrupt the state of the branch predictor and other predictors that are used in a pipeline with aggressive speculation. This ensures that the branch prediction accuracy does not drop after we resume normal execution. The other advantage is that we use the addresses of valid memory instructions in runahead mode to fetch data from the memory system. This in effect prefetches data for the normal mode, which is what we want.

Helper Threads

Let us now look at a different method of doing what runahead execution does for us. This method uses *helper threads*. Recall that a thread is defined as a lightweight process. A process can typically create many threads, where each thread is a subprocess. Two threads share the virtual memory address space, and can thus communicate using virtual memory. They however have a separate stack and program counter. Programs that use multiple threads are known as multithreaded programs.

Definition 49

A thread is a lightweight process. A parent process typically creates many threads that are themselves instances of small running programs. However, in this case, the threads can communicate amongst each other via their shared virtual address space. Each thread has its dedicated stack, architectural register state, and program counter.

The basic idea of a helper thread is as follows. We have the original program, which is the parent process. In parallel, we run a set of threads known as helper threads that can run on other cores of a multicore processor. Their job is to prefetch data for the parent process. They typically run small programs that compute the values of memory addresses that will be used in the future. Then they issue prefetch requests to memory. In this manner, we try to ensure that the data that the parent process will access in the future is already there in the memory system. Let us elaborate.

First, let us define a *backward slice*. It is the set of all the instructions that determine the value of the source operands of an instruction. Consider the following set of instructions.

```
1  add r1, r2, r3
2  add r4, r1, r1
3  add r5, r6, r7
4  add r8, r4, r9
```

The backward slice of instruction *4* comprises instructions *1* and *2*. It does not include instruction *3*. Of course, the backward slice of an instruction can be very large. Nevertheless, if we consider the backward slice in a small window of instructions, it is limited to a few instructions.

Definition 50

The backward slice of an instruction comprises all those instructions that determine the values of its source operands. It consists of the producer instruction of each operand, the producers of the operands of those instructions, and so on.

We can create small subprograms for loads that may most likely miss in the L2 cache, and launch them as helper threads way before the load gets executed. To figure out which loads have a high likelihood of missing in the L2 cache, we can use an approach based on profiling, or prediction based on misses in the past. Each helper thread runs the backward slice of such a load instruction, computes its address, and sends it to the memory system for prefetching the data.

7.8 Summary and Further Reading

7.8.1 Summary

Summary 6

1. Most programs exhibit temporal and spatial locality.

2. Given that large memories are too slow and too inefficient in terms of power consumption, we need to create a memory hierarchy.

   (a) A typical memory hierarchy has 3-5 levels: L1 caches (i-cache and d-cache), L2 cache, L3 and L4 caches (optional), and the main memory.

   (b) The cache hierarchy is typically inclusive. This means that all the blocks in the L1 cache are also contained in the L2 cache, and so on.

   (c) The performance of a cache depends on its size, latency, and replacement policy.

3. The salient features of a cache are as follows.

   (a) A cache has a tag array and a data array.

   (b) We first search for an entry in the tag array, and only if there is a tag match, we get an index for the entry in the data array.

   (c) A direct mapped cache maps a block address to only one cache line. However, a k-way set associative cache maps each block address to a set of k lines (a set). In a fully associative cache, a block can be stored in any cache line.

   (d) A direct mapped cache and a set associative cache are made of 6-transistor SRAM cells, whereas the tag array in a fully associative cache uses 10-transistor CAM cells.

   (e) Every memory cell is connected to two bit lines. Before reading the value, we precharge the bit lines and then monitor the difference in the voltages using a sense amplifier. This is done to increase performance, and reduce the susceptibility to noise.

4. It is necessary to have support for virtual memory.

   (a) Solves the size and overlap problems.

   (b) The virtual to physical address mapping is stored in the page tables.

   (c) The TLB (Translation Lookaside Buffer) acts as a small and fast hardware cache for the page tables. The TLB is accessed before sending a memory request to the cache.

5. We can use the Cacti tool to model and design a cache.

   (a) We replace each element in the cache by an equivalent RC circuit. This helps us estimate the latency and power.

   (b) We calculate the time constant of each element using the Elmore delay model.

   (c) Subsequently, we divide large arrays into banks, subbanks, mats, and subarrays based on the objective function: we can either minimise power, minimise latency, or minimise area.

6. *Modern caches are pipelined and are non-blocking. They have miss status handling registers (MSHRs) that do not allow secondary misses to be sent to the lower levels of the memory hierarchy. We record a secondary miss in the cache, when at the point of detecting a miss, we find that we have already sent a request to the lower level for a copy of the block. Such misses are queued in the MSHR.*

7. *We can use skewed associative caches, way prediction, loop tiling, and VIPT (virtually indexed, physically tagged) caches to further increase the performance of a cache.*

8. *The trace cache stores traces, which are commonly executed sequences of code. We can read decoded instructions directly from it, and skip the fetch and decode stages altogether.*

9. *There are three kinds of misses: compulsory, conflict, and capacity. For all these types of misses, prefetching is helpful.*

10. *We can prefetch either instructions or data. We learn patterns from the miss sequence of a cache, and then leverage them to prefetch data or code blocks.*

11. *For instruction prefetching, next line prefetching is often very effective. However, modern approaches prefetch at the level of functions or groups of functions. They take the high-level structure of the code into account.*

12. *For prefetching data, we studied stride based prefetching for regular memory accesses and pre-execution based methods for irregular memory accesses. The latter class of techniques is very important for code that uses linked lists and trees.*

7.8.2   Further Reading

For a basic introduction to caches and virtual memory, we recommend the textbook by Sarangi [Sarangi, 2015]. For more advanced concepts, readers can refer to the book titled, "Multi-core Cache Hierarchies", [Balasubramonian et al., 2011] by Balasubramonian, Jouppi, and Muralimanohar.

For cache modelling, arguably the best references are Cacti's design manuals: Cacti 1.0 [Wilton and Jouppi, 1993], Cacti 2.0 [Reinman and Jouppi, 2000], Cacti 3.0 [Shivakumar and Jouppi, 2001], Cacti 4.0 [Tarjan et al., 2006], Cacti 5.0 [Thoziyoor et al., 2007], and Cacti 6.0 [Muralimanohar et al., 2009]. For additional details, we recommend the book by Jacob et al. [Jacob et al., 2007]. Readers interested in analytical models can consult the papers by Guo et al. [Guo and Solihin, 2006] and the Roofline model [Williams et al., 2009]. The Roofline model is a general model that correlates compute and memory performance. We shall look at it separately in Chapter 10. For a better understanding of the popular LRU and FIFO replacement schemes including their mathematical underpinnings, we recommend the book by Dan and Towsely [Dan and Towsley, 1990]. In this chapter, we have only explained inclusive caches; however, making caches inclusive is not necessary. Gaur et al. [Gaur et al., 2011] present an alternative design where it is possible to bypass the last level cache in the memory hierarchy.

For additional details on prefetching, readers can refer to the survey paper by Mittal [Mittal, 2016b] and Callahan et al.'s survey paper on software prefetching [Callahan et al., 1991].

Exercises

Ex. 1 — A cache has block size b, associativity k, and size n (in bytes). What is the size of the tag in bits? Assume a 64-bit memory system.

Ex. 2 — Does pseudo-LRU approximate the LRU replacement scheme all the time?

Ex. 3 — From the point of view of performance, is an i-cache miss more important or is a d-cache miss more important? Justify your answer.

Ex. 4 — Why do write buffers and victim caches work?

Ex. 5 — Is it a good idea to have an L4 and L5 cache as well?

Ex. 6 — Why is it necessary to read in the entire block before even writing a single byte to it?

* **Ex. 7** — Assume the following scenario. An array can store 10 integers. The user deliberately enters 15 integers, and the program (without checking) tries to write them to successive locations in the array. It will cross the bounds of the array and overwrite other memory locations. It is possible that if the array is stored on the stack, then the return address (stored on the stack) might get overwritten. Is it possible to hack a program using this trick? In other words, can we direct the program counter to a region of code that it should not be executing? How can we stop this attack using virtual memory based techniques?

Ex. 8 — Assume we have an unlimited amount of physical memory, do we still need virtual memory?

* **Ex. 9** — Does the load-store queue store physical addresses or virtual addresses? What are the trade-offs. Explain your answer, and describe how the load-store queue needs to take this fact (physical vs virtual addresses) into account.

Ex. 10 — In a set associative cache, why do we read the tags of all the lines in a set?

Ex. 11 — What is the key approximation in the Elmore delay model? Why do we need to make this assumption?

Ex. 12 — Show the design of an MSHR where every load checks all the previous stores. If there is a match, then it immediately returns with the store value (similar to an LSQ).

Ex. 13 — Does the VIPT scheme place limits on the size of the cache?

Ex. 14 — Why was it necessary to store a trace in consecutive sets? What did we gain by doing this?

** **Ex. 15** — Consider an application that makes a lot of system calls. A typical execution is as follows. The application executes for some time, then it makes a system call. Subsequently, the OS kernel starts to execute, and then after some time, it switches back to the application. This causes a lot of i-cache misses. Suggest some optimisations to reduce the i-cache miss rate.

* **Ex. 16** — Can you design a piece of hardware that can detect if an OOO processor is traversing a linked list?

** **Ex. 17** — Suggest an efficient hardware mechanism to prefetch a linked list. Justify your answer. Extend the mechanism to also prefetch binary trees.

Design Questions

Ex. 18 — Understand the working of the CACTI tool. Create a web interface for it.

Ex. 19 — Implement way prediction in an architectural simulator such as the Tejas Simulator.

Ex. 20 — Implement a trace cache in an architectural simulator.

Ex. 21 — Implement different prefetching techniques and compare their performance.

8

The On-chip Network

Because of the relentless improvement in transistor technology predicted by Moore's law, processors from 1965 onwards steadily kept on getting more complex. Their performance kept on increasing, and this was the main driver of efforts in the computer architecture community. However, by 2005 it was clear that single core performance will not increase anymore. The signs of saturation were visible on the horizon. There were two big reasons for this. The first was that power dissipation was becoming a very important factor. It was becoming very hard to limit the on-chip power dissipation and consequent temperature rise. As a result, the cores had to be made simpler. The second reason was that the phenomenon of diminishing returns had set in. We were already exploiting as much of ILP as we could, and the benefits of increasing the issue width or investing in creating better predictors was marginal. As a result, the efforts centred around increasing the on-chip cache size. Caches increased in complexity, and very soon became large multi-banked caches, where the timing was dominated by the time it takes to reach the banks that are the farthest away in terms of distance. This also placed a limit on the performance gains.

Over the next few years cores became simpler and the attention shifted to parallel processing. Multicore processors that arose out of this effort have gradually created the space for manycore processors, where the cores are even more simpler and more numerous.

As a result of these trends, a modern processor chip is a mix of 10-20 cores, and an equivalent number of cache banks. Additionally, there are other active elements such as memory controllers and specialised accelerators. The typical layout of a manycore processor die looks like one of the sub-figures in Figure 8.1. The cores and cache banks are either organised as a chess board, or the cores are on the rim and the cache banks are in the centre.

The memory controllers are always located on the periphery. Dedicated accelerators can either be in the centre if their primary job is to perform computations or can be towards the periphery if they need to communicate a lot with memory.

All of these elements inclusive of cores and cache banks need to send messages between each other while executing a program. For example, if core A wants to read a memory location that is in cache bank B, then A needs to send a read-miss message to B. Subsequently, B needs to send the value stored in the cache line back to A, which is another message. We can have different types of communication between the nodes. To manage all of these senders, receivers, and data packets, we need to implement an on-chip network. The on-chip network or NoC (network on-chip) needs to route messages from senders to receivers. Unlike the internet, **we are not allowed to drop messages** in an on-chip network. As a result, we need to have complex protocols to ensure timely and reliable message delivery.

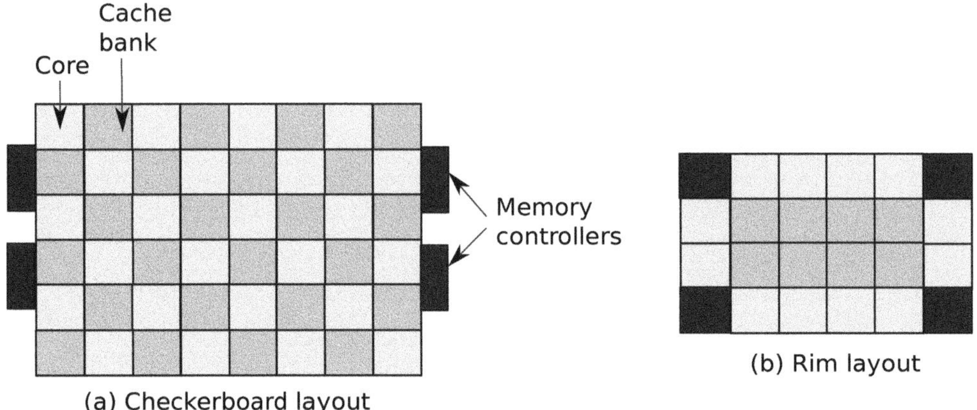

Figure 8.1: Different kinds of multicore layouts

Definition 51
An on-chip network (or network-on-chip or just NoC) is a network that connects cores, cache banks, accelerators, and memory controllers within the chip.

We can think of a processor as a small city, where instead of cars, network packets flow between the cores and cache banks. Akin to a city, we can have traffic jams, queuing, and congestion. The same way that we have a system of lights, and traffic police to manage traffic in cities, we need to have something similar in the form of protocols to manage the on-chip traffic. Additionally, there are other problems that also happen in modern cities. In situations with heavy traffic, it is possible that we can have a gridlock where cars are not able to move because a circular dependence forms between the cars. Car A needs car B to move, car B needs car C to move, and finally car C needs car A to move. Such circular dependences can lead to long jams and gridlocks. We can have a similar situation in an NoC as well. We can have *deadlocks*, where a set of packets simply cannot reach their destination because a circular loop of dependences forms among them. We also can have *starvation*, where a given packet is not able to reach its destination because other packets are causing it to stall. We can also have the case where the packet moves round-and-round in circles and never reaches its final destination – this is known as a *livelock*.

Along with solving the issues of deadlock and starvation, we need to ensure that we are able to maximise the throughput of the network, and minimise the average or worst-case latency. All of these are difficult problems, and to solve these problems a full field of on-chip networks has emerged over the last few years. In this chapter, we shall look at some of the key results in this field and motivate the student to study further.

8.1   Overview of an NoC

Let us quickly summarise all our learning till now. We have made the case for an NoC by observing that today's multicore processors have a multitude of cores and cache banks. A core or cache bank can communicate with another core or cache bank. To support all possible communication patterns, it is necessary to design an NoC that can support a high throughput and also have a low latency.

8.1.1 Nodes and Links

Let us start with creating an abstract model of the system. Let us model an NoC as a graph (defined in Section 2.3.2) that has a set of nodes and a set of edges. A *node* is a generic and abstract component that can send or receive a message. An *edge* is a communication channel between two nodes. A node can be attached to a core, a cache bank, a memory controller, I/O controller, or any other component that is capable of transmitting or receiving a message. Let us define a message as a set of bytes. We shall look at it in detail in Section 8.2.1. For the time being, it is a set of bytes that needs to be atomically sent from the sender node to the receiver node. An *atomic delivery* implies that either the entire message is delivered or nothing is delivered. The sender and the receiver know how to understand the message.

Given that almost all the major components within a chip need to communicate with each other by sending messages, we need not have separate communication systems for different components. All of them can use a generic communication unit that sends and receives messages – this can be thought of as a node in the NoC. A realisation of such a generic communication unit or a node is called a *router*. A router is always attached to a component such as a core or a cache bank. Nowadays, a few adjoining cores and cache banks are typically grouped into a *tile*; there is one router per tile. It transmits and receives messages on its behalf. Additionally, the routers coordinate among themselves to send messages on the network. Henceforth, when we shall refer to a *node*, we will actually be referring to a router in the NoC. These terms might be used interchangeably as well.

Definition 52

A router is a generic communication unit in an NoC. Every component that wishes to communicate using the NoC needs to have access to a router that sends and receives messages on its behalf. In addition, in modern networks a message is sent from a source to a destination by passing it from router to router. The routers cooperate and coordinate among themselves to deliver the message at the final destination.

Unlike connections of yesteryear where all the routers were connected to a single set of copper wires (known as a bus) this method does not scale for modern NoCs. In modern NoCs, the connections are one-to-one, which means that every copper wire is connected to only two nodes. Such connections, known as *links* (or *edges* in the graph), connect a pair of nodes. We can have two types of links: buffered and unbuffered.

Buffered and Unbuffered Links

Assume we have a wire of length l. Its delay is equal to κl^2, where κ is a constant of proportionality (refer to Section 7.3 for the derivation). If the delay is a quadratic function of the length of the wire, then it can become very large. Let us instead split the wire into segments of fixed length, and insert a buffer between consecutive segments. The buffer is a latch or flip-flop that simply reads the bits sent on its incoming link, and then sends them out on its outgoing link. Such buffers are also called *repeaters*. Assume that the delay of a repeater is d.

We claim that by splitting a long wire into segments, and by introducing repeaters, we can reduce the overall delay of the wire. Let us do the math.

Let s be the number of segments, where the length of each segment is l/s. We shall thus require $s - 1$ repeaters. The net delay D is given by

$$D = (s - 1)d + s \times \kappa \frac{l^2}{s^2}$$

$$= (s - 1)d + \kappa \frac{l^2}{s}$$

Let us now find the optimal value of s.

$$\frac{\partial D}{\partial s} = d - \kappa\frac{l^2}{s^2} = 0$$

$$\Rightarrow s^2 = \kappa\frac{l^2}{d}$$

$$\Rightarrow s = \sqrt{\frac{\kappa}{d}} \cdot l$$

Thus the optimal value of the number of segments s is $\sqrt{\frac{\kappa}{d}} \cdot l$. The optimal delay is given by

$$\begin{aligned}
D &= (s-1)d + \kappa\frac{l^2}{s} \\
&= \left(\sqrt{\frac{\kappa}{d}} \cdot l - 1\right)d + \kappa\frac{l^2}{\sqrt{\frac{\kappa}{d}} \cdot l} \\
&= \sqrt{\kappa d} \cdot l - d + \sqrt{\kappa d} \cdot l \\
&= 2\sqrt{\kappa d} \cdot l - d
\end{aligned} \tag{8.1}$$

The important point to observe in Equation 8.1 is that the delay is now a linear function of the length of the wire. As a result a repeated or a buffered wire is significantly faster as compared to a wire that does not have repeaters. Most long wires, also called *global wires,* in the chip are buffered. Such repeaters sadly do not come for free. They have an associated area and power cost. Hence, we do not use them for interconnects that are over short distances. Such interconnects are called *local wires.*

8.1.2   Network Topology

Let us now look at the network topology: the way the nodes and links are laid out. In most books on computer architecture, the authors spend a lot of time discussing different kinds of network topologies including their mathematical properties. However, in modern processors, the network topology is typically very simple. If the number of cores is limited to four, then we often have a bus (see Figure 8.2), which is at its core a set of parallel copper wires. Unfortunately, buses have severe limitations in terms of scalability and bandwidth. All the routers compete for the same bus and this causes a lot of contention. As a result, buses are typically not considered good candidates for networks in large chips.

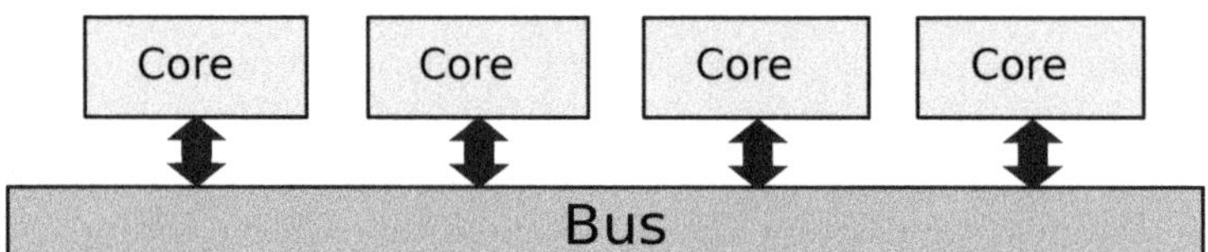

Figure 8.2: A bus connecting four cores

Hence, for large chips with a lot of cores and cache banks, the most common topology is a mesh (2D matrix) or a torus (2D matrix with the ends of each row and column connected). It is possible to have more complex high-radix structures that have more than 4 incoming and outgoing links per router; however, this is rare. High-radix structures have a large number of links per node such as Clos networks and hypercubes [Sarangi, 2015]. Additionally, they have additional properties such as immunity to multiple link failures, which is not of particular concern in on-chip networks. Such topologies are thus more commonly used in large cluster computers.

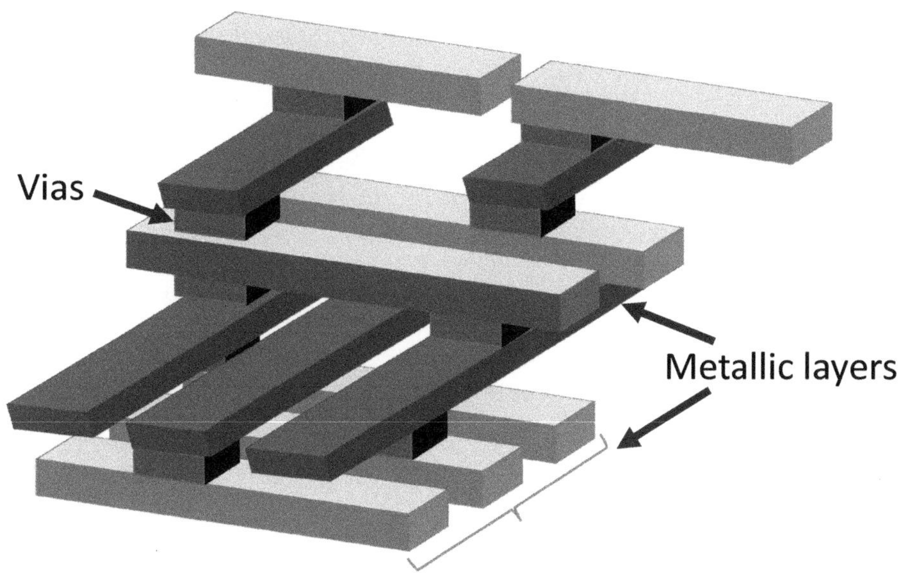

Figure 8.3: Metal layers in a modern chip

Metal Layers in a Modern Chip

In a modern VLSI chip we need to have a complex network of wires between communicating nodes. A simple bus is not enough. If we have an elaborate network, then the wires will intersect each other. However, if two copper wires intersect each other then they do not remain separate wires any more. A conducting path forms between all the senders and the receivers. As a result, we need to design a more complicated structure where we have several layers of wires such that all the wires that we want can be placed on the chip.

To realise this goal, a VLSI chip is composed of multiple layers. The lowest layer is made of silicon. On this layer we create all the transistors. However, this layer does not have enough space to connect all the sender-receiver pairs with copper wires. As a result there is a need to create additional layers on top of this layer that exclusively contain wires. These are known as the *metal layers*. Modern chips as of 2020 have 10-15 such metal layers, where consecutive layers are separated by an insulating layer that is made of silicon dioxide (SiO_2). The lower metal layers have local wires and the higher layers have global wires. Each layer is made of a dielectric material with a low dielectric constant such that the capacitance between wires is reduced to a minimum: this reduces crosstalk noise. In such layers, we can fabricate a wire by creating a trench in the layer and depositing copper in it. We can thus think of a wire as something like a filled trench in the layer. Modern VLSI processes allow us to create thousands of wires on a layer in this fashion.

This is shown in Figure 8.3, where we can see small wires in different layers. Let's say that we need to connect a functional unit A with a functional unit B. Then it is necessary to connect them with a wire. It might not be possible to connect them with a wire that fully resides on the first metal layer. We thus need to create small segments of wires in different layers, and connect them with vertical links made of copper. These vertical links (see Figure 8.3) are known as vias, or trans-silicon vias (TSVs). Hence, a long wire between a source and a destination can traverse through multiple metal layers and vias.

Further, notice that in Figure 8.3 the wires in consecutive layers are perpendicular to each other. This is a standard wire routing technique. If we assume that the wires in one layer are oriented along the x-axis, then in the layer above it they are oriented along the y-axis. This automatically ensures that all the wires in a layer do not intersect with each other. Secondly, if we have enough space, two layers are enough to connect any sender and receiver. However, this does not happen in practice because we run out of space in layers and thus 10-15 metal layers are required.

For the sake of completeness it is necessary to mention that every chip has three additional layers: power, ground, and clock. The power and ground layers are arranged as a grid. They are connected to the supply and the ground terminals respectively. Another layer that does not have any role in signal routing is the clock layer, where the external clock signal is distributed to all the functional units. The clock distribution network is typically arranged as an H-Tree (see Section 7.3.2). Recall that an H-Tree ensures that the distance from the source (located at the centre), and each of the receivers is the same. This ensures that all the users of the clock receive the transitions in the clock signal at almost the same time, which leads to minimal clock skew: difference in the time of arrival of the clock signal across different functional units.

Let us summarise.

Way Point 8

- *A simple bus is not enough for connecting multiple cores and cache banks in a modern chip – there is a lot of contention.*

- *We need to have complex interconnections between the communicating routers.*

- *It is thus necessary to create multiple metal layers, where the layers close to the silicon are for local wires, and the layers farther away contain longer interconnects known as global wires.*

- *A connection from a given source to a destination might have segments in different layers.*

- *Copper wires across different layers are connected by trans-silicon vias (TSVs).*

Let us now use a multi-layer VLSI chip to create more complex interconnections.

Mesh and Torus

Figure 8.4 shows the mesh topology. A mesh is a simple 2D matrix, where we connect two adjacent nodes on the same row or the same column with a link.

The mesh is a very popular structure in on-chip networks because it is very easy to create. It uses rectilinear links that are either horizontal or vertical. Fabricating such structures is very easy in modern VLSI processes. In comparison, it is fairly difficult to fabricate wires that are at oblique angles (neither vertical nor horizontal). Most VLSI fabrication processes do not allow designers to create such wires.

One of the major problems with mesh networks is that the network diameter – maximum delay between two nodes if we are following the shortest path between them – is high. If we are considering an $N \times N$ mesh, then the diameter is $2N - 2$ (distance between two diagonally opposite corners). This is measured in terms of the number of links that we need to traverse. Let us further reduce this. We can use the torus topology in this case (refer to Figure 8.5).

The only addition is the long wires between the ends of reach row and the ends of each column. They effectively reduce the diameter. In this case, the nodes that are the farthest apart are the centre and any of the corners. The diameter is $N/2 + N/2 \ (= N)$. Note that the assumption is that N is even. We have thus reduced the effective diameter roughly by a factor of 2. However, we have also increased the number of wires and introduced a few very long wires that span the length of the chip. Such long wires

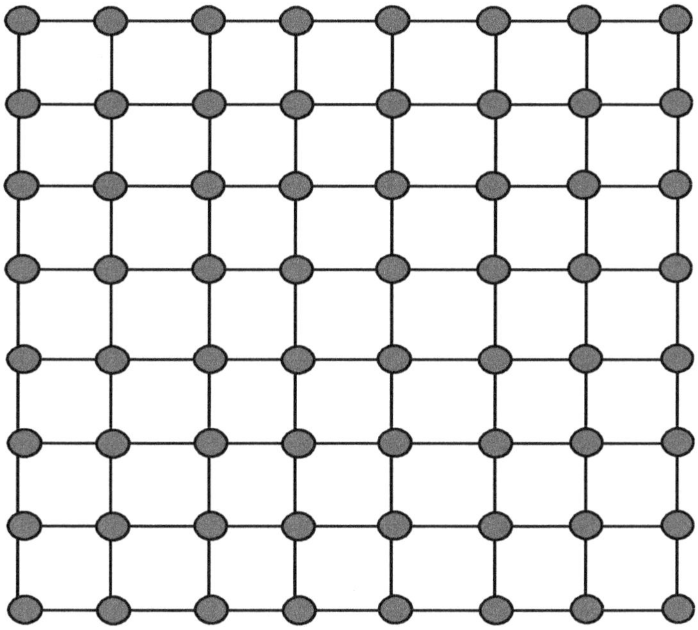

Figure 8.4: The mesh topology

will have very large delays and may not give us any significant advantage. Thus, most designs use the folded torus design shown in Figure 8.6.

Note that the design shown in Figure 8.6 is equivalent to the torus shown in Figure 8.5. However, the connections have been made in a different manner. A node in a row is not connected to the node that is directly adjacent to it (in the next column). Instead it is connected to the node (on the same row) that is two columns away. We have a similar connection pattern for the nodes in each column. Even though such designs increase the timing delay between adjacent nodes by a factor of 2; however, they eliminate long wires completely.

High-Radix Networks

Each node in a torus or a mesh is connected to 2 to 4 other nodes. These are examples of low-radix networks, where each node is connected to a few other nodes. In comparison, if we increase the number of links per node, we shall have a high-radix network. Such networks have some favourable properties such as a low diameter and higher path diversity. The term "path diversity" refers to the diversity of paths between a given source-destination pair. The advantage of increased path diversity is that we can react better to network congestion. Let us consider some of the common high-radix networks that are commonly used in cluster computers. They are difficult to fabricate using current VLSI technologies that do not allow oblique wires. However, there is some ongoing research that focuses on using these networks in NoCs by creating versions of the network that can be fabricated with current technology. In such networks we rearrange the nodes on a 2D plane such that it is easy to route wires between them. These are known as *flattened networks*.

Hypercubes

Figure 8.7 shows the hypercube topology. A hypercube refers to a family of network topologies that are constructed recursively. An order 0 hypercube H_0 is a single node. To construct an order 1

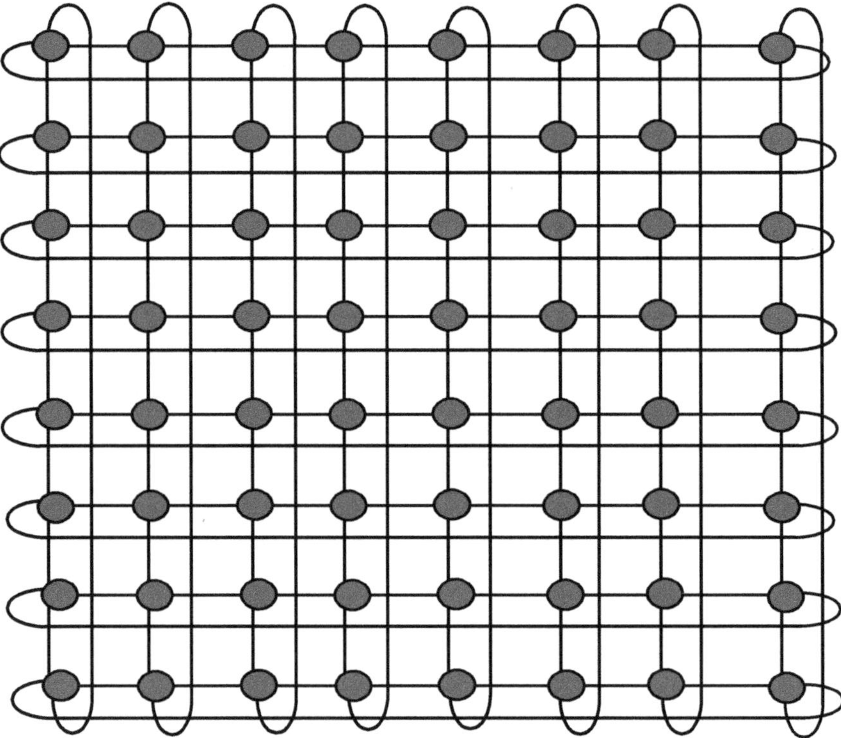

Figure 8.5: The torus topology

hypercube H_1 we take two copies of order 0 hypercubes and connect them together (see Figure 8.7(b)). Similarly, to create H_2 we take two copies of H_1 and connect the corresponding nodes together. Observe that we can number the nodes as binary numbers. For example, the nodes in H_2 can be numbered 00, 01, 11, and 10 respectively.

Now, to construct H_3 we take two copies of H_2, and connect the nodes with the same numbers with each other. For example, we connect the nodes numbered 00 in each hypercube with each other. We then add a prefix the nodes in one copy of H_2 with a 0 and the nodes in the other copy of H_2 with a 1. The numbers for the nodes labelled 00 in the two copies of H_2 become 000 and 100, respectively, in H_3. We follow the same process for the rest of the nodes. On similar lines, we can create H_4, H_5, and so on.

Let us now summarise some properties of this network, which are also easy to derive. In a hypercube with N (power of 2) nodes, each node is connected to $log_2(N)$ other nodes. This is easily visible in Figure 8.7 where we see that in a hypercube with N nodes, each node is labelled with a $log_2(N) - bit$ binary number. When we traverse a link, we flip only one of the binary bits. Given that we can change any one of the $log_2(N)$ bits in the label, it automatically follows that every node has $log_2(N)$ neighbours.

We can extend this result to prove that the diameter of a hypercube is $log_2(N)$. Consider two nodes with labels L and $\bar{L}$ (bitwise complement of L) respectively. To send a message between the nodes we need to traverse a sequence of links. In each traversal we flip a single bit in the label. Given that all the $log_2(N)$ bits differ between the labels of the nodes, we need to flip (complement) all the bits, and this means that we need to traverse $log_2(N)$ links. Note that the diameter is not more than $log_2(N)$ because the Hamming distance (number of corresponding bits that differ) between two labels is limited to the size of the labels, which is $log_2(N)$ bits. Since in every link traversal, we complement a single bit, we will never need to perform more than $log_2(N)$ traversals if we are proceeding on the shortest path.

Clos Network

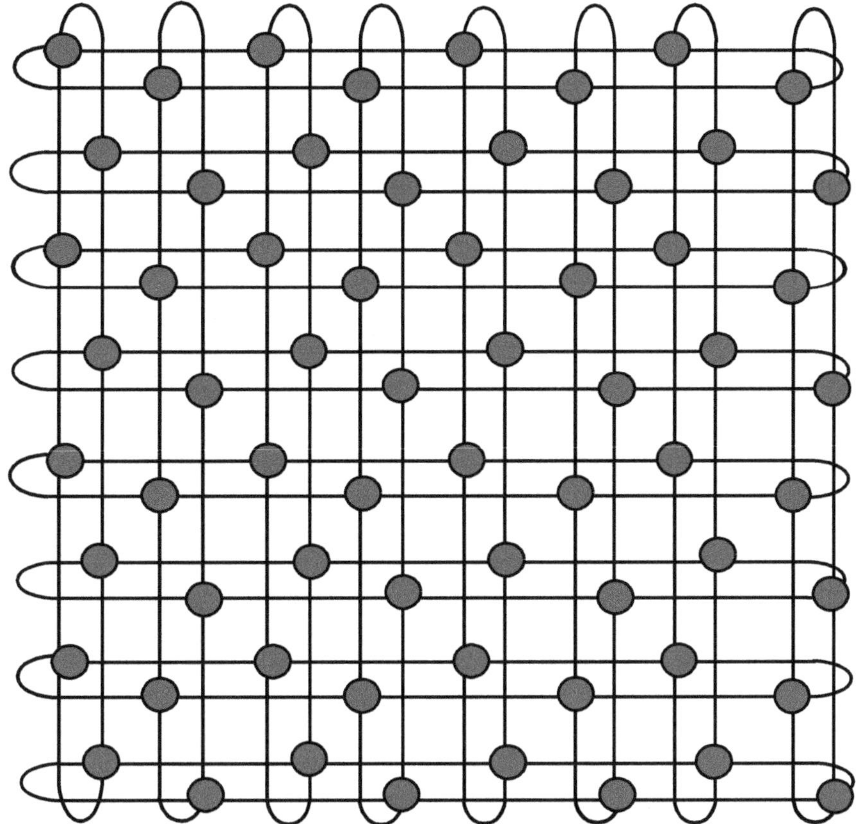

Figure 8.6: The folded torus topology

In Figure 8.8 we show a Clos network. Typical three-layer Clos networks are traditionally described using three parameters: n, m, and r. The first (leftmost) layer or the ingress layer contains r $[n \times m]$ switches. An $n \times m$ switch has n inputs and m outputs. It implements an all-to-all connection where any input can be connected to any output. However, the caveat is that at any given point in time any output of the switch can be connected to only one input, and any input can be connected to only one output.

In Figure 8.8 we show an example with $n = 4$, $m = 4$, and $r = 3$. The ingress layer accepts the input messages. The messages are then sent to switches in the middle layer. The middle layer contains m $[r \times r]$ switches. Note that there is a pattern in the interconnections. Consider a switch in the ingress layer. It has m outputs. Each of these outputs is connected to a different switch in the middle layer.

Finally, consider the third layer or the egress layer. This consists of r $[m \times n]$ switches. Each of the outputs of a switch in the middle layer is connected to a different switch in the egress layer. The output terminals of the egress layer are the outputs of the entire Clos network.

We thus have a total of nr inputs and nr outputs. Note that any message on any input terminal can be routed to any output terminal in the Clos network. Furthermore, it is possible that the input and output terminals might be connected to the same set of routers. This means that we can have nr routers, where if they need to send a message, they drop a message at the corresponding input terminal of the Clos network. Similarly, we can connect each router to an output terminal of the Clos network. If we connect the routers in this fashion, then the Clos network ensures that we can send a message from any router to any other router. Such a network is known as the folded Clos network.

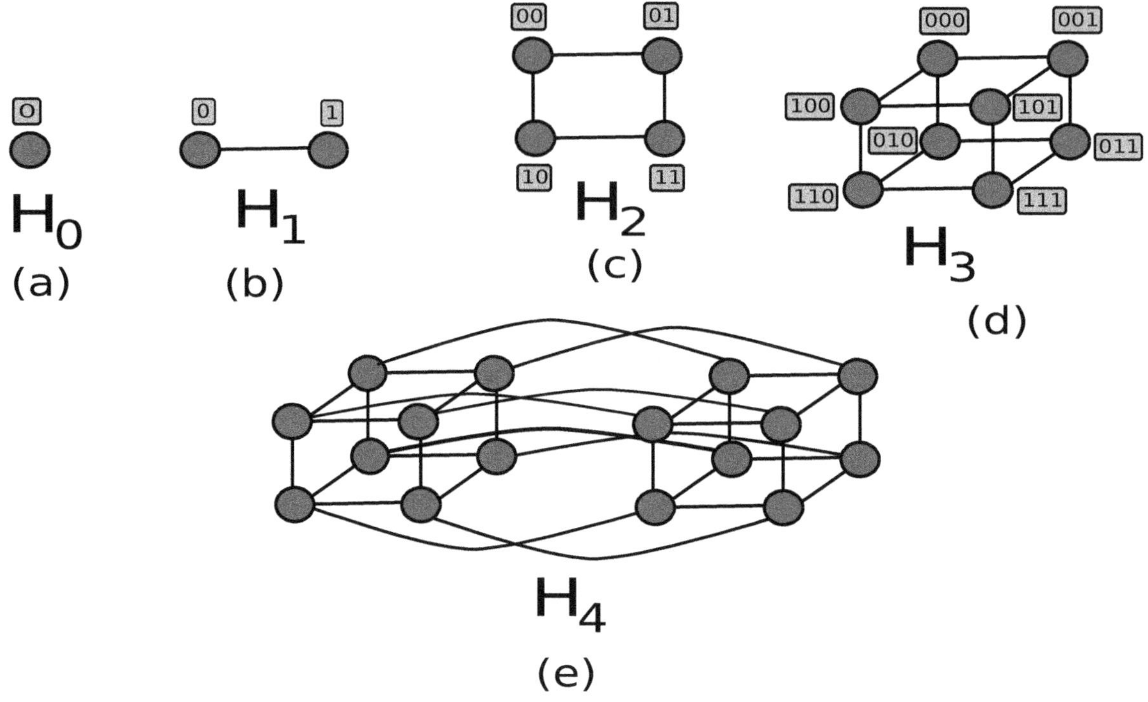

Figure 8.7: The hypercube topology

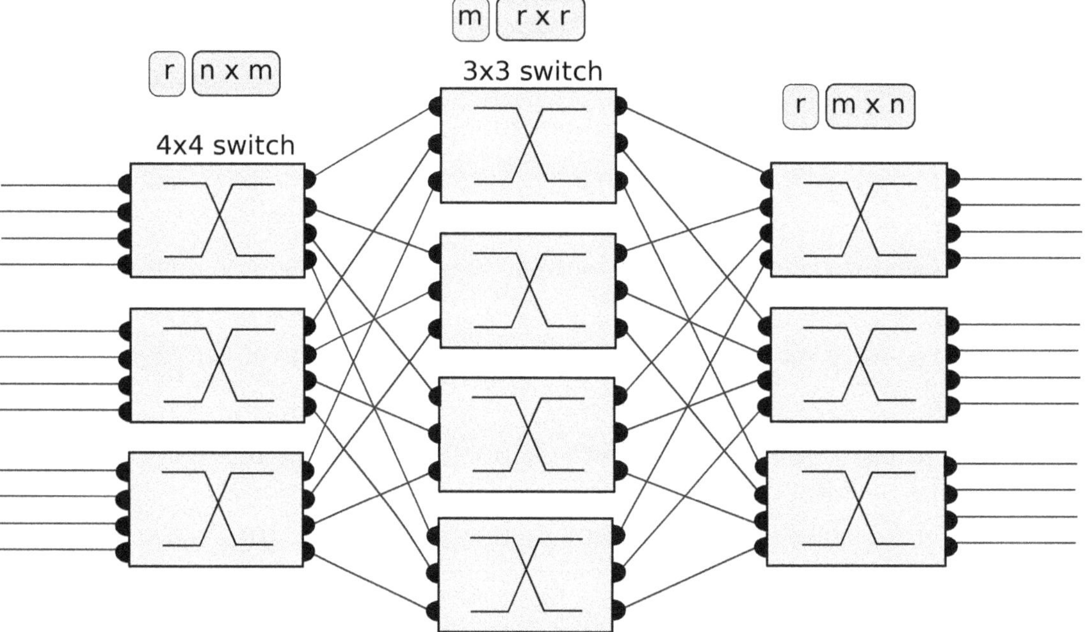

Figure 8.8: The Clos network

Clos networks have some more beautiful properties. Let us quickly list them without going through the proofs. Interested readers can refer to [Clos, 1953].

1. If $m \geq n$, we can always connect an unused ingress terminal with an unused egress terminal by rearranging the rest of the connections. We will not encounter a case where either the new message transfer or any of the existing message transfers have to be terminated because some switches and terminals along the way are fully busy.

2. If $m \geq 2n - 1$, we can always connect an unused ingress terminal with an unused egress terminal to send traffic without rearranging the rest of the connections between the network's input and output terminals.

Butterfly Network

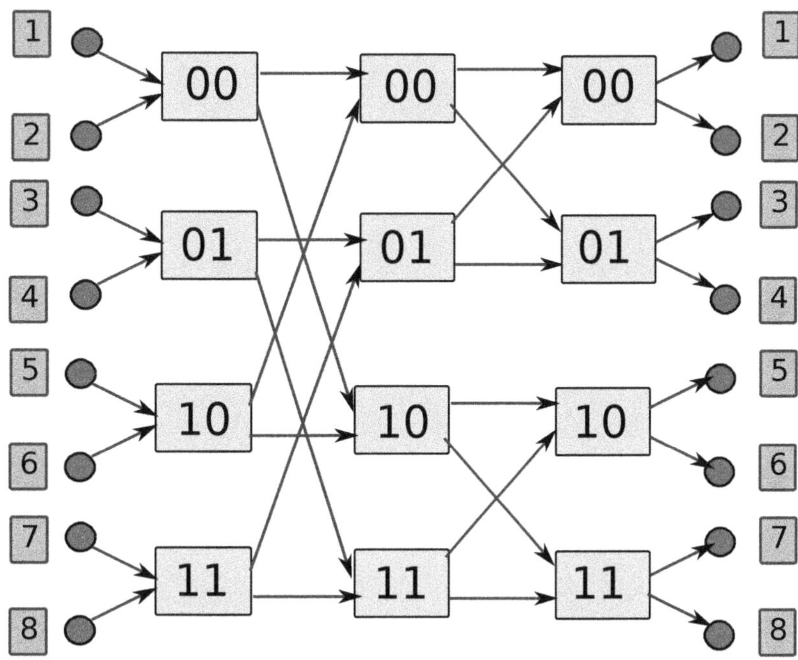

Figure 8.9: The Butterfly network

In the Clos network we have different kinds of switches with different numbers of input and output terminals. Fabricating such heterogeneous structures represents a challenge. Hence, homogeneity is preferred. Variants of the Clos network exist that have multiple intermediate layers with this property. A famous network in this class is the Benes network ($m = n = 2$) that uses only 2×2 switches. Note that in this case we are creating a low-radix network out of a high-radix network.

Let us look at a similar network called a Butterfly network that uses low-radix switches. High performance implementations of Butterfly networks can use high-radix switches; however, they are not covered in this book. Interested readers can refer to [Kim et al., 2007].

The design of a basic Butterfly network is shown in Figure 8.9. The network has N input and N output terminals, and $log_2(N)$ layers of 2×2 switches. Consider the leftmost layer of switches. Each switch has two input terminals, which are connected to two nodes respectively. In our example network, we have 8 nodes. The first layer of switches decide whether the destination lies in the set of first four nodes (1-4) or the set of last four nodes (5-8). The message is routed accordingly. The next layer does another round of filtering. They look at a set of 4 nodes and divide it into two halves. Then the message is routed to the right set of nodes – first half or second half. Finally, the third (rightmost) layer of switches route the message to one of the two destination nodes.

Note that the input and output nodes can be the same. This is similar to the way we connected them in the folded Clos network. Such a topology is also known as a *folded* Butterfly network. Note that as compared to the Clos network, a Butterfly network lacks path diversity. For a given input-output pair of terminals, there is a single path. If we compare this with a torus, then the latter seems to be more efficient. However, let us compare the number of links. For a torus with N nodes we have $2N$ links. However, for a Butterfly network with N nodes we have $(N + Nlog_2(N))$ links: we have $log_2(N)$ levels with $N/2$ switches each. Given that we have more links for large N, the effects of congestion are reduced. In addition, the diameter is $log_2(N) + 1$, which is significantly better than the diameter in tori[1], which is roughly N.

8.2 Message Transmission

Let us look at methods to send messages in a network from a given source to a given destination. To keep the description simple, we shall assume a mesh based topology in this section. The results are generic and hold for all kinds of topologies.

8.2.1 Basic Concepts

Let us first describe some basic concepts. Assume that the sender can send any number of bytes to the receiver. A sequence of bytes that forms one logical unit is called a *message*. Higher protocol layers operate exclusively at the level of messages.

However, at the level of the NoC, a single message might be too big to handle in entirety. We thus divide it into a set of fixed size *packets*. For the purpose of transmission in an NoC, a packet is a consolidated unit. This means that all the bits in the packet flow along the same path; we do not send different parts of a packet along different routes. Moreover, note that in general in an on-chip network we do not drop packets, as we do in conventional networks. However, there are some rare examples of on-chip networks where packets are occasionally dropped and then we have two options: either we retransmit the packet or the entire message.

The size of packets also can be fairly large for on-chip networks. It is thus necessary to break a packet into units of information that the routers can treat as a basic unit for the purpose of storage and transmission. We thus divide a packet into several flow control digits, referred to as *flits*. As of 2020, most on-chip networks use 8 or 16-byte flits. A packet can be 64 to 128 bytes long; it thus contains a sequence of flits. The first flit in the packet is known as the *head flit*. Subsequently, we have a sequence of *body flits*, and the last flit in the packet is known as the *tail flit*. The head flit typically contains the id of the destination router, details of the route (if it has been precomputed), and other information of interest that we shall describe in subsequent sections. The routers analyse the contents of the head flit and compute the routing information. The subsequent body and tail flits follow the same route as the head flit. It is never the case that different flits of the same packet are sent along different routes. This will make the design of the entire on-chip network very complex and this level of complexity is not desirable from the point of view of power consumption. Additionally, the area overhead of routers will become prohibitive because we need to keep track of a lot of additional state.

The flits are physically sent on copper wires that connect two routers. To send a 64-bit flit, we would ideally like to have 64 parallel copper wires between the two routers. However, this is often not desirable with long high-speed links. This is because it is hard to ensure that electrical signals are synchronised across the wires. It is possible that all the signals may not arrive at the same time at the receiver. There

---

[1]plural of torus

might be tiny mismatches in the lengths of the wires, or due to ageing, the RC delays of the wires might change over time. We need circuits to compensate for this drift in timing. The typical approach that is used is that the data transmission is synchronised with respect to a clock signal. The maximum possible delay across wires is thus limited to some fraction of the clock cycle period. With wider links it becomes more difficult to design such circuits. Hence, the only option that remains is to reduce the bandwidth and the transmission rate. This is why most long, high-speed links are serial nowadays: send signals using a single wire.

However, these links are typically several centimetres long, whereas we are talking of links that are limited to a few hundred microns long. In this case, we can afford a limited-width parallel link. For example, we can have a link with 16 or 32 wires. Let's say that we have 32 wires, and the flit size is 8 bytes (= 64 bits). In this case, we need to make two successive transfers: 32 bits each. Each such group of 32 bits is known as a *phit* (physical digit). Therefore, in this case a flit consists of 2 phits. Note that it is necessary to transmit all the phits in a flit consecutively on the link. A flit cannot be split across routers. The routers do not recognise phits. They expect full flits to be transmitted and received. They have small circuits that do the job of breaking down flits into phits, and reconstructing them.

Definition 53

Message *A message is a stream of bytes that makes sense at the level of the application.*

Packet *A message is divided into a sequence of packets where the NoC treats a packet as a consolidated unit. All the bytes in the packet follow the same path.*

Flits *Packets are further subdivided into flits of the same size. All the flits in the packet follow the same route. Additionally, each router has buffers, where each entry can store a single flit.*

Phits *Due to limitations in the signalling technology, it is not possible to have very wide links between two neighbouring routers. We thus have narrow links and send a flit over multiple clock cycles. We thus divide a flit into multiple phits, where a phit (physical digit) represents the set of bits that are sent in a single clock cycle.*

Let us summarise.

Way Point 9

1. *We have discussed messages, packets, flits, and phits. They need to be sent from a sender to a destination through a sequence of routers.*

2. *Each router needs to read in the message, a flit at a time, temporarily store the flits, and forward them on its outgoing links to a neighbouring router.*

Basics of Flow Control

To send a message from a source to a destination, it is necessary to reserve resources along the way. These resources are buffer space in the routers, and the permission to transmit along the links that comprise the path from the source node to the destination node. Note that in this section we shall use the terms *node* and *router* interchangeably to denote a network entity that can send, receive, and forward flits.

There is thus a need to setup a path between the source and the destination, which basically involves allocating and deallocating buffer space on the way. There are three ways that this can be done. We can either do it at the granularity of the entire message, or at the granularity of a packet, or at the level of flits. This process is known as *flow control*.

Definition 54

Management of the flow of flits between nodes in an NoC is known as flow control. It often deals with reserving buffer space in routers and reserving the right to transmit flits.

8.2.2   Flow Control across a Single Link

Let us first consider a very simple scenario, which is sending a message across a link from router A to router B. We can reserve space in B at several levels: at the level of a full message, at the level of packets, or at the level of flits. These will lead to different flow control schemes in an NoC, which differ significantly. However, for sending messages along a single link, the schemes are not very different. At the abstract level, they use the same set of mechanisms. Let us describe a basic problem in this space. Without loss of generality, let us assume that we are performing flow control at the level of flits. At this point, let us introduce the term *channel*, which is defined as a unidirectional link between two adjoining nodes in an NoC. Typically, the term *link* refers to a physical connection, and the term *channel* refers to a logical connection. The connotation will be clear from the usage.

Consider a situation in which we need to send 20 flits from A to B. It is possible that B has buffer space for only 10 flits. When the buffers fill up, it is necessary for A to stop sending flits. Since we are not allowed to drop flits, we need to ensure that every single flit is buffered in the downstream router: B in this case. This implies that before we send a flit, we need to ensure that we have space for it in the downstream router B. This forms the basis of flow control at the level of a single link. The mechanisms are similar for flow control at the level of flits, packets, and messages.

Let us outline the basic structure of a solution. A needs to have a precise idea of the buffer space in B. It can underestimate, however it cannot overestimate. This means that if B has 4 free buffers, then A can estimate that B has 2 free buffers. In this case, A will only send 2 flits. It can send 2 more flits, yet it will not send because it will think that B will run out of buffer space. This will hurt performance. The reverse case, which is when A assumes that B has 5 free buffers might lead to situations where we need to drop a flit.

In a conventional network such as the internet, packets are dropped, and there are retransmissions. However, we cannot afford this luxury at the level of an on-chip NoC, where power and performance are very critical issues. Our protocols also need to be rather simple.

Credit based Flow Control

The simplest approach is credit based flow control, where A maintains an estimate of the number of free buffers at B. This estimate is known as the *credit*. When B frees a buffer, it sends a message to A, and A increments its credit. Subsequently, A can send more flits to B. The exact mechanism is as follows.

Every router has a module to process credits. It maintains the number of credits for each outgoing link. Initially the number of credits is equal to the number of buffers in the downstream router, B. Subsequently, when A sends a flit, it decrements its credit count. Now if we look at B, it sends a message to increment the credit count to A whenever it frees a buffer for the $A \rightarrow B$ link. If A runs out of credits, then it stops sending messages. Here, the overhead is the number of additional credit messages: one per freed buffer. Figure 8.10 shows an example of flow control using credits.

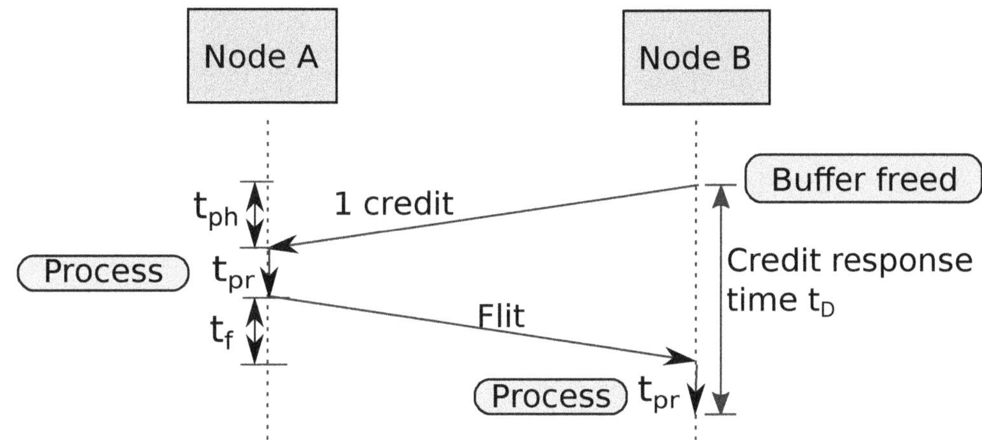

Figure 8.10: Credit based flow control

Let us mathematically analyse this protocol. Let the time it takes a single phit to traverse the link be t_{ph} cycles. This means that to send a credit message (1 phit) it will take t_{ph} cycles. Subsequently, this needs to be processed. Let us assume that the time it takes to process any message (single-phit or multi-flit) be t_{pr} cycles, and the time it takes to send a flit be t_f cycles. Thus the credit round trip delay, t_D (see Figure 8.10), is given as follows:

$$t_D = (t_{ph} + t_{pr}) + (t_f + t_{pr}) = t_{ph} + t_f + 2t_{pr} \tag{8.2}$$

The unit of t_D is in cycles. Typically, the cores and the router share the same clock. However, if this is not the case, let "cycles" in this case mean router cycles. We would ideally want t_D to be zero, which means that the moment a buffer is free, it is immediately filled up. However, because of signal propagation delays, this will not be the case.

Let us look at t_D from B's point of view. In this period, it could have received a maximum of t_D/t_f flits from A subject to the availability of buffer space. The denominator is t_f because A takes t_f cycles to send a single flit. Assume that when a credit was sent, at least t_D/t_f buffers were free. In this case, A would not have stalled even if it sent a phit every cycle. However, if less than t_D/t_f buffers were free, then there is a possibility of a stall on A's side. It is possible that it would run out of credits and not be able to send phits leading to idle cycles.

We can view this result slightly differently as well. Assume that B is able to send its flits as soon as possible. Whenever it sends a flit, it also sends the corresponding credit message to A. In such a situation, if we want A to never stall, then it means that A should always have enough credits available. After it sends a message, its credit count gets decremented. We never want this credit count to become zero. If its starting count is t_D/t_f, then in this setting its credits will never become zero because of the following reason. If it sends a flit at cycle 0, then it will reach B, t_f cycles later, B will process it and send the flit downstream (as per our assumption), and send a credit back to A. This entire process will take t_D cycles. Given that credits come back to A after t_D cycles, if it has t_D/t_f starting credits then it will never run out of them. This would also mean that B needs to have at least t_D/t_f buffers.

On-Off Flow Control

The main disadvantage of credit based flow control is that we need to send a message when every buffer is freed. This increases the load on the NoC, and it is also not power efficient. To increase the power efficiency we need to send messages sparingly. One trivial approach is to send a message once for every k buffers freed ($k > 1$). This will decrease the number of messages; however, it will make A less responsive.

On these lines, let us propose a protocol called on-off flow control, where we propose a set of rules that A can use to decide whether it can send a flit to B. Let us create two thresholds: N_{ON} (on threshold) and N_{OFF} (off threshold). If the number of free buffers in B becomes equal to N_{OFF}, then it sends a message to A to stop sending. Once A receives this message, it stops sending flits. On the flip side, when the number of free buffers becomes equal to N_{ON}, B sends a message to A to start sending flits. Figure 8.11 shows an example of flit transmission using on-off flow control.

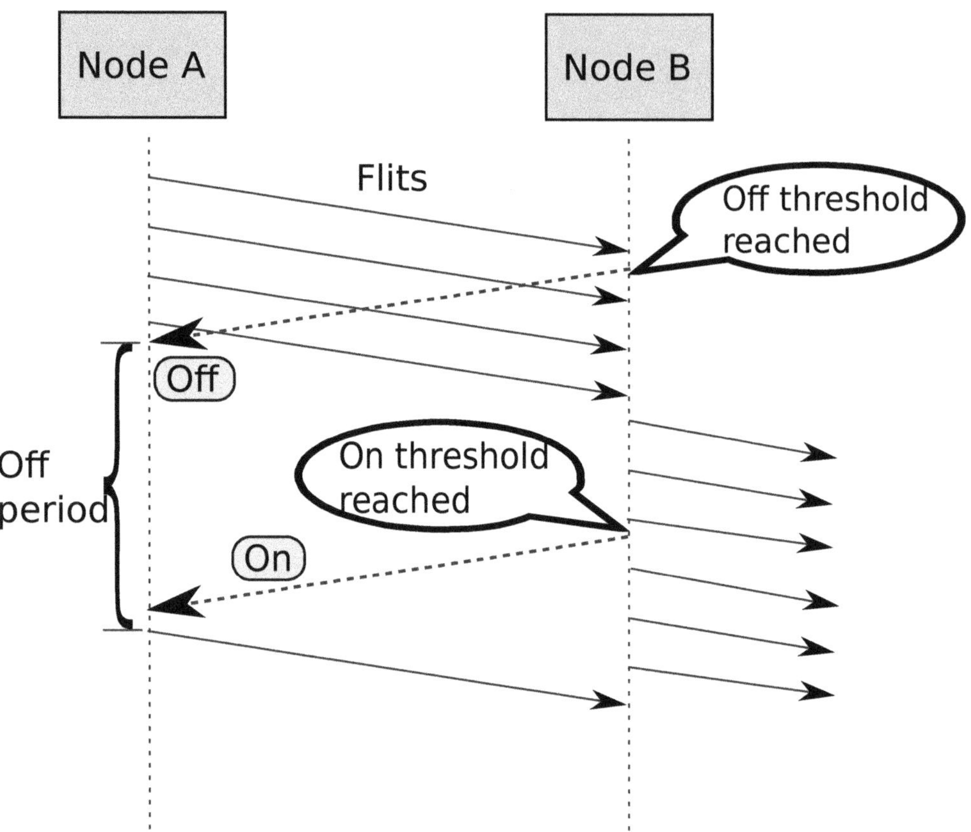

Figure 8.11: On-off flow control

Let us analyse this protocol using the same method and same terminology that we used for credit based flow control. In this case, we need to define two thresholds: N_{OFF} and N_{ON}. Let us first look at N_{OFF}, which is one less than the minimum number of free buffers that B needs to have for A to be allowed to transmit. Note that the key constraint is that we are never allowed to drop a packet.

Assume that B sends an *off* message at time t (assume it is a single phit). It takes an additional $t_{ph} + t_{pr}$ cycles for the *off* message to reach A and get processed. At that point, A stops sending new flits. However, we need to ensure that we do not run out of buffers at B because of flits in flight – flits sent by A before it was asked to turn itself off. The number of messages in flight can be estimated as follows.

B sent the *off* message at time t. The earliest that the next flit can arrive is in the next cycle. It must have been sent at time $t + 1 - t_f - t_{pr}$.

Moreover, the time at which the *off* message reaches A is $t + t_{ph} + t_{pr}$. Let us now focus on the time interval $[t + 1 - t_f - t_{pr}, t + t_{ph} + t_{pr}]$. During this time interval, A can send flits to B. These flits will be received by B after it has sent the *off* message. It needs to have enough buffers to store them. So how many buffers do we need?

If you haven't noticed it yet, the duration of the time interval is $t_f + t_{ph} + 2t_{pr}$. We have seen this expression before. It is the expression for t_D (see Equation 8.2). This means that during this period, when A has not seen the *off* message, it can send t_D/t_f flits. All of them have to be buffered at B because we are not allowed to drop a flit. The N_{OFF} threshold thus needs to be at least t_D/t_f.

$$N_{OFF} \geq \frac{t_D}{t_f} \tag{8.3}$$

Let us now find N_{ON}, which is the threshold at which B can allow A to send messages. The reason that B sometimes does not allow A to send messages is because it may run out of buffers. Once its buffers start clearing up, it can get in more flits. Let us assume that all the flits in the buffers for channel $A \rightarrow B$ need to go from B to C. If the $B \rightarrow C$ channel is blocked, then a back pressure will be exerted on the channel $A \rightarrow B$. Once, B gets an *on* message from C, it can start sending its flits to C. Now, when should it send an *on* message to A?

There is clearly no hard and fast rule. This is an engineering decision and needs to be taken based on simulation results. However, let us look at some general principles. We want to reduce the number of *on* and *off* messages. Hence, we would like to set $N_{ON} > N_{OFF}$ such that if we are sending flits, we keep on sending them for some time. We do not want A to frequently turn off and turn on – this is wasteful in terms of messages and power consumption.

We thus have:

$$N_{ON} > N_{OFF} \tag{8.4}$$

Regarding the value of N_{ON}, let us see what happens if is equal to $N_{OFF} + 1$. In this case, B sends an *on* message, and when A processes it, it dispatches a flit. If by the time B receives the flit it has freed some more buffers, then there is no problem. Otherwise, if no buffers are freed, then the number of free buffers will become equal to N_{OFF}, and an *off* message has to be sent. All the in-flight flits will take up buffers at B. Subsequently, when the number of free buffers rises beyond N_{ON}, A can start sending flits again.

If we do not want the cycle to repeat too frequently, we need to set a large value of N_{ON} such that if A is transmitting flits, it will continue to do so for a longer duration. This will reduce the number of *on* and *off* messages. The exact number needs to be determined after conducting exhaustive simulations. However, this protocol places a lower bound on the total number of buffers at B. Let us elaborate.

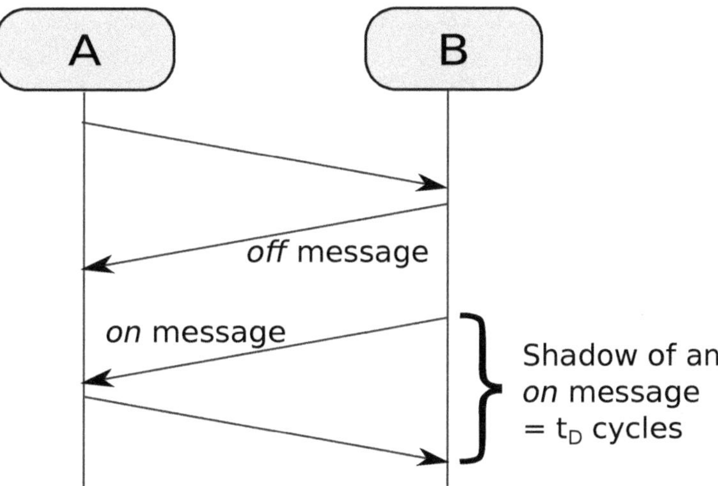

Figure 8.12: The shadow of an *on* message

Consider the communication shown in Figure 8.12. Let us assume that N_{ON} is equal to the total number of buffers at B. If B has N buffers, we are assuming that $N = N_{ON}$. Additionally, let the interval between sending an *on* message and receiving a flit because of it, be referred to as *the shadow of the on message*. Since N_{ON} is assumed to be equal to the total number of buffers, which means that we send an *on* message when all the buffers are free, B will be idle in the shadow of the *on* message. It will not have any flits to send to any downstream router. This is a suboptimal situation.

To ensure that B is able to utilise the shadow of the *on* message to transmit flits to other downstream routers, we need to set $N > N_{ON}$. In this case, B will have $N - N_{ON}$ flits with it when it sends the *on* message. Let us see what happens if $N - N_{ON} \geq t_D/t_f$. Note that the shadow of the *on* message is t_D units of time. During this period, t_D/t_f flits can be transmitted by B to downstream routers. Hence, if $N - N_{ON} \geq t_D/t_f$, it means that B can fully utilise the shadow of the *on* messages to send flits to downstream routers.

Now let us collate all our equations.

$$N \geq N_{ON} + \frac{t_D}{t_f} > N_{OFF} + \frac{t_D}{t_f} \geq \frac{t_D}{t_f} + \frac{t_D}{t_f} = 2\frac{t_D}{t_f} \tag{8.5}$$

We thus have

$$N > 2\frac{t_D}{t_f} \tag{8.6}$$

Thus, the total number of buffers, N, needs to be at least $2t_D/t_f + 1$. This will ensure that in the shadow of an *on* message, B is not idle.

8.2.3 Message Based Flow Control

The classic approach to do this is to use a method called circuit switching that has been around since a long time. Recall the early days of telephony[2]. In those days, to place a call from one number to another it was necessary to first reserve the entire route. The person trying to make the call used to first call the operator. Then the operator used to manually compute the route, call other operators and reserve the lines for the entire route. Once the route was reserved, the operator would call the person trying to make the call, and then the call would be connected. This entire procedure took minutes to hours. All of us should thank modern technology that has made life so much better!

We can do something very similar in NoCs. We can reserve the entire path from the source to the destination. In this case, the router at the source can compute the entire path, and reserve buffer space as well as the right to transmit along all the routers on the way. Once the circuit (path from the source to the destination) has been reserved, the entire message can be sent. This method is known as *circuit switching* because we are reserving the full path (the full circuit).

Let us elaborate. After computing the route we send a packet, known as a *probe packet* along the circuit. We always reserve some amount of bandwidth for probe packets. The probe packet sets up the path (or the route). It tells all the routers along the way that they should expect a given message transmission for which they need to have enough free buffers available as well as provide access to send the flits along the desired outgoing links. Once the probe packet reaches the destination, the process of setting up the path is complete. Then the destination sends an acknowledgement to the source indicating that the path has been set up. After the source receives the acknowledgement, it can start sending the message. After it has sent the message, it needs to tear down the path. An easy way of doing this is to set an additional bit in the last flit of the message indicating that it is the last flit in the message. Routers on the way can see this bit and dismantle the path that has been set up.

This is by itself a fairly simple mechanism. However, it is associated with large overheads in terms of the path setup delay. Let us derive the time it takes for transmitting the entire message, assuming

---

[2]Those who were too young those days can always look up the internet to find out how the good old days used to be!

best case conditions. We shall assume in the subsequent discussion and even in later protocols that one message consists of just one packet. The reason is that for long messages, the total time is simply the ratio of the length of the message and the bandwidth of the link regardless of the protocol (subject to reasonable assumptions). The differences between the protocols arise when we consider the time associated with sending the first packet. Furthermore, given that most message transfers in practical NoCs are single packets that contain a few flits, this is a valid assumption.

Let the length of a packet be L flits, and the bandwidth of a link be B flits per cycle. Furthermore, let the destination be K hops away and let it take 1 cycle to traverse each hop. The total time thus required for the probe packet to reach the destination, and for the acknowledgement to come back is $2K$ cycles. In this case, we are assuming that the probe packet is 1 flit (1 cycle per hop), and the acknowledgement is sent instantaneously. Once the acknowledgement reaches the source, the data transmission starts. To put the last byte on the first link, it takes L/B (size of the packet divided by the bandwidth) cycles. Assume for the sake of simplicity that B divides L and $B \geq 1$.

Subsequently, we require $K - 1$ cycles for the last byte to reach the destination node. We subtract 1 from K because we are already accounting for its transmission time in the expression L/B. The total time thus required is $3K + L/B - 1$ cycles. Let us visualise the process of transmitting the message in Figure 8.13. This diagram is known as a space-time diagram. The columns represent cycles, and the rows represent hops. Such diagrams are used to visualise the actions of a given flow control or message transmission protocol. We shall find them to be very useful while describing different flow control mechanisms.

Before proceeding further, let us differentiate between the terms: *throughput* and *bandwidth*. They are often confused; however, they do not mean the same. Refer to Definition 55.

Definition 55

- *The* bandwidth *is defined as the largest possible rate (measured as bytes per unit time) at which we can send data through a channel or between two points in a network.*

- *On the other hand, the* throughput *is defined as the data rate that we practically observe in a given setting across a channel, or between two nodes in a network. The throughput is always less than or equal to the bandwidth. It is limited by congestion, nuances of the transmission protocol, errors, and any other phenomenon that retards the flow of flits.*

Now, let us consider the average case. We might require much more time. This is because the probe packet might get stuck at any point. In this case, we need to wait. The same can happen to the acknowledgement as well. Moreover, at any point of time while propagating the probe packet, we might run out of buffer space in routers along the way. We need to wait till buffer space is created.

While transmitting the message, we need to pretty much reserve buffer space in routers for at least an entire packet along the entire path. This is unnecessarily conservative. We are essentially reserving the routers for more time than is actually required. The duration of time from the point of reserving buffer space in a router till the point at which the resources in the router are released is not characterised by continuous data transmission. We need to wait for the acknowledgement to reach the source, data transmission to begin, and reach the routers on the way. During this time, it would have been very much possible to send other messages. However, in this protocol, we refrained from doing so. This reduced the net throughput of the system.

In addition, freezing a route in advance is not always a good idea. It is possible that there might be many more messages that might want to use parts of the route. They will not be able to traverse the route till it is released.

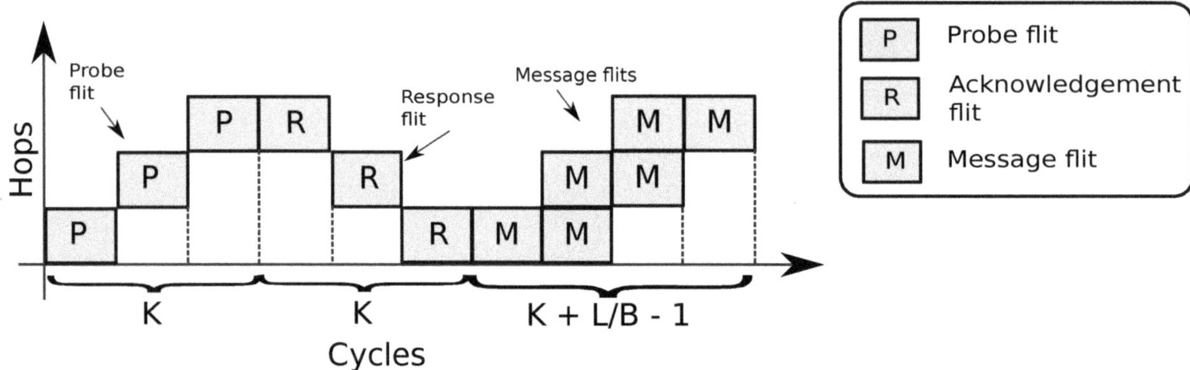

Figure 8.13: Space-time diagram for circuit switching. $K = 3$ cycles, $L = 2$ flits, $B = 1$ flit/cycle. Assume each packet contains a single flit. The y-axis is the hop count (measured from the source).

Now that we have discussed the negative aspects of the protocol, let us briefly enumerate its advantages. Any kind of a circuit switching protocol is always very simple, and works well in a scenario with less contention. They can also be implemented and verified easily. To understand the performance advantages, let us consider the latency once again. We had computed it to be $3K + L/B - 1$ cycles. If L/B is significantly greater than K, we can assume that the net latency is equal to L/B cycles. This means that if we need to send a very long message, the additional timing overhead of the probe packet, and the acknowledgement appear to be negligible. Since we have reserved the full path, the entire message can be sent without any subsequent delays. One more advantage of this system is that we can use routers with very few buffers that are just needed to hold in-transit regular flits and probe/acknowledgement flits. In fact, such schemes can also be used with bufferless router designs. Once a path is setup, we do not need any long term packet storage structures in the routers. The routers just need to read data from the input ports, and write the data out at the relevant output ports. They need not buffer the data beyond the flits that are either not fully read or fully written. This will make our routers smaller, and more power efficient.

To conclude, circuit switching is simple, straight forward, yet is not efficient. It is suited for scenarios that have less contention in the network and very long message lengths.

8.2.4 Packet Based Flow Control: Store and Forward (SAF)

Instead of doing flow control at the level of messages, let us do it at the level of packets. As we shall see, this will give us far more flexibility in scheduling the reservation of resources, and will increase the net message transfer bandwidth among nodes in a chip.

In this case, we do not reserve a full path for a message. Instead, we transmit individual packets separately. There are different mechanisms for choosing the path (route) that each packet will take. This can be done either statically or dynamically. We shall study routing mechanisms in detail in Section 8.3. However, for all of these mechanisms, we need to ensure that we have enough resources in terms of buffer space along the way. We do not ever want to lose a flit because we were not able to transmit it to the neighbouring node. We assume that each router has several flit buffers. To store an entire packet, we need multiple flit buffers – one per each constituent flit.

This is shown in Figure 8.14, where we show two nodes A and B, and a channel from A to B. Every channel has an associated set of flit buffers at its destination. The $A \rightarrow B$ channel has 4 dedicated flit buffers in node B. Any flit that is transmitted on the channel is first buffered in the channel's flit buffers in B, and then B forwards them to their destination. We can see in the figure that out of the four flit buffers, two are empty, and two are occupied. A channel can be thought of as the combination of a link and a set of flit buffers at the destination node. A point to note is that each set of flit buffers is actually a first-in-first-out queue (FIFO queue). We shall use the term "flit buffers" and "flit queue" interchangeably.

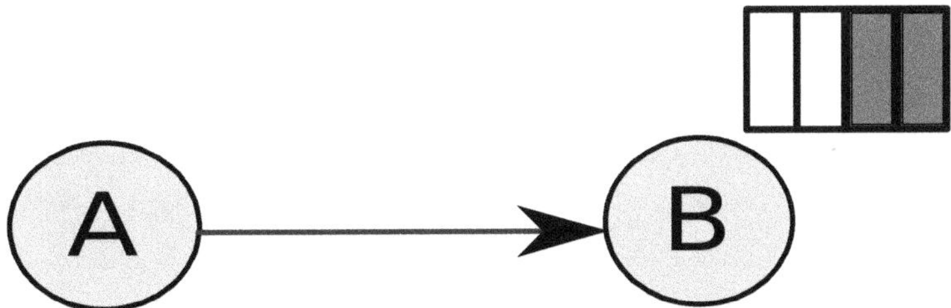

Figure 8.14: A channel and flit buffers

The simplest flow control algorithm for packets is known as the *store and forward* (or SAF) protocol. In this case, we forward the entire packet from one node to the next node on the path. In the next node, we wait for the entire packet to arrive before we transmit the first flit of the packet to the subsequent node on the path. The corresponding space-time diagram is shown in Figure 8.15.

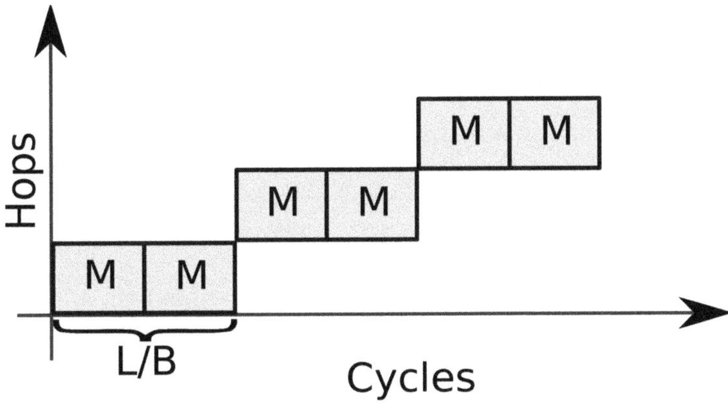

Figure 8.15: Space-time diagram for the store-and-forward approach. $K = 3$ cycles or hops, $L = 2$ flits, $B = 1$ flit/cycle. We are assuming that a packet has 2 flits. The space-time diagram is shown for a single packet.

From Figure 8.15, let us compute the time that is required for a packet transmission. Let us use the same assumptions and the same parameters as we had used for the computation for circuit switched networks. Recall that the three parameters were L (length of the packet) B (bandwidth of a link), and the number of links or hops (K) between the source and the destination. We assume that it takes one cycle to traverse a single hop. As we can observe in Figure 8.15, the total time that is required is $L/B \times K$ cycles. This is because it will take L/B cycles to traverse each hop, and there are K such hops.

Let us compare this formula with what we had derived for a circuit switched network. In that case, the total time taken for a single-packet message transfer was $3K + L/B - 1$ cycles. We can quickly observe that the total time required is much more for our current approach, SAF flow control: the time required is $L/B \times K$ cycles. This is because we wait at every node for the entire packet to arrive, and only then we transmit the packet to the neighbouring node. This is clearly inefficient and negates the benefits accrued out of a packet switching scheme.

8.2.5   Packet Based Flow Control: Virtual Cut Through (VCT)

It is a much better idea to pipeline the packets such that the head flit does not have to wait for the tail flit to arrive at the router. If the head flit can make progress and move to the next node, it should be allowed to do so. This will increase performance because in this case unless there is any congestion, the flits in the packet will never wait. This method of flow control is known as the *virtual cut through* (VCT) approach.

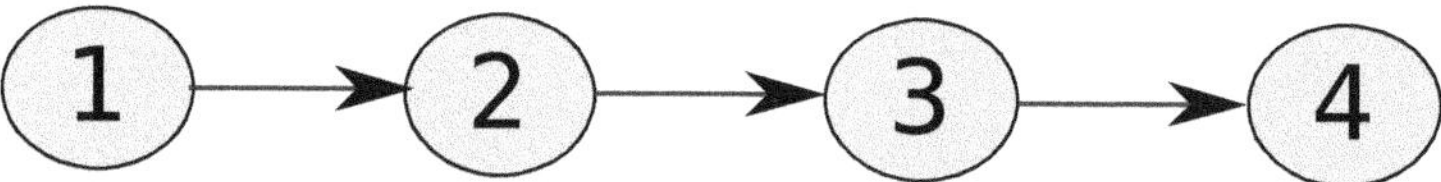

Figure 8.16: Simple network with 4 nodes

Let us show an example of such a transmission in Figure 8.16. Let's say that we need to send a message from node 1 to node 4. At a given instant of time, the flits of the message can be in the nodes 2, 3, and 4. This would not have been possible with the SAF method. However, in this case, it is possible to get more performance because we are transmitting the flits of a packet as soon as possible. Note that there is a caveat: the flow control is still packet based. This means that whenever node A sends the head flit to node B, we need to ensure that in node B, we have enough buffer space to store the entire packet. This is because if the head flit gets blocked at B, the rest of the flits in the packet will continue to arrive, and we need adequate buffer space to store them.

The advantage of this scheme is that we retain the simplicity associated with packet based flow control, and in addition, we do not unnecessarily need to block the head flit if a few of the body flits have still not arrived. Let us draw a sample space-time diagram for message transmission using this kind of flow control. It is shown in Figure 8.17.

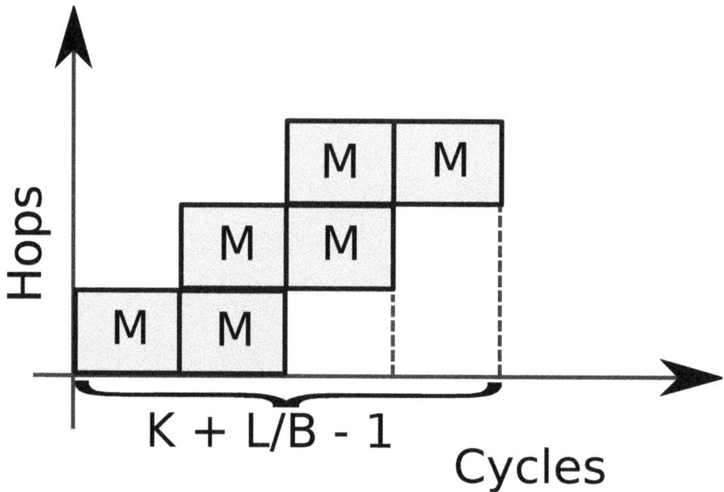

Figure 8.17: Space-time diagram for the VCT approach. $K = 3$ hops or cycles, $L = 2$ flits, $B = 1$ flit/cycle. A packet has 2 flits.

The total time required to send a packet that is L flits long can be derived from Figure 8.17. It is $L/B + K - 1$ cycles. This is because it will take L/B cycles for the source to transmit the last byte. Subsequently, the last flit needs to travel through $K - 1$ hops to reach the destination. Hence, the total time is equal to $L/B + K - 1$ cycles.

Let us now comment on the relative advantages and disadvantages of this scheme. The advantage is that it is the fastest scheme that we have seen up till now (refer to Table 8.1). We observe that VCT is clearly the fastest. For large messages, the time it takes to transmit a message with VCT is similar to the time it takes with circuit switching because $L/B \gg K$. However, circuit switching has other problems, notably the difficulty in reserving resources along a path, and also the fact that it has the potential to keep large parts of the network idle.

Scheme	Time (cycles)
Circuit switching	$3K + L/B - 1$
Store and forward (SAF)	$K \times L/B$
Virtual cut through (VCT)	$K + L/B - 1$

Table 8.1: Single-packet message transmission times using different schemes (assuming no congestion)

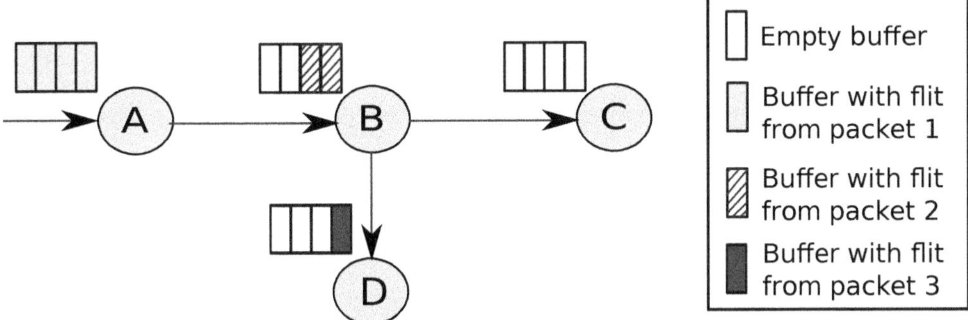

Figure 8.18: Stalls in the VCT scheme

The disadvantages of flow control at the level of packets are several. The biggest disadvantage is that we need to reserve space at the granularity of packets. For example, consider the case where a packet consists of 4 flits. If we have buffer space in the next router for only 3 flits, then we will not be able to transmit any flit in the packet. This means that we will have to wait till one more flit buffer in the next router on the path is free. This is a waste of time because we could have transmitted flits to the next router, and it is possible that in the time being another flit buffer in the next router would have been freed.

Let us illustrate this situation with an example shown in Figure 8.18. Here, we want to transmit a 4-flit packet (packet 1) from node A to C. However, in node B, we do not have enough buffer space available for the entire packet. This is because a packet (packet 2) in B needs to be sent to D. It occupies 2 buffers, and 2 buffers are free. Since packet 1 contains 4 flits, and we reserve space for entire packets, the transmission from A to B cannot proceed. We thus have to wait for 2 cycles for both the flits in packet 2 to leave B and get buffered in D. Then only, we can transmit flits from packet 1.

8.2.6   Flit based Flow Control: Wormhole Flow Control

The only way to solve this issue is to go for flit based flow control, where we decide whether to transmit or not at the level of flits. In other words, it is not necessary for subsequent routers on the path to reserve buffer space at the granularity of packets. This definitely will improve performance at the cost of added complexity.

By removing the restriction of reserving space at the level of packets, we can get a higher throughput, and reduce the latency of message transmission. Let us reconsider the example in Figure 8.18, and see what happens if we reserve space at the granularity of flits. This is shown in Figure 8.19. In this figure, we avoid the problems that we had with VCT based flow control. We always transmit a flit to the next router on the path, if it is possible to do so. Recall that with VCT based flow control, we were not able to transmit any flits of packet 1 till all of B's 4 flit buffers were empty. However, in this case, we need not be constrained by this. Figure 8.19 shows the situation, 1 cycle later. We sent one flit of packet 2 from B to D. At the same time, we sent one flit of packet 1 from A to B. As a result, in the flit buffers of B, we have flits from both packets 1 and 2. Henceforth, for the next 3 cycles we can keep sending a flit from A to B, and thus there are no stalls as far as the traffic from A to B is concerned. This assumes that we send the remaining flit of packet 2 from B to D within this period.

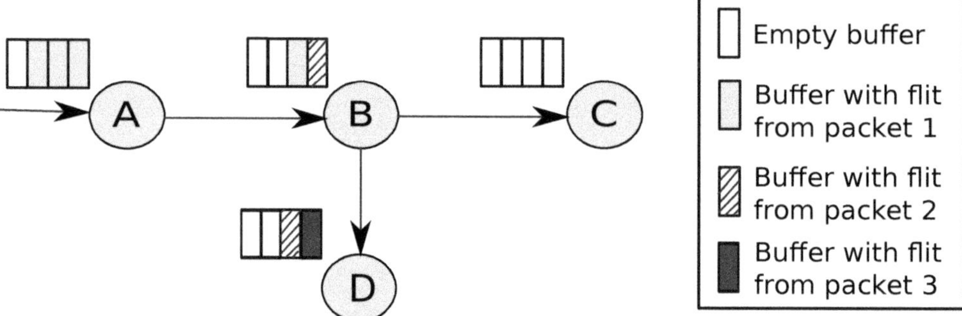

Figure 8.19: Wormhole flow control

The best case time for transmitting a single packet still remains the same: $L/B + K - 1$ cycles. However, in this case, we can deal with congestion much better. If there is congestion and we do not have enough buffer space to store an entire packet, we can still forward some flits of the packet and wait till more space is created. This mechanism is known as *wormhole flow control*. A wormhole is a hole that a worm or an insect makes by burrowing through wood or mud. The way that flits in a packet flow through the network is similar. We can visualise this as a worm moving through its burrow.

Let us quickly go through the advantages of wormhole flow control.

1. Routers can be smaller. They do not need to have space to buffer multiple, large packets. They can have less storage space, and fewer flit buffers.

2. Furthermore, as compared to the SAF and VCT techniques, it propagates flits sooner because of the reduced waiting times.

Wormhole routing is far from perfect. The problems can be illustrated in Figure 8.20. Consider the following scenario. Packet 1 needs to traverse nodes A, B, and C. Simultaneously, packet 2 needs to traverse nodes A, B, and D. Assume that there is congestion at node D, and this stalls packet 2. In wormhole switching we do not allow later flits to overtake earlier flits because they are all in the same queue. Hence, as we see in Figure 8.20, flits from packet 2 block the queue at node B. This blocks the flits of packet 1, even though they can make progress and can be sent to C, whose buffers are empty. For the flit queue at node B, we have head-of-line blocking, also known as HOL blocking, which means that the flit at the head of the queue is blocked, and as a result the rest of the flits in the queue are also blocked, even though some of the flits in the queue could make progress.

Definition 56
Head-of-line (HOL) blocking is a phenomenon in on-chip networks where a sequence of flits is stuck because the flit at the head of the queue cannot move to another node, even though other flits in the body of the queue can traverse their routes.

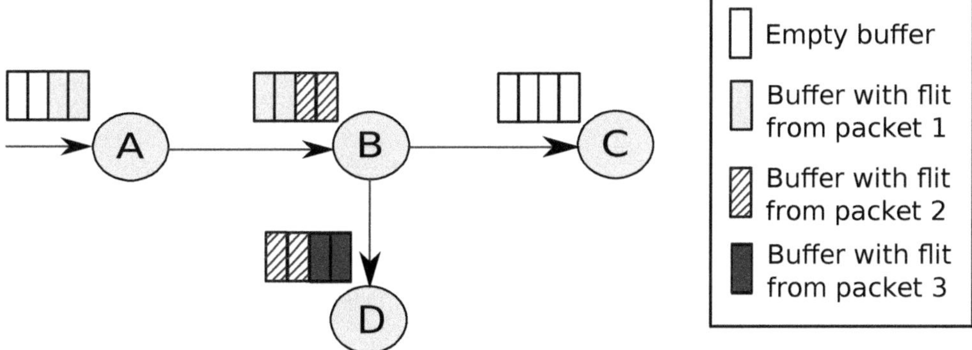

Figure 8.20: Problems with wormhole flow control

8.2.7 Flit based Flow Control: Virtual Channel Based

The main problem with wormhole flow control is HOL blocking. Reconsider the fact that the flits of packet 1 could have made progress in the example shown in Figure 8.20, but they got blocked by flits of packet 2. Let us try to fix this problem by proposing some simple solutions.

What if we had two channels from node A to node B? We could allocate one channel to packet 1 and the other to packet 2. This would solve our problem. Since each channel has its dedicated set of flit buffers, there would be no HOL blocking. Regardless of packet 2, packet 1 could make progress and reach its destination node C. We can do slightly better in terms of reducing the overheads. We can still have two sets of flit buffers, but we can use a single physical link; we can multiplex the transmission of packets 1 and 2 through the link. From a conceptual standpoint, the entire system works as if there are two channels between nodes A and B.

To multiplex a physical channel across different packet transmissions, it is necessary to keep track of the flits that belong to each packet. For example, if we are multiplexing between packets 1 and 2, then we need to have a method of marking the flits that belong to each of these packets. It should never be the case that we are not exactly aware of which packet a given flit belongs to. This means that if N packets are waiting to be transmitted on a channel, we assign a $\log(N)$-bit id to all the flits in each packet. This will help us correctly group the flits into packets. However, just numbering the flits and packets isn't all that is there to physical channel multiplexing. Choosing the flits that need to be transmitted next is equally difficult. Previously, we always sent flits belonging to the same packet, hence, in terms of choice there was nothing to choose. However, now since we have multiple packet flows, we need to make choices. This logic introduces some complexity and increases the overheads.

Virtual Channels

Figure 8.21 summarises our discussion. We started with the picture on the top, where we proposed multiple physical channels: one per packet. The overheads were prohibitive; we then proposed a single channel that is multiplexed between packets. Conceptually, each packet is assigned to a *virtual channel* that has its own set of flit buffers (or a flit queue). *Virtual channels*, abbreviated as VCs, form the core of the routers of modern NoCs.

A virtual channel is like virtual memory in some sense. It provides an abstraction or illusion of a physical channel. As we can see in Figure 8.21, we have multiple flit queues at the input ports of every router. This means that if there is a link from A to B, we have multiple flit queues at B's input ports for the channel $A \rightarrow B$. Each flit queue represents a different virtual channel (VC). When A transmits a flit to B, it indicates the id of the virtual channel that it is using. Assume that we have 4 flit queues at B. Then, when a flit is sent from A to B, we need to mark the id of the VC on the flit. If A says

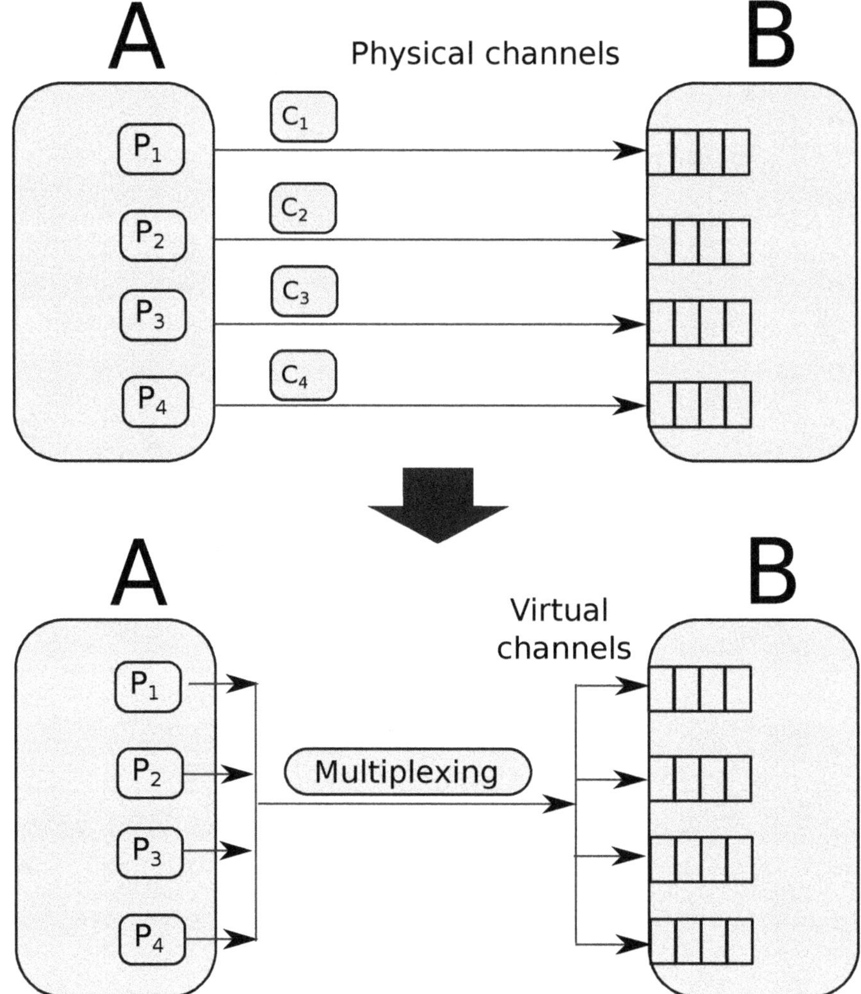

Figure 8.21: Replacing a single physical channel with multiple virtual channels

that a given flit belongs to VC 2, then B reads that information and queues the flit in the second flit queue for the $A \rightarrow B$ channel. Similarly, if A were to stamp a given flit with the VC id 3, then B needs to buffer that flit in the queue corresponding to the third VC of the $A \rightarrow B$ physical channel. Let us look at the other side. Every cycle, A needs to pick a flit from the set of packets that need to be sent to B; it might have multiple choices. It might have let's say four different packets in its buffers ready to be sent to B. In all the previous schemes that we have seen, the only option that A had was to pick a packet, send all of its flits, and then switch to another packet.

However, in this case, it can choose flits from different packets, and send them across different virtual channels to B. It can use different heuristics to decide which flit needs to be sent along the multiplexed physical channel. Again, the best case latency to route a full packet is $L/B + K - 1$ cycles, which is similar to the wormhole and VCT techniques.

However, this method does avoid the HOL blocking problems of wormhole flow control. Let us consider the same example as we had shown in Figure 8.20. Let us show its operation with VCs (virtual channels). We assume that we have two VCs per physical channel. The operation of the protocol is shown in Figure 8.22. We observe that in this case, node B is not a bottleneck any more. It processes

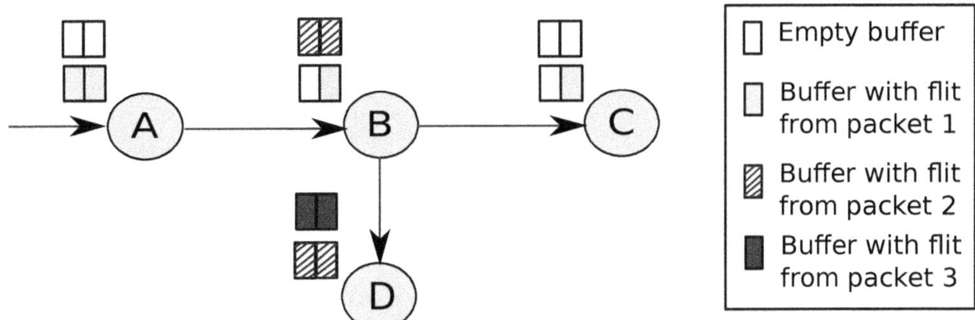

Figure 8.22: Virtual channel based flow control

two separate flows simultaneously: $A \to B \to C$, and $A \to B \to D$. In this case, packet 2 does not block packet 1 because packet 1 is on a different VC. Furthermore, node A multiplexes the $A \to B$ channel between both the packets, and thus flits for both the packets can be sent in the same time window. As a result, flits in packet 1 make progress, even though the flits in packet 2 are blocked at nodes B and D.

This is precisely the greatness of the VC based approach, which is that we do not allow packets taking one route to block packets taking another route. We allot them to separate VCs, and this allows us to ensure that we can move as many flits in the network as possible. This reduces the effects of congestion, decreases the end-to-end latency, and improves the overall throughput. There are a few more advantages of virtual channels such as deadlock avoidance. We shall take a look at such issues in Section 8.3.

8.3   Routing

Let us quickly recapitulate some of the basic concepts.

A network can be visualised as a graph with a set of nodes and links. A *node* is defined as an entity that can transmit and receive messages over the NoC. A node is connected to other nodes as defined by the network topology. For example, in a mesh, a node in the centre of the network is connected to four other nodes via links, where a link is a physical channel via which we send a message. The links are a set of parallel copper wires in conventional NoCs. In a typical scenario, given two nodes in the network, we need to send a message between them. We can have many paths between these nodes. The process of choosing a path between two nodes is known as *routing*. The route (path) between two nodes can either be decided in advance (static), or it can be computed as the message travels from the source to the destination (dynamic routing).

Definition 57

The process of choosing a path between two nodes in an on-chip network is known as routing. *Routing can primarily be of two types: static and dynamic. When the path between two nodes is known in advance, we refer to this method as static routing. In contrast, when the path is not fixed, and is decided as the message is travelling from the source to the destination node, we refer to this method is known as dynamic routing.*

Given a network topology, a source, and a destination, let us understand what are the properties of a good route. Once we know what a good route looks like, we can design a routing algorithm to compute it.

Let us draw an analogy with real life. If we are going from point A to point B in a city, then what are our priorities? We would always like to reach the destination as quickly as possible – in the shortest time. This typically means that we would like to traverse the minimum number of links while going from the source to the destination. The implicit assumption here is that the time it takes to traverse a link is always the same, and we do not spend time doing anything else. This method is known as shortest-path routing, where we would always like to traverse the shortest path with the minimum number of links.

If links have variable delays, then also we can use shortest-path based routing. In this case, we choose the route that requires the least amount of time to traverse. Shortest path based routing is typically a good choice when we are performing static routing. We can use the Djikstra's shortest path algorithm [Cormen et al., 2009] for computing the shortest path between a pair of nodes.

Even though such algorithms seem very simple, straightforward, and optimal; however, in practice they are not very effective. Again let us come back to the analogy of a crowded city. If we always take the shortest route between two points, it might not always take the shortest time. This is because we might enter a crowded intersection, where we might get stranded for a long time. Sometimes it is necessary to take some diversions such that we will reach our destination sooner even though the route might be longer. We thus learn our first lesson: whenever there is congestion in a network, the shortest route in terms of the distance or expected traversal time need not be the shortest in terms of the actual traversal time. In fact, if there is congestion, it is possible that a message might wait at one of the intermediate nodes for a long time until the congestion reduces.

Hence, to reduce the time that it takes to go from point A to point B, the shortest route is not always the best route. We need to take appropriate diversions and go via alternative paths, the same way an experienced cab driver navigates his way through a busy city.

Let us now look at some of the problems that can happen in automated routing algorithms. It should not be the case that we keep going round and round in circles. In this case, we are not waiting at one particular point; however, we are also not making any real progress and reaching the destination. Such a scenario is known as a *livelock*. We need to ensure that livelocks never happen in practice. There is nothing wrong if a message goes round and round in cycles a few times, nevertheless, it should ultimately reach its destination. If we have the possibility of livelocks, then a message can be stuck in the network for an indefinite period. In addition, it is also possible that a given message is not able to make progress because we continuously give preference to other messages. As a result, we are either in a position where we cannot inject it into the network, or the message is stuck at some intermediate node because it is giving way to other messages. Such a scenario is known as *starvation*.

Definition 58 *A* livelock *is defined as a general condition where the state of the system changes continuously; however, there is no long term progress. The classic example of a livelock is two people approaching each other in a corridor. Both of them try to cross each other; however, the moment one person moves to his left, the person on the other end moves to his right (and vice versa). Hence, they continue to face each other, and even though they are moving, they fail to make progress and reach their destinations!*

Starvation is defined as a situation where a message is not able to make progress because routers chose to transmit other messages in its place for an indefinite period. Either it fails to get injected into the network or it gets stuck at an intermediate node because other messages are transmitted in its place.

What else can happen in a city? Let us look at Figure 8.23. It shows an image of typical city traffic where there is a gridlock. If we look closely we can conclude that no car is able to move. Car 1 is trying to go north, it is blocked by car 2 that is trying to go west, which in turn is blocked by car 3 that is trying to go south, which is blocked by car 4 that is trying to go east, and finally this car is blocked by car 1. There is a circular wait where no car is able to make progress. Such a situation in computer

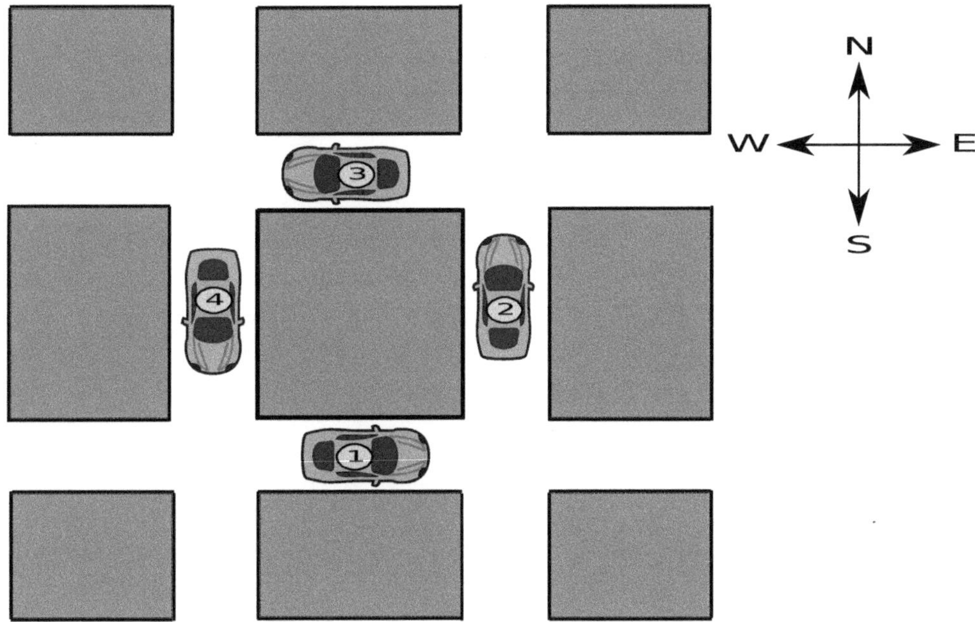

Figure 8.23: Gridlock in a roundabout

science is known as a *deadlock*. It can lead to an infinite wait, and the entire system can stall. In such a situation we have a circular wait, where no car driver is willing to give up. If we have a system where we can fly a helicopter and pick a waiting car and drop it at its destination, then we will never have a deadlock! However, in the normal case, a deadlock is possible, unless one of the cars is willing to back out and try a different route.

Definition 59
A deadlock is defined as a situation where multiple nodes try to send messages, yet none of them are successful because there is a circular wait. Assume that the nodes are numbered $V_1 \ldots V_n$, and node V_i waits on node V_{i+1} for it to free some space such that it can send a message to it $(V_i \rightarrow V_{i+1})$. We also try to send a message from node V_n to V_1. We thus have a circular wait of the form: $V_1 \rightarrow V_2 \ldots \rightarrow V_n \rightarrow V_1$. It is possible to resolve such a deadlock only if we can remove some messages from the nodes and send them along different paths.

We can have a very similar situation while sending messages as shown in Figure 8.24. Note that each node has a finite message storage capacity, and it cannot accept newer messages. Assume that a node can only store one message at a time (for the ease of explanation), and a message is not sent until there is free space available in the destination node. Further, assume that we have four adjoining nodes that have one message each and they want to move in the directions as shown in the figure. It is clear that there is a deadlock situation because the message at node A cannot move to node B because node B does not have the space to store it. For the same reason, the message at node B cannot move to node C. We have a circular wait, and since no message can be dropped, we have a deadlock. Such kind of deadlocks have to be avoided at all costs.

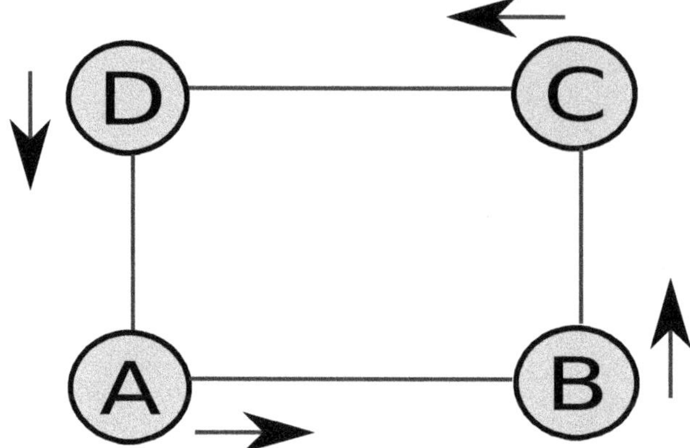

Figure 8.24: A deadlock in a 4-node system

Way Point 10

- *Our main aim while trying to route a message between two points of the NoC is that we want the message to reach in the shortest possible time. Often we would like to maximise the throughput of the network, which means that we should be able to transport the maximum number of bytes per unit time between all pairs of transmitting sources and destinations.*

- *If there is no congestion in the network, then the shortest path between two nodes is also the path that takes the least amount of time. However, if we have congestion at the nodes, then the problem becomes complicated. We need to take the network congestion into account, and this creates the need to often take longer paths in terms of the number of links traversed.*

- *In all cases, we would like to avoid starvation, livelocks and deadlocks. If routers do not transmit a flit yet continue to transmit other flits in its place for an indefinite period, then this condition is known as* starvation. *In contrast, a livelock is a situation where flits move through the network; however, they move around in circles and do not reach the destination in a finite amount of time. Whereas, a deadlock refers to a situation where in a set of nodes, we have flits that are stuck and cannot make any progress. This typically happens when we do not have enough storage (buffer) space available at the nodes and we have a circular wait.*

8.3.1 Handling Starvation and Livelocks

Let us look at avoiding and recovering from starvation and livelocks. This is far simpler than dealing with deadlocks.

For avoiding starvation, we need to have fair routers that do not hold a set of flits for an indefinite duration while transmitting other flits. They need to have a priority scheme, where they transmit flits in a fair manner. We shall discuss such schemes when we discuss the design of routers in Section 8.4.

Handling livelocks is also easy. We can take inspiration from traditional computer networks. We add a *hop count* field with the head flit of each packet. As the head flit traverses each router, we increment the hop count. We can define a threshold for the hop count, which can be a function of the shortest distance between the source and the destination. For example, if the length of the shortest path between the source and the destination is 6 hops, we can set the threshold to be 12 hops. After we have crossed the threshold, we can instruct the routers along the way to only route the message along the shortest path to the destination. They are not allowed to *send* the packet along other paths. Another variation of this approach is to give more priority to packets with a higher hop count in routers. This will ensure that the probability that they will take the shortest path to the destination increases over time.

8.3.2 Deadlocks in Routing Algorithms

Before we look at routing algorithms in depth, it is important to understand the notion of deadlocks in more detail. This is because avoiding deadlocks will be one of our primary objectives while designing routing algorithms. We shall see that taking care of livelocks and starvation is relatively easier. However, designing protocols that are provably deadlock-free is difficult.

A *deadlock* is defined as a situation where we have a set of flits that are not able to make progress because of a circular wait. This means that we are trying to send a flit on a given channel, that channel is not free, the flit blocking that channel is not able to make forward progress, and so on.

Dependence Graphs

Let us explain the notion of deadlocks by developing a set of theoretical tools. Consider a system of four nodes as shown in Figure 8.25. Assume we have a single virtual channel (VC) per physical channel. Here, packet P_1 at node A is trying to use channels 1 and 2, P_2 at node B is trying to use channels 2 and 3, P_3 at C is trying to use channels 3 and 4, and P_4 at D is trying to use channels 4 and 1. Assume that at a given point of time P_1 holds channel 1, P_2 holds channel 2, P_3 holds channel 3, and P_4 holds channel 4. If a packet occupies at least one flit buffer of a channel, it is said to *hold* it. There is a circular wait here if we assume that we do not have enough buffer space for even transmitting a single flit. As a result, none of the packets will be able to make forward progress. This situation represents a deadlock, and needs to be avoided in all cases.

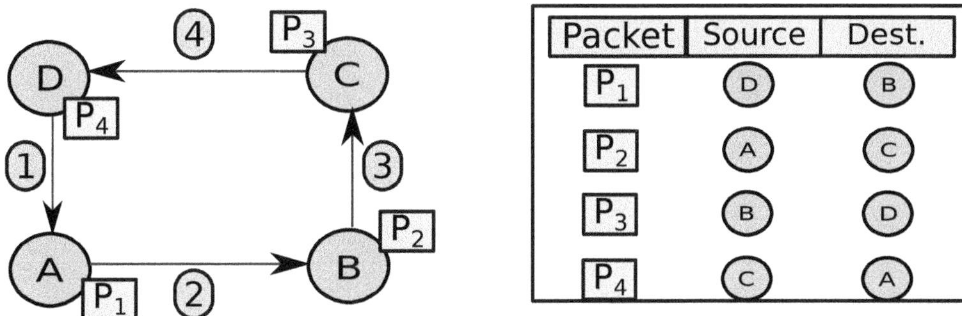

Figure 8.25: Deadlock in an NoC (single VC per channel)

To model this situation and even more complex situations, we need to introduce a new theoretical tool called the *Resource Dependence Graph (RDG)* shown in Figure 8.26 (a graph is defined in Section 2.3.2). Let us have two kinds of nodes: agents and resources. In this case an agent is a packet and the resource is a channel. We add an edge (hold edge) from resource R to agent A, if A holds R. Similarly, we add an edge from A to R (wait edge) if A is waiting for R to become free. Note that the *hold* and *wait* edges are in opposite directions. A resource dependence graph (RDG) for the scenario shown in Figure 8.25 is shown in Figure 8.26. Consider the case of packet P_1. It holds channel 1, hence there is an arrow from channel 1 to P_1. P_1 waits for channel 2 to become free. Hence, there is an arrow from P_1 to channel 2. The rest of the edges are added in a similar manner.

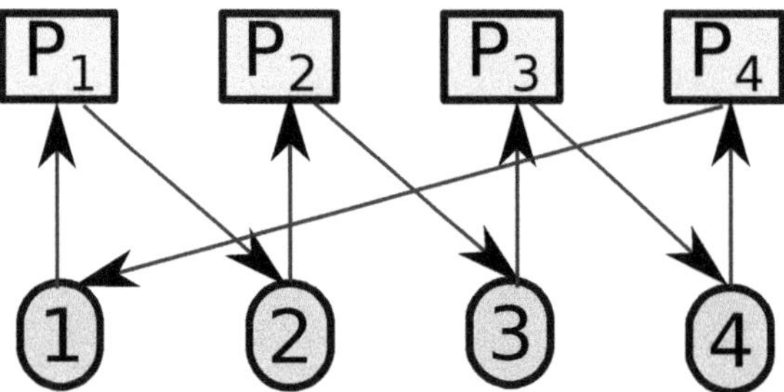

Figure 8.26: Resource dependence graph for Figure 8.25

This graph can be further simplified into a *channel dependence graph* or CDG. In this case, we remove the agents (packets), and just have the channels (physical or virtual) as the nodes. There is an edge from channel C to channel C' if an agent that holds channel C waits for channel C' to become free. The equivalent CDG for Figure 8.25 (and Figure 8.26) is shown in Figure 8.27. Note that we are assuming that channels are *unidirectional*, and the buffer space associated with the channel is at the receiver node. This means that if there is a connection between nodes A and B then there are two channels for message transfer: $A \rightarrow B$ and $B \rightarrow A$. The channel $A \rightarrow B$ has buffer space at node B.

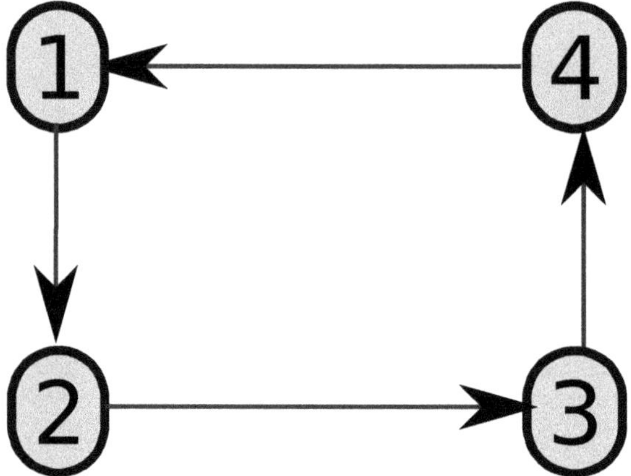

Figure 8.27: Channel dependence graph

Let us quickly observe that there is a cycle in the graph. This hold-and-wait cycle indicates the same situation as Figure 8.24, where we have a deadlock. We claim that whenever we have a cycle in the CDG, we have a deadlock, and vice versa. This is easy to prove. Consider the fact that every edge in the graph indicates that the agent holding a source node is waiting for the agent holding the destination node. This means that in a cycle all the agents (packets in this case) form a cyclic dependence (circular wait), which represents a deadlock. The converse is also true; if there is a deadlock then the circular wait between the channels will be visible in the CDG as a cycle.

Having multiple virtual channels does not fix the issue. Let us consider the same example with two virtual channels per physical channel. In this case, let us number the virtual channels corresponding to each physical channel with the subscripts 0 and 1 respectively. Even if a a packet is allowed a choice between the virtual channels, then also we can have a deadlock (see Figure 8.28). We simply need to consider two sets of packets flowing along the same route, and with the same set of dependences as we have seen before. In this case, both the sets of packets will not be able to progress due to the lack of virtual channels. We shall thus have a deadlock regardless of the number of virtual channels.

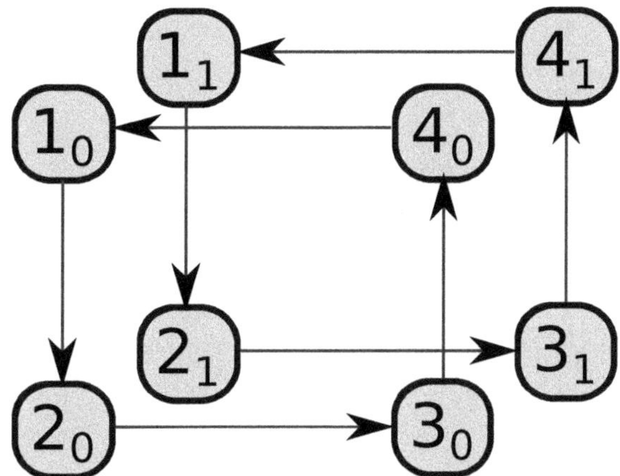

Figure 8.28: Deadlocks in an NoC with 2 virtual channels

Turn Graph

The channel dependence graph (CDG) is the classical tool that is used to detect deadlocks. We just need to check for cycles. However, it is not very useful beyond this. This is because the information about the orientation (or direction) of the channel is lost. Let us thus create another theoretical tool – a turn graph abbreviated as TG. We create a TG from the original topology of the NoC and a subset of the CDG.

In the CDG, let us consider a path $\mathcal{C}$ that may contain cycles as well. $\mathcal{C}$ is an ordered set of channels $(C_1, \ldots C_n)$, where channel C_i is dependent on channel C_{i+1}: the end node of channel C_i has to be the starting node of channel C_{i+1}. The TG allows us to visualise the cycles in $\mathcal{C}$ better in terms of the orientation of the channels that make the cycle.

To define the TG, let us first define $\mathcal{G}$, which is a graph that represents the topology of the network. This graph has nodes (representing the routers) and directed edges (channels). The orientation of the edges is the same as that in the actual NoC. For example, the graph for a 2D mesh is a rectangular grid of nodes connected via edges. If an edge goes from north to south in the actual NoC, then its orientation in $\mathcal{G}$ is the same.

The TG for $\mathcal{C}$ is a sub-graph of $\mathcal{G}$ that contains all the channels in $\mathcal{C}$ and no other channel. Additionally, we insert a new node called the *channel node* in the middle of each edge or channel. This means that if there is an edge from node A to node B in the original graph $\mathcal{G}$, then in the TG we have an edge from A to the channel node C_{AB} and then an edge from C_{AB} to B.

Before looking at an example, let us appreciate the key insights that were used to construct the TG. The first insight is that the turn graph captures the orientation of a channel in the actual NoC. The second insight is that for channels C_i and C_{i+1} in $\mathcal{C}$, where C_i depends on channel C_{i+1}, there is a path from the channel nodes corresponding to C_i and C_{i+1} in the TG. This can be generalised as follows. For $C_i \in \mathcal{C}$ and $C_j \in \mathcal{C}$, where $i < j$, there is a path from the channel nodes corresponding to C_i and C_j in the corresponding turn graph.

Let us consider an example in Figure 8.29. Figure 8.29(a) shows the network topology ($\mathcal{G}$) of a 2D mesh. Figure 8.29(b) shows a CDG with circular (cyclic) waiting for 4 channels: 1, 2, 3, and 4. Then we create a turn graph for these channels, and orient the channels in exactly the same directions as they are oriented in $\mathcal{G}$. We then add the four channel nodes. This creates the turn graph for this set of channels as shown in Figure 8.29(c) (note the positions of the channel nodes).

Let us quickly understand the benefit of having a turn graph. Consider an edge between two channels in the CDG such as the edge between channels 1 and 2. This translates to a *turn* in the TG between nodes A, B, and C. In fact, we can make some general observations here. Consider an edge between

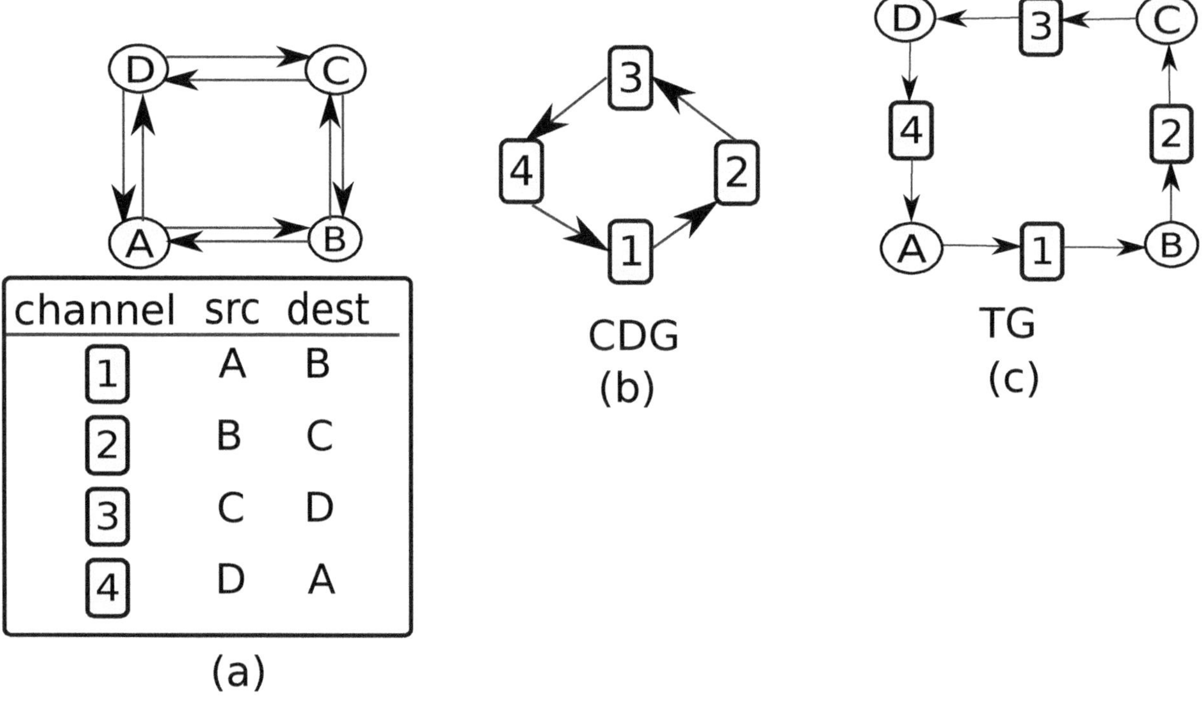

Figure 8.29: (a) Graph $\mathcal{G}$, (b) CDG with a cycle, and (c) its equivalent TG.

any two channels C_i and C_{i+1} in the CDG. Let C_i be between nodes N_i and N_{i+1} and C_{i+1} be between nodes N_{i+1} and N_{i+2}. Note that the channels have to share a node in common if there is a dependence. This translates to a sequence of three nodes (N_i, N_{i+1}, and N_{i+2}) connected via edges in the equivalent turn graph with channel nodes in the middle. Either all three nodes are collinear, or we make a *turn* while going from N_i to N_{i+2}. For us the **turns are of interest**, and we shall see that a study of such turns underpins the development of deadlock-free routing algorithms.

Let us now look at the most important property of a TG. Consider a CDG with a cycle. We can always consider a path $\mathcal{C}$ in the CDG that contains the cycle. We can then construct a TG for this path. Given that each channel in $\mathcal{C}$ has an associated channel node in the TG, and for any two channels $C_i, C_j \in \mathcal{C}$ ($i < j$), there is a path from the channel node corresponding to C_i to the channel node corresponding to C_j, we can say that we shall have a cycle in the TG as well. This path will comprise the same set of channels that have the cyclic dependence in the CDG. We can also say that if for a given routing protocol, we cannot construct a TG with a cycle, then we cannot have a path in the CDG that has a cycle – this means that the routing protocol is deadlock-free.

Important Point 15

If for a given routing protocol ,we can never construct a TG with a cycle, then we cannot have a path in the CDG that has a cycle – this means that the routing protocol is deadlock-free.

Avoiding and Recovering from Deadlocks

Let us look at methods to handle the issue of deadlocks. There are two important concepts in this field.

Deadlock Avoidance or Prevention The first is that we avoid or prevent deadlocks by design[3]. This means that we design the routing protocol in such a way that deadlocks do not happen. Such approaches are also known as pessimistic approaches because we deliberately constrain the routing protocol to avoid deadlocks. This means that we somehow ensure that in all possible turn graphs that we can create for executions with a given routing protocol, there are no cycles. We sacrifice some performance in this process.

Deadlock Recovery The other approach is an optimistic approach. Here we choose the most efficient method of routing and allow deadlocks to happen. If we detect a deadlock, then we initiate a process of recovery. The process of recovery involves either deallocating resources by aborting a packet transmission or allocating some additional temporary storage to deadlocked flits such that they can progress.

Let us initially focus on deadlock avoidance mechanisms using specialised routing protocols. Subsequently, we shall look at deadlock recovery mechanisms.

8.3.3 Dimension-Ordered Routing

Let us consider the simplest class of deadlock-free routing protocols called dimension-ordered routing, the simplest of which is X-Y routing. Consider a mesh of nodes as shown in Figure 8.30. Each node has an x coordinate and a y coordinate. Let us describe the algorithm for routing a message from node A (x_1, y_1) to node B (x_2, y_2).

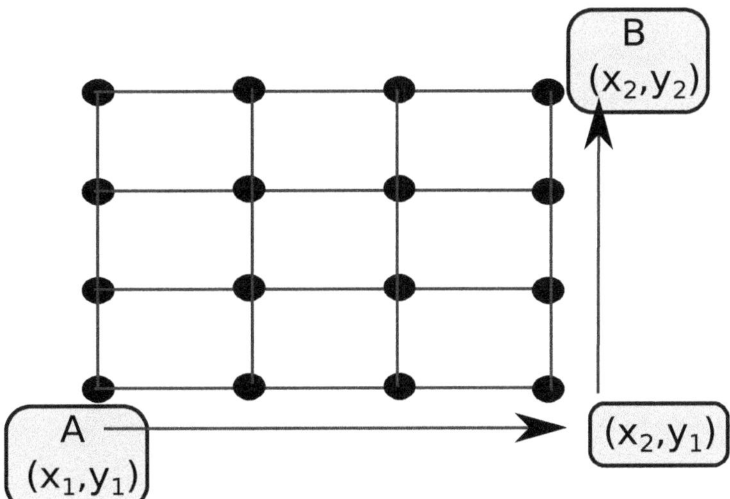

Figure 8.30: X-Y routing in a mesh

We first traverse in the x direction from (x_1, y_1) to (x_2, y_1). Then we traverse in the y direction from (x_2, y_1) to (x_2, y_2). In other words, we always give preference to the x direction over the y direction.

Let us evaluate this routing protocol using the three metrics that we have learnt: number of links traversed, livelocks, and deadlocks.

This algorithm clearly yields the shortest path. We traverse the minimum number of links in both the axes. There is also no potential for a livelock because we never go round and round in circles. We move along the y direction only after we have completed all our moves in the x direction. In each axis,

---

[3]Some texts separately define the terms: deadlock avoidance and deadlock prevention. However, we shall combine the concepts and use a single term – deadlock avoidance.

if we take the shortest route to the same row or same column as the destination, we are guaranteed to traverse through the shortest path.

Now, let us prove that such a routing strategy is also deadlock-free. Let us prove by contradiction. Assume that there is a deadlock. This means that there must be a cycle in the channel dependence graph (CDG). Let us consider the smallest cycle in the CDG. Since packets are not allowed to make a U-turn, we need to have some channels along the x-axis in the cycle. Let the channels (physical or virtual) be $C_1 \ldots C_n$, where the cycle is $C_1 \rightarrow C_2 \rightarrow \ldots C_n \rightarrow C_1$. Without loss of generality, let us assume that C_1 is along the x-axis. Let us visualise the channels as a turn graph (see Figure 8.31). We have annotated each channel node with the number of the channel.

First, assume that C_1 is oriented towards the east and the cycle is anti-clockwise. Now, for the cycle to complete in Figure 8.31, we need to have the following turns: $E \rightarrow N$ (east to north), $N \rightarrow W$ (north to west), $W \rightarrow S$ (west to south), and $S \rightarrow E$ (south to east). The turn that we are interested in is between channels C_k and C_{k+1} (the $N \rightarrow W$ turn). This is not allowed in X-Y routing because it means that a packet first traverses along the y-axis, then moves along the x-axis. Such turns (packet movements) are strictly disallowed in X-Y routing. We thus have a contradiction, and this means that we cannot have a cycle in any TG, and by implication in any CDG with such cycles.

If C_1 is oriented towards the west, we can prove a similar result, and we can do the same for clockwise cycles. This means that the equivalent TG and CDG are always cycle-free.

Hence, deadlocks are not possible and the X-Y routing protocol is deadlock-free. This protocol is ordered by the dimension: first x and then y. If we have more dimensions such as in a 3D mesh network (in a 3D chip), then we can also use this approach by first ordering the dimensions.

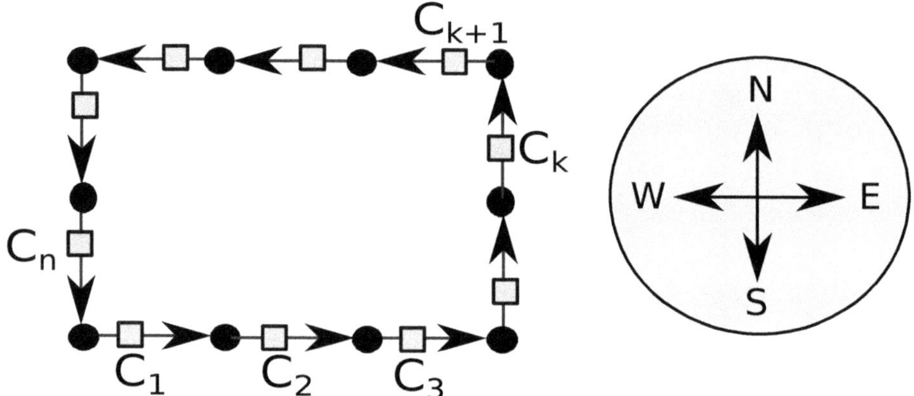

Figure 8.31: A cycle in the turn graph. The nodes are shown with filled, dark circles and the channel nodes are shown with squares.

8.3.4 Oblivious Routing

The main problem with X-Y routing is that the path between every source-destination pair is fixed. This is a desirable feature if we want simplicity; however, it does not allow us any flexibility and if there is congestion in the network, there is no way to route around it. As a result, such algorithms do not perform well when we have congestion in networks. Their lack of flexibility can prove to be a major detriment in networks with some degree of congestion in nodes.

There is thus a need to create an algorithm that provides far more flexibility. This is only possible when we do not have a fixed path between each source-destination pair. Let us thus describe the Valiant's algorithm. The algorithm is very simple; the steps are as follows.

1. Assume we want to route a message from point A to point B. Choose a random point P in the mesh. Let us call it the *pivot point*.

2. First route the message from A to P using a provably deadlock-free algorithm such as X-Y routing.

3. Then route the message from P to B using a similar algorithm as used in the previous step.

Let us understand the pros and cons of this algorithm. The obvious advantage is that we are randomising the route. By choosing an intermediate point we are ensuring that we do not have a deterministic route between the source and the destination. As a result, it is much easier to not get stuck in hotspots. In addition, because of the randomisation, the traffic will uniformly spread throughout the chip. It will be hard for traffic hotspots to even form in the first place.

On the flip side, the main shortcoming of this algorithm is that it lengthens the path from the source to the destination. This is because the pivot point might be far away from both the source and the destination. While sending a message from A to B, we need to incur the additional latency involved in sending the message from A to P and then from P to B. We thus observe a trade-off between the probability of avoiding network congestion and the end-to-end latency. Such kind of routing is known as *oblivious* routing because the source and the destination nodes are effectively unaware of each other. The source just needs to be aware of the pivot point, and the pivot point simply needs to be aware of the destination. This algorithm is otherwise free of deadlocks because in each step we use a provably deadlock-free algorithm such as X-Y routing.

Minimally Oblivious Routing

Let us try to address the main shortcoming of oblivious routing by introducing a more efficient version known as *minimally oblivious routing*. Here, we place restrictions on the pivot point. We do not allow it to be randomly placed at any point in the network. Instead, we demarcate a region around the source or destination and constrain the pivot point to only be within that region. This will ensure that the additional detour involved in going from the source to the destination via the pivot point gets reduced as much as possible.

Let us consider the case where the pivot point is placed in the vicinity of the destination. This situation is shown in Figure 8.32. In this case, we first route the message from A (source) to the pivot point P. Now, given the fact that P is in the vicinity of B (destination), we do not incur a very significant penalty (in terms of latency) by using this method.

This method represents an intermediate point between fully oblivious routing, and deterministic shortest path routing. There is a trade-off between the degree of congestion experienced by a packet, and the length of the path that it takes. Note that it is not necessary that the routing protocol be a variant of X-Y routing. We can use any routing algorithm that has deadlock freedom as one of its properties.

At this point, let us briefly glance back. We first looked at X-Y routing, which is provably deadlock-free. It is however very restrictive in its choice of paths. There is no *path diversity*, which is defined as the set of paths that can be taken from a source node to reach a given destination node. As a result, even if there is congestion along the way, nothing can be done. To a certain extent, this problem is solved with oblivious routing; however, we need to limit the path diversity such that we can avoid extremely long and circuitous routes between the source and destination. Hence, we proposed minimally oblivious routing that achieves a trade-off between these conflicting requirements.

Definition 60
Path diversity *is defined as the number of paths from a source node to a given destination node.*

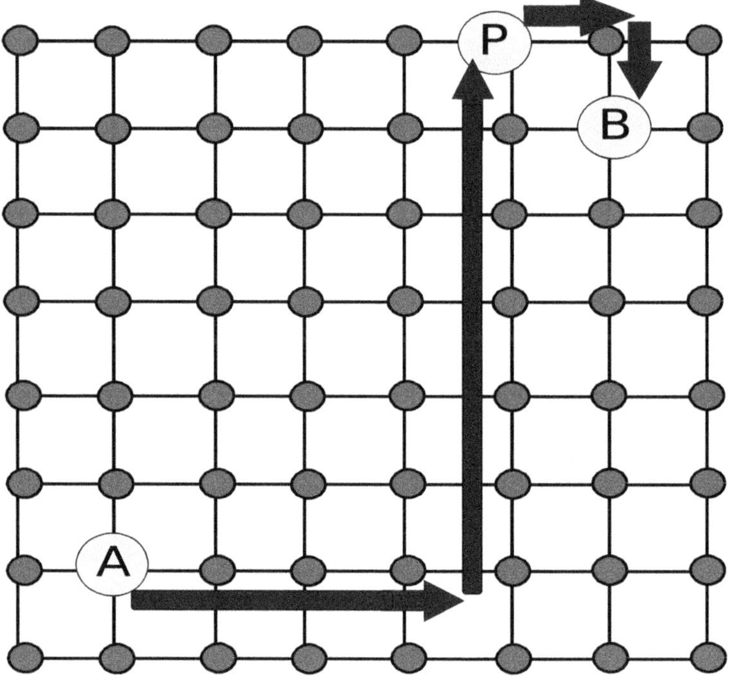

Figure 8.32: Minimally oblivious routing

8.3.5   Adaptive Routing

Whenever we make a routing decision at a router, we run the risk of creating an edge in the CDG between two VCs (virtual channels): the input VC (VC_1), and the output VC (VC_2). An edge will be created in the CDG if a flit coming in via VC_1 is not able to leave the router via VC_2 because the latter does not have enough space in its buffers.

There are two ways in which VC_1 and VC_2 can be related. Either they are in the same direction, or they are in perpendicular directions (turn). For the time being, let us not consider U-turns. Moreover, since all the flits in a packet flow along the same path, if the head flit takes a turn, the rest of the flits do the same.

In this section, we shall argue that if we do not restrict turns in our routing algorithm, then there is a possibility of deadlocks. Let us thus look at the notion of turns in some detail.

Notion of Turns

Traditionally, the directions in a mesh based network are represented as *north*, *south*, *east*, and *west*. They are abbreviated as N, S, E, and W respectively (also see Figure 8.33).

Every router in a mesh or torus has five input ports and five output ports. The five input ports (ingress ports) are N, S, E, W, and local. Recall that we divide a chip into a set of *tiles*, where each tile consists of a few adjoining cores and cache banks. Each tile has a router associated with it. When any core or cache within a tile desires to send a packet on the network, it sends a message to its local router. The local router accepts the message via the *local* port. It then sends the message via its output (or egress) ports. On similar lines, it has 5 output ports: N, S, E, W, and local. To deliver a message to the attached tile, the *local* output port is used.

A flit can either continue straight through a router, or take a turn. There are four possible ways of going straight: continue north, south, east, or west. Going straight by itself is not a problem and does

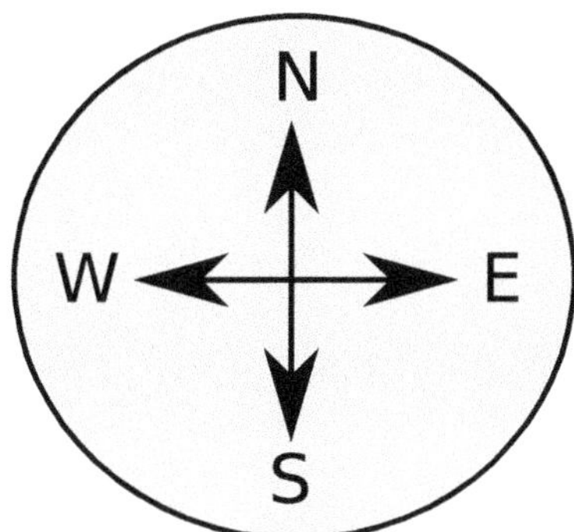

Figure 8.33: Directions used in routing

not lead to deadlocks. We have deadlock situations when flits take turns because only then a situation with a circular wait can form. Let us thus look at the space of turns.

A flit going north can take two possible turns: go west, or go east. Let us designate these turns as $N \to W$ and $N \to E$ respectively. Similarly, for all the other directions, there are two possible ways in which we can take turns. There are thus 8 possible turns that a message can take. Let us quickly look at the number of turns that are allowed in X-Y routing (see Section 8.3.3). Recall that when a flit is travelling along the y-axis, it cannot take a turn in the x direction. This means that if we are going north or south, we cannot take a turn. This automatically precludes 4 turns: $N \to E$, $N \to W$, $S \to E$, and $S \to W$. The only 4 turns that are allowed are $E \to N$, $E \to S$, $W \to N$, and $W \to S$. This is precisely why we have maintained that the X-Y routing algorithm is very restrictive in terms of paths: it allows only 4 out of 8 turns. Let us propose algorithms that allow more turns and also guarantee deadlock freedom.

Cycles

We can always take a complex cycle in the TG and simplify it by fusing a chain of dependences to form a single dependence till it becomes equivalent to one of the cycles shown in Figure 8.34. The cycle is either clockwise or it is anti-clockwise. The rest of the edges do not matter. We are the most interested in the specific turns that create these cycles.

The key learning here is that in a clockwise cycle, we shall definitely have 4 turns: $E \to S$, $S \to W$, $W \to N$, and $N \to E$. Similarly, in an anti-clockwise cycle, we shall also have these 4 turns: $W \to S$, $S \to E$, $E \to N$, and $N \to W$. From each cycle, if we can eliminate at least one turn, then we are sure that cycles will not form: clockwise or anti-clockwise. If cycles do not form in the TG, then as we have discussed earlier, there is no possibility of a deadlock.

If we consider the X-Y routing protocol again, we observe that it prohibits 4 turns. Two of these turns, $N \to E$ and $S \to W$, are present in a clockwise cycle. Since we are not allowed to take these turns, we shall never have a clockwise cycle. Similarly, two other turns that are prohibited and are part of an anti-clockwise cycle are $S \to E$, and $N \to W$. Hence, we shall also never have an anti-clockwise cycle. As a result, the TG with an X-Y routing protocol is acyclic, and the protocol is thus deadlock-free.

We can clearly do better than X-Y routing. We need not prohibit that many turns. We just need to prohibit one turn each in the two cycles – clockwise and anti-clockwise. This means that by allowing 6 out of the 8 turns, we can create deadlock-free routing algorithms.

Deadlock-free Routing Algorithms with 6 Turns

For each cycle, we need to prohibit one turn. We have four possible choices for each cycle (clockwise and anti-clockwise), and thus there are 16 possible choices overall. We can thus design 16 possible routing

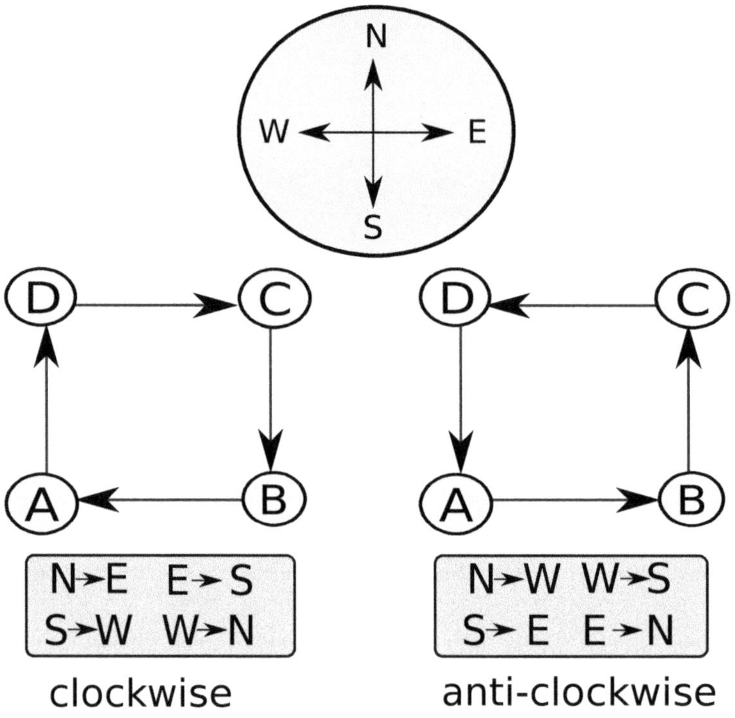

Figure 8.34: Basic turns in a turn graph

algorithms that allow 6 out of 8 turns. Some of these routing algorithms have a name. Let us review a few of them in Table 8.2.

Name	Turns disallowed	Allowed turns
West-first	$N \to W,\, S \to W$	
North-last	$N \to W,\, N \to E$	
Negative-first	$N \to W,\, E \to S$	

Table 8.2: Routing algorithms with 6 allowed turns

In the West-first algorithm we always go west first. The second direction is never west. This is why we disallow the turns $N \to W$, and $S \to W$. On similar lines, we have the North-last protocol, where we always go north at the end. In the Negative-first protocol we go in the negative directions – west or south – at first. We can create many more such algorithms and assign names to them. The key idea is that with such protocols, we have armed ourselves with more turns such that we have a choice of more routes and we consequently have more path diversity. This will also allow us to deal with congestion better.

The entire family of such protocols is deadlock-free. We just need to avoid two turns and it is guaranteed that we shall not have any deadlocks. The next question that arises is, "How do we ensure that we always choose the best possible route in the face of congestion?" This question will be answered in Section 8.4 when we discuss the design of the router.

8.3.6 Preventing Deadlocks by using Virtual Channels

We have discussed a host of routing algorithms where we prevent deadlocks by disallowing a certain set of turns. This ensures that we do not form cycles: clockwise or anti-clockwise. However, there are other methods to ensure that we do not have deadlocks, and some of these mechanisms are based on innovative uses of virtual channels. A historical note is due here. Virtual channels were originally proposed to prevent deadlocks, and they later on got adapted for a host of other things as we have been seeing in the last few sections.

Let us try to understand why VCs are well suited to avoid deadlocks. VCs are channels in their own right because they have their own set of buffers and all physical channels are multiplexed between their VCs. Hence, in the channel dependence graph, we have VCs and not physical channels. Restricting turns is one of the ways in which we can solve a cycle forming among the VCs; however, we can also prevent cycles by placing other kinds of restrictions on the way we select and use VCs.

Routing in a 4-Node System

Let us consider a very simple example in Figure 8.35. In this case, we have 4 nodes (A, B, C, and D) and 4 channels with 2 VCs per channel. As we have seen in Figure 8.28, we can have a deadlock in such an NoC.

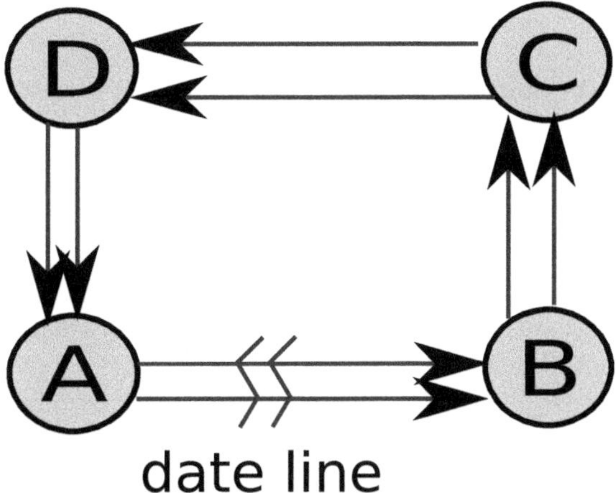

Figure 8.35: Network with 4 nodes and 2 VCs per channel

Let us number the two VCs corresponding to each physical channel as 0 and 1. The two VCs from node A to B are named AB_0 and AB_1 respectively. Other VCs are named in a similar manner. Now, between nodes A and B let us draw an imaginary line called the *date line*[4]. The VC assignment algorithm is as follows. Whenever we inject a packet into a router, we always inject it into VC 0. It travels only via the VCs numbered 0 till it either reaches its destination or till it crosses the date line. Once it crosses the date line, it transitions to the VCs numbered 1. For example, when it traverses through the VC AB_0, the next VC that it needs to be allocated is BC_1. Henceforth, the message will remain in the VCs numbered 1 till it reaches its destination. A flit will never move from a VC numbered 1 to a VC numbered 0. Let us prove that this algorithm is free of deadlocks.

---

[4]This is conceptually inspired from the international date line on the globe.

Theorem 8.3.6.1 *The routing algorithm using a date line in a 4-node system with 2 VCs per channel is deadlock-free.*

Proof: Assume that this protocol leads to a deadlock. Let us show prove by contradiction that this is not possible. There are three cases: we have a cycle with only channels numbered 0, we have a cycle with channels numbered 1, or we have a cycle with channels numbered both 0 and 1.

Case I: We have a cyclic dependence with VCs numbered 0. Since U-turns are not allowed, the cycle will consist of 4 edges: AB_0, BC_0, CD_0, and DA_0. Now there cannot be an edge between AB_0 and BC_0 in the CDG because by the definition of the date line, there can only be an edge between AB_0 and BC_1 in the CDG. Hence, such a cycle is not possible.

Case II: In this case, all the channels in the cycle are numbered 1. Consider the case of the edge between channels AB_1 and BC_1. This means that a flit has acquired the VC AB_1 and wishes to acquire the VC BC_1, which is busy. This is not possible. To acquire a channel numbered 1, it must have already traversed the channel AB_0 before. This means it must have moved through only channels numbered 1, and visited the rest of the nodes before traversing the physical channel between A and B once again. If a flit has visited all the nodes in an NoC (as in this case), it must have visited its destination also. Therefore, the flit should not have been in circulation any more, and thus there is no way in which it is possible to have a dependence between the channels AB_1 and BC_1 in the CDG. This case is thus not possible.

Case III: Consider a cycle with channels that are numbered both 0 and 1. There has to be an edge in the CDG between a channel numbered 1 and a channel numbered 0. This is not allowed in our routing protocol. Hence, this case will never happen.

Thus, we prove by contradiction that it is not possible to have a cycle in the CDG.   ■

Even though this approach looks easy, it has two important drawbacks.

1. Creating a date line in a simple 4-node network is easy. However, a similar mechanism in a larger network with a complex topology is difficult.

2. The VCs numbered 1 are relatively less utilised as compared to the VCs numbered 0. This design choice unequally utilises the system, and is thus wasteful in terms of resources.

The key learning in this scheme is as follows.

> To avoid creating deadlocks, impose an order in which resources are acquired.

Routing in Rings

Let us now extend this result to an N-node ring, where naive protocols can have deadlocks (see Example 7). Moreover, X-Y routing cannot be used in rings because a y-axis does not exist.

We can use a similar date line based approach by using two virtual channels. Let us arbitrarily define a date line between nodes 1 and 2. In this case, it is easy to extend the proof of Theorem 8.3.6.1 to show that a similar algorithm using two virtual channels is free of deadlocks.

Example 7 *Show that it is possible to have deadlocks in a ring where the routing protocol always constrains a flit to move in the clockwise direction. Assume that we have a single VC per physical channel in the clockwise direction and each VC has k buffers.*

Answer: *Consider the following communication pattern. Node i tries to send k flits to node $(i + 2)\%N$ (numbers increase in a clockwise direction). Let us introduce the operator $+_N$, which is defined as follows: $a +_N b = (a + b)\%N$. Here '%' is the remainder or modulo operator.*

Now consider the following sequence of events. Each node i sends k flits from node i to $i +_N 1$. All the nodes do this simultaneously. Subsequently, any given node i will not be able to make progress because the channel between $i +_N 1$ and $i +_N 2$ is occupied by the flits being sent from node $i +_N 1$. Thus the flit gets blocked. In the equivalent CDG there is an arrow between the channel $\langle i, i +_N 1\rangle$, and $\langle i +_N 1, i +_N 2\rangle$. Note that we have such dependences for all i, and this leads to a cycle in the CDG. No flit will be able to move to its second channel in the route because that channel is blocked. This is a deadlock.

Routing in Tori

Let us now consider a torus (see Section 8.1.2). If we consider the traffic pattern along a single row or column, which is arranged as a ring of nodes, deadlocks are possible as we saw in Example 7.

To avoid such deadlocks, let us define two date lines: one along the x-axis, and one along the y-axis. The date lines intersect every row and every column. These ensure that while traversing a row or column in the torus, deadlocks are not possible. We can then use X-Y routing as the overall scheme albeit with the additional constraint that when we cross a dateline we transition to the VC numbered 1. With both of these protocols, we can ensure that routing in tori is free of deadlocks.

Escape VCs for Deadlock Recovery

Let us now look at a radically different idea. Consider a simple example with two VCs per physical channel. Let the message be ordinarily constrained to VC 0. Let us use a fast shortest path based routing protocol for the set of edges that use VC 0. This sub-network gives us efficiency, yet it can lead to a deadlock.

Let us propose a method for deadlock recovery. This can be easily achieved by associating a counter with every flit in a router. When it enters the router, we initialise the counter. Every cycle we increment the counter. Once the flit leaves the router we reset the counter. However, if the counter reaches an upper threshold, then it means that the flit is stuck at the router for a long period of time. This can possibly indicate a deadlock. For practical purposes, let us assume that this does represent a deadlock situation and try to recover from it.

Deadlock recovery in conventional networks involves dropping packets. However, in the case of on-chip networks, we are not allowed to drop packets. Hence, we need to find another method of recovering from deadlocks. Let us have another set of VCs (numbered 1). Consider the sub-network comprising of VCs numbered 1. In this sub-network, let us use a different routing protocol that is provably deadlock-free such as X-Y routing. Any flits that gets possibly stuck in a deadlock moves to the sub-network with VCs numbered 1, and travels to the destination in this sub-network. Since the routing process is deadlock-free in this sub-network, it is guaranteed that the flit will reach its destination.

Now, if we consider the entire system, it is also free of deadlocks. The sub-network with VCs numbered 0 can suffer from a deadlock. However, flits will not wait for an indefinite period. After a certain amount of time has elapsed, they will transition to the other sub-network (VCs with number 1). In the latter sub-network, the flits are guaranteed to reach their destination because we use an algorithm that will not have deadlocks.

The advantage of this network is good performance. We use a high performing sub-network (VCs numbered 0) to route flits. However, occasionally we might have a deadlock. In such cases, we move the flits to a much slower sub-network (VCs numbered 1) that guarantees the delivery of flits to the destination without the possibility of deadlocks. The only disadvantage of this design is that the VCs with number 1 are relatively less frequently utilised as compared to the VCs with number 0. This represents a wastage of resources.

We can further extend this idea to a network that has 4 or 8 VCs per physical channel. We can divide the VCs into different classes, and have different routing algorithms for each class of VCs. We can use the same idea. If we discover a deadlock in the network, we move the flit to a VC in another class that uses a provably deadlock-free routing algorithm.

8.4   Design of a Router

Let us now look at the design of a router. A router is arguably the most important component in the NoC. It includes all the logic and state to store, forward, and route flits. It also includes the logic to allocate virtual channels, detect deadlocks, and perform flow control. In a certain sense, we will combine everything that we have learnt in the past few sections in this section.

A router in a modern NoC is a highly complex pipelined structure. The reason we need to pipeline it is because the latency of a router is fairly high, and thus to sustain a high throughput, pipelining is required. In this section, we shall first describe a quintessential 5-stage router and then propose optimisations to reduce the number of stages. We shall show in later subsections that it is possible to reduce the number of stages from 5 to 3 by making sophisticated optimisations.

Let us explain the design of a router that can be used in a 2D mesh or torus. Akin to normal in-order pipelines, it also has 5 stages.

8.4.1   Input Buffering

Consider the start of the packet transmission process. A core or cache bank decides to send a message over the network. It creates a packet and then sends the sequence of flits to its nearest router. Each router has a dedicated input port for local traffic. This input port can be used by all the senders and receivers in its tile (a set of cores and cache banks). If we are using a packet or circuit switched network, then we need a single buffer queue. Otherwise, the input port will have multiple buffer queues, where each such queue is a VC. The requests can be allotted to VCs in a fair manner such that we do not have starvation.

Now, consider an intermediate node in the network. If we have a packet or circuit switched network, there will be a single set of buffers associated with each physical channel (refer to Figure 8.36(a)). We simply start writing the packets to the buffer queue associated with the physical channel at the destination router. However, in the case of flit based switching with VCs, the situation is slightly more complicated. In this case, we shall have multiple queues associated with the same physical channel. Each queue corresponds to a VC. Hence, every flit that enters the router needs to know the id of the VC that it is using. Assume a system with 2 VCs per physical channel as shown in Figure 8.36(b), which are numbered 0 and 1 respectively. Every flit entering router B from router A needs to know the id of the VC that it belongs to. If it is using VC 0, it gets queued in the queue for VC 0 in router B, and likewise if it is using VC 1, it gets queued in the buffer queue corresponding to VC 1.

The process of writing flits to buffer queues, is known as *input buffering*. This ensures that we are able to store flits in the downstream router (B in this case). There are two possible ways of implementing input buffering. The first is to use separate queues (SRAM arrays in hardware) for each VC. This is a very easy and simple solution. However, it suffers from several drawbacks. The first is that it limits the storage capacity at the routers. Even if the other queues (for other VCs) are free, we will not be able to use their space.

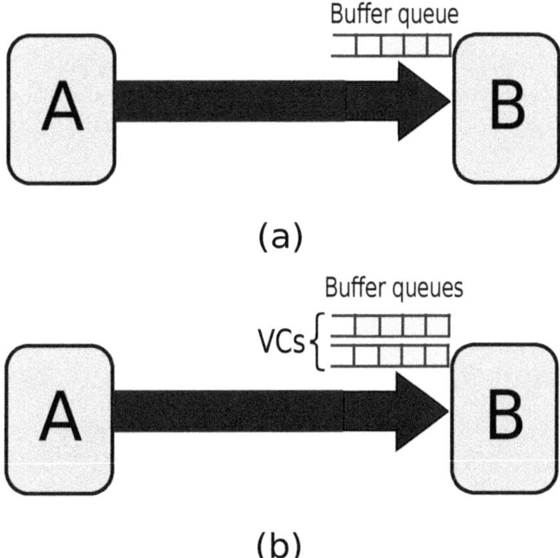

Figure 8.36: Input buffering: (a) without virtual channels, (b) with virtual channels

Hence, if storage space is our primary concern, we can use a shared buffer based approach as shown in Figure 8.37. In this case, we have a single, large array of flits. Different VCs are assigned to different non-overlapping regions of this array. Conventionally, the two ends of a queue are referred to as the *head* and *tail* respectively. The only state that we need to maintain in this case for each VC is the id of its corresponding *head* and *tail* pointers. Whenever we insert or remove a flit from a queue, we need to update these pointers. The advantage of this design is that the storage structure is more flexible. If a given VC needs a lot of space at any given point in time, and the rest of the VCs are unutilised, then it is possible to accommodate this requirement using this design.

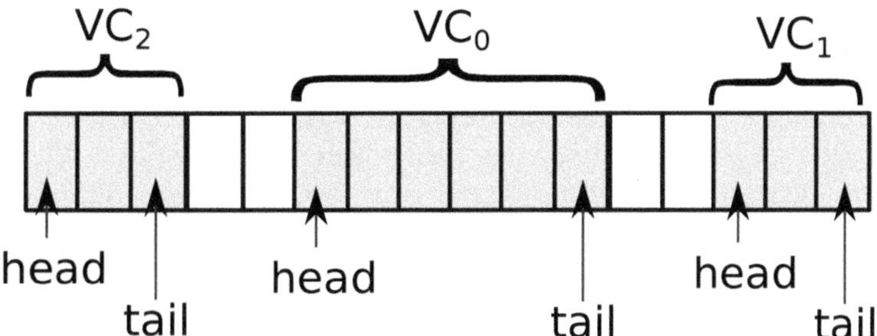

Figure 8.37: All the VCs using a single shared buffer

8.4.2 Route Computation

The next stage of packet processing is to compute the route that the packet will take. This needs to be done once, only for the head flit. The rest of the flits in the packet will follow the same route. The head flit needs to have the id of the destination node. In addition, as discussed in Section 8.3.1, it can have more information such as the number of hops it has already traversed to avoid livelocks.

A dedicated route computation (RC) engine needs to compute the id of the next router. There are

4 possible directions in which the packet can be sent: north, south, east, and west. There are several issues that we need to keep in mind. In general, we should always try to send a packet on the shortest path to its destination. However, there can be issues related to congestion, and thus sometimes taking longer paths can save time, and avoid network hotspots. Let us look at some of the common methods for computing routes.

Source Routing

In this case, the entire route is computed a priori. The route is then embedded into the head flit. At every node, the router checks the contents of the head flit. The route is stored as a queue of directions in the head flit. It removes the head of the queue, and sends the packet along that direction. Ultimately when we arrive at the destination, the queue of directions in the head flit becomes empty.

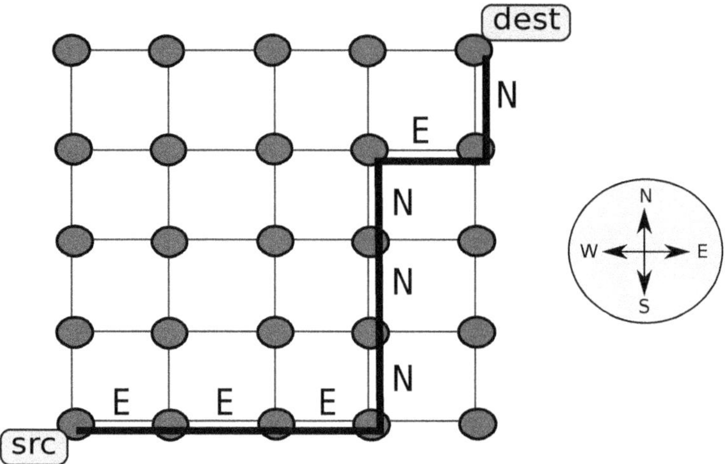

Figure 8.38: Example of source routing in a mesh network

Figure 8.38 shows an example of source routing. In this case, the original route from the source to the destination is computed to be $EEENNNEN$. Each letter in this route represents the direction the flits should take. In every node we remove the head of the queue, which is a direction D, and send the packet along direction D. The disadvantages of this scheme are obvious. We always compute static routes, and we have no means to deal with congestion in the network or take dynamic decisions. Some times it is possible that the temperature of a given zone within the chip rises to unacceptable levels. It is necessary to turn off all activity in the area, and also route NoC packets around it. Such strategies are not possible with source routing. In addition, there are overheads to store all the routing information in the head flit, and modify the head flit at every router. The head flit needs to be modified because we need to remove the entry at the top of the queue that stores the list of all the directions in which the packet needs to be sent.

However, the scheme is not completely devoid of advantages. It is simple, and we do not need to compute the routes dynamically. This saves power. To create path diversity we can store multiple routes for the same destination, and randomly or on the basis of expected congestion, choose between them.

Routing based on Node Tables

Let us explore a different kind of approach. Instead of doing the entire routing at the source, let us instead do the job of routing at the routers. This means that every time a packet reaches a router, we simply compute which outgoing link the packet is going to take. In the case of a 2D torus or mesh, we have four choices: N, S, E, and W.

We keep a table at each router, known as the *node table*. For each destination, we store the directions that the packet needs to take at the egress (exit point) of the router (refer to Example 8). Note that in a routing algorithm based on turns, it is also necessary to have multiple rows in this table: each row corresponds to a direction from which the packet has arrived. For each pair of direction and destination, we have an entry in the table. This contains the direction that the packet needs to take as it exits the router. Note that in some cases, it might be possible to send the packet along multiple directions.

Example 8
For the given network, compute the node table at node 5 for the North-last routing algorithm. Instead of showing all the columns, show only the column for a flit coming from the local tile. Note that we always prefer the shortest path.

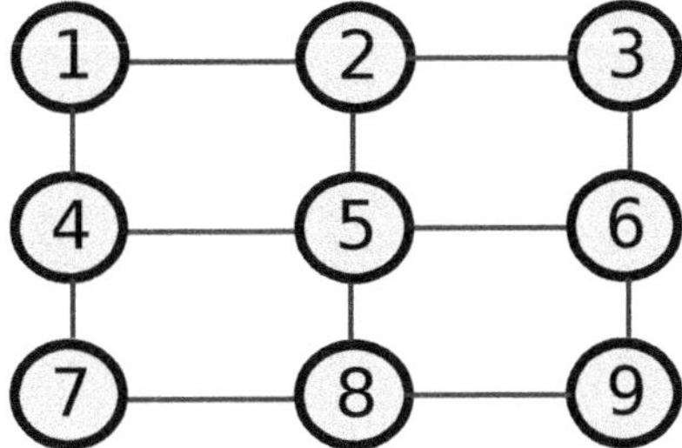

Answer: *Since we are using the North-last routing algorithm, the $N \to W$ and $N \to E$ turns are disallowed. The node table without these turns is as follows. Here, the operator '|' stands for 'OR' (any of the specified routes can be taken).*

Destination	Direction
1	W
2	N
3	E
4	W
6	E
7	S | W
8	S
9	S | E

Note that for nodes 1 and 3, we could have proceeded north as well. However, since the turns $N \to W$ and $N \to E$ are disallowed, we discarded these routes from the node table.

When we have a choice of multiple directions we need to base our routing decision on several considerations.

1. The first is livelocks. If a packet has already traversed a given number of hops, it should be sent preferably along the shortest possible path to its destination. Otherwise, we will have a scenario where the packet will be moving around in circles and not reaching its destination.

2. If livelocks are not an issue, then we should try to minimise the time it will take to reach the destination. When there is no congestion, the least-time path is the shortest path. However, in the presence of congestion, alternative routes become more favourable. We can use the flow-control circuitry to get an idea of the average buffer usage/occupancy at the neighbouring routers. Once

we have this information, we can choose the next hop based on a combination of the following information: distance to the destination, number of free virtual channels in the next hop, and the rate of buffer usage for each virtual channel. We can also use a weighted sum of these quantities (appropriately normalised). The individual weights need to be determined by conducting exhaustive simulation studies. We can also use multi-hop information if we have it with us such as the congestion in local or remote neighbourhoods.

Note that it is not always necessary to maintain tables. It takes space to store the tables, and it also requires energy to access a given row and column in the table. In some cases, where simplicity is required, we can use a simple combinational circuit to compute the route that a packet needs to take. This is very easy to do with schemes such as X-Y routing or some simple turn based schemes.

8.4.3   Virtual Channel Allocation

After computing the route, we need to start the process of sending the packet across the computed outgoing link. A given link or physical channel will have many VCs associated with it. There is a need to allocate a virtual channel to the packet. This process is known as VC allocation. Note that the problem of virtual channel allocation is not simple, because it is possible that different packets that would have arrived on other physical channels could be vying for the same set of virtual channels.

Thus, the prime goals of the VC allocator are as follows:

- The VC allocation process should be fair. No request should be made to wait for an indefinite period. This will lead to starvation.

- It should be done quickly in less than one cycle.

The VC allocator can be modelled as a black box. In every cycle it takes a set of requests, and returns the number of the VC that was allotted to each request. We shall look at the general problem of resource allocation in Section 8.4.6. Hence, we are not discussing VC allocation separately.

The design of the router as described till this point is shown in Figure 8.39. We are assuming two VCs per physical channel. In the first stage, we store the flit in the input buffers corresponding to the VC. Then in the next stage we send the data to the route computation unit via a pipeline register. After we have computed the route, we allocate a VC in the next cycle. We do not have a pipeline register at the end of this stage because we assume that the allotted VC is written to the head flit of the packet.

8.4.4   Switch Allocation

Once we have allotted a virtual channel, the packet is ready to be transmitted via an outgoing link (physical channel). However, this is a complex process. Consider a representative example. Assume we have two VCs per physical channel. For the N, S, E, and W incoming channels we have a total of 8 VCs. In addition, we shall have 2 more buffer queues (same as VCs from our point of view) for local traffic. We thus have 10 input VCs. It is possible that all of these VCs have flits in them, which are waiting to be transmitted via outgoing links. In this case, we have 5 outgoing links: local, N, S, E, and W. Thus, the problem of resource allocation is as follows. We have 10 input channels and 5 output channels. To effect a packet transmission, we need to map an input to an output. Such a hardware structure is known as a *switch*. The 10×5 switch for our router is shown in Figure 8.40.

Realise that it is possible that all 10 packets at the input VCs might want to pass through the same outgoing channel. However, at any one time, only one flit can pass through an outgoing channel. Hence, there is a need to choose one out of the several flits that are possibly interested to traverse an outgoing channel. At this stage, we can multiplex a physical channel among several virtual channels. This is where we need to be *fair* and ensure that every flit gets transmitted within a possibly bounded amount of time. If the switch allocator is fair, then starvation is not possible.

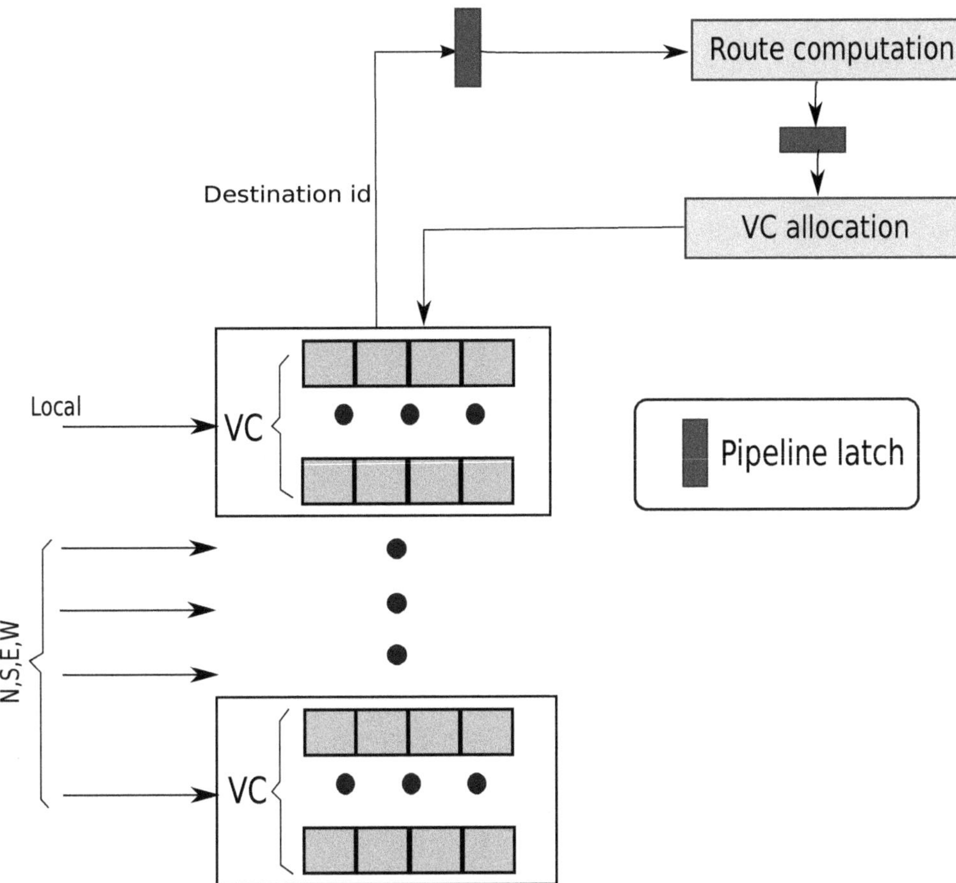

Figure 8.39: Router with the first three stages: input buffering, route computation, and VC allocation

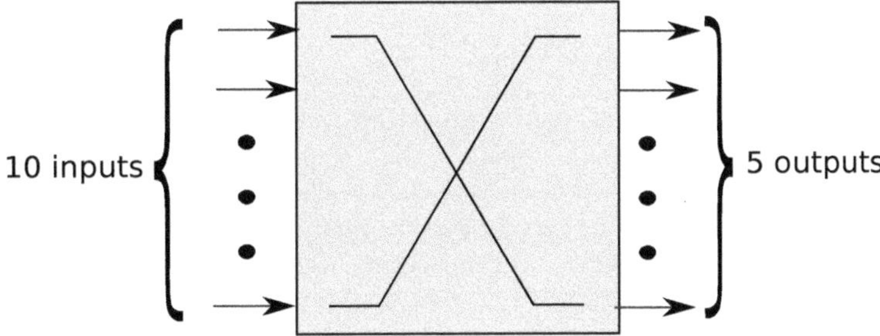

Figure 8.40: 10×5 switch

In addition, it is possible to define several conditions of optimality in this case. Consider a system where we have a priority associated with each packet. If we wish to ensure that all the high priority packets are routed first, then our switch allocator needs to give preference to flits in such packets. Thus, the objective function here is to minimise the end-to-end latency of high priority packets. If we want to increase the system throughput by freeing VCs, then the strategy should be to quickly send all the body and tail flits, after a head flit has been sent. This will ensure that the VC and the associated buffers clear up as soon as possible.

Alternatively, if we wish to minimise the average end-to-end latency, then the best strategy is to often give preference to the smallest packets (least number of flits). In many cases it can be proven that this is indeed the most optimal strategy, and a better strategy does not exist. There are many more kinds of optimisation strategies for different classes of networks and objective functions. Refer to the survey paper by Gabis et al. [Gabis and Koudil, 2016].

8.4.5 Switch Traversal

Once a port in the switch has been allocated an outgoing channel, the only thing that remains for a flit is to traverse the switch, and reach the outgoing link. This process is known as switch traversal. There are several ways to design a switch. Let us look at one of the simplest possible ways (refer to Figure 8.41).

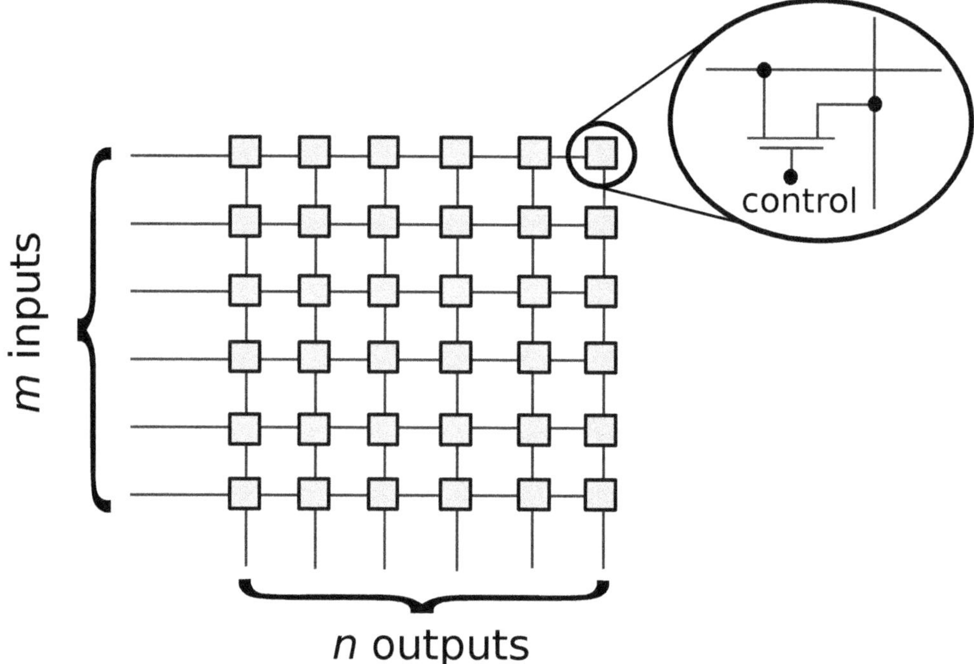

Figure 8.41: An $m \times n$ switch with pass transistors (a connection is made if *control* = 1)

We normally design a switch as an array of pass transistors, where the number of rows is equal to the number of input ports, and the number of columns is equal to the number of output ports. Here, each input port corresponds to an input VC, and each output port corresponds to an outgoing link (physical channel). We connect an input to an output by enabling the transistors between the horizontal and vertical wires. This creates a connection and data can thus be transferred from the input to the corresponding output. Note that any outgoing link can transfer a flit for only a single input VC at any given point of time. Each flit that is being transferred on a channel also contains the virtual channel id that it belongs to. Recall that the VC is allocated earlier in the VC allocation stage, and furthermore all the flits in the same packet are allocated the same outgoing link and the same VC.

The process of switch traversal is fairly simple. A connection is made between the horizontal and vertical connections by programming the transistors. The flit travels seamlessly towards the output port. From the output port, the flit proceeds on the outgoing link. In almost all routers as of 2020, output buffering is not used. This means that at the outputs we do not have any buffers. As soon as a flit exits the switch, it is directly placed on one of the outgoing links. Such kind of a switch that looks like a 2D matrix is known as a *crossbar*.

Optimised Designs of Crossbar Switches

Sadly, large crossbars are not considered to be optimal designs. The chief reasons are the usual suspects namely high power consumption, high area, and increased latency due to larger circuits. However, the key advantage is simplicity and support for high throughput. Given that the overheads often outweigh the advantages, typically a monolithic design is not preferred.

This means that if there are N input VCs and M output channels, an $N \times M$ switch is not preferred. It is considered to be expensive in terms of power, area, and latency. Let us create an approximate metric for area and latency. The area is proportional to the product $N \times M$, and the latency is proportional to the distance the flits travel, which is $M + N$. Let us define these metrics as the area cost and the latency cost respectively.

Thus, for a 10×5 router, the area cost is 50, and the latency cost is 15. It has full flexibility: any input can be connected to any output.

There are several strategies that could be adopted for creating a more efficient design. The first is that we use a hierarchical approach. Out of the 10 VCs, we can first choose 5: one for each incoming link. Then we can have a 5×5 switch. This hierarchical strategy is shown in Figure 8.42. We first have a set of five 2×1 switches, and then we have a single large 5×5 switch. The area cost is the sum of 5 times 2×1, and 25 (5×5), which comes to 35, and the latency cost is $2 + 1 + 5 + 5$, which is 13. The main problem with this design is that it does not allow both the VCs of a single physical channel to send flits simultaneously when they are destined for different outgoing channels.

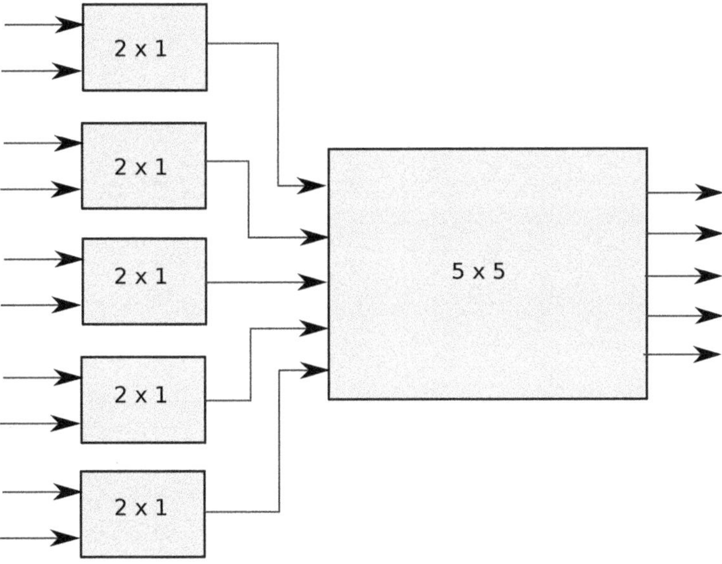

Figure 8.42: Hierarchical switch with 10 inputs and 5 outputs

Let us try to solve the problem with the hierarchical switch by creating a different kind of grouping. Let us again create a 2-level hierarchy, where the first level has two 5×2 switches. The insight here is that we do not always have enough traffic to keep all the 5 links busy. We can safely assume that for an overwhelming majority of time, a maximum of 4 packets are simultaneously flowing through the outgoing links. The second level has one 4×5 switch. The area cost is 40 and the latency cost is 16. This represents a point between a fully hierarchical design and a fully flexible design in terms of the overall area (see Figure 8.43). Many more such designs are possible. Depending upon how we want to optimise area, power, and latency, we choose the appropriate design.

The three switch designs are summarised in Table 8.3. Let us now look at a different way of creating switches.

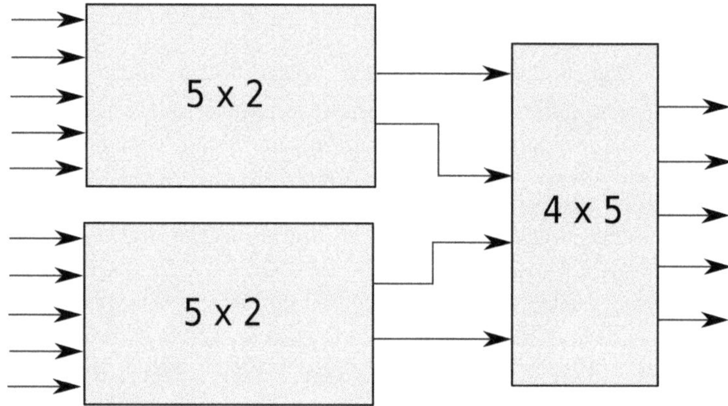

Figure 8.43: Hierarchical switch with wider internal switches

Design		Area cost	Latency cost
Level 1	**Level 2**		
10×5	-	50	15
Five 2×1	5×5	35	13
Two 5×2	One 4×5	40	16

Table 8.3: Area and latency costs of different switch designs

Dimension Slicing

This approach is suitable for protocols that use X-Y routing or other forms of dimension-ordered routing. Let us start out by noting that there is an asymmetry in the directions that a packet can take with this routing protocol. Packets travelling in the x direction can either go straight or take a turn. However, packets travelling in the y direction can only travel straight. Let us use this fact to design a more efficient switch.

First consider a switch that has three inputs: E, W, and *local*. Packets can be sent along any of its outgoing links. This switch has three outgoing links: E, W, and a link to another switch. It is thus a 6×3 switch as shown in Figure 8.44. Note that we are assuming two VCs for each physical channel. Now, all the packets that are travelling along the x axis can go straight through this switch. However, if they are destined for other outgoing links, then they need to go to the second switch as shown in Figure 8.44. The second switch has five inputs: one from the first switch, two VCs each corresponding to the N and S directions. There are three outputs: N, S, and *local*. This is a 5×3 switch. Quickly note that the only directions that the packet can take are north, south, and local. This is a direct consequence of the X-Y routing protocol. A packet from the north or south cannot take a turn towards the east or west. This helps us reduce the number of outgoing links.

The costs of this pair of switches are as follows: area cost = 33 and latency cost = 17. This is clearly the most area efficient solution that we have seen so far (refer to Table 8.3). We were able to design an efficient scheme because our routing protocol constrains the routes and thus some connections could be avoided.

Through this small example, we would like to highlight the fact that it is possible to co-design the routing protocol and the design of the switch.

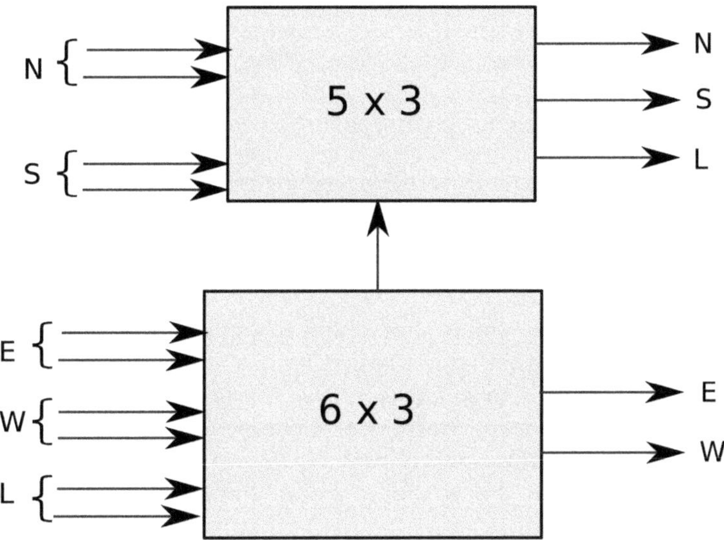

Figure 8.44: Dimension-sliced switch

8.4.6 Allocators and Arbiters

Given that we have discussed the need for VC allocation and switch allocation, let us look at the process of allocation in some detail. First, let us define some terms rigorously. An allocator creates a one-to-one match between N requests and M resources. For example, a virtual channel allocator has M virtual channels at its disposal for a given physical channel. In any given cycle, for a particular physical channel, it might get N requests, and it needs to allocate them M resources (VCs). If $N \leq M$, then there is no problem. We can do a simple one-to-one mapping for the N requests. However, the problem arises when $N > M$. In this case, we need to first choose a subset of requests that we are going to allocate, and then we can map them to the M resources. The process of choosing a subset of requests needs to be fair, in the sense that it should never be the case that a request is kept waiting for an indefinite period. This will lead to starvation.

The other important concept is *arbitration*. In this case, an arbiter chooses one out of N requests.

Definition 61
An allocator *creates a one-to-one mapping between a subset of N requests and M resources, whereas an* arbiter *is far more specific: it chooses one out of N requests for resource allocation.*

Theoretical Fundamentals

Let us generalise the problem of allocation. If we have N requests and M resources, then there are many possible ways of mapping the requests to the resources. We have been assuming that any request can be mapped to any resource. However, this need not always be the case. It is possible that a given request can only be mapped to a specific subset of resources. This is the general problem of allocation, where we need to find a *matching* between resources and requests.

In a system with N requests and M resources, let us define an additional function, f, that indicates if a given request can be mapped to a resource or not. Let the requests be $R_1 \ldots R_n$, and the resources be $S_1 \ldots S_m$. The function $f(R_i, S_j)$ is true if R_i can be mapped to S_j, otherwise it is false. Let us now define the conditions that we shall use to map requests to resources.

Condition 1 Every request is mapped to at most a single resource.

Condition 2 Every resource is mapped to at most a single request.

Condition 3 Request R_i is mapped to resource S_j if $f(R_i, S_j)$ is true.

Let us look at a simple example in the figure below, where we have requests and resources. There is an edge (with a dotted line) between a request and a resource if the request can be mapped to the resource. An edge with a solid line means that the request is mapped to the resource.

Note that the final mapping needs to follow the three conditions that we have enumerated. In this case, we have two requests and two resources. R_1 can be mapped to S_1 only, whereas R_2 can be mapped to S_1 or S_2. If we map R_2 to S_1, then we cannot map R_1 to any other resource. The only resource that R_1 can be mapped to is S_1 and that has already been mapped to R_2. Hence, we shall have a single mapping (see Figure 8.45(b)).

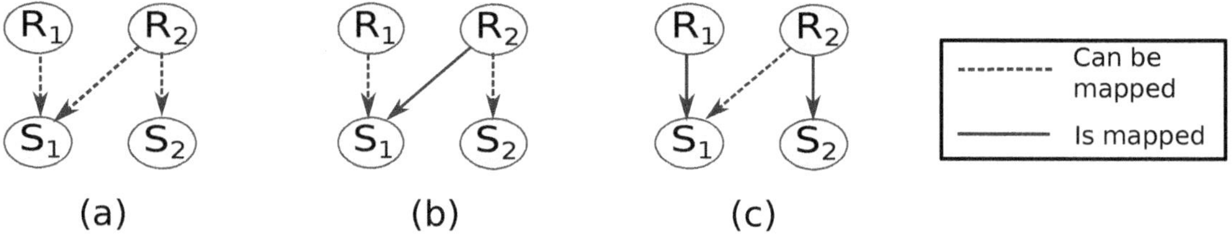

Figure 8.45: Mappings between requests and resources

Now, if we map R_1 to S_1, then S_2 is free. At this stage, the mapping is not *maximal*, which means that it is possible to create more mappings. We thus create another mapping between R_2 and S_2 (see Figure 8.45(c)). In this case, we were able to create two mappings as opposed to the previous case, where we created a single mapping. This is thus a more optimal solution. There is a theoretical name to this problem. It is called the *maximum matching* problem in bipartite graphs. The graph that we have drawn in Figure 8.45(a) is a bipartite graph because we have two classes of nodes – requests and resources – that have no edges between them. We only have edges between a request and a resource.

The aim is to match (or map) the maximum number of requests to resources. This problem is solvable and there are excellent algorithms for finding maximum matches; however, the solutions are slow from the point of view of hardware and are difficult to realise using a simple circuit. Hence, we most of the time try to compute a *maximal matching or mapping*, where it is not possible to create any additional mappings. The solutions shown in Figure 8.45(b) and 8.45(c) are both maximal. However, the solution in Figure 8.45(c) is better because we map more requests to resources.

Let us now discuss a few simple arbiters and allocators.

Round Robin Arbiter

The simplest method of performing arbitration is round robin arbitration. In this case, the resource is distributed among the requesting agents in a round robin fashion. This means that at the outset the resource is given to requesting agent 1, then to agent 2, till we reach agent N. The assumption is that the total number of agents in the system is equal to N. After agent N finishes using the resource, we again come back to agent 1, and continue in the same fashion.

Figure 8.46 shows a simple round robin arbiter. We assume that there are N request lines and N grant lines. Each request line is connected to a requesting agent. If the agent needs to place a request, it raises the voltage of its request line to a logical 1. On similar lines, there are N grant lines. Whenever

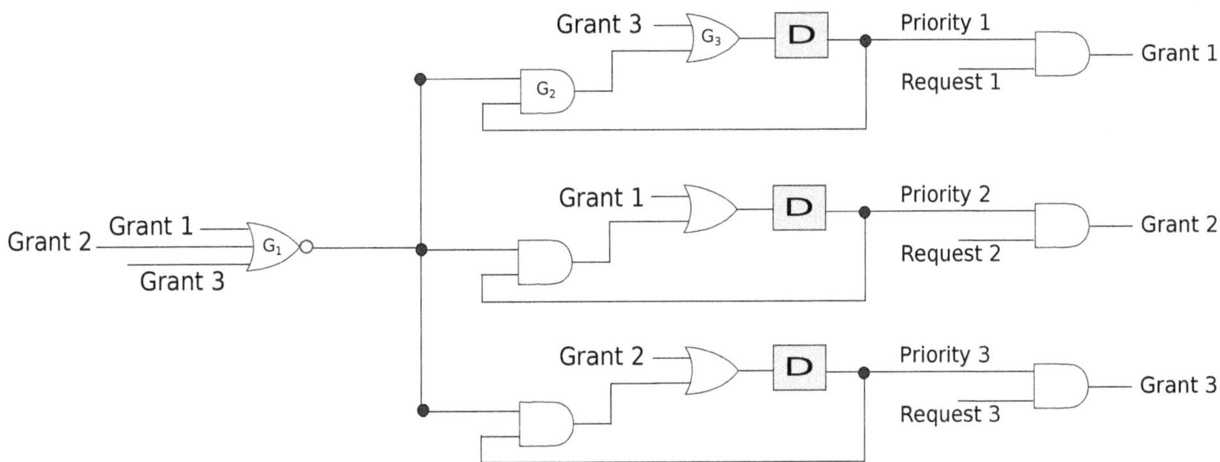

Figure 8.46: A simple round robin arbiter

a request is granted to the ith agent, the ith grant line is set to 1. The rest of the grant lines are set to 0.

In Figure 8.46, we have three requesting agents. They assert the lines *Request 1*, *Request 2*, and *Request 3* respectively. Each request line is connected to an AND gate, whose other input is a priority line. For example, we have an AND gate that has two inputs: request line 1, and a priority for the first input (*Priority 1*). The output is the grant signal for the first input, *Grant 1*. The grant signal is only asserted when the corresponding request and priority lines are both high. We have similar AND gates for the other two request and priority lines.

Let us now come to the main circuit. Gate G_1 is a NOR gate that computes a logical NOR of all the grant lines. If any of the grant lines is equal to 1, then the output of G_1 is 0. This means that the output of G_2 is also 0, because it is an AND gate. This further implies that the output of G_3 is *Grant 3*. If the value of the grant line for the third input (*Grant 3*) is 1, then this value gets recorded in the D flip-flop. At the beginning of the next cycle, the value of the *Priority 1* line is set to 1. This means that the request for the first agent can be granted. This is according to the round robin policy, which says that after agent 3 gets a chance, it is time for agent 1 to get a chance. Hence, its priority line is set to high. At this stage, the reader needs to convince herself that the round robin strategy is indeed being followed. After agent 1 gets a chance, its grant line is set to 1, then agent 2 gets a chance and so on.

Now, let us look at the uncommon cases. Assume that *Grant 3* is equal to 0. If any one of *Grant 1* or *Grant 2* would have been set, then the output of G_2 would have been 0, and the output of G_3 would also have been 0. This means that *Priority 1* would also be 0. This is the correct behaviour. The *Priority 1* line should only be 1 after *Grant 3* has been asserted (as per our round robin policy).

Finally, consider another case where all the grant lines are deasserted (set to 0). In this case, the output of G_1 is 1. The output of G_2 is the value of *Priority 1*, which is also the output of G_3 (because *Grant 3* is 0). This means that *Priority 1* maintains its previous value. The same holds for the rest of the priority lines: *Priority 2* and *Priority 3*. In other words, if no grant lines are asserted, then the priorities maintain their prior values. However, if there are sufficient requests, then the grant lines are asserted using a round robin policy.

The main drawback of this approach is that we are constrained to using a round robin policy. Even if an agent is not interested in acquiring a resource, it still needs to be a part of the algorithm. As long as it does not assert its grant line, the next agent cannot win the arbitration (be granted a request). In a practical scenario, it is possible that a given agent might not have requests even though its priority line may be set to high. To stop indefinite waits, we can add extra logic that asserts the grant line of an agent whose priority is high, if it does not receive any requests for a given period of time.

Matrix Arbiter

The round robin arbiter works for small systems; however it is not very flexible. If some of the agents are not interested in the resource, then there is no way of removing them from the protocol. Let us look at the matrix arbiter, which is more flexible in this regard.

In this case, we create an $N \times N$ Boolean matrix, $\mathcal{W}$, where N is the number of requesting agents. The properties of the matrix $\mathcal{W}$ are as follows.

1. $\forall i, \mathcal{W}[i, i] = \phi$. All the diagonal entries have null values.

2. $\forall i, j, \mathcal{W}[i, j] \neq \mathcal{W}[j, i]$ if $i \neq j$.

This means that the diagonal entries have null values. Secondly, $\mathcal{W}[i, j]$ and $\mathcal{W}[j, i]$ have dissimilar values when $i \neq j$. In this matrix, $\mathcal{W}[i, j] = 1$ means that agent i has a priority over agent j. This implies the following:

> If all the entries in the ith row are 1 (other than the diagonal element), then the ith agent has the highest priority. It can be granted the resource.

The basic steps in the arbitration algorithm are as follows.

1. If a given agent is not interested then it sets all the entries in its row to 0, and all the entries in its column to 1 (other than diagonal elements).

2. In every cycle, the request is granted to the agent, which has ones in all of the entries in its row other than the diagonal element.

3. Once the ith agent is done servicing its request, it sets all the entries in its row to 0, and sets all the entries in its column to 1 (other than the diagonal elements). This means that it relegates itself to the lowest priority.

Figure 8.47 shows an example. In this case, agent 1 is assigned the resource first because all the non-diagonal entries in its row are 1. Subsequently, it resets all the entries in row 1, and sets all the entries in column 1. Since agent 2 is not interested in acquiring the resource, the next agent that should be granted the resource is agent 3 (all the entries in its row are 1). After agent 3 is done, it follows the same procedure. The next agent that should be granted the resource is agent 4. After agent 4 is done, it sets all the entries in column 4 to 1.

Even though agent 2 was not interested, we end up with a situation where the rest of the agents are done with processing their requests, and all the entries in the second row are equal to 1. At this point, only agent 2 can satisfy its request, and none of the other agents can. We thus see that we are constrained to provide every agent a single chance in a cycle of N requests. This algorithm is more flexible than round robin allocation in the sense that we do no have to stick to a pre-defined order. However, we still need to take care of the situation that has been created with agent 2.

An intuitive way of solving this problem is as follows. When agent 2 can acquire the resource, yet it does not have a valid request, it simply follows the protocol of relegating itself to the lowest priority (set the row to zeros, and column to ones).

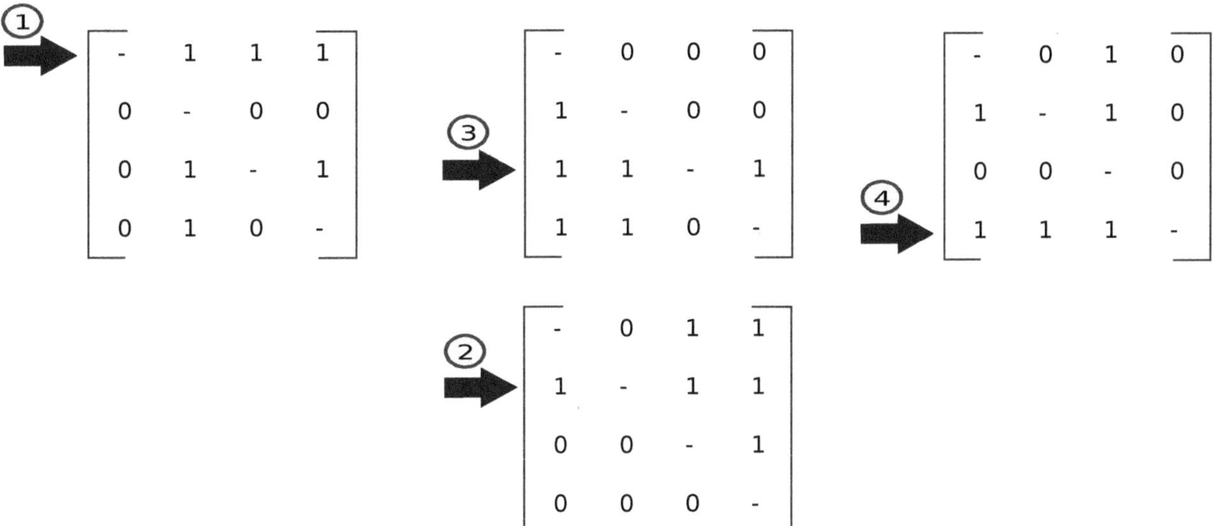

Figure 8.47: Matrix arbiter. The '-' symbol represents a null value.

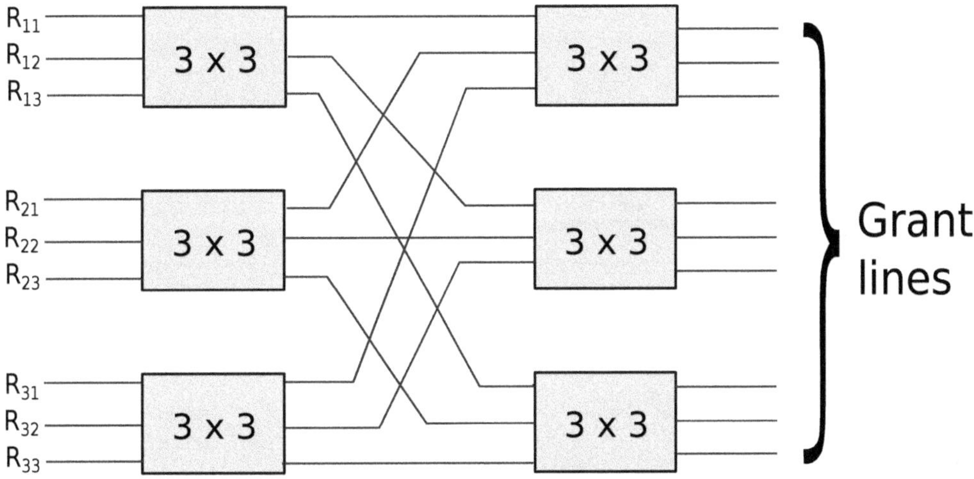

Figure 8.48: A separable allocator

Separable Allocator

Both the round robin and matrix arbiters have limited flexibility. Furthermore, they cannot be used to allocate N agents to M resources. For such scenarios, we need a more general allocator. Let us first look at a naive design, where we have 3 agents, and we have 3 resources. Each agent produces three inputs, which are the request lines for the three resources. We set R_{ij} equal to 1 if the ith agent wishes to acquire the jth resource. We can then create a separable allocator as shown in Figure 8.48.

The separable allocator has two columns of arbiters. An arbiter in the first column chooses one request from each agent. Recall that we cannot allocate two requests issued by the same agent at the same time. We need to choose one of the agent's requests. This is done by the 3×3 arbiters in the first column. Since we have three agents, we have three arbiters. Consider the first arbiter in the first column. It has three inputs: R_{11}, R_{12}, and R_{13}. There are three grant lines as outputs – one corresponding to each request. Let us number them G_{11}, G_{12}, and G_{13} respectively. At most one of them can be asserted (set to 1). If none of the request lines are set, then all the grant lines (G_{11}, G_{12}, and G_{13}) need to be set to 0.

The outputs of the first three arbiters are inputs to the arbiters in the second column. Consider the first arbiter in the second column. Its inputs are the grant signals generated by arbiters in the first column: G_{11}, G_{21}, and G_{31}. They correspond to all the requests for the first resource. Only one of the requests can be chosen (or granted). We follow the same logic here as arbiters in the first column, and choose one of the requests. The outputs of the arbiters in the second column are the final grant lines, which are routed to the agents.

The separable allocator can lead to sub-optimal allocations. Assume that we have a situation where each agent is interested in all the resources. This means that in any maximal matching, we can assign each agent to a distinct resource. However, in a separable allocator it is possible that in the first column, we only choose requests for let's say resource 1. In this case, we can only map one agent to one resource (resource 1). This is clearly sub-optimal. Instead of three mappings, we are creating just one. We need an arbiter with a more global view.

Wavefront Allocator

Let us develop an algorithm where we can simultaneously allocate resources to the requesting agents. This will not create situations where we have different rounds with sub-optimal choices being made.

Consider a matrix, $\mathcal{W}$, where the rows represent the agents and the columns represent the resources. Assume for the sake of simplicity that the number of agents N is equal to the number of resources M ($M = N$). Let us give two tokens to each diagonal element $\mathcal{W}[i, i]$. One of them is called a *row token*, and the other is called a *column token*. The row token propagates along a row, and the column token propagates along a column.

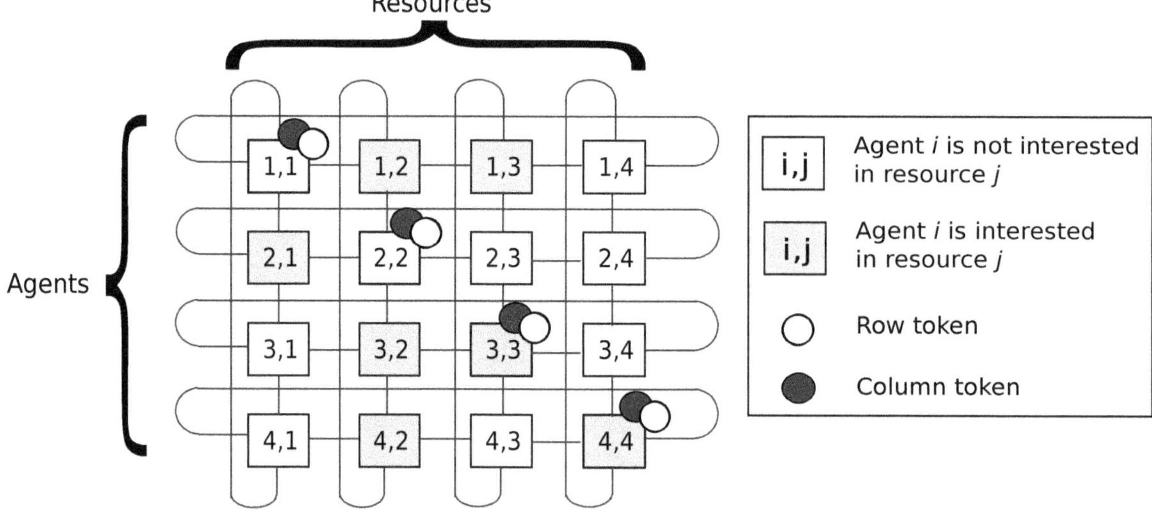

Figure 8.49: The matrix $\mathcal{W}$ with agents, resources, and connections between neighbouring cells

In the matrix $\mathcal{W}$ (shown pictorially in Figure 8.49), we start out with giving one row token and one column token to each of the diagonal elements. If agent i is interested in acquiring resource j then we mark the cell $\mathcal{W}[i, j]$. It is shown with a shaded colour in Figure 8.49.

The matrix is connected like a torus, where neighbouring cells in a row and column are connected, and there is a connection between the first cell of a row and the last cell of the row (likewise in a column).

The algorithm consists of multiple rounds. In each round, each cell executes the following steps.

1. If a given cell in the matrix has a row token and a column token, and is interested in acquiring a resource, then it is allotted that resource. Cell $\mathcal{W}[i, j]$ is interested in acquiring a resource if agent i is interested in getting access to resource j. This cell *consumes* both the tokens, and removes them from the system.

2. If a cell is not interested in a resource, and it has a token, then it sends the token to a neighbouring cell such that it can be processed in the next round. If it has a row token it sends it to the cell on the left, and if it has a column token then it sends it to the cell that is just below it.

3. If a token reaches an edge of the matrix, it traverses the long edges to wrap around the matrix and start from the other end of the matrix (same row or same column) in the next round.

Consider the same matrix $\mathcal{W}$ as shown in Figure 8.49, where all the cells are not interested in acquiring any resource. Let us understand the movement of tokens across rounds (refer to Figure 8.50).

The initial state is round 1, where all the tokens are given to the diagonal elements. Before the next round, all the row tokens move one step to the left. If a token is at the edge of the matrix, it wraps around the matrix. For example, the row token on cell (1,1) goes to cell (1,4). The row tokens in the other cells move one step to the left. Similarly, the column tokens move one step down, and the token in the bottom-most row wraps around. For example, the column token in cell (2,2) moves to (3,2), and the column token in cell (4,4) moves to (1,4) (wraps around).

Observe that in the second round, we have two kinds of cells: cells with two tokens (one row and one column) or no tokens. In the subsequent rounds (round 3 and round 4), the same property holds. Even after the tokens wrap around, we never have the case that a cell has a single token. We would like to advise the reader to manually verify that this property holds across the four rounds, and also if we consider a bigger matrix.

Let us now consider all the cells in a round that have both the tokens (shown using dotted lines in Figure 8.50). It is like a wavefront that is propagating towards the bottom-left. Parts of the wavefront wrap around the edges. The wavefront propagates one step diagonally in each round. Let us look at some features of this wavefront. In the example shown in Figure 8.50, the size of the wavefront is exactly N (in an $N \times N$ matrix). It never has two cells in the same row or in the same column. Any cell on the wavefront, which has two tokens, can consume both the tokens if it is interested in the resource. Henceforth, no other cell in that row or in that column can acquire any resource in the future. In other words, if an agent is allocated a resource, it cannot be allocated any other resource, and likewise if a resource is allocated to an agent, then it cannot be allocated to any other agent. This is precisely the property of allocation that we needed to ensure.

Let us define a cell to be *free* if no other cell in the same row or column has been allocated a request. Our observation is that all *free* cells either have two tokens or do not have a token.

Let us now see if this observation holds true for a case where a few of the agents are interested in acquiring resources. This situation is shown in Figure 8.51, where cells (2,2) and (3,1) are interested in acquiring a resource. In the first round, cell (2,2) consumes both the tokens, thus all the cells in the second column and second row are not free after the first round. For example, the cells (2,1) and (3,2) are not free in the second round. Also observe that they have a single token each.

The remaining tokens propagate as per the rules that we have defined. Again in round 3, the cell (3,1) consumes the two tokens that it gets. Finally, we have 4 tokens left in round 4.

Let us look at the cells that are free in each round. We observe that our earlier observation still holds. All the free cells either have two tokens or do not have any token. We never have a situation where a free cell has a single token. This is not possible because for a cell to have a single token, one of the tokens in its row or column must have been consumed. This means that the cell is not free anymore.

From both these examples (Figures 8.50 and 8.51), we can conclude that the mapping that is produced is correct – no agent is allocated more than one resource, and no resource is allocated to more than one agent. Is it maximal?

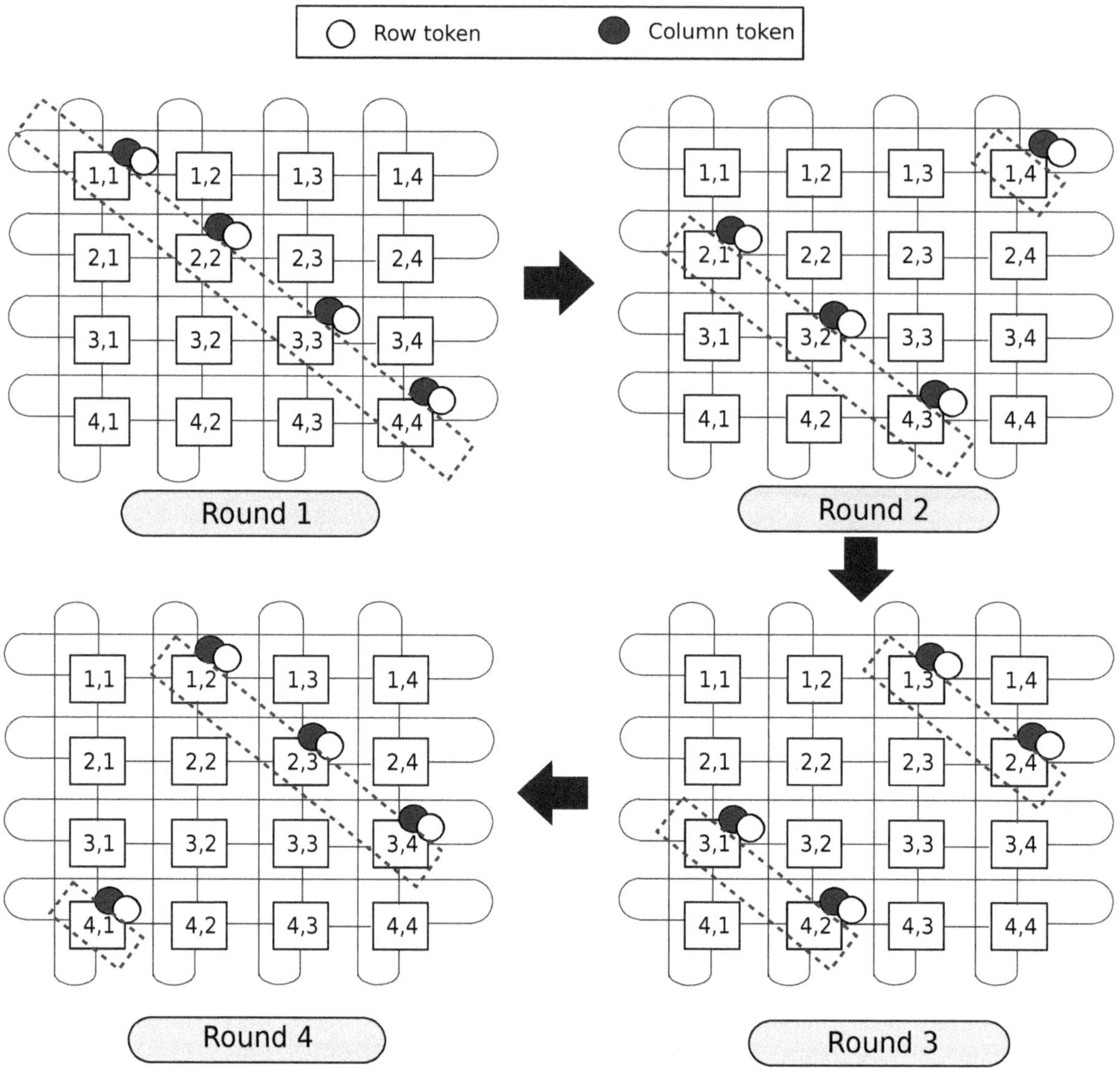

Figure 8.50: The movement of tokens in different rounds

If the mapping is not maximal, then it means that there is an agent-resource pair that can be still mapped after all the rounds are over. If it can be mapped, it must be the case that the corresponding cell was always free. At some point, the wavefront must have crossed it, and at that point the cell should have consumed both the tokens. Since this has not happened, there is a contradiction, and it is not possible to have a free cell after all the rounds are over. Thus we have proven that a wavefront allocator produces a maximal mapping. It is not necessarily optimal though.

Summary

Figure 8.52 shows the full design of the router. Note the credit computation unit that processes the credits received from neighbouring routers and forwards credits when buffers get freed.

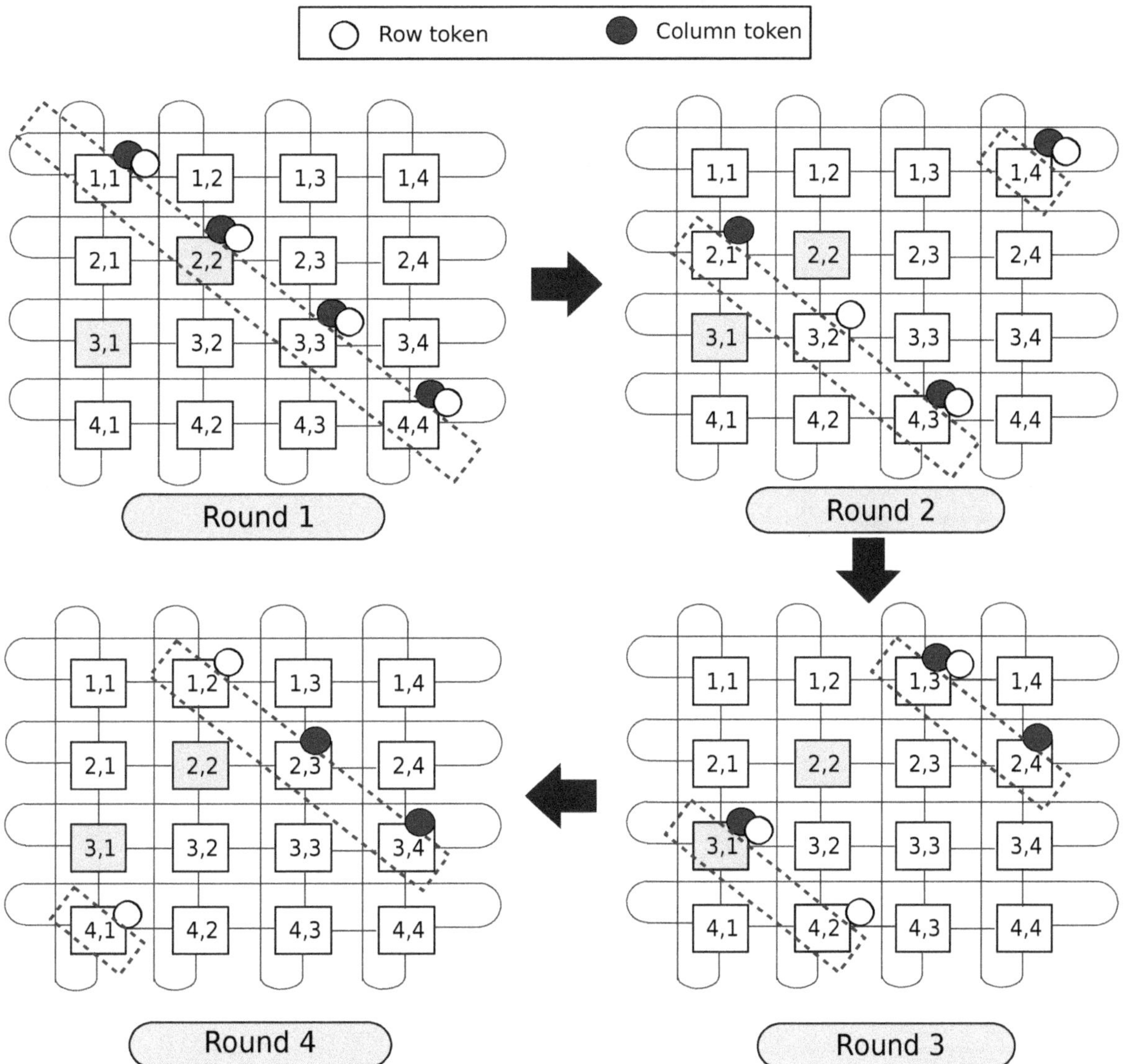

Figure 8.51: The movement of tokens in different rounds when two cells are interested in acquiring a resource

8.4.7 The Router's Pipeline

We have described the five stages of processing a packet at a router: BW (buffer write), RC (route computation), VA (VC allocation), SA (switch allocation), and ST (switch traversal) (see Table 8.4). Note that the head flit needs to go through these 5 stages. However, for the rest of the flits (body and tail), they need not go through all of these stages because they will follow the same route as the head flit and also use the same virtual channel. Hence, for these flits we can skip the RC and VA stages. For them the router's pipeline has only three stages: BW, SA, and ST. However, the critical path is still determined by the head flit because the body and tail flits are not allowed to overtake the head flit.

Similar to processor pipelines, we can make a simplistic assumption that they take roughly the same amount of time. This can also be ensured by sizing the buffers and structures appropriately. As we assume in a standard in-order pipeline, each stage takes 1 cycle to traverse. Thus to traverse the entire

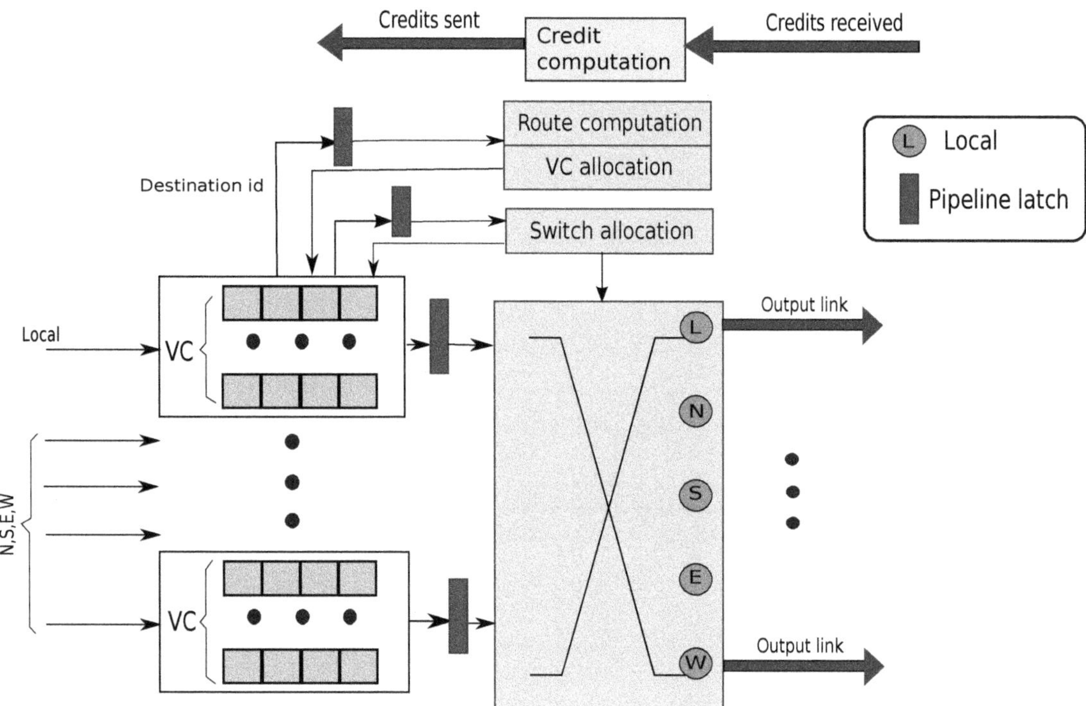

Figure 8.52: Design of the router

Name	Abbreviation
Buffer Write	BW
Route Computation	RC
VC Allocation	VA
Switch Allocation	SA
Switch Traversal	ST

Table 8.4: Stages in a router's pipeline

pipeline in a router, it will take 5 cycles.

This pipeline can be thought of as a simple 5-stage in-order pipeline where a train of flits enter, and leave via the outgoing channels in the same order in which they arrived. It is possible that a flit F in packet P may stall because of the lack of availability of resources such as VCs or switch ports. In this case, there will be a stall in the router's pipeline and we will not be able to transmit the flit, or any subsequent flit in packet P.

This situation is depicted in the space-time diagram in Figure 8.53. Unlike a processor, where one stall stops all the instructions in the earlier stages of the pipeline from making progress, in this case flits in other VCs can proceed. They are not blocked. The only flits that are blocked are flits in the current packet. Here also, there is an important difference. In a processor, two instructions can never be in the same pipeline stage; however in this case, two flits of the same packet can be in the same router pipeline stage. Let us elaborate. It is possible for flit $F3$ to be written into a buffer when flit $F2$ is in the buffer write stage waiting for flit $F1$ to make progress. This means that two flits of the same packet can be in the buffer write stage (either being written into a buffer or waiting to progress to the next stage). We have however not shown this in our space-time diagram in Figure 8.53 for the sake of readability and simplicity. In the figure, we assume that flit $F3$ enters the BW stage after $F2$ leaves it.

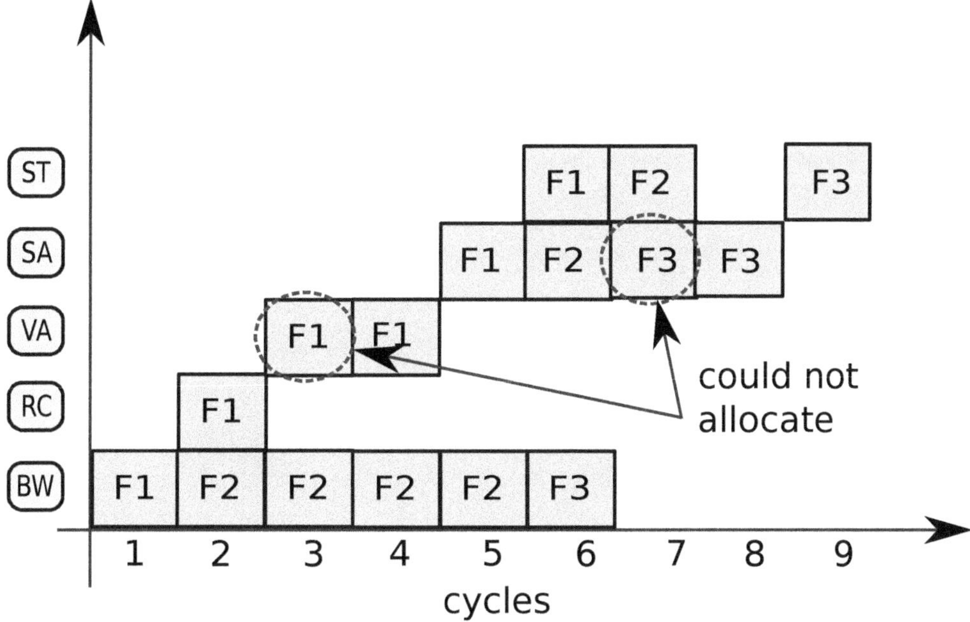

Figure 8.53: Space-time diagram of a 3-flit packet being sent through a router's 5-stage pipeline

Let us now point out an irony. It takes roughly 1 cycle to traverse a link and it takes 5 cycles to traverse a router's pipeline! This means that the delay in the routers is 5 times the time it takes to propagate through all the links. This further means that the latency of routers is the primary determinant of the on-chip transmission delay. Let us consider some representative numbers. Consider a system with 32 cores and 32 cache banks. We can arrange them as a 8×8 chessboard. The worst case delay between two points in a 2D mesh can be calculated as follows. Assume that we always take the shortest path. In this case, the worst case delay is incurred when we send a message from one corner to the diagonally opposite corner. We need to traverse through 14 hops and 15 routers. The total time required is $14 \times 1 + 15 \times 5$ (=89) cycles. Now, if we want a reply from the cache bank at the diagonally opposite corner, the total transmission delay for the request and the reply is equal to two times 89 cycles, which is 178 cycles. This is significant, and is of the order of the main memory access time, which is typically between 200 and 300 cycles.

Hence, there is an urgent need to reduce the time of propagation within a router such that the total latency can also commensurately decrease. It is necessary to speed up the NoC. We cannot reduce the speed of the links themselves because we are constrained by basic physics. The only option that is available to us is to make the routers faster. We need to somehow compress the 5-stage router pipeline to a shorter pipeline. Let us look at some pipeline optimisations to speed up the NoC by reducing the number of stages.

Lookahead Routing

The first stage, buffer write, is required. Without this stage the packet will get lost. Let us thus look at the next stage, Route Computation (RC). We have assumed that this stage takes 1 cycle. Can we move this stage out of the critical path? The answer is No, because the subsequent stage, VC allocation, needs this information. Unless we know the route (the outgoing physical channel), we will not be able to allocate a VC. It does indeed look like that we we need to have the RC stage as the second stage, and this needs to be on the critical path. However, we can do something ingenious.

Let us compute the route one hop in advance. Consider Figure 8.54, where we show the route from nodes 1 to 6 (nodes along the route are numbered 1, 2, 3, 4, 5, and 6). Before sending the head flit to the starting node (node 1), we compute the next hop. Thus, the portion of the route, $1 \rightarrow 2$, is known. Then the head flit enters the pipeline of the router. Since the route is known, the process of route computation is off the critical path. We can assign virtual channels, and switch ports in the router's pipeline, and in parallel compute the route that should be taken after exiting node 2. We compute this to be node 3. After leaving node 1, when the head flit reaches node 2, the subsequent route is known in advance. We know that the next hop is $2 \rightarrow 3$; hence, we can start assigning virtual channels. Similar to the process followed in node 1, we can compute the route to be followed after leaving node 4, which is $3 \rightarrow 4$.

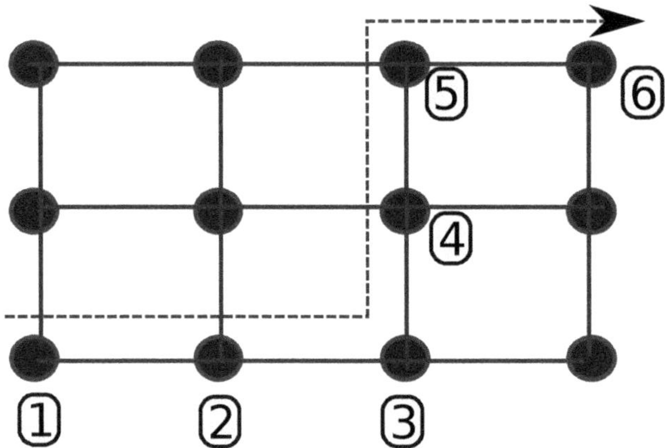

Figure 8.54: Route from nodes 1 to 6

Our 5-stage pipeline thus becomes a 4-stage pipeline because we have removed the RC stage off the critical path. It executes in parallel, and it simply needs to compute its result before the head flit leaves the router. The resultant pipeline is shown in Figure 8.55 for both head flits and body/tail flits.

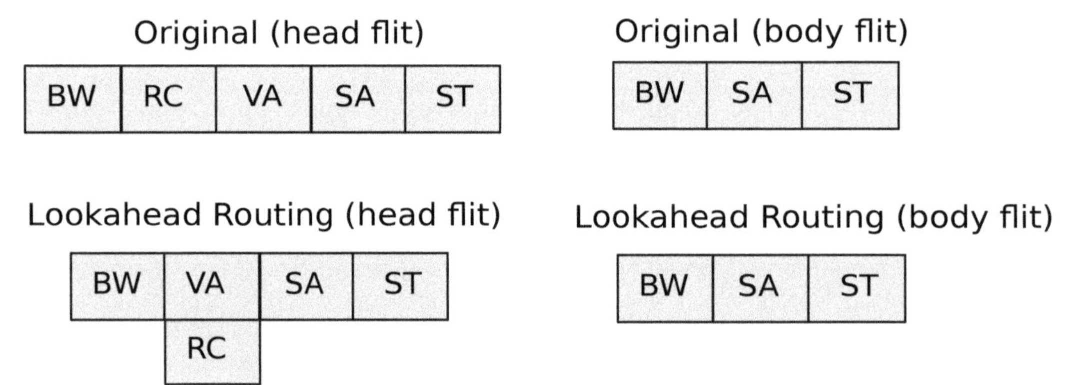

Figure 8.55: Pipeline stages in lookahead routing

Bypassing

Assume a router is very lightly loaded, which means that very little traffic flows through the router. In this case, we need not increase the overhead of the process of routing by first writing the flit to a buffer, and then looking for free ports in the switch. If we make an optimistic assumption that the switch is free, and we can get access to its ports without contention, then we can further shorten the length of the router pipeline. This is called *bypassing* [5]. The pipeline is shown in Figure 8.56. We skip the buffer write (BW), and switch allocation (SA) stages.

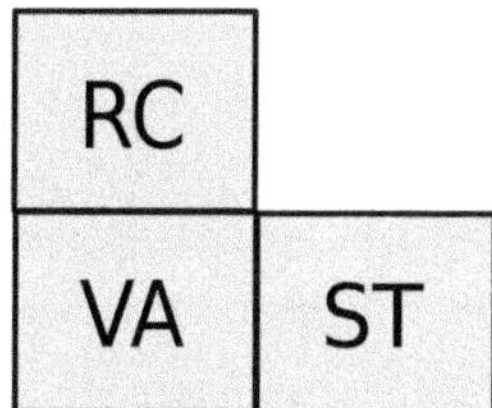

Figure 8.56: 2-stage pipeline in the case of bypassing (for the head flit)

Whenever we decide to adopt this technique, there are several things we must take into consideration. First, it is possible that two flits are trying to enter the same ingress (input) port of the switch (assuming that we do not have one port for each VC). In this situation one of the flits needs to wait. We can write that flit to a buffer, and make it traverse through the regular pipeline. It is also possible that we might have contention at the output links. For example, two flits might be trying to leave the router via the westward outgoing link. In this case, we have a conflict, and one of the flits needs to wait, and get buffered.

As we can observe from Figure 8.56, in the best case, the router pipeline gets compressed to just two stages, which is the best that can be done with our current model. We need at least one cycle for computing the route even with lookahead routing; we allocate a VC in parallel. Subsequently, we need one more cycle for traversing the switch.

Speculative VC Allocation

Even though bypassing can effectively reduce a 5-stage pipeline to a 2-stage pipeline, it cannot be done always. Bypassing can only be done when the amount of traffic in the network is low. This is non-deterministic in nature, and its applicability is limited in scenarios with high NoC traffic. Such schemes are called speculative schemes, because we are making a guess – speculating – that a switch port, and the outgoing link is free.

Let us instead speculatively perform VC allocation (VA stage) by assuming that we shall find one free VC. This will help us remove this stage from the critical path. VC allocation can be done simultaneously with switch allocation and route computation as shown in Figure 8.57 (combined with lookahead routing). By the time we have allocated a VC, the head flit will be in the switch traversal stage. Just before it is sent on the outgoing link, we can add the VC information and send it on the link. This represents the best case scenario where we are able to allocate a VC. However, this need not be the case always, particularly if the load on the network is high. In this case, it is possible that we might run out of VCs. As a result, speculative VC allocation will not succeed. Similar to the case of bypassing, we need to make the head flit follow the rest of the stages of the regular pipeline without resorting to any form of speculation.

The advantage of speculative VC allocation is that it reduces a 5-stage pipeline to a 3-stage pipeline as shown in Figure 8.57. This will not be possible all the time; however, the likelihood of its success is in general much more than the success with bypassing. This is because in this case, we just need a free VC, whereas in the case of bypassing we need a free input port in the switch and a free outgoing link as well. Of course, the final answer depends on the number of VCs per physical channel, the size of

---

[5]Note that bypassing is a router optimisation. It is not the same as forwarding and bypassing in pipelines. These are different terms.

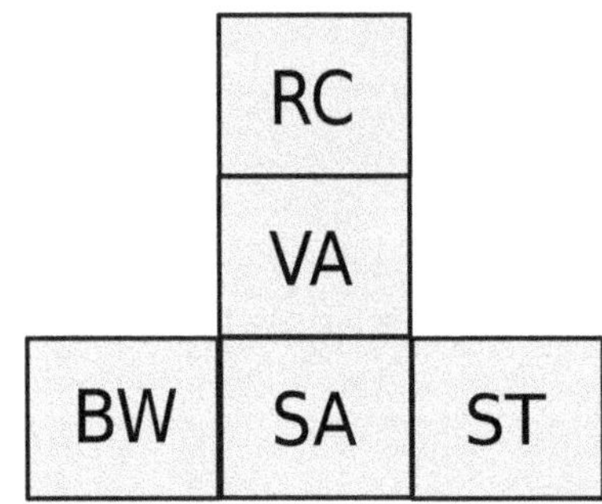

Figure 8.57: Speculative VC allocation

the switch, and the nature of the traffic. This question is best answered with architectural simulation studies.

Late VC Selection

Let us introduce another approach, where we remove the VA stage altogether. Once switch ports are allocated, let us send the head flit through the switch. In the time being, let us try to allocate a VC using a very simple allocator. Let us maintain a queue of free VCs for each outgoing link. Whenever we need to allocate a VC for the head flit, we simply select the head of the queue. The VC information is appended to the head flit after it traverses the switch; the head flit along with the VC is then sent to the next router on the path. Subsequent flits in the packet use the same VC. The reason that we can afford a simple allocator such as a queue is because only one flit traverses a link at any time, and thus there is no need for arbitration across multiple requests.

Let us now look at the finer points. If a head flit is allocated a switch port in the SA stage, then we are making the assumption that it will find a free VC. If it does not find a free VC, then we cannot send the flit. Note that in this case we are speculating, which means that we send the head flit through the switch in the hope of finding a free VC for the outgoing link similar to speculative VC allocation. If the speculation fails, then we have to cancel the process and make the head flit go through the regular pipeline.

We can opt for a slightly more conservative option. We check if the queue has entries before entering the switch allocation stage. If there are no free entries, then the head flit does not enter the SA stage in the first place, we wait to be allocated a VC.

The next question that we need to answer is when do we return a VC to the queue. This can be done when the VC is deallocated – when the tail flit of the packet leaves the router.

8.5 Non-Uniform Cache Architectures

After the complexity of single cores reached saturation, the additional transistors were used to increase the number of cores and the sizes of the caches. The sad part with increasing the sizes of the caches is that they become very large to manage. Hence, as we have seen in Section 7.3, to keep the delays in check, we divide a large cache into banks, and we further divide banks into subarrays. There is a trade-off between the time that a circuit takes to locate and route the signal to the right subarray and the access time of the subarray.

Such conventional designs worked very well when the size of the on-chip cache was of the order of hundreds of kilobytes. However, such designs fail to scale when the cache size exceeds a few megabytes. The main reason for such caches failing to scale is the delay incurred in routing the request to the right subarray. As we have argued, it is thus necessary to create an on-chip network (NoC).

An NoC allows a bank based design, which allows parallel accesses to different banks. Even though this method increases the throughput, let us understand the effect on latency. Consider a chessboard based design with 32 cores and 32 cache banks (8×8) with a mesh based NoC. To move a flit from one corner to the diagonally opposite corner we need to traverse through 15 routers and 14 links. Traversing the links is fast (typically less than a cycle); however the routers are slow (3-5 cycles) in spite of the numerous optimisations that are used to speed up router pipelines.

Moreover, the delays of different banks are not the same. Proximate (nearby) banks take a lesser amount of time to access as compared to banks that are far away. NoC delays can typically vary from 5 to 50 cycles to access different banks. Whenever we have variance to such an extent, we are presented with a huge opportunity for proposing optimisations to cache access protocols. We should strive to somehow place data closer to the requesting cores.

Consequently, let us look at a set of proposals called non-uniform cache architectures [Kim et al., 2003]; they are also referred to as *NUCA* architectures. These schemes propose to manage large L2/L3 caches such that the mean access time is reduced in caches with elaborate NoCs and variable bank access times.

We shall introduce two main types of architectures in this space.

S-NUCA Cache blocks are allotted to banks statically.

D-NUCA Cache blocks are allotted to banks dynamically. Blocks can migrate between banks at run time.

8.5.1   Static NUCA(S-NUCA)

The basic idea is very simple. If we have K cache banks, we use $log_2(K)$ bits from a block's address to address the bank. Let us consider a representative example. Assume a 32-bit addressing scheme, a 64-byte block size, and 256 sets per cache bank. We will thus have to dedicate 6 bits to address a byte within the block. The block address is thus 26 bits. In addition, we need to use 8 bits to address the set. The remaining 18 bits are the tag. Next, assume that we have 32 banks. This means that we need 5 bits to decide the bank. Which 5 bits should these be?

Let us answer this question by considering multiple designs. Consider the two alternatives shown in Figure 8.58. We show two schemes: S_{LSB} and S_{no-LSB}. In the S_{LSB} scheme, we choose the 5 LSB bits (bits 1 to 5) of the block address to uniquely address each bank. Bits 6-13 are used to address the set. In the S_{no-LSB} scheme, we use the 8 LSB bits (bits 1 to 8) of the block to address the set, and then we use bits 9-13 to address the bank. These are the two most popular schemes.

To understand which design is better, let us appreciate a basic fact. We expect the randomness in the least significant bits to be more as compared to the more significant bits in any address. This is because of spatial locality. Most of the time we will be accessing different cache blocks in the same region of memory. Thus, the lower order bits will vary more. Since the memory region remains the same, the higher order bits that determine it will remain the same. For example, if most of the accesses are within the same page then all the bits that determine the page id shall remain the same.

Let us now use this understanding to answer our question. In the S_{LSB} scheme, we shall have more randomness (more uniformity) in choosing the bank; however, the access pattern for sets within a bank will not be that uniform. In the S_{no-LSB} scheme, we shall have the reverse effect. The accesses to sets within a bank will be more uniform, but bank accesses will be less uniform. What do we want to optimise? Essentially, there is a trade-off between bank conflicts and set conflicts. The answer is dependent on the traffic pattern and requires simulation studies.

8.5.2   Dynamic NUCA(D-NUCA)

The main disadvantage of an S-NUCA protocol is that we are not taking the usage of blocks into account. We should ideally place a frequently used block close to the requesting core. This is not

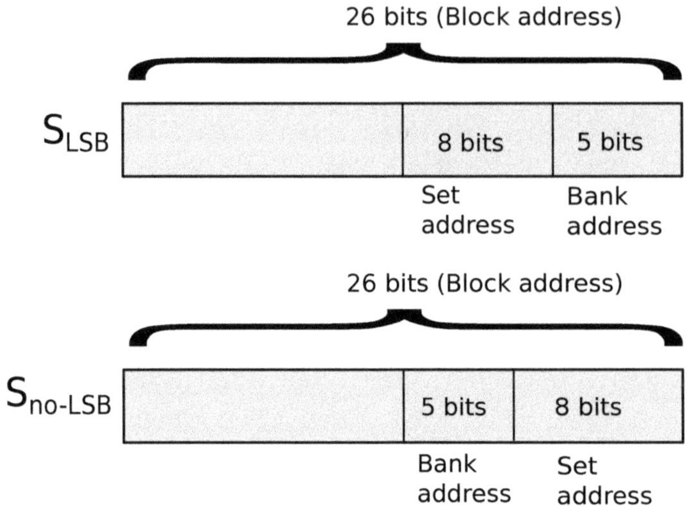

Figure 8.58: Two methods to address a bank and a set in the S-NUCA protocol

happening. Hence, let us propose the D-NUCA protocol that places blocks close to the requesting cores and migrates blocks based on the access pattern.

The key idea is to divide the set of banks into columns as shown in Figure 8.59. We call each such column a *bank set*. A block can be present within any bank of the bank set. There is no replication though.

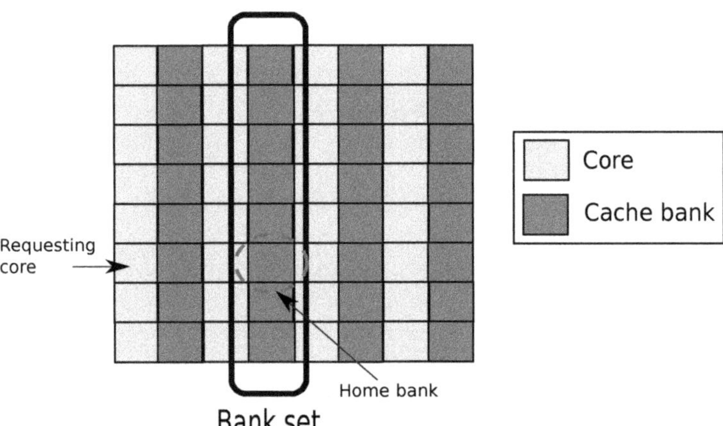

Figure 8.59: Bank sets in D-NUCA. The cores and cache banks are organised in columns.

In Figure 8.59 we have 4 bank sets. We can use 2 bits from the block address to determine the bank set. This is where we need to do something to ensure that we are able to achieve our objective of placing data close to the requesting cores. Let us designate one of the banks within the bank set as the *home bank*. There is no hard and fast rule regarding how we designate the home bank. However, most research proposals in this area designate the bank in the bank set that is the closest to the requesting core (shortest routing path) as the home bank [Arora et al., 2015]. This is shown in Figure 8.59. The requesting core sends the memory request to the home bank first; it has a separate home bank in each bank set.

Search Policies

Once the request reaches the home bank, we need to search for the block. We first search within the home bank. If there is a hit, then we send the value back to the requesting core. If there is a miss, then we need to search the rest of the banks within the bank set. In this case each bank set is a column – a linear sequence of banks. We need to search the rest of the banks according to a given search policy. As described by Arora et al. [Arora et al., 2015] there are three types of commonly used search policies as shown in Figure 8.60. Note that in this scheme, we never replicate a block across banks; every block has a single location. The search policies are as follows.

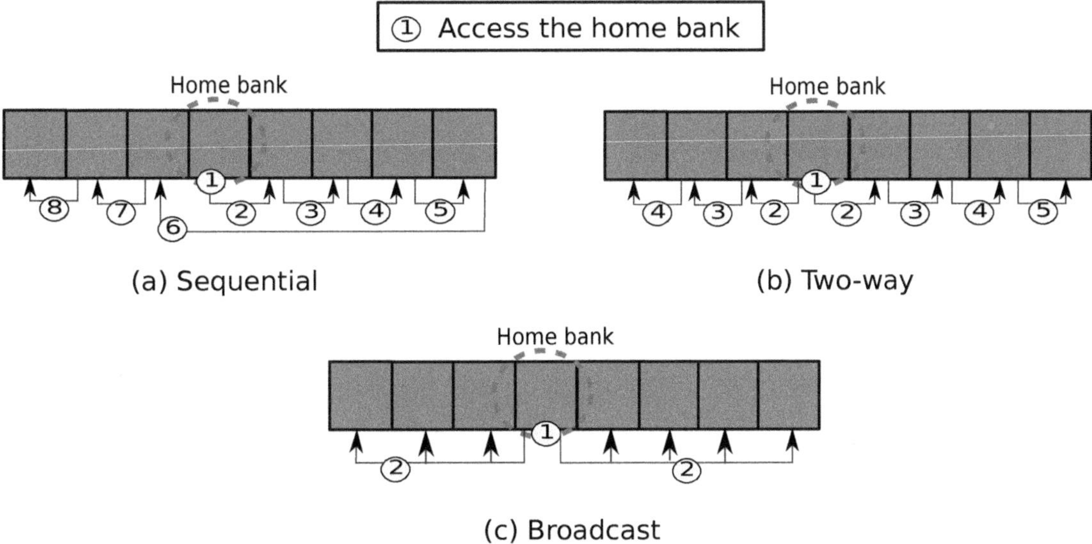

Figure 8.60: Different search policies within a bank set

Sequential We search all the banks in one direction and go till the end. If we do not find the block, then we start searching in the other direction till we reach the end.

Two-Way In this scheme, we send two parallel messages in both the directions. If the block is present in the bank set, then it will be found in only one bank. As compared to the *Sequential* scheme, we are expected to get a response sooner.

Broadcast In this scheme, we broadcast a message to all the banks. On an average, we have a lot of additional bank accesses. However, this is also the fastest scheme if we do not take the contention within banks and the NoC into account. We do not have to waste time searching banks that do not contain the block.

As we can see in Figure 8.60, there is a trade-off between the number of messages we send, the number of banks we search, and the overall latency. Note that *Broadcast* is not necessarily a better scheme. It increases the rate of bank utilisation significantly, and this increases the amount of contention. In a highly loaded system this can decrease the overall performance as well. It is thus necessary to choose the search policy wisely.

Finally, after we locate the block, we send it back to the requesting core. If we don't find it, we signal a miss and a request is sent to the lower level of the memory hierarchy.

Migration

The real magic of a dynamic NUCA cache lies in migration. Upon a hit, we try to bring the block closer to the requesting core. Note that the home bank of the block (from the point of view of the requesting core) is the closest bank in the bank set. If we have a hit in the home bank, then nothing needs to be done because the block resides in the closest possible bank.

Otherwise, we migrate the block towards the home bank. Figure 8.61 shows an example. Initially, we have a hit in bank A, which is not the home bank. We move the block one hop towards the home bank. This means that the next time the same core requests for the same block, the request has to travel one hop less. Ultimately, the block will migrate to the home bank, and remain there assuming that there are no conflicting requests from other cores with different home banks.

By migrating blocks towards the home bank, we are in effect reducing the cache access latency for that block. We are also reducing the number of bank accesses in the *Sequential* and *Two-way* search policies.

When there is an eviction from a bank, we have two choices. Either we write the block to the lower level, or we write it to a bank that is further away from the home bank. In the latter scheme, a block is finally evicted from the cache and written to the lower level when it is evicted from the last bank (rim of the chip) in the bank set. The negative aspect of this scheme is that if a block is not going to be used anymore, it lingers on in the cache for a much longer time. However, on the flip side, the positive aspect is that if the block will be used again, it can found in a bank that is further away in the bank set. Ultimately, the choice of the scheme depends on the nature of the workload.

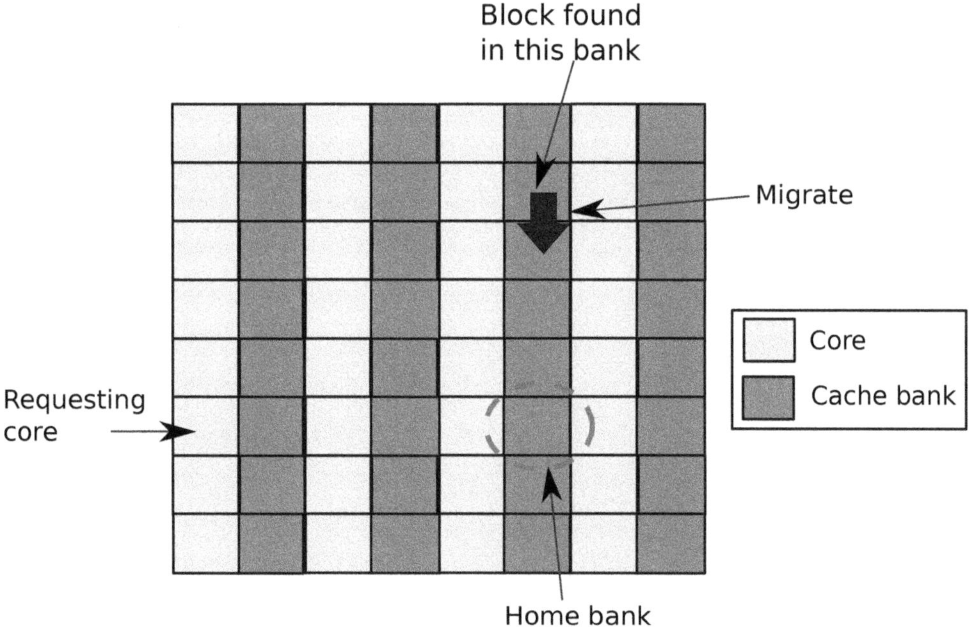

Figure 8.61: Block migration in a D-NUCA cache

This feature helps us reduce the effects of NoC delay in a big way. Even if the chip has a very large NoC, we always try to bring the frequently accessed cache blocks to banks that are the closest to the respective requesting cores subject to the constraint that they remain within their bank sets. This can decrease the latency of cache accesses significantly, and thus is the method of choice in most designs that use NUCA schemes.

Afterthoughts

We can think of a bank set as one large virtual cache bank that all the cores can use. One advantage of having such banks set as opposed to the S-NUCA design is that such bank sets can absorb non-uniformities in bank accesses very effectively. In S-NUCA if there is high contention in one bank, then this will lead to large memory latencies. However, in the case of D-NUCA, blocks will just get distributed in the bank set as per our migration and eviction policies. This will ensure that as a whole, D-NUCA performs better than S-NUCA.

The other advantage of a bank set is that it allows migration of blocks towards proximate banks. This helps us nullify the effect of NoC delays significantly because we reduce the access time of blocks that are the most frequently used.

8.5.3   Advanced Schemes

Till now we have been making the cardinal assumption that blocks are not replicated across banks in the bank set. Otherwise, there will be a need to keep all of these replicas synchronised. This means that whenever we write to one replica of the block, we need to write to the other replicas as well. This increases the complexity, and in addition, we need a lot of additional state to keep track of all the replicas.

However, this is not a very bad idea as long as we can confine this technique to cache blocks that are read-only. Such cache blocks are of two types: instruction blocks and read-only data blocks. In most programs we never modify the cache blocks that contain instructions while the program is running. Hence, as far as we are concerned, they are read-only blocks. In addition, cache blocks containing data can also be read-only, particularly when they contain constants. All of these read-only blocks can be replicated across banks in the bank set, and thus we can further reduce the access latency. However, detecting read-only blocks is difficult in hardware. Even if we can establish that a given block has not been written to in the last N cycles (N being a very large number), it does not mean that it will not be modified in the future. The only way to do this is by using compiler analyses at the time of program compilation. The compiler can place all the constants in a virtual memory page, and mark it as read-only. We can have an additional bit in the TLB and the page table that marks the page as read-only. Once the hardware is aware of this, it can replicate blocks in the read-only page across cache banks.

For blocks that may be modified, it is not possible to do this unless we invest in a lot of hardware to synchronise the different replicas. We shall devote Chapter 9 to precisely study this problem. We shall conclude that it is possible to do this for smaller caches such as the L1 cache. Maintaining synchronisation across replicas is very difficult at the L2 and L3 levels.

Optimisations for Private Data

Assume that a given core is running a thread. Every thread has some private data, which is not accessed by any other thread. This includes the contents of the stack, and the contents of memory areas predefined as thread local storage (TLS) areas. The compiler is aware of the memory regions that are allocated to such areas; hence, it can add instructions to define these memory regions as *private*. In addition, in many architectures, the hardware is also aware of the addresses of these regions. It too can set the *private* bit in the corresponding entries of the TLBs and page tables.

Once we access the TLB, we instantly become aware if the block is in a *private* region or not. If it is, then some more optimisations are possible. Since this data will not be required by any other core, we should not allow the blocks to migrate to a cache bank that is far away. There are several possible strategies.

- We initially load all the blocks in the private region of a thread to the home bank of its core, and thereafter we discourage their eviction by increasing their priority.

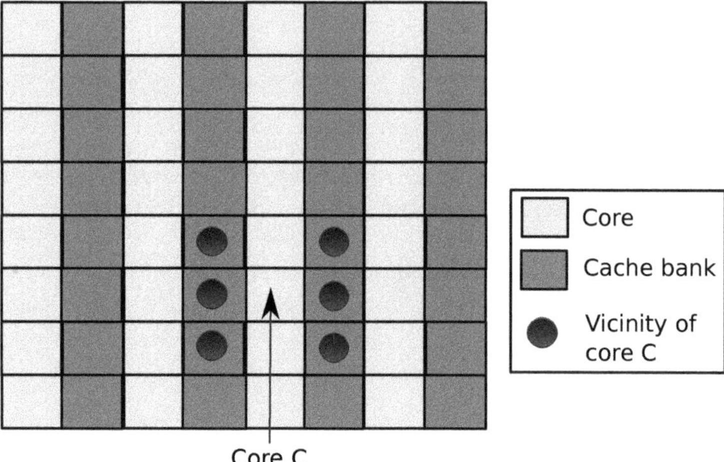

Figure 8.62: Placing private data in the vicinity of core C

- We define a small window of banks in each bank set on both sides of the corresponding home bank. We put private cache blocks in these banks while initialising a thread. To further discourage their eviction, we always try to evict a block that is not private.

- We do not use the concept of bank sets for private data. Instead we store all the blocks in banks around the requesting core C (see Figure 8.62). This means that we consider the banks that are closest to the requesting core (irrespective of their bank set), and store all the private cache blocks in them. Even though this approach is correct because these blocks are never shared, there will be a problem if the thread is migrated to another core. The other core needs to know about the location of the private blocks. We can have severe correctness issues unless we migrate all the private data to the vicinity of the new core. This is very expensive.

8.6 Performance Aspects

Let us now look at some of the ways in which we measure the performance of an NoC. We need to start with a disclaimer that the nature of evaluation depends on the type of optimisations that are proposed and the final use case. For example, if we are designing the NoC for a low power processor, then we should be interested in measuring power consumption. If we are designing the NoC for a high performance processor, then we should be interested in latency and throughput. To assess the performance of an NoC, it is necessary to simulate network traffic and observe the behaviour of the NoC. Let us first describe the metrics of interest and then we shall discuss popular simulation techniques.

8.6.1 Evaluation Metrics

Here is the list of metrics that are used to evaluate an NoC.

Latency One of the simplest metrics is the latency (measured in terms of clock cycles), which is the time that a packet takes to go from a source to a destination. This can be affected by the choice of the route and the degree of congestion in the network. Now, if we consider multiple source-destination pairs, then there are several ways in which we can aggregate this information. We can either consider the mean latency, the variance of the latency divided by the mean, or the mean latency per hop. The mean latency per hop is independent of the distance from the source to the destination – it just indicates the average number of cycles the packet took to traverse each router and the outgoing link. This gives an indication of the degree of congestion in the network.

Throughput The *throughput* of a network is simply defined as the number of bytes that are transferred per unit time throughout the network. A simple way to measure it is to simulate the network for a large number of cycles and compute the throughput over time. Finally, we can report the mean value. Note that the throughput is not the same as the bandwidth. The latter is a theoretical maximum; however, the throughput is a value that is practically observed. The throughput points to the overall efficiency of data transfer in a network.

Energy/Power In modern NoCs, energy and power consumption are important issues. We would like to minimise the energy that the NoC consumes. This can be done by reducing the size of the routers, powering down parts of a router when they are not in use, and minimising the length of routes.

Area and Routing Complexity An NoC requires on-chip resources for all the links (wires) and the routers. We need to ensure that we have enough space to place all the wires, and also ensure that existing connections between circuit elements do not get lengthened. This requires very sophisticated NoC wire placement algorithms. Additionally, we need to minimise the area that the routers take such that we have enough space left for cores and caches.

8.6.2   Simulation Methodologies

The standard way of simulating the performance of an NoC is to use an NoC simulator. In such a simulator, we completely simulate the behaviour of all aspects of the NoC including the routers, the links, and the logic to perform flow control. An NoC simulator can either be standalone, or can be coupled with an architectural simulator that also simulates the processor and the memory system. A standalone NoC simulator needs to be provided inputs regarding the traffic that needs to be simulated. The inputs can be of two types: statistical or trace based.

Standalone Simulators

Statistical inputs specify the probability of injecting a packet in a given node in a cycle. This is known as the *injection rate*. For example, if the injection rate is 0.1 (per cycle) at a node, then it means that there is a 10% probability that the node will start the transmission of a packet to any destination in a cycle. In most network simulations, we typically vary the injection rate and study the behaviour of the network. In addition, it is possible to change the uniform probability distribution of packet injections to either a normal distribution, or a Weibull distribution. Now, for a given a packet source, let us look at the different methods to determine the destination. These are also known as different types of traffic.

Types of Traffic

It is necessary to choose a destination node for a given source node while synthetically generating traffic with statistical injection rates. Let us assume a network that is either a torus or a mesh. Each node has a x-y coordinate (each n bits). Then the location of each node can be specified with a $2n$ bit number: $x_{n-1} \ldots x_0, y_{n-1} \ldots y_0$. Let us now discuss different traffic patterns. Refer to Figure 8.63, where for the sake of readability we only show the traffic from the shaded cells. In the following descriptions, we assume that we send a message from the source, S, to the destination, D. Both S and D are $2n$-bit vectors, where the upper (more significant) n bits represent the x coordinate, and the lower (least significant) n bits represent the y coordinate. We shall represent the x and y coordinates of S using the terms S_x and S_y respectively. Likewise, we define the terms D_x and D_y for the destination. Let $S[i]$ indicate the ith bit in S, where we start counting from 0 (similar definition for $D[i]$). The LSB is always bit 0.

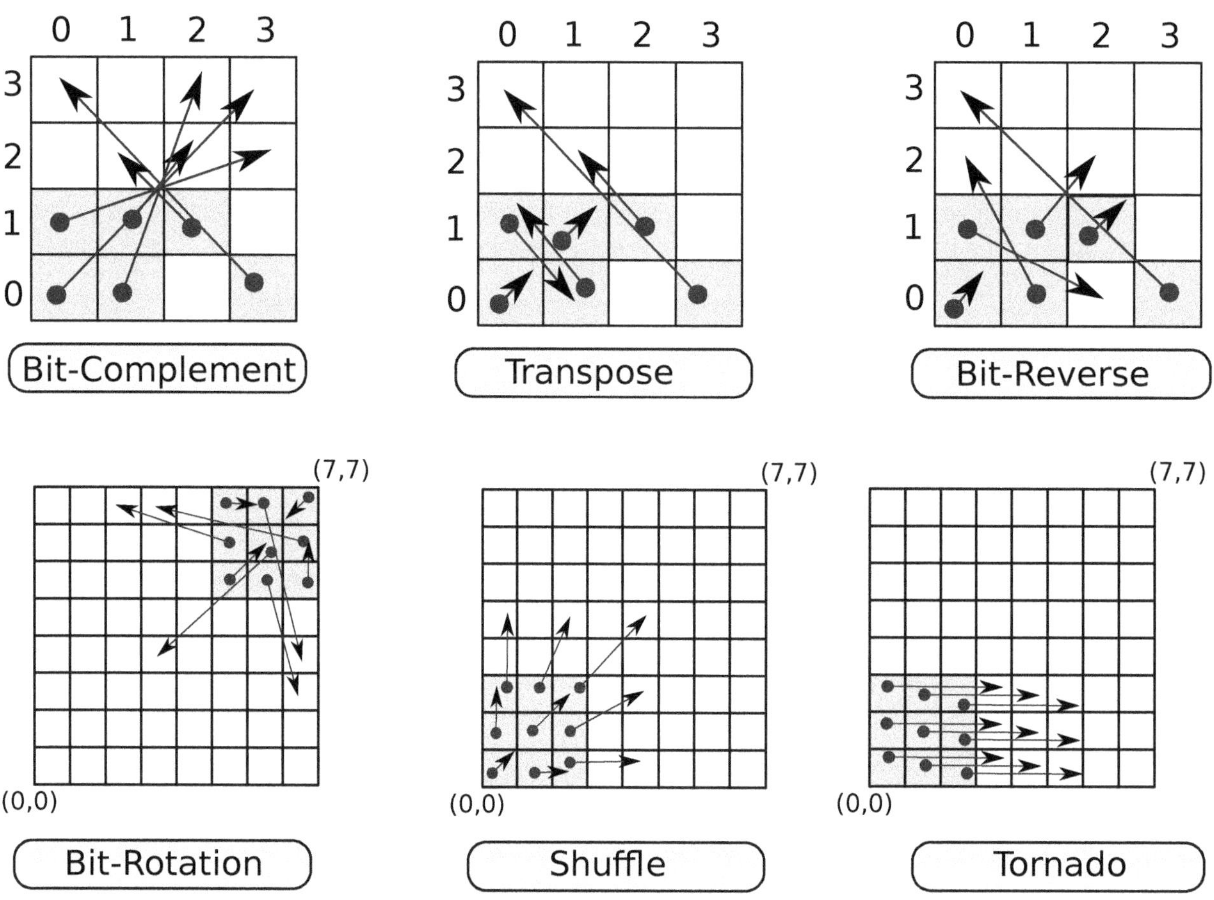

Figure 8.63: Types of traffic

Random In this case, we randomly choose one of the rest of the nodes with a uniform probability distribution. This kind of a simulation method is used when we expect to run workloads without any known communication pattern.

Bit-Complement We consider the 1's complement of each of the coordinate values. The destination is equal to $(\bar{S}_x, \bar{S}_y)$. For example, if the source is $(0,1)$, the destination is $(3,2)$ in a (4×4) 16-node network. As we can see from Figure 8.63, in this communication pattern, messages try to move towards the diagonally opposite corner. This is a good pattern to test the overall throughput of the network because messages typically tend to traverse long distances.

Transpose The destination is (S_y, S_x) (x and y coordinates of the source interchanged). Such a communication pattern is typically found in linear algebra applications that compute functions on transposed matrices. Here the source and the destination are the same for all the elements on the diagonal $((0,0)$ to $(3,3))$. This is shown in Figure 8.63, where the source and the destination are in the same cell for the diagonal elements. The rest of the messages try to cross the diagonal and reach a point that is as far from the diagonal as the source. As compared to Bit-Complement, most of the movement of messages happens in a direction that is perpendicular to the diagonal.

Bit-Reverse In this case, we just reverse the binary bits of the source to get the destination. Formally, we have $D[i] = S[2n - 1 - i]$. Such a communication pattern is found in some implementations of the FFT (Fast Fourier Transform) algorithm. Even though the pattern looks similar to Bit-Complement and Transpose; however, it is far more irregular in nature, with both short distances, and very long distances.

Bit-Rotation This pattern is based on shifting the bits of the source to get the destination. We right shift the $2n$ bits of the source to get the destination. The LSB that is shifted out becomes the MSB of the destination (see Figure 8.64) and the following equations.

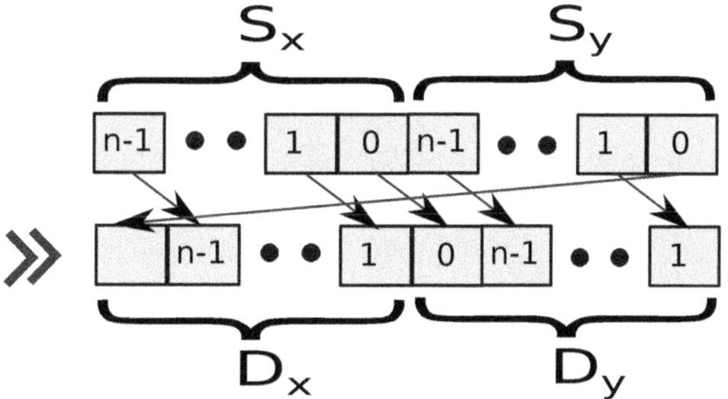

Figure 8.64: Bit-Rotation Pattern

$$D_x = [S_y[0], S_x[n-1], \ldots S_x[1]]$$
$$D_y = [S_x[0], S_y[n-1], \ldots S_y[1]]$$

(8.7)

The logic is as follows. After we right shift S_x, we are left with $n-1$ bits: $S_x[n-1] \ldots S_x[1]$. These are the lowest $n-1$ bits of D_x. The MSB is set to the LSB of S_y, which is $S_y[0]$. We follow a similar procedure for generating D_y. In simple terms, D_x (or D_y) is generated by shifting S_x (or S_y) one position to the right. The MSB is equal to the LSB of S_y (or S_x). As we see in Figure 8.63, a right shift by 1 position reduces the value of the x and y coordinates in most cases and brings the point closer to the origin (left bottom). However in some cases, the results are not quite as expected, the reason is that the MSBs that we set can be equal to 1, and thus the net effect is that the points might move further away from the origin. For example, if S_x is odd, then we will shift in a 1 into the MSB of D_y, and thus it may not decrease; however, if S_x is even, then the value of D_y will roughly halve (right shift by 1).

Shuffle This is the reverse of Bit-Rotation. Instead of shifting to the right, we shift to the left. This pattern of communication is frequently seen while computing FFTs (refer to Figure 8.63 for a visualisation).

$$D_x = [S_x[n-2], \ldots S_x[0], S_y[n-1]]$$
$$D_y = [S_y[n-2], \ldots S_y[0], S_x[n-1]]$$

(8.8)

The value of the MSB that is shifted out of S_x is made the LSB of D_y and vice versa. The intuition here is that we are roughly doubling the coordinates for the destination, when we are moving away from the origin. This allows us to quickly broadcast messages in a direction away from the origin. Many algorithms use this pattern to quickly divide the work and map it to the nodes.

Tornado In an $N \times N$ matrix, the destination is $((S_x + \lceil N/2 \rceil - 1)\%N, S_y)$. This basically means that we send a message that is roughly $N/2$ nodes away on the same row. If we reach the end of the mesh, then we wrap around. Such kind of patterns are typically seen while solving a system of differential equations, where a core computes the result of some computation and passes it to a subset of its neighbours.

Trace Based Simulators

A trace based NoC simulator does not use any statistical models. We can create traces using processor emulators or synthetic traffic generators. The traces contain details of the packets that each node needs to inject and their destinations. The NoC simulator can then read in these traces and simulate the NoC. The advantage of such kind of simulation is that we can simulate the NoC for specific applications. Generic statistical models do not model specific applications very well.

Architectural Simulation

Most generic architectural simulators such as the Tejas Simulator (see Appendix B) also contain NoC simulators. Such simulations are very accurate because we are additionally modelling the cores and the memory system as well. The exact timing gets simulated more accurately, and the NoC gets the right inputs at the right time. The NoC simulation module by itself is very similar to standalone NoC simulators. Architectural simulators are however much slower than NoC simulators because they need to simulate the rest of the components such as the cores and the memory system as well.

8.7   Summary and Further Reading

8.7.1   Summary

Summary 7

1. *In modern multicore processors, we have tens of cores and cache banks. It is necessary to connect them with an on-chip network (NoC).*

2. *We typically divide a chip into tiles, where each tile contains a set of co-located cores and cache banks. We assign one router to each tile.*

3. *A router is the most basic element in an NoC. Its job is to route messages between neighbouring routers or accept/initiate messages on behalf of its local tile. It mainly does routing (finding the path to the destination) and flow control (managing the flow of bits between neighbouring routers without any information loss).*

4. *A router is also called a* node *in a network, and two nodes are connected by a* link *– a set of parallel copper wires to carry multiple bits simultaneously.*

5. *The sender node sends a message to a receiver node. A message is typically broken down into packets, where an entire packet is routed as one atomic unit. Each packet is further subdivided into flits (flow control units) and a flit is divided into phits (physical bits). All the bits in a flit are stored together in routers, and all the bits in a phit are transmitted together on the physical copper wires.*

6. *The two flow-control schemes for transmission across a single link are credit based flow control and on-off flow control. They ensure that a message is sent to the destination only when it has the space for it.*

7. *For the entire NoC, we can do flow control at the level of messages, packets, or flits. A common message based flow control method is circuit switching, where we reserve an entire path from the source to the destination. Even though the path setup overhead is high, we can amortise the costs if the messages are long and the contention is low.*

8. *The two most common methods for flow control at the level of packets are store and forward (SAF) and virtual cut through (VCT). In the SAF approach, we first store an entire packet in a router, and then send its head flit to the next router. In the VCT based approach, we don't have to wait for the entire packet to be buffered at a router before we send its head flit to the next router along the way. Note that in both cases, we need to have enough space to buffer the entire packet in each router.*

9. *In flit based flow control, buffering at routers is done at the level of flits. We need not buffer the entire packet; however, all the flits in a packet are constrained to travel along the same route. The two most common algorithms for flit based flow control are wormhole flow control and virtual channel based flow control.*

10. *Virtual channel based flow control is more efficient than wormhole flow control because it multiplexes a physical channel between different packet transmissions. It conceptually breaks a physical channel into different virtual channels (VCs), where the different VCs have their dedicated set of buffers.*

11. *The three main concerns in routing flits across the NoC are deadlocks, livelocks, and starvation.*

12. *Livelocks and starvation can be avoided by adding the notion of a timeout to a message. If we augment each message with a hop count, and then send it along the shortest path to the destination after the hop count crosses a threshold, we will avoid the possibility of livelocks. Similarly we can avoid starvation if we can ensure that a packet or a flit has the highest priority for being allocated a resource if it has waited for more than a given number of cycles.*

13. *Avoiding deadlocks is far more involved. We use two theoretical tools to reason about protocols that are engineered to avoid deadlocks: channel dependence graph (CDG) and turn graph (TG). A channel dependence graph shows the dependence between physical or virtual channels. There is an edge from channel C_1 to C_2 if the flit that holds C_1 is waiting for C_2 to become free. A turn graph is a subset of the graph representing the network. We typically build a turn graph with a small subset of nodes, and links (channels), when we want to take a deep look at the nature of dependences in a given region of the network. Since a dependence in the channel graph is a turn in the turn graph, we can characterise situations such as deadlocks in terms of the turns that the flits want to take.*

14. *X-Y routing is a simple routing algorithm (provably deadlock-free), where we traverse along the x direction first and then traverse along the y direction.*

15. *To increase the path diversity in X-Y routing, we can use oblivious routing, where we first route a message to an intermediate node, and then route it from the intermediate node to the destination. This helps us deal with congestion better.*

16. *Adaptive routing is a more efficient solution where we avoid 2 out of 8 possible turns: one from a clockwise cycle and one from an anti-clockwise cycle.*

17. *We can use the notion of virtual channels to design deadlock free protocols by either ensuring that we get VCs in a certain order (using date lines) or by using escape VCs.*

18. *A router has 5 stages: buffer write (BW), route computation (RC), VC allocation (VA), switch allocation (SA), and switch traversal (ST).*

19. *An allocator matches N requests with M resources, whereas an arbiter is far more specific; it matches N requests with just 1 resource. We discussed the round robin arbiter, the matrix arbiter, the separable allocator, and the wavefront allocator.*

20. *Several strategies can be used to reduce the latency of a router's pipeline.*

    (a) *We can remove the RC stage from the critical path in lookahead routing by computing the route taken by the packet from the next router on the path towards the destination.*

    (b) *If the contention is low, we can directly try to access the switch and send the packet on the outgoing link. This method is known as bypassing.*

    (c) *If the VCs are normally free, we can try to allocate a VC speculatively. In this case, the VA stage can be moved off the critical path.*

21. *NoC delays can vary between 5 and 50 cycles. This makes the latency of accesses to the last level cache (LLC) quite nondeterministic. To reduce performance losses associated with such variable delays, researchers have proposed NUCA (non-uniform cache architectures) schemes for large caches.*

22. *In an S-NUCA (static NUCA) cache, we distribute all the blocks of the LLC among a multitude of cache banks spread throughout the chip. This scheme does not counteract the effect of large NoC latencies.*

23. *In a D-NUCA (dynamic NUCA) cache, we divide banks into non-overlapping bank sets. We search for a block in the home bank: the bank that is closest to the requesting core in the bank set. If we do not find the block, then we search the rest of the banks in the bank set. If there is a hit, we migrate the block towards the home bank, otherwise we access the lower level of the memory hierarchy.*

24. *The method of choice for assessing the performance and throughput of an NoC is simulation.*

    (a) *We can generate traffic synthetically. These are statistical models that have been derived from many real-world applications.*

    (b) *We can collect traces and feed them to NoC simulators.*

    (c) *Most architectural simulators also contain NoC simulators that take inputs from the memory system and realistically simulate the NoC traffic.*

8.7.2 Further Reading

For an alternative perspective, readers can consult the textbook by Dally and Towles [Dally and Towles, 2004]. The e-book by Jerger [Jerger et al., 2017] describes many contemporary developments in the field. Other sources of information are survey papers on on-chip optical networks such as [Bjerregaard and Mahadevan, 2006, Salminen et al., 2008].

Some major contributions and novel ideas in the design of on-chip networks are as follows: bufferless routing [Moscibroda and Mutlu, 2009], network for a 80-tile chip [Vangal et al., 2007], Garnet network simulator [Agarwal et al., 2009], and express virtual channels that bypass routers [Krishna et al., 2008].

Finally, in the future it is expected that non-conventional interconnects using optical or wireless technology might replace traditional copper based electrical interconnects. A general introduction to the area is given by Karkar et al. [Karkar et al., 2016]. For optical NoCs, readers are referred to the survey paper by Bashir et al. [Bashir et al., 2019] and for wireless NoCs, readers can refer to the report by Li [Li, 2012].

Exercises

Ex. 1 — How does the number of stages in the butterfly topology affect the packet drop rate?

Ex. 2 — Design a modified butterfly topology for 12 nodes using 3 switch stages. Note that in this design, no switch port should be left unused and the radix of all the switches in the same stage should be the same.

Ex. 3 — What is the advantage of flow control at the level of flits?

Ex. 4 — How does a virtual channel increase the throughput of an NoC?

Ex. 5 — Is it possible for a routing protocol with 7 allowed turns to be deadlock-free? Justify your answer.

Ex. 6 — Consider the following routing protocol in a 2D mesh, where the columns are numbered from 1 to N.

- A packet in an even column is not allowed to make the following two turns: east to north and east to south.

- A packet in an odd column is not allowed to make the following two turns: north to west and south to west.

- A packet cannot make a U-Turn.

Prove that this protocol is free of deadlocks.

Ex. 7 — Consider a routing scheme for a 2D mesh where all routes are restricted to at most three right turns, and left turns are not allowed. Is this scheme free of deadlocks? Justify your answer.

Ex. 8 — Among the various routing algorithms described in this chapter, which algorithm is bested suited for the following?

1. Minimum message latency.

2. Maximum throughput.

Ex. 9 — List the typical optimisations that are done in a router's pipeline. Explain their benefits.

* **Ex. 10** — Propose a scheme where we can vary the number of VCs per physical channel based on the traffic pattern.

Ex. 11 — Assume we are using the credit-based flow control mechanism. Propose a scheme to plan the allocation of VCs and switch ports for a few cycles in the future such that these stages can be moved off the critical path.

** **Ex. 12** — Let us say that based on historical data some pairs of nodes and cache banks tend to communicate a lot. Can we leverage this fact to design an NoC that can quickly deliver messages between these pairs of nodes? How can we ensure that messages can quickly bypass the router's pipeline and traverse from the sender to the receiver (for some source-destination pairs only).

Ex. 13 — Do we need a NUCA cache if we have an ultra-fast interconnect such as an on-chip optical or wireless network?

* **Ex. 14** — Consider the following situation in a NUCA cache. We send a request and there is a miss. However, the block is there in the cache. The *search* message did not find the block because the block was at that moment in transit between two cache banks. How do we detect and prevent such race conditions?

** **Ex. 15** — Instead of designing NUCA caches where each bank set is arranged as a column, can we create other arrangements? Suggest a few and comment on their pros and cons.

Design Problems

Ex. 16 — Design the circuit of a wavefront allocator using a hardware description language (HDL) such as VHDL or Verilog.

Ex. 17 — Design a pipelined router with all the optimisations using an HDL. The final circuit should give higher priority to flits that have been in flight for a longer time.

Ex. 18 — Implement the odd-even routing protocol in the Tejas architectural simulator.

9

Multicore Systems: Coherence, Consistency, and Transactional Memory

In the preceding chapters on the design of caches, and the design of the on-chip network, we have been introduced to the incredibly complex and intricate nature of cache design. The chip is a sea of cores, cache banks, and network elements. Moreover, a cache is no more a simple matrix of memory cells. It is rather a complex structure that can be distributed all over the chip. It does not have a homogeneous access latency. Instead, the access latency is dominated by the latency of the routers' pipelines and wire delays. We need to have an elaborate on-chip network to route messages to the desired cache bank, which can be at the opposite end of the chip. Additionally, blocks migrate between different cache banks in NUCA caches such that we can increase the proximity between the cache block and the requesting core. To make matters more complicated, we have at least three levels of caches in a modern server processor (L1, L2, and L3) and we also have MSHRs (miss status handling registers) at each level. Just the task of locating a block can be fairly difficult in modern memory systems, because we need to search through many memory structures and send a lot of messages to different units on the chip. Instead of a simple matrix of cells, an on-chip memory system looks like a busy city with a maze of roads, where we can draw an analogy between the hundreds of cars, and memory request messages.

Writing a parallel program in such an environment with multiple cores is difficult. Recall that a *core* is defined as a full OOO pipeline that can run a program on its own. It is often accompanied with its own L1 cache and write buffers. In a multicore system, a simplistic view of the memory space ceases to hold. The view of the memory space or rather the virtual memory space that we are used to is that the memory space is a linear array of bytes. We can read or write to any location that a program is allowed to access. This abstraction holds very well for a sequential program. However, the moment we consider a parallel program, this abstraction begins to break. This is because as we have argued, the memory system is a complex microcosm of links, buffers, routers, and caches. Memory operations have variable latencies, and it is possible that the same memory operation might be visible to different cores at different points in time depending on where they are placed on the chip. For example, in modern memory systems, it is possible that if core 1 writes to a given memory address, core 2 might see the write earlier than core 3 because of the relative proximity to core 1. As we shall see in this chapter, this can lead to extremely non-intuitive behaviour. There is thus a need to understand all such issues that can arise in a multicore system, and create a set of standards and specifications that both software and hardware must adhere to.

415

Definition 62
A core *is defined as a full OOO pipeline that has the capability to independently fetch instructions and run a program. A chip with multiple cores is known as a* multicore chip *or a* multicore processor.

The organisation of this chapter is as follows. We shall first understand the different ways to write parallel programs in Section 9.1. In specific, we shall look at the two most common paradigms: shared memory and message passing. Once we have understood how parallel programs are written, we will appreciate the fact that even defining what it means for a program to execute correctly on a multicore system is very tough. The same program can produce multiple results or outcomes across runs – some of these may be non-intuitive (described in Section 9.2).

It is thus necessary to create a theoretical foundation of parallel computing and explain the notion of memory models. A *memory model* specifies the rules for determining the valid outcomes of a parallel program on a given machine. This will be described in Section 9.3. We shall further split our discussion into two parts: the rules for specifying the valid outcomes while considering accesses to only a single variable, and similar rules for multi-variable code sequences. The former is called *coherence* and the latter is called *memory consistency*.

To create a high-performing multicore system, it is necessary to associate a small, private L1 cache and possibly an L2 cache with each core. However, this design choice will break the notion of a unified memory system, unless we make it behave in that manner. We shall observe that if an ensemble of small caches obeys the axioms of coherence, it will behave as a large, unified cache (described in Section 9.4). This will allow us to improve the latency and bandwidth of the memory system significantly without compromising on correctness. On similar lines, we shall describe different types of memory models in Section 9.5. There is a trade-off between the types of behaviours a memory model allows and performance. We shall appreciate such issues in this section.

We shall subsequently look at the phenomenon of data races in Section 9.6: a data race is a potential bug in parallel programs that typically is avoided with the programmers' assistance. Along with discussing advancements in hardware, we shall discuss concomitant advances in programming languages for writing such programs. We shall look at one such novel paradigm called transactional memory in Section 9.7 and look at two approaches: one purely in software and one that requires some hardware support.

9.1 Parallel Programming

Let us now explain the methods of programming multiprocessors. For ease of explanation, let us draw an analogy here. Consider a group of workers in a factory. They cooperatively perform a task by communicating with each other orally. A supervisor often issues commands to the group of workers, and then they perform their work. If there is a problem, a worker indicates it by raising an alarm. Immediately, other workers rush to his assistance. In this small and simple setting, all the workers can hear each other, and see each other's actions. This proximity enables them to accomplish complex tasks.

We can alternatively consider another model, where workers cannot necessarily see or hear each other. In this case, they need to communicate with each other through a system of messages. Messages can be passed through letters, phone calls, or e-mails. In this setting, if a worker discovers a problem, he needs to send a message to the supervisor such that she can come and rectify the problem. Workers need to be typically aware of each other's identities, and explicitly send messages to all or a subset of them. It is not possible any more to shout loudly and communicate with everybody at the same time. However, there are some advantages of this system. We can support many more workers because they do not have to be co-located. Secondly, since there are no constraints on the location of workers, they can be located at different parts of the world and be doing very different things. This system is thus far more flexible and scalable.

Inspired by these real life scenarios, computer architects have designed a set of protocols for multiprocessors following different paradigms. The first paradigm is known as *shared memory*, where all the individual programs see the same view of the memory system. If program A sets the value of the shared variable x to 5, then program B immediately sees the change. The second setting is known as *message passing*. Here multiple programs communicate among each other by passing messages. The shared memory paradigm is more suitable for strongly coupled multiprocessors, and the message passing paradigm is more suitable for loosely coupled multiprocessors. A strongly coupled multiprocessor refers to a typical multicore system where the different programs running on different cores can share their memory space with each other, which includes their code and data. In comparison, a loosely coupled multiprocessor refers to a set of machines that are connected over the network, and do not share their code or data between each other. Note that it is possible to implement message passing on a strongly coupled multiprocessor. Likewise, it is also possible to implement an abstraction of a shared memory on an otherwise loosely coupled multiprocessor. This is known as *distributed shared memory* [Keleher et al., 1994]. However, this is typically not the norm.

9.1.1 Shared Memory

Let us try to add n numbers in parallel using a multiprocessor. The code for it is shown in Example 9. We have written the code in C++ using the OpenMP language extension.

It is easy to mistake the code for a regular sequential program, except for the directive *#pragma omp parallel*. This is the only extra semantic difference that we have added in our parallel program. It launches each iteration of this loop as a separate sub-program. Each such sub-program is known as a *thread*. A thread is defined as a sub-program that shares its address space (the heap and global variables) with other threads. It communicates with them by modifying the values of memory locations in the shared memory space. Each thread has its own set of local variables that are not accessible to other threads.

Example 9
Write a shared memory program to add a set of numbers in parallel.

Answer: *Let us assume that all the numbers are already stored in an array called numbers. It has SIZE entries. Assume that the number of parallel sub-programs that can be launched is equal to N.*

```
/* variable declaration */
int partialSums[N];
int numbers[SIZE];
int result = 0;

/* initialise arrays */
...

/* parallel section */
#pragma omp parallel {
        /* get my processor id */
        int myId = omp_get_thread_num();

        /* add my portion of numbers */
        int startIdx = myId * SIZE/N;
```

```
            int endIdx = startIdx + SIZE/N;
            for(int jdx = startIdx; jdx < endIdx; jdx++)
                    partialSums[myId] += numbers[jdx];
    }


    /* sequential section */
    for(int idx=0; idx < N; idx++)
            result += partialSums[idx];
```

The number of iterations or the number of parallel threads that get launched is a system parameter that is set in advance. It is typically equal to the number of processors. In this case, it is equal to N. Thus, N copies of the parallel part of the code are launched in parallel. Each copy runs on a separate processor. Note that each of these copies of the program can access all the variables that have been declared before the invocation of the parallel section. For example, they can access *partialSums* and the *numbers* arrays. Each processor invokes the function *omp_get_thread_num*, which returns the id of the executing thread in the range $[0 \ldots (N-1)]$. Each thread uses the thread id to find the range of the array that it needs to add. It adds all the entries in the relevant portion of the array, and saves the result in its corresponding entry in the *partialSums* array. Once all the threads have completed their job, the sequential section begins. This piece of sequential code can run on any processor. This decision is made dynamically at runtime by the operating system or the parallel programming framework. To obtain the final result, it is necessary to add all the partial sums in the sequential section.

Definition 63
A thread *is a sub-program that shares its address space with other threads. It has a dedicated program counter and a local stack that it can use to define its local variables.*

A graphical representation of the computation is shown in Figure 9.1. A parent thread spawns a set of child threads. They do their own work and finally *join* when they are done. The parent thread takes over and aggregates the partial results.

There are several salient points to note here. The first is that each thread has its separate stack. A thread can use its stack to declare its local variables. Once it finishes, all the local variables in its stack are destroyed. To communicate data between the parent thread and the child threads, it is necessary to use variables that are accessible to both the threads. These variables need to be globally accessible by all the threads. The child threads can freely modify these variables and even use them to communicate with each other as well. They are additionally free to invoke the operating system, and write to external files and network devices. Once, all the threads have finished executing, they perform a *join* operation and free their state. The parent thread takes over and finishes the role of aggregating the results. Here, *join* is an example of a *synchronisation operation* between threads. There can be many other types of synchronisation operations between threads. The reader is referred to [Culler et al., 1998] for a detailed discussion on thread synchronisation. All that the reader needs to understand is that there are a set of complicated constructs that threads can use to perform very complex tasks cooperatively. Adding a set of numbers is a very simple example. Multithreaded programs can be used to perform other complicated tasks such as matrix algebra, and even solve differential equations in parallel.

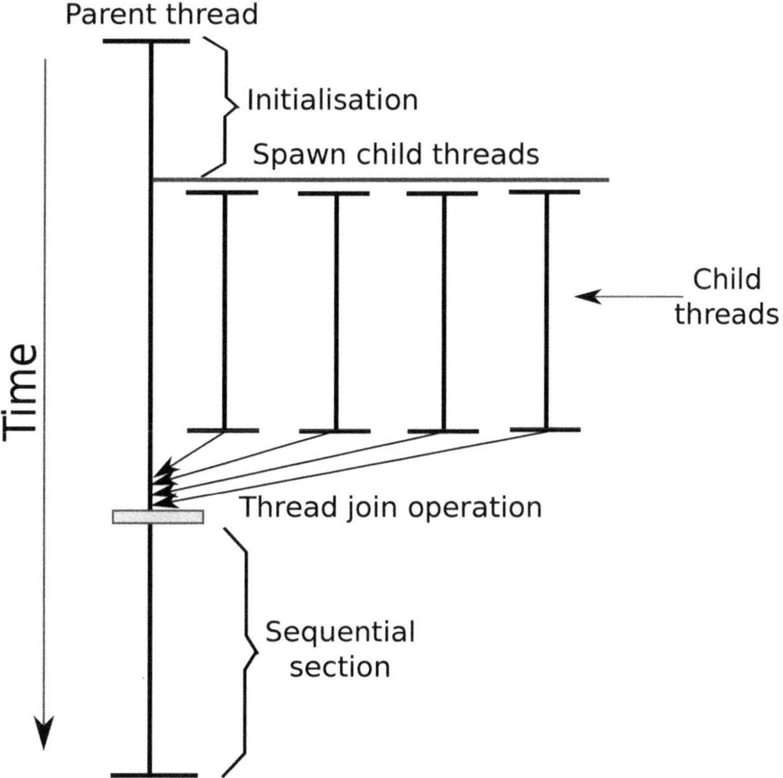

Figure 9.1: Graphical representation of the program to add numbers in parallel

9.1.2   Message Passing

Let us now briefly look at message passing. Note that message passing based loosely coupled systems are not the main focus area of this book. Hence, we shall just give the reader a flavor of message passing programs. Note that in this case, each running program is a separate entity and does not share code or data with other running programs. It is an OS *process*, where a process is defined as a running instance of a program. Typically, a process does not share its address space with any other process.

Definition 64

A process *represents the running instance of a program. Typically, it does not share its address space with any other process.*

Let us now quickly define our message passing semantics. We shall primarily use two functions *send* and *receive* as shown in Table 9.1. The *send(pid, val)* function is used to send an integer (*val*) to the process whose id is equal to *pid*. The *receive(pid)* is used to receive an integer sent by a process whose id is equal to *pid*. If *pid* is equal to ANYSOURCE, then the receive function can return with the value sent by any process. Our semantics is on the lines of the popular parallel programming framework MPI (Message Passing Interface) [Gropp et al., 1999]. MPI calls have many more arguments and their syntax is much more complicated than our simplistic framework. Let us now consider the same example of adding n numbers in parallel (refer to Example 10).

Function	Semantics
send (pid, val)	Send the integer *val* to the process with an id equal to *pid*.
receive (pid)	(1) Receive an integer from process pid. (2) The function blocks till it gets the value. (3) If the pid is equal to ANYSOURCE, then the *receive* function returns with the value sent by any process.

Table 9.1: *send* and *receive* calls

Example 10
Write a message passing based program to add a set of numbers in parallel. Make appropriate assumptions.

Answer: *Let us assume that all the numbers are stored in the array numbers and this array is available to all the N processors. Let the number of elements in the numbers array be SIZE. For the sake of simplicity, let us assume that SIZE is divisible by N.*

```
/* start all the parallel processes */
SpawnAllParallelProcesses();

/* For each process execute the following code */
int myId = getMyProcessId();

/* compute the partial sums */
int startIdx = myId * SIZE/N;
int endIdx = startIdx + SIZE/N;
int partialSum = 0;
for(int jdx = startIdx; jdx < endIdx; jdx++)
            partialSum += numbers[jdx];

/* All the non-root nodes send their partial sums to the root (id 0) */
if(myId != 0) {
        /* send the partial sum to the root */
        send (0, partialSum);
} else {
        /* for the root */
        int sum = partialSum;
        for (int pid = 1; pid < N; pid++) {
                sum += receive(ANYSOURCE);
        }

        /* shut down all the processes */
        shutDownAllProcesses();

        /* return the sum */
        return sum;
}
```

9.1.3   Amdahl's Law

We have now taken a look at examples for adding a set of n numbers in parallel using both the paradigms namely shared memory and message passing. We divided our program into two parts: a sequential part and a parallel part (refer to Figure 9.1). In the parallel part of the execution, each thread completed the work assigned to it and created a partial result. In the sequential part, the root or master or parent thread initialised all the variables and data structures and spawned all the child threads. After all the child threads completed (or joined), the parent thread aggregated the results produced by all the child threads. This process of aggregating results is also known as *reduction*. The process of initialising variables and reduction are both sequential.

Let us now try to derive the speedup of a parallel program vis-a-vis its sequential counterpart. Let us consider a program that takes T_{seq} units of time to execute. Let f_{seq} be the fraction of time that it spends in its sequential part and $1 - f_{seq}$ be the fraction of time that it spends in its parallel part. The sequential part is unaffected by parallelism; however, the parallel part gets equally divided among the processors. If we consider a system of P processors, then the parallel part is expected to be sped up by a factor of P. Thus, the time (T_{par}) that the parallel version of the program takes is equal to

$$T_{par} = T_{seq} \times \left(f_{seq} + \frac{1 - f_{seq}}{P} \right) \tag{9.1}$$

Alternatively, the speedup S is given by

$$S = \frac{T_{seq}}{T_{par}} = \frac{1}{f_{seq} + \frac{1-f_{seq}}{P}} \tag{9.2}$$

Equation 9.2 is known as the Amdahl's Law. It is a theoretical estimate (or rather the upper bound in most cases) of the speedup that we expect with additional parallelism.

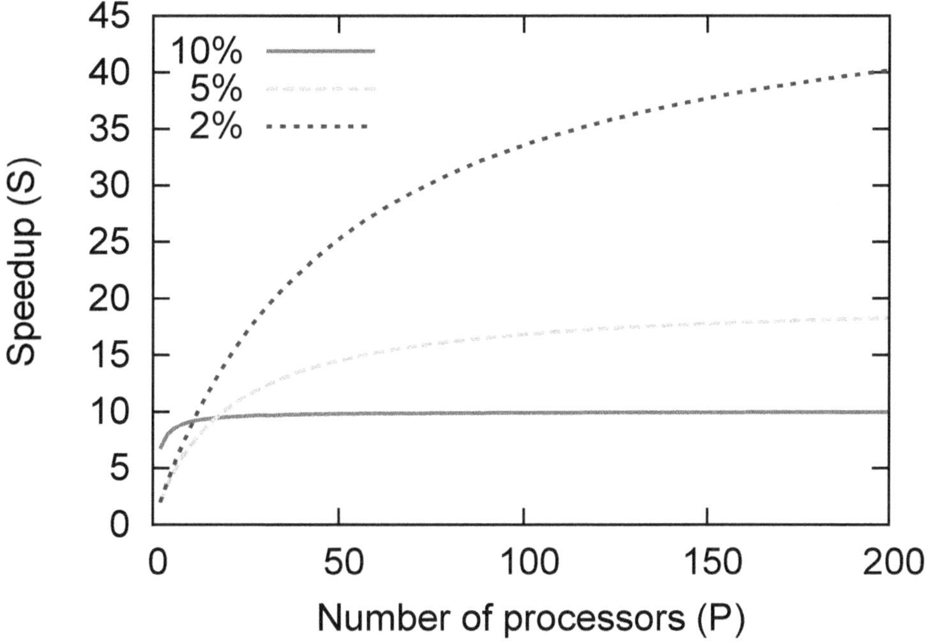

Figure 9.2: Speedup (S) vs number of processors (P)

Figure 9.2 plots the speedups as predicted by Amdahl's Law for three values of f_{seq}: 10%, 5%, and 2%. We observe that with an increasing number of processors, the speedup gradually saturates and tends to the limiting value, $1/f_{seq}$. We observe diminishing returns as we increase the number of processors beyond a certain point. For example, for $f_{seq} = 5\%$, there is no appreciable difference in speedups between a system with 35 processors and a system with 200 processors. We approach similar limits for all three values of f_{seq}. The important point to note here is that increasing speedups by adding additional processors has its limits. We cannot expect to keep getting speedups indefinitely by adding more processors because we are limited by the length of the sequential sections in programs.

To summarise, we can draw two inferences. The first is that to speedup a program it is necessary to have as much parallelism as possible. Hence, we need to have a very efficient parallel programming library and parallel hardware. However, parallelism has its limits and it is not possible to increase the speedup appreciably beyond a certain limit. The speedup is limited by the length of the sequential section in the program. To reduce the sequential section, we need to adopt approaches both at the algorithmic level and at the system level. We need to design our algorithms in such a way that the sequential section is as short as possible. For example, in Examples 9 and 10, we can also perform the initialisation in parallel (reduces the length of the sequential section). Secondly, we need a fast processor that can minimise the time it takes to execute the sequential section.

9.1.4 Gustafson-Barsis's Law

While deriving the Amdahl's law, we assumed that the size of the problem remains the same with an increasing amount of computational power. However, this is not the case in practice. When we have more resources, the problem size also increases. For example, if we are simulating an airplane wing, then we consider finer and finer meshes as we increase the number of processors. This increases the overall accuracy of the simulation.

Let the total workload be W. It has a sequential part Wf_{seq} and a parallel part $W(1 - f_{seq})$. It is the parallel part that is going to be sped up with additional processors. The speedup of the parallel part is equal to P, where P is the number of processors. We can thus do additional work in the same time. We can scale the parallel portion of the workload by a factor of P; the new workload W_{new} is as follows.

$$W_{new} = f_{seq}W + (1 - f_{seq})PW \tag{9.3}$$

The execution time on a single processor is proportional to the workload. Let the constant of proportionality be α. We thus derive the single processor execution time T_{seq} and the P-processor execution time T_{par} as follows. Note that the parallel part of the execution time gets divided by the number of processors.

$$
\begin{aligned}
T_{seq} &= \alpha W_{new} = \alpha(f_{seq}W + (1 - f_{seq})PW) \\
T_{par} &= \alpha(f_{seq}W + (1 - f_{seq})PW/P) = \alpha W
\end{aligned}
\tag{9.4}
$$

The speedup S is equal to T_{seq}/T_{par}.

$$
\begin{aligned}
S &= \frac{T_{seq}}{T_{par}} \\
&= \frac{f_{seq}W + (1 - f_{seq})PW}{W} \\
&= f_{seq} + (1 - f_{seq})P
\end{aligned}
\tag{9.5}
$$

Let us understand the implications of this equation. As we increase the number of processors P, the speedup increases. Ultimately $(1 - f_{seq})P$ will significantly exceed f_{seq}. Thus the speedup for large P

will be $(1 - f_{seq})P$. This means that the only role that f_{seq} plays is in determining the slope of the curve for large P. If $f_{seq} = 0$, then the speedup is P times, which is expected when we do not have a sequential portion.

For all other values of f_{seq} where we are scaling the parallel part of the problem by a factor of P, the slope of the line is given by $(1 - f_{seq})$. Even if we are scaling the problem, we need to still limit the size of the sequential section because the absolute difference in execution times for different values of f_{seq} will be significant for large values of P.

9.1.5　Design Space of Multiprocessors

Michael J. Flynn proposed the famous Flynn's classification of multiprocessors in 1966. He started out by observing that an ensemble of different processors might either share code, data, or both. There are four possible choices – SISD (single instruction single data), SIMD (single instruction multiple data), MISD (multiple instruction single data), and MIMD (multiple instruction multiple data).

Let us describe each of these types of multiprocessors in some more detail.

SISD This is a standard uniprocessor with a single pipeline as described in Chapter 2. A SISD processor can be thought of as a special case in the universe of multiprocessors.

SIMD A SIMD processor can process multiple streams of data using a single instruction. For example, a SIMD instruction can add 4 sets of numbers with a single instruction. Modern processors incorporate SIMD instructions in their instruction set and have special SIMD execution units also. Examples include x86 processors that support the SSE and AVX instruction sets. Vector processors and, to a lesser extent, GPUs are examples of highly successful SIMD processors.

MISD MISD systems are very rare in practice. They are mostly used in systems that have very high reliability requirements. For example, large commercial aircraft typically have multiple processors running different versions of the same program/algorithm. The final outcome is decided by voting. For example, a plane might have a MIPS processor, an ARM processor, and an x86 processor, each running different versions of the same program such as an autopilot system. Here, we have multiple instruction streams, yet a single source of data. A dedicated voting circuit computes a majority vote of the three outputs. For example, it is possible that because of a bug in the program or the processor, one of the systems can erroneously take a decision to turn left. However, both of the other systems might take the correct decision to turn right. In this case, the voting circuit will decide to turn right. Since MISD systems are hardly ever used in practice, other than in such specialised situations, we shall not discuss them any more in this book.

MIMD MIMD systems are by far the most prevalent multiprocessor systems today. Here, there are multiple instruction streams and multiple data streams. Multicore processors, and large servers are all MIMD systems. Examples 9 and 10 also showed the example of a program for a MIMD machine. We need to carefully explain the meaning of multiple instruction streams. This means that instructions come from multiple sources. Each source has its unique location and associated program counter. Two important branches of MIMD paradigms have formed over the last few years.

The first is *SPMD* (single program multiple data) and the second is *MPMD* (multiple program multiple data). Most parallel programs are written in the SPMD style (Examples 9 and 10). Here, multiple copies of the same program run on different cores or separate processors. However, each individual processing unit has a separate program counter and thus perceives a different instruction stream. Sometimes SPMD programs are written in such a way that they perform different actions depending on their thread ids. We saw a method in Example 9 on how to achieve this using OpenMP functions. The advantage of SPMD is that we do not have to write multiple programs for different processors. Parts of the same program can run on all the processors, though their behaviour might be different.

A contrasting paradigm is MPMD. Here, the programs that run on different processors or cores are actually different. They are more useful for specialised processors that have heterogeneous processing units. There is typically a single master program that assigns work to slave programs. The slave programs complete the quanta of work assigned to them and then return the results to the master program. The nature of work of both the programs is actually very different, and it is often not possible to seamlessly combine them into one single program.

From the aforementioned description, it is clear that the systems that we need to focus on are SIMD and MIMD. MISD systems are very rarely used and thus will not be discussed any more. Let us first discuss MIMD multiprocessing. Note that we shall only describe the SPMD variant of MIMD multiprocessing because it is the most common approach.

9.1.6 Multithreading in Hardware

Up till now we have discussed multithreading in software, where a *thread* has been defined as a lightweight process that shares its address space with other threads. A multithreaded program contains multiple threads that run in parallel to complete a large task.

However, the concept of multithreading exists in hardware as well, albeit in a different form. We have very wide issue processors nowadays. It is often not possible to completely saturate the issue width. As a result, a lot of hardware resources get wasted. It is a better idea to run two parallel threads, which are not threads in the software sense – they need not share the address space. These threads may be separate processes.

High-performance processors typically run several hardware threads in parallel. If one thread is waiting for a value to return from main memory and the pipeline is getting stalled, during that time the other threads can execute. This increases the throughput of the entire system. We need to have a separate program counter and rename table for each thread. Furthermore, the id of the thread needs to be a part of the instruction packet to correctly enforce dependences. A simple idea called hyperthreading proposes to partition the resources such as the physical registers, instruction window entries, issue slots, functional units and the ROB equally among the threads. A more sophisticated approach referred to as simultaneous multithreading (SMT) proposes to flexibly allocate the resources depending upon runtime conditions and the priority of threads.

There are several kinds of multithreading. Let us discuss a few popular variants. We would like to reiterate the fact that we are discussing "hardware threads" here.

Coarse-grained multithreading In this case, we time-multiplex the pipeline. For k cycles we run thread 1, and for the next k cycles we run thread 2, and so on. If a given thread gets stalled because of an event that has a long latency such as an L2 miss or an I/O event, then we schedule another thread. In this case, k is of the order of tens of cycles. Scheduling another thread after stopping the execution of the current thread is known as "switching the context".

Fine-grained multithreading The idea is similar to coarse-grained multithreading; however, in this case, k has a much lower value. This approach is typically used when we can change the context quickly and we would like to run another thread as soon as we detect an operation such as an L1 miss, which will take tens of cycles to execute. This approach is more responsive, yet it has more overheads in terms of switching the context between the threads.

Simultaneous multithreading (SMT) This is the most flexible approach, which is also the most complex. In this case, we fetch instructions from several threads in parallel. At runtime, the resources are dynamically partitioned between the threads. This automatically allows other threads to use as many resources as possible when one of the threads is stuck. As of 2020, a lot of server processors implement SMT.

9.2 Overview of Issues in Parallel Hardware

Now that we have an understanding of parallel programs, let us look at the hardware support that is required to run such parallel programs. Note that in the following discussion we need to reconcile two perspectives: the software perspective and the hardware perspective. The software perspective is from the point of view of programs, which have an ideal view of resources. In comparison, the hardware perspective is from the point of view of implementation. The overall aim is to ensure that software programs execute correctly without sacrificing performance. Before proceeding, the reader should thoroughly recapitulate the concept of a software *thread*, and the fact that different threads share parts of the virtual address space.

9.2.1 Shared and Distributed Caches

Let us consider two aspects of such a design – performance and correctness. Let us look at the L1 level. In a single core or a dual core system, we can have a single L1 cache. However, as the number of cores increases, having one large, shared L1 cache is not practical. If we have 16 cores, and we want to support two memory requests per core per cycle, then we need a 32-port L1 cache, which is impossible to fabricate. We can create a NUCA like organisation as we had studied in Section 8.5; however, given the multicycle wire delays and increased chances of bank conflicts, this also is impractical. Hence, we cannot afford a large, shared L1 cache for all the cores in a multicore system.

For similar reasons, it is often difficult to afford a large L2 cache in a server-class multicore system. Since we cannot afford a shared cache because of performance issues, let us consider a design with distributed caches. In such a design, each core has a *private L1 cache*. The ensemble of L1 caches acts like one large shared L1 cache, albeit conceptually. We get the advantage of performance by having one small and fast L1 cache per core. It can be a very small and power efficient structure. It will allow us to take advantage of temporal and spatial locality.

Let us compare the designs with a shared L1 cache and a distributed L1 cache in Figure 9.3. Figure 9.3(a) shows a design with a shared L1 cache, and Figure 9.3(b) shows a design where each core has a private L1 cache. The L1 caches are connected using a shared bus.

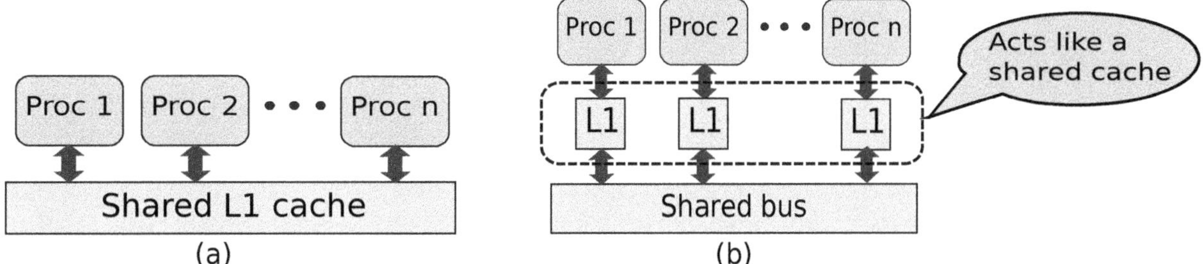

Figure 9.3: (a) Shared cache, (b) A distributed cache that conceptually acts as a single shared cache

Let us now come to the second problem – *correctness*. In a distributed cache, we need to ensure that the ensemble of L1 caches behaves as a single cache. Otherwise, the compiler needs to generate different types of code for machines that use different kinds of caches. The compiler has to be aware of the fact that the machine has a distributed L1 cache, and a write to a shared variable on one core may not be visible to the other core. This is outright impractical. Hence, to an external observer such as the programmer or the compiler, a shared and a distributed cache should look the same from the point of view of program correctness, or the outcomes of a program's execution. Ensuring the correctness of a distributed cache is known as the *cache coherence problem*. Recall that we had used a similar line of reasoning when we designed the OOO processor; we had argued that to an external observer, an OOO processor and an in-order processor should appear to be the same (from the point of view of a program's execution).

Let us elaborate on some of the issues that we shall encounter while designing a distributed cache. Consider two cores, A and B, that are running two threads of the same application. If both the threads decide to write to variable x, then we have a problem. The memory address associated with x will be the same for both the threads. A will write to that address and keep the value in its private L1 cache. B will also do the same. If both the writes happen at more or less the same time, then we have a complex situation in our hands. We will not be in a position to find out which write operation is newer. After some time, if instructions on cores A and B start reading the value of x from memory, then they stand to read different values, even though the read operations are happening at the same time without any intervening writes. Such behaviours need to be handled properly. The reason that such problems can happen is because we have two separate physical locations for the same memory address that contains the value of the variable x. In comparison, a shared cache does not have this problem because the value of a variable (or its associated memory address) is stored in only one physical location.

The correctness issues in a distributed cache such as the one we just described, arise from the fact that for a single memory address, there are multiple locations across caches at the same level. The updates to these locations need to be somehow synchronised, otherwise this will lead to non-intuitive program behaviours. To ensure that all of these caches present a unified view of the physical address space, we need to design a *cache coherence* protocol to solve such problems. Note that all cache coherence issues and definitions are in the context of the behaviour of a multithreaded program with respect to accesses to any **single memory address**. For example, in our current discussion, we only looked at all the accesses to the variable x. This definition is crucial and will be used repeatedly in later sections.

Definition 65

- *A shared cache is one large cache where we have only one physical location for a given memory address.*

- *A distributed cache comprises a group of small caches located at different places on the die. This ensemble of caches may have correctness problems because there are multiple physical locations for a given memory address.*

- *The aim is to make a distributed cache indistinguishable from a shared cache to an external observer in terms of correctness properties with regards to the outcome of memory operations. This is known as the cache coherence problem.*

- *To solve the cache coherence problem, we need a cache coherence protocol.*

Even though in most designs as of 2020, we have a shared L2 cache; however, this is not a strict necessity. We can have a private L2 cache per core, or have one private L2 cache for a group of cores. Whenever we have a distributed cache at any level, we need a cache coherence protocol.

9.2.2 Memory Consistency

Let us look at another aspect of multiprocessor memory systems that deals with accesses to multiple memory addresses. Consider the simple piece of parallel code.

Thread 1	Thread 2
x = 1;	$t1 = y$
y = 1;	$t2 = x$

x and y are global variables in a multithreaded program; assume that all our variables are initialised to zero. Here, Thread 1 is setting both x and y to 1. Thread 2 is reading y into local variable $t1$, and then is reading x into local variable $t2$.

Let us look at what is happening at the level of the NoC and cache banks. When we are updating global variables, we are essentially performing memory writes to their addresses in memory. A write to a memory address is a complex series of events. We need to create a write message and send it on the NoC to the corresponding cache bank such that the value can be written to the correct physical location. It is like sending a letter by post from New Delhi to Moscow. The writes to x and y get converted to such letters that are sent through the NoC. The same is true for a read request to memory, where the basic operation is to inject a read message into the NoC. It needs to be routed to the correct physical location, and then we need to send the value that was read back to the requesting core or cache.

In this complex sequence of messages, it is very well possible that the message to update x might get caught up in network congestion, and the message to update y might reach its destination earlier. This can happen for a myriad of reasons. Maybe the message to update y takes a different route that is less congested, or the cache bank that holds y is closer to the core that is issuing the write request. The net summary is that the updates to x and y need not be seen to be happening one after the other, or even in the same order by other cores. This can lead to pretty anomalous outcomes, which are clearly non-intuitive. Sadly, given the complex nature of interactions inside multicore processors, such occurrences are perfectly normal, and in fact many commercial processors allow many such behaviours.

For example, it is possible for a thread running on another core to read $y = t1 = 1$, and then read $x = t2 = 0$. Recall that the assumption is that all global variables such as x and y are initialised to zero. This observation would be very anomalous and non-intuitive indeed, because as per program order, we first update x and then y. The core that performs these updates sees them in that order. However, because of the non-deterministic nature of message delivery times in a realistic NoC such a situation is perfectly possible.

Even though the outcome $(t1, t2) = (1, 0)$ ($t1 = 1$ and $t2 = 0$) for Thread 2 looks to be plausible, it somehow manages to bother us and tell us that the outcome is not intuitive and hence undesirable. This is simply not how we want programs to behave. It appears that different cores are seeing different views of memory operations, and their perception of the relative order of memory operations is different. This was not happening in a single-threaded system, and thus we are not used to such outcomes. Writing correct parallel programs with such outcomes is going to be very difficult. Reasoning about their behaviour and writing optimising compilers that can possibly reorder memory accesses becomes even more difficult.

We thus need a theoretical framework that will allow us to reason about the possible and valid outcomes of multithreaded programs in large multicore processors with complex NoCs. We need to find ways to rein in the complexity of the behaviours of multithreaded programs on multicore systems and enforce certain policies. These policies are known as *memory consistency models* or simply *memory models*, which explicitly specify the rules for generating the valid outcomes of parallel programs. They preserve our notion of intuitiveness, provide a formal correctness framework, and simultaneously allow the programmer, compiler, and architecture to maximise performance.

Definition 66

Let us informally define a memory consistency model as a policy that specifies the behaviour of a parallel, multithreaded program. In general, a multithreaded program can produce a large number of outcomes depending on the relative order of scheduling of the threads, and the behaviour of memory operations. A memory consistency model restricts the set of allowed outcomes for a given multithreaded program. It is a set of rules that defines the interaction of memory instructions between each other.

We shall take a detailed look at memory consistency models in Section 9.5 including their implementation aspects.

9.2.3 Difference between Coherence and Consistency

The difference between *coherence* and *consistency* is often not fully understood. There are conflicting definitions in literature. Hence, there is a need for a clarification. *Coherence* refers to the behaviour of the memory system with respect to accesses to a single variable or memory address: informally, it provides the illusion that there is a single physical location for every memory address. If coherence is defined in the context of caches, we refer to it as cache coherence. Nevertheless, note that coherence is a general concept.

In comparison, *consistency* is literally defined as *adherence to specifications*. When we talk of memory consistency, we refer to the behaviour of the memory system as a whole, and the fact that the outcome of every parallel program, defined in terms of the set of the results of all memory read operations, is *valid* as per the specifications. In other words, a *memory consistency model* or just a *memory model*, considers accesses to multiple memory locations. Moreover, we can have different kinds of memory models depending upon the underlying architecture. As of 2020, almost all popular memory models obey the rules of *coherence*.

Before an astute reader asks why coherence needs to be treated separately, and why cannot it simply be considered as a subset of the memory model, let us answer this question. When we delve into the practical aspects of coherence and consistency, we shall observe that enforcing coherence requires the maximum amount of hardware as compared to other aspects of a memory model. Hence, this is a special subset. Also, historically, these concepts have been developed somewhat independently.

Let us first provide a formal, mathematical framework to specify and analyse memory models before discussing the practical aspects. This is presented next.

9.3 Theoretical Foundations of Memory Models

Let us summarise the knowledge that we have gained up till now (see Waypoint 11).

Way Point 11

- *Creating one large shared cache for a parallel program is infeasible. It will be too large, too slow, and too inefficient in terms of power.*

- *Hence, it is a much better idea to have an ensemble of small caches. This is known as a distributed cache. The distributed cache however needs to appear to be a single, unified cache. If its behaviour obeys the rules of coherence, this will be the case.*

- *Coherence is only one among several set of properties that modern architectures need to guarantee when it comes to correctly executing parallel, multithreaded programs. In general, the behaviour of parallel programs on a machine needs to be specified by a memory model.*

- *The memory model treats each thread as a sequence of instructions and typically only considers the reads and writes. The outcome of a program is defined as the values read by all the read instructions across the threads. The memory model specifies the set of valid outcomes for a program on a given machine.*

9.3.1   Sequential and Parallel Executions

A shared cache contains a set of blocks, where each block contains a set of bytes. We normally do not access the memory at the level of bytes; instead, we divide the block into a set of memory words, where each word is either 4 or 8 bytes. Let us assume that every variable requires a single memory word, and we only access memory at the granularity of words. We can also say that a memory location corresponds to a single memory word. We are primarily interested in the sequences of reads and writes to memory words issued by different threads, and their associated correctness properties. Let us try to model such sequences formally. We shall introduce a set of concepts that will help us in creating a mathematical model that can accurately explain the concepts of coherence and consistency.

Point of View

Consider a single shared cache. Let us place a hypothetical observer at a specific memory word that we are interested to monitor. We will see a series of read and write accesses made by possibly different threads (running on different cores). Since all of them are to the same location, we can order them sequentially. In this sequence of reads and writes, the correctness criteria is that each read operation returns the value of the latest write operation. The write might have been performed by the same thread, or a different thread running on a different core. A memory operation can be broken down into a request and a response. The request is typically issued by a core and the memory system issues the response. For a load, the response is the value, and for a store the response is typically empty, indicating that the store has completed successfully.

Let us now explain a very important concept in the design of parallel systems. It is the *point of view*. This basically captures what a hypothetical observer placed at a given location inside the memory system observes. This is her point of view.

The observer that sits on the memory location (let's say on the SRAM cells) sees a very simple view of the memory operations (see Figure 9.4). Every memory operation has three points of time associated with it: a time at which it starts (t_{start}), a time at which it completes (t_{comp}), and a time at which it ends (t_{end}). We shall use the generic term *memory operation* in our subsequent discussion – its exact definition depends on the observer. In this case, t_{start} refers to the time at which the request to start the operation arrives at the memory location, or alternatively, the time at which the operation to access the memory location starts. t_{end} refers to the point of time when all the actions with respect to the memory operation cease from the point of view of the memory location. t_{comp} refers to the time when the memory operation completes its action. This is a tricky concept, and needs to be explained in the context of reads and writes. A read operation completes when we have read the final value, and the value will not change henceforth. A write operation completes when we have written the value to the memory location. In this case, $t_{start} < t_{comp} < t_{end}$.

Let us explain with an example. Assume we have a core and a shared cache. The core issues a read request to read 4 bytes (a single memory word) from the memory location 20. The request is sent to the shared cache that has a single first-in first-out queue of memory requests as shown in Figure 9.4. Once the cache receives the request, it is enqueued in a dedicated queue. This time is t_{start}. Once the cache is free, we dequeue the head of the queue and send the address to the decoder of the SRAM array. The array access starts. Once we read the value of the SRAM cells at the sense amplifiers, we are sure that their values are stable, and will not change in the lifetime of the current operation. This is the completion time t_{comp}. Finally, when the response is written on the bus, this time can be treated as t_{end}.

To summarise, from the point of view of this observer, operations arrive sequentially, they complete their action (read or write), and then the responses are sent back. Operations never overlap. One operation finishes, and the next operation starts. This pattern is an example of a *sequential execution*, which is a basic concept in the concurrent systems literature. Let us summarise.

1. A point of view is defined as the set of events that a hypothetical observer sees at a particular

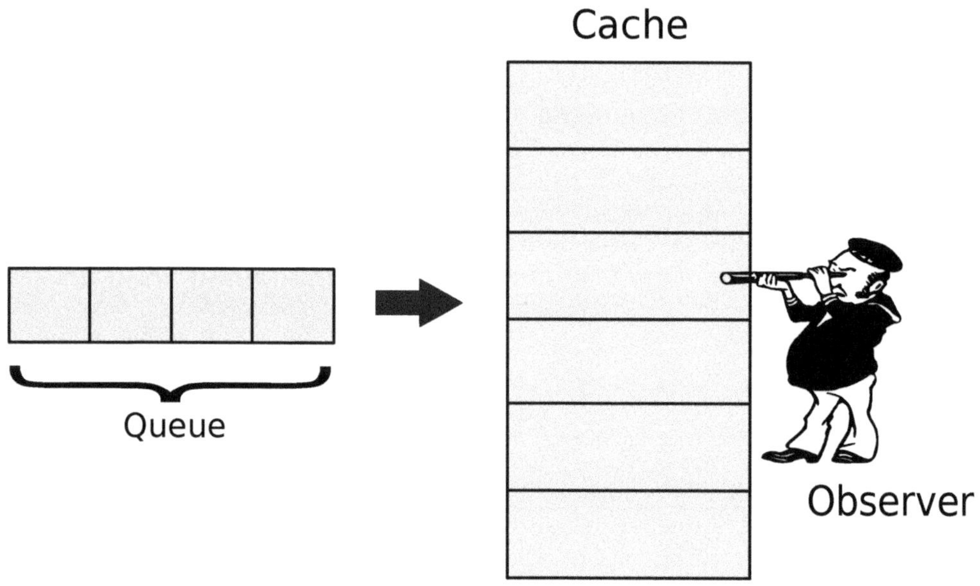

Timeline of memory requests seen by the observer:

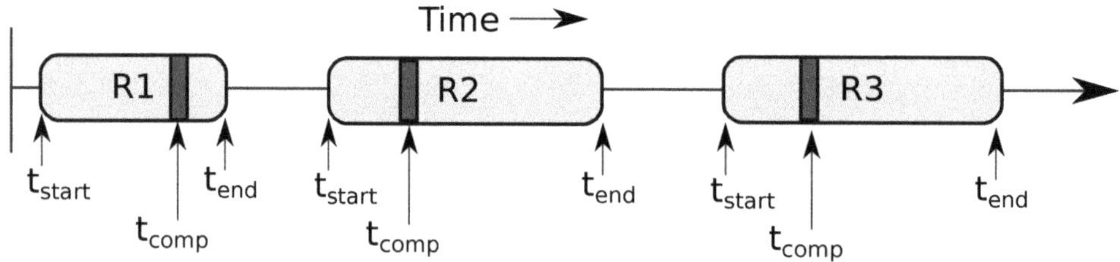

Figure 9.4: Observer at a memory location

point in the memory system.

2. The observer sees a set of memory operations, where a memory operation can either be a read or a write. Note that the exact definition of a memory operation depends on the observer.

3. Each operation has three times associated with it: t_{start}, t_{comp}, and t_{end}. The start and end times represent the times at which the observer sees the processing of the operation start and end respectively.

4. t_{comp} is the time at which the memory operation actually takes effect. For a read, it is the time, when we finally read the value, and there are no chances of the value changing for the current operation. For a write, it is the time when the value gets written, and it is potentially visible to all subsequent operations. Regardless of the observer, this relation always holds: $t_{comp} \geq t_{start}$. The relation between t_{comp} and t_{end} is slightly more tricky – it depends on the observer. Let us keep reading.

Sequential Executions

Let us recapitulate. In a shared cache, an observer sitting on a memory location sees a list of memory operations: reads or writes. Let us formally argue about what constitutes correct behaviour in this case. Even though it is obvious, let us still formalise it because we will use it as a foundation for later sections.

In formal terms, an *execution* is a set of memory operations. Each operation is a 6-tuple of the form $\langle tid, t_{start}, t_{end}, type, addr, value \rangle$. *tid* is the id of the thread that has initiated the operation. t_{start} and t_{end} have been explained before. The *type* indicates if the operation is a read or a write, *addr* is the memory address, and the *value* indicates the datum that is read or written to memory. We have not include the completion time in the definition, because it is often not known. Now, we can either have an ordered execution or a partially ordered execution.

We shall call an ordered execution a *sequential execution* where all the operations are ordered. This is not the case in partially ordered executions – there is at least one pair of operations, where an ordering between them is not specified.

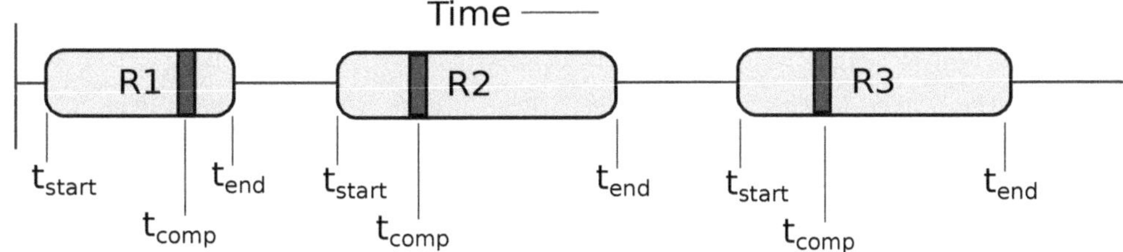

Figure 9.5: A sequential execution with three memory operations: $R1$, $R2$, and $R3$.

To understand sequential executions better, let us reproduce the relevant part of Figure 9.4 in Figure 9.5. The operations in Figure 9.5 are seen by an observer at the memory location. The end time of one operation is strictly less than the start time of the subsequent operation – they have no overlaps. This is a sequential execution where the operations are ordered by their start times (and also the completion times).

It is not necessary for operations to be non-overlapping to be part of a sequential execution. For example, we can have a pipelined cache, where before the previous operation has ended, a new operation may begin. In this case, the operations do overlap, nevertheless, there is still a sequential ordering between them – they are ordered in the ascending order of their start times.

Let us additionally define a property that establishes the *correctness* of a sequential execution. Since it consists of only read and write operations, let us take a look at all the values that are read by read operations. Each of these values needs to be correct, which means that a read operation needs to get the value of the *latest write* to the same address in the sequence. Guaranteeing that read operations get the correct values is enough because write operations do not return a value. It is only the read operations that read values from the memory system and pass them to other instructions. Let us call such a sequence where all the read operations read the correct values (latest writes) as a *legal* sequence. Also note that a legal sequence guarantees the fact that the final value of a variable is equal to the value that was last written to it. This is because if the system remains henceforth quiescent and then we decide to read a variable a long time later, we expect to get the value of the last write.

In simple terms, a sequential execution is just an ordered sequence of memory operations. If the values that are read are correct (from the latest writes), then the execution is *legal*.

Observer at a Core

It is now clear that an observer sitting on a memory location in a shared cache observes a sequential execution, which is also legal. Let us now change the observer, and consider her point of view. Let the new observer be seated on a core that executes a single-threaded program. In this case, a memory operation from the point of view of the observer is actually a memory instruction: load or store. She can see the core executing instructions. Let us consider her point of view. For it, the *start time* is when the memory instruction is fetched, and the *end time* is when the instruction leaves the pipeline.

The *completion time* is the time at which the operation actually performs its operation in the physical memory location: read or write.

In the case of a load instruction, the relation $t_{start} < t_{comp} < t_{end}$ still holds. Now, in the case of a store, the relation $t_{comp} < t_{end}$ does not necessarily hold because the value may reach the desired cache bank much later; recall that we declare that the instruction has *ended* when it leaves the pipeline.

Let us explain this with a simple analogy. Assume that I want to send a letter. I leave my house at t_{start}, then I drop the letter in the post box at t_{end}. As far as I am concerned the operation ends when I drop the letter in the post box. Note that at that point of time, the letter has not yet reached its destination. The letter reaches the destination at the completion time t_{comp}, which happens much later. In this case, we instead have the following relation: $t_{start} < t_{end} < t_{comp}$. In fact, something similar has happened to your author once. Once he dropped a cheque in a drop box, and then assumed that his account has been credited a few days later when he was performing an online transaction. The transaction got declined because the cheque had not been picked up by the bank because of a snow storm – a real life example of t_{comp} being greater than t_{end}!

Nevertheless, in this case also the observer observes a legal sequential execution regardless of the degree of sophistication of the core. Let us prove it. Note that the order of start times (fetch times) is the same as the program order because we fetch instructions in program order. Now, we have already argued in Chapter 2 that to an external observer, the execution of an OOO processor, and an advanced in-order processor are identical (in terms of correctness) to that of a simple single-cycle processor that picks an instruction in program order, completely executes it, and then picks the next instruction. A single-cycle processor thus generates an operation stream that is a legal sequential execution – a read always gets the value of the latest write. Because the executions are identical, it means that regardless of the core, the outcome of every read operation is the same (same as the outcome in a single-cycle processor). Hence, in this case as well, we have a legal sequential execution, even though we have $t_{comp} > t_{end}$ for stores.

The implications are profound. It means that even if we speculate as much as we want, an external observer will always observe a legal sequential execution, which is a simple linear order of operations where every read gets the value written by the latest write.

Definition 67

- *An execution is a set of memory operations. Each operation is a 6-tuple of the form $\langle tid, t_{start}, t_{end}, type, addr, value \rangle$.*

- *In a sequential execution, operations are arranged in an ordered sequence. They need not be non-overlapping.*

- *A sequential execution or in general a sequence of operations is* legal, *if every read operation returns the value of the latest write operation to the same address before it in the sequence. In addition, the final values of all the variables are equal to the their last-written values.*

- *In a single-threaded program, if we order all memory operations in program order, then we arrive at a legal sequential execution.*

Parallel Executions

Up till now, we have only considered executions that have a single observer. Let us now consider a system with multiple observers. We define a *parallel execution* as follows. It extends a regular execution by also including the order of operations recorded by each observer. The set of operations recorded by the observers is mutually disjoint. Furthermore, each observers records a sequential execution. Unlike sequential executions, there is no ordering between all pair of operations. Hence, we have a partial order here. Note that in a parallel execution, unless we know the completion times at which the operations take effect, we do not know how to verify the execution. We cannot create a legal sequence.

We show one such example in Figure 9.6, where we have 3 threads that access two memory locations x and y. We have one observer per core or per thread that sees the entry and exit of instructions. The start and end times are defined in the same way as was defined for the previous example that considered a single-threaded system.

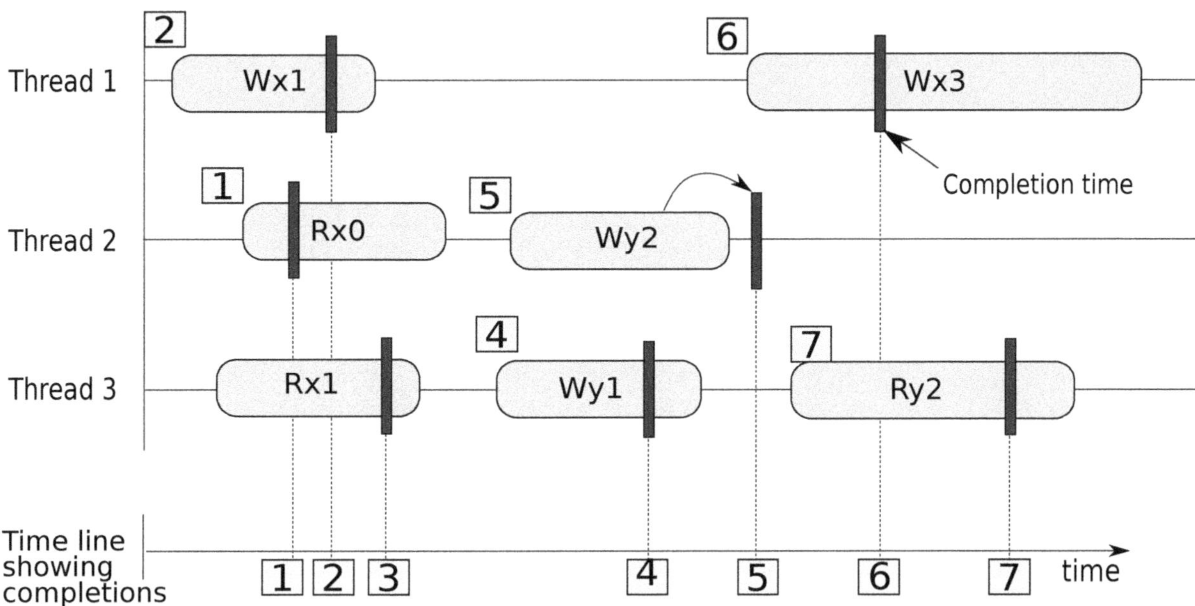

Figure 9.6: A parallel execution with 3 threads. The small vertical lines represent the completion times.

To understand this figure, let us define a standard terminology for read and write operations. Assume we are accessing the memory location corresponding to variable x. Let Rxi mean that we are reading the value i from location x. Similarly, let Wxi mean that we are writing the value i to the location x.

Let us start out by noting several interesting features of this execution. The first is that different threads running on different cores issue memory operations: reads and writes. They operations take effect based on their completion times. These times are shown with small vertical lines in the figure. Other than for $Wy2$, the rest of the completion times are between t_{start} and t_{end} in this execution. For the time being, assume that we somehow know the completion times of each operation. We shall reconsider this assumption later. Given that all the operations are ordered by their completion times, we can verify the execution.

Assume that the variables x and y are initialised to 0. In fact, we shall make this assumption for all examples henceforth – all variables stored in memory are assumed to be initialised to 0. The first instruction to complete is instruction 1 ($Rx0$). This reads the default value of x, which is 0. Subsequently, instruction 2 completes, and writes 1 to x. Then instruction 3 completes and reads $x = 1$. Let us now take a look at instructions 4 ($Wy1$) and 5 ($Wy2$). Even though they overlap, their times of completion are such that 4 completes before 5. Hence, instruction 4's write gets overwritten by the write of instruction 5. Also, note that instruction 5 is an example of an instruction where $t_{comp} > t_{end}$. Instruction 6 is the last write to x and instruction 7 reads the latest write to y ($Wy2$).

Here, each operation has a completion time, at which it appears to **take effect instantaneously**.

This property is known as *atomicity*, where each memory operation appears to take effect instantaneously at its completion time. If we arrange the operations in an ascending order of their completion times, then the operations appear to take effect in that order. We can thus order the operations (*1-7*) by their completion times in a linear timeline as shown in the bottom of the figure, and verify the correctness of the execution.

Definition 68

A memory operation is said to be atomic *if it appears to execute instantaneously at some time t. It is pertinent to underscore the point that all the threads should perceive the fact that the operation has executed instantaneously at t. We refer to this time t as the operation's completion time.*

Problems with Parallel Executions

Unfortunately, an observer sitting on the core will not be able to perceive the completion time. She will only observe the start and end of an operation. In Figure 9.6, we assumed that we somehow know the completion time of each operation, which is impractical.

Let us ask a question to ourselves. What have we gotten by creating a parallel execution? Unlike a sequential execution, it does not allow us to arrange all the memory operations in a sequence. A sequence has some very nice properties; for example, it allows us to define a key correctness property called legality – every read returns the value of the latest write. In a parallel execution, we cannot do this. Specifying the order of operations issued by the same thread might help us visualise the execution better, but other than that, a parallel execution seems to be useless. Unlike a sequential execution, we cannot prove that it is legal or correct because the term "latest write" is not defined. The only solace is that it conveys what each observer records.

Then, why did we describe all of this discrete math to just arrive at a concept called a parallel execution that is mostly useless? The only way that we can do justice to our hard work is if we can somehow **convert** or **map** a parallel execution to a sequential execution. We know that a sequential execution is a good thing: it can be analysed very easily, and it has some good properties like legality that is essentially a correctness property.

Equivalence between Serial and Parallel Executions

Let us introduce the notion of the *equivalence* of two executions. We will use this theoretical tool to create an equivalent sequential execution from a parallel execution.

Consider two executions P and S. Let the notation $P \mid T$ refer to all the operations in P that were issued by thread T. We similarly define $S \mid T$. This basically means that we extract all the operations from S and P that were issued by the same thread T and also preserve their order. $P \mid T$ and $S \mid T$ are thus ordered sequences. Let us use the $\equiv$ operator to denote equivalence. The task at hand is to define the conditions when $P|T \equiv S|T$.

Consider Figure 9.7. It shows the parallel execution P (originally shown in Figure 9.6) and a sequential execution S. They have the same number of operations; there is a one-to-one mapping between operation i in P and operation i' in S. Both the operations have the same type, address, thread id, and read/write the same value. They only differ in their start and end times. The start and end times of the operations belonging to S do not matter – only their relative order matters.

We say that for a given thread T, $P \mid T \equiv S \mid T$, if and only if the two ordered sequences have the same number of operations and there is a one-to-one mapping between the operations for each position in the sequences. For example, consider all the operations issued by thread 3 (T_3). $P|T_3 = \{3,4,7\}$. $S|T_3 =$

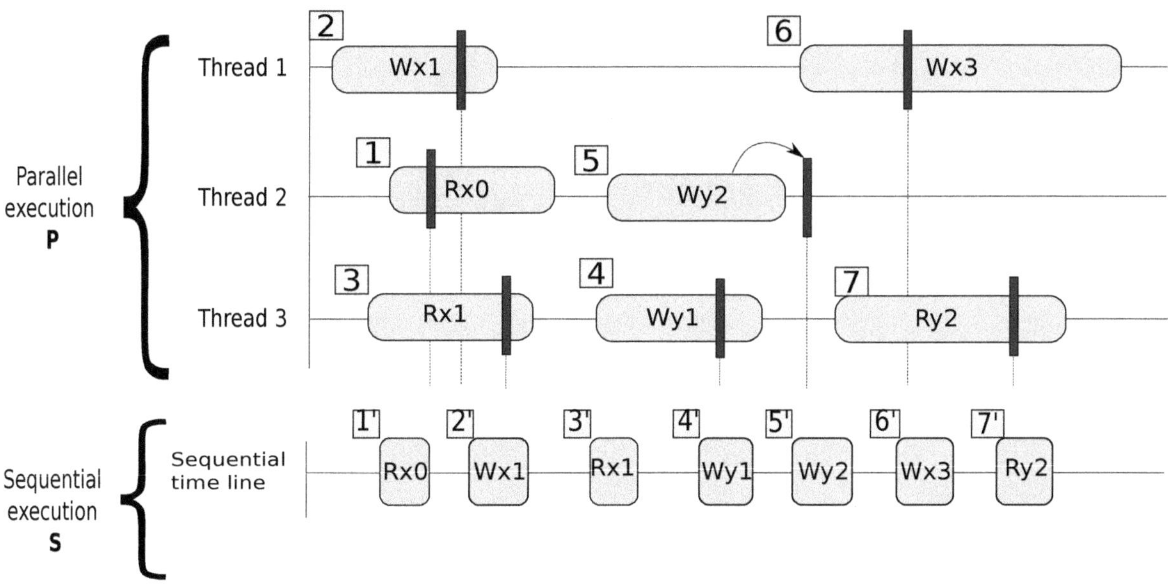

Figure 9.7: Equivalence between a sequential and parallel execution

{3', 4', 7'}. Notice the one-to-one mapping between the two sequences $P \mid T$ and $S \mid T$. Two executions P and S are said to be *equivalent*, i.e., $P \equiv S$ if for all T, $P|T \equiv S|T$. Let us quickly convince ourselves that the two executions shown in Figure 9.7 are equivalent based on our definition of equivalence.

Now note that P is a parallel execution and S is a sequential execution. The parallel execution is equivalent to a sequential execution. The readers might not have realised it yet; we have actually stumbled across one of the most effective tools in concurrency theory. We have established an equivalence between a parallel execution and a sequential execution. Hence, even if we have a parallel execution, and we do not know the completion times, there is nothing to worry. We just need to map it to an equivalent sequential execution. If the sequential execution is *legal*, then we define the parallel execution to also be *legal*. This aligns with our intuitive notion of correctness of parallel executions. The reader needs to convince herself of this fact.

Can we always map a parallel execution to a legal sequential execution? Let us find out.

9.3.2 Sequential Consistency

Consider a parallel execution where the order of operations as recorded by each observer is the same as the per-thread program order. As we saw earlier, this is the case with observers seated on cores or when the observers are the threads themselves watching their instructions get executed. This is also the default case when we are looking at the execution of a thread from the point of view of software. In such a parallel execution, each thread observes its instructions getting executed in program order.

If we can map this parallel execution to an equivalent legal sequential execution, then it means that we have a virtual ordering between all the instructions across all the threads. This is captured by the sequential execution. We can execute the instructions from the parallel threads one at a time, and arrive at the same outcomes. Even if we do not know the actual completion times, it does not matter, we can verify the equivalent sequential execution, and see if each read returns the value of the latest write to the same address.

Any such parallel execution that can be mapped to an equivalent legal sequential execution is said to be *sequentially consistent*. Sequential consistency abbreviated as *SC*, is thus a property of a parallel execution. We can however extend the definition to programs and machines. Any program that only produces sequentially consistent parallel executions or just executions is said to be sequentially consistent.

We also say that the program is in SC. Similarly, if a machine only produces sequentially consistent executions, it is said to be a sequentially consistent machine.

If we think about it, sequential consistency is intuitive. The human mind always thinks sequentially, and it is thus difficult to visualise the execution of a parallel program, and consequently argue about its correctness. However, with the notion of sequential consistency, we can do this very easily. For a parallel execution, if we can show that it is equivalent to a legal sequential execution, then we can actually think of the parallel program as a regular sequential program. We can then visualise it in our mind's eye much better and also reason about its correctness. Additionally, it is a boon to software writers particularly assembly language programmers. If the underlying architecture allows non-SC executions, it will become very difficult to write correct programs. Furthermore, programs written on one machine will not run on another. If the underlying architecture somehow guarantees only SC executions, software writers can easily write correct code that will execute seamlessly.

Definition 69
Sequential consistency has several equivalent definitions. Let us list a few popular ones.

- *If a parallel execution is equivalent to a legal sequential execution where the program order between all the operations issued by the same thread is preserved, then we say that the parallel execution is in SC.*

- *An execution is said to be sequentially consistent, or in SC, if the memory accesses of all threads can be put in a sequential order. In this sequential order, the accesses of a single thread appear in program order, and furthermore every read fetches the value of the latest write.*

- *If it is possible to interleave the memory operations of all the threads and generate a single sequence of memory operations where the operations of each thread appear in program order and the sequence is legal, then we say that the execution is sequentially consistent.*

- *Let us visualise a single-cycle processor that executes instructions from different threads by picking an instruction in program order, executing it, and writing back the results to the architectural state of the thread. We can use it to simulate the execution of parallel threads. If it is possible for it produce the same set of outcomes as a parallel execution using this sequential method of execution, then we say that the parallel execution is sequentially consistent.*

Examples: Single-variable programs

To appreciate the implications of our definitions, let us consider a few examples. First, let us consider executions that access only a single variable. These can arise out of executing multithreaded code snippets that just access a single variable, or we can extract all the accesses to a single variable from the execution of a multi-variable program.

T_1	T_2	T_3
Wx1	Rx0	Rx1
Wx2	Rx2	Rx2

Figure 9.8: SC execution

T_1	T_2	T_3
Wx1	Rx1	Rx2
Wx2	Rx2	Rx1

Figure 9.9: Execution that is not in SC

Figure 9.8 shows an SC execution (variables initialised to 0). It is possible to order the memory accesses sequentially. We can order them as follows: $Rx0 \rightarrow Wx1 \rightarrow Rx1 \rightarrow Wx2 \rightarrow Rx2\ (T_2) \rightarrow Rx2$ (T_3). Here, the arrow ($\rightarrow$) represents a *happens-before* relationship between operations A and B meaning that A needs to happen before B such that B can see its result.

Now consider one more execution that is not in SC in Figure 9.9. The readers need to convince themselves of this fact by trying all possible ways to create an equivalent legal sequential execution.

There is something that we fundamentally do not like in Figure 9.9. $Wx2$ comes after $Wx1$. All other threads should respect this order. However, thread T_3 does not respect it. It reads $Rx2$ before $Rx1$, which means that it sees the writes in the reverse order. This is not intuitively acceptable to us. If there are no more writes to x, threads T_2 and T_3 will have different final values of x, which breaks the notion of x being a shared variable. Hence, let us rule out this behaviour – we do not like it.

One simple way to do this is to constrain **the parallel execution that corresponds to all the accesses to a single location to be sequentially consistent**. This will automatically allow the execution in Figure 9.8 and disallow the execution in Figure 9.9.

We shall discuss such issues in detail later. However, we have already started to form an opinion on what seems intuitive, and what does not. The execution in Figure 9.9 does not seem to be intuitively correct. Why do we say so? This is because it violates per-location sequential consistency (abbreviated as PLSC), which means that if we consider all the accesses to a single location (x in this case), the execution is not sequentially consistent. For now, let us assume that PLSC is a desirable property. We shall continue to look at PLSC in later sections, and keep commenting about its desirability.

Definition 70 *Consider an execution $\mathcal{E}$. For a given location x, let $\mathcal{E} \mid x$ be an execution that only contains all the accesses to x in $\mathcal{E}$. Note that we preserve the order of all memory operations. If for all x, $\mathcal{E} \mid x$ is sequentially consistent, then we say that $\mathcal{E}$ is per-location sequentially consistent or $\mathcal{E}$ is in PLSC.*

Examples: Multi-variable programs

Now let us consider the general case: executions that access multiple memory locations.

T_1	T_2
Wx1	Wy1
Ry0	Rx0

Figure 9.10: An execution that is not in SC

For the execution shown in Figure 9.10, we cannot find a sequential schedule that ensures that we read both x and y to be 0. Let us try different ways of arranging the operations:

$$Wx1 \rightarrow Wy1 \rightarrow Ry0 \rightarrow Rx0$$
$$Wx1 \rightarrow Ry0 \rightarrow Wy1 \rightarrow Rx0$$
$$Wy1 \rightarrow Rx0 \rightarrow Wx1 \rightarrow Ry0$$

All of these are **illegal** sequential executions because a read does not return the value of the latest write. The original parallel execution is thus not in SC. We interpret PLSC in this case as follows. We create two parallel executions: one for accesses to x and one for accesses to y. They are shown in Figures 9.11 and 9.12 respectively.

$$\begin{array}{c|c} T_1 & T_2 \\ \hline Wx1 & \\ \hline & Rx0 \\ \hline \end{array}$$

Figure 9.11: Accesses with respect to x

$$\begin{array}{c|c} T_1 & T_2 \\ \hline & Wy1 \\ \hline Ry0 & \\ \hline \end{array}$$

Figure 9.12: Accesses with respect to y

The reader can easily verify that both the executions are in SC. For example, the execution with respect to x is equivalent to the sequential execution $Rx0 \to Wx1$. Similarly, the execution with respect to y is equivalent to the sequential execution $Ry0 \to Wy1$. These executions thus satisfy PLSC. There is an important learning for us here.

> PLSC does not guarantee SC.

We have already said that PLSC is a desirable property, because without it, executions become extremely non-intuitive. What about SC? Should we demand sequential consistency from every execution? It is easy to design a system that preserves SC and simultaneously guarantees high performance?

To answer this question, let us conduct a small experiment. Let us take a multicore processor such as a regular Intel or AMD machine and write the following piece of code using two threads: T_1 and T_2.

$$\begin{array}{c|c} T_1 & T_2 \\ \hline x = 1 & y = 1 \\ t1 = y & t2 = x \\ \hline \end{array}$$

Here, x and y are global variables. Let us assume that all our global variables are initialised to 0. $t1$ and $t2$ are local variables stored in registers. The convention that we shall henceforth use is that all local variables that are stored in registers are of the form ti, where i is an integer.

Is the outcome $(t1, t2) = (0, 0)$ allowed? This behaviour is not intuitive. We are in a better position to answer this question now. This is the same execution as that shown in Figure 9.10. This was proved to be not in SC.

Let us now run this piece of code on a real Intel or AMD machine where the two threads are assigned to two different cores. We shall observe that the outcome $(0, 0)$ is indeed observed! This is because almost no practical systems today are sequentially consistent. SC is a good theoretical concept and makes program executions appear intuitive. However, to support it we need to discard most architectural optimisations. For example, on Intel machines the write-to-read memory order (for dissimilar addresses) does not hold. This means that in Thread 1, the core can send the instruction $t1 = y$ to memory before sending $x = 1$. This will indeed happen because loads are immediately sent to memory, once the address is resolved. However, stores are sent at commit time and take effect later when they actually update the memory location.

Recall our discussion on start, end, and completion times. It is time to use these concepts now. In all likelihood, in an OOO core, the address of the succeeding load instruction $t1 = y$ will get resolved before the preceding instruction $(x = 1)$ commits. As soon as the address of the load to y is resolved, we will send the load instruction to memory. Hence, the completion time of the load to y will most likely be before the completion time of the store to x. This clearly violates program order but is a direct consequence of an OOO design, where we send loads to the memory system as soon as their address is resolved. This improves performance significantly because loads are often on the critical path. Unfortunately, this ensures that the completion times of these two instructions – an earlier write and a later read to a different address – are not in program order. This ensures that a parallel execution is not in SC, even though this does not create any issues with single-threaded executions. In fact, almost all architectural optimisations starting from write buffers to caches to complex NoCs reorder the execution of memory instructions in a program. For example, a write buffer allows later loads to go directly to the cache, but stops earlier stores from being written to the cache. Hence, in a multicore machine with

OOO cores, SC often fails to hold. In general, whenever we advance the completion time of instructions on the critical path such as load instructions to increase performance, we are essentially violating SC. We celebrated such optimisations when we were considering a single core running a single thread, sadly, they are singularly responsible for making executions non-SC in multicore systems.

We thus see that SC is the enemy of performance – it precludes the use of advanced architectural optimisations. Even though SC is a gold standard of intuition and correctness, it is difficult to enforce it in modern architectures. We need to disrespect it if we wish to use all our architectural tricks. Now, if SC is not respected, how do programs work? Why did we explain so much about SC, if SC is not meant to be enforced?

We need to read the next few sections on consistency and data races to precisely answer this question. Our basic philosophy is that even though SC is not respected at the architectural level, we somehow want to *trick* the high level programmer into believing that SC is indeed respected as long as she follows some rules.

So, where are we now? We have appreciated that SC is a great theoretical tool that unfortunately cannot be fully enforced in practice. However, it does give us a powerful method of reasoning about the correctness of parallel executions. We also looked at PLSC that is somewhat less restrictive and holds for some executions that are not in SC. We have till now not commented about the practicality of PLSC. Let us analyse it further before tackling the question of how to deal with architectures that do not enforce SC. Keep in mind that the final goal is to somehow trick the programmer into thinking that the underlying architecture only produces SC executions.

9.3.3 Exploring PLSC Further: Non-atomic Writes

Let us now complicate our situation even more. Consider a non-atomic write that does not appear to execute instantaneously from the point of view of the programmer. It does not have a single completion time (again from the point of view of the programmer). Rather it appears to execute at different points of time to different threads. We clearly do not have the issue of non-atomic writes in single-threaded systems.

However, in multithreaded programs that run on multiple cores it is possible that a write to x might be seen at different times by threads on other cores. One core might see it earlier than others. This will particularly be a problem when we are considering a distributed cache. The location for x might actually correspond to different physical locations on different caches within this large distributed cache. If we cannot keep all of them synchronised and propagate updates instantaneously, then it is possible that different threads running on different cores will perceive different completion times.

T_1	T_2	T_3
Wx1	while(x != 1){}	while (y != 1){}
	Wy1	Rx0

Figure 9.13: Non-atomic writes

Let us consider one such execution in Figure 9.13. Assume that the *while* loop terminates in the first iteration. The memory operations that the system observes are captured in the execution shown in Figure 9.14.

Thread T_1 writes to x ($Wx1$). Thread T_2 observes this write ($Rx1$), and then writes to y ($Wy1$). Then, T_3 observes the write to y ($Ry1$), and finally reads the value of x. Assume that the *while* loop introduces a happens-before relationship between the condition that it reads and the code after the loop. This should be the case because we cannot terminate a loop unless its exit condition is true.

We have seen the following happens-before relationships till now: $Wx1 \rightarrow Rx1 \rightarrow Wy1 \rightarrow Ry1$.

Let us now consider $Rx0$. This takes effect after $Ry1$ because of the *while* loop. We thus have $Wx1 \rightarrow Rx1 \rightarrow Wy1 \rightarrow Ry1 \rightarrow Rx0$. If we remove the operations in the middle, we end up with $Wx1 \rightarrow Rx0$.

T_1	T_2	T_3
Wx1	Rx1	Ry1
	Wy1	Rx0

Figure 9.14: Non-atomic writes

This is not possible. The sequence of operations is not legal. Instead of $Rx0$, we should have had $Rx1$. However, since this is not the case, we can conclude that this execution is not in SC. Furthermore, the write to x is not atomic. It is visible to T_2, yet is not visible to T_3 at a later time – it is not associated with a single completion time.

Now the important question that we need to answer is, "Do we allow such an execution?" Whenever, we have non-atomic writes, we will be confronted with similar issues. There is no straight answer. However, before taking a decision, we need to keep in mind that many commercial systems such as IBM PowerPC and ARM v7 machines [Alglave, 2012] do not enforce write atomicity. In these architectures, writes to global variables are non-atomic, which basically means in this context that the write to x reaches Thread 3 late. In such systems, this execution will be correct. Even though this execution is not sequentially consistent, the architecture will allow this. Given that commercial systems exist that do not enforce write atomicity, we have no choice but to accept this execution.

How can this happen? This can happen if the variable x is stored at multiple locations in a distributed cache. Thread 2 receives the update to x ($x = 1$), yet Thread 3 does not receive it because the message to deliver the update gets stuck in the NoC. Thread 3 thus ends up reading the older value of x.

Let us use the gold standard, PLSC, that we had developed in the case of atomic writes to analyse this execution. It stated that if we consider the execution with respect to a single memory location, then it should be sequentially consistent. Let us see if this property holds. Let us breakdown the execution shown in Figure 9.14 into two sub-executions (see Figures 9.15 and 9.16), where the operations in each sub-execution access just a single location.

T_1	T_2	T_3
Wx1	Rx1	Rx0

Figure 9.15: Accesses with respect to x

T_1	T_2	T_3
	Wy1	Ry1

Figure 9.16: Accesses with respect to y

Even though the overall execution is not in SC, PLSC holds for each location. This is tempting us to declare PLSC a necessary condition for intuitive behaviour in the case of non-atomic writes as well. Before we do so, let us consider one more execution in Figure 9.17.

T_1	T_2	T_3
Wx1	Rx1	Rx2
Wx2	Rx2	Rx1

Figure 9.17: Execution with non-atomic writes for a single location

Here, Threads 2 and 3 successively read from the same location, x. T_2 reads 1 and then 2. T_3 reads 2 first and then 1. This execution is clearly not in SC. Since writes are non-atomic, we can always argue that this execution should be allowed, because we have after all accepted the non-SC execution in Figure 9.13 that had non-atomic writes. We can say that the write $Wx1$ propagated to T_2 quickly, and then took a long time to reach T_3. We will have a reverse situation with $Wx2$. It arrived at T_3 early and arrived at T_2 late.

So, should this execution be allowed? In this case, the situation is slightly different. We have two successive writes to x: $Wx1$ and $Wx2$. They are made by the same thread, and two other threads see them in different orders. This means that x is perceived to have two different final states: 2 according to T_2, and 1 according to T_3. How can the same variable have two different final states? Let's say that after a long time T_2 and T_3 read the value of x, and if there are no intervening writes to x, they will still read different values. This should not be allowed. This is breaking the notion of memory completely. x is no more associated with a single logical location. It is as if the two threads saw two different variables. Hence, let us conclude that this behaviour should not be allowed. This is indeed the case. No commercial processor allows this.

Now why is this behaviour different from the earlier example shown in Figure 9.13, where we decided to allow non-atomic writes? Let us try to answer this question using the PLSC constraint. The reader needs to convince herself that the execution shown in Figure 9.17 is not in SC and neither in PLSC. This means that even if an execution is not in SC because of non-atomic writes, some architectures still allow it because it satisfies PLSC. However, if the execution does not satisfy PLSC, it is not allowed.

What makes PLSC holier than SC? This has to do with the fact that ensuring SC is difficult at an architectural level mainly because of the fact that it disallows many architectural optimisations. However, to enforce PLSC, we just need to ensure that an observer observing all the accesses to a memory location perceives a sequentially consistent order. This is simpler.

SC is like eating salad and doing exercise very day. This is ideal yet impractical! It is far better to somehow *trick* the body into believing that the person is actually doing this. PLSC is like popping a pill everyday to keep cholesterol levels in check – this is far easier and doable !!!

Let us look at the PLSC vs SC issue further.

PLSC vs SC

What does sequential consistency entail? There are two aspects. We need to ensure that the operations issued by each thread take effect in program order and secondly they appear to execute atomically or instantaneously (appear to have a single completion time). Sequential consistency is essentially program order + atomicity – this will allow us to arrange the operations of all the threads in a legal sequential order where intra-thread program order is respected. Note that reads to single memory words are always atomic because we can never have a *partial read* unlike a *partial write*, where some threads have received the updated value and some haven't. Hence, we normally say that SC = program order + write atomicity.

In OOO cores, ensuring program order for all memory accesses is difficult. However, it is far easier to ensure PLSC. We simply need to ensure that accesses to the same address are not reordered by the pipeline or the memory system. This is anyway the case as far as we have seen. We do not allow a load to go to the memory system if there is a prior store that writes to the same address. Loads always check the LSQ and write buffer to see if there are writes to the same address. Hence, our pipeline does not reorder memory accesses to the same address – later memory accesses do not overtake earlier memory accesses. The NoC may however do it. For example, two store operations to the same address issued by the same core may be reordered by the NoC – this needs to be stopped.

Now, let us look at write atomicity, which can be viewed in a different way. Given a write operation W and any other memory operation X, the order of completion times of W and X as perceived by all the threads should be the same. This means that all the threads should agree that W either completed before X, or after X, or the relative ordering does not matter – two threads should never make different conclusions.

Ensuring this for different memory locations is not easy because different parts of the memory system manage the accesses to different memory locations. For example, the different locations might be in different cache banks with their own controllers. However, ensuring this for a single location is much easier – in this case, we only care about the point of view an observer that is looking at accesses to a single memory location only. We can simply ensure that the accesses are serialised – appear to execute one after the other. This will ensure atomicity.

An astute reader may argue that if writes are atomic from the point of view of a single location, they should be atomic from all other points of view, even when we are considering accesses to multiple locations. However, as we have seen in our examples, this need not be the case. As we saw in Figure 9.14, it is possible that when we consider multiple locations, writes to a single location might appear to be non-atomic; however, if we consider writes to any given location, they appear to be atomic. It is all about the point of view. For a single memory location, the observer sits on the memory location, and for multiple locations, the observer sits on the core. They see different things.

Let us now summarise. Given that PLSC is much easier to enforce than SC, PLSC has been accepted as a correctness criterion that all shared memory architectures need to provide. SC, on the other hand, is desirable but impractical. We nevertheless need to give the programmer an *illusory assurance* that the architecture somehow ensures sequential consistency. We will take up this problem after we wrap up the discussion on PLSC.

9.3.4   From PLSC to Coherence

It is time to wrap up the discussion on PLSC and provide a set of guidelines to hardware designers. PLSC at this point appears more mathematical than architectural.

PLSC has two properties: program order and write atomicity (all the from the point of view of a single memory location). The program order aspect is complicated by the fact that the NoC may reorder messages sent by the same core (for the same address). However, most memory access protocols have easy fixes for this issue. They serialise such accesses. The other property is write atomicity; this is from the point of view of an observer who is only interested in accesses to the same memory address. We will discuss coherence protocols in subsequent sections that ensure a global order of writes (the atomicity aspect of PLSC) to the same address.

However, before doing so, let us understand the implications of PLSC on the behavior and broad design of hardware and software.

Software Implications of PLSC

For software writers, PLSC clearly specifies the executions that are allowed and the executions that are not. PLSC tells the software writer that regardless of the underlying implementation, each memory location is updated in program order, and if we do not consider other addresses, writes are atomic even on non-atomic machines. We can then write programs accordingly.

Hardware Implications of PLSC

The implications on hardware design are more important. It is easily seen that PLSC is both a necessary and sufficient correctness criterion for specifying the behavior of a cache or memory. Any external observer perceives a single physical location associated with a given memory address, regardless of the internal implementation.

PLSC thus provides a theoretical framework to create a distributed cache. If a given memory address has multiple associated memory locations in a distributed cache, then as long as we can maintain PLSC at the high level, the distributed cache will act as a unified cache. An observer on the memory location in a unified cache will see a legal sequential execution. If it sees the same for accesses to the same address in a distributed cache, then it will have no way of knowing whether the cache is unified or distributed. We can thus realise the gains of a distributed cache without changing our notions of correctness.

What does it mean for cache design? A distributed cache should look like a black box to the upper and lower levels. For example, if we hypothetically consider a design where the L1 cache is shared, the L2 cache is distributed, and the L3 cache is shared, then there should be no way for the programmer, or even the L1 and L3 caches to know that the L2 cache has a distributed design. This is a rather bad design from the point of view of performance, but it should still work correctly.

For this L2 cache, program order does not make a lot of sense; it does not perceive the existence of threads on the cores. Each of its constituent caches (known as *sister* caches) has a FIFO (first-in-first-out) queue that is used to accept memory requests. The requests in each FIFO queue are processed and completed in FIFO order, which is the program order from the point of view of the L2 cache. Hence, its only job is to maintain write atomicity when we consider accesses to a single location.

What exactly does this mean from the standpoint of hardware that can see all the accesses to all locations? Let us go back to observers and points of view. Let us define a hypothetical external observer $\mathcal{O}$ that sees the accesses for only a specific memory location (as we have defined before). By PLSC, $\mathcal{O}$ sees a legal sequential execution. Next, let us attach an observer with each sister cache; with the ith sister cache, let us attach observer $\mathcal{S}_i$. It creates a sequential execution for each address based on the times at which it receives messages on the NoC; unlike $\mathcal{O}$ it does not have a global view; it conveys the perspective of real hardware.

Let us analyse four sub-cases where we discuss the ordering between read and write operations to the same address that are issued by different sister caches.

Case I: Consider two read operations R_i and R_j to the same address that read the value produced by the same write (as per $\mathcal{O}$). Let us use the operator $\to$ to indicate the order of the accesses in a sequential execution. Does the order between R_i and R_j matter across the sequential executions recorded by the sister caches? The answer is NO. This is because they read the same value.

Case II: Consider two write operations W_i and W_j. If $\mathcal{O}$ records $W_i \to W_j$, then all the sister caches need to record the same order. Otherwise, read operations stand to get the wrong values, and the final value of the memory location will also be undefined. Since this does not happen in PLSC, the order of writes is *the same* across the sister caches.

Case III: Consider a read and a write operation: R_i and W_j. Assume that R_i returns the value written by W_j. As per PLSC, $\mathcal{O}$ will observe the order $W_j \to R_i$. If we have atomic writes, all the sister caches will also observe the same order. However, if we have non-atomic writes this need not be the case. It is possible that some sister caches may see the write *early* and thus not record $W_j \to R_i$. This means that for them, the completion time of the read will be before the completion time of the write. A write is said to complete when its value reaches all the sister caches and no subsequent read can read an older value. Hence, all the sister caches may not agree on such a write-to-read ordering.

Case IV: Consider a read and a write operation, R_i and W_j, where R_i reads its value from W_i, and W_j is ordered after W_i. As per PLSC, $\mathcal{O}$ will observe $R_i \to W_j$. Will the rest of the sister caches also record this order? Let us prove by contradiction. If a sister cache recorded $W_j \to R_i$, it would have been forced to return the value written by W_j or a newer value. This has not happened. Hence, all the sister caches must have recorded $R_i \to W_j$.

Let us summarise what we just learnt. We learnt that for a distributed cache that is built using FIFO queues, the way that we described, all that it needs to additionally do is ensure that for accesses by different threads to the same address, the read-to-write and write-to-write orders are *global* (all sister caches agree). This is captured by cases II and IV. Alternatively, this means that all the constituent sister caches view the *same order of writes to the same address*. The read-to-write ordering discussed in case IV is subsumed within this definition.

Axioms of Cache Coherence

Let us go a step forward and define the axioms of cache coherence as follows.

> **Write Serialisation (WS) Axiom** All the writes to the same address are seen in the same order by all the threads. This is derived from cases II and IV. This is also known as the **Order Axiom**.
>
> **Write Propagation (WP) Axiom** A write is eventually seen by all the threads.

The write serialisation axiom (WS axiom) captures the relevant part of PLSC in the context of a distributed cache. *Serialisation* means a process where we observe a set of events, such as the writes to the same address, as a *sequence*. The write propagation axiom is new; it has not been discussed before. It is rather trivial in the sense that all it says is that a write never gets lost. It is ultimately visible to all the threads. We shall make use of these axioms to create cache coherence protocols in Section 9.4.

9.3.5   SC using Synchronisation Instructions

Given that we have been able to manage the correctness of accesses to the same memory address with PLSC and cache coherence, we need to revisit the issue of sequential consistency that we have kept pending. It is sad that we have to make a choice between architectural optimisations that we worked so hard to design and SC. If we had SC, we could have executed the piece of code shown in Figure 9.18 seamlessly. This is one of the most common primitives in parallel programming: it allows a producer thread to communicate a value to a consumer thread.

T_1	T_2
value = 3;	while(status != 1){}
status = 1;	temp = value;

Figure 9.18: Communicating a value between threads

This piece of code will work perfectly in a sequentially consistent system. *temp* will always be set equal to *value*. Furthermore, thread T_2 will wait for thread $T1$ to set *status* = 1. Unfortunately, if SC does not hold, specifically if program order does not hold, then we may exit the *while* loop prematurely. We are not guaranteed to see *temp* = *value*. This is the primary mechanism that is used to communicate values between threads. The *while* loop is known as a *spin lock* or a *busy wait loop*.

Let us outline a software solution to ensure that this piece of code works correctly.

Synchronisation Instructions

The most common synchronisation instruction is the *fence* instruction, which is a special instruction that is present in almost all multiprocessor systems as of 2020. It artificially introduces an ordering between instructions. The orderings enforced by a fence instruction are as follows.

$$\text{read} \rightarrow \text{fence}$$
$$\text{write} \rightarrow \text{fence}$$
$$\text{fence} \rightarrow \text{read}$$
$$\text{fence} \rightarrow \text{write}$$
$$\text{fence} \rightarrow \text{fence}$$

This means that all read and write instructions before the fence instruction (in program order) need to fully complete before the fence instruction completes. A read fully completes when it gets its value. Similarly, a write fully completes, when it reaches all the cores and the value cannot change henceforth. Handling reads is easy. We can consider it to be fully completed, when the value reaches the core. However, for a write, the only way to ensure that it has fully completed is to wait for an acknowledgement from the memory system. Secondly, later instructions (after the fence in program order) cannot start until the fence instruction has completed. Once a core decodes a fence instruction, it stops sending later instructions to memory. Once all the preceding instructions are deemed to have completed successfully, the core executes the fence instruction. A vanilla[1] fence instruction merely introduces an ordering. Once we commit a fence instruction, we can then start executing later read,

---

[1]ordinary or standard

write, and synchronisation instructions. Note that if we just consider the execution of fence instructions, it is in SC.

Along with the basic fence instruction, there are other kinds of synchronisation instructions that do other things as well such as atomically reading, modifying, and writing to one or more memory addresses. Nevertheless, almost all such variants still include the functionality of the fence operation that essentially ensures that all the instructions before it in program order fully complete before any instruction after it in program order completes – it enforces an ordering of completion times.

Use of Synchronisation Instructions

A trivial solution is to make every instruction additionally behave like a fence if we would like an execution of a program to be in SC. ISAs such as x86 provide this facility by having a *lock* prefix, which makes some instructions additionally behave as a fence. However, such fences make the program very slow. Tudor et al. [David et al., 2013] estimate that executing a *fence* instruction takes 100-300 cycles, which is prohibitive. Hence, our aim is to insert the minimum number of fences in a program such that the behaviour is predictable. Note that problems arise only while accessing shared variables. If we are accessing thread-local variables, then there is no need to add fences. We can use such insights to reduce the number of fences.

Let us explain with an example. Consider the piece of code that was originally shown in Figure 9.18. Let us now add fences such that all executions are in SC irrespective of the underlying memory model. The code is shown in Figure 9.19.

T_1	T_2
value = 3;	while(status != 1){}
fence;	fence;
status = 1;	temp = value;

Figure 9.19: Communicating a value between threads. The code has fences to make the code behave in a sequentially consistent fashion.

Irrespective of the underlying memory model, the execution will always be in SC. For example, if we do not respect the *write* → *write* order, it does not matter. Because of the fences, first the write to *value* will complete, and then the write to *status* will complete. When we exit the *while* loop we will be sure that *value* has been set correctly. We can happily set *temp = value*.

In general, figuring out the locations where we need to add fences, such that the number of fences is minimised and each execution is in SC, is a computationally intractable problem. It is often easy to find a sub-optimal solution, where we insert more fences than necessary.

Acquire and Release Synchronisation Operations

There are a few other kinds of restricted fence operations that provide a subset of the functionality of the basic fence instruction.

Acquire instruction No instruction after the acquire instruction in program order can complete before it has completed. Note that an acquire instruction allows instructions before it to complete after it has completed.

Release instruction The release instruction can only complete if all the instructions before it have been fully completed. Note that the release instruction allows instructions after it to complete before it has completed.

Memory barriers Memory barriers are restricted fence operations, which disallow particular types of reorderings. For example, a write barrier such as *stbar* in the SPARC® ISA prevents $write \rightarrow write$ reordering. We have similar memory barriers for different kinds of instruction reorderings.

9.3.6 Theory of Memory Models

An important question that we need to ask ourselves is, "Should we give up on sequential consistency?" We did try to force SC in Section 9.3.5 with fence instructions. Even though this solution can guarantee SC, the overhead is prohibitive. A fence instruction takes 100-300 cycles and we cannot add many such instructions.

We thus need to adopt a more nuanced approach and look at other methods to reason about parallel executions. So let us try to generalise the approach that we used to map a parallel execution to a legal sequential execution. Let us introduce an intermediate step. We first convert a parallel execution into some form of an intermediate representation, and then convert that to a sequential execution (not necessarily *legal*). An intermediate representation, which we shall refer to as an *execution witness*, can *map* a parallel execution to many sequential executions. We can use it to prove the correctness of a piece of parallel code, and also write parallel code that runs on a non-SC machine. This conceptual view is shown in Figure 9.20. An important point to note here is that the mapped sequential execution may or may not be legal. This is dependent on whether writes are atomic or not. Notwithstanding this limitation, the method of execution witnesses is a powerful technique that can be used to reason about memory models.

Figure 9.20: Parallel execution $\Rightarrow$ Intermediate representation $\Rightarrow$ Sequential execution

The rules for converting a parallel execution to an execution witness are dependent on the nature of program orders that are preserved in executions and whether stores are atomic or not as we saw with SC and PLSC. These rules pretty much govern the behaviour of the memory system with respect to accesses to multiple memory locations. They comprise the *memory consistency model*, or in short, the *memory model*.

Let us summarise. The goal is to reach a sequential execution by any means. This is because as human beings, we find it far easier to reason about sequential executions. A sequential execution has the notion of an earlier write and a later read. It essentially captures the view of an omniscient observer that is aware of the completion times of all the operations. Of course, given a parallel execution we will never be able to guess the completion times with certainty. Nevertheless, a mapped sequential execution represents one possible order of completion times that is consistent with the parallel execution and the memory model. We might have many such mapped sequential executions that all read and write the same values. The important point is that it should be possible to find at least a single one such that we can argue that there is some order of completion times that can explain the parallel execution. If we can map a parallel execution to a sequential execution as per a memory model, the parallel execution is said to be *feasible* under that memory model. Furthermore, if a piece of parallel code satisfies a certain property such as a given variable should always be set to 1, then all the parallel executions will satisfy the same property, and all mapped sequential executions will do the same too. It does help if the mapped sequential execution is legal – it makes the execution seem more intuitive. Even if it is not, the sequential execution still provides important insights and can be used to verify if a machine follows a given memory model or not.

Memory Consistency Models

> **Definition 71**
> *The rules governing the behaviour of cores and the memory system while accessing multiple memory locations is known as the* memory consistency model *or the* memory model. *It defines the set of valid outcomes for any program: sequential or parallel.*

Given the importance of the memory model in a computer architect's life, it is essential that she understands the basics of a memory model really well. There are two ways in which we can study memory models: from a hardware designer's point of view and from a programmer's point of view. The earlier approach, which is from the hardware designer's point of view was far more common till 10 years ago (as of 2020). In this case, researchers focused on the way that we implement different memory operations in the memory system, and what exactly is allowed, and what is not. The problem with this line of approaches is that it does not convey the big picture to students, and it does not arm them with theoretical tools that they can use to analyse programs, executions, and hardware systems.

Hence, the other approach, which is to just look at program behaviour from the programmer's point of view is far more prevalent these days particularly with programming language researchers and members of the verification community. We shall adopt this line in our book and present a theoretical framework to understand different memory models. In specific, we shall use the framework proposed by Alglave et al. [Alglave, 2012]. Her model covers all existing memory models as of 2020, and is fairly generic enough to be extended for future models as well.

An Execution Witness

Let us introduce the basic terminology proposed by Alglave [Alglave, 2012]. Given a parallel program, let us only consider the different types of memory operations: read, write, and *synch* (synchronisation) operations.

The rest of the operations need not be considered. Since the cores that execute the parallel threads do not run in lockstep, they can get delayed for indefinite periods, and thus we cannot guarantee the relative timing of the operations. As a result in different runs, we may have different outcomes. The space of all possible outcomes is determined by the memory model. A single run is a parallel execution or just an *execution* (formally defined in Section 9.3.1). For example, the code in Figure 9.21(a) can have two different executions (on an SC machine): see Figures 9.21(b) and 9.21(c).

T_1	T_2
1: x = 1	3: y = 1
2: t1 = y	4: t2 = x

Execution 1

```
1: x = 1
2: t1 = y
3: y = 1
4: t2 = x
```

Execution 2

```
1: x = 1
3: y = 1
2: t1 = y
4: t2 = x
```

    (a)   (b)   (c)

Figure 9.21: Two different SC executions of a parallel program

The space of all possible executions for a given program in a given system is known as the space of *valid executions*. For each execution, we can create a graph called the *execution witness*. Recall from

Section 2.3.2 (Definition 11) that a graph is a data structure with nodes and edges, where nodes or vertices are connected with edges (similar to a network of roads where cities are the nodes and the roads are the edges).

In the case of an execution, the nodes are the memory accesses (read, write, or synch), and the edges are the relationships between the nodes, which we shall define shortly. We can use this information to create the execution witness for the execution, which can be further analysed to understand the features of the execution, and its interaction with the memory model. An execution witness is a nice graphical tool that can be used to understand if an execution is valid or not, and the limitations that a memory model imposes on the architecture (and vice versa). We shall primarily use four kinds of edge labels in the execution witness: rf, po, ws, and fr. Note that we can have multiple execution witnesses for an execution, in that case, we only consider that witness (if there is one) that is allowed as per the memory model. In most of our examples, we will only have a single execution witness for a given execution, and thus this problem will not arise.

For defining these edges we will show examples of parallel code and their associated execution witnesses. The conventions that we shall use are as follows.

1. All global variables start with alphabets (other than 't'), and are initialised to 0.

2. All thread-local variables that are restricted to a given thread, start with 't'. They are typically stored in registers.

Nature of Edges: Global and Local

Before introducing the different kinds of edges, let us define a crucial property of the edges. We add an edge between two nodes (memory accesses) in the execution witness if we believe that a memory access (generalised as an *event*) happened before the other. When we want to say that event A happened before event B, we write $A \xrightarrow{hb} B$, and add an edge from event A to event B. Consider an example in Figure 9.22 for a sequentially consistent system, where we show a parallel program with two statements, an execution that shows that operation $Wx1$ executed or completed before (happened before) operation $Wy1$, and then an execution witness. The execution witness has two nodes, $Wx1$ and $Wy1$, and an edge between them that indicates the happens-before relationship between them.

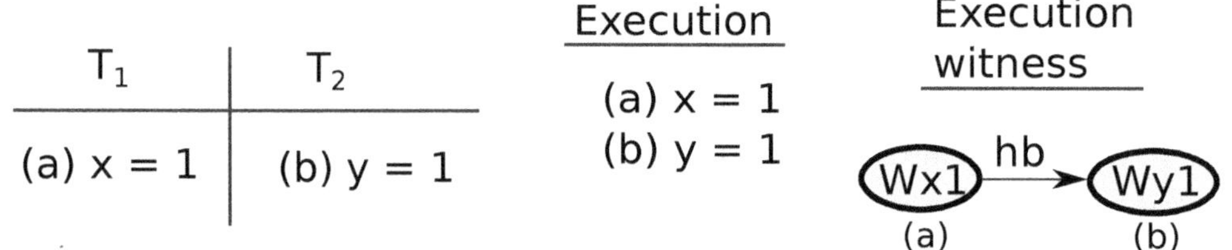

Figure 9.22: Example of an execution witness (assume a sequentially consistent system)

A happens-before relationship can be of two types: local or global. If a thread believes that event A happened before event B, then we can write $A \xrightarrow{lhb} B$ (A happened before B). From the point of view of that thread (T_1), this relationship holds. We can alternatively write, $A \xrightarrow{hb} B \in lhb_{T_1}$. In this case it is possible that another thread T_2 might have a different view and might observe $B \xrightarrow{lhb} A$. This is the local view of T_2. To summarise, a local view does not necessarily hold across threads. There is no global consensus.

When we say that the relation $A \xrightarrow{hb} B$ is global, it means that all the threads agree that A happened before B. There is no disagreement between two threads. In this case, we can write $A \xrightarrow{ghb} B$ or $A \xrightarrow{hb} B \in ghb$.

Further, note that the $\xrightarrow{hb}$ relationship does not indicate if the relationship is local or global – this has to be interpreted from the context. In this book, we shall use the symbol $\xrightarrow{hb}$ if its scope (local or global) can be interpreted from the context or if it does not matter.

Definition 72

- *A is said to globally happen before B, if all the threads agree with the fact that A has happened before B.*

- *Every thread has a view of the events. It is possible that a given thread T_1 may feel that $A \xrightarrow{hb} B$, and another thread T_2 may feel that $B \xrightarrow{hb} A$. In this case, the relationship $A \xrightarrow{hb} B$ is local to T_1 and is not global. We thus write $A \xrightarrow{lhb} B$.*

- *If the happens-before relationship holds globally (across all threads), then we write $A \xrightarrow{ghb} B$.*

All variants of the $\xrightarrow{hb}$ relationship are transitive relationships, which means that $A \xrightarrow{hb} B$ and $B \xrightarrow{hb} C \Rightarrow A \xrightarrow{hb} C$. A set of happens-before edges between events recorded by the same observer cannot have a cycle. This means that we cannot have a set of relationships as follows: $A \xrightarrow{hb} B$, $B \xrightarrow{hb} C$, and $C \xrightarrow{hb} A$. This would automatically imply that $A \xrightarrow{hb} A$, which is not possible (using the transitivity property). The fact that a graph with happens-before edges cannot have a cycle will be used extensively to understand multiprocessor systems. For similar reasons, any graph with just $\xrightarrow{ghb}$ edges cannot have a cycle: it would imply that an event happened before itself, which is not possible.

Relations and Union/Intersection Operations

In Computer Science a relation is a set of tuples, which in this case is defined as a pair of events. Consider a set of memory operations. Let us refer to each memory operation as an event. Let the events be A, B, C, D, and E. Assume that there is a happens-before relationship between them, and this fact can be represented as: $A \xrightarrow{hb} B \xrightarrow{hb} C \xrightarrow{hb} D$. We can say that the $\xrightarrow{hb}$ operation defines a relation hb, which is simply a set of tuples of events of the form $\langle X, Y \rangle$, where $X \xrightarrow{hb} Y$. For this particular example, the relation $\xrightarrow{hb}$ is defined as a set of the following tuples (note the happens-before relationship in each pair).

$$\langle A, B \rangle, \langle A, C \rangle, \langle A, D \rangle, \langle B, C \rangle, \langle B, D \rangle, \langle C, D \rangle$$

Specifying a relation such as $\xrightarrow{hb}$ using a list of tuples of events is another way of defining the relationship. This is however very cumbersome; nevertheless, it helps in understanding it from a theoretical perspective. We can similarly define another relation xy with the following tuples: $\langle B, C \rangle$, and $\langle B, E \rangle$.

Now, we can define a union of relations, which is similar to a union of sets, where the result contains all the tuples that are contained in at least one of the relations. The symbol for union is $\cup$.

$$hb \cup xy = \langle A, B \rangle, \langle A, C \rangle, \langle A, D \rangle, \langle B, C \rangle, \langle B, D \rangle, \langle C, D \rangle, \langle B, E \rangle$$

We can similarly define intersection, where the intersection of two relations consists of only those tuples that are present in both the relations. The symbol for intersection is $\cap$.

$$hb \cap xy = \langle B, C \rangle$$

Let us now discuss the different kinds of edges we add in an execution witness. All of these are happens-before edges.

Definition 73

A relation (R) between two sets A and B is defined as a set of pairs (2-tuples) of elements, where the first element is from set A and the second element is from set B. A and B can also refer to the same set. Consider an example. Let us have a relation $IsTallerThan$ defined over the set of students in a university. Each student is represented by her name (assume it is unique). Then if we write $IsTallerThan(Harry, Sofia)$, it means that Harry is taller than Sofia.

We can define all kinds of set operations between relations such as union and intersection. These are similar to union and intersection operations on regular sets.

We can also say that a relation R_1 is a subset of relation R_2, if all the tuples that belong to R_1, also belong to R_2, but not necessarily the other way. We write $R_1 \subset R_2$. If there is a possibility that R_1 and R_2 might be the same, then we write $R_1 \subseteq R_2$.

Consider an example. Let us define a relation $IsTallerBy2ft$, which contains all pairs of people where the first person is taller than the second person by at least 2 feet. It is clear that $IsTallerBy2ft \subseteq IsTallerThan$.

Program Order Edge: *po*

The program order (*po*) edge is a happens-before edge between memory operations issued by the same thread. They need not have the same address. In an SC execution, where operations complete in program order, we add *po* edges between consecutive operations issued by the same thread. In other memory models, we add edges depending upon the kind of orderings that are allowed. There are six kinds of *po* edges.

1. po_{RW} (read to write): This edge is between two memory operations, where the first operation is a load and the second is a store.

2. po_{WW} (write to write): *po* edge between two store operations.

3. po_{WR} (write to read): The first operation is a store, and the second operation is a load.

4. po_{RR} (read to read): *po* edge between two load operations.

5. po_{IS} (read/write to synch operation): Edge between memory operations and a subsequent synch operation.

6. po_{SI} (synch operation to read/write): Edge between a synch operation, and subsequent memory operations.

We are reiterating the fact that these dependences can be between operations with different memory addresses. The only thing that matters is their relative order within the thread. We shall see in subsequent sections that different memory models give different degrees of importance to different types of program order edges. For example, in the x86 memory model, po_{WW} edges are global, whereas they are not global in the PowerPC and ARM memory models. Depending upon the subset of *po* edges that are global, we can afford different kinds of optimisations in the pipeline and the memory system. We shall use the symbol $\xrightarrow{po}$ to refer to *po* edges in an execution.

However, if there are synch operations in the program, there is an edge between the synch operations and other regular read/write operations. These edges are global in nature. This means that there needs to be a consensus among all the threads that the synch operation completes only after all the operations before it in program order, and furthermore, all the operations after the synch operation complete after the synch operation completes.

Figure 9.23 shows an example of program order edges in an execution witness. We show the execution of a single-threaded program on an SC machine, which preserves the ordering between the operations. The rounded and shaded box with the text $t1 = 1$ shows the outcome of the execution, which is that $t1$'s value is 1.

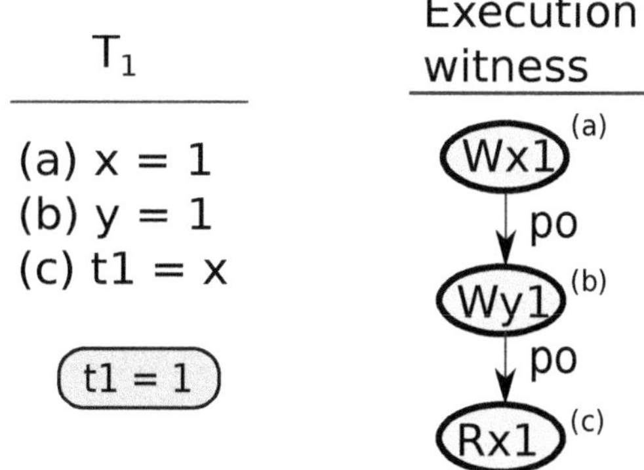

Figure 9.23: Example of program order (po) edges (execution of a single-threaded program on an SC machine)

Read-from Edge: rf

The rf (read from) edge captures a data dependence for reads/writes to the same address either in the same thread or across threads. If we have a read operation R, and a write operation W, where the read operation reads the value written by the write operation, then we have a dependence between the read and the write. It is a happens-before relationship because the write W needs to complete first, before the read operation can read its value. Since the read operation has read its value, we can automatically infer $W \xrightarrow{hb} R$. This is called a read-from relationship or an rf relationship and can be captured with a new type of edge in the execution witness. Let us refer to this as the rf edge, and denote it by $\xrightarrow{rf}$. We thus have $W \xrightarrow{rf} R$.

Figure 9.24 shows an example of a dependence where a write operation sends data to a read operation in a different thread. It is not necessary that the read operation belong to a separate thread, it can also belong to the same thread. In both cases, we shall have a read-after-write or an rf dependence, which is a happens-before relationship.

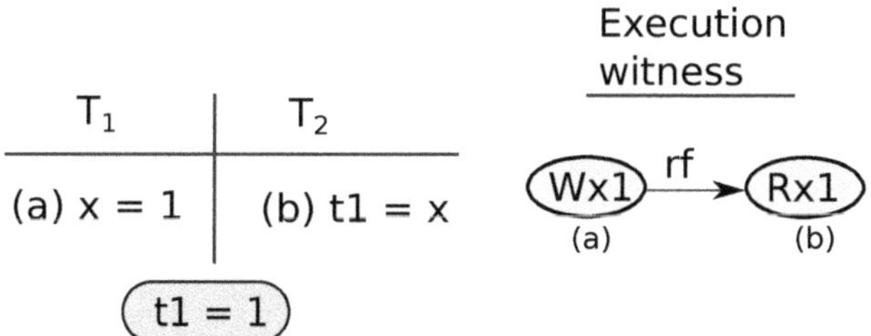

Figure 9.24: An execution witness with the rf edge

Let us divide the relation rf into two sub-relations: rfi and rfe. The rfi relation (read from internal) is a write to read dependence in the same thread. In other words, the read and the write are operations issued by the same thread. The rfe relation (read from external) also represents a write to read dependence; however, in this case the read and write operations are issued by different threads. We have $rf = rfe \cup rfi$, where $\cup$ stands for set union.

The two rf relations, rfi and rfe, need not be global. This depends on the memory model. For example, if a write is non-atomic, it will be visible to some threads earlier than it is visible to other threads. This would automatically mean that the rfe relationship does not hold globally because all the threads will not agree on the order of operations. We shall explore the intricacies of such issues along with their architectural implications in later sections. Finally, note that in many places we shall use the generic term rf which can stand for either rfe or rfi or both. The nature of the usage will be clear from the context.

Write Serialisation Edge: ws

Let us now look at the edges that we need to add because of PLSC and cache coherence. As we had discussed in Section 9.3.4, there is a global order of writes to the same address – all the threads agree with this order.

Let us thus add an edge between two write accesses to the same address and call it a write serialisation edge, or a ws edge, denoted as $\overset{ws}{\rightarrow}$. It is a global happens-before relationship (follows from the write serialisation axiom of coherence).

Figure 9.25 shows an example of the ws relationship, where we have two writes to the same variable x. Even though the writes are performed by different threads, there is still an ordering between them to satisfy PLSC, and thus we add a $\overset{ws}{\rightarrow}$ edge between them.

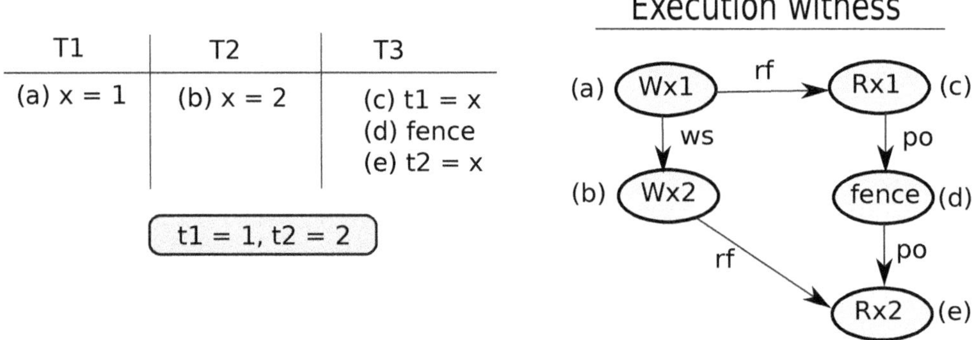

Figure 9.25: An execution witness with the ws edge

From-read Edge: fr

Let us now discuss another kind of edge that arises as a natural consequence of PLSC and the axioms of coherence (this was discussed in Section 9.3.4). We shall refer to it as the $read \rightarrow write$ or simply the fr (from-read) edge.

Consider the piece of code shown in Figure 9.26 and its associated execution witness, where we have two writes to a variable, and one read. In this case, we have a ws dependence between operations $Wx1$ and $Wx2$ because they write to the same variable x and the write operation $Wx2$ is the later write.

However, in this case, we have an intervening read operation $Rx1$ that reads the value of the first write operation $Wx1$. There is an rf edge between the operations $Wx1$ and $Rx1$. However, between $Rx1$ and $Wx2$, we have a dependence. $Wx2$ needs to happen after $Rx1$, otherwise we would read the value of x to be 2, which is not the case. Since there is an order between $Wx1$ and $Wx2$ due to PLSC,

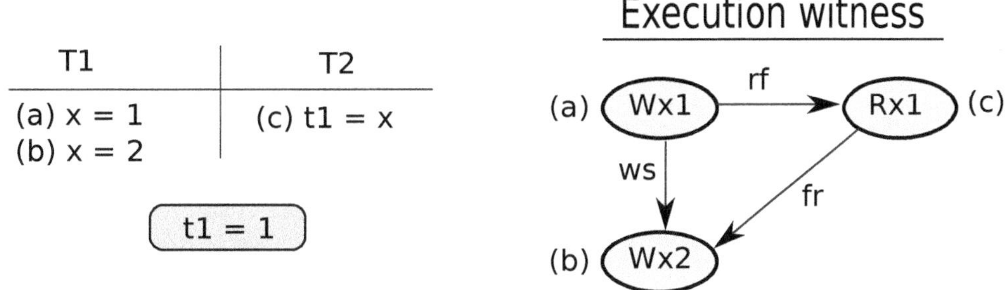

Figure 9.26: An execution witness with the fr edge

by implication, we have an order between $Rx1$ and $Wx2$ as well. Let us create an edge to represent such a read-to-write relationship, and name it the fr edge (represented as $\xrightarrow{fr}$). Akin to the ws relationship, the fr relationship is also global. Otherwise, PLSC will not hold (proved in Section 9.3.4).

Synchronisation Edge: *so*

We assume that all synchronisation operations are globally ordered with respect to each other. If we just consider all the synch operations, the execution is sequentially consistent. Recall that along with fence operations, we can have many more synch operations that additionally read or write to memory addresses (synch variables). For synch operations, we assume that rf and po are global. Furthermore, because of PLSC, ws and fr are also global.

Whenever we show an execution witness, we shall indicate the regular variables and the synchronisation variables (exclusively accessed by synch operations). ws, rf, and fr edges between accesses to the synchronisation variables will always be added. In some cases, it will be necessary to highlight the fact that we are adding an edge between accesses to a synchronisation variable. In this case, we will additionally annotate the edge with the symbol, *so* (or $\xrightarrow{so}$).

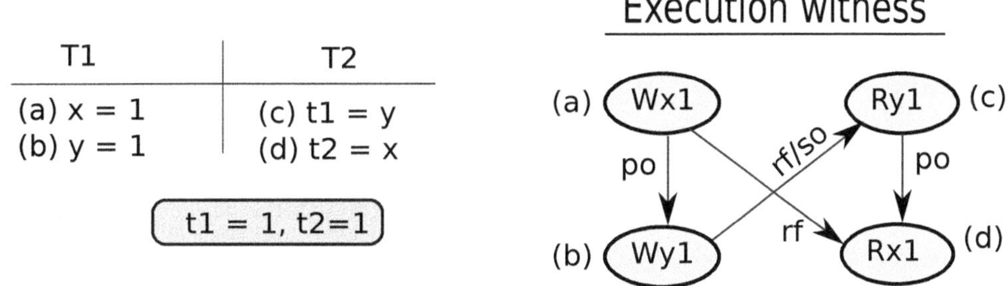

Figure 9.27: An execution witness with the *so* edge

Figure 9.27 shows an example. Here, x is a regular variable and y is a synchronisation variable. We have an rf edge from $Wy1$ to $Ry1$. We additionally annotate the edge with the *so* symbol.

Conditions for Correctness

We have four types of relationships: po, ws, rf, and fr. ws and fr originate from PLSC; they are global relationships. The po and rf relationships might have some global and some local components (sub-relationships). Let $gpo \subseteq po$ be the subset of po that is global and similarly let $grf \subseteq rf$ be the subset of rf that is global. A relation R_1 is a subset of relation R_2, if we can say with certainty that a tuple (pair of events) that is a part of R_1 is also a part of R_2. The reverse may not be true (see Definition 73). For example, it is possible that the po_{SI}, po_{IS}, and po_{WW} relations are global, yet the po_{WR}, po_{RW}, and po_{RR} relations are local. In this case, $gpo = po_{SI} \cup po_{IS} \cup po_{WW}$. Similarly, we may have a model where the rfe relation is global, but the rfi relation is local. In this case, $grf = rfe$.

Let us now define a correctness condition for an execution witness. If we have an execution witness with the edges from gpo, grf, fr, and ws, there should be no cycle. This is because we cannot have a cycle of global happens-before edges. A cycle of the form $A \overset{ghb}{\to} B \overset{ghb}{\to} C \overset{ghb}{\to} A$ implies that $A \overset{ghb}{\to} A$, which is not possible.

Alternatively, the overall global happens-before relation ghb can be written as

$$ghb = (gpo \cup grf \cup fr \cup ws) \tag{9.6}$$

ghb needs to be acyclic for every valid execution witness: it precisely characterises the memory model.

Sequential Consistency

Sequential consistency is rather special when it comes to the four relations that we have defined. Since program order needs to be respected, $gpo = po$. Similarly, we have atomic writes; hence, $grf = rf$. The other two relations, fr and ws, need to hold anyway because they hold for all systems that respect PLSC.

Hence, we can write

$$SC = (po \cup rf \cup fr \cup ws) \tag{9.7}$$

Implications of an Acyclic Execution Witness

Let us recount our journey. We realised that we will not be able to create an equivalent legal sequential execution for every parallel execution on a non-SC machine. Hence, from a parallel execution we created an execution witness. Note that the execution witness need not be unique. However, the execution witnesses that we create have to be acyclic. This is because we cannot have a cycle of happens-before edges. This is a necessary property of a valid execution witness.

However, we have still not looked at the elephant in the room. If we are able to create an acyclic execution witness, where do we go from there? What does it give us? This is where we need to use a very important result from computer science: Theorem 9.3.6.1. We state the theorem without its proof.

> **Theorem 9.3.6.1** *In any acyclic graph, we can lay the nodes one after the other in a sequence such that if there is a path from node A to node B in the graph, then A appears before B in the sequence. The topological sort algorithm can be used to create such a sequence.*

There we go! We can create a sequential execution out of an execution witness. It will respect all the ordering relationships of the memory model and the execution witness. If there is a path of happens-before edges from operation A to operation B, then A will appear before B in the sequence. Since this sequence captures global orders, it may not be *legal*, particularly if the rf relation is not global. Nevertheless, it is a sequential order of operations, which is what we wanted to create – a sequential order presents a possible order of completion times of the instructions. It proves that an execution is *feasible* under a certain memory model. In fact, one of the classic ways of showing that a given memory model will not lead to a certain outcome of an execution is by showing that all execution witnesses will have a cycle – we will not be able to construct a sequential execution from them.

What we can we use this sequential execution for? Given a piece of parallel code, we can find all the sequential executions for a memory model, either manually or using an automated tool. We can then use them to reason about the set of valid outcomes and check if a given property holds across all possible executions.

Let us reconsider this equation again: $SC = (po \cup rf \cup fr \cup ws)$. The *po* relation essentially means that in the mapped sequential execution, all the instructions of a thread appear in program order. Furthermore, $rf \cup fr \cup ws$ ensures that this sequential execution will be *legal* – there will be a global order of writes that appear to be atomic, and every read will get the value of the latest write.

9.3.7 Safety Conditions for Accesses to a Single Location

Let us now create a similar theoretical framework for the PLSC criterion based on the concepts that we have learnt.

Correctness Conditions for Single-Threaded Programs

We have till now discussed the execution of multithreaded programs. We need to ensure that single-threaded programs still work properly when running on a multicore system. The execution of single-threaded programs needs to be independent of the underlying system and its memory model. In fact, a programmer should not be able to know if the program is running on a uniprocessor or multiprocessor system. To ensure that this abstraction is met, we need to add some more edges and constraints to ensure that this genuinely happens. Let us consider a single-threaded program as shown in Figure 9.28.

```
1   x = 1;
2   x = 2;
3   y = 3;
4   z = x + y;
5   x = 4;
```

Figure 9.28: Example program to show memory access constraints in uniprocessors

In this case, we are setting the value of z, after reading x and y (see Line 4). The variable x is initialised to 1 and then set to 2. In a single-threaded execution, from the point of view of the programmer, our requirements are as follows for computing z.

1. In the statement $z = x + y$, we read the value of x to be 2.

2. In the statement $z = x + y$, we read the value of y to be 3.

We can say that in every statement, we need to read the latest value of each operand (as per program order). As far as we are concerned there is no other requirement. As long as this condition holds for all variable and array accesses, we are fine. After all, the only basic actions that we perform are memory read, memory write, branches, and ALU operations. Branches and ALU operations are independent of the memory model. As long as we read the latest value that was written, the execution is correct.

Let us look at the happens-before edges that we need to have to ensure that this happens. Consider the variable x. We set it to 1, then to 2, we read its value to compute z, and then we finally set it to 4. These statements need to execute in program order, at least from the point of view of the current thread. If the order gets mixed up, then the final execution will be incorrect. Note that we can reorder the write to y (Line 3) with respect to the writes to x as long as it is done before y is read in Line 4. The execution will still be correct.

Let us now try to derive a pattern from this observation. For an execution to be correct on a uniprocessor, every read has to get the correct value, which is the value of the latest write to the same address. This means that we cannot reorder accesses to the same variable where at least one of them is a write. For the sake of simplicity, let us constrain all the accesses to the same variable to appear to an external observer as if they are happening in program order. Let us refer to this as the *uniprocessor access constraint where accesses to the same variable in a thread are not reordered and furthermore they take effect in program order.* This is the same as PLSC in the context of a single thread.

We can always reorder accesses to different variables such as reordering accesses to x and y in Figure 9.28.

Now, let us take this single-threaded program and run it on a multiprocessor. As long as the uniprocessor access constraint holds, the program will yield the same output irrespective of the memory model. All the reads will get the values of the latest write, and thus the execution will be the same. Let us thus create a new edge called a *up* edge (uniprocessor edge) that we can add between two operations that belong to the same thread and access the same address. We shall assume that the *up* edge is global when we are considering the point of view of an observer sitting on the memory location. She only observes the accesses to that specific memory location. We shall represent this edge with the symbol $\xrightarrow{up}$.

Access Graphs

An access graph is in principle similar to an execution witness. It can be used to deduce the correctness of programs running in multithreaded environments. Like the execution witness it also needs to be acyclic. The key differences in an access graph are that it contains accesses for only a single location, and the edges that we consider are *up*, *ws*, *fr*, and *rf*. The *up* edge enforces the uniprocessor access constraint for each thread. The rest of the edges show the constraints governing the communication of values across threads or the data flow. An observer sitting on a memory location will see all of these edges.

An example access graph is shown in Figure 9.29 for the code shown in Figure 9.28. Note the positions of the $\xrightarrow{up}$ edges that are added to ensure the uniprocessor access constraints.

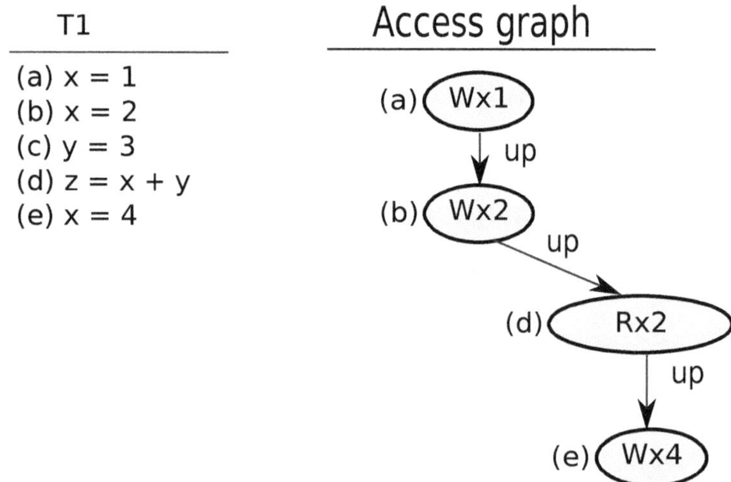

Figure 9.29: An access graph for the code shown in Figure 9.28

PLSC

Consider the four types of edges in the access graph: the uniprocessor access constraint up, and the three edges (ws, fr, and rf) that reflect the data flow between threads. They represent the behaviour of the program from the point of view of a single memory location. Irrespective of the way these accesses interact with accesses to other locations, we would like all these four orderings to hold from the point of view of the single location. This is because they are required to ensure PLSC. In this case, the up relation represents the program order in executions that access a single location, the same way the po relation represented the program order in general programs. We have proven that $SC = po \cup rf \cup fr \cup ws$. We can define something similar for PLSC. The proof is on similar lines. For SC we considered multi-variable executions, for PLSC we shall consider executions that access a single variable. After replacing po with up we get

$$PLSC = up \cup rf \cup fr \cup ws \tag{9.8}$$

Example 11

Consider the code in Figure 9.30(a). Here, the two threads see the two updates to x in different orders. This is not allowed as per PLSC and coherence. To disallow an execution in our framework we need to find a cycle in the access graph.

Consider the access graph in Figure 9.30(b). We have a cycle between the nodes (c), (e), and (f). Since we cannot have a cycle with happens-before edges, this execution is not allowed. This execution is not in PLSC.

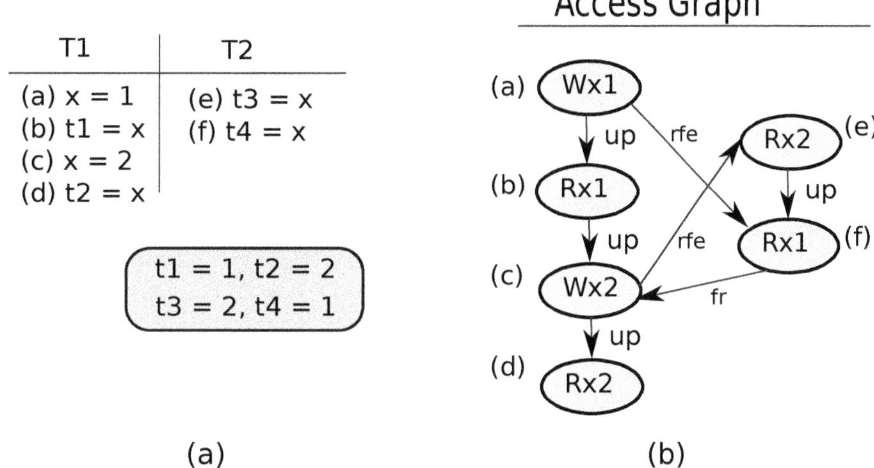

Figure 9.30: An access graph that shows an execution that does not satisfy PLSC

9.3.8 Safety Conditions for Data and Control Dependences

Even in models that do not respect program order, there is some causal dependence. A causal dependence is between a producer and a consumer (cause-effect relationship). It is not possible for a consumer to use a value before it has been produced. Till now we have not captured such dependences. This can lead to extremely non-intuitive behaviour.

Consider the execution in Figure 9.31(a) and the execution witness in Figure 9.31(b). In this case, $Rx1$, the *if* statement, and $Ry0$ are causally related: there is a cause-effect relationship. $Rx1$ is the producer of $t1$, the *if* statement is the consumer, and its consumer is $Ry0$. We can think of the *if*

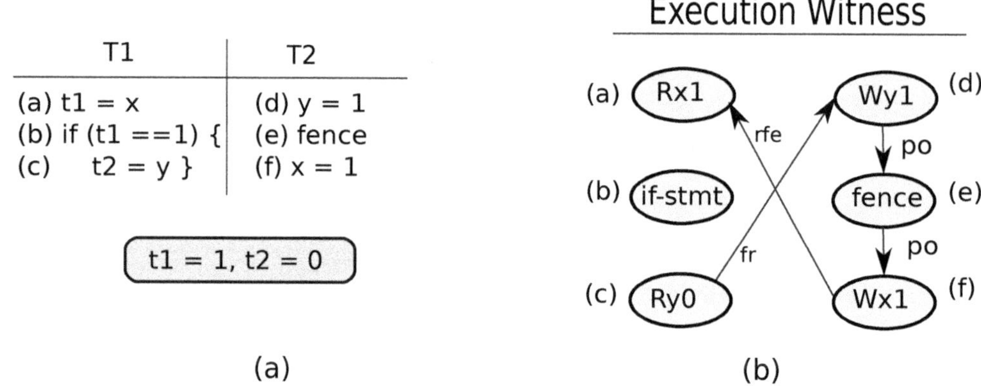

Figure 9.31: Non-intuitive execution when there is a data dependence

statement creating the permission for $Ry0$ to execute. Since our memory model does not respect read-after-read dependences, and does not treat *if* statements in a special manner, we have not added edges between $Rx1$, the *if* statement, and $Ry0$. However, in our memory model, we respect program orders between normal instructions and fences, and the rfe relation is global. Hence, we have added the corresponding edges. This execution witness does not have cycles and thus satisfies the memory model. However, it is not intuitively correct.

Instruction $Rx1$ produces the value of $t1$, which determines the direction of the *if* statement. Since in our execution $t1 = 1$, $Ry0$ executes. $Ry0$ reads $y = 0$ and thus there is an fr edge between it and $Wy1$ (in thread 2). The three instructions in thread 2 have to be executed in program order because the second instruction is a fence. After collating the dependences, we can conclude that $Wx1$ should complete after $Rx1$ because of the causal dependences, fr edge, and the fence. However, this is not what is happening. $Wx1$ produces the value for $Rx1$. Intuitively, we have a cycle even though we cannot see it in Figure 9.31(b). It appears that we have read $Rx1$ much before we should have actually read it. This is known as a *thin air read*. This can indeed happen in modern systems that use value prediction. If we would have predicted the value of x to be 1, we would have later on found the prediction to be correct because of $Wx1$ and the execution would have been deemed to be absolutely fine!

Definition 74
A thin air read is defined as a read, where we read a value without seeing its preceding write.

Let us thus introduce a new edge called a dependence edge (*dep*) (symbol: $\xrightarrow{dep}$) that represents both data and control dependences. We add this edge between a read and a subsequent instruction that uses its value in the same thread or between a conditional statement and its body.

Let us thus create a new kind of graph to model causality. Let us call this a *causal graph* that only contains edges to model producer-consumer relationships. We have three kinds of edges in such a graph: rf edges, gpo edges and *dep* edges. gpo edges are program order edges that hold globally ($gpo \subseteq po$). Akin to the execution witness and access graph, the causal graph should also be acyclic.

Now, if we add these edges to the execution in Figure 9.31, we have the execution shown in Figure 9.32. We have added *dep* edges between $Rx1$, the *if* statement, and $Ry0$. Here, there is a cycle and thus the execution is not valid.

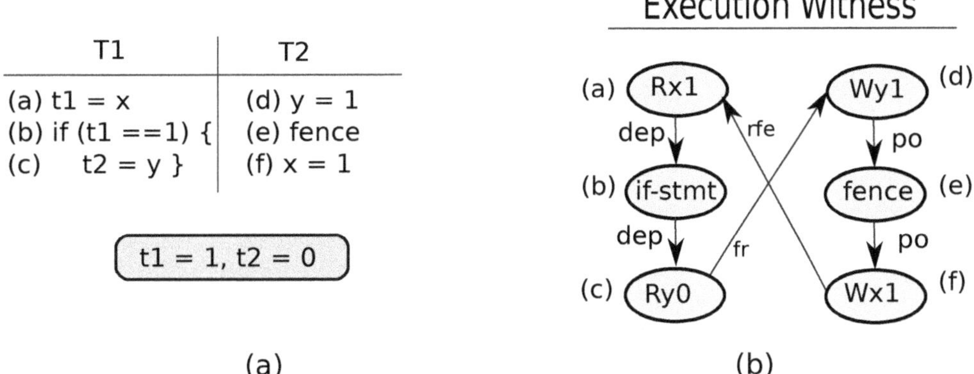

Figure 9.32: Example of an execution with the $\xrightarrow{dep}$ edge

Let us thus define a new condition that precludes thin air reads.

$$NoDepCycle = acyclic(rf \cup gpo \cup dep) \tag{9.9}$$

9.3.9   Correctness of Executions

Now we are in a position to answer the question, "When is an execution correct?" This is in general a tricky question because this depends on how exactly different systems, programming languages, and runtime environments exactly define correctness. Let us however take the liberty of providing a definition that enjoys a broad consensus in the technical community and is as per our discussion.

An execution is correct if all the following conditions in Table 9.2 hold.

Condition	Test
Satisfies the memory model	The execution witness is acyclic
PLSC holds for all locations	The access graphs are acyclic
NoDepCycle holds	The causal graph is acyclic

Table 9.2: Correctness conditions for an execution

9.4   Cache Coherence

Recall our discussion in Section 9.3.4 where we motivated the need for PLSC and showed how the axioms of coherence arise as a natural corollary of PLSC. In this section, we need to design a practical cache coherence protocol that ensures that the two cache coherence axioms hold: there is a global order of writes (write serialisation), and a write is never lost (write propagation).

9.4.1   Write-Update Protocol using a Bus

Let us consider a simple system. Consider Figure 9.33, where the set of caches are connected using a bus. Recall that a bus is a set of copper wires that can support only one sender at any point of time; however, we can have any number of receivers. Such buses naturally support broadcast based traffic. It is possible for any cache to snoop on the bus – read all the writes that are made on the bus even if the writes are not meant for it. Such kind of a bus is known as a snoopy bus. Cache coherence protocols that use snoopy buses are known as *snoopy protocols*.

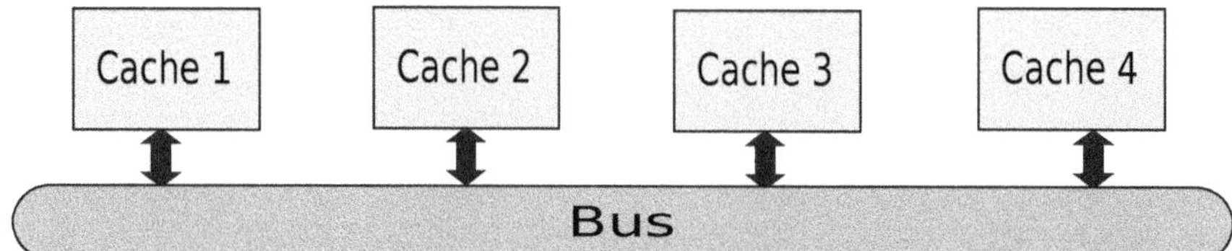

Figure 9.33: A broadcast bus

We shall discuss two kinds of snoopy protocols: write-update and write-invalidate. Let us describe the simpler protocol write-update in this section. The key idea is that every write is broadcast on the bus such that the rest of the caches can snoop it and take some action.

Each constituent sister cache, $C_1 \ldots C_n$, in the distributed cache is a complete cache in itself. It can store any block. It can supply a copy of the block if it receives a request. However, to ensure that the set of caches follow coherence, we need to observe some rules. Before framing the rules, let us understand the constraints. Since $C_1 \ldots C_n$ are mostly independent caches, they can have different copies of the same block. In this case, ensuring write serialisation (WS) is difficult because we might update the copies in any order. It is necessary to thus add restrictions to the process of writing such that the WS axiom is not violated. In addition, it is possible that because there is a single bus, a cache might get continuously denied access to the bus, and thus it might not get a chance to let other caches know about a write request that it has received. This will violate the write propagation (WP) axiom. There is thus a need to ensure some fairness such that the WP axiom is not violated – a write is ultimately visible.

Reads

Let us outline a simple protocol.

Whenever a cache receives a read request, if there is a read hit, we are sure it is the correct value, and thus we quickly forward the value to the requester. However, if there is a read miss, then there is a need to search for the value in other sister caches first. Recall that in a conventional system, we would have sent the request to the lower level. In this case, we will not do that. We will first ask other sister caches. Only if all of them indicate that they do not have the block, then only we send the request to the lower level. To send a request to the rest of the sister caches, the cache that has a read miss needs to first get control of the bus. Once it has exclusive access to the bus, it needs to broadcast a read miss request – denoted as RdX. We assume a bus controller that gets requests from different caches, and then in a fair manner allocates the bus to them. This ensures that our protocol follows the WP axiom.

After the cache broadcasts the read miss message, the rest of the sister caches get the message by snooping on the bus. If any of the sister caches has a copy of the block, then it sends it over the bus to the requesting cache. There is a subtle point that has to be made here. Assume three sister caches have a copy of the block. It should not be the case that all three of them send back a copy of the block. This will not happen in a bus based system, because the cache that gets control of the bus first will send a copy of the block. The rest of the caches will see this and decide not to send a response (with a copy of the block) to the requester.

Let us thus propose a simple protocol known as the MSI protocol to implement this high-level idea. In this protocol, each cache line has three states: modified (M), shared (S), and invalid (I). The protocol is as follows. When a given cache line is empty, it is said to be in the invalid state I. When it gets a copy of the block after a read miss, it transitions from the I to the S state. S refers to a shared state, where it is known that the block is possibly shared with other caches. This means that other sister caches might have the same copy of the block with them. This part of the protocol is shown with a state machine in Figure 9.34. The standard method of annotating a state transition is to create an event-action pair separated with the '|' symbol. For example, the notation "*Evict* | −" means that whenever we need to evict a block, we just evict it and do not do anything else. However, if we need to read a cache line, when it is in the invalid state (block not present in the cache), we send a read miss message (RdX) on the bus. Once the block arrives, we transition to the shared state. The action in this case always means that a message is sent on the bus, which every sister cache can read.

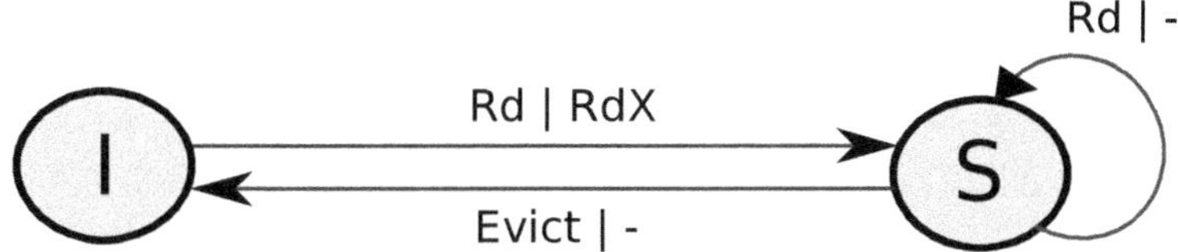

Figure 9.34: State transitions in the write-update protocol: S and I states

Note the transitions from the shared state. If we need to read a line that is already in the shared state, then we can just go ahead and read it. There is no need to send a message to any sister cache. This transition is shown as "Rd | −" in Figure 9.34.

Next, consider evictions from the cache when the line is in the S state. The S state basically means that we have not written to the block. We are only reading it. Since the current cache has not modified the block, it can seamlessly evict the block. We will not lose any data.

Writes

Let us now consider the tricky case of writes. Assume that we have a write miss. This means that the block is not present in the cache. We need to first request the rest of the sister caches for a copy of the block, and the write can be effected only after we get a copy of the block (like regular caches). This is similar to the case of a read miss. We send a write miss message WrX to the rest of the caches. If we do not get a reply within a specific period of time, or we get a negative response from the sister caches, then it means that the block must be fetched from the lower level. This part is exactly similar to the case of a read miss. Once we get a copy of the block, we transition to the modified (M) state. This is shown in Figure 9.35. Note that till this point we have not performed any read or write yet, we are merely requesting a copy of the block from other caches. Once, we have made the $I \rightarrow M$ transition after receiving a copy of the block, we can then proceed with the read or write operation.

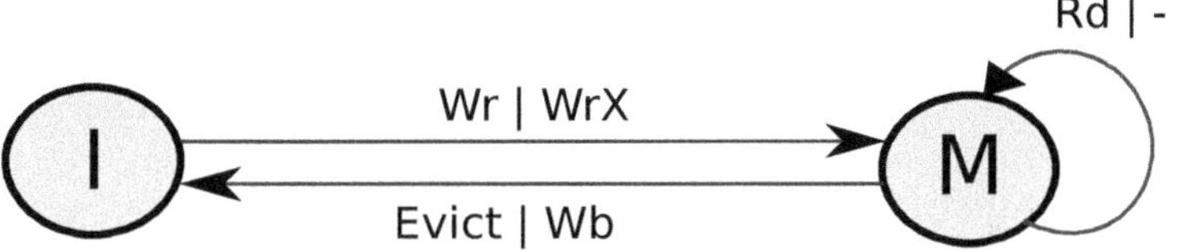

Figure 9.35: The $I \rightarrow M$ and $M \rightarrow I$ transitions (writes in the M state are not shown)

Once, the block is in the M state, reads are seamless. This is indicated by Rd | − in Figure 9.35, which means that no message needs to be sent on the bus. We can go ahead and read a copy of the block. However, if we evict the block we need to write a copy to the lower level, because we have modified its contents. If we do not write back a copy to the lower level, then it is possible that we might lose our updates because no other sister cache may have a copy of the block. Hence, to be on the safer side, every time we evict a block in the M state, we should write back the block to the lower level such that updates are not lost. We use the term Wb in Figure 9.35 to denote a write back. We can thus conclude that unlike the S state, in the M state, evictions are more expensive.

Let us now look at writes in the M state, which is the only event-action pair that is not shown in Figure 9.35. This is where we need to ensure that the WS (write serialisation) axiom is not violated.

Let us first consider a simple solution that might appear intuitive yet is wrong. Our algorithm could be that we write to the block, and then broadcast the write on the bus to the rest of the sister caches such that they can update the copy of the block that they may have with them. This will ensure that at all points of time, all the caches have the same contents of the block. However, this is not correct. Assume cache C_1 writes 1 to x, and at the same time cache C_2 writes 2 to x. Then they will try to broadcast the values. Whoever (C_1 or C_2) gets control of the bus the last will end up writing the final value. Assume C_1 broadcasts first and then C_2 broadcasts. It is perfectly possible that on C_1 two successive reads will read the following values: first 1 and then 2. Now, on C_2 we might have a read operation that arrives after we have just written 2 to x, and not performed or received any write messages on the bus. In this case, we will read $x = 2$. After C_2 receives the broadcast from C_1 and updates x to 1, the second read operation on x by C_2 will return 1. Thus, the order of writes perceived by C_2 is (2,1), whereas for C_1 it is (1,2). This clearly violates the WS axiom. The writes are not serialised.

Let us thus try to fix this. Let us make writes atomic, where a write is visible to all the caches at the same time. This can be done very easily. When we need to write to a block, which is present in the cache, we wait to get control of the bus. Then we broadcast the write. All the sister caches **update the copy of the block** if they have a copy of it. This includes the requesting cache as well, which effects the write when it is broadcasted successfully. This process ensures that we can implement an atomic write operation, where all the caches see it at the same time. This will ensure write serialisation.

Figure 9.36 shows the final diagram for the transitions in the M state. The flow of actions on a write miss is as follows: broadcast a WrX message on the bus, wait to receive a copy of the block, transition to the M state, and then effect the write.

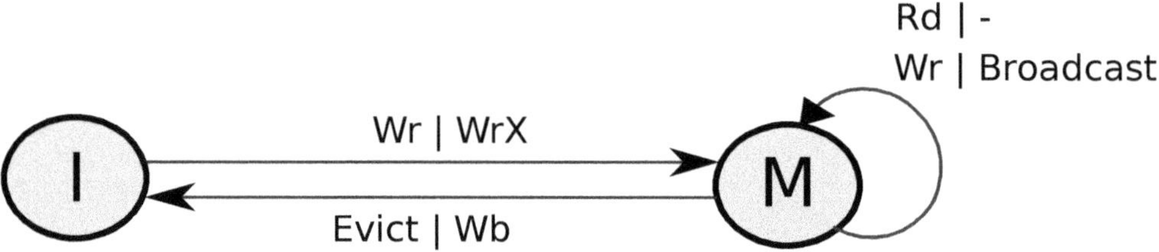

Figure 9.36: $I \to M$ and $M \to I$ transitions

Till now we have looked at transitions from the I state to the S and M states. We now need to look at transitions between the S and M states. In the write-update protocol, we never make a transition from the M state to the S state. This is because if we have write access to the block, then it automatically implies that we have read access to the block. However, we do need to make a transition from the S state to the M state if there is a write request. This would indicate that we have modified a copy of the block. The final state diagram for the protocol with all the three states is shown in Figure 9.37.

Transitions due to events received from the bus

There are three kinds of events that a cache can receive from the bus: RdX (read miss), WrX (write miss), and $Broadcast$ (a write being broadcasted to the rest of the caches). We need to process these messages for each of our valid states: S and M. The state transition diagram is shown in Figure 9.38.

Whenever we get a read miss or a write miss from the bus, it means that some other sister cache needs to be sent a copy of the block. One of the caches that contains a copy of the block needs to reply with the copy, and when the rest of the caches see the reply they need not send their own copies to the requesting cache. In terms of messages, when we receive the RdX and WrX messages from the bus, we need to start the process of sending a copy of the block over the bus to the requesting cache. This is denoted by the $Send$ action in Figure 9.38. The fact that the $Send$ action may be suppressed because a sister cache already sent a copy of the block is not shown in the figure.

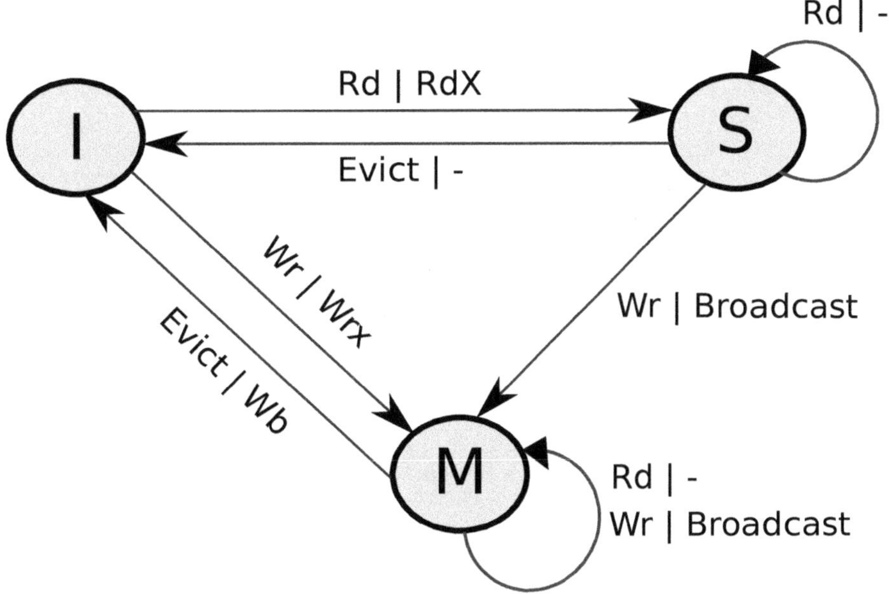

Figure 9.37: The write-update protocol: state transitions due to read, write, and evict events

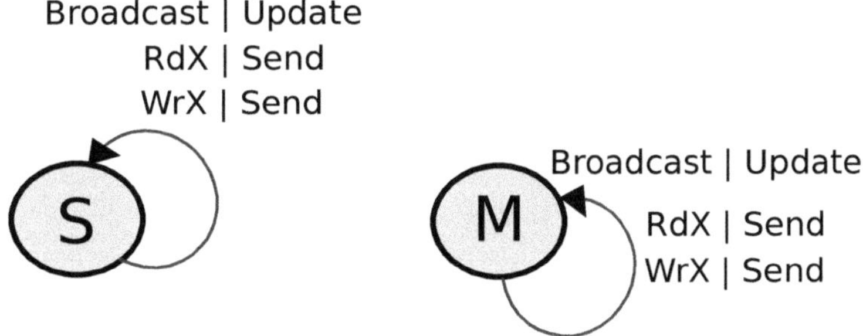

Figure 9.38: The write-update protocol: state transitions due to events received from the bus

The other message that a cache can receive is a *Broadcast* message, which means that a sister cache has written to a block. The caches that contain a copy of the block need to update their local copies with the values being sent over the bus. This is an *Update* action.

Summary

The axioms of coherence hold because of the following reasons. The WS axiom holds because all the writes are atomic, and they are instantaneously visible to all the caches. Alternatively, the caches see the same order of writes, which is also the same as the order in which the caches get access to the bus. The WP axiom needs to be guaranteed by the bus master – circuit that controls access to the bus. It needs to ensure that all the caches get access to the bus in finite and bounded time. This way writes will not be lost. Every cache will be able to place its requests on the bus without waiting indefinitely.

Even though we have guaranteed the axioms of coherence, significant performance and power issues still remain mainly because a write is very expensive. Let us elaborate.

1. For every write operation, we need to broadcast the values on the bus. This increases the bus

Term	Meaning
States	
I	Invalid state. This means that the block is not present in the cache.
S	Shared state. The block can be read and evicted seamlessly. However, we cannot write to the block.
M	Modified state. We can read or write to the block.
Cache actions and events	
Rd	Read request
Wr	Write request
$Evict$	Eviction request for a block.
Wb	Write back data to the lower level.
$Update$	Update the copy of the block with values sent on the bus.
Messages on the bus	
RdX	Read miss
WrX	Write miss
$Broadcast$	Broadcast a write on the bus.
$Send$	Send a copy of the block to the requesting cache.

Table 9.3: Glossary of terms used while describing coherence protocols

traffic and power utilisation significantly.

2. Whenever a write is broadcast on the bus, every cache needs to check whether it contains the cache block or not. If it does, it needs to update its contents. This increases the contention at every cache and also increases the power utilisation significantly.

Before proceeding to discuss more efficient protocols, let us conclude this section by providing a glossary that defines all the terms used for the states and transitions. We shall use the same terminology later as well. Refer to Table 9.3.

9.4.2   Write-Invalidate Protocol using a Bus

The main drawback of the write-update protocol is that we need to send a message on every write. This increases the power utilisation and the bus occupancy significantly. The write-invalidate protocol does not suffer from this problem. To keep matters simple, let us keep the model of the system the same: all the caches are connected to each other using a shared bus. Since every cache can snoop on the bus, this is another example of a *snoopy protocol*. This protocol has the same three states albeit with different connotations.

Basic Insights

The insights for this protocol are as follows. The reason that we need to broadcast writes to the rest of the caches is because the rest of the caches need to be kept up to date. Hence, their state needs to be kept updated all the time. The cost of ensuring this is significant, and it encumbers every single write operation. To solve this problem, we need to constrain the process of reading and writing to copies of the same block. Let us thus propose the following set of rules.

Single Writer At any point of time, we can at the most have only a single writer for each block and no readers.

Multiple Readers If no cache has the permission to write to the block, then multiple caches can read the block simultaneously. In other words, we can support multiple readers at a time.

Either we have a *single writer* situation or a *multiple readers* situation. We never have a case where we have two caches that can write to different copies of the same block simultaneously. We also do not have a case where one cache is writing to the block, and another cache is concurrently reading it. This is very different from the conditions that we had in the case of the write-update protocol. However, because we allow a single writer at a time, we shall show that we can design a protocol where we do not need to send a message after every write operation.

Let us define the term *conflicting access*. Memory instructions A and B that access the same block are said to be conflicting if one of the following conditions is true.

- A is a write and B is a write.

- Or, A is a read and B is a write.

- Or, A is a write and B is a read.

We can express the set of rules (single writer or multiple readers) that we have seen before in another way:

> In the write-invalidate protocol, we do not support concurrent and conflicting memory accesses.

Write-Invalidate Protocol: Read, Write, and Evict events

In the write-invalidate protocol, the shared (S) state represents the multiple-readers scenario, and the M state represents the single-writer scenario. The state transitions for read, write, and evict events are shown in Figure 9.39.

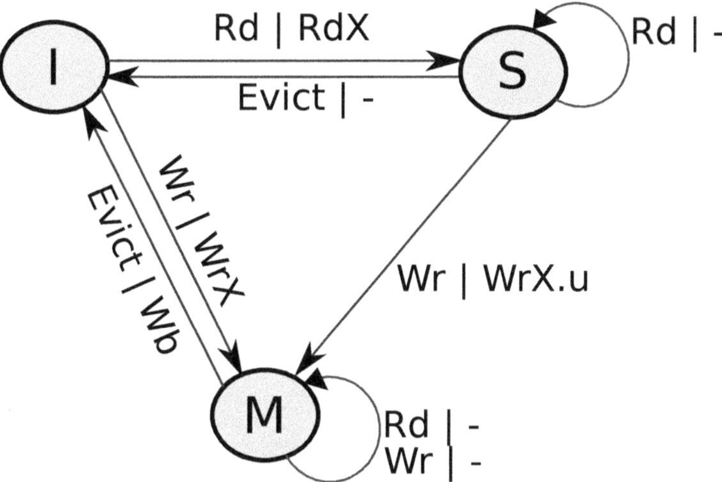

Figure 9.39: MSI protocol (messages from the higher level)

We make a transition from the I state to the S state, when there is a read request. In this case, we send a read miss RdX on the bus, and get a copy of the block. If it is there with a sister cache, then we get that copy, otherwise we get it from the lower level. The logic for avoiding multiple responses is the same as that in the write-update protocol, which is that once a response is sent, the rest of the sister caches that have the data discard their responses.

In the S state, we can read as many times as we want. However, we are not allowed to write to the block. It is necessary to transition to the M state, and for that it is necessary to seek the permission from the rest of the sister caches. Recall that we can only support a single writer at a time. If there is a need to write to the block in the S state, then the cache places a write miss, $WrX.u$, message on the bus. It is important to make a distinction between a regular write miss message WrX, and a write miss upgrade message, $WrX.u$. We have seen the WrX message in the write-update protocol as well. We send a WrX message when the requesting cache does not have a copy of the block. A copy of the block needs to be supplied to it by a sister cache if it is present with it. However, when we are transitioning from the S state to the M state in the write-invalidate protocol, we already have a copy of the block, we do not need one more copy. Instead, we wish to let the sister caches know that they need to discard their copies such that the requesting cache can perform a write. Discarding copies of a block is known as *invalidation*. This is why this protocol is called the write-invalidate protocol. As a result, we send a different message that informs the rest of the caches that the state of the block is being upgraded to the M state. This is why we introduced a new message called the write miss upgrade message $WrX.u$.

Subsequently, we can transition to the M state. In the M state, the cache is guaranteed to have an exclusive copy of the block. No other cache has a copy. The cache is thus free to perform its reads and writes. There is no need to <u>inform the other caches</u>. This is the crux of this protocol. In the M state, a cache can read or write a block any number of times without placing messages on the bus because no sister cache has a copy of the block. This is where we save on messages.

Now consider the $I \rightarrow M$ transition. This happens, when the block is not present in the cache, and we wish to write to the block. In this case, we place a write miss message WrX on the bus. A sister cache, or the lower level forward a copy of the block, and then we directly transition to the M state.

Let us now look at evictions. If a block gets evicted in the S state, then we transition to the I state. Since we were only reading the block, its contents have not been modified. We can thus seamlessly evict the block. Nothing needs to be done. However, an eviction in the M state is more expensive. This is because we have modified the contents of the block, and we are sure that there are no copies of the block in other sister caches. If we seamlessly evict it, then the updates to the block will be lost. It is thus necessary to write-back a copy of the block to the lower level. Then it can be evicted and we can make an $M \rightarrow I$ transition.

Write-Invalidate Protocol: Messages from the Bus

Let us now see how a cache needs to react to messages coming from the bus (see Figure 9.40). Consider the S and M states because considering the I state in this case is pointless. In the S state, if we get a read miss message, we can prepare a response with a copy of the block. If no other cache has sent a response already, then the response can be immediately sent. However, if we get a write miss, it is necessary to transition to the I state; recall that only one cache can have the permission to write to the block at any point of time.

In the M state, if we receive a read miss, then it means that another cache is requesting for read-only access. Since it is not possible for two copies of the block to be in the M state simultaneously, or for one copy to be in the M state and the other copy to be in the S state, we need to do several things.

1. Provide a copy of the block. This needs to be done because no other cache, or even the lower level of memory contains an up to date copy of the block.

2. Transition to the S state ($M \rightarrow S$). The cache will at least be able to seamlessly read the data in the future.

3. Write back a copy of the block to the lower level. This needs to be done because we wish to have seamless evictions in the S state. Assume that we make an $M \rightarrow S$ transition, and we do not write-back a copy. Subsequently, if the copies get evicted, the updates will be lost, because we support seamless evictions from the S state. Hence, a write-back is required upon an $M \rightarrow S$ transition.

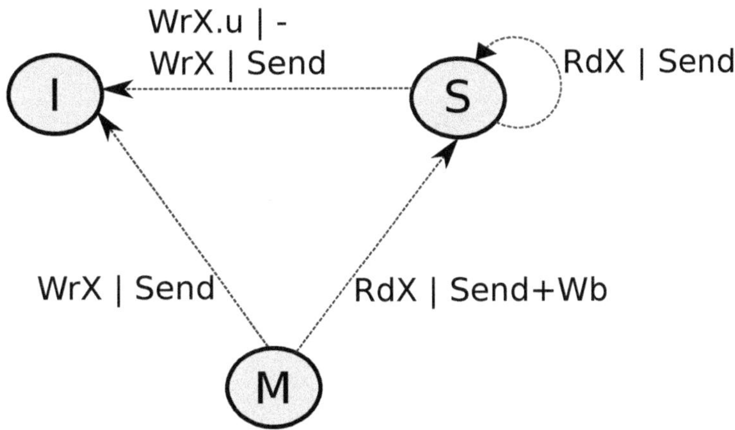

Figure 9.40: MSI Protocol with invalidate messages (messages from the bus)

Let us now consider write miss messages. In the S state, if we get a write miss message then it means that we need to transition to the I state. This is because when a cache writes to a block, it needs to do so exclusively. If the message is WrX, we need to forward a copy of the block to the remote cache because it does not have a copy. However, if the message received is of type $WrX.u$, which is just an announcement that the requesting cache is transitioning the state of the cache line containing the block from the S to the M state, we do not have to send a copy of the block. The requester already has a copy of the block in the S state. On the same lines, we need to transition to the I state from the M state upon receiving a write miss. Since the block was in the M state, the remote cache does not have a copy of it; it is thus necessary to forward a copy.

Summary of the Write-Invalidate Protocol

Let us summarise our discussion. The write-invalidate protocol either allows a single writer or multiple readers to simultaneously exist for each cache block at any single point of time. Since we do not have multiple writers at a time, the order of writes to a single location can be clearly established. It is the order in which we enter the M state across the caches. This ensures that the WS axiom holds. For the WP axiom, we need to ensure that if a cache needs to write to a block, it ultimately gets write access to it. This is possible to ensure by having a fair bus that gives every cache a fair chance to send messages on the bus. Once a waiting cache gets access to the bus, it can send a write miss message on the bus and subsequently get write access to the block. Note that some corner cases are possible. For example, it is possible that before the cache is able to write the data, it receives a write miss on the bus from a sister cache. In such cases, the pending operation – write operation in this case – needs to complete first. Such policies will ensure that the axioms of coherence hold.

9.4.3 MESI Protocol

Let us now make the snoopy protocol slightly more efficient. Assume that a cache has a read miss, and it tries to read the data from other sister caches. If none of the sister caches have the block, then there is a need to go to the lower level in the memory hierarchy. Once the block is fetched, the cache is sure that it holds an exclusive copy of the block, and no other sister cache has a copy of the block. Now, if it desires to write to the block it needs to follow the same procedure that entails broadcasting a write miss on the bus, and waiting for other caches to invalidate their copies. This is not required given the fact that we already know that no other cache has a copy of the block. The MSI protocol has no way of dealing with the situation. It will always broadcast a message when we need to transition from the S to the M state. This can be fixed by adding an extra state called the exclusive state – E state. This state will indicate that the given cache can read the block and no other sister cache has a copy.

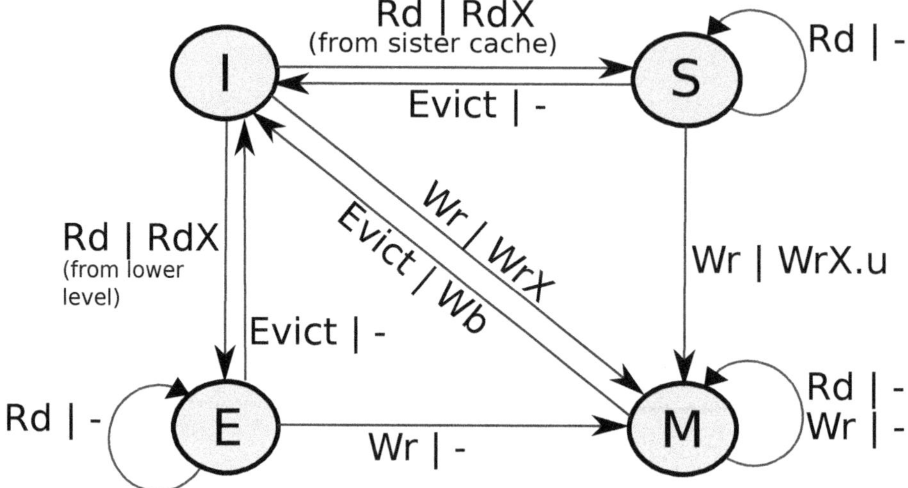

Figure 9.41: MESI protocol (read, write, and evict)

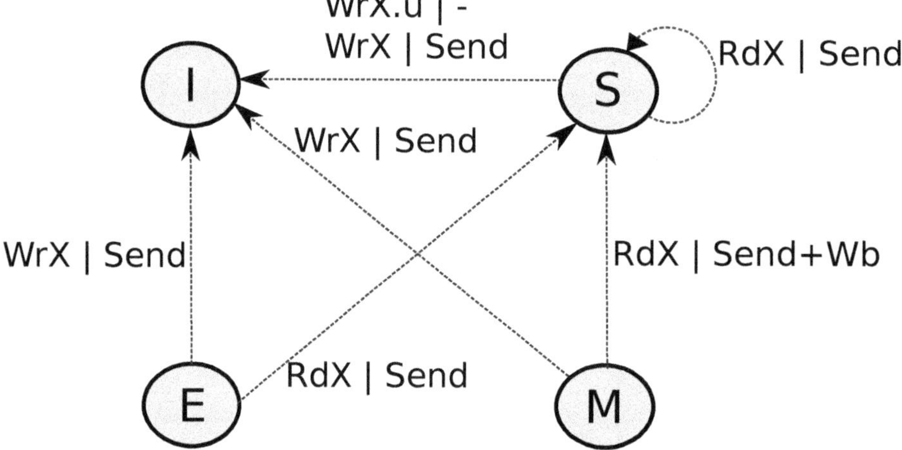

Figure 9.42: MESI protocol (bus events)

Let us explain the E state in the context of the state diagram that only considers reads, writes, and evicts. Refer to Figure 9.41. Let us start from the I state. If we have a read miss (denoted by Rd), there are two possible choices. Either the data is present in a sister cache, or we need to fetch it from the lower level. Initially we do not know. We place an RdX message on the bus. If we get a reply from a sister cache, then we transition to the S state, because we know that there are multiple copies of the block. However, if we do not get a reply from any sister cache, then it is necessary to fetch the block from the lower level. After fetching a copy, we can transition to the E (exclusive) state because we are sure that no other cache has a copy.

The S and M states behave in the same manner as the original MSI protocol. Let us thus solely focus our attention on the E state. We can seamlessly read a block that is in the E state because no other cache is writing to it. However, the key advantage of having the E state is that we can silently move from the E to the M state if we need to write to the block. There is no need to send a message on the bus. This is because there is no need to send any invalidate messages to any of the other sister caches (they do not have a copy of the block). Eviction from the E state is also seamless (no messages are sent) because the data has not been modified.

Let us now look at the state transitions due to events received from the bus (see Figure 9.42). The transitions for the M, S, and I states remain the same. Let us divert our attention to the transitions from the E state. We can receive two kinds of messages from the bus: RdX and WrX. RdX indicates that another sister cache wants to read the data. In this case, we need to send the data and then transition to the shared state. This is because at this point of time two caches contain a copy of the block; it is not *exclusive* to any single cache. Second, if we get a write miss message, WrX, on the bus, then we need to make an $E \rightarrow I$ transition and also send the data to the requester. This transition is similar to the $M \rightarrow I$ transition.

Let us summarise.

1. The MESI protocol adds an extra E (exclusive) state. The state transitions for the M, S, and I states remain mostly the same.

2. The main advantage of the E state is that we can take advantage of codes where we access a lot of blocks that are not shared across the caches. In such cases, we should have the ability to silently write to the block without sending invalidate messages on the bus. The E state allows us this flexibility.

The MESI protocol reduces the traffic on the bus as compared to the MSI protocol. However, both the protocols suffer from the same problem, which is that we need to perform frequent write-backs to the lower level, when we have a transition from the M to the S state. Note that this is a very frequent pattern for shared data. Write-backs to the lower level are required to ensure that we can perform seamless evictions from the S state. Let us try to fix this issue by introducing one more state, where the explicit aim is to reduce the number of write-backs to the lower level.

In addition, we need to solve one more problem. Whenever we have a read miss or a write miss, a sister cache needs to forward a copy of the block. If multiple caches have a copy, then all of them will try to send a copy; however, we want only one of them to succeed. Our current solution is that all of them create their responses, and the moment they see a response on the bus sent by a sister cache, they discard their responses. This is time consuming, and requires additional hardware support. It is possible to do something better such that most of the sister caches do not create such responses in the first place. The process of choosing one candidate among a set of interested candidates, like sister caches in this case, is known as *arbitration*; our aim is to ease this process or eliminate its need by proposing a more efficient cache coherence protocol.

Definition 75
The process of choosing one entity among a plurality of interested entities (software or hardware) is known as arbitration. *For example, in this case, multiple sister caches compete amongst each other to send a response to the requesting cache. There is thus a need for arbitration.*

9.4.4 MOESI Protocol

We need to solve two problems:

1. Minimise the number of write-back messages that write data back to the lower level. These messages are slow and time consuming.

2. Eliminate (as far as possible) the need for arbitration while forwarding a copy of the block to the requesting cache.

We shall achieve this by creating an additional state called the owner, O, state, and two more temporary states – St and Se. If a cache contains a block in the owner state then it is by default responsible to forward the data. This ensures that caches do not compete among each other to supply data to the requesting cache. Furthermore, caches do not have to prepare responses, and discard them. A lot of effort will get reduced by just adding this extra state. In addition, the O state can contain data that has been modified. The aim is to eliminate write-backs as far as possible.

Let us thus create a MOESI protocol, where we have the MESI states, and an additional owner state. The state transition diagrams are shown in Figures 9.43 and 9.44 for messages received from the bus and regular read/write/evict events respectively. We shall argue later that we need the two temporary states St and Se for the sake of correctness.

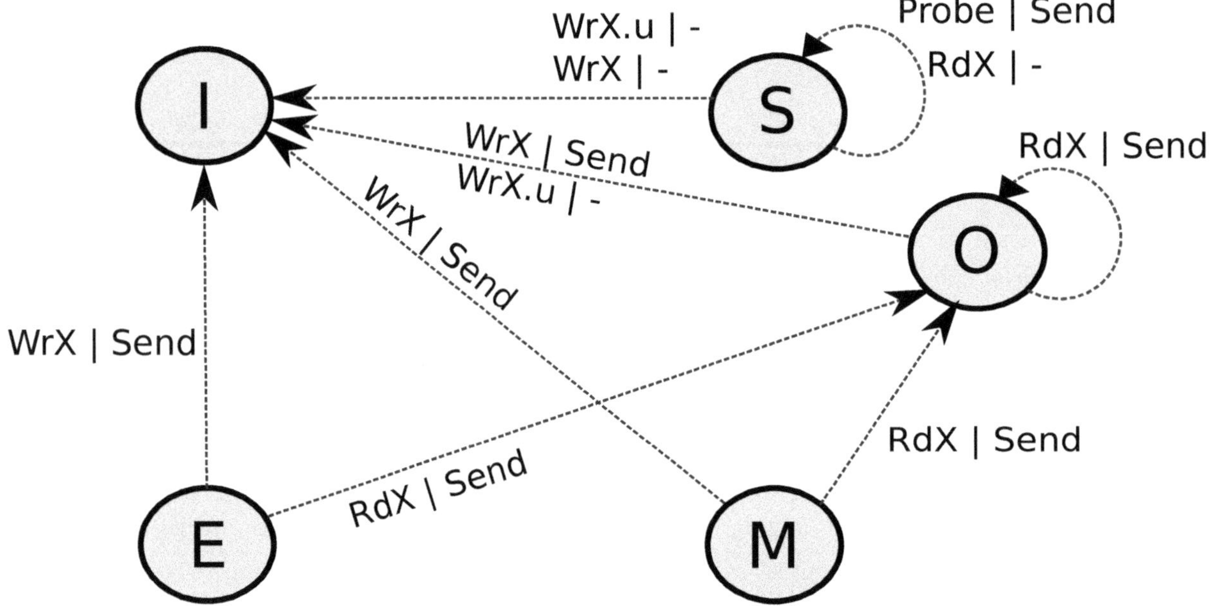

Figure 9.43: MOESI protocol (bus events)

Let us first focus on Figure 9.43 that shows the state transitions after receiving a message on the bus. We can transition to the O state from either the E state or the M state. Whenever a block is in the E state and an RdX (read miss) message is received from the bus, it means that another sister cache is interested in reading the block. In the MESI protocol, we would have transitioned to the S state. However, in this case, we set the new state as the O state. After this operation, there are two caches that contain a copy of the block: one has the block in the S state and the other has it in the O state. Henceforth, if another sister cache has a read miss and requests for a copy of the block, arbitration is not required. The cache that has the block in the S state simply ignores the read miss message. The only cache that responds is the one that has the block in the O state. It responds with the contents of the block. Thus there is no need for arbitration.

The other interesting feature of the O state can be observed by taking a look at the $M \rightarrow O$ transition. We make an $M \rightarrow O$ transition when we receive an RdX message on the bus (instead of transitioning to the S state). The cache with the block in the O state subsequently keeps supplying data to requesting caches. Note that in this case, the block's contents are possibly modified, yet we do not perform a write-back. If another cache wishes to write to a block by sending a WrX (write miss) or $WrX.u$ (write upgrade) request, then the block simply transitions from the O to the I state. In the former case, there is a need to send the contents of the block; however, in the latter case, there is no need to send a copy.

We add one more message called the *Probe* message. If in the S state, a *Probe* message is received, then we send a copy of the block. The reasons will be clear later. The rest of the transitions remain the same.

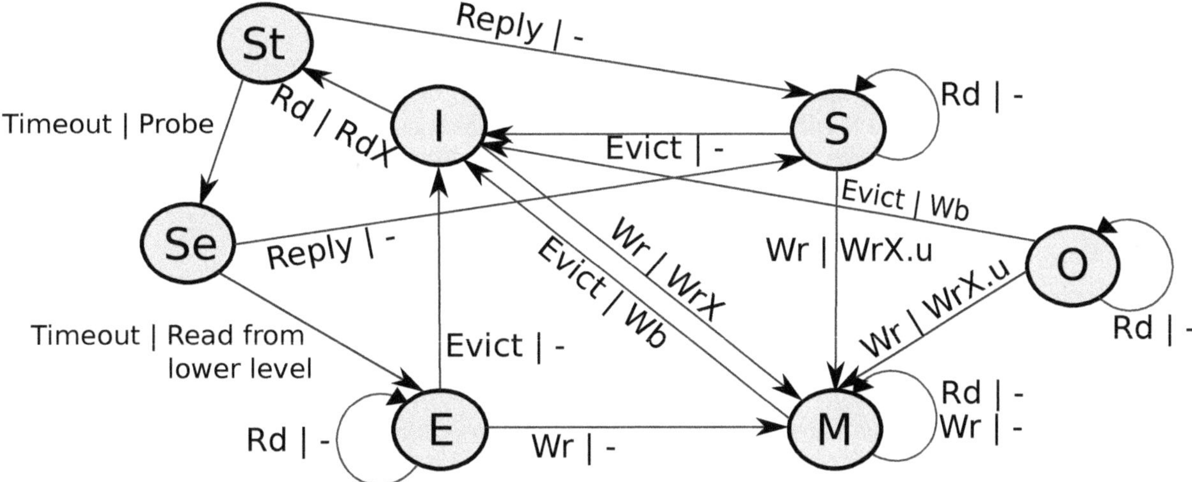

Figure 9.44: MOESI protocol (read, write, and evict)

Let us now look at regular reads, writes, and evict operations (see Figure 9.44). The transitions in the M, E, S, and I states are the same other than the $I \rightarrow S$ and $I \rightarrow E$ transitions; they require new intermediate states, which we shall discuss later. The main addition is the O state. In the O state, we can seamlessly read data. However, we are not allowed to write to the block. In this case, there is a need to invalidate the rest of the copies by sending a write upgrade message $WrX.u$, and to transition to the M state. In the M state, we can seamlessly read and write to the block.

Let us now consider the case in which we evict a block in the O state. Since the O state can possibly contain modified data, we need to write the data to the lower level. A write-back is obvious in the $M \rightarrow I$ transition because no other cache has a copy of the block. However, in an $O \rightarrow I$ transition because of an eviction, there is theoretically no need to perform a write-back if another cache has a copy.

There is space for a new optimisation here. If a sister cache has a copy of the block, then we need not write the data to the lower level upon an eviction in the O state. We should simply transfer ownership. However, this requires arbitration because the block might be present with multiple sister caches. This overhead is justified if it is significantly lower than accessing the lower level. The MESIF protocol that introduces a new F state (on the lines of our O state with some differences) has the notion of transfer of ownership. We can introduce this notion in our MOESI protocol as well. The reader is advised to look up the details of the MESIF protocol on the web. For the sake of simplicity, let us not introduce this state and continue without it.

In the vanilla MOESI protocol, we do not transfer ownership, instead we write-back the block upon an eviction in the O state. Assume that there are other caches that have a copy of the block in the S state. Now if a new cache requests for a copy of the block, it will not find a cache that has the block in the O state. It will thus be forced to read a copy of the block from the lower level, which is inefficient. There is a correctness problem as well. When a cache that does not contain a copy of the block reads the block from the lower level, what is its state: E (exclusive) or S (shared)? We do not know if sister caches have a copy or not. Either they have the block in the S state only, or none of them have a copy. We have no way of distinguishing between these two situations.

Hence, we introduce two temporary states: St and Se (see Figure 9.44). Let us focus on the tricky corner case when there is a read miss from the I state. We send a read miss (RdX) message on the bus and transition to the *St* state. This is a temporary state, because we need to make a transition from it in finite time. Then we wait for a reply. If we get a reply from a sister cache (*Reply* in the figure), we transition to the *S* state. Otherwise we wait till there is a timeout. We assume that there is a timeout period after which we can conclude that none of the caches have a copy of the block in the *O*, *E*, or *M* states. After a timeout, we transition to the second temporary state, *Se*, and simultaneously we send a *Probe* message on the bus.

If any cache has the block in the shared state, it prepares a response with a copy of the block. The cache that gets control of the bus first sends the response. Once we get this message (*Reply* in the figure), we can transition to the *S* state because another sister cache also has a copy of the block. However, if we have a timeout in the *Se* state, we can conclude that no sister cache has a copy of the block in any state. We thus need to read the block from the lower level. We do this, and then transition to the *E* state because we are sure that no other cache has a copy of the block.

To summarise, we observe that even though the MOESI protocol solves an important problem by introducing an additional state, there is a need to add two temporary states to solve resultant correctness problems.

9.4.5   Write-Invalidate Protocol using a Directory

Let us now try to make the write-invalidate protocol even more efficient and scalable. Recall that we proposed the invalidate protocol in the place of the update protocol to reduce the number of bus accesses; we wanted to reduce the contention on the bus. Let us go one step forward and try to improve the performance even more.

The biggest problem with bus based protocols is the bus itself. The bus is by definition a centralised structure and can only handle one message at a time. It is true that a protocol using a bus naturally places an order on all the requests based on the order in which they get access to the bus. This proves beneficial while ensuring the axioms of coherence. However, at the same time, it reduces the communication bandwidth, and thus does not scale with the number of constituent caches. For 2-4 caches, using a bus is a good idea. However, as we increase the number of constituent caches, the bus fails to scale. We need to use a network-on-chip (NoC) as we studied in Chapter 8. In an NoC we can sustain many parallel read-write operations between pairs of nodes, and thus the net bandwidth is much larger.

Sadly, we lose the most important advantage of a bus with regards to the cache coherence axioms – ensuring an order between write operations. Ensuring the write propagation axiom is still easy because we can always design an underlying network that provides fairness guarantees.

To solve these issues, let us *centralise* our NoC. This means let us add a new node in the NoC whose job is to provide an order between write operations – *serialisation*. Let us refer to this structure as the *directory*. It provides serialisation along with a few more services to the set of caches in a distributed cache. The conceptual diagram of the system is shown in Figure 9.45. A cache coherence protocol that uses the directory is known as a directory protocol.

Structure of a Directory

The main role of a directory is to keep track of the sharing status of all the blocks in a cache. It is organised as a cache where we have a standard tag array and a data array. It contains a list of entries known as directory entries, where an entry corresponds to a single block. The structure of a directory entry is shown in Figure 9.46. We have a state field that stores the state of the block, and then we have a list of sharers. The state indicates if the block is shared, or held exclusively by a single cache. The list of sharers is a list of cache ids that contain copies of the block.

The state field is similar to the state fields that we maintain in the MSI based protocols that we have already seen. However, unlike the snoopy protocols where we never maintain a list of caches that contain a copy of the block, in this case we need to maintain an explicit list. Since we do not have a

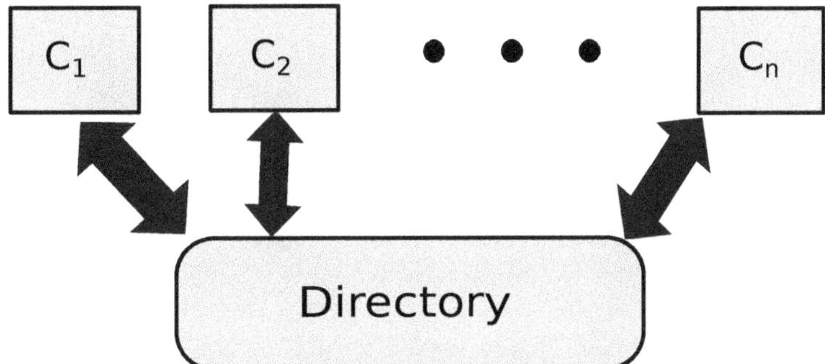

Figure 9.45: Conceptual view of a directory. $C_1 \ldots C_n$ are the sister caches connected to the directory via the NoC.

Figure 9.46: Structure of a directory entry. The tag part of the block address is not shown.

bus based configuration, a broadcast is a very expensive proposition in an NoC, and thus it is necessary to maintain an explicit list and send point-to-point messages the the *sharers* of a block. A *sharer* is a sister cache that has a copy of the block.

The simplest way for storing a list of sharers is to have a bit vector where each bit corresponds to a sister cache. If the ith bit is set, then it means that the ith sister cache has a copy of the block. If there are N sister caches in a given distributed cache, then each entry in its directory contains N bits (1 bit per cache). This is known as the *fully mapped* scheme. We shall discuss more schemes to optimise the list of sharers after discussing the cache coherence protocol.

Definition 76
A scheme in which we have an entry for each sister cache in the list of sharers is known as a fully mapped scheme.

Protocol

Let us design a MESI protocol. Let us keep the same set of states: M, E, S, and I at the level of each constituent cache. The only difference is that whenever we evict a block we need to send an *Evict* message to the directory. We were not doing this in the case of the snoopy protocols. Moreover, all the read and write miss messages are sent to the directory first, not to the sister caches.

Taking this account, let us list the messages that a cache sends on the NoC. They are as follows: RdX (read miss), WrX (write miss), $WrX.u$ (write upgrade), and *Evict* (block evicted from a cache). The rest of the state transition diagram for read, write, and evict messages remains the same. Hence, we do not show the modified state diagrams for these events. Let us instead focus on the **state transition of a given directory entry** as shown in Figures 9.47 and 9.48. We use three states: U (uncached), E (a sister cache contains a copy of the block in either the E or M state), and S (one or more sister caches have the block in the S state).

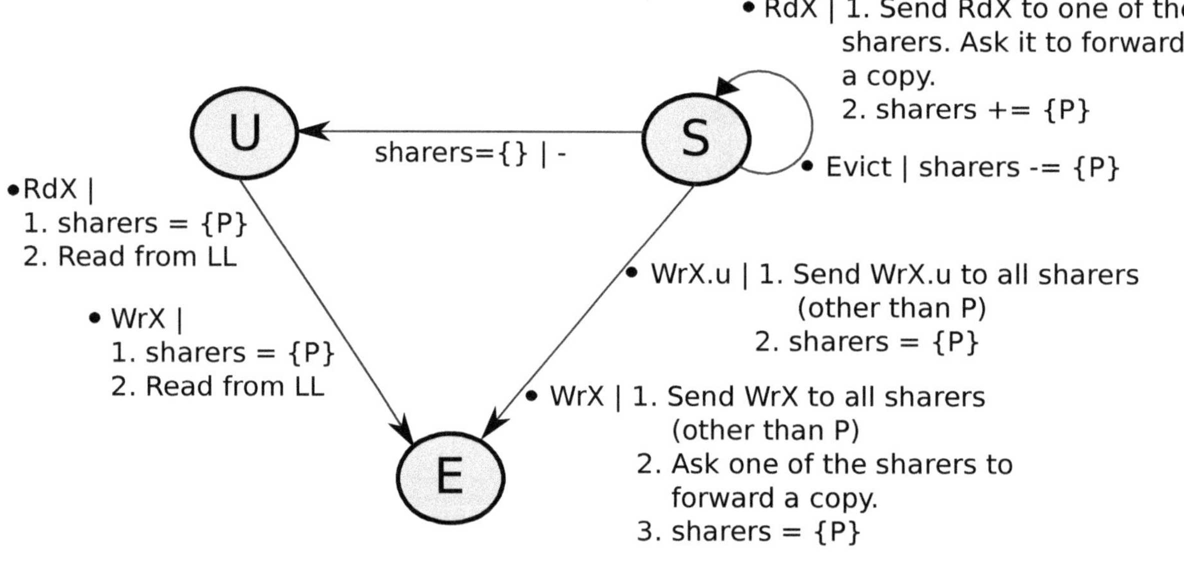

Figure 9.47: State transitions in a directory entry (from the U and S states)

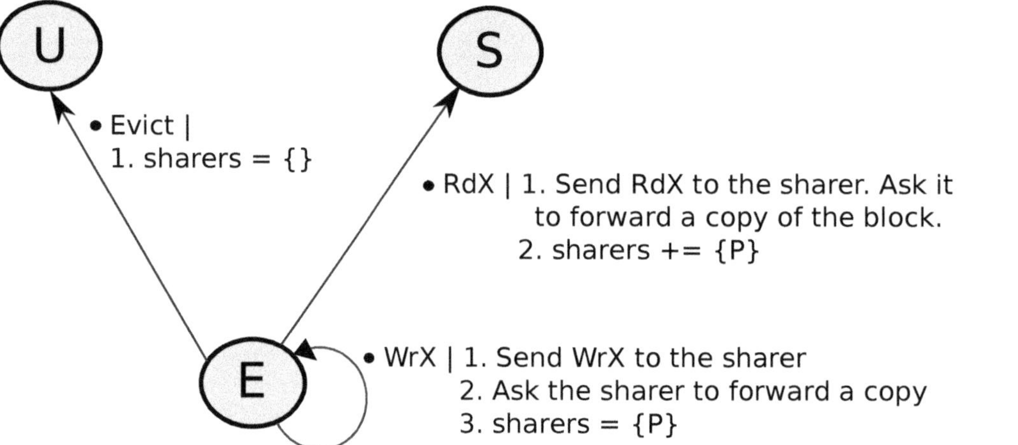

Figure 9.48: State transitions in a directory entry (from the E state)

Let us focus on Figure 9.47 that shows all the transitions from the U and S states. Initially, we start from the uncached (U) state. In this state there are no sharers – no sister cache contains a copy of the data. Whenever the directory gets an RdX message from a cache, it transitions to the E (exclusive) state: only one sister cache contains a copy of the block in either the E or M state. For this $U \rightarrow E$ transition, the directory can initiate a read from the lower level (LL in the figure) to get a copy of the block and forward it to the requesting cache. Let us adopt a convention to designate the id of the sister cache that is sending an event to the directory as P. In this case we add P to the list of sharers, which hitherto was empty.

We have an S state, which has the same connotation as the S state in the MESI protocol. It represents the situation where the block is present in one or more sister caches in the shared state. In the S state, we can keep on receiving and responding to read miss (RdX) messages from caches. In each case, we forward the read miss message to one of the sharers, and ask it to directly send a copy of the block to the requesting cache. The response need not be routed through the directory. Subsequently, we add P

to the list of sharers. If we get an evict message, then we remove P from the list of sharers. If the list of sharers becomes empty, then it means that a copy of the block is not present in any sister cache, and we can thus change the state to U.

Next, let us consider the write miss messages: WrX and $WrX.u$. We need to transition to the E state. The E state indicates that only one cache contains a copy of the block, and the block in that cache can either be there in the E state or M state. Recall that $E \to M$ transitions are silent, and thus the directory will never get to know if the block has transitioned from the E to the M state in a sister cache. Hence, we have just one state to denote exclusivity with possible write access in the directory entry. First consider the $U \to E$ transition. This happens when we get a WrX message from a sister cache. In this case, there is a need to read a copy of the block from the lower level because no other cache contains a copy, and forward it to the requesting cache P. In addition, we make P the only sharer because it has an exclusive copy of the block. We transition from the S to the E state upon receiving two kinds of messages: WrX and $WrX.u$. In the case of the upgrade message $WrX.u$, the requesting cache already has a copy of the block. It is just requesting for write permission. We thus need to send invalidate messages ($WrX.u$) to all the sharers other than P, and make P the only sharer. In the case of the WrX message, it means that the requesting cache does not have a copy of the block. Hence, it is necessary to additionally ask one of the existing sharers to forward a copy of the block to the requesting cache P.

Now consider Figure 9.48, which shows the transitions from the E state. Upon an eviction, the list of sharers will become empty, and we need to transition to the U state. This is because no sister cache will contain a copy of the block after the block is evicted. If there is a read miss (RdX), then we make an $E \to S$ transition. Additionally, we send an RdX message to the lone sharer such that it can move to the S state, and also provide a copy of the block. The requesting cache, P, is then added to the list of sharers.

For a write miss (WrX) message, we do not need to change the state. The state can remain to be E. However, we need to invalidate the sharer, forward the requesting cache a copy of the block, and update the list of sharers to contain only the requesting cache P.

Let us summarise. A directory has taken the place of a snoopy bus. It acts as a point of serialisation where the order of writes is determined by the order in which the directory chooses to process them. This ensures the WS axiom. To ensure the WP axiom, it is necessary to ensure that the directory is fair – it does not delay write requests indefinitely. This can easily be achieved with a FIFO queue.

Let us now look at some optimisations and consider corner cases.

9.4.6 Optimisations and Corner Cases in the Directory Protocol

Evicting an Entry from the Directory

The directory needs to have a finite size. It cannot have an entry for every single block in the memory system. If we have 32 GB of main memory, and each block is 64 bytes, then we need half a billion entries, which is clearly not practical. The directory is thus organised as a set associative cache, where each way contains directory entries. When we access the directory, we first search for the entry, and if there is no entry for the block address, then it is necessary to allocate a new entry.

Let us now consider the case when an entry needs to be evicted. Note that we need to evict the state of the block (stored in the directory entry) and the list of sharers. One option is to keep a copy of the directory entries in main memory or in secondary storage. The other option is to discard the contents of the entry altogether after it is evicted. The first option necessitates a lot of storage in the memory system and in secondary storage. It is thus not practical. The only feasible solution is to forget about the contents of the directory entry after it is evicted. However, this will cause problems. We will forget the list of sharers. Next time if the block associated with the entry is accessed, we will not be able to run the state machine correctly because we would have no record of its previous state and the list of sharers.

The only way out of this quagmire is to invalidate all the sharers once a directory entry is evicted. If the block has been modified, then we write it back to the lower level. This ensures that the next time we access the block, the directory entry can be initialised to the pristine U state. Sadly, the process of invalidation and write-back increases the overheads significantly and makes the protocol slow. There is however no choice, and thus our strategy should be to reduce the number of evictions from the directory as far as possible. We thus need a very good replacement algorithm.

Multiple Directories

If we have a single large directory, then we need many read and write ports to cater to different requests every cycle. Thus we will require a large multiported storage structure in the directory. This will be slow and consume a lot of power. Hence, an effective idea is to split the physical address space into disjoint subsets, and associate a directory with each subset. For example, we can create 8 such subsets by considering the 3 LSB bits of the block address. A subset corresponds to a distinct combination of bits. This way we can create subsets that are mutually disjoint. We can then create 8 separate directories: one for each subset. This is similar to creating a banked cache and the reasons for doing this are the same. Each directory will be smaller, and hence faster; additionally, it will also suffer from less contention. Note that there is no correctness issue here.

Managing the List of Sharers

Let us now consider the list of sharers. In a large server processor we can have tens of cores. Often it is possible to add more processors and cores using expandable slots in the motherboard at runtime. If we were to design for the worst case, then we have to create space for the maximum possible number of sharers, which is the maximum possible number of cores in the system if we are considering a distributed L1 cache. In large servers, this can be a fairly large number such as 256. Adding 256 bits to every entry in the directory is a significant overhead. This should thus be avoided.

Thankfully we can leverage some patterns here. It is very unlikely that a single block will be accessed by all the threads running on all the cores. The degree of sharing is limited to 4 or 8 sister caches in an overwhelming majority of cases. Thus instead of having a bit-vector based scheme for storing the list of sharers, we can optimise the space by explicitly storing a few sharers: 4 or 8. If the maximum possible number of sharers is 256, then it takes 8 bits to represent each sharer; therefore, we need to store 32 or 64 bits in each directory entry depending on the number of sharers that we wish to support. Note that storing 32 or 64 bits as compared to 256 bits is a significant reduction in the number of bits that need to be stored. Hence, a significant savings in storage space is possible. Such a scheme is known as a *partially mapped* scheme.

Definition 77
A partially mapped scheme in a directory refers to a method where we explicitly store the ids of a limited number of sister caches in the list of sharers. We do not have a dedicated entry in the list of sharers for every single sister cache in the ensemble of caches.

If the number of sharers is less than the maximum number of entries that we can store, then there is no problem. However, if the number of sharers exceeds this number, then there is an overflow. We did not have this problem in a fully mapped scheme, where we had a single bit for every sister cache. However, in the partially mapped scheme, we shall have the problem of overflows. There are several strategies to deal with this situation.

Replace: Assume that a directory entry can store up till K sharers. If it is full, and we need to add an additional entry to the list of sharers, we have the problem of overflow. In this case, we select one of the K sharers and invalidate its contents. It does not remain a sharer anymore. In its place, we can store the id of the requesting cache for the current request.

Invalidate All: The other option is to have an overflow bit. This bit indicates that we were not able to fit the ids of all the sharers in the list of sharers, owing to space constraints. If the overflow bit is 1, then it means that we have had an overflow. This is not a problem for read accesses; however, it is a problem for write accesses because every single copy needs to be invalidated. The most feasible solution in this space is to send invalidate messages to all the sister caches that are a part of the distributed cache after receiving a write miss. This is undoubtedly a slow and time consuming process.

Coarse Grained Coherence: Another solution is to change the granularity of the information. Assume that we store the ids of 8 caches in a system with 256 caches. In this case, the id of each cache is 8 bits long, and since the list of sharers stores 8 such ids, it needs 64 bits of space. Now assume that a block is present in 9 caches. This situation represents an overflow. Let us change the granularity of information that is stored. Let us divide the set of 256 caches into 128 sets that contain 2 caches each (with consecutive ids). Since we have 128 sets, we require 7 bits to uniquely identify each set. In these 64 bits, let us store the ids of 9 such sets containing two caches each.

The advantage of this scheme is as follows. In this case, 9 sets can potentially cover up to 18 caches. Even in the worst case when we do not have two caches in the same set, we can still cover 9 caches, which is one more than what we could do before. We can increase the granularity of this scheme further and cover more caches. In the worst case, we can have one large set containing 256 caches. The advantage of this scheme is that all the sharers are mapped to at least one set. The disadvantage is that we have no way of recording which caches in a set are genuine sharers and which caches are not. This means that if we need to send an invalidate message, we need to send it to all the caches in a set. Those that have a copy of the block will invalidate it, and the rest of the caches will ignore the message. This adds to the overheads of the scheme.

However, this scheme is very flexible. If a block is stored in a single cache then we use a granularity of 1, and in the worst case if is contained in all the caches, then we use a granularity of 256. We can easily adopt the resolution of our sharing vector (list of sharers) depending on the degree of sharing of a block.

Race Conditions

Till now we have assumed that the transition between states is atomic: appears to be instantaneous. However, in practice this is not the case. Assume we are transitioning from the S to the M state. In this case, the requesting cache needs to first send a message to the directory, and then wait. The directory in turn needs to first queue the request, and then process it when it is the earliest message for the block. The directory then sends write miss (invalidate) messages to all the sharers, and waits for them to finish their state transitions. In most practical protocols, the sharers send acknowledgements back to the directory indicating that they have transitioned their state. After collecting all the acknowledgements, the directory asks the requesting cache to change its state and perform the write access.

To support this long chain of events, we need to add many more waiting states that indicate that the respective caches and directories are waiting for some message or some event. Furthermore, modern high performance protocols try to break the sequence of actions and interleave them with other requests. These are known as *split transaction* protocols. In an environment with so much complexity, we need to effectively deal with race conditions (concurrent events for the same block).

Let us elaborate. Assume cache A has a block in the modified state. Cache B wishes to read a copy of the block. Cache B sends a message to the directory and the directory initiates the process of getting a copy of the block from A. However, assume that before the messages reach A, it decides to evict the block. In this case, there is a race condition between the read miss and the evict. The relative ordering of the actions is important. If A evicts the block before a copy is sent to B, then the directory will search for the copy of the block in A, and it will not find it. If it goes to the lower level, here also there is a race condition. We need to ensure that an earlier write-back reaches the lower level before we search for a copy of the block in the lower level later. Since these messages are sent via the NoC, their ordering cannot be guaranteed, and there is a chance that a reordering may happen. One option is that we do not allow A to evict the block till it gets a final confirmation from the directory; this will happen after B completes its operation. Such design choices are overly conservative and restrict performance. To get more performance, protocols typically add more states, transitions, and messages (see the Cray X1 protocol [Abts et al., 2003]) such that we can achieve a better overlap between different operations on different copies of the same block. The main idea behind such protocols is that we add more waiting and pending states where the caches and directories wait for parts of their operations to complete. This adds more states to the protocol and more transitions. It is not uncommon for protocols in modern processors to contain more than 20-30 states and 100+ transitions.

To summarise, while designing correct cache coherence protocols in the presence of simultaneous requests and resultant race conditions, we need to add more states and transitions to a protocol. Vantrease et al. [Vantrease et al., 2011] report the existence of cache coherence protocols that have up to 400 state transitions. Verifying these protocols requires exhaustive testing and massive formal verification efforts. There is a trade-off between correctness and performance, and thus such complex protocols are necessary for performance reasons, even though they require a significant design and verification effort.

False Sharing

Our cache coherence protocol operates at the granularity of cache blocks. A typical cache block is 64 or 128 bytes wide. However, a typical access to memory is for 4 or 8 bytes.

Let us now look at another problem that will only happen with multiprocessor coherence. Consider a block with 64 bytes where the bytes are numbered from 1 to 64. Assume core A is interested in bytes $1 \ldots 4$, and core B is interested in bytes $33 \ldots 36$. In this case, whenever core A writes to bytes $1 \ldots 4$, it will invalidate the copy of the block that is there with B. Similarly, when B writes to bytes $33 \ldots 36$, it will invalidate the copy of the block with A. Even though there is no actual overlap between the data that is accessed by cores A and B, they still end up invalidating copies of the same block in each other's caches. Such a phenomenon is known as *false sharing*. Here, we have cache misses and invalidations because two separate cores are interested in different sets of bytes that are a part of the same block. As opposed to false sharing, we can also have true sharing where invalidations happen because two cores access the same data bytes. In this case, there is a need to genuinely invalidate a copy of the data residing in the other core's cache. False sharing is a consequence of the fact that an entire block is treated as one atomic entity.

Definition 78

When two threads running on separate cores have conflicting accesses for the same set of data bytes, the associated cache lines will keep getting invalidated, and the data block will keep moving between caches. Such cache misses are known as true sharing *misses, because the cause of the misses is data sharing between threads.*

As opposed to true sharing, we can have false sharing*, which is defined as follows. In this case, both the threads make conflicting accesses to disjoint sets of bytes within the same cache block. Note that the sets of data bytes do not have any overlap between them. In spite of this, because of the nature of our coherence protocol that tracks accesses at the level of blocks, we shall still have invalidations, and block migration. This is an additional overhead, and will also lead to an increased number of read and write misses.*

A lot of misses in parallel programs can be attributed to false sharing. The common approaches for handling false sharing are as follows.

1. Use a smart compiler that lays out data in such a way that multiple threads do not make conflicting accesses to the same block. It is necessary for the compiler to find all overlapping accesses between threads, and ensure that data is laid out in such a way in memory that the probability of false sharing is minimised.

2. Use word-level coherence tracking. In this case, we modify the invalidate protocol to allow conflicting accesses to different non-overlapping parts of a block. We maintain multiple copies and explicitly keep track of the words within the block, which have been modified by the thread accessing the cache. This approach is expensive and complicates the hardware significantly. The compiler based approach is significantly simpler.

9.4.7 Atomic Operations

Till now we have been using the coherence protocol to implement the cache coherence axioms. However, let us now use it to implement advanced functionalities that most parallel applications require. Let us consider a realistic scenario, where we are running a multithreaded banking application. The code for updating the balance in an account will be similar to that shown in Listing 9.1. We shall prove that this code is erroneous when run in a multithreaded setting, and we need *atomic operations* to ensure that this code works correctly. Let us devote this section to the study of such operations.

Listing 9.1: Code to update the balance in an account

```
void update (int amount) {
    balance += amount;
}
```

This code for the *update* function looks simple; however it is not safe in a multithreaded environment. To understand the reasons for this, let us look at an expanded version of the same code, where each line corresponds to a statement in assembly. Here, all the variables starting with a 't' stand for temporary variables that are assigned to registers.

```
1  void update (int amount) {
2      t1 = balance;      /* load instruction */
3      t2 = t1 + amount;  /* add instruction */
4      balance = t2;      /* store instruction */
5  }
```

We replaced one C statement with three instructions: one load, one add, and one store. Let us now see what will happen when two copies of the same code run on two different threads. The execution is shown in Figure 9.49. For the ease of understanding, in thread T_2, we use a different set of temporary variables: $t3$ and $t4$. The instructions are numbered *1*, *2*, and *3* respectively for thread T_1, and *1'*, *2'* and *3'* for thread T_2.

If the set of instructions in T_1 run before or after the set of instructions in thread T_2, then there is no problem. However, in Figure 9.49, both the threads are trying to credit a value of ₹100 to the account[2]. We have assumed that the starting balance is ₹0. In this case, the final balance should be ₹200 irrespective of the order in which the threads credit the amount. However, because of the overlap in the execution of the functions, it is possible that both the threads read the value of the *balance* variable to

---

[2]₹is the symbol for the Indian rupee

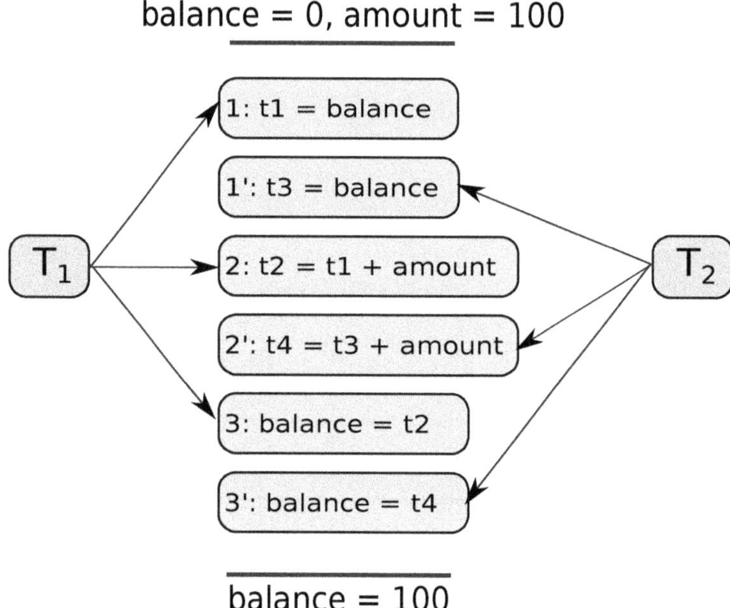

Figure 9.49: Two threads executing the code to update the balance at the same time

be 0. As a result, $t1$ and $t3$ are 0. Subsequently, $t2$ and $t4$ are set to 100, and the final balance is set to 100. This is clearly the wrong answer and this is happening because we are allowing an overlap between the executions of the *update* function in both the threads. There is a need to *in some way* lock the set of instructions such that we do not allow the same set of instructions to be executed concurrently by another thread. No two threads should be executing the instructions in the *update* function concurrently. We need a mechanism to ensure this.

A piece of code that does not allow two threads to execute it concurrently is known as a *critical section*. In this case, we need to create a critical section and insert these three statements in it such that only one thread can execute them at one time. Almost all languages today that support parallel programming also support the notion of critical sections. Without supporting critical sections it is not possible to write most parallel programs.

Definition 79

A critical section is a region of code that contains contiguous statements, and all the statements in the critical section execute atomically. After thread t starts executing the first instruction in a critical section, it is not possible for another thread to execute an instruction in the same critical section till t finishes executing all the instructions in the critical section.

Lock and Unlock Functions

Most critical sections use the lock-unlock paradigm. Here the idea is that we *lock* a memory address before entering the critical section. Locking a memory address is often tantamount to setting its value to 1 from 0. Then, when a thread leaves the critical section, it needs to unlock the memory address, which means setting its value back to 0 from 1. Let us call this memory address as the *lock address*.

However, if the lock is acquired (value set to 1), which means that there is already another thread executing the critical section, then in that case, we need to wait till that thread has left the critical section and released the lock: performed an unlock operation. The thread that is trying to acquire the lock keeps trying to acquire the lock till it is free. Let us represent this situation pictorially in Figure 9.50. Here, we observe a call to the lock and unlock functions before we enter and exit the critical section respectively.

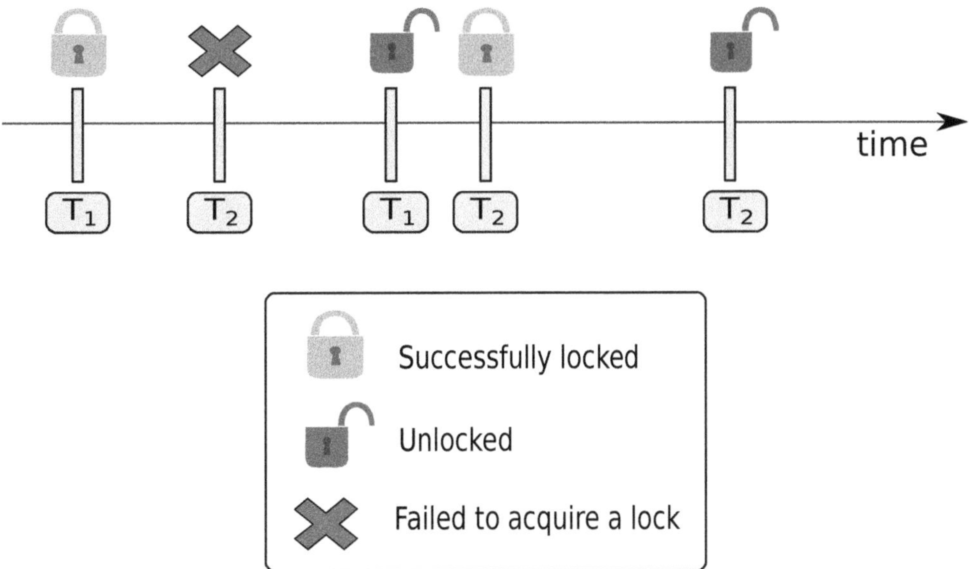

Figure 9.50: A time line that shows two threads acquiring and releasing a lock

Before discussing the details and corner cases, let us look at the implementation of the lock and unlock functions. Let us make a simplistic assumption that there is one lock address in the entire system, and the associated lock needs to be acquired before we enter the critical section. The assembly code for the lock and unlock functions is as follows. Let us assume that the address of the lock is in the register $r0$. The *bne* instruction means branch-if-not-equal.

```
1   .lock:
2        mov   r1, 1
3        xchg  r1, 0[r0]
4        cmp   r1, 0
5        bne   .lock
6        ret
7
8   .unlock:
9        mov  r1, 0
10       xchg   r1, 0[r0]
11       ret
```

The key instruction in the lock function is the atomic exchange instruction called *xchg*. Note that till now we have not introduced this instruction. The atomic exchange instruction atomically exchanges the contents of a register and a memory location. The keyword here is *atomic*. This operation appears to happen to other threads instantaneously. No thread can interrupt the operation in the middle or observe any intermediate state. Let us now explain how to use this instruction to realise a lock function.

We first set $r1$ to 1, and then atomically exchange the contents of $r1$ with the lock variable (address stored in $r0$). If the lock is free, which means that no thread has currently acquired it, then the contents of the lock variable will be 0. After the exchange, the lock variable will contain 1, because we are exchanging its contents with register $r1$'s contents, which was set to 1 in Line 2. The interesting thing is that after the exchange operation, $r1$ will contain the earlier value of the lock variable. We compare it with 0 in Line 4. If the comparison is successful, which means that the lock variable contained 0, then it means that the current thread changed its value from 0 to 1. It has thus acquired the lock by successfully changing its status. In the other case, when the comparison fails, it means that the lock was already acquired – the value was already equal to 1. If we find that we have not acquired the lock, then there is a need to try this process again, and thus we loop back to the beginning of the lock function. If we have successfully acquired the lock function, we return back to the caller function and start executing the critical section.

The unlock function is comparatively simpler. In this case, we just need to release the lock. This is as simple as setting the value of the lock variable to 0. Other threads can then acquire the lock by setting its value to 1. The key point here is that instead of using the regular store instruction, we use the atomic exchange instruction that also contains a fence. The idea here is that the fence ensures that when other threads see the unlock, they will also see all the reads and writes that have happened within the critical section, regardless of the memory model.

First, let us convince ourselves that this mechanism genuinely ensures that only one thread can execute the critical section at a given point in time. This property is also known as *mutual exclusion*. Let us try to formally prove this.

Theorem 9.4.7.1 *The algorithm with the lock and unlock functions ensures mutual exclusion.*

Proof: Assume that two threads T_1 and T_2 are in the critical section at the same time. With no loss of generality, let us assume that T_1 got the lock first and then T_2 got it. This means that T_1 set the value of the lock address to 1 from 0. When T_2 executed the atomic exchange instruction, it must have seen the value of the lock to be 1, which was set by T_1. There is thus no way that it could have seen the lock's value to be 0, because T_1 is still there in the critical section. If T_2 had seen the value of the lock to be 1, it could not have entered the critical section. Hence, the hypothesis is wrong and we thus have a proof by contradiction. ∎

Implementing Atomic Operations

Let us now look at implementing atomic operations like atomic exchange in cache coherent systems. Irrespective of the atomic operation, the method to implement it is roughly the same. The first step is to get write access to the block that contains the lock variable. In an invalidate protocol with a directory, which is the standard, the processing begins with a write miss received at the directory. It invalidates all the copies of the block, and after collecting acknowledgements from all the sharers it sends a message to the requesting cache. Once the requesting cache receives a go-ahead from the directory, it sets the state of the line to M (modified).

Instead of doing a write, in this case we proceed with the atomic operation. Most atomic operations are read-modify-write operations. We read the value of a memory location, compute the new value, and write it to the memory location. We proceed with all the steps once the line's state is set to M. The ideal case is where all the steps complete without interruption and the atomic operation completes.

The worst case is when in the middle of the execution of the atomic operation another cache sends a read miss or write miss. We clearly cannot abandon an atomic operation in the middle. There are several strategies to deal with this. The simplest strategy is that the cache and the core executing the atomic operation hold off sending the acknowledgement to the directory till the atomic operation completes. Another idea is a lease based approach. The directory assumes that a cache requesting for a block in the M state should at least get κ cycles to work on the contents of the block. Meanwhile, if the directory receives any other request, it simply queues it. If κ is enough for an atomic operation to execute, then we need not rely on acknowledgements.

Atomic operations are often synchronisation operations (see Section 9.3.5). This means that they also act as fence instructions. This is required because such operations are typically used to implement critical sections or implement other important parallel programming primitives: this requires them to behave like a fence and enforce some memory orders for the instructions before and after them in program order. This aspect of their execution further increases their overhead.

Efficient Spin Locks

Our simple lock-unlock algorithm does indeed guarantee mutual exclusion. However, it is not a very efficient algorithm because it keeps on trying to acquire the lock in a loop – such a pattern is known as a *spin lock.*. Let us look at some of the flaws of such naively implemented spin locks.

1. Each attempt requires the thread to perform memory, arithmetic, and synchronisation operations repeatedly. This consumes a lot of power and is slow.

2. The other problem with a spin lock is that threads basically do useless work when they are waiting for a lock. Even though the processor might perceive them to be busy; however, they are actually not doing any useful work. Most processors will not be able to detect this pattern, and thus will not schedule instructions from other threads. In modern locks used by the Linux operating system, the code of the lock is written in such a way that after a certain number of iterations, the thread notifies the OS that it is ready to sleep. The OS can then schedule another thread or another process on the core.

3. There is a possibility of *starvation*, which means that a thread might never be able to acquire a lock. It might always lose the competition to another thread. Modern locking algorithms have a notion of fairness, where they ensure that a thread does not have to wait forever. However, they are far more complex as compared to the simple code that we have shown. Interested readers can take a look at the book by Herlihy and Shavit [Herlihy and Shavit, 2012] for a discussion on modern algorithms to implement locks.

Creating a fair locking algorithm is out of the scope of this book. This requires a complex locking algorithm, where we maintain an order between the requests, or ensure that the system somehow increases the priority of threads that have been waiting to get a lock for a long time. Let us instead focus on the time and power overheads.

In Linux, locks typically wait for a fixed duration, typically 100 μs, and then automatically send an interrupt to the OS kernel. The OS kernel puts the thread to sleep and schedules some other thread. This ensures that threads waiting for a lock do not unnecessarily tie up a core. Furthermore, this reduces the power overheads of spin locks significantly. The sad part is that this also makes our parallel programs slower. Let's say we have 10 threads, and we want all of them to finish a critical section, before we can make progress. If one of the threads gets swapped out of the core by the OS, then it will not be able to execute even if the lock becomes free. We need to wait for the OS to reschedule the swapped thread. This will unnecessarily block the entire set of 10 threads. Let us thus slightly speed up the execution of the basic lock primitive.

The main problem with a basic spin lock that uses the exchange instruction is that in every iteration, we try to set the value of the lock variable using an expensive synchronisation instruction. This means that we need to send a write miss message on the bus, and wait till we get the data in the M state. Recall that in the M state, a cache owns the block exclusively and it can modify its contents. The main problem with modern write-invalidate protocols is that their performance dips if multiple threads are desirous of writing to a block simultaneously. Because of exclusive ownership in the M state, the block keeps bouncing between caches, and this causes a lot of network traffic as well as slowdown. This can be reduced by creating an optimised version of a spin lock.

Let us create an algorithm that tries to write to a block only if it feels that there is a high probability of the atomic exchange operation being successful, which alternatively means that there is a high probability of lock acquisition. To achieve this, let us first test if the value of the lock variable is 0 or not, and only if it is 0, let us make an attempt to acquire the lock. This will drastically reduce the number of invalidate messages and the number of times we need to use synchronisation instructions such as atomic exchange. The code to implement this concept is as follows.

```
1   /* the address of the lock is in r0 */
2   .lock:
3       mov  r1, 1
4
5   .test
6       /* test if the lock is 0 */
7       ld   r2, 0[r0]
8       cmp  r2, 0
9       bne  .test
10
11      /* attempt an exchange only if the lock is free */
12      xchg r1, 0[r0]
13      cmp  r1, 0
14      bne  .test
15      ret
16
17  .unlock:
18      mov r1, 0
19      xchg  r1, 0[r0]
20      ret
```

In this case, we have added three extra lines: Lines 7 till 9. The aim of these lines is to first read the value of the lock variable, check if it is equal to 0, and then exit the loop if the value of the lock variable is found to be equal to 0. Assume that another thread has acquired the lock. Then it will have the lock variable in the M state. The first time that the current thread reads it, the blocks in both the caches will transition to the S state. This requires a read miss message. However, after that the current thread will keep on reading the block, and since it is in the S state, this will not require any messages to be sent to the directory nor do we need to use the atomic exchange instruction to test if the lock is free or not. This is far more power efficient and also the messages on the NoC will reduce significantly. This method is called test-and-exchange (TAX). Once, we read the value of the lock variable as 0, we are sure that the thread that was holding the lock has released it.

We can then proceed to Line 12, where we try to perform the atomic exchange. Here, if we are successful, then we are deemed to have acquired the lock. Note that it is possible that two threads may have realised that the lock is free, and both of them may try to execute the atomic exchange operation in Line 12 concurrently. In this case, only one thread will be successful. The other thread needs to start the entire operation of trying to acquire the lock once again.

It is true that this algorithm increases the time it requires to acquire a lock if there is no contention. This is because of the additional test step. However, in the case of a contended scenario, we will need to execute multiple exchange instructions using the basic algorithms that we have proposed. This is slow because of the inherent fence operation and will cause many write misses. With the TAX mechanism, we have replaced write misses with read hits because till a thread owns the lock, the rest of the threads will continuously read the lock variable, and find it to be in their caches in the S state: no messages are sent to the directory. A read hit is power efficient and does not lead to NoC traffic. Once we have some hope of getting the lock, we issue the expensive atomic exchange instruction.

Definition 80

A spin lock is a locking algorithm where we repeatedly check the value of a lock variable stored in memory, in a loop. The advantage of a spin lock is that the threads get to know very quickly when a lock is released. However, the disadvantage is that a thread keeps on executing the same code over and over again in a loop without doing any other useful work. This wastes power. Furthermore, the CPU and system software also falsely believe that a thread is doing useful work and thus do not schedule other threads on the same core.

Other Atomic Operations

We have seen the atomic exchange operation, and we have also seen how we can implement a lock with it. This is not the only kind of atomic operation. There are many more types of operations that can be used for many different kinds of operations. Implementing a lock is one of the simplest operations in the field of parallel and concurrent algorithms. There are far more complicated algorithms (refer to [Herlihy and Shavit, 2012]) that require more complicated atomic operations. Let us list some such atomic operations with a snippet of pseudo code describing their operation in Figure 9.51.

Figure 9.51 shows a set of atomic operations starting from the simple test-and-set operation to the elaborate LL/SC operation. Here, LL stands for load-linked and SC stands for store-conditional. In an LL-SC pair, each of these operations are atomic operations. They work as follows. An LL operation loads a value from memory like a regular load operation. However, in addition to this, it also sets a flag in the cache line containing the local copy of the block indicating that an LL operation has been executed. Subsequently, we can execute other instructions depending upon the logic of the program. It is necessary to execute an SC operation at a later point in time. This operation is mostly similar to a regular store operation with one critical difference. The operation returns a value and is conditional. If the block has not been modified after the last LL operation, then the paired SC operation returns 1, and also completes its operation. However, if the block has subsequently been modified by the same thread or another thread then SC returns 0 and does not execute the store operation. We can easily implement a lock using the LL/SC operations as shown[3] in Example 12.

We can implement all the operations by slightly modifying the cache coherence protocol such that we finish the execution of the atomic operation by acquiring the lock variable in the M state. For LL/SC we need to set a bit in the cache line that contains the lock variable. Whenever a write miss arrives from another cache, we set this bit to 0, otherwise this bit continues to remain 1. Now, when we subsequently perform the SC operation, we check the bit in addition to getting write access to the block. If the bit is still set to 1, the SC operation is successful. If the bit is 0, or if the block has been evicted, then the SC operation fails: this means that there may have been an intervening write by another thread. If the SC operation is successful, the write operation to update the lock variable is effected. Both LL and SC operate atomically.

Example 12 *Implement the lock and unlock functions using the LL/SC primitive and fence instructions. Assume that the address of the lock is stored in register r0. Reduce the number of NoC messages by first testing the value of the lock.*

Answer:

---

[3]The code for acquiring and releasing a lock for obvious reasons cannot use locks.

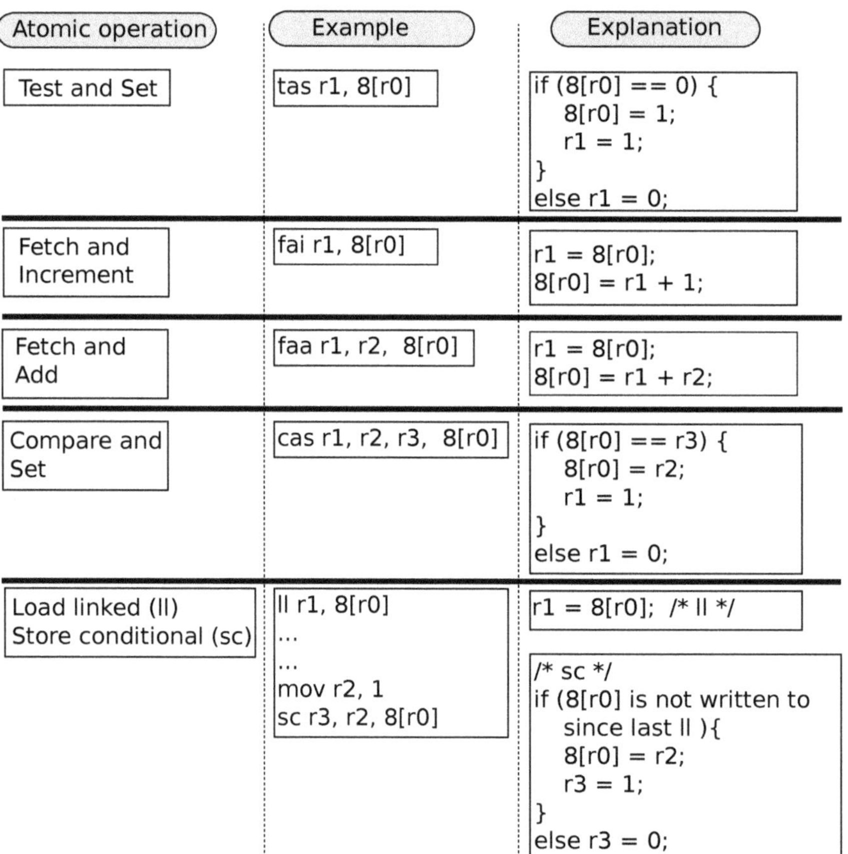

Atomic operation	Example	Explanation

Test and Set	`tas r1, 8[r0]`	`if (8[r0] == 0) {`
		`    8[r0] = 1;`
		`    r1 = 1;`
		`}`
		`else r1 = 0;`

Fetch and Increment	`fai r1, 8[r0]`	`r1 = 8[r0];` `8[r0] = r1 + 1;`
Fetch and Add	`faa r1, r2, 8[r0]`	`r1 = 8[r0];` `8[r0] = r1 + r2;`

Compare and Set	`cas r1, r2, r3, 8[r0]`	`if (8[r0] == r3) {`
		`    8[r0] = r2;`
		`    r1 = 1;`
		`}`
		`else r1 = 0;`

Load linked (ll)
Store conditional (sc)
	`ll r1, 8[r0]`
	`...`
	`...`
	`mov r2, 1`
	`sc r3, r2, 8[r0]`
		`r1 = 8[r0];  /* ll */`
		
		`/* sc */`
		`if (8[r0] is not written to`
		`    since last ll ){`
		`    8[r0] = r2;`
		`    r3 = 1;`
		`}`
		`else r3 = 0;`

Figure 9.51: Different types of atomic operations

---

lock function

```
.lock:
    ll   r1, 0[r0]
    cmp  r1, 0
    bne  .lock      /* If the lock is not free
                       iterate once again */

    mov  r2, 1
    sc   r3, r2, 0[r0]
    cmp  r3, 1
    bne  .lock      /* iterate if sc is not
                       successful */
    ret
```

unlock function

```
.unlock:
    mov  r1, 0
    fence
    st   r1, 0[r0]
```

```
    ret
```

On similar lines, we can use other atomic operations to implement locks. Before the reader asks the question, "Why do we have so many types of atomic operations?", let us answer this question. The trivial answer that comes to the mind is that some operations do some computations with fewer lines of code. For example, we can always implement a fetch-and-add operation with a compare-and-set (CAS) operation. However, this will be cumbersome. As a result, having more instructions will allow us to write simple and elegant code. This is however just the superficial part of the story. There is a much deeper answer, which is that different atomic operations have different amounts of power. This means that some operations are less powerful and some other operations are more powerful. We can always implement a less powerful operation with a more powerful operation; however, we cannot do the reverse.

For example, operations such as test-and-set and atomic exchange are regarded as the least powerful. In comparison, compare-and-set and LL/SC are the most powerful. There is a spectrum of atomic operations whose power lies between them. Let us elaborate.

9.4.8 Lock-free Algorithms using Atomic Operations

Consider the problem of updating the bank balance once again. The crux of our argument was that if we use multiple RISC instructions to update the balance, then it is possible that due to conflicting operations by different threads, the final result can be wrong. Hence, we decided to wrap the code in a critical section such that only one thread can access it. Each critical section begins with a call to a lock function, where we set the value of the lock (memory address that contains it) to 1, and then it ends with a call to the unlock function. To ensure that we atomically update the value of the lock, we introduced atomic operations (see Figure 9.51).

Locks unfortunately have their share of problems. The biggest problem is that they do not allow *disjoint access parallelism*. This means that even if two threads need to update the balance of two separate accounts, only one thread can be in the critical section at any point in time. Note that if the accounts are different, it is possible for both the threads to execute their critical sections concurrently – this is not allowed. To solve this, we can have different lock addresses for different bank accounts. This solution will work for a simple update of a bank account. However, if we are implementing a parallel data structure such as a concurrent queue where multiple threads can enqueue and dequeue items concurrently, such approaches will not work. In general, using locks will ensure that only one operation can be done at any single time. Hence, using locks with a concurrent queue will effectively make it a sequential queue. Other disadvantages of locks include the possibility of starvation where a thread never gets the lock.

Additionally, with locks we can have deadlocks (no thread makes progress) as follows. Assume that there are two locks: A and B. Consider a situation where thread 1 holds lock A and tries to acquire lock B. Similarly, thread 2 holds lock B and tries to acquire lock A. In this case, none of the threads will be able to make progress. This situation is a deadlock. Furthermore, in most practical systems, instead of wasting power by continuously testing the value of a lock (spin locks), most operating systems put the thread to sleep. It takes a disproportionately long time to wakeup the thread later.

It is possible to do better by using a set of algorithms known as non-blocking or lock-free algorithms that do not use locks at all. Most concurrent libraries are today written using such non-blocking algorithms. There is a general result that all operations on data structures such as stacks, queues, etc., can be implemented using lock-free algorithms (see [Herlihy and Shavit, 2012]. Note that even though lock-free algorithms are very promising, they are very hard to code and debug.

Let us show a simple lock-free algorithm for updating the bank balance with the compare-and-set (CAS) primitive. The format of the special CAS instruction is as follows: $CAS\langle reg4\rangle, \langle reg3\rangle, \langle reg2\rangle, \langle mem\rangle$.

If the contents of the memory location are equal to the value of $reg2$, then the value stored in the memory address is atomically set to the value of $reg3$. If the CAS is successful, then we set the value of $reg4$ to 1, else we set it to 0.

```
/*  address of balance is in r0
    the additional amount is in r1 */

.start:
    ld   r2, 0[r0]       /* r2 contains the balance */
    add  r3, r2, r1      /* r3 contains the final balance*/
    CAS  r4, r3, r2, 0[r0]   /* if (r2 == 0[r0]) 0[r0] = r3*/

    cmp  r4, 0           /* test the result */
    beq  .start          /* retry if the CAS fails */
```

In this case, we do not use locks. We repeatedly invoke the CAS instruction to set the value of the variable *balance*. If the CAS fails, then it means that some other thread has succeeded in updating *balance*, and we try again. In this case starvation is possible; however, this implementation is more efficient. If the lock is free, we need 5 instructions to finish the operation using the lock-free algorithm. Whereas in the implementation using locks, we require 5 instructions for the lock, 3 instructions for the unlock, 3 instructions for updating the balance, and 2 function calls.

Wait-free Algorithms

Lock-free algorithms are typically much faster than their lock based counterparts for implementing concurrent data structures. However, they have the problem of starvation. We can use *wait-free algorithms* that additionally guarantee that every operation completes in finite time. Wait-free algorithms are more complicated than their lock-free counterparts, and on an average are slower.

They work on the principle of helping. If any thread is not able to complete its operations, then other threads help it complete its operation. This ensures that there is no starvation.

Definition 81

- *A* lock-free *algorithm does not use locks. With such algorithms we can have starvation where a given thread may never complete its operation because other threads successfully complete their operations.*

- *A* wait-free *algorithm provides more guarantees. It guarantees that a given thread will complete its operation within a finite or bounded number of internal steps.*

Consensus Numbers and the Power of Atomic Operations

Definition 82 *The* consensus *problem is as follows. Let us assume that we have n threads. Each thread proposes a value. Ultimately all the threads choose a value that is one among the set of proposed values.*

The consensus problem is a very basic problem in concurrent systems. Its definition for an n-thread system is as follows. Let each thread propose a value. Eventually, all the threads need to agree on a single value that is one among the proposed values. It can be shown that a lot of real world problems are basically different variants of consensus problems. In fact, the heart of modern cryptocurrencies such as Bitcoin is a consensus problem. The basic problem that most transaction processing systems such as online payments solve is a consensus problem. As a result, solving the consensus problem is of paramount importance in concurrent systems, and moreover, it can be shown that many problems of interest can be mapped to equivalent consensus problems. The power of different atomic operations is based on who can efficiently solve the consensus problem in finite time in different settings.

This is quantified by the *consensus number* of an atomic operation, which is defined as follows. It is the maximum number of threads for which we can solve the consensus problem using a wait-free algorithm that uses the atomic operation and simple read/write operations. If the consensus number is k for a given atomic operation, then it means that it is theoretically not possible to write a wait-free algorithm that solves the consensus problem in a $k+1$ thread system.

Let us look at the consensus numbers of some of the common atomic operations.

Type of operation	Consensus number
Atomic exchange	2
Test and set	2
Fetch and add	2
CAS (compare and set)	∞
LL/SC	∞

From the definition of consensus numbers, it is clear that an operation with a lower consensus number cannot be used to implement an operation with a higher consensus number. This automatically implies that we cannot use test-and-set to implement CAS using a wait-free algorithm. The most powerful operations are CAS and LL/SC.

9.5 Memory Models

Let us quickly summarise what we have learnt in the preceding sections with respect to memory models.

Way Point 12

- *There are four kinds of relationships between regular memory operations: ws, fr, po, and rf.*

- *ws and fr orders are global in most systems today because of the requirements imposed by PLSC.*

- *Different processors relax different orders within po and rf. They thus have different memory models. If a given order is not global, it is said to be* relaxed.

Given that we can relax different orders that are a part of rf and po, we can create a variety of memory models. Different models have different trade-offs between flexibility and performance. Let us look at each of these relaxations from an architectural perspective.

9.5.1 Relationships in rf

Let us look at cases where we need to relax the rfi and rfe relationships. Recall that the rfi relationship is between a write and a successive read to the same address in the same thread, whereas the rfe

relationship is between a write and a read to the same address across threads. The rfe edge will be global if we have atomic writes because the write will appear to happen instantaneously and thus all the threads will agree on the write-to-read order.

When we use a write buffer (see Section 7.1.7), we are breaking the rfi order. Consider the situation, where we have a write and a subsequent read from the same address (in the same thread). The write operation is not made visible to the rest of the cores immediately. The write is sent to the write buffer and is not immediately broadcast to the rest of the cores. However, a later read operation can read its value and make progress. This effectively means that the read is visible globally, before its earlier write. The earlier write operation is visible to the rest of the cores, when it is ejected from the write buffer. From the point of view of the rest of the cores, the write executes after the read. Hence, the rfi relation in this case is not global. We have a similar case when we have forwarding in the LSQ. A later read gets the value from the LSQ and moves ahead, whereas the write needs to wait till the instruction gets committed.

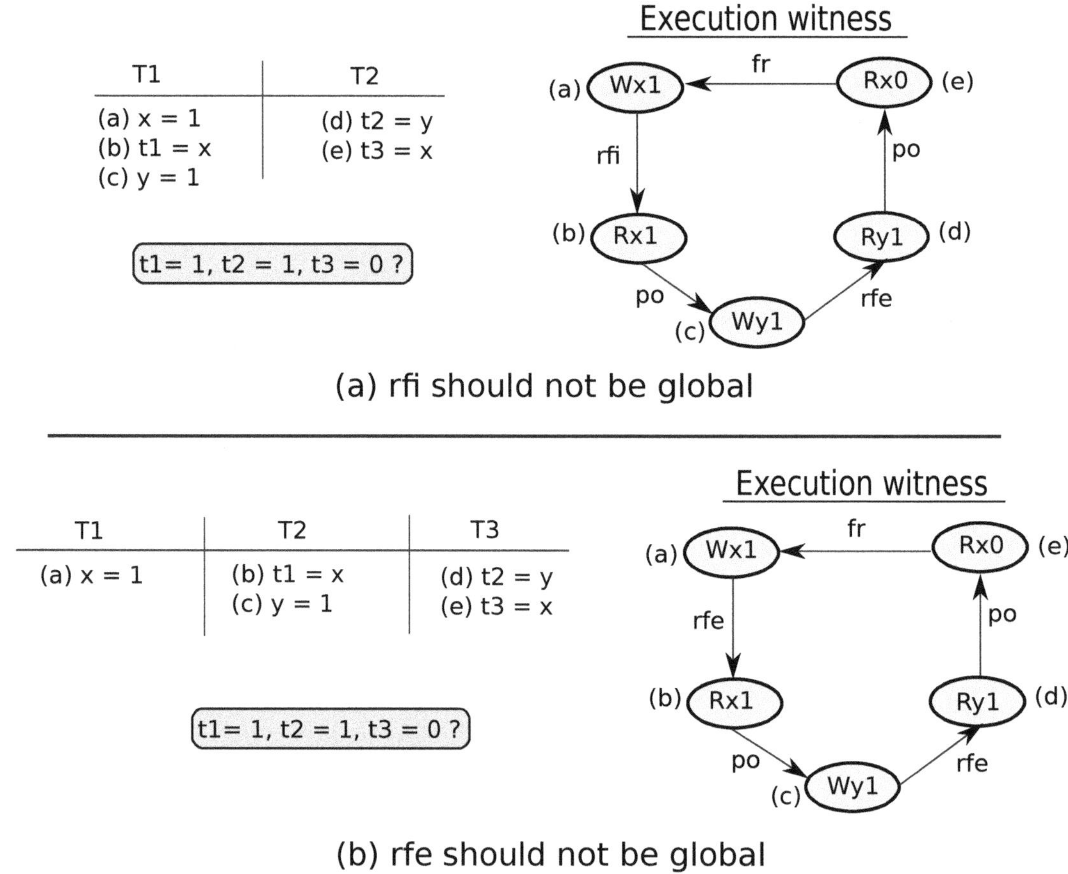

Figure 9.52: Execution witnesses: rfi and rfe orders

Consider the execution witness as shown in Figure 9.52(a). In this case, the read and write are a part of the same thread. Let us assume that the rfi relation is global. Additionally, the rfe edge, which is a write to read edge across threads is also assumed to be global because we are assuming atomic writes in this example. Now, assume that we do not have a program order edge between a write and a read. In We can thus add only an rfi edge between $Wx1$ and $Rx1$. Then we add a po edge between $Rx1$ and $Wy1$ because in this case we assume that a read to write program order is global. We then add an rfe

edge between $Wy1$ and $Ry1$. Finally, we add a program order edge (po_{RR}) between $Ry1$ and $Rx0$, and then an fr edge between $Rx0$ and $Wx1$. The reason that we add an fr edge is because the instruction $Rx0$ reads an earlier value of x. Now, we see that we have a cycle in the execution witness. Since many processors obey the RR and RW program orders, fr is global, and we have assumed rfe to also be global because of atomic writes, the only relation that we can relax is rfi for this execution to be valid.

In almost all OOO processors with atomic writes, this execution will be valid because the rfi edge is not respected. We say that an order is *respected* if it holds globally. In fact, whenever we delay earlier writes and use structures like write buffers, rfi is not global: this execution will be valid.

Now consider the example in Figure 9.52(b). Assume that the RW and RR program orders hold. Since the fr edge is global, the only edge in the graph that can be relaxed is the rfe edge. To avoid a cycle, the rfe order needs to be relaxed. This means that this execution is valid in a system with non-atomic writes. If we have atomic writes, this execution is not allowed.

9.5.2 Write-to-Read Program Order

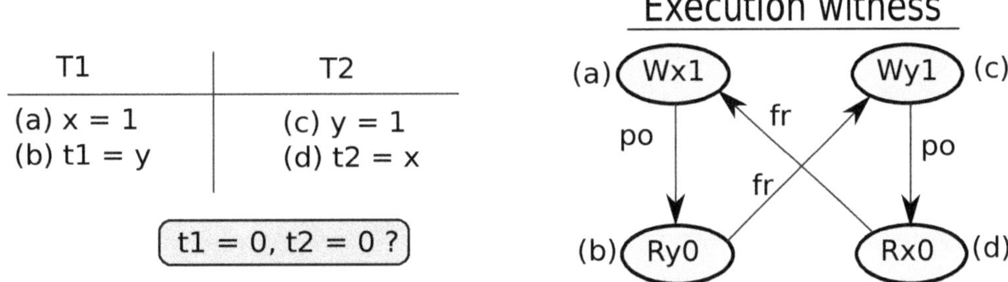

Figure 9.53: Execution witness: po_{WR} should not be global

In most conventional OOO pipelines, we send stores to the memory system once they reach the head of the ROB and are ready to be committed. We, however, do not stall later loads to different addresses. If there is no chance of a forwarding in the LSQ, the loads are sent to the memory system. This means that later loads can overtake earlier stores. In other words the $W \to R$ program order is not respected. In fact, the key aim of having an LSQ is to allow later loads to overtake earlier stores. Hence, in almost all practical memory models this ordering is relaxed. Figure 9.53 shows an example along with its execution witness, where the $W \to R$ program order edge needs to be relaxed for the execution to be valid. Readers are welcome to run this code on any multicore machine. We claim that they will see the output $((t_1, t_2) = (0, 0))$ at least once.

9.5.3 Write-to-Write Program Order

Let us now consider the write-to-write ($W \to W$) program order. If we have writes to different addresses, there is no requirement for them to take effect in program order for a single-threaded program. The correctness of the thread is not dependent on the order in which these writes are executed. However, for the rest of the cores, the order matters.

Such an order can break for a variety of reasons. It is true that from the point of view of the core, we commit write instructions in program order. However, it does not mean that they are sent to the memory system in that order. Consider the write buffer. Let's say we have two writes, W_1 and W_2, in a thread where W_1 is before W_2 in program order. If there is a write buffer entry for the address of W_1, then the write will be written to the write buffer entry. However, if the entry for W_2 is not there in the write buffer, we have an option of sending it directly to memory, instead of freeing a write buffer entry. In this case, W_2 appears to happen before W_1 to other cores, which is not true.

The $W_1 \overset{po}{\to} W_2$ relation can also break because of messages in the NoC. It is possible that the write messages might get reordered. Thus the $W \to W$ order will not remain global.

A guaranteed way to ensure that the write to write order is maintained is to make use of acknowledgement messages. The assumption is that an acknowledgement message is sent to a core after the write becomes globally visible. This means that the write is visible to all the threads. In the case of $W_1 \overset{po}{\to} W_2$, we wait for the acknowledgement of W_1 and then send the write W_2 to memory. The main problem with such acknowledgements is that they make a write more expensive. The write unnecessarily blocks the pipeline till its acknowledgement arrives. This delays later instructions ultimately reducing the IPC.

There are other mechanisms as well that ensure that the memory system is designed in such a way that later writes do not overtake earlier writes. These require changes to the write buffers, MSHRs, and the NoC. This is why most weak memory models in use today do not ensure the $W \to W$ order. The Intel TSO model is an exception to this rule. It obeys the $W \to W$ ordering.

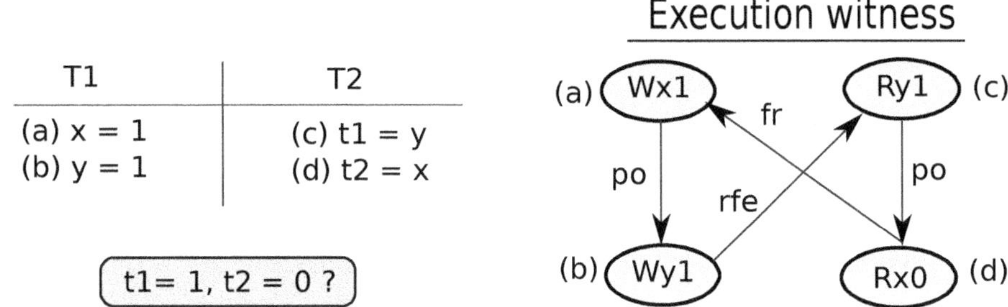

Figure 9.54: Execution witness: po_{WW} edges should not be global

Consider the example in Figure 9.54. The execution witness has a cycle. If we assume that rfe is global (writes are atomic), and fr is also global, then we have two more edges left: po_{WW} and po_{RR}. Assume that po_{RR} holds. Then the only edge that we can relax is the po_{WW} edge between $Wx1$ and $Wy1$ to make this execution valid. In most modern processors that have a weak memory model, such $W \to W$ program orders are not global. Hence, this execution is valid. However, in processors that follow the *total store order* memory model (mostly Intel processors), where the order of writes (stores) is global, this execution is not allowed.

9.5.4 Read-to-Read Program Order

The read-to-read ($R \to R$) order is also not respected by many OOO processors as of 2020. To ensure that this ordering holds we need to issue load operations in program order. Note that this decreases performance because it is possible that the address of a later load might be computed before the address of an earlier load. In this case, it is not fair from a performance point of view to make the later load wait for the earlier load. Recall that we are considering loads to different addresses.

Even though ensuring this order is easy, which is by making modifications to the LSQ, we should realise that we would be sacrificing some amount of performance. This is not acceptable in high performance processors.

Let us understand this order with an example (refer to Figure 9.55). We have three threads running on a machine with atomic writes (rfe is global). Assume that the po_{RW} edge is global, which is hard to relax even in OOO processors (discussed in the next subsection). Given that the fr edge is always global, the only edge that we can relax is the po_{RR} edge. On a machine with weak ordering that does not respect the *read* $\to$ *read* program order, this execution would be valid. However, if the LSQ ensures a strict ordering between reads, this execution is not possible.

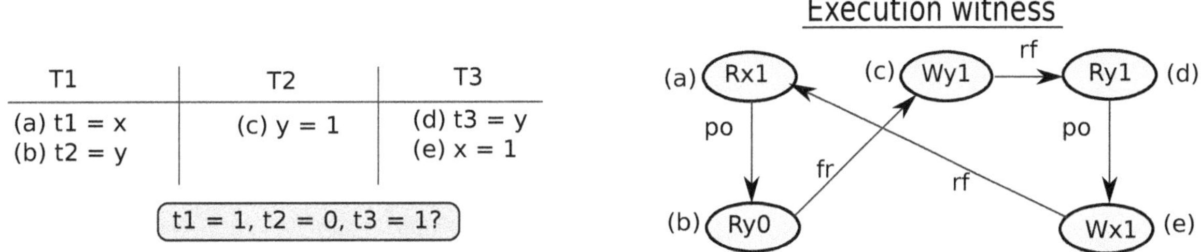

Figure 9.55: Execution witness: po_{RR} edge should not be global

In an OOO processor, we ideally do not want to stall later reads because of earlier unresolved reads (address is not computed). We would ideally like to send read operations to the memory system as soon as possible. This is because many instructions are typically dependent on the result of a read operation. Hence, the program order between read operations to different addresses is seldom respected.

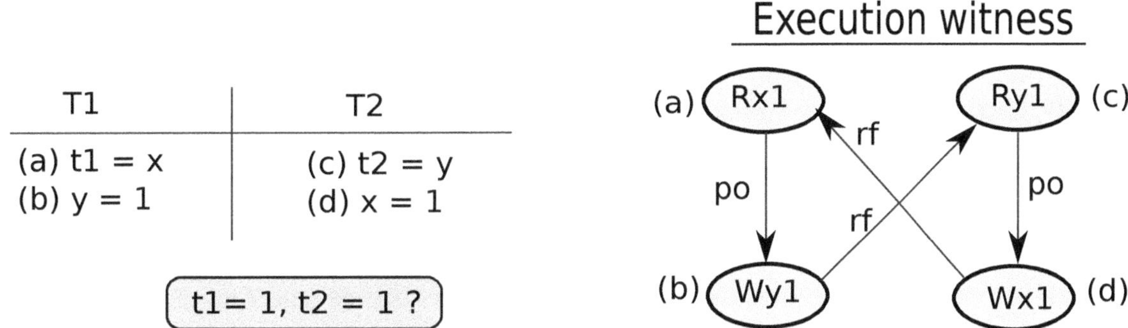

Figure 9.56: Execution witness: po_{RW} edge should not be global

9.5.5   Read-to-Write Program Order

In most OOO processors, this order is maintained; however, there are exceptions. In a conventional OOO processor the earlier read needs to have read its value and left the pipeline before the later write can write its value at commit time. To reverse the order, we need to think of a situation where the read operation appears to read its value after the write. This can happen in systems where writes are sent to the memory system early. We can design systems where an instruction can go ahead and write to an entry in the write buffer after we know that it is on the correct branch path. In this case, writes can be visible before earlier reads have read their value. Another case is when we use load-value prediction, where the prediction is validated after the load has committed. Such a situation is shown in Figure 9.56, where we assume atomic writes (rfe is global). The only edge that we can relax to avoid a cycle is the po_{RW} edge. Now that we have understood the implications of relaxing different orderings, let us look at the orderings that are relaxed by different memory models.

9.5.6   The Special Case of *rfi* in SC

Consider a sequentially consistent machine. What will happen if the rfi edge is not global? Will it still remain sequentially consistent? This will allow us to use LSQ forwarding in an SC machine. A core or thread can effectively read its own write *early*.

Consider a write operation W and a later read operation R that accesses the same address. They belong to the same thread. Let there be intervening operations of the form $O_1 \ldots O_n$. Furthermore, let us assume that none of $O_1 \ldots O_n$ are read operations that access the same address and there are no rfi dependences between them (we can always find such a pair if W and R access the same address). Then we can write $W \xrightarrow{ghb} O_1 \xrightarrow{ghb} O_2 \ldots O_n \xrightarrow{ghb} R$ because program order holds in SC for the cases that we consider. This means that $W \xrightarrow{ghb} R$. In this case, it does not matter if rfi is global or not because they are globally ordered anyway. Hence, rfi being global only matters when W and R are consecutive operations – there are no intervening operations. Note that in this case, we do not add a po or rfi edge between them. The question is whether the execution will still be in SC?

SC will be violated only when other threads see the read by R before seeing the previous write by W. Note that this problem will not happen in the same thread because as far as future operations in the thread are concerned – R is taking effect in program order. Now, consider the first operation O in another thread, which is reachable from R in the execution witness. It is either reachable via an $R \xrightarrow{fr} O$ edge or from an edge from another instruction O' in the same thread where we have $R \xrightarrow{po} O' \xrightarrow{ghb} O$. We use the $\xrightarrow{ghb}$ edge here because the nature of the edge between O' an O does not matter. Now, consider the first case. We need to also have $W \xrightarrow{ws} O$ (by the definition of fr). In the second case, we will have $W \xrightarrow{po} O' \xrightarrow{ghb} O$. In both cases, we will have $W \xrightarrow{ghb} O$. Hence, as far as O is concerned, both W and R happen before it, and R appears to have executed after W because it returns the value written by it. The fact that we relaxed the rfi edge between consecutive instructions is not visible to the same thread or to other threads. Hence, the execution still is in SC because the rest of the conditions for SC hold.

We can thus conclude that in SC, a thread can read its own writes *early*.

Model	Program order (po)				rf	
	po_{WR}	po_{WW}	po_{RR}	po_{RW}	rfe	rfi
SC						✓
TSO	✓					✓
PC	✓				✓	✓
PSO	✓	✓				✓
Weak const.	✓	✓	✓	✓		✓
RC	✓	✓	✓	✓		✓
PowerPC	✓	✓	✓	✓	✓	✓
ARM	✓	✓	✓	✓	✓	✓
A ✓ indicates that the ordering is relaxed						

SC	Sequential consistency	Weak const.	Weak consistency	
TSO	Total store ordering	RC	Release consistency	
PC	Processor consistency	PowerPC	PowerPC's memory model	
PSO	Partial store ordering	ARM	ARM v7 memory model	

Table 9.4: Popularly used memory models (adapted from [Adve and Gharachorloo, 1996])

9.5.7 Popular Memory Models

Table 9.4 lists some common memory models. Other than SC, each model relaxes some order in pursuit of better performance. Each memory model can be characterised by the orderings that it respects and the orderings that it relaxes. To find if a given execution is allowed by a memory model or not, we simply need to create an execution witness, add the edges that are a part of the memory model, and see if there is a cycle or not. If there are no cycles, then the execution is allowed by the memory model, otherwise it is not allowed. For SC we need to add all the po, ws, rf, and fr edges, whereas for other models we add fewer edges. They thus allow more executions.

Note that memory models are not necessarily artefacts of a hardware design, they can be used to describe software systems as well. Consider the comments on a news story. It is non-intuitive to see replies to comments before seeing the comments themselves. This is an example of consistency in the software world. We have defined memory models from the point of view of threads. Hence, the underlying substrate does not matter – it can either be software or hardware.

Consider a system such as the Java virtual machine (JVM), which runs Java programs by dynamically translating Java byte code to machine code. It also needs to implement a memory model such that programmers know what orderings are preserved in the final execution. In fact a lot of compiler optimisations are dependent on the memory model. For the purposes of increasing efficiency, compilers routinely reorder instructions subject to the uniprocessor access constraints. This reordering can violate the program order relations of the memory model. Hence, the memory model interacts with compiler optimisations as well. As a thumb rule, readers should assume that any entity in the stack starting from the compiler to the virtual machine to the actual hardware can reorder instructions. Given the way that we have defined memory models, the point of view of the programmer and the final outcome of the program determine the memory model. Let us proceed with these assumptions in mind.

The gold standard of memory consistency models is sequential consistency (SC), which is mainly a theoretical model and is used to reason about the intuitive correctness of parallel programs and systems. Implementing SC is expensive in terms of performance, and thus is almost always impractical. Almost all optimisations are precluded in SC, and thus very few mainstream processors support SC. The only exception to this rule has been the MIPS R10000 processor that provided sequential consistency. We shall see in Section 9.6 that there are methods to give the programmer an illusion of sequential consistency even though the underlying hardware has a relaxed memory model.

As compared to SC, the second model, TSO (total store ordering), has seen more commercial applications. The Intel x86 and the Sun Sparc v8 memory models broadly resemble TSO [Alglave, 2012]. This model relaxes the po_{WR} and rfi relations. TSO can thus be supported by OOO processors and we can seamlessly use LSQs and write buffers. Note that the rest of the program orders still hold and writes are atomic.

Many multiprocessor systems (particularly software systems) relax the TSO model to allow for non-atomic writes even though they do not relax the po_{WW} edge. This means that writes from the same thread are seen in program order, even though a thread can read the value of a write (issued by another thread) before all the threads see it – a thread can read another thread's write early. Implementing atomic writes is actually difficult in large systems where we can have a large number of cached copies. Thus, it sometimes makes sense to relax the requirements of write atomicity. The Processor Consistency (PC) memory model falls in this class; it supports non-atomic writes.

The PSO (partial store ordering) model on the other hand supports atomic writes but relaxes the po_{WW} edge. It was supported by some of the Sun SPARC v8 and v9 machines. The advantage of relaxing the $write \rightarrow write$ order is that we can support non-blocking caches. A later write can be sent beyond the MSHR to the lower levels of the memory systems, while an earlier write waits at the MSHR. This optimisation allows write operations to be reordered in the NoC as well. Note that read and write operations are fundamentally different. A read operation is synchronous, which means that the core gets to know when the value arrives. It is thus easy for it to enforce an order between a read instruction and any other instruction. However, writes are by nature asynchronous. Unless we have a system that sends write acknowledgements, a core has no idea when a write takes effect. Thus, enforcing an order between writes and other operations is difficult. Hence, PSO relaxes both the po_{WR} and po_{WW} orders. This simplifies the design of the memory system and the NoC.

The next model is called *weak consistency*, which is a generic model where all the orderings are relaxed other than write atomicity. A large number of RISC processors that are used to implement large multicore systems use some variant of weak ordering. Note that here write atomicity is the key; it is not compromised.

All the memory models that we have seen up till now define synchronisation instructions, and all of them respect the ordering between normal instructions and synch instructions. This means that they respect the following orders:

$$synch \xrightarrow{ghb} (read \mid write \mid synch)$$

$$(read \mid write \mid synch) \xrightarrow{ghb} synch$$

Let us now introduce another model called release consistency (RC) that was designed to implement critical sections efficiently. It supports the same orderings as weak consistency. However, it defines two additional synchronisation operations – *acquire* and *release*. In other words, a synch operation can be an acquire, release, or any other synchronisation operation. The orderings between these operations are as follows:

$$acquire \xrightarrow{ghb} (read \mid write \mid synch)$$

$$(read \mid write \mid synch) \xrightarrow{ghb} release$$

This means that we need to wait to complete an acquire operation, before any subsequent instruction can complete. This operation can be used for example to acquire a lock, where no operation in the critical section can begin till the lock is acquired. Similarly, we complete a release operation, only when all the operations before it have completed. This can be used to release a lock.

The last two models – ARM v7 and PowerPC – relax all orders including write atomicity. They thus allow for the maximum number of optimisations at the level of the compiler and architecture. They do have synchronisation instructions though that enforce strict orders between synch instructions and the rest of the instructions.

Note that relaxing orders beyond a certain point is not necessarily a good thing. It can make the design of software more complicated. We might have to insert a lot of synchronisation instructions and fences to make the code behave in a certain way. This has its performance implications. These issues will be dealt with in Section 9.6.

9.5.8 Summary

Let us now summarise our discussion. A memory model, MM, is characterised by the orderings that it respects. It needs to respect ws and fr because of PLSC. Then it needs to respect a subset of po and rf. Let it respect $gpo \subseteq po$ (program orders) and $grf \subseteq rf$ ($write \rightarrow read$ orders).

We thus can write,

$$MM = (gpo \cup ws \cup fr \cup grf) \tag{9.10}$$

9.6 Data Races

We discussed lock and unlock functions in Section 9.4.7. These are required to ensure that parallel code executes correctly. Otherwise, we will not be able to implement critical sections, which are required to correctly execute parallel code. Furthermore, in Section 9.4.7, we had considered an example where parallel threads try to update an account's balance. We concluded that two concurrent updates to the *balance* variable of the same account might lead to an incorrect state. To fix this situation, we had decided to enclose the update in a critical section.

9.6.1 Critical Sections, Concurrency Bugs, and Data Races

Now, if we forget to use critical sections, will we always have an error? The answer is NO. Let us look at an example.

```
counter++;
```

In this case, we are just incrementing a global counter. The correctness of this piece of code depends on how it is implemented in assembly (see the code snippets below). If we implement it as three instructions, where we first read the value of the *counter* from memory, increment the value that has been read, and then write the value to the memory location that holds the variable, *counter*, then there is a possibility of an error, a concurrency bug. This is because another concurrent update operation can also read the same initial value of the *counter* variable. This will lead to one update getting lost. However, if this statement is mapped to a fetch-and-increment atomic operation, then there is no possibility of an error because it is an atomic operation – not a *regular* read or write. Both the updates to the counter will get reflected in the final state of the program.

Multiple instructions

```
t1 = counter;
t2 = t1 + 1;
counter = t2;
```

Single instruction

```
fetch_and_increment(counter);
```

Note that in these code snippets $t1$ and $t2$ represent temporary variables that are mapped to registers. The first example with multiple instructions might clearly lead to incorrect execution, whereas the second example will not. Before proceeding further, we need a far more precise definition of what is an error in a parallel program, and how do we deal with it.

In general, in a parallel program, if we run it multiple times, the order of operations will be different because of the complex interplay of messages in the NoC and the memory system. However, we want the parallel program to be correct in all cases. For example, if it is multiplying two matrices, then the result should always be correct irrespective of the order in which the instructions are executed. To ensure that this genuinely does happen we need to regulate the behaviour of concurrent accesses to the same variable. If both are reads, then there is no problem. However, if at least one of them is a write, then there is a problem; the order of accesses to the variable become important. Different orders might lead to different outcomes. A pair of accesses to the same address where at least one of them is a write are said to be *conflicting accesses*.

> **Definition 83**
> *A pair of accesses to the same address, where at least one of them is a write, are said to be conflicting accesses.*

Let us reconsider our example with the *counter* variable. If it is implemented with regular load/store assembly instructions, then there is a possibility that the execution might be incorrect. This is because it uses regular reads and writes, and this is where there is a possibility of an error because of concurrent and conflicting accesses by the two threads. Let us characterise this scenario by defining the term *data race*. A *data race* is informally defined as a situation where we have regular, concurrent, and conflicting accesses to a variable by different threads, where at least one of them is a write access. If we can eliminate data races in our program, then we can at least claim that between any two conflicting accesses to the same variable, there is some kind of an order. Such an *order* must have been enforced by the programmer using program logic and synch instructions. This order ensures that the accesses are ordered sequentially and such kind of errors do not happen. This means that one thread will finish its updates, and then somehow signal another thread to begin. If we were to enclose the counter update function within lock and unlock functions, then such an order will automatically be imposed. It will not be possible to incorrectly update the *counter* variable. However, we can always make concurrent and conflicting accesses using synchronisation operations such as *fetch_and_increment*. They update the *counter* variable atomically and correctly.

We have deliberately not defined the term *concurrent accesses* precisely. In computer architecture parlance, it does not mean "at the same time". It has a deeper meaning, which we shall explore in the subsequent sections.

From our informal discussion, we have learnt several things. Two conflicting accesses need to be somehow *ordered* if we are using regular loads and stores. Otherwise, the output of the program may be wrong as we saw with the example to update the *counter*. This order can be enforced by wrapping the code in a critical section (demarcated by a lock and unlock function), otherwise we need to use atomic operations such as *fetch_and_increment*. Let us formalise this.

9.6.2   Data Races in the Context of Memory Models

A Formal Model of Data Races

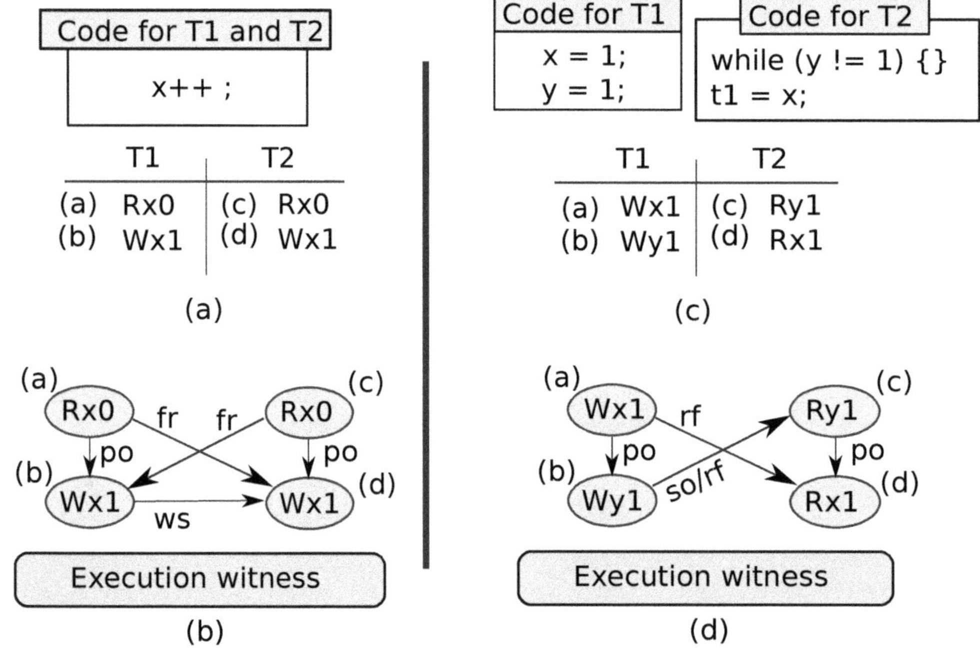

Figure 9.57: (a) and (b): Code and execution witness of a program that updates a counter. (c) and (d): Code and execution witness of a program that transfers the value of variable x across threads. Assume that y is a synch variable.

Assume an SC machine. Consider the code and execution witness in Figure 9.57 (a) and (b). It shows the code of a regular counter update where there is a data race (as we have defined, albeit, informally). The value of x (counter in this case) is finally set to 1, which is wrong. We need to disallow such executions. Now consider the code in Figure 9.57(c) and (d). Further assume that x is a regular variable and y is a synch variable, and the *while* loop exits in the first iteration. This piece of code basically transfers the value of x from thread T1 to thread T2. This execution seems to be correct. Until the value of y has not been read to be 1 by T2, it will keep looping. Once it reads $y = 1$, it has to read $t1 = x = 1$. This is correct execution on an SC machine. In fact all executions will yield the same output, which is correct.

So what is wrong in the execution witness shown in Figure 9.57(b) and what is correct in the execution witness shown in Figure 9.57(d)? Look closely. Consider only regular variables: x in both cases. The answer is that between two conflicting accesses in Figure 9.57(b), there is a path that has no synchronisation order (*so*) edges. For example, between the instructions (b) and (d) (both $Wx1$), we only have a path with a *ws* edge. Now, focus on the execution witness shown in Figure 9.57(d). The path from $Wx1$ to $Rx1$ has an *so* edge. This is the crux of the definition of *concurrent accesses*. Consider two accesses to the same regular variable in the execution witness. If there is no path between them with an *so* edge, they are said to be *concurrent*. Let us now define a data race with the concepts we have just learnt.

Definition 84
Consider two accesses to the same regular variable across threads. If there is no path between them in the execution witness with an so edge, they are said to be concurrent. *Whenever we have a pair of such conflicting and concurrent accesses, we* refer *to this situation as a* data race.

Let us appreciate the definition. We want that at least one path should exist with an *so* edge between conflicting accesses to the same variable, and this edge should be across threads. When we had such an edge, we saw that the execution was correct, and the lack of such an edge led to an incorrect execution. Can we generalise this?

When there is a path with an *so* edge, it means that synchronisation instructions of the program are involved in enforcing a dependence between two conflicting accesses to the same variable. It will allow us to regulate conflicting accesses. Of course, here we need to differentiate between regular and synchronisation variables. We do allow concurrent and conflicting accesses to synchronisation variables: we assume that they are always updated in a sequentially consistent fashion. However, when it comes to regular variables, if we want the program to be free of data races, then if there is a rf, fr, or ws edge between any two operations on regular variables in the execution witness across threads, there has to be another alternative path between them that has *so* edges. This would mean that the operations are ordered by other instructions; they are not *concurrent*.

Does SC Imply Data-Race-Freedom?

Let us look at the examples shown in Figure 9.58.

We observe in Figure 9.58 that for the same code, we can have many different sequential executions on an SC machine. The first execution (Figure 9.58(a)) is free of data races because there is a happens-before relationship between $Rx0$ and $Wx1$ with an *so* edge; however, the second execution has a data race because there is no happens-before ordering between the accesses $Wx1$ and $Rx1$ with an *so* edge. Now from our point of view, this *code* has a concurrency bug because it is possible to have an execution that has a data race. Hence, SC does not guarantee data-race-freedom.

Does Data-Race-Freedom Imply SC?

Let us ask the reverse question now. Assume an execution does not have any data races. Is it in SC? Let us look at a few theorems.

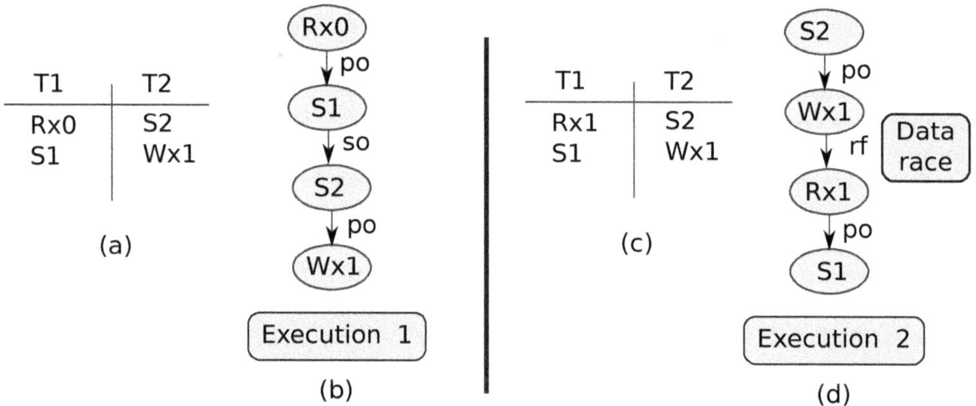

Figure 9.58: Different SC executions of the same program. $S1$ and $S2$ are synchronisation operations.

Theorem 9.6.2.1 *Consider two conflicting accesses e_1 and e_2 in two different threads T_1 and T_2, where $e_1 \xrightarrow{hb} e_2$. If the execution is data-race-free, then there have to be two synchronisation operations s_1 and s_2 with the following properties.*

- *$s_1 \in T_1$ and $s_2 \in T_2$*

- *$e_1 \xrightarrow{hb} s_1$, $s_2 \xrightarrow{hb} e_2$, and $s_1 \xrightarrow{hb} s_2$*

- *The paths from $e_1 \to s_1$ and $s_2 \to e_2$ will each have a po edge.*

Proof: Given that the execution is data-race-free, there will always be a path from e_1 to e_2 that has at least one *so* edge in the execution witness. Let us name this path $\mathcal{P}$. Assume that there are two threads in the system: T_1 and T_2.

By the definition of data-race-freedom, in the path $\mathcal{P}$, we will find two accesses s_1 and s_2 to a synch variable. This will be an *so* edge.

Given that we will find such an edge from $s_1 \in T_1$ to $s_2 \in T_2$, we see that we have satisfied all the conditions. We have $e_1, e_2, s_1, s_2 \in P$. From the definition of a synch operation, it follows that $e_1 \xrightarrow{hb} s_1$, $s_1 \xrightarrow{hb} s_2$, and $s_2 \xrightarrow{hb} e_2$. Note that since e_1 and s_1 access different addresses, there has to be a *po* edge between them. The same holds for s_2 and e_2.

This argument can easily be extended to the case of multiple threads. ∎

Now, the time has come to expose the magic of data-race-freedom. We shall prove that it implies SC execution regardless of the memory model.

Theorem 9.6.2.2 *A data-race-free execution is in SC regardless of the memory model.*

Proof: Consider a data-race-free execution E. Let us add all the edges to the execution witness that an SC execution needs to have namely po, rf, fr, and ws edges. If there is no cycle, the execution is in SC. Assume there is a cycle.

First consider the case of two threads. There have to be at least two edges in E with the following properties. The first edge has to be from $e_1 \in T_1$ to $e_2 \in T_2$. The second edge has to be from $e_3 \in T_2$ to $e_4 \in T_1$. Without loss of generality, assume that the cycle is of the form: $e_1 \overset{hb}{\to} e_2 \overset{hb}{\to} e_3 \overset{hb}{\to} e_4 \overset{hb}{\to} e_1$. As proven in Theorem 9.6.2.1, for any edge of the form $e_1 \overset{hb}{\to} e_2$, we need to have an edge of the form $s_1 \overset{hb}{\to} s_2$, where $e_1 \overset{hb}{\to} s_1$, and $s_2 \overset{hb}{\to} e_2$. $s_1 \in T_1$ and $s_2 \in T_2$. s_1 and s_2 are synch instructions. Similarly, we will have $s_3 \overset{hb}{\to} s_4$, where $e_3 \overset{hb}{\to} s_3$ and $s_4 \overset{hb}{\to} e_4$. Here, $s_3 \in T_2$ and $s_4 \in T_1$.

Since we have a cycle comprising $\langle e_1, e_2, e_3, e_4 \rangle$, and program orders hold between synch operations issued by the same thread, we shall also have a cycle comprising the accesses $\langle s_1, s_2, s_3, s_4 \rangle$. However, we have assumed that synch instructions' execution is sequentially consistent. Hence, they cannot form a cycle. This proves by contradiction that we cannot have a cycle in the execution witness between e_1, e_2, e_3, and e_4. This result can be extended to consider multiple threads. Hence, the execution is in SC.

∎

Herein lies the greatness of data-race-freedom – it implies SC. Let us quickly recapitulate what we have proven.

Property	Reference
SC does not imply data-race-freedom	Figure 9.58
Data-race-freedom implies SC	Theorem 9.6.2.2
Non-SC execution implies data races	Contrapositive of Theorem 9.6.2.2
What do data races imply?	–

Let us now see what does having data races imply? Let us say that we have data races in a given execution with a certain memory model. Can we say something more? It turns out that we can. See the following theorem.

Theorem 9.6.2.3 *If we have a data race in a program, then it is possible to construct a sequentially consistent execution that also has a data race.*

Proof: Assume a multithreaded program has an execution, E, that exhibits a data race. This execution is as per the memory model of the machine. Let us construct an SC execution from it that also has a data race.

Let us keep running the program until we detect the first data race. Assume that just after executing the memory operation e_j, we observe the first data race. We stop there. Let us refer to this partial execution as $\hat{E}$. Till this point ($\hat{E} - e_j$), the execution has been data-race-free. By Theorem 9.6.2.2, the execution $\hat{E} - e_j$ is sequentially consistent because it is free of data races. Let us now add e_j to the execution.

Is execution $\hat{E}$ still sequentially consistent? Assume it is not. Then there will be a cycle involving c_j. Let $e_j \in T_j$ and let the cycle be of the form $e_{j-1} \overset{hb}{\to} e_j \overset{hb}{\to} e_1 \ldots \overset{hb}{\to} e_{j-1}$. If the cycle has any other node that is in thread T_j, then we need to have a synchronisation edge, because before adding e_j, no data races were detected. If the synch operation in thread T_j is after e_j in program order, then it should not have executed in the first place because e_j had not completed. This is a contradiction. If it is before e_j in program order, then also we cannot have a cycle involving e_j because there will be a path from e_1 to e_j containing *so* edges. This means that e_j is globally ordered after e_1 and there can be no path from e_j to e_1. Hence, the only option is that there are no other nodes of the cycle in T_j.

Assume e_j is a write. Note that because SC has held up till now, no node in $\hat{E} - e_j$ has read the value written by e_j. Hence, we can treat e_j as the latest write to its location. Thus, no rf or ws edges will emanate from it and it cannot complete a cycle.

Now, assume that e_j is a read. This means that an rf edge will enter it, and an fr edge will exit it. Let the rf edge be from e_i to e_j, and let the fr edge be from e_j to e_k. By definition, we will also have a ws edge from e_i to e_k. For the cycle to complete, there needs to be a path from e_k to e_i that does not have e_j. This means that there will be a cycle that does not involve e_j. This would have existed even before e_j was considered. Given that SC held up till now, this is not possible. Hence, there is a contradiction in this case as well.

Hence, there are no cycles and the execution $\hat{E}$ is in SC. Furthermore, this execution has a data race. Let the equivalent sequential order be $\mathcal{S}$.

Is the execution $\hat{E}$ complete? This means that if a given operation of a thread is present, are all of its previous operations (in program order) there? If they are not there, let us add them. Let us refer to all the operations that are missing as the set of *skipped operations*. For every such *skipped operation*, there is some memory operation $e \in \hat{E}$ that succeeds it in program order. Because $\hat{E}$ is in SC, the backward slice (all the operations that determine the values of the operands) of every operation in $\hat{E}$ is present in it. Furthermore, because of PLSC all the preceding instructions of $e \in \hat{E}$ in the same thread that access the same address are also present in $\hat{E}$. This means that adding the skipped instructions is not going to change the outcome of memory operations in $\hat{E}$.

Now, let us add the skipped instructions to the equivalent sequential order, $\mathcal{S}$. Note that given that we are at liberty to set their outcome and moreover their outcome does not influence the values read or written in $\hat{E}$. For each thread we add its earliest skipped instruction at the appropriate point (as per program order) in $\mathcal{S}$. It reads the latest value in the sequence. Similarly, for a write, we also add it at an appropriate point in $\mathcal{S}$. We assume it is the latest write for the location. Given that we are ensuring that the resultant sequence of instructions is in SC after each step, we can prove by induction that after adding all the skipped instructions, the final sequence is still in SC, and still has data races.

We can then simulate the rest of the execution in a sequentially consistent manner.

This proves that it is possible to construct an SC execution that also contains a data race, if the original program has a data race with any memory model.

■

From the results of Theorem 9.6.2.3, we can say that **a program has a data race, irrespective of the memory model**. We can complete the table now.

Property	Reference
SC does not imply data-race-freedom	Figure 9.58
Data-race-freedom implies SC	Theorem 9.6.2.2
Non-SC execution implies data races	Contrapositive of Theorem 9.6.2.2
A program with a data race has an SC execution with a data race	Theorem 9.6.2.3

9.6.3 Properly Synchronised Programs

Can we guarantee that all executions of a program are data-race-free? Such a program is called a data-race-free or a DRF program.

Let us first answer this question. Consider a program where every shared variable is accessed within a critical section, and the same shared variable is always protected by the same lock. Recall that a critical section is demarcated by lock and unlock functions – these functions access synch variables. This automatically disallows concurrent accesses to the same shared variable because only one thread can hold a lock at a time, and thus it is not possible for two threads to concurrently access the same shared variable – one of them will not be able to acquire the corresponding lock for the shared variable. This program is thus data-race-free. Let us refer to such programs as *properly synchronised programs* or PS programs.

Definition 85 *In a properly synchronised program (PS program), every shared variable is accessed within a critical section, and throughout the program, the same shared variable is protected by the same set of locks. This ensures that we cannot have concurrent accesses by two threads to the same shared variable. Such programs are free of data races.*

Discussion

We thus observe that any properly synchronised program is data-race-free and always produces sequentially consistent executions. It is thus a DRF program. In other words, properly synchronising a program ensures that our executions are both data-race-free and in SC regardless of the underlying memory model! This is arguably one of the most impactful results in modern parallel computing and parallel architecture, and allows hardware designers to pursue all kinds of performance enhancing optimisations while maintaining the intuitiveness of the high level code.

Regardless of the memory model, all that programmers need to do is that they need to enclose all the accesses to shared variables in critical sections (individually or in groups), and always ensure that the same shared variable is protected by the same set of locks. Once this is done, the execution is in SC, and thus it is very easy to write parallel programs. Additionally, our executions do not exhibit data races, as a result we avoid many classes of concurrency bugs.

Regarding performance, this depends on the proportion of shared variables that are accessed. In most modern parallel programs, shared variable accesses are relatively infrequent. Most of the accesses are to private data (private to a thread), therefore there is no additional overhead in terms of synchronisation instructions while accessing such data. Given this pattern, the overheads of properly synchronising are considered to be rather modest, and it is by and large possible to reap the advantages of a relaxed memory model.

The main challenge now is to ensure that a given program is properly synchronised. This is unfortunately computationally undecidable, and thus it is not possible to write a tool to find this out. However, we can analyse programs and their executions for evidence of data races. If we find a data race, we can conclude that the program is not properly synchronised, and we can also pinpoint the regions of the code the programmer should look at based on the addresses involved in the data race. Note that the absence of data races in a few sample runs does not indicate that the program is properly synchronised, however, this approach has proven to be an extremely efficient and successful method for finding bugs in parallel programs.

9.6.4   DRF Memory Models

The main aim is to "properly synchronise" a program. This will give us the best of all worlds: relaxed memory models, SC execution, and data-race-freedom.

Now how do we do this? As discussed, one way is to enclose all accesses to shared variables within critical sections. This means that the high level language needs to give us the facility for creating critical sections. We can thus define a memory model at the level of a high level language such as C++ or Java that specifies a set of orderings similar to memory models in hardware. Additionally, this model needs to specify what a programmer needs to do to produce data-race-free executions. Such memory models are known as DRF memory models. They are defined for programming languages.

They can be of different kinds because we can have many kinds of synch operations. For example, a synch operation need not be a regular fence operation. We can instead use the acquire and release operations defined in release consistency (see Section 9.5.7). Theorem 9.6.2.1 only says that the following relations need to hold: $e_1 \overset{hb}{\to} s_1$, $s_2 \overset{hb}{\to} e_2$, and $s_1 \overset{hb}{\to} s_2$. s_1 and s_2 need not be regular fence operations; s_1 can be a release and s_2 can be an acquire. The theorem will still hold. We can then prove that with such acquire and release operations, data-race-freedom implies SC. A DRF model that provides such acquire and release operations will be different from a DRF model that just provides regular fences. Modern languages such as C++and Java have many such synchronisation constructs and thus provide a complex DRF model.

9.6.5   Lock Set Algorithm

We have concluded that by ensuring that there are no data races, we will not face issues with different memory models, particularly models that have non-atomic writes. All that we need to ensure is that the code is properly synchronised and consequently data-race-free. Even though such theoretical models have taken us very far, still in practice, it is possible that programmers might forget to "properly synchronise" their programs. In this case, we might encounter data races, and this will give rise to a new class of bugs called *concurrency bugs*.

Hence, there are several algorithms in both software and hardware to ensure that the code is properly synchronised. Let us discuss one of the simplest algorithms in this class known as the *Lock Set Algorithm* [Savage et al., 1997]. The basic idea is as follows. We associate a set of locks with each memory location v (the lock set). When we initialise the program, we assume that the lock set for each location contains all the locks that the program uses.

Additionally, each access (read or write) is also associated with a lock set. It is defined as a set of locks held by the thread that is issuing the memory access.

To summarise, there are two lock sets that we are considering: one held by the memory location ($L(v)$), and the other held by the thread, T, while accessing the memory location (represented as $L(T)$). Now it is possible that several locks protect a given memory location, however we do not know them. Hence, we need to instrument reads and writes to the shared variables, and find the set of locks that protect each shared variable (its lock set). Hence, after each access we compute

$$L(v) = L(v) \cap L(T) \tag{9.11}$$

This further narrows down the set of locks that protect each variable. In every step, we keep iterating and refining the lock set till we reach the end of the program. At this point of time, there are two possible scenarios. The first scenario is that the lock set is non-empty. This means that for the variable (and its associated memory address), we have found a set of locks that protect it. The other scenario is when the lock set is empty. In this case, it means that we were not able to find a set of locks that protect a given location. This means that most likely there is a data race associated with this location.

The standard approach for implementing this technique is in software. In this case, we augment each access to a shared variable with additional code that refines the lock set for the variable. At the end, we analyse the lock sets for all the shared variables, and find those variables with empty lock sets. We can then report these variables to the programmer, and then she can check if the code that accesses these variables is properly synchronised or not. This is thus a method for *data race detection*.

This basic mechanism is however suboptimal as pointed out by Savage et al. [Savage et al., 1997]. There are three important patterns in modern programming languages that are falsely reported to be data races, whereas these patterns are perfectly safe.

Initialisation We often initialise shared variables without using any locks.

Read-only variables A program might use many read-only variables that are written once during initialisation, and later they are read many times. This algorithm will report such accesses to be data races. This is however not the case.

Reader-writer pattern Such access patterns allow multiple readers to read the same variable concurrently. Multiple concurrent read accesses do not lead to data races. However, this algorithm will find the different read accesses to contain different lock sets, and thus might report a few of them to be data races.

It is thus necessary to refine the basic algorithm.

Improved Version of the Basic Lock Set Algorithm

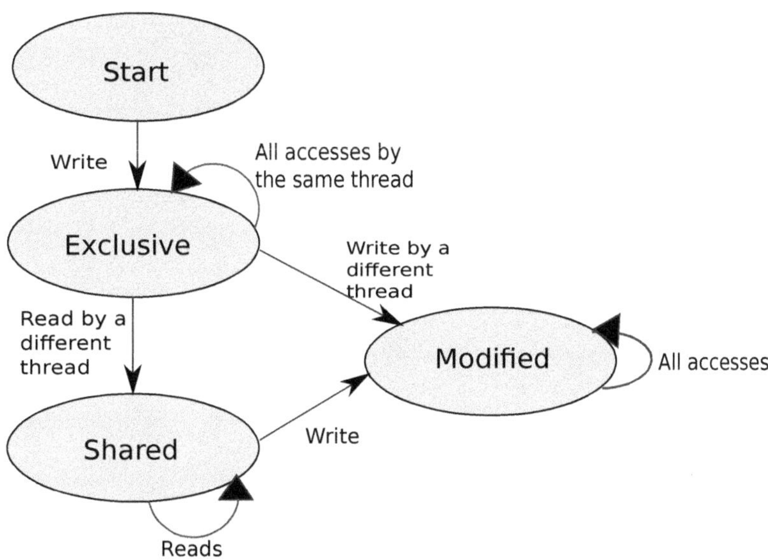

Figure 9.59: States in the advanced version of the lock set algorithm

Figure 9.59 shows the state diagram for the advanced version of the algorithm. We start in the *Start* state. The first access to a memory location has to be a write because we need to set its initial value. After it is initialised with the write, the initialising thread will continue to make accesses (reads or writes). This should be kept out of the purview of the data race detection algorithm. We refer to this state as the *Exclusive* state. Subsequently, we need to track the accesses made by other threads.

If there is a read by another thread, we transition to the *Shared* state. This captures the multiple-readers scenario. At this point, even if multiple threads are reading the variable, we do not report a data race. However, if there is a write, then we need to start using the regular lock set-based data race reporting algorithm. We transition to the *Modified* state. On similar lines, if we have a write access by another thread in the *Exclusive* state, we transition to the *Modified* state. Subsequently, we remain in this state and keep using the regular lock set algorithm, where we continue refining the lock set. Only in this state, we detect and report data races.

9.6.6   Data Race Detection with Vector Clocks

Let us now discuss one more approach that uses a mechanism called vector clocks. Most approaches in this space are in software, where a compiler or a module at runtime, instruments the reads and writes to record their dependences. If we find some unusual patterns symptomatic of data races, then an error is flagged. There are approaches in hardware to detect dynamic data races; however, they are expensive and at best only make probabilistic guarantees.

Theoretical Preliminaries

Let us now look at a more general mechanism for detecting data races.

The key question that we need to answer is how do we find if two events are concurrent? Recall that in the world of concurrent systems, two concurrent events need not take place at the same time. In fact, when we are considering multiple cores, with their own clocks, the definition of time itself is fuzzy. We need to come up with an alternative definition.

Till now we have been saying that two events e_1 and e_2 are concurrent if there is no happens-before ordering between them. We have however not dwelt on how to find if there is a happens-before ordering between two events. To do so, we will use results from classic distributed systems literature – vector clocks.

Consider n processes. There is no global clock. All the processes have their separate clocks, and the relationship between these clocks is not known. There are two kinds of events: internal and external. Internal events are local to a process. They are not visible to other processes. However, external events are visible to other processes. They are modelled as send-receive messages, where one process sends a message to another process.

Let every process contain an n-element vector, which is a *vector clock*. The ith process's vector is denoted as V_i. The ith element of V_i represents the local time of process i. We increment the local clock, $V_i[i]$, before sending a message, and after receiving a message. $V_i[j]$ $(i \neq j)$ represents i's best estimate of j's local time.

Let us see what happens when processes send and receive messages. Before sending a message, process i increments $V_i[i]$, and sends the message along with its vector clock, V_i. When j receives the message, it first increments its own time, $V_j[j]$, and then sets V_j as follows.

$$\forall k, V_j[k] = max(V_i[k], V_j[k]) \tag{9.12}$$

We refer to this as the *union* operation of V_i and V_j: $V_i \cup V_j$.

Here, the symbol $\forall$ stands for *"for all"*. This operation gives j the most up to date estimate of the local times of the rest of the processes. Given two vector clocks, we can define a few relationships between them. Two vector clocks, V_i and V_j, are equal if and only if all their elements are pairwise equal.

$$V_i = V_j \Leftrightarrow \forall k, V_i[k] = V_j[k] \tag{9.13}$$

Let us now look at the conditions where we can say that event e_i (by process i) happened before event e_j (by process j). Let us define a precedence relationship, $\prec$, between vector clocks. Let us say that $V_i \prec V_j$ if the following relationship holds (note that $\wedge$ stands for logical AND).

$$V_i \prec V_j \Leftrightarrow (V_i \neq V_j) \wedge (\forall k, V_i[k] \leq V_j[k]) \tag{9.14}$$

The first term in Equation 9.14 means that the two vector clocks are not equal (both the arrays are not exactly equal). The second term means that each entry in the first vector clock V_i is less than or equal to the corresponding entry in V_j. This alternatively means that there is some k' for which $V_i[k'] < V_j[k']$. Let us understand the logic behind comparing vector clocks in this manner.

Causal Ordering

Let us list some classic results in distributed systems. Let event e_i happen at time V_i and event e_j happen at time V_j.

Theorem 9.6.6.1 $V_i \prec V_j \Rightarrow e_i \xrightarrow{hb} e_j$

Theorem 9.6.6.2 $e_i \overset{hb}{\to} e_j \Rightarrow V_i \prec V_j$

By considering both the theorems, we can say that the following relationship holds.

$$e_i \overset{hb}{\to} e_j \Leftrightarrow V_i \prec V_j \tag{9.15}$$

Two events, e_i and e_j, are said to be concurrent if none of the following relationships hold: $V_i \prec V_j$ or $V_j \prec V_i$. We write $V_i || V_j$ or $e_i || e_j$ to indicate concurrency.

Definition 86 *A vector clock is defined as an n-element vector, where there are n processes in the system. Whenever, process i sends a message to process j, it also attaches its vector clock along with the message. The vector clock of each process is initialised to all zeros.*

Before process i sends a message, it increments, $V_i[i]$. When process j receives the message, it first increments its own time, $V_j[j]$, and then sets V_j as follows.

$$\forall k, V_j[k] = max(V_i[k], V_j[k])$$

Two vector clocks can be compared with a precedence relationship.

$$V_i \prec V_j \Leftrightarrow (V_i \neq V_j) \wedge (\forall k, V_i[k] \leq V_j[k])$$

For vector clocks, we have the following relationship.

$$V_i \prec V_j \Leftrightarrow e_i \overset{hb}{\to} e_j$$

Two events, e_i and e_j, are said to be concurrent if none of the following relationships hold: $V_i \prec V_j$ or $V_j \prec V_i$.

Data Race Detection using Vector Clocks

If we have n threads, we assign an n-element vector clock to each thread (*process* in theoretical parlance). Additionally, each memory location, v, is assigned two vector clocks: a read clock R_v and a write clock W_v. Let C_T be the vector clock of the current thread, *tid* be its thread id, and let C_L be the vector clock associated with the acquired lock.

Algorithm 1: Lock acquire
1 $C_T[tid] \leftarrow C_T[tid] + 1$
2 $C_T \leftarrow C_T \cup C_L$
3 $C_L \leftarrow C_T$
4 $C_T.inLock \leftarrow$ **True**

Let us first consider the lock acquire function. In this case, we are using synch variables, and since the system ensures an SC execution for such variables, we have allowed data races between their accesses. Whenever, a given thread acquires a lock, it is necessary to set both the vector clocks to the same time because this point is a rendezvous point for the thread and the lock. Hence, we first increment the local clock $C_T[tid]$ of the current thread, compute the union of both the vector clocks (C_T and C_L), and set both of them to the computed union. Finally, we set the *inLock* bit of the current thread to 1, which indicates the fact that the current thread is inside a critical section.

Algorithm 2: Lock release
---
1 $C_T.inLock \leftarrow$ **False**

On similar lines, when we release the lock we set the *inLock* bit to 0. A thread may make accesses to shared variables without a lock, some of these will be data races.

Algorithm 3: Read operation
---
1 **if** $\neg C_T.inLock$ **then**
2 | $C_T[tid] \leftarrow C_T[tid] + 1$
3 **end**
4 **if** $W_v \preceq C_T$ **then**
5 | $R_v \leftarrow R_v \cup C_T$
6 **end**
7 **else**
8 | **Declare Data Race**
9 **end**

Let us now discuss the read operation. If the current thread does not hold a lock, then an access is being made outside a critical section. We are not in a position to detect if this variable is shared or not. However, to indicate that this is a separate event, we increment $C_T[tid]$ (local clock of the current thread).

For any read operation, all the writes to location v should precede it or be equal (denoted by the $\preceq$ symbol) in terms of logical time. We explicitly verify this by comparing the write clock W_v with the current time. If W_v precedes the current time or is equal to it, then we replace the read clock R_v with $R_v \cup C_T$. This ensures that the read clock is up to date as per the semantics of standard vector clocks. Note that we do not require the read clock to precede or be equal to the current time because we allow concurrent reads in our system – they are not classified as data races.

However, if we find that $W_v \| C_T$ or $C_T \prec W_v$, then there is a data race, and it is immediately flagged.

Algorithm 4: Write Operation
---
1 **if** $\neg C_T.inLock$ **then**
2 | $C_T[tid] \leftarrow C_T[tid] + 1$
3 **end**
4 **if** $(W_v \preceq C_T) \wedge (R_v \preceq C_T)$ **then**
5 | $R_v \leftarrow R_v \cup C_T$
6 | $W_v \leftarrow W_v \cup C_T$
7 **end**
8 **else**
9 | **Declare Data Race**
10 **end**

Finally, let us consider the write operation. Here also, we first check if the access is made within a critical section or outside it. This is handled on the same lines as the read operation.

For a write, we need to ensure that both the read clock and the write clock either precede or are equal to the current time. This follows from the way we have defined data races. Writes need to be totally ordered with respect to prior reads and writes. If this is not the case, then we can immediately flag a data race. Otherwise, we proceed to update the values of R_v and W_v with information contained in the current time using the union operation.

This notion of vector clocks can thus be very easily used to create data race detectors in software.

9.7 Transactional Memory

We had discussed critical sections in Section 9.4.7, and then connected them to data races in the previous section. It should not be possible for other threads to see the values written by instructions in the critical section before it has ended and the lock has been released. Also, instructions within the critical section should not be able to see values written by concurrent writes. This means that the entire block of code within the critical section needs to appear to execute as a single statement. Either it appears to other instructions that the entire block of code has executed, or it appears that the execution of the block has not begun. This property as we have seen in the case of write operations is known as *atomicity*. It basically signifies an all-or-none behaviour. We need atomicity at the level of critical sections as well.

Let us now also consider how we implemented critical sections. We created a special pair of *lock* and *unlock* functions, where the lock function uses an atomic exchange instruction to atomically exchange the contents of a register and a memory location. This instruction does the atomic exchange in such a manner that no other instruction can interrupt it in the middle or can view any intermediate state. The atomic exchange instruction is supported by almost all instruction sets as of 2020, and more sophisticated locking algorithms use other primitives such as atomic fetch-and-increment, and atomic compare-and-set. All of these atomic primitives are implemented by modifying the coherence protocol. We delay sending acknowledgements to the directory till the atomic operations complete.

Such simple modifications to the coherence protocol allow us to implement atomic instructions, which in turn allow us to implement critical sections in parallel programs. All parallel programming libraries including *pthreads* and *OpenMP* implement a variety of locking mechanisms that allow us to create many kinds of critical sections. Additionally, they ensure fairness by providing a guarantee on how long it will take a thread to acquire a lock.

However, there are problems with such conventional mechanisms. Consider the following C code snippet to credit or debit money from a bank account referred to as *account*. In this case, the bank account is an instance of a class of type *Account*. Let the *Account* class have a single field called *balance*. The way we present the following code snippet is similar to the way we presented the notion of critical sections in Section 9.4.7, where each line corresponds to a line of assembly code.

Listing 9.2: Java code to update the balance in a bank account. Assume that *account* is passed by reference (a pointer to it is passed).

```
void updateBalance(int amount, Account account){
    lock();

    int temp = account.balance;
    temp = temp + amount;
    account.balance = temp;

    unlock();
}
```

In this case, we lock all three lines. However, if a bank has a lot of accounts, then it is not necessary that two accesses to the *updateBalance* function access the same data. In fact they might be accessing different sets of data (different accounts). There will be no overlap in terms of memory addresses between the two sets of accesses; however, given the nature of our critical section, we will only allow one of the threads to proceed. In other words, with conventional locks, we do not allow *disjoint access parallelism*. This means that if different threads access different accounts, we do not execute them in parallel. In the conventional code that we show, irrespective of the data being accessed, we encapsulate the statements accessing shared data in a critical section, and force threads to execute the critical section in sequence. This is good because it ensures correctness; however, it is bad because it limits opportunities for parallel execution.

Let us look at the term disjoint access parallelism in some more detail. It is defined as a property of a parallel program, where two threads can execute the same set of statements concurrently if they access different sets of data. A critical section as shown in Listing 9.2 that is enclosed between a lock and an unlock statement, does not allow disjoint access parallelism.

Definition 87
Disjoint access parallelism is defined as a property of a parallel program, where two threads can execute the same set of statements concurrently if they access different sets of data.

Now, to enable disjoint access parallelism, we can change the locking logic. Instead of having one single lock for the entire function, we can associate a different lock with each account. Before accessing an account, we need to acquire the lock associated with the account, and then once we are done with the processing, we can release the lock. The modified code is shown below.

```
void updateBalance(int amount, Account account){
    account.lock(); /* account specific synchronisation */

    int temp = account.balance;
    temp = temp + amount;
    account.balance = temp;

    account.unlock();
}
```

Having a separate lock for each account takes care of the problem of an absence of disjoint access parallelism. However, it introduces other problems. Let us consider realistic code where we might be accessing different accounts. In this case, before executing the code of the critical section, we need to lock all the accounts that might be accessed beforehand. At the end we release all the locks. For example, if we want to write a function to transfer money from one bank account to the other, then we need to lock both the accounts.

Sadly, we may have a deadlock situation. Assume that there are two accounts A and B. It can so happen that similar to deadlocks in an NoC, we have a situation where thread 1 holds the lock for A and waits for the lock for B, and there is a reverse situation with thread 2. Then no thread will be able to progress, because there is a circular wait between threads A and B. A wants a resource that B has and at the same time B wants a resource that A has. Similar to ordering virtual channels, we can use the same algorithm here. If we acquire the locks in order, for example, if we acquire the lock for A before we acquire the lock for B, it is not possible to have a deadlock.

Again this approach creates a few more problems. This means that we need to be aware of all the locks that a given critical section is going to acquire at the beginning of the critical section. This might not always be possible in critical sections with a complex control flow. In fact, when the address of the account is computed dynamically, we might not be aware of the lock variable's address till we execute the relevant statements at runtime. We can always be conservative by prohibiting certain kinds of code within the critical section, particularly, code that dynamically computes the addresses of locks, and also ensure that we acquire a superset of locks at the outset – more than what we actually require.

Many such techniques unnecessarily restrict our freedom in writing parallel code and also reduce performance. It is thus essential to look at a solution beyond locks such that we can write critical sections with ease, and without bothering about how we acquire locks and avoid deadlocks. We can borrow inspiration from the world of database design and introduce the notion of *transactions*. A transaction is defined as a block of code that executes atomically and allows disjoint access parallelism. This is exactly the property that we want, where in a certain sense the entire block of code executes as if it is a single instruction. Let us motivate our discussion by looking at how our running example will look like with support for transactions.

```
void updateBalance(int amount, Account account){

    atomic {  /* an atomic transaction */
        int temp = account.balance;
        temp = temp + amount;
        account.balance = temp;
    }
}
```

We create an *atomic* block where we assume that the code encapsulated within it executes atomically as a transaction – all or nothing. Moreover, it executes like a critical section and also allows disjoint access parallelism. This means that two instances of this code that access different variables can execute in parallel. The benefits of such an approach are obvious: ease of programmability and support for disjoint access parallelism. We need not bother about low level issues such as how locks are implemented.

Transactions have a notion of succeeding or failing. If a transaction succeeds, then it means that it was able to complete the execution of all the statements encapsulated within it. On the other hand, if there was interference from other threads meaning that different transactions clashed with each other by accessing the same set of addresses in a conflicting manner, the transaction might need to fail or *abort*. In this case, the transaction is said to have *failed* or *aborted*. In either case – success or failure – the transaction should appear to execute instantaneously; moreover, its partial state (before completing) should not be visible to other threads. Formally, a transaction is expected to possess the four ACID properties.

Atomicity: Either the entire transaction completes or if there is a problem (discussed later) the entire transaction fails. If a transaction fails, no traces of its execution are visible to the same thread or other threads. This is also known as all-or-nothing semantics.

Consistency: Let us define a valid state of a system as a state that has been created by following all the rules of program execution, coherence, and consistency. If the state of the system is valid before a transaction starts its execution, then the state is valid after the transaction finishes its execution. The transaction might either succeed or fail; irrespective of the outcome, it should appear that after the transaction is over, the state of the system is valid. For example, if a failed transaction leaves back some of its updates in the system, the state would be invalid. We need to ensure that this does not happen.

Isolation: Transactions are executed concurrently with other transactions and regular read/write instructions. Particularly with respect to other transactions, we wish to have a property akin to sequential consistency. The property of isolation states that a parallel history of transactions is equivalent to some sequential history of transactions, where transactions initiated by different threads execute one after the other. This further means that it appears that each transaction has executed in isolation.

Durability: Once a transaction finishes or *commits*, it writes its memory updates to stable storage. This means that those updates will not get lost.

Most transactional memory systems as of 2020 follow these four ACID properties. This ensures that each transaction looks like a large single instruction that executes atomically.

> **Definition 88**
>
> *A transaction is defined as a block of code that executes atomically. It acts like a critical section; however, it also allows disjoint access parallelism. The transaction appears to execute instantaneously to other transactions. A software or hardware mechanism that has support for transactions is a* transactional memory *system.*
>
> *A software-only mechanism is known as* software transactional memory *(abbreviated as STM). On similar lines, a hardware based mechanism is known as* hardware transactional memory *(abbreviated as HTM).*
>
> *If a transaction executes successfully, then it is said to finish normally, and the finish operation is called a* commit. *However, if it fails for some reason, then it is said to have* aborted.

9.7.1 Fundamentals of Transactional Memory

Let us now define some basic terminology with respect to transactions. Consider an atomic block of code. If we need to run it as a transaction, then we need support for transactions either exclusively at the level of software, or at the level of both hardware and software. At runtime, software or hardware entities will create transactions that will execute the instructions within an atomic block.

Conflicts

Consider a scenario, where we have two threads executing an atomic block. We thus have two transactions: TS_A and TS_B. If they access disjoint sets of variables, then they cannot affect each other's execution, and both the transactions can proceed in parallel. However, if there is an overlap in the set of variables that they access, then they are not executing in isolation. We would ideally like sequential consistency to hold among transactions, which means that they should appear to execute serially. Either TS_A sees the state written by TS_B or vice versa. However, if they are executing concurrently on different cores, and modifying the same set of variables, this will not happen. One of the transactions needs to be either stalled or it needs to abort.

If such a scenario arises, we say that the transactions are conflicting, or they have a conflict. A conflict is defined as follows. Let the set of variables that a transaction reads be defined as its read set ($\mathcal{R}$), and let the set of variables that a transaction writes be defined as its write set ($\mathcal{W}$). Let the read and write sets of transaction TS_A be $\mathcal{R}_A$ and $\mathcal{W}_A$ respectively. Similarly, let the read and write sets of transaction TS_B be $\mathcal{R}_B$ and $\mathcal{W}_B$ respectively.

We say that TS_A and TS_B *conflict* if and only if any one of the relations (shown below) is true.

$$\mathcal{R}_A \cap \mathcal{W}_B \neq \phi \tag{9.16}$$

$$\mathcal{W}_A \cap \mathcal{R}_B \neq \phi \tag{9.17}$$

$$\mathcal{W}_A \cap \mathcal{W}_B \neq \phi \tag{9.18}$$

In simple terms, if one transaction writes something that another transaction reads, then they have a conflict. Or, if two transactions write to the same variable, then also they have a conflict. However, if their read sets overlap ($\mathcal{R}_A \cap \mathcal{R}_B$), then this is not a conflict because we can read the same data in any order – it does not matter. At this stage, please realise that the notion of conflicts among transactions is similar to dependences between instructions. If two instructions have a dependence, they cannot execute in parallel.

Concurrency Control

With each conflict, we define three events of interest: occurrence, detection, and resolution. A conflict is said to have *occurred*, when the conflicting memory accesses happen (read-write, write-read, or write-write). It need not be *detected* immediately, it can be detected later. However, we are not allowed to detect a conflict after the transaction finishes – it will be too late. After we detect a conflict, we must *resolve* it. We can either roll back one of the conflicting operations and stall the transaction that issued it, or we can kill one of the conflicting transactions. Killing a transaction is also known as *aborting* a transaction. Sometimes aborting a transaction is the best choice, otherwise if we stall transactions, we might create a deadlock.

The timing of these events varies with the TM (transactional memory) system. It depends on the type of concurrency control, which is defined as the way in which we deal with accesses to shared variables. There are two common kinds of concurrency control: pessimistic and optimistic.

Pessimistic Concurrency Control In this type of concurrency control, conflict occurrence, detection, and resolution happen at the same point of time. In other words, this means that we do not execute any instructions after we detect a conflict, and this saves wasted work. However, we need to work harder to detect conflicts every time there is a memory access. In software-only schemes, this is hard to do; however, in hardware based systems, this approach does not have significant overheads.

Optimistic Concurrency Control In this case, we allow transactions to execute without performing a lot of checks while they are accessing memory variables. When a transaction completes, we check if it has completed successfully, and if there are any conflicts. If there are no conflicts, then the transaction commits, otherwise it aborts. This kind of concurrency control is well suited for software transactional memory systems, because this minimises the work that needs to be done for each memory access. We simply need to check for conflicts at the end, which involves fewer instructions.

Conflict Detection

With pessimistic concurrency control, we detect conflicts as soon as they occur. This is also known as eager conflict detection. There are many flavours of eager conflict detection. We can either detect the conflict when the transaction accesses a variable or a cache block for the first time or when its coherence state changes, or we can detect conflicts every time the variable is accessed. The latter is a very inefficient approach, and thus is typically not preferred.

The other paradigm of conflict detection is lazy conflict detection, where we detect a conflict after it has occurred. This happens in systems with optimistic concurrency control. Here also, we have many different approaches. We either detect a conflict at the time of committing a transaction, or we can detect it at specific points in the transaction known as *validation* points. The validation points can be inserted by the compiler, or can be decided dynamically by the hardware. At these validation points a dedicated thread or hardware engine checks for conflicts.

Conflict detection has some subtle complications. Assume that transactions TS_A and TS_B conflict. However, later TS_B gets aborted. It would have been wrong to abort TS_A based on the conflict, because its conflicting transaction TS_B ultimately got aborted. Hence, many systems have dedicated optimisations to take care of such cases.

Version Management

To ensure that a transaction executes in isolation, we need to ensure that all of its updates are not visible to other threads. This means that it needs to create a new *version* of memory for itself. This version of memory contains the values of all the variables/memory locations before it started, and the changes it has made to the variables in its write set. The changes that a transaction makes to memory is known as the transactional state, and this needs to be made visible only after the transaction commits. Managing the transactional state is also known as version management.

Eager Version Management

There are two kinds of version management: eager and lazy. In eager version management, we directly make changes to memory. The write set is not separately buffered in any software or hardware structure. A thread goes ahead and changes the values of variables in memory, this reduces the read or write time. To safely recover the state if the transaction is aborted, we need to maintain an undo log. The first time that the thread writes to a variable in a transaction, it saves its previous value in an undo log, which can be a structure in hardware or software. Subsequent changes need not be logged because if there is an abort, we only need the value that existed before the transaction began.

Eager version management is very efficient for large transactions that abort very infrequently. All the updates to variables are directly sent to memory. Commits are fast because the changes are already there in memory. In comparison, aborts are very slow. We need to read all the values from the undo log and restore the memory state. However, the most important problem is maintaining isolation. If the values are written directly to memory, then other threads can see data written by the transaction before it has committed. This violates the property of isolation.

There are two ways of dealing with this problem. In software based systems, we add a version number to each variable in the write set. At commit time, we increment the version of each variable in the write set. Additionally, we lock each variable before writing to it. This ensures that other transactions cannot write to the variable at the same time. For transactions that read the variable, they record the version number, and also check the version number when they commit. If the version numbers do not match, then it means that some other transaction has written to the variable in the meanwhile. We shall discuss such schemes later in Section 9.7.3.

For hardware based systems, we augment each cache line with additional bits that indicate whether a variable has been read or written by an active transaction. The system does not supply the values of such variables to memory accesses made by other threads. This ensures isolation. Once a transaction commits or aborts, it is necessary to clear all such bits. There is a fast method in hardware to clear such bits. It is known as *flash clearing*. Flash clearing can be used to quickly set or unset a given bit in all the lines of a cache. We can then discard the undo log.

If a transaction with eager version management aborts, then we need to read each entry in the undo log, and send the corresponding write to the memory system. This ensures that the changes made by the transaction are not visible to any other thread. Note that as compared to commits, aborts are more expensive in terms of time.

Important Point 16

Let us provide the main insight regarding flash clearing. The reader might want to go through the relevant background in Section 7.3 before reading this paragraph. If a cache line is 64 bytes, only one or two additional bits are used to store transactional state, and they may need to be flash cleared after a transaction commits or aborts. It is often a good idea to create a separate subarray to store the bits that need to be flash cleared. We need to support two kinds of accesses for this subarray. We need to read/write the bits, and flash-clear them. For reading and writing, we can use the same mechanism as the data array, where the decoder drives the corresponding word line to high, and then we read the value through the bit lines. For flash clearing, we need to ensure that all the cells in the entire subarray store a logical 0 after the operation is over. One solution is to enable all the word lines, set one bit line to a logical 0, and the other to a logical 1. By using this approach, we can write a logical 0 to all the memory cells in a single cycle. Another approach is to create a 2-ported memory, where we have two word lines. One word line can be used for regular access, and the other can be used for the purpose of flash clearing (writing a 0 to the cell). These approaches

> *have different trade-offs in terms of the complexity of the decoder and the overheads in creating an additional memory port.*
>
> *Regardless of the design, simultaneously writing to an array of memory cells is difficult. We typically need a large amount of current to charge or discharge so many transistors. This places an unreasonable demand on the power grid. Hence, a lot of practical flash clearing systems [Miyaji, 1991, Rastegar, 1994] propose to divide the subarray into different continuous groups of memory cells. We clear them in stages. We first clear the bits in the first group, then after a given time delay we move to the next, and so on. This ensures that at no point of time, we place an unreasonable demand on the power grid of the chip. This does increase the latency of the entire operation; however, faults related to an excessive current draw do not happen.*

Lazy Version Management

In lazy version management, we have a redo log that unlike an undo log stores data written by the transaction. All the variables in a transaction's write set have an entry in the redo log. Whenever, a transaction writes to a variable for the first time, it adds an entry for it in the redo log. Any subsequent read request made by the transaction needs to check for the variable in the redo log first. If the variable is present, then we treat its value as the current value of the transactional variable. If we do not find an entry, then we need to read the value of the variable from the regular memory system.

In this case, commits are more expensive than aborts. While committing a transaction, we need to write its entire redo log to memory. Moreover, all read requests in a transaction now have to be routed through the redo log. If they find their data in the redo log, then they need to use it. However, if they do not find their data, they need to read it from the regular memory system. The redo log basically acts like a cache. In the case of aborts, we simply need to discard the redo log; nothing else needs to be done.

The redo log per se can be stored as a software structure or as a separate hardware buffer. The good thing about a redo log is that it is more flexible, and allows us to support very large transactions. Since buffering the transactional state is an issue with eager version management, this approach is more scalable.

> **Way Point 13**
>
> - *The methods to manage concurrent transactions are collectively known as concurrency control mechanisms. There are two broad families of approaches: optimistic concurrency control and pessimistic concurrency control.*
>
>   - *In optimistic concurrency control, we detect and recover from a conflict possibly after it has occurred. This means that we execute instructions after the conflicting accesses, and fix any resultant problems later.*
>
>   - *In pessimistic concurrency control, whenever a conflict occurs, we immediately detect it and try to resolve it.*
>
> - *There are two ways for detecting conflicts: eager and lazy. Eager conflict detection implies that we detect a conflict as soon as it occurs, as opposed to lazy conflict detection where we detect it much later.*

> - *On similar lines, we have two kinds of version management: eager and lazy.*
>
>   - *Eager version management implies that we write directly to the memory system. We maintain an undo log. We flush it if the transaction commits, and restore the state upon an abort. With this scheme commits are much faster than aborts. The main problem is maintaining the isolation property, where we need to ensure that other transactions are not able to read the temporary state of a transaction.*
>
>   - *Lazy version management requires a redo log. While a transaction is active, all the writes are sent to the redo log. It acts as a temporary cache for the transaction, which the read operations need to check first. In this case, aborts are fast because we just need to discard the redo log; however, commits are slow because the entire contents of the redo log need to be written to the program's permanent state.*

9.7.2 Correctness Conditions

The same way we defined correctness conditions for parallel programs, we need to define some correctness conditions for transactions. There are a few widely used models for transactional correctness. Let us discuss a few of them. Note that in the following subsections, we only discuss correctness models for transactions. We do not discuss the interactions of transactions with non-transactional instructions. These are known as *mixed mode accesses*, and will be discussed later.

Serialisability

This is a direct import from the world of databases with the same meaning. It states that a parallel execution with transactions should be equivalent to a serial execution with the same set of transactions. In other words, it should be possible to order the transactions in some sequence such that the results of both the executions are the same. In general, it is assumed that the transactions issued by the thread take effect in program order, hence, we shall use this as a necessary property in the definition of serialisability. This is like sequential consistency at the level of transactions. Furthermore, the property of serialisability does not specify the behaviour of transactional accesses with respect to non-transactional accesses.

Strict Serialisability

This is an extension of serialisability, where we consider the real-time order as well. If transaction TS_A created by thread 1 completes before transaction TS_B (created by thread 2) starts, then the property of serialisability does not say anything about how they should be ordered in the equivalent sequential order. TS_A can be ordered before TS_B or vice versa. However, strict serialisability says that if TS_B begins after TS_A completes, then TS_B has to be ordered after TS_A in the sequence. If TS_A and TS_B are concurrent, which means that they overlap in time, then they can appear in any order in the equivalent sequence. For non-concurrent transactions, this property effectively enforces a real-time order on the transactions.

Opacity

The main problem with strict serialisability can be seen in the following example (see Figure 9.60). Here, we read from two variables x and y. Initially, both of them are initialised to 0. The transaction by thread 2 sets both of them to 5. Now, assume that we have lazy conflict detection (at commit time), and eager version management. If we take a look at the transactions, we can quickly conclude that $t1$ should always be equal to $t2$. If the transaction of thread 2 executes first, then both x and y are equal to 5, otherwise both of them are equal to 0. It will never be the case that $t1 \neq t2$. Thus, thread 1 will never go into an infinite loop.

Listing 9.3: Thread 1

```
atomic {
    t1 = x;
    t2 = y;
    while (t1 != t2) {}
}
```

Listing 9.4: Thread 2

```
atomic {
    x = 5;
    y = 5;
}
```

Figure 9.60: A code snippet showing the need for opacity (adapted from [Harris et al., 2010])

This argument is correct for committed transactions because committed transactions need to follow all the ACID properties. However, we cannot say the same for aborted transactions that can read incorrect data, and then as a consequence get aborted. In this case, we use eager version management, which means that as soon as we effect a write, the value is visible to the rest of the transactions. They can access the variable; however, they may get aborted in the future. Here, thread 2 writes 5 to x. Then transaction 1 begins. It reads $x = 5$ and $y = 0$. In this case, thread 1 needs to get aborted. This will only happen when it reaches the end of the transaction. Sadly, before it reaches the end, we check if $t1 = t2$. This turns out to be false, and thus thread 1 goes into an infinite loop and never aborts. This behaviour was not expected.

The reason that we have this behaviour is because we did not define the correctness semantics for aborted transactions. We only defined them for committed transactions. Given that the transaction by thread 1 is aborting, we assumed that it need not follow any rules. This however lead to an infinite loop, and as far as the entire system is concerned, this execution is incorrect. We thus need to define a correctness model for aborted transactions as well. This model is known as *opacity*, which extends strict serialisability by saying that it should be possible to order all transactions – committed, running or aborted – in a linear sequence. Every transaction Tx, committed or aborted, needs to see a consistent state, which is defined as the state produced by all the committed transactions ordered before Tx in the linear sequence. Furthermore, no transaction should be able to see the writes made by an aborted transaction. The execution in Figure 9.60 will not lead to an infinite loop if the TM system follows opacity.

Mixed Mode Accesses

Till now we have only discussed correctness models for transactions. We have not included non-transactional accesses in our discussion. Let us now consider non-transactional accesses as well. Since we are considering both transactional as well as non-transactional accesses, let us refer to such accesses as *mixed mode accesses*.

Single Lock Atomicity

The simplest correctness model in this space is known as *Single Lock Atomicity* or SLA. We assume a hypothetical lock variable that has a global scope. Let us consider an execution to be valid if all the transactions *appear to* first acquire the hypothetical global lock, and then release it at commit/abort time. If an execution or a TM system follows this property, then we say that it satisfies single lock atomicity.

This model takes mixed mode accesses into account very well. We can borrow all the results from an equivalent lock based program, where we replace each transaction begin event with an acquire operation that acquires the global lock, and we replace the completion (abort/commit) of each transaction with a lock release operation. For example, in a TM system with SLA we have a data race, if the equivalent lock based execution has a data race.

The main problem with SLA is that it does not allow disjoint access parallelism, and creates unnecessary dependences between all the transactions in the system. Now, all of them need to acquire the same global lock. This defeats the purpose of having a TM system.

Disjoint Lock Atomicity

The problem of an absence of disjoint access parallelism in SLA is readily solved by adopting another correctness criterion called *Disjoint Lock Atomicity* or DLA. Here, a transaction acquires all the locks for the variables that it accesses before hand. Then the transaction progresses. It finally releases all the locks when the transaction finishes. This model allows disjoint access parallelism, and we can realise many of the expected gains of transactional memory.

Even though DLA sounds very appealing, its biggest drawback is that we need an exact knowledge of the locks that a transaction needs. Later transactional models (see Section 9.7.3) have relaxed this requirement to make the DLA model more practical. They require the transaction to acquire locks for all the variables that it accesses just before the first access to each variable. We thus need not know which variables a transaction is going to access a priori.

Transactional Sequential Consistency

Transactional sequential consistency (TSC) is defined as an extension of sequential consistency for TM systems. It is defined on the same lines as opacity and traditional sequential consistency. It says that we can order all transactions (committed or aborted) and all non-transactional instructions in a linear sequence. In this sequence, all the instructions including the ones within transactions appear in program order.

We have the notion of transactional data race freedom (TDRF), which prohibits races between non-transactional accesses, and races between transactional and non-transactional accesses. On similar lines, we can prove that TDRF programs obey TSC.

9.7.3 Software Transactional Memory

Software Transactional Memory (STM) is a popular paradigm for implementing transactional memory systems. An STM is easy to use and it requires changes to just the compiler or the runtime. Unlike hardware transactional memory, it does not suffer from limitations of space. We shall describe two commonly used STM algorithms in this section. They are at different points in the design space of transactional memory technologies.

First, we need to augment each variable used in transactions with some additional data called *metadata*. This metadata is used to track different versions of a variable, check for conflicts, and effect commits and aborts. Different algorithms use different kinds of metadata. In addition, each transaction maintains a read set and a write set. The read set contains the set of variables read by the transaction, and the write set contains the set of variables written by the transaction.

Finally, the compiler or the runtime convert every read or write operation into equivalent *readTX* and *writeTX* operations. In addition to performing regular reads and writes, these operations execute additional code to check for conflicts, and also buffer either speculative data, or data that has been overwritten. Let us look at two popular designs in this category.

Bartok STM

The Bartok STM [Harris et al., 2006] uses optimistic concurrency control for reads, with eager version management (an undo log), and lazy conflict detection.

Figure 9.61: Structure of a transactional variable

Every transactional variable has three fields (see Figure 9.61): value, version, and lock. The *value* field (as the name suggests) is the value of the variable. The version is a monotonically increasing integer that indicates the version of the variable. Every time we write to the variable, the version number is incremented. Finally, the *lock* field is a 1-bit value that indicates if the variable is locked or not.

Read Operation

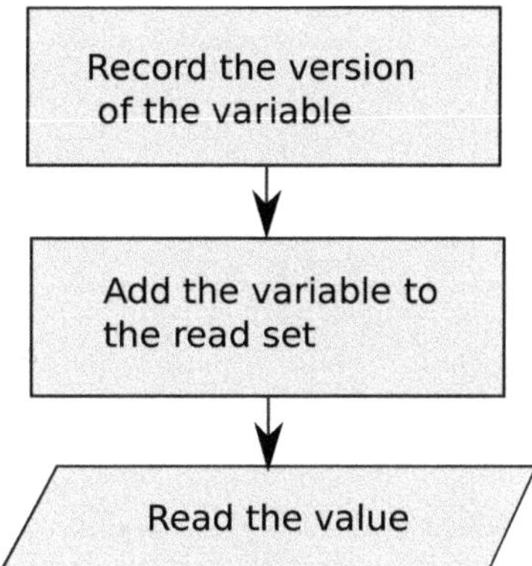

Figure 9.62: A read operation in the Bartok STM

A basic read operation is very simple as shown in Figure 9.62. We first record the version of the variable, then we add it to the read set of the transaction, and finally we read the variable and return its value. The main reason for recording the version of the variable is to use this information to detect a conflict later. If it is found out that we read an outdated version, then the transaction needs to be aborted. We shall see later that the version of a variable is incremented if a write to that variable commits.

Write Operation

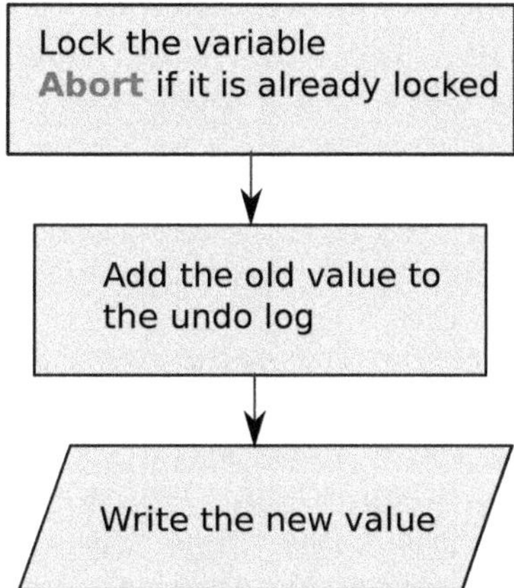

Figure 9.63: A write operation in the Bartok STM

In the write operation, we first try to lock the variable. This is to ensure that no other thread modifies the variable during the transaction. If the variable is already locked by another transaction, then we abort the transaction. In other words, this means that the current transaction cannot proceed. If we are successful in getting the lock, then we add the old (previous) value of the variable to the undo log. The *undo log* in this case is a region in software that stores the old values of variables. Once, we have added the value to the undo log, we proceed to effect the write. In this protocol, both the read and write operations are simple. Let us now look at the commit operation. Figure 9.63 shows the flow of actions.

Commit Operation

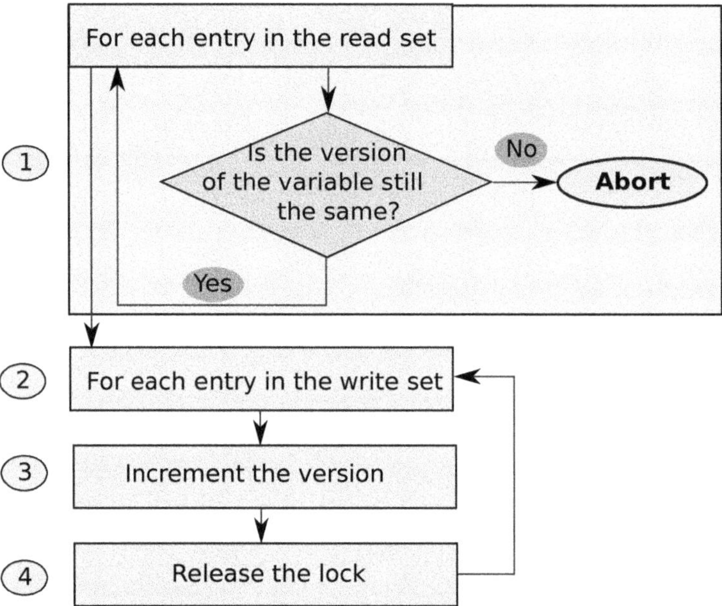

Figure 9.64: The commit operation in the Bartok STM (the numbers indicate the sequence of actions)

We commit a transaction when we finish executing the last instruction in the transaction. The commit protocol is shown in Figure 9.64. We have separate actions for the read set and the write set. For each entry in the read set, the protocol is as follows. For each variable, we compare its recorded version (at the time it was read by the transaction for the first time), and the current version. If the versions are not the same, then we can conclude that there was an intervening write by another transaction. Thus, the current transaction needs to abort because in this case the two transactions are conflicting. After we abort the transaction, we release all the locks.

For each entry in the write set, we first increment the version, and then release the lock. This ensures that all other transactions see the results of this transaction, and also perceive the fact that the variable has been updated. Once we have committed a transaction, we can discard its undo log. Let us now understand why this protocol works.

Consider a read operation for variable x. Between the time that it is read for the first time in the transaction, and when we commit the transaction, we are sure that no intervening write has committed. A transaction that writes to x is thus ordered after the current transaction. Hence, a read-write conflict is handled correctly. Now consider write operations. We need to lock a variable during the lifetime of its use within a transaction. We lock it the first time that we use it, and keep it locked till we are ready to commit the transaction. This ensures that no other transaction can write to the variable. Any transaction that will write to the variable has to wait till the current transaction is over. This ensures that we do not have write-write conflicts in our system.

Let us now consider the pros and cons. This approach is simple, and read operations simply need to record the version of the variable. However, write operations are expensive. It is necessary to lock the variables, and this increases their delay. Since this method uses lock and unlock operations, the performance is dependent on how many variables within a transaction need to be locked, and how long it takes to acquire a lock.

Since this protocol uses eager version management, commits are fast because nothing needs to be written to memory. The final state has already been written to memory. However, aborts are more expensive because we need to restore the state of all the variables that have been written to. This is done by reading the undo log, and replacing the contents of each entry with the value stored in the undo log.

From the point of view of correctness, this protocol provides a strong semantics for transactions in the sense it ensures that all the transactions are serialisable. However, it does not provide opacity, which also mandates that aborted transactions see a consistent state.

TL2 STM

Let us now look at another STM solution that works very differently, yet provides opacity. It is known as the TL2 STM [Dice et al., 2006]. Unlike the Bartok STM, it uses lazy version management, which means that it requires a redo log. In this transaction memory protocol, we have a monotonically increasing atomic global counter that provides a timestamp to every invoking process. Every time a transaction Tx starts, it reads and increments the global counter. The timestamp provided by the global counter is stored as $Tx.rv$ (field called rv (read version) in the transaction). In addition, the metadata corresponding to each transactional variable contains two additional fields: a timestamp and a lock.

Read Operations

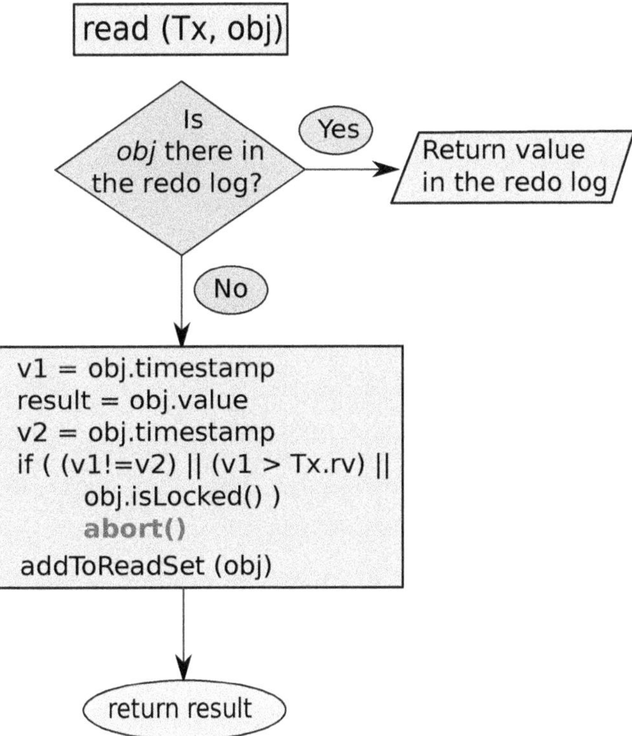

Figure 9.65: The read operation in the TL2 STM (adapted from [Harris et al., 2006, Harris et al., 2010])

Figure 9.65 shows the flow of the read operation. Since we have a redo log, whenever we read a value, we need to check in the redo log first. The redo log is a software structure that keeps the values of transactional variables till the transaction is over. If the variable is present in the redo log, then we return the value, otherwise we need to follow a complex protocol.

We first record the timestamp of the variable in $v1$. Then we read the value of the object, and then we read the timestamp of the variable once again, and store it in $v2$. Then we check a couple of conditions. If any one of them is true, we need to abort the transaction. The reasons are as follows.

[$v1 \neq v2$] This means that the variable has possibly changed between the time that it was read and the time that we are checking the timestamp for the second time. This algorithm is known as an *atomic snapshot*. The reason we need to do this is as follows. We are reading the value of the variable and the timestamp at the same time. It is possible that we read the timestamp first and then the variable changes. Then both the pieces of information will be out of sync. There is thus a need to read the timestamp once again and verify that it is the same. We will be sure that we have atomically collected a snapshot of both the variable and its timestamp. This is a standard technique that is used to read an object that spans multiple memory words. We read the timestamp twice – once before reading the variable and once after reading the variable.

[$obj.isLocked()$] If the variable is locked by some other thread, then this variable is in the process of getting updated. Its value cannot be read at the moment. Thus, the current transaction needs to abort.

[$v1 > Tx.rv$] This means that some other transaction has incremented the timestamp of the variable, after the current transaction began. We cannot guarantee the isolation of transactions, and thus the current transaction has to abort.

Note that in this case all the checks are being done at the time of reading. We are ensuring that a value that is being read is safe to read. We then add the variable that was read to the read set and proceed.

Write Operations

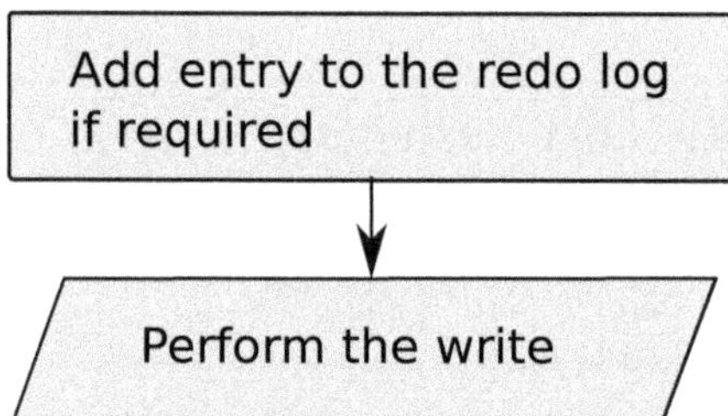

Figure 9.66: The write operation in the TL2 STM

A write operation is far simpler (see Figure 9.66). We just add an entry into the redo log if it is not already there, and we go ahead and perform the write. Note that in this case, the value that is written is sent to the redo log. Writes are made permanent only while committing.

Commit Operation

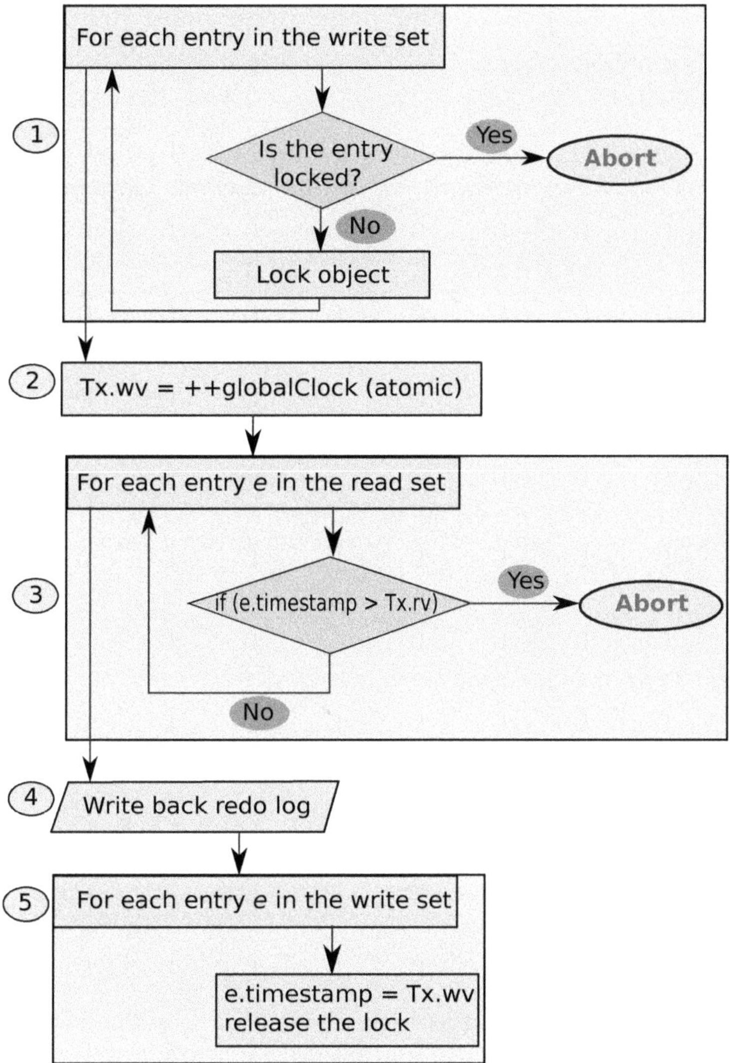

Figure 9.67: The commit operation in the TL2 STM (adapted from [Harris et al., 2010, Harris et al., 2006])

Figure 9.67 shows the flow of actions while performing a commit. For each entry in the write set, we lock the variable. If we are not able to lock any variable, then we need to release all the locks that we have obtained, and abort.

Now, assuming that we have gotten all the locks, we increment the global timer and get a new timestamp for the current transaction, which is stored in the variable $Tx.wv$ (write version). Next, we validate the read set. Note that in this protocol reads are expensive. We did a round of validations while reading a variable for the first time, and we need to do another round of validations at the time of validating the read set.

As shown in Figure 9.67, we compare the timestamp of each variable with the read timestamp of the transaction, $Tx.rv$. Recall that we had collected the read timestamp when the transaction began. This comparison checks if the variable has been updated after the current transaction began. If it has, then we need to abort the current transaction.

At this point, the read set and the write set have been validated. We can thus proceed with performing the writes. We read all the entries in the write set, get their values from the redo log, and write them to memory. These writes make the transaction visible. Once we are done with the writes, the redo log can be discarded.

Finally, we set each variable's timestamp to $Tx.wv$, and then we unlock all the variables in the write set. This finishes the commit process. We need to note a couple of subtle points in this algorithm.

1. With a redo log, commits are more expensive than aborts. If we need to abort the transaction, we just need to release all the locks and discard the redo log. Commits in comparison are more expensive.

2. We use two timestamps per transaction: $Tx.rv$ and $Tx.wv$. $Tx.rv$ is set at the beginning of a transaction by reading the value of the global counter, whereas $Tx.wv$ is set at the time of committing the transaction. $Tx.wv \geq Tx.rv + 1$.

3. We first write the variables to permanent state and then we update their timestamps. This ensures that if another transaction sees an updated timestamp, it is sure that the changes have been made to the permanent state.

4. As compared to Bartok STM, we do not hold locks for very long. They are only held for the duration of the commit operation. This is expected to be a short duration since the commit operations are a part of the transaction manager library and large delays are not possible by design.

9.7.4   Hardware Transactional Memory

Software transactional memory (STM) systems have numerous shortcomings. They essentially convert reads and writes into function calls. For every read and write in a transaction, it is necessary to call a function that records the version of the variable that is read/written, makes changes to the undo/redo log, and acquires a lock. Furthermore, at the end of a transaction, it is necessary to look at every single read and write in the read and write sets and take appropriate action. This can involve releasing the locks, comparing versions, and aborting the transaction (if necessary). Coming to correctness, even in models that provide opacity, they do not guarantee safety against data races when one of the accesses is outside the scope of a transaction. It is thus necessary to create support for supporting transactional operations in hardware.

Hardware transactional memory (HTM) has numerous advantages over STMs. Individual operations such as reads, writes, transaction begin and end events are much faster. In addition, maintaining undo and redo logs is done at the level of hardware, which can be done very efficiently. Along with performance advantages, hardware transactional memory requires little software support other than additional instructions to mark the beginning and end of transactions, and methods to indicate if a transaction has aborted or committed.

Coming to disadvantages, HTM systems have plenty of them. As is common in hardware based implementations, such augmentations increase the complexity of hardware and increase power consumption. Furthermore, hardware has more resource constraints. For example, if we wish to maintain undo or redo logs in hardware then this limits the size of a transaction. If a transaction requires more storage for storing values, then we need to either abort the transaction or create a complex mechanism to dynamically allocate more memory to the transaction from the regular memory space.

Let us appreciate these trade-offs by looking at the design of a HTM, which is inspired by LogTM [Moore et al., 2006] [4].

ISA Support

We need to add some extra instructions to the ISA. These instructions mark the beginning and end of transactions. Most versions of hardware transactional memory typically add three instructions: *begin,*

---

[4]The protocol that we describe is not exactly similar. Some simplifications and modifications have been made.

commit, and *abort*. An *abort* instruction is required to enable the software to automatically kill a transaction if a special circumstance arises. By default, the compiler or programmer place a *commit* instruction at the end of a transaction.

If we have nested transactions (transaction within a transaction), then the *begin* instruction increments the nesting level, and the *abort* and *commit* instructions decrement the nesting level. Transactions typically contain simple processor instructions that only make changes to memory and the registers. Most implementations of transactional memory do not allow transactions to make system calls or write to I/O devices.

Version Management

In any HTM protocol, we have a choice between eager and lazy version management. From the point of view of performance, using eager version management with an undo log is better, particularly if we have large transactions. In this case, values can be read and written directly to memory. We do not have to maintain a separate data structure to hold the values of transactional variables.

In our HTM, we shall use eager version management. Each thread creates an undo log in its virtual memory space. This log is stored in the physical memory space and can be cached. The algorithm for reads and writes is as follows. Whenever a transaction begins, the core sets a bit and remembers the fact that it is in a transaction. Till the transaction ends, we need to keep track of the read set and the write set. This is required to detect conflicts.

To help in this process our HTM adds two bits to every L1 cache line: R (read) and W (write). The R bit is set when we read a word in the line. When we write to a word in the line, we set the W bit. We need not set it all the time; we can set it only once at the time of the first write access. At this point of time, it is also necessary to write the previous value to the undo log, which is a dedicated memory region in the process's virtual address space. For subsequent writes to the same block, it is not necessary to modify the undo log. Once the transaction is over, there are fast mechanisms to quickly clear all the R and W bits within a few cycles. These are known as *flash clearing* mechanisms in caches [Miyaji, 1991, Rastegar, 1994] (see Point 16).

The main advantage of the R and W bits is that they identify the variables that have been read and written in a transaction. This information can then be used to detect conflicts. They implicitly represent the read and write sets.

Conflict Detection

The main advantage of using hardware is eager conflict detection. Unlike software based methods, where we need to perform elaborate checks, a hardware based conflict detection scheme can leverage the coherence protocol. Eager conflict detection saves a lot of wasted work. Secondly, since all processors support coherence, a minor modification to the coherence protocol to support transactions does not represent a significant overhead.

Whenever a given word is not there with a core, it sends a request to the directory asking for either read access or write access. If it is a read request, the directory forwards it to the cache that has a copy of the block. If it is a write request, then the directory needs to invalidate all the copies of the block that are there with other sister caches. In both cases, it needs to send a message to a set of sister caches, indicating that one of their blocks needs to be read or written by another cache.

This is where we can detect a conflict. For the subsequent discussion, let us assume a system with coherent L1 caches; it forwards all the directory messages to the cores, which forward them to their attached L1 caches after some processing. There are two kinds of replies that a core can send to a directory: *ack* and *nack*. It sends an acknowledgement (*ack*) if the access does not conflict with its read set or write set; otherwise, if there is a conflict, then it sends a *nack* message. This lets the directory know that a conflict has occurred; the directory then forwards this message to the requesting core. Once a conflict is detected it needs to be resolved, which means that one of the transactions involved in the conflict needs to either wait or get aborted.

The main problem with such kind of conflict detection is that if a cache evicts a block, and if the directory also removes its corresponding entry, then we will have no record of the fact that a given block is in the read or write set of a given core. This means that if a cache evicts a block that is a part of the transactional state of the core, the directory still cannot remove it completely. It can be removed from the list of sharers; nevertheless, its state still needs to be kept in the entry of the directory.

There are two cases: the block was in the M state or in the S state. When core C replaces a block that was in the M state, its corresponding entry in the directory transitions to the state $M@C$ (referred to as a *sticky* state). For example, if core 2 replaced a block, then the state is set to $M@2$. In addition, C sets its overflow bit – assume that each core has a dedicated *overflow* bit, which is initialised to 0, and reset to 0 when a transaction ends (commit or abort). The state $M@C$ means that currently there are no sharers for this block; C does not have a copy of it in its cache, even though this block is in its write set. When another core requests for the block, the directory forwards the request to core C with its current state ($M@C$). C infers that this block must be in its write set. If the transaction is still going on, then there is a conflict, otherwise core C can return an acknowledgement (refer to Figure 9.68).

Now, consider the second case: the block in core C was in the S state. Depending upon the protocol, we can either have silent evictions (no messages sent) or the core might send a message to the directory. Consider the more difficult case, where the eviction is silent. In this case, the directory has no record of the fact that C is no more a sharer. The next time it gets a write miss request from another core, it forwards the request to C. This is where a conflict can be detected (similar to the earlier case with writes).

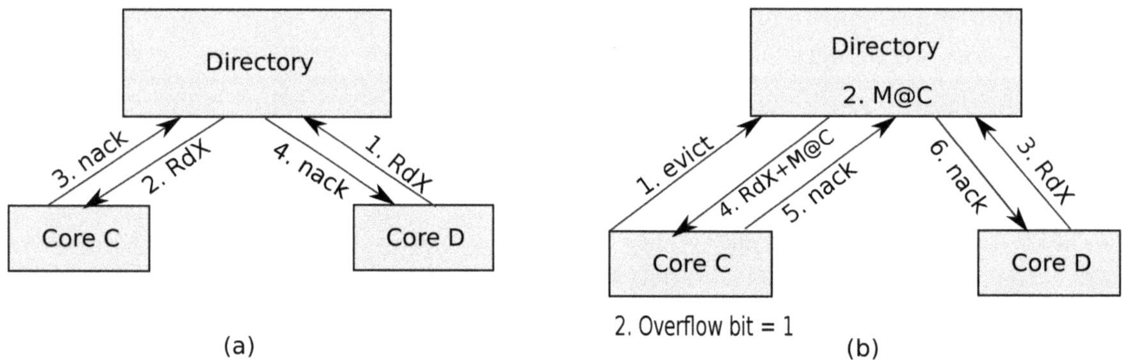

Figure 9.68: (a) Detection of a conflict (block present in the cache), (b) Detection of a conflict using the overlap and $M@C$ bits.

Subtle Correctness Issues

Let us conclude with looking at subtle correctness issues when it comes to evictions. If there is an eviction, then we need to send the block to the lower level. This means that we are also polluting the lower levels of the memory hierarchy with data that might belong to an aborted transaction.

Read and Write Sets

Let us first consider *what happens to the read and write sets* when a block is sent to the L2 cache from the L1 cache. In this case, we are maintaining the read/write sets implicitly using the R and W bits. If the block is evicted, this information is also gone.

However, we can avoid correctness issues by using the sticky states in the directory. They ensure that processing another access (transactional or non-transactional) will not lead to errors. If the other access is transactional, one of the transactions needs to abort because C will send a *nack* message. In this case, either the transaction on C will abort, or it will continue to run (other transaction will abort). In the former case, the read and write sets need to be discarded anyway, and in the latter case, the status quo will continue. Now, if the other access was non-transactional and we do not want it to wait, then the transaction running on core C needs to abort. This is because that other access cannot be rolled back because it is not a part of a transaction. The read and write sets will be discarded and this is the correct behaviour.

Contents of Evicted Blocks

The other issue that we need to account for is the contents of evicted blocks that are possibly written to the lower levels of memory. If a transaction is active, then no other transactions or non-transactional reads/writes can make conflicting accesses to the locations in its read and write sets.

There are two cases here: the original transaction commits or aborts. If the original transaction commits, then there is no issue. However, if it aborts, then we may end up with incorrect data populating the L2 cache. Fortunately, this will not cause a problem because we *need to write back the contents of the undo log*. Consider a block b that was evicted by core C, and this block was written to the L2 cache. If the transaction aborts, then the old contents of b will be written to the L1 cache, and thus the correct state of the memory system will be restored. Note that if L1 contains a block in the modified state (because of a write from the undo log), then the contents in the L2 cache do not matter. It is anyway assumed to have a stale copy of the data.

Commits and Aborts

With eager version management, commits are always easy. We need to flash clear all the R and W bits, reset the overflow bit of the core, and clear the undo log. In this case, an additional action that needs to be taken is that we need to ensure that all the sticky states created in the directory because of the committed transaction are cleared. One easy option is to send a message to the directory with the core id, C. The directory can then walk through all the entries whose state is $M@C$, and clear their states. If the write set is very small, we can send messages for all the blocks in the write set as well.

If a transaction aborts, we need to restore each entry stored in the undo log. The time taken for this step is proportional to the size of the undo log. After restoring the memory state, we need to flash clear all the RW bits, and reset the rest of the states as we had done in the case of committing a transaction.

9.8 Summary and Further Reading

9.8.1 Summary

Summary 8

1. *There are two major paradigms in parallel programming: shared memory and message passing.*

    (a) *In the shared memory paradigm, we assume that all the threads share the memory space and communicate via reading and writing variables.*

    (b) *In the message passing paradigm, threads communicate explicitly by sending messages to each other.*

    (c) *The shared memory paradigm is typically used in strongly coupled systems such as modern multicore processors, whereas message passing is used in loosely coupled systems such as cluster computers.*

2. *The speed up with parallel execution as a function of the number of computing units, and the sequential portion of the benchmark is governed by the Amdahl's law.*

$$Speedup = \frac{1}{f_{seq} + \frac{1 - f_{seq}}{P}}$$

Here, f_{seq} is the fraction of the execution that is sequential, and P is the number of processors.

3. *The Amdahl's law assumes that the size of the workload remains fixed as we scale the number of processing units. This is seldom true. The Gustafson-Barsis's law fixes this problem, and assumes that the parallel portion of the work scales with the number of processing units. The net speedup is thus as follows:*

$$Speedup = f_{seq} + (1 - f_{seq})P$$

4. *The Flynn's taxonomy defines the spectrum of multiprocessing systems: SISD (uniprocessor), SIMD (vector processor), MISD (redundant processing units in mission critical systems), and MIMD (multicores). MIMD processors can further be divided into two types: SPMD (master-slave architecture) and MPMD (regular multithreaded programs).*

5. *Hardware multithreading is a design paradigm where we share the pipeline between multiple concurrently running threads. Each thread has its PC, architectural registers, and rename table. The rest of the units are partitioned between the threads.*

6. *A typical multicore processor contains multiple processing cores that use the shared memory paradigm to communicate with each other. In such a system, having a single shared cache is not efficient in terms of performance, hence we need to have a distributed cache.*

7. *If a distributed cache follows the properties of coherence, then it appears to the program as a single shared cache. A distributed cache has a low access time and can support many parallel accesses by different cores.*

8. *A key correctness property of a memory system is PLSC (per location sequential consistency). This means that all the accesses to a single location can be laid out in a sequence such that each access is legal – every read gets the value of the latest write. PLSC needs to hold even in systems with non-atomic writes.*

9. *There are two fundamental axioms of cache coherence that naturally arise out of PLSC and the fact that in practical systems writes are never lost.*

   Write Serialisation Axiom *A write to the same location is seen in the same order by all the threads.*

   Write Propagation Axiom *A write is eventually seen by all the threads.*

10. *The behaviour of a memory system for multiple locations is governed by the memory model (or memory consistency model).*

11. *Sequential consistency (SC) is the gold standard for memory models. An execution is said to be in SC, if the memory accesses made by all the threads, can be put in some sequential order subject to the fact that in this sequential order the accesses of each thread appear in program order, and each read gets the value of the latest write.*

12. *SC forbids most optimisations such as write buffers, LSQs that send reads to the cache before earlier writes, complex NoCs that reorder messages, MSHRs, and non-blocking caches.*

13. *Hence, in practice, most memory consistency models relax the program order constraint because of performance issues. Many modern models such as those provided by IBM and ARM also allow non-atomic writes.*

14. *The standard theoretical tool to model executions is the method of execution witnesses. In an execution witness, we have four kinds of edges: a subset of program order edges (po), write $\rightarrow$ read dependence edges (rf: rfe and rfi), write serialisation edges (ws), and read $\rightarrow$ write edges (fr). ws and fr edges are a direct consequence of PLSC, and are present in almost all systems. However, the po and rf edges are relaxed (not present in the execution witness) to different degrees in different memory models. In an execution witness, we add all the edges corresponding to a memory model, and if there are no cycles, then it means that the execution is consistent with the memory model.*

15. *We also need to obey uniprocessor access constraints such that single-threaded code executes correctly on a multiprocessor machine and PLSC is not violated.*

16. *Most systems prohibit thin-air reads. This means that some data and control dependence relations need to be respected by the memory model.*

17. *To implement coherence we need a cache coherence protocol. If we have a small number of cores, then we prefer snoopy protocols, where all the cores are connected with a single bus. Otherwise we prefer the directory protocol, where the directory is a dedicated structure that is reachable via the NoC.*

18. *The two most common snoopy cache coherence protocols are the Write-Update and Write-Invalidate protocols.*

    (a) In the Write-Update protocol, we broadcast every write to the rest of the sisters caches. Even though we broadcast writes very quickly and eagerly, this protocol has a large overhead due to the frequent write messages.

    (b) The Write-Invalidate protocol solves this problem by broadcasting messages to the rest of the sister caches only when there is a write miss.

19. *We typically use the MESI protocol to implement the Write-Invalidate protocol. Each cache line has four states: Modified (M), Exclusive (E), Shared (S), and Invalid (I). In the Shared state, the cache can only read the block, in the Exclusive state we are sure that no other sister cache has a copy of the block (read-only access), and in the Modified state the cache is allowed to both read and write to the block. These protocols have elaborate state transition diagrams that determine the rules for transitioning between the states. We can additionally add an O (Owner) state that designates a given cache as the owner of a block – it supplies a copy of the block if there is a remote request.*

20. *In the directory protocol, we typically have a few centralised directory structures that maintain the list of sharers for each cache block. Whenever there is a read miss, a message is sent to the directory, it adds the new cache to the list of sharers, and asks one of the sharers to send a copy of the block to the new cache. If there is a write miss, then the directory sends an invalidate message to all the sharers, and ensures that a copy of the block is sent to the cache that wishes to write to it.*

21. *Atomic instructions that are used to implement locks and critical sections, are implemented using extensions of the coherence protocol. Different atomic instructions are powerful to different degrees; this is captured by the* consensus number.

22. *To implement different memory models, we need to explicitly enforce different orderings. This often requires sending acknowledgements for write completion and ensuring that the ordering of regular instructions with respect to synchronisation instructions is respected.*

23. *A* data race *is defined as a conflicting access of a regular variable by two concurrent requests across threads. When two requests access the same variable, where at least one of them is a write, they are said to be* conflicting. *Two requests are said to be* concurrent, *when there is no path between them in the execution witness that contains a synchronisation edge (edge between two synch operations).*

24. *Data-race-freedom implies SC. However, it is possible for an SC execution to have a data race. If we enclose all accesses to shared variables in critical sections and consequently disallow concurrent accesses, we can prevent data races. Such programs are said to be* properly synchronised.

25. *If a program has a data race on a machine that uses a non-SC memory model, then we can construct an execution of the program that has a data race and is in SC.*

26. *There are two common approaches for detecting data races: the lock set algorithm, and the algorithm based on vector clocks.*

27. *Traditional programming that uses critical sections is difficult for most programmers, and many desire simpler abstractions. Hence the paradigm of transactional memory was developed, where all that a programmer needs to do is mark a block of code as* atomic. *The runtime ensures that the block runs atomically, and it is not possible for any other thread to see a partial state (state in the middle of an atomic block's execution). Such atomic blocks are known as* transactions, *and such a system is known as a* transactional memory system.

28. *There are two kinds of transactional memory systems: STMs (in software) and HTMs (in hardware).*

    (a) *Transactions typically have a begin and end operation.*

    (b) *Every transaction has a read set and a write set – the set of variables read and written respectively. Two transactions T_i and T_j are said to conflict if either $R_i \cap W_j \neq \phi$, or $R_j \cap W_i \neq \phi$, or $W_i \cap W_j \neq \phi$.*

    (c) *If a transaction executes correctly without any conflicts (concurrent conflicting accesses), then it can commit (make its changes visible to the rest of the threads), else it needs to abort (none of the changes made by it are visible).*

    (d) *We can either detect conflicts eagerly or lazily (when the transaction ends).*

    (e) *Every transaction needs to temporarily buffer its state till it commits. There are two approaches in this space. Either it can eagerly write to the memory system, and rollback changes later if there is an abort (using an undo log). Conversely, it can adopt a lazy approach and buffer its writes in a redo log during its execution. The entries in the redo log can then be written to the memory system (permanent state), if the transaction commits.*

> 29. *STM systems instrument the transaction begin, end, commit, and abort operations to track the version of each variable, perform book keeping, and in some cases lock a few variables. When the transaction ends, they check if there have been any conflicting accesses during the lifetime of the transaction, and if there have been, then one of the conflicting transactions needs to abort. Otherwise, the changes are made permanent (committed). We discussed two STMs in this chapter: the TL2 and Bartok STMs.*
>
> 30. *Hardware transactional memory (HTM) systems modify the coherence protocol to track conflicting accesses to variables within the scope of transactions, and use this information to abort or commit transactions.*

9.8.2   Further Reading

Readers should start this chapter by first learning how to write parallel programs. They can refer to the book by Quinn [Quinn, 2017]. If they would like to get a better understanding of the material on the theory of memory models, then it is advisable that they read the first few chapters of the book by Herlihy and Shavit [Herlihy and Shavit, 2012]. This will teach them all about sequential and parallel executions, legal sequences, lock-free algorithms, and consensus numbers.

For cache coherence readers can start with a survey of implementations of cache coherence protocols by Stenstrom [Stenstrom, 1990] and then proceed to read the book by Sorin [Sorin et al., 2011]. For an early implementation of the directory protocol in the Stanford Dash multiprocessor, the paper by Lenoski et al. [Lenoski et al., 1990] is the most definitive reference. Modern implementations are described in the references [Abts et al., 2003, Vantrease et al., 2011].

For memory consistency models, readers should first read the tutorial by Adve and Gharachorloo [Adve and Gharachorloo, 1996] followed by the theses of the authors [Adve, 1993, Gharachorloo, 1995]. These references are at a fairly high level, to get a deeper theoretical understanding, it is necessary to read papers with more formal methods such as the papers by Alglave [Alglave, 2012], and Wickerson et al. [Wickerson et al., 2017]. For a micro-architectural perspective, we recommend the papers by Arvind et al. [Arvind and Maessen, 2006] and Lustig et al. [Lustig et al., 2014]. An important work in this space that generates tests for different memory models is the work by Mador-Haim et al. [Mador-Haim et al., 2011].

Much of the theory of DRF memory models was developed by Adve in her thesis [Adve, 1993]. Subsequently two papers discussed lockset based data race detection in software [Savage et al., 1997] and hardware [Zhou et al., 2007] respectively. Readers can refer to Prvulovic et al. [Prvulovic, 2006] for a method to detect races in hardware using simple timestamps.

For transactional memory, the book by Harris, Larus, and Rajwar [Harris et al., 2010] is a comprehensive reference. For important theoretical results refer to the work by Guerraoui [Guerraoui and Kapalka, 2008, Guerraoui and Kapałka, 2010].

Exercises

Ex. 1 — Write a shared memory program to perform merge sort in parallel.

Ex. 2 — What are the pros and cons of the shared memory and message passing schemes.

Ex. 3 — Why is it often better to use the Gustafson-Barsis's law in place of the Amdahl's law?

Ex. 4 — Why do we write the block back to the lower level on an $M \rightarrow S$ transition?

Ex. 5 — What is false sharing? How can we avoid it?

Ex. 6 — What are the advantages of the directory protocol over a snoopy protocol.

Ex. 7 — Consider a regular MESI based directory protocol, where if a line is evicted, we do not inform the directory. What kind of problems will this cause? How do we fix them?

* **Ex. 8** — In the MOESI protocol, we may have a situation where a block does not have an owner. This is because we do not have a mechanism for transferring the ownership. Propose a solution to this problem that has the notion of ownership transfer.

** **Ex. 9** — We need to create a new instruction called MCAS (multi-word CAS). Its pseudocode is as follows.

```
boolean MCAS (int* addresses[N], int oldValues[N], int newValues[N]) {
      int i, flag = true;
      for (i=0; i < N; i++) {
            if (*addresses[i] != oldValues[i]) {
                  /* old value does not match */
                  flag = false;
                  break ;
            }
      }

      /* at least one of the old values did not match */
      if (flag == false) return false;

      for(i=0; i<N; i++)    /* set all the new values */
            *addresses[i] = newValues[i];
      return true;
}
```

1. Provide a hardware implementation of MCAS that makes it appear to execute atomically. What changes do we need to make to the ISA, the pipeline, and the memory system. Note that we have to introduce a simple RISC instruction called MCAS. How do you give it so many arguments?

2. Given two variables stored in different locations in memory, we need to read an atomic snapshot where the snapshot contains a pair of values (one for each variable) that were present at the same point of time. We cannot use normal reads and writes (values might change in the middle). How can we use MCAS to do this? [Hint: Use timestamps]

3. Use MCAS to implement lock and unlock functions. Show the code.

* **Ex. 10** — Assume a cache coherent multiprocessor system. The system issues a lot of I/O requests. Most of the I/O requests perform DMA (Direct Memory Access) and directly write to main memory. It is possible that the I/O requests might overwrite some data that is already present in the caches. In this case, we need to extend the cache coherence protocol that also takes I/O accesses into account. Propose one such protocol.

Ex. 11 — Does PLSC guarantee SC? Does SC guarantee PLSC?

* **Ex. 12** — How does the method of execution witnesses provide an illusion of sequential execution?

* **Ex. 13** — You are given a machine with many cores. You don't know anything about the memory model that it follows. You only know that the rfe order is *global*. You are allowed to write parallel

programs, give them as input to the machine, and note the outcomes. If you run the program for let's say a million times, it is **guaranteed** that you will see all the possible outcomes that the memory model allows.

Write four programs to find if each of these four orders hold: $W \to R$, $W \to W$, $R \to W$, $R \to R$ (R means read, W means write). Prove that your approach will work using the method of execution witnesses. Try to minimise the number of instructions.

** **Ex. 14** — Consider the following relations between two loads, L and L', in a multiprocessor system.

$$\begin{aligned}
loc(L) &= loc(L') \quad (same\ location) \\
&\wedge (A, L) \in ghb \\
&\wedge (A, L') \in ghb \\
&\wedge (source(L), B) \in ghb \\
&\wedge (source(L'), B) \in ghb
\end{aligned}$$

$loc(L)$ refers to the memory address of L. Consider A and B to be two other memory accesses. ghb is the global happens before order. $(X, Y) \in ghb$ means that X needs to happen before Y. $source(L)$ refers to the store that produces the value for load L ($source(L) \xrightarrow{rf} L$).
Does $(A, B) \in ghb$ hold for all standard memory models, or only for some?

** **Ex. 15** — What changes should be made to the pipeline and the memory system to ensure that thin air reads do not happen with value prediction?

** **Ex. 16** — Consider the following code for the Peterson lock with two threads. The threads are numbered 0 and 1 respectively. For a thread, we assume that the function $getTid()$ returns the id of the thread. It can either be 0 or 1. If $(getTid() = t)$, then t is the id of the current thread, and $(1 - t)$ is the id of the other thread. *turn* and *interested* are global variables. Rest of the variables are local.

```
void lock(){
    int tid = getTid();
    int other = 1 - tid;

    interested[tid] = true;
    turn = tid;

    while ( (interested[other] == true) && (turn == tid))
        { /* keep looping */ }

    /* lock acquired */
}

void unlock(){
    int tid = getTid();
    interested[tid] = false;
}
```

1. Prove that this algorithm is correct in a sequentially consistent system.

2. Will this algorithm work in a system with weak consistency? Explain your answer.

3. Consider the TSO memory model that Intel uses. It has atomic writes, and the only ordering that is relaxed is the $Write \to Read$ ordering. Where do we need to add fence instructions? Explain the correctness of the code with fences.

For all the three problems preferably use execution witnesses.

** **Ex. 17** — In any execution witness with a cycle, and different addresses, is it possible to have a single *po* edge? Justify your answer.

** **Ex. 18** — Is it true that a memory model = atomicity + ordering? Prove your answer.

Ex. 19 — Consider the *RCpc* memory model. *RC* stands for release consistency. However, the only extra feature in this case is that the synchronisation operations follow the *pc* (processor consistency) memory model instead of sequential consistency. Prove that for properly synchronised programs, *RCpc* leads to PC executions.

Ex. 20 — How do lazy and eager conflict detection mechanisms differ from each other? What is the effect of these schemes on the overall system performance?

Ex. 21 — Prove that the TL2 system algorithm is correct.

Ex. 22 — Can transactional memory systems suffer from livelocks? If yes, how do you prevent them.

* **Ex. 23** — Define opacity. How do we ensure opacity in STM systems? Does hardware transactional memory guarantee opacity?

Ex. 24 — When we want to commit a transaction in an STM, we lock all the locations that were written. Can this lead to deadlocks? If yes, how will you avoid deadlocks?

Design Problems

Ex. 25 — Understand the working of cache coherence protocols in the Tejas architectural Simulator.

Ex. 26 — Design a circuit to implement the directory protocol in Verilog or VHDL.

Ex. 27 — Understand the memory models of different programming languages such as C++ 17 and JAVA.

Ex. 28 — Download a popular STM library. Use it to write parallel programs.

10

Main Memory

Till now we have been treating the main memory as a static and passive array of bytes. We have been assuming that once there is a miss in the last level cache (LLC), we send a request to main memory. It takes 100-300 cycles to get the answer back, and thus sending a request to main memory should be avoided at all costs. Unfortunately, the main memory is just not a block of DRAM. There is much more to designing main memory these days. In fact, inside the main memory we have a microcosm of DRAM banks, interconnections, and controllers. There is a small component of the main memory within the CPU chip as well. It is called the *memory controller*. The role of the memory controller is to take all the memory requests from the caches, queue them, schedule them, and send them to the main memory. We shall see in this chapter that the scheduling algorithm for the memory controller is very crucial. It is a very important determinant of the overall performance.

There are several challenges in managing large memories. As of 2020, it is not uncommon to find 1 TB memories in server class systems. Managing such a large memory in terms of scheduling accesses, and distributing the bandwidth among different cache banks and I/O devices is in itself a fairly complex problem. We need to understand that memory capacity has been increasing with Moore's law (refer to Section 1); however, DRAM access latency has traditionally reduced very slowly. Hence, there is a need to design effective strategies to bridge this gap – known as the *memory wall*.

Moreover, DRAM based memories sadly lose all their data once the system is powered down. The next time that we turn on the system, all the data needs to be read from the hard disk once again. This causes an unacceptable delay. Additionally, we need to periodically refresh a DRAM, which means that we need to periodically read all the blocks, and write them back again. If we do not refresh the values, the capacitors that hold the values will gradually lose their charge and the stored data will be lost. In modern DRAMs the refresh operation causes unacceptable delays, and thus there is a need to create memory that is nonvolatile in nature, which means that it maintains its state even after the system is powered off. Such modern memories are already being used in USB drives and many chips containing them are being produced commercially. In the future, we expect them to become commonplace in computing systems starting from small embedded systems to large servers. The latter half of the chapter will focus on such nonvolatile memories.

10.1 Dynamic RAMs: Devices, Circuits, and Systems

10.1.1 DRAM Cell

Recall our discussion in Section 7.3.1 where we created a 6-transistor SRAM cell; let us do something similar here. The most significant drawback of an SRAM cell is that each cell requires 6 transistors and thus the storage capacity is limited. If we could design a memory with a much smaller cell, then we could store more bits per unit area. Keeping this in mind, let us design a very simple memory structure, which is known as a dynamic memory cell or DRAM cell. It is shown in Figure 10.1. Note that the subsequent discussion assumes that the reader is well versed with the material presented in Chapter 7.

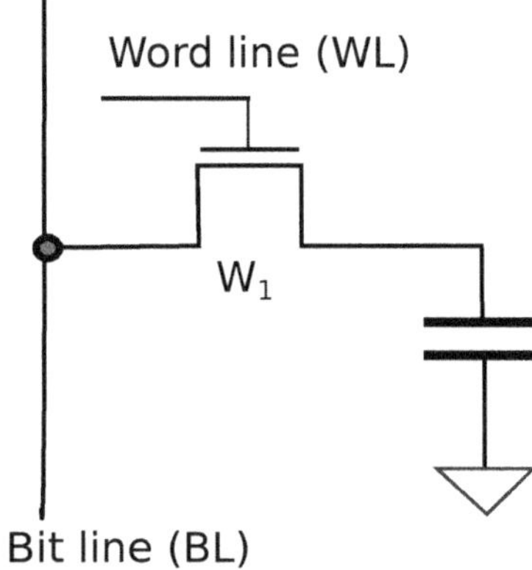

Figure 10.1: A DRAM cell

The charge is stored across a single capacitor and there is only one access transistor: W_1 in Figure 10.1. This is controlled by the word line. Recall that in the case of an SRAM cell there were two access transistors that were controlled by the word line. This is because the inverter-pair had two outputs. In this case, the capacitor has only one input/output terminal. Hence, only one word line transistor and one bit line are required.

The capacitor is particularly very important in this case because it is the charge storage device. Moreover, unlike an SRAM cell, a capacitor cannot maintain a steady voltage for a long period of time. Due to some current leakage between the parallel plates, ultimately all the stored charge will leak out. Even if the leakage current is very small, these capacitors will ultimately lose their stored charge. It is thus necessary to reduce the leakage current to as small a value as possible. The standard technique to handle this situation is that we periodically read the value of a DRAM cell and write it back. This ensures that even if the potential has dropped due to a leakage of charge, the voltage across the capacitor can be restored to the ideal level. This process is known as a *refresh*, and DRAM cells require periodic refresh operations to ensure that we do not lose any data.

Definition 89
The process of periodically reading the values of blocks in DRAM memory and writing them back is known as a refresh *operation. The capacitors in the DRAM cells gradually lose their stored charge; hence, it is necessary to periodically read their state and then restore the voltage across the capacitors to the ideal values.*

Keeping these considerations in mind, let us quickly look at the technology used to build capacitors for DRAM cells.

10.1.2   Capacitors used in DRAM Cells

To create a capacitor in silicon, we need to create two parallel plates and put a dielectric material in between. Given that we wish to maximise the density of DRAM devices, we need to make the capacitor as small as possible. Note that if the capacitor is very small, there is a possibility that its charge might leak out very quickly and we will need more refresh operations. Hence, there is a need to strike an optimal trade-off between storage density and the maximum time between two refresh operations issued to the same cell. There are two main methods that are used to create capacitors for DRAM processes. The first type of capacitor is called a trench capacitor that is embedded in the silicon substrate. The second type is called a stacked capacitor that is above the silicon surface.

Trench Capacitors

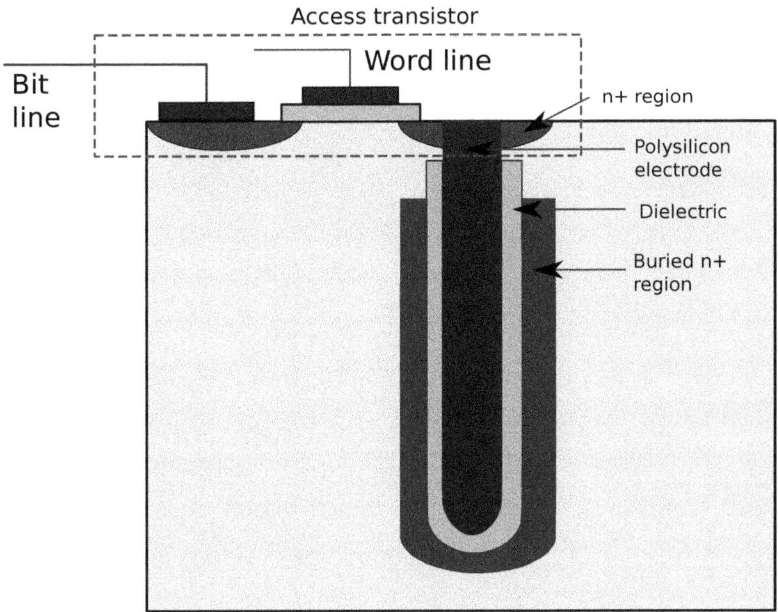

Figure 10.2: A trench capacitor along with the word line transistor.

The structure of a trench capacitor is shown in Figure 10.2. It is literally shaped as a trench or rather a deep hole in silicon. The hole is filled with a conducting material such as polysilicon. This acts like one of the plates of the capacitor, which is connected to a terminal of the access transistor of the DRAM. Often one of its electrodes is embedded within one of the terminals of the access transistor such that we do not need additional metallic connections between them. The next inner layer is made of an insulating dielectric such as Al_2O_3, HfO_2, or Ta_2O_5. This dielectric layer is typically very thin. For a 40 nm wide trench, it is typically in the range of 15-20 nm [Gutsche et al., 2005]. The only way to scale such designs is to have very deep trenches and have thin layers of dielectrics such that we can pack more capacitors per unit area. For a feature size of 40 nm, the trenches can be several microns deep (typically 4 to 6 microns), which means that the trench is 100 times as deep as it is wide! This allows us to increase its capacitance. The advantage of this design is that we can pack many such deep trenches in silicon without increasing the cross-sectional area. The dielectric is enclosed by a buried plate (or a region) made of n-type doped silicon. This acts as the other electrode, which is connected to the ground terminal.

Such trench capacitors are embedded in silicon and are ideal for embedded DRAMs in 3D chips.

We can have transistor layers or metal layers over the memory layer. These layers can have their own connections. The memory layer will not introduce any congestion or wire routing problems because it is below them.

Stacked Capacitors

Even though trench capacitors have many advantages, they have a few disadvantages as well. The major disadvantage is that the trench is hard to fabricate. Particularly at the deepest point, it is hard to guarantee the parameters of the trench. Hence, for many commercial processes, a stacked capacitor is preferred even though it requires more area and has structures above the silicon layer.

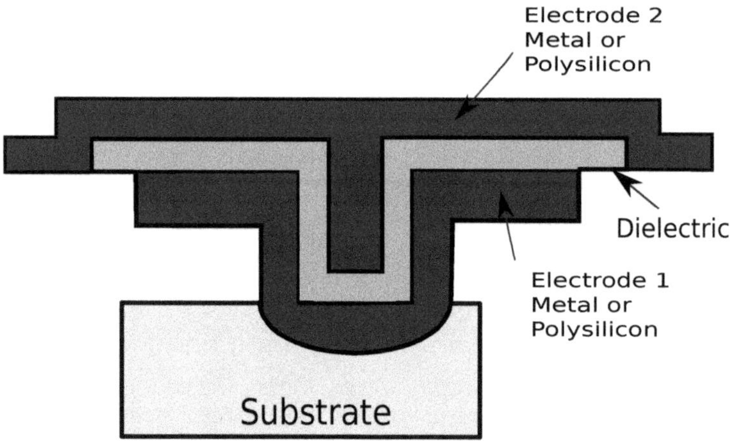

Figure 10.3: A stacked capacitor. The electrode touching the substrate is connected to one of the terminals of the word line transistor.

As shown in Figure 10.3, the stacked capacitor does not have deep trenches. It is a 3D structure, where the capacitor is fabricated in layers above the access transistor. One of the terminals of the access transistor is connected to a polysilicon electrode that is vertically stacked above it. The other electrode is also a polysilicon electrode, which is separated by a dielectric. Note that it is possible to replace polysilicon with metallic electrodes as well (depends on the process).

A stacked capacitor is still much better than a regular planar capacitor that is made on silicon because it is a 3D structure. The capacitor can be fabricated above one of the terminals of the access transistor and thus we can increase density. Modern avatars of stacked capacitors have multiple fins and some designs have a cylindrical structure. Such designs increase the density such that we can store more bits per unit area in a DRAM.

10.1.3 Array of DRAM Cells

Let us now create an array of DRAM cells on the same lines as an array of SRAM cells. Note that in this section we shall refrain from describing the basic underlying concepts of the design of an array of memory cells. The reader is referred to Section 7.3.1.

Recall that in an array of cells, the address is first sent to a row decoder, which enables one of the word lines in the 2D array of DRAM cells. This enables all the cells in a given row, which is also called a *page*[1]. They can then be accessed by the bit lines. Note that in this simplistic design we have a single bit line per memory cell. Each bit line is connected to a sense amplifier that senses the voltage and converts it to a logical 0 or 1. Unlike SRAM arrays, in a DRAM array we can only read a single column

---

[1]This is different from a page in virtual memory

in one cycle. We have a column multiplexer/demultiplexer (mux/demux) that chooses the right column to read or write. It is controlled by a column decoder that takes as input a set of bits from the address. The column mux/demux is connected to read and write buffers that buffer the values that are read or need to be written. The value that is read then needs to be sent on the CPU-memory bus.

An important point to note here is that in DRAM arrays the sense amplifiers appear between the bit lines and the column mux/demux. This was not the case in SRAM arrays. In SRAM arrays the bit lines were directly connected to the muxes/demuxes, and this structure was then connected to the sense amplifiers. The reasons for this will gradually become clear over the next few sections.

Important Point 17
A row in a DRAM array is also called a page.

Read Access

Figure 10.4 shows an array of DRAM cells. Let us consider a read access. The address first arrives at the row decoder. Recall that a decoder takes n inputs and produces 2^n outputs. The n inputs encode, in binary, the number of the output that needs to be set to a logical 1. For example, if $n = 3$, and the input bits are equal to 101, then it means that the 5th output (word line) is set to 1 (count starts from 0). This enables the corresponding word line, which enables all the cells in its row. The cells start setting the values of their attached bit lines. In a DRAM array we typically read an entire row at a time and buffer its contents.

Here also we can use the precharging trick, where we first set all the bit lines to a fixed voltage, which is typically half of the supply voltage ($V_{dd}/2$). Subsequently, we monitor the direction in which the voltage on the bit line is gravitating towards. If it is gravitating towards a logical 0, then we declare the bit to be 0, much before the voltage actually reaches 0 Volts, and vice versa for the case when the cell stores a logical 1. The advantage of precharging (see Section 7.3.1) is that we do not have to wait for the voltage to swing to either 0 or V_{dd}). We simply need to ensure that the voltage difference between the current voltage and the precharged voltage is more than the noise margin. This helps us significantly speed up the operation of a memory array. The reason that we can precharge the bit lines quickly is because we can use strong precharge drivers to pump in current into the bit lines; however, we do not have this luxury when a bit line's voltage is set by a feeble DRAM cell.

Now, consider the case where the capacitor in the DRAM cell stores a logical 1. When we enable the access transistor via the word line, the capacitor starts to charge the bit line. This means that stored charge from the capacitor flows towards the bit line and increases its voltage. This further means that the voltage across the capacitor in the DRAM decreases. The next time that we read this cell, the voltage across it might not be enough to infer a logical 1. This means that the DRAM cell will lose its value, which is not desirable. This phenomenon is known as a *destructive read*. The only way to avoid this situation is to ensure that we rewrite the value after it is read. This is known as *restoring* the value that has been read. This is essential in a DRAM and adds to the latency of a read operation.

Definition 90 *Once a DRAM cell is read, its capacitor loses its charge, and the cell cannot be read again. This phenomenon is known as a* destructive read. *It is thus necessary to* restore *the potential across the capacitor if it stored a logical 1.*

The circuit to detect these small voltage swings is called a sense amplifier (similar to sense amplifiers in SRAM arrays). Recall that a sense amplifier is a differential voltage amplifier that converts a small

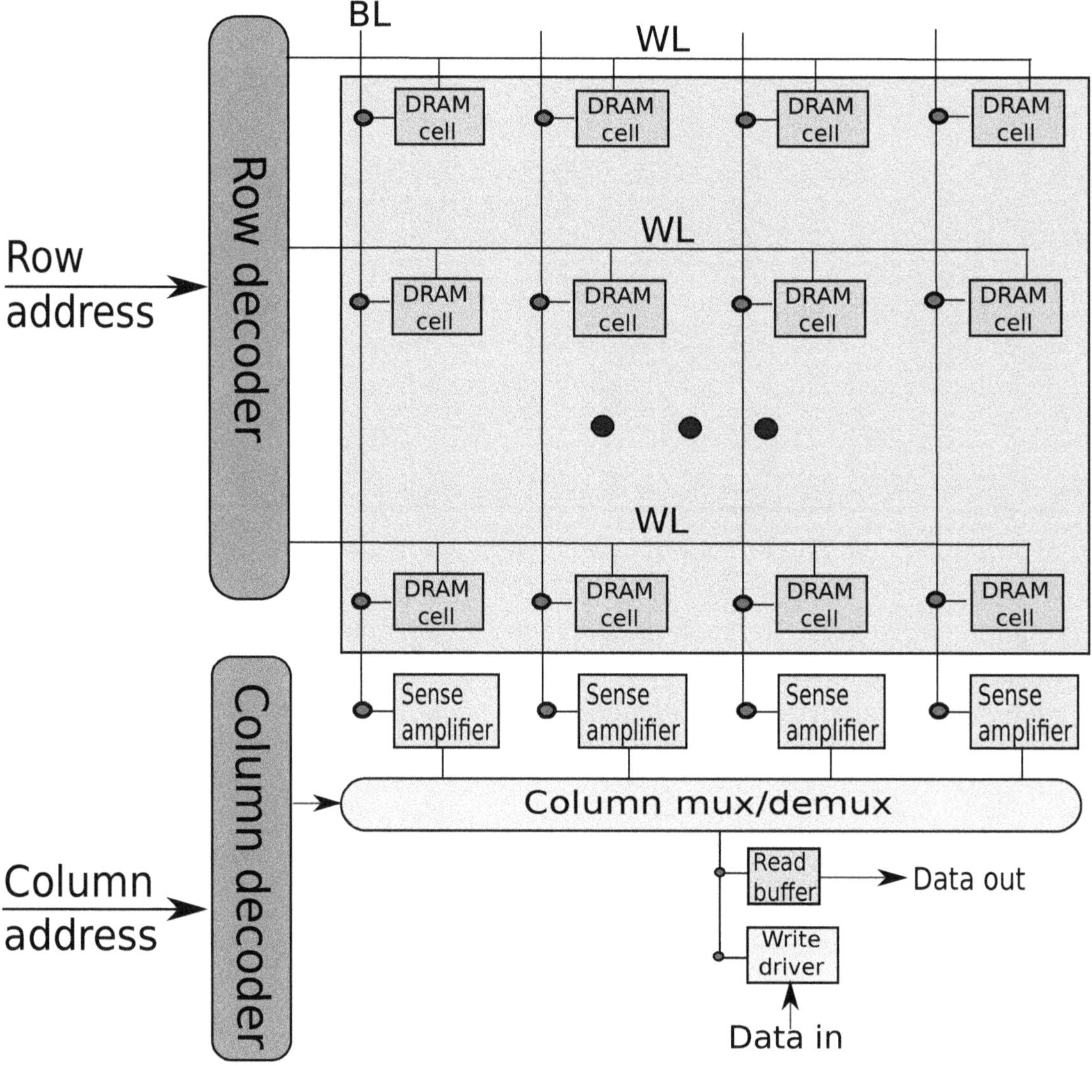

Figure 10.4: Array of DRAM cells

voltage swing to a logic level: 0 or 1. Once we have read the data and converted it into appropriate logic levels, it is buffered in the sense amplifiers. DRAM sense amplifiers are special in the sense that they function both as differential amplifiers as well as buffers. We can then choose the subset of the DRAM row that we are interested in. In a quintessential DRAM array, we typically choose a single bit to read or write to. This bit is selected using a column mux/demux that internally uses a column decoder. This data is sent to powerful driver circuits that send the data over the bus to the CPU.

Sense amplifiers for SRAM arrays have been discussed extensively in Section 7.3.1; however, DRAM sense amplifiers are slightly different. The specific differences are as follows. In an SRAM array, the sense amplifiers are placed after the column multiplexers. We first choose the appropriate set of columns, and then we sense their logic levels. However, in a DRAM array, sense amplifiers are placed before the column multiplexers. We first convert all the voltage values on the bit lines to logical 0s or 1s, and then we choose a subset of these values. The reasons for this are as follows. In a DRAM array, along with sensing the values, the sense amplifiers are also used to buffer the data, and even restore the values. Since we need to buffer the entire row of data, we need a sense amplifier for each column. As compared to an SRAM array, this design choice does increase the number of sense amplifiers that are required; however, this is a necessity in a DRAM array because a lot of DRAM access schemes try to serve data directly from the sense amplifiers as opposed to accessing the DRAM row once again. The sense amplifiers thus act as a small cache that is much faster to access as compared to making a fresh DRAM access. With this vision in mind, let us discuss sense amplifiers next.

DRAM Sense Amplifiers

A sense amplifier has two inputs. It compares the voltage difference between them and senses the direction in which the voltage difference is progressing. If the voltage difference exceeds a positive threshold, then we can infer a logical 1, and likewise if it decreases beyond a negative threshold, then we infer a logical 0. In the case of SRAM arrays, the bit lines BL and $\overline{BL}$ were the inputs to a sense amplifier. However, in this case, we have a single bit line and thus we have a single input. It is thus necessary to add an additional input. The naive solution is to use a line with a fixed voltage, which is the base voltage that all the bit lines are precharged to. However, this is expensive in terms of area and wiring overhead. Since we never activate two rows in the same array at once, we can divide each bit line into multiple subsections. We can then use these *bit line segments* as inputs to the sense amplifiers. Let us elaborate by discussing the two broad design paradigms in this space.

Open Bit Line Array Architecture

In this design, we split the entire array by dividing each bit line into multiple segments as shown in Figure 10.5. We then connect the bit lines for segments i and $i + 1$ to the same sense amplifier. Recall that since we never activate two rows of the array at the same time, at most one sense amplifier will be activated at any given point of time. This design has two advantages: each sense amplifier is connected to two inputs without adding any additional wires, and the number of transistors connected to each bit line can be kept within limits. The latter effect is important because it limits the capacitive loading and consequent latency of each bit line.

In the DRAM world, we typically describe the area of a memory cell as a function of the feature size, F, which is the minimum size of a feature that can be reliably fabricated in a given process. The area of each cell is at least $4F^2$. This is because the DRAM cell's minimum dimensions are $F \times F$. In addition, it needs to be separated by a distance of at least F from the nearest cell. This means that the area that needs to be apportioned for each cell is $2F \times 2F$. However, we need to additionally account for the area taken by bit lines, circuitry, and also the fact that the capacitor and the transistor cannot be completely vertically stacked. Taking all of these overheads into account, the area of each cell in the open bit line architecture is around $6F^2$.

The main disadvantage of this design is that it has reduced noise tolerance. Bit lines are large structures that can pick up a lot of inductive noise. Since the bit lines that are inputs to a sense amplifier are not co-located, they can pick up different degrees of noise. Thus, this design is susceptible to more noise-induced errors.

Folded Bit Line Array Architecture

Such noise-induced errors are mitigated by folded bit line architectures that try to co-locate the bit lines that are inputs to the sense amplifiers.

Figure 10.6 shows an architecture that twists two bit lines to cover a column of DRAM cells. Counting from the top, cells 1, 2, 5, and 6 are connected to the first bit line, whereas cells 3 and 4 are connected to the second bit line. The bit lines change their direction, and intersect in the figure after every two DRAM cells in a column. Note that they do not actually intersect – they just seem to do so when viewed from the top. This ensures that for every group of two cells, one bit line is connected and the other is disconnected. The disconnected bit line always runs parallel to the connected bit line.

The advantage of this design is that both the bit lines are in close proximity to each other. As a result,

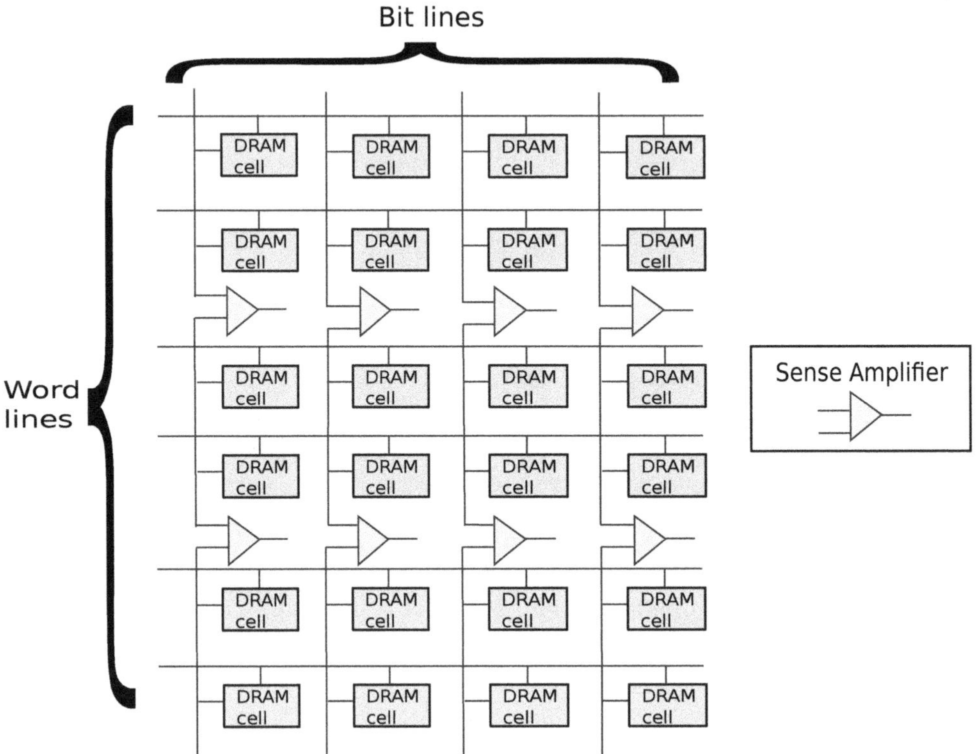

Figure 10.5: Open bit line array architecture.

they accumulate roughly the same amount of noise. Since the sense amplifier senses the difference in voltage between the bit lines, any noise that is common will get rejected. As a result, the noise tolerance of this design is much more than the architecture with open bit lines.

However, there are several shortcomings of this design as well. The first is that we need additional area for the second bit line that is disconnected. This increases the cell area even though the design is not planar. The area increases to $8F^2$ (from $6F^2$ in the the open bit line array architecture). Secondly, the number of cells connected to each bit line is roughly equal to half the number of rows. This can increase the capacitance of a bit line significantly and slow it down.

Many designs for bit line array architectures have been proposed to extend these schemes and use different combinations of splitting the bit lines and folding.

Design of a Sense Amplifier

Sensing the voltage difference is a two-stage process. We first equalise the voltages of the two bit lines. This is done using the circuit shown in Figure 10.7. This is a very simple circuit that is connected to the two bit lines. When the EQ line is set to a logical 1, transistor $T1$ gets enabled. After this the potential difference between the two bit lines (1 and 2) becomes roughly zero. Next, we need to ensure that it is equal to the precharged voltage: $V_{dd}/2$. Look at transistors $T2$ and $T3$. After EQ is set to V_{dd}, transistors $T2$ and $T3$ will turn on and the bit lines will get set to the voltage $V_{dd}/2$. Once this is done, both the bit lines are said to be precharged.

Then in the second stage, we enable a row of the DRAM array and allow the bit lines to gradually get charged or discharged. Next, we need to sense the difference in the voltages between Bit line 1 and Bit line 2 (see Figure 10.8). Note that we are deliberately avoiding the notation BL and $\overline{BL}$ over here because these are two separate bit lines that are connected to different sets of DRAM cells. Assume that

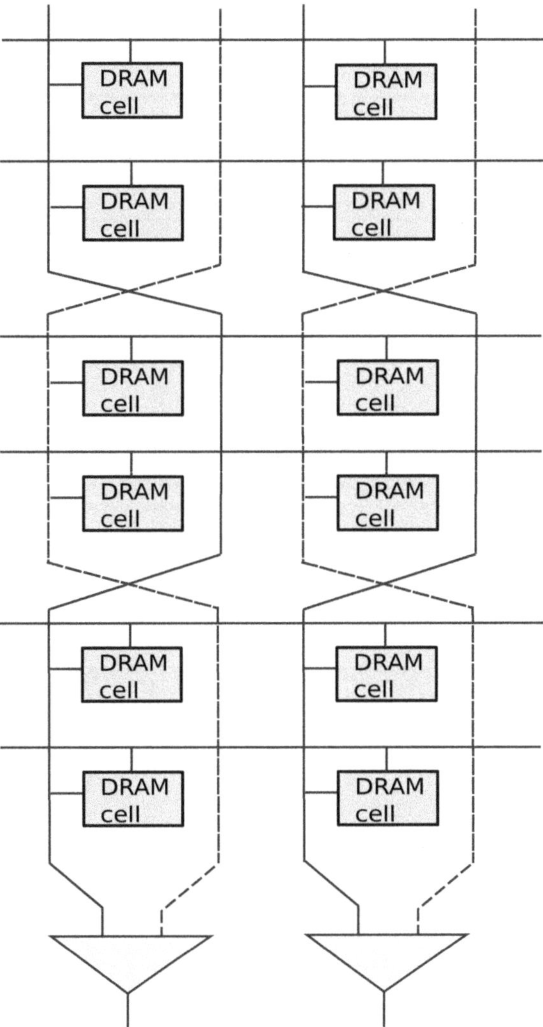

Figure 10.6: Folded bit line array architecture

the voltage on Bit line 1 (V_1) is slightly higher than the voltage on Bit line 2 (V_2), where $V_2 = V_{dd}/2$. At this point of time let us set the voltage on SAN to 0 V and the voltage on SAP to V_{dd} (assume logical 1 is V_{dd} volts). This enables the sensing operation.

The sequence of actions is as follows. Gradually, $T2$ starts becoming more conducting. As a result, the voltage on Bit line 2 dips because SAN is set to 0 V. Because of this, the voltage at the gate of $T3$ also starts dipping and this makes $T3$ more conductive. Since SAP is set to V_{dd}, the voltage on Bit line 1 starts to increase. Very quickly the voltage on Bit line 1 reaches V_{dd} and the voltage on Bit line 2 reaches 0 V. At this point, the voltages on the bit lines have reached the maximum and minimum levels respectively. We have a reverse case when the voltage on Bit line 1 stays at $V_{dd}/2$ and the voltage on Bit line 2 increases slightly. We leave it as an exercise for the reader to reason about what happens when the voltage on any bit line decreases slightly from the reference value $(V_{dd}/2)$ because the value stored in the DRAM cell is a logical 0. In all cases the bit lines swing to the maximum and minimum voltage values. Also note that they always have complementary voltages. This is a stable state for the sense amplifier. The bit lines will continue to maintain their state. This design of a sense amplifier has thus

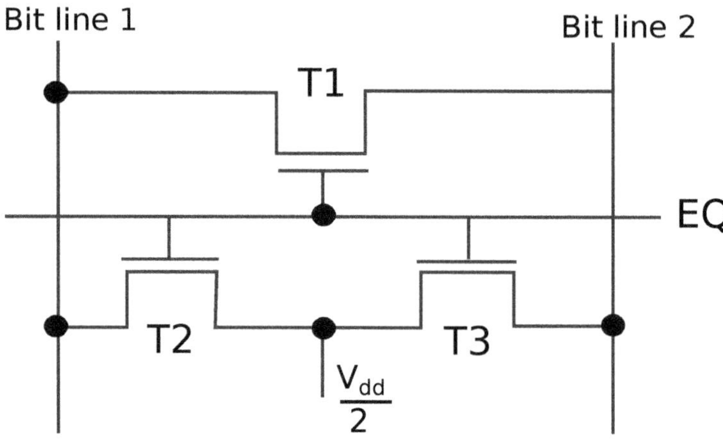

Figure 10.7: A voltage equaliser

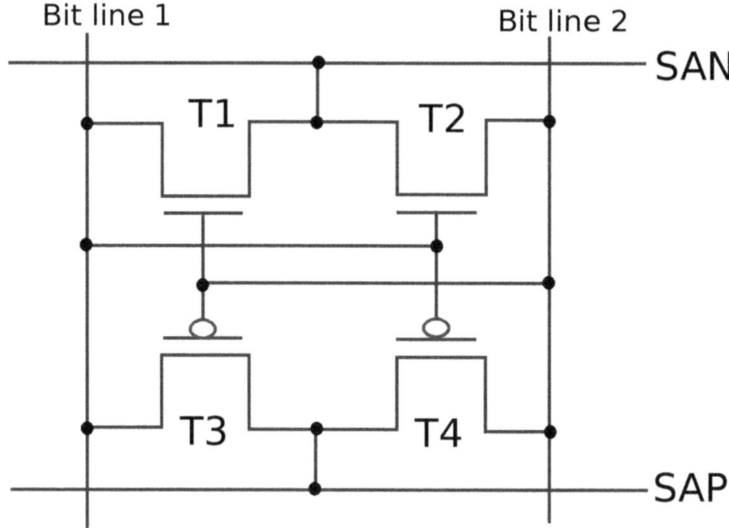

Figure 10.8: A DRAM sense amplifier

helped us to store a bit as well. Finally, note that once the respective bit line gets charged or discharged, the DRAM cell can also "restore" its value. For example, if the cell stored a logical 1, the charged bit line can restore the charge of the capacitor.

We thus see that the sense amplifier serves several purposes at the same time. First, it senses small changes in the voltages of the bit lines and amplifies the difference such that the bit lines quickly get fully charged or discharged. Once, the voltages of the bit lines have been set, they will remain that way and keep restoring the value of the DRAM cell till we disable the word line. For accessing a new row, we need to activate the equaliser circuit once again and set the voltages of both the bit lines back to the precharge voltage: $V_{dd}/2$. To disable the sense amplifier at this point, we can set the voltages of SAN and SAP to $V_{dd}/2$; this will ensure that all the four transistors are in the cut-off state.

The sense amplifier and the precharge circuit are connected to powerful write drivers via access transistors as shown in Figure 10.9. The access transistors are controlled by a chip select line (CS), which effectively enables the DRAM chip. To summarise, to read a row we perform the following actions in sequence.

1. Precharge the bit lines. Set the voltages on the SAN and SAP lines to $V_{dd}/2$.

2. Enable the corresponding word line.

3. Set the values of the SAN and SAP lines.

4. Enable the "Chip select" and "Read enable" signals.

5. Send the column address to the column decoder within the column mux/demux unit. Read the data out.

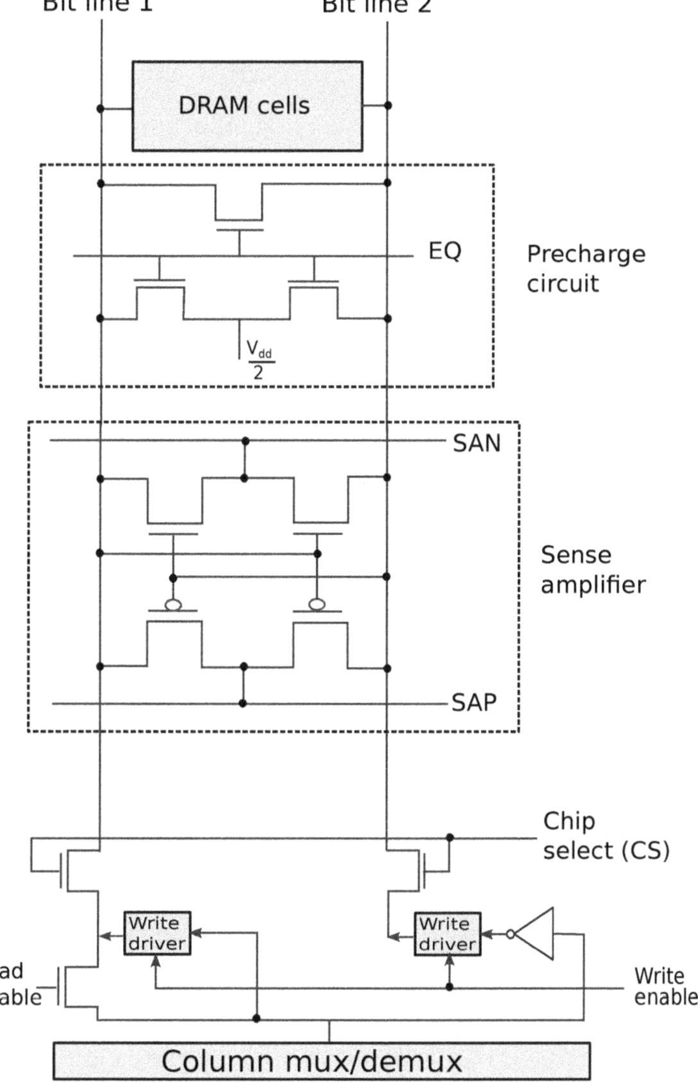

Figure 10.9: Layout of a part of a DRAM array with the precharge circuit, sense amplifier, and write drivers

Write Access

The process of writing in DRAMs is different as compared to SRAMs. We can divide the overall process into two broad stages. The first stage is the same as most of the read process where we precharge the bit lines, send the address to the row address decoder, enable the row, sense and restore all the values.

The actual write part is the second stage of this process. After all the cells in a row have been sensed and restored, the column address is sent to the column decoder. Then we enable the two write drivers (refer to Figure 10.9). It is assumed that the write drivers are strong enough to override the sense amplifiers. They set the state of the corresponding bit lines, the DRAM cell, and the corresponding sense amplifier. This finishes the write. The additional time required to do this is known as the write recovery time.

Refresh Operation

It is necessary to refresh the values of DRAM cells periodically (once every 32 to 64 ms), otherwise any charge stored across the capacitor will gradually leak out and the cell will lose its value. Thankfully, the refresh operation by itself is very simple – it is just the regular sense and restore operation. Recall that the sense and restore operations read the values of all the cells in a row, then use the sense amplifiers to set the values of the bit lines to either the maximum or minimum voltage. This process in effect refreshes the value that is stored in each cell by restoring the charge on the capacitor to the ideal value. Just in case some charge has leaked out, the corresponding capacitor gets fully charged after this operation. Hence, a refresh can be thought of as a dummy read operation. Note that we do not need to use the column decoder or enable the chip select line.

There are two types of refresh operations: burst and distributed. In the *burst* operation, we freeze the entire DRAM array and refresh all the rows one after the other. During this time, it is not possible for the DRAM array to process any requests. This is inefficient, hence, advanced processors use the *distributed* refresh mode. In this case, refresh accesses are interspersed with regular memory accesses. This is done to hide the overhead of refresh operations as much as possible. Moreover, it is possible to further optimise this process by not refreshing the rows that do not contain any valid data. Additionally, in modern DRAMs it is possible to slightly overshoot the maximum refresh interval without causing any correctness issues. This allows us to schedule critically important read requests.

10.1.4 A Computer System with DRAM Arrays

Since DRAM arrays have a very high storage density, they are typically used as off-chip memories. They can be used to store a large amount of data off chip and are thus ideally suited for a last level memory system. They are not particularly suitable for on-chip caches because SRAM arrays tend to be faster. There are several reasons for this.

1. A DRAM cell is very feeble. It has a single capacitor that needs to charge a very long bit line. In comparison, in an SRAM, the bit line is connected directly to either the ground or supply terminals via the transistors in the SRAM cell. As a result, it is possible to supply much more current and thus charge the bit lines more quickly.

2. In a DRAM, a read access is *destructive*. This means that we need to write the original value back to the cell that we read from. This requires additional time because in a DRAM array a read is actually a read and a write. This overhead is absent in an SRAM.

3. We need to spend some time doing a refresh on a compulsory basis, otherwise we run the risk of losing data.

Given these factors, it is almost always advisable to have a large off-chip DRAM memory, which is typically at the lowest level in the memory hierarchy. Recently, embedded DRAM (eDRAM) devices have arrived where we can integrate DRAM memory into the same die as the processor or have a separate module within the same package. The main advantage of eDRAM devices is that they allow shorter and higher bandwidth connections between the LLC (last level cache) and the eDRAM memory.

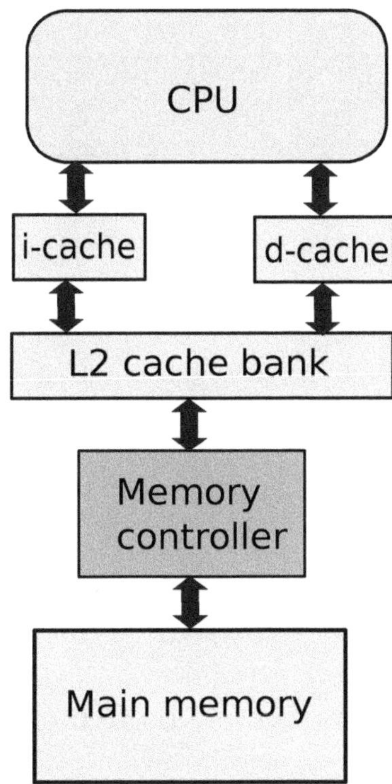

Figure 10.10: Processor + memory controller + DRAM

Generic Architecture

In this section, let us discuss a generic architecture for all kinds of DRAM devices that are used with modern processors (refer to Figure 10.10). The processor is connected to a memory hierarchy that consists of layers of caches of increasing sizes. The i-cache and the d-cache occupy the highest levels, then we have the L2 cache, and some processors might optionally have an L3 or L4 cache. The last layer of caches in a processor is known as the last level cache – abbreviated as *LLC*. The layer below the LLC is the off-chip memory, which is made of DRAM arrays. In a chip we have multiple memory controllers, which act as mediators between the LLC and the DRAM memory. If we have a miss in the LLC, then a request is sent to a memory controller, whose job is to interact with the DRAM arrays and complete the memory access.

Let us look at this in some more detail. A processor can have many memory controllers. The physical address space needs to be partitioned across these memory controllers. For example, we can use the MSB bits of the memory address. Consider a system with two memory controllers. If the MSB is 0, we access memory controller 0, else if it is 1, we access memory controller 1. Each memory controller is connected to a set of DRAM arrays via a set of copper wires. These sets of wires are known as *channels*. A channel is typically 32-128 bits wide. Channel widths are getting shorter with time mainly because if we are sending data at a high frequency, it is hard to keep the data across the different copper wires in the channel synchronised. The channels are connected to a set of printed circuit boards (PCBs) that contain DRAM chips. These PCBs are known as DIMMs (dual inline memory modules). The picture of a DIMM is one of the most recognisable images for DRAMs. It is shown in Figure 10.11. Note that both sides of a DIMM have DRAM chips. The DIMMs are inserted into the motherboard, which has dedicated slots for them. Refer to Figure 10.12 that shows a motherboard having multiple DIMMs installed in its slots. Installing a DIMM is as simple as aligning the DIMM with the slot and then pressing it such that it fits snugly in the slot. Many desktops and servers are often sold with a few empty DIMM slots such that if later on there is a need, the user can buy new DIMMs and install them. This will increase the memory capacity. If some DIMMs develop faults, they can be replaced as well.

Figure 10.11: Photograph of a DIMM (Photo by Franck V. on Unsplash)

Each DIMM contains a set of DRAM chips. We typically divide a DIMM into multiple ranks (typically 1 to 4), where each *rank* contains a set of DRAM chips that execute in lockstep. Moreover, it is assumed that the chips in a rank are equidistant from the memory controller: it takes the same amount of time for signals to reach all the chips from the memory controller. Typically, the memory controller issues a command to a given rank. All the DRAM chips that are a part of the rank work in lock-step to execute the command. The main advantage of grouping DRAM chips together is to provide a high bandwidth memory. For example, if we need to supply 64 bits every cycle, then it makes sense to create a rank of 16 chips, where each chip supplies 4 bits. This keeps each individual DRAM device small and power efficient.

Subsequently, each rank has multiple *banks* (grouped into bank groups in the DDR4 protocol). A bank is a set of arrays within a DRAM chip that operates independently with respect to other banks on the same chip. A bank typically contains multiple arrays that cannot be independently addressed.

The arrays within each bank work in synchrony. For example, if we have 4 arrays in a bank, we access the same row and column in each array while performing a bank access. We read 4 bits in parallel.

Figure 10.12: Photograph of a motherboard with DIMM slots (Photo by Stef Westheim on Unsplash)

This is conceptually the same as assuming that we have one large array where each cell or each column is 4 bits wide. Using more arrays increases the bandwidth of a DRAM device because we can read more bits in parallel. In a DRAM chip all the banks have the same number of arrays.

This is typically specified as follows. When we say that we have an x4 DRAM, this means that we have 4 arrays in a bank, and we read and write 4 bits at a time. An xN DRAM has exactly N arrays in a bank. As of 2020, x16 to x128 DRAMs are there in the market. x64 and x128 configurations are typically only present in 3D DRAMs (we shall study them later in Section10.5.6).

Each array is a matrix of DRAM cells. We first access the row and then the column to read or write a single bit. The entire hierarchy of structures in a DRAM is as follows: channel $\rightarrow$ DIMM $\rightarrow$ rank $\rightarrow$ chip or device $\rightarrow$ bank $\rightarrow$ array $\rightarrow$ row $\rightarrow$ column. This is shown in Figure 10.13.

Topology

There are several methods to connect a memory controller to memory modules (DIMMs). The simplest possible arrangement is that we connect one memory controller to one DIMM using a dedicated channel. Typically on a channel, we send four kinds of information: address, data, command, and chip-select. The first three are self explanatory, the *chip select signal* is used to enable a specific rank of devices. If we have 4 ranks in a DIMM, then we need a 2-bit chip select signal to select the specific rank. The address and command buses are unidirectional, and so is the chip select bus. However, the data bus is bidirectional because data can flow either from the processor to the memory or in the reverse direction. We can either use separate address and command buses, or have a single bus to carry the information for both memory addresses and commands. It is possible to fuse them because we typically send the address and commands at different points of time.

It is additionally possible to connect multiple DIMMs per channel. There are several advantages of doing this.

1. To increase the bandwidth, we can split the channel across the DIMMs. For example, if we have a 128-bit wide data bus, we can split it into two equal halves across two DIMMs that read or

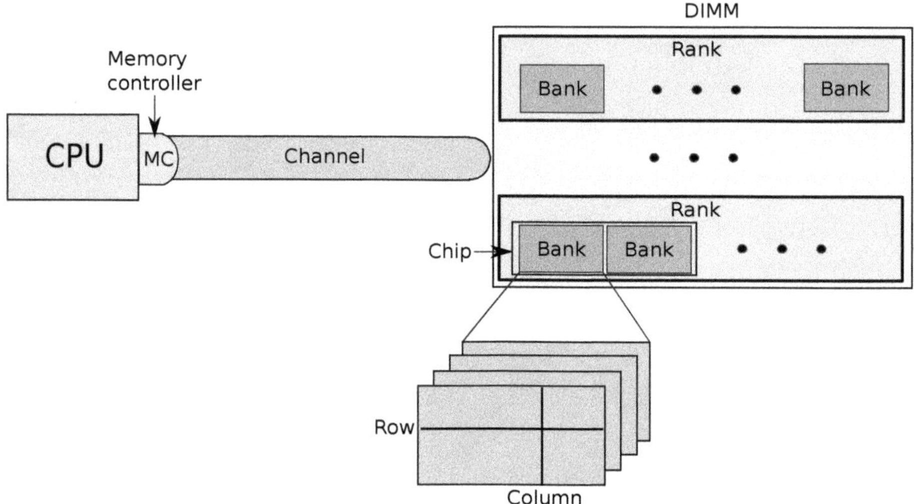

Figure 10.13: Hierarchy of elements in DRAM memory

write 64 bits at a time. Both the DRAMs can operate in lockstep. This will effectively double the bandwidth of the channel assuming the maximum amount of data that we can transfer from each DIMM per cycle is 64 bits.

2. We can also connect different DIMMs that are not similar. For example, if our data bus is 64 bits wide, we can use one DIMM that has a 64-bit interface and another DIMM that has a 32-bit interface. Such topologies can be used to support legacy systems that use older technologies. In this case, we cannot use both the DIMMs simultaneously. We need to interleave their accesses and the achieved bandwidth is the maximum of the bandwidths of the individual DIMMs.

3. If the channel is not being kept busy all the time because the DIMMs take time to perform their accesses, we can use this time to access other DIMMs connected to the same channel. The total bandwidth in this case depends on the degree to which we can interleave the accesses. It can theoretically scale with the number of DIMMs per channel till we are limited by the channel capacity.

Now, let us see how we connect the address, data, command, and chip select buses to the DRAM chips within each DIMM. One of the most common topologies is shown in Figure 10.14. In this topology, the DRAM chips are arranged as a 2D matrix. DRAM chips in the same rank are the columns, and corresponding chips across ranks form the rows. The address/command bus is routed to every DRAM chip, and the chip select lines are connected to each rank separately. The latter are used to either enable or disable the entire rank in one go. The data bus is split into four *lanes* (one-fourth the width of the data bus). Each of these lanes is connected to a row of banks across the ranks. Only one of the ranks can use the lanes of the data bus at a given point in time, and thus this ensures that we can read 32 to 128 bits in parallel from all the banks in the rank.

Important Point 18
There is a very important point to note here. Note that the address/command bus is connected to all the banks across the ranks. In this case, it is connected to 16 banks. Whereas, each data bus lane is connected to only 4 banks. This means that the capacitive loading *on the address/command bus*

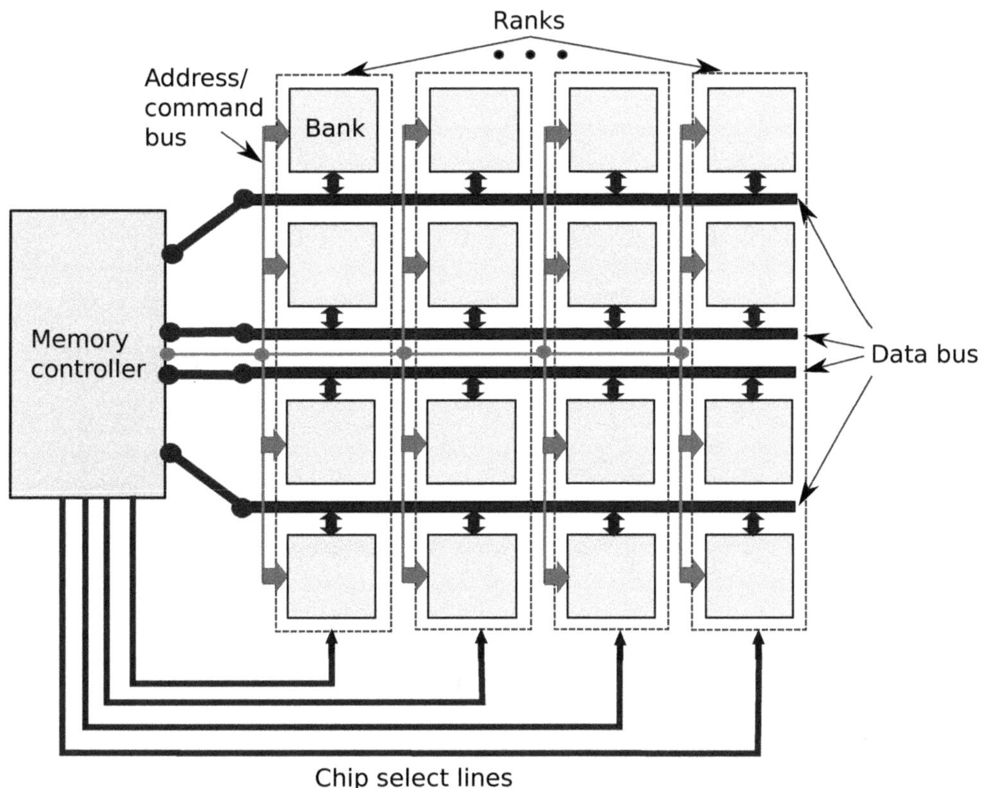

Figure 10.14: Organisation of memory banks

> *is 4 times more than that of a data bus lane. As a result, its RC delay is more, and thus it is a*
> *slower bus. In comparison, the data bus is faster, because each of its lanes is connected to a fewer*
> *number of devices. It can thus sustain a higher data transfer frequency. This is a* **crucial insight**,
> *which we shall use while designing DDR (double data rate) memory later on.*

10.2 Design Space of DRAMs

10.2.1 DRAM Access Protocols

DRAM memories are passive memories. There are no computing elements embedded inside the memory. As a result, the entire job of scheduling all the accesses, ensuring that there are no conflicts, and providing fairness is left to the memory controller. The memory controller needs to be aware of the timing details of the memory devices and then it needs to schedule all the requests that it gets from the cores and the cache banks. Previously, the memory controller used to reside in a separate chip on the motherboard; however, nowadays the memory controller is placed on the same die as the CPUs and caches. It needs to be aware of the details of the devices that are attached to the memory channels, for example, their timing and the commands that they support. Let us look at DRAM devices now in some more details.

Over the last two decades, DRAM technology has been improving at a significant pace. Initially, they were asynchronous devices. The advantage was that they could be connected with any memory controller because there were no strict constraints on the timing. However, this also introduced additional complexities in orchestrating the data transfer and it also made buffering commands difficult. Hence, gradually DRAM technology has moved towards synchronous devices where the DRAM devices have their own clocks, and there is some degree of synchrony between the DRAM clock and the clock of the core. This has paved the way for modern synchronous DRAM access protocols that are fast and reliable. In the next few sections, let us look at the evolution of DRAM access protocols over the last two decades.

Asynchronous Transfer

The first memory transfer protocols were asynchronous protocols, where the CPU and the memory did not share a clock. In an asynchronous mechanism there is no common time base, hence, the sender needs to let the receiver know when it can read the data.

Let us first explain a simple scheme. Let us have two buses to transfer data: one each way (simplex mode). The two buses carry two signals: a strobe signal (DQS) and the data signal (DQ). The reason we need a strobe signal is as follows. Whenever the sender sends data, the receiver needs to read the data and store it in a latch. Such latches are typically edge triggered (read data in at a clock transition). Since the sender and receiver do not share a clock, synchronisation is an issue. There needs to be a mechanism for the sender to let the receiver know when it can read the data. This is where the strobe signal is used. The receiver monitors the strobe, and whenever there is a transition in its voltage level, it reads the data bus (DQ signal).

If we assume that a transition in the strobe signal happens at $t = 0$, then no transition is allowed in the data bus in the time interval $[-t_{setup}, +t_{hold}]$. The data signal (DQ) needs to be steady in this time window, otherwise we shall have a phenomenon called metastability that leads to unpredictable behaviour. t_{setup} and t_{hold} represent the setup time and hold time respectively. Refer to Figure 10.15 for the timing diagram. It is not necessary for strobe signals to always convey information via transitions, many times the level is also used to convey some information such as whether a given unit is enabled or disabled. Note that we can latch data at either the falling edge of the clock (as shown in Figure 10.15(b)) or the rising edge of the clock.

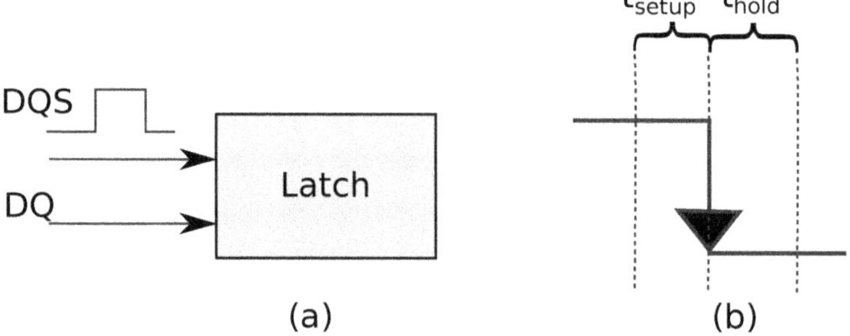

Figure 10.15: Storing a value in a latch with a strobe input

Let us now slightly complicate the scheme and consider two half-duplex buses (only one side can send at a time) between the memory controller (MC) and the DRAM. One of these buses is an *address bus* to carry row or column addresses and the other is a *data bus*, also called DQ. In an asynchronous memory, we have two strobe signals: $\overline{RAS}$ and $\overline{CAS}$. RAS stands for *row address strobe* and CAS stands for *column address strobe*. These are active low signals and are said to be asserted when the voltage is a logical 0. To indicate this fact, we use the symbols $\overline{RAS}$ and $\overline{CAS}$ in our diagrams. They mean that the signals are said to be asserted when the voltage is equal to a logical 0. This can be slightly confusing. Readers should make a note of this. They need to understand that the signals that are being transmitted are $\overline{RAS}$ and $\overline{CAS}$, which are said to be asserted or active when they are equal to a logical 0.

The first action that the memory controller needs to perform is that it needs to activate the DRAM row. This is done by sending the row address on the address bus, and then after some time asserting the $\overline{RAS}$ signal (setting it to 0). The reason that we do this is as follows. We want the data on the address bus to be stable before the device starts reading it. The device will start reading it when it sees the $1 \rightarrow 0$ transition of the $\overline{RAS}$ signal (refer to Figure 10.16). Once the DRAM device sees the row address and the $\overline{RAS}$ signal set to 0, it activates the row decoder, and then activates the row.

Subsequently, the memory controller sets the $\overline{CAS}$ signal to 0, and then after some time sends the column address on the address bus. Along with this, it can send one bit indicating if it wants to read or write. This activates the column decoder, which then prepares the column for reading or writing.

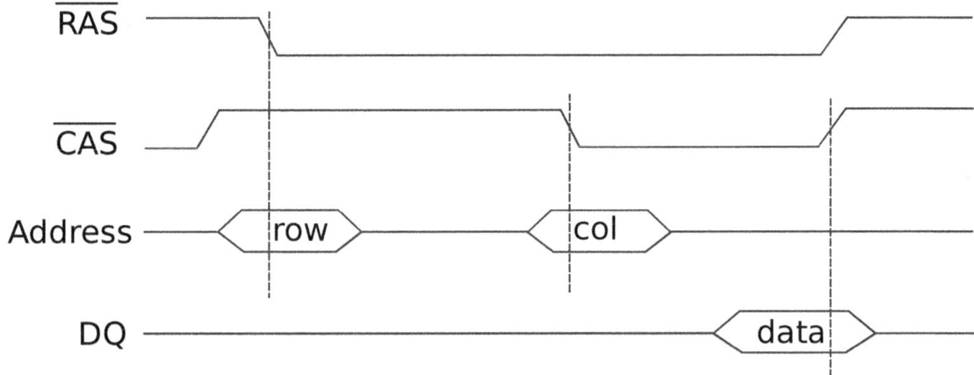

Figure 10.16: Timing diagram of an asynchronous DRAM

Consider a read access. The DQ bus is set to the value of the column by the DRAM device when the data is ready to be sent to the memory controller. After that the device sets $\overline{CAS}$ to 1, which indicates to the memory controller that it can start reading the DQ bus.

In the case of a write access, after sending the column address, the memory controller sends the data bit, which is then written to the device. In some protocols, after a write is done, an acknowledgement is sent to the CPU. The timing of the write is also managed by the strobe signals.

Fast Page Mode (FPM)

The basic asynchronous DRAM protocol is inefficient because we need to send the row and column address for every data transfer. This can be improved by operating the DRAM devices in *fast page mode*. In this mode, an entire row of data (page) is stored in the sense amplifiers, and then read over subsequent cycles. It is not necessary to send a separate row address for reading a different set of columns. This process is shown in Figure 10.17. The same holds for writes.

We first send the row address by asserting (setting to 0 in this case) the $\overline{RAS}$ signal. The DRAM banks read the entire row (page) and store the contents in the sense amplifiers. Subsequently, we send a sequence of column addresses to the DRAM banks. Each bank then chooses the right column using the column multiplexers and sends the data back. Since the entire page is stored in the sense amplifiers, it is not necessary to send the row address again if we intend to read more data from the same row, which is often the case because we read an entire 64-byte block at a time. In this case, we just need to send subsequent column addresses, and the banks can quickly transmit the data. Since this process is asynchronous, we need a strobe signal. We use the $\overline{CAS}$ signal to provide the timing for this process.

The key insight in this scheme is that we are using the sense amplifiers as a buffer. A typical FPM device can have 1024 columns per row, where each column is 16 bits wide. We can realise such a design by having a total of 16 arrays in each rank. We first read the entire row and store it in the sense amplifiers. We then select one column at a time, and in each array we read a single bit. The entire rank can thus provide 16 bits at a time, and we do not need to incur the overhead of row activations several times. We activate the row only once, and then read out all the columns that we are interested in.

We shall henceforth not discuss how we handle writes because they are handled in a very similar manner.

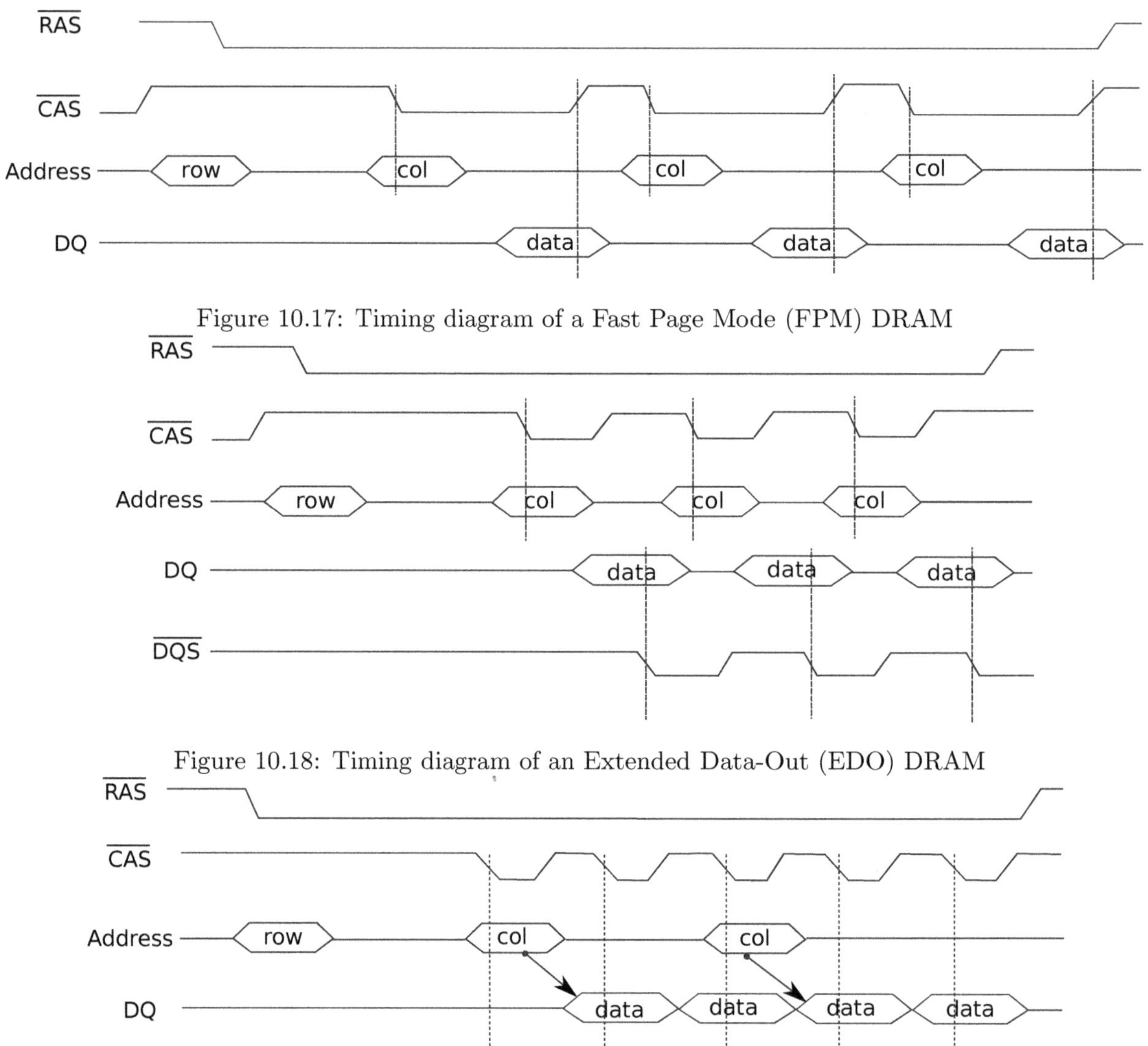

Figure 10.17: Timing diagram of a Fast Page Mode (FPM) DRAM

Figure 10.18: Timing diagram of an Extended Data-Out (EDO) DRAM

Figure 10.19: Timing diagram of a Burst Extended Data-Out (BEDO) DRAM

Extended Data Out (EDO)

In the FPM protocol, we send the column address, then we wait for the data to be read, and then we send the next column address, and so on. This process can be optimised further. We can send a column address, internally buffer the data that has been read, and while that data is being transferred, send the address of the next column. This process is shown in Figure 10.18.

This will however require another strobe signal ($\overline{DQS}$) as shown in the figure. This strobe signal indicates to the memory controller that the data is available on the data bus. If we compare Figures 10.18

and 10.17, we observe that the throughput has increased because of a reduced column-to-column delay.

Burst Extended Data Out (BEDO)

Most of the time, we do not access DRAM devices with random addresses. We typically wish to read consecutive columns because we transfer 64-byte blocks to the CPU. This takes multiple cycles, where we issue reads to consecutive columns by sending separate column addresses. It is not necessary to send the column addresses for consecutive sets of bytes in a 64-byte block. They can be generated internally.

In a certain sense, the DRAM device prefetches data words (groups of data bits) and sends them to the CPU via the memory controller. Since most accesses read contiguous sequences of data words, this access pattern is very common in practice. Hence, as shown in Figure 10.19, after one column address is sent, we can generate the next k column addresses internally, read those columns, and send their data over the data bus. We do not have to waste time in sending column addresses separately. In Figure 10.19, our prefetch length is 2 (read two columns after sending a single column address). We do not need a separate strobe signal, we can use the $\overline{CAS}$ signal to provide the timing.

The *prefetch length* or *prefetch width* is the number of bits we read in one go from each DRAM array. For example, if we read 8 bits in one go, the prefetch length is 8. In a clocked bus, we need 8 bus cycles to send these 8 bits (1 bit per cycle).

Synchronous DRAM

Even though asynchronous memory devices became very efficient, they still had numerous drawbacks. In general, maintaining timing is difficult, particularly in complex DRAM systems. As a result, almost all of the memory devices today use synchronous DRAM (*SDRAM*). In such devices, the memory controller and the DRAM devices use a common time base, which means that they use the same clock. All the latencies are specified in terms of clock signals, and all the messages are aligned with respect to clock boundaries. This simplifies the communication to a large extent and makes it possible to create elaborate and scalable protocols. Some of the other advantages of synchronous communication are as follows.

1. A synchronous system is simple to design and verify.

2. In asynchronous memory, the $\overline{RAS}$ and $\overline{CAS}$ signals directly control the banks. It is not possible to add additional programmable logic within the DRAM devices. However, with synchronous memory, it is possible to simply send commands to the devices, and let the devices implement them in different ways.

3. SDRAM devices are more configurable. For example, it is possible to switch the mode of an SDRAM device, and also dynamically change its prefetch length (typical values: 1, 2, 4, or 8).

4. SDRAM devices contain multiple banks. It is possible to send different commands to different banks. For example, it is possible to pipeline commands where we can read one bank while precharging another bank.

It is possible that there is a phase difference between the clock of the memory controller and the internal clock of the DRAM device. To ensure clock synchronisation, most SDRAM devices have a DLL (delay locked loop) circuit within them. This ensures that the clock of the DRAM devices and the memory controller remain synchronised and the phase difference is reduced to a minimum. The clock of the memory controller can either be recovered from transitions in the data or from a dedicated strobe signal sent by the memory controller.

Figure 10.20 shows the timing diagram for a typical SDRAM device. We have four buses: *CLK* (clock), *Command*, *Address*, and *DQ* (data). The commands and the addresses are latched into the SRAM device at the rising edge of the clock.

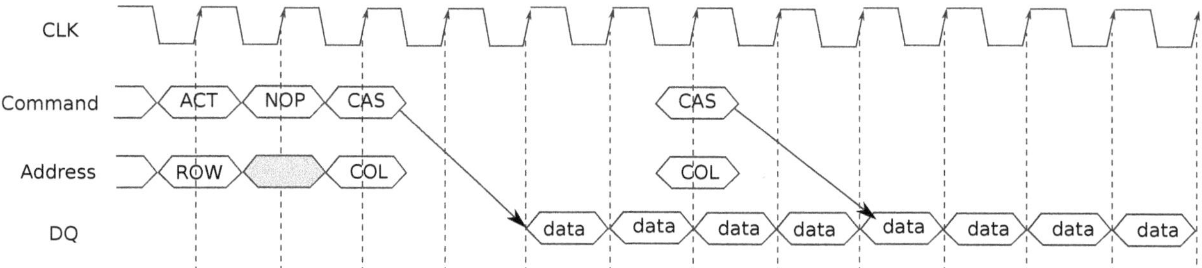

Figure 10.20: Timing diagram of synchronous DRAM memory

We first activate the row by sending the row activate ACT command along with the row address on the address bus. Subsequently, we assume that it takes one cycle to activate the row, then we send the column activate command CAS, along with the column address. After sending the column address, we wait for one clock cycle, then the memory controller starts receiving data from the DRAM device. In the case of a read transaction, the data transmission starts at the rising edge of the clock. In this case, the prefetch length is 4. Similar to BEDO DRAM, we can send additional column addresses to read other data words from the row (opened page) in subsequent clock cycles. The advantage here is that we do not need to send the row address and activate the row again.

Note two things. We shall sometimes issue the NOP command indicating that we are not issuing any command; this will be done whenever it is necessary to show inactivity on the command bus. Second, a shaded hexagon on the data or address bus means that we do not care about the data or address being sent.

10.2.2 DDR Generations and Timing

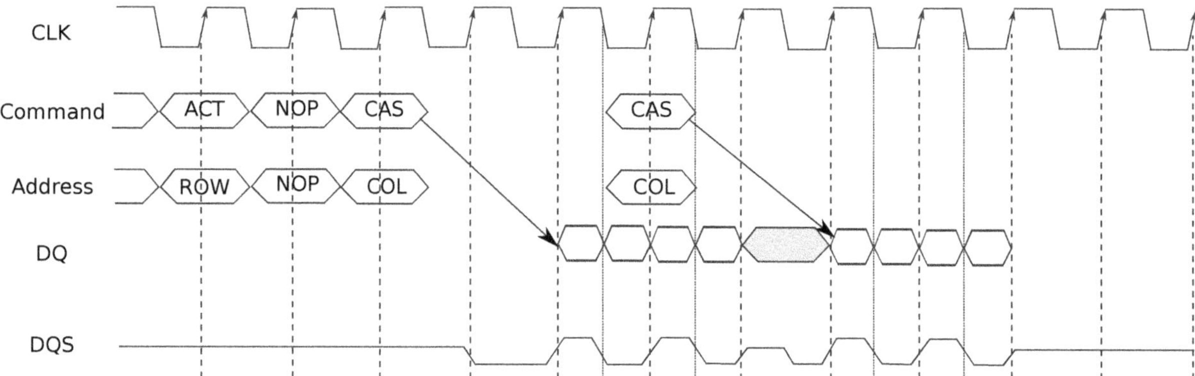

Figure 10.21: Timing diagram of DDR memory

Recall that we had argued that the command and address buses have a much higher capacitive loading, and are consequently much slower because they are connected to all the DRAM banks. In comparison, the data buses are connected to far fewer banks, and thus the loading on each bus is significantly lower (refer to Figure 10.14). Given that the data bus is expected to be much faster than the address or command bus, we can use this fact to further speed up our memory access protocol.

Because of the fundamental asymmetry in the speeds of the data bus and the address and command buses, double data rate memory (DDR memory) was developed. In this memory, the data bus runs at twice the speed of the address and command buses.

Figure 10.21 shows the timing diagram of a DDR memory device. The clock, command, and address buses have the same functions. The major difference is that we transmit data at twice the rate. Additionally, we have a new signal, a data strobe signal DQS, that is sent along with the data. This is because we can have minor clock skews, and for the receiver to read the data correctly, it needs to use the DQS signal for clock synchronisation. This method of transmission is known as *source synchronous transmission*. As we can see from Figure 10.21 this signal can take three values: logical 0, logical 1, and an intermediate voltage that represents the undefined state. Furthermore, its voltage can be set by either the memory controller or the DRAM device depending upon the direction of data transmission.

Let us now study some of the subtle aspects of the design of DDR memory. We see a one-cycle bubble between the two data bursts. In this case, we assume that the second burst of data in the figure is provided by another rank of DRAM devices whose corresponding row has been activated in the past. To switch the rank it takes one cycle because the new rank has to re-synchronise its clock with the data strobe.

When we are using this protocol to write data to the DRAM devices, the memory controller sends data such that transitions of the strobe signal happen at the middle of transmitting each bit. This makes it easier for the DRAM device to latch the data. However, it increases the complexity of the circuit at the end of the memory controller. This is acceptable because we want DRAM devices to be simple, and we want to migrate the complexity to the memory controller where we can afford it.

It is important to understand that while reading data, this is not necessary. This is because while reading data, the DRAM device is the sender. It is much easier for it to transmit data at clock boundaries. The memory controller can then recover the clock from the strobe and latch the data at the correct time instants. This requires more circuitry but is an acceptable overhead at the side of the memory controller.

Note that the data bus in this case runs in half-duplex mode, Which means that it does not allow simultaneous transmission of data in both directions. Thus DDR memory is the most efficient when we either have only reads, or only writes. To remedy this problem, QDR (quad data rate) memory was proposed that has two data buses: one read bus and one write bus. This allows us to effectively achieve a higher bandwidth by interleaving reads and writes.

DDRX Memory

After the basic DDR memory was proposed, no fundamental changes to the paradigm were made. Instead, there were subsequent improvements in the process and signalling technologies to realise faster memories. Thus, we have several DDR generations: DDR2 to DDR4. They are collectively known as DDRX technologies.

Technology	Bus clock speed	Prefetch length	Transfer rate (MT/s)	Voltage	Maximum DIMM size
DDR	100-200 MHz	2	200-400	2.5-2.6 V	1 GB
DDR2	200-400 MHz	4	400-800	1.8 V	4 GB
DDR3	400-1066 MHz	8	800-2133	1.35/1.5 V	16 GB
DDR4	800-2133 MHz	8	1600-4266	1.2 V	64 GB

Table 10.1: Description of the different DDR technologies

Table 10.1 describes the different DDR technologies. In the list of technologies, DDR is the oldest standard, and DDR4 is the newest standard (as of March, 2020). As of March 2020, DDR5 is still in the process of standardisation. Each DDR device has an internal clock that runs at a much lower clock speed as compared to the bus frequency. For example, in DDR4, the internal clock can vary from 200 MHz to 533 MHz (increasing in units of $33\frac{1}{3}$ MHz). However, the bus frequency varies from 800 MHz to 2133 MHz.

Note that the bus frequency is always more than the devices' internal clock frequency. This is because buses have gotten faster over the years, whereas DRAM devices have not sped up at that rate. Consider DDR once again, for a bus frequency of 800 MHz, the internal clock is 200 MHz. There is thus a rate mismatch, which can only be equalised if the internal bus width of the DRAM devices is more. Given that we are transmitting data at both the edges of the clock, the DRAM devices need to provide $2 \times 800/200 = 8$ times more data per cycle. This means that, internally, the rank needs to produce data at 8 times the rate per cycle by parallelising the read/write operations among the arrays and by reading more data per clock cycle.

Let us do the math for this example. In all DDR technologies, the channel width is 64 bits (72 bits with ECC), and we send 64 bits in parallel in each half-cycle. This set of 64 bits is known as a *memory word* and each half-cycle is also known as a *beat*. If the internal frequency is 200 MHz and the bus frequency is 800 MHz, then as argued before, DRAM devices need to produce more data per cycle. Let us consider 8 beats, which is equal to the length of a DRAM device's clock cycle (internal cycle). In 8 beats, we need to transmit 512 bits. If we have 64 arrays in a rank, then we need to read 8 bits in every internal cycle. This can be done by prefetching columns as we had discussed before in the case of BEDO DRAM. The number of bits we prefetch per internal cycle is known as the *prefetch length* in the case of synchronous DRAM. This needs to be equal to 512/64, which is equal to 8.

The prefetch length scales with the ratio of the bus frequency to the internal DIMM frequency. It was 2 for DDR, 4 for DDR2, 8 for DDR3 and DDR4. For example, if the prefetch length is 8, then we will require 8 beats to transmit all the data that has been read from the DRAM devices. This means that the minimum data transfer size in DDR4 is 64 bytes (8×64 bits). A sequence of bits being transmitted is known as a *burst*. In this case, the minimum burst length is 8.

This unfortunately has negative consequences. This stops us from transmitting data that is less than 64 bytes in DDR3 and DDR4. Hence, in DDR3 the *burst chop* mode was introduced. It is possible to program the DRAM devices such that they disregard the second half of a 8-beat burst. We can thus effectively reduce the minimum burst length to 4 beats, even though we are not sending useful data in place of the disregarded beats.

The next column in Table 10.1 shows the transfer rate of the DRAM device measured in millions of transfers per second (MT/s). A *transfer* is defined as the transfer of a 64-bit data packet (equal to the channel width) from the memory controller to DRAM or vice versa. In a DDR memory, the number of transfers per second is equal to twice the bus frequency. For example, if the bus frequency is 400 MHz, then we perform 800 million transfers per second (MT/s) because of double data rate transmission. The standard nomenclature that we use to label DRAM devices is of the form ($\langle Technology \rangle - \langle Transfer\ rate \rangle$). For example, a DDR3-1600 technology means that we are using the DDR3 technology and we perform 1600 million transfers per second.

The next column shows the transmission voltage. It has steadily decreased from 2.6 V to 1.2 V. As we lower the voltage, we also reduce the time it takes to transmit a message. However, the susceptibility to noise and crosstalk increases. These need to be managed with technological innovations. Subsequent DDR generations are expected to reduce the supply voltage even further.

Furthermore, due to increased miniaturisation and improvements in fabrication technology, the density of bits is increasing. The maximum capacity of a DIMM has also been steadily increasing from 1GB (DDR) to 64 GB (DDR4).

10.2.3 Buffered DIMMs

An important shortcoming of conventional memory systems is that there is a trade-off between the frequency of the memory bus, the frequency of the DIMMs, and the number of DIMMs that we can connect to each channel. As we connect more DIMMs to the channel, the capacitive loading on the address, command and data buses increases, which adversely impacts their RC delay. Recall that the RC delay or the time constant is the time that it takes to charge the bus to 63% percent of its final value. This means that with more connected devices, it takes more time to effect voltage transitions on the bus, and this directly places limits on the bus frequency. For the different DDR generations, this is what is happening. For example, in DDR2 where the bus frequency was 400 MHz, we could connect 8 devices to each memory channel, whereas in an 800 MHz DDR3 bus, we can only connect 2 devices. Such trade-offs limit DRAM scaling to a large extent.

As a result, it became necessary to think of new bus technologies that can circumvent such limitations. On the flip side, there are very strong business reasons to keep DIMMs unmodified. The DRAM business is very competitive; therefore, vendors have been averse to adding additional circuitry to the devices. In addition to that, it is necessary for all memory controllers and the RAM chips to be compliant with the DDR standards. Hence the space for innovation is very restricted.

Keeping all of these constraints in mind, a set of buffered memories were proposed. These classes of DIMMs contain a buffer with every DIMM chip that buffers either the data or the control messages. The effect of such buffers is that it reduces the net capacitive loading on the memory channel. It thus allows for faster data transfer, and we can connect more devices to a channel. There are many classes of buffered memories. We shall discuss two of the most popular classes in this section: fully buffered DIMMs and registered memory.

Fully Buffered DIMMs (FB-DIMMs)

In the 2000-2005 time frame, there was an increasing realisation that traditional DDR based memory technologies will not scale. We are limited by the frequency of the bus, and since these are multidrop buses (many DIMMs are connected), the capacitive loading on the command and address buses is a key limiting factor. There was a need to create large server-based systems that could sustain large memories and provide robust communication. At that point of time, an audacious attempt was made to completely re-architect the memory system. One such attempt was the proposal to create Fully Buffered DIMMs (FB-DIMMs). Given that this idea involved significant changes to the memory system, DIMMs, memory controllers, and the motherboards, the industry was not very enthusiastic, and thus this technology is not very popular as of 2020. However, from an educational perspective, this technology has immense theoretical value and provides insights into what it takes to create robust and scalable DRAM based memory systems.

AMBs

The crux of the idea behind FB-DIMMs was a custom chip called the Advanced Memory Buffer (AMB) that was supposed to be a part of each DIMM. A representative diagram of the system is shown in Figure 10.22. The CPU has a dedicated FB-DIMM memory controller, which is connected to the AMB of the first DIMM chip. The AMB is connected to all the DRAM devices within the DIMM. The AMB can use traditional DDR protocols to communicate with the DRAM devices. They need not be aware of the fact that a different protocol is being used.

The AMB in the first DIMM chip is connected with the memory controller via a set of lanes. Akin to high-speed I/O protocols such as USB and PCI-X, each lane is a high-speed serial bus, whose timing is independent of other parallel lanes. The memory controller sends data and commands to the first AMB via a set of lanes known as the southbound lanes. The AMB sends responses to the memory controller via another set of lanes known as the northbound lanes. The advantage of using lanes is as follows.

1. Since each lane is a high-speed serial bus, its timing need not be synchronised with other lanes, and thus we can raise the transmission frequency significantly.

2. The communication architecture is more immune to failures. Assume that a given lane fails, or the timing on a lane changes due to ageing, the system remains unaffected. In the first case, we can simply disregard the lane and transmit on the remaining lanes that are functional. In the second case, since the transmission on the different lanes happens independently, this will not lead to a failure.

The AMBs are connected in a chain using point-to-point links. The role of each AMB is as follows.

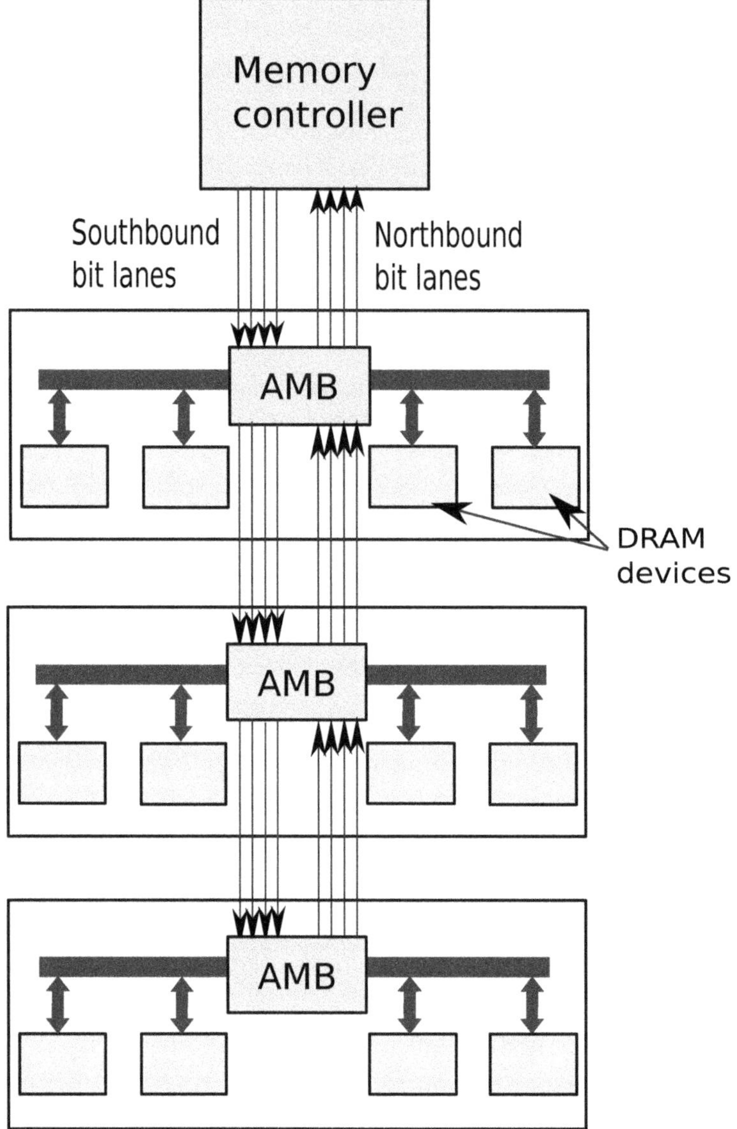

Figure 10.22: An FB-DIMM system

1. Receive data from southbound lanes (from the memory controller).

2. If the data is meant for the DIMM associated with the AMB, then reconstitute the packet by reading data from the serial bit lanes, and send it to the constituent DRAM devices. If the data is meant for an AMB downstream, then forward it to the next AMB in the chain.

3. Get data from northbound lanes, and send it towards the memory controller (northward).

A few of the advantages are obvious.

Scalability This is a scalable system, because we can add a large number of DIMMs.

High-speed The loading on buses is minimised and this ensures that we can have high-speed buses. Furthermore, since we use a set of serial bit lanes, they can use very high-speed signalling to transfer data as quickly as possible.

Reduced Pin Count The increasing number of pins associated with memory controllers was an issue because they needed to support many channels. There are limits to the pin count due to packaging issues. This protocol reduces the number of pins that are required in memory controllers.

Reliability Because we can use a variable number of bit lanes, and the loading per lane is deterministic, the overall reliability is enhanced.

The FB-DIMM technology was unfortunately not adapted at a large scale because of the complexity of the AMB. It needs to act as a router, serialise/deserialise data, buffer data, run the DDR protocols between itself and the DRAM devices, and monitor the reliability of transmission. Instead of being relatively passive devices, which can be produced in bulk, FB-DIMMs are active devices with elaborate AMBs. This increased the cost. However, FB-DIMMs are still attractive solutions for large servers.

Let us now discuss some of the specific technologies that are used in FB-DIMMs.

High Speed Transmission

Normally, we have 10 bit lanes in the southbound channel and 14 bit lanes in the northbound channel. We have more bit lanes in the northbound channel because they are used to transmit data for read operations, which are often on the critical path. Because all of these bit lanes are high-speed serial buses, we can afford to transmit data at a much higher clock rate. On each lane, we can transport 12 bits per DRAM clock cycle. This means that on the southbound channel with 10 bit lanes, we can transmit 120 bits in one DRAM clock cycle. On the northbound channel, we can transmit 168 bits in one DRAM clock cycle. This includes status bits, commands, and bits to perform error correction. The FB-DIMM protocol uses the CRC (Cyclic Redundancy Check) error detection and correction scheme that is particularly useful for detecting a burst of errors.

Let us compare this approach with a DDRX protocol. In such a protocol, we can transmit 144 bits in one DRAM cycle, assuming that the bus is 72 bits wide (64 bits for data and 8 bits for error correction bits). With FB-DIMMs, we can send one write command with 64 bits of data and 8 error correction bits every cycle on the southbound channel. On the northbound channel, we can simultaneously transmit 144 bits of read data inclusive of error correction bits. Thus the total amount of useful data that we can transfer between the memory controller and the FB-DIMMs is 144+72 = 216 bits. This is one and half times the bandwidth of a DDRX channel. Hence, there is an advantage in terms of bandwidth.

Along with this, we can support more FB-DIMM devices per channel, and more memory channels per memory controller because the number of pins required by each channel is much lower in this case.

Resample and Resync

Recall that AMBs also forward commands, addresses, and data to adjacent AMBs. We can use two methods. The first method called *Resampling* is as follows. An AMB directly forwards the data to the next AMB on the chain. In this case, it is possible that there would be some skew between the signals being sent on the different bit lanes. The skews will tend to accumulate over several hops. Even though this scheme is fast, we can still end up having a large amount of skew between different bit lanes. Note that at the destination, we need to wait for the slowest signal to arrive. We can however be slightly lucky if over the long transmission across several AMBs, the skews get balanced. This is not uncommon; however, we still need to be prepared for the worst case.

The other method is to read the entire data frame sent on the bit lanes, remove all the skew, and then retransmit the entire data frame to the downstream AMB. This method is known as *resync*, and introduces more delay in the protocol. It is good for a network with large skews that are unbalanced across the bit lanes.

Bit Lane Steering

Reliability is a key advantage of FB-DIMMs. Note that reliability is a key requirement of servers that typically use a lot of DRAM memory. Faults can often develop while replacing DIMMs or due to temperature induced stresses.

Let us assume that at some point of the transmission, we find that we are having too many errors (detected with the CRC error detection code). We shall first attempt a channel reset, which means that both ends of the channel discard their state, and try to resynchronise themselves. However, if this is not successful, we need to conclude that one of the bit lanes has developed a fault. FB-DIMMs have various BIST (built-in self test) mechanisms that allow us to determine which bit lanes have developed faults.

We can then use the bit lane steering mechanism to use the rest of the lanes for the communication. This will have a minimal effect on the bandwidth of the bus, however it will increase the reliability significantly.

Summary of the Discussion on FB-DIMMs
Undoubtedly, FB-DIMMs incorporate many technological advances. Their most important advantages include reducing the pin count, tolerating a high amount of skew during transmission, reducing the capacitive load on the bus, and using bit lane steering to use only those lanes that are fault-free. However, any revolutionary technology is still a slave of market economics, and if significant changes need to be made to the memory controller, DIMMs, and the channels on the motherboard, it is necessary for all of those vendors to adapt this technology. This sadly did not happen in the 2005-10 time frame, hence as of today such memories are not very popular. However, simpler variants of FB-DIMMs such as registered memories have become commonplace (as of 2020), and it looks like that the industry is making evolutionary changes in this direction.

Registered Memory

As compared to FB-DIMMs that have large overheads, registered memory is a much simpler technology that is in use today, and in many ways has taken over the space that FB-DIMMs were supposed to occupy. Registered memory modules (RDIMMs) have a register associated with a DIMM. This buffers memory addresses and commands, effectively reducing the capacitive loading on the address and command buses. Some variants of RDIMMs called LRDIMMs (Load-Reduced DIMMs) also place buffers on the data bus as well. Other than placing simple buffers on regular DDRX buses, they do not have any of the sophisticated features of FB-DIMMs.

Given that reads and writes are delayed by an extra cycle, there is an associated performance penalty. However, this is offset by the fact that buses can run at a higher frequency when using RDIMMs and can support more DIMMs. RDIMMs are very popular in the server market. The pitfalls of this technology are that motherboards need to be designed differently to support RDIMMs. Moreover, it is typically not possible to have a mix of regular DIMMs and RDIMMs.

10.3 DRAM Timing

The memory controller and the DRAM banks communicate via an elaborate set of commands. These commands have their own timing requirements, and there are rules that dictate when a command can be issued after another command. In this section, let us look at the world of DRAM commands and the DRAM access protocol in general.

We primarily perform three simple operations: read, write, and refresh. However, to support these operations we need a large portfolio of commands such that we can extract the maximum possible throughput from today's complex DRAM systems. We can divide the life cycle of every operation into four distinct stages: (1) transporting and decoding the command, (2) performing the actual read or write in the DRAM array, (3) moving the data within the DRAM chip, and (4) transmitting the result on the bus back to the processor. Each of these stages has its own set of commands and timing requirements. We shall broadly describe the latest DDR4 protocol in the next few sections and abstract away many of the details for the ease of explanation. Note that many simplifications have also been made for the sake of clarity. For an accurate description of the DDR4 protocol readers can refer to the corresponding JEDEC standard [JEDEC Solid State Technology Association, 2020]. This section presents only a very small subset of the overall protocol. Note that all the copyrights belong to JEDEC. The material in this section is reproduced with permission from JEDEC.

We assume a single DRAM device (DRAM chip) with 16 banks divided into groups of banks. We can create groups of 4 banks each or create groups with 8 banks each. Assume that all delays are in terms of bus cycles.

10.3.1 State Diagram

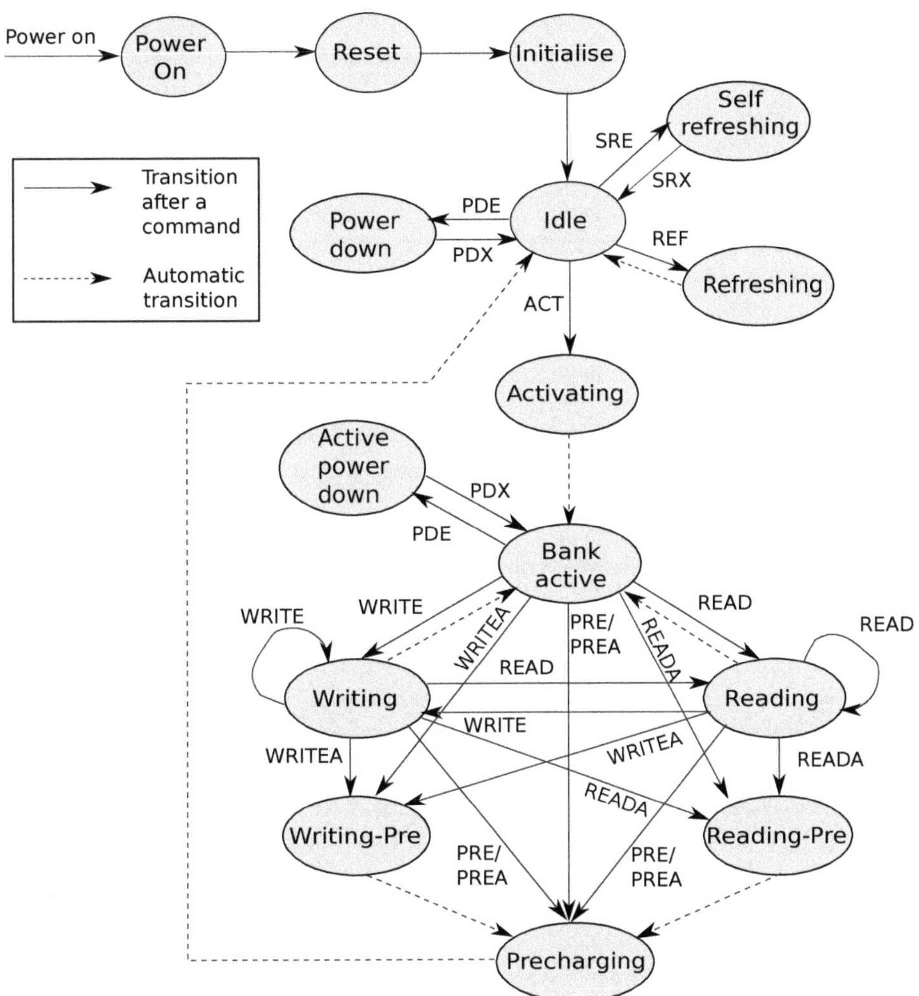

Figure 10.23: State diagram of the DDR4 protocol. Copyright JEDEC. Reproduced with permissions from JEDEC. Source: [JEDEC Solid State Technology Association, 2020]

Figure 10.23 shows the state diagram of the DDR4 protocol from the point of view of a DRAM device (DRAM chip). There are two kinds of arrows: solid and dashed. The solid arrows indicate a state transition that happens because we either receive a command from the memory controller or a command is generated internally. The dashed arrows indicate a state transition that happens automatically.

We first power the device on, reset its state, initialise it, and then reach the *Idle* state. Along with commands for reading and writing, there are many commands for managing the device. Let us look at them first.

Modern DRAMs support two kinds of refresh modes: external refresh and self refresh. An *external refresh* means that the memory controller sends the *REF* command to the device, and then it enters the *Refreshing* state. However, if the CPU is powered down, the DRAM can still maintain its values by using the self refresh mechanism. In this case, it has a built-in timer that generates two commands *SRE* (self refresh enter) and *SRX* (self refresh exit). These are used to enter and exit the *Self refreshing* state respectively. If there is no activity, we can save power by entering the *Power Down* state.

Before accessing any row, it is necessary to activate it first. The controller sends the *ACT* command to the device, the device activates the corresponding row and transitions to the *Bank active* state. In this state, we can also power the device down and transition to the *Active power down* state upon receiving the *PDE* command and later exit this state after receiving the *PDX* command.

For reading and writing, there are two kinds of commands: one without auto-precharge and one with auto-precharge. The former class of commands keep the row open, which means that it is possible for subsequent reads and writes to access columns in the same row. The contents of the row are buffered in the sense amplifiers. In this class, there are two commands: *READ* and *WRITE*. Upon receiving them, the state transitions to the *Reading* and *Writing* states respectively. After the operations are over, the device switches back to the *Bank active* state. The row remains open for future accesses. In the *Writing* state, if the device gets a *READ* command, it transitions to the *Reading* state and vice versa.

The next set of commands automatically precharge the DRAM array after the commands finish executing. These commands are *READA* and *WRITEA* for reading and writing respectively. Whenever, the device receives a *READA* command, it executes the read and also transitions to the *Reading-Pre* state. It behaves in a similar manner when it receives a *WRITEA* command: it transitions to the *Writing-Pre* state along with performing the write. From both of these states, an automatic transition is made to the *Precharging* state where all the bit lines are precharged, and made ready for a subsequent memory access to another row.

From any state, it is possible to enter the *Precharging* state directly by issuing the *PRE* (precharge one bank) and *PREA* (precharge all banks) commands.

This state diagram determines the operation of each DRAM device. The memory controller also keeps a copy of the state of each DRAM device and also tracks the transitions. This is done such that the memory controller can issue the right commands at the right instances of time.

Next, let us look at the major commands used for controlling and operating DRAM devices, and their associated timing constraints.

10.3.2   Activate and Precharge Commands

Activate Command

The activate command *ACT* is used to activate a given row in a bank, read all the columns into the sense amplifiers, and wait for a subsequent read or write access. Note that each row (or page) can be fairly large: 1024 or 2048 bits. Whenever we activate a row, all of this data is brought into the sense amplifiers, and subsequently the column multiplexers choose a subset of the bits. This is thus an expensive operation.

The timing parameters associated with the *ACT* command are shown in Table 10.2. The way to interpret this table is as follows. The first column indicates a pair of events, and the second column shows the minimum time interval between the first event and the second event. The events can either be external commands or internally generated commands. For example, the parameter $tRAS$ refers to the minimum amount of time that needs to elapse between issuing an *ACT* command and subsequently

Consecutive pair of commands	Time interval
$ACT \rightarrow PRE$	$tRAS$
$ACT \rightarrow \langle IntREAD/IntWRITE \rangle$	$tRCD$
$ACT \rightarrow ACT$	tRC
$ACT \rightarrow REF$	
Relationships: $tRC > tRAS > tRCD$	

Table 10.2: Timing constraints for the ACT command

issuing the PRE (precharge) command. We can also specify the minimum time interval between a command, and issuing an internal command such as $IntREAD$. The second row means that we issue the internal read command $IntREAD$ at least after $tRCD$ (row to column delay) units of time after issuing the ACT command. An internal read command is issued to read the values stored in the sense amplifiers. The internal write command $IntWRITE$ is defined on similar lines.

Next, let us consider tRC (row cycle time). It is the largest among the three parameters because it specifies the duration of the entire process: activate a row, close the row, and precharge.

Precharge Command

The precharge commands, PRE and $PREA$, are used to precharge the bit lines in a given bank, or in all the banks respectively. The row is subsequently deactivated and the bank enters the $Idle$ state. For a subsequent access, we need to activate a row first.

Consecutive pair of commands	Time interval
$PRE \rightarrow ACT$	tRP
Relationships: $tRC = tRAS + tRP$	

Table 10.3: Timing constraints for the PRE command

The timing parameters associated with the precharge command PRE are shown in Table 10.3. The minimum time interval between issuing the PRE command and a subsequent ACT command is tRP. We thus have $tRC = tRAS + tRP$ (refer to Tables 10.2 and 10.3). In other words, the minimum row cycle time is equal to the sum of the time it takes to issue a precharge command after activation and the minimum duration of precharging.

Timing Constraints for Limiting Power Consumption

Consecutive pair of commands	Time interval
Different bank group: $ACT \rightarrow ACT$	$tRRD_S$
Same bank group: $ACT \rightarrow ACT$	$tRRD_L$
Four-bank Activation Window	$tFAW$
Relationships: $tFAW \geq 4 * tRRD_S$ and $tRRD_L \geq tRRD_S$	

Table 10.4: Timing constraints added for limiting power consumption

In modern DRAM systems, power and temperature are important issues. Hence, it is necessary to limit the power consumption of DRAM devices. As a result, there are two timing parameters to limit the power usage of DRAM devices (refer to Table 10.4). Both these parameters target row activations, because a row activation is an extremely power-hungry operation. We need to read an entire row of 512-2048 cells, and store their contents in the sense amplifiers. Furthermore, since reads are destructive, the data needs to be restored. Consequently, we need to have a minimum delay between row activations such that we can limit the power consumption.

The first is the row-to-row delay (t_{RRD}). This is the minimum time interval between activating a given row and activating another row. There are two types of row-to-row delays: $tRRD_S$ (short) and $tRRD_L$ (long). $tRRD_S$ is the minimum delay when the rows are in different bank groups. Whereas, $tRRD_L$ is the minimum delay when the rows belong to different banks in the same bank group. $tRRD_L \geq tRRD_S$ because we wish to enforce a power constraint for each bank group. Here *same* means *same as the previous access*, and the term *different* is defined likewise. This definition holds for the rest of the commands that use the same nomenclature. This means that we are discouraging consecutive row activations in the same bank group, which needs to be done to limit power consumption and local temperature rise.

Another parameter that limits the device-wide power consumption is $tFAW$ (Four-bank Activation Window). This means that in any sliding window of time that is $tFAW$ cycles wide, we can have at most four row activations. For example, if this window is 50 cycles wide, then there is no 50-cycle window of time in which there are more than four row activations. This limits the overall power consumption of the DRAM device.

10.3.3   Read Operation

To initiate a read, the memory controller sends the $READ$ command along with the number of the column (on the address bus), and the address of the bank group. Subsequently, the device starts to read the values by issuing the internal read command $IntREAD$.

Preamble and Postamble

Modern DRAM devices have extremely high frequencies and thus recovering the clock signal is difficult. We thus have a data strobe signal, DQS, that helps the receiver properly latch the data. However, with extremely high frequencies this also proves to be difficult. Hence, there is the notion of adding a preamble to the data transmission. The preamble is a set of cycles in which we do not transmit data. We allow the receiver to synchronise its clock with the transmitted data. This is known as the *read preamble*.

The read preamble is typically 1-2 cycles. This process of adjusting the clocks before a read operation is known as *read levelling*.

Similar to the preamble, we also have the option of adding a postamble where we wait for a given number of cycles after transmitting the last data bit before starting the next transmission. This allows the receiver to latch all the bits correctly. The preamble and postamble are graphically shown in Figure 10.24.

We have two timing parameters defined for these operations: $RPRE$ and $RPST$ (see Table 10.5). In a burst of read and write commands, the requirement of the preamble and postamble is sometimes relaxed because there is no need to synchronise the clock.

Operation	Duration
Read preamble	$tRPRE$
Read postamble	$tRPST$

Table 10.5: Timing constraints for the preamble and postamble

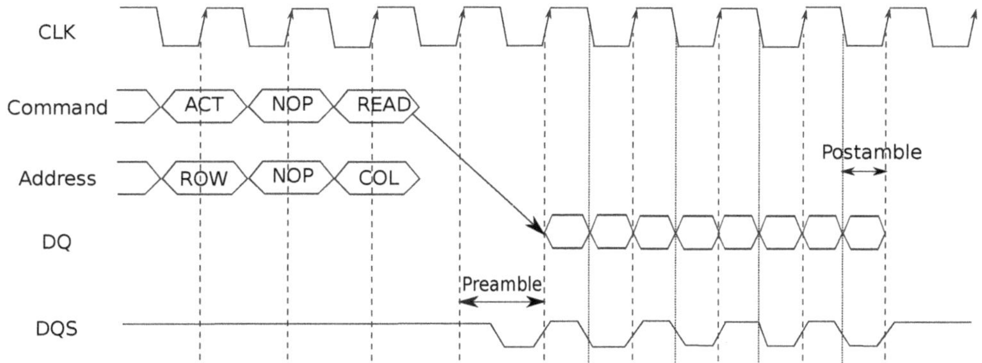

Figure 10.24: The read preamble and postamble in the DDR4 protocol

Consecutive pair of commands	Time interval
$READ \rightarrow \langle$First data bit on the bus$\rangle$	RL
$READ \rightarrow IntREAD$	AL
$IntREAD \rightarrow \langle$First data bit on the bus without parity checking$\rangle$	CL
Time to verify the parity	PL
$IntREAD \rightarrow PRE$	$tRTP$
Relationships: $RL = AL + CL + PL$	

Table 10.6: Timing constraints for the read operation

$READ$ command

The parameters for the read operation are shown in Table 10.6. The time between issuing the $READ$ command and getting the first data bit is the read latency RL. Subsequently, we get 1 bit every half-cycle (beat) depending upon the burst length. The read latency can be broken down into three components: additive latency (AL), CAS latency (CL), and the parity latency(PL). We have $RL = AL + CL + PL$.

The DDR4 protocol allows us to issue a $READ$ command immediately after an ACT command. However, we need to wait for $tRCD$ time units before we can start an internal read operation. This means that the $READ$ command needs to be internally buffered till the device is ready to issue an internal read. This delay is known as the additive latency (AL). Once an internal read command is issued, the time it takes to put the first data bit on the bus is the CAS latency CL. Furthermore, we can program the device to check for any parity errors before the data is sent on the bus. This takes some additional time, which is known as the parity latency (PL). We thus have $RL = AL + PL + CL$.

Finally, we define $tRTP$ as the delay between an internal read command and the precharge command. This is the amount of time that it takes to complete the read operation and send the data to the buffers of the bus. After this operation is done, the precharge command can be issued. We can infer that the minimum spacing between an external read command $READ$ and the PRE command is $AL + tRTP$ time units.

Burst of Read Commands

Till know we have considered a single read command. Let us now consider a burst of read commands for different columns in the same row (see Table 10.7).

We define the column-to-column delay for access to the same bank group as $tCCD_L$, and for access to different bank groups as $tCCD_S$. This is the minimum duration between issuing two $READ$ commands

Consecutive pair of commands	Time interval
Column to column delay (same bank group)	$tCCD_L$
Column to column delay (different bank group)	$tCCD_S$
Relationships: $tCCD_L \geq tCCD_S$	

Table 10.7: Timing constraints for the column-to-column delay

to two different columns across the same or different bank groups. It is faster to access a different bank group than the same bank group ($tCCD_L \geq tCCD_S$). This is a standard feature of DDR4. The reason is that the same bank group (one that is being currently used) has many resources allocated for the current transfer, whereas, a different bank group has more resources available and is thus faster to access. Additionally, we wish to limit localised power consumption.

10.3.4   Write Operation

The write operation is similar to the read operation. It is initiated by sending a $WRITE$ command. At the same time, we send the column address on the address bus and the address of the bank group. Let us discuss the specifics.

Preamble and Postamble

Similar to the $READ$ command we also have a preamble and postamble (refer to Table 10.8) for the $WRITE$ command. The reasons are similar – detecting the relative skews between the data, strobe, and the internal clock of the DRAM. Once we detect the skews, we can correctly latch the data. This process of training the circuit for correctly latching the data is known as *write levelling*.

Operation	Duration
Write preamble	$tWPRE$
Write postamble	$tWPST$

Table 10.8: Timing constraints for the write preamble and postamble

$WRITE$ command

The $WRITE$ command is similar to that $READ$ command in terms of the way it is issued. In this case, we define a term called the write latency (WL). It is the sum of the additive latency (AL), the parity latency (PL), and the CAS write latency (CWL). Refer to Table 10.9 for a description of the parameters that are relevant to the write operation. We have $WL = AL + PL + CWL$.

Consecutive pair of commands	Duration
$WRITE \rightarrow \langle$First data bit on the bus$\rangle$	WL
$WRITE \rightarrow IntWRITE$	AL
Time to compute the parity	PL
$IntWRITE \rightarrow \langle$First data bit on the bus$\rangle$	CWL
Relationships: $WL = AL + PL + CWL$	

Table 10.9: Timing constraints for the write operation

Burst of Write Commands

In a write burst, we use the same timing constraints as the $READ$ command for issuing different $WRITE$ commands. The parameters $tCCD_S$ and $tCCD_L$ are relevant (with the same meanings) for writes as well.

10.3.5   Interaction between the Read, Write, and Precharge Operations

The $READ$ and $WRITE$ commands have several interactions between them. The timing constraints are shown in Table 10.10.

Consecutive pair of commands	Time interval
$READ \rightarrow WRITE$	$tRTW$
$WRITE \rightarrow READ$	$tWTR$
Burst length	tBL
$WRITE \rightarrow PRE$	tWR

Table 10.10: Interaction between read and write operations

$tRTW$ (read to write) is the minimum time interval between a $READ$ and a subsequent $WRITE$ command. Similarly, $tWTR$ (write to read) is the minimum time interval between a $WRITE$ command, and a subsequent $READ$ command. We also define the parameter tBL, which is the burst length – the number of beats used to transmit data for a single command. As we have discussed in Section 10.2.2, for DDR3 and DDR4, it is normally equal to 8 beats. If the burst-chop mode is used, it is equal to 4 beats.

Read to Write Delay

Let us derive the timing relationship between issuing a $READ$ command and issuing a $WRITE$ command. This is shown in Figure 10.25. Let us make a simplistic assumption that $PL = 0$ for the ease of explanation.

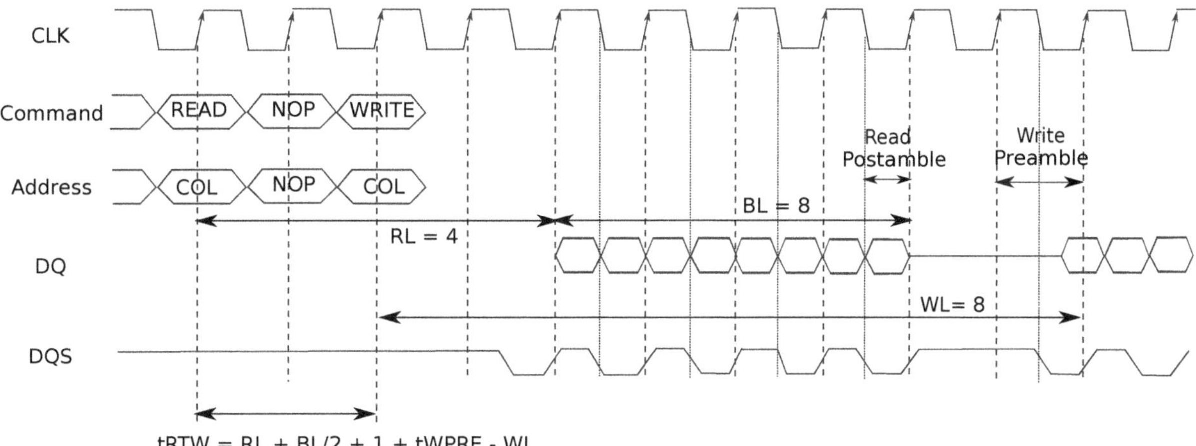

Figure 10.25: Read to write delay ($tRTW$)

If the $READ$ command is issued at the beginning of cycle 0, then the earliest we can write data to the bus is cycle $RL + BL/2 + tWPRE + 1$ (refer to Figure 10.25). The reason we add $BL/2$ is because we are assuming that the unit of BL is half-cycles. In most DDR4 devices, we need to add the additional 1 cycle delay because for starting a write operation we need to change the direction of the data transmission on the bus. Given that the write latency is WL, the minimum spacing between the $READ$ and $WRITE$ commands is therefore equal to $RL + BL/2 + tWPRE + 1 - WL$. Note that in this case the read postamble is getting subsumed within the read burst. Otherwise, we needed to add a component of it as well.

Write to Read Delay

The $tWTR$ (write to read) parameter is defined differently. It refers to the minimum interval between the end of a write operation (including its postamble) and a subsequent $READ$ command. Here also, we can define two parameters $tWTR_S$ (different bank group) and $tWTR_L$ (same bank group). We have the same relationship: $tWTRL_L \geq tWTR_S$. A write operation is slightly slower as compared to a read because after every write we need to do some more work. $tWTR$ cycles are needed to ensure that we are able to write the correct state to the sense amplifiers and the DRAM cells. This requires time because some of the bit lines need to undergo voltage transitions.

Write Recovery Time

The write recovery time tWR is defined in a similar manner as the write-to-read time. Its corresponding interval starts from the end of a write (including its postamble). It is the minimum duration from this point till we can issue a precharge command. The reason for the write recovery time is similar to the extra time required for starting a read operation after a write operation ($tWTR$).

10.3.6 Refresh Operation

Every time that the memory controller requires a refresh, it issues the REF (refresh) command. DDR4 memories require a refresh cycle once every $tREFI$ cycles. Before a refresh command is sent, all the banks need to be precharged and be idle for at least tRP cycles. Every DRAM device has an internal refresh controller that generates a list of all the addresses that need to be refreshed. The entire process takes $tRFC$ cycles (refresh cycle time). All the banks are set to the idle state and can be accessed.

Modern memory protocols provide some flexibility in scheduling refresh commands particularly if the memory traffic is high. They allow us to postpone refresh commands subject to a maximum limit.

Along with an external refresh mode, most DDR devices also have a self-refresh mode that allows them to retain their data even when the CPU is powered down. The process is similar to that of an external refresh. The timing constraints are summarised in Table 10.11.

Interval	Duration
Maximum refresh interval	$tREFI$
Refresh cycle time	$tRFC$

Table 10.11: Timing constraints for the refresh commands

10.3.7 Example of a Protocol

Let us enumerate the parameters of the DDR 1600 protocol. It can support 1600 transfers per second with a 800 MHz clock rate. The clock cycle time is thus 1.25 ns. Table 10.12 lists all the parameters. The unit is clock cycles.

Parameter	Mnemonic	Value (cycles)
Row cycle time	tRC	38
ACT to PRE command period	$tRAS$	28
PRE to ACT command period	tRP	10
ACT to internal read or write	$tRCD$	10
CAS latency	CL	10
CAS write latency	CWL	9
Column to column delay (same bank group)	$tCCD_L$	5
Column to column delay (different bank group)	$tCCD_S$	4
Row to row delay (same bank group, 1Kb page size)	$tRRD_L$	5
Row to row delay (different bank group, 1Kb page size)	$tRRD_S$	4
Four-bank activation window (1Kb page size)	$tFAW$	20
Write to read latency (same bank group)	$tWTR_L$	6
Write to read latency (different bank group)	$tWTR_S$	2
$IntREAD$ to PRE command period	$tRTP$	6
Write recovery time	tWR	12

Table 10.12: Parameters for the DDR 1600 protocol

10.4 Memory Controller

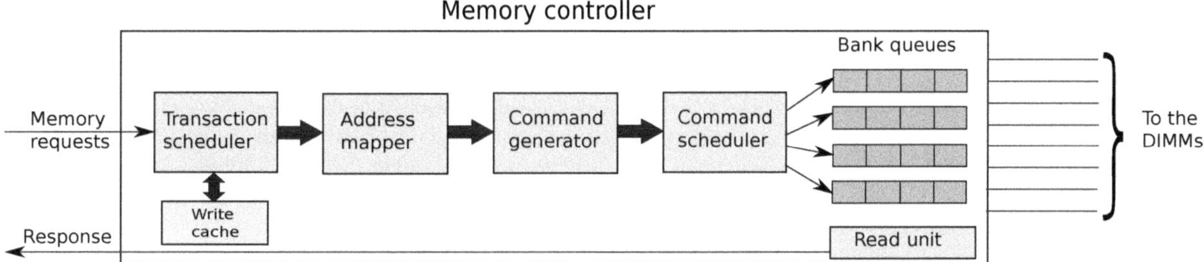

Figure 10.26: Structure of the memory controller

The general structure of the memory controller is shown in Figure 10.26. We typically have one memory controller per channel.

It receives requests from different cache banks. All the requested memory transactions are first handed over to the transaction scheduler. It ascertains the priority of the transaction with respect to other transactions that are being processed. For example, at this stage it can decide that a much-needed refresh operation should have the highest priority. The second stage, address mapper, maps the physical memory address to addresses on the DRAM devices. For a given physical address, this stage maps it to a given rank and a set of banks. There are a range of possibilities here depending on the number of DRAM devices, the number of arrays within each device, and the request pattern. After the address mapping stage, the memory request is converted to a sequence of DRAM commands by the command generator, which are then inserted into a set of bank-specific queues. Finally, we have a command scheduler, that dispatches the commands to the banks. This needs to follow the timing rules that we discussed in Section 10.3.

To summarise, the main components in the memory controller are as follows.

1. A high-level read/write transaction scheduler.

2. Address mapping engine.

3. DRAM command generation unit.

4. Command scheduling unit.

Let us revisit the notion of the *rank*. Multiple DIMMs are connected to each channel, and we have multiple DRAM devices on each DIMM. All of them share the same address and command buses. This makes life complicated. This is because in principle all the devices can have different clock skews because their distance from the memory controller might vary. However, this is not allowed because ensuring proper timing would become a very onerous task. Hence, we divide the set of devices into ranks. All the devices in each rank have roughly the same degree of clock skew and are equally distant from the memory controller in terms of timing. As a result, it is possible to run all the DRAM devices in a rank in unison.

In the DDR4 protocol, we specify three pieces of information with each command: chip-select id, bank group id, and bank id. The chip select signal selects the rank. The rest of the ranks are disabled for that command. This signal is routed to all the devices within the rank such that they all get enabled. The bank group and bank id bits are used to choose a specific bank within each device. Then the command is delivered to all the chosen banks across the DRAM devices. Let us consider a concrete example. Assume we have 8 DRAM devices in a rank with 4 banks per device and 8 arrays per bank. Thus each bank can read 8 bits at a time (one bit from each array). When we send the read command, we also send the id of the bank (and the bank group, if we have bank groups). For example, if we send bank id 2, then this selects all the banks with id 2 in all the 8 DRAM devices. The read access commences. Once the data is ready each selected bank produces 8 bits (1 bit per array). Since we have selected 8 banks (1 bank per device), all 8 of them produce 64 bits in a single cycle. These bits can then be sent to the memory controller.

Since read accesses take time, we can utilise the time in the middle to activate and schedule requests on other banks. Note that in most memory systems, *accessing a bank* means accessing the same bank id across all the devices. Some advanced memory protocols such as DDR4 do allow commands to be sent to individual devices in a rank; however, that is mainly for setting specific electrical parameters.

Important Point 19

It is important to note that the reason we organise memory devices into a rank is such that we can increase the amount of parallelism and read or write a large number of bits in a single cycle. Furthermore, each memory device has multiple banks where only one bank is allowed to process a command from the bus in a given cycle. For any memory request, we enable one bank from each device, and then send a read/write/activate request to the set of enabled banks across the devices in a rank; they work in lockstep.

10.4.1 DRAM Transaction Scheduling

Each DRAM controller receives memory requests from the NoC. An overwhelming majority of them are either read or write requests. Sometimes it can also generate its own requests such as refresh operations.

The first part of transaction scheduling is to decide the relative priorities of the operations. Typically, memory controllers prioritise read requests because they are most of the time on the critical path, whereas write requests can be deferred. Additionally, in the DDR4 protocol, back-to-back read requests are much faster than request pairs in which the first request is a write. Recall that we need time to recover from a write because along with writing to the sense amplifier array, we also need to write to the memory cells.

As a result, it is a much better idea to schedule write operations when the DRAM devices are relatively free.

Write Caching

Sadly reordering reads and writes can introduce correctness and consistency problems. This can be easily solved by adding a write cache (similar to a write buffer). This stores all the outstanding writes. A read operation first checks for its address in the write cache. If there is a hit, then it returns with the value stored in the write cache, otherwise if there is a miss, then the read operation is sent to the DRAM devices.

Open-Page Access Policy

One major advantage of having a sense amplifier array is that it can store an entire row (512, 1024, or 2048 bits). Recall that we refer to a row as a page as well, and the storage part of the sense amplifier array is synonymously referred to as the *row buffer* or the *page buffer*. In every access, we typically need to access a subset of these bits. Here, the advantage is that we need not perform a precharge operation after every read or write, instead if there is temporal and spatial locality, then this row buffer can be used as a cache. This saves us unnecessary activate and precharge operations. This is efficient in terms of both time as well as power.

This policy is known as the open-page access policy where after a read or write operation completes, we do not set the bank to the *idle state*. Instead, we keep the row open such that it can serve later requests that map to the same row. Because of temporal and spatial locality, we expect a lot of hits to the open row (or page). To ensure that the hit rate is high, most memory controllers reorder the requests such that contiguous requests map to the same open page.

Once we run out of requests, we precharge the bank and set its state to the *idle* state.

Close-Page Access Policy

The close-page access policy closes the row after it has been accessed once. This favours a random-access pattern, where there is very little spatial and temporal locality. The memory controller issues the $READA$ and $WRITEA$ commands that immediately issue a precharge after completing the read or write respectively.

Hybrid Access Policy

Most memory controllers as of today use a hybrid access policy, where they decide when the row should be kept open and when it should be closed. They monitor the sequence of memory accesses and if they predict that a given row is unlikely to be used again in the near future, then it is immediately closed after the access.

Managing Refreshes

A typical DRAM row can hold its data for 32 to 64 ms. It needs to be refreshed at least once during this period. Let us assume that it can hold its data for 64 ms and we have 8192 rows. Then we need to send a refresh command to the devices once every $64,000/8192 = 7.8$ μs. Each refresh command refreshes a given row. During that period (refresh cycle time: $tRFC$), the bank cannot be used for any other purpose.

Modern DRAM devices have refresh modes: self refresh and external refresh. The self refresh mode is useful when the CPU is powered down or is not in a position to send refresh commands. Otherwise, we rely on external refresh commands, where the memory controller explicitly sends refresh commands to each row. Sometimes it is possible that we may have to delay critical read and write requests to accommodate a refresh. The DDR4 protocol does give us some flexibility in this regard. We can defer a refresh message by up to 8 refresh intervals (a refresh interval is 7.8 μs in our example). During this period we can finish sending critical read and write messages. After that we need to quickly finish all the pending refresh operations.

10.4.2 Address Mapping

Every physical address needs to be mapped to an equivalent DRAM address. A DRAM address is a combination of the channel id, the rank, the bank, the row, and the set of columns. This determines the available parallelism, number of bank conflicts, and the time it takes to wait between consecutive accesses. The address mapping scheme is dependent on the technology that is used, latencies of different operations, and the memory access pattern.

Basic Terminology

Symbol	Description
c	Channel id
k	Rank id
g	Bank group id
b	Bank id
r	Row id
l	64-byte block id in a row

Table 10.13: Symbols used in address mapping

Table 10.13 shows the symbols that we shall use to describe the address mapping scheme. Let us first go over our main assumptions.

1. We read or write data at the granularity of 64-byte blocks.

2. We assume that each row stores an integral number of 64-byte blocks. The id of a block in a row is denoted by the symbol l.

3. All the counts start from zero.

4. We assume that a physical address given to the DRAM memory controller points to the starting address of a 64–byte block. In each beat, we transfer 64 bits.

5. If the paging mechanism has indicated that a given frame is present in the DRAM, then we are guaranteed to find the frame. Unlike a cache, there are no misses in main memory. We would like to reiterate that a page in DRAM is not the same as a virtual memory page.

We can deduce that the address of each 64-byte block in the DRAM memory is uniquely specified using $c + k + g + b + r + l$ ($= N$) bits. To operationalise this, once the memory controller gets the address of the block, it retrieves N bits from the address, and discards the rest of the bits. These are typically the least significant bits of the block address. The virtual memory system needs to ensure that no two blocks who have these N bits in common in their physical addresses are present in the DRAM memory at the same time. This will remove the need for having a tag array. This further ensures that our DRAM structure can be used in modern processors very easily. Note that this design choice is not a significant issue when it comes to performance because main memories are typically very large and we have a lot of locality at the page level.

Now we need to decide which bits we need to use to address the channel, which bits we need to address the rank, and so on. Any addressing scheme can be described using the following format. Let's say we have a scheme, $c : k : g : b : r : l$. This means that in the N-bit block address, we use the least significant l bits to address the block in the row, the next r bits to address the row in the bank, and so on. In comparison, the addressing scheme $k : b : r : l : g : c$ means that we use the least significant c bits to address the channel, the next g bits for the bank group id, and so on.

Let us create addressing schemes for the open-page and close-page policies.

Addressing for the Open-Page Policy

The key insight is that the least significant bits tend to vary more, and there is more randomness in them. In comparison, the more significant bits vary less. If for some reason we want to distribute the accesses, we should use the least significant bits.

Out of the six parameters – c, k, g, b, r, l – we need to first decide which parameter we should map to the least significant bits. Let us look at the most common access pattern, which is accessing the next block address. Most of the time we tend to read consecutive blocks because this is the typical pattern of both instruction accesses and data accesses, notably array or stack accesses. Hence, we should optimise the addressing method for this pattern.

Switching between channels is the cheapest operation in terms of time. We typically have different memory controllers for different channels, and it is possible to operate them independently. We can even read consecutive blocks in parallel if they are mapped to different channels. Hence, our addressing scheme should be of the form $x : x : x : x : x : c$. Here, x, refers to a parameter that is unspecified as of now.

Since we are considering the open-page access policy, the row buffer will continue to maintain the contents of the entire row unless it is explicitly precharged. We can leverage this fact and read the next block from the row buffer. Hence, the next set of bits should be mapped to the parameter l (block id in a row). The addressing scheme thus becomes $x : x : x : x : l : c$.

Let us now make a choice between a different bank and a different rank. We shall discuss why we are discarding the row id at this stage slightly later. To send an access to a different rank, we need to resynchronise the timing of the processor-memory bus. Recall that different banks have different timing requirements and have different clock skews. Some re-synchronisation, read levelling, and write levelling needs to be done. This will take time. Consequently, let us reduce the priority of switching the rank.

Let us thus maximise locality at the level of the banks by switching to another bank in the same rank. Recall that banks are independent of each other. We can activate bank 2, while bank 1 is completing a read operation. This feature can be leveraged to send consecutive accesses to other banks. Recall from Section 10.3 that the delay is larger if we send a request to another bank in the same bank group; therefore, we need to send a request to a different bank group. To achieve more randomness in this regard, let us map the next set of bits to the bank group g. After this, let us consider the bank id b. Thus our addressing scheme now looks like $x : x : b : g : l : c$.

We are now left with the choice of the rank id and row id. We have already discussed that switching to a new rank involves costly re-synchronisation. However, switching to a new row is even more expensive. We need to close the row buffer by performing a precharge operation, and then activate the new row. This is very expensive in terms of time. Hence, let us prefer switching to a new rank.

The final addressing scheme is $r : k : b : g : l : c$.

Addressing for the Close-Page Policy

Here also the first priority should be the channel because it is very easy to switch between channels, and requests can be sent to different channels in parallel. Since we do not intend to reuse the row, we need to look at increasing bank-level parallelism. We thus map the next few bits to b and g. The addressing scheme at this stage is $x : x : x : b : g : c$.

Next we can switch the rank because that is much faster than precharging and accessing a new row. Hence, the scheme becomes $x : x : k : b : g : c$.

We now have a choice between the id of the block in a row (l), and the row id (r). Since we close the row after an access, we cannot leverage any locality at the level of the row buffer. However, we can always take advantage of caching schemes at the memory controller, if we stick to the same row. Hence, we map the next few bits to l.

Therefore, the final addressing scheme is $r : l : k : b : g : c$.

10.4.3   Command Scheduling

After the address mapping stage, we generate the DRAM commands and store them in a set of queues. The queues are typically bank specific, which means that each bank has a set of queues. Furthermore, for each bank we can have three separate sub-queues: a read queue, a write queue, and a refresh queue. Let us discuss different scheduling mechanisms for the different bank queues.

Bank Round-Robin (BRR)

This is one of the simplest scheduling mechanisms. For a given rank, the scheduler follows a round-robin algorithm. It visits each bank queue, picks a request, and sends it to the DIMMs. At this stage, several optimisations are possible. For example, we can prioritise reads as compared to writes. The DDR protocols allow us to send a *READ* command immediately after an *ACT* command. This can be done at this stage. This is a beneficial feature because we need to otherwise wait for a long time before we revisit the same bank queue once again.

Once we are finished with processing the requests of a given rank, we move to the next rank. Note that at this stage, the memory controller also maintains some state regarding the timing of the commands such that no timing constraints are violated.

Rank Round-Robin (RRR)

The rank round-robin algorithm (RRR) differs slightly from the bank round-robin algorithm (BRR) in terms of the order of accessing the queues.

We first access the same bank id in each rank, and then go to the next bank id. This approach distributes requests between ranks more uniformly as opposed to BRR. Note that the choice of the command scheduling algorithm and the addressing scheme are related. In practice, memory controller designers take all of this into account, conduct extensive simulations, and then create a design that provides the highest aggregate speedup for a wide variety of memory access patterns.

Greedy

Both the scheduling algorithms, BRR and RRR, are relatively oblivious of the timing constraints while making their scheduling decisions. Their main aim is fairness across banks and ranks. Note that they still need to observe timing constraints, and this is done after the scheduling decision has been made.

As opposed to this philosophy, the greedy algorithm works very differently. Out of all the bank queues we choose that request that can be issued (sent to the DIMMs) as soon as possible. This ensures that our system waits as little as possible to issue commands. Even though this approach works well in a lightly loaded system, there can be issues with starvation and fairness in a moderate to heavily loaded system.

Most practical scheduling algorithms in modern processors try to maximise performance by minimising the waiting time, and simultaneously also try to not compromise on fairness significantly.

10.5 Emerging Memory Technologies

The single largest criticism of modern DRAM memory is that it is *volatile* in nature. This means that when we turn the power off, a DRAM chip loses all of its data. It thus cannot be used as a persistent storage medium. The next time that we restart the machine, it will be necessary to repopulate the DRAM by reading all the pages that it needs to have from the disk. This increases the system startup time and induces page faults during execution. Wouldn't it be nice to have a memory that is *nonvolatile* in nature? This means that it will not lose its data when the power is switched off. In this section, we shall look at the basic physics, and the design of such nonvolatile memories, henceforth referred to as NVMs.

To design a nonvolatile memory device, it needs to have two distinct permanent states. As long as we can switch the device from one state to the other and back, we have a functional memory cell. These memory cells can then be interconnected to create a memory array, which can then be connected to the CPU via a set of memory channels. In this section, we shall look at different kinds of nonvolatile memories.

Please note that a nonvolatile memory is a storage device, which is meant to permanently store data. We still require regular DRAM memories for speed and efficiency. Nonvolatile memories compete with hard disks and other forms of slow secondary storage. Moreover, a nonvolatile memory can be used as a fast cache for a hard disk. Additionally, it can be used in critical applications where we do not want to spend any time in reading *cold data* from the disk.

Definition 91

- *A memory is said to be* volatile *when it loses its data after the power is switched off. DRAM memory is an example of a volatile memory.*

- *In comparison, a memory is said to be* nonvolatile *if it does not lose its data when the power is switched off. The most popular example of such memory is flash memory that we have in USB sticks. Nonvolatile memories will be referred to as NVMs henceforth.*

10.5.1 Flash Memory

Hard disks and optical drives are fairly bulky, and need to be handled carefully because they contain sensitive mechanical parts. An additional shortcoming of optical storage media is that they are very sensitive to scratches and other forms of minor accidental damage. Consequently, these devices are not ideally suited for portable and mobile applications. We need a storage device that does not consist of sensitive mechanical parts, can be carried in a pocket, can be attached to any computer, and is extremely durable. Flash drives such as USB pen drives satisfy all these requirements. A typical pen drive can fit in a wallet, can be attached to all kinds of devices, and is extremely robust and durable. It does not lose its data when it is disconnected from the computer. We have flash based storage devices in most portable devices, medical devices, industrial electronics, disk caches in high end servers, and small data storage devices. Flash memory is an example of an EEPROM (Electrically Erasable Programmable Read Only Memory) or EPROM (Erasable Programmable Read Only Memory). Note that traditionally EPROM based memories used ultraviolet light for erasing data. They have been superseded by flash based devices.

Let us look at flash based technology in this section. The basic element of storage is a floating gate transistor.

The Floating Gate Transistor

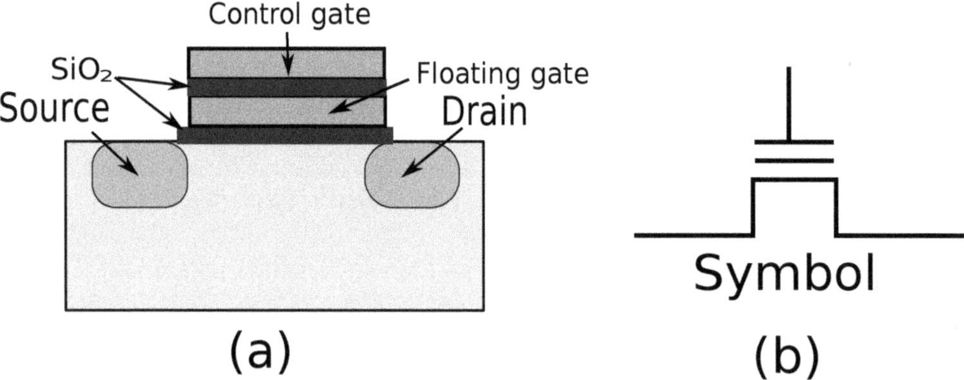

Figure 10.27: A floating gate transistor

Figure 10.27 shows a floating gate transistor. The figure shows a regular NMOS transistor with two gates instead of one. The gate on top is known as the *control gate*, and is equivalent to the gate in normal MOS transistors. The gate below the control gate is known as the floating gate. It is surrounded on all sides by an SiO_2 based electrical insulation layer. Hence, the floating gate is electrically isolated from the rest of the device. By some means if we are able to implant a certain amount of charge in the floating gate, then the floating gate will maintain its potential for a very long time. In practice, there is a negligible amount of current flow between the floating gate and the rest of the components in the floating gate transistor under normal conditions.

Let us now consider two scenarios. In the first scenario, the floating gate is not charged. In this case, the floating gate transistor acts as a regular NMOS transistor. In the second scenario, the floating gate has accumulated electrons containing negative charge (we will discuss how this can happen later). Then we have a negative potential gradient between the channel and the control gate. Recall that to create an n-type channel in the transistor, it is necessary to apply a positive voltage to the gate, where this voltage is greater than the threshold voltage. In this case, the threshold voltage is effectively higher because of the accumulation of electrons in the floating gate. In other words, to induce a channel to form in the substrate, we need to apply a larger positive voltage at the control gate.

Let the threshold voltage when the floating gate is not charged with electrons be V_T, and let the threshold voltage when the floating gate contains negative charge be V_T^+ ($V_T^+ > V_T$). If we apply a voltage that is in between V_T and V_T^+, then the NMOS transistor conducts current if no charge is stored in the floating gate. Otherwise if charge is stored, the threshold voltage V_T^+ of the transistor is greater than the gate-to-source voltage, and thus the transistor is in the *off* state. It thus does not conduct any current. We typically assume that the default state (no charged electrons in the floating gate) corresponds to the 1 state. When the floating gate is charged with electrons, we assume that the transistor is in the 0 state.

Now, to write a value of 0 or *program* the transistor, we need to deposit electrons in the floating gate. This can be done by applying a strong positive voltage to the control gate, and a smaller positive voltage to the drain terminal. Since there is a positive potential difference between the drain and source, a channel gets established between the drain and source. The control gate has an even higher voltage, and thus the resulting electric field pulls electrons from the n-type channel and deposits some of them in the floating gate.

Similarly, to *erase* the stored 0 bit, we apply a strong negative voltage between the control gate and the source terminal. The resulting electric field pulls the electrons away from the floating gate into the substrate and source terminal. At the end of this process, the floating gate loses all its negative charge, and the flash device comes back to its original state. It now stores a logical 1.

To summarise, programming a flash cell means writing a logical 0, and erasing it means writing a logical 1. There are two fundamental ways in which we can arrange such floating gate transistors to make a basic flash memory cell. These methods are known as NOR flash and NAND flash respectively.

NOR Flash

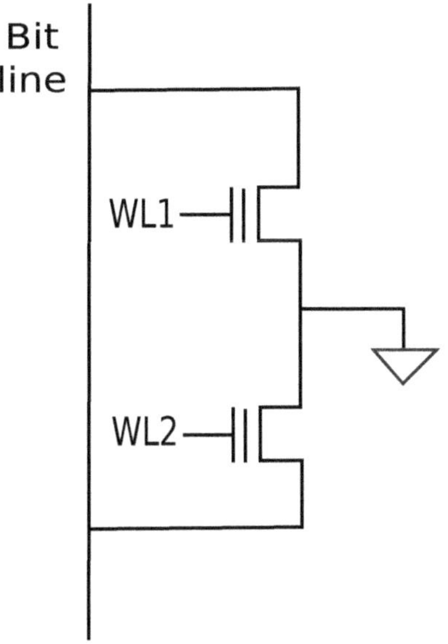

Figure 10.28: NOR Flash Cell

Figure 10.28 shows the topology of a 2-transistor NOR flash cell that saves 2 bits. Each floating gate transistor is connected to a bit line on one side and to the ground on the other side. The control gates are connected to distinct word lines. After we enable a floating gate transistor (set the voltage of the control gate to somewhere between V_T and V_T^+), it pulls the bit line low if it stores a logical 1, otherwise it does not have any effect because it is in the *off* state. Thus the voltage transition in the bit line is logically the reverse of the value stored in the transistor. The bit line is connected to a sense amplifier that senses its voltage, flips the bit, and reports it as the output. Similarly, for writing and erasing we need to set the word lines and bit lines to appropriate voltages. The advantage of a NOR flash cell is that it is very similar to a traditional DRAM cell. We can build an array of NOR flash cells similar to a DRAM array.

NAND Flash

A NAND flash cell has a different topology. It consists of a set of NMOS floating gate transistors in series similar to series connections in CMOS NAND gates (refer to Figure 10.29). There are two dedicated transistors at both ends known as the *bit line select transistor* and *ground select* transistor, respectively. A typical array of transistors connected in the NAND configuration contains 8 or 16 transistors. To read the value saved in a certain transistor in a NAND flash array, there are three steps. The first step is to set the gate voltages of the ground select and bit line select transistors to a logical 1 such that they are conducting. The second step is to set the voltages of the control gates of the rest of the floating gate transistors other than the one we wish to read by setting their word line voltages to V_T^+. Finally, we

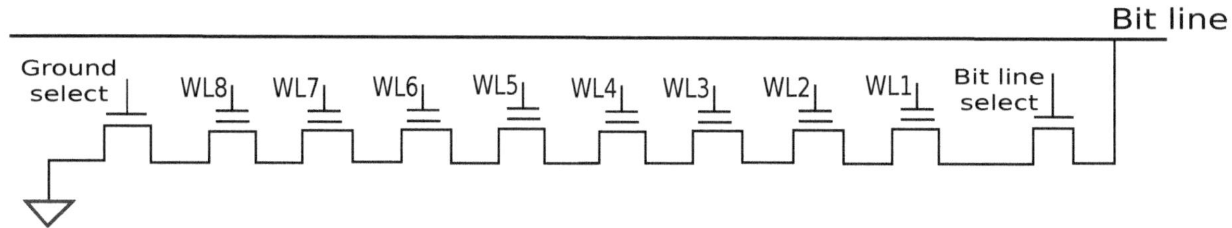

Figure 10.29: NAND flash cell

need to read the specific transistor by setting its word line voltage to some value between V_T and V_T^+. If the cell is not programmed (contains a 1), it drives the bit line low, otherwise it does not change the voltage on the bit line. Sense amplifiers infer the value of the logical bit saved in the transistor. Such arrays of floating gate transistors known as NAND flash cells are connected in a configuration similar to NOR flash cells.

This scheme might look complicated at the outset; however, it has a lot of advantages. Consequently, most of the flash devices in use today use NAND flash memories instead of NOR flash memories. The bit storage density is much higher. A typical NAND flash cell uses a lesser number of wires than a NOR flash cell because all the floating gate transistors are directly connected to each other, and there is just one connection to the bit line and ground terminal. Hence, NAND flash memories have at least 40-60% higher density as compared to NOR flash cells. Of course, accessing a single cell is more complicated. Nevertheless, given the advantages in storage density, market economics has chosen the NAND flash cell.

Blocks and Pages

The most important point to note here is that a (NAND) flash memory device is not a memory device, it is a storage device. Memory devices provide word-level access. In comparison, flash devices typically provide page-level access, where a page's size can be between 512-4096 bytes. Note that a page as defined here is different from a page in virtual memory. Due to temporal and spatial locality in accesses to flash media, the working set of most programs is restricted to a small number of pages.

Page-level access to flash media is typically not very inefficient. This is because of the following reason. To reduce the number of accesses to storage devices, most operating systems have in-memory storage caches such as hard disk caches. Most of the time, the operating system reads and writes to the in-memory caches. This reduces the I/O access time. Such caches are typically large contiguous regions in physical memory, and thus they can be read or written in bulk – at the level of pages. This naturally aligns with the page-level access paradigm of flash devices. Let us look at an example.

After certain events, it is necessary to synchronise the cache with the underlying storage device. For example, after executing a *sync()* system call in Linux, the hard disk cache writes its updates to the hard disk. Depending on the semantics of the operating system, and file system, writes are sent to the underlying storage media after a variety of events. For example, when we right click on the icon for a USB drive in the "My Computer" screen on Windows and select the eject option, the operating system ensures that all the outstanding write requests are sent to the USB device. This is a bulk operation and uses page-level I/O.

On a humorous note, most of the time users simply unplug a USB device. This practice can occasionally lead to data corruption, and unfortunately your author has committed this mistake several times. This is because, when we pull out a USB drive, some uncommitted changes are still present in the in-memory cache. Consequently, the USB pen drive contains stale and possibly half-written corrupted data. Hence, don't do this !!!

Data in NAND flash devices is organised at the granularity of pages and blocks. Note: the connotation of the term *block* is different here, its definition is specific to flash devices. As we have discussed, a *page* of data typically contains 512 – 4096 bytes (in powers of 2). Most NAND flash devices can typically read or write data at the granularity of pages. Each page additionally has extra bits for error correction based on CRC codes. A set of pages are organised into a block. Blocks can contain 32 – 128 pages, and their total size ranges from 16 – 512 KB. Most NAND flash devices can erase data at the level of blocks.

Let us now look at some of the salient points of NAND flash devices.

Program/Erase Cycles

Writing to a flash device essentially means writing a logical 0 bit since by default each floating gate transistor contains a logical 1. In general, after we have written data to a block, we cannot write data again to the same block without performing additional steps. For example, if we have written 0110 to a set of locations in a block, we cannot write 1001 to the same set of locations without erasing the original data. This is because, we cannot convert a 0 to a 1 without erasing data. Erasing is a slow operation and consumes a lot of power. Hence, the designers of NAND flash memories decided to erase data at large granularities, i.e., at the granularity of a block. We can think of accesses to flash memory as consisting of a *program phase*, where data is written at the granularity of pages, and an *erase phase*, where the data stored in all the transistors of the block is erased. After an erase operation, each transistor in the block contains a logical 1. We can have an indefinite number of read accesses between the program phase, and the erase phase. Let us define a new term here: a pair of program and erase operations is known as a program/erase cycle or P/E cycle.

Unfortunately, flash devices can endure a finite number of P/E cycles. As of 2020, this number is between 50,000 to 150,000. This is because each P/E cycle damages the silicon dioxide layer surrounding the floating gate. There is a gradual breakdown of this layer, and ultimately after hundreds of thousands of P/E cycles it does not remain an electrical insulator anymore. It starts to conduct current and thus a flash cell loses its ability to hold charge. This gradual damage to the insulator layer is known as *wear and tear*. To mitigate this problem, designers use a technique called *wear levelling*.

Wear Levelling

The main objective of *wear levelling* is to ensure that accesses are uniformly distributed across blocks. If accesses are non-uniformly distributed, then the blocks that receive a large number of requests will wear out faster, and develop faults. Since data accesses follow both temporal and spatial locality, we expect a small set of blocks to be accessed most often. This is precisely the behaviour that we wish to prevent. Let us further elaborate with an example. Consider a pen drive that contains songs. Most people typically do not listen to all the songs in a round robin fashion. Instead, they most of the time listen to their favourite songs. This means that a few blocks that contain their favourite songs are accessed most often and these blocks will ultimately develop faults. Hence, to maximise the lifetime of the flash device, we need to ensure that all the blocks are accessed with roughly the same frequency. This is the best case scenario, and is known as *wear levelling*.

The basic idea of wear levelling is that we define a logical address and a physical address for a flash device. A *physical address* corresponds to the address of a block within the flash device. The logical address is used by the processor and operating system to address data in the flash drive. Every flash device contains a circuit that maps logical addresses to physical addresses. Now, we need to ensure that accesses to blocks are uniformly distributed. Most flash devices have an access counter associated with each block. This counter is incremented once every P/E cycle. Once the access count for a block exceeds the access counts of other blocks by a predefined threshold, it is time to swap the contents of the frequently accessed block with another less frequently accessed block. Flash devices use a separate temporary block for implementing the swap. First, the contents of block 1 are copied to it. Subsequently, block 1 is erased, and the contents of block 2 are copied to block 1. The last step is to erase block 2, and copy the contents of the temporary block to it. Optionally, at the end, we can erase the contents of the temporary block. By doing such periodic swaps, flash devices ensure that no single block wears out faster than others. The logical to physical block mapping needs to be updated to reflect the change.

Definition 92

A technique to ensure that no single block wears out faster than other blocks is known as wear levelling. *Most flash devices implement wear levelling by swapping the contents of a block that is frequently accessed with a block that is less frequently accessed.*

Read Disturbance

Another reliability issue in flash memories is known as *read disturbance*. If we read the contents of one page continuously, then the neighbouring transistors in each NAND cell start getting programmed. This is because the control gate voltage of the neighbouring transistors needs to be greater than V_T^+ such that they can pass current. Note that in this case, the voltage of the gate is not as high as the voltage that is required to program a transistor, and it also lasts for a shorter duration. Nonetheless, a few electrons do accumulate in the floating gate. After thousands of read accesses to just one transistor, the neighbouring transistors start accumulating negative charge in their floating gates, and ultimately get programmed to store a 0 bit.

To mitigate this problem, we can start out with having a read counter with each page or block. If the read counter exceeds a certain threshold, then the flash controller needs to move the contents of the block to another location. Before copying the data, the new block needs to be erased. Subsequently, we transfer the contents of the old block to the new block. In the new block, all the transistors that are not programmed start out with a negligible amount of negative charge in their floating gates. As the number of read accesses to the new block increases, transistors start getting programmed. Before we reach a threshold, we need to migrate the block again.

10.5.2 Ferroelectric RAM (FeRAM)

Basic Physics

Ferroelectric RAM (or FeRAM) is a strong competitor of flash memory. It was commercialised way back in 1998, and it has been available ever since. It is in principle similar to a DRAM cell. Each FeRAM cell has one transistor and one capacitor. However, the capacitor is special, instead of using a normal dielectric material, it uses a ferroelectric dielectric. A ferroelectric dielectric is made of a ferroelectric material such as lead zirconate titanate ($PbZrO_3 + PbTiO_3$), popularly known as PZT, barium titanate ($BaTiO_3$), or strontium bismuth tantalate $SrBi_2Ta_2O_9$ (SBT).

These materials exhibit the phenomenon of ferroelectricity. Its explanation is as follows. In general, when we apply an electric field across a dielectric, the electrons get displaced towards the positive pole and the positively charged ions get displaced towards the negative pole. As a result, there is a net electrical dipole moment. This means that the centre of the positively charged elements and the centre of the negatively charged elements do not coincide. There is a separation between them, which results in an electric field. The product of the charge (positive or negative) with the distance is known as the *dipole moment. Polarisation* is defined as the dipole moment per unit volume.

For most materials, the degree of polarisation that is induced by an externally applied electric field is linearly proportional to it. Additionally, when the electric field is removed the polarisation becomes zero. However, ferroelectric materials are an exception to this rule. As shown in Figure 10.30, there is a certain degree of hysteresis in the relationship between the applied electric field and the degree of induced polarisation. Particularly, it is possible that even when the electric field is zero, the material can have an inherent polarisation. Here, the degree of polarisation depends on the history of how the electric field across the medium has varied in the past, we say that there is a certain degree of hysteresis to it, which is clearly visible in Figure 10.30.

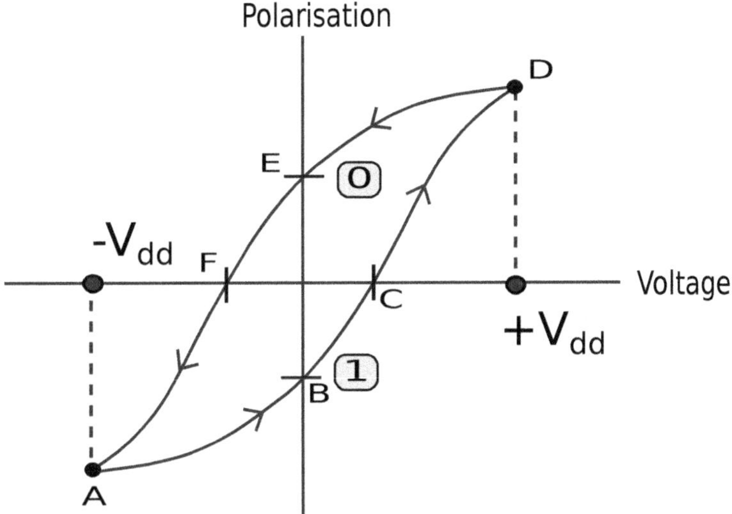

Figure 10.30: Hysteresis loop of polarisation vs voltage in a ferroelectric capacitor

Consider a point of time when we are at point A (in Figure 10.30). The applied voltage is $-V_{dd}$. Then as we increase the voltage and the voltage becomes zero, we arrive at point B. Note that at this point, the applied voltage is zero, still there is an inherent polarisation. Then as we increase the voltage towards $+V_{dd}$, we arrive at point C where the degree of polarisation is zero, and finally when the voltage is $+V_{dd}$, we arrive at point D. Now as we decrease the voltage we do not follow the same path, rather we follow a different path. This is a characteristic of all systems that exhibit some degree of hysteresis. For example, as we reduce the voltage to 0, we start arriving at point E. At this point, there is a certain amount of inherent polarisation, which the device seems to remember. Finally with a further decrease in the voltage across the capacitor, we first arrive at point F, and then when the voltage reaches $-V_{dd}$, we arrive at point A (the same point at which we started).

The key point to note here is that there is a notion of a state associated with the dielectric material. When the electric field is zero there are two states B and E, where it can either have a positive polarisation or a negative polarisation: these can correspond to different logical states (0 and 1). FeRAMs use this property to store data: a negative polarisation is a logical 1 (point B) and a positive polarisation is a logical 0 (point E).

FeRAM Cell

Now that the basic physics has been established, the next step is to create a functioning device out of an FeRAM cell. Figure 10.31 shows the design of an FeRAM cell. Akin to a DRAM cell, each FeRAM cell has a bit line and a word line. The bit line is connected to one of the terminals of the access transistor, which is controlled by the word line. The other terminal of the access transistor is connected to the ferroelectric capacitor, which is made by sandwiching a layer of ferroelectric material with two metal electrodes typically made of platinum or iridium.

Note that here there is a major difference as compared to DRAM cells. The other terminal of the ferroelectric capacitor is connected to a plate line (PL), instead of being connected to ground. We can independently control the voltages on the bit line and the plate line. Furthermore, note that the convention is that the voltage across the capacitor is considered to be positive if the voltage on the plate

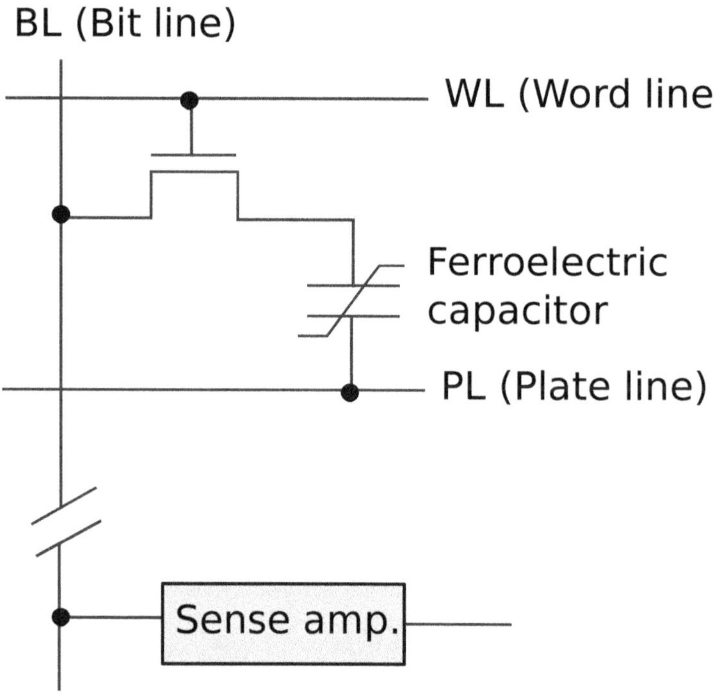

Figure 10.31: An FeRAM Cell

line is greater than the voltage on the bit line. It is necessary to have a separate plate line because we need to create both positive and negative voltages across the capacitor.

Let us now look at the basic read and write operations. We shall describe the write operation first because it is easier.

The Write Operation

To write a value, all that we need to do is set appropriate voltages on the bit line (BL) and the plate line (PL), after setting the word line. For example, when we want to write a 0, we need to ensure that the dielectric is positively polarised. This can be done by increasing the voltage of the plate line to V_{dd}, and setting $BL = 0$ V. To write a logical 1, we need to do the reverse. We need to set $BL = V_{dd}$, and $PL = 0$ V, which also means that as per our convention, the voltage across the two terminals of the capacitor is equal to $-V_{dd}$. After doing this, if we set the word line to 0, the dielectric will move to any one of the stable states: logical 0 (point E) or logical 1 (point B).

The Read Operation

The read operation is slightly more tricky. In this case, we set $PL = V_{dd}$, and set the voltage on the bit line (BL) to 0 V. After this, we enable the word line. There are two choices: either the cell stores a logical 0 or a logical 1. Assume it stores a logical 0, then it will move from point E to D, and this will increase the polarisation of the capacitor. This will cause a net current outflow from the cell into the bit line, which will increase its voltage. Let this increase in voltage be ΔV_0.

Next, let us consider the other case where the cell stores a logical 1. In this case the movement will be from B to D. This will lead to a reversal in the polarisation. This can happen only if there is a net current flow down the bit line, which will charge a few capacitors along the way and raise the potential of the bit line to ΔV_1. We expect that $\Delta V_1 > \Delta V_0$ from the shape of the hysteresis curve as shown in Figure 10.30.

The sense amplifier can thus be tuned to sense a voltage that is between ΔV_0 and ΔV_1. Akin to a DRAM array, subsequent stages can buffer the logical values that were read and send them on the bus to the memory controller.

We have a special case if the cell contained a logical 1. In this case, we will move from point B to D. Once the electric field is removed, because of the nature of the hysteresis curve, we will arrive at point E, which actually corresponds to a logical 0. We thus observe that when the cell stores a logical 1, we have a destructive read. However, if the cell stores a logical 0, we move from E to D, and back to E again when the access transistor is disabled. Thus in this case, the read is not destructive. Sadly, in the former case, when the cell stores a logical 1, it is necessary to write the value back again (similar to DRAMs).

Comparison vis-a-vis DRAM and Flash

Even though FeRAM memories have been around for a long time, they have not gained the kind of popularity that flash memories have gained. There are many reasons for this. Let us analyse some of the important ones.

The first is that flash memories use the regular silicon fabrication process to a large extent. They are not dependent on special fabrication processes or special materials. However in this case, we need to integrate materials such as PZT or SBT in the fabrication process. This requires us to create new fabrication facilities and also these materials are associated with a lot of contamination issues. Another important factor that prevented the FeRAM technology from scaling is that researchers could not build an analogue for trench capacitors or very small stacked capacitors using PZT-based dielectrics, thus preventing their further miniaturisation. Moreover, it was observed that as we reduce the size of the dielectric, its ferroelectric properties diminish significantly.

The FeRAM technology however does have its advantages. Unlike DRAM arrays it does not need periodic refreshes, which helps save a lot of power. Furthermore, unlike flash where writing is a very expensive operation, in this case we can write to cells very easily and the energy difference between writes and reads is minimal. FeRAM also has much more endurance than flash memories. An FeRAM cell can support at least up to 10^{12} read/write cycles as compared to just 10^5 cycles for flash memory cells as of 2020.

10.5.3   Magnetoresistive RAM (MRAM)

MRAMs stand for magneto-resistive random access memories.

MRAM Cell

An MRAM cell has three layers: two ferromagnetic layers that are separated by a very thin layer made of an electrical insulator. One of the ferromagnetic layers is known as the *pinned layer* because the direction of its magnetisation is fixed. The other layer is known as the free layer because the direction of its magnetisation can be changed by applying a magnetic field. This is shown in Figure 10.32. There are thus two states of this device. If the magnetic fields of both the ferromagnetic layers are aligned, then we call this the *parallel* state, otherwise if the fields are in opposite directions, then we call this the *anti-parallel* state. Figure 10.32 shows an avatar of the device where the magnetic field lines are in the same plane as the thin film separating the ferromagnetic layers. These devices are increasingly giving way to devices where the direction of magnetisation is perpendicular to the plane of the film. For the sake of simplicity, we shall describe the former approach. Note that the method of operating the cell is the same for both the approaches.

Since the insulating layer (often made from MgO) is very thin, typically 1-2 nanometers thick, a quantum mechanical effect called tunnelling magnetoresistance (TMR) is seen. It is possible for electrons

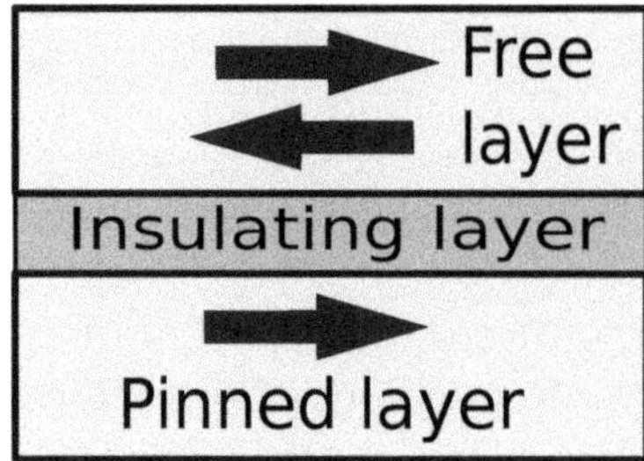

Figure 10.32: Structure of an MRAM cell

to jump from one ferromagnetic layer to the other layer, even though this is forbidden by the rules of classical physics. This means that if there is a voltage difference between the two ferromagnetic layers, a current can flow through the MRAM cell. Specifically, the current through the insulator will flow because of the TMR effect, which acts as a resistive element. The greatness of this device is that the resistance of the cell is a function of the orientation of the magnetic field of the free layer. If the cell is in the parallel state (the pinned layer and the free layer have the same direction of magnetisation), then the resistance is low, and if the cell is in an anti-parallel state (opposite directions of magnetisation), then the resistance is high. We assume that low resistance means a logical 1 and high resistance means a logical 0. Measuring the resistance is easy (sense the voltage with a fixed current or vice versa) and thus reading the value stored in the cell is fairly straightforward.

However, the main challenge is to create a mechanism such that we can write to the cell efficiently, which means that we need to be able to generate a magnetic field that can set the direction of the magnetic field in the free layer. The traditional approach was to create a magnetic field by passing a very high current; the main problem is that such approaches do not scale with decreasing feature sizes and it is possible that the value stored in the nearby cells gets perturbed. Hence, a new avatar of such devices has been proposed that also relies on nanoscale effects, albeit in a different manner.

STT-MRAMs

These are called spin-transfer torque (STT) devices, or STT-MRAMs. Recall from high school physics that electrons are associated with an angular momentum, which is known as the *spin*. In quantum mechanical terms, the spin can take two values: $+1/2$ and $-1/2$. Furthermore, if any charged particle like an electron has an associated angular momentum, then it also has an associated magnetic moment. In general, if we consider electric current as a stream of electrons flowing along the wire, half of them will have a positive spin $(+1/2)$ and half of them will have a negative spin $(-1/2)$. However, if we pass an electric current through a magnetised medium such as the pinned layer of an MRAM cell, we can produce spin-polarised current, where a majority of electrons have the same type of spin. Furthermore, when this current passes through the insulating layer and reaches the free layer, it is possible for it to transfer some of its spin (or angular momentum) to the electrons in that layer. This can flip the direction of its magnetic field, and we can thus program the memory cell. The process of transferring this angular momentum is also known as applying a *torque* to the electrons in the free layer. Hence, the name of this device is a spin-transfer torque device. In terms of both latency and power, this technique is far superior to previous approaches that use large magnetic fields to set the state of an MRAM cell. Let us delve into the details.

The Write Operation

Figure 10.33 shows the design of an MRAM cell. The free layer of an MRAM cell is connected to the bit line, and the pinned layer is connected to the *select line* via an access transistor. Let us look at

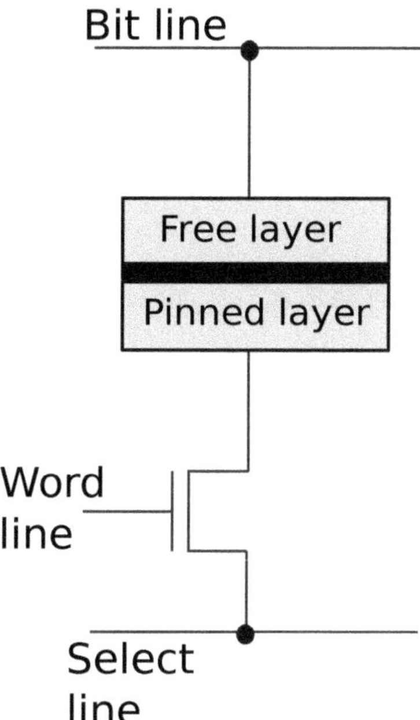

Figure 10.33: Design of an MRAM cell [Kawahara et al., 2012]

the process of programming a cell. Recall that when the cell is in the parallel (P) state (directions of magnetisation are the same), we store a logical 1; when the cell is in an anti-parallel (AP) state (high resistance), we store a logical 0.

To switch from the AP to the P state, electrons need to flow from the pinned layer to the free layer. This is because as they pass through the pinned layer their spins get polarised (most of them in one direction). Subsequently, as they tunnel through the MgO layer, and enter the free layer, they transfer some of the spin torque to magnetise the free layer in the direction of the pinned layer. To achieve this, we need to have the bit line at a higher potential as compared to the select line such that current flows from the bit line to the select line.

Now to move from the P to the AP state, we pass electrons in the reverse direction – from the free layer to the pinned layer. This is achieved by setting the potential of the select line higher than the bit line. In this case, the electrons pass through the free layer first. The electrons that have the same spin direction as the direction of magnetisation in the pinned layer seamlessly pass through. However, a fraction of electrons that do not have the same spin direction, bounce back. They get reflected from the MgO-pinned layer boundary. Gradually, more and more such electrons accumulate in the free layer. They transfer their torque to electrons in the free layer, and the direction of the magnetisation in the free layer gets reversed. Thus the free layer's magnetisation changes its direction, and the cell enters the AP state.

Pros and Cons

The STT-MRAM cell has several advantages. The leakage current, which is the current that flows through the cell even when it is inactive is almost zero. As we shall see in Chapter 11, this is not the case in conventional SRAM and DRAM memories. For them, the leakage power is a major component of the overall power consumption. Additionally, the current requirements to read or write an STT-MRAM cell are low.

A major disadvantage of this device is that it is not as fast as a traditional DRAM cell. The reason is that a DRAM cell relies on fast electrical switching, whereas in this case, there is an interaction of magnetic and quantum mechanical effects. For example, to write a value it is necessary to wait till the magnetic field in the free layer reverses and reaches a certain strength. Similarly, to read a value it is necessary to sense the resistance of the cell, where the main issue is that the difference in the resistances of the two states might be as low as 20%. This requires a sophisticated sensing circuit. In addition, thermal stability of such memory cells is an issue, particularly, when there are large variations in die temperature.

Notwithstanding such concerns, STT-MRAMs as of today are considered fairly mature technology; they have relatively fast read and write times and a very high endurance. There are challenges in large-scale production (as of 2020), however it is expected that in the coming years many of these issues will be solved.

10.5.4 Phase Change Memory (PCM)

Basic Physics

Another popular memory technology is Phase Change Memory (known as *PCM*). It encodes information in the phase of a material, which is typically a chalcogenide glass. A *chalcogenide glass* is an amorphous solid that is made of one or more chalcogen elements such as sulfur, selenium, or tellurium. One of the most popular materials for making phase change memory is *GeSbTe* (germanium-antimony-tellurium) abbreviated as GST.

Unlike the memory cells that we have seen up till now, the PCM memory cell changes its state based on its temperature. It has two states: amorphous and crystalline. In the amorphous state, it has a high resistance (logical 0), and in the crystalline state it has a low resistance (logical 1). The reason that a material made of GST has a low resistance in the crystalline state is because there is a lot of order in the structure and there are a lot of free electrons to carry current. The situation in the amorphous state is the reverse, hence it has a high resistance.

Given that the PCM cell has two states, we need a method to switch between the states. All previous technologies have relied on the injection of electric current to either deposit charge, or induce magnetism in a material. A PCM cell also relies on current injection, however the current is required to change the temperature such that the material melts and then either transforms to the amorphous state or to the crystalline state. Whenever we apply a short and high amplitude current pulse, the material melts quickly and then rapidly transitions to the amorphous state. This sets the value stored in the cell to a logical 0, and *resets it*. On the other hand, if we apply a low amplitude and long current pulse, then the material crystallises. The cell stores a logical 1. This current is known as the *set current*, which *sets* the value stored in the cell.

Let us quickly deduce the properties of a PCM cell from its basic physics. Given that it stores data in the phase of the material, it can hold its data for a very long time. Commercially available PCM devices as of 2020 can hold their data for at least 10 years. In addition, it allows us to directly overwrite the value of a cell, quite unlike flash memory where we erase data at the level of blocks. Finally, unlike DRAM and FeRAM cells, reads are not destructive. The structure of a basic cell is shown in Figure 10.34.

Several improvements have been proposed to the basic PCM cell. For example, it is possible to store multiple bits in a single cell. Between a fully crystalline and a fully amorphous state, we can have two more partially crystalline states, and thus we can realise a total of four states, which are sufficient to encode two Boolean bits. This further increases the density of storage.

Read and Write Operations

A PCM cell is typically a 1T1R (1 transistor, 1 resistor device) as shown in Figure 10.35. The access transistor (controlled by the word line) is connected to one end of the cell, and the other end of the cell is connected to the bit line.

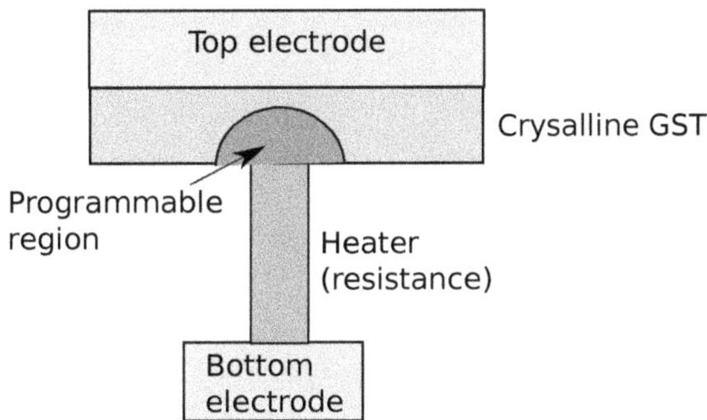

Figure 10.34: Design of a PCM cell

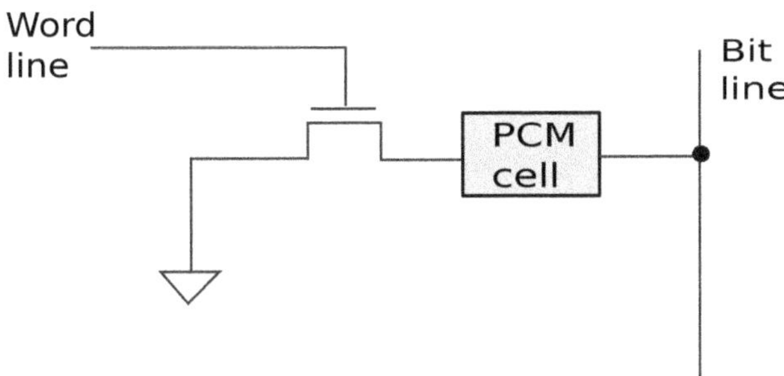

Figure 10.35: A PCM cell connected to the word line and bit line

The read process is simple. We precharge the bit line, and then enable the access transistor. If it is in the low resistance state, then the bit line discharges quickly. This can be sensed using sense amplifiers. Conversely, if it is in the high resistance state, then the voltage after a certain period of time is much higher.

The write operation is dependent on whether we are setting (writing a 1), or resetting the cell (writing a 0). If we are writing a logical 1, then we need to move the state of the chalcogenide material to the low-resistive crystalline state using a low current for a relatively long time. However, if we are resetting the state of the cell (setting to a logical 0), then we need to provide a short high-amplitude current pulse. Finally, note that unlike DRAMs, reads in PCM are not destructive, and there is no need for restoring the state.

Dealing with Slow Writes

In PCM, writes are slow. It takes time to change the state of the chalcogenide material. Particularly, if we are changing the state from the amorphous to the crystalline state, then we need to supply a write current for a long duration of time. During this time the bank cannot be used for servicing any other request. Often writes are not on the critical path, however reads are very often on the critical path.

At the level of the memory controller, we can reduce the priority of writes, implement a DRAM based write cache, and discard ineffectual writes. An ineffectual write operation has no effect. For example, if we are successively writing two values to the same location, then the first write operation is ineffectual.

There are two more sophisticated methods of dealing with slow write operations: write cancellation and write pausing. Assume that a write operation is in progress, and a high-priority read arrives. We can immediately cancel the write in the middle of the operation by deasserting the write enable signal of the PCM device. This will stop the write midway, and the state of the cell will be in a non-deterministic state. This is not necessarily a problem because we always know what we were writing, and this value can be stored in a write buffer till the write is finally completed at a later point of time. This allows us to immediately service the read request.

Another method in this space is write pausing. In modern PCM cells, the time of a write operation becomes more and more non-deterministic over time because of the varying rates of crystallisation of the devices based on how much they have been used. Moreover, if we are using a PCM cell that can store multiple logic levels, this process is even more complicated. Hence, the conventional approach to deal with this problem is that we perform a write iteratively. For one iteration, we apply the write current, and then *verify* if the value has been correctly written. If it has not been correctly written, then we start the next iteration, and keep doing this till the value is correctly written. Let us say that when we have completed an iteration, a high-priority read arrives. Then we can *pause* the next iteration of the write, service the read, and then come back and complete the rest of the iterations for the write operation. This allows us to service requests with minimal delay.

Reliability and Endurance

High write currents and thermal cycling in the chalcogenide material reduce the reliability of the PCM device significantly. Similar to flash memory, the standard approach for dealing with such problems is *wear levelling*. This means that we ensure that all the banks in the PCM array are equally accessed. We need to create a mapping between the CPU generated addresses, and the internal PCM addresses, and keep updating this mapping to ensure that all the PCM blocks are roughly equally accessed. Note that we care about writes more than reads, because writes are more intense operations in PCM memory.

An important approach in the space is start-gap wear levelling. In this technique, we periodically move each block L to another block L', where there is a one-to-one mapping between them. It can be proven that if we do this, all the locations are roughly equally accessed. A simple function can be $L' = L + 1$. It is possible to work out more complicated functions that are based on cryptographic primitives and provide better guarantees.

10.5.5 Resistive RAM (ReRAM)

Basic Physics

ReRAMs or resistive RAMs rely on the *resistive switching phenomenon*. This phenomenon is observed in several metal oxides (such as NiO or TiO_x), where the resistance is a function of the history of the voltage applied across the material. To create a nonvolatile memory, we need to have two physical states that are stable. For such materials we can have a high resistance state (HRS) and a low resistance state (LRS).

Similar to the other nonvolatile memory cells, a ReRAM cell also contains a metal oxide layer sandwiched between two electrodes (see Figure 10.36). The metal oxide layer is typically a transition metal oxide or titanium nitride, and the electrodes are made of Pt (Platinum), Ir (Iridium), or Ag (silver). Depending upon the history of the voltage that is applied between the electrodes, the resistance varies. The I-V curve of such devices typically shows a certain degree of hysteresis, this is why we observe two distinct physical states (explained later). The HRS state corresponds to a logical 0, and the LRS state corresponds to a logical 1. The process of changing the state from HRS to LRS ($0 \rightarrow 1$) is known as the *set* process. The reverse process ($1 \rightarrow 0$) is known as the *reset* process.

Reading such a cell is easy; we just need to apply a small voltage and measure the current. Let us now discuss the two main types of ReRAM cells: Redox ReRAMs, and CBRAMs.

Redox ReRAMs

The most important charge transport mechanism in such ReRAMs is the *filamentary conduction mechanism*. As per this mechanism, when we apply a large voltage across the electrodes, tiny conducting

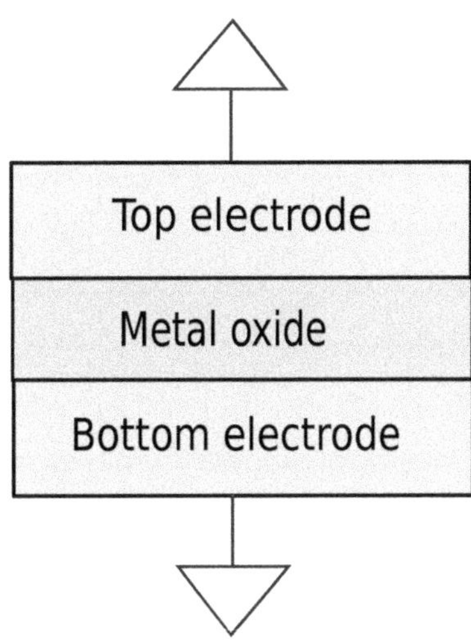

Figure 10.36: Basic ReRAM cell

filaments form between the two electrodes; these filaments can carry current and thus the cell enters the low resistance state. If we can somehow destroy these filaments, the cell will enter the high resistance state. Let us elaborate.

In a Redox ReRAM, the mechanism is as follows. Let us assume that the material in the middle metal oxide layer is of the form VO_2. Here, V is a transition metal. Similar to electrons and holes, here also we have two kinds of charge carriers: O^{2-} ions and oxygen vacancies (V_o). An oxygen vacancy is similar to a hole in device physics, and is a positively charged quantity. Let us now look at the different phases of a Redox ReRAM.

At the beginning, the density of oxygen vacancies is low. Then each cell needs to go through the forming phase. In this case, we apply a large potential across the electrodes. Dielectric breakdown takes place and the negatively charged O^{2-} ions move towards the anode. Meanwhile the oxygen vacancies stay back in the metal oxide layer. Near the anode we have an excess of negatively charged oxygen ions. If the material of the anode electrode reacts with oxygen ions then an oxide layer forms on top of the anode. These ions are thus effectively removed from the metal oxide layer.

The oxygen vacancies in the metal oxide layers align themselves along the electric field and form a *conductive filament*. This is a conducting path that can carry current, and thus the cell enters the low resistance state (LRS). This is shown in Figure 10.37. This is the *set* process. Typically, the oxide layer at the anode is amorphous in nature and has large-sized grains. The filaments form at the grain boundaries.

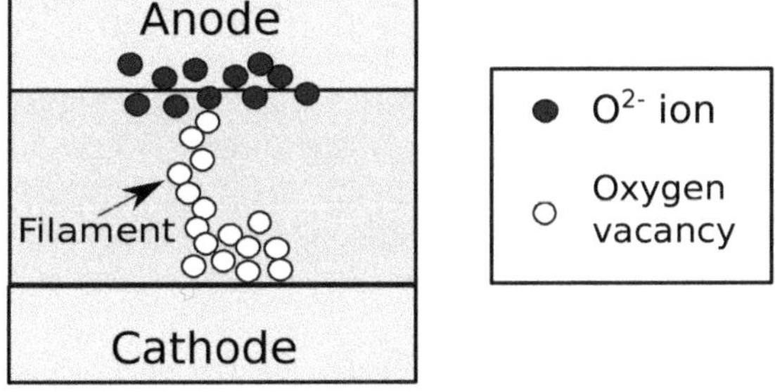

Figure 10.37: Filament in a Redox ReRAM cell

Let us now look at the *reset* process. In this case, we need to break the filaments that have been created such that the cell enters the high resistance state. There are two mechanisms in this space. We can either have unipolar switching or bipolar switching. In unipolar switching only the magnitude of the voltage is important, whereas in bipolar switching the sign of the voltage (positive or negative) is also important. In the case of unipolar switching, we send a high reset current through the conducting filament. This causes localised heating (Joule heating). The O^{2-} ions that are trapped at the anode get displaced and they combine with the oxygen vacancies in the filament effectively rupturing it.

In the case of bipolar switching we have a smaller reset current. We apply a negative voltage at the anode, which pushes the O^{2-} ions towards the metal oxide layer. They combine with oxygen vacancies and rupture the filament. The cell thus enters the high resistance state (logical 0). The next time that we want to set the value of the cell, we apply a positive voltage at the anode again. This attracts the negatively charged oxygen ions leaving oxygen vacancies in the metal oxide layer. The filament forms again. Given that we have a series of Redox (oxidation-reduction) reactions, this cell is known as a *Redox ReRAM*.

Let us quickly summarise what we have learnt in Point 20.

Important Point 20

- *In a Redox ReRAM, to enter the low resistance state, we apply a positive voltage to the cell. The negatively charged oxygen ions migrate towards the anode and get deposited over there. In some cases, they might also react with the material in the anode electrode and form an oxide layer. In the metal oxide layer, the remaining oxygen vacancies align themselves along the electric field and form a conductive filament.*

- *To rupture this filament there are two mechanisms: unipolar switching and bipolar switching.*

- *In unipolar switching we apply a large positive voltage to the anode. Because of the large current flow and resultant Joule heating, some of the oxygen ions get dislodged and move towards the conducting filament. They combine with oxygen vacancies and break the filaments. The cell thus enters the high resistance state.*

- *In bipolar switching, we apply a negative voltage at the anode; this sends back oxygen ions back to the metal oxide layer. There they get combined with oxygen vacancies in the filament. The filament thus gets ruptured.*

CBRAMs

A *conductive bridging RAM* or a CBRAM is another kind of a ReRAM cell that also relies on the filamentary switching mechanism. The basic structure of this cell is the same as that of the Redox ReRAM cell. We have two electrodes and a thin electrolyte layer in between.

However in this case, the electrodes play a very significant role and provide the material for the filament. One of the electrodes is called an electrochemically active electrode and is made of Ag (silver), Cu (copper), or Ni (nickel). The other electrode is called the inert electrode and is made of Pt (platinum), or Ir (Iridium). In between both the electrodes, we have a thin layer of an electrolyte: Ge_xS_y, SiO_2, TiO_2, Ta_2O_5, or ZrO_2.

The process for programming the cell is as follows. If we apply a highly positive voltage to the active electrode (typically Ag), it dissolves into the electrolyte. The positively charged silver ions(Ag^+) drift into the thin electrolyte and get pushed towards the inert electrode by the electric field. Some of them finally reach the inert electrode (cathode), absorb an electron $(Ag^+ + e^-)$ and get deposited on the surface of the inert electrode. Gradually a channel of Ag atoms forms between the anode and the cathode (see Figure 10.38). Once this is fully formed, this becomes a conducting filament, which can carry current. The cell subsequently enters the low resistance state. Even after turning off the voltage source, the filaments remain. This state of the cell thus represents a logical 1.

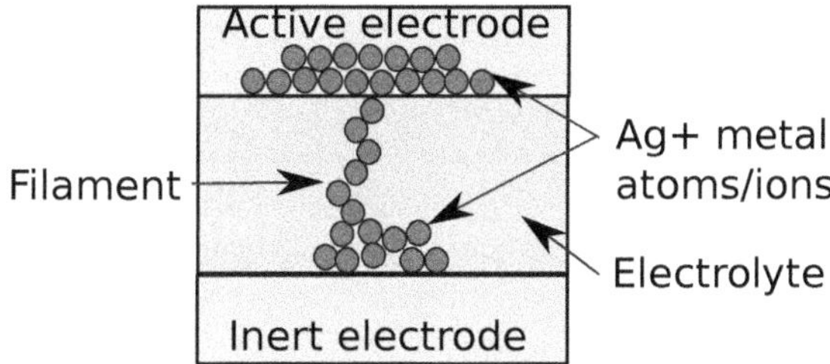

Figure 10.38: Filament in a CBRAM cell

To reset the cell, we need to apply a negative voltage to the active electrode (bipolar switching). Positively charged silver ions (Ag^+) migrate towards the active electrode, absorb an electron, and get deposited on the active electrode. This resets the state of the cell. Subsequently, the filament gets ruptured and thus there is no conductive path between the two electrodes; the cell enters the high resistance state (logical 0).

Applications in Neural Networks

Resistive devices have an interesting property – they can work as a multiplier. In a modern ReRAM, we just don't have one high resistance state, and one low resistance state, we can create several intermediate states with different levels of resistance. If the conductance of a ReRAM device is G, then we have $VG = I$ from the Ohm's law. This means that for a variable voltage, this device works as a multiplier.

Moreover, if we have an array of ReRAM cells, then we can compute a dot product by adding the currents (according to Kirchhoff's law). We shall see in Chapter 14 that this is the most performance-sensitive operation in deep neural networks. We can directly implement such operations in ReRAM based hardware and achieve significant speedups.

10.5.6   3D and Embedded Memory Technologies

Typically, the memory system proves to be the bottleneck for many high-bandwidth applications. Hence, there is a need to adopt futuristic memory technologies. A few of the technologies that stand out in this regard are 3D memory technologies such as High Bandwidth Memory (HBM) and Hybrid Memory Cubes (HMC). They use DRAM devices; however, instead of a single 2D layer, they are composed of multiple 2D layers stacked over each other.

The underpinnings of all these memory technologies are the same. The core idea is that we have a 3D stack of DRAM memory arrays. The memory arrays are connected to each other via TSVs (trans-silicon vias) or microbumps that form high-bandwidth connections across the layers. Microbumps are small metallic structures that are used to connect to the layer below. Furthermore, we divide each layer into a set of blocks and we consider a column of blocks to be one unit. It is known as a *vault*. There are several ways of integrating such 3D memory stacks. The most common method is a configuration where the silicon die and the 3D memory are placed side by side on the motherboard. They are connected via a high-bandwidth connection known as an *interposer*, which typically consists of several 128-bit wide links to connect the 3D DRAM memory and the chip.

The reason for the high bandwidth is two-fold. The first is that we can read many bits in parallel from each vault. The second is that because of the close proximity between the CPU chip and the 3D memory chip, we can afford a very wide bus.

Another technology that allows for high-bandwidth connections is embedded DRAM (eDRAM). Here, the DRAM module is integrated into the same die as the chip or is present in a multi-chip module configuration (within the same package). There are process challenges because we typically use different processes to fabricate logic and to fabricate DRAM. Hence, 2.5D integration, where we fabricate separate dies for the processor and the DRAM, respectively, and place them in the same package is considered to be a more feasible and practical solution. Here, of course, there is a need to create a high-bandwidth network within the package, something similar to an interposer.

10.6   Roofline Model

In this chapter we have introduced a large number of techniques to optimise the memory system. They need to work in conjunction with the techniques that we proposed to optimise the design of the OOO pipeline. Let us now look at modelling and understanding the performance of such systems. We have discussed basic performance equations in Section 2.2 and Section 7.1.6. In this section let us present a simple method for modelling the performance of such systems using simple diagrams. We shall introduce the *Roofline* model [Williams et al., 2009] in this section.

10.6.1   Overview

It is possible to propose many models that relate the DRAM throughput with the performance. Many such models have been proposed in the literature that extend the performance equation and incorporate the effect of different kinds of off-chip memory technologies. The main drawbacks of all of these models is that they are dependent on the workload and use too many constants. This makes the models hard to use and they are also not very intuitive. The quest for such models ended with the Roofline model that proposes a simple technique to find out the limitations of a workload – is it memory bound or compute bound or both?

Using this model it is possible to understand how the peak off-chip memory bandwidth and peak performance interact. It is also possible to find out how much a given set of workloads can be optimised till they reach the limits imposed on them by the system. Furthermore, with this model, it is possible to study the effects of different performance enhancing optimisations in the pipeline and the memory system.

At the outset, let us define three terms.

Operational Intensity This term captures the crux of the model – it is defined as the average number of floating point operations a processor can perform for every single byte read from off-chip memory. In other words, it represents the processing power of the CPU and the efficiency of the caches. An increased operational intensity means that the CPU can very effectively make use of the information that it reads from main memory. We typically measure this using performance counters that give us an estimate of the number of floating point operations and the number of off-chip memory accesses.

Memory Bandwidth For a given system (processor + off-chip memory), this quantity represents the observed off-chip memory bandwidth. This includes the effect of caching, memory controller optimisations, and prefetching. It is measured with the help of performance counters.

Performance The performance in this case is defined as the number of arithmetic operations performed per second. Typically, in the high-performance computing world, it is measured in the unit of FLOPS (floating point operations per second). It is possible to use other measures as well such as the number of integer operations per second; however, this is not very common and is not relevant in a high-performance computing context.

Hence, we shall go with FLOPS. Note that we shall use the term "FLOP" (floating point operation) to indicate a single floating point operation, the term "FLOPs" as its plural, and the term "FLOPS" to denote the number of floating point operations per second. The performance of a program is measured using dedicated performance counters to compute the number of floating point operations per second (FLOPS).

It is very easy to relate these three quantities – operational intensity, memory bandwidth, and the performance. The relation is shown in Equation 10.1. This follows from the definition of these quantities.

$$\underbrace{\frac{FLOPs}{second}}_{Performance} = \underbrace{\frac{bytes}{second}}_{Memory\ bandwidth} \times \underbrace{\frac{FLOPs}{byte}}_{Operational\ intensity} \tag{10.1}$$

We thus observe that the performance at any point of time is a product of the memory bandwidth and the operational intensity. The performance and the operational intensity can be varied by changing the benchmark and by making architectural optimisations. Hence, let us plot a graph where the performance is on the y-axis and the operational intensity is on the x-axis. In this graph, let us consider all the points that have a constant memory bandwidth B.

The equation for this line is $y = Bx$ (from Equation 10.1). This is a line with constant slope B and passes through the origin. For different memory bandwidths we shall have lines with different slopes as shown in Figure 10.39. We can make improvements to Figure 10.39 to make it look more intuitive. Let us plot the same data in the log-log scale.

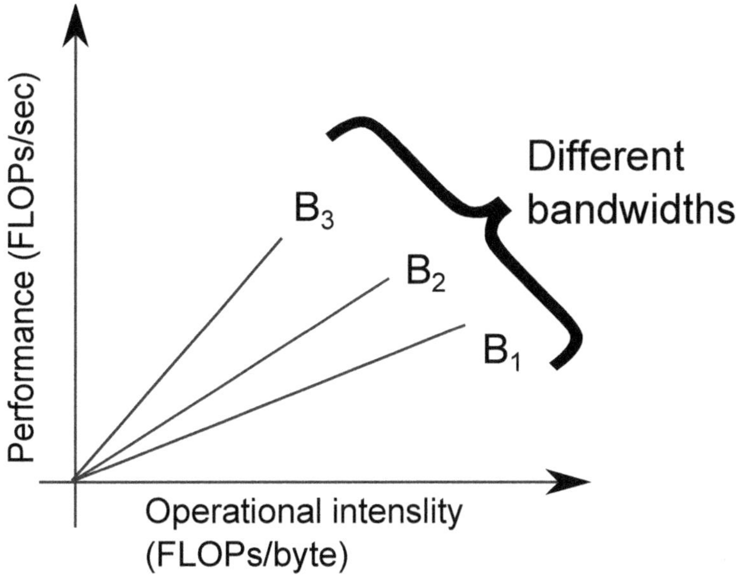

Figure 10.39: Different memory bandwidths

We have:

$$y = bx$$
$$\Rightarrow log(y) = log(x) + log(B) \tag{10.2}$$

In this case, all the constant-bandwidth lines have a slope of 45°. They are all parallel lines. This is shown in Figure 10.40. Points P and Q require a memory bandwidth that is less than B_1, and points R and S require a memory bandwidth that is more than B_3. Finally, note that for representing a line corresponding to another memory bandwidth, B', we just need to draw a line at 45°. If $B' < B$, the new line for bandwidth B' will be below the line for B. Otherwise, it will be above it.

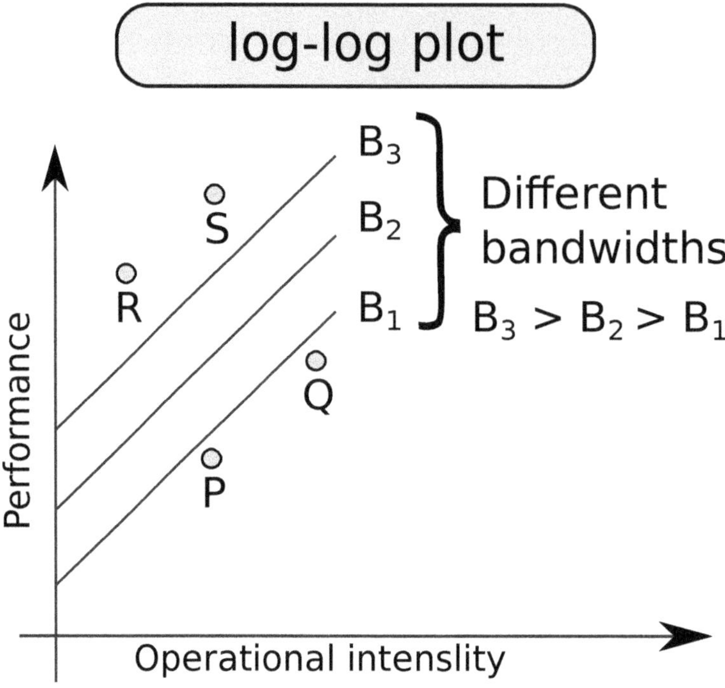

Figure 10.40: Log-log plot of performance vs operational intensity

10.6.2 Adding Ceilings

Now that we have explained the justification for the log-log plot, and also explained how to draw lines that contain all the points that need the same memory bandwidth, let us proceed to add computation ceilings.

Consider the peak performance (measured in terms of FLOPS). There are two ways to measure the peak performance in a system. First, we compute the theoretical maximum by looking at the processor's data sheets, or we write dedicated micro-benchmarks to stress the processor to the maximum limit. We can then find the peak performance using dedicated performance counters.

The peak performance can be represented as a horizontal line in the log-log plot. It is not possible to exceed the peak performance unless we change the configuration of the system, i.e., enable new architectural optimisations or increase the frequency.

On similar lines, we can define the peak memory bandwidth. It is a 45° line in the log-log plot. If we consider both of these constraints (also known as ceilings), then we have a trapezoidal region in which any workload can lie. It will always use less memory bandwidth than the maximum, and its computational throughput will be limited by the peak performance. This is shown in Figure 10.41. Since these ceilings establish limits on the performance and memory bandwidth, they are also known as *Rooflines*. Such a diagram is known as a *Roofline diagram*.

We can have several ceilings corresponding to different architectural and compiler configurations. If we consider the memory bandwidth, we can have different 45° lines corresponding to different memory system optimisations. Figure 10.42 shows three different lines for different configurations: theoretical-maximum, with-prefetching, and without-prefetching. All of these are memory bandwidth ceilings.

Similarly, we can add computational ceilings. These are parallel horizontal lines on the log-log plot. Examples of the computational ceilings are as follows. (1) The peak performance for a default configuration without SIMD instructions such as Intel SSE, (2) performance with SIMD instructions, and (3) the peak theoretical computational capacity. These are shown in Figure 10.42 . We thus observe

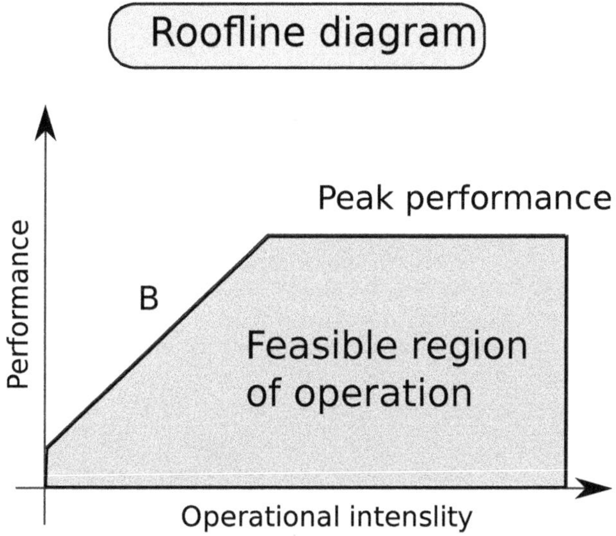

Figure 10.41: Performance vs operational intensity (with Rooflines)

different feasible regions of operation for different kinds of ceilings.

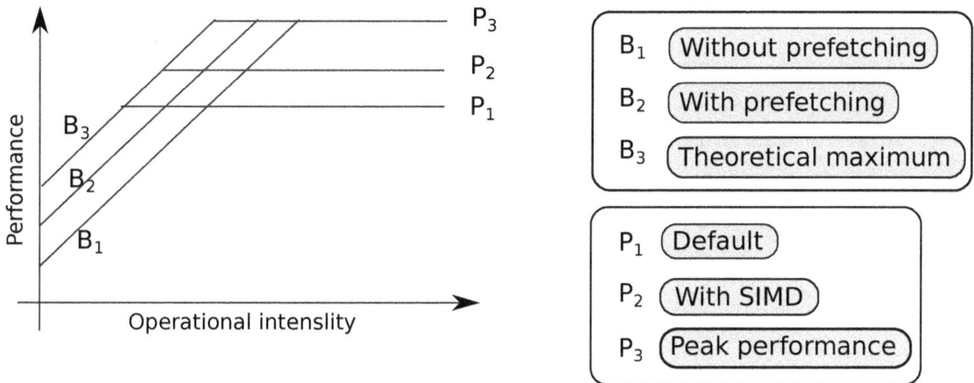

Figure 10.42: Roofline diagram with many ceilings

10.6.3 Uses of the Roofline Model

The Roofline model is a very simple tool to reason about the bottlenecks in an application. Let us consider Figure 10.43. In this figure we show several points: P, Q, and R. Point P is close to the memory bandwidth ceiling. In this case, we cannot get additional performance without increasing the memory bandwidth. Hence, any additional investment should be made in increasing the available memory bandwidth. In comparison, point Q is close to the performance ceiling. This means that it has saturated all the computational power, and memory bandwidth is not an issue because this design is not using all the bandwidth that it can use. In this case, we need to enable newer architectural optimisations for increasing the computational power. Finally, let us consider point R, which is far away from both the memory bandwidth and performance ceilings. In this case, the design can be modified to use far more memory bandwidth, and much more computational capacity as compared to the current

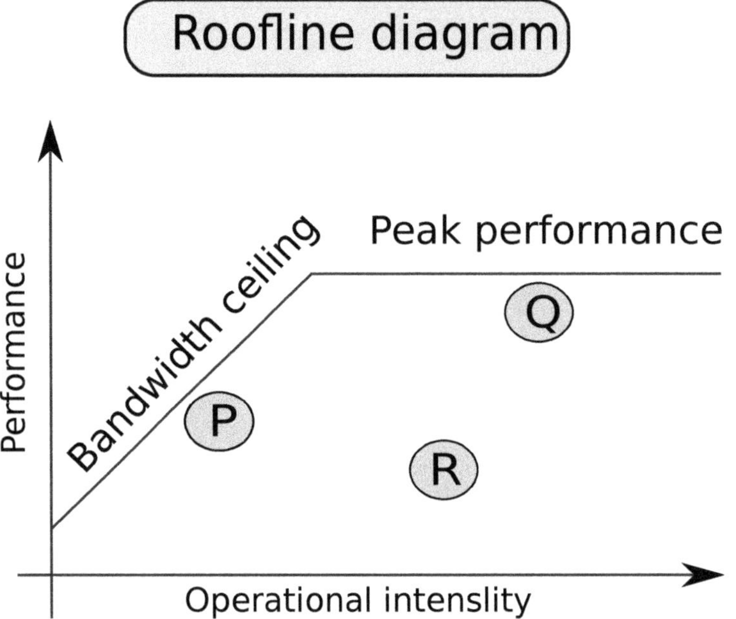

Figure 10.43: Three different operating points in the Roofline diagram

implementation.

We thus see from these three examples that given any workload or architectural configuration, we can easily find out the bottlenecks by finding the proximity of the point to different ceilings. We can use these models in many different ways. For example, it can tell us that given a certain value of the operational intensity, what is the minimum memory bandwidth that is needed to sustain a given performance.

Additionally, we can also define a lower threshold for the performance, which means that we are guaranteed a certain level of performance. Now between the upper and lower ceilings, we can reason about the bandwidth that is required to sustain a given level of performance. Researchers have proposed numerous extensions to this model to include different kinds of additional effects, notably energy [Choi et al., 2013].

10.7　Summary and Further Reading

10.7.1　Summary

Summary 9

1. *A typical DRAM cell is very simple; it has a single transistor and a single capacitor.*

2. *Two kinds of capacitors are used to create modern DRAM cells: a trench capacitor and a stacked capacitor.*

3. *Akin to SRAM cells, we can create an array of DRAM cells. The major difference is that in this case, the sense amplifiers appear before the column multiplexer/demultiplexer. The sense amplifiers are also designed differently. They are designed to also buffer data for the entire row (page) of cells, and drive the voltages of the bit lines.*

4. *It is typically necessary to split each bit line into multiple segments. There are two architectures in this space: open bit line array architecture and folded bit line array architecture. The latter design is more tolerant to noise, at the cost of lower storage density.*

5. *DRAM reads are destructive in the sense that once a row is read, the contents of the cells that store a logical 1 are destroyed. Hence, it is necessary to restore their values. Since the contents of the row are stored in the array of sense amplifiers (row buffer), if subsequent reads are to the same row, then their values can be supplied from the row buffer.*

6. *Each DRAM cell can maintain its state for at the most 32 to 64 ms. The charge stored across the capacitor gradually leaks out. Hence, it is necessary to periodically refresh (read and then write) every single cell in the DRAM array.*

7. *The earliest versions of DRAM used asynchronous transfer. The row address was synchronised with the $\overline{RAS}$ strobe signal and the column address was synchronised with the $\overline{CAS}$ strobe signal. Even though pure asynchronous transfer is a generic solution; however, it has low performance and scalability.*

8. *Given that we often fetch a sequence of bytes from DRAM memory, a more efficient method of transfer is the fast page mode (FPM). After sending a row address, the controller sends a series of column addresses for that row. We read the sequence of bits corresponding to the column addresses. A shortcoming of this method is that we wait to receive the data and then only we send the next column address.*

9. *The next generation of DRAM technology was called extended data out (EDO). This overcomes the shortcoming of the FPM technology, by overlapping the transmission of data and column addresses. To provide the timing for the data signals, an additional data strobe signal $\overline{DQS}$ is used*

10. *EDO was succeeded by the burst extended data out (BEDO) technology. In this case, for a single column address, we read multiple bits – essentially prefetch the next few bits. This reduces the need to send additional column addresses.*

11. *All of these technologies have been superseded by synchronous DRAM technologies. The DRAM devices have a clock that is synchronised with the clock of the memory controller prior to a message transmission.*

---

12. *The command and address buses are connected to every single device; this increases the capacitive loading on them. In contrast, the data buses are only connected to a subset of DRAM devices. Hence, they are faster. To leverage this, the double data rate (DDR) memory was proposed where we transfer data at both the edges of the clock.*

13. *There are multiple DDR generations: DDR1, DDR2, DDR3, and DDR4. Over the generations, there has been an increase in the bus frequency and storage density, whereas the supply voltage has reduced.*

14. *The topology of a DDR4 memory is as follows.*

    (a) *The CPU is connected to memory modules via a set of channels. Each channel is a set of copper wires that are used to transmit memory addresses, data, and commands. Each channel has its dedicated memory controller that is co-located with the cores and cache banks.*

    (b) *Several DIMMs (dual inline memory modules) are connected to each channel.*

    (c) *Each DIMM is divided into ranks, where each rank is a set of DRAM devices (chips). All the devices in each rank operate in lockstep. They perceive the same amount of clock skew and signal delay.*

    (d) *Each device has multiple banks, where each bank can operate independently of the others. In modern DRAM devices, these banks are organised into bank groups.*

    (e) *When sending a command, we specify the rank, the bank group id, and the bank id. All the banks across the devices in the rank, with the specified bank group id and bank id, get activated (one bank per device).*

    (f) *Each bank consists of multiple memory arrays that are always accessed together. Each array has a set of rows and columns.*

    (g) *We can either read 1 bit (single column) at once, or read multiple bits. If the latter is the case, and we read n contiguous columns, then the prefetch length or prefetch width is said to be n.*

15. *The DDR4 protocol is associated with different timing parameters. Some of the major parameters are as follows.*

Parameter	Mnemonic
Row cycle time	tRC
ACT to PRE command period	$tRAS$
PRE to ACT command period	tRP
ACT to internal read or write	$tRCD$
CAS latency	CL
CAS write latency	CWL
Column to column delay (same bank group)	$tCCD_L$
Column to column delay (different bank group)	$tCCD_S$
Row to row delay (same bank group, 1Kb page size)	$tRRD_L$
Row to row delay (different bank group, 1Kb page size)	$tRRD_S$
Four-bank activation window (1Kb page size)	$tFAW$
Write to read latency (same bank group)	$tWTR_L$
Write to read latency (different bank group)	$tWTR_S$
IntREAD to PRE command period	$tRTP$
Write recovery time	tWR

16. *The memory controller schedules and orchestrates all the memory accesses. It has the following components:*

(a) A high-level transaction scheduler that reorders read and write operations. It also has a write cache that services later reads.

(b) An address mapping engine that maps the physical address to internal DRAM addresses.

(c) A DRAM command generator. There are two broad strategies. Either we can keep a row open after it has been accessed once such that later accesses to the row can read or write to the row quickly using the row buffer. This is known as the open page access policy. The other option is to immediately close the row and precharge it. This is the closed page access policy.

(d) A command scheduler that chooses DRAM commands from multiple bank queues. The commands are scheduled based on fairness criteria, priorities (e.g. refresh), and the timing requirements of the DRAM devices.

17. *Nonvolatile memories that maintain their state even after the system is powered off are becoming increasingly popular. It is a storage technology that has replaced hard disk drives in almost all mobile and hand held devices. The main types of nonvolatile memories are as follows:*

Flash memory *Such kind of a memory uses a novel transistor that traps charge in an additional gate called the* floating gate. *The presence and absence of charge in the floating gate represents its two permanent states. Flash memory is easy to manufacture and reads are fast. Sadly, writes are slow because to write a page, it is necessary to first erase an entire set of pages (block). Moreover, it has a relatively low shelf life because it can tolerate roughly 10^5 to 10^6 program-erase cycles.*

FeRAM *FeRAM uses a ferroelectric dielectric in the capacitor, as opposed to using a normal dielectric. This dielectric has two polarisation states when no voltage is applied across the capacitor. To switch between these two states, we need to change the direction of the potential across the parallel plates of the capacitor. Similar to a DRAM, the reads are destructive. However, both reads and writes are very fast and the endurance is much more than flash memory.*

STT-MRAM *In an STT-MRAM cell we have two magnetic layers: pinned layer (fixed direction of magnetisation) and the free layer (direction of magnetisation can change). They are separated by a thin film made of MgO. This cell has two permanent states based on the directions of magnetisation of the pinned and free layers: parallel (low resistance) and anti-parallel (high resistance). Reading is very fast because we just need to sense the resistance of the cell. However, writing is a slower process because electrons need to transfer their spin torque to the electrons in the free layer and appropriately change their direction of magnetisation. Unlike flash memory, we can access individual words and the leakage current is negligible.*

PCM *PCM (phase change memory) relies on the state of a chalcogenide material: amorphous or crystalline. If we apply a large current quickly, then because of Joule heating, the material melts and enters the amorphous state. This state has a high resistance. However, if we apply a relatively lower current for a longer time, then the material crystallises and this state is associated with a lower resistance. PCM memory has fast reads and slow writes. Two methods to deal with slow writes are write cancellation and write pausing, where the process of writing a value is terminated midway to give way to scheduling read operations. Endurance is an issue, hence there is a need to ensure that all the locations are equally accessed.*

ReRAM *Resistive RAM (ReRAM) is a family of technologies where the instantaneous resistance of the cell depends upon the history of voltages applied to the terminals of the cell.*

> *In Redox ReRAMs, a conductive channel forms in an oxide layer sandwiched between two electrodes when a positive voltage is applied to the anode. This conductive channel is a filament that is made of oxygen vacancies after oxygen ions migrate to the anode. This conductive channel can be ruptured by either applying a large voltage (unipolar switching), or reversing the voltage across the cell (bipolar switching). On similar lines, a CBRAM also forms a conductive filament of Ag^+ ions that migrate towards the cathode. Off late, ReRAMs are increasingly being used to implement neural networks because they basically work as multipliers.*
>
> *18. The Roofline model is used to study the limits of performance in a system. It is a log-log plot with the operational intensity (FLOPs/byte) on the x-axis and the performance (FLOPs/sec) on the y-axis. A $45°$ line represents a set of points that have a fixed memory bandwidth, and a line parallel to the y-axis represents constant performance. Using these two lines – memory bandwidth and performance – we can define a feasible region of operation, and study the effect of different architectural optimisations.*

10.7.2   Further Reading

The references that we have used for the topics on DRAMs are as follows: the book by Jacob, Ng, and Wang [Jacob et al., 2007], the design of the DRAMsim simulator [Wang et al., 2005], and the JEDEC standards [JEDEC Solid State Technology Association, 2003, JEDEC Solid State Technology Association, 2008a, JEDEC Solid State Technology Association, 2008b, JEDEC Solid State Technology Association, 2020]. We have used the same symbol names as the JEDEC standards. Readers can consult them for a deeper understanding of technologies related to DRAMs particularly the DDR4 protocol that we have described in great detail.

The following references [Yu and Chen, 2016, Chen, 2016, Feng et al., 2010] give an overview of NVM technologies and future directions. For understanding the physics and the operation of FeRAMs, readers can refer to the FeRAM guide book [Fujitsu Semiconductor Limited, 2010] from Fujitsu. A thorough description of spin transfer torque mechanisms is provided by Khvalkovskiy et al. [Khvalkovskiy et al., 2013], Kawahara et al. [Kawahara et al., 2012], and Apalkov et al. [Apalkov et al., 2013]. For phase change memories, we would recommend the seminal paper by Lee et al. [Lee et al., 2009] and the e-book by Qureshi et al. [Qureshi et al., 2011]. Finally, for ReRAMs the following references [Wouters, 2009, Akinaga and Shima, 2012, Yu, 2016, Wang et al., 2018] will prove to be useful.

Exercises

Ex. 1 — Why is the sense amplifier placed after the column mux/demux in SRAMs? In comparison, why is it placed before, i.e., between the array and the column mux/demux in DRAMs?

Ex. 2 — Compare the open and folded bit line array architectures.

Ex. 3 — Calculate the refresh rate for a DRAM cell with a capacitor of capacitance 1 fF and a transistor whose leakage current is 1 pA . Assume that the voltage across a fully charged capacitor is 1.5 V and the cell needs refreshing before the voltage drops below 0.75 V.

Ex. 4 — Define a DRAM *rank*. Why is it required?

* **Ex. 5** — Why do we typically avoid multi-ported DRAM arrays? Furthermore, why do we typically access the DRAM array at the level of single columns, where a column usually stores a single bit.

Ex. 6 — Why is it typically necessary to use a strobe in high-speed DRAM protocols?

Ex. 7 — What is the advantage of using active low signals?

Ex. 8 — Prove that $tRC = tRAS + tRP$.

Ex. 9 — Why is the $ACT \rightarrow ACT$ delay less for a different bank group?

Ex. 10 — Why is a preamble and postamble required?

Ex. 11 — Prove the formula for the read to write delay. Modify the formula to include the parity latency as well.

Ex. 12 — Can the algorithm followed by the DRAM memory controller cause any memory consistency issues?

Ex. 13 — Create an addressing scheme for an FB-DIMM DRAM system. Make your own assumptions.

Ex. 14 — Why is NAND flash called NAND flash? How is it superior to NOR flash?

Ex. 15 — Design a memory controller for a 3D memory.

Ex. 16 — Can we use the Roofline model to compare a CPU and a GPU? Assume that they use the same off-chip DRAM-based memory system. What insights will we get?

Ex. 17 — How can we model software prefetching, hardware prefetching, and NUCA caches using the Roofline model?

Design Problems

Ex. 18 — Design the sense amplifier circuit using any popular circuit simulator.

Ex. 19 — Understand the working of the memory controller in DRAMSim2 or the Tejas architectural simulator.

Ex. 20 — Design a DDR4 DRAM memory controller using Logisim, Verilog, or VHDL.

Part III

Advanced Topics

11

Power and Temperature

In the last two parts of the book we have studied the design of a modern out-of-order processor, on-chip network, and memory system in detail. We started with a simple 5-stage in-order processor, and increased its performance several times by using sophisticated optimisations to enhance all aspects of the design. The natural question that we need to ask now is, "Are there any limits to doing this?" If there were indeed no limits, then we can keep on proposing newer and better optimisations, and keep on increasing the performance. However, nature has its way of applying brakes. For at least the last 15 years, the single largest factor that has kept processors from scaling in terms of additional features and complexity is the issue of high power consumption and consequent temperature rise. Both these issues are connected, and have effectively stymied many design features.

Let us motivate the reader by providing some facts that indicate the extent of the problem. While running a floating point application the die temperature of a CPU exceeds $100°C$, which is enough to boil a cup of water, or fry an egg. If the CPU remains at this temperature long enough, then the wires and transistors can get seriously damaged. As we shall see in Chapter 12, the probability of failure is an exponential function of the die temperature. The problem of high temperature not only bedevils large processors that are used in desktops and servers, it is also important for mobile phones. Imaging using a mobile phone that feels like a warm face pack in a hot and humid climate. A consistently high temperature increases the probability of the battery of the mobile phone exploding!

Let us now look at energy/power consumption. We all have been in situations, where we just have 3% of the total battery charge left in our phones, and we have to either finish a call, or go back home using Google Maps^{TM}, and there is no charger in sight. In such cases, one would wish that she had a phone that consumed very little energy such that she could finish all her work with the remaining energy in the battery. Nobody likes to charge their phones or laptops very frequently.

In the case of large server processors, we might be misled to believe that temperature rise and power consumption are not an issue because the servers are isolated in a server room or a data centre. Since we are not physically present in the building, temperature rise is not an issue, and since there is no battery, energy usage is also not a concern. However, this is not correct. The energy required to maintain the optimal temperature in a large data centre is roughly 20-40% of the total energy consumption. For a large corporation such as Facebook® or Google® this can translate to billions of dollars. Even for a much smaller setup, the electricity bill is a large part of the operating expenditure of a data centre, and thus reducing the energy consumption by even 10% is significant. Consider the fact that in 2017, data centres in the US consumed 90 billion units (kilowatt-hours) of energy, and globally 3% of the energy was used to power data centres. This number is growing and is expected to double by 2021, which will put a significant strain on the planet's resources [Danilak, 2017].

There are two major components of power consumption: dynamic power and static (or leakage) power. The dynamic power is dependent on the clock frequency, and the activity inside the CPU. However, temperature-dependent leakage power is dissipated by transistors via mechanisms that are normally considered to be associated with no power dissipation. As of 2020, leakage power is roughly 20-40% of the total power dissipation in high-end processors. The relationships between power and temperature are complex: an increase in dynamic power increases the total power, which increases the temperature, which increases the leakage power, which increases the total power, which increases the temperature (and so on). There is thus a cyclic dependence between power and temperature, which means that a small increase in power leads to a small increase in temperature, which further leads to a small increase in power, and so on. In most cases, this process converges; however, in some cases it does not and this leads to a very dangerous condition called *thermal runaway*. The system needs to be immediately shut down if such a situation arises. Let us thus summarise what we have learnt up till now.

Way Point 14

1. *The dynamic power consumption of a processor is dependent upon its design and the workloads that execute on it.*

2. *An increase in dynamic power increases the temperature, which increases the leakage power. The leakage power further increases the temperature. There is thus a cyclic dependence between temperature and leakage power.*

3. *It is necessary to limit the power consumption for controlling the peak temperature.*

We shall proceed as follows in this chapter. We shall first look at methods to model power and temperature in Sections 11.1 and 11.2 , then describe methods for power management in Section 11.3, and finally conclude by briefly discussing methods to reduce temperature in Section 11.4.

11.1 Power Consumption Model

There are many power dissipation mechanisms in modern processors. The mechanisms can broadly be divided into two types: dynamic power dissipation and static power dissipation (also known as *leakage power* dissipation) [1]. Dynamic power refers to traditional power consumption where power is consumed because of the current flow between transistors in the circuit whenever an input changes. The resistive loss in the different circuit elements leads to this kind of power dissipation.

Starting from the early 2000s, static power (or leakage power) has increasingly become more important. In the ideal scenario, we only expect current flow between the drain and source of a transistor when it is switching its state. However, this is often not the case. For example, in modern transistors and capacitors there is a small amount of current flow between the drain and source even in the off state. This is not expected, and is thus categorised as *leakage power*. Similarly, we never expect any current flow between the gate of a transistor and the body; however, this also is not true in practice. When we integrate the effects of such small sources of power dissipation over billions of transistors, the total amount of power dissipated can be significant. As of 2020, static power accounts for roughly 20-40% of

---

[1] In this book the terms *leakage power* and *static power* will be used synonymously and interchangeably.

the overall CPU power budget. The important point to understand is that even though the leakage current and the resultant leakage power in a given transistor are at least an order of magnitude lower than the dynamic power, they become significant when we consider the cumulative sum across the billions of transistors. Additionally, note that a rather small fraction of transistors are active or switching their state at a given point of time. The total number of transistors is actually an order of magnitude more. If we take both of these effects into account, the leakage power becomes disproportionately important.

It is important to mention that to understand the rest of the discussion in this section, it is necessary to go through Section 7.3.3, and also understand the basic structure of a transistor. For the latter, interested readers can refer to a standard text on digital electronics [Taub and Schilling, 1977].

11.1.1   Dynamic Power

The Notion of Voltage Transitions

As we discussed in Section 7.3.3, a lot of circuits in modern processors including memories can be approximated as RC networks. Every circuit element can be replaced with an equivalent RC model and the subsequent calculations are reasonably accurate – at least to get a broad estimate and get an idea of the overall trends. Consider a pair of two inverters in series as shown in Figure 11.1. The gates of the two transistors in inverter I_2 have an associated gate capacitance. These capacitors need to be charged if we need to set the voltage at the gates of I_2 to a logical 1. If they were at a logical 0, then current needs to flow via the PMOS transistor (T_1) of inverter I_1 to charge these capacitors. Whenever there is a current flow in a circuit, it leads to power dissipation across the resistive elements. Even though we cannot see any resistor in the circuit diagram of Figure 11.1, however the equivalent circuit of these transistors has resistive elements (described in detail in Section 7.3.3). In general, whenever there is a current flow across any device (transistor or capacitor), we shall encounter an associated resistance. We observe a resultant power dissipation – I^2R loss.

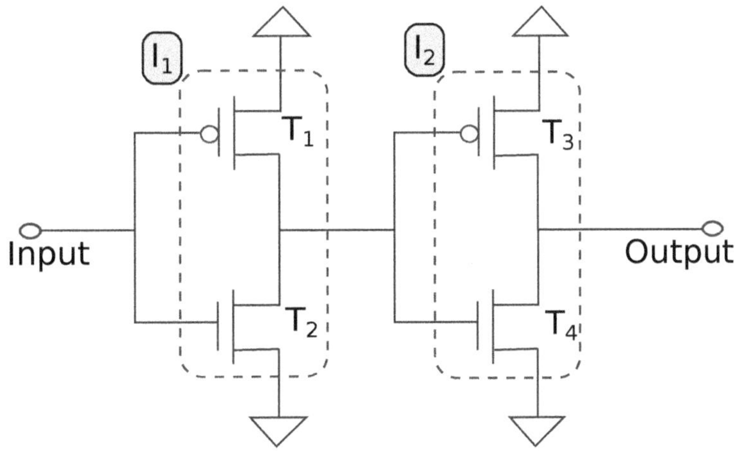

Figure 11.1: Circuit with two inverters in series

We can make a generalised observation here. Whenever there is a current flow in a circuit to effect a transition in the voltage level (logical $0 \rightarrow 1$, or $1 \rightarrow 0$), there is some amount of dynamic power dissipation because of the passage of current through resistive elements in the circuits and in the devices themselves. Hence, to compute the dynamic power dissipation of a circuit, we need to locate all the voltage transitions in a cycle, compute the current flow required to effect the transitions, and then compute the sum of the resistive (I^2R) losses throughout the circuit.

Let us consider a functional unit that has n input and m output terminals. In a cycle if none of the

n inputs change, which means that they maintain their previous values, then there will be no transitions within the circuit because none of the inputs changed. If a point inside the circuit was charged to a logical 1, it will continue to maintain that voltage (assuming no leakage). Likewise is the case for points at a logical 0. There will be no transitions because the inputs did not change, and thus the dynamic power dissipation will be zero. We can thus conclude that the dynamic power dissipation of a circuit is dependent not only on its inputs but also on the previous inputs and the previous state of the entire circuit. Essentially, the only thing that we care while computing dynamic power is the locations of all the *voltage transitions in the circuit.*

The power dissipated per voltage transition also depends on the values of resistances and capacitances in the vicinity of the point at which there was a voltage transition. Given the sheer complexity of this problem with the multitude of variables, it is necessary to analyse simple situations to understand the broad trends that affect power consumption. Let us thus look at a simple model for computing the effect of voltage transitions.

Mathematical Model of Power Dissipation

Consider the circuit shown in Figure 11.2. It has a resistor and a capacitor in series.

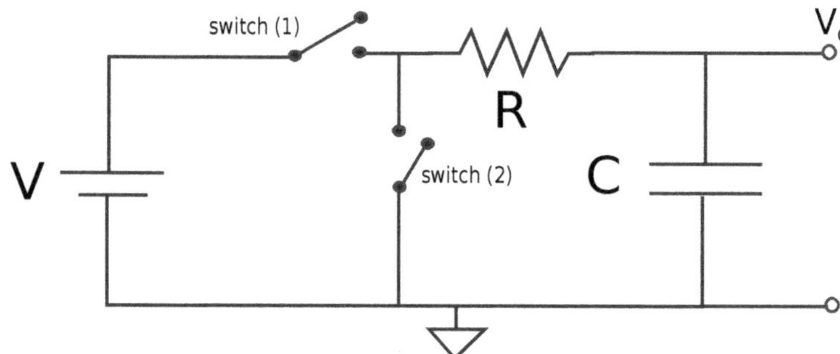

Figure 11.2: A simple RC circuit

Let's say at $t = 0$, we connect the voltage source V to the circuit. The current across the capacitor at any point of time is $I = CdV_o/dt$, where V_o is the voltage at the upper terminal of the capacitor. From Kirchhoff's laws we have $V_o = V - IR$.

Let us solve for the current I.

$$\begin{aligned}
I &= C\frac{dV_o}{dt} \\
\Rightarrow I &= C\frac{-dIR}{dt} \\
\Rightarrow I &= -RC\frac{dI}{dt} \\
\Rightarrow \frac{dI}{I} &= -\frac{dt}{RC} \\
\Rightarrow \int \frac{dI}{I} &= -\int \frac{dt}{RC} \\
\Rightarrow ln(I) &= -\frac{t}{RC} + k \\
\Rightarrow I &= e^{-\frac{t}{RC}} \times e^k
\end{aligned} \tag{11.1}$$

Here, k is the constant of integration. At $t = 0$, $I = \frac{V}{R}$, because the voltage across the capacitor is 0. We thus have $e^k = \frac{V}{R}$.

The final solution is given by

$$I = \frac{V}{R}e^{-\frac{t}{RC}} \tag{11.2}$$

Let us now compute the total energy provided by the voltage source in a typical charging cycle.

$$\begin{aligned}
P_{tot} &= \int V \times I \\
&= V \times \frac{V}{R}\int_0^\infty e^{-\frac{t}{RC}}\,dt \\
&= CV^2 \int_0^\infty e^{-\frac{t}{RC}}\,d\frac{t}{RC} \\
&= CV^2
\end{aligned} \tag{11.3}$$

Thus the total energy that is provided is CV^2. Out of this energy, some of it is dissipated as heat via the resistor and the rest is stored as energy across the capacitor. The final voltage across the capacitor is equal to V. From basic physics, we know that the energy stored across a capacitor is equal to $\frac{1}{2}CV^2$. This means that the energy lost as heat via the resistor is equal to the difference: $\frac{1}{2}CV^2$.

Now while discharging, the current flows along the discharge path (via switch(2) in the figure with switch(1) turned off). The capacitor will lose all of its charge and its stored energy. By the simple rules of energy conservation, we can deduce that all this energy will be dissipated as heat via the resistor. This energy is $\frac{1}{2}CV^2$.

We can thus make several important conclusions.

- The total energy provided by the voltage source to charge the capacitor is equal to CV^2.

- Half of this energy is dissipated as heat while charging the capacitor, regardless of the value of the resistance, R.

- The rest of the energy is also dissipated as heat while discharging the capacitor. This is also equal to $\frac{1}{2}CV^2$.

- The total energy dissipated in a charge-discharge cycle is equal to CV^2.

Given that $\frac{1}{2}CV^2$ units of energy are dissipated in every cycle (charging or discharging), the power consumption is equal to $\frac{1}{2}CV^2/\tau$, where τ is the cycle time. $1/\tau = f$, where f is the frequency. Thus, we arrive at the most important equation in dynamic power consumption. The dynamic power consumption, P_{dyn}, is given by

$$P_{dyn} \propto CV^2 f \tag{11.4}$$

Here, the proportional sign $\propto$ is very important. For a simple RC network, it is equal to half assuming that in every cycle either we charge or discharge the capacitor. However, in a complex circuit we might have hundreds of transistors and many of them would be switching their state in a cycle. Additionally, all the transistors will not be switching their state in a given cycle. We thus need to factor in the level of activity of the circuit. Hence, we need to modify Equation 11.4 as follows:

$$P_{dyn} \propto \beta CV^2 f \tag{11.5}$$

Here, β, is the activity factor, which is a number between 0 and 1. A value of "1" indicates that all the transistors in the circuit change their state in any given cycle, and a "0" means that none of the transistors change their state. The activity factor basically determines the mean fraction of transistors that change their state every cycle.

If we know the constant of proportionality, then we can find the exact value of power for the functional unit, and we can also find the total power dissipation of the processor by summing up the values for each functional unit.

However, even without knowing the constant of proportionality, Equation 11.5 is extremely valuable. If we know the power for a given level of activity (β), we can easily estimate the power consumption at a different level of activity. This will tell us how the power consumption of a functional unit changes as we vary the activity. Using this insight we can design micro-architectures that modify β dynamically such that the power consumption changes.

Sadly changing the activity factor, β, isn't always possible. It is far more practical to tune the voltage and frequency, which are arguably the most powerful knobs to contain power consumption.

Dynamic Voltage and Frequency Scaling (DVFS)

The key learning from Equation 11.5 is that the power consumption is dependent on the voltage and the frequency. It is possible to change the power consumption by tuning the voltage and frequency, which is known as Dynamic Voltage and Frequency Scaling (DVFS).

In the early days when the behaviour of transistors was governed by very simple equations, the time it took for a transistor to change its state was roughly inversely proportional to the supply voltage. Hence, we assumed that the relation $V \propto f$ is roughly true. This can be intuitively reasoned as follows. More is the voltage, higher is the current, and thus it will take a proportionately lesser amount of time to charge and discharge capacitors in the circuit. However, this simple relationship has ceased to hold. The relationship is now governed by the Alpha Power Law [Sarangi et al., 2008].

$$f \propto \frac{(V - V_{th})^\alpha}{V} \tag{11.6}$$

V_{th} is the threshold voltage and α is a constant. We observe that if $V \gg V_{th}$ and $\alpha = 2$, then the traditional relation $f \propto V$ holds. However, in modern technologies V/V_{th} is between 4 and 6, which is a comparatively much smaller ratio. Secondly, the value of α has reduced. It is now between 1.1 and 1.5 [Sarangi et al., 2008].

In practice, modern processors do not use such formulae. They have a table that contains a few voltage and frequency settings. These are known as the DVFS settings. The processor is only allowed to operate in any one of these settings.

ED^2 Metric

Let us first understand the traditional view of thinking when people assumed that $f \propto V$. We can still use this model to derive many insights and results. Assuming a constant activity factor and no leakage power. We have,

$$\begin{aligned} P_{dyn} &\propto CV^2 f \\ &\propto Cf^2 \times f \quad (V \propto f) \\ &\propto f^3 \end{aligned} \tag{11.7}$$

We thus have: $\boxed{P_{dyn} \propto f^3}$.

The key result that we derive is that the dynamic power is proportional to a cube of the frequency. If we double the frequency, the power will increase by 8 times. This explains why the processor frequency was not able to cross 4 GHz: the power consumption was prohibitive.

Let us also look at one more key metric that has survived from the old days. Consider the product ED^2, which is alternatively $P_{dyn}D^3$. Here, E is the energy, and D is the delay; we are assuming that there is no leakage power. If we consider the power for the entire system, we need to sum up the per-component dynamic power. Since the factor $V^2 f$ is common to all the power values for the components we can write that $P_{dyn} \propto V^2 f$, where the constant of proportionality incorporates all the activity factors and capacitances. Let us make one more simplifying approximation that is not exactly correct, however it still can be used to derive an approximate relationship between the frequency(f) and the delay(D) (program execution time). We assume that $f \propto 1/D$, which is approximately true for programs that are CPU-bound – we need to discount the effect of the main memory latency, which does not scale with the frequency.

We thus have,

$$\begin{aligned}
ED^2 = P_{dyn}D^3 &\propto V^2 f \times D^3 \\
&\propto f^3 \times D^3 \quad (V \propto f) \\
&\propto \frac{f^3}{f^3} \quad (D \propto 1/f) \\
&\propto 1
\end{aligned}$$
(11.8)

The key result is that ED^2 is a constant with respect to any DVFS based scaling. In other words, regardless of the values of the frequency and voltage, ED^2 remains a constant as long as the voltage and frequency are scaled according to our assumptions. ED^2 is essentially a function of the activity factors, the capacitances, and other artefacts of the architecture and the circuit. It is an inherent property of an architecture, and is immune to voltage and frequency scaling.

This discussion answers a very important question in computer architecture. Let us say that we have two designs: A and B. As compared to design A, B is 10% faster yet consumes 20% more energy. Which design is better? We previously did not have any method to answer this question, however we can answer this question now using the ED^2 metric (see Example 13). The lower is the ED^2, better is the design.

Example 13

We have two designs: A and B. As compared to design A, B is 10% faster, yet consumes 20% more energy. Which design is better in terms of its ED^2?

Answer: *Let the ED^2 of design A be 1 (arbitrary units). Then the ED^2 of B is 1.2×0.9^2, which is equal to 0.97. The ED^2 of design B is lower, hence it is a better design.*

In all of this discussion, one fact should always be kept in mind that such metrics are approximate and date back to an era where many of these assumed relationships used to strictly hold. However, the reason that they are still used today is because they provide a very intuitive method of approximately comparing two designs that have different power consumption and performance values.

Short-Circuit Power

Let us now specifically discuss a minor component of the dynamic power, which is known as the short-circuit power. It is typically 10% of the overall dynamic power [Li et al., 2009], however in some designs where the threshold voltage is relatively high as compared to the supply voltage, this can increase to roughly 25% [Nose and Sakurai, 2000].

A typical inverter as shown in Figure 11.3 has two transistors: the pull-up PMOS transistor and the pull-down NMOS transistor. When it is going through an input transition there is a brief period when both the transistors are conducting. During this time there is a short circuit between the supply

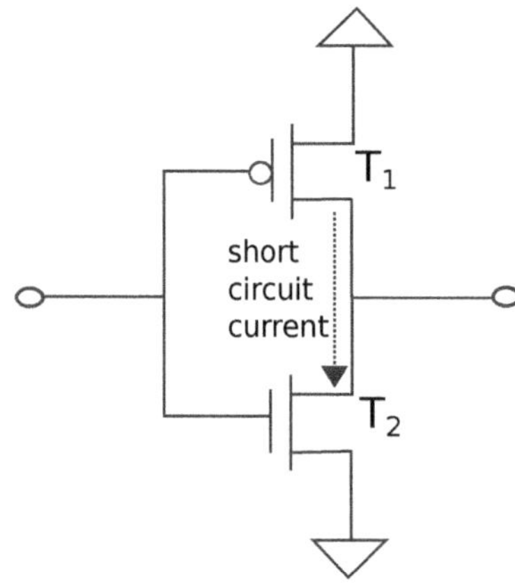

Figure 11.3: A single CMOS inverter (note the short circuit current)

and the ground. The corresponding current that flows is known as the *short-circuit current*, and the corresponding power is known as the *short-circuit power*.

11.1.2 Leakage Power

Sadly dynamic power dissipation is not the only power dissipation mechanism. 20-40% of the overall power dissipation is accounted for by leakage power in high-end processors.

Leakage (or static) power is any source of power dissipation that is not present in an ideal transistor. For example, in a typical NMOS transistor we do not expect any current to flow from the gate to the substrate, or from the drain to the substrate. However, real devices have such non-idealities, and thus they *leak* some power via interfaces that are assumed to be perfect insulators in simplistic models.

If we add the effect of these small sources of power dissipation across all the transistors in the chip, then the net power dissipation can be significant. Leakage is particularly an issue in the large L2 and L3 caches. There are several different leakage power dissipation mechanisms, and their relative predominance depends on the transistor technology.

Overview of Different Leakage Mechanisms

Figure 11.4 shows the diagram of an NMOS transistor. It shows six different leakage mechanisms: currents I_1 to I_6 in the figure. Let us discuss them one by one.

I_1: P-N Junction Reverse-Bias Current

A p-n junction is said to be reverse-biased if the p side is connected to a low voltage source, and the n side is connected to a high voltage source. Most of the time during the operation of an NMOS transistor, this is the case for the drain to body junction. The drain voltage (connected to the n-type doped region) is much higher than the body voltage. This makes the drain-body junction reverse-biased. The main component of the reverse-biased current is band-to-band tunnelling (BTBT).

Band-to-Band Tunnelling
Typically in today's transistors, there is a very high electric field across the drain-to-body p-n junction. This high electric field causes electrons to "tunnel" from the valence band of the p-type doped region to the conduction band of the n-type doped region.

It is necessary to explain the terms *valence band* and *conduction band* here. As per the rules of quantum mechanics, an electron in a system of atoms can only occupy a fixed set of energy levels. It is

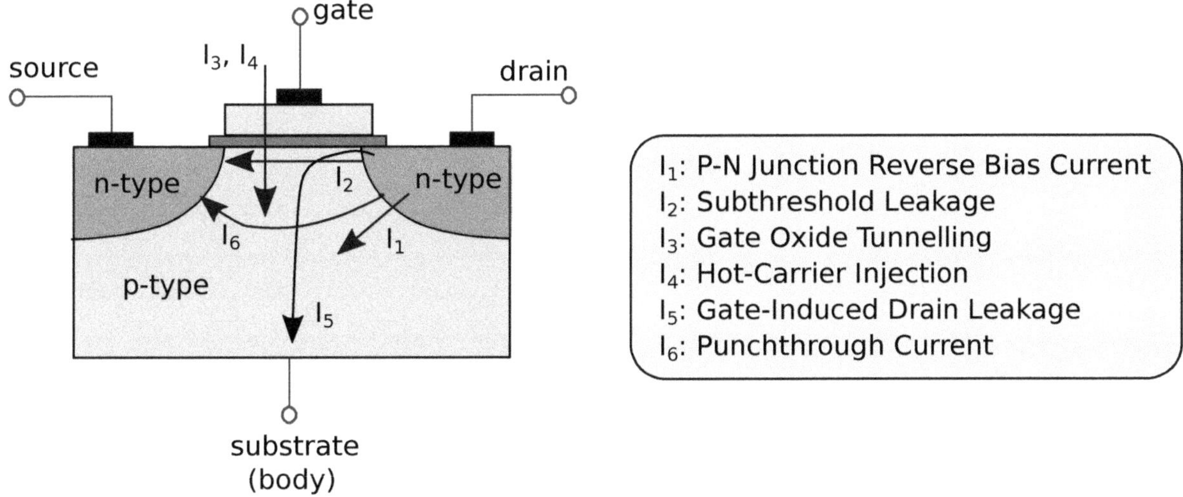

Figure 11.4: Different leakage mechanisms

not possible for it to occupy any intermediate energy level because quantum state is discrete. Over the long run any material's electrons will migrate into the low-energy states. However, by Pauli's exclusion principle two electrons cannot have the same state. As a result, some electrons will have to be in high-energy states. Now, every solid-state material can be characterised by the *Fermi level*, which is defined as follows. When the temperature is 0 K (absolute zero) all the energy levels below the Fermi level are occupied with electrons, and no energy level above the Fermi level is occupied with an electron. At higher temperatures, a fraction of electrons occupy energy levels *above* the Fermi level.

The *valence band* is a range of energy levels just below the Fermi level. Likewise, the *conduction band* is a range of energy levels just above the Fermi level. In semiconductor materials, typically there is a band gap between the valence and conduction bands. An electron can only act as a charge carrier if it gets transferred to the conduction band, and likewise is the case for holes. If the energy supplied to an electron because of the potential difference across the drain-body junction is more than the band gap between the conduction and valence bands, then it is possible for the resultant electric field to accelerate the electrons and move them into the conduction band of the n-type region. They can then flow towards the positively charged drain terminal.

I_2: Subthreshold Leakage

Till a few years ago (before 2015) subthreshold leakage used to be the dominant mechanism for dissipating leakage power.

As we can see in Figure 11.4, this current flows from the drain to the source via the channel. When the gate voltage is lower than the threshold voltage (V_{th}), we traditionally assume that there is no current flow between the drain and the source. However, a small amount of current still flows and this is known as the subthreshold leakage current [Roy et al., 2003]. The subthreshold current, I_{ds}, is given by the following equation.

$$I_{ds} = \mu_0 C_{ox} \frac{W}{L} (m-1) v_T^2 \times e^{(V_g - V_{th})/m v_T} \times \left(1 - e^{-\frac{V_{DS}}{v_T}}\right) \quad (11.9)$$

The terms are defined as follows.

Term	Meaning	Term	Meaning
μ_0	Zero bias mobility	C_{ox}	Gate oxide capacitance
W	Width	L	Length
m	Subthreshold swing coefficient	v_T	kT/q
V_g	Gate voltage	V_{th}	Threshold voltage
V_{DS}	Drain-source voltage	k	Boltzmann's constant
q	1.6×10^{-19} C	T	Temperature (in Kelvins)

One of the most important terms in this equation is $v_T = kT/q$, which is known as the thermal voltage that is proportional to the temperature. We see that I_{ds} is proportional to the square of v_T via the term v_T^2, and is exponentially dependent on it via the two terms that have v_T as a part of the exponent. Because of these relationships, for a long time it was assumed that the leakage current is an exponential function of the temperature. However, this relationship is not strictly true as of 2020.

Sultan et al. [Sultan et al., 2018] in their study show that in most cases a linear model of leakage is reasonably accurate (within 6%) in the temperature range 40°C-80°C. This is because Equation 11.9 is approximately linear in this temperature range. For more accuracy it is wise to either use a piecewise linear model or a quadratic model. The errors for both models are within 1%.

In short-channel devices the source and drain regions are relatively close to each other. As a result, the threshold voltage of the transistor becomes dependent on the drain-source voltage, V_{DS}. This effect is known as drain induced barrier lowering (DIBL). As V_{DS} increases, it reduces the threshold voltage, which further increases the subthreshold leakage current as per Equation 11.9.

The subthreshold leakage current is also dependent on the body to source voltage (body bias). If it is reverse biased, then the threshold voltage increases, and this reduces the leakage current. Likewise, if we forward bias this junction, then the threshold voltage reduces – the transistor becomes faster at the cost of a higher leakage current. The exact relation between the threshold voltage and the body bias is dependent on the transistor technology. Most circuit simulation tools including Spice can model body bias. Body biasing is an important technique to modulate the leakage power consumption in circuits.

I_3: Gate Oxide Tunnelling

With increasing miniaturisation, the thickness of the gate oxide is reducing, and this is increasing the electric field across the gate oxide. This causes a quantum mechanical effect known as *tunnelling*. Here, electrons (or holes) in the channel can directly escape into the gate oxide or the gate. Any flow of electrons (or holes) is associated with a current. In this case, it is a leakage current because in an ideal transistor the gate oxide is assumed to be a perfect insulator.

There are two mechanisms for gate oxide tunnelling: Fowler-Nordheim tunnelling and direct handling.

In Fowler-Nordheim tunnelling, electrons move into to the conduction band of the oxide layer because of the external electric field. Note that in the conduction band, electrons have significant mobility and can be used to conduct current.

The other mechanism is known as direct tunnelling, which is becoming increasingly more prevalent as the gate oxide size thickness reduces to a few nanometers ($<$ 3-4 nm). In this case, electrons and holes tunnel directly from the surface of the silicon layer to the gate (typically made of polysilicon).

I_4: Hot-Carrier Injection

This is similar to Gate Oxide Tunnelling in terms of the fact that here also electrons or holes escape across the $Si\text{-}SiO_2$ (silicon and gate oxide) interface. However, the mechanism is different. Because of the large electric field, some electrons gain sufficient kinetic energy (become *hot carriers*) to cross the interface and move from the substrate to the gate (in the case of a positively charged gate). In Chapter 12, we shall study the effect of such hot carriers on the reliability of the gate, and appreciate how hot carrier injection gradually causes a breakdown of the gate oxide. This phenomenon is also associated with transistor ageing where the parameters of the transistor gradually change over time.

I_5: Gate-Induced Drain Leakage (GIDL)

Gate-Induced Drain Leakage (GIDL) is particularly concerning when the gate-to-drain voltage ($V_{GD} < 0$). In this case, positively charged holes migrate towards the gate oxide and get accumulated on the surface of the silicon. Holes get crowded at the drain-gate boundary. Because of this, minority carriers (holes in this case) migrate into the substrate (body of the transistor), where their concentration is relatively lower. This causes a current flow from the drain to the substrate. This is a leakage current, and happens because of the negative gate-to-drain voltage.

I_6: Punchthrough Current

In transistors with short channels we see this effect. It is possible that the drain-substrate and source-substrate interfaces are reverse biased. If the channel is short enough, then it is possible that the depletion regions of both of these regions can *merge*. This causes a breakdown in the substrate because now the drain and source are connected by a single and large depletion region. This decreases the potential barrier between the source and drain allowing carriers to flow between the source and drain terminals. Note that this current is very poorly controlled by the gate voltage because the conductive path is located deep within the substrate. This gets added to the subthreshold leakage current.

11.1.3 Summary

Let us summarise this section by going through the definitions of the key concepts once again.

Definition 93

- *Most of the power in a digital circuit is dissipated when we have* voltage transitions *at different points in the circuit. Whenever we have a transition there is a current flow across a CMOS transistor, and the resultant resistive power loss is known as* dynamic power.

- *A subclass of dynamic power consumption is short-circuit power consumption that specifically refers to the power that is dissipated when both the NMOS and PMOS transistors in a CMOS circuit are in a conducting state (while going through a state transition).*

- *Ideally we assume that the current flow in a CMOS transistor is only between the source and drain terminals, and that too when the gate or drain-source voltage changes. However, a small amount of current* leaks *through interfaces such as the drain-body junction, and body-gate junction, even when the transistor is in the* off *state. If we aggregate these small sources of power consumption across the billions of transistors, the total power consumption is sizeable. This is known as* leakage power *or* static power.

11.2 Temperature Model

11.2.1 Overview of the System

Figure 11.5 shows the diagram of a semiconductor package. The silicon die itself is fairly small. The typical die size for a server processor is 400 mm^2. Most of the power is dissipated in the logic layer (layer that contains transistors) of the chip. It is thus beneficial if the chip is placed upside down – transistor layer on top and metal layers at the bottom. Moreover, it is possible that temperature hotspots might form inside the chip that may adversely impact the reliability. Hence to homogenise the

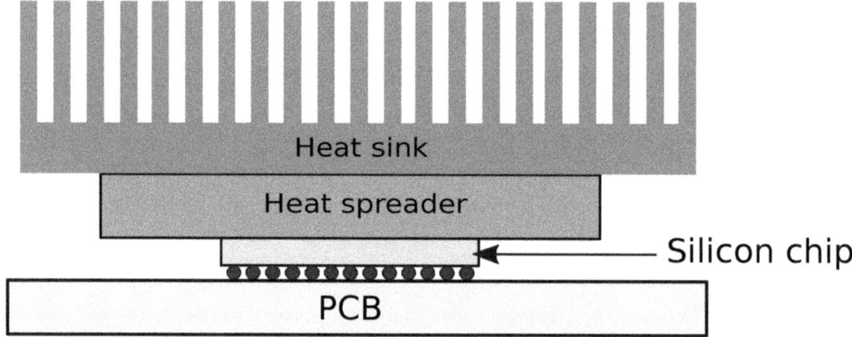

Figure 11.5: A semiconductor package

temperature profile, most packages have a heat spreader that is made of a copper-nickel alloy. A typical heat spreader's area is 4cm by 4cm, and it is roughly 5 mm thick. Subsequently, to dissipate the heat we need a structure with a large surface area such that the heat can be dissipated to the surrounding environment. For this purpose, we use a heat sink with a large number of fins as shown in Figure 11.5. The fins increase the effective surface area and the resultant cooling capacity. Adjoining structures are separated by a thermal interface material (TIM). The role of the TIM is to ensure proper conductive heat transfer between the structures. For example, we have a TIM layer between the chip and the spreader, or the spreader and the heat sink. It needs to be a gel like material to ensure that it has good contact with the solid structures that it connects.

At the bottom, the semiconductor package is connected to the printed circuit board (PCB) via a ball-grid array. Each ball is a metallic connector that is used to transfer I/O signals or transfer current to the power and ground grids.

Most of the heat is transferred via the top surface (through the heat sink). The heat transfer through the sidewalls or via the PCB is comparatively much lower.

The goal of thermal modelling is to predict the temperature on the silicon die for a given power profile. In other words, if we know the topology of the chip and its power consumption, it should be possible to compute the temperature map of the entire silicon die. In this process some standard assumptions are made. We assume that the bottom surface (the side that touches the PCB) and the sides are *adiabatic*, which means that there is no heat flow across the boundary. The heat sink dissipates power to the *ambient* (surrounding environment), which is assumed to have a constant temperature that is known as the *ambient temperature*. This is an isothermal boundary (having a constant temperature). Note that these are idealistic assumptions, and in practice they are not completely true; however, for the sake of architecture level thermal modelling they are sufficient.

Definition 94
There is no heat flow across an adiabatic boundary. We have heat flow through an isothermal boundary where one of the sides has a constant temperature such as the boundary between the heat sink and the surrounding air (in a simplistic model that is suitable for architectural simulation).

Steady-state and Transient Analysis

While computing the temperature map, there are two kinds of analyses that can be done. The first is *steady-state analysis* where we assume that the power profile remains constant for a long period of time, and we are interested in finding the steady-state temperature. This is the most common kind of analysis that is performed. In comparison, we might be interested in *transient analysis*. Here we are interested in the variation of temperature across time. For example, we might be interested to know how long it takes the temperature to rise to a given value after the power consumption of a functional unit is increased. Thermal time constants are typically of the order of milliseconds, and thus whenever we are interested in finer timescales we opt for transient analysis. Note that transient analysis is far more expensive in terms of time and computational resources as compared to steady-state analysis.

Definition 95

When the power profile does not vary and we are interested in the temperature profile after it has stabilised, we perform steady-state analysis. In comparison, if we wish to compute the variation of temperature over time, we opt for transient analysis. This is more expensive than steady-state analysis in terms of both computational time and computational resources.

11.2.2 Basic Physics

It is necessary to provide a brief overview of the physics of heat transfer to understand how temperature is modelled in modern chips. There are three primary mechanisms for heat transfer.

Heat Transfer Mechanisms

Conduction This is a process of heat transfer between objects that are in direct contact. Heat is transferred from the object that has a higher temperature to the object that has a lower temperature. For example, if we touch a hot electric iron, heat is transferred from it to our fingers. In a semiconductor chip, this is the primary mode of heat transfer within the package.

Convection This kind of heat transfer occurs within a fluid (liquid or gas). For example, near an active volcano, hot air and hot gases rise up into the atmosphere, effectively heating up the upper reaches of the atmosphere. Cold air takes its place, its temperature rises, and then it rises up in the same manner. The heat sink behaves in a similar manner. When the processor is running, the temperature of the heat sink rises which further increases the temperature of the nearby air. This hot air expands and moves through the cabinet, and cold air takes its place. The heat sink is effective because of this process of convective cooling. Sometimes, it is necessary to increase the velocity of air such that this process becomes more efficient, and this is why fans are required in laptop, desktop, and server processors.

Radiation Radiative heat transfer happens in free space. Any heated object emits radiation at different frequencies, and when this radiation is absorbed by remote objects their temperature rises. This method of heat transfer sustains our life. This is how the sun transfers its energy to our planet!

In semiconductor chips we are mostly interested in conductive cooling. There are two kinds of conductive processes in modern systems.

Vertical and Lateral Heat Conduction

Most of the heat escapes *vertically*, i.e., through the heat spreader and the heat sink. This is a desirable feature because the rest of the boundaries are mostly adiabatic. However, we do have some *lateral* heat conduction, where the heat flows sideways. This can happen either through the silicon die, or via the heat spreader. Even though lateral heat conduction is not as large as vertical heat conduction, it is still an important heat transfer mechanism and determines the placement of tasks and components on the chip as we shall see in Section 11.4.

> **Definition 96**
> *Vertical heat conduction via the heat spreader and heat sink is the dominant heat transfer mechanism in packages. However, from the point of view of temperature management, a lesser mechanism called lateral heat transfer is also very important, where heat is transferred laterally on the silicon die.*

Fourier's Law of Heat Conduction

The basic law that governs heat conduction is the Fourier's law. Consider an infinitesimally small rectangular area A (see Figure 11.6(a)). Let the temperature on the left side be T_1 and the temperature on the right side be T_2 ($T_1 > T_2$). Assume that the region's normal vector is along the x-axis, and the thickness of the region is Δx. Let the power entering the left side be q_x units. Then the Fourier's law of heat conduction says that $(T_1 - T_2)/\Delta x$ (temperature gradient) is proportional to q_x/A (heat flux).

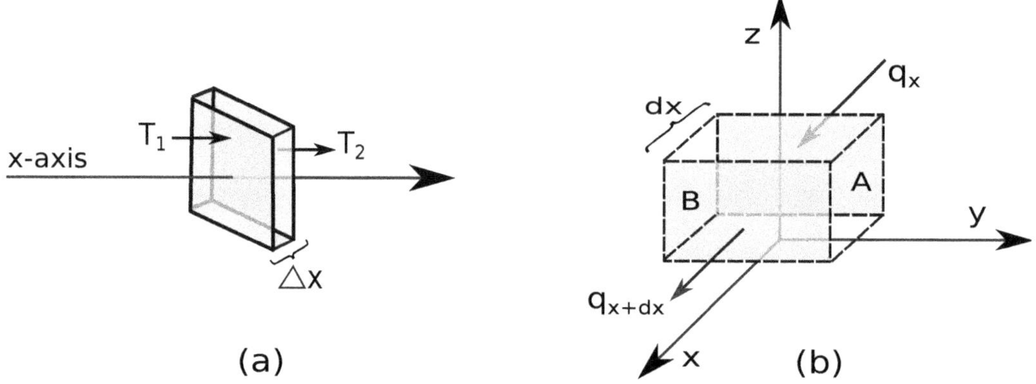

Figure 11.6: Setting for explaining the Fourier's law of heat conduction (a) rectangular slab whose normal vector is oriented along the x-axis, (b) A small 3D region

Given that the temperature gradient, and the direction of heat flow are in opposite directions, we can write the following equation, where k is the constant of proportionality. Note the negative sign.

$$q_x = -kA\frac{dT}{dx} \tag{11.10}$$

Now consider a very small three-dimensional volume with dimensions dx, dy, and dz in Figure 11.6(b). We show the heat transfer on the x-axis (likewise is the case for other dimensions). q_x units of thermal power (in Watts) enter face A (normal vector along the x-axis), and q_{x+dx} Watts leave face B. The difference is $q_x - q_{x+dx}$, and the area of the face is $dydz$. Let us now use Equation 11.10. We have,

$$q_x = -k.(dydz).\frac{\partial T}{\partial x} \tag{11.11}$$

Here the "." operator is used to denote multiplication. Note that we use a partial derivative because we are only interested in the temperature difference along the x-axis. Let us use this result in the following derivation.

$$\frac{q_x - q_{x+dx}}{dx} = -\frac{\partial q_x}{\partial x}$$

$$\Rightarrow q_x - q_{x+dx} = -dx.\frac{\partial}{\partial x}\left(-k.dy.dz.\frac{\partial T}{\partial x}\right) \quad (by\ Equation\ 11.11) \tag{11.12}$$

$$\Rightarrow q_x - q_{x+dx} = k.dx.dy.dz\frac{\partial^2 T}{\partial x^2} = kd\mathcal{V}\frac{\partial^2 T}{\partial x^2}$$

We will use the term $\mathcal{V}$ to represent volume and the term V to represent voltage.

In Equation 11.12, the term $q_x - q_{x+dx}$ is the heat that remains within the volume if we only consider heat flow along the x-axis. Note that we assume that k is a constant in all directions and $d\mathcal{V} = dx.dy.dz$. If we sum up the power that remains within the volume because of heat flow along all the three axes, we arrive at the expression $kd\mathcal{V}\left(\frac{\partial^2 T}{\partial x^2} + \frac{\partial^2 T}{\partial y^2} + \frac{\partial^2 T}{\partial z^2}\right)$. Let the operator $\left(\frac{\partial^2}{\partial x^2} + \frac{\partial^2}{\partial y^2} + \frac{\partial^2}{\partial z^2}\right)$ be represented as ∇^2. Thus the thermal power that remains within the volume is $k.d\mathcal{V}.\nabla^2 T$.

Let us now consider the internal heat generation. It is possible that we have a power source within the volume that generates Q' units of energy per unit volume and per unit time. It can be alternatively described as the internal power generated per unit volume. Thus the total power generated is $Q'd\mathcal{V}$. Note that we will use the term Q' to denote the internal heat generation rate and the term Q for denoting the charge in an electrical circuit.

Hence, the sum of the total power that enters the volume and is generated within it equals $P_{st} = (k.\nabla^2 T + Q').d\mathcal{V}$. All of this stored thermal power, P_{st}, must increase the temperature of the small volume that we are considering. Let ρ be the density. Thus, the mass of the region is equal to $\rho.d\mathcal{V}$. The relation between the temperature rise per unit time, $\frac{\partial T}{\partial t}$, the mass, the specific heat (c_p), and the net thermal power entering and being generated within the volume is given by

$$P_{st} = \rho.d\mathcal{V}.c_p.\frac{\partial T}{\partial t} \tag{11.13}$$

From the laws of the conservation of energy, the total power entering and being generated within the volume equals the value of P_{st} shown in Equation 11.13. After cancelling the common factor $d\mathcal{V}$, we have,

$$k\nabla^2 T + Q' = (\rho c_p)\frac{\partial T}{\partial t} \tag{11.14}$$

This can be simplified to:

$$\nabla^2 T + \frac{Q'}{k} = \frac{1}{\alpha}\frac{\partial T}{\partial t} \tag{11.15}$$

Here, $\alpha = k/\rho c_p$. If we consider only the steady state problem we have,

$$\nabla^2 T = -\frac{Q'}{k} \tag{11.16}$$

Here, T is the temperature map and Q' is the power map. We now need to find a general solution to this differential equation, and then need to factor in the effect of boundary conditions.

11.2.3 The Finite Difference Method (FDM)

Let us convert Equations 11.15 and 11.16 into a set of simple algebraic equations. Consider the silicon die and adjoining structures; let us break it into a 3D grid consisting of very small cube-shaped cells. Assume that the cells are numbered with an integer.

Consider cell i at time t. Assumption: cells $i-1$, and $i+1$ are the neighbours of cell i on the x-axis.

$$\left.\frac{\partial^2 T}{\partial x^2}\right|_{i,t} \approx \frac{\left.\frac{\partial T}{\partial x}\right|_{i+1,t} - \left.\frac{\partial T}{\partial x}\right|_{i,t}}{\Delta x}$$

$$\approx \frac{\frac{T_{i+1,t}-T_{i,t}}{\Delta x} - \frac{T_{i,t}-T_{i-1,t}}{\Delta x}}{\Delta x} \tag{11.17}$$

$$= \frac{T_{i+1,t} - 2T_{i,t} + T_{i-1,t}}{\Delta x^2}$$

We can create a similar set of equations for the y and z axes. The important point to note is that these are all *linear equations*, and these equations hold for a point that is not on the boundary. We need to formulate special equations for points that lie on the boundary based on the boundary conditions. Then we can solve the entire system of equations using standard linear algebra techniques.

As an example, consider the steady-state problem. We need not consider the time axis. We thus have a set of linear equations where the only set of variables are of the form T_i as shown in Equation 11.17. i varies from 1 to N, where N is the number of cells. Let us create an N-element vector representing the power map, $\mathbf{P}$ (one entry for each cell). On similar lines, let $\mathbf{T}$ (N elements) represent the temperature map. We now know that we can obtain $\mathbf{T}$ from $\mathbf{P}$ (Equation 11.16) by applying a linear transformation. Assuming these are column vectors, we can write this relationship as follows (note that a linear transformation can be written as a matrix-vector product):

$$\mathbf{T} = \mathbf{AP} \tag{11.18}$$

$\mathbf{A}$ is an $N \times N$ matrix. It can either be derived from first principles by creating a set of algebraic equations (see Equation 11.17), or this matrix can be learnt from sample values.

Transient Analysis

Let us now solve the transient problem by creating a similar matrix based formulation. Let us first start with the Fourier equation with the terms slightly rearranged.

$$k\nabla^2 T + Q' = \frac{k}{\alpha}\frac{\partial T}{\partial t} \tag{11.19}$$

As per Equation 11.17 $k\nabla^2 T$ is a linear transformation, which can be represented as the product of a matrix and the vector of N temperatures. Let us refer to the time derivative of temperatures as $\mathbf{T}'$, which is also an N-element vector. We are multiplying each of its elements with a scalar, which can be different for each element because it depends on its density and specific heat. We can thus represent this product as the product of a diagonal matrix $\mathbf{C}$ with an N-element vector $\mathbf{T}'$. Finally, note that Q' is the internal power generated per unit volume across the chip, which we are representing by the vector $\mathbf{P}$. We can thus write Equation 11.19 as a linear equation.

$$\mathbf{GT} + \mathbf{P} = \mathbf{CT}' \tag{11.20}$$

Here, $\mathbf{G}$ and $\mathbf{C}$ are matrices, $\mathbf{P}$ and $\mathbf{T}$ represent the power and temperature vectors respectively. This equation can be solved using numerical methods.

For example, we can divide time into discrete time-steps, and starting from $t = 0$ we can keep solving Equation 11.20 using standard linear algebra techniques. We can replace $\mathbf{T}'$ with an expression of the form $(\mathbf{T_{k+1}} - \mathbf{T_k})/\Delta t$, where $\mathbf{T_k}$ is the temperature at all the points in the kth time step.

11.2.4   Electrical Analogue of the Heat Transfer Problem

Closely take a look at Equation 11.20: $\mathbf{GT} + \mathbf{P} = \mathbf{CT}'$. We can replace the thermodynamic quantities with analogous electrical quantities that have similar relationships. We can replace temperature with voltage, and power with current. This is know as the electrical analogue of a thermal problem. Let us now try to map the rest of the terms.

The matrix $\mathbf{G}$ can be thought of as conductance matrix. Recall from high school physics that conductance is the reciprocal of resistance. By the Ohm's law the product of conductance and voltage is equal to the current (power in this case). The second term in the LHS, $\mathbf{P}$, can be thought of as a the output of a set of current sources. Thus, the sum of the two terms on the left-hand side indicates the total amount of current being injected into the circuit. In an electrical circuit when current is injected the voltage rises, which is being captured by the expression on the right-hand side.

To understand the right-hand side, let us consider the equations related to capacitance: $Q = VC$ (Q is the stored charge, V is the voltage, and C is the capacitance). If we differentiate it, we get $dQ/dt = I = CdV/dt$. The time derivative of voltage can be equated with the time derivative of temperature T'. The matrix $\mathbf{C}$ in Equation 11.20 can thus be thought of as the thermal capacitance.

Let us now describe the electrical analogue in a simpler setting. Consider a 1-dimensional rod. By Equation 11.10 the temperature difference across its ends $T_1 - T_2$ is equal to the inlet power multiplied by the term $\Delta x/kA$ (ignoring the negative sign). Here, Δx is the length of the one-dimensional rod. This is very similar to the formula for electrical resistance: $\rho l/A$ (ρ is the resistivity, l is the length, and A is the cross-sectional area). We can interpret the constant k as the thermal conductivity.

Similarly, for capacitance let us start with the equation: $P_{st} = \rho.d\mathcal{V}.c_p\frac{\partial T}{\partial t}$. In this case, P_{st} can be mapped to the electrical current and $\frac{\partial T}{\partial t}$ to the time derivative of voltage (dV/dt). Since $I = CdV/dt$, the thermal capacitance can be represented by $\rho.d\mathcal{V}.c_p$. Note that this is a capacitance to ground.

The advantage of this approach is that we can replace a thermal problem with an analogous electrical problem, and then we can use traditional circuit simulators to find the voltages and currents at different places. These values can then be mapped to temperature and power values. Since there are very efficient methods to simulate circuits, this method is very efficient.

Consider an example in Figure 11.7. The cell in the centre is connected to the neighbouring cells via thermal resistances. Additionally, note the capacitance to ground. For cells at the edges we will not add a resistance to the ambient if the boundaries are adiabatic (no heat flow).

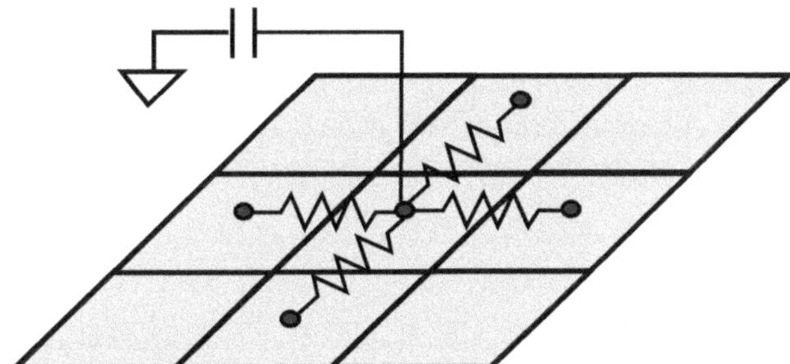

Figure 11.7: The electrical analogue of a thermal problem

11.2.5   The Finite Element Method (FEM)

The main advantage of the finite difference based approaches is that they are simple. However, for complicated thermal models that consider a variety of heat transfer paths, the effect of the thermal interface materials and heat transfer via the PCB, often finite element-based methods are found to be more accurate. Along with the effect of capturing complex geometries, this method is also very effective when the properties of materials tend to vary over space. The cost of such additional accuracy is slower speed.

Let us now provide an outline of the basic steps that are involved. For a deeper discussion readers can refer to the book by Logan et al. [Logan, 1986].

1. The first step is to convert the differential equation into an integral equation. This is an analytical exercise and is done by multiplying the original differential equation with a test function, $v()$, which has continuous derivatives till a certain point.

2. The next step is to discretise the domain, which means dividing it into a set of triangles, rectangles, cuboids or tetrahedrons. This process is known as *meshing*. Consider a triangular mesh. Here, the size of each triangle determines the accuracy of the solution and the time the method takes to complete. Each such triangle is called an *element*, and the points at which elements are connected are known as *nodes*. We can choose an appropriate subset of elements to reduce the size of the problem.

3. We take the integral equations generated in step (1) and convert them into a set of algebraic equations. Here we consider different values of the function v for each node. These are known as basis functions, and typically satisfy several desirable properties. For example, we can have linear basis functions, where v is a linear function of the coordinates of the nodes around an element. We can also use quadratic or polynomial basis functions. The intuition is as follows.

   We wish to represent $f(x)$ (where f is the function to be evaluated) as $\sum_{k=1}^{n} f_k v_k(x)$. Here, $v_k(x)$ is the basis function corresponding to node k and f_k is the value of $f(x)$ at node k. The assumption here is that the values of $f(x)$ within an element are only a function of the values at the nodes surrounding the element and the functions of the form $v_k(x)$ (basis function for node k). We have essentially assumed that the final solution is a weighted sum of simple basis functions multiplied by the values of the function at the nodes. If there are other functions in a differential equation, they can be represented with a similar sum.

4. Given this assumption, the task that remains is to find the values of the function f at the nodes. We convert the set of equations derived in step (3) into linear equations in the matrix form, and solve them using standard linear algebra techniques. We thus get an estimate of the function $f()$ at all the nodes.

It is important to note that the final accuracy is dependent upon the choice of basis functions. There is a very rich area of research for determining the right set of basis functions for different problems. However, given the slow speed of such methods they are seldom used in architectural simulation.

11.2.6   Green's Functions

Let us now consider the fastest methods in the space, Green's functions. We can use some unique features of the thermal problem to design a very fast method to compute the temperature profile. The key features that we use are *linearity* and *shift invariance*. Linearity means that if T_x is the thermal profile for the power profile P_x, and T_y is the thermal profile for the power profile P_y, then the thermal profile for the power profile $P_x + P_y$ is $T_x + T_y$. This can be easily derived from Fourier's heat equation, which is a linear equation. Shift invariance means that the thermal profile generated at any point because of a point power source remains the same with respect to the power source, even if the power source is shifted. A disclaimer is due here. Shift invariance does not hold if the power source is applied too close to the boundary of the chips. For the rest of the points if the power source is small enough, we can assume that they are very far away from the boundaries and thus the localised temperature spread is roughly the same.

To use these relationships, let us proceed as follows. Let us divide the entire silicon die into a set of very small square grid-shaped cells (an $N \times N$ grid). For a cell at the centre, let us apply 1W of power. Let its temperature profile be given by the function $G(x, y)$. Consider this cell at the centre as the origin. Because of the property of shift invariance we will have the same thermal profile if the power source is applied at any other point (x_p, y_q). For a set of power sources and by the properties of linearity and shift invariance we have,

$$T(x_p, y_q) = \sum_{i=1}^{N} \sum_{j=1}^{N} P(x_i, y_j) G(x_p - x_i, y_q - y_j) \tag{11.21}$$

This considers the cumulative effect of a set of power sources on the temperature at a single point (x_p, y_q). Let us consider the integral form of this equation at the point (x', y').

$$T(x', y') = \int_x \int_y P(x, y) G(x' - x, y' - y).dxdy \tag{11.22}$$

This is precisely the convolution operation $(\star)$, and we can thus simplify this equation to,

$$T = P \star G \tag{11.23}$$

If we consider an infinitesimally small cell, the power source becomes the Dirac delta function $\delta(x)$. The Dirac delta function is defined for a point x_0, and has a value of 0 elsewhere. It satisfies the property $\int \delta(x)dx = 1$. The Green's function thus becomes the temperature profile of the Dirac delta function, which is known as its *impulse response*.

The Green's function can be computed analytically or can be estimated by simulating the thermal profile of a very small power source using a traditional FEM or FDM based tool. Computing the temperature profile is as simple as computing a simple convolution operation using Equation 11.23. Most methods convert Equation 11.23 into the Fourier transform domain, where a convolution becomes a multiplication. This is a very fast operation as compared to finite difference based methods.

Definition 97
The Green's function is the impulse response of a power profile that is a Dirac delta function. The temperature profile is the power profile convolved with the Green's function.

Note that this approach has its limitations because it is applicable to cells that are not at the edges and corners. At the rim of the chip the heat does not dissipate through the side walls because they are considered to be adiabatic. Hence, there is a disproportionate temperature rise. Here, we use the method of images. If a power source is x units away from a side wall, then we add another power source of the same magnitude at the point $-x$, which is x units away from the side wall on the opposite side. This is known as an *image source*. The temperature profile is approximately a superposition of both the temperature fields.

11.3   Power Management

11.3.1   Managing Dynamic Power

DVFS

As discussed in Section 11.1.1, the relationship between voltage and frequency in modern processors is not linear. Most processors define a set of power states, where each state is a voltage and frequency pair. The CPU can move between these states depending upon the ambient temperature, BIOS settings, and the power usage of the application. In most power efficient processors it is possible to run different cores in different power states. The only problem of doing so is that it becomes hard to send a message across voltage-frequency boundaries. We need a special circuit that shifts the level of the voltage, and synchronises the transfer. Once this is done we can achieve a fine grain control of the voltage and frequency of each core. It is possible to extend this idea further and have separate DVFS (dynamic voltage and frequency scaling) settings at the level of individual functional units. However, given the overheads, such choices are often not justified.

The DVFS settings for the Intel® Pentium® M Processor are shown in Table 11.1. It has six different power states. It is also possible for the operating system to make the CPU migrate between power states if the architecture makes special instructions available. The advantage of having software control is that we can leverage the additional visibility that is there at the level of the operating system. This can also be done at the level of individual programs. For example, in Linux, the *cpufreq* utility allows us to adjust the voltage and frequency on-the-fly. Many software applications use such facilities to reduce their power consumption.

Frequency	Voltage
1.6 GHz	1.484 V
1.4 GHz	1.420 V
1.2 GHz	1.276 V
1.0 GHz	1.164 V
0.8 GHz	1.036 V
0.6 GHz	0.956 V

Table 11.1: Voltage and frequency settings for the Intel Pentium M processor [Intel, 2004]

In any such processor, to transition from one state to the other it is necessary to do the following.

Higher frequency We first increase the supply voltage by programming the voltage regulators on the motherboard. Note that the process of increasing the voltage takes time because the capacitors associated with the chip's power grid, and power pins need to be charged. After this is done, we pause the execution and re-tune the PLL (Phase locked loop) based clock generator of the processor to generate the new high-frequency clock signal. On the motherboard we typically have a quartz-based oscillator that generates a clock signal at a fixed frequency – typically 133 MHz. Based on the frequency setting we multiply this clock signal with a fixed value and set the PLL to oscillate at that frequency. After the PLL locks to the new frequency, we can start the execution.

Lower frequency In this case, we first pause the system, and then relock the PLLs to the new clock frequency. After that the voltage regulators gradually reduce the voltage.

Note that the process of changing the DVFS settings is asymmetric in nature. We never have a situation where the frequency is higher than what the supply voltage can support. This can cause unpredictable behaviour in the circuits. Furthermore, the process of changing the voltage takes time because large capacitors in the on-chip power grid need to be charged or discharged. Additionally, it takes time for the PLL to relock to the new frequency. In very aggressive implementations, this process takes roughly 10-20 μs. During most of this period, the chip is not operational. Hence, DVFS is an expensive optimisation and power states should be changed infrequently.

DVFS is done at the level of a core or at the level of the entire chip. Additionally, it is dependent on the behaviour of an application and the expectation of the end-user. For example, if we are playing a video we want every frame to be processed within 33 ms. Assume that it takes only 20 ms to process a frame. In this case, we can apply DVFS to deliberately slow down the processor such that it takes roughly 33 ms, and we reduce power as much as possible. In this case, it is clearly known that the user wants to see jitter-free video; hence, there is a strict deadline for processing a frame. As long as we stay within that, we can use DVFS to lower the voltage and frequency and consequently save power. In mobile phones, DVFS can be applied based on the user's requirements and the available battery power. We can apply DVFS more aggressively if the user wants to be in a power save mode.

Let us next look at the space of decisions that can be taken at a much lower level – at the level of functional units.

Clock Gating

Clock gating is a simple technique where we simply disable the clock of a functional unit (see Figure 11.8) that is not expected to be used in the near future. Here, we can either follow a deterministic policy or a non-deterministic policy. In the first case, we know for sure that a given functional unit is not going to be used. For example, if we see a divide instruction we can be very sure that the functional unit for subtraction is not going to be used till we execute one more instruction. In this case, we can confidently gate the clock of the subtract unit.

However, in some cases we might not be very sure (non-deterministic). In such cases it is necessary to design a predictor, which can predict if a functional unit is expected to be used in the near future or not. If it predicts that a functional unit will remain idle then its clock can be gated. By gating the clock we are not allowing the latches that feed data to the functional unit to change their values. This means that there will be no voltage transitions in the inputs of the functional unit and thus there will be no current flow or resultant dynamic power dissipation. Even if the inputs remain the same, then also there is a benefit because the clock is routed to all the latches in a circuit, and we need to periodically charge and discharge the clock inputs of the latches. This is also avoided.

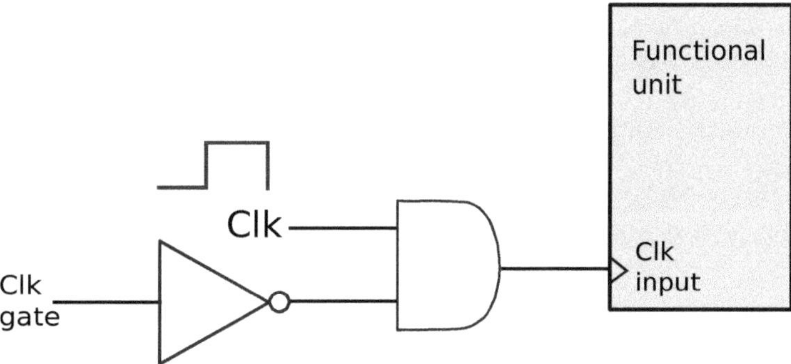

Figure 11.8: A simple clock gating circuit

There are different micro-architectural techniques to find out when a unit is going to be used or not. We can embed a small counter within a unit. If the unit is idle, the counter starts counting down to 0. Once it reaches 0, we can gate the clock of the associated functional unit. We can also find the usage of functional units in the select stage, where we know which execution units are not going to be used. The clocks of the unused functional units can be gated. Similarly, after decoding instructions we know which parts of the rename and dependence check logic will be used. The remaining parts can also be clock gated. For the caches, we can predict cache activity and clock gate the decoders.

The primary problem with clock gating is that it makes the circuit complicated. For example, we need to be very careful with regards to when we gate the clock. If the value of the clock is being set to 0 when its value is 1, we are introducing a clock transition. The rest of the circuit will perceive a negative edge prematurely. No correctness problem should be created by this. Secondly, verifying the design becomes more complex, because it is possible that when an input arrives at a functional unit, its clock is gated. We need to wait till the unit is enabled. This can lead to many unforeseen errors. To avoid such situations many processors only opt for deterministic clock gating where no such delays are introduced.

Issue and Fetch Throttling

Let us now consider an even simpler mechanism that does not involve major changes to the circuit, and does not introduce correctness errors. We can simply reduce (*throttle*) the issue or fetch rate. Instead of issuing six instructions per cycle, we can issue four instructions per cycle. This will reduce the dynamic power consumption immediately. Additionally, implementing this is very simple and requires minimal changes to the select logic. On similar lines, we can throttle the fetch and commit rates as well.

Even though this mechanism is very effective in reducing dynamic power, it has a direct impact on the performance. It slows down the program and does not necessarily reduce the total energy requirement. There is an important point to note here with regards to leakage power. See Example 14.

Example 14

Consider two designs A and B. Assume they require the same amount of dynamic energy (power × delay). The dynamic power of design A is 50% more, and it is 3 times faster than design B. Which design should we prefer?

Answer: *The temperature is a mildly super-linear function of the dynamic power. If temperature is a concern then we should prefer design B. However, if we want to reduce the total amount of energy then we need to consider the energy consumed by leakage as well. The leakage energy is equal to the leakage power multiplied by the program's execution time (delay). In this case, A consumes more leakage power because of the higher temperature, however we cannot say the same about the leakage energy. This is because A's total delay is one-third of B's delay. It is possible that the sum of the dynamic energy and leakage energy for A is less than that of B. In this case, we will prefer design A.*

If we also want to bring the performance into the picture, then we should minimise the energy-$delay^2$ or (power-$delay^3$) product. If the power of design B is P and delay is D, then the power-$delay^3$ product for design B is $1.5 \times P \times (D/3)^3 = 0.05PD^3$. The corresponding product for design A is PD^3. We would clearly prefer design B with these metrics.

11.3.2 Managing Leakage Power

Power Gating

The most effective way of controlling leakage power is *power gating*. If we stop the flow of current into the circuit, then there will be no leakage, and consequently no leakage power dissipation.

There are three ways of implementing power gating. We either disconnect the supply voltage, V_{dd}, disconnect the connection to the ground, or disconnect both. In all the three cases we are breaking the connection between the supply and the ground and thus ideally there will be no current flow. Out of these approaches, disconnecting the supply voltage or disconnecting both the supply and ground are more common. Disconnecting only the ground terminals does eliminate most sources of leakage power, however in a large circuit we always have some leakage paths to ground via the package. Some current can leak through them.

The design of both the circuits is shown in Figure 11.9. The idea is very simple. We have two grids for supplying and removing current: one for the supply voltage (power grid), and one for ground (ground grid). If a chip has higher power requirements then we can have multiple grids for the supply voltage and ground. However, for the sake of simplicity let us assume that we have a single grid for each type of voltage, and each grid has its dedicated VLSI layer. The reason that we need a grid is such that if a given functional unit needs more power, it can draw current from other parts of the grid. Having a grid helps us balance the current flow across the power and ground pins of the chip. Furthermore, a large grid has a large capacitance, which can further be augmented by adding additional capacitors called decoupling capacitors to limit voltage fluctuations.

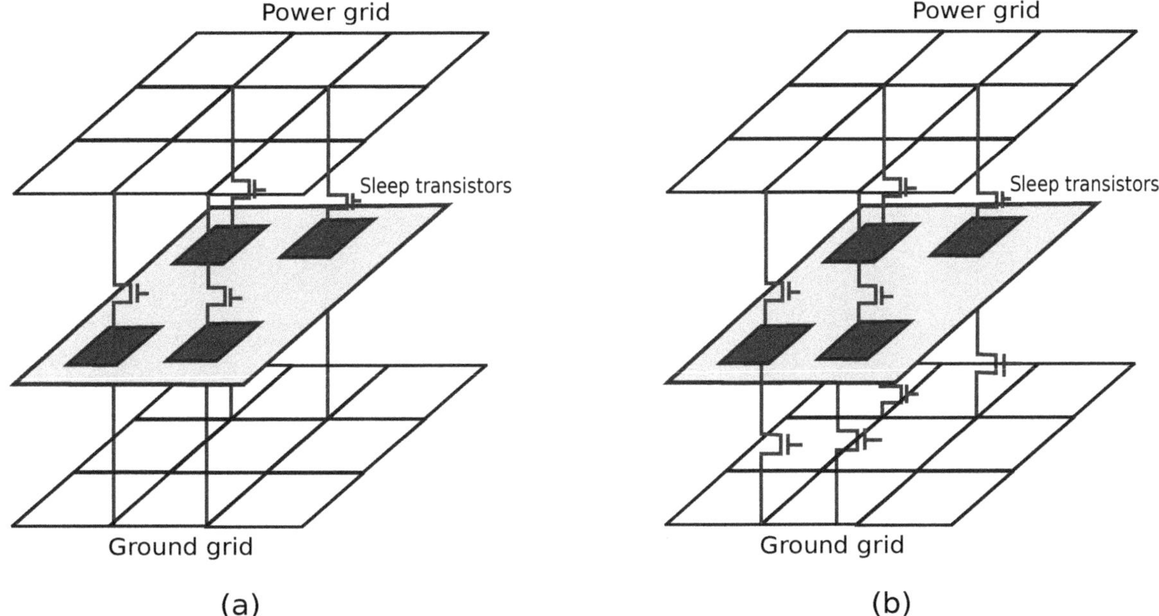

Figure 11.9: Power gating. (a) Disconnecting the supply voltage, (b) Disconnecting the supply and ground

Each functional unit has several connections to the power and ground grids respectively. To effectively decouple the functional unit we need to add pass transistors on all these connections. To power gate the functional unit all that we need to do is disable these transistors, which are also commonly known as *sleep transistors*. When a circuit is power gated, it is said to be in the *sleep state*. However, this is easier said than done. We need to keep several things in mind.

1. The current that is available to a functional unit should not reduce after adding sleep transistors. This means that to carry the requisite amount of current these transistors have to be large.

2. The problem with large transistors is that they take a long time to switch on and switch off. This puts a limit on how frequently we can power gate a circuit and then enable it back again.

3. There will invariably be some amount of leakage through the sleep transistors. In most designs this is expected to be insignificant though.

4. When we enable and disable power gating, the current flow in the power and ground grids changes rather abruptly. As per Lenz's law, any electrical conductor opposes the change of current through it by introducing a back EMF – referred to as the *power gating noise*. To taper the effect of such voltage fluctuations, we need to add large decoupling capacitors to the power grid and also slow down the process of entering and exiting sleep states. The decoupling capacitors will also increase the leakage power rather disproportionately.

5. The sleep transistors will also have a potential difference across their terminals. This will decrease the effective supply voltage for the transistors in the functional unit. As a result, the supply voltage needs to be increased to compensate for this reduction.

6. When a functional unit is power gated, it loses its state. As a result, functional units need to be designed keeping this in mind, which is sometimes difficult.

7. We are assuming that we know for sure when a functional unit is not expected to be used. We need a predictor for this purpose, and if the predictor is not accurate, then there will be a loss in performance. We will waste valuable cycles in waking up the functional unit from the sleep state.

8. Cycling between the active and sleep states is associated with drawing in large currents from the power grid. The resultant dynamic power consumption needs to be taken into consideration.

To summarise, the support for power gating does not come for free, it has its associated costs. As a result, we need to take a very judicious decision regarding whether a functional unit should be power gated or not. An important point to note is that we need to have a reliable predictor, which can predict long periods of inactivity in the future based on either past history or from programmer/compiler inputs. It does not make sense to power gate a circuit for a short period of time because the overheads of doing so might overshadow the gains in a reduction of leakage power. Over the past decade, many algorithms have been proposed for effective prediction of inactive periods, and this is still an area of active research.

Drowsy Caches

A major limitation of power gating is that we completely turn off the supply voltage and this leads to a complete loss of state. Power gating is thus not a very effective approach for cache banks, which take up a large amount of area on the die. The issue is that when we turn off the supply voltage, the caches lose all their data, which is not acceptable. Hence, it is a much better idea to define an intermediate *drowsy state* [Kim et al., 2004], where the supply voltage is reduced but it is not so low that the state elements lose their values. The state elements can be either regular latches or SRAM arrays.

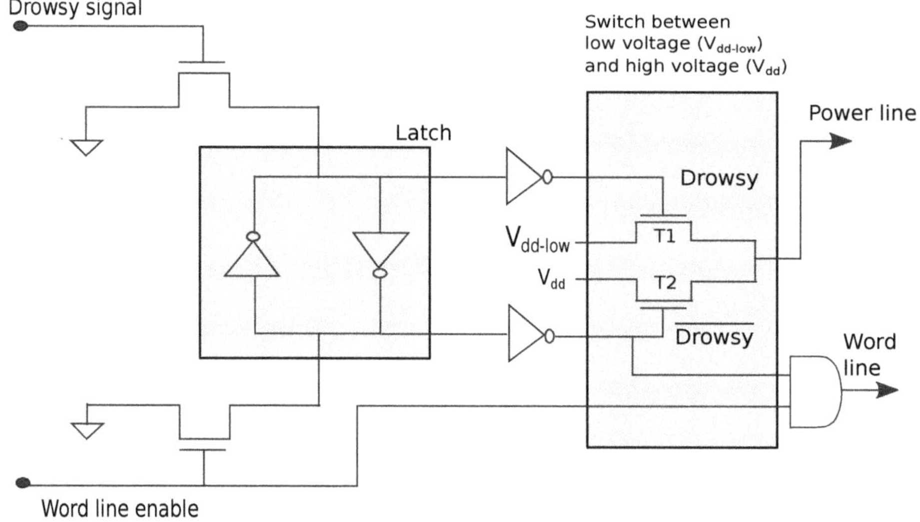

Figure 11.10: Voltage regulator of a drowsy cache (adapted from [Kim et al., 2004])

Figure 11.10 shows the changes that need to be made to make a regular cache bank a *drowsy cache bank*. We have a set-reset latch made of an inverter-pair where the drowsy signal sets the latch, and the word line enable signal resets the latch. It is assumed that when the cache is in drowsy mode, the word line enable signal is off. In other words, we do not access the cache. Similarly, when we intend to access the cache by setting the word line enable bit, the cache should not be in drowsy mode (the drowsy signal should be reset). Let us elaborate.

Consider the case when the drowsy signal is a logical 1, and the word line enable bit is a logical 0. In this case the gate voltage of transistor $T1$ is a logical 1, and this transistor is enabled. However, transistor $T2$ is disabled. Thus the voltage of the power line (powering the cache bank) is V_{dd-low}, which means that the cache bank is in the drowsy state. On similar lines, we can argue that when the drowsy signal is a logical 0, and the word line enable signal is 1, transistor $T2$ is enabled and the cache bank gets the full supply voltage, V_{dd}. This is when the bank can be accessed. The AND gate also enforces the condition that a word line in a bank can be enabled only if the drowsy signal is 0, and the word line enable signal is 1.

Finally, note that in the default state when both the signals are a logical 0 the latch maintains its value. If the cache bank is in a drowsy state, it continues to be in that state.

There are several design decisions that need to be made here. We need to decide the granularity at which we add this circuitry. Starting from an individual cache line to an entire cache bank we can create groups of lines and together assign them to the drowsy state. There is a trade-off between area and flexibility here.

The second design decision that needs to be made is regarding prediction. At one end of the spectrum we have an on-demand approach, where we might decide to set every cache line to the drowsy state and only make it active when there is an access. If we disregard the power required to enter and exit the states, then this is the most power efficient approach. However, the cache access time increases because we need to allocate at least one cycle to changing the state of the cache line. This results in a slow down. The other option is to predict periods of inactivity for groups of cache lines, and then collectively set them to the drowsy state. In this case the accuracy of the predictor is very important.

Multiple V_{th} Designs

The leakage power is a function of the threshold voltage. If the threshold voltage is low, the leakage power is high and vice versa. Moreover, lower is the threshold voltage, faster is the transistor. This property can be exploited in many different ways.

In a typical circuit all the transistors are not on the critical path (the longest path that determines the overall timing). There are many paths in the circuit that can be slowed down without changing the length of the critical path. On such paths we can have transistors with higher threshold voltages. They will be slower, yet will be more power efficient. Let us say that in a given circuit, the length of the critical path measured in terms of the time it takes a signal to propagate is 300 ps. If we have a path in the circuit, which is 200 ps, we can slow the transistors down such that the length of the path becomes equal to 300 ps. By slowing down the transistors we will save on leakage power.

There are different methods to slow down the transistors. One of the most popular methods is body biasing. In this case we set the voltage of the body of the transistor to a given value. If the body-to-source voltage is positive, then this is known as forward body biasing. In this case the threshold voltage reduces. Likewise if the body-to-source voltage is negative, then this is known as reverse body biasing, and this leads to an increase in the threshold voltage. It is possible to create islands of transistors where their bodies are connected to a single voltage source, and we can thus change the threshold voltage (speed and power) of a group of transistors by just adjusting the body voltage.

Static techniques to change the threshold voltage include changing the dopant density, and the dimensions of the transistors.

Regardless of the approach, the overarching idea is that we can deliberately slow down transistors to save leakage power, when the transistors are not on the critical path.

11.4   Temperature Management

In general any power management scheme is effective for temperature as well. Since the overall power decreases, the temperature and the leakage power also decrease. However, sometimes temperature hotspots can form if a functional unit is being heavily used. For example, it is possible that in some workloads a given core or a given functional unit such as a multiplier may be very heavily used. Coupled with other factors, this can cause a local temperature rise, which can be detrimental to the health of the chip in the long run. Hence, it is necessary to monitor the temperature in as many places as possible and take appropriate action. In this case, the action would be to either move the computation to another core or another multiplier, or throttle the computation rate. Both of these would be effective in reducing the intensity of the temperature hotspot. A common approach is called stop-and-go, where we stop the execution for some time till the chip cools down, and then we restart it. This is an extreme case of throttling.

Hence, for a long time we did not have separate schemes for temperature reduction. Additionally, most of the heat transfer happens in a vertical direction (through the heat sink) and thus the spatial location of activity was not that important because lateral heat conduction was less of an issue.

However, off late this problem has been receiving more attention because of increasing power density, and process variation where localised regions of the die can have a very high leakage power with large non-linear effects. Let us elaborate.

1. The power density is increasing, and transistors are getting smaller and more unreliable. In addition, because of process variations (variation in transistor dimensions caused due to imperfections in the fabrication process), the leakage power tends to vary across the chip, and thus it is possible to have some areas of the chip where the leakage power is very high. Because of this, the probability of forming temperature hotspots is also elevated.

2. Modern hardware such as GPUs and neural network accelerators consume a lot of power (typically 2X that of server processors), hence for such settings, temperature issues are far more important.

3. We are moving into an era of 3D chips that will have multiple transistor and DRAM layers. Here heat transfer is an issue for the inner layers where the temperature can increase significantly. Hence, there is a need to lay out the computations in such a manner such that at all points the temperature is below a specified threshold. Nowadays, the GPU has also come into the package; this further increases the power dissipation and causes temperature problems.

4. For 3D chips traditional air cooling might not be sufficient. There is a lot of research underway in creating water based cooling solutions and microchannel based cooling. A microchannel is a very small tube (cross-sectional area: $50 \times 100 \mu m^2$) within the chip that carries a coolant. The idea is to create an array of microchannels to carry a cooling fluid, particularly for cooling the inner layers of a 3D chip, where modelling and mitigating temperature hotspots is of vital importance.

Given these reasons, mapping jobs to cores has become an important problem. Such problems are known as mapping or job placement problems.

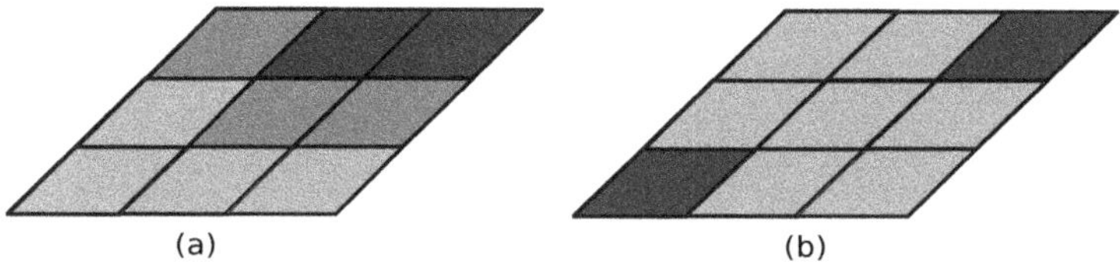

Figure 11.11: Effect of the placement of jobs. (a) Two hot jobs placed side by side, (b) The hot jobs placed at opposite corners

11.4.1 A Typical Placement Problem

A typical job placement problem in this space as follows. Assume we have N jobs and N cores. The power consumption of each job (thread) is known. We can have many objective functions. Consider a simple one: minimise the peak temperature subject to a constraint on the minimum performance.

First consider a problem where the performance is not dependent on the placement. Then we have several options. We can either place the hot jobs (high power consumption) side by side as shown in Figure 11.11(a). In this case, there is an unacceptable temperature rise in the nearby cores because of lateral heat conduction and additional leakage. However, if the hot jobs are placed far apart as in Figure 11.11(b) then the temperature rise is much lower, and the leakage power is also commensurately lower.

Let us complicate this situation by bringing in performance constraints. Let's say that some jobs need to be placed in close proximity because they access similar data. Now if they are placed far apart, performance will suffer. We can thus add additional performance constraints.

Now, we can further complicate this picture if we consider DVFS, more jobs than cores, variability in leakage power, and dynamic migration of jobs. We thus have a very rich research area in this space.

11.5   Summary and Further Reading

11.5.1   Summary

Summary 10

1. *Power consumption is a very significant issue in modern processors. There are two primary modes of power consumption: dynamic power consumption and leakage power consumption.*

   (a) *Circuits consume dynamic power when there is a transition in the voltage levels ($0 \rightarrow 1$ or $1 \rightarrow 0$). Upon a transition there is a flow of current to charge or discharge gate capacitances and the resulting resistive loss is known as dynamic power consumption.*

   (b) *An important component of the dynamic power is the* short-circuit *power. When there is a transition in a CMOS transistor's input voltage, there is a short period of time when both the NMOS and PMOS transistors are conducting. For this brief period, there is a short circuit from the supply to the ground. The resultant current flow and power dissipation is known as the short-circuit power consumption.*

   (c) *In a transistor, we typically assume that many interfaces are ideal, which means that there is no current flow through them. However, this is not the case in modern transistors. Some amount of current* leaks through *such interfaces and this is known as the* leakage current. *The resulting power consumption is known as leakage power.*

2. *The dynamic power consumption is proportional to $\beta CV^2 f$, where β is the activity factor (varies from 0 to 1), C is the lumped capacitance, V is the supply voltage, and f is the frequency.*

3. *The relationship between the voltage and frequency is typically given by the Alpha-power law.*

$$f \propto \frac{(V - V_{th})^\alpha}{V}$$

   V is the supply voltage, V_{th} is the threshold voltage, and α is a constant between 1.1 and 1.5.

4. *The process of changing the voltage and frequency to either increase performance or reduce power is known as dynamic voltage frequency scaling (DVFS).*

---

5. *To compare systems that have different frequencies, typically the energy-delay-square (ED^2) metric is used. It is independent of the DVFS setting if some simplistic assumptions are made.*

6. *There are six main sources of leakage power: P-N junction reverse bias current, subthreshold leakage, gate-oxide tunnelling, hot-carrier injection, gate-induced drain leakage, and punch-through current.*

7. *There is a feedback loop between the temperature and leakage power particularly the subthreshold leakage power. If the temperature increases, the leakage power also increases, and the resultant increase in overall power increases the temperature.*

8. *The basic equation in temperature modelling is the Fourier's equation: the heat flux (power per unit area) is proportional to the gradient of the temperature.*

9. *The final form of the Fourier's equation in Cartesian coordinates is:*

$$k\nabla^2 T + Q' = \rho c_p \frac{\partial T}{\partial t}$$

k is a constant, Q' is the rate of internal power generation, T is the temperature field, ρ is the density, and c_p is the specific heat.

10. *The finite difference approach for solving this equation is to convert it to a linear transformation. The Fourier equation can be simplified as follows for the steady-state case.*

$$\mathbf{T = AP}$$

11. *An equivalent expression for the transient case is as follows where $\mathbf{C}$ is a diagonal matrix.*

$$\mathbf{GT + P = CT'}$$

12. *We can create an electrical analogue of the problem where we can designate the constants of proportionality in our equations as equivalent* thermal resistances *and* thermal capacitances. *Voltage can be mapped to the temperature, and current to power. We can use a standard circuit simulator to compute the thermal profile.*

13. *Using the properties of linearity and superposition, we can define the Green's function that is the impulse response of a unit power source. The temperature profile is given as $T = P \star G$. Here, $\star$ is the convolution operator.*

14. *The common approaches to manage dynamic power are voltage-frequency scaling, clock gating (setting the clock equal to 0), and issue/fetch throttling (reducing the issue or fetch rate).*

15. *For reducing leakage power we can opt for power gating, which means disconnecting the circuit from the power and ground lines. Another approach for reducing leakage in caches is to implement the* drowsy *mode, where the supply voltage is reduced such that the stored value can be maintained but the cell cannot be accessed.*

16. *In general, any approach that reduces power reduces temperature as well. However, there are dedicated schemes to reduce temperature hotspots as well. For example, we can stop the execution completely, or map the jobs in such a manner that high-temperature hotspots do not form. This can lead to very interesting optimisation problems where we can place constraints on the performance and reduce the peak temperature as much as possible. We can additionally couple these problems with energy and DVFS based constraints.*

11.5.2 Further Reading

For power estimation techniques, readers can refer to the extensive survey by Sultan et al. [Sultan et al., 2014], and the following books: [Kaxiras and Martonosi, 2008, Själander et al., 2014]. To get a better understanding of the tools, readers can refer to the design of the Wattch [Brooks et al., 2000] and McPAT [Li et al., 2009] tools. For modelling leakage power one of the most authoritative references is a paper by Roy et al. [Roy et al., 2003].

For temperature estimation, readers can refer to another survey paper by Sultan et al. [Sultan et al., 2019]. Along with this, readers can look at the popular temperature estimation tools such as HotSpot [Huang et al., 2006], HS3D [Hung et al., 2006], and 3D-ICE [Sridhar et al., 2010]. To understand how Green's function based methods are used in temperature estimation, readers can refer to [Sarangi et al., 2014, Park et al., 2010]. For estimating temperature in 3D chips using the Green's function, readers can find the following reference useful: [Sultan and Sarangi, 2017].

Finally, for understanding power management schemes, some of the most comprehensive references are the e-books [Kaxiras and Martonosi, 2008, Själander et al., 2014], and for dynamic thermal management schemes these references [Kong et al., 2012, Coskun et al., 2008] can be consulted.

Exercises

Ex. 1 — Understand the working of a thermal simulator such as Hotspot or 3D-ICE. Use an architectural simulator to generate the power profile of a 32-core chip running the Parsec benchmarks. Generate the temperature map of the chip for the power profile.

Ex. 2 — Write an algorithm for dynamically assigning threads to cores based on temperature and leakage power in an architectural simulator.

Ex. 3 — Implement clock gating and power gating in an architectural simulator.

Ex. 4 — Implement DVFS for GPUs in an architectural simulator such as GPUTejas.

12

Reliability

Till now we have assumed that all our elaborate designs and protocols work flawlessly. This is sadly not the case and unfortunately modern hardware suffers from a variety of faults, which can impact its correctness and ultimate lifetime. This chapter is devoted to studying the different aspects of hardware reliability, and how we can detect and recover from faults.

Before we proceed further, it is important to differentiate between three terms here: fault, error, and failure. A *fault* refers to a defect: a part of the architecture, implementation or protocol that deviates from the ideal specification. Note that a lot of faults can be benign in the sense that they do not manifest into wrong internal states. However, some of them lead to erroneous internal states of the system – these are known as *errors*. Even if an internal state such as the value of a register is wrong, it does not mean that the final output is wrong. It is possible that the value may get *masked*. For example, we might have an instruction the divides the value in the register by itself. In this case the final output will still be correct even if the value in the register is incorrect. However, in many other cases the final output will be wrong. This is known as a *failure*. A failure is basically defined as any change in the operation of the system (observed externally) that deviates from ideal specifications. Note that a failure is not limited to a wrong output, even a system crashing is a failure.

Definition 98

Fault *A fault is a defect in the system. It is an aspect of the hardware or software that is undesirable. Note that all faults do not necessarily lead to erroneous results. Many faults can be* masked *(their effects are not visible).*

Error *An error is an internal state of the system that is perceived to be incorrect. Similar to the case of faults, errors do not necessarily lead to wrong outputs. They can get masked.*

Failure *A failure is an externally visible event, where the behaviour of the system deviates from its specifications and this is visible to the user of the system. It can include an erroneous output, an unresponsive system, or the case of a system going down. Most of the time we assume a* fail-stop *failure mode, where sub-systems are capable of checking themselves and simply cease their operation if their outputs are wrong. However, there are other failure modes as well*

> *where sub-systems produce erroneous outputs often maliciously, and deliberately confuse other sub-systems. In this case it is also possible for sub-systems to collude and send potentially confusing and erroneous messages. Such malicious failures are known as Byzantine failures. They are relatively rare in hardware systems.*

There are a few well known reliability metrics in the context of failures that need to be explained first: FIT, MTTF, MTBF, and MTTR. The FIT metric measures the expected number of failures per billion hours of operation. MTTF is defined as the mean time to failure, which essentially represents the expected time it will take for the system to fail. The assumption here is that the system is not repairable; however, if we make the assumption that the system can be repaired then typically the metric MTBF (mean time between failures) is used. This measures the expected duration between two failures. Once the system has failed, there is a need to repair its state, and restore it. The time it takes to repair the state is known as the mean time to repair (MTTR).

We will keep on referring to these metrics throughout this chapter.

Definition 99

- *Failure rates are typically measured in the units of FITs (failures in time). One FIT is one failure per billion hours.*

- *MTTF is the mean time to failure (assuming the system cannot be repaired).*

- *MTBF is the mean time between failures (assuming a system that can be repaired).*

- *MTTR is the mean time to repair (fix the state of the system).*

Given this understanding, we shall delve into the different sources of erroneous execution in this chapter. Notably, we shall look at two kinds of faults: transient and permanent. Transient faults are ephemeral in nature, come in to existence for a very short period of time and then disappear. However, permanent faults never disappear. We can further divide permanent faults into two types: congenital and ageing related. Congenital faults are there since the time of fabrication, and are typically caused because of imperfections in the fabrication process. However, ageing related faults happen because of a gradual deterioration of transistors' properties. Over time transistors or wires can fully deteriorate and either become open circuits or closed circuits. In this case, these faults can permanently alter the operation of the processor, and unless there is some redundancy, the computer system needs to be decommissioned.

We shall first look at three sources of transient errors/faults: soft errors, faults due to inductive noise, and faults due to non-determinism. Then we shall consider congenital faults: process variation and RTL-level bugs. Finally, we shall consider ageing related faults that lead to permanent breakdowns.

12.1 Soft Errors

12.1.1 Physics of Soft Errors

In the 60s and 70s, engineers noticed a strange phenomenon. A lot of electronic devices in the proximity of nuclear sites, and in space missions were mysteriously crashing. They thus set out to find the reason and also understand the connection between such failures. They found that high-energy particles such as neutrons and alpha particles that are a part of nuclear or cosmic radiation collide with the silicon die at great speed. These particles displace charge, which causes a temporary current pulse. The current pulse is strong enough to flip the value of bits, particularly in memory cells. In the early 80s, engineers started noticing failures in DRAM devices even at sea level. With increased miniaturisation, such failures started affecting SRAM cells and even logic gates. Such errors are known as *soft errors* that are mostly single-event upsets (SEUs), which means that a particle with a very high momentum makes an impact, and the resulting current pulse flips the value of a bit in the circuit.

It should be noted that such single event upsets are not radiation-induced all the time, we can have several intrinsic factors such as power supply noise and inductive noise, which we shall consider in Section 12.2. However, in this chapter we shall limit ourselves to extrinsic factors, which are particle strikes because of cosmic radiation, or because of inherent impurities present in the packaging material.

Sources of Radiation

In the early 70s, alpha particles (two neutrons and two protons) were the most common sources of radiation-induced soft errors. They were emitted by trace uranium and thorium impurities in the packaging material. These are radioactive elements and spontaneously emit alpha particles. Alpha particles have a high mass, and consequently they need to have a high energy to penetrate deep into silicon. The particles generated by these impurities have energies in the range of 4-9 MeV, and thus the maximum penetration range is limited to 100 μm. Hence, we need not worry about alpha particles that are generated outside the package.

Another source of alpha particle emissions is an unstable isotope of lead, ^{210}Pb. It decays into ^{210}Po, which emits alpha particles. These alpha particles can displace a lot of charge. With sophisticated fabrication technologies the proportion of such impurities has gradually decreased and as of today high-energy cosmic rays that comprise mostly of neutrons are the primary source of radiation-induced soft errors.

Next, let us consider a secondary source of radiation, which materialises due to the interaction of neutrons with a relatively rare isotope of boron called ^{10}B. Boron is heavily used in creating p-type materials and is also a part of boron phosposilicate glass that is used as a dielectric material. Whenever a neutron impacts such a boron atom, it breaks it into an alpha particle and a lithium nucleus that travel in opposite directions. Both the alpha particle and the lithium nucleus are capable of inducing soft errors is in the circuit.

Dynamics of a Particle Strike

Whenever a particle strikes the silicon substrate it approaches it with a very high momentum and gradually loses momentum. Most approaches model the loss of energy as a linear process, and the rate of energy loss per unit distance is known as the LET (linear energy transfer) rate. It is often divided by the density of the target material. Normally in CMOS circuits, transistors are most susceptible to such single event upsets (SEUs) in the *off state*. An LET rate of more than 20 MeV-cm^2/mg [Wang and Agrawal, 2008] is sufficient to create a current pulse that can propagate in the circuit and change the value stored in a latch.

The mechanism is as follows. Whenever there is a particle strike, it displaces charge and creates a lot of electron-hole pairs. If the trajectory of the particle strike passes through the depletion regions in a transistor, carriers get rapidly collected over there. This collection phase lasts for tens of picoseconds. The resultant displacement in charge creates a current pulse. The initial phase of charge collection is because of drift, and later on the amount of current reduces and the mechanism of the movement of carriers changes to diffusion. A representative current pulse with the drift and diffusion dominated regions is shown in Figure 12.1. Typically, the entire current pulse lasts for roughly 200-600 ps, which accounts for the majority of the clock period (with a 3GHz clock). Most of the charge collection, henceforth denoted as Q_{total} happens within 2-3 μm of the junction region. Q_{total} depends on the energy of the particle, nature of the particle, the trajectory, the impact site, and the voltages of the different terminals. The current pulse can be approximated by an equation of the form [Wang and Agrawal, 2008]:

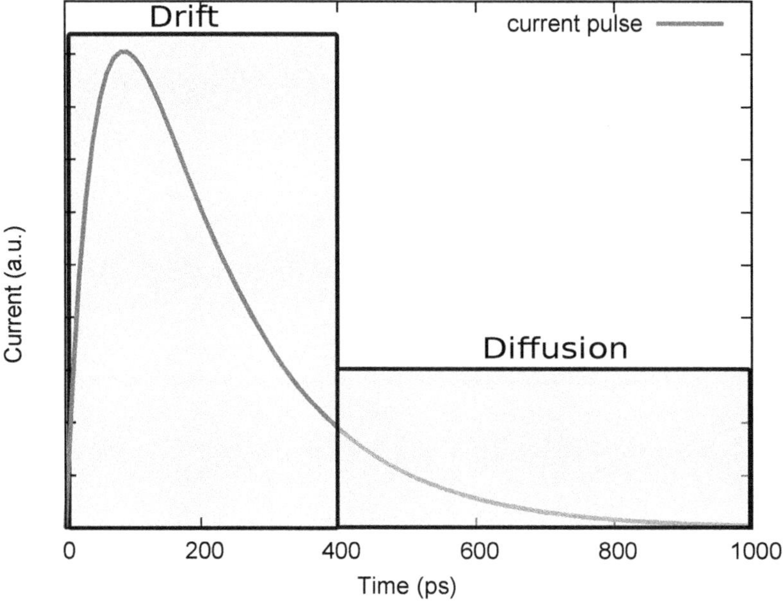

Figure 12.1: Representative current pulse. (a.u. stands for arbitrary units)

$$I(t) = \frac{Q_{total}}{\tau_\alpha - \tau_\beta}(e^{-\frac{t}{\tau_\alpha}} - e^{-\frac{t}{\tau_\beta}}) \tag{12.1}$$

Note that this equation is a difference of two exponential functions. Typically, τ_α is dependent on the properties of the transistor and represents the charge collection time, whereas τ_β is relatively independent of the manufacturing process and depends on the trajectory of the particle strike. As mentioned in [Wang and Agrawal, 2008] typical values are 164 ps for τ_α and 50 ps for τ_β. The value of Q_{total} is somewhere between 50-500 fC (femto coulombs) depending on the nature of the particle.

Alternative one-parameter models also exist [Hazucha and Svensson, 2000] for the current pulse (η is a single empirically determined parameter here).

$$I(t) = \frac{2}{\eta\sqrt{\pi}}\sqrt{\frac{t}{\eta}}e^{-\frac{t}{\eta}} \tag{12.2}$$

Hazucha-Svensson Model

Unfortunately just computing the total collected charge is not enough to estimate the soft error rate. This is because the output terminals of the transistor have an associated capacitance, which can attenuate the current pulse significantly. While computing the soft error rate, it is necessary to take into account the environment in which the particle strikes. For the purposes of calibration and comparison, we typically consider soft errors in the context of simple 6-transistor SRAM cells.

The Hazucha-Svensson model to estimate the soft error rate is as follows.

$$SER = F * CS \tag{12.3}$$

Here, SER is the rate of soft errors. It is typically measured in the unit of FITs (failures in time), where one FIT is one failure per billion hours. F is the neutron or alpha-particle flux (depends on the type of particle we are considering). CS (critical section) is the effective area that is susceptible to particle strikes. We can think of it as the relevant part of the transistor's structure that is vulnerable to particle strikes. It is given as follows.

$$CS \propto A \times e^{-\frac{Q_{crit}}{Q_S}} \tag{12.4}$$

It is unfortunately hard to compute the size of the critical section exactly. Hence, Equation 12.4 uses a proportional sign. CS is clearly proportional to the area of the circuit that is sensitive to particle strikes (around the junctions and so on). Additionally, it is a negative exponential function of the ratio of two variables: Q_{crit} and Q_S. Q_{crit} is the minimum amount of charge that needs to be displaced to generate a current pulse that is large enough to flip the value stored in the SRAM cell. Q_S is known as the charge collection efficiency, which is a measure of the charge generated by a particle strike (units in fC). If $Q_S \ll Q_{crit}$ then the term $e^{-\frac{Q_{crit}}{Q_S}}$ tends to 0. This means that the rate of soft errors tends to 0. Whereas, if $Q_S \gg Q_{crit}$ then the rate of soft errors is proportional to the area.

Note that Equation 12.4 was derived empirically by Hazucha and Svensson based on experiments and observations. This was valid for their setting with a gate length of 600 nm. For different technologies this equation will have a different form, and thus for any upcoming technology it is necessary to perform similar experiments to derive a new soft error model. We can either perform experiments on a device simulator, where we can irradiate the device with different particle streams that have different velocities and trajectories, and measure the resultant soft error rate. Another approach is to conduct a physical experiment where we have a neutron source. It is used to bombard a test circuit with neutrons and then measure the rate of bit flips.

12.1.2 Circuit and Device Level Techniques to Mitigate Soft Errors

Device Level Techniques

Reducing the susceptibility of a device to soft errors is known as *radiation hardening*. Radiation hardening techniques at the device level are the most preferred, particularly if there is no concomitant cost. This is because it reduces the amount of effort that is needed at later stages: the circuit and architectural levels. At the device level, the first approach is to eliminate all those materials that are involved in soft errors: uranium and thorium impurities, and impurities with the ^{10}B or ^{210}Pb isotopes. The use of the BPSG dielectric that contains ^{10}B can also be curtailed and it can be limited to layers that are not close to the silicon layer.

Another set of approaches focus on radiation hardened transistor technologies. Here, the main aim is to reduce Q_S. A common approach is to use the triple well structure as shown in Figure 12.2(a). Here, there is a deep n-type doped region below the substrate to reduce the total amount of collected charge.

The other popular approach is to use the silicon-on-insulator (SoI) technology. In this case, there is a buried oxide layer below the channel that effectively cuts it off from the rest of the substrate (see Figure 12.2(b)). This reduces the volume in which charge can be collected. As a result, the chances of a soft error reduce drastically.

Let us now discuss a few approaches to increase Q_{crit}. It primarily depends on the transistor size, supply voltage, and output capacitance. With an increase in any of these quantities, the critical charge increases. Sadly, if we increase these quantities the circuit takes up more area and dissipates more power. On the flip side, we observe that with increasing miniaturisation, the critical charge will continue to decrease and this will increase the susceptibility to soft errors.

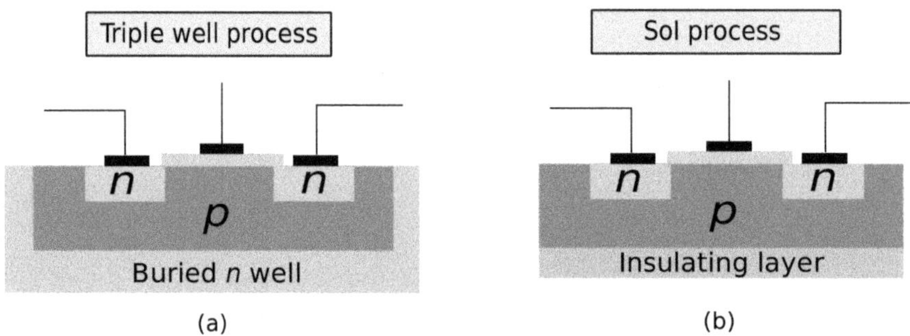

Figure 12.2: (a) A triple well process, (b) An SoI process

Circuit Level Techniques

While studying the effect of soft errors, we typically differentiate between memory and logic circuits. Soft errors in memory such as SRAM and DRAM arrays are easy to model and detect.

Let us thus first look at the effect of soft errors in a combinational logic circuit. Recall from our discussion on in-order pipelines that we typically break a large circuit into smaller chunks and pipeline them. To achieve this, we need to add a pipeline latch after a block of logic to store its value at the end of the clock cycle. Let us look at the effect of soft errors on logic circuits in this setting. We will consider a particle strike as leading to a soft error only if a bit in the pipeline latch gets flipped. Furthermore, this can only happen if a particle strikes a transistor in the logic circuit, and the current pulse reaches the pipeline latch, where it flips a bit. For example, instead of storing a logical 0, we might end up storing a logical 1.

Masking Mechanisms

The good news is that most current pulses are not potent enough to flip a stored bit. There are various reasons why such current pulses can get *masked*. Let us look at some of the most common masking mechanisms. The first masking mechanism is known as *electrical masking*. Assume that a particle strikes a transistor in a combinational logic circuit. As the disturbance propagates towards the pipeline latches, the pulse passes through a multiplicity of logic gates, and it gradually gets attenuated. By the time it reaches the latches, its strength reduces considerably and thus may not be potent enough to change the state. This is known as electrical masking (see Figure 12.3(a)).

Now, consider *logical masking* (see Figure 12.3(b)). Look at the first input of the AND gate in the figure. Assume it makes a transition from a logical 0 to a logical 1. Since the value of the other input is a logical 0, this transition does not have any effect on the output. This is because the final output continues to remain a logical 0 because of the input that continues to remain at 0. Hence, regardless of the transition made by one of the inputs (because of soft errors), the final value still remains the same. This is where the potential error is said to be logically masked.

The third category of masking is known as *timing window masking* (see Figure 12.3(c)). Note that for a latch to actually change its value, the updated value has to appear only in a critical time window around the negative edge of the clock (between the setup time and the hold time). At any other time the changed input does not lead to a change in the stored state of the latch. This means that if there is a particle strike, the resultant current pulse has to reach the output latch only during this critical period. If this does not happen then the changes will not flip the value of any stored bit, and thus the error will get masked. Due to a combination of these three mechanisms, the actual probability of a bit flip reduces significantly.

Reducing the probability of soft errors in memory arrays is relatively easy. We just need to add ECC (error correction codes) bits to each line. These can be used to detect and correct bit flips. In comparison, bit flips in logic circuits are much harder to detect and correct. Some of the most effective

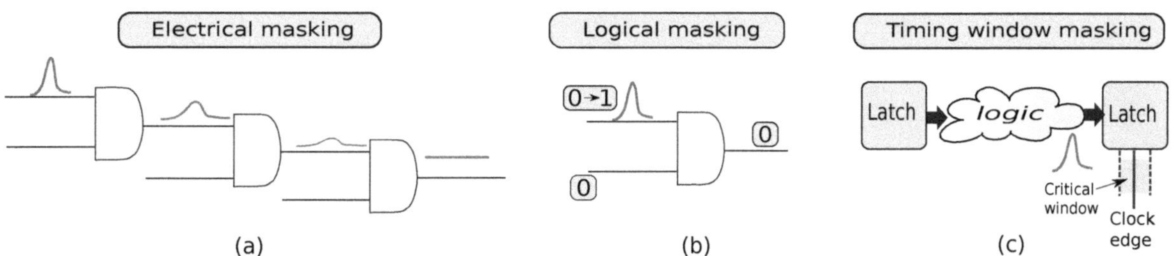

Figure 12.3: Different masking mechanisms. (a) Electrical masking, (b) Logical masking, (c) Timing window masking

approaches actually try to reduce the probability of the current pulse propagating to the latches. This can be done by identifying *sensitive paths* in the circuit (paths that are more susceptible to propagating current pulses). The transistors on the sensitive paths can then be modified to reduce their susceptibility. There are several ways of doing this: increase the size, increase output capacitance, or increase the supply voltage (if there is a choice).

12.1.3 Architectural Techniques to Mitigate Soft Errors

Basic Concepts

There are numerous architectural techniques to mitigate the damage caused by soft errors. First we need to understand the basic mechanisms by which soft errors can impact architectural state. We should first note that not all errors will actually impact the architectural state. For example, if the unit is not being used or if the value of an instruction's result gets corrupted, but the instruction itself is on the wrong path, then the error is not visible. There can be many such instances where the effect of soft errors does not lead to failures: the final output is not wrong, and the program does not crash.

To model the failure rate, SE_{fail}, correctly let us consider the following equation.

$$SE_{fail} = SER \times TVF \times AVF \tag{12.5}$$

SER is the soft error rate. TVF is a factor (between 0 and 1) known as the timing vulnerability factor, which captures the effect of the unit being off (unused at that point of time). AVF is the architectural vulnerability factor, and is defined as the probability that the soft error leads to an erroneous output.

Let us understand the architectural vulnerability factor in detail (refer to Figure 12.4). The aim here is to find if a given bit is vulnerable or not, which means that if it gets flipped, whether it affects the final architectural state or not. If the bit is not read, clearly it is not vulnerable. There is thus no error in this case. However, if it is read then it is possible that it is protected by parity or ECC bits. For example, in many modern processors even small structures such as the register file are protected by ECC bits. If the bit is protected then it is possible that the error is only detected and not corrected. This can happen if we are only using parity bits, or if let's say we can correct only one-bit errors, and there are errors in two bits. Such errors are known as Detected but Unrecoverable Errors (DUE errors). Whereas, if we can correct the bit flips then there is no error.

Now let us consider the case when the bit is not protected. In this case, we need to assess if the bit is relevant to the architectural state or not. If it is a part of the architectural state and helps in determining the output then the resultant bit flip is known as Silent Data Corruption (SDC).

The good news is that a lot of errors happen in parts of the circuit that do not determine the final output. For example, we have numerous bits in the ALU logic, decode logic, and pipeline latches that are not used. If any of these bits get flipped, then there are no errors. Additionally, there are a lot of structures in the pipeline that impact performance but do not affect correctness. Consider the branch

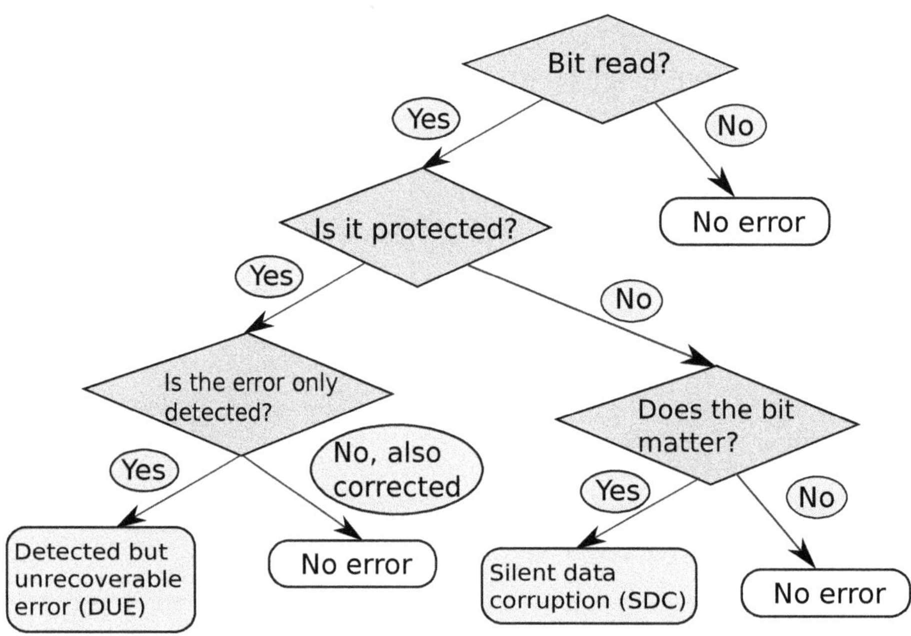

Figure 12.4: Components of the AVF

predictor, the prefetch buffers, and entries in the instruction window for issued instructions. Even if there is a bit flip in the contents of these structures, correctness is not affected. Moreover, there are many instructions in the pipeline that are either dynamically dead (do not affect the output), are on the wrong path, fetch the value of performance counters, or are a part of some misspeculated state – the contents of all of these instructions are immune to soft errors. For example, the AVF of a branch predictor entry is 0. The AVF of an instruction window entry is between 0 and 1 (depending on the behaviour of the program).

Design Space of Checkers

Soft errors do not pose much of a problem in regular desktops and laptops. However, they are very serious issues in large servers and supercomputers. The single bit flip can have catastrophic consequences. Imagine a bank account where a bit flip converts a billionaire to a pauper – all because of a single neutron! Additionally, radiation induced soft errors are serious issues in aircrafts and definitely in components that go to space. Even with extensive shielding soft errors do happen, and thus we need architectural techniques to mitigate their pernicious effects.

Given that there is no way to predict soft errors, we need checkers that can be dedicated software or hardware units whose job is to check the execution of a program (particularly SDC errors); if they detect any kind of a transient fault, then they can initiate a process of recovery. We shall use the same terminology as originally used in the survey paper by Kalayappan et al. [Kalayappan and Sarangi, 2013] to classify the design space of checkers based on their degree of coverage.

Complete In this case the execution of the entire thread is checked. Such approaches are typically very expensive. However, in most cases where we cannot take a risk, this approach is required.

Subset Here we check the results of a subset of instructions.

Invariant In this case we check if certain properties (invariants) hold for the outputs. For example, if it is always the case that regardless of the values, the sum of the outputs is equal to a known value, then all that we need to do is add the outputs and check if it is equal to the expected value.

Symptom Here we check if something went wrong during the execution of a thread. For example, if we do not expect a segmentation fault (illegal memory access), and if there is one it might point towards a bit flip.

Let us now look at another axis where we focus on the structure of the checker. Here we can have three different configurations: *MultiMaster*, *SingleSlave*, and *MultiSlave*. In this case, a *Master* is an independent computing unit that executes the program as it would have executed on a regular system. The *Slave* on the other hand is a system that is impaired either in terms of hardware resources or performance. It is often used to check for invariants, or check for error symptoms. Note that we did not list the SingleMaster configuration because it simply represents the default implementation, which does not have any in-built checking mechanism.

MultiMaster Systems

The *MultiMaster* configuration uses redundant threads. In this case, we have parallel threads either running on the same core or on different cores that perform exactly the same computations. We can then periodically compare the results. If there is a discrepancy, we can infer a soft error. One of the earliest designs in this space was the IBM G5 processor [Slegel et al., 1999] that used two parallel pipelines that executed instructions from the same thread. They compared the values for all the stores and register writes every cycle. If a discrepancy was detected, the pipeline was flushed. It is important to note here that when we have only one redundant checking unit (a parallel pipeline in this case), it is not possible to determine which value is correct. Hence, it is necessary to flush both. Here, the error remains confined to the pipeline, it is not allowed to propagate to the memory system. We are also making the implicit assumption that the memory system is protected with ECC bits, and DUE errors are not an issue.

Let us now analyse the problems in the scheme. In this case, we have a straightforward 100% overhead in terms of hardware. Furthermore, non-trivial changes need to be made to an OOO pipeline to support this feature. We need to log every single value that changes the architectural state; these values need to be compared at commit time. To minimise the communication overhead, we can run both the threads on the same core (simultaneous multithreaded execution) by partitioning its resources between the threads; however, this will halve the computational throughput of the core and result in a significant slowdown. Hence, the other approach is to run the second thread on a different core. In this case, we will solve the issue of the slowdown, but add two more problems. The first is that values need to be communicated at the end of every cycle. This will place a substantial load on the NoC. The second is that it is in general very difficult to run two cores in lockstep in modern multicores with complex NoCs. Hence, we need to occasionally spend additional time and effort to ensure that the cores remain in synchrony.

Because of these issues, later approaches such as the HP NonStop [Bernick et al., 2005] systems allow errors to propagate to the memory system. Instead of comparing values every cycle, they only compare the values of I/O operations that are visible to the external world. This minimises the communication overhead, and allows us to utilise the full computational throughput of the cores. Furthermore, the different checking threads can run in separate address spaces (as separate programs) and there is no need for lockstepped execution. This is by far a more practical and efficient setup.

Now, in this configuration we have some unique challenges and opportunities as well. The first is that if we detect a discrepancy, then we still cannot find out which core is at fault. This is because we have only two cores, which means we have dual modular redundancy (DMR). If we detect a transient fault, we need to rollback both the threads on the two separate cores to a safe checkpoint. The *checkpoint* in this case is defined as an earlier point in the execution, which is deemed to be correct; moreover, it is possible to restore the state to that point in the execution. Recall that we have discussed various checkpointing schemes in Section 9.7. Any of them can be used here.

In this case rollback and recovery is a fairly expensive operation. The good news is that soft errors are very rare, hence in practice this does not represent a large overhead. However, in specialised cases such as in environments with a high particle flux such as in aircrafts or in space, where either we cannot afford the long recovery time or the check pointing overhead is prohibitive, we need to opt for triple modular redundancy (TMR). In this case, we run three parallel threads on three separate cores and if there is a discrepancy, then the results are decided on the basis of voting. The implicit assumption here is that since soft errors are rare, the chances of an error happening simultaneously in two threads is also very rare. Hence, if we have three threads, the probability that two of them will simultaneously be afflicted by a soft error and that too in the same checkpointing interval is extremely improbable. Hence, it is expected that voting will be successful almost all the time.

There are variations of this scheme, where we divide time into fixed size intervals called *epochs*, and for every epoch we compute a hash of all the values that a thread computes (known as its signature). At the end of an epoch, different threads compare their signatures. Here again, a DMR or TMR based mechanism can be used.

To summarise, with a variety of interventions it is possible to reduce the time overhead of such checking schemes by a significant amount, however, the hardware overhead is still significant. The next two families of approaches that we shall describe will help us in reducing that.

SingleSlave Systems

In *SingleSlave* systems, there is a smaller processor known as the slave processor that takes some inputs from the master and tries to verify the master's computed results. The aim is to finish the verification process quickly such that the critical path is not lengthened. The key insight here is that verification can be a faster process than the computation itself. Consider a simple example. Finding the roots of a set of non-linear equations with multiple variables is a very difficult problem. However, given a solution we can always verify it very quickly. Such *SingleSlave* systems are built on similar lines. In some cases we check for invariants, which means that the master sends its computed results to the slave, which simultaneously checks if the solution is correct or not.

Let us now describe a general system that is based on the original research idea called *DIVA* presented by Austin [Austin, 1999]. Here, the assumption is that the checker is made of larger transistors that are by far more immune to soft errors.

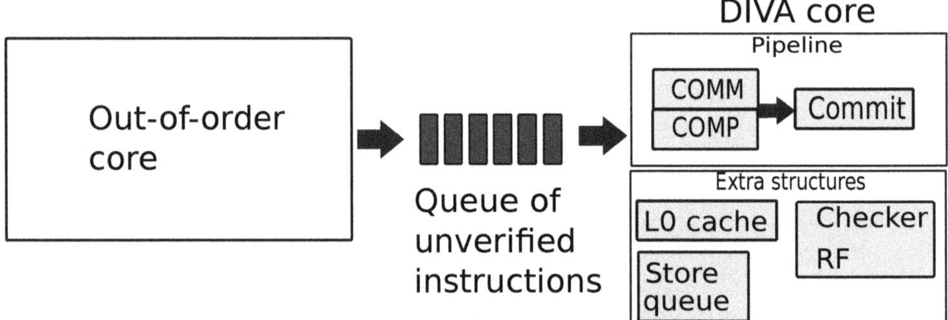

Figure 12.5: The DIVA checker core

Figure 12.5 shows the schematic of a master-slave system. The master core sends an instruction packet to the slave core, which contains the program counter, opcode of the instruction, the values of the operands, and the computed result. The checker processor is a small 2-stage in-order processor that maintains a copy of the architectural register file. The first stage of this pipeline is broken into two sub-stages: communication and computation. These sub-stages run in parallel. The communication sub-stage checks if the operand values and the memory values have been read correctly. There is a need to read the register values again from the architectural register file in the checker, and for memory values the addresses need to be read again from the cache. Accessing the L1 cache again will increase the pressure on the cache, and this can cause severe performance issues. Hence, later versions of DIVA have proposed to have a small L0 cache within the checker itself that can cache many of the frequently read values.

Next, let us consider the computation sub-stage. Here, a dedicated ALU in the checker re-computes the result and verifies if it is the same as the result passed by the master. If the values are the same, then this means that the computation is correct, otherwise we can infer an error. After the computation and communicate are verified, the instruction proceeds through the DIVA core's pipeline and gets *committed* – writes the results to the architectural state.

If there is any mismatch in the operands' values or results, then there is a need to flush the pipelines. A few more subtle points need to be considered here. Instructions in the master remain within the ROB and the store queue till the checker verifies them. This means that we need to have larger ROBs and store queues to support DIVA. This is indeed an overhead. Furthermore, the store queue is used as a temporary cache to store values written to memory by uncommitted instructions. This is required by both the master and the checker and it is not a good idea to make the checker access the store queue of the master. Hence, we need to replicate the store queue in the checker as well. For the values written by uncommitted stores, the checker can access entries in its private store queue.

Let us now consider another core issue. The checker needs to match the master in terms of IPC. If the checker is slower, the master will also get slowed down. The good news is that even in cores with a large issue width, for many integer codes the average IPC is never more than 1.5 in practice. Hence, a 2-issue in-order pipeline in the checker is sufficient. If there are temporary peaks in the IPC of the master, a queue between the master and slave can be used to buffer some instructions. However, if we are running floating point code in the master and the IPC is high (let's say more than 3), then a simple checker will not be able to keep up. It will thus slow the system down. Hence, we need to look at another set of designs known as *MultiSlave* systems.

MultiSlave Systems

In a *MultiSlave* system we have multiple checkers. A representative execution is shown in Figure 12.6.

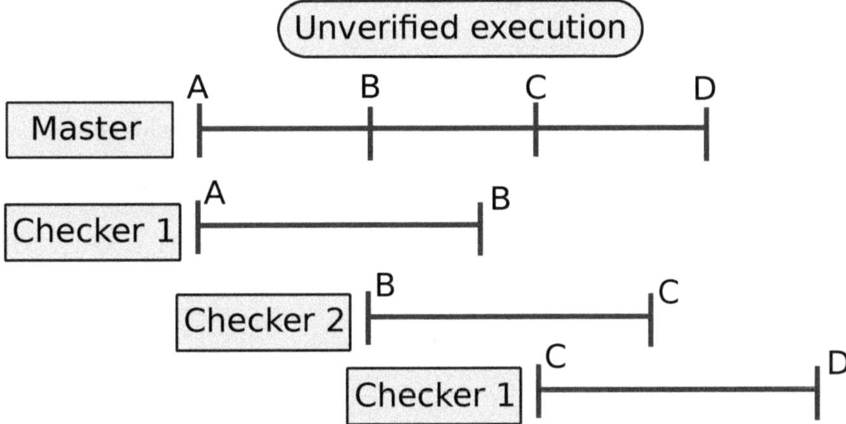

Figure 12.6: Single master, multiple checkers. Here each individual checker is slower than the master.

In such a design we divide the execution into multiple fixed size intervals called *epochs*. Consecutive epochs are checked by different checkers. This solves the problem of matching the rates of the master and the checker. In this case, we have several checkers that simultaneously verify the results of different epochs. This allows the master to continue at its regular pace, and the checkers can carry on with their work in parallel. If the IPC ratio is four times, then we simply need to have four checkers for each master. Note that in this case rolling back may not be as simple as flushing the pipeline, a slightly more complicated checkpoint recovery mechanism is necessary.

12.2 Inductive Noise

12.2.1 Basic Physics

Recall that we discussed in Section 11.3 that processors have a complex power delivery mechanism. Every processor has a power grid that is connected to the external power supply using hundreds of pins. The reason we need to have a power grid is because if there is a sudden current requirement, the additional current can come from many pins at the same time. Now we have assumed that this is an *ideal voltage source*, which means that it can provide any amount of current while maintaining a constant voltage. Furthermore, we have assumed that the internal impedance of this voltage source is zero. This is sadly not true. Let us now describe the constraints of realistic power grids. For following the rest of the discussion a basic understanding of concepts such as reactance and impedance is required.

The power grid has a lot of wires connected in a grid like fashion, which also means that it has a large inductance. Any inductor opposes the flow of current through it by creating a back EMF (Lenz's law). This means that if there is a sudden current requirement, the power grid will take some time to actually provide it. To offset this effect, designers typically add capacitors known as *decoupling capacitors* that can provide the additional current and also maintain the voltage level. A power grid can thus be replaced by an equivalent RLC circuit. In any such circuit, the behaviour is dependent upon the frequency of the variation of the voltage or current. For the purposes of analysis, we typically assume it to be a sinusoidal variation, and quantify it in terms of its angular frequency ω. The reactance of the capacitors and inductors in the circuit is a function of ω. The final impedance takes into account the complex reactances of the inductors and capacitors, and the real-valued resistances.

Any such RLC circuit has an interesting property known as *resonance*. Here, the impedance typically becomes real (imaginary component is zero), and the impedance as a whole reaches an extremum (maximum or minimum). In other words at this point the circuit offers either the maximum resistance to the flow of current or the minimum. In either case, we will have large voltage spikes and these spikes can indeed induce errors in the circuit. Hence, the job of a processor designer is to ensure that the power delivery mechanism never operates close to its *resonance point*. Maintaining the stability of the operating voltage at this point is difficult. To ensure that we are always off resonance the frequency of variation in the current requirement of the CPU should be far away from the resonant frequency. Secondly, the amplitude of variation in the current requirement should be commensurately small to eliminate large voltage fluctuations.

12.2.2 Pipeline Damping

The resonant frequency is typically between 10-100 MHz [Powell and Vijaykumar, 2003a]. If we are unlucky we can have code snippets that run in a loop, and the frequency of the resultant current variation is close to the resonant frequency. In such cases, it is necessary to perform *pipeline damping* – deliberately homogenise the activity by reducing the rate of computation at some point in time (damping). It has been observed that the front end of the pipeline (fetch and decode logic) has a fairly homogeneous power usage (across time), and thus its activity does not have to be damped.

However, there is a need to monitor the activity of the back end: issue, execute, and commit logic. Here the primary aim is to reduce the amplitude of the fluctuation in the current requirement across fixed size intervals of time (known as epochs). Even if the frequency of variation is close to the resonant frequency, because of the homogenisation of activity (stability in the current demand), the voltage fluctuations are limited. To implement this, the idea is as follows. The manufacturer needs to create a model that links the activity of different structures within the CPU (ALU operations, selection operations, instruction issue, etc.) with the current requirement. Every epoch a dedicated circuit keeps a count of all the activity and computes a dynamic estimate of the current drawn since the beginning of the epoch. The aim is to limit the difference in the current drawn across epochs to a value Δ. This can be done by throttling the select rate or issue rate, or by introducing extraneous (fake) instructions to just draw more current. Both of these approaches allow us to introduce a degree of controlled jitter in the execution, which limits the occurrence of large voltage spikes.

12.3 Faults due to Inherent Nondeterminism

Till now we have assumed deterministic latencies for all the components inside the chip inclusive of the cores, the caches, and the network on-chip. This assumption has helped us design systems that are simple, easy to model, and easy to debug. However, as we shall see in this section, this abstraction breaks down in most practical systems that are in use today because of various sources of nondeterminism. Sadly, getting an accurate, deterministic snapshot of the system is a vital requirement for debugging the chip. Most modern chips have scan chains, which are serial buses that can be used to read out the entire internal state of the chip after a given event. To ensure that such debugging data is deterministic (same data produced for the same input) we need to make a lot of changes to the processor. Otherwise, if we observe different internal states in each run and that too for the same input, debugging a processor will be very difficult. To accurately detect faults, it is necessary to get an exact idea of the internal state of the processor and assess if it is on expected lines or not. In this section, we shall analyse the sources of nondeterminism in a system (with a CPU, memory, and buses), and discuss solutions to increase the amount of determinism.

12.3.1 Sources of Nondeterminism

Nondeterminism in CPUs and Caches

Some of the sources identified by your author in one of his previous papers [Sarangi et al., 2006a] are as follows: random replacement policies in caches, random choices made by bus arbiters, and uninitialised state elements in the processor. Furthermore, power gating, clock gating, and voltage-frequency scaling can introduce more nondeterminism.

This means that when these mechanisms are turned on, we cannot guarantee that the internal state of the processor will be the same even if we start from a known state and apply the same input. In the debug mode these features need to be turned off. Even if a few of these mechanisms are turned on such as clock gating, we need to somehow ensure that the internal state remains the same.

Nondeterminism in DRAM Memory

The two most common reasons for nondeterministic behaviour are DRAM refresh operations, and ECC scrubbing. As we have noted in Chapter 10, refresh operations are scheduled opportunistically based on the memory traffic. Furthermore, in many modern systems refresh operations are scheduled based on runtime conditions, and thus the refresh times tend to vary across runs. The other reason is called *ECC scrubbing*, which means fixing the errors in a DRAM row based on errors indicated by the ECC bits. Such errors can happen because of soft errors. Since such errors cannot be predicted, the time we shall spend on ECC scrubbing is fundamentally nondeterministic.

Nondeterminism in I/O and Interrupts

Systems with mechanical components such as hard disks are extremely unpredictable when it comes to exact timing. Their rotational delay and seek time is dependent on many factors, and cannot be reliably predicted at the nanosecond level.

Nondeterminism in Buses

This is a major source of nondeterminism at the board level. For example, the buses connecting different chips on the motherboard, or the buses connecting a chip on the motherboard with main memory, can have nondeterministic delays for a variety of reasons. Because of ambient conditions we might see some degree of jitter in the transmission. Additionally, it is possible that the clock of the sender and the clock of the receiver might gradually drift (relatively). Because of such jitter and drift issues, it is possible that let's say in one run we get a message in cycle 10, and in the next run we get a message in cycle 11.

Nondeterminism due to Faults

Lastly we can have nondeterminism due to faults in the circuit such as faults due to inductive noise or soft errors that lead to rollbacks and restarts.

12.3.2   Methods to Enforce Determinism

Deterministic CPUs

There should be a method to set a CPU's internal state to a known state such that a given sequence of inputs will always lead to the same output state. Note that here we are differentiating between the outputs of a program, and the CPU's internal state. Even if the program's outputs are the same, the internal state might still be different for different inputs. Even though this will make no difference externally, it is significant from the point of view of verification and validation engineers. Many processors already have debugging instructions to reset the state of all flip-flops, flush the caches and clean the TLBs. In addition, if we wish to deterministically replay a set of inputs, then we need to also log the exact nature and timing of nondeterministic events such as interrupts, voltage-frequency changes, and clock gating.

Events in the memory and the I/O subsystem can be handled in a similar manner. We simply need to log the exact time of different events, and replay them in a CPU debug run if there is a need.

Deterministic Buses

Ensuring determinism in buses is a hard problem. This is because the sender and receiver might have different clocks that are loosely synchronised with each other and the transmission process itself might have some jitter. First consider the case where their frequencies are the same. In this case, the standard approach is that the sender sends its local cycle count to the receiver. Let us say that the sender's time is t_s as per its local clock, and due to nondeterminism the time at which the receiver gets the message (receiver's local time) can be anywhere between $t_s + \theta_1$ and $t_s + \theta_2$. Then the idea is to delay the message till $t_s + \theta_2$ (the absolute worst case delay) at the receiver. If the receiver reads the message at its own time $t_s + \theta_2$, it is guaranteed to do so in all runs with the same inputs. Note that this approach does increase the latency of a message at the cost of ensuring determinism. It is indeed much easier for engineers to debug and perform post-silicon validation (validate the design after it has been fabricated) if determinism is ensured.

There are however two problems with this scheme. The first is that the two clocks need not have the same frequency. In this case, there are various proposals [Sarangi et al., 2006a, Chen et al., 2012] that slightly modify the basic idea to factor in the effects of different frequencies as long as their ratio remains more or less the same. The second shortcoming is that we need to send a large number (current cycle count) with every message. Note that given that the relative clock skew is a bounded quantity (between θ_1 and θ_2) we can significantly reduce the number of bits that are sent (refer to [Sarangi et al., 2006a]).

12.4 Design Faults

How many of us have actually heard of a bug or a mistake in hardware? The answer is probably very few or maybe none. On the other hand, we all can recount horror stories of software bugs. We all remember that time when our screen went blue, the system was frozen, and maybe the file system crashed – all before an assignment deadline. We have grown up thinking that hardware is always correct. This is sadly not true. Hardware is after all a very long piece of code written in a high-level synthesis language such as Verilog or VHDL. If we can make mistakes in C++ or Java code, we can make mistakes in Verilog or VHDL code as well. With software the vendor can issue patches, but with hardware once there is a bug, almost nothing can be done. Such faults are known as design faults.

Given that faults in hardware are very expensive primarily because they cannot be fixed, or have very expensive workarounds in software, designers spend a disproportionate amount of time in trying to verify and validate their designs. Incidentally, the terms *verification* and *validation* are two widely used terms in this space, and thus they deserve to be more accurately defined. Verification is the process of checking whether a certain part of the design conforms to specifications. It is typically done at design time. In comparison, validation is an activity that is performed after the chip has been fabricated. In this case, we typically provide several arrays of test vectors to a chip as inputs and test to see if the outputs are according to published specifications or not. Validation engineers often test a chip in extreme scenarios and rate its fitness in the field.

After the verification and validation stages, processors are released in the market. Unfortunately, some bugs nevertheless manage to slip through into the final product. Even though we do not get to hear about design faults a lot; however, when they happen, they cause major losses to the company. One of the most widely documented events was a bug in the division unit of Intel's Pentium® processor [Pratt, 1995]. In some rare cases, floating point division produced an error in the fourth (or beyond) decimal digit, which was ultimately traced to incorrect entries in an internal lookup table. This was considered a very serious bug particularly because of the fact that division is used by almost all of Intel's customers and such errors tend to accumulate over time. As a result, Intel had to recall all the defective processors and provide replacements. Way back in 1994, Intel had to spend 475 million US dollars to replace all the defective processors. This was a substantial penalty. Another widely reported incident was a bug in AMD's Barcelona and Phenom™ processors, which caused the processors to lock up. The bug was traced to the TLB.

For most bugs of this type, vendors often issue "patches", which are updates to the BIOS, OS, or compiler. They are really invasive in nature, and thoroughly constrain the behaviour of the system such that it is not affected by the bug. The resulting performance penalty can be very severe. Hence, it often makes commercial sense to just recall the processors and deliver a new one without the bug – totally free of cost. Given the risks, it is very important for companies to thoroughly vet their designs before releasing a processor. In this section, we shall first look at some of the common verification and validation steps, then we shall understand the nature of design bugs and how they can be detected in the field, and finally discuss solutions.

12.4.1 Verification and Validation

Verification

Unlike traditional software design, verification and validation are very important steps in hardware design. It is not uncommon to find that 50-60% of the time and a majority of team members are devoted to just checking the correctness of the hardware.

Once the architecture has been decided, and the high level design has been planned, each of the individual components are assigned to different teams. Some companies even outsource this job to third parties. The specifications of each module, and its interaction with other modules needs to be specified very accurately. It is the job of each team to thoroughly verify its module before releasing it to the rest of the company. Many small circuits such as floating point units or adders are formally verified, which is the gold standard for verification. In this case, the operation of the unit is first described in a formal language that clearly specifies the relationship between the outputs and the inputs. Subsequently, either the circuit or some abstracted version of it is checked to see if the specifications (relationship between the inputs and outputs) hold or not.

There are two approaches in this space: automated theorem proving and model checking. In automated theorem proving we start with a set of axioms, define a theory, and then we check if it is possible to prove that a given circuit obeys a certain property. For example, we can use this approach to prove that the output of an adder is correct. Sadly, such approaches require a lot of skills, and are often very slow. Hence, methods based on model checking are preferred. In this case we create a model of the system using a theoretical language. We start from a known state, and the aim is to show that a given set of states that satisfy a certain property are reachable. The main advantage of this technique is that it produces counterexamples – starting states that lead to finishing states that don't satisfy a certain property. This is a very useful debugging tool because the designers can then see what is wrong with the circuit, and for which inputs a wrong output is produced.

After model checking was proposed in the early 1980s, different methods have been proposed to substantially speed up the process. However, formal verification techniques are still plagued by their slow speed. Hence, it is very common to also test small subsystems via generating test vectors.

For each test vector (initial state), we simulate the circuit and verify if the output is equal to the ideal output or not. The simplest method of verification uses random test vectors. However, now we have many automatic test pattern generators that try to intelligently generate test vectors to maximise the overall coverage. The coverage is defined as the fraction of the input space that has been verified to generate correct outputs. There are two ways to simulate the behaviour of circuits with test vectors: RTL simulation, and FPGA prototyping. The latter is a much faster approach as compared to the former.

Validation

After the chip has been manufactured we still need to test it for manufacturing defects. This process is known as *validation*. The first step of testing happens at the wafer level. After the wafer is ready, special probes are attached to dedicated points in the fabricated dies and test vectors are applied. If all the outputs are correct for a given die in the wafer, it is marked to be correct. Here, the main aim is to verify the properties of the fabricated transistors and do some high-level tests on the generated outputs. The next phase of testing is known as burn-in testing. Here the packaged die is tested at elevated temperatures. If it works correctly, it means that it can operate in extreme conditions and is ready to proceed to the next level.

For the next phase a special purpose motherboard is used that allows us to arbitrarily vary the clock frequency, pause the execution, read the internal state of the processor, and reset the processor to a known state. Subsequently, a wide range of test vectors are applied to the chip that are often generated by automatic test pattern generation software. In this phase we use scan chains. A *scan chain* is simply a serial bus that is connected to most of the flip-flops in the chip. It is possible to set their values by sending bits along the scan chain. Furthermore, after setting the initial state of the flip-flops, we can run the chip with representative inputs, and again use the scan chain mechanism to read the state of all the connected flip-flops. We can thus verify if the internal state is correct or not. If there is a discrepancy, this mechanism will accurately tell us which flip-flop's state is erroneous. Another test that is performed in this stage is known as Iddq testing. Here, we verify that in the quiescent state (no switching activity) the supply current (Idd) that is drawn is roughly equal to the total estimated leakage current. If this is not the case, then it means that there is a short circuit from the supply to the ground.

The next phase of validation is called characterisation. In this phase, the chip is run at different voltages and frequencies (known as *shmooing*), and a plot is generated for the voltage-frequency pairs at which the chip executes correctly. This is used to characterise the chip and set its operating frequency and voltage along with its DVFS settings. For example, it is possible that different chips produced in the same fabrication facility run at different frequencies because of minute variations in the fabrication environment. This process of setting the voltage and frequency is also known as *binning*.

Till now all the tests have been *structural*; they basically tested if the circuit was fabricated correctly or not. However, we can also have *functional testing*, where we test if the behaviour is as per existing specifications. Regardless of whether the internal state is correct or not, the outputs that are visible to external observers should be correct. Here, the idea is to first set the state of the chip to a deterministic state and then apply test vectors that are possibly associated with long executions. The final output should be correct, only then is the chip deemed to be executing correctly, and is ready to be shipped. After this discussion, the reader should be able to appreciate why it is so important to remove nondeterministic effects.

Sadly, in spite of so much of verification and validation, design faults still slip into products that are in the market. Hence, almost all processor vendors release extensive errata sheets, where they document the nature of the defects, the factors that trigger them, and possible workarounds.

12.4.2   Nature of Design Faults

Types of Faults

To understand the nature of design faults, let us look at a few and try to appreciate the broad patterns. Table 12.1 lists a few design faults taken from publicly released errata sheets.

	Processor	Defect
Fault 1	IBM G3	If the L1 cache suffers a miss, at the same time the processor is flushing the L2 cache, and power management is turned on, then some L2 lines may get corrupted.
Fault 2	Pentium 4	If the following conditions are simultaneously true – there is a cache hit on a line in the M state, a snoop access is going on, there are pending requests to reinitialise the bus – then this can lead to a deadlock.
Fault 3	AMD Athlon 64	If within a window of 4 instructions we have two adjust-after-multiply (AAM) instructions or within a window of 7 instructions we have a DIV instruction and a following AAM instruction, the ALU might produce incorrect results.

Table 12.1: Three design faults [Sarangi et al., 2006b]

Sarangi et al. divide such design faults into three classes: non-critical, critical-complex, and critical-concurrent.

Non-critical Such faults do not affect the correctness of the program. Faults in the performance counters, and debug registers fall in this category.

Critical-concurrent Look at Fault 1 and Fault 2 in Table 12.1. They are fundamentally different from Fault 3 in the sense that all the events need to happen concurrently. For example, for Fault 1, at the very same time we need the L1 cache to be processing a miss, the L2 cache should be in the process of flushing itself, and power management should be turned on. Hence, these are concurrent faults because multiple conditions are active at the same time. In other words, these are simple Boolean combinations of signals, where a *signal* is defined as a micro-architectural event such as an L1 cache miss or the fact that power management is enabled. We typically think of a signal as a Boolean event, hence, we shall make the same assumption here.

Critical-complex Fault 3 is an example of such a fault. Here, we have a dependence in terms of time. The relationship is not purely combinational, there is a temporal dependence. For example, we say that event A needs to happen within n cycles of event B. Such defects are difficult to detect and debug.

We can alternatively classify the defects based on their root cause as proposed by Constantinides et al. [Constantinides et al., 2008].

Logic design faults These faults are caused because of errors in the RTL code, which lead to erroneous logic.

Algorithmic faults Here, the faults are deeper. It means that there are major algorithm (design level) deviations from the specifications. The fixes are not limited to fixing the output of a logic gate, or changing a value from a logical 0 to 1. The workarounds typically involve major modifications to the circuit.

Timing faults In this case the timing paths are not analysed properly. It is possible that signals either do not reach the latches at the right time, or are sometimes latched too early. We need to either reduce the frequency, make modifications to the circuit to add extra flip-flops or fix the signal latching logic.

Note that the two types of classifications are orthogonal. It is possible that performance counters have timing faults, and critical-complex faults have logic design faults. Whenever, we detect the conditions that might lead to an error we also need to consider if the error has already manifested or not. In many cases, we can stop the error in its tracks before the value propagates to the memory or the register file. In some cases, the error might be restricted to the pipeline, and in this case we simply need to flush the pipeline. However, if the error has propagated to the memory system or the I/O ports, then there is a need to invoke higher level checkpointing mechanisms, or simply let the OS know that there is a need to restart the system.

Type of Workarounds

Once a processor is released with such design faults, they remain with it forever. One option for the vendor is to recall all the processors and then provide the customers with fault-free versions of the processors. This is a very expensive exercise as we have seen in the case of the Intel Pentium bug. As a result, it is a much better idea to anticipate that we will have design faults, and to create circuits within the processor that can be activated to provide fixes and workarounds to these faults as and when they are detected. This implies that even after the processor is released, the vendor continues to verify and validate the design. If any fault is detected there is a need to characterise it, and find the cheapest possible workaround. Often, the faults can be fixed in software. For example, it is possible to instruct the compiler and operating system writers to ensure that certain conditions are avoided.

Let's say that a certain bug is triggered if prefetching is enabled while the power management module is computing the next DVFS configuration, then the operating system can be instructed to not let this happen. It can simply turn off prefetching while computing the next DVFS configuration.

Similarly, in the case of Fault 3, the compiler can just ensure that such instruction sequences are not there in any program. However, note that this is only possible for programs that are compiled after this particular defect has been characterised. To ensure that released codes work correctly on processors with this defect, it is necessary for the vendor to issue periodic patches that change the parts of the binary that have such error-prone instruction sequences. In general, handling design faults in software (OS or compiler) is easy, particularly if the resultant performance loss is limited.

However, in many cases such as Fault 1 and 2, it is not possible to provide fixes in software. There is a need to make changes to the hardware itself. After the processors have been released the hardware cannot be changed. However, if it is possible to at least detect that the conditions for an error are about to get enabled, we can then try to turn one of the conditions off. Note that this is far more efficient than permanently turning off one of the conditions such as permanently turning off power management or prefetching; in this case the conditions are only turned off for a very short duration of time. Hence, the net impact on the performance loss is minimal.

Even though such approaches look promising, they are bedevilled by the fact that we at least need to add the circuitry to collect all the signals (events of interest) from the chip at design time. This means that the designer needs to anticipate, which part of the chip will suffer from more faults, and then she needs to tap the signals. Examples of such signals are an L1 cache miss, ALU add operation, receiving a snoop message from the bus, etc. Once the signals are available, then it is possible to configure programmable logic arrays that can compute Boolean functions over the signals and give an indication if certain errors are going to happen or not in the near future. If there is a chance of an error, then it is possible to turn off one of the enabling conditions, and then turn it back on after some time. This is essentially a mechanism to provide a *hardware patch*, where even after the processor is released, we can ensure that the triggering event-combinations of certain hardware faults do not occur.

Even though this idea [Sarangi et al., 2006b, Constantinides et al., 2008] is promising; however, it is dependent on the signals that are tapped and furthermore this approach is the most useful for critical-concurrent bugs. To detect conditions that have a temporal relationship between them is hard. Another way of looking at this is that this mechanism can be thought of as a sophisticated scan chain where instead of reading a large number of flip-flops via a serial bus, we focus our attention to a small number of Boolean events known as signals. If there is a high likelihood of a fault happening in the areas where the signals are tapped, then we can detect the combination of signals before an error actually manifests. For example, many studies have shown that the power management and cache coherence subsystems typically have a lot of bugs given their complexity. Hence, we can tap more signals from these units.

However, as of 2020 this is primarily a research idea mainly because we have thousands of potential signals on the chip, effectively tapping them and computing Boolean combinations on them is prohibitively expensive. However, interventions are now made at the level of the microcode array and the firmware. Recall that in a CISC instruction set, complex instructions are translated into a sequence of microcodes, and these translations are stored in a microcode array. By changing these translations it is possible to avoid the conditions that activate a design fault.

12.4.3   Using Signals for Debugging and Post-Silicon Validation

The notion of tapping signals can also be used for post-silicon validation and subsequent debugging. The basic insights are the same, which is that we need to create an intelligent version of scan chains where we can tap more signals in regions of the chip that are difficult to verify, and it is expected that they would be involved in a disproportionate number of design faults. For many such situations using traditional scan chains is difficult because we wish to do at-speed debug – run the CPU at native speeds without stalling in the middle. This means that we cannot stall the processor while reading out the scan chain. To run the processor at its native speed, designers insert design-for-debug (DfD) hardware units throughout the chip. These are a network of buffers called *trace buffers*, which are circular buffers that store the values of specific signals and any associated data. If an error is detected, the contents of the trace buffers can be inspected to figure out the set of conditions that led to the error. This is a reverse problem as compared to detecting errors early. In this case we wish to find the conditions that led to a certain error as a part of post-silicon validation.

Here, the most important issue is that the trace buffers have a limited size and they very soon start to overflow. Hence, there are proposals to only log a subset of signals [Xu and Liu, 2010, Ma et al., 2015] – those that are deemed to be important. We can additionally have runtime techniques where we dynamically filter [Neishaburi and Zilic, 2011] the information that is collected and discard information that is not relevant. Another approach is to compress [Anis and Nicolici, 2007] this information using traditional compression techniques.

Out of this family of approaches, the most popular set of techniques try to filter the information and only store the values of relevant signals in the trace buffers. This process is known as *summarisation*. We can either have *spatial summarisation*, where a single trace is filtered, or we can have *temporal summarisation* where we jointly filter all the traces that have roughly been collected at the same point in time. Note that for both these types of summarisation, it is necessary for the validation engineer to indicate the nature of filtering that is desired. The debug hardware has dedicated circuits to filter out this information. For example, for spatial summarisation the debug engineer can specify the set of signals that she is interested in. She can also specify the regions of activity that may be of interest. Such regions typically begin with a known signal pattern, and have a similar signature when they end. The DfD hardware can track such regions by monitoring the signals.

In the case of temporal summarisation, the approaches for spatial summarisation still work. In addition, it is possible to also filter out a lot of events if the processor reaches a given state. For example, let us say that the processor goes to sleep, and this is the expected behaviour. Then we can flush all the events in the trace buffers that led to this action. On similar lines, we can define other properties and the trace events that help ensure them. If the property is verified we can delete the corresponding trace events from all the trace buffers.

12.5 Faults due to Parameter Variation

12.5.1 Introduction to Different types of Parameter Variation

Process Variation

Before reading this section it is advisable that the reader gets a very broad idea of the VLSI fabrication process, particularly photolithography. The reader can consult [Glendinning and Helbert, 2012].

In the VLSI fabrication process we create structures on silicon such as wires and transistors. To start with, we coat the silicon wafer (thin circular slice of silicon 200-300 mm in diameter) with a photoresist, which is a light-sensitive material, and then illuminate the photoresist with a *pattern* by placing a photomask in front of a light source. When the photoresist is exposed to light, the parts of it that are exposed change their chemical structure. Subsequently, a solvent is applied to remove those areas that were not exposed to light (the reverse is also possible). This process is known as *etching*. We can then spray dopants (p-type or n-type) that permeate into the exposed regions, and thus we can create doped regions in the silicon substrate. This process can be used to fabricate billions of transistors. Moreover, we need to repeat this process several times for creating a multilayered VLSI chip.

For creating the metal layers, a similar technique can be applied where we deposit metallic vapours into the areas that were not exposed. We can also deposit insulating materials such as silicon dioxide between the layers and etch vias (vertical metallic connections) through it for creating connections across layers.

We need to understand that we are trying to create very small (nanometre level) features on silicon. The dimensions of a transistor as of 2020 are in the range of 10 to 20 nm, whereas the light that is used to etch patterns has a wavelength of 193 nm. This is like trying to make a fine engraving with a very blunt knife. It is obvious that we will not be completely successful and the patterns that will actually be created on silicon will be non-ideal. Additionally, because of the particle nature of light the number of photons that strike different regions of the die will not be uniform, and there will be fluctuations in the dopant density. All of these effects will cumulatively introduce a degree of variation into the transistors' geometrical characteristics. We can have inter-die variation (die-to-die or D2D variation) and within-die (WID) variation. D2D variation happens because of a slight variation in the process parameters across dies. However, we are typically more concerned about WID variation, which can further be classified into two types: systematic variation and random variation. The former is more predictable, and has a degree of spatial correlation, whereas the latter type of variation is of a random nature even at the level of neighbouring transistors.

Regardless of the source of process variation, the end result is that the physical and electrical properties of transistors and wires vary across the chip. Most notably, the threshold voltages of transistors change. If the threshold voltage reduces, the transistors become faster and more leaky, and vice versa. We thus have problems of increased leakage power dissipation in some regions of the die and an increased susceptibility to timing faults in other regions because of slow transistors.

Systematic Variation

There are two reasons for systematic variation: CMP (chemical mechanical polishing), and photolithographic effects.

The surface of the wafer has structures with different mechanical properties such as silicon dioxide layers that are hard and the silicon substrate that is soft. As a result, the topography – thickness of the copper and silicon dioxide structures – of a given region of the wafer is dependent on the relative ratio of the amount of silicon dioxide and copper. This amounts to a degree of variation in the geometry and thickness of the devices across a fabricated chip. It is possible to predict the nature of this variation to a large extent, however the mathematical models and the resultant computation is very complex. To reduce this type of variation, designers typically fill up unused regions of the die with metallic fills, such that the regions become more uniform. Subsequently, it is necessary to polish the surface of the wafer using a rotating pad and a mix of chemicals to even out the surface. This is known as chemical mechanical polishing, abbreviated as CMP. This process does not eliminate the degree of variation in transistors' dimensions completely. The residual variation is nonetheless predictable to some extent.

The second reason for systematic variation is because of the relatively high wavelength of light as compared to the size of the fabricated feature. The size of the smallest feature that we can fabricate with adequate quality guarantees is known as the *resolution*. By the Rayleigh criterion, the resolution is proportional to λ/NA, where λ is the wavelength of light, and NA is the numerical aperture. Sadly, despite intensive efforts we have not been able to reduce the wavelength of light beyond 193 nm. Because of this, the features that are fabricated are inaccurate (see Figure 12.7(a)). For example, we observe the rounded corners of shapes that should have been perfectly rectangular. Efforts to reduce the wavelength of light such as extreme ultraviolet (EUV) lithography using light with a wavelength of 13.5 nm have not proven to be successful yet. Because of this limitation, we suffer from effects that are a consequence of the wave nature of light such as diffraction. The photomask essentially contains millions of tiny slits, and light propagating through these slits has a high degree of diffraction, which makes it hard to print sharp features on silicon. This problem is by far more serious than CMP based variation.

Random Variation

We have had an issue with the wave nature of light; we unfortunately also have an issue with the particle nature of light! When we are trying to fabricate a straight line on silicon we want the photon flux to be uniform on the silicon surface. At the nanometre level, there is a certain uncertainty with regards to whether a photon will strike a given region or not in a given window of time. Because of this it is possible that there will be a certain degree of non-uniformity in the photon flux, and thus the corresponding areas of the photoresist where we want to fabricate a straight line will also have a varying degree of exposure. Additionally, during the process of etching it is possible that because of non-uniform acid diffusion, the photoresist is not removed uniformly. Both of these effects lead to *rough lines* as shown in Figure 12.7(b).

There are other problems as well. Current feature sizes are close to 10 nm. They are expected to go down to 5 nm or maybe even 3 nm over the next few years. Since the size of a silicon atom is roughly 0.22 nm, the number of atoms that will be used to build a transistor will be in the tens and not in the thousands or millions. Placing atoms so accurately is very hard and a few errors are bound to happen. When transistors were large (of the order of microns), these errors had no significance. However, for nanometre scale transistors, they can affect the dimensions of the transistors by as much as 10 to 20%, which can lead to large deviations in the electrical parameters. Unfortunately, we do not have a very accurate way of placing atoms. For example, we have fluctuations in the dopant density and thus a varying number of dopant atoms diffuse through the silicon. This causes random variations even at the

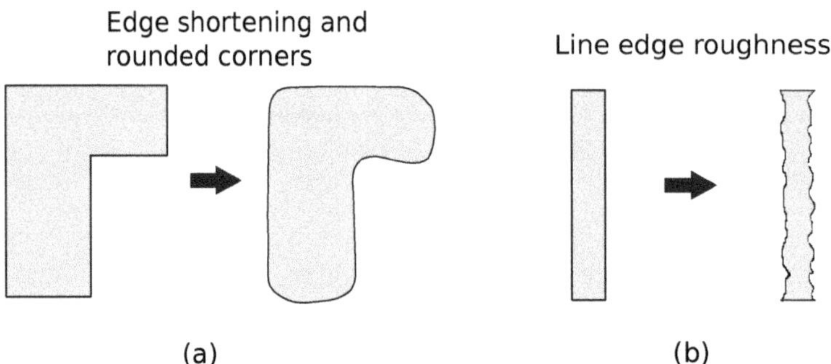

Figure 12.7: (a) Edge shortening and corner rounding and (b) Line edge roughness

level of neighbouring transistors. We see a similar effect also in the case of the thickness of the gate oxide, which is of the order of several nanometres. Both of these effects are modelled as random processes.

Voltage and Temperature Variation

Process variation is not the only reason for the electrical characteristics of transistors to change. They can change because of other reasons as well. Two of the notable reasons are variations in the operating temperature and the supply voltage. As we have studied in Chapter 11, the temperature of the chip can vary depending on several factors such as the dynamic power and the ambient temperature. Because of temperature variability, the speed and leakage power can also change. This will lead to the same kind of problems as process variation such as high leakage power and timing faults.

Along with temperature variations, because of the fact that the current requirements change very rapidly we can have voltage variations on the chip as we studied in Section 12.2. Changes in the supply voltage can affect the speed of transistors. For example, an increase in the supply voltage makes transistors faster and vice versa. All these sources of variation inclusive of process variation comprise *parameter variation*.

12.5.2   A Mathematical Model of Parameter Variation

We shall describe the Varius [Sarangi et al., 2008] model in this section.

Model for the Gate Delay

The switching time of a gate, T_g, is given by the following equation known as the Alpha power law.

$$T_g \propto \frac{L_{eff}V}{\mu(V - V_{th})^\alpha} \tag{12.6}$$

Here, L_{eff} is the effective channel length, V is the supply voltage, V_{th} is the threshold voltage, α is roughly 1.3 (between 1.1 and 1.5 in general), and μ is the mobility of carriers. In this equation process variation affects V_{th} and L_{eff}. It is also obvious to see the effect of the variation of the supply voltage; however, the effect of the variation in temperature applies indirectly. The mobility is typically a function of temperature. In silicon $\mu(T) \propto T^{-1.5}$, which means that with an increase in temperature the mobility decreases and the gate delay increases. Additionally, the threshold voltage, V_{th}, also reduces with increasing temperature (typically at the rate of 2.5mV/°C). We can thus see that with increasing temperature, V_{th} reduces, $V - V_{th}$ increases, and the gate delay reduces. In general, the first factor (mobility) dominates, and thus with increasing temperature the gate delay increases.

Components of Process Variation

We can divide the components of process variation into three parts: die to die, intra-die systematic and intra-die random variation. They are modelled as additive components. Let ΔP denote the deviation in a given parameter such as the threshold voltage due to process variation. Then we have,

$$\Delta P = \Delta P_{D2D} + \Delta P_{WID} = \Delta P_{D2D} + \Delta P_{rand} + \Delta P_{sys} \tag{12.7}$$

The first component is a constant additive component for a given die; hence, most of the modelling effort is focused on the intra-die systematic and random variation. They are modelled as normal distributions.

Systematic Variation

To model systematic variation, we divide the entire chip into a two-dimensional grid. Each point has an x-coordinate and a y-coordinate. Furthermore, we assume that the following parameters have a systematic variation component: the threshold voltage (V_{th}) and the effective channel length (L_{eff}). For the case of systematic variation we assume that V_{th} and L_{eff} are linearly related. The Varius model further assumes that the relative variation in L_{eff} is half of the variation in V_{th}. However, this is a technology dependent effect and might change in future technologies. Given that the systematic variation in these quantities is linearly related we can first compute a systematic variation map that stores the deviation with respect to the mean for each grid cell. Let the mean threshold voltage be V_{th0} and the computed deviation for a grid cell be d. The threshold voltage at the grid cell is given by

$$V_{th} = V_{th0} + d \times V_{th0} \tag{12.8}$$

We typically model the dimensionless quantity d using a two-dimensional multi-variate normal distribution. The formula for such a normal distribution is as follows. Let us consider a k-element vector $\mathbf{X}$ that contains the values of the deviation for each grid cell.

Its probability density function is given by the following equation:

$$pdf(\mathbf{X}) = \frac{1}{\sqrt{(2\pi)^k \mid \boldsymbol{\Sigma} \mid}} exp\left(-\frac{1}{2}(\mathbf{X} - \boldsymbol{\mu})^T \boldsymbol{\Sigma}^{-1}(\mathbf{X} - \boldsymbol{\mu})\right) \tag{12.9}$$

Here, $\boldsymbol{\mu}$ is a vector that contains the mean value for each grid cell. We can assume that all its elements have a value equal to 0. The covariance matrix $\boldsymbol{\Sigma}$ is of special interest to us because it represents the covariance of the deviations across two grid cells. The systematic variation is dependent on its structure. Lastly, the symbol $\mid \boldsymbol{\Sigma} \mid$ refers to the determinant of the $\boldsymbol{\Sigma}$ matrix.

We make two simplifying assumptions. The first is that the covariance is isotropic (does not depend upon the direction), and second assumption is that it only depends on the Euclidean distance between the grid cells. With these assumptions, we can simplify the modelling as follows. We first note that the covariance is related to the correlation as follows for two random variables U and V.

$$\boldsymbol{\rho}(U, V) = \frac{\boldsymbol{\Sigma}(U, V)}{\sigma_U \sigma_V} \tag{12.10}$$

Here $\boldsymbol{\rho}$ is the correlation matrix, $\boldsymbol{\Sigma}$ is the covariance matrix, σ_U is the standard deviation of random variable U, and σ_V is the standard deviation of random variable V. Let U and V represent the deviations at grid cells u and v respectively. If we assume that the standard deviations are the same (equal to σ), which is normally the case, then we have the following formula.

$$\boldsymbol{\Sigma}(U, V) = \sigma^2 \boldsymbol{\rho}(U, V) \tag{12.11}$$

σ^2 is the variance, which is assumed to be a constant. It is a measure of the systematic variation and will be denoted henceforth as σ_{sys}. The other important takeaway from this equation is that the correlation matrix and the covariance matrix are related by a factor σ_{sys}^2. It is often easier to compute the correlation matrix, and then use it to compute the covariance matrix.

Many experimental studies have indicated that the correlation matrix has a spherical structure, which means that if the Euclidean distance between two grid cells is r, then their correlation is given by Equation 12.12. Here we consider a function ρ, which yields the correlation between the deviations at two grid cells separated by a distance r. We normalise the distance to the chip's width, which is assumed to be 1.

$$\rho(r) = \begin{cases} r < \phi & 1 - \frac{3r}{2\phi} + \frac{r^3}{2\phi^3} \\ r \geq \phi & 0 \end{cases} \tag{12.12}$$

ϕ is a constant and can be anywhere from 0.1 to 0.5 (assumptions in the Varius model). This means that the correlation is 1 at the grid cell, decreases linearly when r is small, then it decreases sublinearly, and finally becomes 0 (uncorrelated) when $r \geq \phi$. We can consider many different such correlation functions to model different kinds of processes. Statistical packages can be used to generate samples from such a multivariate distribution. Each such sample is a variation map.

Random Variation

Random variation in comparison to systematic variation occurs at a far smaller scale – at the level of individual transistors. Furthermore, the variations in V_{th} and L_{eff} are not linearly related any more. They are modelled as independent quantities.

We typically model both these quantities as univariate normal distributions. The formula for a regular univariate normal distribution is comparatively much simpler.

$$pdf(x) = \frac{1}{\sigma\sqrt{2\pi}} exp\left(\frac{-(x-\mu)^2}{2\sigma_{rand}^2}\right) \tag{12.13}$$

Here, σ_{rand} is the standard deviation for the randomly varying component.

Putting it all Together

We can use the standard formula for adding the variance of two normal distributions.

$$\sigma_{total} = \sqrt{\sigma_{rand}^2 + \sigma_{sys}^2} \tag{12.14}$$

This will give the net variance for any quantity of interest (V_{th} or L_{eff}). For different values of σ_{total}/μ (standard deviation/mean) we can generate different kinds of variation maps. Most researchers as of 2020 perform simulations assuming $\sigma_{total}/\mu = 0.09$, and $\sigma_{sys} = \sigma_{rand}$.

Given a logic circuit we can create a timing model for it by considering the effects of both random and systematic variation. If the circuit is small we can consider the systematic component to be a constant, and then we can add the delays of each wire and gate on the critical path of the circuit to compute its delay, which in this case will not be a single value because of random variation – it will be a probability distribution instead.

To start with, we model the delay of each gate as a normal distribution. This makes computing the delay of the critical path of the circuit easy because the sum of normally distributed variables also follows a normal distribution. We thus have a distribution for the time taken by a circuit. However, if there are multiple critical paths, then the analysis is more complicated because the time that the circuit will take to compute its result is the time taken by the slowest critical path. Given that the delay in this case is actually a distribution we a priori do not know which critical path will turn out to be the slowest. We thus need to compute the maximum of several normally distributed variables. Even though the delay of each path can be modelled as a normal distribution, the maximum of several normally distributed variables is not normally distributed. It follows the Gumbel distribution. Furthermore, if the circuit is large and different parts of the circuit have different systematic components, then this effect also needs to be factored. After considering all of these effects we typically arrive at the distribution of the delay of the circuit.

Comparatively, it is far easier to compute the statistical distribution of the delay of an SRAM array. It has a regular structure. Similar to the Cacti model (introduced in Chapter 7), we can break down the components of the total delay, model each one separately, and then add them up to compute the final distribution of the delay of the memory array.

Let us now describe how this model can be used to mitigate the effects of parameter variation.

12.5.3 Methods to Mitigate Parameter Variation at the Architectural Level

Random Variation

We use the inputs of the variation model to compute the distribution of the delay of a circuit (either logic or memory). This is known as statistical static timing analysis (SSTA). Once this is done, we need to place an upper bound on the maximum expected delay of the circuit in a real setting. This means that we need to be conservative and ensure that we give sufficient time to the circuit to compute its result under all kinds of runtime conditions. Hence, while designing the chip we need to ensure that the delays of each unit (in terms of clock cycles) are calculated correctly and account for the worst case.

Systematic and Die-to-Die Variation

Techniques at the Lithographic Level
There are a host of techniques to reduce the amount of process variation because of photolithographic effects. Please refer to Figure 12.8.

Optical Proximity Correction(OPC) The key idea here is that we pre-distort the shape on the photomask such that the shape that is actually printed on silicon resembles the desired output. In Figure 12.8 we show an example where we actually try to print a distorted structure; however, because of the wave nature of light we get the desired rectangle on silicon. Figuring out these OPC features is a very computationally intensive process.

Off-Axis Illumination Here light from the source is incident on the photomask at an oblique angle (it is not perpendicular). Higher diffraction orders strike the surface of the silicon, and thus in layman's terms the pattern on silicon receives more light.

Sub-resolution Assist Features (SRAFs) These are very small structures that we place beside isolated lines on the photomask. Since they are smaller than the resolution limit, they themselves do not get printed on silicon, however the light passing through them forms an interference pattern with the light passing through the main structure and can thus enhance the accuracy of the printing process.

Phase Shift Masking (PSM) It is possible that the light passing through two adjacent lines can constructively interfere and also print a pattern in the intervening space. To avoid this we shift the phase (often by 90°) of the light passing through adjacent structures such that they destructively interfere in the intervening space and do not form any patterns there. To shift the phase we increase the optical path length by changing the transmission properties of adjacent regions in the mask.

Architectural Solutions
Both systematic as well as die-to-die variation affect the chip at the macroscopic level. This also means that different chips fabricated using the same technology will have different speeds. This is taken care

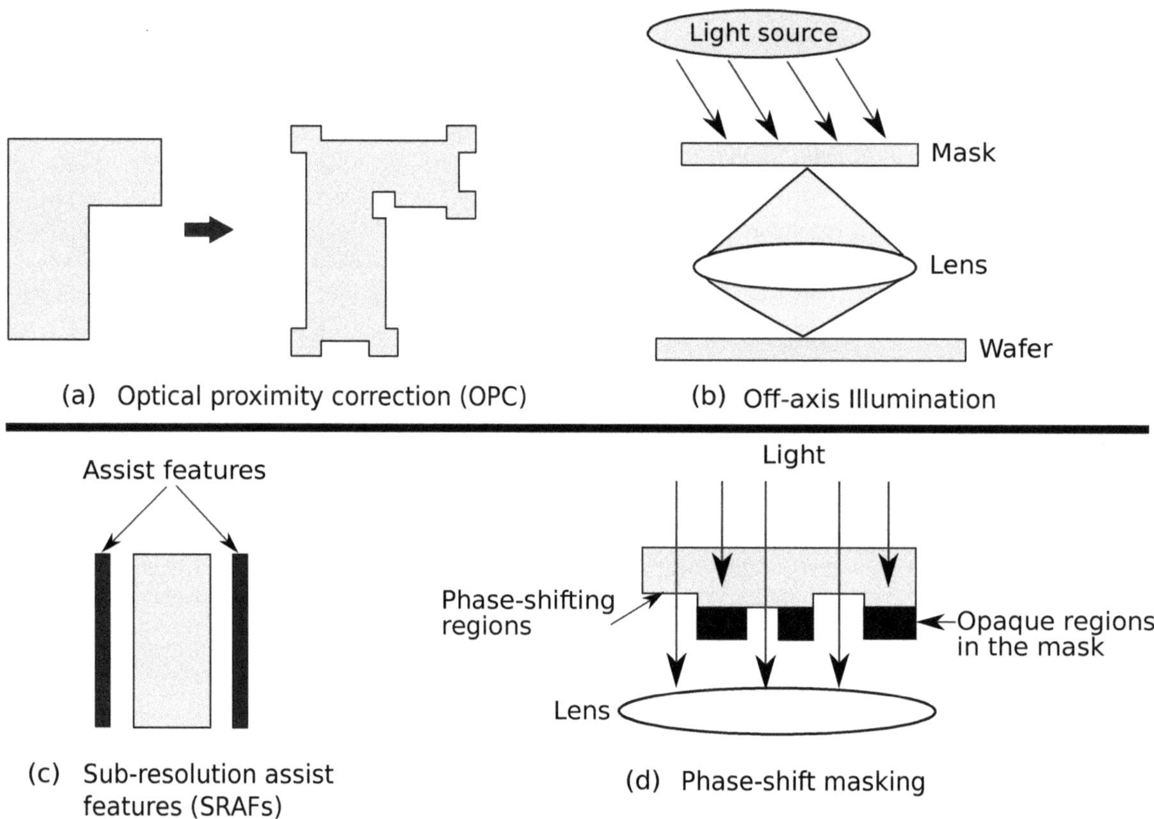

Figure 12.8: Different types of mechanisms to correct variations due to photolithographic effects

of during post-fabrication testing where the operating frequency of the chip is determined. As discussed in Section 12.4.1 this process is known as frequency binning. We need to ensure that the chip safely operates at a given frequency regardless of the ambient parameters such as the temperature or the supply voltage (as long as they stay within certain predefined limits). It is further possible to leverage systematic variation by assigning different frequencies to different cores. For example, it is possible that a given region of the chip is faster than other regions. Cores located in the faster regions can have a higher frequency as compared to cores located in the slower regions. However, this is easier said than done because cores in the high frequency regions may also need a higher supply voltage, and furthermore it is hard to synchronise data between cores from the different frequency regions. Finally, with different such voltage-frequency islands within the chip, verification and validation become far more challenging.

12.6   Hard Errors and Ageing

Similar to human beings, processors also *age* and finally end up developing permanent faults. Such faults lead to *hard errors*, which means that the circuit suffers from some permanent damage. The damage is not limited to the transistors alone, it is possible that some of the wires get snapped or some of the I/O connectors develop a very large resistance. This happens gradually over time (*ageing*) and ultimately renders the processor non-functional. In this section we shall understand the basic physics underlying the development of hard faults, and the ageing processes. Then we shall provide a brief overview of the techniques used to slow down the ageing processes and still keep the processor running in the presence of hard errors.

12.6.1   Ageing

Negative Bias Temperature Instability (NBTI)

Hydrogen is extensively used in the semiconductor fabrication process. It is not known to react significantly with silicon or change its characteristics, hence it is preferred. However, the effects of hydrogen can be very important at the boundary of the channel and the gate. Recall that the channel is made of silicon with some dopants (depending upon the type of the transistor), and the gate is made of silicon dioxide (SiO_2). Given that silicon has four valence electrons, in the crystalline state it is bonded with four other silicon atoms. However, atoms at the surface have a few dangling bonds, and this is where $Si - H$ bonds form. This is as such a stable state and does not pose any threat to the operation of the transistor.

However, this can induce an ageing effect in PMOS transistors [Mahapatra and Parihar, 2018a, Rashkeev et al., 2002]. The mechanism is as follows. When the transistor is enabled, the gate-to-source voltage is negative. This causes some of the hydrogen atoms to get dislodged and H^+ ions (basically protons) start moving towards the gate. It is however hard to cross the Si-SiO_2 barrier. Hence, they start getting accumulated at the interface. Subsequently, the protons interact with the Si-H bonds, remove the hydrogen nucleus and form a stable hydrogen molecule H_2. This leaves a positive charge at the silicon atoms. Because of a combination of such effects, we have an accumulation of positive charge at the Si-SiO_2 interface. Now, it is possible to have Si-H bonds within the dielectric (SiO_2 layer) that can be filled with holes coming from the channel. This process creates positive charges within the dielectric.

Because of a combination of these effects, the effective threshold voltage rises and thus the transistor degrades. This is known as the *stress phase*. However, the good news is that once the transistor is turned off or disconnected from the power lines, a large part of this effect can be reversed. This is known as the *recovery phase*. However, the reversal is not complete and there is a long-term degradation primarily because H^+ ions get *trapped* at the interface. Many of these traps go away in the recovery phase, however the degradation in terms of an increase in the threshold voltage continues to get worse over time. Traditionally the change in the threshold voltage has been assumed to be proportional to $t_{stress}^{0.25}$, where t_{stress} is the time that the PMOS transistor is under stress (negative gate-to-source voltage) [Tiwari and Torrellas, 2008]. The recovery (in terms of the threshold voltage) is proportional to $(1 - \sqrt{\eta \times t_{rec}/(t_{rec} + t_{stress})})$ where t_{rec} is the time under recovery and η is a constant (assumed to be 0.35 in [Tiwari and Torrellas, 2008]).

Please bear in mind that many of these models are approximate and empirical; they tend to change with changes in technology. In general, we can assume that most of the degradation happens early on, and the degradation rate subsequently slows down (modelled as a power-law relationship). Such effects are particularly important for analog circuits where we need to match the electrical characteristics of neighbouring transistors. If the characteristics change then the quality of the output may also change.

Hot Carrier Injection(HCI)

Recall that hot carrier injection is a form of leakage current (Section 11.1.2) where carriers gain sufficient kinetic energy such that they can overcome the potential difference at the channel-gate boundary. This happens with electrons when they gain sufficient kinetic energy because of a positive potential at the gate. They tunnel through the channel-gate boundary and get permanently lodged or trapped in the SiO_2 layer within the gate. This increases the threshold voltage in NMOS transistors. Additionally, charged electrons can also collide with Si-H bonds and change the chemical structure of the Si-SiO_2 interface. This also leads to a change in the transistor's parameters. The rate of degradation (measured as the change in the threshold voltage) is for obvious reasons proportional to the activity factor and the frequency. However, the most important point to note in existing models is that $\Delta V_{th} \propto t^{0.5}$ (t is the time). Unlike NBTI, the recovery is very little, and changes mostly accumulate over time.

12.6.2 Hard Errors

We shall heavily refer to the RAMP reliability model [Srinivasan et al., 2004, Srinivasan et al., 2005] in this section.

Electromigration

In copper and aluminium based interconnects that carry DC current within a chip electrons flow from one direction to the other. Gradually over time because of this mass transport, some of the momentum gets transferred to the metal atoms and a few of them also start moving along with electrons. This is as such a very slow process but after years of use a wire will appear to thin at the source of electrons and fatten up at the destination. This increases the resistance of the wire at one end gradually over time; the wire can ultimately get snapped and develop a permanent fault. Additionally, atoms can also drift towards nearby conductors causing short circuits (known as *extrusions*). Such failures lead to erroneous internal states that are aptly referred to as hard errors.

This mechanism is known as electromigration. The mean time to failure is given by the following equation, which is known as the Black's equation [Black, 1969].

$$MTTF_{em} \propto (J - J_{crit})^{-n} e^{\frac{E_{aEM}}{kT}} \qquad (12.15)$$

J is the current density, J_{crit} is a constant for a given wire and is known as the critical current density, E_{aEM} is the activation energy needed for electromigration, k is the Boltzmann's constant, and T is the absolute temperature in Kelvin. n and E_{aEM} are assumed to be 1.1 and 0.9 respectively for copper interconnects in the RAMP model.

The important point to note is the relationship with temperature. As the temperature increases the mean time to failure reduces. The relationship with the reciprocal of the absolute temperature is exponential.

Stress Migration

Another failure mechanism in interconnects is *stress migration*. First note that in a modern interconnect its contacts are made of different materials, and they have different thermal expansion rates. Because of this some stresses tend to accumulate in the body of the interconnect, and this causes a migration of metal atoms. The subsequent ageing and failure mechanism is similar to electromigration. Its MTTF is given by the following equation.

$$MTTF_{sm} \propto | T_0 - T |^{-n} e^{\frac{E_{aSM}}{kT}} \qquad (12.16)$$

Here, T_0 is a very high baseline temperature (typically 500 K), n and E_{aSM} are constants (2.5 and 0.9, respectively, for copper interconnects in the RAMP model), and the connotation of k and T is the same as that for the equation for electromigration. As the temperature increases, $| T_0 - T |^{-n}$ increases. However, there is a reverse effect where $e^{\frac{E_{aEM}}{kT}}$ decreases. The latter compensates for the former, and thus the overall MTTF reduces. Here also note the dependence with temperature.

Time-dependent Dielectric Breakdown

As the dielectric layer gets thinner because of miniaturisation, the tunnelling current through it has an increasing impact. It ultimately changes its chemical structure till it ultimately fails and forms a conductive path. The MTTF is inversely proportional to the voltage, V, and a complex function of the temperature, T.

$$MTTF_{tddb} \propto \frac{1}{V}^{a-bT} e^{\frac{X + \frac{Y}{T} + ZT}{kT}} \qquad (12.17)$$

The RAMP model uses the following values for the constants: $a = 78$, $b = -0.081$, $X = 0.759\,eV$, $Y = -66.8\,eVK$, $Z = -8.37 \times 10^{-4}\,eV/K$ (eV stands for electron volts).

Thermal Cycling

The chip goes through many thermal cycles. Some of these represent major events such as powering up or powering down the processor (low frequency cycles), and many of these represent minor events that correspond to variations in the temperature because of the variation in the dynamic power consumption (high frequency cycles). The low frequency cycles have a greater effect on the solder joints in the packaging. They alternately expand and contract; this constant thermal cycling causes metal fatigue and the joints fail over time. The resulting MTTF is given by the Coffin-Manson equation [Coffin Jr, 1954, Manson, 1953].

$$MTTF_{tc} \propto \left(\frac{1}{T - T_{ambient}} \right)^q \tag{12.18}$$

T is the average temperature of the packaging, $T_{ambient}$ is the ambient temperature, and q is a material dependent parameter (assumed to be 2.35). Again note the polynomial dependence with temperature.

12.6.3 Failure Rate of the Entire System

Estimating the failure rate of the entire system is difficult because we need to understand how the failures are distributed over time. In general, we assume that the processor is a series-failure system, which means that if one component fails the entire processor is deemed to have failed. There are several models that have been considered for representing failure rates across time. There are studies that have used the exponentially distributed failure rate model or the log-normal failure rate model. This is a complex function of the technology and the usage pattern.

One reason why the academic community has particularly not been very interested in modelling hard errors over time is because most failures in an electronic system follow a bath-tub curve as shown in Figure 12.9. This curve has three components. At the outset, the failure rate is high because processors have many manufacturing defects whose effects are further exacerbated during the burn-in phase (see Section 12.4.1). Once these defects are detected, the processors are discarded. This explains the elevated failure rates in the first phase of the processors' operation, which is basically post-silicon validation. Subsequently, once the processors are released to the market (second phase) they have a period of relatively stable operation. During this time hard errors are not particularly concerning because in most cases processors become obsolete before they actually start developing permanent faults. Towards the end (third phase) of the lifetime of a processor – typically 7 to 10 years after it is first put to use – some of the processors start developing faults and then they get finally decommissioned. Sadly, most processors become obsolete before they reach this stage; hence, for most customers hard errors are not particularly concerning.

12.6.4 Methods to Reduce or Tolerate Hard Errors

The silver bullet for reducing the probability of developing such permanent faults is to reduce the operating temperature. As we have seen, most of the failure rates are exponentially dependent on linear functions of the temperature, and thus any temperature management technique will help reduce the incidence of such hard errors.

In addition, there are many solutions at the level of the fabrication process to reduce the effects of failure mechanisms such as electromigration. For example, we can coat copper wires with materials such as TaN (Tantalum nitride). Such protective coatings stop the diffusion of copper atoms to nearby structures.

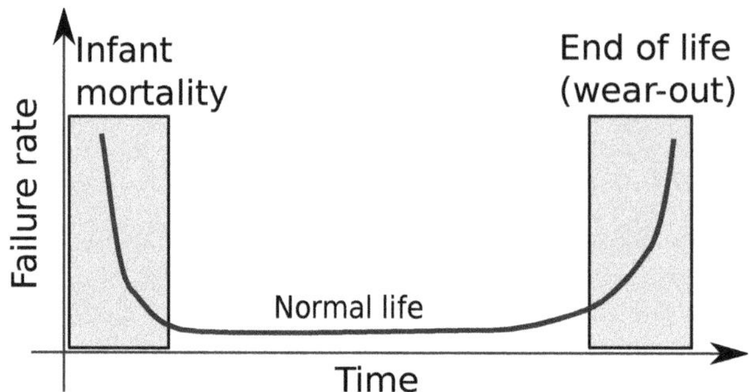

Figure 12.9: Bathtub curve for failures

At the architectural level, most modern processors do not have the level of redundancy that is needed to tolerate such hard errors simply because processors are expected to get obsolete before they develop such problems. The only exception is the memory system, where we always keep a set of spare rows. Whenever, we have a permanent fault in a row we remap it to a spare row.

12.7   Summary and Further Reading

12.7.1   Summary

Summary 11

1. *The three most important terms while studying processor reliability are fault, error, and failure.*

   (a) *A fault is defined as a defect in the system, which might or might not manifest into an erroneous internal state or output. It can either be permanent or transient.*

   (b) *An error is an incorrect internal state.*

   (c) *A failure is an externally visible event where the output or the behaviour of the system deviates from its specifications.*

2. *We typically quantify the error rate using the following metrics.*

   FIT *A FIT is defined as one failure per billion hours.*

   MTTF *It is the meantime to failure, assuming that the system cannot be repaired.*

   MTBF *If the system can be repaired, this metric represents the mean time between failures.*

   MTTR *This is the mean time to repair the system.*

3. *We can divide the set of faults into three types: transient, congenital, and ageing related faults. Transient faults are ephemeral in nature, whereas congenital faults are present in the processor right after it is fabricated and packaged, and faults related to ageing develop gradually over time.*

4. *Soft errors that are caused by particle strikes lead to transient faults. Earlier the main sources of soft errors were uranium and thorium impurities, and unstable isotopes such as ^{210}Pb and ^{10}B in the materials used to fabricate the chip. Nowadays the primary sources of soft errors are impacts from alpha particles and neutrons.*

5. *Soft errors are caused because the particle strike displaces charge causing a current pulse. If this pulse propagates to the latches then it can flip the value of the bit that needs to be stored. It is dependent on the velocity, angle of incidence, and the critical charge Q_{crit}. Q_{crit} is a function of the transistor's characteristics and the output capacitance.*

6. *There are three masking mechanisms for soft errors in circuits: electrical masking (pulse gets attenuated), logical masking (the bit being flipped does not matter), and timing window masking (the pulse does not reach the latch near the relevant clock edge). The process of redesigning circuits to reduce the probability of bit flips due to particle strikes is known as radiation hardening.*

7. *At the architectural level we define two terms: TVF (timing vulnerability factor) and AVF (architectural vulnerability factor). The TVF indicates the probability of the functional unit being turned on, and the AVF is the probability that the soft error leads to an erroneous output.*

8. *Another source of transient errors is the fluctuation in the voltage because of the varying impedance of the power grid (inductive noise). When the variation of the on-chip power requirement matches the resonant frequency, the supply voltage fluctuations are the highest, and this can lead to faults. We thus need to ensure that the resultant voltage fluctuations are limited by throttling activity, or by inserting dummy instructions.*

9. *While trying to debug a processor, we need to ensure that its behaviour is deterministic such that the observed errors are reproducible. There are inherent sources of non-determinism in processors such as clock gating in CPUs, scrubbing in memories, jitter in transmission, and delays due to inductive noise or soft errors.*

10. *Design faults (bugs in the RTL) slip into production silicon in spite of extensive verification and post-silicon validation. Such bugs can be classified into three classes: non-critical (defects in performance monitors and debug registers), critical-concurrent (several signals need to be enabled at the same time), and critical-complex (time-dependent relationships such as signal A needs to be enabled k cycles after signal B). A signal is defined as an event that can be tapped from a functional unit, and it often has a Boolean value.*

11. *We can use tapped signals to characterise design faults and also detect them as soon as they happen.*

12. *Another set of congenital faults are because of parameter variation, which has three components: process variation, supply voltage variation, and temperature variation.*

    (a) *Process variation is defined as the deviations in transistors' parameters such as the channel length and threshold voltage because of errors induced due to random effects (dopant density fluctuations and line edge roughness) and systematic effects (CMP and photolithographic effects).*

    (b) *The supply voltage and temperature can vary due to inductive noise and due to a change in the dynamic power dissipation respectively.*

    (c) *All the sources of parameter variation can affect the switching speed and leakage power of transistors. The former can cause timing faults.*

13. *Process variation has three components: die to die variation, intra-die systematic variation and intra-die random variation.*

14. *We model systematic variation as a spherically correlated multivariate normal distribution and we model random variation as a univariate normal distribution.*

---

15. *The four techniques to address photolithography based systematic variation are optical proximity correction, off-axis illumination, sub-resolution assist features and phase shift masking. For addressing random variation we perform statistical timing analysis and set our timing margins accordingly.*

16. *Two prominent ageing mechanisms are negative bias temperature instability (NBTI) and hot carrier injection (HCI). The former is seen in PMOS transistors when positive charges accumulate at the gate-channel interface. The latter is seen in NMOS transistors where charged electrons change the chemical structure of the interface and lead to charge trapping in the dielectric layer. Both increase the threshold voltage and change the electrical properties of the transistor.*

17. *The prominent mechanisms for inducing hard errors are electromigration, stress migration, time-dependent dielectric breakdown and thermal cycling. All of them are strongly dependent on temperature.*

12.7.2 Further Reading

The original model for soft errors was created by Hazucha and Svensson [Hazucha and Svensson, 2000]. For a slightly better understanding of soft errors, readers can refer to [Baumann, 2005, Wang and Agrawal, 2008]. For an even more deeper and holistic treatment of this area, the most comprehensive reference is the book by Mukherjee [Mukherjee, 2011].

For inductive noise some of the original papers in the area on pipeline damping [Powell and Vijaykumar, 2003a] and muffling [Powell and Vijaykumar, 2003b] are good references. There are similar papers for GPUs [Leng et al., 2014, Leng et al., 2015] as well.

For non-determinism one of the seminal papers is by your author [Sarangi et al., 2006a]. This work has been extended by Chen et al. [Chen et al., 2012]. Similarly, for design faults the first impactful work in the area was also by your author [Sarangi et al., 2006b]. Subsequently, the work was extended to consider signals in a real processor by Constantinides [Constantinides et al., 2008] and Chandran et al. proposed a method to capture critical-complex faults by proposing a theoretical framework [Chandran et al., 2017].

Your author had the good fortune to be involved in creating the first publicly available toolkit to simulate parameter variation. It is the Varius toolkit [Sarangi et al., 2008]. For work on the circuits side, readers can refer to the work by Kuhn et al. [Kuhn et al., 2011], where they propose techniques to measure the degree of variation, and present a detailed characterisation of the results. There are many architectural techniques to deal with process variation. Mittal's survey [Mittal, 2016a] is a comprehensive reference in this space.

One of the early papers in the area of ageing was Facelift [Tiwari and Torrellas, 2008] that introduced NBTI and HCI. However, the models and mechanisms have subsequently changed. A more recent reference in this area is a paper by Mahapatra et al. [Mahapatra and Parihar, 2018b]. For hard errors the two classic references are the papers by Srinivasan [Srinivasan et al., 2004, Srinivasan et al., 2005].

Exercises

Ex. 1 — Let us consider a processor that has a large physical register file (let's say 150 entries). The designers considered it a very expensive idea to have ECC (error correcting code) protection for each entry because of area constraints. However, they later realised that they would like to have some protection against soft errors for register operands as well. The protection mechanism need not cover all the accesses, but covering 60-70% of the accesses is desirable. How can we ensure this?

Ex. 2 — Assume that a bit has been flipped because of a soft error. How can we recover the state if the error has propagated to any of the following components?

1.Logic in the same functional unit.

2.Other stages in the pipeline.

3.L1 cache.

4.L2 cache.

Ex. 3 — The dynamic instruction verification architecture (DIVA) is a checker architecture in which a small checker processor is used to verify the execution of the master processor. Implement the DIVA architecture using the Tejas architectural simulator and quantify the loss in performance for the SPEC benchmarks.

Ex. 4 — Extend the Varius toolkit to model hard errors and ageing.

13

Secure Processor Architectures

Up till now we have assumed that all the components that we use are trustworthy. Of course, they can develop faults and they can fail; however, they will not deliberately introduce faults, or leak sensitive data to unauthorised outsiders. Sadly, these assumptions are not valid in today's complex world. Modern computing systems have to be designed to be immune to various kinds of attacks. Otherwise, it is possible that sensitive data such as passwords and credit card numbers can be stolen and used by malicious adversaries. Hence, gradually security is becoming an important criteria in designing processors and computing systems in general.

In this chapter, we shall primarily look at two important aspects of security namely *confidentiality* and *integrity*. The former ensures that data is encrypted and is not visible to outsiders. The latter ensures that it is not possible to maliciously change the contents of data or instructions, and remain undetected. First, we shall discuss the cryptographic primitives that are necessary to enforce these properties. Then, we shall design architectures that use basic cryptographic hardware and protect different aspects of the processor and the memory system.

Definition 100

Confidentiality *Data is encrypted, and the original data cannot be inferred from the encrypted data.*

Integrity *The data has not been tampered with.*

13.1 Data Encryption

Given a piece of text known as the *plaintext*, the aim is to encrypt it to an encrypted form. The resulting text is known as the *ciphertext*, which typically has the same size as the original plaintext. Any algorithm that encrypts data is known as an *encryption* algorithm. In general, the algorithm is not kept hidden, instead we protect the key, which is a small 128-256 bit number that determines the result of the encryption. All encryption algorithms rely on such a *secret key*, and may also use multiple keys for encryption and decryption respectively.

We can divide the space of encryption algorithms into two types: block ciphers and stream ciphers. Block ciphers encrypt data block by block, where a block is between 128 bits and 1024 bits, and stream ciphers encrypt data at smaller granularities. It is typically possible to parallelise the implementation of block ciphers, however, stream ciphers have a predominantly sequential character.

There are two properties that such ciphers should normally satisfy namely *confusion* and *diffusion* (see Definition 101).

Definition 101

Confusion *If we change a single bit of the key, most or all of the ciphertext bits will be affected. This ensures that the key and ciphertext are not correlated (in a statistical sense), and thus given the ciphertext, it is hard to guess the key.*

Diffusion *This property states that if we change a single bit in the plaintext, then statistically half the bits in the ciphertext should change, and likewise if we change one bit in the ciphertext then statistically half the bits in the plain text should change. This reduces the correlation between the plaintext and the ciphertext.*

Many of the algorithms have interesting confusion-diffusion trade-offs, which we shall study in this section.

13.1.1 AES Block Cipher

The most popular block cipher algorithm as of 2020 is the AES algorithm (Advanced Encryption Standard). The AES algorithm typically has a block size of 128 bits, and it uses three different key sizes (depending upon the degree of security that is required): 128, 192, or 256 bits. The AES algorithm is divided into a sequence of rounds, where in each round we perform simple substitution and permutation operations. The number of rounds depends on the key size as shown in Table 13.1.

Key size	Rounds
128	10
192	12
256	14

Table 13.1: AES key sizes and rounds

Consider a sequence of 128 bits or 16 bytes of plaintext. Let us number the bytes as $B_0, B_1 \ldots B_{15}$. We can represent the 16 bytes as a 4×4 matrix of byte-sized blocks as shown below.

$$\begin{bmatrix} B_0 & B_4 & B_8 & B_{12} \\ B_1 & B_5 & B_9 & B_{13} \\ B_2 & B_6 & B_{10} & B_{14} \\ B_3 & B_7 & B_{11} & B_{15} \end{bmatrix}$$

This matrix is known as the *state* of the algorithm. The state is initially set equal to a block of plaintext. Subsequently, in each round we perform a subset of the following operations. They modify this matrix. After all the rounds, this matrix contains the bytes of the ciphertext.

AES Operations

SubBytes In this stage we replace (or substitute) each byte B_i with another byte C_i. The relationship between the two is determined algebraically; however, we shall not discuss the math in this section because it is out of the scope of this book. The basic idea is that we represent each byte by a polynomial, and then perform arithmetic on polynomials. It is typically not required to do this at runtime. For each combination of 8 bits, we can store the result in a lookup table known as the S-box. The aim of this step is to increase the distance between the plaintext and ciphertext as much as possible.

ShiftRows In this stage we shift the contents in each row. This is also known as left rotation because the byte that is shifted out enters the row at the rightmost end. The rows are numbered 0, 1, 2 and 3. We left shift the ith row by i positions.

MixColumns In this step we take the four bytes of each column, and multiply it with a fixed matrix. The multiplication however uses modular arithmetic (defined over a Galois field [Howie, 2007]). The aim of the **ShiftRows** and **MixColumns** step is to *diffuse* the bits of the plaintext.

AddRoundKey This is the last stage. In AES, we derive a key for each round from the original encryption key. The size of the round key is the same as the size of the state (128 bits in this case). We compute a byte-by-byte XOR with the round key. This helps us mix the key with the data.

Key Schedule

The algorithm for generating multiple round keys in different AES rounds is known as the key schedule. The basic operations for generating each round key are as follows:

RotWord We perform a left rotation: $B_0B_1B_2B_3 \rightarrow B_1B_2B_3B_0$.

SubWord We substitute the value of each byte using the **SubBytes** operation defined in the previous section.

XORWord For a word of the form $B_0B_1B_2B_3$, we replace B_0 with $B_0 \oplus RC[i]$. The array RC is known as the round-constant array. We have $RC[1] = 1$ and for $i > 1$, $RC[i] = 2 * RC[i-1]$.

Let us now create a *key matrix* (assuming a 128-bit key) where each element is a single byte. It is constructed in exactly the same way as we constructed the *state* of the algorithm out of plaintext bytes. In this case, we initially use the original key to create the key matrix. It is shown below. This matrix is updated in each round to generate a new round key.

$$\begin{bmatrix} K_0 & K_4 & K_8 & K_{12} \\ K_1 & K_5 & K_9 & K_{13} \\ K_2 & K_6 & K_{10} & K_{14} \\ K_3 & K_7 & K_{11} & K_{15} \end{bmatrix}$$

Let us use the superscript to specify the round number, for example, K_j^i is the jth key in the matrix for round i. Let us use the mnemonics $\mathcal{R}$, $\mathcal{S}$, and $\mathcal{X}$ for the functions **RotWord**, **SubWord**, and **XorWord** respectively. The key matrix is initialised with the AES key (round 0), and for every subsequent round it changes according to the key schedule, which is as follows (reference: [Padhye et al., 2018]).

$$K_j^i = \begin{cases} K_j^{i-1} \oplus K_{j-4}^i & 4 \leq j \leq 15 \\ K_0^i K_1^i K_2^i K_3^i = \mathcal{X}(\mathcal{S}(\mathcal{R}(K_{12}^{i-1} K_{13}^{i-1} K_{14}^{i-1} K_{15}^{i-1}))) \oplus K_0^{i-1} K_1^{i-1} K_2^{i-1} K_3^{i-1} \end{cases} \tag{13.1}$$

Complete Algorithm

The complete algorithm is as follows. Assume that the protocol consists of N rounds. The first step also known as the 0th round is called *pre-whitening*. In this stage, only the `AddRoundKey` operation is performed. For the rest of the $N - 1$ rounds, all the four operations are performed, and in the last round (N^{th} round), the `MixColumns` operation is skipped. Finally, the state of the algorithm becomes the ciphertext. We can convert the matrix back into a string of 16 bytes.

Decryption

All the operations in AES are invertible. We start from the final state and perform a reverse order of operations. During this process, we will need the round keys at each stage. To aid this process, the round keys can be generated first, and then stored in a lookup table.

AES Modes

An AES block can only encrypt 128 to 256 bits (16 to 32 bytes) at a time. For longer plaintext messages we need to use one of the following *encryption modes*.

The key idea here is to divide the entire plaintext message into a set of 128-256 bit blocks, and encrypt each plaintext block separately using a piece of hardware called an *encryption block*. Each such encryption block incorporates one AES block and some additional logic. The encryption blocks can either operate serially or in parallel. Depending upon the encryption mode an encryption block can provide some information to the subsequent encryption block. The overall goal is to increase the parallelism of encryption/decryption as well as ensure good confusion/diffusion properties.

Electronic Codebook

This is a naive encryption method, where we divide the plaintext into blocks, and encrypt them with the same key. The main problem with this method is that identical blocks of plaintext produce the same ciphertext. This can reveal significant details about the structure of the plaintext, and thus this is not preferable. Even though we can ensure high levels of confusion, the levels of diffusion will be low.

Cipher Block Chaining

Let us solve the problem with the electronic codebook method (see Figure 13.1).

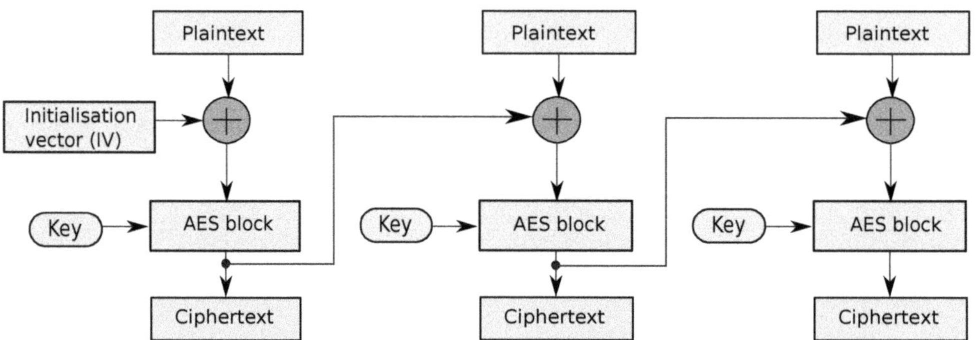

Figure 13.1: Cipher block chaining

In the first block on the left we compute a XOR between the plain text and a pre-decided initialisation vector. We encrypt this block using the secret key. The important feature of this algorithm is that the encrypted cipher is used as the initialisation vector for the second block, which means that the plaintext for the first block determines the ciphertext for the second block. The encryption proceeds in a similar fashion. If we flip a single bit of the plaintext, then the ciphertexts for all the subsequent blocks change.

This is considered a default implementation of AES as of 2020. The other advantage of this algorithm is that the decryption can be parallelised even though encryption is a strictly sequential operation. The reason for this is left as an exercise for the reader.

Output Feedback Mode

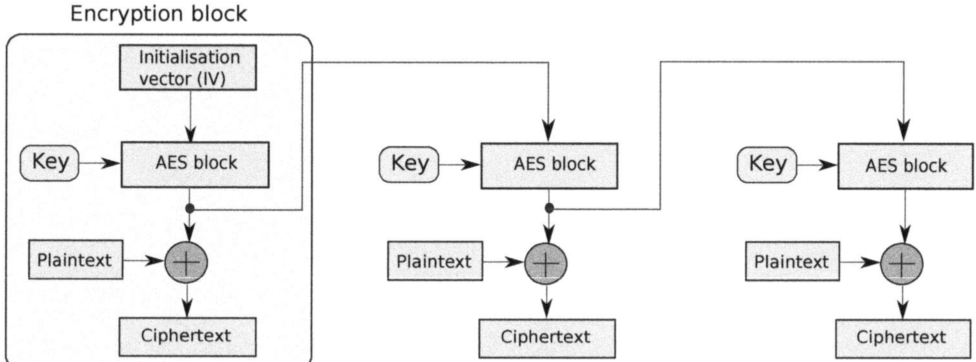

Figure 13.2: Output feedback mode

Having a high diffusion rate has its problems as well. It limits parallelism and introduces a degree of sequentiality in the computation. In addition, if there are errors in the plaintext, then the entire ciphertext is damaged. One approach that fixes the second problem (not the first w.r.t. parallelism) is the output feedback mode (see Figure 13.2). Here, the first encryption block takes the initialisation vector (IV) as input, the second encryption block takes the output of the first AES block as input, the third encryption block takes the output of the second AES block as input, and so on. This approach sequentialises the encryption and decryption processes. The output of each AES block is known as an one-time pad (OTP).

For each encryption block, the ciphertext is a XOR of the output of the AES encryption block (OTP) and the plaintext, which is a very fast operation. This means that if there is an error in a single bit of the plaintext, then there is an error only in a single bit of the ciphertext. The other interesting thing is that given a key we can compute the output of all the AES blocks that are chained together. In parallel, we can perform error correction on the plaintext (if there is a need). Once these parallel tasks complete, we can then quickly compute the ciphertext with a XOR operation.

Off late this approach has been superseded by counter mode encryption because it provides more parallelism.

Counter Mode Encryption

The main problem with output feedback mode encryption is the lack of parallelism. Counter mode (CTR) encryption fixes this (see Figure 13.3).

The key innovation here is that the encryption blocks are not chained. Instead, their constituent AES blocks use different inputs. Each input is a combination of two numbers: major counter and a minor counter. The major counter remains the same for all the encryption blocks. This means that if we are encrypting a long message we can have a single major counter for all of its constituent plaintext blocks. The value of the major counter should remain confidential. It can be thought of as an encryption key for the entire message.

Now, if we have k blocks in the plaintext, then we need k minor counters. They can be of the form $0, 1, 2, 3, \ldots (k-1)$. Each AES block takes in a major+minor counter pair, encrypts it with a secret key that is hard-coded, and produces a one time pad (OTP). This is similar to the OTP that we had generated in the output feedback mode. Subsequently, we compute a XOR between the OTP and a

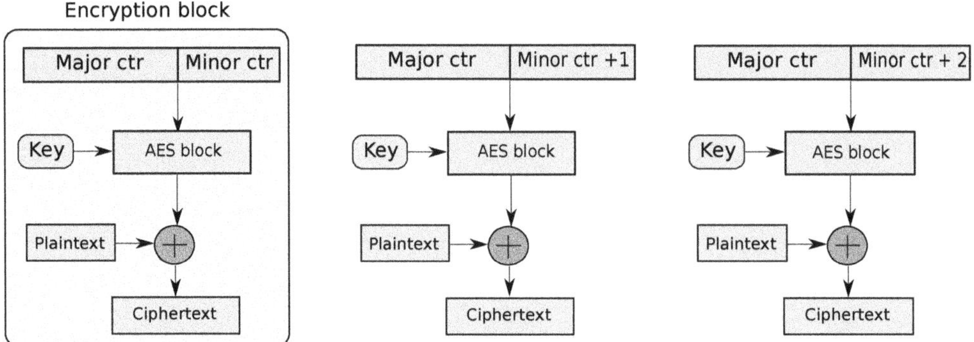

Figure 13.3: Counter mode encryption

block of plaintext to produce a block of ciphertext.

The key advantage of having this major-minor counter mechanism is that we just have to store the major counter, the minor counters can simply be generated at runtime. Second, as compared to the output feedback mode, the encryption blocks are not chained together. In this case, both encryption and decryption can be done in parallel across the encryption blocks. We can also simultaneously correct errors in the plaintext.

Finally, note that because the AES algorithm itself has good confusion/diffusion properties, the OTPs are random in nature and extremely hard to predict if the major counter is kept confidential. Even if two blocks of plaintext are the same, they will produce different blocks of ciphertext because their minor counters will be different. Hence, we are not significantly sacrificing on any cryptographic guarantees by using counter mode encryption.

We shall see in later sections that counter mode encryption is the basis of modern secure architectures.

13.1.2 RC4 Stream Cipher

RC4 (Rivest Cipher 4) is the most popular stream cipher algorithm as of 2020. As compared to a block cipher, a stream cipher has a different philosophy; it works at the level of individual bytes or small blocks of bytes. It is useful in situations where the length of the plaintext message is not known beforehand such as many wireless communication scenarios.

The key idea of the RC4 cipher is that it generates a sequence of pseudo-random bits known as the *keystream*. We can treat each byte in the keystream as a one-time pad that can be used to compute a XOR between itself and a plaintext byte. The main features of the algorithm are as follows.

The most important structure is the state vector, S, which has 256 entries. Here also we have a *key* that is an array of 5 to 16 bytes. The constant *key_length* is the length of the key in bytes. We first have an initialisation phase, and then we have a pseudo-random number generation phase.

Initialisation Phase

We first set $S[i] = i$ $(0 \leq i \leq 255)$. Then we run the following code (either in software or in hardware) .

```
1  j=0;
2  for (i=0; i<=255; i++){
3          j = (j + S[i] + key[i%key_length])%256;
4          swap(S[i],S[j]);
5  }
```

Line 3 helps increase the confusion and Line 4 helps increase the diffusion within the vector S.

Pseudo-random Number Generation

```
1  i=0; j=0;
2
3  while (1){
4          i = (i+1) % 256;
5          j = (j+S[i]) % 256;
6          swap (S[i],S[j];
7          output (S[(S[i] + S[j]) % 256]);
8  }
```

In this case, we are basically computing complex permutations of the bytes in the state vector, and then returning a randomly generated byte that can be used as an OTP. Recall that since each location in S is just one byte, we have 256 possible combinations, which have been stored in S in the initialisation phase. In this phase, we just permute the values and produce one of the values in each iteration as the output. This is a pseudo-random number and can be used as the OTP. We need to compute a XOR between the OTP and a plaintext byte to compute the ciphertext. The process of decryption is very easy. We just need to compute the OTP and compute a XOR with the corresponding byte of the ciphertext to obtain the plaintext byte.

13.1.3   Hardware Implementation

Let us briefly discuss the hardware implementations of the AES and RC4 algorithms. For encrypting 128 bits, AES uses 10 rounds with added overheads for initialisation and computing the key schedule. However, the advantage is that all the 128 bits (16 bytes) are encrypted at once. Since all the rounds (other than the last one) do the same computation, we can in principle unroll the loop and have multiple units where each unit computes the result for several rounds as shown in Figure 13.4(a).

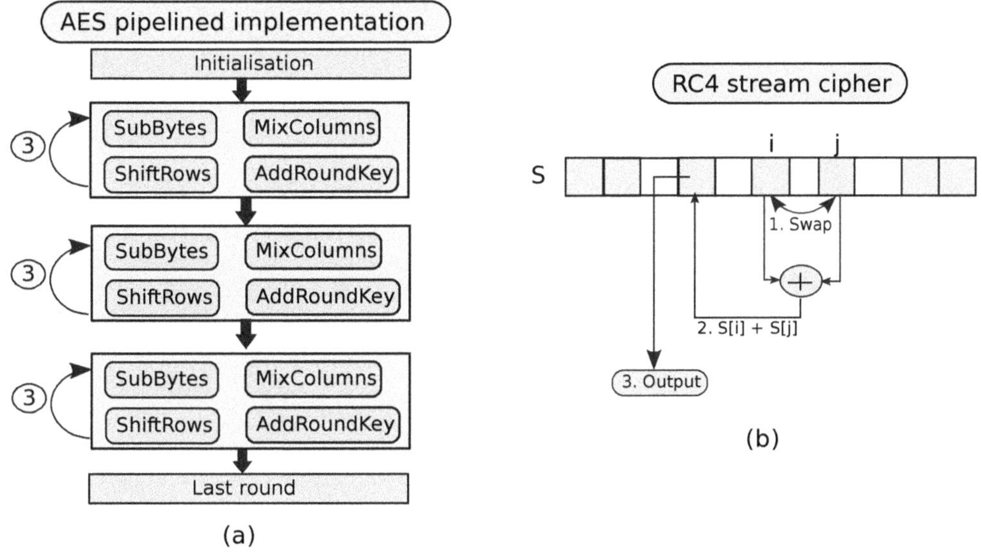

Figure 13.4: (a) Pipelined AES implementation, (b) RC4 stream cipher

If we look closely at Figure 13.4(a) we can discern that we have divided the process of computing the encrypted ciphertext using the AES algorithm into five stages. Each of the three intermediate stages processes three rounds of the algorithm. The advantage is that this structure can be pipelined because there are no dependences across the stages. This can help us tremendously increase the performance of the AES algorithm.

In comparison, the implementation of the stream cipher as shown in Figure 13.4(b) is sequential. We need to read two locations i and j, access the state vector S, perform a swap (step 1), add the values in $S[i]$ and $S[j]$ (step 2), access that location and read the output (step 3). Even though this process is fast it is nevertheless still sequential and not pipelined – we need to process the data byte by byte. However, it is still possible that RC4 is more power efficient (depends upon the implementation details though).

In modern power-constrained devices used in the internet of things, researchers have developed fast and power efficient block and stream ciphers. This is an active area of research as of 2020.

13.1.4   Symmetric and Asymmetric Ciphers

RC4 and AES are examples of symmetric ciphers because we use the same key for encryption and decryption. This means that we need to share the key between the sender and the receiver. This might not be desirable in some cases.

Hence, in this case we opt for asymmetric ciphers that have two keys – a public key and a private key. The RSA (Rivest Shamir Adleman) algorithm is the most prominent in this space. It is typically not used in CPUs because it is at least 1-2 orders of magnitude slower than AES. We shall explain the basic principles in this section. The users should keep in mind that even though RSA is seldom used in secure hardware; however, it is most often the target of attackers because RSA is used extensively in the internet to securely access web pages (HTTPS, SSL, and TLS technologies). Nevertheless, there are exceptions. For example, many technologies built on RSA are used to initialise the secure state of the processor.

Basics of the RSA Protocol

Let us first define the modular congruence relation between two integers a and b, $a \equiv b \ (mod\,n)$, which means that the positive integer n divides $(a - b)$.

Instead of describing all the math, let us explain the protocol with an example.

1. Choose two distinct prime numbers p and q. Let us choose $p = 59$ and $q = 67$. Compute $n = pq$. $n = 3953$.

2. Compute $\lambda(n) = lcm(p - 1, q - 1) = lcm(58, 66)$, where lcm is the least common multiple. We have $\lambda(n) = 1914$.

3. Let us choose a number e $(< \lambda(n))$ such that e and $\lambda(n)$ are coprime. Let us choose $e = 31$.

4. Compute a number d such that $d \times e \equiv 1 \ (mod\ 1914)$. We can choose $d = 247$. The readers needs to manually verify that $247 \times 31 \equiv 1 \ (mod\ 1914)$.

5. The public key is $(n = 3953, e = 31)$. The encryption function is $\mathcal{E}(m) = m^e \, mod\, n$.

6. The private key is $(n = 3953, e = 247)$. The decryption function is $\mathcal{D}(m) = m^d \, mod\, n$.

Here, is the magic! Let us consider a plain text message and convert it to a number. Say the number is 54. We can easily compute:

$$54^{31} \ mod \ 3953 = 3574$$
$$3574^{247} \ mod \ 3953 = 54$$

What is even more interesting is that the following relationship also holds!

$$54^{247} \ mod \ 3953 = 1011$$
$$1011^{31} \ mod \ 3953 = 54$$

Given a key $K = (n, e, d)$ the operation $\mathcal{E}_K = m^e \ mod \ n$ is known as public key encryption and the operation $\mathcal{D}_K = m^d \ mod \ n$ is known as private key encryption. What is intriguing is that the following relationships also hold.

$$\mathcal{D}_K(\mathcal{E}_K(m)) = m \tag{13.2}$$
$$\mathcal{E}_K(\mathcal{D}_K(m)) = m \tag{13.3}$$

Encryption and Decryption

Using RSA for encryption is very easy. We simply compute the triplet $K = (n, e, d)$. There are very efficient algorithms to do this. Then we compute the function $\mathcal{E}_K$, which involves modular exponentiation. We can simply use the following property to speedup up our algorithm if $a \equiv b \,(mod \ n)$ and $c \equiv d \,(mod \ n)$, then $ac \equiv (bd \ mod \ n) \,(mod \ n)$. We invite the reader to prove this.

Decryption is a similar process. Note that the numbers e and d are not shared. The only number that is shared is n. Furthermore, given n and e, it is computationally very hard to compute d if these numbers are large enough. Even though these are commutative operations, the convention is that one pair of numbers (n, e) is known to all – it is referred to as the public key. The other pair (n, d) is private and is only known to one entity (it is known as the private key). We can have implementations where both the pairs of numbers are private (only known to their respective owners).

It is important to appreciate that in RSA, encryption and decryption are essentially the *same operations*. They just use different pairs of numbers (or different keys).

Digital Signatures

How do we ensure that a message sent from Alice to Bob is actually sent by Alice? Again this is very easy. We simply encrypt the message with Alice's private key. Bob can then use Alice's public key to retrieve the original message (recall that $\mathcal{E}_K$ and $\mathcal{D}_K$ are commutative operations). If Bob knows some part of the original message, and that part matches, then the message has indeed been sent by Alice. This can be formalised as follows. Alice publishes her public key and a known message. Then she encrypts the known message with her private key – this is known as her *digital signature*. Anybody (including Bob) can validate the digital signature by decrypting it with Alice's public key. They should get the known message back. Whenever a message contains some information that allows us to establish the identity of the sender, the message is said to be *authentic* – this property is known as *authenticity*.

A modern approach to ensure the authenticity of a given piece of hardware is to use a physically unclonable function (PUF). Because of process variations (see Chapter 12), every fabricated chip has a unique signature in terms of the properties of its transistors. It is possible to place sensors at different locations within a chip, measure the values of parameters related to process variation such as the leakage current or temperature, and use them to generate a unique hardware fingerprint (32 to 128-bit number) called the PUF. This serves as a unique id of the device, and as long as the parameters used to generate the PUF remain stable, the PUF uniquely identifies the device. There are several algorithms that use PUFs for authentication, software license management, and secure communication.

13.1.5 Session Keys

The main difference between communication on the internet and within a processor is that the latter does not allow us to use algorithms like RSA that are very slow. We need to be able to encrypt and decrypt messages quickly. For that purpose the AES algorithm and faster variants are used. However, the main problem that arises here is how to distribute a common key to the sender and the receiver. During the process of key distribution an attacker can try to read it, particularly, in modern systems-on-chip where different hardware modules are made by different vendors. In such cases, malicious behaviour cannot be ruled out.

We can think of slow solutions at boot time, where some trusted hardware circuit generates and distributes the key using a separate network. It is the job of the system integrator to ensure that this process works correctly in spite of malicious hardware or software. Another slow solution is to use RSA based public-private key communication at boot time to establish a secure connection with a trusted entity and securely obtain an AES key. Then a sender-receiver pair can use such a dedicated key to establish a fast AES-based secure communication channel. Such keys are typically valid for a single session (from power up to power down); they are known as session keys.

There is a faster method to compute a session key. It is known as the Diffie-Hellman key exchange protocol, which is as follows.

1. Alice and Bob decide on two prime numbers p and q. These numbers need to be exchanged between them only once. If they are hardware entities, then this can be done at the time of fabrication.

2. Alice generates a secret number a, computes $A = q^a \ mod \ p$, and sends A to Bob.

3. Bob does the same, generates a secret number b, computes $B = q^b \ mod \ p$, and sends B to Alice.

4. Alice computes $K = B^a \ mod \ p = q^{ab} \ mod \ p$.

5. Bob computes $K = A^b \ mod \ p = q^{ab} \ mod \ p$.

6. Once the reader has verified the math, she will quickly realise that now both have computed the same value of the key K unbeknownst to any entity snooping the channel!

Definition 102

RSA encryption and decryption *Encryption and decryption in the RSA algorithm are commutative operations. They use the same algorithm albeit with different keys.*

Digital signature *A message encrypted with the private key of the sender can be used to establish its* authenticity. *Any receiver can decrypt the message with the sender's public key and if it gets a piece of known plaintext then the message is* authentic.

Session key *Slow algorithms such as RSA are often used to establish a session key between a pair of communicating nodes. If the nodes have exchanged some information at an earlier point of time, then we can use the faster Diffie-Hellman key exchange algorithm. The nodes can then use this session key and the AES algorithm to exchange encrypted messages.*

13.2   Hashing and Data Integrity

13.2.1   Common Cryptographic Attacks

Sadly, encrypting data is not enough. We also need to ensure *data integrity* – messages are not tampered. Consider Alice and Bob again. Alice sends a message to Bob (see Figure 13.5).

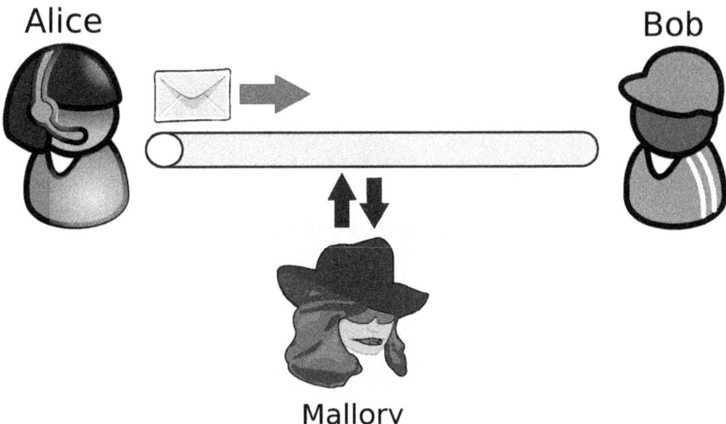

Figure 13.5: Alice trying to send a secure message to Bob. Mallory is the attacker.

If Mallory is a passive attacker who can just eavesdrop on the messages being sent on the channel, then there is no issue. This is because we are assuming that Alice has already encrypted the message. Thus, even if Mallory gets copies of the ciphertext, she will not be able to get any useful information. However, the problems begin if she is an active attacker. This means that she can insert and remove messages from the channel.

One of the classic attacks in this space is called the man-in-the-middle (MIM) attack. In this case, she establishes a secure channel with Alice and masquerades as Bob. She gets the message from Alice, then decrypts and reads the message. Then, she maliciously modifies the message and sends the modified message to Bob. Bob again thinks that the message is coming from Alice. Unbeknownst to both of them the messages are being modified by Mallory. This is not acceptable. Such MIM attacks can be easily thwarted with digital signatures as described in Section 13.1.4. This will establish the authenticity of the sender. It is not possible for Mallory to mount such attacks, which are also known as *spoofing attacks*, where Mallory pretends to be someone else such as Alice or Bob.

Alternatively, Mallory can mount a *splicing attack*, where she captures legitimate encrypted commands and responses from another communication between Bob and another user Carlos. She can then join (or splice) the relevant messages that she has captured with plaintext message headers that Alice uses to communicate with Bob. The spliced message can be sent to Bob. If Alice and Carlos use the same key for creating digital signatures then Bob will get tricked. To avoid such splicing attacks, Alice and Carlos need to use separate keys. This seems reasonably obvious in this case. However, the implication here is that if Alice and Carlos are different memory locations, then we need to encrypt them with different keys.

Let us look at the problem of digital signatures. They need to be sent along with every message. This increases the size of the message. If the size of the signature is k bits, then the probability of mounting a successful spoofing attack can be shown to be 2^{-k}. To ensure that this probability is vanishingly small, k should be more than 64 bits at least – this increases the message size quite a bit. Second, it takes a lot of time to compute these signatures because we need to perform RSA encryption. We thus need a much faster solution that does not involve sending a digital signature.

13.2.2 SHA-based Hashing

Secure Hash Algorithms (SHA) are the de facto standards as of 2020 for hashing a block of data. The main idea of hashing is as follows. We take a piece of text (the message), thoroughly permute and mutate the bits, and finally arrive at a string that is 160 to 512 bits long. This is a one-way hash function, which means that it is not possible to recover the original text from the hash. This hash serves as a signature of the message. Given a message and its hash, the receiver can recompute the hash. If the computed hash matches the hash that the sender has sent, then the message is correct with a very high probability. If the length of the hash is 160 bits, then the probability of two messages having the same hash tends to 2^{-160}, which is vanishingly small.

Let us now compare this approach with digital signatures, where the key idea is to embed a piece of ciphertext in the message, which is a known piece of text encrypted with the sender's private key. The entire message itself might be encrypted with a session key. The idea is that even if a single bit is tampered, the embedded digital signature will not match with a very high likelihood. However, if we have some other way of enforcing authenticity, and we just want to ensure message integrity, we simply send the hash after the message. The size of the hash will be much smaller than the size of the message, and computing it also will be very fast.

Most secure processors use hashes from the SHA family that as of 2020 has three versions: SHA1, SHA2, and SHA3. SHA2 produces hashes that are between 224 bits and 512 bits. The broad approach is as follows. We break the message into 512-bit chunks. Each chunk is divided into 16 words that are 32 bits each. The processing of each chunk is divided into 64 rounds (same philosophy as AES). In each round we compute a complicated function of the bits in the message that involves permutation, shifting, rotation, and Boolean operations involving round constants. After processing all the chunks, we finally arrive at a hash that is anywhere from 224 to 512 bits (depending upon the variant of the algorithm). The probability of two pieces of text having the same hash is roughly 2^{-l}, where l is the length of the hash.

13.2.3 Message Authentication Code (MAC)

We have seen two solutions: digital signatures and hashes. Both have their flaws. Digital signatures take too long to compute yet provide authenticity; in comparison, hashes can be computed quickly yet do not ensure authenticity. We thus use a message authentication code (MAC) that provides both.

There are many ways to compute a MAC. One of the common approaches used in architectures is to first compute the hash of a message, and then use an encryption algorithm based on a session key to encrypt the hash. The hash of the message needs to be computed anyway, and thus the consequent delays incurred are unavoidable. Since computing hashes is a much faster process than encrypting the entire message this is a tolerable overhead. In the same time, we can use a shared session key to generate a one-time pad (see Section 13.1.1). This will be relatively fast because we are not encrypting the entire message, we are typically encrypting a 256 or 512-bit vector. The MAC is a XOR of the hash and the OTP.

Once the receiver gets the message and the MAC, it proceeds as follows. It proceeds to decrypt the message and the MAC by recomputing the OTP using the shared session key. It then computes the hash of the message, and compares it with the decrypted MAC. If they match, then the message has not been tampered with. Furthermore, it is not possible for a third party to maliciously modify the message or the MAC and still go undetected, because it does not have the shared session key. The reader needs to convince herself of this fact.

There is still a problem unfortunately. Mallory can read a set of (message, MAC) pairs and store them. Later on it can simply *replay* the sequence of messages. If the sequence of messages were to withdraw money from Alice's bank account (Bob being the banker), Mallory can ensure that Alice goes bankrupt! This is a *replay* attack where legitimate commands are recorded and replayed at a later point in time.

13.2.4 Preventing Replay Attacks

The sad news is that in spite of ensuring confidentiality and integrity we have the possibility of replay attacks. Thankfully, there are a set of known techniques to prevent replay attacks that are as follows. All of them try to ensure the *freshness* of data, which means that the data that is received is not old data.

One-time Session Keys Change the session key for every communication round. This is possible to do with counter mode encryption (Section 13.1.1). This means that the sender and receiver have a pre-decided arrangement where the keys change according to a particular set of rules. Thus replaying messages encrypted with an older key will not work.

Timestamps The sender can include its local time in the message. If there is clock synchronisation between the sender and receiver, the receiver can reject messages that were sent before a certain time.

Nonces The problem with timestamps is that we need to have large timestamps and also ensure that they do not overflow. We can achieve the same result with *nonces*, which are integers embedded in the message. Every time the sender sends a message it can increment the nonce. The receiver needs to maintain a state variable that stores the last value of the sender's nonce. Here, the assumption is that messages are delivered in FIFO (first-in first-out) order.

Definition 103

Security properties *We are primarily interested in ensuring four properties in a system for guaranteeing secure communication: authenticity, confidentiality, integrity, and freshness. Let us refer to these properties as the ACIF properties or ACIF guarantees. Many texts also mention* availability *as another property, where attackers can simply try to make a system unavailable by keeping it busy. However, this is not very relevant for processor architectures, and thus we shall not consider it.*

Eavesdropping *Eavesdropping is a passive attack where the* eavesdropper *can read the contents of the message. If the message is encrypted then the eavesdropper cannot extract any meaningful information.*

Man-in-the-middle Attack *It is possible for an intermediary like Mallory to masquerade as Alice or Bob, and establish a secure communication channel with both of them. She can then read and modify all the messages. This is prevented by using digital signatures that guarantee authenticity (establish the identify of the sender).*

Hashing *Hashing using the SHA family of algorithms generates short 224 to 512-bit hashes for arbitrarily large pieces of plaintext. These are one-way functions. The message cannot be regenerated from the hash.*

MAC *A MAC is an encrypted hash that additionally authenticates the sender.*

Replay attack *It is possible for an intermediary to replay both the original message and its MAC. To prevent this, we can either embed timestamps or nonces in the message, or use time-varying session keys. For the latter, counter mode encryption is a very effective technique.*

13.3 Secure Architectures

13.3.1 Security in Traditional Processors

There are several things that we need to keep in mind before we design a secure architecture. The first is that systems are already designed to be reasonably secure. This means that starting from wearable computers to servers, it is very hard to get unauthorised access to data or maliciously modify a program's execution. The most important security enforcing mechanisms in modern computer systems are the virtual memory sub-system and the file system.

Virtual memory and the paging mechanism ensure that one process cannot read or modify the data of another process in the caches or main memory. Unless intended otherwise, the memory spaces of two processes are separate. It is thus not possible for one process to access (read or write) the memory space of another process. Similarly, for data stored on the disk there are strict file access policies. They ensure that users without the right permissions are not able to access a given file. For critical hardware resources including I/O devices, all the accesses need to go through the operating system, which decides the legitimacy of the requests. This means that for most normal users, most security requirements are taken care of. However, this is not enough for commercial users such as banks and cloud computing providers. Moreover, defence installations and military hardware also have an increased need for security, which traditional mechanisms typically do not provide. Let us give an example of a simple attack that can be mounted on software by providing special input sequences.

Traditional Attacks on Software

The most common approach in this space is the *buffer overflow* technique. Assume that a program requires a password, which is stored in an array of characters. Instead of entering the password, we enter a very large string. If the program does not check the length of the input, it will store all the characters in an array (known as the *buffer*). There will be an overflow in terms of the size allocated to the buffer. As a result, the data that we enter will get stored on the heap or stack and overwrite previous data. This is where we can play a little trick. In many systems including Intel x86 the function return addresses are stored on the stack. If we carefully craft our input, we can ensure that the overflowed bytes overwrite the return address and make it point to a location of our choosing, which can be the starting address of another section of the large string array. We can thus execute any code that we like including custom code that we inject into the process's virtual memory space using this approach. This would be an example of a *code injection attack*.

Let us look at a simple example in Figure 13.6. In this case, the expected behaviour is that the function returns seamlessly (Figure 13.6(a)). However, it is possible for us to mount a code injection attack, where we overwrite the return address. Figure 13.6(b) shows a situation where the return address points to a location in the buffer.

Stopping such a code injection attack based on a buffer overflow is easy. The simplest solution is to check every input and ensure that no buffer ever overflows. A more generic way that does not rely on programmers' skill is as follows. Recall that the new instructions are stored on the stack, which is essentially *data*. We just create a method to separately mark data and code pages. A data page is not allowed to contain code. Even if malicious users are able to modify the return address and direct the control flow to an address within a data page, they will not be able to execute the corresponding code.

Alternatively, we can direct the control flow to existing functions within the code of the running program (Figure 13.6(c)). It has been shown that it is possible to string together many such existing functions in the code (known as *gadgets*) to implement a custom logic. This is a *code reuse attack*, and marking data pages as non-executable will not fix this problem. We thus randomise the layout of the virtual address space on every run. This means that the starting addresses of the stack and heap, dynamic linked libraries, and memory-mapped files change with every run. To compute the actual memory address in virtual memory, the code relies on certain base addresses in each of the aforementioned regions. Specifically, for each memory access, we need to add an offset to the corresponding base address.

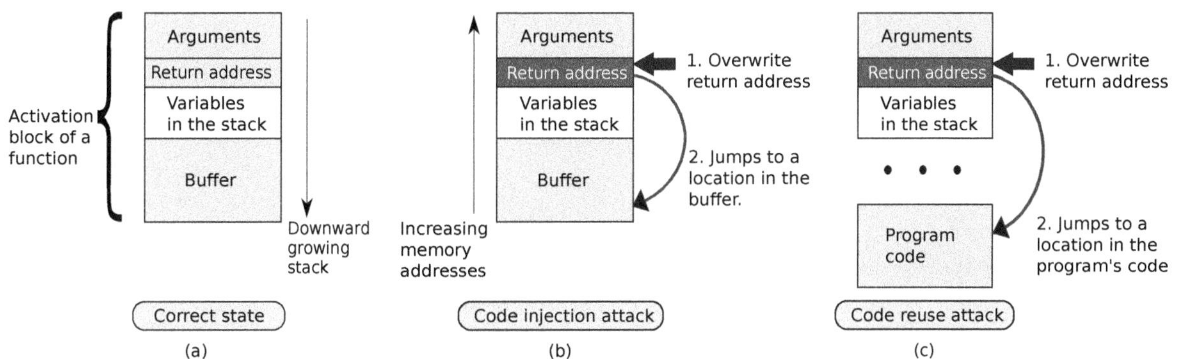

Figure 13.6: (a) Correct execution, (b) Code injection attack, (c) Code reuse attack

These starting addresses are set by the operating system in a random fashion. The main advantage of this approach is that the attacker does not know the exact addresses of the return address or of functions in the code. This technique is a standard as of 2020. It is known as ASLR (address space layout randomisation).

13.3.2 Hardware Security: Key Concepts

Our aim in this section is to introduce some of the concepts that form the bedrock of hardware security: Trusted Computing Base (TCB), Attack Surface, threat model, Trusted Execution Environment (TEE), Trusted Platform Module (TPM), Root of Trust, measurement, remote attestation, and sealing.

Trusted Computing Base (TCB)

Whenever we consider a computer system inclusive of the software, CPU, off-chip memory, and storage modules, we need to define the set of entities that we want to secure. This is known as the *Trusted Computing Base*, abbreviated as TCB. It contains a set of hardware and software components that we assume to be secure. In other words, it means that the components of a TCB together guarantee certain security properties, which are often the ACIF properties (see Section 13.2.4).

There are two important principles that are used in designing the TCB.

Kerckhoff's Principle This states that the design of the TCB should be open and publicly known. The only secret should be a set of keys. They should ensure the security of the entire system. The reason is that sooner or later the secrets of the design leak out. Hence, there is no point in keeping the design a secret.

A chain is only as strong as the weakest link Security is typically thought of as a series-failure system – if one component in the TCB succumbs to an attack, the entire system is compromised. It is assumed that an adversary will always find the weakest part of the TCB and try to attack it.

Attack Surface

We can next define the term *attack surface*, which is defined as the set of all the attack mechanisms that can be mounted on the TCB. The larger is the TCB, the larger is the attack surface. Note that attacks can be mounted both by untrusted hardware and malicious software that are outside the TCB. Attacks can either be passive that are limited to eavesdropping, or they can be active where the attacker tries to change the state of the system such as spoofing, splicing and replay attacks as discussed in Section 13.2. Alternatively, the term "attack surface" broadly refers to all the vulnerabilities in the TCB that can be targeted by attacks.

Threat Model

A *threat model* is a precise set of attacks that the designers expect to be mounted on their system. They essentially consider a subset of the attack surface and then provide countermeasures against expected attack mechanisms (also known as *attack vectors*). Note that every architecture is designed with a specific threat model in mind. Most commercial architectures typically do not provide countermeasures against all possible threats because this increases the hardware overheads significantly. Designers and architects consider the most realistic scenarios and design an appropriate threat model to thwart most attacks. This is where a trade-off needs to be made between security guarantees and the overheads of providing security.

Trusted Execution Environments (TEEs)

After the TCB and threat model are defined, it is the job of the hardware vendor to create an environment where secure code can run. This is known as the *Trusted Execution Environment* or *TEE*. The TEE allows users to create secure processes. The TCB guarantees the security of these processes in accordance with the threat model. The TEE creates an execution environment for a secure program that is known as an *enclave*. In most secure processors, we can have multiple enclaves running in parallel.

Root of Trust

The key question that we need to ask is, "Who sets up the TEE?" If the operating system is malicious, then it can trick secure programs into thinking that they are actually executing within a TEE. It can then steal their secrets such as passwords or credit card numbers. In fact, there are a large number of events that happen before setting up a TEE: the BIOS boots the processor, it initialises the firmware and the I/O devices, the OS is loaded, the TEE is set up, and then the secure program is run in the TEE. If any of these steps is compromised, then the TEE may not be setup correctly. Consider the case of a fake TEE created by the OS. In this case, the secure application should first be able to verify if the TEE is genuine or not. This means that it needs to verify if the entire chain of actions that lead to the creation of the TEE are secure or not.

Let us first consider a *secure boot* process. In the beginning, we need to run a small program called the BIOS (Basic Input/Output System) to initialise and test all the hardware components. The BIOS typically runs in firmware (code stored in a ROM). There is a need to verify if the BIOS has been tampered with. A simple way to do this is to read the code of the BIOS, compute a hash, and verify it with a stored hash. Now, who does this? That module needs to be infallible. Every secure system needs to have such a module that is known as the *root of trust* (RoT), which is assumed to be immune to attacks and is fully trustworthy. It is typically a small secure coprocessor that runs along with the main processor. Such a processor is also known as a *Trusted Platform Module*. The root of trust can alternatively be a piece of software, firmware or even a remote device – depends on the threat model.

The job of the root of trust hardware at boot time is to verify the BIOS by computing its hash and comparing it with a known value. The RoT also offers other cryptographic services to the rest of the system such as encryption, secure storage, and the facility to create digital signatures. It typically maintains a public-private key pair that allows it to *attest* a given piece of data (digital signature). Remote machines that have access to the processor's public key can subsequently verify the digital signature. The key pair can optionally be generated from the processor's PUF.

Finally, note that a system can have multiple RoTs and TPMs.

Measurement and Chain of Trust

The hash of a piece of code or data that is computed by the RoT is known as a *measurement*. To ensure that the TEE is setup correctly, the RoT can compute a measurement of the BIOS code, which can subsequently compute a measurement of the code of the OS loader. The OS loader can do the same for the OS, and the OS can finally compute the measurement of the secure application. Similar to cipher block chaining (Section 13.1.1), we can combine all the hashes to form a *chain of trust*. The final hash is the measurement of the entire TCB. The RoT can compare this with a stored value, and not allow the system to establish a TEE if the values do not match. If the hashes do not match, then it means that someone has tampered with the system.

The process of measurement starts from the BIOS and ends in the last module that is assumed to be within the TCB. If the OS is a part of the TCB, then the entire chain of trust will contain all the elements of the boot process including the OS. However, if the OS is not a part of the TCB, then the chain of trust will stop at at an earlier point such as the BIOS or the boot loader.

Remote attestation

The process of verifying the measurement can be done remotely as well. A secure software can request the processor to generate a digitally signed measurement of the TEE. This can then be sent to a remote machine, which can obtain the public key of the processor from a trusted third party. It can then validate the digital signature and verify if the measurement is correct or not. Such remote machines typically maintain a set of acceptable values of measurements for different configurations. If the measurement that was sent matches one of the stored values, then the remote machine can send data back to the secure software by encrypting it with the processor's public key. This can be decrypted by the RoT for the secure software.

Sealing

Secure programs use a lot of data that needs to be written to the hard disk. This data needs to be stored in an encrypted format and should be accessible to only the secure program at a later point in time. We thus need to somehow *tie* the key used to encrypt the data to a measurement. This process is known as *sealing*. Once the secure program is about to write to the disk or other forms of stable secondary storage, it asks the RoT to generate a measurement. This measurement is used to derive a key that is used to encrypt the data. The next time that we read this data back, we can derive the decryption key from the measurement. As long as the measurement is valid, we can read the data; otherwise we cannot read it.

13.3.3   Design of a Secure Processor

Let us create a reference design of a secure processor that is loosely inspired by the Intel® SGX (Software Guard Extensions) [Costan and Devadas, 2016] technology.

Design of the System

The first thing that needs to be decided while creating a secure processor is the TCB. This is shown in Figure 13.7. We assume that everything within the processor package inclusive of the cores, NoC, and the caches is secure. The processor-memory traffic is visible to an adversary. The threat model is that the adversary can read and write to all the memory locations, snoop and modify the data being sent on the memory bus. In fact this is very easy to do in practice, and is known as a *cold boot attack*. If we lower the temperature by dipping the motherboard in liquid nitrogen, then the DRAM can retain its data for a reasonably long time. This time is enough to translocate the DIMM chips to another motherboard. There we can boot an untrusted OS, read and modify all the data in main memory.

Given the threat model, it is obvious that we need to encrypt the traffic on the memory bus, and store all data in the DRAM memory in an encrypted form. We also need to provide the ACIF guarantees (Section 13.2.4).

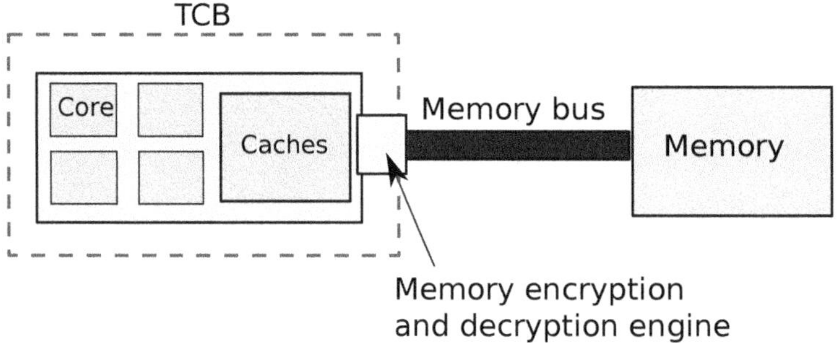

Figure 13.7: The TCB in a typical secure processor

Secure Memory Architecture

The aim is to secure the main memory and the memory bus by successfully avoiding snooping (eavesdropping), spoofing, splicing, and replay attacks. We assume that each memory controller has a dedicated unit called a Memory Encryption Engine (MEE) that implements all the security functionality.

We need to ensure the ACIF properties. Let us consider them one by one in a different order. First consider *confidentiality*, which can simply be ensured by encrypting all the data that is sent on the memory bus. If we always encrypt the same data with the same key, then this is leaking some information to the adversary and is thus unwise. Hence, we need to use a succession of different encryption keys. Next, consider *integrity*. We need to store a hash of every line that we read from memory. For ensuring *authentication,* we can encrypt the hash with a secret key. An encrypted hash is referred to as a Message Authentication Code (MAC). Once the MEE decrypts the hash and compares it with the hash of the data block, it also implicitly verifies the authenticity property. Finally for ensuring *freshness*, we need to avoid replay attacks. This can happen if we encrypt the same block every time with a different key, and the key is stored within the TCB. If any old data is sent by the attacker, the MEE will try to decrypt it with the stored secret key and then verify its hash. The verification process will fail. Note that this paragraph is loaded with concepts, and is fairly difficult to understand for beginners. Hence, we would like to request the reader to read this paragraph several times, understand the ACIF properties, and go through the entire section on cryptographic attacks (Section 13.2). It would be unwise to proceed to the rest of the text without meditating on this paragraph for quite some time.

Counter Mode Encryption

The key idea of our discussion up till now has been that we cannot encrypt the same piece of plaintext repeatedly with the same key. Even though the attacker cannot figure out the plaintext from the ciphertext, she can at least figure out that the same data is being used repeatedly. This behaviour can be used to mount many successful attacks. Hence, every time we encrypt a block of plaintext, we need to use a different key. This makes our task very complicated because now we need to manage millions of keys.

Instead of using so many separate encryption keys, we can use counter mode encryption that uses different counters in a systematic fashion. The effect is the same as using different encryption keys (see Section 13.1.1). We use two counters: a 64-bit major counter, and a 6-bit minor counter. We store one major counter per physical page (frame), which is assumed to be 4 KB, and we store one minor counter per 64-byte block. A frame contains 64 blocks, and thus we need to store 64 minor counters for each major counter. We cache the *counters* in a dedicated on-chip cache called the *counter cache* that the MEE has access to. Each entry in this counter cache is indexed by the physical page id and the line size is 448 bits. These bits are divided as shown in Figure 13.8. We store a 64-bit major counter and 64 6-bit minor counters.

At this point it is important to recapitulate the concepts in counter mode encryption. Recall that we encrypt the counter-pair with a secret key. The result is the one-time pad (OTP). We compute a XOR of the OTP and a block of plaintext to compute a block of ciphertext.

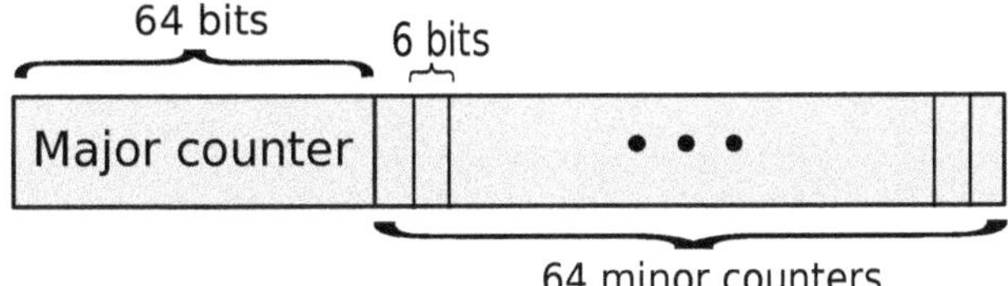

Figure 13.8: 64-bit major counter, and 64 6-bit minor counters (total: 448 bits)

The input to each counter mode encryption block for generating the one-time pad is a combination of the major counter (64 bits), minor counter (6 bits), and the block address (58 bits[1]). This is a total of 128 bits (or 16 bytes). The important point to note here is that we have concatenated the block address with the major+minor counter-pair. The reason is that if two blocks have the same data, they will have the same encrypted contents for the same counter-pair. This can leak some information. To avoid this, we also include the block address along with the counter-pair.

The secret key used in each AES block is a combination of the PUF, a random number generated at boot time, and the id of the enclave. This ensures that other enclaves cannot read the data of the currently running enclave, and every run of the same program produces different encrypted data. This part of the counter mode encryption algorithm is shown in Figure 13.9. After generating the OTP (16 bytes), we need to compute a XOR with a 16-byte plaintext block. The next task is to use four such encryption blocks to encrypt an entire 64-byte line.

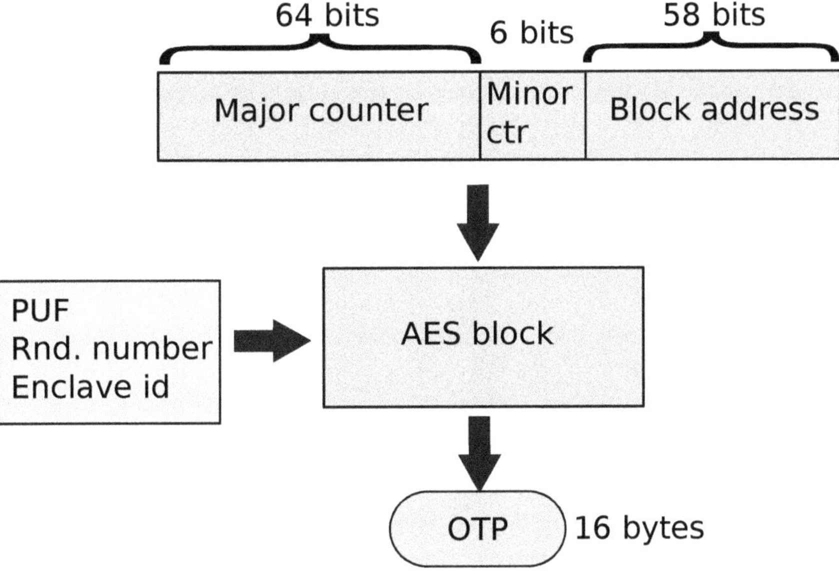

Figure 13.9: Encryption in a secure processor

Let us divide a 64-byte line into four 16-byte chunks, and encrypt them in parallel. The problem is that if two 16-byte chunks are the same, they will produce the same ciphertext. This problem can be avoided by computing a XOR between the 128-bit combination of the $\langle majorcounter, minorcounter, blockaddress \rangle$ and an enclave-specific randomly generated initialisation vector (IV) that is different for each 16-byte

---

[1] Assume a 64-bit address space. With a 64-byte block size, the block address becomes 58 bits.

chunk. The IV is generated when the enclave is created. This will ensure that two chunks with the same contents are encrypted differently.

Finally, for computing the MAC we can use one of the known hashing algorithms, and the same AES hardware with counters for encrypting it. This method of computing the MAC is known as the Carter-Wegman construction [Wegman and Carter, 1981].

Read Operation

Every time we have a miss in the last level cache (LLC) we need to send a request to main memory. We read the 64-byte data block, and its associated 64-bit MAC using two separate memory requests. This process takes a long time – typically 100-300 cycles. During this time we use the counter mode decryption algorithm to compute the OTP. The key innovation here is that the latency of this entire operation, computing the OTP, gets hidden in the shadow of the LLC miss. The decryption operation is thus not on the critical path. Once we get the encrypted data and its MAC, we decrypt them using the computed OTP. We can either wait to compute and verify the hash, or we can speculatively send the data to the LLC. Note that whenever we detect an ACIF violation, it is a catastrophic event, and we need to shut the processor down. Hence, there is no harm in sending the data to the LLC and verifying the hash at the same time. If there is no integrity violation (hashes match) then there is no problem, and if the hashes do not match then also sending the data early to the LLC does not matter because we shall lose all the erroneous volatile state by turning off the processor.

Since we verify the MAC, we can detect spoofing attacks – attacker cannot send arbitrary data. The block address is a part of the OTP; we can thus detect splicing attacks – attacker cannot replace the contents of memory locations (A, B) (data, MAC) with the contents of memory locations (C, D). Finally, since we use different counters each time we write a block to main memory, the attacker cannot mount a replay attack.

Evict Operation

Whenever, we evict a modified block from the LLC and write it to main memory, we need to encrypt it. This is done as follows. We first increment the minor counter in the counter cache; this creates a new encrypted version of the block. This will ensure that every time a block is written to memory it gets a new OTP (same effect as changing the encryption key). We can increase randomness further by initialising each major counter to a random value. The minor counters can still be initialised to 0.

Corner Cases

What happens if a minor counter overflows? This means it reaches $2^6 - 1$ (63). We would not like to reuse counter values – this enlarges the attack surface. Thus, we can reset all the minor counters to 0, and increment the major counter. The major counter is 64-bits long, and in practice will never overflow. This further implies that we need to read all the blocks in the page that are there in main memory, re-encrypt them with the new pair of counters, and write them back. This is an expensive operation. Fortunately, it is rather infrequent.

Important Point 21

The important point to note here is that if all the counters are stored correctly, then the system provides all ACIF guarantees, or the system stops because an ACIF violation is detected. Using counters and MACs prevents eavesdropping, spoofing, splicing, and replay attacks. The reader needs to convince herself of this fact.

Integrity Verification: Merkle Tree

Classical Approach

Our entire architecture's security only depends on the integrity of the counters. As long as they are deemed to be correct, we can say that the entire execution is secure. If we find a counter in the counter cache, which is located within the chip, then the counter will always be correct because the chip is assumed to be secure. However, the counter cache has a finite capacity and it will be necessary to evict counters to main memory. This is where an attacker might try to change the values of the counters. Hence, we also need to compute and store a hash of the counter values. This will ensure their integrity.

It is unfortunately possible to mount a replay or splicing attack that can simultaneously replace a set of counters and their corresponding hashes or MACs. The classical way of dealing with this problem is to create a structure known as a *Merkle tree*. This is a k-ary tree (k children per parent), where each parent contains the hash of each child's contents. The leaf nodes of this Merkle tree are the major and minor counters used to encrypt the data blocks in a single page (total: 448 bits).

We can compute the hash of these counters, and store the hash in the parent node. We can add one more level by again following the same procedure: compute the hash of the contents of each child, and store it in the parent. We can proceed in a similar manner to create a tree with $log_k(N)$ levels (see Figure 13.10). The most interesting property of the Merkle tree is that we can store the value of the root within the TCB: within a register in the MEE. As long as the root of the tree is stored correctly, the entire tree is correct. This is the key property of a Merkle tree that we would like to use. The reader needs to convince herself of this fact before proceeding forward. Any tampering anywhere in the tree can be easily detected.

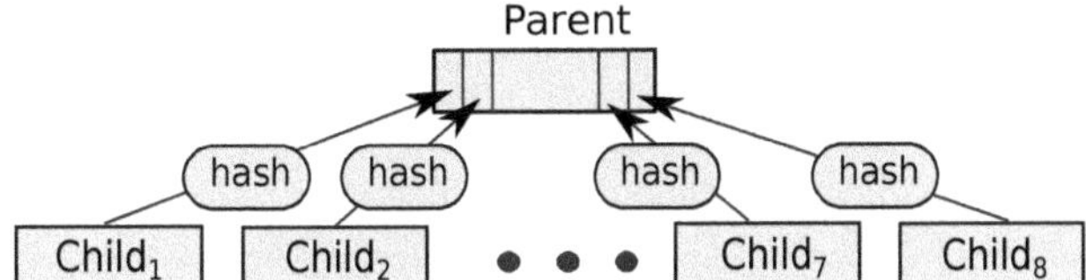

Figure 13.10: A k-ary Merkle tree

In a practical implementation, we can cache nodes of the Merkle tree in the processor's caches. Any cached value is deemed to be correct because it is within the TCB. Now assume that we need to verify the value of a certain counter, we first compute the hash of the major and all the minor counters, and check the hash at the parent node. If the parent node is in the CPU's caches, then it is deemed to be correct, and we need not proceed further. If this is not the case, then we need to verify the contents of the parent – this operation proceeds recursively until we reach a node that is either cached or is the root of the Merkle tree.

Likewise, for writing a group of major-minor counters to main memory, we need to traverse the Merkle tree towards the root, and update all the hashes on the way. This process can terminate when we reach a node that is cached in the CPU (again the reader needs to justify this). The entire process is reasonably inefficient because if a hash is 8 bytes (64-bits) then a 64-byte cache line can only contain 8 such hashes. Thus, k is restricted to 8. For a 1-GB secure memory space we need 7 levels, which is a significant overhead [2].

Efficient Approach

It turns out that we can use the same Carter-Wegman construction to compress the size of the Merkle tree.

First, recall that the size of the major and minor counters put together was 448 bits for a physical page. This means that we still have 64 bits left in a 64-byte (512-bit) line in main memory. Let us use these bits productively.

Should we use them to store the hash of the counters? This will unfortunately not work because the Merkle tree relies on a parent-child connection – parent stores the hash of the child's contents. This connection is not being established with this technique. Instead of storing the hash, let us store the

---

[2] A 1-GB memory has 2^{18} 4-KB pages. There are thus $log_8(2^{18})$ (=6) internal levels plus one level for the leaves. This makes a total of 7 levels.

encrypted hash – the MAC – in these 64 bits, and store the counters used to generate this MAC at the parent node. This solves all our problems – we have a parent-child connection, and the long 64-bit MAC is stored in the leaf node itself.

Let us elaborate. Consider the leaf nodes first. We first compute a 64-bit hash of the contents of a leaf node (major counter + all the minor counters). Then we use the Carter-Wegman approach to read the relevant counters from the parent, and encrypt the hash to produce the MAC. The assumption here is that the parent node is structured in a similar manner: it has one 64-bit major counter, 64 6-bit minor counters, and the space for a 64-bit MAC. Once we compute the MAC of the leaf node, it is stored in the leaf node itself (recall that we had kept 64 bits of space in a line for storing the MAC). The MAC is dependent on the rest of the contents of the leaf node (its counters) and the corresponding major-minor counter pair that is stored in the parent node. We can see the parent-child relationship here, and the way in which integrity is maintained.

We can now generalise this design. Given the fact that the structure of the leaf node and the parent node is the same in terms of the space apportioned for storing the major counter, the 64 minor counters, and the MAC, we can extend this design to all the levels of the tree. All of them are structured in this manner. A node at level i has 64 bits to store its MAC, which is computed using the major-minor counter pair stored in its parent level (level $i - 1$). Refer to Figure 13.11.

Note that it is not possible to mount a splicing or replay attack because the parent stores the counters that keep changing with every update. The logic is similar to the reasoning we had used to design our system for storing regular data blocks.

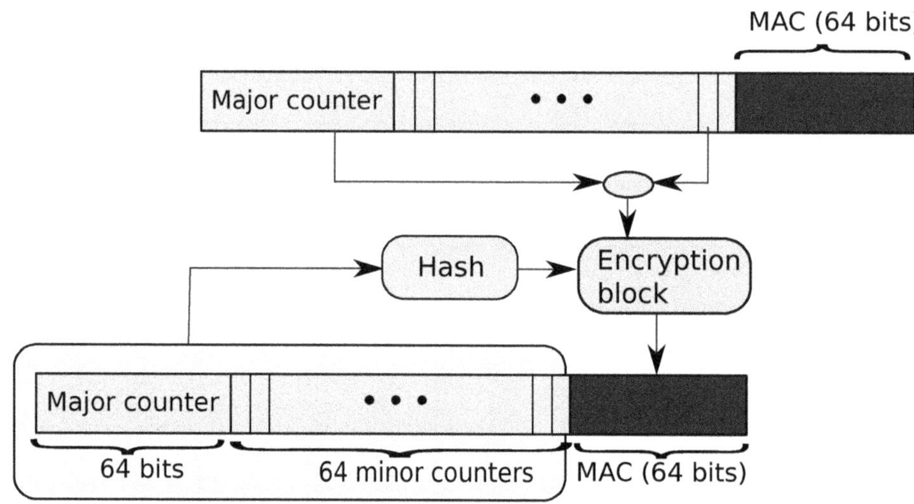

Figure 13.11: Counters and MAC stored in main memory

It is important to stress that we still have a parent-child connection, and here also, the root of the Merkle tree captures the values of all the counters in the system. We can have similar optimisations here also, where we can cache the nodes in the Merkle tree such that every time we do not have to traverse the tree till the root. Let us quantify the advantage.

Recall that the parent node has the same counter structure as the child node; we can thus create a 64-ary tree. For a 1-GB secure memory, we just need 4 levels (including the level that contains all the leaves). If a minor counter overflows in an intermediate node, we need to increment the major counter, set all the minor counters to zero, and recompute the MACs for all the child nodes. Given that nodes at higher levels are expected to receive relatively more updates, the tree can have a lower arity at higher levels.

13.3.4 The Software Environment

Most secure processors assume that the OS is not trusted. They provide security guarantees in spite of an untrusted OS, and even assign the OS key responsibilities such as issuing privileged instructions to manage secure execution environments and managing the page tables. This may sound somewhat contradictory, but it is possible to do so.

Creating and Initialising an Enclave

A secure processor needs to provide a set of instructions that can be used by the secure program or the operating system to create and manage enclaves (secure execution environments). The typical configuration is that a regular process known as the *host process* creates these enclaves, executes code in it, and ultimately tears it down.

Most secure processors such as Intel SGX provide an `ECREATE` instruction that creates the data structures for an enclave. At boot time, we partition the physical memory into a non-secure part and a secure part. The frames in the secure part can only be used by active enclaves. Furthermore, for every secure process (running instance of a program), we also partition the virtual address space into two parts: secure and non-secure. When an enclave is created a portion of the secure part of the physical address space (frames) and a set of contiguous pages from the virtual address space of the secure process are assigned to it.

Subsequently, we need to provide an `EADD` instruction that adds code and data to the secure enclave. The OS needs to copy code/data from non-secure pages to secure pages. Once the starting state has been set up, we need an `EINIT` instruction to launch the enclave. Before an enclave is launched, the TPM computes its measurement, and digitally signs it. Sometimes, the process of generating an authenticated measurement is very complicated, and thus processors have a dedicated enclave known as the *quoting enclave* that performs cryptographic operations on the measurement in software. The signed measurement is then stored in dedicated control structures. It has several uses. It can be used by an enclave to prove its identity to other secure enclaves running locally, or it can be used to convince a remote third party with regards to its identity.

Execution within an Enclave

Subsequently, the enclave starts executing the secure code. During this process the operating system manages the enclave's page tables, and the core running the secure enclave gets the address translations from the TLB. If the OS is not trusted, it can mount an *address translation attack*. This means that it can make a virtual page in the secure region point to a frame in the non-secure region. The secure program will not get to know and it will get tricked into writing secure information to non-secure pages. The OS can thus steal the secure program's secrets unbeknownst to it.

To prevent such attacks, it is necessary to maintain a mapping within secure memory. This is usually an inverted page table (IPT) that is indexed by the physical frame number where each entry contains the virtual page ids that point to it. The reason for using an IPT is because in this case we are more concerned about all the virtual pages that point to a given physical frame; it should never be the case that a secure and non-secure virtual page point to the same frame unless we explicitly want this to be the case. Whenever, pages are added to an enclave by `EADD` instructions, entries in the IPT are created. Before the enclave is launched, we need to check that all the entries in the IPT point to valid pages and frames. A page is valid if it is a known code or data page, and it lies within the portion of the virtual address space marked as secure. A frame is valid if it falls within the secure region of the physical address space. Subsequently, after the enclave is launched, we monitor all the updates to the TLB. Whenever a mapping is created that involves either a secure page or frame, the mapping needs to be first checked in the IPT. If it is an invalid mapping or the same frame is mapped to a different page, then we need to generate a fault and terminate the operation. This ensures that address translation attacks cannot be mounted because any change to the TLB needs to be validated by looking up the IPT first. The crux of this idea is that all updates to the TLB are monitored and we do not allow any update to the TLB to go through without consulting the IPT first. We can implement custom logic in this phase.

Note that we can still have page faults and TLB misses. Page faults need to be handled by the OS. For a TLB miss, we have two options: a dedicated hardware unit can populate the TLB by accessing the page tables or the TLB can be populated by a software module. Since the OS populates the page tables, this process can expose several security risks. They are handled as follows.

1. For secure pages, the hardware needs to zero out the bits that point to the exact memory word in the page that caused a miss, and just report the page id. The OS will thus not be able to see the word-access sequence. It can still see the page-access sequence because it can induce page faults and TLB misses by deliberately clearing the TLB or by swapping out pages.

2. We cannot simply allow a secure page to be swapped out from main memory. The OS can tamper with its contents. Hence, before swapping a page out it is necessary to perform some bookkeeping. First, we need to create a tree akin to the Merkle tree that we used for memory data. Second, we need to compute a MAC for the page with a nonce based scheme (see Section 13.2.4) that preserves the ACIF guarantees and store the $\langle key, nonce \rangle$ pair at a dedicated location in the secure physical address space. When the page is swapped in, we verify its contents.

   Highly flexible implementations can also allow the metadata pages that contain such page-specific nonces and keys to be swapped out. Again, we need to follow the same process and maintain the encryption information in the secure space. This approach allows us to support large enclaves, and also many enclaves simultaneously.

In spite of such measures, the OS can definitely see the page-access sequence upon a page fault. Furthermore, if a TLB miss is handled in software, the OS can see the page id for that too. It has been shown that, from just the page-access sequence, it is possible to derive important information in some cases. Most secure processors do not protect against such *page fault snooping attacks*.

System Calls and Interrupts

Interrupts can be delivered to cores executing secure enclaves. In this case, they need to store a *secure context* of the running thread in the secure region. This will include the values of all the registers, the PC, and all encryption information including the enclave id. For such asynchronous enclave exits, it is necessary to flush the TLB such that subsequent accesses cannot be made to the secure region. A dedicated hardware mechanism is required for this.

We also need to support enclave enter (**EENTER**) and enclave exit (**EEXIT**) instructions that can be used to voluntarily enter an enclave and exit it, respectively. Normally, the **EENTER** instruction is issued by the host process to enter an enclave and resume its execution. In this case, the OS can treat this as a regular context switch and store the context of the host process. Additionally, the hardware needs to record the fact that a given secure enclave is executing on the core.

The enclave code needs to issue an **EEXIT** instruction if there is a need to temporarily leave the enclave and execute code in the host process. For example, enclaves are not allowed to issue system calls because we wish to limit their interaction with the OS. Hence, an enclave needs to send the relevant system call arguments to the host process via a shared page, and then issue an **EEXIT** instruction. After the secure context is stored and the TLB is flushed, the OS can resume the host process, which can execute the system call on behalf of the enclave code. The host process can then invoke the **EENTER** instruction to resume the execution of the enclave.

Tearing Down an Enclave

It is necessary to provide an **EREMOVE** instruction to tear down an enclave. The OS can invoke it to dismantle the enclave. A dedicated hardware units clears the state of the secure thread including its pages in memory and pages swapped to the disk.

13.3.5 Oblivious RAM

Till now we have only focused on protecting the data that is sent or received from main memory. Unfortunately, addresses need to be sent to main memory in an unencrypted form. Conventional DRAM does not support encrypted addresses. An attacker can easily snoop these addresses and gain a lot of information about the execution of the program in terms of the data it is accessing and the code it is running. An attacker can further increase the information content of this process by executing a few instructions of the secure code, and then causing an enclave exit by sending an interrupt. Until DIMMs start supporting encrypted addresses this problem will be there. This is a generic problem and afflicts any bus that carries addresses.

We need to thus create an *oblivious RAM* or *ORAM*, which is a virtual layer over DRAM that obfuscates the access sequence in such a manner that an attacker gets as little information as possible by studying the sequence of addresses. An absolutely naive approach will be to access all the locations in the DRAM for every single access. The CPU can then only choose that value, which it actually needed. Another equally impractical idea is to randomly permute all the addresses at the beginning, and then subsequently when we read a memory line, we write it to a new location. This means that at the memory line level we need to maintain a long list of mappings. These impractical ideas do give us two important insights though. The first is *redundancy* – we need to access a set of locations for every single access. The second is *permutation* – it is necessary to permute the memory locations such that the physical location for a memory address keeps changing. In fact both are required (the proof is beyond the scope of the book).

ORAM as proposed in the original paper by Goldreich and Ostrovsky [Goldreich and Ostrovsky, 1996] was considered to be very slow to be used in practical settings. Off late a practical implementation known as *Path ORAM* [Stefanov et al., 2013] has been proposed, which still is associated with large slowdowns (2 to 10 times), yet can be used if there is a dire need.

Path ORAM

Assume that N is the size of the secure memory in terms of blocks. The block addresses are between 0 and $N - 1$. This algorithm proposes to maintain a small local cache at the memory controller known as the *stash(S)*, and a *position map(posMap)* that maps each block address to a unique position in the range $0 \ldots (N - 1)$. Given an address a, let $S[a]$ represent its entry in the stash, and if $S[a] = \phi$, then it means that address a is not present in the stash. Before presenting the algorithm let us define all the terms and subroutines (read it very carefully).

In the main memory we maintain a complete binary tree with 2^L leaves and $L + 1$ levels, where $L = log_2(N)$. Each node stores a bucket containing B blocks. These can be real memory blocks or dummy blocks. We assume a function $readPath(k)$ that returns the contents of all the blocks in the path from the root of the tree to the kth leaf. Here the *position* of the leaf is k. Let $P(k)$ represent the path from the root (level 0) to the kth leaf (level $L + 1$), and let $P(k)[l]$ represent the bucket at the lth level in this path. Let us define the function $getCousins(k, l)$ that returns a set W of block addresses, where each address $a' \in W$ satisfies the following property: $P(k)[l] = P(posMap[a'])[l]$ and $S[a'] \neq \phi$. This function essentially returns all the addresses whose corresponding leaves(positions) are in the subtree rooted at $P(k)[l]$ and whose data is present in the stash. Finally, assume a function *trim* that takes the set W (output of $getCousins$) and selects a random subset of B elements (adds dummy elements if $| W | < B$).

The key insight is that the data for address a can be present in any bucket along the path $P(posMap[a])$. We thus need to fetch the entire path, and then slightly permute and rearrange the data in the tree. The pseudocode for a memory access to address a is as follows [Stefanov et al., 2013]. The proof is beyond the scope of this book.

```
1   /* op is the operation, a is the address, new_data is the data to be written (
        if op==write) */
2   access(op, a, new_data):
3
4   /* Read the mapping of the address from posMap and compute the new random
        position */
5   pos ← posMap[a]
6   posMap[a] ← random (0 ... (N-1))
7
8   /* Add all the blocks on the path (pos to root) to the stash S */
9   S ← S ∪ readPath(pos)
10
11  /* Implement the read or write. For a write add the <address,data> to the stash
        . */
12  old_data ← S[a]
13  if (op == write) S[a] ← new_data
14
15  for l ∈ (L, L-1, ..., 1, 0) {
16          W ← getCousins(pos, l) /* get all cousin nodes that are in the stash */
17          W ← trim(W)                        /* |W| = B   */
18          S ← S - W                  /* remove W from S */
19
20          /* Add all the addresses in W to the bucket at level l in P(pos), along
                  with their data */
21          ∀a′ ∈ W, P(pos)[l].add (a′, S[a′])
22  }
```

13.4 Side-Channel Attacks

Recently, your author was narrated a story by a cybercrime investigator. A lady in France was being blackmailed by a kidnapper to pay ransom money. The kidnapper used to call her on WhatsApp and one day as she was moving around with the phone in her house, the kidnapper told her that she was currently in her living room, and was moving towards the kitchen. She got totally unnerved and got convinced that her apartment was bugged. This is why she did not call the police immediately. The fun part is that the kidnapper had not placed any camera in her apartment. He was a known person who knew the layout of her apartment and was guessing her position based on the strength of the Wi-Fi signal, which could again be guessed from the Whatsapp call quality! This is an example of a *side channel* where information leaks out in unusual and unforeseeable ways. We have many such side channels in the CPU and the memory system. Note that such channels have an extremely low information content and bandwidth, yet they can give us very crucial information.

In this section, we present a brief introduction to such attacks. For more details, readers can refer to a survey paper by Szefer [Szefer, 2019]. There is a related term known as a *covert* channel where a process running in a secure environment communicates with a process outside the environment via such a mechanism, particularly, when they are not supposed to communicate. We will focus our attention on side channel based attacks in this section, and use the generic terms *victim* and *attacker*.

13.4.1 Classification of Side Channels

Figure 13.12(a) shows a taxonomy for side-channel attacks. Figure 13.12(b) shows the key part of the RSA algorithm where we perform a modular exponentiation. We will use this code as a running example throughout this section. Note that the number of iterations of the loop is dependent on the number e.

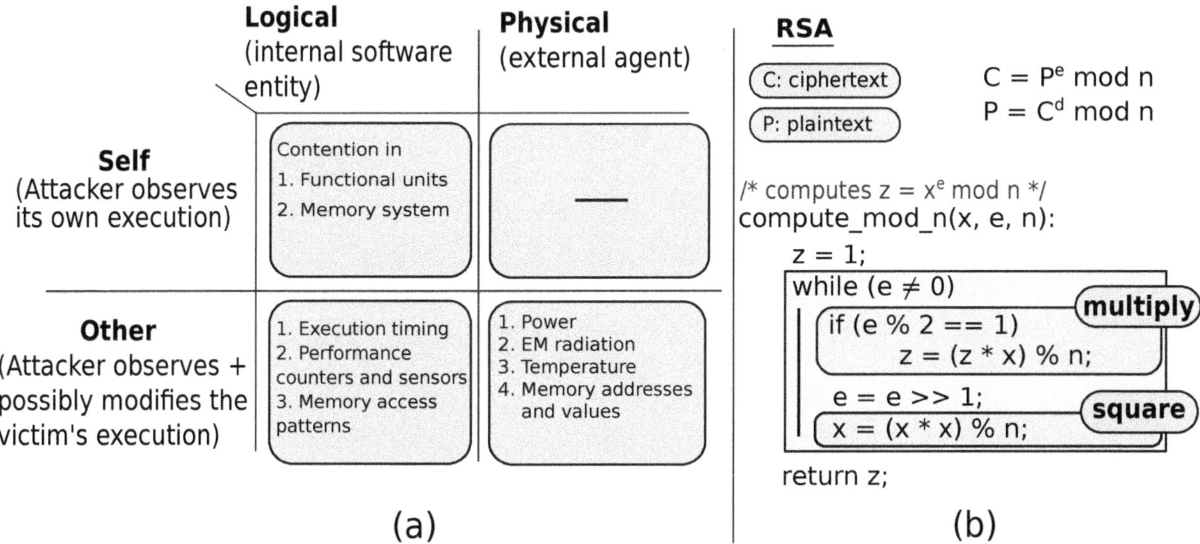

Figure 13.12: (a) Classification of different kinds of side channels [Szefer, 2019], (b) Running example: the binary modular exponentiation operation in the RSA algorithm

Furthermore, each iteration has two basic operations: modular square and modular multiply. Whenever the LSB of e is 1, we execute the instructions for the modular multiply operation. Just by monitoring this operation, which has a unique signature in terms of instruction latencies, power consumption, and i-cache line addresses, we can figure out all the bits in the key, e!

Let us now go through the different types of side-channel attacks. The square at the top left refers to scenarios, where the attacker monitors its own execution. Note that whenever there is a contention between two threads in a shared structure, it is possible for one thread's behaviour to influence the behaviour of the other thread. Thus, a thread can monitor its own behaviour and get some valuable information about the other thread (explained later). The second row refers to scenarios where the attacker monitors the victim and tries to also modify the environment in which the victim operates. Such channels can be of two types: one in which the attacker is a software entity, and the other in which it has physical access to the processor.

13.4.2 Type 1: Attacker Monitoring Itself

Whenever there is contention at a shared structure such as the branch predictor, BTB, floating point unit, d-cache, i-cache, L2 cache, interconnect, directory, or the memory controller, we can deduce important information from the nature of the destructive interference.

For a large number of contention-based attacks the key idea is very similar. They rely on *data-dependent accesses*, which means that the addresses of memory instructions (instruction or data) are dependent on data values such as bits in the key. If such an access has been made, then its corresponding data will be present in the cache, and a subsequent access will result in a cache hit. We can use a high-resolution timer to measure the latency of a memory operation and infer if there is a hit in the cache or not. Alternatively, we can check if the contents at an address have been evicted or not by inferring if there is a cache miss. Both these approaches will help us detect and characterise data-dependent accesses. There are many ways of implementing this in practice.

Let us explain how to do this in the context of cache-based side channels for our running example: RSA encryption.

The most popular example in this space is the Prime+Probe technique. Here the attacker thread accesses all the cache lines in the L1 or L2 levels. This is the *priming* phase. Subsequently, it yields the processor to the victim thread. After the victim has executed for some time, the attacker starts to execute again. It measures the time of accessing each cache line with a high resolution nanosecond-level timer (*probing* phase). It can automatically infer the lines that have suffered a cache miss because it takes longer to access them – they need to be fetched from lower levels. In this case, there will be a cache miss if the victim has evicted the block. This can give the attacker some idea about the memory addresses accessed by the victim. For example, if we can execute the victim for very short intervals of time, then in our running example we can find out if it executed the modular multiply operation (a data-dependent instruction access) or not. This will give us the value of one bit in the key.

A similar technique is the Flush+Reload technique that can be used when we have shared pages between the attacker and the victim. Here the attacker first flushes a given set of cache lines from the caches. Many processors already provide such flush instructions. It is alternatively possible to do so by accessing another memory space that is as large as the cache. After this is done, the attacker allows the victim thread to run for a short duration. Then it checks if any of the flushed lines are back in the cache using a high-resolution timer by checking for cache hits and misses. This is a practical technique when the code pages of a cryptographic library such as RSA are shared between the attacker and the victim. The attacker can use this approach to find out which instruction blocks the victim accessed. It can thus find out if the victim executed the modular multiply operation or not.

We can on similar lines exploit contention at the functional unit level. For example, if the victim and attacker are running as simultaneous hardware threads, then the attacker can just issue multiply instructions and analyse the slowdown. If the victim is also issuing multiply instructions, then the attacker will perceive a slowdown because of structural hazards (limited number of multiply units). We can do very similar things with the branch predictor where we try to create an aliasing between the *if* statement in the modular multiply operation and a conditional branch statement in the attacker's code.

Another very interesting attack type in this category is the *Rowhammer attack*. If a given DRAM row is accessed repeatedly, it causes the neighbouring row to leak faster, and the neighbouring row ultimately has bit flips. Any subsequent access to the neighbouring row takes more time because error correction needs to be done; the time required for a memory access operation can be measured with a high resolution timer. To leverage this effect, the attacker first accesses two neighbouring DRAM rows: R_0 and R_1. We assume that it can control the page-to-frame mapping process. It first repeatedly accesses R_0 to increase the probability of R_1 developing a bit-flip fault in the future. Just before R_1 has bit flips, it schedules the victim. Assume that row R_0 is the target of a data-dependent access by the victim thread. Subsequently, if R_0 is accessed, R_1 will see bit flips. This can be detected with a high-resolution timer, and thus we can get an idea of the victim's memory access pattern.

13.4.3   Type 2: Attacker Monitoring or Manipulating the Victim using Software Techniques

This is another class of attacks where the aim is to measure different aspects of the victim's execution.

Here the Evict+Time technique is typically used to exploit cache based side channels. We first measure the execution time of the victim program. Then we evict all the lines from certain cache sets by accessing other data that maps to the same sets. We measure the time of the victim program again. In this case, if the difference in times is more than a certain threshold, then we can conclude that the victim accessed some of the evicted cache sets. Even page fault snooping attacks (Section 13.3.4) by the OS fall in this category.

Similarly, an attacker can use instruction level timing information to learn some features of the victim program. For example, if it has access to accurate timing information such as detailed statistics regarding the execution of functional units, then it can estimate the number of modular multiply operations that have been performed. This will give it an estimate of the number of 1s in the key.

Performance counters that measure the total number of cache hits, misses, memory accesses, and overall instructions can be a very important source of information as well. In the case of our running example, we can also use this information to predict the number of 1s in the key by counting the number of arithmetic operations.

Recently a new class of attacks known as *speculative execution attacks* or *transient execution attacks* have been proposed such as Spectre [Kocher et al., 2019], Meltdown [Lipp et al., 2018], and Foreshadow [Van Bulck et al., 2018]. These attacks extract information from memory read accesses made in the wrong path of a conditional branch. Consider the following code snippet that needs to be a part of the victim program.

```
if (val < threshold)
        v = array1[array2[x]];
```

Assume in this case that *val* is in the control of the attacker – it is an input that can somehow be modified. The attacker can deliberately set it to be greater than the threshold. The double array access may still go through to memory because such wrong-path memory read instructions can still get executed (not committed) before the branch instruction of the *if* statement reaches the head of the ROB. The address that will be accessed is $array2[x] * 4 + array1\_base$ assuming the size of each array element is 4 bytes, and the starting address of $array1$ is $array1\_base$. This access is clearly against the semantics of the victim program. Sadly, we can find this address using the Prime+Probe technique. From this address, we can find the value of $array2[x]$. Furthermore, if the attacker can control x, we can read any memory location. It could contain a secret key!

13.4.4 Type 3: Attacker Monitoring the Victim by Physically Accessing the System

If the attacker has physical access to the system, then it can monitor the power consumption signature, temperature profile, and the electromagnetic (EM) radiation. If we consider our running example then we can clearly see that the modular multiply and modular square operations will have very distinct power and EM profiles. These can be analysed using sophisticated signal processing algorithms to identify several bits of the key. Temperature of course has a much larger time scale. However, by running the victim program repeatedly, we can get an estimate of the aggregate power consumption and possibly estimate the number of 1s in the key.

The attacker can also physically insert probes into the memory bus and read out all the addresses. Unless ORAM is used, the address pattern will be visible to the attacker.

13.4.5 Countermeasures

There are three generic countermeasures used to reduce the probability of such attacks.

1. Partition the on-chip resources to eliminate contention. For example, if there are two threads, we can partition all the cache sets between them. Likewise can partition other structures such as the branch predictor or the floating point unit. This will eliminate destructive interference and stop the attacker from getting any information regarding the victim's behaviour.

2. Deliberately add noise to the computation such that we can eliminate data-dependent accesses. This means that we access many more locations than what is required such that the attacker cannot derive any information from the access pattern.

3. Turn off features such as the high-resolution timer or speculative execution. This is most of the time very expensive.

13.5 Summary and Further Reading

13.5.1 Summary

Summary 12

1. The goal of any hardware security architecture is to provide the ACIF guarantees: authenticity, confidentiality, integrity, and freshness.

2. A good cryptographic cipher should have both the properties of **confusion** (a single bit of the key determines a large number of ciphertext bits) and **diffusion** (if we change a single bit in the plaintext, roughly half the bits in the ciphertext change).

3. The AES algorithm is divided into four rounds that shift, substitute, and permute the bits. The default AES algorithm typically operates on 16 bytes of data. To encrypt larger pieces of text we need to use one of the AES modes. The most relevant mode is counter mode encryption. Here two counters – a major counter and a minor counter – are concatenated and encrypted with the private key to produce a one-time pad (OTP). This is XORed with the plaintext to produce the cipher text.

4. RC4 is the most common stream cipher that produces one byte at a time.

5. The RSA algorithm uses two keys: a public key and a private key. Both encryption and decryption rely on modular exponentiation to produce their results. They can be used to create digital signatures to verify the authenticity of the sender, which is tantamount to encrypting a message with the sender's private key. The third party can decrypt this message with the sender's public key and thus verify its identity.

6. To verify the integrity of the message, we typically need to compute a short 1-way hash. Sometimes this hash is encrypted with a key to establish authenticity. Such a keyed hash is known as a MAC.

7. We can have different kinds of attacks in secure architectures.

    Snooping or Eavesdropping An attacker reads the data. This can be avoided by using encryption.

    Spoofing An attacker masquerades as some other node. Solution: use digital signatures.

    Splicing A part of one message is replaced with a part of another message. Use sender specific MACs to establish integrity and identity.

    Replay Old messages including their hashes are replayed. We need to add nonces or sequence numbers to messages, or use counter mode encryption.

8. The most common attack on software is based on buffer overflows.

9. In any secure hardware architecture, we need to assume a trusted computing base, an attack surface, and a threat model. These will be used to create the specifications of a trusted execution environment (TEE). It is necessary to ensure that such a TEE is setup correctly. We need a root of trust (RoT) that first verifies the boot process and provides some cryptographic services that are assumed to be correct. Subsequently, we need to establish a chain of trust from the RoT to the TEE. This is established by computing hashes (measurements) of the relevant code

> *and data of the TCB, and then verifying the overall measurement with known values (locally
> or remotely). Secure data can also be stored outside the TCB, however it needs to be sealed –
> encrypted with the correct measurement as the key.*
>
> 10. *We can design a secure architecture that uses counter mode encryption to provide the ACIF
> guarantees for blocks in main memory. We just need to protect the integrity of all the counters,
> which can easily be done with a Merkle tree. For the sake of efficiency, these counters can be
> stored in a dedicated on-chip counter cache, and a few of the Merkle tree nodes can be stored
> in the L1/L2 caches. The root of the Merkle tree however needs to always be kept on chip.*
>
> 11. *It is necessary to provide a set of instructions to create and manage secure enclaves. Even
> though the OS is typically not trusted, it still manages the secure applications' page tables. It
> cannot mount address translation attacks because any update to the TLB needs to be vetted by
> an inverted page table stored in the secure memory region of each enclave.*
>
> 12. *Oblivious RAM (ORAM) introduces redundant memory accesses and permutes the locations
> to obfuscate the memory access pattern.*
>
> 13. *Side-channel attacks are mostly based on deriving information out of destructive interference
> in contended shared structures. The most common side channels are the caches. In most
> side-channel attacks on caches, the attacker first runs and sets the state of the cache, then
> the victim accesses specific caches lines, and finally the attacker runs once again. The timing
> differences between the first and third runs often yield the set of cache lines that are accessed.
> If they are dependent on the data, then we can derive useful information about the victim's
> secrets.*
>
> 14. *We can also mount a set of attacks by analysing the victim process's power, EM radiation, or
> temperature traces. They provide important information regarding the set of instructions that
> must have executed, which can give us an idea about the secret data.*
>
> 15. *Effective countermeasures seek to either partition the hardware resources among the threads,
> or deliberately introduce noise into the computation.*

13.5.2   Further Reading

To work on hardware security a strong foundation in applied cryptography is essential. We would
recommend a standard text on cryptography such as the book by Padhye [Padhye et al., 2018] or
Stallings [Stallings, 2006]. The e-book by Lee [Lee, 2013] is also very comprehensive. Students should
also educate themselves about techniques in light-weight cryptography [Eisenbarth et al., 2007] and
study the PRESENT algorithm [Bogdanov et al., 2007].

For hardware security one of the best resources is the e-book by Szefer [Szefer, 2018] and his survey
on side-channel attacks [Szefer, 2019]. For papers published in academia, readers should start with some
of the seminal papers such as XOM [Thekkath et al., 2000], Aegis [Suh et al., 2005], Bonsai Merkle
trees [Rogers et al., 2007], Ascend [Ren et al., 2017] (contains secure ORAM), Bastion [Champagne and
Lee, 2010] (support for trusted software), and Vault [Taassori et al., 2018]. Reading the description of
Intel SGX [Costan and Devadas, 2016] by Costan et al. is mandatory in this area, along with relevant
literature on ARM® Trustzone® [Ngabonziza et al., 2016, Pinto and Santos, 2019]. For ORAM, readers
should start with Goldreich and Ostrovsky's paper [Goldreich and Ostrovsky, 1996] and then study Path
ORAM [Stefanov et al., 2013].

The survey paper by Szefer on side-channel attacks [Szefer, 2019] is a good starting point in this
area. Some of the most publicised exploits today use speculative execution such as Spectre [Kocher

et al., 2019] (transient execution attacks), Meltdown [Lipp et al., 2018] (read kernel data), and Foreshadow [Van Bulck et al., 2018] (read data in an SGX enclave). Readers should also make themselves familiar with power analysis attacks [Ors et al., 2004] and attacks based on analysing electromagnetic emanations [Sehatbakhsh et al., 2020].

Exercises

Ex. 1 — Design an LLC replacement policy that prevents eviction-based attacks.

Ex. 2 — Design a scheme that prevents the denial-of-service attack at the DRAM level. For mounting such an attack, an attacker sends a flurry of requests to the DRAM, and this causes other threads to starve. How can we incorporate fairness in the DRAM memory controller to ensure that this does not happen?

Ex. 3 — Most secure architectures such as Intel SGX have a threat model that assumes that the processor is trusted and the OS is untrusted. Such Trusted Execution Environments ensure that the applications run securely even in the presence of a malicious OS. However, it lacks trusted I/O paths, and thus I/O messages need to pass through the OS. It is possible for the OS to maliciously read and modify I/O data. Propose a solution to this problem.

Ex. 4 — Design a scheme that improves the performance of integrity trees used to prevent replay attacks. The access frequencies of different blocks in the memory space is non-uniform. How can we design our integrity trees to take this into account?

Ex. 5 — Simulate a secure architecture such as Intel SGX in an architectural simulator.

14

Architectures for Machine Learning

Traditional paradigms of computing are undergoing a tectonic shift. This is primarily because many conventional methods including the algorithms that we study in our early years of college have proven to be inadequate to solve today's problems. For example, we still do not have good algorithms for complex tasks such as face recognition, feature recognition in images, and speech synthesis. These tasks are traditionally associated with the human brain; training machines to do them using current techniques is very difficult. Such tasks were almost impossible to successfully complete in the 2010-2015 time frame with old school artificial intelligence technologies. However, off late the scenario has changed. With the advent of technologies like deep learning that mimic the processes in the human brain like never before, it is possible to solve many of these complex problems to some degree. We are far from getting the accuracies that even a 2-year old can get; however, many steps have been taken in this direction in the last 5 years (as of 2020). In fact the way your author has written most of this book is by using a speech to text translation software! Typing for long hours places a strain on the wrists and shoulders; hence, to reduce the associated risk of injury and to significantly increase the speed and pleasure of writing this book, your author simply spoke in to a microphone, and a computer software did the rest!

All of these extremely interesting things are possible because instead of using traditional algorithms based on data structures and graphs, such speech recognition software use methods known as *deep learning* or *deep neural networks*. A deep learning system is nothing but a hierarchy of simple learners that increasingly learn more and more complex concepts – this is inspired by the way the human brain learns new concepts. It is thus possible to transcribe an entire piece of speech with the right spellings and punctuation. Deep learning technologies are the norm now when it comes to image recognition, image analysis, speech recognition, natural language processing, self-driving cars, and robotic systems. In fact last night your author went for dinner and to book a table he used a chatbot that asked him for his preferences including the time and the number of people, and then dutifully booked the table in the right restaurant. What technology did the chatbot use? **Answer: Deep learning**.

Any deep learning system is divided into a set of layers. Each layer processes the inputs by computing a function over the set of inputs. They can either be linear or nonlinear functions. Designers typically alternate the linear and nonlinear layers to learn extremely complex functions. The layers learn increasingly complex concepts, and ultimately they are able to recognise faces or transcribe speech into text. Note that this kind of computation is very different from the kind of computation that happens in normal integer or floating point programs. Furthermore, the computation is massively parallel and requires a very high memory bandwidth. This is one reason why deep learning methods were not popular before 2010 primarily because we did not have the hardware to run these algorithms. But with the advent of large-scale parallel processing frameworks such as FPGAs and GPUs, large memories and storage devices, it is now possible to run deep learning algorithms on massive amounts of data. Just consider the vast amounts of data that social networking sites process on a daily basis. To analyse all this data, we need very large data centres that essentially run deep learning algorithms.

Let us make it clear that this chapter is not about teaching the fundamentals of deep learning or discussing popular software implementations. Readers can refer to the book by Goodfellow, Bengio, and Courville [Goodfellow et al., 2016] to get a thorough understanding of deep learning technologies. Some popular deep learning frameworks such as Caffe [Jia et al., 2014], TensorFlow [Abadi et al., 2016], and Keras [Gulli and Pal, 2017] are extensively documented and readers can go through them. This chapter is devoted to novel computer architectures that are designed exclusively for accelerating deep learning algorithms. We shall first provide a very brief introduction to some popular deep learning architectures, then discuss the process of mapping the code to an architecture, and finally discuss the design of custom deep learning hardware.

14.1 Basics of Deep Learning

The aim of any learning system is to learn a function that is hidden. The learner is given a set of inputs and their corresponding outputs. Based on them it needs to estimate the function that computes the outputs given the inputs. The process of trying to learn this function is known as *training*. Once the learner (also known as the *model*) has been trained, it can be used to predict the output of an hitherto unseen input. This process is known as *testing*. Since we do not know the actual process that converts the inputs to the outputs, the function that is estimated will be an approximation of the real function. Hence, it is expected that there will be some error in the output. Better learners minimise this error over a set of test inputs. In the learning literature there are several ways to measure the error: absolute value of the difference, mean square error, and so on. Regardless of the way that the error is measured, the main aim of any learning process is to minimise the error for unseen test inputs.

14.1.1 Formal Model of the Learning Problem

A learning system typically takes an n-element vector $\mathbf{x}$ as input and returns an output y, which can be a floating point value or an integer. We shall use the bold font for vectors and matrices, and use the regular font for scalars. In addition, let the real output be $\hat{y}$ in this case. The error is thus a function of y and $\hat{y}$. Furthermore, following convention let $\mathbf{x}$ be a column vector. We traditionally write $\mathbf{x} \in \mathcal{R}^n$, which means that $\mathbf{x}$ is a vector that contains n real numbers. In general, the training algorithm is given a set of inputs and a set of outputs. Let us represent the set of inputs as $\mathbf{X}$, where the ith column is the ith input vector, and the set of outputs as a column vector $\mathbf{y}$ (the ith entry is the ith output). We want to find the relationship – function f^* – between the set of inputs and the set of outputs. Given that we will never get to know what the real relationship actually is, we have two make an intelligent guess from the training data that has been provided to us: $\mathbf{X}$ and $\mathbf{y}$. It is important to note here that the hidden function f^* does not take into account the order of inputs. It is in a sense memoryless – does not remember the last input.

The main aim of the learning problem is to find a good estimate for f^*. The number of possible functions is very large, and unless we simplify the problem, we will not arrive at a good function. The simplifying assumption is that in this case we desire a *universal approximator*. A universal approximator is an algorithm that does not rely on any a priori estimate of f^*. It can be used to approximate any continuous function with inputs in $\mathcal{R}^n$. Every such approximator takes in a list of parameters that completely specify its behaviour; it is possible to approximate different hidden functions just by changing the parameters. This method simplifies the learning problem significantly; all that we need to do is simply estimate the parameters of a universal approximator.

Definition 104

A universal approximator is an algorithm that does not rely on any a priori estimate of the function to be learnt (f^* in this case). Moreover, it can be used to approximate any continuous function with inputs in $\mathcal{R}^n$, and its behaviour can be fully controlled by a list of parameters.

Most of the initial learning algorithms were not universal approximators; hence, they failed for many classes of learning problems. Let us outline the journey from simple linear models to deep neural networks.

Linear Regression

The simplest approach is to assume that f^* is a linear function. We can thus estimate y as follows:

$$y = \mathbf{w}^T\mathbf{x} + b \tag{14.1}$$

Here, $\mathbf{w}$ is a *weight vector* and b is a bias parameter. Even though this approach is very simple, however its main shortcoming is that if f^* is not linear then the estimate can turn horribly wrong. For example if f^* consists of *sine*, *cos*, *tan*, and other transcendental functions then a linear estimate will give us a very low accuracy. Such a linear approach is not a universal approximator because of this issue.

ML using Nonlinear Models

Given that linear models are associated with significant limitations, much of the research in machine learning has moved towards nonlinear models. Here we consider complex nonlinear functions that are parameterised by a set of constants. The task of the learning algorithm is to find an appropriate set of constants that minimise the error.

In this space, support vector machines and support vector regression are very popular. A support vector machine (SVM) is used for binary classification. Here it is assumed that each input data point is associated with a binary bit: 0 or 1 (its class). We can assume that each input vector is a point in an n-dimensional space. We can increase the number of dimensions by mapping each point to an even higher dimensional space where it is easy to segregate the points labelled 0 and 1 respectively. SVM based approaches try to fit an imaginary hyperplane (surface in a high dimensional space) that separates both the classes of points. It is not necessary to compute the equation of this plane directly, we can instead describe its behaviour by considering a set of points that are the closest to it (known as *support vectors*). This basic approach can be extended for classification with multiple classes, and can even be used to estimate real values instead of discrete class labels. The main problem of SVMs are the difficulty in finding functions to map points to higher dimensional spaces and their limited accuracy as compared to neural networks.

14.1.2   Neural Networks

Modelling Nonlinearity with Neural Networks

The main issue that constrained prior approaches was that there was no effective way to model nonlinearity. Given that the space of functions that we want to approximate is potentially infinite, the learning model should be general enough such that we can achieve a low error with almost any data set. Neural networks (inspired by the human brain) are universal approximators and also generalise very well.

The key idea here is to introduce nonlinear transformations along with linear transformations such that the relationship between the input and the output can be captured accurately. We introduce a function g such that the output can be represented as $g(\mathbf{w}^T\mathbf{x} + b)$. The function g is typically one of the following functions.

Sigmoid function This was one of the earliest functions used in the design of neural networks. It is defined as,

$$\sigma(x) = \frac{1}{1 + e^{-x}} \tag{14.2}$$

tanh function This is the hyperbolic tangent function.

$$tanh(x) = \frac{e^x - e^{-x}}{e^x + e^{-x}} \tag{14.3}$$

ReLU activation function "ReLU" stands for *Rectified Linear Unit*. The function associated with it, also known as the activation function, is as follows:

$$f(x) = \begin{cases} 0, & (x < 0) \\ x, & (x \geq 0) \end{cases} \tag{14.4}$$

Let us visualise all the three functions in Figure 14.1.

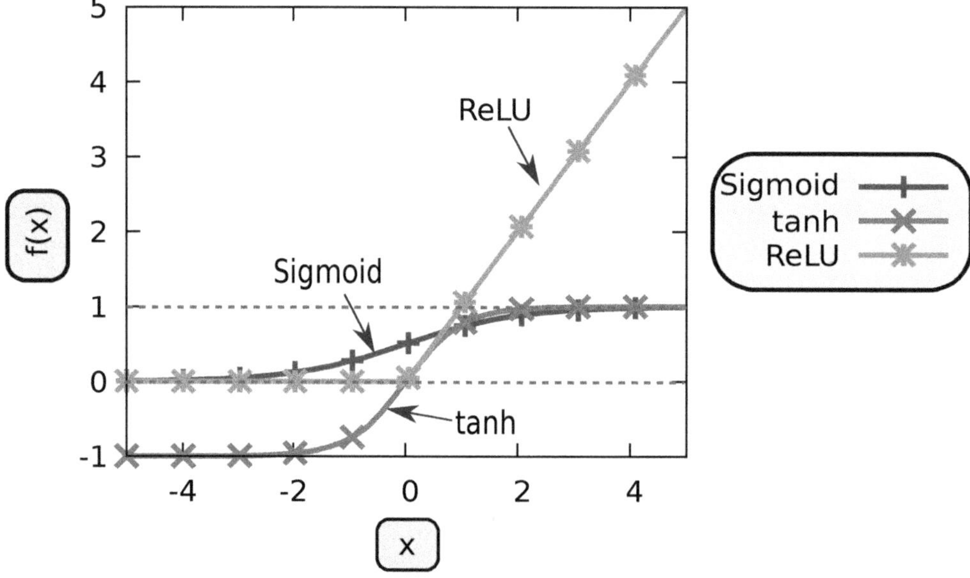

Figure 14.1: The Sigmoid, *tanh*, and ReLU activation functions

Let us now look at an example that uses such nonlinear units. Let us solve a problem that is not possible to solve with purely linear approaches. We wish to create a network that evaluates the XOR function. Consider the input to be a column vector $[a, b]$, where the output is $a \oplus b$. The reader needs to convince herself that simply by multiplying weights with a and b and adding the results, it is not possible to realise a XOR function. Note that for the sake of readability we will be writing the column vectors horizontally. For example, as per our representation $[a, b]$ is a column vector and $[a, b]^T$ is a row vector.

Let us focus on the Karnaugh map in Figure 14.2(a). The aim is to identify and "somehow nullify" the inputs when $a = b$. Let us compute the vector product $[1, -1]^T[a, b]$ (dot product of $[1, -1]$ and $[a, b]$)

where $[1, -1]$ is the weight vector. This is arithmetically the same as computing $a - b$. The results are shown in Figure 14.2(b). For the inputs $(0, 0)$ and $(1, 1)$, the result of this operation is 0. For the inputs where $a \neq b$, the result is non-zero (1 and -1). The final output needs to be the modulus of this result. Computing $|x|$ is easy. It is equal to $ReLU(x) + ReLU(-x)$. The resulting neural network is shown in Figure 14.2(c). Note that we have two functional units in the first linear layer. Each unit computes a dot product between a weight vector and the input vector. For the first functional unit the weight vector is $[1, -1]$, and for the second functional unit it is $[-1, 1]$. The second weight vector is generated by multiplying $[1, -1]$ with -1 because we wish to compute $ReLU(-x)$ in the next nonlinear layer. The rest is self-explanatory.

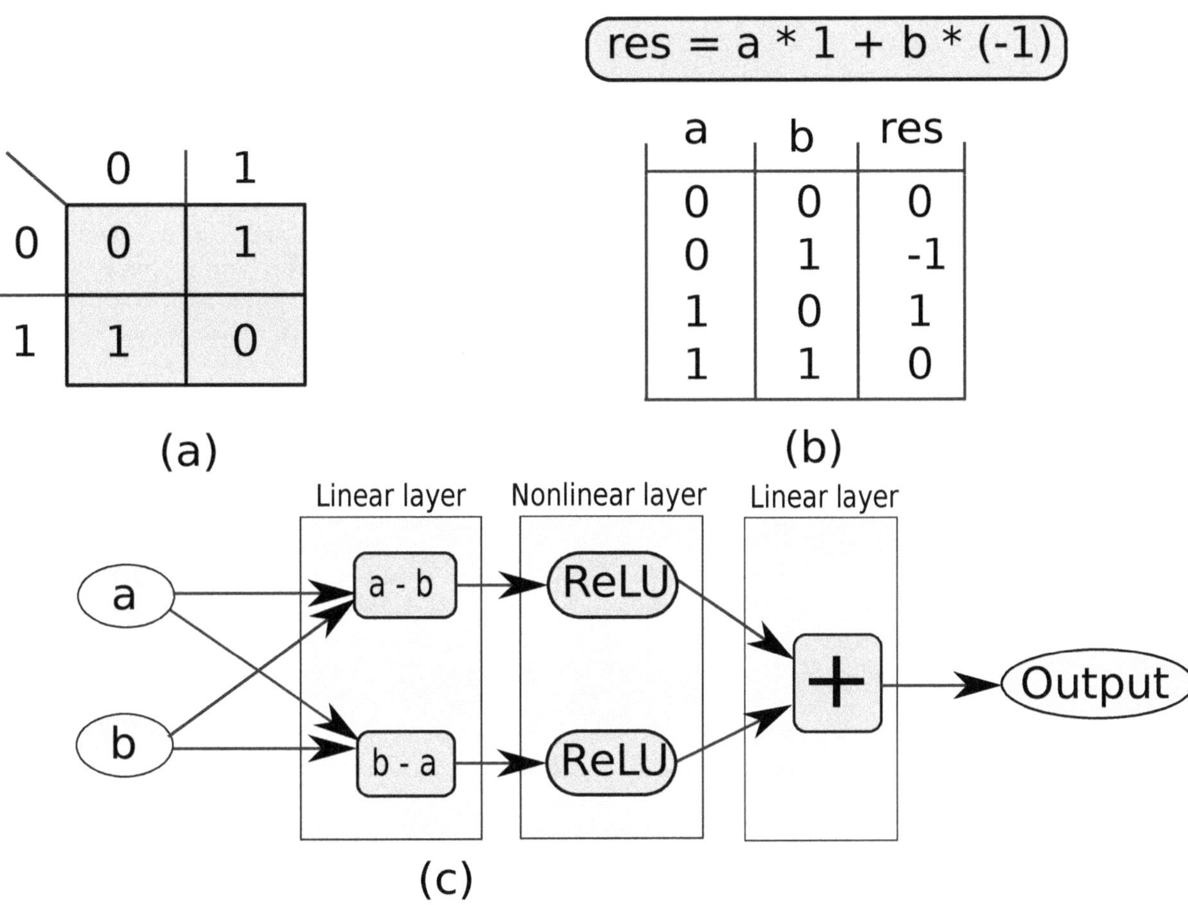

Figure 14.2: Computation of the XOR function. (a) Karnaugh map, (b) Outputs after computing a dot product with [1,-1], (c) Structure of the network

The structure of the network has an interesting property: it has alternating linear and nonlinear layers. The inputs are fed into the first linear layer, which computes dot products with different weight vectors. Subsequently, the outputs of this layer are passed to a nonlinear layer that uses the ReLU function. Finally, the outputs of the nonlinear layer are passed to a linear layer that generates the final output of the neural network. In this case, this network implements a XOR function. Even though this network appears to be very simple, readers will be surprised to know that for a very long time it was not possible to come up with such a network! This had stalled the development of neural networks for decades. Gradually, neural networks increased in terms of complexity: this led to an increasing number of layers and weights within a layer.

Note that this was a specific example for a simple function. In general, it is possible to take such neural networks and train the weights to compute any given function. The architecture is fairly generic, and we can learn functions by simply changing the weight vectors. There are two important terms that we need to introduce here: training and inferencing. While *training* a neural network we are provided a set of known inputs and outputs, and then we try to compute the weights such that the outputs of the network match the given outputs as far as possible. Almost all neural networks use the *backpropagation algorithm* [Goodfellow et al., 2016] for computing the weights in the training phase. It is important to note that the architecture of a neural network in terms of the number and type of layers, and the nature of functional units within the layers is decided a priori. Subsequently, these parameters do not change. The training phase is used to only compute the weights in the network. This phase is carried out offline and there is typically no need to accelerate this phase in hardware.

However, for hardware designers, the *inferencing part* where given an unknown input we try to predict the output, is far more important. Almost all neural architectures as of 2020 focus exclusively on accelerating the inferencing.

Note that the expressive power of a neural network is dependent on the number of layers and the number of functional units within each layer. Hence, for learning complex functions it is typically necessary to have deeper neural networks with more layers. Previously, neural networks used to be fairly small with 3 to 4 layers as we showed in Figure 14.2. With an increase in compute power, the rise of GPUs and FPGAs, and also a concomitant increase in memory capacity, we can now afford to have large neural networks with a few hundred layers. This has spawned the revolution in the design of large deep neural networks.

Deep Neural Networks

The simple example that we saw in Figure 14.2(c) had three layers: two linear layers and one nonlinear layer. Such small networks are good for learning small and simple functions. However, to identify far more complex patterns such as the number of faces in an image or perform face recognition, we need many more layers. Neural networks with a large number of layers are known as *deep neural networks* or simply *DNNs*. It is not uncommon for a modern neural network to have 100+ layers with millions of weights. Such deep neural networks have a series of layers that progressively learn more and more complex concepts. For example, if we would like to classify the images of different animals, the first few layers serve to identify local features such as the paws, the head, the body and the tail. Subsequent layers try to aggregate all this information and identify global features. For example, it is hard for a computer to differentiate between a dog and cat by just looking at the tail or the legs. However, when we consider the image in entirety, the difference between a dog and a cat is very obvious. This is the job of the later layers that aggregate all the information that has been learnt by the earlier layers and then try to infer high-level concepts.

Before proceeding forward, let us define some terms.

Input Feature Map or *ifmap* The input feature map is an input to a functional unit in a layer. For DNNs processing images, it is a 2D matrix. It can also be a 1D vector or a 3D matrix (if we are considering a set of images).

Output Feature Map or *ofmap* It is an output of a functional unit in a layer. Note that a layer typically has a multitude of functional units. It thus takes several *ifmaps* as inputs, and produces several *ofmaps* as outputs. For a given layer, all the *ifmaps* (or *ofmaps*) typically have the same dimensions; however, the dimensions of an *ifmap* and an *ofmap* need not be the same.

Pixels We refer to each entry of an *ifmap* or *ofmap* as a *pixel*.

In such neural networks we never have two linear layers adjacent to each other. This is because two adjacent linear layers are equivalent to a single linear layer. DNNs typically have alternating linear and nonlinear layers. As we have seen, the linear layer simply computes a dot product between the *ifmaps* and a vector of weights. Additionally, DNNs also use different types of nonlinear layers that are either ReLU, Sigmoid or pooling layers. A *pooling layer* takes a region of $K \times K$ pixels in an *ifmap*, and replaces it with a single value. This can either be the mean of the values or the maximum. The latter is known as *max pooling*. The advantage of pooling is twofold: we reduce the size of data by K^2, and secondly, if there is some translation in the feature (displacement by a few pixels) then this operation successfully mitigates its effect.

Before an astute reader asks how the layers are connected, let us answer the question. The most common category of networks is the deep feed-forward network. Here, the layers are organised as a linked list, one after the other. The output of the ith layer is the input of the $(i + 1)^{th}$ layer. This however need not always be the case. We can have back edges, where a later layer feeds its outputs to an earlier layer. Such cyclic connections make the process of training and inferencing harder. However, they also increase the expressive power of the neural network. Let us now look at the most popular variants of DNNs in use today, which are known as Convolutional Neural Networks (CNNs).

14.1.3   Convolutional Neural Networks (CNNs)

Let us reconsider the linear layers in Figure 14.2 once again. In each functional unit of a linear layer we compute a dot product between the *ifmaps* and weight vectors. In most modern neural networks that process complex images or analyse speech, the *ifmaps* are very large. In each linear layer in particular, we need to store large weight vectors and then compute the dot products. If we have millions of pixels in an *ifmap*, which is incidentally not that uncommon, we also need to store millions of weights just for each layer. The storage complexity, memory access overheads, and compute time will make the process of training and inferencing intractable. Additionally, for training we will need a prohibitive number of examples, which in most cases will prove to be impossible. We thus need to simplify the problem. Hence, we typically create two kinds of linear layers: one that has a lot of weights, and a layer that uses a small set of weights.

Fully Connected Layer This is a traditional linear layer where we simply multiply each element in an *ifmap* with a weight. If the *ifmap* has N elements, then we also need N weights. We cannot afford many such layers given the amount of computation that is needed to generate a single output value. Typically, the last layer in a DNN is a fully connected layer. This layer is presented with a lot of high-level concepts identified by earlier layers, and it simply needs to make the final decision. It has very high memory requirements as well. Given that there are a very few such layers, their total contribution to the computational time is small ($\approx 10\%$).

Convolutional Layer For intermediate linear layers we do not store large weight vectors. Instead, we store a very small set of weights known as a *filter*. We compute a convolution between typically two-dimensional *ifmaps* and the filter to compute an *ofmap*.

Before going into the details, let us explain the high level idea. Consider a neural network that needs to classify the image of an animal. We need to first identify small features such as the mouth, horns, and paws. Even before identifying them we need to identify the edges and make a distinction between points within the image and outside it. For detecting edges, and simple shapes, we do not need to compute a dot product with a weight vector that is as large as the *ifmap*. Conceptually, this is a local operation, and computing a localised dot product with a small weight vector should suffice. This is precisely the idea. We consider a small filter with R rows and S columns and a portion of the *ifmap* with the same dimensions and just compute a dot product. This is known as the *convolution operation*. We can extend our definition of a dot product of two vectors to a dot product of two n-dimensional matrices. Here, we multiply corresponding elements, and the value of the final dot product is a sum of the individual element-wise products.

The Convolution Operation

Consider Figure 14.3. It shows an *ifmap* with H rows and W columns, and a given position within it (h, w). The convention that we adopt is that we list the row number first and then the column number (similar to addressing a matrix). We draw an $R \times S$-element shaded rectangle whose left top is at (h, w). We then compute a dot product between the elements of the filter and the shaded rectangle in the *ifmap*. Let us represent the *ifmap* by the matrix $\mathbf{I}$, the *ofmap* by the matrix $\mathbf{O}$, and the filter by the matrix $\mathbf{F}$. We can then write this formally as

$$\mathbf{O}[h][w] = \sum_{r=0}^{R-1} \sum_{s=0}^{S-1} \mathbf{I}[h+r][w+s] \times \mathbf{F}[r][s] \tag{14.5}$$

This is not a traditional convolution operation that we learn in a signal processing course – this is an element-wise dot product. However, we can modify the classical convolution equations to become equivalent to Equation 14.5 by changing the sign of some variables. Basic insight: note that $\sum f(x - y)g(y) = \sum h(z + y)g(y)$, if we consider $z = -x$ and $h(x) = f(-x)$. We will thus henceforth refer to expressions listed in Equation 14.5 as convolutions.

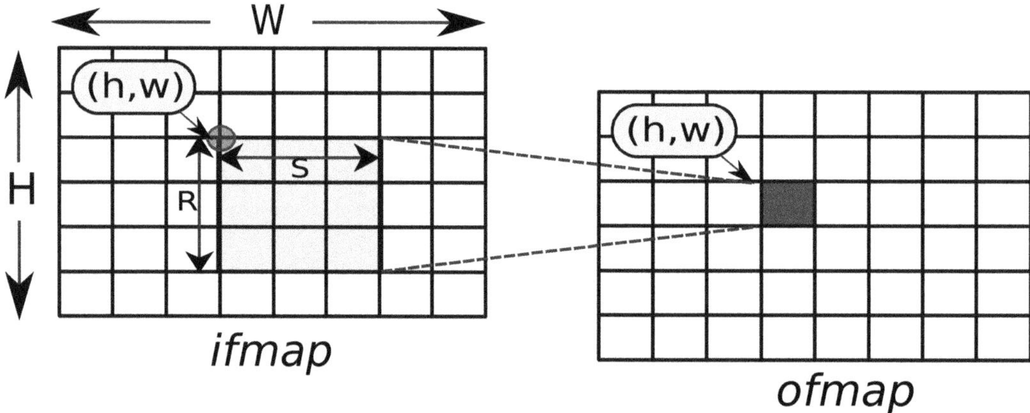

Figure 14.3: A convolution operation

The main advantage here is that we need not store very large weight vectors. We can just store small filters. Let us now complicate Equation 14.5 and make it more realistic. Here are some of the crucial insights. First, an *ofmap* is typically dependent on multiple *ifmaps*, and there is a unique filter for each *ifmap-ofmap* pair. Second, we typically compute a set of *ofmaps* in each layer, and finally to maximise the reuse of inputs and filter weights, we process a *batch* of input images in one go. Let us thus introduce some additional terminology. Consider a layer that takes as input C *ifmaps* (each *ifmap* is called a *channel*), and produces K output *ofmaps*. Additionally, the entire neural network processes N input images in a batch. For the sake of simplicity, let us assume that all the *ifmaps* and *ofmaps* have the same dimensions: $H \times W$ (row-column format). The terminology is summarised in Table 14.1. Please thoroughly memorise the terms. We shall be using them repeatedly in the next few sections.

Variable	Symbol	Iterator
Number of input images	N	n
Number of input channels	C	c
Number of *ofmaps* produced	K	k
Dimensions of the *ifmaps/ofmaps*	$H \times W$	h and w
Dimensions of the filter	$R \times S$	r and s

Table 14.1: Terminology used to describe a convolution operation

We can thus represent a convolution operation as follows:

$$\mathbf{O}[n][k][h][w] = \sum_c \sum_r \sum_s \mathbf{I}[n][c][h + r][w + s] \times \mathbf{F}[k][c][r][s] \tag{14.6}$$

We make several simplifications in this equation. We omit the ranges of the iterators, and secondly we assume that the operation is defined for pixels at the edges of the image. Consider the pixel at the bottom right $\mathbf{O}[H - 1][W - 1]$. The convolution operation is not defined for this pixel because most of the pixels that need to be considered for the convolution do not exist. In this case, a simplifying assumption is typically made where we assume the existence of additional elements beyond the bottom and right edges that contain zeros. This is known as *zero padding*.

Moreover, we observe that for each input image, we compute a convolution. Each pixel of an *ofmap* is dependent on all the input *ifmaps* (general case), and for each *ifmap-ofmap* pair we have a filter. This is the basic equation for a convolution, which allows us to avoid heavy computations with large weight vectors. Such convolutional neural networks are known as CNNs, and they have proved to be extremely useful in very diverse fields.

Design of a CNN

We have four kinds of layers in a CNN: convolutional layer, fully connected layer, ReLU layer, and pooling layer. The latter two layers are nonlinear layers. An illustration of a CNN's design is shown in Figure 14.4 that shows all these layers.

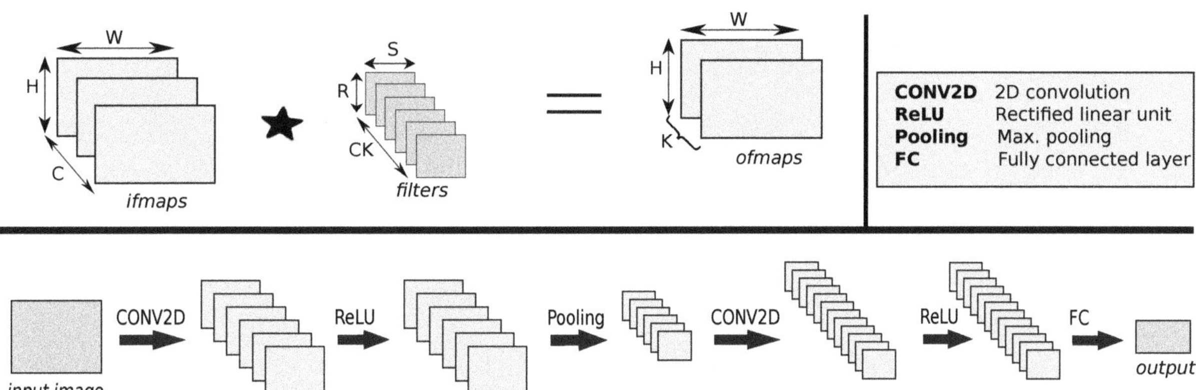

Figure 14.4: Design of a CNN

From the point of view of computation, the ReLU and pooling layers are very easy to handle. We require very little logic to realise their functionality, and their execution is a very small fraction of the total execution. The fully connected layer is heavy in terms of its memory footprint and computational overhead. However, since we have only one such layer in a deep neural network and its generate a few outputs, its execution time is not particularly concerning. Almost all the research in CNNs has been devoted to accelerating the convolutional layers that account for more than 90% of the total execution time. We shall thus henceforth focus on the convolutional layers and discuss various methods to optimise their execution.

14.2   Design of a CNN

14.2.1   Overview

As far as we are concerned, the only computation that we need to do is compute all the outputs as per Equation 14.6. Let us reproduce it again for the sake of readability.

$$\mathbf{O}[n][k][h][w] = \sum_c \sum_r \sum_s \mathbf{I}[n][c][h+r][w+s] \times \mathbf{F}[k][c][r][s] \tag{14.7}$$

We can alternatively write this equation as a piece of code with 7 nested loops (see Listing 14.1).

Listing 14.1: 2D Convolution

```
for (n=0; n<N; n++) {   /* input images */
  for (k=0; k<K; k++) { /* outputs */
    for (c=0; c<C; c++) { /* input channels */
      for (h=0; h<H; h++) { /* rows of the ifmap/ofmap */
        for (w=0; w<W; w++) { /* cols of the ifmap/ofmap */
          for (r=0; r<R; r++) { /* rows of the filter */
            for (s=0; s<S; s++){ /* cols of the filter */
              O[n][k][h][w] += I[n][c][h+r][w+s]
                                * F[k][c][r][s];
}}}}}}}
```

The code in Listing 14.1 has several important features, which are as follows.

1. The order of the loops does not matter. Since there are no dependences between the loop variables, we can reorder the loops in any way we wish. We will see that this has important implications when it comes to cache locality.

2. For each output pixel, we perform $C \times R \times S$ multiplications and the same number of additions. We thus perform a total of $2C \times R \times S$ operations. Most ISAs provide a multiply-and-accumulate operation (MAC) that performs a computation of the form $a\ +=\ b \times c$ similar to what we are doing. The number of operations in such algorithms is typically mentioned in terms of the number of MAC operations. We thus observe that per output pixel we perform $C \times R \times S$ MAC operations where we add partial sums to the output pixel (initialised to 0). Here, the product $I[n][c][h + r][w + s] \times F[k][c][r][s]$ is referred to as a *partial sum*.

3. We are essentially defining a 7-dimensional space where the dimensions are independent. This space can be *tiled* – broken down into subspaces. Let us explain with an example. Assume that we change the increment for the loop iterators w and h from 1 to 3. It means that we are considering 3×3 tiles of output pixels. Then we need to add two inner loops that traverse each tile (3×3 space) and compute the corresponding partial sums and add them to obtain the *ofmaps*.

4. Given that the computations are independent, we have a great opportunity to run this code on a set of parallel processors, where each processor is given a fixed amount of work. This also naturally fits with our notion of tiling the loop where a small amount of work can be given to each processor. Furthermore, since these processors only have to perform MAC operations and iterate through a loop, we do not need regular processors. Akin to a GPU, we can create an array of very small and simple processors. Let us call such a small and simple processor as a processing element or a PE.

A Reference Architecture

Let us think about this problem from the point of view of software first. We can reorder and tile loops, and moreover also embed directives in the code to run all the iterations of a loop in parallel – map each iteration to a separate PE or a separate group of PEs.

A high level reference architecture is presented in Figure 14.5 that will allow us to achieve these objectives. Such an architecture typically has a 1D array or a 2D matrix of PEs, some local storage in each PE (akin to the L1 cache), a large L2 cache, and an off-chip main memory (see Figure 14.5). In the figure, the local buffer (LB) in each PE is analogous to the L1 cache and the global buffer (GB) is analogous to the L2 cache. The PEs are interconnected with an NoC. Note that the small, filled circles represent the connections between wires. The horizontal and vertical links are not connected in this figure (no filled circles at the intersections).

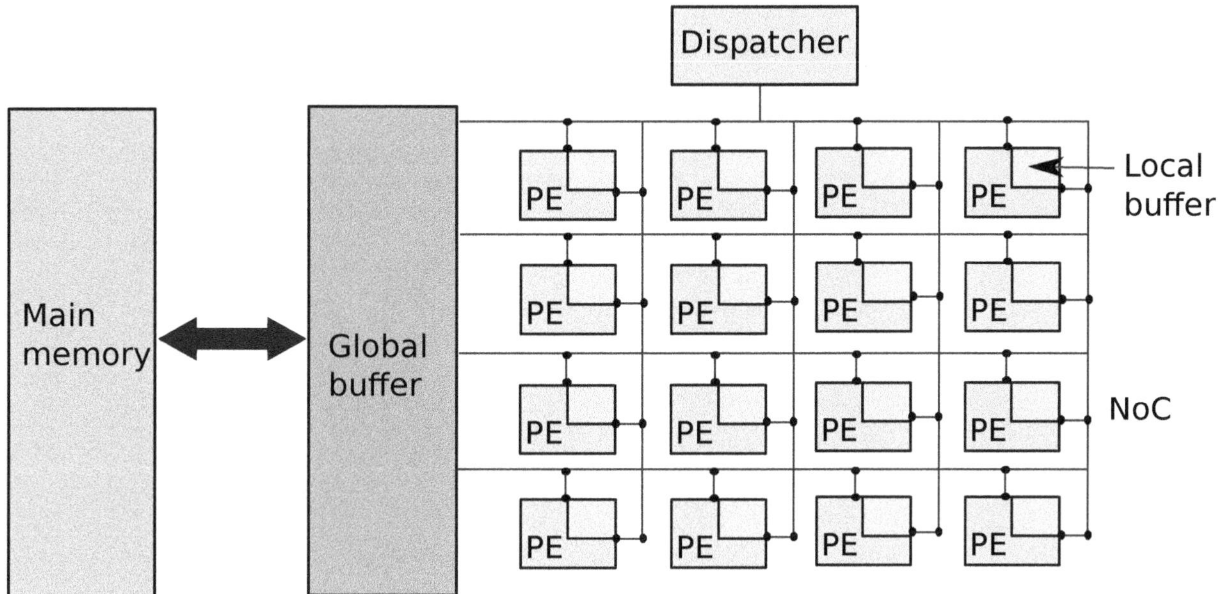

Figure 14.5: Reference architecture with a matrix of PEs

From the point of view of software we need at least one complex processor that we refer to as the *dispatcher*. It controls and orchestrates the entire computation. This includes dividing the work amongst the PEs, sending fetch and prefetch commands to memory, and moving outputs from the global buffer to the main memory. We can reorder, tile, and parallelise the loops in many different ways. There are implications in terms of data locality in the GB and LBs. Additionally, we need to consider the overhead of moving data over the NoC, sending multicast messages, and computing the final output value for a pixel after adding the partial sums. The latter operation is also known as *reduction*.

To understand the space of loop transformations, let us describe a formal representation to represent a transformation. It will be easy to understand different optimisations subsequently.

Formal Representation of the Nested Loops

For the loops shown in Listing 14.1, let us represent them by the notation $n \triangleright k \triangleright c \triangleright h \triangleright w \triangleright r \triangleright s$, which represents the temporal order of loops. Let us refer to this as a *mapping* because we are in essence mapping the computations to PEs. In this case it is a single PE; however, very soon we shall introduce directives to parallelise this computation. Here, the operator $\triangleright$ indicates a temporal relationship. The loops on the right hand side are strictly nested within the loops on the left hand side. In the context of this notation, it means that we process one input image at a time. Then for an input image, we process the *ofmaps* one after the other, and so on.

Let us introduce another operator to denote the possible parallel execution of a loop (distributed across the PEs) with the symbol $\|$, where the notation $n\|$ means that we can process all the N input images in parallel. It does not mean that we necessarily have adequate hardware to actually run all the iterations in parallel; it just says that it is possible to do so if we have enough hardware. If we do not have enough hardware then each PE needs to run several iterations. Furthermore, if we have two consecutive $\|$ symbols then it means that both the corresponding loops run in parallel. For example $h\|w\|$ means that each (row,column) pair is processed in parallel. We can also enclose it in square brackets for readability such as $[h\|w\|]$. This notation denotes a single level of parallelism. We create $H \times W$ parallel copies of loops and map them to the PEs.

We might however wish to implement hierarchical parallelism. This means that we might first want to parallelise the loop with iterator h, map each iteration to a group of PEs, and then assign one PE in each group to an iteration of w. This would be represented by $h\| \triangleright w\|$. This provides a structure to the parallel execution. The rule of thumb here is that $\triangleright$ represents a sequential order and $\|$ represents parallelism.

There is an important point to note here. The $\|$ operator indicates that we "can parallelise a loop" by distributing its iterations among the PEs. Assume a case where the loop has 1024 iterations and we just have 256 PEs. In this case, we can run the first 256 iterations in parallel, then schedule the next 256 iterations and so on. The way that we interpret the $\|$ operator is that the loop corresponding to the loop iterator preceding the operator can be executed in parallel if we have enough PEs. However, if we do not have enough PEs then the execution will be a hybrid of parallel and sequential execution. In this case, we say that the execution is *folded* (as we just described). Our representation is conceptual and conveys the perspective of a software writer.

Example 15

What is the difference between $[h\| \triangleright n \triangleright w\|]$ (S_1) and $[h\| \triangleright w\|n\triangleright]$ (S_2)?

Answer: *In both S_1 and S_2, we partition the iteration space for h, and assign each iteration to a group of PEs. However, the difference arises after that. In S_1 we consider an input image and process its pixels in parallel. An image is loaded only once. After that we process its pixels by dividing the values of w across the PEs in each group. Even if the execution is folded, the image is nevertheless loaded only once. However, in S_2 if W is more than the number of PEs in a group, then we need to cycle through the images. This means that if the execution is folded, then we need to load an image into memory many times. Note that if the execution is not folded, then both the representations are equivalent from the point of view of loading the input images (iterator: n).*

Now consider loop tiling (see Section 7.4.5). Let's say we decide to tile the loops with the iterators h and w, then we have to create two loops per iterator – one where we increment h by the tile size T_h, and an inner loop where we iterate in the range $[h, h+T_h-1]$. We introduce two variables h' and h'': h' is incremented by the tile size T_h (outer loop), and h'' (inner loop) is a temporary variable that is used to iterate through the tile – it is incremented by 1 in each iteration. Now if we decide to tile the loops corresponding to the iterators h and w, a possible mapping can be $n \triangleright k \triangleright c \triangleright h' \triangleright w' \triangleright h'' \triangleright w'' \triangleright r \triangleright s$. One advantage of doing this is that we can have a multitude of parallel processing elements (PEs), where each PE can compute the results for a tile represented by the computation $h'' \triangleright w'' \triangleright r \triangleright s$. To realise this, we can run the outer loops for the iterators h' and w' in parallel. This will leverage the effect of locality in the LBs (local buffers). The mapping will thus be $n \triangleright k \triangleright c \triangleright h'\|w'\|h'' \triangleright w'' \triangleright r \triangleright s$. Note the parallel execution of the tiles.

In this case, we run H/T_h parallel instances of the loop for h' and W/T_w parallel instances for the loop for w'. We can visualise this as running $\frac{HW}{T_h T_w}$ parallel copies of the tile.

Way Point 15

- *We can reorder loop iterations. Different reorderings have different implications in terms of the temporal locality of data in the LBs and GB.*

- *The $\|$ operator indicates that we can parallelise the iterations of a loop across the PEs. If the number of iterations is more than the number of PEs, then we need to fold the loop – each PE runs multiple iterations.*

- *The $\triangleright$ operator determines the order of nesting of the loops. If we write $n \triangleright k$, then it means that for each value of n, we consider all the values of k.*

Software Model

Our formalism for describing the nested loops predominantly captures the control flow of the CNN program, and the nature of parallelism. For the same control flow we can have different types of data flow. For example, we can cache some data in the local buffer (LB) of the PE, move some data from the GB to the PEs, and also move some data values between PEs. To capture the intricacies of the data flow we need to unnecessarily complicate our model. Hence, to a large extent we shall avoid doing so.

The only extension that we propose is to encompass some loops in a shaded box to indicate that the corresponding data is cached locally within a PE. For example the mapping $- n \triangleright k \triangleright c \| h \triangleright w \triangleright \boxed{r \triangleright s} -$ indicates that the entire filter ($R \times S$ elements) is cached locally within a PE. Think of this as a software *hint* given to the hardware asking it to cache certain types of data. This is an example of *temporal reuse* where a given piece of data is cached within a PE.

The way that we shall interpret such mappings is as follows. Each PE runs a thread that computes partial sums according to the mapping. We split the iteration space among the threads, and each PE executes a set of threads (iterations) *mapped* to it. Secondly, we assume very coarse grained synchronisation among the threads. For the mapping $n \triangleright k \triangleright c \| h \triangleright w \triangleright \boxed{r \triangleright s}$ where we parallelise the loops on the basis of input channels, after every iteration of k, we insert a barrier (see Section 6.3.2 for a definition). This means that after we have processed all the channels for a given value of k, we encounter a barrier (a synchronisation point for all the threads). The threads otherwise need not run in lockstep, and we assume that they do not suffer from data races while computing the values of output pixels.

14.2.2 Design Space of Loop Transformations

In this section, we shall look at different methods of reordering and tiling the loops to maximise locality at each PE. Moreover, we shall also like to leverage the fact that we have a parallel array of PEs. The aim is to consider different types of architectures where we keep different types of data cached in each PE. Caching data in local buffers is known as *stationarity*. We shall discuss a few reference designs in this section, and it should be kept in mind that the designs are suggestive in nature. More efficient designs are possible.

The key idea behind stationarity of any data is to use it as **frequently as possible** when it is resident in the local cache, and then **minimise** the number of times the data needs to be reloaded into the cache. This means that the stationary data should be reused as much as possible and then **replaced**.

Note that it is possible to design architectures where there is no stationarity. Such architectures are known as No Local Reuse (NLR) architectures.

Weight Stationary (WS) Architecture

Let us now look at a few of the common ways in which the basic 7-loop structure can be transformed. Consider our example from the previous section: $n \triangleright k \triangleright c \triangleright h' \| w' \| h'' \triangleright w'' \triangleright r \triangleright s$. This means that we compute the results for each *ifmap-ofmap* pair and image sequentially. Next, we divide an *ofmap* (and corresponding *ifmap*) into small tiles and distribute them across the 2D PE array. Each PE computes the output pixels for each tile. It reads the corresponding inputs, and repeatedly accesses the filter weights. In this case, it makes sense to cache the filter weights for a given *ifmap-ofmap* pair in each PE. This is an example of *filter reuse* or *weight reuse*. We can keep the filter weights *stationary* at each PE and this will ensure that we only need to stream the inputs and outputs to and from each PE. This is an example of a *weight stationary* or *WS* architecture.

Let us make the mapping more efficient. The aim is to reuse the filter weights as much as possible. This means that we need to load them once, finish all the computations that require them, and then load the next filter. This is equivalent to maximising the distance between the iterations that change the filter; this also maximises the number of iterations that use the filter in the mapping. One such mapping is as follows.

$$k \triangleright c \triangleright n \triangleright h' \| w' \| h'' \triangleright w'' \triangleright \boxed{r \triangleright s} \tag{14.8}$$

The parameters k and c change the filter and thus they are the iterators of the outermost loops. The loops traversing the filter are the innermost. Note the shaded box $\boxed{r \triangleright s}$. In this case it indicates that the entire filter (dimensions $R \times S$) is cached within a PE.

Let us analyse the execution described in Equation 14.8. We cache the entire filter (dimensions: $R \times S$) in the LBs of the PEs. The filter depends on k and c, which are incremented in the two outermost loops. Each PE is assigned a tile ($h'' \triangleright w''$). At runtime, each PE can read the part of the *ifmap* that corresponds to its tile, and keep computing the convolution. Note that to compute the partial sums for a tile with dimensions $T_h \times T_w$, we actually need to read $(T_h + R - 1) \times (T_w + S - 1)$ input pixels. We assume that all of these reads are performed by the system. For the sake of simplicity, we shall not go into the details now. Finally, when there is a change in the iterators c or k, each PE reads the filters corresponding to the new values of c and k.

This mapping is inefficient. This is because even though we are maximising filter reuse, computing the outputs is slow. For the same (c, k) combination we first compute all the partial sums for all the images, and then move to a new value of (c, k). Recall that every time we compute a partial sum we need to read the relevant entry from the *ofmap*, add the partial sum to it, and write it back. The next time we reuse the output is after we have processed entries from all the images. Processing *ofmaps* thus has very little temporal locality. Furthermore, we also need a lot of space to store all of these partial sums (across all the images).

Let us instead create a different mapping (see Equation 14.9).

$$n \triangleright k \| c \| h \triangleright w \triangleright \boxed{r \triangleright s} \tag{14.9}$$

In this case we also cache the filter weights. However, we allocate work to the PEs in a different manner. Each PE is responsible for a (c, k) (*ifmap-ofmap*) combination. For this combination, the filter remains the same. Then we process all the elements of an *ifmap* to generate all the partial sums. Given that we aggregate the partial sums, it is best to process an entire image in one go before loading the next image. Note that in general, it is a good idea to finish the computations for one large image before loading the next one from the point of view of locality and the space required to store the partial sums. Hence, we set the loop that increments n to be the outermost loop. This design is frequently used. We learnt an important lesson.

> Trying to maximise the locality of one block of data can adversely impact the locality of another block of data and the space required to store temporary results. Often there is a

trade-off. We would like to opt for a balanced choice that maximises the performance of the system as a whole.

Input Stationary (IS) Architecture

Consider another kind of mapping where we distribute parts of the *ifmaps* (inputs) to every PE, and keep them stationary in the LB there. We tile the loops with iterators h and w. We thus break the *ifmap* into tiles of dimensions $(T_h + R - 1) \times (T_w + S - 1)$. Given that there are C input channels, we can store C such tiles in every PE assuming we have the space for them. Note that in this case, the tiles stored across the PEs have an overlap. This had to be done to ensure that we can efficiently compute the convolutions for pixels at the right and bottom edges of each tile. Otherwise, we need to communicate values between the tiles. Such pixels at the bottom and right edges of the tile for which we need to store or communicate extra information are known as *halo pixels*.

In this case, the mapping is as follows for such an *input stationary* or *IS* architecture.

$$n \triangleright h' \| w' \| k \triangleright r \triangleright s \triangleright \boxed{c \triangleright h'' \triangleright w''} \tag{14.10}$$

The input *ifmaps* are stationary. In each PE we store C *ifmap* tiles. Each PE reads the relevant filter weights and computes the corresponding partial sums. Finally, it adds the partial sums for the corresponding output tile and computes the output; then it moves to the next image. This limits the number of partial sums that need to be stored. Given that a PE stores tiles for all the C channels, it can compute all the convolutions locally. There is no need to handle halo pixels in a special manner.

Output Stationary (OS) Architecture

On similar lines we can define an *output stationary* or *OS* architecture. Here we distribute the output pixels across the PEs. They read the relevant inputs and filter weights, and then compute the partial sums.

$$n \triangleright h' \| w' \| c \triangleright r \triangleright s \triangleright \boxed{k \triangleright h'' \triangleright w''} \tag{14.11}$$

Row Stationary (RS) Architecture

We can alternatively distribute rows of the *ifmap* and the filter across the PEs. They can compute the relevant partial sums. For a given *ofmap* row one of the PEs can take up the role of aggregating the partial sums. The rest of the PEs that have computed partial sums for that *ofmap* row, albeit with different filter weights and *ifmap* rows, can send the partial sums to the aggregating PE. A possible mapping is as follows.

$$n \triangleright k \triangleright c \triangleright h' \| r' \| w \triangleright s \triangleright \boxed{h'' \triangleright r''} \tag{14.12}$$

Important Point 22

The important point to note here is that there are many ways of creating stationary architectures. Even for a given type of architecture, there are many ways of distributing the computations and organising the data flow. The examples given in this section were of a generic and simplistic nature. Let us now create data flow mechanisms for such architectures.

14.2.3 Hardware Architectures

In Section 14.2.2 we described loop transformations from the point of view of a generic software model. We only described temporal reuse, where we keep some data stationary in the PEs such that it can be used by later computations. However, for building an efficient hardware implementation, we also need to consider efficient *spatial reuse*, which means that we read a block of data once from memory and try to reuse it as much as possible. For example, this can be done by multicasting it to a set of PEs. The PEs do not have to issue separate reads to memory. Alternatively, data values can flow from one PE to the next along the same row or column. Again this reduces the memory bandwidth requirement. Any hardware implementation has to consider such kinds of spatial reuse to reduce the pressure on the global buffer.

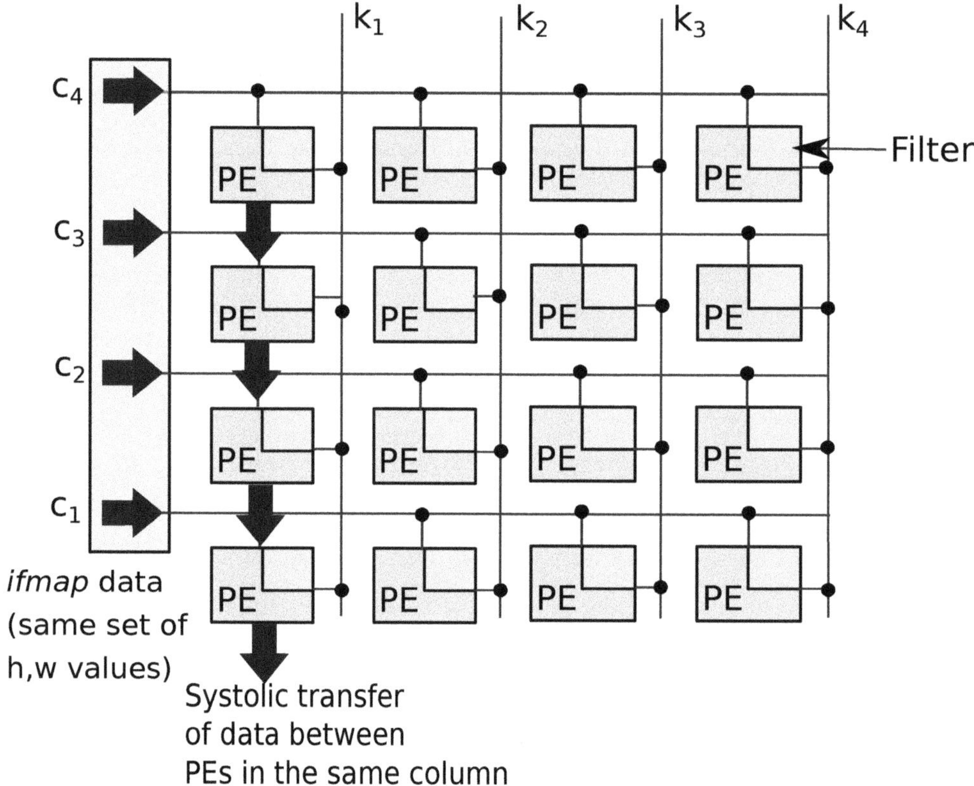

Figure 14.6: A weight stationary architecture

Weight Stationary Architecture

Consider the following mapping that we derived in Section 14.2.2. We need to realise this on a 2D array of PEs, which is the most generic architecture in this space. Each PE has a filter stored for an *ofmap-ifmap* (k, c) pair.

$$n \triangleright k \| c \| h \triangleright w \triangleright \boxed{r \triangleright s}$$

For a 2D-matrix of PEs, we need to structure the matrix in such a way that it allows us to aggregate the outputs. We thus assign the rows to channels, and the columns to *ofmaps*. The mapping thus becomes,

$$n \triangleright k \| \triangleright c \| \triangleright h \triangleright w \triangleright \boxed{r \triangleright s} \tag{14.13}$$

The steps are as follows (keep referring to Figure 14.6). In Figure 14.6, there are no connections between the vertical and horizontal wires. Note that there are no connection symbols (filled dark circles) at their intersections. For systolic transfer between the PEs, the vertical links are used. Note that the arrows between PEs (denoting systolic transfer) are conceptual: they are only showing the direction of the flow of data.

Phase I First for a given (k, c) pair we need to load the filter weights in the PEs. Each PE can issue reads to the GB via the NoC. We arrange the filters as follows. Each row of the 2D-array corresponds to one channel ($c_1 \ldots c_4$), and each column of this array corresponds to a given *ofmap* (total of K ($= 4$) such *ofmaps*). We thus have C rows and K columns.

Phase II For each channel, we send a block of values from the corresponding *ifmap* along the rows. We have a choice here, either we can send data byte by byte, pixel by pixel, or as a tile of pixels. Normally the last approach (a tile of pixels) is preferred. In this case, we send a tile of pixels for each channel. The important point to note is that all the tiles have the same coordinates (same h and w values).

Phase III Each PE computes the convolutions between the input data and the filter data.

Phase IV Note that all the partial sums computed in each column need to be added to get the value of the corresponding output pixels. We need to sum up the values columnwise. This can be done in two ways. We can either have a tree of adders at the end of each column. All the values can be sent to the adder tree via the NoC. This is known as *parallel reduction*. The other option is to opt for a *systolic transfer*. A PE in the highest row transfers its partial sums to the PE below it (in the same column). This PE adds the received partial sums with the partial sums it has computed, and transfers the result to the PE below. This process continues and finally the result leaves the PE array via the last row of PEs (bottom row in Figure 14.6).

Input Stationary Architecture

We derived the following mapping in Section 14.2.2.

$$n \triangleright h' \| w' \| k \triangleright r \triangleright s \triangleright \boxed{c \triangleright h'' \triangleright w''}$$

The aim was to map C input tiles with the same coordinates to a PE. We just need to stream all the filters and the PE can compute all the K outputs. These outputs can then be streamed out via the vertical links. This is shown in Figure 14.7.

Note that we are running the PEs independently in this case. We can do better. We can parallelise the computations in a different way. Consider the following mapping where we split the channels for each *ifmap* tile across the rows.

$$n \triangleright h' \| w' \| \triangleright c \| k \triangleright r \triangleright s \triangleright \boxed{h'' \triangleright w''} \tag{14.14}$$

The corresponding data flow is shown in Figure 14.8. In each column we store the inputs for the same *ofmap* tile: one *ifmap* tile per channel. Then we send the filter weights down the rows. For channel c and *ofmap* k, we send $\mathbf{F}[k][c][\ldots]$ on the row corresponding to channel c. The PEs compute a convolution between the filter weights and the stored input tile to get a set of partial sums. Note that all the PEs in each column compute partial sums for the same *ofmap* tile; hence, all that we have to do is send the partial sums down the column. Each PE adds its computed partial sums to the values it receives from its neighbour above it. It passes the result to the PE below it. This is an example of a *systolic transfer*.

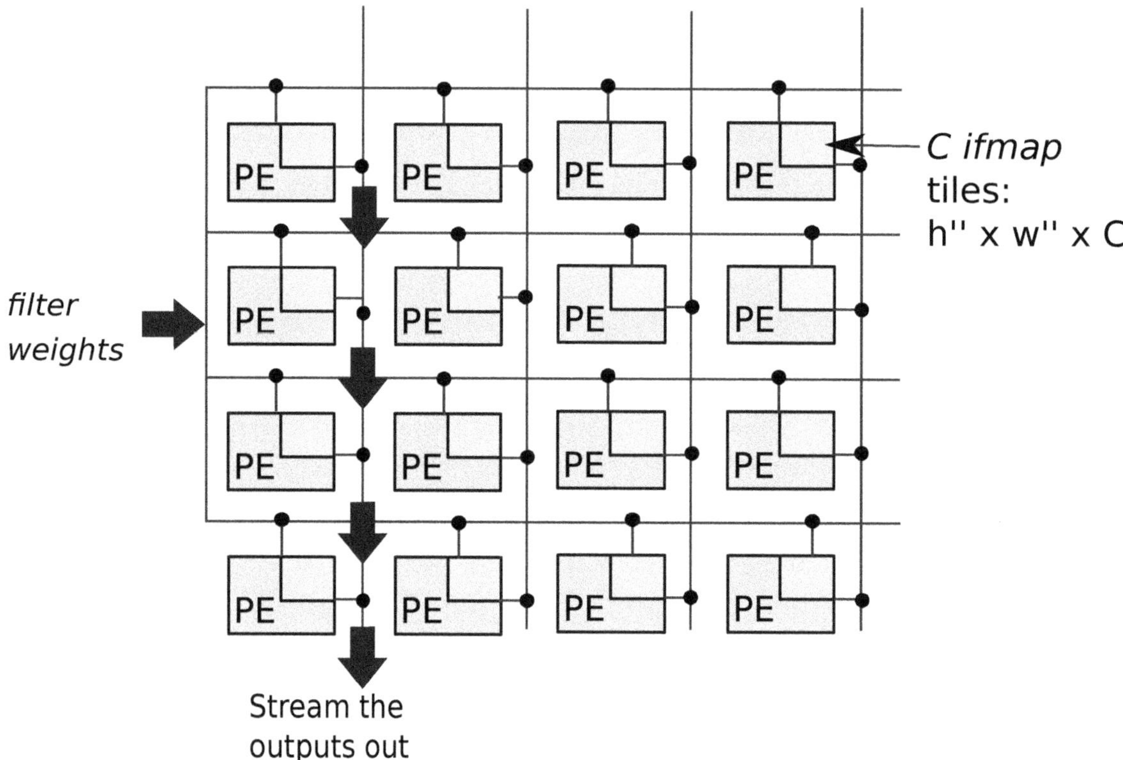

Figure 14.7: An input stationary architecture. The thick dark arrows represent the conceptual flow of data from one PE to the one below it (via vertical links).

Output Stationary Architecture

Let us consider the order of loops that we derived for a software-only implementation. It was as follows.

$$n \triangleright h'\|w'\|c \triangleright r \triangleright s \triangleright k \triangleright h'' \triangleright w'' \tag{14.15}$$

The idea here was simple, we simply parallelise the computation by assigning a set of output pixels to each PE. The PE computes the output pixels for a $T_h \times T_w$ tile for all the *ofmaps*. It does so by reading the corresponding input pixels and filters. This is indeed an effective mechanism; however implementing this scheme in hardware is difficult. The memory bandwidth requirements will be high. We ideally want to read some data and reuse it as much as possible by multicasting it to a set of PEs. This is what we have done in the WS and IS architectures. Let us change the mapping to enable more spatial reuse.

If we compute $k \triangleright h'' \triangleright w''$ in a PE, it means that only that PE will get the inputs corresponding to the $h'' \triangleright w''$ tile. This cuts the opportunities for spatial reuse of *ifmap* input data. Let us thus organise the computation differently. Let us assign all the PEs in a column to an *ofmap* (refer to Figure 14.9).

Consider a single row first. In the new organisation, the order of computation will look like $k\| h'' \triangleright w''$ for a single row. All the PEs in the row share the input tile but produce output pixels for different *ofmaps*. We can cache a tile for a single *ofmap* in each PE in the column. Next, we stream the inputs corresponding to the tile $h'' \triangleright w''$ along the row for all the input channels one after the other (horizontal direction). At the same time, we stream the filters along the columns. The mapping thus becomes $k\|c \triangleright r \triangleright s \triangleright h'' \triangleright w''$.

Each PE reads the corresponding input tile for channel c and the filter for the (k, c) pair, and then computes the partial sums. Finally, across the rows we need to stream a set of input tiles. For example,

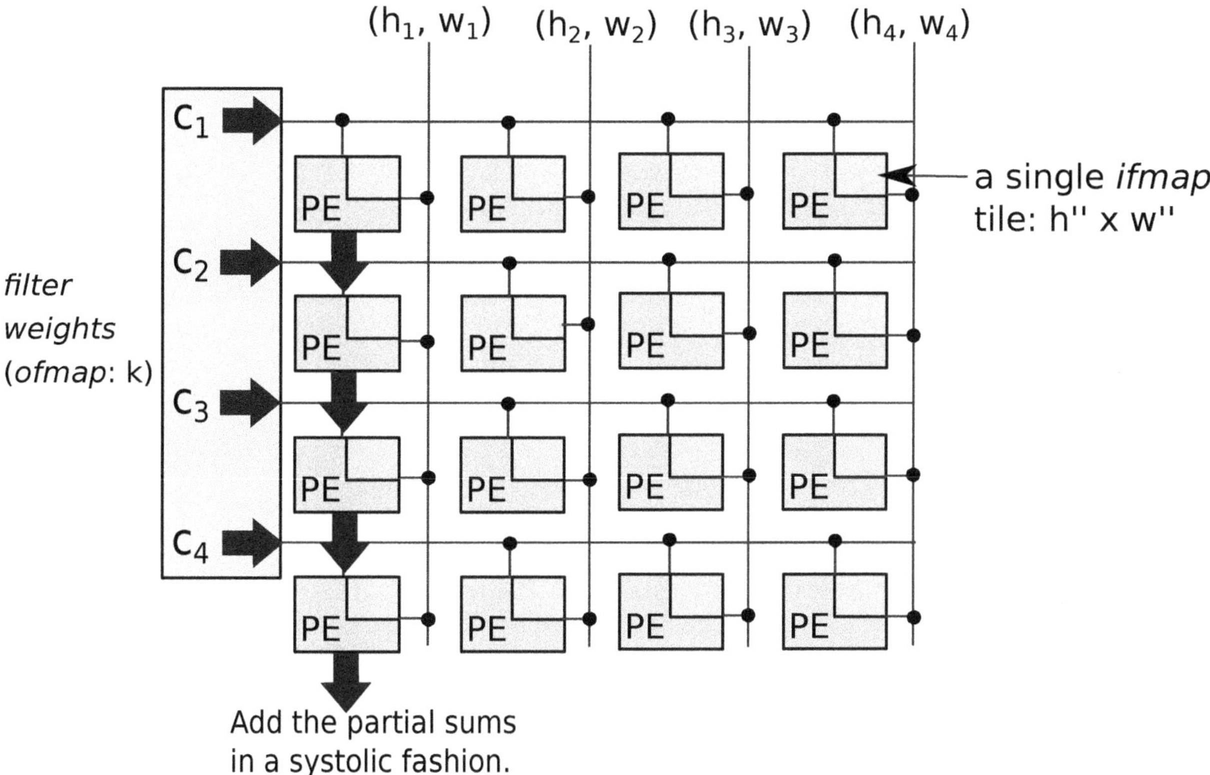

Figure 14.8: An input stationary architecture that performs a column-wise reduction. The thick dark arrows represent the conceptual flow of data from one PE to the one below it (via vertical links).

if we have 10 rows, then we can stream 10 different input tiles along these rows. The final mapping is thus as follows.

$$ n \rhd h'\|w'\| \rhd k\|c \rhd r \rhd s \rhd \boxed{h'' \rhd w''} \tag{14.16} $$

Figure 14.9 realises this mapping. The key idea can be summarised as follows. Each column corresponds to a specific output channel (*ofmap*). Each row corresponds to an input/output tile. We transmit input tiles along the rows and filter data along the columns corresponding to the respective *ofmaps*. At each PE assigned to *ofmap* k, *ifmap* data for channel c and filter data for the (k, c) pair arrive simultaneously; it subsequently computes the output pixels for a single tile in an *ofmap*. At the end of a round of computations, the output pixels are read out through the columns.

Row Stationary Architecture

Let us create a row stationary or RS architecture where we keep rows of the inputs and the filters stationary. We derived the following mapping in Section 14.2.2.

$$ n \rhd k \rhd c \rhd h'\|r'\|w \rhd s \rhd \boxed{h'' \rhd r''} $$

Consider a 3×3 filter, and a tile size of 1 for the *ifmap* and filter rows. It means that for computing an output pixel in the context of a single channel, we need to consider three rows. These rows are cached in different PEs. We need to read the partial sums that they have computed and aggregate them. We

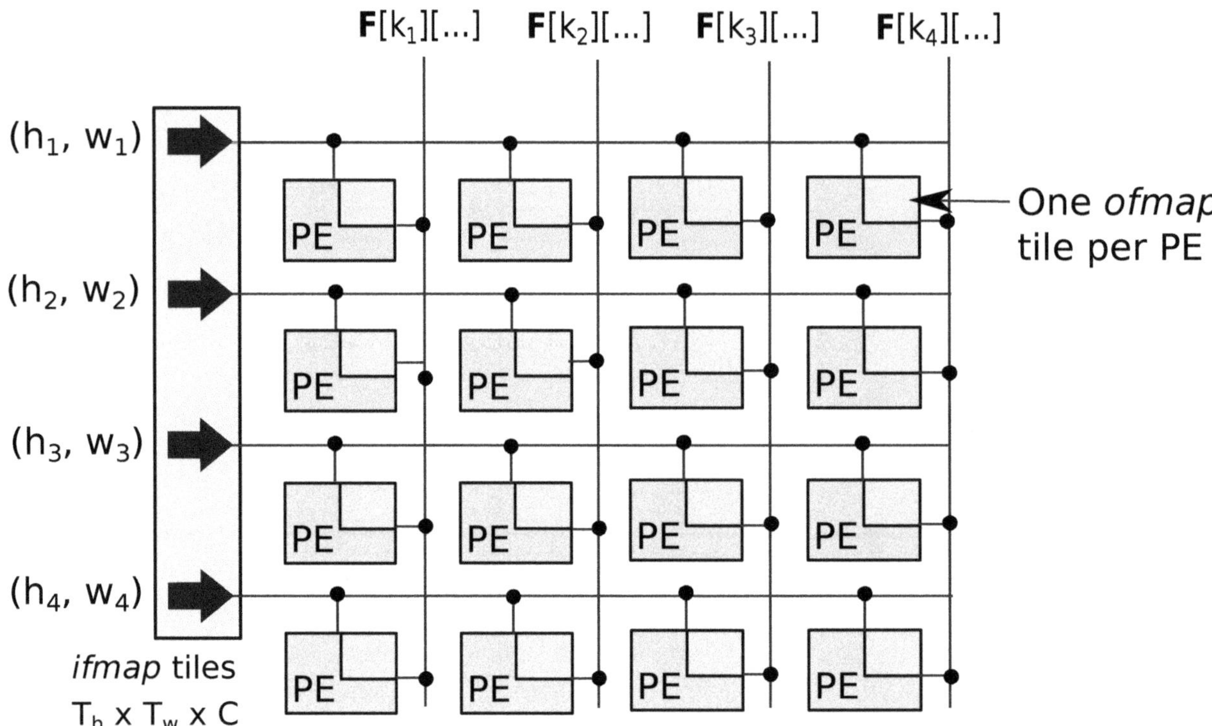

Figure 14.9: An output stationary architecture

thus need to organise pairs of *ifmap* and filter rows such that it is possible to do so very easily. One of the representative organisations (refer to [Chen et al., 2016]) is as follows.

Let us number the rows in the *ifmap* $h_1, h_2, h_3, \ldots$, and the rows in a filter $r_1, r_2, r_3, \ldots$. Figure 14.10 shows a simplified representation of a row stationary (RS) data flow for a filter with 3 rows. All the PEs in each row keep a row of the filter stationary. We then distribute rows of the input among the PEs such that each column computes the partial sums corresponding to the top row. For example, in the first column we store the *ifmap* rows h_1, h_2, and h_3. We compute the convolutions $h_1 \star r_1$, $h_2 \star r_2$, and $h_3 \star r_3$ in the first column. We need to aggregate the partial sums by transferring them down each column to compute the aggregated partial sums for all the output pixels that correspond to row h_1.

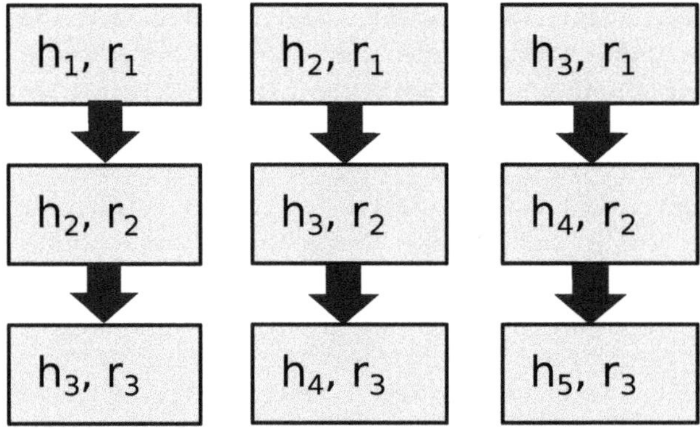

Figure 14.10: A row stationary data flow

The stored *ifmap* rows can be represented by a matrix as follows.

$$\begin{bmatrix} h_1 & h_2 & h_3 \\ h_2 & h_3 & h_4 \\ h_3 & h_4 & h_5 \end{bmatrix}$$

In the next round, the filter weights remain the same, we just change the *ifmap* rows to the following matrix.

$$\begin{bmatrix} h_4 & h_5 & h_6 \\ h_5 & h_6 & h_7 \\ h_6 & h_7 & h_8 \end{bmatrix}$$

Note that this computation is happening for only one input channel. To compute the final values of the output pixels, we need to add the partial sums across all the channels. An issue with this design is that the filter, which is kept stationary, also determines the *ifmap-ofmap* pair. We cannot change the input channel without changing the cached filter rows. Hence, we propose to partition the 2D matrix of PEs into 2D blocks. The partitioning will be based on the input channel c and the output *ofmap* k. For each (c, k) pair, we implement an RS data flow. Then for each row of output pixels, we simply need to add the partial sums computed by each group of PEs. This can be done either by storing the partial sums in a dedicated set of buffers, or by reading them from memory. Hence, the mapping for a full RS system will look something like this.

$$n \triangleright k \| c \| \triangleright h' \| r' \| w \triangleright s \triangleright \boxed{h'' \triangleright r''} \tag{14.17}$$

Let us critique this design. There is clearly a degree of redundancy. We store multiple copies of filters, and multiple copies of input rows. Additionally, for multiple *ifmap-ofmap* pairs, we need to create 2D blocks of PEs. The IS, WS, and OS architectures were comparatively more elegant. However, in those architectures, we were computing 2D convolutions within each PE, and in this RS architecture we need to compute only a 1D convolution, which is comparatively far easier to compute. Secondly, whenever we have more redundancy, we have more flexibility. In this case, there is no information exchange between the columns of PEs; hence, they need not run in lockstep. Secondly we can achieve an overlap between adding partial sums and loading rows of PEs with new data. When the bottom row is adding partial sums, the top row of PEs can be getting loaded with new data (*ifmap*-filter row pairs).

No Local Reuse (NLR) Architecture

The NLR architecture does not allocate any local storage to a PE for caching data; all the inputs, filters, and partial sums are either read from the global buffers or passed between PEs in a systolic fashion. An advantage is that we can create architectures with a large number of PEs; however, to compensate for this we need a large memory that can quickly supply data to the PEs via a very efficient NoC. An example of such an architecture with a 1D array of PEs is shown in Figure 14.11. In this case, the parallelisation is across the channels. Each PE computes the partial sums for each channel; each such partial sum is sent to the neighbouring PE on the right. We can parallelise along other axes also, and also create a 2D array of PEs by juxtaposing such 1D arrays.

14.3 Intra-PE Parallelism

Up till now we have been discussing parallelism at the level of PEs. We observed that it is a good idea to divide large chunks of computations amongst the PEs such that they can work independently. We created rather loose synchronisation mechanisms across the PEs. This allowed us to scale the design without relying on very tight clock synchrony. As we shall see later, such design choices will allow us to make use of different optimisations such as using 0-valued pixels to reduce the number of computations

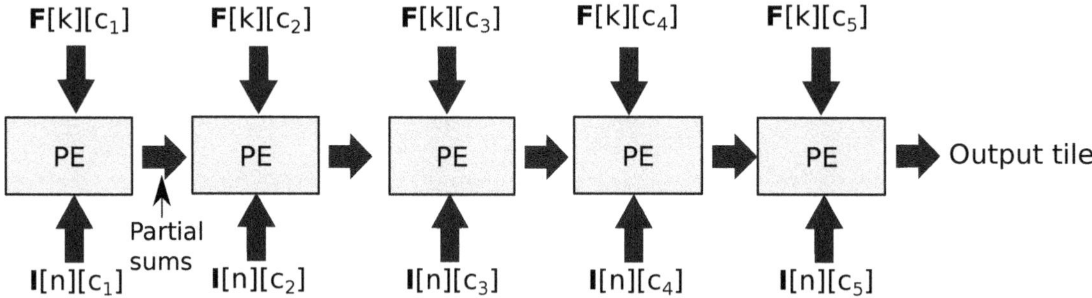

Figure 14.11: An NLR data flow

within the PEs. Let us now focus on the design of a PE. As far as a PE is concerned, it receives a set of inputs and filter weights. It needs to compute a 2D-convolution in most architectures, and a 1D convolution in the row stationary architecture.

Let us first focus on 1D convolution, which is simpler.

14.3.1 1D Convolution

Let us first introduce simpler terminology. We shall use the variables $\mathbf{w}$, $\mathbf{x}$, and $\mathbf{y}$ to represent the weight vector, a row of inputs, and a row of outputs respectively. Let the length of the weight vector be n. For referring to individual elements we shall use a subscript. For example, w_i refers to the ith element of $\mathbf{w}$. The convolution operation that we wish to compute is of the form,

$$\mathbf{y} = \mathbf{w} \star \mathbf{x}$$
$$\Rightarrow \forall i, \ y_i = \sum_{j=0}^{n-1} w_j \times x_{i+j} \tag{14.18}$$

Such circuits contain only two kinds of basic elements: logic elements for computing the result of addition and MAC operations, and registers. Let us explain with some examples. We shall first introduce semi-systolic arrays in this context. Please note that in the diagrams shown in the subsequent sections, we start the count from 1 for the sake of simplicity. All the definitions remain the same; there is a slight abuse of notation.

Semi-systolic Arrays

Stationary Weights

Consider the design shown in Figure 14.12. In this case, we have four weights: w_1, w_2, w_3, and w_4. They are kept stationary in four registers respectively. Then inputs start flowing in from the left. The inputs are numbered $x_1, x_2, \ldots$. Consider time $t = 1$ (see the timeline on the right side). Each of the combinational elements computes a product. The products are $w_1 \times x_1$, $w_2 \times x_2$, $w_3 \times x_3$, and $w_4 \times x_4$. All of these products are computed in parallel. We then assume the existence of an adder tree that adds all these *partial sums* in a single cycle. If we now consider the timeline we see that in the first cycle we compute y_1, then we compute y_2, and so on. The computation can be visualised as a sewing machine where the cloth (representing the inputs) passes through the needle.

Every cycle each input moves one step to the right. Note the placement of a register between two multiply units. We assume that it takes an input one cycle to pass through a register. This pattern of

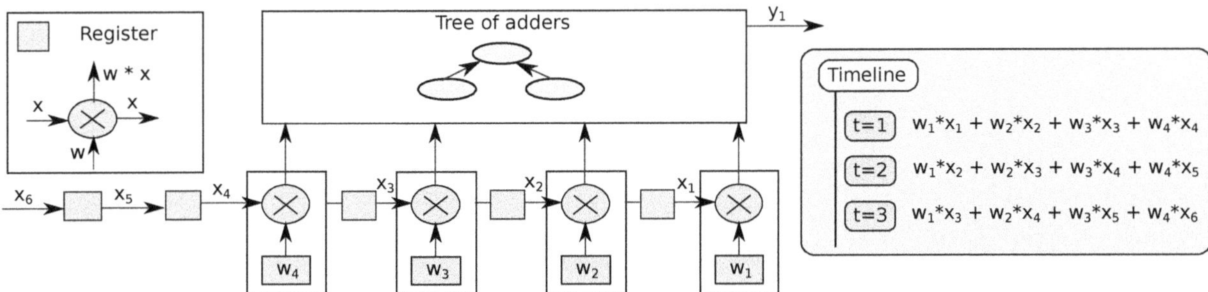

Figure 14.12: The weights remain stationary, the inputs pass through them, and the output is computed by an adder tree.

computation where in every cycle the inputs or partial sums move to a neighbouring register is known as *systolic computation*. Such systolic circuits typically use an array of registers, MAC/multiply elements, and adders. We can have many kinds of systolic machines. This is an example of a semi-systolic array. Whenever two combinational elements are directly connected without an intervening register then we call this structure a semi-systolic array. In this case, there are no registers between each multiply element and the adder. However, if we have a register between every two combinational elements, then the structure is known as a *systolic array*.

Definition 105

- *An array is defined as a structured network of registers and combinational elements. In a systolic computation, values flow from one register to adjacent registers every cycle.*

- *In a semi-systolic array there need not be any intervening registers between adjacent combinational elements. Combinational elements A and B are said to be adjacent if from the output of one to the input of the other, there is a path comprising only of wires and registers.*

- *In a systolic array we always have a register between any two adjacent combinational elements.*

Semi-systolic arrays have their fair share of shortcomings. Let's say we have 25 weights, then we need to add all the 25 partial sums in a single cycle. This may not be possible. We need to unnecessarily slow down the cycle time. In such semi-systolic architectures a single cycle needs to accommodate a lot of Boolean computations, which may result in a slowdown. To convert this architecture into a systolic architecture, we can pipeline the adder tree by adding an array of registers at each level.

Now instead of keeping the weights stationary, let us create another semi-systolic architecture where we broadcast the weights. This avoids having the costly adder tree.

Broadcasting the Weights

In this case, we keep the outputs stationary, and broadcast the weights one after the other in successive cycles (refer to Figure 14.13). We compute a set of outputs in parallel ($y_1 \ldots y_6$). Consider the computation from the point of view of output y_1. In the first cycle, we broadcast w_1 to all the MAC units. We set $y_1 = w_1 \times x_1$. In the next cycle, the input x_2 arrives from the left, and simultaneously we broadcast w_2. The MAC unit then computes $y_1 = y_1 + w_2 \times x_2$. Likewise, in the next few cycles we compute and add the rest of the partial sums to y_1. At the end of 4 cycles, y_1 is correctly computed. In

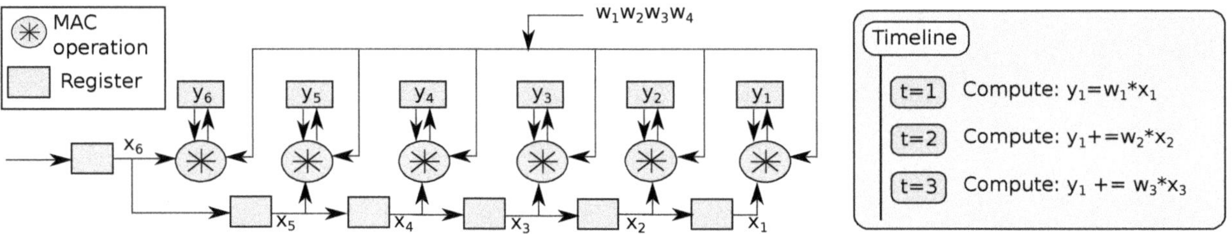

Figure 14.13: The weights are broadcast to all the MAC units

parallel, we would have computed the rest of the partial sums: $y_1 \ldots y_6$. All of them can be written to the output memory. We can then compute the next 6 outputs and so on. This is also an example of a systolic computation, but the array is semi-systolic because we are broadcasting the inputs – there are no registers between the inputs and the MAC units. Here again, the broadcast operation can be slow if we have a large number of weights. We need to take into account the RC delay of the wires and the input capacitance values of the registers.

We looked at two examples of performing 1D convolution using semi-systolic arrays in this section. Many more architectures are possible. In fact there is a lot of theoretical work on automatically converting a set of loops into a systolic computation [Lavenier et al., 1999, Lam, 2012]. Discussing this is beyond the scope of this book.

It is possible to automatically convert a semi-systolic array into a systolic array using the Retiming Lemma [Leighton, 2014]. Hence, many designers initially create a semi-systolic array for their problem because it is often easier to design it. Then they use the Retiming Lemma to automatically convert the architecture to one that uses a systolic array, which effectively bounds the amount of computation that needs to be done in a single clock cycle. This is because of the mandatory placement of registers between combinational units.

The Retiming Lemma

We will not explain this in great detail in this chapter. We will just present the basic idea. We represent the array as a graph $\mathcal{G}$, where each combinational element is a node, and if there is a connection between two combinational elements (even via some registers), we add an edge between them. The weight of each edge is equal to the number of registers it contains. If there are no registers on an edge, its weight is zero. We next compute $\mathcal{G} - 1$ by subtracting the weight of each edge by 1. Now, we present a few results without proofs.

1. For any node, we can move k registers from each of its input edges and add them to each of the output edges. The results will remain the same and the rest of the nodes will not perceive this change. This is known as *retiming*. This is a purely local operation.

2. If $\mathcal{G} - 1$ does not have any negative weight cycles, we can successfully *retime* it to produce an equivalent systolic array. If there are negative weight cycles, we typically slowdown the array by a factor of k by multiplying the number of registers on each edge with k (we produce the graph $k\mathcal{G}$). For small values of k, $k\mathcal{G} - 1$ typically does not have a cycle.

3. We set the *lag* of a vertex/node as the weight of the shortest path from it to the output in $k\mathcal{G} - 1$. For an edge from u to v, we set the new weight as follows. $weight_{new} = weight_{old} + lag(v) - lag(u)$. The result of this operation is that we add extra registers to different edges – we delay different values flowing in the array to varying extents.

We introduced multiplicative slowdowns (to avoid negative weight cycles), and additive delays by adding more registers to edges. This additional timing overhead may be prohibitive in some cases, and thus we may prefer a semi-systolic array if it is faster. This determination needs to be done on a case-by-case basis.

Systolic Array

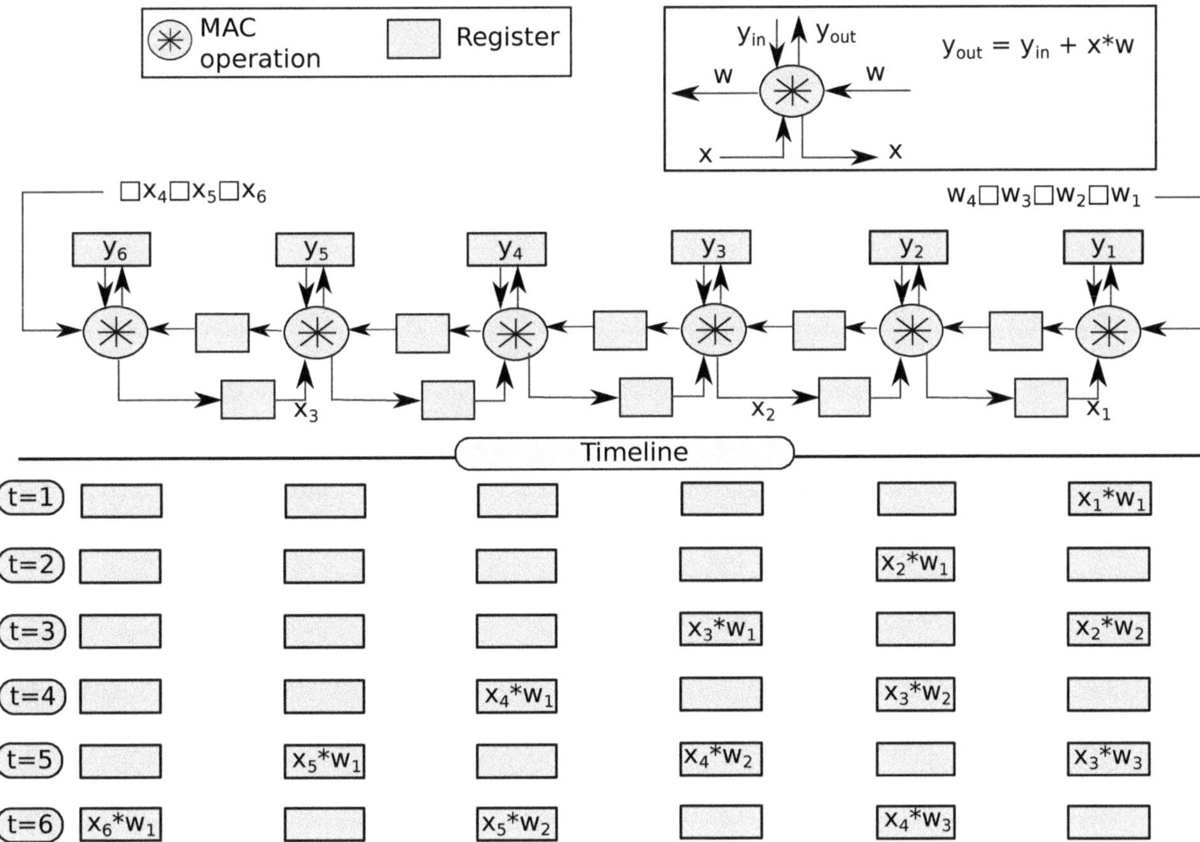

Figure 14.14: A systolic array for 1D convolution

Let us take the semi-systolic array presented in Figure 14.13 (architecture that broadcasts weights) and use the Retiming Lemma to create a systolic version of it. This is shown in Figure 14.14. First, note that it is indeed a systolic array because there is always a register between any two adjacent combinational elements. Second, we have slowed down the array by a factor of 2 in accordance with the Retiming Lemma (to eliminate negative weight cycles). Hence, the inputs and the weights are provided to the array every alternate cycle. In this context, the symbol $\square$ represents an empty cycle – no inputs or weights are provided to the array in that cycle.

Now consider the structure of the systolic array. The inputs and weights traverse the array from opposite sides. The array is designed in such a way that whenever an input *collides* with a weight, it produces a partial sum and this sum is added to the value in output register y_i. The pictorial description at the bottom of the figure shows the timeline, where each rectangle corresponds to an output register (registers storing $y_1 \ldots y_6$). Here, we can see that a separation of one cycle between the inputs or weights is necessary. This is because if the previous input is two columns away, in the next cycle it will only be one column away, which is where it needs to be to compute the partial sum correctly. Using a similar argument we can reason about the spacing between the weights. The reader should convince herself about the correctness of this design.

Now, an important criticism of this design can be that we are halving the throughput. On the flip side, we are gaining regularity, we can most likely afford a much higher clock speed, and we are avoiding costly broadcasts. However, for all of these advantages, sacrificing 50% of the throughput does not seem to be justified. This problem can be solved very easily. We can compute two convolutions at the same time. The second convolution can be scheduled in the empty cycles. The different convolutions will not interfere with each other as long as we have separate output registers for each convolution. This is the conventional technique that is used to ensure that we do not sacrifice on throughput. This can easily be done in a CNN because we typically need to compute the results of a lot of convolutions.

Direct Product

If we are willing to use a lot of resources, then there is a simple and direct method. Instead of a traditional systolic style computing, we can instead directly compute the convolution as follows. Let us say that we want to convolve the 1D input vector x with the filter vector w that contains n elements. We load $x_1 \ldots x_n$ into a buffer B_1, and simultaneously load $w_1 \ldots w_n$ into another weight buffer W. At the same time, we load the elements $x_2, \ldots, x_n, x_{n+1}$ into buffer B_2. We can use combinational logic to select the elements $x_2 \ldots x_n$ while they are being loaded into B_1, shift them by one position, and separately load x_{n+1} from memory. We can do the same for more buffers such as B_3 and B_4 that start with x_3 and x_4, respectively. For this design we can have 4 PEs; each PE reads the contents of one input buffer and the weight buffer, computes the convolution, and writes the output to an output array. All the convolutions can be computed in parallel. Furthermore, each PE can have an array of MAC units and an adder tree.

This is a very simple algorithm and can easily be implemented on an FPGA. It does not require the sophistication or coordination that a systolic array requires. In terms of the resources required, we need more storage space because now a single input element is stored in multiple buffers and we also need more hardware to handle data movement.

14.3.2　2D Convolution

Systolic Approaches

Let us now extend our results to perform a 2D convolution. The simplest approach is to divide it into a sequence of 1D convolutions, compute each convolution separately, and add the partial sums. Given that we have a fairly robust architecture for computing 1D convolutions, we can easily reuse it in a 2D scenario.

To describe this, let us use similar terminology where $\mathbf{X}$ represents the input. In this case, $\mathbf{X}$ is a 2D matrix. We shall use the term $row(x_i)$ to refer to the ith row of $\mathbf{X}$. Similarly, we shall use the notation $row(w_i)$ to refer to the ith row of the filter, and $row(y_i)$ to refer to the the ith row of the output.

To compute all the output pixels for the ith row of the output *ofmap*, we need to compute the following convolutions: $row(w_i) \star row(x_i)$, $row(w_{i+1}) \star row(x_{i+1})$, ..., $row(w_{i+R-1}) \star row(x_{i+R-1})$. We are assuming that the filter has R rows. We need to add these partial sums column-wise to compute all the output pixels for the ith row. We then need to start from the next row and again compute a similar set of partial sums. This is a very classical design that was originally proposed in [Kung and Song, 1981].

Figure 14.15 shows a representative scheme. We assume that the filter has 3 rows. We first compute the output pixels for $row(x_1)$ by sending three rows as input to the first convolutional block. We simultaneously feed in the filter weights (not shown in the figure) and compute the three 1D convolutions. We then need to add the three partial sums (computed by each 1D convolution) to get the final result $row(y_1)$. Then we stream the input rows $row(x_2)$ and $row(x_3)$ to the second convolutional block. Additionally, we stream $row(x_4)$ to this block. This convolutional block computes $row(y_2)$. We can similarly have many more cascaded convolutional blocks. It is also possible to reuse a block to perform multiple convolutions one after the other. This can be done by feeding two input rows back into the block once the convolution is done. Simultaneously, we stream in a new input row.

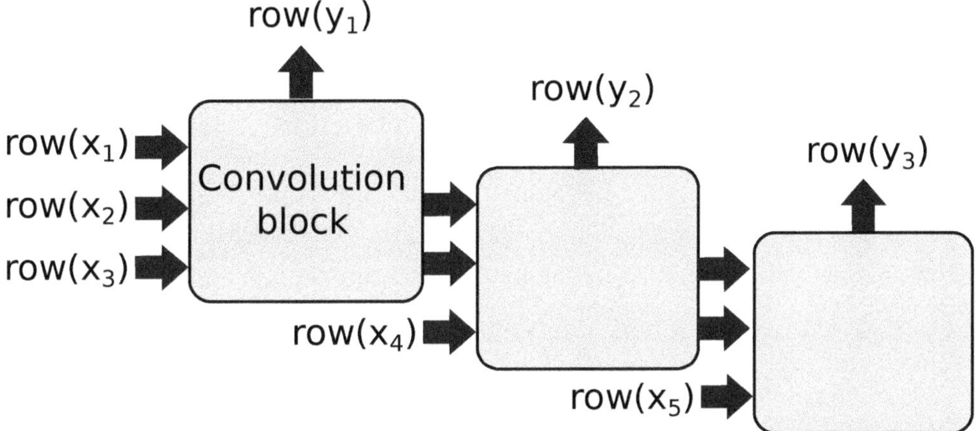

Figure 14.15: A set of systolic arrays for 2D convolution

Matrix-Vector Product

Convolution can also be represented as a matrix-vector product. Let us explain with a small example. Assume we want to compute the following convolution. We have a 2D weight matrix $\mathbf{W}$ with elements w_{ij}, and a 2D input matrix $\mathbf{X}$ with elements x_{ij}.

$$\mathbf{W} = \begin{bmatrix} w_{11} & w_{12} \\ w_{21} & w_{22} \end{bmatrix} \qquad\qquad \mathbf{X} = \begin{bmatrix} x_{11} & x_{12} & x_{13} \\ x_{21} & x_{22} & x_{23} \\ x_{31} & x_{32} & x_{33} \end{bmatrix}$$

The convolution $\mathbf{W} \star \mathbf{X}$ can be converted into a matrix-vector product as follows.

$$\mathbf{Y} = \underbrace{\begin{bmatrix} w_{11} & w_{12} & 0 & w_{21} & w_{22} & 0 & 0 & 0 & 0 \\ 0 & w_{11} & w_{12} & 0 & w_{21} & w_{22} & 0 & 0 & 0 \\ 0 & 0 & 0 & w_{11} & w_{12} & 0 & w_{21} & w_{22} & 0 \\ 0 & 0 & 0 & 0 & w_{11} & w_{12} & 0 & w_{21} & w_{22} \end{bmatrix}}_{\hat{\mathbf{W}}} \times \begin{bmatrix} x_{11} \\ x_{12} \\ x_{13} \\ x_{21} \\ x_{22} \\ x_{23} \\ x_{31} \\ x_{32} \\ x_{33} \end{bmatrix}$$

$\hat{\mathbf{W}}$ is known as a *doubly block circulant matrix*. Each row is generated by flattening the weight matrix and inserting an adequate number of zeros. Each subsequent row is generated by shifting the previous row by either 1 position or by 2 positions (relevant only for this example). The reader needs to convince herself that the matrix-vector product is indeed equal to the convolution of the matrices $\mathbf{X}$ and $\mathbf{W}$. We can extend this framework to compute a matrix-matrix product for calculating the respective convolutions of several input blocks in one go.

One of the advantages of this approach is simplicity. Moreover, matrix multiplication is a classical problem, and there are a lot of highly optimised hardware circuits to compute the product of two matrices. Such circuits can be incorporated into commodity processors that contain CNN accelerators. As a matter of fact, modern CPUs and GPUs have already started incorporating matrix and tensor processing units as of 2020.

These units can be used to compute such convolutions by converting them into standard linear algebra operations such as matrix-vector or matrix-matrix products. Even though we need to create additional redundancy in this scheme by storing multiple copies of the weights, and we need to flatten matrices into vectors, sometimes using standard matrix multiplication hardware that has been rigorously verified and optimised is a worthwhile design decision.

14.4 Optimisations

We can perform a wide variety of optimisations while designing CNN accelerators. For example, we may have 0-valued weights or inputs. In this case, we need not compute any MAC operations that involve them. Such operations are known as *ineffectual operations.* In some other cases we have repeated weights or repeated input values. We can leverage such patterns to reduce the number of arithmetic operations that we perform.

Typically a systolic array based system is rather rigid. It does not allow us to take advantage of such patterns in the inputs or in the weights. However, if we are using reconfigurable hardware such as FPGAs or if there is some scope for reconfigurability within our ASIC circuits, then we can leverage many such patterns. Let us look at some of the common methods that are used to reduce the computation time, and then we shall move on to techniques that optimise the usage of the memory system.

14.4.1 Reduction of the Computing Time

Common Subexpression Elimination

One of the common techniques in this space is common subexpression elimination. Assume that w, w' and w'' are filter weights. While computing the convolution we might encounter an expression of the form: $(wx_1 + wx_2 + w'x_3 + w'x_4 + w''x_5 + w''x_6 + w''x_7)$. In this case, we can group the elements as follows: $w(x_1 + x_2) + w'(x_3 + x_4) + w''(x_5 + x_6 + x_7)$. In this case, we can create circuits to compute the sum of the first two inputs elements (x_1 and x_2), the next two input elements (x_3 and x_4), and then the input elements from positions 5 to 7. By doing this we save a few multiplications. To compute $wx_1 + wx_2$, we need one addition and two multiplications. Whereas, to compute $w(x_1 + x_2)$, we need only one addition and one multiplication. We thus save a multiplication over here. The savings are even more if we have more repeated weights. Furthermore, the sum of the inputs that we compute can be used across filters if they also have a similar pattern of weight reuse.

Zero and Negative Values

Next, we can consider zero-valued weights or inputs. We can add additional circuits to detect those weights or inputs whose value is below a certain threshold. Subsequently, we can generate a mask that is essentially a bit vector, which contains a '1' for those positions that have a non-zero weight or input. We can only fetch those values into the PEs and then compute a convolution. Alternatively, we can fetch all the values into the PEs, and only compute convolutions for the non-zero values. Performing such optimisations using direct products is easier than other methods that rely on the fixed structure of hardware such as systolic arrays.

Most convolution layers feed their output to ReLU layers, which filter out all the negative values. If we are aware of this, then in the process of the convolution itself, we can terminate the computation and set the value of the output pixel to 0, if we are sure that the final output is going to be negative. To get a quick estimate of the final sign of the output, we can compute an approximate value only using the more significant bits of the inputs and the weights. This will give us an estimate of the final value. If we find it to be negative, then we can skip the entire convolution process.

One of the main criticisms of such approaches has been that the time taken to compute a convolution becomes nondeterministic. Since we need to wait for all the blocks to finish their convolutions, the slowest block determines the total computation time. This is not desirable. Hence, in this case we need to dynamically apportion the work among the PEs such that all the parallel computations roughly finish at the same time.

14.4.2 Reduction of the Memory Access Time

Compression

In general, it is very easy to compress images because they have a fair amount of redundancy. For example, a large scenery might have a lot of blue pixels because they represent the blue sky. We can take advantage of such patterns and optimise this process. We can use traditional image compression techniques to compress the *ifmaps*, and then load compressed versions of these *ifmaps* into higher levels of memory such as the global buffer or the local buffers. When the input data is ready to be processed, we can uncompress the *ifmaps*. Such techniques effectively increase the memory bandwidth and reduce the time it takes to load a set of *ifmaps*.

One of the common techniques that is used in such compression strategies is base-delta compression [Wang et al., 2016]. Here, we compute the mean value for a block of filter weights or inputs. This is known as the *base*. Then we compute the offset of each value (the *delta*) about the mean. If all the values are clustered roughly in the same zone, then we need far fewer bits to represent all the offsets. For example, if the values are 10, 11, 12, and 13, the delta values will be -2, -1, 0, and 1 assuming the base is equal to 12. These values will only require 2 bits to be represented. We thus need a total of 8 (2×4) bits to store all the deltas and 4 bits to store the base, whereas we would have needed 4×4 (16) bits to store all the original values. We observe a space savings of 25%. Of course, this scheme does make the implicit assumption that all the deltas are in the range of [-2,1]. If the possible values of delta were more spaced apart from the mean, we might not have seen any savings in storage space.

Dynamic Detection of Zero-Valued Weights and Inputs

We can detect zero-valued weights and inputs either statically or dynamically. Almost always, the latter is preferable if we can find an efficient method. We can scan the weights or inputs and create a bitmap or a bit vector that stores a 1 if the corresponding weight or input element is non-zero. Such bitmaps can be stored in a separate region in memory and treated like an indexing structure. Whenever we need to read in an *ifmap*, we first access the index (in the bitmap or bit-vector) and only fetch those elements that have non-zero values.

Reduction of Precision

Different layers of the neural network do not need the same level of precision. We can reduce the precision of values in some layers if the resulting error is insignificant. Of course, this depends on the nature of the input, the nature of the features we are trying to detect, and the architecture of the network. Sometimes by studying the interaction of all three, it is possible to identify layers where the precision of the stored values can be reduced significantly. In this case, we can reduce both the computation time as well as the memory access overheads because the data values now are significantly narrower. One of the most important criticisms of such architectures is that the functional units are typically designed for a fixed operand width in mind. If the operand width is changed, then the functional units need to be changed as well. This is not possible in an ASIC architecture, and is also hard to implement in reconfigurable architectures because they typically incorporate fixed-width adders and multipliers. Hence, reducing the computation time with reduced precision is hard.

Bit-serial Multipliers

It is possible to use bit-serial multipliers that read in the input bit by bit to implement this functionality. The key insight here is that each of the two numbers that we wish to multiply (input and weight) can be represented as bit vectors. We claim that the product of two numbers is equal to the convolution of the bit vectors. This is very easy to visualise if we think about how we actually multiply the numbers using the standard primary-school multiplication algorithm. Figuring out a proof for this is left as an exercise for the reader.

We can use a standard systolic architecture to compute the convolution. Since it is independent of the number of elements (operand width in this case), we can use it to implement a bit-serial multiplier that multiplies two operands bit by bit completely disregarding the width of the operands. The multiplier can thus scale to any precision. Even though we gain a tremendous degree of flexibility by using such bit-serial multipliers, the latency suffers. Such multipliers take $O(N)$ time, whereas a conventional parallel multiplier takes $O(log(N))$ time. Here, N is the operand width. This can be offset by the fact that such multipliers have a very low area and power footprint.

Bit-serial architectures can additionally make optimisations based on zero-valued bits. The key idea is to break a large n-bit number into several smaller m-bit numbers. For each of these numbers we compute the length of the prefix and suffix that contain all zeros. These are ineffectual bits, and need not be considered in the multiplication. We then multiply these m-bit numbers with the filter weight using a bit-serial multiplier, and then left-shift the result according to the length of the zero-valued suffix and the position of the m-bit number within the larger number. We can then use a traditional adder tree to add all of these partial sums.

14.5 Memory System Organisation

Up till now we have only discussed the design of the compute engines of CNN accelerators. However, the design of the memory system is also equally important. This is because a large array of PEs also requires a very high memory bandwidth. We need to supply all the inputs, partial sums, and weights to the large array of PEs. This requires a very high-bandwidth connection to memory. Latency is not particularly important here. The most important metric that we are concerned with is the achieved throughput.

14.5.1 DRAM+SRAM based Organisation

The traditional approach uses DRAM banks for off-chip memory, and SRAM technology for the global buffer and the on-chip local buffers. Consider the output stationary (OS) architecture presented in Figure 14.9. In such architectures we typically stream the inputs from one side, and stream in the filter weights from another side of the 2D array. Consider a 16×16 PE array. This means that we typically need to read 16 different input streams, and 16 different filter streams in parallel. The only way of sustaining such a high degree of parallelism is to have a 32-banked global buffer. We dedicate 16 banks to store the inputs, and we dedicate 16 banks to store the filter weights. Every cycle we access all the banks and stream in data from them.

There are two ways to manage the process of loading the local buffers and the global buffers. The first method is to use the traditional cache eviction and replacement mechanisms to fill any data that the local buffer or global buffer may require. This is the traditional *pull*-based mechanism. However, in the case of a CNN, since the entire computational process is deterministic, we can have a *push*-based mechanism where we have a dedicated finite state machine that loads data from the lower levels of memory at appropriate times and effectively acts as a data prefetching engine. This process can be automated where the FSM figures out the data access pattern automatically, or it can use hints embedded in the code. The latter approach is preferred in high-performance designs.

Let us show an example for an OS architecture. Its mapping was as follows.

$$n \triangleright h' \| w' \| \triangleright k \| c \triangleright r \triangleright s \triangleright h'' \triangleright w''$$

Listing 14.2 shows a piece of code (using a traditional software paradigm) that represents this mapping. The code does not capture the finer aspects of the data flow; we use it for explaining the role of prefetching. It introduces the *parallel for* statement to represent the $\parallel$ operator. h' is represented by $h1$ and h'' is represented by $h2$. We have omitted the code to prefetch data. For the ease of readability, we have put comments in its place.

Listing 14.2: 2D Convolution with directives to load data from memory

```
for (n=0; n<N; n++) {  /* input images */
// load the nth image I[n] in the DRAM

 parallel for (h1=0; h1<H; h1+= Th) {/*rows: ifmap/ofmap */
  parallel for (w1=0; w1<W; w1+= Tw) {/*cols: ifmap/ofmap */
// load the output tile at O[n][k][h1][w1] (for each k) in a separate LB

    parallel for (k=0; k<K; k++) { /* outputs */
     for (c=0; c<C; c++) { /* input channels */
// load the filter F[k][c] in the GB
// load the input ifmap at I[n][c] in the GB

      for (r=0; r<R; r++) { /* rows of the filter */
       for (s=0; s<S; s++) { /* cols of the filter */

        for (h2=h1; h2<h1+Th; h2++) {
         for (w2=w1; w2<w1+Tw; w2++) {
          O[n][k][h2][w2] += I[n][c][h2+r][w2+s]
                            * F[k][c][r][s];
}}}}}}}
```

The key point to note is the comments that we have added for loading data into different memory structures. We can at the beginning load an entire image into the DRAM. Since we keep the output pixels stationary in the local buffers (LBs), we can immediately load them once we have partitioned the pixel space. They remain stationary until we move to a new set of output pixels. Then, when we change the channel, c, we load the corresponding input pixels and filters into the GB. Such hints can be made more sophisticated, and we can prefetch values into the GB, and also add a streaming component – as old data leaves, new data moves in to take its place. Something similar can be implemented in hardware as well. It needs to capture the finer aspects of the data flow and accurately synchronise the data transfer with the computation.

Traditional DRAM memory typically proves to be a bottleneck in terms of bandwidth. Hence, for implementing CNNs we typically prefer high-bandwidth memory technologies such as embedded DRAM, HBM memory, or Hybrid Memory Cubes (see Section 10.5.6). We typically assign a PE to each vault. We can think of a vault as a high-bandwidth bank in 3D memory.

14.5.2 Processing in Memory

Till now, our approach has been to stream values to the array of PEs, compute the results, and write them back. Processing in memory (PIM) approaches propose to take the computation to the memory system. This means that we make the memory *smarter* such that we can easily perform addition or multiplication operations in situ. We can use traditional memory technologies such as SRAMs, and DRAMs, or even use modern NVM based technologies.

Overview

The basic idea is the same for all the PIM designs. To compute a dot product between two vectors, we need to first perform an elementwise multiplication, and then add the partial sums. Let us consider a typical array-based memory design, where each row of memory cells is activated via the word line, and each column of memory cells is connected to at least one bit line. Let the voltage on each word line correspond to the value of an input. The assumption is that the weight is embedded within the memory cell, and we use a column of cells to compute a single dot product between a vector of inputs and a vector of weights.

There are two broad paradigms in this space: *charge sharing* and *current summing*. In the charge sharing approach each memory cell has a capacitor, whose stored charge is proportional to the product of the input and the weight. This is done for all input-weight pairs, and it is further assumed that all such capacitors are connected to the same bit line via switches (see Figure 14.16(a)). Then, to add the values we just need to connect all the capacitors to the bit line by closing all the switches. The stored charge will redistribute. Since for each capacitor $Q = VC$ [1], we can think of this as a multiplication operation. There are two design choices here. Either we can keep C the same and use an analog multiplier to generate V or think of C as the weight and V as the input. Regardless of the design choice, the charge Q_i for memory cell i represents the product of an input pixel and a weight. When we connect all the switches we shall have $\sum Q_i = V_{bitline} C_{lumped}$. Here, $V_{bitline}$ is the voltage of the bit line, and C_{lumped} is the lumped capacitance of the entire set of memory cells and the bit line – this is known a priori. Hence, the voltage on the bit line can be a very good estimate of the dot product. This can be measured with an ADC (analog to digital converter).

Next, let us consider the current summing approach. If we look at the basic Ohm's law equation, $V/R = I$, here also we are performing a multiplication between the voltage and the conductance $1/R$. If there is some way to configure the conductance then we can realise a multiplication operation between an input (voltage V) and a weight (the conductance). Furthermore, if we add the resultant current values, then we effectively realise an addition operation. The magnitude of this current can again be detected by measuring the voltage across a register using an ADC (see Figure 14.16(b)).

In both cases, we perform an approximate computation where we get an estimate of the dot product. In such cases, we are embedding the weight into the memory cell either as a capacitance or a conductance. It is possible to use modern nonvolatile memory technologies to also dynamically configure these values. There are criticisms for both these approaches. Any analog computation of this nature is associated with a certain degree of error caused by noise and process variation. Hence, for such architectures designers typically use either binary weights, or significantly reduce the precision of the weight values. Over the years many optimisations have been proposed to get acceptable accuracies with such neural networks that use such reduced weights. Furthermore, many advances have been made particularly over the last five years (as of 2020) to increase the noise tolerance. Charge sharing approaches are in general more tolerant to noise than current summing approaches.

Implementations

We typically use a voltage multiplier circuit for charge sharing based schemes and a variable resistance in a current summing based scheme.

Let us first look at options in traditional CMOS logic. For binary-valued inputs and weights, we can use an AND gate to effect a voltage multiplication. Another way of creating such a multiplier in traditional CMOS logic is to operate a transistor in the linear mode of operation. In this case, the current is proportional to the drain-source voltage. This mechanism can be used to create a configurable current source. We can alternatively keep the drain to source voltage constant, and instead vary the gate voltage. This will change the drain current, which we can approximate as a linear relationship. This approach is typically preferred while using regular CMOS transistors where the word line voltage is set to be proportional to the input. We use a DAC (digital to analog converter) to generate these voltages for each word line. We can then use any of the approaches – charge sharing or current summing – with appropriate modifications.

Nonvolatile memory technologies such as resistive RAMs (ReRAMs) are ideally suited for this purpose. Here, we can easily vary the resistance as discussed in Section 10.5.5. Then we can use the current

---

[1] Q is the charge, V is the voltage, and C is the capacitance

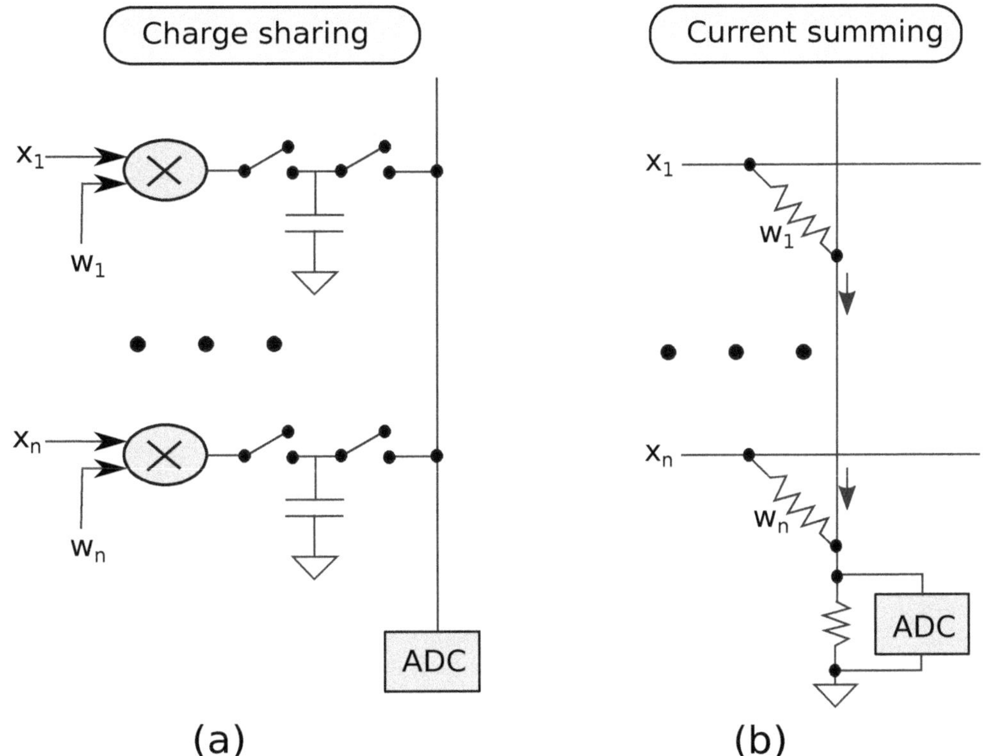

Figure 14.16: (a) Charge sharing, (b) Current summing

summing approach. Given that such devices are very easily configurable, we can change the weights at run time. Researchers have created variable resistance states with almost all known NVM devices and used them to realise such computations. Such circuits are also known as *neuromorphic circuits*.

In all such architectures, dealing with negative weights is not possible. However, they can be easily incorporated into such designs by computing two dot products: one with positive weights (negative weights are zeroed), and one with negative weights (positive weights are zeroed). Subsequently, we can subtract the second dot product (one with negative weights) from the first one (one with positive weights).

14.6   Summary and Further Reading

14.6.1   Summary

Summary 13

1. *In any learning problem, we try to figure out the relationship between a set of inputs and the corresponding outputs. We can either assume a linear relationship or a nonlinear relationship.*

2. *Since the relationship is not known a priori, we typically use a class of learners known as universal approximators, where we simply need to change the parameters to realise different functions. The aim of the learning problem is to learn these parameters.*

3. *Early approaches were based on linear and nonlinear regression, where it was assumed that the relationship is a polynomial curve and the main aim was to learn the coefficients.*

4. *Neural networks are one of the most popular universal approximators that are composed of a set of layers. The input to a layer is called an* ifmap, *and the output is called an* ofmap. *A layer typically takes in multiple* ifmaps *as inputs and generates multiple* ofmaps *as outputs. Each element of an* ifmap *or an* ofmap *is called a* pixel. *The layers either compute a linear function over the inputs (outputs of the previous layer) by multiplying the input vector with a dedicated weight vector, or by computing a nonlinear function over the inputs such as the Sigmoid function, the tanh function, or the ReLU function. In modern deep neural networks we can have hundreds of such layers with millions of weights.*

5. *In convolutional neural networks (CNNs) we typically consider 2D* ifmaps *and* ofmaps. *We avoid costly vector or matrix products, and instead compute the convolution of a set of* ifmaps *with a very small weight matrix known as the* filter. *To reduce the size of the inputs, we perform an operation known as* max pooling, *where we replace a set of pixels with its maximum value for translational invariance. A typical CNN consists of four types of layers: convolutional, max pooling, ReLU, and a traditional fully connected linear layer that computes a dot product between an input vector and an equal-sized weight vector.*

6. *The operation of the CNN can be represented as a nested loop with seven iterations. Some of these iterations can further be tiled, and also be parallelised across a set of functional units known as processing elements or PEs. We designed a custom notation to represent such computations.*

7. *In this notation, the symbol $\|$ indicates that the loops of the iterator preceding it can be parallelised, and the operator $\triangleright$ refers to sequential execution.*

8. *We initially proposed a software model where we model each PE as a separate thread that has some local storage space. We can decide to keep some data stationary within the local storage space. In this space we proposed all kinds of architectures: input stationary (IS), weight stationary (WS), output stationary (OS), and row stationary (RS).*

9. *We can simply take the software abstraction and map it to hardware, where each thread is a separate processing element. In this case, we need to consider the connection between the PEs. The PEs are typically arranged as a 2D matrix interconnected via an on-chip network. Depending upon the type of the architecture we stream in one kind of data from one side (inputs, filters, etc.) and another kind of data from another side. Additionally, we also have the option of storing some data within the local buffers of each PE. We can realise all the four kinds of architectures using such hardware designs.*

10. *We typically distribute work at a coarse grain among the PEs because it is very hard to make all the PEs work in lockstep. To further achieve the benefits of parallel execution we can leverage intra-PE parallelism. In general, to compute a 2D convolution, we break it into a series of 1D convolutions.*

11. *We first discussed semi-systolic arrays, where we have a set of combinational units (CUs) arranged in a linear sequence. In every cycle we can either broadcast a value to all the CUs, or make a set of values flow between adjacent CUs. Because of the lockstep nature of the execution such execution patterns are known as* systolic execution *patterns.*

12. *In a semi-systolic architecture we at least have one pair of adjacent CUs without registers in between. This makes it hard to maintain the timing, manage clock skew, and also increases*

> *the cycle time. Hence, we may prefer systolic architectures, where we always have intervening registers between a pair of adjacent CUs. We can use the Retiming Lemma to convert a semi-systolic architecture to a systolic architecture. However, while doing so, it is typically necessary to introduce k stall cycles every time we stream in one input. This slows down the computation by a factor of k, and additionally we need to add many extra registers throughout the array. The problem of stall cycles can be solved by solving multiple problems concurrently. We can then clock such systolic networks at a very high speed without wasting cycles.*
>
> 13. *In many reconfigurable architectures we use a direct method, where we load large overlapping sections of the* ifmaps *into different memory arrays at the same time. For each array, we have a dedicated set of MAC units and a tree of adders to compute a dot product with the filter weights. This approach does require more resources because of the added redundancy, however, it is fast and simple to implement if we have the required hardware.*
>
> 14. *We can also convert a convolution into a matrix-vector product. The* ifmap *can be flattened into a vector, and we can convert the filter matrix into a doubly block circulant matrix. Their product is equal to the 2D convolution.*
>
> 15. *For designing a memory system we typically use a large multi-banked global buffer. We can alternatively use modern 3D stacked memory technologies such as High Bandwidth Memory (HBM) or Hybrid Memory Cubes (HMC). They are integrated into the same package and connected using an interposer.*
>
> 16. *We can make memory cells smarter and use them to compute dot products. Two common approaches to compute dot products using an array of memory cells (traditional or NVM) are the charge sharing and current summing techniques. This is an analog computation that yields an estimate of the dot product of an input vector (typically expressed as word line voltages) and the weight vector (typically embedded as a conductance or capacitance within each memory cell).*

14.6.2   Further Reading

To understand all the concepts presented in this chapter and to pursue research in this area, it is necessary to first get a good idea of machine learning. Readers should first consult a standard textbook on machine learning such as [Bishop, 2006]. Before moving on to deep learning, it is important to thoroughly understand linear algebra [Cooperstein, 2015], and also understand matrix calculus [Turkington, 2013]. Subsequently, readers can move on to the classic text on deep learning by Goodfellow, Bengio, and Courville [Goodfellow et al., 2016].

After appreciating deep learning, the next step is to cover some of the basic literature on systolic arrays. Most of these papers were published in the early 80s. Some of the early papers in this area are as follows: [Kung and Song, 1981, Kung, 1982, Kung and Picard, 1984, Ersoy, 1985, Kwan and Okullo-Oballa, 1990]. A large number of semi-systolic and systolic architectures are covered in the book by Leighton [Leighton, 2014]. Please refer to this book to learn more about the Retiming Lemma. The paper by Lam discusses algorithms for designing a compiler for systolic architectures [Lam, 2012].

Now, coming to architectures for CNNs, the reader should first take a look at the survey paper by Moolchandani et al. [Moolchandani et al., 2020] and follow up with the e-books by Reagen [Reagen et al., 2017] and Sze et al. [Sze et al., 2020]. Then interested readers can read a few highly cited papers in this area such as the papers on Neuflow [Farabet et al., 2011], Diannao [Chen et al., 2014], Cnvlutin [Albericio et al., 2016], Flexflow [Lu et al., 2017], Google TPU [Jouppi et al., 2017] and Eyeriss [Chen et al., 2016].

Some recent progress has been made in designing software simulators for hardware neural networks (the Scale-Sim project [Samajdar et al., 2020]), and in modelling the power and performance of CNNs [Wu et al., 2019, Parashar et al., 2019, Kwon et al., 2018]. These tools can be used to quickly estimate the overheads of implementing different CNN architectures in hardware.

Exercises

Ex. 1 — Implement a CNN accelerator using a hardware description language such as Verilog or VHDL.

Ex. 2 — Create an architecture for an RNN or LSTM using the techniques that we have learnt in this chapter.

Ex. 3 — In this chapter, we described the architecture for inferencing. Create an architecture for neural network training.

Ex. 4 — Design and simulate a ReRAM based convolution layer.

Part IV

Appendix

SimpleRisc ISA

In this book, all the examples that use assembly code have been written in the *SimpleRisc* assembly language. It is a toy assembly language that was originally introduced by Sarangi [Sarangi, 2015].

Inst.	Format	Inst.	Format
add	add rd, rs1, (rs2/imm)	lsl	lsl rd, rs1, (rs2/imm)
sub	sub rd, rs1, (rs2/imm)	lsr	lsr rd, rs1, (rs2/imm)
mul	mul rd, rs1, (rs2/imm)	asr	asr rd, rs1, (rs2/imm)
div	div rd, rs1, (rs2/imm)	nop	nop
mod	mod rd, rs1, (rs2/imm)	ld	ld rd, imm[rs1]
cmp	cmp rs1, (rs2/imm)	st	st rd, imm[rs1]
and	and rd, rs1, (rs2/imm)	beq	beq offset
or	or rd, rs1, (rs2/imm)	bgt	bgt offset
not	not rd, (rs2/imm)	b	b offset
mov	mov rd, (rs2/imm)	call	call offset
ret	ret		
$rd \rightarrow$ destination register id, $rs1 \rightarrow$ first source register			
$rs2 \rightarrow$ second source register, $imm \rightarrow$ immediate			

Table A.1: The *SimpleRisc* instruction set

Its main features are as follows.

1. It is a 32-bit ISA. It has 16 registers numbered $r0, r1, \ldots r15$.

2. The first 14 registers are general purpose registers. $r14$ is the stack pointer; it is also referred to as *sp*.

3. $r15$ is the return address register (also referred to as *ra*).

4. There is a special *flags* register that is set by the *cmp* (compare) instruction. Later conditional branches use it to make their decisions.

5. It has 21 instructions. The format of the instructions is shown in Table A.1.

6. Most arithmetic and logical instructions are in the 3-address format. The destination comes first, and the sources come later.

An example program to compute the factorial of a number stored in $r0$ is as follows.

```
.factorial:
/* input stored in r0, output in r1 */
/* Assume that the value in r0 is greater than 0 */
mov r1, 1    /* prod = 1 */

/* loop */
.loop
        /* check the iterator */
        cmp r0, 0
        beq .exit

        /* multiply */
        mul r1, r1, r0   /* prod = prod * r0 */

        /* loop */
        sub r0, r0, 1 /* r0 = r0 - 1 */
        b .loop

.exit:
```

B

Tejas Architectural Simulator

B.1 Overview

For proposing and evaluating architectural features, designers and researchers typically use an architectural simulator. It is a large software program that simulates all the features of a processor including the memory system, on-chip network, and off-chip DRAM. We can think of it as a *virtual processor* that can run a full program including an operating system and the programs running on it. Along with providing overall execution statistics such as the total number of simulated cycles, cache miss rates, energy, and power consumption values, we can also use architectural simulators to implement new protocols and processor designs. We can accurately assess their advantages and overheads. Note that in this case, the main task is to just simulate the overheads in terms of time and power while ensuring that the program running on the processor executes correctly. Correctness of the program is not being verified here.

As compared to implementing novel features in a hardware description language, using an architectural simulator is much faster. Its simulation speed is typically 100 times more, does not require sophisticated software or FPGA boards, and can also be easily parallelised. There are four types of commonly used architectural simulation methods.

Cycle-accurate Simulation Such simulators are typically tightly coupled with the real hardware. They model latencies exactly. It is expected that the time a program will take to run on an architectural simulator will be the same as the corresponding hardware implementation (in terms of simulated execution cycles). Such simulators are typically very slow and we we also need access to a hardware implementation to calibrate the simulator.

Cycle-approximate Simulation Simulators in this category are not coupled with a specific hardware implementation. They assume a piece of generic hardware and provide numbers that are internally consistent. They are much faster and are the most popular as of today.

Sampled Simulation In this case, we do not simulate all the instructions. We separate the actual execution of the instructions from the simulation. We execute all the instructions; however, we only simulate small sequences of dynamic instructions. These sequences are periodically extracted from the running program. The final simulation results are obtained by extrapolating the results obtained by considering the size of the sequences and the total number of dynamic instructions in the program.

Statistical Simulation Such approaches typically extend sampled simulation to incorporate statistical and machine learning based models. We can simulate small snippets of the execution or collect a few metrics from hardware performance counters, and then try to used a learned model to predict the rest of the outputs of the simulation. This method admits statistical approaches and machine learning based techniques that try to estimate the final execution statistics.

B.2 Tejas Architectural Simulator

Let us now describe the Tejas architectural simulator [Sarangi et al., 2015], which is a cycle-approximate simulator and can simulate regular programs, operating systems, Java programs, and CUDA programs. It can be freely downloaded from `http://www.cse.iitd.ac.in/tejas`.

B.2.1 Design of Tejas

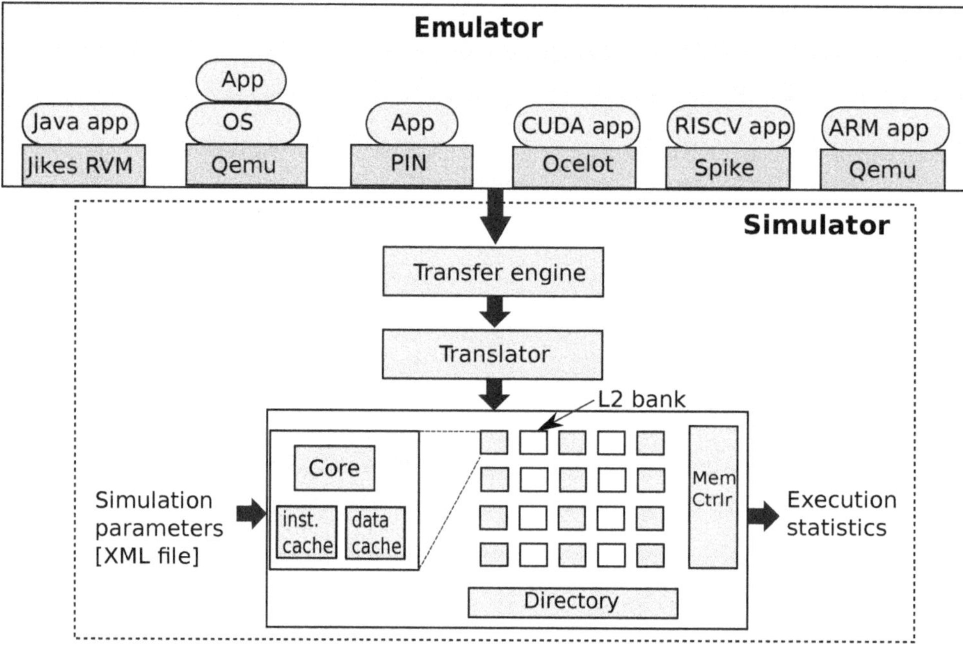

Figure B.1: Design of Tejas

While talking about an architectural simulator, we need to distinguish between two key concepts: *emulator* and *simulator*. The emulator executes the program instruction by instruction. This can either be a sequential program or a parallel program. In the latter case the emulator spawns parallel threads. The emulator is presumed to be always correct. It collects *instruction traces*, which include the PC of the instruction, its contents, the branch direction, and the load/store addresses. The instruction traces are sent to the simulator, which simulates the behaviour of the processor including its timing and power. Specifically, the simulator is responsible for implementing the pipeline, NoC, caches, and the entire memory system.

Tejas can use different emulators as shown in Figure B.1. By default, it uses Intel PIN [Luk et al., 2005], which runs x86 binaries and collects traces. Tejas supports other emulators as well such as the Jikes virtual machine [Alpern et al., 2005] for Java programs, the Qemu [Bellard, 2005] virtual machine for full fledged operating systems, Ocelot [Farooqui et al., 2011] for CUDA programs, Spike for RISC-V programs, and Qemu's ARM version for ARM programs. The traces have the same high-level format.

Subsequently, the transfer engine is used to transfer traces to the simulator, which is written in Java. It is a separate process. Standard IPC (inter-process communication) mechanisms such as shared memory, sockets, and pipes can be used. Once the traces reach Tejas, it simulates the synchronisation behaviour of threads, and once a thread is unblocked, its traces are transferred to the Translation Engine. The Translation Engine has separate modules for each ISA. Tejas defines a virtual instruction set known as VISA (virtual ISA). Regardless of the original ISA, its traces are internally converted to the VISA ISA. The instructions are sent to the pipeline simulator for the corresponding core. This allows us to design a generic core that is ISA-independent.

Tejas simulates the pipeline within each core, its caches, the NoC, L2/L3 banks, the directories, and the memory controllers that send messages to off-chip DRAM modules. The simulator is fully configurable. Its input is in the form of an XML file, which includes the configurations of all the hardware structures and the number of instructions that need to be simulated. The final output includes detailed statistics for each hardware structure, the number of simulated cycles, the details of stalls, and power consumption statistics. Tejas includes the Cacti [Muralimanohar et al., 2009] and McPat [Li et al., 2009] tools to simulate power consumption.

B.2.2   Semi-event Driven Simulation

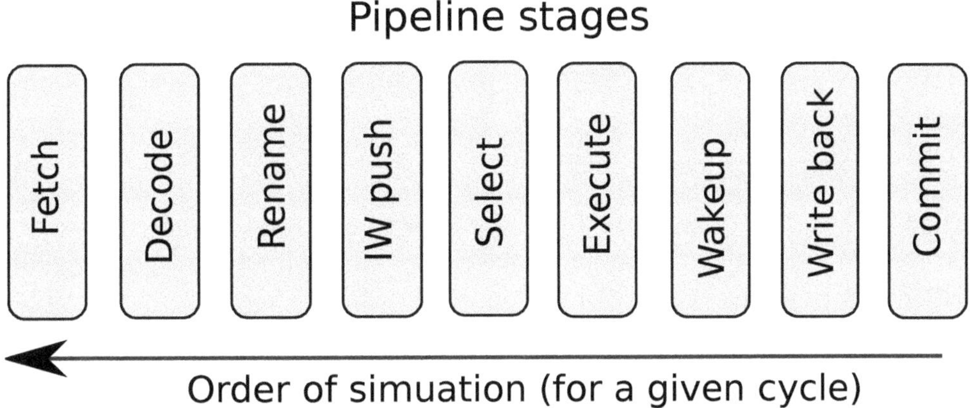

Figure B.2: Sequence of pipeline stages that are simulated

There are two ways of performing architectural simulations. The first is an *iterative approach*, which is primarily used to simulate in-order processors. For a given cycle i, we start from the last stage (write-back stage), find instructions that are ready to execute on it in cycle i, and simulate their execution. Then we move to the second last stage and do the same. This process continues till we reach the first stage. This process can be extended to out-of-order processors; however, in this case, we need to deal with large non-deterministic delays and thus the bookkeeping overhead is substantial. Hence, this approach is in general considered to be a fast scheme when it comes to simulating the pipeline only.

Consequently, to simulate the memory system and NoC of OOO processors, we typically use an event queue (event driven model), which is a priority queue ordered according to the time at which events get *activated*. Consider an example. Let's say that the response to a memory request is expected 10 cycles later. If the request was issued in cycle 100, the response needs to be processed in cycle 110. We then add an event to the event queue with its timestamp set to 110.

The general idea is that in cycle i, we fetch all the events from the event queue that have a timestamp equal to i. The assumption is that in previous cycles, all the events for this cycle would have been added by all the event producing units. While processing an event, we may insert new events into the event queue. Once all the events for cycle i have been processed, we move to the next event in the event queue (in increasing order of timestamps). This approach is more flexible than the iterative approach, yet it is far slower.

Tejas thus uses a hybrid approach known as a semi-event driven model. It uses the iterative approach to simulate the traditional OOO pipeline as shown in Figure B.2. Here also, we start from the commit stage and work our way back to the fetch stage. For the memory system, NoC, directory, and memory controllers that have rather non-deterministic delays, the event queue based mechanism is used. This design strategy provides the best of both worlds.

B.2.3   Optimisations and Corner Cases

To sustain a simulation throughput of 100 KIPS (100 kilo instructions per second), we need a very efficient memory manager. For every instruction and every operand, we cannot allocate memory on the heap. Given that Java uses a garbage collector, the overhead of managing so many objects will become prohibitive. Hence, Tejas uses pools – set of pre-allocated objects. Whenever we need an object of a certain type, we just fetch it from its pool, and for de-allocating an object, we return it to its pool.

Since an architectural simulation approximates a real execution, it also needs to take care of corner cases and race conditions. Simulating relaxed memory models, managing MSHRs, and simulating cache coherence are particularly complex because of the large number of intermediate states. For the purposes of architectural simulation, we need to focus on the common case primarily because we are simulating for timing and power. Let's say, if a case arises once every 100,000 cycles, we need not handle it in a special way. We can just use a brute force solution, where for example we can disable parallel updates to the same hardware structure by using locks or just forcibly fix the global state.

Tejas tries to reuse event objects as much as possible. A core event can lead to a cache event, which can lead to an event destined to the memory controllers. Instead of creating separate events, Tejas uses the same event and keeps on changing its type and its fields. The same event is reused for completing subtasks of a request in the core, caches, and the memory system.

B.2.4   Parallelisation

Tejas has been parallelised by assigning different cores to different threads [Malhotra et al., 2017]. In this case, we cannot have a global notion of time nor afford a global event queue. Threads have a local notion of time where the timeline is viewed as an array of slots. Consider an example. Let's say that if a message is sent from unit i to unit j at time 10 (local time of i), it would have been processed at $t = 15$ at unit j, if they shared a global clock. In this case, we search for free time slots at or after $t = 15$ at unit j (as per its local time). The request is processed at the earliest such time slot. We thus need to maintain a slot array for each thread that can be updated in parallel. The authors use lock-free data structures to implement such a fast, parallel, and scalable slot array.

Another approach is as follows. Emulation is typically 1-2 orders of magnitude faster than simulation. If we need to simulate a billion instructions, we can start 10 emulators, and move each one of them very quickly to a point after 100 million, 200 million instructions and so on. Then we pair a simulation thread with each emulator and begin simulating. In this case, we just simulate 100 million instructions per thread and finally combine the results. Disregarding the time it takes the emulators to reach the starting points, we can obtain a roughly 10X speedup here. The problem is that other than the first thread, the rest of the threads will not be starting from the correct architectural state. This can be solved by including a small *warm up* phase – simulate 10-25 million instructions before the starting point. The ideal speedup for this example is 10X, in practice it is much lower because of the overheads of parallel execution, memory contention, overhead of threading, and the time spent in warmup phases.

B.2.5   Evaluation

Tejas has been validated against native hardware, and the error is limited to 1-11% for the sequential SPEC CPU2006 (`http://www.spec.org`) benchmarks and 4-33% for parallel benchmarks (Splash2 suite [Woo et al., 1995]). The errors for architectural simulation are typically in that range. The main aim is to ensure that the numbers are internally consistent.

Also note that we typically simulate the single-threaded SPEC benchmarks either individually or as an ensemble (bag of tasks: one thread mapped to each core), when we wish to simulate a set of sequential workloads. For parallel workloads, we normally use the Splash 2 [Woo et al., 1995] and the Parsec benchmark [Bienia et al., 2008] suites. For getting stable results, it is a good idea to simulate at least a billion instructions from each distinct program phase. Program's typically exhibit phase behaviour, where their behaviour remains stable for a period of time, and then as they move to a different region of code, their behaviour changes, yet remains stable for some time. We need to ensure that our simulation captures all the phases and the results attain their steady state values.

Intel Processors

C.1 Sunny Cove Microarchitecture

Intel released the details of the Sunny Cove microarchitecture in December, 2018. It is meant to be fabricated using a 10 nm process and will be the architecture of its state-of-the-art server chips for the next few years (as of 2020). The aim was to increase the IPC by increasing the fetch and issue widths, and improve the performance of cryptographic applications by adding a set of custom ISA extensions.

C.1.1 ISA Extensions

Intel added a few new instructions to the 512-bit SIMD AVX instruction set, which primarily focused on the performance of cryptographic operations. The reason is that gradually, security is becoming a first-order concern in the design of processors and thus it is necessary to support a wide variety of cryptographic operations such as AES and primitives that use Galois field arithmetic.

Improvements in the memory system target large shared memory systems and NVM memory such as Intel's 3D XPoint memory. It was necessary to add support for large physical and virtual address spaces because now the physical memory space can be extended by adding NVM modules. Additionally, the architecture has better support for cloud computing by having dedicated storage for storing up to 32K encryption keys; these can be distributed to individual virtual machines or applications.

C.1.2 Processor Design

Front End

The design of the front end of the processor, which includes the fetch logic, branch predictors, micro-op caches and the decoder has not been disclosed publicly. Let us thus explain the design of the Intel Skylake architecture, which precedes the Sunny Cove architecture.

Intel Skylake has a 8-way 32 KB L1 i-cache that provides 16 bytes per cycle. After pre-decoding, the instructions are stored in a 50-entry instruction queue. Subsequently, five macro-instructions (variable length CISC instructions) are sent to the decode unit that contains five decoders. There are four simple decoders and one complex decoder. A complex decoder typically produces multiple micro-ops (μOPs) for a single macro-instruction. Overall, the decoders can supply 5 μOPs per cycle. There are other sources of μOPs as well. Intel has a μOP cache that is connected to the branch predictor. It can supply

6 μOPs per cycle, and the microcode ROM can supply 4 μOPs per cycle (refer to Figure C.1). The microcode ROM is used to translate very long and complex CISC instructions. These μOPs then enter the decode queue. Every cycle, the decode queue can send 6 μOPs to the rename table and ROB.

These μOPs are subsequently renamed, added to the ROB, and physical registers are allocated to hold their results. In total, Intel Skylake can send up to 8 such μOPs to the scheduler (instruction window along with the wake-up/select logic). An astute reader will not that the dispatch bandwidth is more than the decode bandwidth. This is a common feature in advanced processors where internal stages have a higher bandwidth to sustain peaks in ILP. This however does necessitate additional buffers between the decode and dispatch stages.

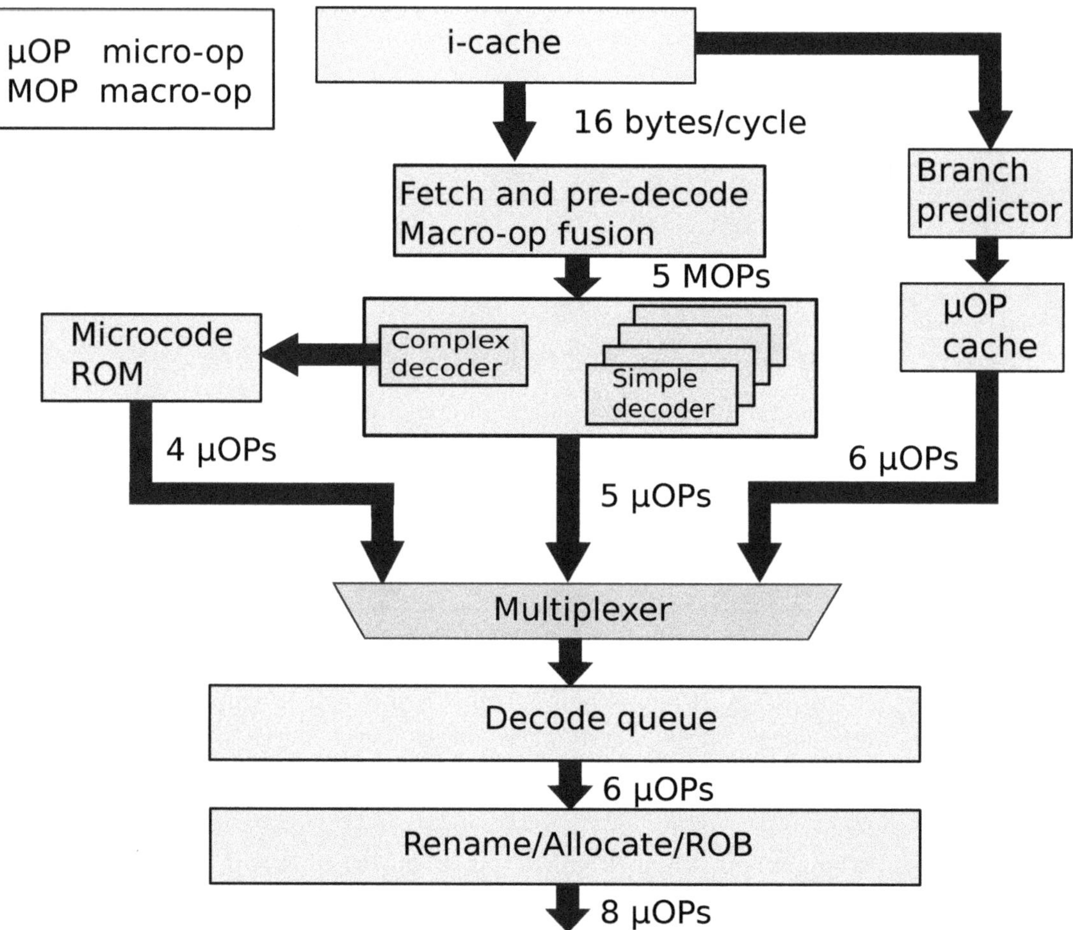

Figure C.1: Front end of the Skylake microarchitecture

Back End

Figure C.2 shows the backend architecture [Kanter, 2019] of Intel Sunny Cove. Sunny Cove's scheduler is split into multiple reservation stations. The reservation stations are connected to a set of execution ports that are in turn connected to a set of functional units. For ALU operations, there are two clusters of functional units: one integer cluster and one vector/floating point cluster. A key feature of this class of architectures is the functional unit for the *LEA* (load effective address) instruction, which transfers the computed memory address to a register instead of the memory contents. It is needed while making

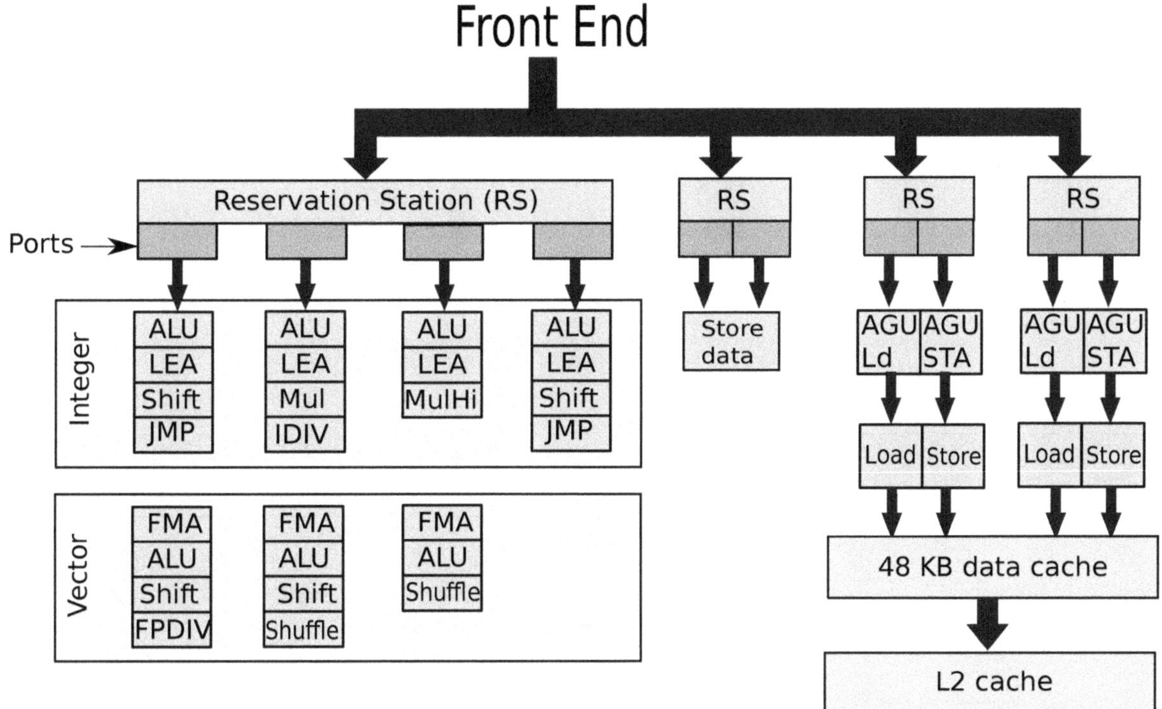

Figure C.2: Back end of the Sunny Cove microarchitecture

indirect accesses via pointers. To get a better understanding of the instruction types shown in the figure, the reader is requested to go through Intel's x86 programming manuals.

The floating point (FP) cluster supports regular arithmetic operations. Also note the functional unit for the shuffle operation that allows us to permute words in a 512-bit SIMD (SSE or AVX) register.

The architecture has six ports for load and store operations that have different functions. The aim was to be able to perform two loads or two stores per cycle. Hence, Intel added 4 AGUs (address generation units): two for loads and two for stores. The role of an AGU is to simply generate the memory address of a load or a store (it is basically an adder). Additionally, there are two ports for storing data in the write buffers or the L1 cache. The L1 cache is a 48-KB cache that is connected to a large L2 cache, which is smaller for desktop processors and much larger for server chips. Finally, note that most processors in this class use a 2-level TLB: an L1 TLB and an L2 TLB. This minimises the TLB miss rate.

It is important to note that most processor vendors typically do not disclose the exact sizes of the units and the bit widths of the ports. Nevertheless, in an architecture such as Sunny Cove it is expected that the SIMD functional units will be able to handle 512-bit data in one go, and furthermore the processor should be able to execute at least a few vector (512-bit) loads and stores in a cycle.

C.2 Tremont Microarchitecture

We have discussed the Intel "Cove" series of microarchitectures that are predominantly aimed towards the server market. Let us now discuss the "Mont" series, which are processors that are aimed for the laptop and mobile markets. Here, of course, the main aim is power efficiency and getting the maximum amount of performance within a limited area and power budget.

Figure C.3 shows the microarchitecture of the Tremont core [Halfhill, 2019]. It is an out-of-order

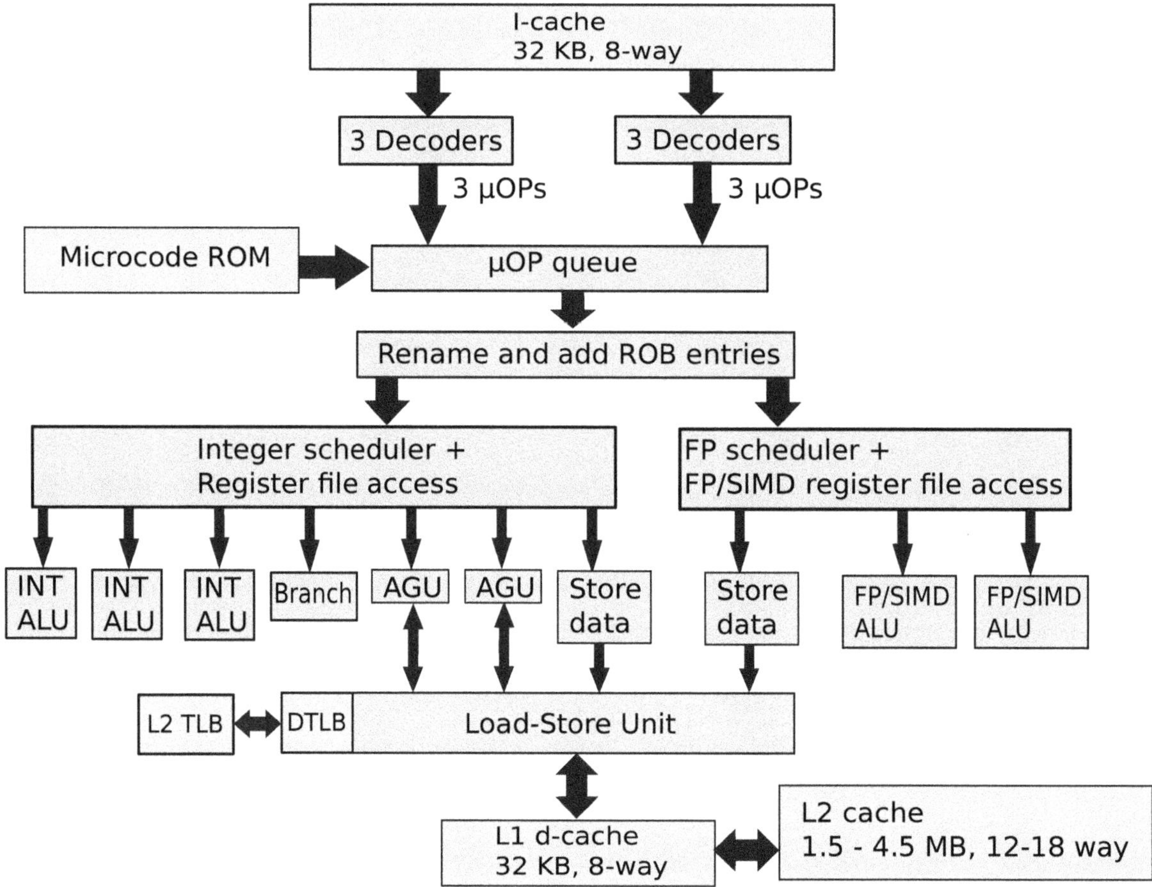

Figure C.3: The microarchitecture of the Tremont core

architecture that supports a single thread at a time. In comparison, most high-end server microarchitectures such as Sunny Cove support multithreading at the hardware level and are able to partition the resources among different parallely running threads. However, this is not very important in the market segment that Tremont targets.

Now let us explain the microarchitecture of the Tremont core. We start out with a 32-KB 8-way instruction cache that feeds two sets of decoders. Each set contains three simple decoders; these two sets of decoders run in parallel. This is a problem for a complex instruction set such as x86 because instruction boundaries are not known in advance; we need to sequentially read all the instructions. There are several standard ways of solving this problem. The first is that we can do pre-decoding and store the instruction boundaries within the i-cache lines. This will allow such parallel decoders to quickly move to the right starting point. The other approach is that we start from a safe point such as a branch target or try to guess the beginning of an instruction using speculative techniques.

These two decoders feed 6 μOPs to the ROB and rename tables. After renaming, they enter one of the eight schedulers (instruction window + wakeup/select). The schedulers are connected to the register files and a set of 10 functional units. The processor has three integer ALUs, one branch unit, two address generation units (AGUs), and one store unit. The load store unit (LSU) contains the LSQ and also interfaces with the level 1 and level 2 TLBs.

This architecture also has a floating point (FP) scheduler. It is connected to two FP/SIMD ALUs and a store unit.

The L1 cache in this design is a 8-way 32 KB cache and the L2 cache can vary from 1.5-4.5 MB (12-18 ways).

As compared to the Sunny Cove microarchitecture, in this design, the size of the fetch unit is reduced, there are fewer ALU units, and we have fewer functional units that are involved in memory accesses – fewer AGUs and store units. This is thus a smaller and more power efficient design.

C.3 Lakefield Processor

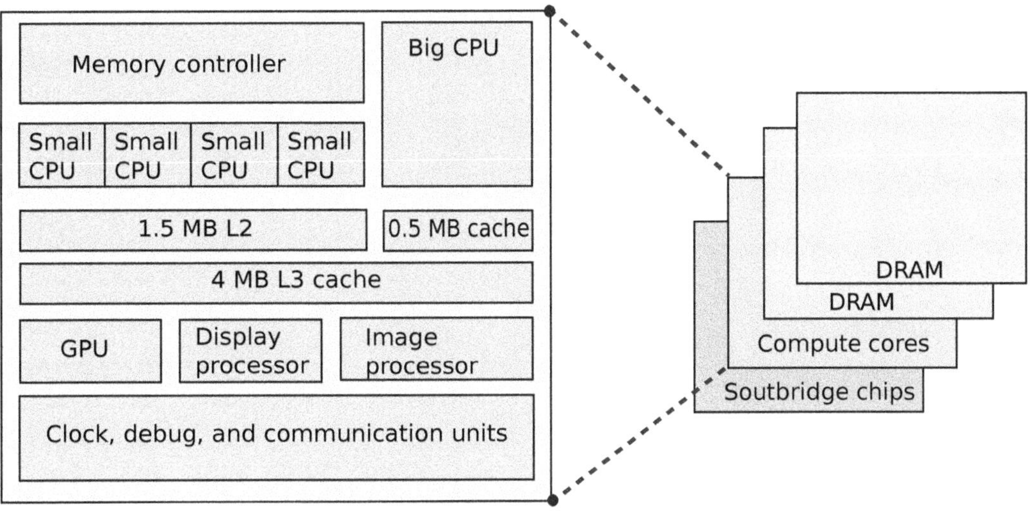

Figure C.4: The design of the Lakefield processor

Intel introduced the Lakefield processor in 2019 that combines a big Sunny Cove core and four small Tremont cores. It has been designed for mobile phones and small computing devices that are expected to run heterogeneous workloads. Its architecture is shown in Figure C.4.

Along with a heterogeneous design, this processor is revolutionary in many other ways. It uses the Foveros 3D stacking technology to stack four layers and create a 3D chip. The bottommost layer encapsulates the functionality of the erstwhile Southbridge chip that contains all the chips in the chipset that control the storage and I/O devices. For example, it has modules to control the USB devices, hard disks, audio controllers, PCI devices, and it also contains dedicated accelerators for cryptographic operations. The next layer contains the cores and the GPU. The top two layers are dedicated to the DRAM modules. The advantage of 3D stacking is that we can realise very fast and high bandwidth connections between the layers. Second, we need less space on the motherboard and this allows the processor to be used in devices with small form factors.

The Foveros technology allows us to connect two adjoining layers with a large array of microbumps (see Section 10.5.6). The layers themselves can be fabricated using different processes and different feature sizes. To connect two such layers that are fabricated using incompatible silicon processes, all that we need to do is vertically integrate them in a 3D package and align the microbumps.

Let us now focus on the layer that contains the cores. There are four small Tremont cores and one big Sunny Cove core. The L1 caches are within the cores, and the small cores are connected to a shared 1.5 MB L2 cache. The big core additionally has a 0.5 MB private cache for itself. All of these caches are connected to a shared LLC (4 MB L3). Intel also placed a wide variety of graphics and vision chips in this layer. This includes a standard GPU, a display processor that can support multiple displays, and an image processor for processing the inputs captured by cameras. We additionally have clock, debug, and communication units in this layer.

The Lakefield processor is a one-of-a-kind design that combines heterogeneous computing, 3D stacking, and DRAM modules embedded in the package. Previously, such designs were not feasible primarily because of power and temperature issues; however, now with improvements in process technology and reduced feature sizes, it is possible to realise such designs. In the future it is expected that in the processor landscape, we shall have many such designs that have a very high degree of 3D integration and diverse computing devices.

AMD Processors

Zen 2 is AMD's latest microarchitecture for desktop and server processors. It is fabricated using TSMC's latest 7nm process. Zen 2 cores are used in the Ryzen 3000 processors meant for desktops, Threadripper processors for high-end desktops, and Epyc processors for servers. We will first discuss the microarchitecture of a Zen 2 core, then discuss the AMD Ryzen 3000 series processors (codenamed "Matisse") that uses such Zen 2 cores to implement an SoC, and finally conclude with a discussion on the AMD Epyc^{TM} 7742 server processor (codenamed "Rome") [Suggs and Bouvier, 2019, Gwennap, 2019b, Advanced Micro Devices, 2017]. Note that an SoC (system-on-chip) contains multiple computing or memory elements within a single chip. These can include cores, caches banks, memory controllers, and GPUs.

D.1 Zen2 Microarchitecture

D.1.1 Fetch and Decode Logic

Figure D.1 shows the microarchitecture of the Zen 2 core. Zen 2 uses an advanced variant of the TAGE branch predictor [Seznec, 2007]. Some of the features of this predictor are as follows. Along with hashing entries, the predictor also stores tags in the entries to eliminate aliasing. Second, it uses variable-sized histories: small histories for easy-to-predict branches and long histories for difficult-to-predict histories.

Zen 2 uses a 8-way 32-KB i-cache that can supply 32 bytes per cycle to the decode unit. The decode unit has four decoders that can process 4 instructions per cycle. Additionally, the core contains a micro-op cache that has 2K to 4K entries. It reduces the need to decode every instruction. Frequently executed instructions hit in this cache, and this saves decode energy. Additionally, the pipeline containing the micro-op cache is shorter, and thus there is an improvement in the overall latency as well. The decoded μOPs (micro-instructions) are stored in a μOP queue.

The fetch logic also contains a three-level BTB (branch target buffer) and a 32-entry return address stack. Most codes have some indirect branches, where the target of the branch changes (it is typically the value of a register). Zen 2 contains an indirect branch predictor that predicts the target based on the history of the branch. We typically use such indirect branches while using function pointers in C and virtual functions in C++.

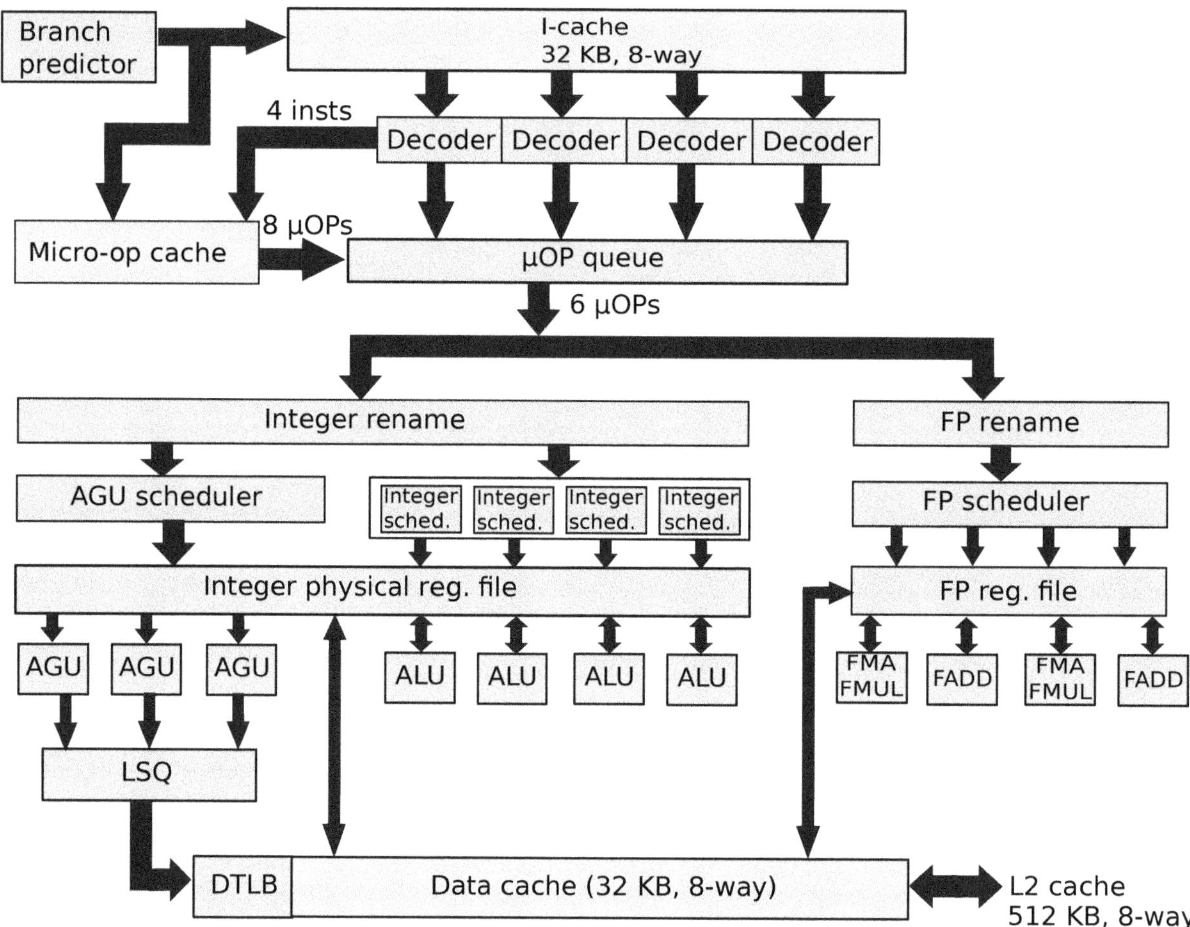

Figure D.1: The microarchitecture of the AMD Zen2 processor (source [Suggs and Bouvier, 2019])

D.1.2   Scheduling and Execution

After register renaming, the instructions are sent to the corresponding schedulers (instruction window + wakeup/select logic). The schedulers can receive up to 6 micro-ops per cycle (the dispatch width is 6). There are four ALU schedulers, one AGU (for loads and stores) scheduler, and one FP (floating point) scheduler.

The AGU scheduler is connected to two load AGUs (address generation units) and one store AGU. Each such AGU can process one μOP per cycle. The floating point (FP) scheduler is similarly connected to two FP multiply and two FP add units. Each FP multiply unit can also process the FMA instruction (fused multiply and add). The SIMD data path is 256 bits in the Zen 2 core. This means that if we have packed single precision floating point numbers, then we can operate on 8 pairs of such numbers in parallel.

Once an instruction is scheduled, it reads the values from the corresponding register file and proceeds towards the execution units. The Zen2 core has an elaborate load-store unit that contains an LSQ that can forward values from earlier stores to later loads, track in-flight cache misses, and support x86's complex addressing modes.

The Zen 2 core has an 180-entry general purpose physical register file for storing integers and memory addresses, and an 160-entry vector register file in the floating point unit. The four integer ALUs and

the three AGUs access the the general purpose register file. It should be noted that each core supports
2-way SMT (simultaneous multithreading). The schedulers incorporate a notion of fairness such that
the threads make similar rates of progress.

D.1.3   Data Caches

Each core has a 8-way 32-KB data cache that can support two 256-bit loads and one 256-bit store per
cycle. It uses a variant of way prediction 7.4.4 to hide the time it takes to convert virtual addresses into
physical addresses. It computes a hash of the last virtual address that was used to access a cache line,
and stores the hash in the cache line itself. Before the physical address is available, the core speculatively
accesses the line that has a matching hash.

The data cache is connected to a 512-KB, 8-way L2 cache. This is connected to an L3 cache (4
MB or 16 MB). Like all processors in its class, the Zen 2 core has a 2-level TLB. The first level has an
I-TLB (for instructions) and a D-TLB (for data). The level 1 TLBs are connected to level 2 TLBs. To
handle TLB misses, the Zen 2 core has two hardware page walkers to service TLB misses. The Zen 2
core supports huge pages (2 MB or 1 GB). A 1 GB page is stored as a set of 2 MB pages in the TLB –
this is known as *smashing*.

D.2   AMD Ryzen 3000 Series Processor (Codenamed Matisse)

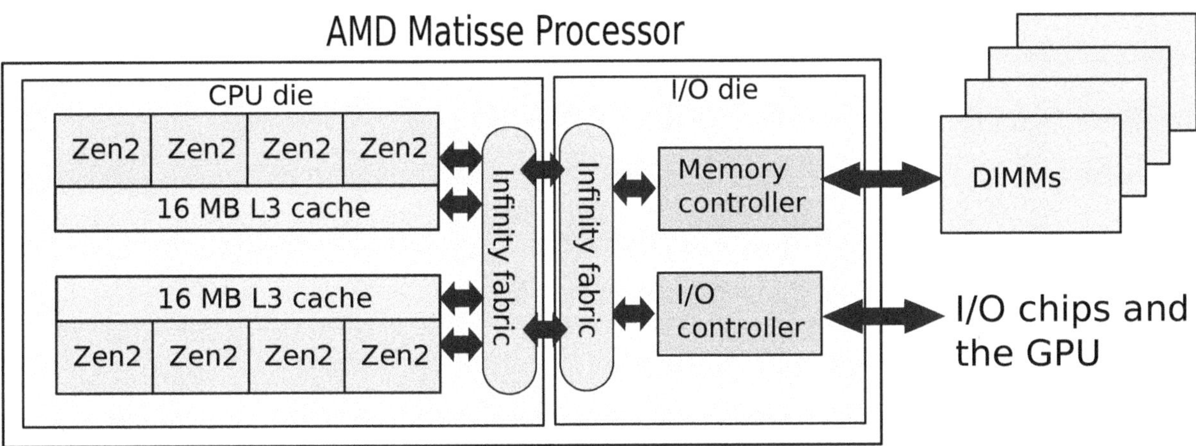

Figure D.2: The layout of the AMD Matisse package (source [Gwennap, 2019b])

Figure D.2 shows the architecture of an SoC targeted at client platforms such as laptop and desktop
computers; it has eight such Zen2 cores (the Matisse chip). The cores are grouped into two clusters; each
cluster has a shared 16-MB L3 cache. This is a chiplet-based design, where multiple dies (fabricated with
different technologies) are integrated into the same package. Figure D.2 shows two chiplets: a core chiplet
with 8 cores and 32 MB of L3 cache, and an I/O chiplet. The latter contains the memory controller
and the I/O controllers. Both are connected with a low-latency and high-bandwidth interconnect, which
AMD calls the *Infinity Fabric*.

D.3   AMD EPYC™ 7742 Processor (Codenamed Rome)

Let us now discuss AMD's latest server processor (as of 2020) that uses the Zen 2 core. It is the AMD
EPYC 7742 processor (codenamed "Rome"). As shown in Figure D.3(a), the chip can be viewed as

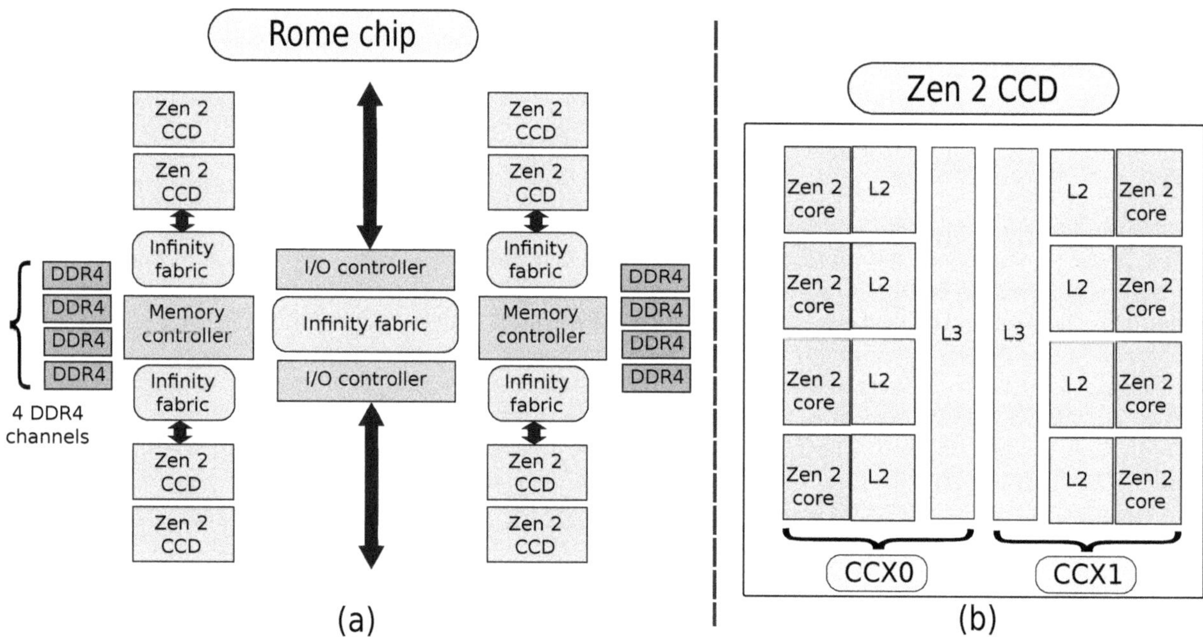

Figure D.3: The Rome chip (source [Suggs and Bouvier, 2019])

comprising four quadrants with two Core-Complex Dies (CCDs) and two memory channels per quadrant. Each CCD in turn consists of a pair of two core complexes: CCX0 and CCX1 (see Figure D.3(b)). Each such core complex consists of 4 cores sharing a 16MB L3 cache. Each core supports 2-way Simultaneous Multi Threading (SMT).

Hence, the entire processor consists of 64 cores (128 hardware threads) with a 256 MB distributed L3 cache and 8 memory channels, where each memory channel can support the DDR4-3200 protocol. The four quadrants can be configured to expose different Non-Uniform Memory Access (NUMA) topologies to the operating system, designated by the Nodes Per Socket (NPS) parameter. NUMA is conceptually similar to NUCA (see Section 8.5), albeit it is at the level of main memory.

The reason for grouping channels together and creating a *NUMA domain* is as follows. Let's say we want to provide high bandwidth to a core. Then we would like the core to be able to access all the memory channels simultaneously and read or write data to the attached DIMMs. Using this technique, we can realise a very high bandwidth connection to memory. However, this technique might not work very well because the latencies to different memory banks are different. Some memory controllers are close to the core; they can be accessed quickly; however, many memory controllers are on the other side of the chip, and it is necessary to traverse the on-chip interconnect. Hence, we might not want to interleave memory accesses across all the channels. We might instead want to create groups comprising 2 or 4 channels and assign them to a core. It can then access these channels in parallel and interleave its memory accesses to maximise the available bandwidth. The NPS parameter allows us to control this behaviour.

Qualcomm Processors

Qualcomm® is famous for its Snapdragon® processors, which are primarily designed for mobile phones. These processors are SoCs (systems on chip) That contain many other elements as well such as GPUs and custom accelerators. In this appendix, we will describe the latest Snapdragon 865 processor [Gwennap, 2019a, Hachman, 2019].

Snapdragon has been released in 2020. It is a futuristic mobile chip where the main focus is on artificial intelligence(AI), high-intensity gaming, and 5G communication. This requires a diversity of cores and accelerators. We cannot have a single kind of core for so many diverse applications. Hence, the designers have opted for what is known as a big.LITTLE™ architecture. This was invented by ARM® Limited. Such an architecture contains a set of *big* cores to provide good single thread performance, and a set of *little* cores that are extremely power efficient. The advantage of such an architecture is that depending upon the workload we can dispatch it to either the big cores or the little cores to achieve an equitable trade-off between power and performance. Most multicore mobile platforms as of today use such an architecture.

Let us split our discussion into two parts. We shall first discuss the general computer architecture, and then move to the application-specific accelerators.

E.1 Compute Cores

The organisation of the cores and caches is shown in Figure E.1. This is an octa-core architecture. It contains three types of cores. It has one large ARM® Cortex®-A77 core, which implements the 64-bit ARM v8 instruction set. This is a fairly wide OOO core with a decode width of 4 and a fetch width of 6. The frequency is set to 2.84 GHz and the L1 I/D cache sizes are set to 64 KB. This core is connected to a large 512-KB L2 cache.

Then it has three other Cortex-A77 cores that run at a lower frequency, 2.4 GHz. The L2 cache allocated for these three cores is limited to 3×256 KB.

Then we come to the third types of cores (little cores): four Cortex-A55 cores. They also support the same version of the ARM ISA; however, these are far weaker superscalar in-order cores with a decode width of 2. Such in-order cores are typically very useful when coupled with accelerators. The in-order cores run the general-purpose code, and offload custom computations to accelerators that provide the speed-up. In comparison to the big cores, we provision only 128 KB of L2 cache for each little core, and also run them at a much lower frequency, 1.8 GHz.

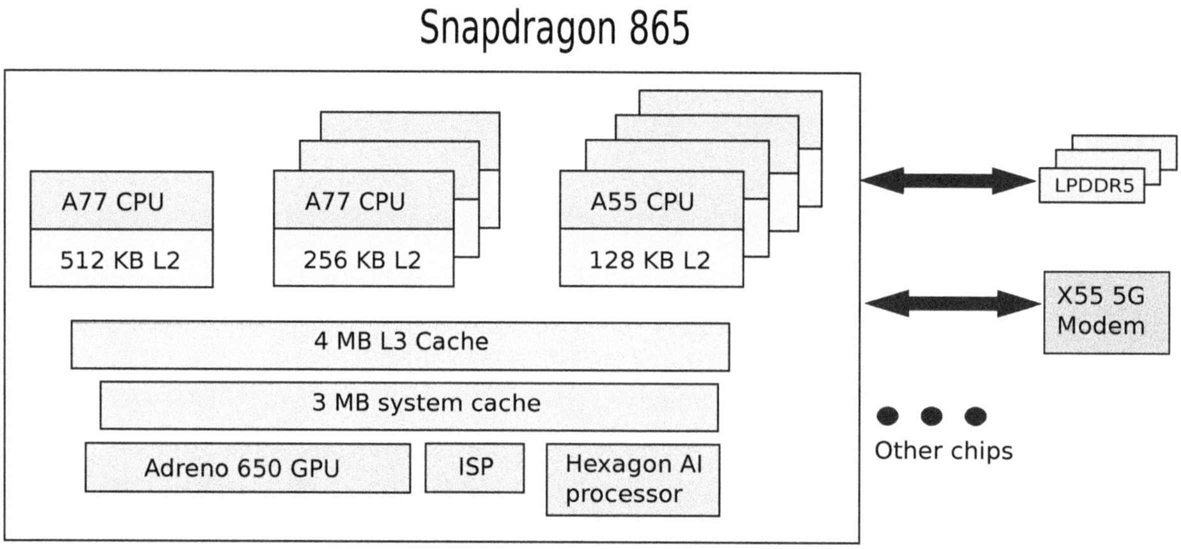

Snapdragon 865

Figure E.1: The Qualcomm Snapdragon 865 processor (many of its components are not shown in the figure)

The cores share a 4 MB L3 cache, and use the low power LPDDR5 protocol to connect to off-chip memory modules. Here, "LP" stands for "low power". Some of the key features that make such protocols more power efficient include a narrow channel width (16 or 32 bits), reduced supply voltage, partial DRAM refresh modes, low power memory states, multiplexed control and address lines, and avoiding transmitting data if it is all zeros or all ones.

Lastly note that whenever we have a set of cores, a GPU, and a set of accelerators, we often need a dedicated memory structure that can be used to transfer data between them. This can either be the last level cache such as the L2/L3 caches, or we can add a separate memory structure for effecting such transfers. This is a standard design technique, and this has been used in the Snapdragon 865 processor as well. It adds a 3 MB system cache for such kind of communication. Think of this as a bespoke L4 cache.

E.2   Accelerators

To support model workloads such as AI, 5G, and advanced video processing, it is necessary to add custom accelerators.

Qualcomm adds an Adreno® 650 GPU, which can support modern 4K displays and high intensity graphics. The key design decision here was to support modern immersive gaming environments. Such gaming environments support a wide diversity of colours and also their screen refresh rate is set to 90-144Hz, which is far more than the typical 50 to 60 Hz refresh rates of modern monitors. To bring complex scenes to life, it is necessary to add a lot of depth information to the image and also support a wide variety of graphics effects. Keeping all of this in mind, futuristic GPUs such as the Adreno 650 have been designed.

Snapdragon 865 also has a dedicated AI processor (Hexagon 698), which is primarily a tensor processing accelerator. Modern smart phones use all kinds of AI technologies such as speech recognition, gesture recognition, and integrate data from all kinds of sensors that include gyroscopes, accelerators, and multiple cameras. They need a sophisticated AI engine to search for patterns in the data, and to effectively analyse it. This necessitates the need for a dedicated accelerator. Using this accelerator,

Snapdragon 865 offers a throughput of 15 trillion AI operations per second.

Qualcomm has a dedicated image signal processor (ISP) in the chip for processing images captured by the cameras. It can process billions of pixels per second. This is typically necessary to generate autofocus points, perform an optical zoom, capture still images and video, and capture slow motion video.

As of 2020, we are entering the era of 5G. 5G can in principle support a peak data rate of 10 Gbps. Most 5G systems are expected to use millimetre waves to transmit data at a very high frequency. As of mid 2020, there are limited 5G deployments in the world; however, the technology is showing a lot of promise. Hence, mobile chip makers need to ensure that their SoCs are 5G ready. Qualcomm has thus added an X55 5G modem into the Snapdragon motherboard (note that it is a separate chip). Along with that, Qualcomm has also integrated other chips along with the Snapdragon processor on the motherboard, which include fast wireless and Bluetooth chips.

While designing a large SoC, designers are typically faced with a dilemma: should they have certain components within the SoC or place them outside it on the motherboard? The former design decision can provide us with greater performance as long as we can ensure that we can fabricate such a large chip with acceptable yield rates, and keep on-chip power dissipation below a certain threshold. If power consumption is an issue or there is a possibility that the chip will become too big and the yield rate will go down, the components may be fabricated as separate chips and placed close by on the motherboard.

Bibliography

[ccs,] Creative commons sharealike license. `https://creativecommons.org/licenses/by-sa/4.0/legalcode`. Accessed on 5th Feb 2019.

[Abadi et al., 2016] Abadi, M., Barham, P., Chen, J., Chen, Z., Davis, A., Dean, J., Devin, M., Ghemawat, S., Irving, G., Isard, M., et al. (2016). Tensorflow: A system for large-scale machine learning. In *12th {USENIX} Symposium on Operating Systems Design and Implementation ({OSDI} 16)*, pages 265–283.

[Abts et al., 2003] Abts, D., Scott, S., and Lilja, D. J. (2003). So many states, so little time: Verifying memory coherence in the cray x1. In *Parallel and Distributed Processing Symposium, 2003. Proceedings. International*, pages 10–pp. IEEE.

[Advanced Micro Devices, 2017] Advanced Micro Devices (2017). *Software Optimization Guide for AMD Family 17h Processors*.

[Adve, 1993] Adve, S. V. (1993). *Designing memory consistency models for shared-memory multiprocessors*. PhD thesis, University of Wisconsin-Madison.

[Adve and Gharachorloo, 1996] Adve, S. V. and Gharachorloo, K. (1996). Shared memory consistency models: A tutorial. *Computer*, 29(12):66–76.

[Agarwal et al., 2009] Agarwal, N., Krishna, T., Peh, L.-S., and Jha, N. K. (2009). Garnet: A detailed on-chip network model inside a full-system simulator. In *2009 IEEE international symposium on performance analysis of systems and software*, pages 33–42. IEEE.

[Aho, 2003] Aho, A. V. (2003). *Compilers: principles, techniques and tools (for Anna University), 2/e*. Pearson Education India.

[Aho and Ullman, 1977] Aho, A. V. and Ullman, J. D. (1977). *Principles of Compiler Design (Addison-Wesley series in computer science and information processing)*. Addison-Wesley Longman Publishing Co., Inc.

[Akinaga and Shima, 2012] Akinaga, H. and Shima, H. (2012). Reram technology; challenges and prospects. *IEICE Electronics Express*, 9(8):795–807.

[Akkary et al., 2003] Akkary, H., Rajwar, R., and Srinivasan, S. T. (2003). Checkpoint processing and recovery: Towards scalable large instruction window processors. In *Microarchitecture, 2003. MICRO-36. Proceedings. 36th Annual IEEE/ACM International Symposium on*, pages 423–434. IEEE.

[Albericio et al., 2016] Albericio, J., Judd, P., Hetherington, T., Aamodt, T., Jerger, N. E., and Moshovos, A. (2016). Cnvlutin: ineffectual-neuron-free deep neural network computing. In *Proceedings of the 43rd International Symposium on Computer Architecture*, pages 1–13.

[Alglave, 2012] Alglave, J. (2012). A formal hierarchy of weak memory models. *Formal Methods in System Design*, 41(2):178–210.

[Alpern et al., 2005] Alpern, B., Augart, S., Blackburn, S. M., Butrico, M., Cocchi, A., Cheng, P., Dolby, J., Fink, S., Grove, D., Hind, M., et al. (2005). The jikes research virtual machine project: building an open-source research community. *IBM Systems Journal*, 44(2):399–417.

[Alpert and Avnon, 1993] Alpert, D. and Avnon, D. (1993). Architecture of the pentium microprocessor. *IEEE micro*, 13(3):11–21.

[Anis and Nicolici, 2007] Anis, E. and Nicolici, N. (2007). On using lossless compression of debug data in embedded logic analysis. In *2007 IEEE International Test Conference*, pages 1–10. IEEE.

[Annavaram et al., 2003] Annavaram, M., Patel, J. M., and Davidson, E. S. (2003). Call graph prefetching for database applications. *ACM Transactions on Computer Systems (TOCS)*, 21(4):412–444.

[Apalkov et al., 2013] Apalkov, D., Khvalkovskiy, A., Watts, S., Nikitin, V., Tang, X., Lottis, D., Moon, K., Luo, X., Chen, E., Ong, A., Driskill-Smith, A., and Krounbi, M. (2013). Spin-transfer torque magnetic random access memory (stt-mram). *J. Emerg. Technol. Comput. Syst.*, 9(2):13:1–13:35.

[Arora et al., 2015] Arora, A., Harne, M., Sultan, H., Bagaria, A., and Sarangi, S. R. (2015). Fp-nuca: A fast noc layer for implementing large nuca caches. *IEEE Transactions on Parallel and Distributed Systems*, 26(9):2465–2478.

[Arvind and Maessen, 2006] Arvind, A. and Maessen, J. (2006). Memory model= instruction reordering+ store atomicity. In *Proceedings. 33rd International Symposium on Computer Architecture*, pages 29–40.

[Austin, 1999] Austin, T. M. (1999). Diva: A reliable substrate for deep submicron microarchitecture design. In *MICRO-32. Proceedings of the 32nd Annual ACM/IEEE International Symposium on Microarchitecture*, pages 196–207. IEEE.

[Bakhoda et al., 2009] Bakhoda, A., Yuan, G. L., Fung, W. W., Wong, H., and Aamodt, T. M. (2009). Analyzing cuda workloads using a detailed gpu simulator. In *Performance Analysis of Systems and Software, 2009. ISPASS 2009. IEEE International Symposium on*, pages 163–174. IEEE.

[Balasubramonian et al., 2011] Balasubramonian, R., Jouppi, N. P., and Muralimanohar, N. (2011). Multi-core cache hierarchies. *Synthesis Lectures on Computer Architecture*, 6(3):1–153.

[Bashir et al., 2019] Bashir, J., Peter, E., and Sarangi, S. R. (2019). A survey of on-chip optical interconnects. *ACM Comput. Surv.*, 51(6):115:1–115:34.

[Baumann, 2005] Baumann, R. C. (2005). Radiation-induced soft errors in advanced semiconductor technologies. *IEEE Transactions on Device and materials reliability*, 5(3):305–316.

[Bekerman et al., 2000] Bekerman, M., Yoaz, A., Gabbay, F., Jourdan, S., Kalaev, M., and Ronen, R. (2000). Early load address resolution via register tracking. In *Proceedings of the 27th Annual International Symposium on Computer Architecture*, pages 306–315.

[Bellard, 2005] Bellard, F. (2005). Qemu, a fast and portable dynamic translator. In *USENIX Annual Technical Conference, FREENIX Track*, volume 41, page 46.

[Benini et al., 1999] Benini, L., Macii, A., Macii, E., and Poncino, M. (1999). Selective instruction compression for memory energy reduction in embedded systems. In *Proceedings of the 1999 international symposium on Low power electronics and design*, pages 206–211. ACM.

[Bergstra et al., 2010] Bergstra, J., Breuleux, O., Bastien, F., Lamblin, P., Pascanu, R., Desjardins, G., Turian, J., Warde-Farley, D., and Bengio, Y. (2010). Theano: A cpu and gpu math compiler in python. In *Proc. 9th Python in Science Conf*, volume 1.

[Bernick et al., 2005] Bernick, D., Bruckert, B., Vigna, P. D., Garcia, D., Jardine, R., Klecka, J., and Smullen, J. (2005). Nonstop advanced architecture. In *2005 International Conference on Dependable Systems and Networks (DSN'05)*, pages 12–21. IEEE.

[Bienia et al., 2008] Bienia, C., Kumar, S., Singh, J. P., and Li, K. (2008). The parsec benchmark suite: Characterization and architectural implications. In *Proceedings of the 17th international conference on Parallel architectures and compilation techniques*, pages 72–81. ACM.

[Bishop, 2006] Bishop, C. M. (2006). *Pattern recognition and machine learning.* springer.

[Bjerregaard and Mahadevan, 2006] Bjerregaard, T. and Mahadevan, S. (2006). A survey of research and practices of network-on-chip. *ACM Computing Surveys (CSUR)*, 38(1):1.

[Black, 1969] Black, J. R. (1969). Electromigration—a brief survey and some recent results. *IEEE Transactions on Electron Devices*, 16(4):338–347.

[Blythe, 2008] Blythe, D. (2008). Rise of the graphics processor. *Proceedings of the IEEE*, 96(5):761–778.

[Bodin and Seznec, 1997] Bodin, F. and Seznec, A. (1997). Skewed associativity improves program performance and enhances predictability. *IEEE transactions on Computers*, 46(5):530–544.

[Bogdanov et al., 2007] Bogdanov, A., Knudsen, L. R., Leander, G., Paar, C., Poschmann, A., Robshaw, M. J., Seurin, Y., and Vikkelsoe, C. (2007). Present: An ultra-lightweight block cipher. In *International Workshop on Cryptographic Hardware and Embedded Systems*, pages 450–466. Springer.

[Brooks et al., 2000] Brooks, D., Tiwari, V., and Martonosi, M. (2000). Wattch: a framework for architectural-level power analysis and optimizations. In *Proceedings of the 27th annual International Symposium on Computer Architecture*, pages 83–94.

[Brown et al., 2001] Brown, M. D., Stark, J., and Patt, Y. N. (2001). Select-free instruction scheduling logic. In *Microarchitecture, 2001. MICRO-34. Proceedings. 34th ACM/IEEE International Symposium on*, pages 204–213. IEEE.

[Budde et al., 1990] Budde, D., Riches, R., Imel, M. T., Myers, G., and Lai, K. (1990). Register scorboarding on a microprocessor chip. US Patent 4,891,753.

[Calder and Reinman, 2000] Calder, B. and Reinman, G. (2000). A comparative survey of load speculation architectures. *Journal of Instruction-Level Parallelism*, 2:1–39.

[Calder et al., 1999] Calder, B., Reinman, G., and Tullsen, D. M. (1999). Selective value prediction. In *Proceedings of the 26th annual international symposium on Computer architecture*, pages 64–74.

[Callahan et al., 1991] Callahan, D., Kennedy, K., and Porterfield, A. (1991). Software prefetching. In Patterson, D. A. and Rau, B., editors, *ASPLOS-IV Proceedings - Forth International Conference on Architectural Support for Programming Languages and Operating Systems, Santa Clara, California, USA, April 8-11, 1991*, pages 40–52. ACM Press.

[Champagne and Lee, 2010] Champagne, D. and Lee, R. B. (2010). Scalable architectural support for trusted software. In *HPCA-16 2010 The Sixteenth International Symposium on High-Performance Computer Architecture*, pages 1–12. IEEE.

[Chandran et al., 2017] Chandran, S., Panda, P. R., Sarangi, S. R., Bhattacharyya, A., Chauhan, D., and Kumar, S. (2017). Managing trace summaries to minimize stalls during postsilicon validation. *IEEE Transactions on Very Large Scale Integration (VLSI) Systems*, 25(6):1881–1894.

[Chen, 2016] Chen, A. (2016). A review of emerging non-volatile memory (nvm) technologies and applications. *Solid-State Electronics*, 125:25–38.

[Chen et al., 1997] Chen, I., Bird, P., and Mudge, T. (1997). The impact of instruction compression on i-cache performance. Technical Report CSE-TR-330-97, Computer Science and Engineering, University of Michigan.

[Chen et al., 2014] Chen, T., Du, Z., Sun, N., Wang, J., Wu, C., Chen, Y., and Temam, O. (2014). Diannao: a small-footprint high-throughput accelerator for ubiquitous machine-learning. In *Proceedings of the 19th international conference on Architectural support for programming languages and operating systems*, pages 269–284.

[Chen et al., 2012] Chen, Y., Chen, T., Li, L., Li, L., Yang, L., Su, M., and Hu, W. (2012). Ldet: Determinizing asynchronous transfer for postsilicon debugging. *IEEE Transactions on Computers*, 62(9):1732–1744.

[Chen et al., 2016] Chen, Y.-H., Krishna, T., Emer, J. S., and Sze, V. (2016). Eyeriss: An energy-efficient reconfigurable accelerator for deep convolutional neural networks. *IEEE journal of solid-state circuits*, 52(1):127–138.

[Choi et al., 2013] Choi, J. W., Bedard, D., Fowler, R., and Vuduc, R. (2013). A roofline model of energy. In *2013 IEEE 27th International Symposium on Parallel and Distributed Processing*, pages 661–672. IEEE.

[Chrysos and Emer, 1998] Chrysos, G. Z. and Emer, J. S. (1998). Memory dependence prediction using store sets. In *Proceedings of the 25th annual international symposium on Computer architecture*, pages 142–153.

[Clos, 1953] Clos, C. (1953). A study of non-blocking switching networks. *Bell System Technical Journal*, 32(2):406–424.

[Coffin Jr, 1954] Coffin Jr, L. F. (1954). A study of the effects of cyclic thermal stresses on a ductile metal. *Transactions of the American Society of Mechanical Engineers, New York*, 76:931–950.

[Constantinides et al., 2008] Constantinides, K., Mutlu, O., and Austin, T. (2008). Online design bug detection: Rtl analysis, flexible mechanisms, and evaluation. In *2008 41st IEEE/ACM International Symposium on Microarchitecture*, pages 282–293. IEEE.

[Cooperstein, 2015] Cooperstein, B. (2015). *Advanced linear algebra*. CRC Press.

[Cormen et al., 2009] Cormen, T. H., Leiserson, C. E., Rivest, R. L., and Stein, C. (2009). *Introduction to Algorithms*. MIT Press, third edition.

[Corporation, 2014a] Corporation, N. (2014a). Nvidia geforce gtx 1080. *White paper, NVIDIA Corporation*.

[Corporation, 2014b] Corporation, N. (2014b). Nvidia's next generation cuda compute architecture: Kepler GK110/210. *White paper, NVIDIA Corporation*.

[Coskun et al., 2008] Coskun, A. K., Rosing, T. ., Whisnant, K. A., and Gross, K. C. (2008). Static and dynamic temperature-aware scheduling for multiprocessor socs. *IEEE Trans. VLSI Syst.*, 16(9):1127–1140.

[Costan and Devadas, 2016] Costan, V. and Devadas, S. (2016). Intel sgx explained. *IACR Cryptology ePrint Archive*, 2016(086):1–118.

[Cover and Thomas, 2013] Cover, T. M. and Thomas, J. A. (2013). *Elements of Information Theory*. Wiley.

[Culler et al., 1998] Culler, D., Singh, J. P., and Gupta, A. (1998). *Parallel Computer Architecture: A Hardware/Software Approach*. The Morgan Kaufmann series in Computer Architecture Design. Morgan Kaufmann.

[Dally and Towles, 2004] Dally, W. J. and Towles, B. P. (2004). *Principles and practices of interconnection networks*. Elsevier.

[Dan and Towsley, 1990] Dan, A. and Towsley, D. (1990). An approximate analysis of the lru and fifo buffer replacement schemes. In *Proceedings of the 1990 ACM SIGMETRICS conference on Measurement and modeling of computer systems*, pages 143–152.

[Danilak, 2017] Danilak, R. (2017). Why energy is a big and rapidly growing problem for data centers. `https://www.forbes.com/sites/forbestechcouncil/2017/12/15/why-energy-is-a-big-and-rapidly-growing-problem-for-data-centers`. Accessed on May 15th 2019.

[David et al., 2013] David, T., Guerraoui, R., and Trigonakis, V. (2013). Everything you always wanted to know about synchronization but were afraid to ask. In *Proceedings of the Twenty-Fourth ACM Symposium on Operating Systems Principles*, pages 33–48. ACM.

[Diaconis et al., 1983] Diaconis, P., Graham, R., and Kantor, W. M. (1983). The mathematics of perfect shuffles. *Advances in applied mathematics*, 4(2):175–196.

[Dice et al., 2006] Dice, D., Shalev, O., and Shavit, N. (2006). Transactional locking ii. In *International Symposium on Distributed Computing*, pages 194–208. Springer.

[Eden and Mudge, 1998] Eden, A. N. and Mudge, T. (1998). The yags branch prediction scheme. In *Proceedings of the 31st Annual ACM/IEEE International Symposium on Microarchitecture*, pages 69–77.

[Eisenbarth et al., 2007] Eisenbarth, T., Kumar, S., Paar, C., Poschmann, A., and Uhsadel, L. (2007). A survey of lightweight-cryptography implementations. *IEEE Design & Test of Computers*, 24(6):522–533.

[Elmore, 1948] Elmore, W. C. (1948). The transient response of damped linear networks with particular regard to wideband amplifiers. *Journal of applied physics*, 19(1):55–63.

[Ergin et al., 2004] Ergin, O., Balkan, D., Ponomarev, D., and Ghose, K. (2004). Increasing processor performance through early register release. In *Computer Design: VLSI in Computers and Processors, 2004. ICCD 2004. Proceedings. IEEE International Conference on*, pages 480–487. IEEE.

[Ersoy, 1985] Ersoy, O. (1985). Semisystolic array implementation of circular, skew circular, and linear convolutions. *IEEE transactions on computers*, 34(2):190–196.

[Eyre and Bier, 2000] Eyre, J. and Bier, J. (2000). The evolution of dsp processors. *IEEE Signal Processing Magazine*, 17(2):43–51.

[Farabet et al., 2011] Farabet, C., Martini, B., Corda, B., Akselrod, P., Culurciello, E., and LeCun, Y. (2011). Neuflow: A runtime reconfigurable dataflow processor for vision. In *Cvpr 2011 Workshops*, pages 109–116. IEEE.

[Farber, 2011] Farber, R. (2011). *CUDA Application Design and Development*. Morgan Kaufmann.

[Farooqui et al., 2011] Farooqui, N., Kerr, A., Diamos, G., Yalamanchili, S., and Schwan, K. (2011). A framework for dynamically instrumenting gpu compute applications within gpu ocelot. In *Proceedings of the Fourth Workshop on General Purpose Processing on Graphics Processing Units*, pages 1–9.

[Federovsky et al., 1998] Federovsky, E., Feder, M., and Weiss, S. (1998). Branch prediction based on universal data compression algorithms. In *Proceedings. 25th Annual International Symposium on Computer Architecture*, pages 62–72. IEEE.

[Feng et al., 2010] Feng, P., Chao, C., Wang, Z.-s., Yang, Y.-c., Jing, Y., and Fei, Z. (2010). Nonvolatile resistive switching memories-characteristics, mechanisms and challenges. *Progress in natural science: Materials international*, 20:1–15.

[Ferdman et al., 2011] Ferdman, M., Kaynak, C., and Falsafi, B. (2011). Proactive instruction fetch. In *Proceedings of the 44th Annual IEEE/ACM International Symposium on Microarchitecture*, pages 152–162. ACM.

[Fujitsu Semiconductor Limited, 2010] Fujitsu Semiconductor Limited (2010). Fram guide book. `https://www.fujitsu.com/downloads/MICRO/fme/fram/fram-guide-book.pdf`. Accessed on 20th November, 2019.

[Gabbay and Mendelson, 1997] Gabbay, F. and Mendelson, A. (1997). Can program profiling support value prediction? In *Proceedings of the 30th annual ACM/IEEE international symposium on Microarchitecture*, pages 270–280. IEEE Computer Society.

[Gabis and Koudil, 2016] Gabis, A. B. and Koudil, M. (2016). Noc routing protocols–objective-based classification. *Journal of Systems Architecture*, 66:14–32.

[Gaur et al., 2011] Gaur, J., Chaudhuri, M., and Subramoney, S. (2011). Bypass and insertion algorithms for exclusive last-level caches. In *Proceedings of the 38th annual international symposium on Computer architecture*, pages 81–92.

[Geer, 2005] Geer, D. (2005). Taking the graphics processor beyond graphics. *Computer*, 38(9):14–16.

[Gharachorloo, 1995] Gharachorloo, K. (1995). Memory consistency models for shared-memory multiprocessors, phd thesis. *Computer System Laboratory, Stanford Univ.*

[Glendinning and Helbert, 2012] Glendinning, W. B. and Helbert, J. N. (2012). *Handbook of VLSI microlithography: principles, technology and applications*. William Andrew.

[Goldreich and Ostrovsky, 1996] Goldreich, O. and Ostrovsky, R. (1996). Software protection and simulation on oblivious rams. *Journal of the ACM (JACM)*, 43(3):431–473.

[Goodfellow et al., 2016] Goodfellow, I., Bengio, Y., and Courville, A. (2016). *Deep learning*. MIT press.

[Gropp et al., 1999] Gropp, W., Thakur, R., and Lusk, E. (1999). *Using MPI-2: Advanced features of the message passing interface*. MIT press.

[GTX, 2014] GTX, N. G. (2014). 980: Featuring maxwell, the most advanced gpu ever made. *White paper, NVIDIA Corporation*.

[Guerraoui and Kapalka, 2008] Guerraoui, R. and Kapalka, M. (2008). On the correctness of transactional memory. In *Proceedings of the 13th ACM SIGPLAN Symposium on Principles and practice of parallel programming*, pages 175–184. ACM.

[Guerraoui and Kapałka, 2010] Guerraoui, R. and Kapałka, M. (2010). Principles of transactional memory. *Synthesis Lectures on Distributed Computing*, 1(1):1–193.

[Gulli and Pal, 2017] Gulli, A. and Pal, S. (2017). *Deep learning with Keras*. Packt Publishing Ltd.

[Guo and Solihin, 2006] Guo, F. and Solihin, Y. (2006). An analytical model for cache replacement policy performance. *ACM SIGMETRICS Performance Evaluation Review*, 34(1):228–239.

[Gutsche et al., 2005] Gutsche, M., Avellan, A., Erben, E., Hecht, T., Hirt, G., Heitmann, J., Igel-Holtzendorff, T., Jakschik, S., Kapteyn, C., Krautheim, G., Kudelka, S., Link, A., Lützen, J., Sänger, A., Schroeder, U., Seidl, H., Stadtmüller, M., and Wiebauer, W. (2005). DRAM Capacitor Scaling. Technical report, Infineon.

[Gwennap, 2019a] Gwennap, L. (2019a). Snapdragon 865 dis-integrates. Microprocessor Report.

[Gwennap, 2019b] Gwennap, L. (2019b). Zen 2 boosts ryzen performance. Microprocessor Report.

[Hachman, 2019] Hachman, M. (2019). Inside the snapdragon 865: Qualcomm reveals the features you'll find in 2020's best android phones. `https://www.pcworld.com/article/3482244/inside-the-snapdragon-865-qualcomm-android.html`. Accessed on 10th August, 2020.

[Halfhill, 2008] Halfhill, T. R. (2008). Intel's tiny atom. *Microprocessor Report*, 22(4):1.

[Halfhill, 2019] Halfhill, T. R. (2019). Intel's tremont: A bigger little core. Microprocessor Report.

[Harris et al., 2010] Harris, T., Larus, J., and Rajwar, R. (2010). Transactional memory. *Synthesis Lectures on Computer Architecture*, 5(1):1–263.

[Harris et al., 2006] Harris, T., Plesko, M., Shinnar, A., and Tarditi, D. (2006). Optimizing memory transactions. In *Proceedings of the ACM SIGPLAN 2006 Conference on Programming Language Design and Implementation, Ottawa, Ontario, Canada, June 11-14, 2006*, pages 14–25.

[Hazucha and Svensson, 2000] Hazucha, P. and Svensson, C. (2000). Impact of cmos technology scaling on the atmospheric neutron soft error rate. *IEEE Transactions on Nuclear science*, 47(6):2586–2594.

[Helkala et al., 2014] Helkala, J., Viitanen, T., Kultala, H., Jääskeläinen, P., Takala, J., Zetterman, T., and Berg, H. (2014). Variable length instruction compression on transport triggered architectures. In *Embedded Computer Systems: Architectures, Modeling, and Simulation (SAMOS XIV), 2014 International Conference on*, pages 149–155. IEEE.

[Henning, 2006] Henning, J. L. (2006). Spec cpu2006 benchmark descriptions. *ACM SIGARCH Computer Architecture News*, 34(4):1–17.

[Herlihy and Shavit, 2012] Herlihy, M. and Shavit, N. (2012). *The Art of Multiprocessor Programming*. Elsevier.

[Hinton et al., 2001] Hinton, G., Sager, D., Upton, M., Boggs, D., et al. (2001). The microarchitecture of the pentium® 4 processor. In *Intel Technology Journal*.

[Hong and Kim, 2009] Hong, S. and Kim, H. (2009). An analytical model for a gpu architecture with memory-level and thread-level parallelism awareness. In *Proceedings of the 36th annual international symposium on Computer architecture*, pages 152–163.

[Horowitz, 1983] Horowitz, M. A. (1983). *Timing models for MOS circuits.* PhD thesis, Stanford University.

[Howie, 2007] Howie, J. M. (2007). *Fields and Galois theory.* Springer Science & Business Media.

[Huang et al., 2006] Huang, W., Ghosh, S., Velusamy, S., Sankaranarayanan, K., Skadron, K., and Stan, M. R. (2006). Hotspot: A compact thermal modeling methodology for early-stage vlsi design. *IEEE Transactions on Very Large Scale Integration (VLSI) Systems*, 14(5):501–513.

[Hung et al., 2006] Hung, W.-L., Link, G. M., Xie, Y., Vijaykrishnan, N., and Irwin, M. J. (2006). Interconnect and thermal-aware floorplanning for 3D microprocessors. In *International Symposium on Quality Electronic Design (ISQED)*. IEEE.

[Hwu and Patt, 1987] Hwu, W.-M. W. and Patt, Y. N. (1987). Checkpoint repair for high-performance out-of-order execution machines. *Computers, IEEE Transactions on*, 100(12):1496–1514.

[Intel, 2004] Intel (2004). Enhanced speedstep® technology for the intel® pentium® m processor, white paper, march 2004. `http://download.intel.com/design/network/papers/30117401.pdf`. Accessed on 10th October 2019.

[Jacob et al., 2007] Jacob, B., Ng, S., and Wang, D. (2007). *Memory Systems: Cache, DRAM, Disk.* Morgan Kaufmann.

[JEDEC Solid State Technology Association, 2003] JEDEC Solid State Technology Association (2003). Double data rate SDRAM specification. Standard JESD79C, JEDEC.

[JEDEC Solid State Technology Association, 2008a] JEDEC Solid State Technology Association (2008a). DDR2 SDRAM specification. Standard JESD79-2E, JEDEC.

[JEDEC Solid State Technology Association, 2008b] JEDEC Solid State Technology Association (2008b). DDR3 SDRAM. Standard JESD79-3C, JEDEC.

[JEDEC Solid State Technology Association, 2020] JEDEC Solid State Technology Association (2020). DDR4 SDRAM. Standard JESD79-4C, JEDEC.

[Jerger et al., 2017] Jerger, N. E., Krishna, T., and Peh, L.-S. (2017). On-chip networks. *Synthesis Lectures on Computer Architecture*, 12(3):1–210.

[Jia et al., 2014] Jia, Y., Shelhamer, E., Donahue, J., Karayev, S., Long, J., Girshick, R., Guadarrama, S., and Darrell, T. (2014). Caffe: Convolutional architecture for fast feature embedding. In *Proceedings of the 22nd ACM international conference on Multimedia*, pages 675–678.

[Jiménez, 2003] Jiménez, D. A. (2003). Fast path-based neural branch prediction. In *Proceedings of the 36th annual IEEE/ACM International Symposium on Microarchitecture*, page 243. IEEE Computer Society.

[Jiménez, 2011a] Jiménez, D. A. (2011a). Oh-snap: Optimized hybrid scaled neural analog predictor. *Proceedings of the 3rd Championship on Branch Prediction.*

[Jiménez, 2011b] Jiménez, D. A. (2011b). An optimized scaled neural branch predictor. In *Computer Design (ICCD), 2011 IEEE 29th International Conference on*, pages 113–118. IEEE.

[Jouppi et al., 2017] Jouppi, N. P., Young, C., Patil, N., Patterson, D., Agrawal, G., Bajwa, R., Bates, S., Bhatia, S., Boden, N., Borchers, A., et al. (2017). In-datacenter performance analysis of a tensor processing unit. In *Proceedings of the 44th Annual International Symposium on Computer Architecture*, pages 1–12.

[Kaeli et al., 2015] Kaeli, D. R., Mistry, P., Schaa, D., and Zhang, D. P. (2015). *Heterogeneous computing with OpenCL 2.0*. Morgan Kaufmann.

[Kalayappan and Sarangi, 2013] Kalayappan, R. and Sarangi, S. R. (2013). A survey of checker architectures. *ACM Computing Surveys (CSUR)*, 45(4):1–34.

[Kallurkar and Sarangi, 2017] Kallurkar, P. and Sarangi, S. R. (2017). Schedtask: a hardware-assisted task scheduler. In *Proceedings of the 50th Annual IEEE/ACM International Symposium on Microarchitecture*, pages 612–624. ACM.

[Kanter, 2019] Kanter, D. (2019). Intel's sunny cove sits on an icy lake. Microprocessor Report.

[Karkar et al., 2016] Karkar, A., Mak, T., Tong, K.-F., and Yakovlev, A. (2016). A survey of emerging interconnects for on-chip efficient multicast and broadcast in many-cores. *IEEE Circuits and Systems Magazine*, 16(1):58–72.

[Kawahara et al., 2012] Kawahara, T., Ito, K., Takemura, R., and Ohno, H. (2012). Spin-transfer torque ram technology: Review and prospect. *Microelectronics Reliability*, 52(4):613–627.

[Kaxiras and Martonosi, 2008] Kaxiras, S. and Martonosi, M. (2008). Computer architecture techniques for power-efficiency. *Synthesis Lectures on Computer Architecture*, 3(1):1–207.

[Keleher et al., 1994] Keleher, P., Cox, A. L., Dwarkadas, S., and Zwaenepoel, W. (1994). Treadmarks: Distributed shared memory on standard workstations and operating systems. In *USENIX Winter*, volume 1994.

[Keltcher et al., 2003] Keltcher, C. N., McGrath, K. J., Ahmed, A., and Conway, P. (2003). The amd opteron processor for multiprocessor servers. *Micro, IEEE*, 23(2):66–76.

[Khvalkovskiy et al., 2013] Khvalkovskiy, A., Apalkov, D., Watts, S., Chepulskii, R., Beach, R., Ong, A., Tang, X., Driskill-Smith, A., Butler, W., Visscher, P., et al. (2013). Basic principles of stt-mram cell operation in memory arrays. *Journal of Physics D: Applied Physics*, 46(7):074001.

[Kim et al., 2003] Kim, C., Burger, D., and Keckler, S. W. (2003). Nonuniform cache architectures for wire-delay dominated on-chip caches. *IEEE Micro*, 23(6):99–107.

[Kim and Lipasti, 2004] Kim, I. and Lipasti, M. H. (2004). Understanding scheduling replay schemes. In *Proceedings of the 10th International Symposium on High Performance Computer Architecture*.

[Kim et al., 2007] Kim, J., Dally, W. J., and Abts, D. (2007). Flattened butterfly: a cost-efficient topology for high-radix networks. In *Proceedings of the 34th annual international symposium on Computer architecture*, pages 126–137.

[Kim et al., 2004] Kim, N. S., Flautner, K., Blaauw, D., and Mudge, T. (2004). Circuit and microarchitectural techniques for reducing cache leakage power. *IEEE Transactions on Very Large Scale Integration (VLSI) Systems*, 12(2):167–184.

[Klaiber et al., 2000] Klaiber, A. et al. (2000). The technology behind crusoe processors. *Transmeta Technical Brief*.

[Kocher et al., 2019] Kocher, P., Horn, J., Fogh, A., Genkin, D., Gruss, D., Haas, W., Hamburg, M., Lipp, M., Mangard, S., Prescher, T., et al. (2019). Spectre attacks: Exploiting speculative execution. In *2019 IEEE Symposium on Security and Privacy (SP)*, pages 1–19. IEEE.

[Kolli et al., 2013] Kolli, A., Saidi, A., and Wenisch, T. F. (2013). Rdip: return-address-stack directed instruction prefetching. In *Microarchitecture (MICRO), 2013 46th Annual IEEE/ACM International Symposium on*, pages 260–271. IEEE.

[Kong et al., 2012] Kong, J., Chung, S. W., and Skadron, K. (2012). Recent thermal management techniques for microprocessors. *ACM Computing Surveys (CSUR)*, 44(3):1–42.

[Krick et al., 2000] Krick, R. F., Hinton, G. J., Upton, M. D., Sager, D. J., and Lee, C. W. (2000). Trace based instruction caching. US Patent 6,018,786.

[Krishna et al., 2008] Krishna, T., Kumar, A., Chiang, P., Erez, M., and Peh, L.-S. (2008). Noc with near-ideal express virtual channels using global-line communication. In *2008 16th IEEE Symposium on High Performance Interconnects*, pages 11–20. IEEE.

[Kroft, 1981] Kroft, D. (1981). Lockup-free instruction fetch/prefetch cache organization. In *Proceedings of the 8th annual symposium on Computer Architecture*, pages 81–87. IEEE Computer Society Press.

[Kuhn et al., 2011] Kuhn, K. J., Giles, M. D., Becher, D., Kolar, P., Kornfeld, A., Kotlyar, R., Ma, S. T., Maheshwari, A., and Mudanai, S. (2011). Process technology variation. *IEEE Transactions on Electron Devices*, 58(8):2197–2208.

[Kung and Picard, 1984] Kung, H. and Picard, R. (1984). One-dimensional systolic arrays for multidimensional convolution and resampling. In *VLSI for Pattern Recognition and Image Processing*, pages 9–24. Springer.

[Kung and Song, 1981] Kung, H. and Song, S. W. (1981). A systolic 2-d convolution chip. Technical Report CMU-CS-81-110, Carnegie Mellon University, Department of Computer Science.

[Kung, 1982] Kung, H.-T. (1982). Why systolic architectures? *IEEE computer*, 15(1):37–46.

[Kwan and Okullo-Oballa, 1990] Kwan, H.-K. and Okullo-Oballa, T. (1990). 2-d systolic arrays for realization of 2-d convolution. *IEEE transactions on circuits and systems*, 37(2):267–233.

[Kwon et al., 2018] Kwon, H., Chatarasi, P., Pellauer, M., Parashar, A., Sarkar, V., and Krishna, T. (2018). Understanding reuse, performance, and hardware cost of dnn dataflows: A data-centric approach. *arXiv preprint arXiv:1805.02566*.

[Lam, 1988] Lam, M. (1988). Software pipelining: An effective scheduling technique for vliw machines. In *Proceedings of the ACM SIGPLAN 1988 conference on Programming Language design and Implementation*, pages 318–328.

[Lam, 2012] Lam, M. S. (2012). *A systolic array optimizing compiler*, volume 64. Springer Science & Business Media.

[Lavenier et al., 1999] Lavenier, D., Quinton, P., and Rajopadhye, S. (1999). Advanced systolic design. *Digital Signal Processing for Multimedia Systems*, pages 657–692.

[Lee et al., 2009] Lee, B. C., Ipek, E., Mutlu, O., and Burger, D. (2009). Architecting phase change memory as a scalable dram alternative. In *Proceedings of the 36th Annual International Symposium on Computer Architecture*, ISCA '09, pages 2–13.

[Lee, 2013] Lee, R. B. (2013). Security basics for computer architects. *Synthesis Lectures on Computer Architecture*, 8(4):1–111.

[Lefurgy et al., 1997] Lefurgy, C., Bird, P., Chen, I.-C., and Mudge, T. (1997). Improving code density using compression techniques. In *Microarchitecture, 1997. Proceedings., Thirtieth Annual IEEE/ACM International Symposium on*, pages 194–203. IEEE.

[Leibholz and Razdan, 1997] Leibholz, D. and Razdan, R. (1997). The alpha 21264: A 500 mhz out-of-order execution microprocessor. In *Compcon'97. Proceedings, IEEE*, pages 28–36. IEEE.

[Leighton, 2014] Leighton, F. T. (2014). *Introduction to parallel algorithms and architectures: Arrays· trees· hypercubes.* Elsevier.

[Leng et al., 2013] Leng, J., Hetherington, T., ElTantawy, A., Gilani, S., Kim, N. S., Aamodt, T. M., and Reddi, V. J. (2013). Gpuwattch: enabling energy optimizations in gpgpus. In *Proceedings of the 40th Annual International Symposium on Computer Architecture*, pages 487–498.

[Leng et al., 2015] Leng, J., Zu, Y., and Reddi, V. J. (2015). Gpu voltage noise: Characterization and hierarchical smoothing of spatial and temporal voltage noise interference in gpu architectures. In *2015 IEEE 21st International Symposium on High Performance Computer Architecture (HPCA)*, pages 161–173. IEEE.

[Leng et al., 2014] Leng, J., Zu, Y., Rhu, M., Gupta, M., and Reddi, V. J. (2014). Gpuvolt: Modeling and characterizing voltage noise in gpu architectures. In *Proceedings of the 2014 international symposium on Low power electronics and design*, pages 141–146.

[Lenoski et al., 1990] Lenoski, D., Laudon, J., Gharachorloo, K., Gupta, A., and Hennessy, J. (1990). The directory-based cache coherence protocol for the dash multiprocessor. In *[1990] Proceedings. The 17th Annual International Symposium on Computer Architecture*, pages 148–159. IEEE.

[Li et al., 2009] Li, S., Ahn, J. H., Strong, R. D., Brockman, J. B., Tullsen, D. M., and Jouppi, N. P. (2009). Mcpat: an integrated power, area, and timing modeling framework for multicore and many-core architectures. In *Proceedings of the 42nd Annual IEEE/ACM International Symposium on Microarchitecture*, pages 469–480. ACM.

[Li, 2012] Li, X. (2012). *Survey of Wireless Network-on-Chip Systems.* PhD thesis, Auburn University.

[Lin, 2011] Lin, M.-B. (2011). *Introduction to VLSI Systems: A Logic, Circuit, and System Perspective.* CRC Press.

[Lindholm et al., 2008] Lindholm, E., Nickolls, J., Oberman, S., and Montrym, J. (2008). Nvidia tesla: A unified graphics and computing architecture. *Micro, IEEE*, 28(2):39–55.

[Lipasti et al., 1996] Lipasti, M. H., Wilkerson, C. B., and Shen, J. P. (1996). Value locality and load value prediction. In *Proceedings of the seventh international conference on Architectural support for programming languages and operating systems*, pages 138–147.

[Lipp et al., 2018] Lipp, M., Schwarz, M., Gruss, D., Prescher, T., Haas, W., Fogh, A., Horn, J., Mangard, S., Kocher, P., Genkin, D., et al. (2018). Meltdown: Reading kernel memory from user space. In *27th {USENIX} Security Symposium ({USENIX} Security 18)*, pages 973–990.

[Logan, 1986] Logan, D. L. (1986). *A First Course in the Finite Element Method.* PWS Engineering.

[Lu et al., 2017] Lu, W., Yan, G., Li, J., Gong, S., Han, Y., and Li, X. (2017). Flexflow: A flexible dataflow accelerator architecture for convolutional neural networks. In *2017 IEEE International Symposium on High Performance Computer Architecture (HPCA)*, pages 553–564. IEEE.

[Luk et al., 2005] Luk, C., Cohn, R. S., Muth, R., Patil, H., Klauser, A., Lowney, P. G., Wallace, S., Reddi, V. J., and Hazelwood, K. M. (2005). Pin: building customized program analysis tools with dynamic instrumentation. In *Proceedings of the ACM SIGPLAN Conference on Programming Language Design and Implementation*, pages 190–200.

[Lustig et al., 2014] Lustig, D., Pellauer, M., and Martonosi, M. (2014). Pipecheck: Specifying and verifying microarchitectural enforcement of memory consistency models. In *Proceedings of the 47th Annual IEEE/ACM International Symposium on Microarchitecture*, pages 635–646. IEEE Computer Society.

[Ma et al., 2015] Ma, S., Pal, D., Jiang, R., Ray, S., and Vasudevan, S. (2015). Can't see the forest for the trees: State restoration's limitations in post-silicon trace signal selection. In *2015 IEEE/ACM International Conference on Computer-Aided Design (ICCAD)*, pages 1–8. IEEE.

[Mador-Haim et al., 2011] Mador-Haim, S., Alur, R., and Martin, M. M. (2011). Litmus tests for comparing memory consistency models: How long do they need to be? In *Proceedings of the 48th Design Automation Conference*, pages 504–509. ACM.

[Mahapatra and Parihar, 2018a] Mahapatra, S. and Parihar, N. (2018a). A review of nbti mechanisms and models. *Microelectronics Reliability*, 81:127–135.

[Mahapatra and Parihar, 2018b] Mahapatra, S. and Parihar, N. (2018b). A review of nbti mechanisms and models. *Microelectronics Reliability*, 81:127–135.

[Malhotra et al., 2014] Malhotra, G., Goel, S., and Sarangi, S. R. (2014). Gputejas: A parallel simulator for gpu architectures. In *High Performance Computing (HiPC), 2014 21st International Conference on*, pages 1–10. IEEE.

[Malhotra et al., 2017] Malhotra, G., Kalayappan, R., Goel, S., Aggarwal, P., Sagar, A., and Sarangi, S. R. (2017). Partejas: A parallel simulator for multicore processors. *ACM Transactions on Modeling and Computer Simulation (TOMACS)*, 27(3):1–24.

[Manson, 1953] Manson, S. S. (1953). *Behavior of materials under conditions of thermal stress*, volume 2933. National Advisory Committee for Aeronautics.

[Martínez et al., 2002] Martínez, J. F., Renau, J., Huang, M. C., and Prvulovic, M. (2002). Cherry: Checkpointed early resource recycling in out-of-order microprocessors. In *Microarchitecture, 2002.(MICRO-35). Proceedings. 35th Annual IEEE/ACM International Symposium on*, pages 3–14. IEEE.

[McNairy and Soltis, 2003] McNairy, C. and Soltis, D. (2003). Itanium 2 processor microarchitecture. *IEEE Micro*, 23(2):44–55.

[Mittal, 2016a] Mittal, S. (2016a). A survey of architectural techniques for managing process variation. *ACM Computing Surveys (CSUR)*, 48(4):1–29.

[Mittal, 2016b] Mittal, S. (2016b). A survey of recent prefetching techniques for processor caches. *ACM Computing Surveys (CSUR)*, 49(2):35.

[Mittal, 2018] Mittal, S. (2018). A survey of techniques for dynamic branch prediction. *CoRR*, abs/1804.00261.

[Miyaji, 1991] Miyaji, F. (1991). Static random access memory device having a high speed read-out and flash-clear functions. US Patent 5,054,000.

[Moolchandani et al., 2020] Moolchandani, D., Kumar, A., and Sarangi, S. R. (2020). Accelerating cnn inference on asics: A survey. *Journal of Systems Architecture*, page 101887.

[Moore et al., 2006] Moore, K. E., Bobba, J., Moravan, M. J., Hill, M. D., and Wood, D. A. (2006). Logtm: Log-based transactional memory. In *The Twelfth International Symposium on High-Performance Computer Architecture, 2006.*, pages 254–265. IEEE.

[Moscibroda and Mutlu, 2009] Moscibroda, T. and Mutlu, O. (2009). A case for bufferless routing in on-chip networks. In *Proceedings of the 36th annual international symposium on Computer architecture*, pages 196–207.

[Moshovos et al., 1997] Moshovos, A., Breach, S. E., Vijaykumar, T. N., and Sohi, G. S. (1997). Dynamic speculation and synchronization of data dependences. In *Proceedings of the 24th annual international symposium on Computer architecture*, pages 181–193.

[Moshovos and Sohi, 1999] Moshovos, A. and Sohi, G. S. (1999). Speculative memory cloaking and bypassing. *International Journal of Parallel Programming*, 27(6):427–456.

[Muchnick et al., 1997] Muchnick, S. S. et al. (1997). *Advanced compiler design implementation*. Morgan Kaufmann.

[Mukherjee, 2011] Mukherjee, S. (2011). *Architecture design for soft errors*. Morgan Kaufmann.

[Muralimanohar et al., 2009] Muralimanohar, N., Balasubramonian, R., and Jouppi, N. P. (2009). Cacti 6.0: A tool to understand large caches. Technical Report HPL-2009-85, University of Utah and Hewlett Packard Laboratories.

[Mutlu et al., 2003] Mutlu, O., Stark, J., Wilkerson, C., and Patt, Y. N. (2003). Runahead execution: An alternative to very large instruction windows for out-of-order processors. In *High-Performance Computer Architecture, 2003. HPCA-9 2003. Proceedings. The Ninth International Symposium on*, pages 129–140.

[Narayan and Tran, 1999] Narayan, R. and Tran, T. M. (1999). Method and apparatus for five bit predecoding variable length instructions for scanning of a number of risc operations. US Patent 5,898,851.

[Neishaburi and Zilic, 2011] Neishaburi, M. H. and Zilic, Z. (2011). Hierarchical embedded logic analyzer for accurate root-cause analysis. In *2011 IEEE International Symposium on Defect and Fault Tolerance in VLSI and Nanotechnology Systems*, pages 120–128. IEEE.

[Ngabonziza et al., 2016] Ngabonziza, B., Martin, D., Bailey, A., Cho, H., and Martin, S. (2016). Trustzone explained: Architectural features and use cases. In *2016 IEEE 2nd International Conference on Collaboration and Internet Computing (CIC)*, pages 445–451. IEEE.

[Nose and Sakurai, 2000] Nose, K. and Sakurai, T. (2000). Analysis and future trend of short-circuit power. *IEEE Transactions on Computer-Aided Design of Integrated Circuits and Systems*, 19(9):1023–1030.

[NVIDIA, 2018] NVIDIA (2018). Cuda toolkit documentation. `https://docs.nvidia.com/cuda/cuda-c-programming-guide/index.html`.

[NVIDIA Inc., 2017] NVIDIA Inc. (2017). V100 gpu architecture. the world's most advanced data center gpu. White Paper: Version WP-08608-001_v1.1, NVIDIA.

[NVIDIA Inc., 2020] NVIDIA Inc. (2020). Cuda compiler driver nvcc. Reference Guide TRM-06721-001_v11.0, NVIDIA.

[Ors et al., 2004] Ors, S. B., Gurkaynak, F., Oswald, E., and Preneel, B. (2004). Power-analysis attack on an asic aes implementation. In *International Conference on Information Technology: Coding and Computing, 2004. Proceedings. ITCC 2004.*, volume 2, pages 546–552. IEEE.

[Padhye et al., 2018] Padhye, S., Sahu, R. A., and Saraswat, V. (2018). *Introduction to Cryptography*. CRC Press.

[Palacharla et al., 1997] Palacharla, S., Jouppi, N. P., and Smith, J. E. (1997). Complexity-effective superscalar processors. In *Proceedings of the 24th annual international symposium on Computer architecture*, pages 206–218.

[Parashar et al., 2019] Parashar, A., Raina, P., Shao, Y. S., Chen, Y.-H., Ying, V. A., Mukkara, A., Venkatesan, R., Khailany, B., Keckler, S. W., and Emer, J. (2019). Timeloop: A systematic approach to dnn accelerator evaluation. In *2019 IEEE International Symposium on Performance Analysis of Systems and Software (ISPASS)*, pages 304–315. IEEE.

[Park et al., 2003] Park, I., Ooi, C. L., and Vijaykumar, T. (2003). Reducing design complexity of the load/store queue. In *Proceedings of the 36th annual IEEE/ACM International Symposium on Microarchitecture*, page 411. IEEE Computer Society.

[Park et al., 2010] Park, J.-H., Shin, S., Christofferson, J., Shakouri, A., and Kang, S.-M. (2010). Experimental validation of the power blurring method. In *SEMI-THERM*, pages 240–244. IEEE.

[Peterson et al., 1991] Peterson, C., Sutton, J., and Wiley, P. (1991). iWarp: a 100-MOPS, LIW microprocessor for multicomputers. *Micro, IEEE*, 11(3):26–29.

[Petric et al., 2005] Petric, V., Sha, T., and Roth, A. (2005). Reno: a rename-based instruction optimizer. In *32nd International Symposium on Computer Architecture (ISCA'05)*, pages 98–109. IEEE.

[Pinto and Santos, 2019] Pinto, S. and Santos, N. (2019). Demystifying arm trustzone: A comprehensive survey. *ACM Computing Surveys (CSUR)*, 51(6):1–36.

[Powell et al., 2001] Powell, M. D., Agarwal, A., Vijaykumar, T., Falsafi, B., and Roy, K. (2001). Reducing set-associative cache energy via way-prediction and selective direct-mapping. In *Proceedings of the 34th annual ACM/IEEE international symposium on Microarchitecture*, pages 54–65. IEEE Computer Society.

[Powell and Vijaykumar, 2003a] Powell, M. D. and Vijaykumar, T. (2003a). Pipeline damping: a microarchitectural technique to reduce inductive noise in supply voltage. In *30th Annual International Symposium on Computer Architecture, 2003. Proceedings.*, pages 72–83. IEEE.

[Powell and Vijaykumar, 2003b] Powell, M. D. and Vijaykumar, T. (2003b). Pipeline muffling and a priori current ramping: architectural techniques to reduce high-frequency inductive noise. In *Proceedings of the 2003 international symposium on Low power electronics and design*, pages 223–228.

[Pratt, 1995] Pratt, V. (1995). Anatomy of the pentium bug. In *TAPSOFT'95: Theory and Practice of Software Development*, pages 97–107. Springer.

[Prvulovic, 2006] Prvulovic, M. (2006). Cord: Cost-effective (and nearly overhead-free) order-recording and data race detection. In *The Twelfth International Symposium on High-Performance Computer Architecture, 2006.*, pages 232–243. IEEE.

[Quinn, 2017] Quinn, M. (2017). *Parallel Programming in C with MPI and OpenMP*. McGrawHill Education.

[Qureshi et al., 2011] Qureshi, M. K., Gurumurthi, S., and Rajendran, B. (2011). Phase change memory: From devices to systems. *Synthesis Lectures on Computer Architecture*, 6(4):1–134.

[Rashkeev et al., 2002] Rashkeev, S., Fleetwood, D., Schrimpf, R., and Pantelides, S. (2002). Dual behavior of $H+$ at $Si-SiO_2$ interfaces: Mobility versus trapping. *Applied physics letters*, 81(10):1839–1841.

[Rastegar, 1994] Rastegar, B. (1994). Integrated circuit memory device having flash clear. US Patent 5,311,477.

[Rathnam and Slavenburg, 1996] Rathnam, S. and Slavenburg, G. (1996). An architectural overview of the programmable multimedia processor, tm-1. In *Compcon'96.'Technologies for the Information Superhighway'Digest of Papers*, pages 319–326. IEEE.

[Rau, 1993] Rau, B. R. (1993). Dynamically scheduled vliw processors. In *Proceedings of the 26th annual international symposium on Microarchitecture*, pages 80–92. IEEE Computer Society Press.

[Rau, 1994] Rau, B. R. (1994). Iterative modulo scheduling: An algorithm for software pipelining loops. In *Proceedings of the 27th annual international symposium on Microarchitecture*, pages 63–74. ACM.

[Reagen et al., 2017] Reagen, B., Adolf, R., Whatmough, P., Wei, G.-Y., and Brooks, D. (2017). Deep learning for computer architects. *Synthesis Lectures on Computer Architecture*, 12(4):1–123.

[Reinman and Jouppi, 2000] Reinman, G. and Jouppi, N. P. (2000). Cacti 2.0: An integrated cache timing and power model. Research Report 2000/7, Compaq Western Research Laboratory.

[Ren et al., 2017] Ren, L., Fletcher, C. W., Kwon, A., Van Dijk, M., and Devadas, S. (2017). Design and implementation of the ascend secure processor. *IEEE Transactions on Dependable and Secure Computing*, 16(2):204–216.

[Rogers et al., 2007] Rogers, B., Chhabra, S., Prvulovic, M., and Solihin, Y. (2007). Using address independent seed encryption and bonsai merkle trees to make secure processors OS and performance-friendly. In *40th Annual IEEE/ACM International Symposium on Microarchitecture (MICRO 2007)*, pages 183–196. IEEE.

[Roy et al., 2003] Roy, K., Mukhopadhyay, S., and Mahmoodi-Meimand, H. (2003). Leakage current mechanisms and leakage reduction techniques in deep-submicrometer cmos circuits. *Proceedings of the IEEE*, 91(2):305–327.

[Rumpf and Strzodka, 2006] Rumpf, M. and Strzodka, R. (2006). Graphics processor units: New prospects for parallel computing. In *Numerical solution of partial differential equations on parallel computers*, pages 89–132. Springer.

[Rupp, 2017] Rupp, K. (2017). Moore's law: Transistors per microprocessor. `https://ourworldindata.org/grapher/transistors-per-microprocessor`. Accessed on 11th August 2020.

[Saini, 1993] Saini, A. (1993). Design of the intel pentium processor. In *Computer Design: VLSI in Computers and Processors, 1993. ICCD'93. Proceedings., 1993 IEEE International Conference on*, pages 258–261. IEEE.

[Salminen et al., 2008] Salminen, E., Kulmala, A., and Hamalainen, T. D. (2008). Survey of network-on-chip proposals. *White paper, OCP-IP*, 1:13.

[Samajdar et al., 2020] Samajdar, A., Joseph, J. M., Zhu, Y., Whatmough, P., Mattina, M., and Krishna, T. (2020). A systematic methodology for characterizingscalability of dnn accelerators using scale-sim. In *International Symposium on Performance Analysis of Systems and Software*. IEEE.

[Sarangi, 2015] Sarangi, S. R. (2015). *Computer Organisation and Architecture*. McGrawHill.

[Sarangi et al., 2014] Sarangi, S. R., Ananthanarayanan, G., and Balakrishnan, M. (2014). Lightsim: A leakage aware ultrafast temperature simulator. In *2014 19th Asia and South Pacific Design Automation Conference (ASP-DAC)*, pages 855–860. IEEE.

[Sarangi et al., 2008] Sarangi, S. R., Greskamp, B., Teodorescu, R., Nakano, J., Tiwari, A., and Torrellas, J. (2008). Varius: A model of process variation and resulting timing errors for microarchitects. *IEEE Transactions on Semiconductor Manufacturing*, 21(1):3–13.

[Sarangi et al., 2006a] Sarangi, S. R., Greskamp, B., and Torrellas, J. (2006a). Cadre: Cycle-accurate deterministic replay for hardware debugging. In *International Conference on Dependable Systems and Networks (DSN'06)*, pages 301–312. IEEE.

[Sarangi et al., 2015] Sarangi, S. R., Kalayappan, R., Kallurkar, P., Goel, S., and Peter, E. (2015). Tejas: A java based versatile micro-architectural simulator. In *International Workshop on Power and Timing Modeling, Optimization and Simulation (PATMOS)*.

[Sarangi et al., 2006b] Sarangi, S. R., Tiwari, A., and Torrellas, J. (2006b). Phoenix: Detecting and recovering from permanent processor design bugs with programmable hardware. In *Proceedings of the 39th Annual IEEE/ACM International Symposium on Microarchitecture*, pages 26–37. IEEE Computer Society.

[Savage et al., 1997] Savage, S., Burrows, M., Nelson, G., Sobalvarro, P., and Anderson, T. (1997). Eraser: A dynamic data race detector for multithreaded programs. *ACM Transactions on Computer Systems (TOCS)*, 15(4):391–411.

[Scheurich and Dubois, 1988] Scheurich, C. and Dubois, M. (1988). The design of a lockup-free cache for high-performance multiprocessors. In *Proceedings of the 1988 ACM/IEEE Conference on Supercomputing*, Supercomputing '88, pages 352–359.

[Sehatbakhsh et al., 2020] Sehatbakhsh, N., Nazari, A., Alam, M., Werner, F., Zhu, Y., Zajic, A. G., and Prvulovic, M. (2020). REMOTE: robust external malware detection framework by using electromagnetic signals. *IEEE Trans. Computers*, 69(3):312–326.

[Settle et al., 2003] Settle, A., Connors, D. A., Hoflehner, G., and Lavery, D. (2003). Optimization for the intel/spl reg/itanium/spl reg/architecture register stack. In *Code Generation and Optimization, 2003. CGO 2003. International Symposium on*, pages 115–124. IEEE.

[Seznec, 1993] Seznec, A. (1993). A case for two-way skewed-associative caches. In *Proceedings of the 20th Annual International Symposium on Computer Architecture*, pages 169–178. IEEE.

[Seznec, 2004] Seznec, A. (2004). Revisiting the perceptron predictor. Technical Report PI-1620, IRISA, France.

[Seznec, 2007] Seznec, A. (2007). A 256 kbits l-tage branch predictor. *Journal of Instruction-Level Parallelism (JILP) Special Issue: The Second Championship Branch Prediction Competition (CBP-2)*, 9:1–6.

[Seznec et al., 2002] Seznec, A., Felix, S., Krishnan, V., and Sazeides, Y. (2002). Design tradeoffs for the alpha ev8 conditional branch predictor. In *Proceedings 29th Annual International Symposium on Computer Architecture*, pages 295–306. IEEE.

[Sharangpani and Arora, 2000] Sharangpani, H. and Arora, H. (2000). Itanium processor microarchitecture. *IEEE Micro*, 20(5):24–43.

[Shivakumar and Jouppi, 2001] Shivakumar, P. and Jouppi, N. P. (2001). Cacti 3.0: An integrated cache timing, power, and area model. Research Report 2001/2, Compaq Western Research Laboratory.

[Silberschatz et al., 2018] Silberschatz, A., Gagne, G., and Galvin, P. B. (2018). *Operating system concepts*. Wiley.

[Själander et al., 2014] Själander, M., Martonosi, M., and Kaxiras, S. (2014). Power-efficient computer architectures: Recent advances. *Synthesis Lectures on Computer Architecture*, 9(3):1–96.

[Slegel et al., 1999] Slegel, T. J., Averill, R. M., Check, M. A., Giamei, B. C., Krumm, B. W., Krygowski, C. A., Li, W. H., Liptay, J. S., MacDougall, J. D., McPherson, T. J., et al. (1999). Ibm's s/390 g5 microprocessor design. *IEEE micro*, 19(2):12–23.

[Sloss et al., 2004] Sloss, A., Symes, D., and Wright, C. (2004). *ARM system developer's guide: designing and optimizing system software*. Elsevier.

[Smith and Sohi, 1995] Smith, J. E. and Sohi, G. S. (1995). The microarchitecture of superscalar processors. *Proceedings of the IEEE*, 83(12):1609–1624.

[Sorin et al., 2011] Sorin, D. J., Hill, M. D., and Wood, D. A. (2011). A primer on memory consistency and cache coherence. *Synthesis Lectures on Computer Architecture*, 6(3):1–212.

[Sprangle et al., 1997] Sprangle, E., Chappell, R. S., Alsup, M., and Patt, Y. N. (1997). The agree predictor: A mechanism for reducing negative branch history interference. In *Proceedings of the 24th annual international symposium on Computer architecture*, pages 284–291.

[Sridhar et al., 2010] Sridhar, A., Vincenzi, A., Ruggiero, M., Brunschwiler, T., and Atienza, D. (2010). 3d-ice: Fast compact transient thermal modeling for 3d ics with inter-tier liquid cooling. In *2010 IEEE/ACM International Conference on Computer-Aided Design (ICCAD)*, pages 463–470. IEEE.

[Srinivasan et al., 2005] Srinivasan, J., Adve, S., Bose, P., and Rivers, J. (2005). Exploiting structural duplication for lifetime reliability enhancement. In *32nd International Symposium on Computer Architecture (ISCA'05)*, pages 520–531. IEEE.

[Srinivasan et al., 2004] Srinivasan, J., Adve, S. V., Bose, P., and Rivers, J. A. (2004). The case for lifetime reliability-aware microprocessors. In *Proceedings of the 31st annual international symposium on Computer architecture*, ISCA '04, pages 276–.

[Stallings, 2006] Stallings, W. (2006). *Cryptography and network security, 4/E*. Pearson Education India.

[Stefanov et al., 2013] Stefanov, E., Van Dijk, M., Shi, E., Fletcher, C., Ren, L., Yu, X., and Devadas, S. (2013). Path oram: an extremely simple oblivious ram protocol. In *Proceedings of the 2013 ACM SIGSAC conference on Computer & communications security*, pages 299–310.

[Stenstrom, 1990] Stenstrom, P. (1990). A survey of cache coherence schemes for multiprocessors. *Computer*, 23(6):12–24.

[Suggs and Bouvier, 2019] Suggs, D. and Bouvier, D. (2019). Zen 2. https://www.youtube.com/watch?v=QU3PHKdj8wQ. Accessed on 17th August, 2020.

[Suh et al., 2005] Suh, G. E., O'Donnell, C. W., and Devadas, S. (2005). Aegis: A single-chip secure processor. *Information Security Technical Report*, 10(2):63–73.

[Sultan et al., 2014] Sultan, H., Ananthanarayanan, G., and Sarangi, S. R. (2014). Processor power estimation techniques: a survey. *IJHPSA*, 5(2):93–114.

[Sultan et al., 2019] Sultan, H., Chauhan, A., and Sarangi, S. R. (2019). A survey of chip-level thermal simulators. *ACM Comput. Surv.*, 52(2):42:1–42:35.

[Sultan and Sarangi, 2017] Sultan, H. and Sarangi, S. R. (2017). A fast leakage aware thermal simulator for 3d chips. In *Design, Automation & Test in Europe Conference & Exhibition, DATE 2017, Lausanne, Switzerland, March 27-31, 2017*, pages 1733–1738.

[Sultan et al., 2018] Sultan, H., Varshney, S., and Sarangi, S. R. (2018). Is leakage power a linear function of temperature? *arXiv preprint arXiv:1809.03147*.

[Sze et al., 2020] Sze, V., Chen, Y.-H., Yang, T.-J., and Emer, J. S. (2020). Efficient processing of deep neural networks. *Synthesis Lectures on Computer Architecture*, 15(2):1–341.

[Szefer, 2018] Szefer, J. (2018). Principles of secure processor architecture design. *Synthesis Lectures on Computer Architecture*, 13(3):1–173.

[Szefer, 2019] Szefer, J. (2019). Survey of microarchitectural side and covert channels, attacks, and defenses. *Journal of Hardware and Systems Security*, 3(3):219–234.

[Taassori et al., 2018] Taassori, M., Shafiee, A., and Balasubramonian, R. (2018). Vault: Reducing paging overheads in sgx with efficient integrity verification structures. In *Proceedings of the Twenty-Third International Conference on Architectural Support for Programming Languages and Operating Systems*, pages 665–678.

[Tarjan et al., 2006] Tarjan, D., Thoziyoor, S., and Jouppi, N. P. (2006). Cacti 4.0. Technical Report HPL-2006-86, HP Laboratories.

[Taub and Schilling, 1977] Taub, H. and Schilling, D. L. (1977). *Digital integrated electronics*. McGraw-Hill New York.

[Thekkath et al., 2000] Thekkath, D. L. C., Mitchell, M., Lincoln, P., Boneh, D., Mitchell, J., and Horowitz, M. (2000). Architectural support for copy and tamper resistant software. In *Proceedings of the Ninth International Conference on Architectural Support for Programming Languages and Operating Systems*, page 168–177.

[Thornton, 2000] Thornton, J. E. (2000). Parallel operation in the control data 6600. *Readings in computer architecture*, page 32.

[Thoziyoor et al., 2007] Thoziyoor, S., Muralimanohar, N., and Jouppi, N. P. (2007). Cacti 5.0. Technical Report HPL-2007-167, HP Laboratories.

[Tiwari and Torrellas, 2008] Tiwari, A. and Torrellas, J. (2008). Facelift: Hiding and slowing down aging in multicores. In *2008 41st IEEE/ACM International Symposium on Microarchitecture*, pages 129–140. IEEE.

[Turkington, 2013] Turkington, D. A. (2013). *Generalized vectorization, cross-products, and matrix calculus*. Cambridge University Press.

[Van Bulck et al., 2018] Van Bulck, J., Minkin, M., Weisse, O., Genkin, D., Kasikci, B., Piessens, F., Silberstein, M., Wenisch, T. F., Yarom, Y., and Strackx, R. (2018). Foreshadow: Extracting the keys to the intel {SGX} kingdom with transient out-of-order execution. In *27th {USENIX} Security Symposium ({USENIX} Security 18)*, pages 991–1008.

[Vangal et al., 2007] Vangal, S., Howard, J., Ruhl, G., Dighe, S., Wilson, H., Tschanz, J., Finan, D., Iyer, P., Singh, A., Jacob, T., et al. (2007). An 80-tile 1.28 tflops network-on-chip in 65nm cmos. In *2007 IEEE International Solid-State Circuits Conference. Digest of Technical Papers*, pages 98–589. IEEE.

[Vantrease et al., 2011] Vantrease, D., Lipasti, M. H., and Binkert, N. (2011). Atomic coherence: Leveraging nanophotonics to build race-free cache coherence protocols. In *High Performance Computer Architecture (HPCA), 2011 IEEE 17th International Symposium on*, pages 132–143.

[Wang et al., 2018] Wang, C., Wu, H., Gao, B., Zhang, T., Yang, Y., and Qian, H. (2018). Conduction mechanisms, dynamics and stability in rerams. *Microelectronic Engineering*, 187:121–133.

[Wang et al., 2005] Wang, D., Ganesh, B., Tuaycharoen, N., Baynes, K., Jaleel, A., and Jacob, B. (2005). Dramsim: a memory system simulator. *ACM SIGARCH Computer Architecture News*, 33(4):100–107.

[Wang and Agrawal, 2008] Wang, F. and Agrawal, V. D. (2008). Single event upset: An embedded tutorial. In *21st International Conference on VLSI Design (VLSID 2008)*, pages 429–434. IEEE.

[Wang et al., 2013] Wang, J., Tim, Y., Wong, W.-F., and Li, H. H. (2013). A practical low-power memristor-based analog neural branch predictor. In *Low Power Electronics and Design (ISLPED), 2013 IEEE International Symposium on*, pages 175–180. IEEE.

[Wang and Franklin, 1997] Wang, K. and Franklin, M. (1997). Highly accurate data value prediction using hybrid predictors. In *Proceedings of the 30th annual ACM/IEEE international symposium on Microarchitecture*, pages 281–290. IEEE Computer Society.

[Wang et al., 2016] Wang, Y., Li, H., and Li, X. (2016). Re-architecting the on-chip memory sub-system of machine-learning accelerator for embedded devices. In *2016 IEEE/ACM International Conference on Computer-Aided Design (ICCAD)*, pages 1–6. IEEE.

[Wegman and Carter, 1981] Wegman, M. N. and Carter, J. L. (1981). New hash functions and their use in authentication and set equality. *Journal of computer and system sciences*, 22(3):265–279.

[Wickerson et al., 2017] Wickerson, J., Batty, M., Sorensen, T., and Constantinides, G. A. (2017). Automatically comparing memory consistency models. In *Proceedings of the 44th ACM SIGPLAN Symposium on Principles of Programming Languages*, pages 190–204.

[Williams et al., 2009] Williams, S., Waterman, A., and Patterson, D. (2009). Roofline: an insightful visual performance model for multicore architectures. *Communications of the ACM*, 52(4):65–76.

[Williamson, 2007] Williamson, D. (2007). Arm cortex-a8: A high-performance processor for low-power applications. *Unique Chips and Systems*, page 79.

[Wilton and Jouppi, 1993] Wilton, S. J. and Jouppi, N. P. (1993). An enhanced access and cycle time model for on-chip caches. Research Report 93/5, Digital Western Research Laboratory.

[Wittenbrink et al., 2011] Wittenbrink, C. M., Kilgariff, E., and Prabhu, A. (2011). Fermi gf100 gpu architecture. *IEEE Micro*, 31(2):50–59.

[Wong et al., 2010] Wong, H., Papadopoulou, M.-M., Sadooghi-Alvandi, M., and Moshovos, A. (2010). Demystifying gpu microarchitecture through microbenchmarking. In *Performance Analysis of Systems & Software (ISPASS), 2010 IEEE International Symposium on*, pages 235–246. IEEE.

[Woo et al., 1995] Woo, S. C., Ohara, M., Torrie, E., Singh, J. P., and Gupta, A. (1995). The splash-2 programs: Characterization and methodological considerations. *ACM SIGARCH computer architecture news*, 23(2):24–36.

[Wouters, 2009] Wouters, D. (2009). Oxide resistive ram (oxrram) for scaled nvm application. *Innovative Mass Storage Technologies-IMST*.

[Wu et al., 2019] Wu, Y. N., Emer, J. S., and Sze, V. (2019). Accelergy: An architecture-level energy estimation methodology for accelerator designs. In *2019 IEEE/ACM International Conference on Computer-Aided Design (ICCAD)*, pages 1–8. IEEE.

[Xu and Liu, 2010] Xu, Q. and Liu, X. (2010). On signal tracing in post-silicon validation. In *2010 15th Asia and South Pacific Design Automation Conference (ASP-DAC)*, pages 262–267. IEEE.

[Yeh and Patt, 1991] Yeh, T.-Y. and Patt, Y. N. (1991). Two-level adaptive training branch prediction. In *Proceedings of the 24th annual international symposium on Microarchitecture*, pages 51–61. ACM.

[Yeh and Patt, 1992] Yeh, T.-Y. and Patt, Y. N. (1992). Alternative implementations of two-level adaptive branch prediction. In *Proceedings of the 19th annual international symposium on Computer architecture*, pages 124–134.

[Yeh and Patt, 1993] Yeh, T.-Y. and Patt, Y. N. (1993). A comparison of dynamic branch predictors that use two levels of branch history. In *Proceedings of the 20th annual international symposium on computer architecture*, pages 257–266.

[Yiu, 2009] Yiu, J. (2009). *The definitive guide to the ARM Cortex-M3*. Newnes.

[Yoaz et al., 1999] Yoaz, A., Erez, M., Ronen, R., and Jourdan, S. (1999). Speculation techniques for improving load related instruction scheduling. In *Proceedings of the 26th annual international symposium on Computer architecture*, pages 42–53.

[Yu, 2016] Yu, S. (2016). Resistive random access memory (rram) from devices to array architectures. *Synthesis Lectures on Computer Architecture*, 6.

[Yu and Chen, 2016] Yu, S. and Chen, P.-Y. (2016). Emerging memory technologies: Recent trends and prospects. *IEEE Solid-State Circuits Magazine*, 8(2):43–56.

[Zhou et al., 2007] Zhou, P., Teodorescu, R., and Zhou, Y. (2007). Hard: Hardware-assisted lockset-based race detection. In *2007 IEEE 13th International Symposium on High Performance Computer Architecture*, pages 121–132. IEEE.

Index